DATE DUE		
MAR - 7 1992	MAY - 6 1993	
MAR 2 8 1992	MAR 1 0 1994	
	APR - 5 1994	
DEC 1 6 1992		
JAN 4 1993		
JAN 2 6 1993		
FEB 1 6 1993		
MAR 1 7 1993		
APR 2 2 1993		

THE ENCYCLOPEDIA

OF

HUMAN DEVELOPMENT

AND

EDUCATION

THEORY, RESEARCH, AND STUDIES

Advances in Education

This is an internationally acclaimed series of Pergamon education reference works. Each volume in the series is thematically organized and aims to provide comprehensive and up-to-date coverage of its own specialist subject area. The series is being developed primarily from the well-received *International Encyclopedia of Education* using the latest electronic publishing technology for data capture, manipulation, and storage of text in a form which allows fast and easy modification and updating of copy. Where appropriate a number of other volumes have been specially commissioned for the series. Volumes that are not derived from *The International Encyclopedia of Education* are indicated by an asterisk.

DUNKIN (ed.)
The International Encyclopedia of Teaching and Teacher Education

ERAUT (ed.)
The International Encyclopedia of Educational Technology

KEEVES (ed.)
Educational Research, Methodology, and Measurement: An International Handbook

LEWY (ed.)
The International Encyclopedia of Curriculum

POSTLETHWAITE (ed.)
The Encyclopedia of Comparative Education and National Systems of Education

PSACHAROPOULOS (ed.)
Economics of Education: Research and Studies

REYNOLDS (ed.)*
Knowledge Base for the Beginning Teacher

TITMUS (ed.)
Lifelong Education for Adults: An International Handbook

WALBERG & HAERTEL (eds.)
The International Encyclopedia of Educational Evaluation

WANG, REYNOLDS & WALBERG (eds.)* (3 volumes)
Handbook of Special Education: Research and Practice

A Related Pergamon Journal[†]

Journal of Child Psychology and Psychiatry, and Allied Disciplines

Joint Editors: Michael Berger, St. George's Hospital, London and Eric Taylor, Institute of Psychiatry, London

[†]Free Specimen copy available on request.

NOTICE TO READERS

Dear Reader

If your library is not already a standing/continuation order customer to the series **Advances in Education**, may we recommend that you place a standing/continuation order to receive immediately upon publication all new volumes. Should you find that these volumes no longer serve your needs, your order may be cancelled at any time without notice.

ROBERT MAXWELL
Publisher at Pergamon Press

THE ENCYCLOPEDIA

OF

HUMAN DEVELOPMENT

AND

EDUCATION

THEORY, RESEARCH, AND STUDIES

Edited by

R. MURRAY THOMAS

University of California, Santa Barbara, USA

PERGAMON PRESS

Member of Maxwell Macmillan Pergamon Publishing Corporation

OXFORD · NEW YORK · BEIJING · FRANKFURT
SÃO PAULO · SYDNEY · TOKYO · TORONTO

U.K.	Pergamon Press plc, Headington Hill Hall, Oxford OX3 0BW, England
U.S.A.	Pergamon Press, Inc., Maxwell House, Fairview Park, Elmsford, New York 10523, U.S.A.
PEOPLE'S REPUBLIC OF CHINA	Pergamon Press, Room 4037, Qianmen Hotel, Beijing, People's Republic of China
FEDERAL REPUBLIC OF GERMANY	Pergamon Press GmbH, Hammerweg 6, D-6242 Kronberg, Federal Republic of Germany
BRAZIL	Pergamon Editora Ltda, Rua Eça de Queiros, 346, CEP 04011, Paraiso, São Paulo, Brazil
AUSTRALIA	Pergamon Press Australia Pty Ltd., P.O. Box 544, Potts Point, N.S.W. 2011, Australia
JAPAN	Pergamon Press, 5th Floor, Matsuoka Central Building, 1-7-1 Nishishinjuku, Shinjuku-ku, Tokyo 160, Japan
CANADA	Pergamon Press Canada Ltd., Suite No 271, 253 College Street, Toronto, Ontario, Canada M5T 1R5

First edition 1990

Library of Congress Cataloging-in-Publication Data

The Encyclopedia of human development and education: theory, research, and studies/edited by R. Murray Thomas.—1st ed.
p.   cm.—(Advances in education)
1. Development psychology. I. Thomas, R. Murray, (Robert Murray), 1921–   II. Series.
BF713.E65   1989
155—dc20 89-26480

British Library Cataloguing in Publication Data

The Encyclopedia of human development and education: theory, research, and studies.—(Advances in education)
1. Man. Development
I. Title II. Series
155

ISBN 0-08-033408-3

Computer data file designed and computer typeset by Page Bros (Norwich) Ltd.

Printed in Great Britain by BPCC Wheatons Ltd, Exeter

Contents

Contents

PART 5   PSYCHO-PHYSICAL DEVELOPMENT

PART 6   **SOCIAL AND CULTURAL INTERACTIONS WITH DEVELOPMENT**

Preface

Although human development has been of interest to scholars for a very long time, the empirical study of human development, and particularly child development, is a relatively recent phenomenon. It was only during the late nineteenth century that researchers on both sides of the Atlantic began to conduct empirical studies on individual development, individual differences, and the learning process, with a focus on the implications of these studies for education. In the last fifty years, however, an increasing number of studies have been carried out in all parts of the world—at universities and at research-and-development centers. As a result of this research, there are now several thousand books on various aspects of human development and hundreds of thousands of journal articles on the subject.

After a century of studies concerned with various aspects of human development, it seems appropriate to take stock of what is known about the basic problems of human development relevant to schooling, child raising, and counseling. *The Encyclopedia of Human Development and Education: Theory, Research and Studies* provides practitioners such as teachers, school psychologists, social workers, school administrators, counselors, and guidance workers, as well as students of education, with state-of-the-art accounts of the various facets of human development and their bearing on education.

1. The Origins of the Encyclopedia

The contents of this *Encyclopedia* derive from articles appearing in the 10-volume *International Encyclopedia of Education: Research and Studies* which was edited by Torsten Husén and T. Neville Postlethwaite and published in 1985. *The International Encyclopedia of Education* was awarded the 1986 Dartmouth Medal for an outstanding reference work by the American Library Association and was also selected by *Choice* as an Outstanding Academic Book of 1987.

In preparing *The Encyclopedia of Human Development*, authors were invited to revise and update their articles which had been published previously in *The International Encyclopedia of Education*. In addition to these articles, eleven articles were newly commissioned to cover recent studies and research in the field.

In the 10-volume parent encyclopedia, all articles were arranged in alphabetical order, with the result that the entries on human development were widely distributed throughout the 10 volumes. In *The Encyclopedia of Human Development and Education,* the entries have been organized thematically, rather than alphabetically. There are six major Parts, with sections organized in a pattern intended to reflect the potential categories of interest to readers. Each Part is preceded by an introduction, written by the Editor, describing the contents and placing them in perspective.

2. Scope of the Encyclopedia

The decision as to which articles should be included in this work was based on three main criteria:

(a) An identification of principal subjects commonly found in textbooks and journals on development in the 1980s. Examples of such entries include: *Genetics and Human Development, Basic Concepts and Applications of Piagetian Cognitive Development Theory, Basic Concepts of Behaviorism, Psychoanalytic Theory of Human Development, Stages of Human Development, Infancy, Adolescence, Cognitive Development, Vision and Visual Perception,* and *Socialization.*

(b) An effort to present traditional, widely-held views of human development not ordinarily found in such books and journals. The most prominent of such entries are accounts of theories of development embedded in such religious/philosophical traditions as those of Christianity, Judaism, Islam, Buddhism, Hinduism, Confucianism, and Shinto.

(c) Consultants' suggestions about problems which have gained interest in the field of development during the late 1980s. Examples of these articles include: *Information-processing Theory, Bilingualism, Drugs and Human Development, Homosexuality and Human Development, Body Image and Body Language, Multiculturalism, One-parent Families,* and *Child Influence on Adults.*

A further criterion used in the selection of articles was that their topics should be linked to education. Once the articles were selected, authors were asked to devote their main attention to explaining the concepts and facts of human development in relation to their topic. In addition they were asked to indicate implications that such concepts and facts could hold for educational practice—school instruction, child rearing, and counseling.

Another important consideration in the choice of articles for this *Encyclopedia* was that the volume should contain both theoretical and practical-empirical information about human development. The reason for this is that theory and research go hand-in-hand, since research is dependent on theory for the selection of variables to be studied and the design adopted. As well as entries devoted primarily to various theories of development, empirical-research entries include both theory and research results. The research reported throughout this volume reflects many investigative approaches—survey and experimental, historical, hermeneutic, psychoanalytic, anthropological, ethnographic, and case-study.

3. Structure of the Encyclopedia

The conceptual framework of the *Encyclopedia* is shown in Fig. 1. It identifies the six major Parts and their relationships. As Fig. 1 suggests, the most general concepts regarding development appear in the first three Parts of the volume, while the most specific information is located in the last three Parts. In effect, Parts 1, 2, and 3 offer theoretical settings in which the more detailed summaries of research and studies described in Parts 4, 5, and 6 can be viewed.

4. The Contents of the Six Parts

Part 1, consisting of five articles, focuses on general development issues and their historical backgrounds, including such concepts as *Life-span Development, Genetics*

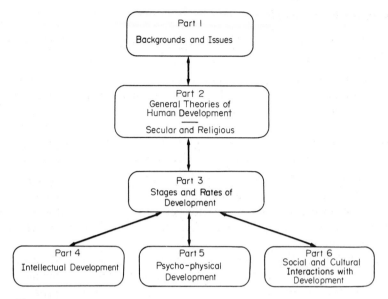

Figure 1
Schematic representation of the *Encyclopedia*'s organization

and Human Development, Maturation and Human Development, and *Individual Differences.*

Part 2, divided into two sections, contains 23 articles describing General Theories of Human Development. Part 2(a), Secular Theories, consists of 16 articles describing scientific and secular models conceived by European and North American philosophers and psychologists. The secular theories described range from *Basic Concepts and Applications of Piagetian Cognitive Development Theory* and *Soviet Theories of Human Development* to behaviorist, psychoanalytic, humanistic, and information-processing conceptions. Part 2(b), Theories Embedded in Religious Traditions, reviews theories derived from major religious traditions, including Jewish, Christian, and Islamic theories, which originate in the Middle East, as well as Hindu, Buddhist, Confucian, and Shinto beliefs, originating in Central and Eastern Asia.

The process of development is often viewed as a series of stages that start with prenatal life and end with old age. Part 3, divided into two sections discusses Stages and Rates of Development. Part 3(a), Definitions of Stage and Rate, contains three articles which analyze concepts of growth stages and developmental rates. These articles serve as an interpretive backdrop to Part 3(b) which consists of seven articles describing characteristics of development at seven successive stages, extending from prenatal life through to old age.

Parts 4, 5, and 6 deal with three major facets into which textbook authors have customarily divided human development—the intellectual, the psycho-physical, and the social-cultural.

Intellectual Development is reviewed in Part 4 which is divided into four sections—Mental Development in General, Learning Processes, Varieties of Intellectual Development, and The Self in the Environment.

The psycho-physical aspects of Development are dealt with in the 15 articles which comprise Part 5. This Part is divided into three sections—Influences on Psycho-physical

Development, Developing Vision and Hearing, and Special Issues in Physical Development.

Finally, Part 6 contains 24 articles dealing with Social and Cultural Interactions with Development. These articles are divided into three sections—Socialization and Acculturation, Prosocial and Antisocial Behaviour, and Factors Affecting Socialization.

5. How to Use the Encyclopedia

This volume is designed to serve both as a reference book and a textbook. A user with a specific subject or question in mind, will find it useful to proceed either via the Contents at the beginning of the book, or via the Subject Index at the end. Should a user require a more general view of a large segment of the field, it would be more useful to start by reading the introductions to each Part. These give helpful overviews and sufficient guidance to the contents of individual entries to assist the reader in deciding where to go next.

Further assistance is provided by a comprehensive bibliography at the end of each article which readers may find profitable for locating further sources of information. In addition to the Subject Index at the end of the volume, there is an Author Index covering all authors cited in articles. A full list of contributors and their affiliations is also included at the back of the volume.

6. Acknowledgements

Robert Maxwell conceived the idea of the parent encyclopedia, while Torsten Husén and T. Neville Postlethwaite took on the enormous task of finding Section Editors and of guiding the publication through its development. Together with Barbara Barrett, the Editorial Director at Pergamon Press, they were largely responsible for initiating and overseeing that remarkable work. As for this single-volume *Encyclopedia of Human Development and Education*, Joan Burks, Editorial Manager and Debra Rosen, Editor were primarily responsible for the more detailed work at Pergamon Press. To all of the above I owe a deep debt of gratitude for their crucial roles in this venture. Finally, I must express my very sincere thanks to the authors of the articles, whose expertise, dedication, and care is reflected in the high quality of their contributions.

March 1990

R. M. Thomas
California, USA

Part 1

Backgrounds and Issues

Part 1

Backgrounds and Issues

Introduction

Part 1 has two main purposes: first, to prepare a foundation for the subsequent parts of this *Encyclopedia* by offering an historical perspective on research on human development, and second, to identify three persistent issues that have influenced both the content and the methodology of studies in this field. The issues are those of conflicting research traditions, heredity-environment interaction, and individual differences in development.

In popular thought, education has been traditionally equated with schooling, and schooling has been regarded as an activity intended for children and youths. Consequently, past studies of the relationship between development and education have focused primarily on child development and schooling. With respect to children below the age of five, research has centered on the way infants and very young children are influenced by child-raising practices in the home and in the nursery school. However, during the 1970s and 1980s the field has extended in such a way that studies of development-and-education in the late 1980s encompass the entire life span and include informal and nonformal learning opportunities in addition to formal schooling. The manner in which the expansion of the concept of development-and-education has evolved is described in Kastenbaum's article on *Life-span Development* which opens Part 1.

In the second article, *History of Research of Human Development*, Dixon enlarges the historical purview of human-development studies by identifying five research traditions that have contributed to current modes of interpreting why people grow up as they do. The traditions are those of organicism, mechanism, psychoanalysis, contextualism, and dialecticism.

Both Kastenbaum and Dixon credit the evolutionist Charles Darwin as a major influence on current views of human growth, views which typically picture development as the consequence of interaction between an individual's genetic inheritance and environmental forces. The third article in Part 1 extends this notion with Matheny and Wilson's more detailed analysis of how genetic structure contributes to development over the life

3

span. The authors illustrate their analysis mainly with findings from studies of twins and siblings.

A fundamental point made by Matheny and Wilson is that all of the genes contained in the human organism at conception do not exert their observable effect on development at the same time. Rather, their effect emerges at different times over the life span. Matheny and Wilson (p. 23) note that:

> This fact of timed gene action has led to the recognition that the core feature of development is the process by which the genetic material in a single fertilized egg ultimately transforms that cell into a multibillion-cell organism of extraordinary differentiation and detail. In this perspective, development is a continuous dynamic process, with episodes of differentiation and growth being switched on and off in accordance with instructions in the genetic program.

Among biologists and psychologists, the term *maturation* has traditionally been used to label this process by which the genetic time clock "switches on" a new aspect of development. How the term *maturation* is currently used and ways in which concepts of maturation can affect educational practices are described briefly in the fourth article of Part 1, *Maturation and Human Development*.

If the proposal that development results from the interaction of heredity and environment is accepted, we may be accused of offering an unnecessary truism when the following observation is made:

Since no two people have identical genetic structure that combines with identical environmental experiences, no two people can be exactly alike. And if no two people are alike, what good does it do to study one person or one group and then expect that the conclusions which are drawn will be useful in explaining someone else's development?

The answer is that even while no two people are exactly alike they have many developmental characteristics in common. Thus, it has been the job of researchers to discover these common characteristics and to describe how they function. As a result of such research, statements about commonalities have come to comprise the bulk of the existing literature on human development, including the contents of this *Encyclopedia*. Yet while the emphasis of researchers is on discovering ways in which people are similar in their growth, it is still important not to lose sight of the ways in which individuals differ. The aim of the final article in Part 1 is to draw attention to this matter of *Individual Differences* and to ways individuality can influence decisions about child care and education.

In Part 1 the stress placed on matters of genetics may give the impression that heredity is to be featured throughout this *Encyclopedia* to the neglect of environmental influences on development. However, such is not the case. Not only do all 24 articles in Part 6 center on specific environmental forces, but environmental variables play a prominent role throughout all the other parts of the *Encyclopedia* as well. For the *Encyclopedia* as a whole, far greater attention is accorded to environmental factors than to genetic variables, particularly because the environmental factors are the ones amenable to alteration by education.

Life-span Development

R. Kastenbaum

The infant obviously differs from the child it will become, who in turn differs from the adolescent, the adult, and the aged adult. Yet, different as the person may be at various phases of life, it is still somehow the "same" person. How are we to understand the shifting relationships between continuity and change as the individual moves forward through time? What is the contribution of environment and experience to the developmental process? These are among the questions addressed by the approach known as life-span development. For perspective on this newly emerged approach it will be useful to touch briefly on its history. (See also Charles 1970, Baltes and Goulet 1970, Havighurst 1973.)

1. The Fixation on Early Development

The first empirical studies of human development concentrated almost exclusively on the period from infancy through adolescence. Both theoretical assumptions and the need for socially useful information motivated this approach. Heredity was assumed to be the dominant force in development—an idea that perhaps owed something to the influence of social class structure in nineteenth century Europe and its growing challenge from the technological revolution. Defenders of the heredity assumption were also defending the social status quo.

Early researchers often considered their major task to be careful description of the way in which genetic patterns unfold during the early years of life. Information on child development was also becoming of increasing importance to educators and, indeed, to all who wished to set future generations on the straight and narrow path mandated by society. One theme after another continued the emphasis on early development. Offshoots of Charles Darwin's theory of evolution led to the belief that, as G. Stanley Hall put it in a much-echoed phrase: "ontogeny recapitulates phylogeny" (Hall 1904). The evolution of the human race, in other words, was thought by some leading scholars to repeat itself in the early development of every individual.

One major implication of this view (known as "genetic psychology") was that the infant and young child are not ready for serious social influence. It is necessary to wait until adolescence when the individual has (supposedly) reached the "social phase of evolution" and is now malleable to cultural influence. Furthermore, Hall and some other influential people of the day held that

the evolutionary advances society might induce in one wave of adolescents would carry over into succeeding generations. While this new conception did extend the developmental spectrum as far as adolescence, it was at the expense of infancy and early childhood, now considered as of secondary interest because only a primitive, nonmalleable type of development was thought to occur in the first years of life.

Meanwhile, however, the eugenics movement directed intense concern toward the physical and mental quality of the young. Francis Galton's innovation of a test battery to evaluate individual abilities was a product of the eugenics movement (Galton 1883), and helped lay the foundation for the now ubiquitous testing of abilities and achievement which our children must endure. Advances in the biological sciences also encouraged attention to the early phases of development. There was no model available for the study of development in adults of any species!

The early emphasis on the first years of development was fostered by society's need to exercise control and guidance over the young during a time of rapid, disconcerting socioeconomic change. This effort was also allied to a belief in the possibility of bettering the human race by timely and appropriate interventions in the developmental process, including even the genetic pool. Many of the scientific and quasi-scientific assumptions that encouraged this view have since been rejected in the wake of improved research. Nevertheless, this social and theoretical context did serve to stimulate research that has added to our understanding of the early phases of human development.

2. Life-span Development and its Social Context

The new life-span approach to development also has its social context. One salient feature is the higher proportion of people surviving into middle and old age. There is a more visible presence of mature and aged adults in society which gradually has increased policy making and scientific attention to the second half of the life span. Another influential factor is the greater diversity of adult careers and life-styles. In past generations, once a child had stepped securely into a pre-established occupational and social track, the likelihood was strong that he or she would continue in a predictable course. Today there is much more variability and unpredictability. Increased geographic mobility, techno-

5

logical change including the current computer revolution, the women's liberation movement, and many other significant social trends have both shaken social stability and opened new opportunities. Where people go from childhood has become a more pertinent question than ever, to which must be added new questions regarding the directions of adult life. Life-span development as an approach to understanding and predicting human behavior has increasing value for a society in which life trajectories and life-styles have grown ever more diverse.

Furthermore, the "greying of societies"—that is, more people living longer—has intensified the concern for quality as well as extension of life. In the research sphere this concern translates itself into the task of differentiating between "pathological" and "normal" aging (not a truly satisfactory distinction in the long run, but a useful starting point). To understand and perhaps modify undesired concomitants of advancing age, it is necessary to analyze and weigh several sets of factors. Some impairments are most accurately attributed to chronic or acute illnesses which are not intrinsically a part of the aging process. Other impairments may be more closely related to the individual's previous life experiences, e.g., hearing deficit that resulted from years of work in a noisy factory. Still again, there are coping difficulties in later life that might be related to early socialization and educational experiences, or to the discontinuity between what was learned when young and what one encounters now in a vastly different society in old age. After these—and other—sources of influence are subtracted from the total picture, it may then be possible to find those components which can be atrributed most appropriately to intrinsic biological patterns of change. Although the attempt to differentiate between pathological and normal aging provides one organizing guideline for life-span research, it is not entirely sufficient. Closely related is the quest to answer questions such as the following:

(a) To what extent is it possible to shape or modify the patterns of change often associated with aging?

(b) For this purpose, what types of intervention are most useful (educational, environmental, health awareness)?

(c) What accounts for the marked individual differences in human development from early through late adulthood? Why do some people continue to grow and mature, while others soon enter upon a routine, relatively fixed life-style?

These are very broad guiding questions that exemplify but do not exhaust the problems addressed by this emerging field. In practice, life-span development, like any field of research, focuses upon more specific questions that one can hope to answer clearly. The answers—and the research strategies as well—produced by life-span developmentalists have implications for more traditional fields of study such as infancy and childhood.

Pioneers of the life-span approach, such as Charlotte Bühler (1933) and Sidney Pressey and Raymond G. Kuhlen (1957), expressed the belief that we could not truly understand any one point in human development without comprehension of the totality. This belief is now embodied in a wide variety of research and a growing number of practical applications.

3. Some Principles of Life-span Development

The following points of emphasis are characteristic of the life-span approach to development, and are best considered as guiding assumptions for theory, research, and practice.

(a) Individual development is most usefully studied within its biocultural context, rather than by artificial separation of person and historical context.

(b) Development through time must be carefully distinguished from changes with time. Many types of experiential and sociobehavioral change can be observed over time, but not all of these should be considered manifestations of development.

(c) New concepts are required to replace or at least supplement the use of chronological age as an index of developmental status. Taken by itself, chronological age often is not a satisfactory datum either for careful research or practical decision making.

(d) New research strategies are required to encompass the entire range of life-span phenomena, and to discover the complex relationships among individual and social factors in development. Methods that have worked well enough for study of limited age groups (e.g., the preschool years) are not always sufficient for approaches that are concerned with larger blocks of age and developmental change.

(e) Existing theories of human behavior must be modified or replaced by models that are both more precise and more encompassing with respect to human behavior and experience throughout the entire lifespan. The issue of continuity versus discontinuity of development, for example, goes beyond the effective limits of traditional theories. Furthermore, life-span developmentalists are alert for the unfolding of phenomena and themes in broader arches and more complex shapes than what is usually observed within more delimited sectors of the life span.

4. Innovative Research Strategies

Life-span developmentalists have started to make good on their promises. This is shown clearly in the innovation of research strategies that are now influencing the design and interpretation of experiments in other areas as well. Three types of research innovation will be described briefly.

4.1 Functional Measures of Age

Numerous investigators have attempted to establish measures that can serve as partial definitions of age based upon how the person functions rather than upon the time elapsed since date of birth. Alex Comfort (1969) specified 55 distinct variables that could yield partial functional measures of age, along with possible methods of assessment. Scientists associated with the Veterans Administration's Normative Aging Project in Boston have conducted longitudinal studies that, while not quite as extensive as Comfort's proposal, do encompass a wide variety of variables, ranging from functions of the retina through a number of behavioral and social aspects (Damon 1972, Fozard 1972). Independently, Kastenbaum et al. (1972) introduced a procedure for studying subjective and interpersonal aspects of functional age. The concept of one overall functional age for an individual is premature at this time. Indeed, it is more likely that a profile of subscores will prove most useful both for research and applied purposes. At present, specific measures of functional age can be grouped usefully under the rubrics of biological, behavioral, subjective, interpersonal, and social ages. These partial functional ages have variable relationships with each other; that is, a person may look older than his chronological age to other people (interpersonal age), while feeling younger (subjective age), while occupying a senior position in family and occupational life (social age), and being just about at the modal point for biological and behavioral functions. Many other configurations are possible.

4.2 Use of Archival and Other Indirect Data

Baltes et al. (1977) are among those who have stimulated the utilization of information obtained from a variety of sources in addition to controlled research designs. These sources include demographic data, especially those illuminating shifts in population structure, archival information on sociocultural phenomena, and retrospective reports. Because the intended scope of life-span development research is so vast and its data-gathering demands so great, investigators in this field continually seek new sources of information that, while having certain limitations, enrich the context from which conclusions are to be drawn.

4.3 Time-lag Research Designs

Until recently, most research designs in the behavioral and social sciences could be classified either as cross-sectional or longitudinal. The cross-sectional design, by far the most common, relies on a single time point for measurement or data collection. If a researcher was interested in age differences, then individuals of several different ages would be studied at the same time. This design is insensitive to actual changes with age. Unfortunately, much of our data base on human development derives from cross-sectional studies which, whatever other considerable merits they might possess, fail to distinguish true age change from age differences. Longitudinal designs are more sensitive to the passage of time, involving two or more time points of measurement for the same individuals. More expensive and difficult to manage than cross-sectional studies, the longitudinal approach often has yielded valuable data when feasible to mount and continue. Despite its advantages, however, the longitudinal approach also has drawbacks which limit the conclusions one can draw (assuming the application of high standards for inference). While the research participants are moving, for example, from age 5 to 75, much else is in motion as well. How do we know how much of the observed changes represent intraindividual variation through time and how much represent sociocultural shift? The answer is simple enough: we don't know!

A spectrum of new research strategies has been introduced by life-span developmentalists both to transcend the limitations of the traditional designs and to acquire more refined and complete data. These designs include some of the most complex ever put forth in the social and behavioral sciences, both on the overall data-plan side, and in the nature of the multivariate analyses required. For nonspecialists in this area, the complexity can seem overwhelming to the point of discouragement, but the approach can be exemplified easily enough in one of its more elementary forms. Suppose, for example, that the initial sample is of research participants who are spread in chronological age at Time 1: for example, 5-year-olds, 10-year-olds, and so on in five-year increments up to age 75. The first data-gathering foray (Time 1) has the semblance of an ambitious cross-sectional study. Additional data will be gathered at future points in time, however, for example, at five-year intervals. This multiple time series places the study in motion and gives it the semblance of a vigorous (and highly expensive) longitudinal study. The new wrinkle introduced now is the periodic addition of fresh participants. At Time 2, the original 5-year-olds will now be 10 years of age. A new set of 5-year-olds is introduced at this point (and the same can be done, at least theoretically, with all the other age groups represented). This time-lag feature makes it possible to sort out the effects of historical time and its possible sociocultural shift from "true" developmental change. If, for example, television were new and had first appeared in American homes in time for the second (but not the first) set of 5-year-olds, it would be possible at least to begin to distinguish differences attributable to television exposure from whatever might be the "basic" or "pure" course of early development. Designs of the time-lag type are powerful and their results may eventually lead to a much altered and expanded view of human development. They are also expensive and complex, as already noted, and so for the present often serve more as ideal than reality. Additional readings on this and related research design topics include Schaie (1977), Nunnally (1973), Baltes and Nesselroade (1973), and Horn and McArdle (1980).

5. Applications to the Educational Process

As a new although rapidly growing field of study, most of life-span development's substantive contributions to the educational process are to be told by the future. A few illustrative suggestions can be made, however, based on data already in hand.

5.1 Expanding the Target Population

The late Gunther Reinert speaks for many in stating that "A life-span educational psychology . . . presumes that *all* people—children, adolescents, adults, and senior citizens—are potential students and have to be educated" (Reinert 1980 p. 10). Less emphasis should be placed on chronological age on the part of both teacher and student: the educational process can work well in both directions. Educational needs continue to emerge throughout the life span, as in beginning second or third careers, learning to function as a single parent, taking advantage of leisure time, and preparing for the problems and opportunities of later life. Peer instruction is one aspect of the total educational process that will repay more extensive and adventuresome use, Reinert believed.

5.2 Expanding the Ecology of Education

Reinert, building on suggestions by Bronfenbrenner (1977), proposed that the educational processes be cultivated in a variety of environments, decisively rejecting the predominantly classroom-only model. Life-span developmental research has provided many examples of the variety of ecologies inhabited and created by people throughout their adult lives: ecologies that are far removed from the formal schooling situation. Expanding the ecologies of education would provide more continuity between instruction and "real life."

5.3 More Attention to Transitional Situations and Challenges

Life-span developmentalists disagree among themselves regarding the degree of continuity between early and later life patterns, with some data available to support the continuity and the discontinuity positions. There is substantial agreement, however, on the importance of transitional situations, such as leaving home, leaving school, taking a job, leaving a job, marrying, separating or divorcing, and facing the death of oneself or loved ones. More attention could well be devoted to the influence of transitional situations and challenges on the educational process itself. Of even greater significance, though, is the potential of education to help people prepare for, cope with, and survive transitional and crisis situations. For this potential to be realized, educational planning will have to take the shape of the total life span into account, whether one is working with young children, adolescents, or mid-life adults. Research conducted and reviewed by Majorie Fiske Lowenthall (1977) offers one useful reference source.

5.4 More Opportunity for Age-heterogeneous Interactions

A side observation in many life-span developmental studies has been the incidental learning, often distinctive and substantial, that takes place when people of various ages have the opportunity to interact. Social trends in the United States in recent years have reduced such opportunities. The educational process might well be enriched by cultivating situations in which individuals functioning at different "developmental stations" in life have the opportunity to learn from each other, "learning" being defined in affective as well as cognitive and instrumental terms.

5.5 Competence Does not Vanish with Age

Many practices in the educational sphere assume that competence diminishes, perhaps vanishes with advancing age. The mandatory retirement provision for teachers is but one example. For another, consider the patronizing that is often evidenced in adult education. Life-span developmental research has made progress in specifying conditions that help older learners perform at their best (Botwinick 1978). Studies using the time-lag "super-designs" have picked away at the stereotype that all intellectual functions decline for all people with advancing age. While we do not yet have a total and definitive picture of ability change with advancing age, it is already clear enough that chronological age is unacceptable as a basis for educational practice and policy regarding the abilities of teacher and learner.

6. Flexibility or Commitment? The Search for Balance

One major lesson from life-span developmental research concerns the need for flexibility and resourcefulness in coping with changed circumstances (changes both internal and external to the individual). It would be tempting to urge more attention to educational experiences that equip the person to interpret and respond resourcefully to the unpredictable, unprecedented challenges that might be encountered in the years ahead. And yet, something should also be said for maintaining self-identity, commitment to enduring values, or whatever term one cares to employ (perhaps "psychological center of gravity"). Consummate adaptability is a questionable outcome of the educational process if it is at the cost of other human values. In the author's work with sick and frail old people, he has admired the strength of purpose that has somehow become entangled with a web of problems that threaten to overwhelm. One would like to reduce the stress and untangle the problems, but this must be done without assaulting the values this person has brought forth through many years of life experience. Educators and life-span developmentalists might become excellent partners in conceiving an optimal balance between flexibility of coping style and strength of identity and purpose.

Long before the current age of psychology and empirical studies of development, L. T. Hobhouse authored a book whose title as well as message bears remembrance today. In *Development and Purpose* (1913), Hobhouse argued cogently that goals and intentions should not be exorcised from our understanding of human experience, even though some would substitute an entirely utilitarian-functionalistic approach in the name of science. His concern for integrating mechanism and teleology is still timely. Both the educational process and the study of life-span development require sensitivity to goals, intentions, and purposes as well as mechanisms, functional abilities, and overt outcomes.

Bibliography

Baltes P B, Goulet L R 1970 Status and issues of a life-span development psychology. In: Goulet L R, Baltes P B (eds.) 1970 *Life-span Developmental Psychology: Research and Theory*. Academic Press, New York, pp. 3–21

Baltes P B, Nesselroade J R 1973 The developmental analysis of individual differences on multiple measures. In: Nesselroade J R, Reese H W (eds.) 1973 *Life-span Developmental Psychology: Methodological Issues*, Proc. 2nd West Virginia University Conf., 1971. Academic Press, New York, pp. 219–52

Baltes P B, Reese H W, Nesselroade J R 1977 *Life-span Developmental Psychology: Introduction to Research Methods*. Brooks/Cole, Monterey, California

Botwinick J 1978 *Aging and Behavior: A Comprehensive Integration of Research Findings*, 2nd edn. Springer, New York

Bronfenbrenner U 1977 Toward an experimental ecology of human development. *Am. Psychol.* 32: 513–31

Bühler C 1933 *Der Menschliche Lebenslauf als Psychologisches Problem*. Hirzel, Leipzig

Charles D C 1970 Historical antecedents of life-span developmental psychology. In: Goulet L R, Baltes P B (eds.) 1970 *Life-span Developmental Psychology*. Academic Press, New York, pp. 24–52

Comfort A 1969 Test battery to measure ageing-rate in man. *Lancet* 1411–15

Damon A 1972 Predicting age from body measurements and observations. *Int. J. Aging Hum. Dev.* 3: 169–74

Fozard J L 1972 Predicting age in the adult years from psychological assessments of abilities and personality. *Int. J. Aging Hum. Dev.* 3: 175–82

Galton F 1883 *Inquiries into Human Faculty and Its Development*. Macmillan, London

Hall G S 1904 *Adolescence: Its Psychology and its Relations to Physiology, Anthropology, Society, Sex, Crime, Religion and Education*. Appleton, New York

Havighurst R G 1973 History of developmental psychology: Socialization and personality development through the life span. In: Baltes P B, Schaie K W (eds.) 1973 *Life-span Developmental Psychology: Personality and Socialization*. Academic Press, New York, pp. 4–25

Hobhouse L T 1913 *Development and Purpose: An Essay Towards the Philosophy of Evolution*. Macmillan, London

Horn J L, McArdle J J 1980 Perspectives on mathematical/statistical model building (MASMOB) in research on aging. In: Poon L W (ed.) 1980 *Aging in the 1980's: Psychological Issues*. American Psychological Association, Washington, DC, pp. 503–41

Kastenbaum R, Derbin V, Sabatini P, Artt S 1972 The ages of me: Toward personal and interpersonal definitions of functional aging. *Int. J. Aging Hum. Dev.* 3: 197–212

Lowenthall M F 1977 Toward a sociological theory of change in adulthood and old age. In: Birren J E, Schaie K W (eds.) 1977 *Handbook of the Psychology of Aging*. Van Nostrand Reinhold, New York, pp. 116–27

Nunnally J C 1973 Research strategies and measurement methods for investigating human development. In: Nesselroade J R, Reese H W (eds.) 1973 *Life-span Developmental Psychology: Methodological Issues*. Academic Press, New York, pp. 87–110

Pressey S L, Kuhlen R G 1957 *Psychological Development Through the Life Span*. Harper and Row, New York

Reinert G 1980 Educational psychology in the context of the human life span. In: Baltes P B, Brim O G Jr (eds.) 1980 *Life-span Development and Behavior*, Vol. 3. Academic Press, New York, pp. 2–31

Schaie K W 1977 Quasi-experimental research designs in the psychology of aging. In: Birren J E, Schaie K W (eds.) 1977 *Handbook of the Psychology of Aging*. Van Nostrand Reinhold, New York, pp. 39–58

History of Research of Human Development[1]

R. A. Dixon

The term human development is a general one, potentially referring to a myriad of aspects and varieties of individual and cultural change. For the purpose of this article, however, the term will bear a more restricted meaning. Henceforth, "human development" shall refer to behavioral ontogeny, that is, to social and psychological processes that occur in a larger context but which are assessed primarily on the individual level and which change or develop across a portion of the life span. While research on human development so defined is thus generally (but not necessarily) of a psychological nature, it may be produced or consumed by representatives of a variety of psychological perspectives, as well as several sociologically or educationally

[1] The author is grateful to U. Bronfenbrenner, R. Lerner, S. Toulmin, and J. Wohlwill for their critical comments on earlier versions of this article.

oriented disciplines. Thus, the present overview of the history of human development examines the origins and lineages of what is presently known most generally as developmental psychology.

The following historical account is organized chronologically. In the first section, after a brief overview of the historical problem, several early (prior to the middle of the nineteenth century) precursors of developmental psychology are identified. It will be seen that during this period the "match" between sociohistorical context and theories produced by individual scientists was imperfect. While several early precursors produced intellectually appealing and cogent models of human development—some of which resonate nicely with contemporary efforts—few had any direct lasting impact. Following this, in the second section, the climate of historicity and temporality surrounding the emergence of evolutionary thought in the middle- to late-nineteenth century is described. While no direct causal attribution is made, it is inferred that this intellectual climate nurtured the subsequent growth of developmental psychology. The third section traces the proliferation of developmental theories that occurred in the twentieth century. For the sake of brevity, the major figures in this expansion, as well as their place in their respective lineages, are portrayed in a skeletal fashion.

1. Overview and Early Precursors

It is apparent that the enterprise of human development did not arise in a vacuum, without antecedent or concurrent contextual influences. Given the contemporary theoretical fragmentation of the discipline, it is somewhat less apparent, but no less certain, that there is no single originative figure directly linked to all present "paradigms" or research traditions of developmental psychology. Further, it is doubtful that the history of even a single variety (or family of theories) of developmental psychology is so clear, unbroken, and unilinear. Indeed, from a truly historical point of view, each antecedent figure or theory was duly installed in a continuing historical progression. Hence, it would appear that all putatively originative developmental psychologists produced theories or systems that were only relatively original. Their historical eminence may be due as much to their creativity, breadth, precision, and personal persuasiveness as it is to their intellectual originality. This suggests yet another important factor in the staying power of early developmental psychologists, namely, their location in sociohistorical time. If it is true that the ideas of originative developmental psychologists were influenced by the extant social and intellectual climate, it is no less true that their ideas influenced that climate in a reciprocal fashion. Insofar as this reciprocity prevailed, they were able to attract a coterie of devotees, advocates, and normal scientists. In this way, their potential systems could grow and their impact on the discipline of human development be maximized.

1.1 Early Precursors

Prior to the nineteenth century, several prefigurative (but discontinuous) steps were taken to investigate behavioral ontogenesis. It is perhaps only natural that the problem of individual development and aging—so obviously a part of everyday life—would attract the attention of scholars (Groffmann 1970). Similarly, given the intellectual climate prior to the scientific revolutions of Galileo Galilei (1564–1642), Francis Bacon (1561–1626), Sir Isaac Newton (1642–1727), and Charles Darwin (1809–1882), it is not surprising that these early efforts derived primarily from philosophical, literary, or theological domains. From Aristotle (384–322 BC) to St. Augustine (354–430) to William Shakespeare (1564–1616) and Jean Jacques Rousseau (1712–1778), many important thinkers wrote about the ages or stages of human life, often speculating on their respective needs and purposes (Dennis 1972).

It was not until the eighteenth century, however, that these theoretical perspectives were attached to empirical investigations. Foremost among the latter group are the following European figures: (a) Johann Nikolas Tetens (1736–1807), who argued that only through natural science was it possible to arrive at general laws regarding human development from birth to death, (b) Dietrich Tiedemann (1748–1803), who produced the first primarily psychological diary of the growth of a young child, (c) Friedrich August Carus (1770–1808), who attempted to develop a comprehensive, general age-oriented science of life-span psychological development, and (d) Adolphe Quetelet (1796–1874), who proposed highly advanced methods to disentangle multiple influences on the course of human development. Other observers (e.g., Baltes 1983, Reinert 1979) have pointed out that, while these efforts had no direct influence on contemporary developmental psychology, and in fact in most circles were only recently rediscovered, they boast several features consonant with recent advances in developmental theory and methodology.

2. Evolutionism and the Proliferation of Developmental Psychology

To propose that Charles Darwin is salient among early figures of developmental psychology is certainly not a novel idea. It should be noted, however, that Darwin is not identified as the singular or even the most influential of originative figures. Rather, a more modest claim—a claim in keeping with our earlier historical overview—is advanced. To wit: the intellectual climate of evolutionism that both preceded Darwin and gained impetus from him—and which was epitomized by him—is one of the originative intellectual cores of many contemporary developmental psychologies. Certainly among early evolutionists it is Darwin whose contributions have been both lasting and most adaptable to the theoretical contours and practical concerns of the developmental human sciences. It is useful to note parenthetically that not all contemporary approaches actively embrace the Darwinian model, and some less visible approaches (not discussed herein) may not have been meaningfully influenced by evolutionary theory.

Partly as a result of the publication of Darwin's *On the Origin of Species* in 1859, the notions of temporality, historicity, and open-ended development began spreading through nineteenth-century science and letters. Scientific inquiry—indeed, most intellectual study—became infused with history. Toulmin and Goodfield (1965) have suggested that this passion for historicizing intellectual inquiry gave the latter half of the nineteenth century a characteristic period flavor. That is, this period, having witnessed the discovery of developmental time, became exemplified by this metaphor.

While Darwin was perhaps the embodiment of historicism in the nineteenth century, he was not without intellectual antecedents and coevals. While it is beyond the task of this article to completely disentangle his multiple intellectual influences, a summary of their interrelated strands may be offered (see also Dixon and Lerner 1984). It is by now well-known that Darwin, relatively originative with regard to the human sciences, owed (and acknowledged) a strong intellectual debt to geology, and in particular the uniformitarian work of Sir Charles Lyell (1797–1875), whose research in natural history led him to confirm the continuous, historical, biographical nature of geological phenomena. Darwin, who was originally trained in the competing faction of geology—progressive catastrophism—took Lyell's monumental *Principles of Geology* with him on his celebrated voyage on the *Beagle*, and returned a confirmed uniformitarian. Lyell's version of uniformitarianism (a) suggested the principle of incessant change, (b) rejected all notions of final causation, (c) suggested a cumulative interpretation of natural history, and (d) began focusing attention on the problem of life. In brief, Darwin's contribution was to adapt the continuous historicism of Lyell and combine it with the mechanisms of evolution absent, or incorrect, in such earlier thinkers as Jean Baptiste de Monet Lamarck (1744–1829). This mechanism, believed to have been adapted from Thomas Robert Malthus's (1766–1834) *Essay on Population* and from Lyell's translation of Augustin de Condolle (1778–1841), was the "struggle for survival" metaphor. This metaphor was gradually transmuted by Darwin into the natural selection hypothesis.

To summarize, the concept of development emerging from evolutionism was characterized by (a) continuity of historical change, (b) multidirectionality of evolution, (c) an ongoing or progressive character, and (d) creativity and emergence. As change and development became the universal principles of historical study, they came to be applied ever increasingly to the study of human societies and human individuals. If, as Darwin (in his *Expression of Emotions in Men and Animals*, published in 1871, and *Descent of Man*, published in

1872) and early comparative psychologists suggested, there was descriptive and explanatory continuity (i.e., homology) between human and animal at a given point in time, and if this continuity could be extended longitudinally through childhood, then the adult of the species was, at least in part, a product of the child. In this way, the early attempts at applying the concept of development to the study of individuals may be viewed as efforts to understand the child within the adult. Further, as several contemporary observers have noted, this understanding was neither motivated from nor designed to remain in purely academic strata (Cairns and Ornstein 1979, Reinert 1979). Rather, it was to be used to enhance the development of individuals (and, by implication, the species and society) by providing, for example, an optimal educational context. Indeed, it appears that some educational administrators and social planners, concerned with the large-scale education of a growing population of children, influenced this emergence.

3. Some Roots of the Contemporary Models of Development

In the previous section it was suggested that Darwinism supported, if not fostered, an interest in the study of behavioral ontogeny. It should be noted that Darwin (1877) himself conducted one of the earliest attempts at careful, observational ontogenetic study. His "Biographical sketch of an infant" was one of the better descriptive, idiographic child diaries to appear in the nineteenth century and certainly bolstered the practical and intellectual appeal of the connection between evolutionism and the individual-level genetic method.

The present section will describe how Darwinism served as a point of origin for five major modes of thought in contemporary developmental psychology. It will show how several early developmental psychologists drew a measure of sustenance from evolutionism and then turned to face the fresh demands of their own social or intellectual milieu. In so doing, the contributions of Darwinism were selected and molded to fit unwonted social, cultural, historical, and intellectual contingencies, as well as personal and political motivations. Darwinism proved to be sufficiently multifaceted and ambiguous to propagate developmental theories that very soon became relatively independent. It is apparent that, while contemporary developmental psychologies share to some extent a common antecedent influence, the early developmentalists exercised selective perception in their adaptation of both their immediate intellectual predecessors and the evolutionary model.

In the following précis, the fundamental assumptive features of five contemporary models or research traditions of developmental psychology—organicism, mechanism, psychoanalytic tradition, contextualism, dialecticism—are briefly described (Pepper 1942, Reese and Overton 1970). Following this, their patterns of development are depicted in the form of intellectual lineages among the major figures representing these models. The system of linkages, especially as they derive from nineteenth-century evolutionism, is of central concern. It should be noted that any given linkage may represent only a limited portion of the full explanation of the variance of any figure's thought. That is, if B is represented as influenced by A, it is suggested only that the portion of B's thought which is developmental in nature is influenced by a given portion of A's thought and is traceable to Darwinism. Finally, as it is not the intent to provide a full causal explanation of the thought of any given figure, only those influences most pertinent to the present discussion are noted.

3.1 Organicism

As described by Pepper (1942), (see also Reese and Overton 1970), the contemporary organismic model is patterned after the prevailing view of biological growth. That is, psychological development is thought to be goal directed and teleological in character. Developmental change is generally characterized as primarily qualitative rather than quantitative, and is unidirectional and irreversible. Following the emphasis on qualitative change, a stage pattern is often employed, thus resulting in a conception of development that is discontinuous and universal in sequence and pattern. The individual is seen as relatively active, constructing the relatively passive environment. From Darwin this line of thought moved via the early G. S. Hall (see below) and James Mark Baldwin (1861–1934) through Pierre Janet (1859–1947) to Jean Piaget (1896–1980) and Heinz Werner (1890–1964) (see Fig. 1).

There are two major intellectual sources to J. M. Baldwin's (1895) genetic psychology. He was fundamentally a Darwinian evolutionist but was also influenced by British Associationism. The former influence is manifested most positively in his devotion to a Darwinian psychology and, less positively, in his endorse-

ment of recapitulation theory. The latter influence is revealed in his stimulus–response system based on pleasure and pain. The child was thought to develop from the simple to the more complex, through first an instinctive biological stage, and second, a plastic or learning stage. The social system, especially the dialectical interactions between the child and the system, was a critical feature of ontogenesis (Cairns and Ornstein 1979). While some of Baldwin's ideas appear to be antithetical to organismic theory, his endorsement of the genetic method and leadership of the genetic psychology movement assures him a place in the history of organicism. Moreover, much of his work prefigures the assimilation–accommodation theory of Piaget. Indeed, the young Piaget was exposed to Baldwin's views on mental development via Edouard Claparède in Geneva.

Pierre Janet developed an historical clinical psychology. From this perspective, the life course was viewed as a succession of adaptive moments, each of which may influence the long-range adjustment of the individual. Hence, to understand the psychological conditions of adulthood, the investigator must explore the childhood and adolescent history. The mental life of the organism is seen as both active and passive (reflective). Piaget took courses from Janet and has noted that Janet had an active appreciation of Baldwin. Indeed, it may be through Janet that Piaget was most influenced by Baldwin (Cairns and Ornstein 1979, Piaget 1978).

Although Piaget's early work does not cite Baldwin, his later publications, as well as those of observers, contained ample acknowledgement of Baldwin's influence (Cairns and Ornstein 1979, Piaget 1978). Piaget took from Baldwin an interest in such processes as imitation and play. Further, the early work of Piaget contained some endorsement of a modified recapitulation theory. Like Baldwin, Piaget proposed a quali-

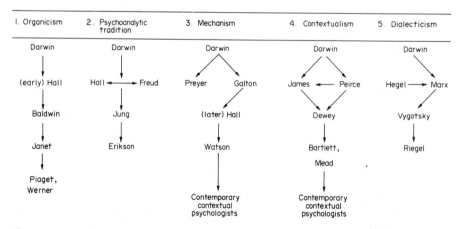

Figure 1
Heuristic scheme representing the Darwinian origins of five research conditions in contemporary developmental psychology

tative stage model of the development of the individual's interpretation of reality. In part, Piaget's genetic psychology was anticipated by Baldwin. Unlike Baldwin, however, early Piaget accorded less emphasis to the influence of the social environment on individual development. Because of Piaget's centrality in modern organismic theory, most of the introductory comments to this section are directly applicable to his present developmental psychology.

Werner's orthogenetic principle—that development proceeds from a lack of differentiation to increasing differentiation, integration, and hierarchic organization—was anticipated by Baldwin and supported by research in embryology. Werner's early work (*Introduction to Developmental Psychology*, first published in German in 1926) was influenced by the genetic–wholistic psychology of Felix Krueger (Baltes 1983). In keeping with his conviction that developmental theory was not systemizable, but rather a way of viewing behavior in general, Werner did not generate a methodical scheme of developmental psychology. In his later writing he considered recapitulation theory (in particular, G. S. Hall's version) and rejected it. He was, however, willing to accept a parallel between evolutionary development and ontogenetic development, but not a one-to-one correspondence. A discontinuous, qualitative stage model of development was proposed (as is characteristic of organicism) with the endpoint in the mature organism being stability or fixity. Further change may only take the form of regression.

3.2 Mechanism

The mechanistic model represents the organism as analogous to a machine in that it is composed of discrete parts interrelated by forces in a space–time field (Pepper 1942, Reese and Overton 1970). Developmental change is quantitative and continuous. The direction of development depends upon the level of stimulation, kind of stimulation, and history of the organism. The organism is viewed as relatively passive (or reactive), whereas the environment is relatively active. From Darwin this line of thought moved via Wilhelm Preyer (1842–1897) and Sir Francis Galton (1822–1911) to G. Stanley Hall (1846–1924) and John B. Watson (1878–1958) (see Fig. 1).

It is to Preyer (1882, 1893), Galton (1883), and Hall (1883) that the origin of the science of developmental psychology is usually traced. Preyer's early publication was the first book devoted to systematic consideration of the development of the mental faculties of the child, and the one to which responsibility for the advent of developmental psychology is often assigned (Hardesty 1976, Reinert 1979). Although much attention was devoted to patterns of physical development, Preyer also observed such psychological phenomena as reflexes, language, spatial knowledge, and memory. Preyer, a physiologist, trained in the scientific biological tradition and was interested in the development of both mind and body. In this way, while in somewhat the

same mold as Darwin's (1877) "Biographical sketch of an infant," Preyer's effort was, from a contemporary point of view, more ambitious. While Preyer (1893) upheld a basically voluntaristic position, the organism must exert some effort to overcome immediate environmental contingencies. Thus, development is seen as a struggle for freedom or emancipation. His principle of competition was inspired by Darwin, but differed in certain respects. Dennis (1972) notes that Preyer's method of response management anticipates much of the reinforcement theory of modern mechanistic psychology.

Galton's investigation of individual differences in psychology formed an intellectual bridge between Darwinian evolutionism and individual psychology. His well-known work on heredity (*Hereditary Genius*, 1869) formulated one of the basic issues of developmental psychology, namely, the nature–nurture question. Galton's consuming interest in this issue, however, was practical as well as theoretical, and thus led to the founding of eugenics, the applied science of heredity. In addition, his classic treatise on human development (Galton 1883) contained an array of essays anticipating both experimental and correlational developmental psychology. Galton's support of gemmule theory and his extreme view on the complete inheritance of mental traits may have reflected partly the political climate of the time.

With G. S. Hall, an American follower of Darwin, a former student of W. Wundt, and receiver of the first doctorate in psychology (under W. James) given in the United States, part of the mechanistic tradition was carried into the twentieth century. An ardent evolutionist and a strong proponent of recapitulation theory, Hall nevertheless placed considerable emphasis on environmental—especially social—factors in later ontogenesis. At separate points, recapitulation theory and environmental influences were incorporated into Hall's life-span perspective. Attempting to extend the work of previous developmentalists beyond childhood, Hall argued that until adolescence the developing child repeats (through both play and fear) the evolution of human society. However, during adolescence environmental factors rise in developmental significance (McCullers 1969). Indeed, one concession to Lamarckian evolution was Hall's belief that during adolescence genetic changes could be affected by the environment.

As a developmental psychologist, Hall lacked a systematic program of thought; in this respect, while his later work generally fits the mechanistic structure, his earlier, nativistic work is more consonant with organicism (Dixon and Lerner 1984). Hall's loose eclecticism is revealed by his attachment to correlational, experimental, and psychoanalytic traditions, in addition to his a priori dedication to the biogenetic law (Cairns and Ornstein 1979). With regard to the latter, Hall represents the peak of the influence of recapitulation theory in psychology; as it was being increasingly discredited in embryology, the foundation of its application to psychology was crumbling (Gould 1977).

Although John B. Watson is not normally identified as a developmental psychologist, he had a lasting impact on the emergence of behavioral or mechanistic developmental psychology. His atomistic, reductionist framework continues to influence the contemporary scene. His subsequent view of development as tantamount to cumulative learning could hardly be more in contrast with the biological, organismic view of Baldwin and Piaget. Today mechanism is represented by the work of such behavioral psychologists as Donald M. Baer, Sydney W. Bijou, and Charles C. Spiker.

3.3 Psychoanalytic Tradition

The dynamic psychology of Freud did not emerge until the last few years of the nineteenth century. A hydraulic model of humans is employed, and developmental change is qualitative, proceeding through tension resolution from one stage to the next. Generally, a direction of development is implied; that is, there is an endstate toward which development progresses. Regression is possible and in some cases frequent; but at any given state, psychological functions are fully determined. The focus of attention is on personality development (especially abnormal personality); little consideration is given to cognitive progression. An explicitly genetic method—primarily retrospective, autobiographical—is employed. This line of thought which may have been influenced by Darwin, and which received American assistance from G. S. Hall, moved from Sigmund Freud (1856–1939) to Carl Jung (1875–1961) (see Fig. 1).

Groffmann (1970) argues that, because psychoanalysts dealt primarily with pathological manifestations of adults, they were outsiders to the early developmental psychology tradition. While psychoanalysis may have been ostracized by mainstream American developmental psychology, McCullers (1969) suggests, however, that the reverse may not have been true; for example, Freud may have been influenced by G. S. Hall, especially in light of the former's active endorsement of recapitulation theory in such seminal works as *Totem and Taboo* (published in 1912–13), *Introductory Lectures on Psychoanalysis* (published in 1916), and *Moses and Monotheism* (published in 1939). On this latter point Gould (1977) argues more strongly: Freud was a devout adherent to the biogenetic law, in part because he was trained as a biologist when it reigned supreme, and in part, because of his unremitting Lamarckian perspective on evolution (and Lamarckism, more than Darwinism, justifies recapitulation theory). In addition, Groffmann (1970) pointed out that psychoanalysis brought the confrontive relationship between the individual and his/her social environment into focus in developmental research. It bears noting that such a characterization of environment–organism interaction (minus Lamarckian inheritance, of course) is not antithetical to Darwin's evolutionary theory. Certainly Freud adopted a genetic biographical approach to the

understanding of his preferred domain of psychological phenomena. In addition, psychoanalytic theory delineates two major mechanisms (fixation and regression) by which early events influence or determine later behavior (Cairns and Ornstein 1979).

Freud's psychosexual theory of development may be viewed as partly mechanistic and partly Darwinian (Groffmann 1970). Significant events (or confrontations) in the life course disposed the individual for particular developmental paths. The indirect Darwinian connection is further supported by noting one point in which Galton appears to have anticipated Freud. Galton (1883) described mental operations and incidents that may appear in childhood and then lie dormant for years, until roused to consciousness. Alternatively, permanent traces of these incidents may continually influence the development of mental operations throughout life. This notion, which appeared prior to Freud, bears a striking resemblance to the latter's theory of the unconscious. One other even more indirect linkage may be noted. Recall that it has been claimed that Darwin influenced Baldwin who in turn influenced Janet and Piaget. As it happens, Freud is another figure (albeit minor) in this equation, for he shared a direct intellectual ancestor with Janet: both Freud and Janet studied under Jean Martin Charcot (1825–1893) in Paris.

Jung's developmental psychology was more explicit, if not more refined, than Freud's. Jung, criticizing both Freud's model of psychosexual development (as too reductionistic) and the Christian view of personal transformation (as lacking applicability to rational modern man), proposed an individuation process consisting of four stages. This constitutes a rather teleological perspective: the goal of such development is the emergence of self. Jung, taking an explicit life-span perspective and also adopting a recapitulation view, may more closely parallel Hall than Freud. Jung, like Freud, was a lifelong supporter of recapitulation theory, although he made less theoretical use of it than Freud. For Jung, few psychopathologies were developed during the childhood period of recapitulation. As did Freud, Jung possessed a Galton connection. In his early work Jung employed the method of associative word reaction, which had been invented by Galton and Wundt. Whereas the latter two researchers were primarily interested in intellectual factors related to word association, Jung demonstrated that the affective dimension was also influential. Further, while Galton had pioneered the psychology of individual differences, Jung took what seemed to be a natural second step: he attempted to classify individuals into types based on selected key differences.

Modern psychoanalytic views of development are represented by Erik Erickson, who has developed a life-span theory of personality. His theory, revolving around a set of sequential psychosocial tasks (note again the confrontation between organism and environment), is also a stage theory. Presently this work informs an active research tradition that is increasingly accepted by mainstream developmental psychology.

3.4 Contextualism

The contextual model of developmental psychology is perhaps the least refined of the five presented in this article. As a philosophical position, however, it is one of the more advanced (Pepper 1942). Recently revived in psychology, it is now one of the more promising interpretive frameworks. Its basic metaphor is change or the historic event. In human psychology the Darwinian attentiveness to the continuing tension between the organism and its surroundings—in short, to the problem of adaptation—is embraced, but shifted slightly to include the interaction between the individual and the social and cultural environments. After Darwin this line of thought was held aloft by William James (1842–1910), Charles Sanders Peirce (1839–1914), and John Dewey (1859–1952), the major figures of pragmatic psychology (see Fig. 1).

James, while disenchanted with the deterministic, evolutionary psychology of Spencer (as in the latter's *Principles of Psychology*), was quite influenced by Darwin's natural selection theory of evolution. James' (1890) psychology was nonreductionistic in character; that is, he argued against the Wundtian analysis of mental events into more primitive parts or complexes. Experience consists of a stream of events, each of which possesses a unique quality or meaning. The novelty of each event is assured by the stream metaphor. The implication which James develops is that the meaning or significance of a mental event is inseparable from the context of its occurrence, which is itself in flux. Development is continuous, "without breach, crack, or division" (James 1890 p. 237); it is composed of quantitative differences rather than qualitatively distinct stages. His approach to psychology may be characterized as historical in that "mental reaction on every given thing is really a resultant of our experience of the whole world up to that date" (1890 p. 234).

As had Darwin, James viewed the human mind as both dynamic (active) and functional, continuously involved in the process of adaptation to a changing ecology. Both James and Peirce sought to infuse the developmental stream (at the individual, phyletic, and cosmological levels) with the element of chance (for instance, Peirce's tychism), so integral to the Darwinian hypothesis. While eschewing the directional or teleological focus of Lamarckian evolutionists and psychologists, the early contextualists were nevertheless historical in method. According to the Darwinian interpretation, a chance event, while not wholly determined by the past, does reflect the character of preceding events. In this way both novelty and developmental continuity are maintained.

To John Dewey's classic paper, "The reflex arc concept in psychology" (1896), the functional approach to psychology is often dated. However, in his *Psychology* (1887) he had already demonstrated a strong dynamic orientation to the study of mental phenomena. At this time, however, Dewey was still casting developmental questions in the framework of a Hegelian telos. Nevertheless, in the early twentieth century Dewey fell under the influence of Darwinism and his subsequent psychological writings stressed the genetic method, the continuous model of developmental change, as well as the Darwinian view of the dynamic organism–environment transaction. Like James, Dewey offered a relatively active organism (and active environment) model of this transaction. In addition, it should be noted that Dewey attributed the discovery of the historical or genetic method to Darwin.

No modern contextual developmental psychologist has produced a system as complete as that of James or, for that matter, even Dewey and Peirce. Indeed, except for the work of F. C. Bartlett (1886–1969) and perhaps George Herbert Mead (1863–1931), and related work in dialectical psychology, contextual developmental psychology appears to have lain dormant for much of this century. Since the early 1970s, however, numerous psychologists have rediscovered contextual thinking and have attempted to articulate its methodological implications for both cognitive (for instance, James J. Jenkins) and personality (for instance, Theodore R. Sarbin) processes. In addition, contemporary efforts by such researchers as Urie Bronfenbrenner to decipher the ecology of human development bear a conceptual relationship to this approach.

3.5 Dialecticism

The dialectical materialism of the nineteenth century has significantly influenced a modern approach to developmental psychology. Under the contemporary dialectical model, the basic metaphor appears to be contradiction or conflict (Riegel 1979). As is the case with the contextual model, the activities of the individual are viewed as being in dynamic interaction with the activities of the environment. The individual, like the society, develops through a continuous process of thesis, antithesis, and synthesis. This model has its principal roots in both the social philosophy of G. W. F. Hegel (1770–1831) and Karl Marx (1818–1883), and the evolutionary biology of the nineteenth century. This culminates in the dialectical model of development psychology of the Russian Lev S. Vygotsky (1896–1934) and, more recently in America, the model of Klaus F. Riegel (1925–1977).

While both Hegel and Marx lacked a specific program of individual development, their views on, in the first instance, ideational change and, in the second, social change have been adapted to the individual–psychological level. Hegel was unquestionably an influence on Marx, although in certain respects his ideas were rejected by the much younger revolutionary. For the purposes of this article, the important point of commonality is the dialectic itself. The influence of Darwin on Marx is difficult to assess, but it is known that the latter was, at certain stages, greatly impressed with the accomplishments of the former. Several scholars have debated whether Marx went so far as to offer to dedicate

Das Kapital to the evolutionist. Nevertheless, it is known that Marx warmly inscribed a copy of the second edition of his magnum opus to Darwin. In addition, Marx's own intellectual companion, Friedrich Engels (1820–1895), vividly portrayed the intellectual kinship of Darwin and Marx in his own notes given at the graveside of Marx.

In point of fact, however, Marx's own evolutionism may have more closely resembled Spencer's or Lamarck's than Darwin's, especially with regard to the Marxist goal directedness of historical change. Nevertheless, both Darwin and Marx shared a concern, emerging on multiple fronts in the nineteenth century with temporality, historicity, and development. It is this shared fundamental concern that in part forms a critical link.

After the Bolshevik revolution in 1917, dialectical psychology in the Soviet Union burgeoned. The most influential of these dialectical developmentalists was Vygostky. Through his students and colleagues (for instance A. R. Luria, S. L. Rubinstein) a strongly Marxist approach to psychology was developed. Among other features, this psychology may be characterized as teleological, cultural, and possessing an active organism model. For both intellectual and political reasons, dialectical developmental psychology was not until recently a noticeable, much less a prominent, force on the American scene. Thus, there is little explicit linkage between Marx and American developmental psychology until after the mid-twentieth century. Riegel, the leading figure in contemporary American developmental dialectics, describes three laws of developmental change based on Marxist theory: (a) the unity and opposition of contradictory principles and their resolution through synthesis; (b) the possibility of transforming basic quantitative change into qualitative change; and (c) the negation of a negation, or the continual process of replacing the old by the new. Developmental psychology is viewed dialectically as the study of the changing individual in a changing world. The utility of the methods involved in a dialectical approach to the empirical study of human development have been debated, but much recent cross-cultural work in developmental psychology has successfully applied pertinent techniques and modes of interpretation.

4. Conclusions

Together the five research traditions described above represent the bulk of research and theory in contemporary human development. Other possible divisions of the contemporary scene—for instance into age-related regions of study, or even into areas defined by the target process—are to some extent subsumed by the present delineation. In recent years the life-span movement in developmental psychology has attained a currency that cuts across both age regions and processes; in this orientation, research is often characterized in terms of metatheoretical position. Recently, this latter movement has been one of the fastest growing research orientations in developmental psychology. Major proponents of this approach include Paul B. Baltes, John R. Nesselroade, and K. Warner Schaie.

This overview of the history of developmental psychology has been necessarily brief. Nevertheless, the compendium of intellectual lineages originating in the nineteenth century may serve a heuristic purpose on at least two levels of analysis. First, it may serve as an orienting feature for future reading in the history of human development. Second, it demonstrates that the history of this discipline is complex and interactive. Darwinism, steeped as it was in its own sociohistorical context, supported the emergence of ontogenetic behavioral research and, eventually, the institutionalization of developmental psychology. Insofar as it emphasized general underlying issues pertaining to ontogeny—and, significantly, insofar as it was sufficiently fertile and grandiose to propagate developmental theories that eventually became relatively independent—it provided an early orienting point for understanding the history of this discipline.

Bibliography

Baldwin J M 1895 *Mental Development in the Child and the Race: Methods and Processes.* Macmillan, New York

Baltes P B 1983 Life-span developmental psychology: Observations on theory and history revisited. In: Lerner R M (ed.) 1983 *Developmental Psychology: Historical and Philosophical Perspectives.* Erlbaum, Hillsdale, New Jersey

Cairns R B, Ornstein P A 1979 Developmental psychology. In: Hearst E (ed.) 1979 *The First Century of Experimental Psychology.* Erlbaum, Hillsdale, New Jersey

Darwin C 1877 A biographical sketch of an infant. *Mind* 2: 285–94

Dennis W (ed.) 1972 *Historical Readings in Developmental Psychology.* Appleton-Century-Crofts, New York

Dixon R A, Lerner R M 1984 A history of developmental psychology. In: Lamb M E, Bornstein M H (eds.) 1984 *Developmental Psychology: An Advanced Textbook.* Erlbaum, Hillsdale, New Jersey

Galton F 1883 *Inquiries into Human Faculty and its Development.* Macmillan, London

Gould S J 1977 *Ontogeny and Phylogeny.* Harvard University Press, Cambridge, Massachusetts

Groffmann K S 1970 Life-span developmental psychology in Europe: Past and present. In: Goulet L R, Baltes P B (eds.) 1970 *Life-span Developmental Psychology: Research and Theory.* Academic Press, New York

Hall G S 1883 The contents of children's minds. *Princeton Rev.* 11: 249–72

Hardesty F P 1976 Early European contributions to developmental psychology. In: Riegel K F, Meacham J A (eds.) 1976 *The Developing Individual in a Changing World.* Aldine, Chicago, Illinois

James W 1890 *The Principles of Psychology,* Vol. 1. Dover, New York

McCullers J C 1969 G. Stanley Hall's conception of mental development and some indications of its influence on developmental psychology. *Am. Psychol.* 24: 1109–14

Pepper S C 1942 *World Hypotheses: A Study in Evidence.* University of California Press, Berkeley, California

Piaget J 1978 *Behavior and Evolution.* Pantheon, New York

Preyer W 1882 *Die Seele des Kindes: Beobachtungen über die Geistige Entwicklung des Menschen in den Ersten Lebens Jahr.* Grieben, Leipzig

Preyer W 1893 *Mental Development in the Child.* Appleton, New York

Reese H W, Overton W F 1970 Models of development and theories of development. In: Goulet L R, Baltes P B (eds.) 1970 *Life-span Developmental Psychology: Research and Theory.* Academic Press, New York

Reinert G 1979 Prolegomena to a history of life-span developmental psychology. In: Baltes P B, Brim O G Jr (eds.) 1979 *Life-span Development and Behavior*, Vol. 2. Academic Press, New York

Riegel K F 1979 *Foundations of Dialectical Psychology.* Academic Press, New York

Toulmin S E, Goodfield J 1965 *The Discovery of Time.* University of Chicago Press, Chicago, Illinois

Genetics and Human Development

A. P. Matheny and R. S. Wilson

The importance of information about genetics for child rearing, education, and counseling should be apparent, since an understanding of the role of heredity in development helps parents, teachers, and counselors to set reasonable expectations for children's growth and performance. Furthermore, such information suggests what sorts of interventions in the growth process are likely to promote desired development.

Understanding of human development has often concentrated on the main developmental themes as depicted by the use of developmental norms, milestones, or more elaborately, stage concepts. The developmental prototype offered by these themes characterizes the human species and serves as a reference for developmental expectations. At the same time, individual variations around the human developmental prototype are equally important, and it is to these variations that genetic explanations are offered as having an important role.

Recent advances in human behavioral genetics have revitalized an interest in a conceptual framework that places genetics as a shaping influence throughout the entire course of development. The purpose of this article is to outline general principles of genetics that underly developmental processes. Because the scope of human genetics is quite broad in its scientific and applied aspects, only the general conceptual framework for understanding the principles of human genetics, and particularly human behavioral genetics as it pertains to development, will be provided. In addition, the citation of specific findings will be selective rather than exhaustive.

1. Basic Concepts

Genetics refers to a branch of the sciences which examines the storage, transmission, and actualization of biologic information with structural, functional, and developmental consequences for related living organisms. The gene is the element for considering the information transmitted, through heredity, as well as the storage and actualization of that information. Human genetics is primarily directed toward understanding genetic influences on humans although, for obvious reasons, a great deal of that understanding has been accomplished by studying infrahuman organisms.

It is possible to examine genetics according to two approaches or paradigms. The first approach is attributed to Mendel (1866) who demonstrated by selective breeding of plants, that it is possible to produce or remove the observable evidence of specific characteristics or traits: the phenotype. This particular emphasis is often referred to as qualitative genetics because the quality of the observed characteristic—phenotype—has a fairly straightforward connection with the inferred underlying genetic complex—the genotype—from which the observed phenotype has derived.

The second approach is associated with Galton (1869) who favored a statistical or biometric approach in order to demonstrate that there are traits that continuously vary and, by inference, the phenotype is the product of small contributions from many genes. The statistical study of genetics is referred to as a quantitative approach. These two approaches are not mutually exclusive and the basic concepts of genetics apply to both.

The fundamental unit of genetics is the gene which is now recognized as a "coded" combination of 20 amino acids: the deoxyribonucleic acids (DNA). Genes are located on chromosomes. Two or more alternate forms of genes (alleles) are found at the same position (locus) on two matching chromosomes—one obtained from each parent. For any given locus on a chromosome, the offspring receives only one gene allele from each parent even though each parent has two alleles available for transmission. When the parent's germ cells (sperm or ova) were initially formed, each cell received only one allele from the available pair of genes, as determined by chance. This same random division of alleles from each pair extends throughout the entire gene complement for the parent, effectively subdividing all pairs of alleles into separate germ cells.

During inheritance, therefore, the allele contributed by each parent becomes segregated from the other allele of that parent (law of segregation). If the new combination of the two segregated alleles, one contri-

17

buted by each parent, is made up of equivalent alleles, the offspring is a homozygote for that form of the gene. However, when the recombined alleles are different, the offspring is a heterozygote.

In the heterozygote condition, the offspring does not express both forms phenotypically, but rather one form or the other. The form expressed is called a dominant and the form unexpressed is called a recessive. The expression of one allele rather than the other allele is in terms of the phenotype; at the genotype level, there has been no alteration in the basic genetic material.

In effect, the phenotypes observed are only the manifest alleles that override others, but there are many alleles unexpressed phenotypically and these have the potential to be transmitted to subsequent offspring. Individuals possessing unexpressed alleles for a given trait are known as carriers for that trait, and essentially, all humans are carriers for one specific trait or another.

The Mendelian law of segregation applies to the separation of alleles responsible for one trait (monohybrid). A second Mendelian law—the law of independent assortment—applies to the inheritance of two or more traits (e.g., dihybrid or trihybrid). In these instances, the alleles responsible for each trait follow the law of segregation with the added provision that the alleles for each gene segregate or assort independently of the other gene(s). With some exceptions (as in the linkages), the segregation of alleles for one gene does not influence the segregation of alleles for other genes; the assortment for each is random.

The usual traits to which these rules apply are dichotomous in that they are phenotypically present or absent, as demonstrated, for example, by the classical approach of studying human pedigrees. Such studies have led to the detection and isolation of a number of traits, many of which are important because of their consequences, as diseases, for limiting "normal" human development. Several examples of these dominant and recessive diseases are listed in Table 1. A more comprehensive list can be found in McKusick (1978).

Most of the traits listed in Table 1 involve a single gene being responsible for a known specific enzyme defect. The term "inborn errors of metabolism," coined by Garrod (1923), describes a group of familial diseases

Table 1
Examples of dominant and recessive traits relevant to behavioral development

Trait	Heredity	Behavioral consequences
Crouzon's syndrome	Dominant	Mental retardation
Huntington's chorea	Dominant	Chronic degeneration of central nervous system affecting motor and mental behaviors
Tuberous sclerosis	Dominant	Mental retardation
Behr syndrome	Recessive	Mental retardation
Galactosemia	Recessive	Mental and motor developmental retardation
Gargoylism (Hurler's syndrome)	Recessive	Progressive mental deterioration; epilepsy
Histidinemia	Recessive	Mental retardation; speech defects
Homocystinuria	Recessive	Mental retardation; deafness; personality disorder
Phenylketonuria	Recessive	Mental retardation; neurological problems; personality disorder; epilepsy
Tay-Sachs disease	Recessive	Progressive neurologic deterioration; personality disorder
Wilson disease	Recessive	Personality disorder
Hyperuricemia	Sex-linked recessive	Psychomotor retardation; personality disorder
Menke's syndrome	Sex-linked recessive	Chronic degeneration of the central nervous system progressing to profound mental retardation
Retinitis pigmentosa	Sex-linked recessive	Behavioral limitations secondary to narrowing of visual fields and blindness

in which the absence or deficiency of an enzyme leads to an impairment in the normal sequence of metabolic processes.

Table 1 also provides examples of sex-linked recessive disorders in which the dominant and recessive phenotypes are associated with genes located on the sex-determining chromosomes. The known sex-linked disorders almost invariably are found for the female or X chromosome, rather than the male or Y chromosome. At fertilization, the female contributes only X chromosomes and the male contributes either an X or a Y chromosome, resulting in a female or male offspring respectively.

It is easy to see that if the female contributes an X chromosome with the phenotypically recessive gene and the male contributes a Y chromosome (which has no allele for that gene), then the offspring will be a male with a phenotypic expression of the recessive gene. In these instances, there is no allele available to override the recessive. In order for female offspring to have the recessive phenotype, the X-connected allele for the recessive must be contributed by the female parent (a carrier), and the male parent. As a consequence, the recessive phenotype is more frequently found among male offspring.

It is interesting to note that most of the human disorders involving single genes are accompanied by impairments of cognitive development and many are accompanied by stunting of physical stature. Combinations of traits attributed to the effect of single genes are considered within the context of genetic pleiotropism.

2. Pleiotropism

With evidence from studies of abnormalities such as those in Table 1, as well as studies of normal traits, it has been demonstrated that there are multiple phenotypic effects from the actions of a single gene. Focusing on abnormalities, one sees that a single gene defect is not expressed in a target anomaly but in a host of anomalies, which in combination constitute the disease syndrome. The multiple effects of a single gene are termed pleiotropy.

The immediate single, specific product of a single gene is an enzyme. In turn, that enzyme will participate in a series of reactions, each of which may have far-reaching functional and structural consequences. Because the sequence of events occurs developmentally over a period of time during which widely disparate organs and tissues become differentiated, the effect of a single gene may promulgate physical or behavioral effects whose relations are not readily apparent.

For example, among mice strains there is an apparent pleiotropic effect linking albinism and higher levels of emotionality as mediated through the visual system. Among humans, the single gene associated with phenylketonuria (PKU) has an effect on a metabolic pathway. During development, this pathway is associated with a variety of evolving systems that, at the highest level of phenotypic measurement, include as their product stunted stature, lighter pigmentation of hair and skin, and intellectual deficits.

Phenotypic correlations as evidence of pleiotropic gene effects should be surveyed with caution, however. Correlated traits derive from a common relation to a single gene, but they can also appear because mating is nonrandom. If individuals high on one trait tend to mate with individuals high on another trait, but without regard to rank order on the first, there will appear to be a correlation between two traits that, in fact, may not be influenced by a single gene.

Two or more traits may also appear correlated because they have a common response to environmental variations, such as improvement of diet and health practices or the like. Similar phenotypes may differ genotypically, and there are instances in which environmental agents can produce phenocopies of phenotypes known to be produced by genes. In these regards, one must be particularly cautious in interpreting correlated human behaviors as representing pleiotropisms.

3. Chromosome Anomalies

Abnormalities in human chromosomal material are a unique aspect of the genetic effects on human development because they represent many genes at the affected chromosome. Therefore they do not represent the qualitative paradigm, but at the same time, the phenotypic expression of chromosomal abnormalities tends to appear in an all-or-none fashion.

In the human there are 46 chromosomes, of which 44—the autosomes—are constituted in 22 pairs of like or homologous chromosomes. The other two chromosomes are sex chromosomes. Two X chromosomes are found for the phenotypic female, an X and a Y chromosome represent the phenotypic male.

Anomalous conditions for any of the 22 pairs of autosomes and the two sex chromosomes can occur; however, among live borns, the most common chromosomal abnormalities are represented by partial or complete trisomies. In these cases there is an extra partial or complete chromosome in one of the 22 pairs, or there is an extra X or Y chromosome. For example, there may be an extra chromosome in the 21st pair of chromosomes and this is called Trisomy 21 or Down Syndrome. Among live borns, trisomies have only been identified for a few of the 22 pairs of autosomes; presumably it is lethal in most cases (see Table 2).

For the sex chromosomes, extra chromosomes can be found for both phenotypic males or females. There have been phenotypic females who have had more than two X chromosomes (up to five Xs) and there have been phenotypic males with more than the single X and Y chromosomes. In the latter case, phenotypic males with the following sex-chromosome complements have been detected: XXXY, XXXXY, XXYY, XYY, and XXXXYY. The most common sex chromosome anomaly for phenotypic

Table 2
Major chromosomal abnormalities and their behavioral consequences

Type of abnormality	Behavioral consequences
Trisomy 22	Severe mental retardation
Trisomy 21 (Down Syndrome)	Developmental retardation in varying degrees (median IQ is 40–50); less difficult temperament
Trisomy 18	Severe retardation
Trisomy 13	Severe retardation
Trisomy 9	Severe retardation
Trisomy 8	Severe retardation
Cri-du-chat (deletion of the short arm of chromosome 5)	Severe retardation
XXY (Klinefelter's syndrome)	IQ levels from the mildly retarded to normal range; evidence of dyslexia; behavioral problems including those involving sexual development
XXXY, XXXXY, XXYY, XXXYY — Klinefelter variants	Severe to mild mental retardation
XO (Turner's syndrome)	Slightly depressed general IQ scores; specific spatial difficulties including space-form blindness, deficits in perceptual–spatial organization; mild deficits in arithmetical reasoning
XXX, XXXX, XXXXX — Extra-X syndromes	Distribution of IQ scores ranges from the normal to severely retarded ranges of intelligence. Generally, intelligence is in the retarded range
XYY	Mean IQ in the 80 to 90 range

males is XXY or Klinefelter's syndrome. Among all of the conditions with extra chromosomal material, there is an increased severity of behavioral and physical symptoms as genetic material is increased.

Partial or complete deletion of chromosomal material represents another class of chromosome anomalies. Complete deletion of one of the autosomes is considered lethal; however a partial deletion of the chromosome material of the fifth chromosomal pair has been found for a specific syndrome called "cri-du-chat" because of the cat-like cry of affected children. These children have severe limitations for developing normally.

Complete deletion of an X chromosome among females has been found; the single X chromosome—symbolized by XO—is called Turner's syndrome, which involves abnormalities in the development of sex characteristics. Female patients with Turner's syndrome do not have appreciable retardation in general cognitive development, but it has been discovered that they have a specific deficit involving spatial skills as measured on perceptual–cognitive tests (Money 1968).

The effects of chromosome anomalies can be com-plicated by the presence of mosaicism in which some cells have one chromosome complement and other cells have a different complement. Most typically, the mosaic individual has a normal chromosome complement in some cells, but a sex-chromosome anomaly in other cells. Mosaic individuals typically have higher IQs.

Extensive research on remedial programs and developmental outcomes has been reported for chromosomal abnormalities. Almost all of the abnormalities are featured by general or specific deficits in cognitive development, and Table 2 summarizes the general behavioral consequences of the major chromosomal abnormalities.

4. Quantitative Genetics

The relation between single genes, or one chromosome with many genes, and abnormal phenotypes does not necessarily mean that the genes in question are responsible for the normal development of the phenotype. Rather, it is possible to consider these isolable genetic defects as impeding or blocking the systematic contribution from a number of other genes, each of which adds a genetic increment to the individual's total phenotype.

Even when the anomalous gene is responsible for errors in the progression toward the normal phenotype, some (although markedly reduced) variation in the total phenotype of the affected person can still exist. For example, all individuals with PKU are not exactly alike in every respect, and in a small number of cases, individuals with biochemical evidence of PKU can be of average or higher intelligence. Within the most serious genetic defects, some individual variability can be detected. It is to this variability from many genetic sources that quantitative approaches are applied. These approaches are particularly useful for the study of human behavior genetics, which does not readily permit isolation of genetic strains and control of environmental conditions. In these instances, individual differences in behavior are almost the basic unit of data because the classical analytical methods suitable for studying qualitative effects are not applicable.

The quantitative—biometric—methods applied to polygenically determined traits make use of statistical procedures, many of which are familiar to investigators of human behavior. The major focus of the procedures is upon variance, a statistical expression representing the difference or deviation of scores from the mean score in a population of scores. For such human characteristics as physical stature, blood pressure, intellectual skills and the like, one establishes the sum of the individual deviations from the average score.

The sum of the deviations, adjusted for the size of the population measured, is the phenotypic variation, or P, which represents three sources: genetic or G, environment or E, and an interaction or $G \leftrightarrow E$ between the two. The general theoretical expression, therefore, is $P = G + E + (G \leftrightarrow E)$, plus some error of measurement. After the expression is put in terms of variance, the subsequent steps involve partitioning the total variance, that is, the phenotypic variance, into different components which may differ according to mathematical models and assumptions employed (Falconer 1960, Kempthorne 1957, Mather 1949).

None of the terms in the general expression provided above can be determined by measuring a single individual; populations of individuals differing in the degree of genetic relationship and in the range of living environments are studied to obtain the estimates of variance needed for each term of the expression. Because varying degrees of genetic relationships are directly ascertained and variations in environment are often not, estimates of genetic variance are more typically reported. These estimates are based on studying twins, other family members, and biologically unrelated members within families.

4.1 Twin Studies

Galton suggested that the measure of twins would be useful for examining genetic effects. Since then, the twin method has been a key source of data for human genetics (Vandenberg 1966). The basic method is dependent on the fact that identical or monozygotic (MZ) twins originate from the division of one fertilized egg into two identical replicas. By contrast, fraternal or dizygotic (DZ) twins originate from the fertilization of two separate eggs. Monozygotic twins are clones in that they are genetically identical; dizygotic twins, either of the same or opposite sex, are not genetically identical and share, on average, about one-half of their genes in common.

The twin method capitalizes on the genetic difference between monozygotic and dizygotic twins, the potential similarities of prenatal and postnatal environmental influences upon both members of each pair, and the fact that differences within monozygotic twin pairs must be due to nongenetic factors. General limitations of the measures obtained by the twin method are due to potential differences between twins and nontwins for the trait being studied, and differences between the environments of monozygotic and dizygotic twins. The severity of these limitations is often debated; however, they do not nullify the power and advantages of the twin method (Husén 1959).

Twin studies of a host of behavioral traits have been reported, but the studies of intelligence represent the largest series. Table 3 provides correlations for twins as well as correlations from other pairings of related and unrelated individuals. The discrepancies between the average correlations reported from a series of studies and the expected genetic correlations are usually interpreted in terms of environmental influences. For example, the average dizygotic correlation of 0.62 is higher than the average genetic correlation of 0.50, and the increment is often attributed to the influence of a common environment in which the twins are raised. By contrast, the average monozygotic correlation is less than 1.00, and the decrement is attributed to differences in environmental effects plus measurement error.

4.2 Other Familial Pairings

Genetically, siblings have the same degree of relationship as dizygotic twins, and they are raised in the same family, but they lack the continuous experience of twinness that may enforce greater similarity among twins. Sibling–sibling correlations are valuable in controlling for this effect while holding others constant, but it is critical that the siblings be matched for age and type of test when measured. Otherwise, variation from these sources may confound the actual differences within sibling pairs. Parent–offspring correlations are particularly susceptible to effects that may accrue from differences in age and in type of test.

Studies of adopted children provide an estimate of environmental and genetic effects, whether the correlations have been obtained for parents and adopted offspring, or for unrelated children reared together in the same family. When the parents and children or siblings are unrelated, the correlations directly reflect environmental effects; however, selective placement of

Table 3
Familial correlations for intelligence[a]

	Average correlation found	Correlation expected
Monozygotic twins reared together	0.86	1.00
Monozygotic twins reared apart	0.72	1.00
Dizygotic twins reared together:	0.60	0.50
Same-sex	0.62	0.50
Opposite-sex	0.57	0.50
Siblings reared together	0.47	0.50
Half-siblings	0.31	0.25
Sibling pairs (one adopted, one maternal)	0.29	0.00
Sibling pairs (both adopted)	0.34	0.00
Single parent—offspring reared together	0.42	0.50
Adopting parent—offspring	0.19	0.00
Parent—parent	0.33	0.00

a After Bouchard and McGue 1981

children would tend to inflate the effects of family environment per se.

Finally, the parent–parent correlation for IQ represents the effects of assortative mating, and to the extent that these correlations are greater than zero, the common genetic variance within families tends to be estimated higher.

Average correlations for all of these pairings are also provided in Table 3. In general, the pattern of the averaged correlations is consistent with a polygenic model applied to measures of intelligence. Equally important, the averaged correlations indicate that environmental effects enter into the pattern as well. Precise estimates of the genetic effect on intelligence are not possible from these summarized data or others

(Erlenmeyer-Kimling and Jarvik 1963, Plomin and DeFries 1980) because there is marked heterogeneity among the correlations from one study to the next.

Behavioral measures which correlate with IQ scores also reflect the same trends as demonstrated by the data from twin studies. Table 4 displays the monozygotic and dizygotic correlations for several studies of academic achievement. Again, parental education and IQ, as well as social class, are known to correlate with education of offspring. Because there is assortative mating for education, the correlations in Table 4 are also confounded to some degree by genetic and environmental effects. Detailed examination of these issues can be found in Vogel and Motulsky (1979).

The pair correlations shown in Tables 3 and 4 illus-

Table 4
Twin studies of academic achievement

Test of achievement	Within-pair correlations: Identical	Fraternal	Source
Reading			
Stanford Achievement Word Meaning	0.86	0.56	Newman et al. (1937)
Sweden Achievement	0.89	0.62	Husén (1960)
Sweden Achievement	0.77	0.50	Husén (1963)
National Merit Test:			Loehlin and Nichols (1976)
English usage	0.74	0.57	
Word usage	0.85	0.64	
California Achievement-total	0.89	0.61	Matheny and Dolan (1974)
Mathematics			
Sweden Achievement	0.82	0.61	Husén (1963)
National Merit Test	0.88	0.54	Loehlin and Nichols (1976)
South Australian Intermediate Examination-Mathematics	0.85 (estimate)	0.42 (estimate)	Martin (1975)

trate the trend for pair similarities to vary according to genotypic similarity. The correlations are not direct indications of the observed variance attributed to heredity. For those indications, two statistical terms are often employed. The most cited term is narrow-sense heritability or h^2, a statistic that describes the ratio of specific genotypic variance to phenotypic variance for a measured characteristic. The specific genotypic variance is additive variance: that part issuing from the cumulative influence of single genes transmitted from parent to offspring. Therefore, estimates of h^2, based on monozygotic and dizygotic twins or other relatives, take into account the degree of relation among the individuals.

Heritability in the broad sense (the degree of genetic determination) takes into account the proportion of phenotypic variance attributed to genotypic variance from all sources: additive, dominance, and interaction between alleles at different loci. The distinction between these two expressions for genotypic variance, as well as their quantitative derivations from twins and other family resemblances, can be found in several references (Cattell 1953, 1960, Falconer 1960, Fulker 1979, Kempthorne 1957, Lush 1949, McClearn and DeFries 1973).

The choice between using heritability in the narrow sense or heritability in the broad sense to estimate genetic influence is problematic. Narrow-sense heritability has more practical consequences for selective breeding of a given character; therefore, it is often employed in studies where experimental controls are more exact and one can determine to what extent traits can be made to "breed true."

Broad-sense heritability, on the other hand, takes into account all sources of genetic variation that might be reflected in phenotypic variation; consequently, it also permits an estimate of phenotypic variation not explained by genetic influences. In effect, it is possible to use broad-sense heritability to estimate the degree of environmental determination as well. For human development, these estimates are of intrinsic interest, particularly when one tries to ascertain the relative extent to which genetics and environment contribute to variations in behavioral development over the entire life span.

5. Genes and Development

Heretofore, discussion of genetic influences on human behavior largely concentrated on the connections between genotypic variations and individual differences at specific points in the life span. Provocative questions remain, however. One of those questions concerns the timing of gene action—all genes are present at conception, but they do not all act simultaneously during development, and many only become expressed in the phenotype at later points in the life span. Apparently, the genetic information transmitted at conception has a long temporal reach, and many aspects of that influence have been traced by noting the similarities in time of

onset for health problems among adult monozygotic twins (Gedda 1951).

This fact of timed gene action has led to the recognition that the core feature of development is the process by which the genetic material in a single fertilized egg ultimately transforms that cell into a multibillion-cell organism of extraordinary differentiation and detail. In this perspective, development is a continuous dynamic process, with episodes of differentiation and growth being switched on and off in accordance with instructions in the genetic program. Insofar as these manifold growth processes are regulated by programs in the genetic code, the resultant behaviors that emerge during childhood must be guided by the same processes.

The implications for behavioral development are far reaching. One influential model has been proposed by Waddington (1957, 1962, 1971, 1975), and his concepts have been profitably employed by other investigators in child development and behavior genetics (Fishbein 1976, Gottesman 1974, McClearn 1970, Scarr-Salapatek 1976, Wilson 1978).

Waddington (1971) remarks on two important features of developmental concepts: first, that such concepts must be ones that involve progressive change over time, or pathways of development; and second, that such pathways are resistant to modification and tend to resume their original course even if deflected. The latter property is often referred to as canalization, a measure of how deeply ingrained a behavior pattern has become during the course of evolution, and how self-correcting it is in the face of disturbances.

Canalization means that certain patterns of behavior are easily, almost inevitably, acquired by all humans under the normal circumstances of life. Such behaviors come with a high degree of preorganization and priming laid down in the brain structure by evolution, and they are actuated in straightforward fashion except in the most extreme circumstances. The acquisition of language is one illustration of a routinely developed capability which depends upon brain structures unique to *Homo sapiens*, and which consistently unfolds except in the most severe circumstances. At a broader level, the growth of mental functions proceeds through successive stages of complexity from infancy to adulthood, and in accordance with a timetable which is consistent for all species members.

In addition to the strong main trend for the species, however, there are marked individual differences in the rate of development and the timing of particular phases. The variation among individuals is most clearly revealed by the timing of the adolescent growth spurt, but these variations ramify throughout every phase of development, physical and behavioral. Patterns of acceleration or delay in growth, of precocity or lag in mental development, may reflect the switching on and off of gene-action systems in accordance with a distinctive schedule for each child.

These points can be illustrated by data for five characteristics measured periodically during the first 6 years

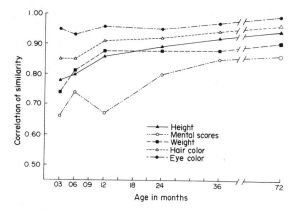

Figure 1
Monozygotic-pair correlations of simlarity for five measured traits of twins aged 3 to 72 months (Matheny and Wilson 1980)

of life. The characteristics are height, weight, hair color, eye color, and twins' mental scores. All of these characteristics provide individual differences at a given age, and for the pattern of changes across ages. Moreover, these characteristics are not likely to share the same degree of canalization. Figure 1 provides the degree of similarity for identical twins' measures at each age; Fig. 2 presents the same material for fraternal twins.

The within-pair correlations for monozygotic and dizygotic twins indicate that the genotypic influences vary according to the trait being measured, and the age of measurement. Thus, genetically influenced similarities for all of the traits are not equivalent; and, from age to age, the genetic correlations are not stably repeated. But, keeping in mind that there are age-to-age changes for each of the traits, it is apparent that there is a gradual increase in monozygotic similarity, which shows the developmental synchronization of

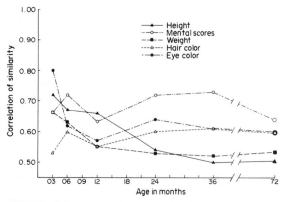

Figure 2
Dizygotic-pair correlations of similarity for five measured traits of twins aged 3 to 72 months (Matheny and Wilson 1980)

change for the monozygotic pairs. Interestingly, estimates of narrow-sense heritability as calculated from the difference between the monozygotic and dizygotic correlations would therefore appear to fluctuate from age to age, because these estimates do not take into account the genetic influence on developmental changes.

Wilson (1978) has presented extensive data from twin pairs to illustrate the genetic influence on the spurts and lags in mental development and physical stature. The spurts and lags were demonstrated by the age-to-age deflections—increases and decreases—as shown by the profile of scores obtained for each twin. The next step concerned the match of the profile of scores for monozygotic twins and for dizygotic twins; and a genetic influence was established by showing that the monozygotic-profile correlations were significantly higher than the dizygotic-profile correlations.

Figure 3 illustrates the profiles of scores for three monozygotic pairs measured several times during the

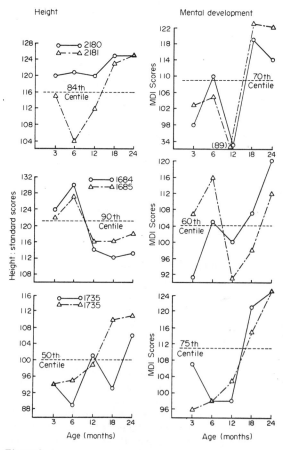

Figure 3
Standardized scores for longitudinal measures of height and mental development for three monozygotic twin pairs (Wilson 1981)

first 2 years of life. It should be noted that there are age-to-age changes in both height and mental scores, and that there is some congruity in the profiles generated by each of the twins in a pair. The trajectory of these developmental pathways seems to be genetically influenced.

Because these paths represent infancy, a time of great change, it can be supposed that similar demonstrations can be made during other periods of developmental change. Indeed, Jarvik and colleagues (1957, 1962) have produced similar evidence for a genotypic influence on the senescent changes in intellectual functions of elderly twins. One might add that the age-related increase in correlations between parents and offspring for intelligence and physical stature may represent the same developmental genetic process.

Inclusion of the idea that developmental genetic processes may "switch on and switch off" behavioral processes leads to greater consideration of the interactions between genotypes and environment, but these considerations are complex, particularly when we have such poor means for matching environments independent of the humans who act in them. It is possible with monozygotic twins to have genetically identical individuals, but it is perhaps impossible to have environmentally identical humans.

It has even been suggested that humans may actively pick some environments—niches—on the basis of genetically influenced characteristics such as personality and intellect (Plomin et al. 1977). Plomin and his colleagues have further suggested that the genotype–environment correlation also changes developmentally because of age-related differences in the degree to which humans can actively pick their environmental niches. For example, infants are more passive recipients of their environments, and adults are more active selectors of theirs.

In this necessarily brief account of genetics as a contributor to the potential understanding of human behavioral development, it is possible to recognize analogous psychological ideas fostered by Gesell (1945), Lenneberg (1967), Piaget (1966), and Werner (1948). The underlying commonality among these ideas is that the life processes concern an evolving, orderly sequence of progressive organizations, each of which is rooted in the genetic constitution, each of which builds upon the last, and each of which becomes increasingly more differentiated and specialized. The basic plan for the entire sequence can be found in the genes—those that lead to the differentiation of structure, and those that govern the chronology of behavioral development.

Although these conceptualizations call for a revision in the explanatory power previously allocated to environment, the ongoing influence of the environment is not ignored. For example, Piaget, in affinity with Waddington's formulations, has traced the progressive adaptations of individuals to the environment as a reflection of the continuous interchange between genotypic and environmental influences. However, by recognizing the continuing influence of the genotype throughout development, it may be worth reconsidering the force of critical periods, environmental deprivation, compensatory programs, or methods of instruction, since they will not have an equivalent effect on all children.

Bibliography

Bouchard T J Jr, McGue M 1981 Familial studies of intelligence: A review. *Science* 212: 1055–59

Burdette W J (ed.) 1962 *Methodology in Human Genetics.* Holden-Day, San Francisco, California

Cattell R B 1953 Research designs in psychological genetics with special reference to the multiple variance method. *Am. J. Hum. Genet.* 5: 76–93

Cattell R B 1960 The multiple abstract variance analysis equations and solutions: For nature–nurture research on continuous variables. *Psychol. Rev.* 67: 353–72

DeFries J C 1972 Quantitative aspects of genetics and environment in the determination of behavior. In: Ehrman L, Omenn C S, Caspari E (eds.) 1972 *Genetics, Environment, and Behavior: Implications for Educational Policy.* Academic Press, New York, pp. 6–16

Ehrman L, Omenn G S, Caspari E (eds.) 1972 *Genetics, Environment, and Behavior: Implications for Educational Policy.* Academic Press, New York

Erlenmeyer-Kimling L, Jarvik L F 1963 Genetics and intelligence: A review. *Science* 142: 1477–79

Falconer D S 1960 *Introduction to Quantitative Genetics.* Ronald Press, New York

Fishbein H D 1976 *Evolution, Development, and Children's Learning.* Goodyear, Pacific Palisades, California

Fishbein S 1979 *Heredity—Environment Influences on Growth and Development During Adolescence.* Gleerup, Lund

Fulker D W 1979 Some implications of biometrical genetical analysis for psychological research. In: Royce J R, Mos L P (eds.) 1979 *Theoretical Advances in Behavior Genetics.* Sijthoff and Noordhoff, Alphen aan den Rijn, pp. 337–76

Fuller J L, Thompson W R 1966 *Behavior Genetics.* Wiley, New York

Fuller J L, Thompson W R 1978 *Foundations of Behavior Genetics.* Mosby, St. Louis, Missouri

Galton F 1869 *Hereditary Genius: An Inquiry into its Laws and Consequences.* Macmillan, London. (Reprinted: 1962, World Publishing, Cleveland, Ohio)

Garrod A E 1923 *Inborn Errors of Metabolism*, 2nd edn. Frowde, Hodder and Stoughton, London

Gedda L 1951 *Studio dei Gemelli.* Orizzonte Medico, Rome

Gesell A L 1945 *The Embryology of Behavior: The Beginnings of the Human Mind.* Harper, New York

Gottesman I I 1974 Developmental genetics and ontogenetic psychology: Overdue détente and propositions from a matchmaker. In: Pick A D (ed.) 1974 *Minnesota Symposia on Child Psychology*, Vol. 8. North Central Publishing, St. Paul, Minnesota, pp. 55–80

Hallgren B 1950 *Specific Dyslexia ("Congenital Word-Blindness"): A Clinical and Genetic Study.* Einar Munksgaard, Köpenhamn

Husén T 1959 *Psychological Twin Research: A Methodological Study.* Almqvist and Wiksell, Stockholm

Husén T 1960 Abilities of twins. *Scand. J. Psychol.* 1: 125–135

Husén T 1963 Intra-pair similarities in the school achievement of twins. *Scand. J. Psychol.* 4: 108–14

Jacob F, Monod J 1961 On the regulation of gene activity. *Cold Spring Harbor Symp. Quant. Biol.* 26: 193–211

Jarvik L F, Kallmann F J, Falek A 1962 Intellectual changes in aged twins. *J. Gerontol.* 17: 289–94

Jarvik L F, Kallmann F J, Falek A, Klaber M M 1957 Changing intellectual functions in senescent twins. *Acta Genet. et Stat. Med.* 7: 421–30

Kempthorne O 1957 *An Introduction to Genetic Statistics.* Wiley, New York

Lamy M, Royer P, Frezal J, Rey J 1968 *Maladies héréditaires du métabolisme chez l'enfant.* Masson, Paris

Lenneberg E H 1967 *Biological Foundations of Language.* Wiley, New York

Lerner I M 1958 *The Genetic Basis of Selection.* Wiley, New York

Lerner I M, Libby W J 1976 *Heredity, Evolution, and Society,* 2nd edn. Freeman, San Francisco, California

Loehlin J C, Nichols R C 1976 *Heredity, Environment, and Personality: A Study of 850 Sets of Twins.* University of Texas Press, Austin, Texas

Lush J L 1949 Heritability of quantitative characters in farm animals. *Hereditas,* suppl. vol.: 356–75

McClearn G E 1970 Genetic influences on behavior and development. In: Mussen P H (ed.) 1970 *Carmichael's Manual of Child Psychology,* Vol. 1. Wiley, New York, pp. 39–76

McClearn G E, DeFries J C 1973 *Introduction to Behavioral Genetics.* Freeman, San Francisco, California

McKusick V A 1975 *Mendelian Inheritance in Man: Catalogs of Autosomal Dominant, Autosomal Recessive, and X-Linked Phenotypes,* 5th edn. Johns Hopkins University Press, Baltimore, Maryland

Martin N G 1975 The inheritance of scholastic abilities in a sample of twins, II: Genetical analysis of examination results. *Ann. Hum. Genet.* 39: 219–29

Matheny A P, Dolan A B 1974 A twin study of genetic influences in reading achievement. *J. Learn. Disabil.* 7: 99–102

Matheny A P, Wilson R S 1980 Synchronies of infant's cognitive and affective development: Structural continuities in the midst of change. *Enfance,* Suppl. 4/5: 32–33

Mather K 1949 *Biometrical Genetics: A Study of Continuous Variation.* Dover, New York

Mayr E 1974 Behavior programs and evolutionary strategies. *Am. Sci.* 62: 650–59

Money J 1968 Cognitive deficits in Turner's syndrome. In: Vandenberg S G (ed.) 1968 *Progress in Human Behavior Genetics.* Johns Hopkins University Press, Baltimore, Maryland, 27–30

Newman H H, Freeman F N, Holzinger K J 1937 *Twins: A Study of Heredity and Environment.* University of Chicago Press, Chicago, Illinois

Piaget J 1966 *Biologie et connaissance: Essai sur les relations entre les régulations organiques et les processus cognitifs.* Gallimard, Paris [1971 Biology and Knowledge. University of Chicago Press, Chicago, Illinois]

Plomin R, DeFries J C 1980 Genetics and intelligence: Recent data. *Intelligence* 4: 15–24

Plomin R, DeFries J C, Loehlin J C 1977 Genotype–Environment interaction and correlation in the analysis of human behavior. *Psychol. Bull.* 84: 309–22

Plomin R, DeFries J C, McClearn G E 1980 *Behavioral Genetics: A Primer.* Freeman, San Francisco, California

Robertoux P, Carlier M 1976 *Génétique et comportements.* Masson, Paris

Rosenthal D 1970 *Genetic Theory and Abnormal Behavior.* McGraw-Hill, New York

Scarr-Salapatek S 1976 An evolutionary perspective on infant intelligence: Species patterns and individual variations. In: Lewis M (ed.) 1976 *Origins of Intelligence.* Plenum, New York, pp. 165–98

Sinnott E W, Dunn L C, Dobzhansky Th 1950 *Principles of Genetics.* McGraw-Hill, New York

Slater E, Cowie V 1971 *The Genetics of Mental Disorders.* Pergamon, Oxford

Vandenberg S G 1966 Contributions of twin research to psychology. *Psychol. Bull.* 66: 327–52

Vernon P E 1979 *Intelligence: Heredity and Environment.* Freeman, San Francisco, California

Vogel F, Motulsky A G 1979 *Human Genetics: Problems and Approaches.* Springer, New York

Waddington C H 1957 *The Strategy of the Genes: A Discussion of Some Aspects of Theoretical Biology.* Allen and Unwin, London

Waddington C H 1962 *New Patterns in Genetics and Development.* Columbia University Press, New York

Waddington C H 1971 Concepts of development. In: Tobach E, Aronson L R, Shaw E (eds.) 1971 *The Biopsychology of Development.* Academic Press, New York, pp. 17–23

Waddington C H 1975 *The Evolution of an Evolutionist.* Cornell University Press, Ithaca, New York

Werner H 1948 *Comparative Psychology of Mental Development,* Rev. edn. International Universities Press, New York

Wilson R S 1978 Synchronies in mental development: An epigenetic perspective. *Science* 202: 939–48

Wilson R S 1981 Synchronized developmental pathways for infant twins. In: Gedda L, Nance W E, Parisi P (eds.) 1981 *Twin Research: Intelligence, Personality and Development,* Vol. 3, Pt. B. Liss, New York, pp. 199–209

Maturation and Human Development

R. M. Thomas

The concept of maturation in the field of human development has been assigned closely related, though not identical, definitions by different authors. The simplest definition proposes that maturation means changes in a person that are not caused by experience (Ljung 1965 p. 28). But other writers have offered more complex meanings. In the opinion of Bee (1978 p. 9), maturation refers to "internally determined patterns of change in such things as body size, shape, and skill" that unfold according to "instructions" which are "presumably part of the genetic code. . . . Maturationally determined development, in its pure form, occurs regardless of practice or training." Berelson and Steiner (1964 p. 38) have called maturation "the biological development of the bodily machinery that does the behaving: the musculature, the nervous system, and so on. It is the underlying process necessary but not sufficient for normal behavioral development." Gesell (1954 p. 355) has written: "The function of the nervous system is to maintain the integrity of the organism and to anticipate the specific demands of the environment with provisional and preparatory arrangements. These forereference arrangements are not determined by stimulation from the outside world. Experience does not create them. . . . We apply the term 'maturation' to this intrinsic and prospective aspect of ontogenetic patterning."

Some confusion exists among lay people about the meaning of maturation because they use the term in a different sense from the above psychological definitions. While psychologists conceive of maturation as being the contribution to development of internal growth processes rather than of experience, the lay public often equates maturation with maturity, as found in such an expression as "That girl is already at a high level of maturation." This layman's usage, in effect, refers to a person's present position along a path or scale leading to a defined mature state of adult development. But in the psychologist's view, the causal forces that have brought the individual to this present state or level are both genetically timed internal growth (the psychologist's meaning for maturation) and experience. Our discussion in the following paragraphs concentrates solely on the psychologists' conception of the term.

While at an abstract level "pure" maturation can be defined as development resulting entirely from internal forces that are uninfluenced by the environment, at the practical level it is not possible to eliminate environmental influences. From the instant of conception until death, each human obviously inhabits a succession of environments that interact with internal-growth factors to fashion the person's observed development. The problem for students of development, then, becomes one of discovering how this interaction takes place at different times during the human life span to determine the myriad aspects of physical structure and of personality. This problem forms the traditional heredity–environment or nature–nurture controversy: a continuing debate over how much and in what manner heredity, by virtue of the maturation process, contributes to development as contrasted to the contributions made by exterior environmental forces.

The debate is clearly not just an academic issue. It carries highly significant consequences for people in the realms of child rearing, education, medicine, and social work. It is the issue behind such practical questions as: What stage of maturation is needed for a child to walk, to be toilet trained, and to feed himself, and how does an adult recognize when such maturation has occurred? At what time in a child's development is she ready to learn to read, and can this time be hastened by special instructional methods or a special diet? What kind of maturation is required before a pupil can grasp complex mathematical concepts, and at what time does such

maturation take place? What mathematics teaching methods are best suited to effecting the mathematics learning that this maturation makes possible? And if a pupil is compelled to study such mathematical concepts before he has matured sufficiently to master them, will he suffer damage in the form of distorted notions about mathematics or of diminished feelings of self-confidence? In the area of sex education, what are the consequences for a girl's development if she is given sex instruction prior to the maturational changes of puberty as compared to her receiving such instruction only after puberty?

For decades biologists and psychologists have studied the interaction of maturation with experience by means of several research methods. One of the most respected has involved the investigation of twins raised in similar and in different environments. By using monozygotic twins who have developed from the same fertilized ovum, scientists have ensured that the pair of children have inherited the same genetic determinants. Thus differences in their development can be attributed to environmental influences. Through such twin studies, investigators have been able to propose how significantly maturation contributes to such characteristics as physical coordination, growth in use of language, intelligence and concept formation, social interaction, separation anxiety, schizophrenia, and others (Bower 1979 pp. 75, 159, 262, 318–20, 401–4). Another popular investigative approach has been that of studying the incidence and time of appearance of a given characteristic among large numbers of children or adults raised in different environments. The more that the form and timing of the characteristic are alike in the various people, the more the characteristic's development is attributed to maturation.

The concept of stages or periods of development is linked to that of maturation. For example, the stages of mental development described by Piaget are postulated on his belief that among the factors causing intellectual growth, the first and most basic is:

> . . . organic growth and especially the maturation of the nervous system and the endocrine systems . . . . Organic maturation is undoubtedly a necessary factor and plays an indispensible role in the unvarying order of succession of the stages of the child's development . . . . (Piaget and Inhelder 1969 pp. 154–55)

It is beyond the scope of this article to catalogue all research about maturation's role in human development. However, the following examples illustrate the nature of research results for several facets of growth. McGraw's (1935, 1940) studies show that the time at which children first walk and can be toilet trained is determined chiefly by maturational factors rather than instruction. For adolescence, Ljung's (1965 pp. 356–57) research supports the results of other investigations showing that "the maturation of the biological correlates" of development accelerate both physical and mental growth in early adolescence, producing a developmental spurt that is preceded and followed by periods of relatively slow growth. The average girl experiences both the physical and mental growth spurts a year or two earlier than the average boy. Lenneberg (1967) has described the biological foundations of language which appear to account for the similarity in language-learning patterns of young children raised in very different cultures.

As practical aids to people concerned with child rearing and education, investigators have proposed age levels or observable signs in children which suggest that sufficient maturation has taken place to make instruction in a given skill feasible. These signs of readiness for learning, which result from a combination of maturation and past experience, are described in books on development and serve as guides for parents and educators in establishing reasonable expectations for children's development. Information about readiness also aids curriculum planners in locating learning tasks at suitable places in the school's curriculum sequence.

Bibliography

Bee H L 1978 *The Developing Child*, 2nd edn. Harper and Row, New York

Berelson B, Steiner G A 1964 *Human Behavior: An Inventory of Scientific Findings.* Harcourt, Brace and World, New York

Bower T G R 1979 *Human Development.* Freeman, San Francisco, California

Gesell A 1954 The ontogenesis of infant behavior. In: Carmichael L (ed.) 1954 *Manual of Child Psychology.* Wiley, New York, pp. 335–73

Lenneberg E H 1967 *Biological Foundations of Language.* Wiley, New York

Ljung B O 1965 *The Adolescent Spurt in Mental Growth.* Almqvist and Wiksell, Stockholm

McGraw M B 1935 *Growth: A Study of Johnny and Jimmy.* Appleton-Century, New York

McGraw M B 1940 Neural maturation as exemplified in achievement of bladder control. *J. Pediatr.* 16: 580–90

Piaget J, Inhelder B 1969 *The Psychology of the Child.* Routledge and Kegan Paul, London

Individual Differences

R. M. Thomas

Educators' most serious instructional problems derive from the fact that no two learners are exactly alike. In every classroom, students differ from each other in a variety of ways that influence how well they learn. Students vary in the acuity of their eyesight and hearing, in their intelligence and style of thinking, in the direction of their interests, in their strength of motivation, in their energy level, in emotional stability, in family background, and much more. A widespread ambition among modern-day educators is to understand these variations among learners so that administrative and teaching arrangements can be created that enable all students to progress satisfactorily despite the differences among them. Clearly this concern about differences is not limited to school personnel, but is shared as well by parents in their child-rearing tasks and by counselors in their efforts to help youths and adults solve life's problems.

If parents, educators, and counselors are to realize their ambition to meet the needs of individuals, then they need information about the following four sets of issues:

(a) The significant differences: for parents, which differences among children seriously influence children's development? For educators, which differences among students have a substantial effect on students' learning? For counselors, which differences among clients determine the clients' success in solving their problems?

(b) Assessment: how and why are differences measured or judged?

(c) Applications: what uses are made of assessments of differences?

(d) Change: which of the differences can and should parents, educators, and counselors try to change?

In the following paragraphs, general answers to each of these questions are offered. Then readers are directed to other entries in the Encyclopedia that provide more detailed answers to particular questions.

1. Determining which Differences are Significant

It is apparent that individuals can differ from each other in thousands of ways—in a great range of physical traits, mental skills and knowledge, emotional responses, and sociocultural conditions. However, only a limited number of these ways are significant for child raising, education, or counseling. Thus the initial task for parents, educators, and counselors is to decide which differences are important in promoting the learner's development. In the process of making this decision, it is useful to recognize that the influence of an individual difference can be either direct or indirect. The influence is direct when a characteristic of the person immediately determines how well the person learns or performs a task. In the following five examples of direct influence, the first two differences have enhanced the learner's performance, while the last three have impeded it: (a) a 16-year-old boy plays football better than his age-mates because he inherited well-formed musculature and because he has received special training in football over the past 10 years; (b) a young woman sings nicely in tune because she has an acute sense of pitch discrimination; (c) a 12-year-old boy fails to master the process of multiplying fractions because he has less mental ability than most 12-year-olds; (d) a 6-year-old girl cannot learn games that require running because her left leg was damaged badly when she was an infant; (e) a college student has failed in a calculus course because he did not previously learn the algebra concepts necessary for understanding the calculus.

Indirect influence occurs when the person's development is not directly determined by some individual difference which he or she possesses, but rather is influenced by the reaction of other people to that difference. In the following four examples, the first illustrates an individual difference that fosters the person's goal attainment, while the other three illustrate differences that obstruct goal attainment: (a) a high-school girl was asked to join the drama club and was given special lessons in acting because the drama instructor considered her the most beautiful girl in school; (b) a black secondary-school graduate did not attain his goal of learning electrical engineering, for he was not admitted to engineering college because the nation's colleges had restricted the enrollment of blacks to 5 percent of the student population; (c) a young woman who wished to become a police officer was denied the opportunity because in her culture police work was regarded as an improper occupation for women; (d) a child born with a malformed lower jaw was kept for years by his family in the house, not permitted to mix with other children or go to school, because the family was embarrassed by the boy's grotesque appearance and faulty speech; so the boy acquired neither social nor academic skills.

The significance that a particular difference assumes is heavily influenced by the cultural setting, that is, by the person's social ecology. A characteristic that is highly significant in one culture, or even in one family, may be of little importance in another. Preliterate societies that depend chiefly on hunting animals for food and clothing do not value the same traits as do societies that depend heavily on electronic-computer technology for their operation. In the society of hunters, differences in visual-perception skills for detecting distant animals and predicting their movement are very significant, while in computer-dependent societies differences in the ability to manipulate abstract symbols and concepts are more important. Within the same culture, one set of parents may value initiative and aggressiveness, while another may prize obedience and submissiveness. Therefore, differences among children in these traits will not have the same meaning in one family as they have in another.

Not only does the significance of differences vary from one social setting to another, but significance can vary with age in the same culture. Numerous ways that children differ are of little or no consequence during the early years prior to their attending school. This is true for such characteristics as certain types of visual and auditory perception, speech articulation, skill in grouping objects and arranging them in series, and many others. But these characteristics assume great importance once the child is in school: (a) a far-sighted boy can see only blurred words in the books he is to read; (b) a girl with a disordered visual-perception system is labeled dyslexic because she cannot learn to read adequately, even though her eyesight is normal; (c) a boy who stammers when required to speak before a group is considered sufficiently deviant to be sent to a speech therapist; (d) a girl who cannot organize objects into correct series and groups, even though her general intelligence appears average, is labeled dyscalculic and she faces a future of difficulty with mathematical tasks.

Besides these changes in significance that occur between ages 4 and 7, other differences change in importance at other stages of life. For instance, variations in the ability to acquire new intellectual or psychomotor skills are far less important for people past age 65 than for youths who are newly entering the vocational world.

A final obvious fact about differences is that some are regarded as desirable and others are not. People who differ in a desirable direction are often termed above average, skilled, talented, gifted, superior, brilliant, and the like. Those differing in an undesirable direction are called below average, slow, disadvantaged, retarded, subnormal, and handicapped. People in between these two sets of categories may be called average or normal. The decision about whether a difference is desirable or undesirable does not depend upon some universal standard valid in all cultures, but upon how the difference is perceived in a given culture, and upon the system of values in a particular family. Some types of difference—such as ones in visual acuity and physical mobility—are valued in such similar ways in various societies that the standards applied to them are virtually universal across cultures. Blindness and lameness are rarely if ever regarded as assets. However, other types of differences—such as levels of assertiveness or frequency of hallucinations (seeing visions not seen by other people)—are not valued the same in all cultures, so their meaning for child raising, education, and counseling varies from one social setting to another. An aggressive, competitive adolescent will be admired and rewarded in one culture, but disapproved and punished in another. An adult who often has visions is revered as a sage in one culture but hospitalized as a mental patient in another.

In conclusion, then, the foregoing line of reasoning about the significance of individual differences leads to the following generalization that may be of use to people engaged in child care, schooling, and counseling: those responsible for guiding an individual's development are better prepared to do their job if they recognize which differences in the particular cultural setting and at the individual's age-level exert the greatest direct and indirect influence (either positive or negative) on that development.

2. Assessing Differences

Measurement or assessment is performed for three main purposes: (a) to determine the extent of difference among people in a given characteristic, such as in intelligence, temperament, or auditory perception; (b) to determine the relationship between types of differences, such as the relationship of finger agility to visual-perception speed; or (c) to estimate causes of people's differences in a given characteristic, such as what causes differences in mathematical ability or in running speed. By comparing these three purposes, we are able to understand what sorts of measuring techniques, research designs, and statistical analyses have been developed for each purpose.

2.1 Measuring the Extent of a Difference

This section will deal with the first of these purposes (to assess the extent of differences among people) by distinguishing between: (a) assessments of achievement or outcome, meaning how well a goal has been attained, and (b) assessments of cause or input, meaning what factors have contributed to or influenced the achievement. In other words, the second of these is intended to explain why the first has occurred.

To identify which kinds of assessments belong to the first type (the measures of achievement or outcome), the question can be asked that is posed in industry: "What is the nature of the final product we desire?" Or, cast in more human terms: "As a parent, what do I want my child to be like? As a teacher, what do I want my students to learn? As a counselor, what characteristics do I expect to see in a counselee whom I consider to be well adjusted?" Typical instruments to measure for such outcomes are tests of physical fitness, of academic achievement, of vocational skills, and of personal–social adjustment. In addition to tests, there are other evaluation instruments in the form of rating devices for recording how well an individual performs some observable skill (singing, playing a sport, speaking, acting, leading a discussion group, solving a problem) or for evaluating the quality of a product the individual has created (a literary work, a research report, a musical composition, a painting, agricultural products, a science exhibit, an architectural design). However varied these instruments for assessing achievement may be, one characteristic they all share in common is that all are measures of the individual himself, not of his environment.

The assessment of causal or input factors is a different matter. To identify the objects of such assessment, the following question may be asked: "What characteristics of the individual or of the individual's environment significantly influence how well the person achieves the desired goals or outcomes?" Two sorts of assessment techniques are used to evaluate such characteristics. The first focuses on the person and the second focuses on that person's environment. Typical measures of the first type—the personal characteristics—are tests of intelligence and aptitude, of interests, of personality or temperament, of attitudes, and of emotional stability. In addition, ratings of the same characteristics and of others (perceptions of reality, social skills, agressivity, dietary habits) can be based upon observations of the individual.

The second type of cause-of-achievement differences lies not in the individual but in the environment. Assessments of significant environmental factors can be made through observations and interviews, with the results recorded as verbal descriptions (anecdotal records, interview summaries) or ratings on a scale or check list. Environmental factors thus evaluated often include parental attitudes and child-rearing practices, family socioeconomic status, the school's classroom environment, teachers' instructional methods and techniques of discipline, the models of behavior set by a child's peers, the types of entertainment in which the individual engages, and the family's health and nutrition habits.

In the foregoing discussion a distinction has been made between achievement and causal variables, as if they were two distinctly different things. Sometimes, however, they are not entirely separate. Some outcomes that parents and teachers want children to achieve can serve also as causal variables that affect other kinds of achievement. Good health and sufficient energy are usually considered to be desirable goals in and of themselves, but they are also regarded as important variables contributing to success in academic, physical, and social activities. The same can be true of a person's physical appearance, verbal skills, and manner of interacting with other people. Therefore, assessments of certain of an individual's characteristics may simultaneously provide information about both the achievement of a desired goal or characteristic (such as physical beauty) and the influence of this characteristic on the achievement of other desired goals (social acceptability and opportunities for employment).

Earlier it was suggested that there were three chief purposes for assessing individual differences: to learn the extent of difference among a group of people, to discover the relationships between different kinds of differences, and to estimate causes for individual differences. However, it is now apparent that in discussing the first of the three—the extent of the differences—the third purpose, cause, has already been focused on. This inevitable interlinking of the three purposes will now become additionally apparent as the second and third purposes are considered together—discovering relationships among kinds of differences and estimating cause.

2.2 Determining Correlations Between Variables

The types of assessments discussed above involve measuring for individual differences in one characteristic at a time. However, the types now being considered involve discovering the amount of relationship or correlation between two or more characteristics or variables, such as how much relationship there is between intelligence and reading skill or how much between parents' methods of discipline and their children's ability to get along well with age-mates. A variety of statistical techniques have been devised over the past century for computing correlations among different sorts of variables.

This article will now consider the use of correlation information for estimating causes. The importance of making such estimates should be obvious. If the cause of a problem in a child's development or in an adult's personal adjustment can be discovered, then there is hope that the cause can be altered so the problem is solved or at least its effects are minimized.

In studying cause, the kinds of correlations that are most significant are ones between achievements (output variables) and factors that influence these achievements (input variables). The achievement may be good health, and the influences may be aspects of diet or physical exercise. Or the achievement may be skill in solving mathematical problems, and the variable apparently influencing this skill may be general intelligence. So the task is to measure each variable separately—problem-solving skill and intelligence—and then compute the relationship between them to discover how much of problem-solving ability appears to be caused by general intelligence.

Frequently educators are not only seeking to locate the direct correlation between an achievement and an apparent causal factor, but they are trying to discover, in addition, the amount of connection between an immediate cause and an underlying cause. To illustrate this, a teacher observes that a 12-year-old girl is unwilling to try new tasks in school—unwilling to engage in new games, to give a speech in front of her classmates, or to attempt painting during an art lesson. The teacher estimates that the cause behind such inadequate achievement is the girl's lack of self-confidence. In other words, the girl's low self-concept causes her to avoid unfamiliar tasks. Thus, low self-concept is estimated to be an immediate cause of the learning difficulties. But the teacher is interested not only in the amount of relationship between self-confidence and a person's attempting new tasks, but also in what has caused the low self-concept. So the teacher is seeking the underlying cause. Let it be assumed that the teacher estimates that the girl's low self-concept is chiefly the result of criticism the child has received from her parents over the years; the mother and father have always found fault with the girl's attempts at new tasks, so the girl now conceives of herself as a person who cannot do new things well. Therefore, the teacher's interest is to learn how much relationship there is between the parent's fault-finding behavior and the girl's lack of confidence when facing new tasks. In short, the search for causes of individual differences can focus either on immediate or on underlying causes.

A principal difficulty with the process of establishing cause is that few achievements are the result of a single causal factor. Nearly all behaviors of interest to parents, teachers, and counselors are the result of multiple factors, with some of the causes exerting more influence than others. Therefore, the task of diagnosing cause consists of identifying not only which factors have been involved, but also in deciding which factors have been most powerful. Although it is likely not to be possible to identify all of the causal variables behind a student's learning difficulty, if at least the most powerful factors can be identified, then there is hope of alleviating the difficulty to a great extent. A variety of investigative methods and statistical techniques have been devised over recent decades to assist with this task of identifying multiple causes and of determining their relative influence in producing individual differences.

One of the most vexing puzzles in the search for causes is that of distinguishing a causal correlation from only an incidental correlation. Simply discovering that two variables are correlated does not mean that changes in one of the variables have been caused by changes in the other. The two sets of changes may be related only incidentally or only casually. By way of illustration, consider the correlation between the number of storks in a community and the number of babies born. In the Low Countries of Western Europe it was reported that there was a positive correlation between storks and babies—the more storks in the community, the more babies born; and the fewer the storks, the fewer the babies. So a correlation existed, but the question becomes: does this mean that storks cause babies? Or that babies cause storks? Or that there is no causal relation between the two variables, so that the relationship is only incidental or "by chance"? Closer inspection of the Low Country example shows that storks prefer rural areas or villages to industrialized cities. Likewise, rural parents have more children than do urban parents. So the correlation between the number of storks and of babies is apparently only incidental, not causal.

Consequently, it is not enough to learn that two variables are correlated. It is also necessary to build a convincing argument that one variable caused the other. One principle traditionally applied in adducing such an argument is that a relationship is not causal unless one of the variables (the effect) never occurs unless the other variables (the multiple causes) have already all occurred in a particular combination. Theories of human development, of learning, and of personality are essentially proposals intended to explain in a reasoned manner the way causal variables and their apparent effects are linked together.

There are two main ways that causal correlations concerning individual differences are studied. One is to investigate the extent of correlations in groups of people. Group studies are conducted to answer such questions as: (a) in general, how much does children's "native intelligence" contribute to their academic success as compared to the contribution of their strength of motivation? (b) On the average, how effective will large doses of vitamin C be in reducing the incidence of influenza? (c) Or, typically, how effective is punishment in teaching adolescents to be honest?

While the thousands of studies carried out to investigate such correlations in groups can be of general guidance to parents and educators, they do not tell precisely how such causes operate in the life of an individual child or adult. This is because nearly all events in a person's life are the result of a combination of causal factors, and the patterning of these multiple causes is somewhat different in one person's life than in another's. Therefore, the results of group studies suggest only "in general" or "on the average" what has caused a given difference in a person's life. To understand that person's condition precisely, the parent or teacher or counselor can use group-research results as general guides, but then must also decide how to fit together the puzzle of the unique individual's pattern of cause and effect. This act of individualizing the explanation of differences goes under such terms as clinical diagnosis, case-study approach, and differential diagnosis. It is the task of estimating how the complex causal factors have operated in that unique person's life.

Although the importance of causal correlations in the study of individual differences has been stressed, it should be recognized that incidental correlations can be of use as well. Their function is to show the degree to which two different measurements of individual differences are actually assessments of the same underlying factor. To illustrate, let it be assumed that two tests are created. The items of one are devised to measure for verbal problem solving and the items of the other to measure for visual memory. After administering the pair of tests to a large number of students and then computing correlations between students' scores on the two, it is discovered that there is a very high positive correlation between the two sets of scores, a correlation of over 0.90. To a great extent, the students who scored high on one test also scored high on the other, and the students who scored low on one also scored low on the other. It can now be concluded that the two characteristics being measured, verbal problem solving and visual memory, apparently have a common base. They are both seated in a more fundamental ability. This information is useful in at least two ways. First, it helps to explain the patterning of such abilities in people. Second, it should be recognized that if one wishes to estimate a given student's ability in either verbal problem solving or visual memory, it is now not essential to administer both tests, but it will be enough to use only one. A student's score on one of the tests will give a fair representation of what his or her score would be on the other. So incidental correlations do have their uses, even though they are not nearly so valuable to the practitioner as are causal correlations.

3. Making Use of Assessment Results

One use of assessment results has already been identified in the foregoing discussion—the use of assessment information for estimating the causes of a developmental or learning difficulty so that the difficulty can be remedied. Three other important ways assessments are used are in (a) setting standards, (b) selecting and grouping people, and (c) measuring progress toward a goal.

3.1 Setting Standards

Of universal interest to people engaged in child raising, education, and counseling is the question of how the individual compares with other people. In other words, how does a person's achievement or ability or attitudes compare with the norm, meaning the "normal" or "standard" or "usual" performance of other people? This norm or standard is commonly established by measuring a group of people on the characteristic of interest, then describing the group's success in some readily understood form. The form may be that of a graph showing how many people scored at each level of the characteristic. Or, as is more often the case, the description consists of statistics which tell at least (a) the group's average performance (a measure of central tendency) and (b) how much the members of the group spread above and below the average (a measure of dispersion or deviation).

Everyone who makes judgments about how well children are developing or how well adults are managing their lives uses such norms as the bases for judgments, that is, as the foundation for standards. However, not everyone agrees on what level of achievement of a given characteristic is most desirable. Some people feel that in academic achievement, athletic skill, or social adaptability it is best for an individual to be average. Others feel that the individual should be "at least average, and preferably somewhat above average." And teachers or parents who hold particularly high ambitions for a child may expect the child to score "in the top 10 percent of the group."

Not only may people disagree on the desired level to be attained in relation to the group's performance, but they can disagree as well on which characteristic, or on which patterning of selected characteristics, should be most significant in judging how well the individual is developing. To illustrate, one mother may highly value academic achievement and social leadership, so she sets a well-above-average standard of achievement in these areas for her children. A second mother may place more value on home-making skills and the child's feelings of happiness, so she holds higher-than-average expectations in these realms. As a result, the two mothers' treatment of their children will differ because of their difference of opinion about which characteristics are most important. The first mother would not be satisfied with a child's scoring near the average in academic studies, whereas the second mother could consider such performance quite satisfactory if the child herself appeared happy with average achievement.

Differences in standards exist not only between individuals within the same culture, as in the case of the two mothers, but between cultures as well. The typical expectation in one society may differ from the typical expectation in another. Consider, for example, the characteristic of academic precocity—the case of a child whose academic skills are more like those of the typical older youth than of the child's own age-mates. In some cultures such precocity is greatly valued, with the precocious child richly rewarded with praise and opportunities, and cited as a model that other children should imitate. In other cultures, displays of intellectual precocity are deemed improper, so the precocious child is criticized and urged to conform more nearly to the group average.

In any society, the particular culture's pattern of values causes precocity in one characteristic to be viewed differently from precocity in another. A culture that prizes rapid growth in physical agility may not prize early sexual maturation and experimentation, so that above-average and early performance in agility is encouraged, but in sexual activities the desired standard is to display only an average level of interest and only at the average time that one's age-mates display it.

Furthermore, the standards held by a given society may differ for subgroups within the society. Perhaps the most obvious examples are those subgroup divisions along sex and age dimensions. In many cultures, tallness and physical strength are more valued in males than in females, probably because assessments of height over the decades have shown that on the average males are taller than females; and this difference has been accepted not only as a description of reality but also as a proper standard—as not only what is but also as what should be. The same line of logic has also appeared in terms of age differences. The typical or average behavior of children of a given age is accepted as the desired, or at least the expected behavior for that age and is therefore regarded as the proper, or at least the accepted behavior. Such a viewpoint is reflected in such comments as "It's all right, because that's normal at her age" or "Don't worry, all children his age do the same thing." Not infrequently, books on child development represent this viewpoint that the average way children perform at a given age is the standard of how they should perform (Gesell and Ilg 1949). But critics of such reasoning contend that people responsible for guiding human development should not equate what is with what should be when they set standards of achievement. An obvious example illustrating this objection is that of selecting average nutrition for the desired standard as measured in a population that is in generally poor health.

In summary, assessments of individual differences, reported as distributions of scores or averages for a group from a population, are frequently used in setting standards of achievement. However, the manner in which these assessments are interpreted for such a purpose can vary between cultures and between individuals within the same culture, depending upon the pattern of values to which they subscribe.

3.2 Selecting and Grouping People

In the field of education, one of the chief roles of evaluation is to select individuals and to assign them to groups. Students are tested at the end of a school term so they can be assigned marks or grades intended to reflect the quality of their achievement. At the end of several years of schooling, students are assessed to determine whether they deserve a school-completion diploma or certificate. Applicants who apply for entrance into a secondary school or college are evaluated to determine whether they are worthy of admission. In each of these instances, the intention of the testing is to ensure the quality of the educational product.

Assessment data also aid educational administrators in answering such questions as: are there enough pupils suffering reading problems to warrant employing a remedial-reading teacher? Is there so much difference between the highest and lowest students in mathematics that three different classes in mathematics should be formed—one high, one medium, and one low—or is the range of mathematics skill so limited that the students can be assigned randomly to classes?

Similar to this administrative use of assessments is the use of evaluation information within the individual classroom. The teacher assesses students to decide how to arrange instruction for the most efficient learning. Can the students read well enough to master the concepts in the textbook, or will the teacher need to explain certain concepts orally? Or is reading the textbook sufficient for some students, but others will need a supplementary explanation? In studying mathematics, should the pupils be divided into four subgroups according to their levels of ability, or can the class be taught as one large group?

Not only are students selected and grouped for purposes of administrative and instructional efficiency, but often they are divided to achieve some social or political purpose. In some societies, or at least in some segments of societies, the criteria for selection are not academic achievement or mental and physical aptitude, but rather are some social characteristic—religion, race or ethnic origin, socioeconomic status, regional or tribal origin, or political affiliation. There are two opposite ways in which information about individual differences along such dimensions have been used. The first and more frequent way is to select individuals who share a characteristic in common so they can be afforded the same educational opportunity, while people without that characteristic are excluded from the opportunity. One school may accept only pupils from families of the Moslem faith, while another may accept only children from Catholic families. Or, race may be the basis of selection, with blacks assigned to one school and whites to another. Socioeconomic status becomes a self-selection factor when the cost of a particular school is beyond the means of families with modest incomes.

In contrast to such long-standing practices of segregating students into different schools or into diverse educational streams is the more recent effort in a variety of societies to ensure the mixing of students who differ in social characteristics. Educators seeking to foster social integration use data about individual differences to help insure that students are not grouped homogeneously in terms of a social trait but, instead, are taught in a group which approximates the same social heterogeneity of the broader society outside of the school.

In virtually all nations today, much of the sociopolitical conflict related to education centers on issues of how data about individual differences are used to determine the selection and grouping of learners.

3.3 Measuring Progress

There are two principal ways in which a person's progress may be judged. The first, termed norm-referenced appraisal, consists of comparing the individual with assessments of a group, such as comparison with people of the same age or of the same school level. The group provides the norm or standard against which the individual is judged. As a consequence, statements can be made about whether the individual is keeping up with the group (continuing to score about average), is consistently ahead of the group (always above average), or is gradually falling behind (earning increasingly lower scores as compared with the group). The second form of comparison, called criterion-referenced appraisal, consists of setting a precise ultimate goal, then measuring periodically to determine how rapidly the individual is approaching the goal. The goal for a runner might be to run a mile in four minutes. The goal for a sixth-grade pupil might be to comprehend all of the words and sentences in the sixth-grade reading textbook. With criterion-referenced appraisal, no comparisons are made between one student and another. Both of these approaches—norm-referenced and criterion- or self-referenced appraisal—are commonly used by parents, educators, and counselors in judging the progress of the children or clients they are trying to guide.

In summary, common applications of assessment information are for setting standards of achievement, for selecting and grouping people, for judging people's progress, and for analyzing the causes of individual differences so people can be guided in achieving their goals. In relation to this last application—analyzing cause—the matter of attempting to change causes of individual differences will be considered.

4. Deciding on what Changes to Attempt

From the standpoint of fostering people's development and learning, the purpose of understanding causes of individual differences is to determine which factors can be changed and should be changed. In considering this matter, it is useful to distinguish between the goals of the scientist who is seeking to learn the nature of life itself and the goals of the practitioner (parent, teacher,

physician, counselor, social worker) who is seeking to help individuals lead more satisfying, constructive lives. This distinction can be explained in terms of what philosophers have called the infinite regress of cause. The notion of infinite regress is that behind each cause is a complex of underlying causes that recede into the past farther than anyone can trace. The mission of "pure" science is to pursue the unending regression of underlying causes so as to explain the complete nature of the universe and of life. In contrast, the mission of the practitioner is to pursue causes back only far enough to identify (a) those underlying factors which feasibly can be influenced or changed in order to promote an individual's welfare and (b) those underlying factors which cannot reasonably be changed, so that the individual must accept the causal factors as they are and must conduct his or her life as well as possible despite these factors.

The following example illustrates this concern of the practitioner. It is the case of a teacher who suspects that four factors are the most prominent causes for an 8-year-old boy's unsatisfactory academic progress. The four estimated causes are poor eyesight, slight mental retardation, a lack of encouragement at home for the boy to succeed in school studies, and an unhealthy diet. To investigate these possibilities, the teacher (a) observed the boy's vision habits in school to detect symptoms of eyesight difficulties, and then had the child's eyesight tested by an oculist, (b) observed the boy's decision-making and memory skills to estimate the child's mental capacity, and then had the school counselor administer an intelligence test to the boy, (c) asked the boy during health-education class what food he ate on a typical day, with the child's answer aiding the teacher in estimating the adequacy of the boy's diet, and (d) interviewed the child's mother to learn whether she encouraged her son to do well in school and whether the boy ate healthy meals at home. From the results of these assessments the teacher concluded that the boy was far-sighted, was probably slightly mentally retarded, and had a diet that was too heavy in carbohydrates and far too light in protein, vitamins, and minerals. But contrary to her initial suspicion, the teacher concluded that the boy was indeed encouraged at home to succeed in school; his mother appeared very anxious that her son do well in his studies.

With the foregoing assessment completed, the teacher now faced the question of which causes she should attempt to change, which ones she could not feasibly hope to change, and which ones needed deeper study in order to understand additional causes that might underlie them. First, there seemed to be no reason to seek changing the attitude of the mother toward school studies, since her attitude was apparently not a cause contributing to the child's problems. Second, the teacher could feasibly change the eyesight problem by having eyeglasses provided so the boy might carry out reading and writing activities without suffering blurred vision. In addition, the teacher could make sure that the boy was seated in an area of the classroom that had clear lighting so he could more easily read and write without eyestrain. Third, it was not feasible for the teacher to try changing the mental retardation that the boy displayed. As far as present-day medical and psychological technology is concerned, there seems to be no way to alter such mental deficiency, so the teacher would not try to change it. Nor would it be useful for the teacher to search for the underlying cause of the child's retardation (such as a possible genetic disorder or an illness the mother suffered while she was pregnant with the child or an injury to the child's brain during his infancy). Searching for causes underlying a mental condition that could not be improved would be a waste of time. However, even though the cause could not be altered, the teacher still could rearrange the boy's school program in ways that would enable him to learn as well as possible despite his handicapping condition. Three of the things that might be done to help accommodate for the slight mental retardation are for the teacher (a) to lower her expectations regarding the level of difficulty of problems the boy is asked to solve, (b) to simplify explanations of new concepts, and (c) to provide more practice with each new skill than is normally required for 8-year-old children. In addition, the teacher could counsel with the boy's parents in order to help them understand the nature of the child's mental abilities and the ways they might best help him to develop.

In summary, the practitioner can profitably distinguish between causes that can be altered and ones that cannot, and then base the treatment of the individual on this distinction.

5. Research on Individual Differences

All of the topics reviewed in this article have been the subject of a great quantity of research. Much of this research is discussed in other entries throughout the Encyclopedia. Theories and empirical studies of individual differences are also treated in detail, particularly for the psychological aspects of differences, in the readings listed below.

Bibliography

Allport G W 1961 *Pattern and Growth in Personality*. Holt, Rinehart, and Winston, New York
Anastasi A 1958 *Differential Psychology: Individual and Group Differences in Behavior*. Macmillan, New York
Bloom B S 1964 *Stability and Change in Human Characteristics*. Wiley, New York
Bloom B S 1976 *Human Characteristics and School Learning*. McGraw-Hill, New York
Buss A R, Poley W 1976 *Individual Differences: Traits and Factors*. Gardner, New York
Cattell R B 1971 *Abilities: Their Structure, Growth and Action*. Houghton-Mifflin, Boston, Massachusetts
Gesell A L, Ilg F L 1949 *Child Development: An Introduction to the Study of Human Growth*. Harper, New York
Tyler L E 1978 *Individuality: Human Possibilities and Personal Choice in the Psychological Development of Men and Women*. Jossey-Bass, San Francisco, California
Westman J C 1973 *Individual Differences in Children*. Wiley, New York
Willerman L 1979 *The Psychology of Individual and Group Differences*. Freeman, San Francisco, California

Part 2

General Theories of Human Development

Part 2

General Theories of Human Development

Introduction

When human development is defined as "the changes that occur in people with the passing of time," then a theory of development can be defined as "a way of identifying changes and of explaining why they occur as they do." Alternately, theory can also be defined in terms of its relation to facts. In this event, facts or data are considered to be either (a) discrete observations and measurements of people and of their actions or (b) summaries of such observations and measurements. In this case theory becomes an explanation of how the facts fit together. More precisely, the process of theorizing means the act of proposing (a) which facts are most important for understanding people's development and (b) what sorts of relationships among facts are most significant for producing this understanding. Theory is what makes sense out of facts. The purpose of the following discussion is not to present any particular theory in detail, but rather to describe several ways in which theories can be analyzed and to direct readers' attention to other articles in the *Encyclopedia* that focus on specific theories.

For educators and parents, the importance of knowing different theories lies in the conviction that everyone's teaching methods or child-rearing practices are founded on his or her assumptions about how and why people grow up as they do. These assumptions collectively form the individual's theory of development. The study of various theories is considered useful to educators and parents not only for aiding them in assessing their own beliefs but also for providing them with other theoretical alternatives that they may wish to adopt. The study of theories can also aid a person in understanding why other people's educational and child-rearing practices differ from his or her own practices.

The facets of human development theories inspected in the following paragraphs are those of (a) explicit versus implicit theories, (b) the terminology of theories, (c) questions of development on which theories focus, (d) descriptive versus prescriptive theories, and (e) criteria to use in judging the goodness of a theory.

The introduction concludes with a brief overview of the articles contained in Part 2 and with a discussion of the implications that the theories presented in this Part hold for educational practice.

1. Explicit versus Implicit Theories

The term *explicit theory* is used here to mean a proposal written specifically to explain either human development in general or else one or more selected aspects of development. A very general theory consists of a collection of integrated principles explaining not only physical and mental development but also social and emotional development over the entire life span. A more specific or less general theory either limits its focus to one segment of the life span, such as to childhood or old age, or else limits its scope to a selected aspect of the person, such as mental growth or speech development, or changes in structure of the neural system. From an historical perspective, the activity of creating explicit theories of development is a relatively recent phenomenon, concentrated mainly within the past 100 years or so. During this period a host of theories and their variants have been produced, particularly in Europe and North America (see *Basic Concepts of Behaviorism*; *Piaget's Theory of Genetic Epistemology*; *Humanistic Theory of Development*; *Ipsative Theory of Human Development*; *Psychoanalytic Theory of Human Development*; *Social Learning Theory*).

In contrast to explicit theories are implicit ones. These are of two types. The first can be labeled as embedded theories, since they consist of segments of belief scattered throughout the contents of some broad philosophical or religious tradition. Such theories can be extracted from their environs by means of a search through the literature in which they are embedded, a search guided by questions that theories of development are expected to answer (see *Jewish Theory of Human Development*; *Christian Theory of Human Development*; *Islamic Theory of Human Development*; *Hindu Theory of Human Development*; *Buddhist Theory of Human Development*; *Confucian Theory of Human Development*; *Shinto Theory of Human Development*).

The second type of implicit theory can be labeled as commonsense or naive theory. It is the set of beliefs that any individual holds about how and why humans develop as they do. Commonsense theory, defined in this manner, is usually not organized into a systematic statement of principles. Instead, it exists as the collection of assumptions about human growth that a person accumulates during the process of daily living. The people who compose a given society can be expected to hold many of the same commonsense notions, since their belief systems are affected by cultural influences that they experience in common. The nature of a person's or a group's commonsense theory can be sought through such techniques as observations of how the individual treats others, by what the person says about people's growth and behavior, and by analysis of belief systems to which the person or group subscribes (folklore, proverbs, religious doctrine, codes of ethics, and laws). Attempts by psychologists to analyze the structure of people's commonsense theories have led to such interpretations as those found in attribution theory (Baldwin 1967 pp. 5–37, Heider 1958, Thomas 1985 pp. 92–109).

2. Terminology of Theories

Writers seeking to explain human development have not always called their explanations theories but have used a variety of other terms. Such terms include model, paradigm, analogue, structure, and system. Some authors use these labels interchangeably, with all of the terms meaning a scheme for identifying the most important facts about development and for interpreting the way facts are interrelated. However, other writers differentiate among the terms, assigning a separate meaning to each. Thus, a model may be defined as a simplified version of the original complex phenomenon, altered in ways that emphasize its most salient features so they become easier to understand. In some cases a model is an exclusively mathematical or graphic representation of the way something operates (Suppes 1969 pp. 10–17). The term paradigm (to rhyme with either *dim* or *dime*) is sometimes used to mean a very general description of the relationships in human development or, at other times to mean a detailed description of the relationships that appear to exist among selected variables. The words analogue and analogy often refer to a comparison between human development and some other aspect of life with which readers are familiar. For instance, in an effort to explain the manner in which the passing of time brings new experiences to alter the child's growth pattern, a theorist may liken development to a river that gradually is expanded and reformed by new tributaries that enter the main stream as it flows along. In another example, the operation of the human brain can be likened to an electronic computer or to a telephone network. The words structure and system frequently carry the same meaning, referring to the elements that comprise human development and an explanation of how the elements interact.

Because not all authors use the foregoing terms in the same way, it is useful while studying a theoretical scheme to discover what meanings the writer attaches to the terminology used.

3. Questions of Development on which Theories Focus

One perspective from which to analyze a theory is in terms of the way the theory answers questions posed under the nine headings of scope, cause, direction, desirable versus undesirable development, moral condition, stages, personality structure, the learning process, and individual differences.

3.1 Scope

The domain encompassed by a theory can be described as answers to three questions.

Firstly, on what segment of the life span does the theory focus? Some theories are designed to explain only one segment of life, such as childhood, or else they place primary emphasis on just one segment (see *Piaget's Theory of Genetic Epistemology*; *Psychoanalytic Theory of Human Development*). Other theories encompass the entire life span from conception until death (see *Basic Concepts of Behaviorism*; *Erikson's Developmental Theory*). Still others have even greater scope, extending beyond the current life span (beyond ontogeny) to explain development before birth or after death, that is, to explain phylogeny or reincarnation (see *Buddhist Theory of Human Development*; *Hindu Theory of Human Development*).

Secondly, on what aspect of life or human existence does the theory focus? As mentioned earlier, some theories propose to explain many aspects of development, while others limit their attention to one or two aspects. Frequently the broad-scale theories attempt to propose general principles of growth that are thought to be true of all facets of human development (Baldwin 1967 pp. 85–166, Gesell 1954 pp. 335–73, Werner 1961). In other cases, broad-scale theories describe the development of many specific facets of human life, such as mental, social, emotional, physical, vocational, moral, and others (Gesell and Ilg 1949, Havighurst 1953). However, far more common than general theories are ones which confine their attention to a particular aspect, such as psychosexual development (see *Psychoanalytic Theory of Human Development*), language (Brown

1973, Chomsky 1957), mental ability (Piaget 1963), religious conviction (Strommen 1971), moral reasoning (Kohlberg 1971), character and social relations (see *Confucian Theory of Human Development*), and many more.

Thirdly, to what population of humans does the theory apply? Most theories appear to be designed for explaining the behavior of all humans, at any place and any time. However, some are intended to describe the development of only a defined population, such as the upper social castes of India (see *Hindu Theory of Human Development*) or middle-class Americans in the mid-twentieth century (Havighurst 1953). While certain theories ostensibly describe development for all humans, the limited sample of people on which the theoretical proposals have been based can cast doubt on how general the proposals really are. Perhaps they may not explain in exactly the same way the growth of people in other places and other times (Gesell and Ilg 1949, Thomas 1985 pp. 120–25, 255–59).

3.2 Causes of Development

Perhaps the most significant question theories can be expected to answer is: what are the causes for developmental changes in human structure and behavior, and how do the causal factors operate?

In Western scientific circles for more than a century the most popular way of answering this question had been in terms of the interaction of heredity and environment. In conceiving this interaction, some theorists have credited genetic factors with greater power in effecting development (Gesell and Ilg 1949, Jensen 1973, Piaget 1963) than have other theorists who have placed more emphasis on environmental factors (Skinner 1974). Differences of opinion among theorists about the relative importance and manner of operation of heredity versus environment has produced a continuing debate in the field known as the nature-versus-nurture or nativism-versus-cultural-relativism controversy.

Another facet of cause on which theorists can disagree is the question of whether a cause must always precede its effect, or can something that lies in the future be considered the cause of present developmental changes. In other words, theories built according to the traditional logic of the physical sciences assume that a cause must come before its effect—a group of conditions that converged yesterday can bring about the changes observed today (see *Basic Concepts of Behaviorism*; *History and Educational Applications of Behaviorism*). In contrast, other theories are founded on the assumption that human development is goal directed, so that it is a person's anticipation of a future reward or condition that determines the direction of present development (see *Humanistic Theory of Development*). Linked to this debate about the location of cause is the issue of teleology: is there an ultimate, predestined condition toward which human development is drawn?

Although heredity and environment have been the factors most often postulated in scientific circles as causes of development, there is a long tradition of attributing developmental changes to a pair of additional sources—human will and supernatural intervention. People who credit will power as a significant force believe that the course of human life is not entirely determined by genetic and environmental variables. Instead, they believe that humans have some measure of control over their destiny, so development can be affected by the free-will choices individuals make and by how hard they strive to implement such choices. This concept of the importance of will power appears in such diverse religions as Christianity, Judaism, Islam, Confucianism, Hinduism, and Shinto, as well as in much of the commonsense psychology of the general public.

The influence of supernatural intervention as a contributor to development is a central theme of most, if not all, religious persuasions. Adherents of such persuasions believe that an individual's developmental fate can be significantly affected by destructive supernatural forces (Satan or other evil spirits) and constructive or salutary powers (Allah, Cosmic Energy, God, or other beneficent spirits). Sometimes the supernatural powers act on their own volition to influence people's lives. In other cases supernatural intercession is solicited by people through prayers, rituals, and offerings.

In effect, an important difference among theories is in the types of causal factors they propose to account for development as well as in the particular role that each source of cause is thought to play.

3.3 Direction of Development

A further question typically answered by theories is: in what direction does development proceed, or from what earlier condition to what later condition does development pass?

Some theorists describe the direction of development in terms of a series of general growth principles. Lewin proposed that the growing person's life becomes increasingly differentiated, expands with regard to both time and space, achieves a more complex organized interdependence of the various parts of personality, and becomes more realistic about what is real and what is fantasy (Baldwin 1967 pp. 85–166). Writers on physical development have identified two major directions in which growth moves: (a) from the center of the body toward the extremities (the proximodistal direction); and (b) from the head toward the tail (the cephalocaudal direction) (Gesell 1954 pp. 335–73). Other theorists have defined the direction of development by describing a series of steps or stages through which a human normally passes between the time of conception and death.

3.4 Desirable–Undesirable, Normal–Abnormal Development

From the viewpoint of parents, educators, and counselors, the way a theory differentiates desirable from undesirable or normal from abnormal development is highly important, since such information suggests whether the growing person is progressing satisfactorily or will need remedial aid or therapy in order to grow up properly.

Confusion sometimes results from authors not using the term normal to convey the same meaning. Some writers intend normal to mean development that is average for an age group or a type of behavior commonly found in an age group. Abnormal, then, is development that is unusual or deviates from the average of the group. In this sense, the two terms carry no intent of desirability or undesirability. A normal or common type of erratic behavior of adolescents may be judged undesirable by society, while an abnormally high level of intelligence on the part of a child may be regarded as desirable. Other writers, however, consider normal to be desirable and abnormal undesirable. From this perspective, normal development is to be allowed to continue undisturbed, while abnormal development should be remedied. Consequently, when theories are analyzed, it is useful to discover whether a theorist distinguishes between desirable and undesirable development, and also to identify the meanings assigned to the terms normal and abnormal if, indeed, such notions appear in the theory at all.

3.5 The Child's Original Moral Condition

A question that usually has been of greater concern in religious traditions than in modern-day scientific approaches to development is: what is the moral tendency of the child at birth—moral, immoral, or amoral? Or, stated another way, is the newborn naturally motivated to act morally, to act immorally, or to be morally neutral?

The issue can be of interest to parents and educators, for the answer offered by a given theory will suggest whether those responsible for child rearing and schooling need to free the growing child to express the child's innate goodness, or to curb the child's innate wickedness, or to teach the amoral child the difference between right and wrong as conceived in his or her society. At least one version of humanistic theory holds that humans are to some degree innately moral (Maslow 1968 pp. 3–4). A fundamental Christian view holds that humans are born immoral, carrying the vestiges of the original sin of Adam and Eve in the Garden of Eden (Thomas 1985 pp. 58–59). A variety of scientific approaches do not address the question of innate morality directly but appear to imply that the children are born amoral, with no moral status, so that their moral development depends entirely upon environmental influences (see *Basic Concepts of Behaviorism; Piaget's Theory of Genetic Epistemology; Psychoanalytic Theory of Human Development*).

3.6 Stage-wise versus Continuous Development

While all writers appear to agree that growth is a gradual day-by-day process, some theorists have proposed that successive segments of the life span display sufficiently different characteristics to warrant their being called stages or periods of growth. The segments that are most obviously marked by physical and social changes are perhaps universally recognized: infancy beginning at birth; early childhood starting when the child can walk independently and manage some measure of oral communication; adolescence starting with the sex changes of puberty; adulthood beginning with the end of growth in height and the beginning of freedom from parental control; and old age starting with the deterioration of physical and mental vigor. More precise than these general stages are the periods of growth identified in specific theories. For the first two decades of life, Freud proposed psychosexual stages, Piaget described mental-growth stages, and Kohlberg identified moral-reasoning stages. Erikson conceived of psychosocial stages for the entire life span, while Hindu theory has posited four periods of development between the time of puberty and death (see *Psychoanalytic Theory of Human Development; Piaget's Theory of Genetic Epistemology; Erikson's Developmental Theory; Hindu Theory of Human Development*).

Although in general behaviorists and social learning theorists have viewed development as continuous growth rather than as steps from one identifiable period to another, Bijou (1976) has identified three stages of childhood and Skinner (1948) has proposed different stages of child-rearing practices to suit the characteristics of the growing child.

Understanding the stages of a given theory is useful to people responsible for child rearing and education, because a particular kind of treatment is more appropriate during one stage than during another.

3.7 Personality Structure

An additional question to be answered from the inspection of a theory is: what components of personality are recognized in the theory, and how do these components change and interact with the passage of time?

In some theories the key elements that compose personality are explicitly described and their interrelationships explained in detail. Such is the case with Freud's psychoanalysis, with its id, ego, and superego as components that perform at both conscious and unconscious levels of awareness (see *Psychoanalytic Theory of Human Development*). In a very different manner, Piaget conceived of personality as being made up of a complex of sensory-motor and cognitive schemes that are generated as the maturing child interacts with the environment (see *Piaget's Theory of Genetic Epistemology*). In other theories the components of personality are not displayed clearly for the reader but must be assembled by the reader from a search of the theory's literature. Such is true of theories derived from religious persuasions and people's commonsense views.

Child-rearing practices, teaching methods, and counseling techniques are typically founded on various assumptions about personality structure and its development. As a result, parents and educators who adopt a particular theory of development to guide their child rearing and teaching can profit from understanding the way personality is conceptualized in the theory.

3.8 The Learning Process

If learning is defined as "changes in structure and behavior as a result of experience," then a further pertinent question to ask about a theory of development is: how is the process of learning portrayed in the theory?

The way conceptions of the learning process differ from one theory to another can be illustrated with three examples.

Firstly, Piaget's genetic epistemology theory proposes that learning depends, first, on sufficient maturation of the nervous system to accomplish a given task and, second, on the opportunities offered by the environment to meet that task. The process of learning consists of the child seeking to match his or her existing concepts of physical-behavior patterns with tasks or phenomena of the environment, then of altering the concepts— that is, learning new concepts—when the match seems unsatisfactory.

Secondly, in Skinner's behaviorism, learning is controlled by the consequences an individual experiences following an action. Those acts whose consequences are experienced as rewarding (or reinforcing) are learned. Those acts experienced as nonrewarding or punishing (not reinforced or punished) are either not learned at all or, if once learned, are subsequently unlearned (extinguished).

Thirdly, in information-processing theory, learning is pictured as a sequence of stages through which a person receives sensations from the environment and from inner stimuli and then comprehends the stimuli in relation to memories.

The differences in the learning component of development theories are important to people concerned with child rearing, education, and counseling, since the theories imply different suggestions for promoting efficient learning.

3.9 Individual Differences

The central concern of theories is to account for the way people in general develop, to identify principles that govern the growth of a typical person in any place and at any time. In thus concentrating on universal tenets or truths, theories sometimes fail to account directly for how the differences among individuals occur in patterns and rates of development. Such a lack of direct attention to individual differences is regarded by some users of theories as a shortcoming, since many practical questions about child rearing and education depend for their answers on a theory's explanations about the causes of significant deviations from the average. As a result, a query often posed in the analysis of a theory is: what individual differences does the theory identify, and what explanation does it propose to account for these differences?

While the forgoing nine categories of questions represent key issues which users of theories often expect the theories to treat, the categories do not exhaust the matters included in theories. Further questions can be listed as well, such as ones relating to the energizing forces that stimulate development, critical periods for the appearance of different characteristics during the life span, the investigative methods on which the theory is founded, philosophical assumptions underlying the theory, the success achieved with child-rearing and teaching practices derived from the theory, and more.

4. Descriptive versus Prescriptive Theories

A descriptive theory is designed to tell how people develop. It is the theorist's picture of current reality. A prescriptive theory proposes how people should develop. It is the theorist's concept of an ideal state of living toward which people should strive. Modern-day theories in the tradition of Western science are usually intended to be descriptive. In contrast, theories embedded in religious and in many philosophical traditions are heavily prescriptive, proposing how a person should grow up in order to achieve religious salvation, earthly happiness, or self-fulfillment.

Some theories are both descriptive and prescriptive, in that the theorist not only seeks to explain how people actually develop but he or she also recommends—either by precept or implication—how they should develop if they are to achieve an optimum state of existence. For example, B. F. Skinner not only produced descriptions of human growth from a radical behaviorist perspective (Skinner 1974) but also wrote a novel (Skinner 1948) picturing a utopian society in which his theory was applied prescriptively to fashion an ideal personal–social existence for its members. In effect, some theories are intended to be explanations of actual human growth, some are proposals of ideal development, and others are both descriptions of typical growth and prescriptions of an ideal pattern of development.

5. Criteria for Judging Theories

Not everyone agrees on which theories of development are the best and which the poorest. The reason for such disagreement is either that the disputants have based their judgments on different criteria or else they have used different sorts of evidence in arriving at their conclusions. The following eight standards illustrate types of criteria frequently used for judging the goodness of a theory. One person may apply only one or two of these, whereas another may use most or all of them. In addition, two people who subscribe to the same set of standards may differ in their overall judgments of a theory because the two have disagreed about which of the standards should be considered the most important.

(a) *The reality standard.* According to this criterion, a theory is more acceptable if it accurately reflects the facts of the real world of child and adult development. Some theories fail to meet this standard because the authors of the theories have drawn generalizations from a small and atypical sample of children or adults. Another possibility is that the theorist has studied one facet of human growth (such as physical development) and then drawn conclusions which he applies to other facets of growth (such as emotional development) without collecting evidence that such an application is appropriate. A third cause for inaccurately reflecting the real world of child and adult development is an author's basing the theory upon his or her own faulty memory or inaccurate observations of past events.

(b) *The internal-consistency standard*. This criterion requires that all of the elements within the theory fit together logically. A person seeking to understand the theoretical system should not have to disregard one segment in order to understand another segment, nor should one aspect conflict with another.

(c) *The parsimony standard*. This law of parsimony or Morgan's canon was proposed by a biologist, Lloyd Morgan, who stated that if two explanations of a phenomenon fit the facts equally well, it is better in the long run to choose the simpler of the explanations.

(d) *The falsifiability standard*. It is a common belief in the scientific world that if a theory's hypotheses can be tested to determine whether they are true, then the reverse should also pertain—it should be possible to test that a hypothesis is false. In effect, many scientists feel that the validity of a theory should not only be confirmable through logic and the presentation of data, but it should also be falsifiable. However, some theories of human development—or at least parts of them—do not appear to be falsifiable. One example is the Hindu theory that the human soul, after the death of the body, transmigrates, that is, it inhabits a new body. Another example is the Freudian contention that children have strong sexual drives. If a child explicitly talks of sex or engages in sexual investigation, then this evidence is considered confirmation of the theory. If a second child does not talk of sex or show sexual curiosity, this too is considered confirmation of the theory, with Freudians proposing that the second case is an instance of reaction formation, meaning that in order to mask an interest in sex, the child forms a reaction in behavior that is the opposite of his or her true desire. In effect, with the concept of reaction formation, Freudians have rendered this aspect of the theory nonfalsifiable.

(e) *The fertility standard*. According to this criterion, a theory is better if it stimulates the creation of new research techniques, generates new questions to investigate, and furthers the discovery of new knowledge.

(f) *The practical-guidance standard*. For many people who are responsible for child rearing, teaching, and counseling, the most important characteristic of a theory is its usefulness in improving their own skills of understanding and treating the children and adults they face. In this sense, a good theory is one that offers practical guidance in solving daily problems of child rearing and education.

(g) *The predictability standard*. Under this standard, a theory is considered more acceptable if it not only explains why past events occurred but also accurately predicts future events. In addition, the theory is better if it enables a person to make accurate predictions about specific behaviors of a particular child or adult rather than only speculations about general growth patterns for a group of people.

(h) *The self-affirmation standard*. Frequently people subscribe to a theory or conviction not simply on grounds of logic or objective evidence but also on intuitive grounds or emotional factors. Ultimately, every theory would appear to depend for its acceptance on the reader's self-affirmation or self-conviction, that is, on the reader's concluding that "it feels right" or "it makes overall sense," with this affirmation founded on both identified and unidentified factors or criteria.

6. The Contents of Part 2

The 23 articles that comprise Part 2 are divided into two sections. The first section contains 16 articles describing Secular Theories that have been created specifically to explain human development. These theories are modern ones, in that all of them have been formulated within the last 100 years or so. The second section, comprised of seven articles, describes Theories Embedded in Religious Traditions. The seven are ancient theories, in that each finds its beginnings many centuries in the past.

An inspection of the titles of articles in Part 2 shows that not all present-day theories of development are included. In other words, Part 2 represents a selection of theories, ones that were chosen by the application of two criteria, those of popularity and of diversity.

The popularity of a theory was judged by either (a) how frequently the theory was mentioned in educational and psychological literature in recent decades or (b) the number of people who apparently subscribe to the theory. Examples of theories that often appear in the professional literature are Piaget's genetic epistemology, behaviorism, social-learning theory, and psychoanalysis. Examples of theories placed in Part 2 because of their large numbers of adherents are the Islamic, Buddhist, Hindu, Christian, Jewish, Confucian, and Shinto conceptions.

A number of theories have been included in this Part, not because of the widespread popularity, but because they represent very diverse perspectives. By adopting a diversity criterion in selecting theories, the Editor sought to illustrate for readers a wide variety of ways in which human development may be interpreted. Such diversity is reflected both in the more popular theories (Piaget's proposals, behaviorism, psychoanalysis, and information-processing models) and in viewpoints not so widely known (ecological theory, ego psychology, Soviet theory, existential and humanistic conceptions, attribution theory, ipsative theory, and developmental-task approaches).

The 16 articles treating secular theories are presented in a sequence that generally reflects their popularity in professional literature in recent times. Thus, the collection begins with the work of Jean Piaget and ends with ipsative theory. The seven articles treating theories embedded in religious traditions are organized into two groups. The first group consists of religions born in the Middle–East (Judaism, Christianity, and Islam) and the second of religions that evolved in South–Central and East Asia (Hinduism, Buddhism, Confucianism, and Shinto).

7. Educational Implications of Human-Development Theories

The theory of development on which an educator bases educational practice can significantly influence each aspect of the process of education—the goals to be achieved, the assumptions about how people learn, the sequence and pace of learning objectives, the methods of teaching, the teaching materials, the ways individual differences among learners are treated, the methods of evaluating student progress, and more. Either explicitly or by implication, all of the articles in Part 2 suggest educational consequences that derive from the theories they describe. The variety of forms that such consequences may take is illustrated in the following examples.

7.1 Educational Objectives

Each theory described in this Part either states or implies its own developmental goals which, in turn, suggest the types of educational objectives that will contribute to the achievement of those goals. For instance, from the viewpoint of Christian theory, the goal of development is for the individual to live on earth in keeping with God's commandments and thereby to achieve a heavenly eternal life-after-death. Consequently, the objectives of Christian education are to teach people the nature of God's dicta and to motivate learners to live according to these principles. In contrast, the goal of development in psychoanalytic theory is for people to advance through a sequence of psychosexual stages in order to achieve an ultimate satisfactory relationship with a partner of the opposite sex. The objectives of education from a psychoanalytic perspective are to guide the growing child toward recognizing and accepting his or her own sexual characteristics and toward developing a "self" or "ego" that adopts constructive methods of adjusting to the demands of the world.

Different still are the educational goals that derive from an existential conception of development. Existentialists typically hold that the reality of life is found in each person's unique inner experience, so a person's developmental goal is to achieve a keen awareness of this inner life and to enhance its richness. Hence, the aim of existential education is to sharpen and expand the individual's self-awareness.

Yet another desired outcome of development is reflected in the dominant theoretical view held in the Soviet Union. As Davidov (p. 97) explains in the article on *Soviet Theories of Human Development:*

> The general results in intellectual development achieved by the end of childhood are expected to match the goals the socialist society sets for the education system. These goals are explicated in terms of the socially accepted image of a young person who is to embark on the life of an adult. In terms of psychology, this ideal image contains the needs and capabilities that a contemporary young man or young woman acquires to fulfill, in a creative and productive manner, the individual's job demands and civic responsibilities.

Thus, the objectives of Soviet education are to teach children and youths the required work skills and attitudes of civic obligation.

In a similar manner, other theories of development imply their own educational objectives.

7.2 *Assumptions About How People Learn*

Theories differ in the way in which they conceive the learning process. To illustrate this point, radical behaviorists propose that the most important factor in learning is the set of consequences a person experiences after carrying out some act. In other words, a person "learns" (meaning that the person "repeats in the future") those actions that are followed by rewards (reinforcement) and does not learn ("does not repeat in the future") actions that go unrewarded.

In contrast, Piaget identified other variables as being the most significant factors in learning. He proposed that, first, the child's nervous system must have become sufficiently mature biologically to prepare the child for the level of complexity that a particular learning task requires. Next, the child needs opportunities to become acquainted with the objects or concepts that the learning will involve. Through such direct acquaintance, children teach themselves. However, some learning also requires instruction, that is, intentional teaching by people who already have acquired the desired knowledge—such people as teachers and parents. Therefore, following the steps of internal maturation and personal acquaintance, the child can profit from instruction offered by others.

An information-processing approach to learning focuses on still different elements. In order for a person to learn and then to display this learning in the form of actions, the individual must accurately see and hear environmental stimuli, must interpret what the stimuli mean, must store the interpretation in memory, must retrieve the information when it is required, and must exhibit the learning in behavior. Hence, if a student's learning difficulties are to be diagnosed, it is necessary to discover where in this chain of events the information-processing system has failed to operate properly.

Likewise, other theories of development identify still other elements as the crucial factors in learning.

7.3 Teaching Methods and Materials

Instructional procedures and learning materials also vary from one conception of development to another. For instance, Islamic theory holds that such holy books as the *Koran* and the *Hadith(Traditions)* serve as the basic teaching materials for Moslem education. Principal methods of instruction consist of guiding learners in rote-memorizing the contents of the holy books and, at more advanced levels of education, of engaging students in discussions about the proper application of doctrine to solving life's problems.

In contrast, social-learning theorists emphasize the importance of imitation and of reward and punishment in the learning process. Imitation means that much of what humans learn is acquired by imitating the behavior of people they observe. In selecting which models to imitate, learners are influenced by the rewards and punishments that those models experience as a result of their actions. Thus, effective teaching depends both on providing desirable models for students to emulate and on manipulating the reward and punishment system in a way that encourages students to acquire the behaviors advocated by the educators.

7.4 Methods of Evaluating Student Progress

Marked differences among theories appear in what the theories imply for methods of evaluating how well a learner is progressing. For instance, behaviorists depend solely on evaluation devices that measure overt actions, such as achievement tests and ratings of observable acts. In contrast, humanistic psychologists place great emphasis on the learners' subjective reports of how they feel they are getting along, that is, of how their "self" or "ego" is gaining strength in its ability to solve life's problems. Still different is a Piagetian perspective, which emphasizes assessments of cognitive development. However, these are not simply measures of whether the learner can get the correct answer to problems about the physical and social world. Rather, they are evaluations of the process the learner has employed in arriving at an answer.

In summary, as the forgoing examples indicate, different theories of human development can imply quite different educational practices. More detailed illustrations of what sorts of child-raising, schooling, and counseling activities derive from specific theories are given in the individual articles that comprise Part 2.

Bibliography

Baldwin A L 1967 *Theories of Child Development*. Wiley, New York
Bijou S W 1976 *Child Development: The Basic Stage of Early Childhood*. Prentice-Hall, Englewood Cliffs, New Jersey
Brown R 1973 *A First Language: The Early Stages*. Viking, New York
Chomsky N 1957 *Syntactic Structures*. Mouton, The Hague
Crain W C 1980 *Theories of Development: Concepts and Applications*. Prentice-Hall, Englewood Cliffs, New Jersey
Gesell A 1954 The ontogenesis of infant behavior. In: Carmichael L (ed.) 1954 *Manual of Child Psychology*. Wiley, New York, pp. 335–73
Gesell A, Ilg F L 1949 *Child Development: An Introduction to the Study of Human Growth*. Harper, New York
Havighurst R J 1953 *Human Development and Education*. Longmans, Green, New York
Heider F 1958 *The Psychology of Interpersonal Relations*. Wiley, New York
Jensen A R 1973 *Educability and Group Differences*. Harper and Row, New York
Kohlberg L 1971 From is to ought. In: Mischel T (ed.) 1971 *Cognitive Development and Epistemology*. Academic Press, New York, pp. 151–235

Langer J 1969 *Theories of Development*. Holt, Rinehart and Winston, New York
Lerner R M 1976 *Concepts and Theories of Human Development*. Addison-Wesley, Reading, Massachusetts
Maier H W 1978 *Three Theories of Child Development: Erik H. Erikson, Jean Piaget, and Robert R. Sears*, 3rd edn. Harper and Row, New York
Maslow A H 1968 *Toward a Psychology of Being*. Van Nostrand, Princeton, New Jersey
Miller P H 1983 *Theories of Developmental Psychology*. Freeman, San Francisco
Piaget J 1963 *The Origins of Intelligence in Children*, 3rd edn. Norton, New York
Skinner B F 1948 *Walden Two*. Macmillan, New York
Skinner B F 1974 *About Behaviorism*. Knopf, New York
Strommen M P 1971 *Research on Religious Development: A Comprehensive Handbook*. Hawthorn, New York
Suppes P C 1969 *Studies in the Methodology and Foundations of Science*. Reidel, Dordrecht
Thomas R M 1985 *Comparing Theories of Child Development*, 2nd edn. Wadsworth, Belmont, California
Werner H 1961 *Comparative Psychology of Mental Development*. Science Editions, New York

Secular Theories

Basic Concepts and Applications of Piagetian Cognitive Development Theory

R. M. Thomas

One of the most influential theories of how intelligence develops in children and adolescents has been that devised by a Swiss, Jean Piaget (1896–1980), who became known as the world's most eminent child psychologist.

Piaget's interest in child psychology was not stimulated simply by a desire to catalog the ways in which children at different age levels think about the world around them. Rather, he was motivated by a desire to pursue genetic epistemology, which he defined as the study of the mechanisms of the growth of knowledge (Piaget 1972 p. 21). By the time of his death, after the pursuit of the self-imposed mission for nearly 60 years, he had published over 40 books and hundreds of articles describing both the data and theoretical interpretations he derived from a great range of empirical studies.

Basic features of Piagetian theory are described in the following paragraphs, along with ways that the theory has been applied in educational settings. Further discussion of epistemological aspects of Piaget's work and a description of his research methods and the rationale behind his growth stages are discussed elsewhere in the Encyclopedia.

1. The Development of Knowledge

Piaget's concept of knowledge differed from that of most other theorists. Whereas many writers have viewed knowledge as a store of information and beliefs, Piaget proposed that knowledge is a process, a repertoire of actions that a person performs. In Piaget's opinion, to know something means to act on that thing, with the action being either physical or mental or both. The 2-year-old child's knowledge of a ball consists of his or her picking it up, pressing it with his or her fingers, tossing it, and observing it bounce. As children grow up, they gain more experience with such direct, physical knowing, while at the same time their nervous systems are maturing. As a consequence, they are gradually freed from having to carry out direct physical behavior in order to know something. They come to produce mental images and symbols (words, mathematical figures) that represent objects and relationships. Hence, the older child's knowledge increasingly becomes mental activity. Older children "think about" things by carrying out interiorized actions on symbolic objects.

The purpose of all behavior or all thought, according to Piaget, is to adapt the organism—in this case the human—to the environment in ever more satisfactory ways. The techniques of adaptation in Piaget's system are called schemes (schemas or schemata). A scheme, as a technique of adjustment, can be biological or mental or both. The grasping movement of the infant's hand is a scheme, a physical organization of actions that the child can generalize to grasp a bottle, a rattle, or the edge of the crib. On the intellectual level, an adolescent child's concept of a series is also a scheme, a mental organization of actions. He or she can apply it in constructing a series of numbers or in arranging a series of colors by their shades. Such schemes, both physical and mental, are always accompanied by feelings which Piaget called affective schemes (Piaget and Inhelder 1969).

From a Piagetian perspective, development can be seen as a progressive elaboration of schemes or knowledge by means of a pair of complementary processes called assimilation and accommodation. Assimilation occurs when a person encounters a new experience in the environment and interprets this experience as being identical or very similar to a scheme already in his or her repertoire of physical or mental acts. A child meets an animal and concludes that it fits a label he or she already knows, dog. A student faces a problem in mathematics and concludes that its form is familiar, that of a quadratic equation.

Sometimes, however, people do not perceive a good match between an experience with the environment and any of their existing schemes. In such instances, one of two things occurs. Either the person fails to comprehend the experience at all, or else he or she must alter existing schemes to produce some new variant that fits the new experience. This latter process of adding to, refining, and elaborating schemes to create new versions is called accommodation.

In Piaget's system this process of development—of generating a growing complex of schemes—is governed by four factors: heredity (internal maturation); physical experience with the world of objects (spontaneous or

53

psychological development); social transmission (education or instruction); and equilibrium (Piaget 1973).

Heredity, in Piaget's view, furnishes the newborn with the initial equipment the infant needs for coping with problems met in the world. Heredity also establishes a time schedule for new development potentials to arise at successive stages of the individual's growing years. However, genetically determined internal maturation does not guarantee that the potential schemes or abilities will materialize. Their fruition depends also on the nature of the person's interaction with the environment.

Unlike many theorists, Piaget separated the child's involvement with the environment into two varieties: direct and generally unguided experience (physical experience or spontaneous development) and the guided transmission of knowledge known broadly as education or instruction. Piaget contended that the first of these varieties must precede the second.

The fourth factor determining development, called equilibrium, is a coordinating force, performing the regulation and compensation among the other three factors that are needed to make the entire system of development a coherent whole.

2. Stages of Development

When Piaget viewed the span of childhood and adolescent years, he was able to distinguish breaks in the process of growing up. These breaks suggested to him that the child had at each such point completed one phase of growth and was now engaged in a further phase, so the Piagetian model of development can be called a stage theory.

Although Piaget identified somewhat different sets of stages for different aspects of growth (one set for physical causality, a second for play, a third for moral development, and others), underlying all of these sets was a basic series that provided the framework for general sensory-motor intellectual development. One of the most familiar versions of this set depicts growth as proceeding through four successive levels: the sensory-motor period; the preoperational-thought period; the concrete-operations period; and the formal-operations period. As children move from the first to the last of these levels, they change from being entirely self-centered infants with no realistic knowledge of their environment to becoming adolescents who employ logic and language with facility, able to manipulate the environment intellectually and thus to comprehend ever more realistically how the world functions.

In the following overview of the stages, the age designations attached to each should be regarded as only approximations, since Piaget stated that the age at which children reached a stage varied somewhat from child to child and from one culture to another. However, the sequence of the stages he considered to be invariant (Piaget 1973 pp. 10–11).

2.1 Sensory-motor Period (Birth to Age 2)

The level is composed of six substages which mark the infant's progress from only performing reflex actions to his or her gradually perceiving the effect of his or her actions on objects, then to distinguishing between self and objects, to anticipating people and objects, and finally to representing objects mentally and thereby cognitively combining and manipulating them.

2.2 Preoperational-thought Period (about Age 2 to Age 7)

The term operations in Piaget's system means manipulating objects in relation to each other. However, it is not just any sort of manipulation. In order to qualify as operations, actions must be internalizable, reversible, and coordinated into systems that have laws that apply to the entire system and not just to the single action itself. By internalizable Piaget meant that the actions can be carried out in thought without losing their original character as physical manipulations. By reversible he meant that they can be readily inverted into their opposite—two groups of apples that are combined (added together) to form a whole group can as easily be reduced (subtracted from the whole) to their original status as two groups. As the phase "preoperational-thought period" implies, the child before about age 7 is not yet able to carry out mental operations in the above sense but is still in the stage of preparation for performing true operations (Piaget 1972 p. 8).

The preoperational period has been divided into two levels. The first, from about age 2 to 4, is characterized by both egocentric speech and primary dependence on perception in problem solving. Egocentric speech is the running oral commentary young children carry on to accompany what they are currently doing, and it is not intended as a vehicle of communication with others. The child's heavy dependence on perception means that in problem solving he or she draws conclusions from what can be directly seen or heard rather than from what he or she might recall about the permanent characteristics of objects and events.

The level of intuitive thought is reached between ages 5 and 7. It is a transition phase between the child's depending solely on perception and depending on logical thought in problem solving. While in earlier years children's thinking suffered from centering (focusing exclusively on one dimension of a situation), during the intuitive period they begin to recognize that more than one factor at a time influences an event in a coordinated manner. A short wide glass holds as much liquid as a tall thin glass, because the short glass's greater width compensates for its lack of height.

2.3 Concrete-operations Period (about Age 7 to Age 11)

In this stage children become capable of performing true operations, ones directly related to objects. Concrete does not mean the child must see or touch the actual objects as he or she works through a problem, but rather that the problem involves identifiable objects that are either directly perceived or imagined.

It is during these years that children's understanding of conservation matures. The phenomenon of children's ideas of conservation is one of Piaget's signal discoveries, and it continues to be the focus of much of the investigation generated from Piaget's work. The term conservation refers to those aspects or events that remain constant when other changes are produced in objects or situations. When a ball of clay is rolled into a sausage shape, the form has been altered but the substance, weight, and mass have been conserved. Distinguishing between what has been changed and what has been conserved during transformations marks a major advance in children's reasoning skills during this stage.

By the end of the concrete-operations period children have markedly increased their abilities to account for the cause of physical events so that they are now ready to solve not only problems that involve objects but also ones concerning hypotheses and propositions about relationships.

2.4 Formal-operations Period (about Age 11 to Age 15)

During adolescence the typical child is no longer limited by what he or she directly sees or hears, nor is he or she restricted to the problem at hand. The adolescent can now imagine the conditions of a problem—past, present, or future—and devise hypotheses about what might logically occur under different combinations of factors. For example, if a child younger than age 12 or so is asked to imagine a problem in which water runs uphill, he or she typically will claim that the problem cannot be solved because water does not run uphill. But by the close of the formal-operations period the adolescent can accept the hypothetical condition of upward flow and can apply it in solving problems that are posed.

By the end of this final stage of mental development the youth is capable of all the forms of logic that the adult commands. Then further experience over the years of youth and adulthood fill in the outline with additional, more complex schemes so that the adult's thought is more mature and freer of lingering vestiges of egocentrism than is the adolescent's.

3. Educational Applications of Piagetian Theory

In recent decades Piaget's writings have exerted a growing influence on educational practice in many parts of the world. Piaget himself frequently suggested educational implications of his model (Piaget 1970). However, far more applications of Piagetian thought to child rearing and schooling have been promoted by others. The applications have treated such a range of educational functions as the choice of learning objec-

tives, curriculum sequencing, grade placement of learning topics, the assessment of mental processes, and teaching methodology.

In selecting learning objectives from a Piagetian viewpoint, educators do not choose concepts and facts because they traditionally have been studied in schools or because they think them important. Rather, educators choose objectives that are recognized as valuable in fostering the development of each successive level of cognitive growth that the child is working toward in the Piagetian model.

Piaget not only proposed, in terms of mental stages, the sequence in which children's general thought processes develop, but he identified specific substages for a variety of subrealms of thought—mathematics, moral judgments, physical causality, and others. Advocates of Piagetian theory contend that in the traditional school curriculum, children are often expected to acquire concepts of mass, weight, volume, space, time, causality, geometry, and speed in a sequence that is at odds with the child's natural pattern of comprehending such concepts. A curriculum founded on Piagetian theory and empirical studies would seek to correct such incoordination between development and school learning activities (Elkind 1976 p. 196).

The studies of Piaget and his followers have not only suggested the sequence in which different topics might most profitably be studied by children, but they have also indicated in a general way the approximate age or grade level at which children can master different modes of thought. As a consequence, curriculum planners receive guidance from Piagetian studies about the suitable grade placement of topics.

Piagetians are critical of the use of traditional intelligence tests for estimating children's cognitive development. The chief criticism is that the typical intelligence test determines whether the child can give a correct answer to questions, but it does not reveal the child's thinking processes, that is, the way the child arrives at answers. Piagetians, therefore, prefer to base their judgments of children's cognitive styles on: (a) how children solve the problems posed in the tasks Piaget used in his research studies and (b) teachers' observations of the level of children's reasoning as they go about the regular activities of the classroom (Elkind 1976 pp. 171–94).

In many of the analyses of teaching methodology based on Piagetian theory, the two most basic responsibilities of the teacher are those of diagnosing the current stage of a child's mental development and offering the child learning activities that challenge him or her to advance to the next higher step in the sequence of sensory–motor–cognitive development. Not all writers have conceived of the teacher's role within the Piagetian model in precisely the same way. Some have recommended that the teacher offer pupils a sequence of activities that can aid them in progressing to the next higher stage of development, but the decision of when and how to use these activities is primarily up to the pupil (Furth and Wachs 1975 p. 46). Others have suggested a more active role for the teacher in guiding the child's studies (Elkind 1976). But in each case the intent is to promote the child's mental growth in keeping with Piagetian theory.

Bibliography

Elkind D 1976 *Child Development and Education: A Piagetian Perspective.* Oxford University Press, New York

Furth H G, Wachs W 1975 *Thinking Goes to School: Piaget's Theory in Practice.* Oxford University Press, New York

Inhelder B, Piaget J 1964 *The Early Growth of Logic in the Child: Classification and Seriation.* Routledge and Kegan Paul, London

Piaget J 1970 *Science of Education and Psychology of the Child.* Orion, New York

Piaget J 1972 *Psychology and Epistemology: Towards a Theory of Knowledge.* Penguin, Harmondsworth

Piaget J 1973 *The Child and Reality: Problems of Genetic Psychology.* Viking, New York

Piaget J 1976 Autobiography. In: Campbell S F (ed.) 1976 *Piaget Sampler: An Introduction to Jean through his own Words.* Wiley, New York

Piaget J, Inhelder B 1969 *The Psychology of the Child.* Basic Books, New York

Piaget's Theory of Genetic Epistemology

J. J. Vonèche

The phrase "genetic epistemology" was coined in 1906 by James Mark Baldwin in his famous book *Thought and Things or Genetic Logic.* For Baldwin, genetic epistemology "concerns itself with the implications of reality at each of the greater stages of conscious process, from the most primitive to the most derived" (Baldwin 1911 Vol. 3 p. 16). Epistemology, for Baldwin, is equivalent to "instrumental logic" or the science of truth by the control of facts in opposition to "axiology" or the science of value or worth covering the whole range of "normative" disciplines. This dichotomy is founded on the fundamental distinction between the two possible controls (according to Baldwin) mediated in the thought content. If the control of fact, then this is epistemology. If the control of the inner sort, then this is axiology, that is to say, "the relative selection and utilization of facts through the mediation of the thought system as means" (Baldwin 1908 Vol. 2 p. 383).

What is essential here is what Baldwin called "genetic modes" according to which nature presents "genetic series" which are qualitative, irreversible, and non-mechanical, movements of progressive change. These genetic series constantly manifest evidence of the rise of new and progressive "genetic modes" or sorts of organization which are each for themselves novel, *sui generis*, and creative. "In passing from one genetic mode to another, nature achieves a real evolution; there is an actual production of novelties" (Baldwin 1911 Vol. 3 p. 258). The logic of this general movement is stated in the "axioms" of genetic sciences (Baldwin 1902) and is interpreted for the movement of mental process in the "canons of genetic logic" (Baldwin 1906 Vol. 1 Chap. 1). This movement is externally guided in accordance with the Darwinian principle of natural selection.

The concept of genetic epistemology was not Baldwin's exclusive property. Mention should also be given to W. Wundt from Germany (Wundt 1880), C. Sigwart (Sigwart 1894–1895), and E. Cassirer (Cassirer 1903–1920) or in the Anglo–Saxon tradition, B. Bosanquet (Bosanquet 1888) and L. T. Hobhouse (Hobhouse 1888, 1912). Thus, the tacit procedural assumption that "genetic epistemology" is, or ought to be, identified with Piaget's specific undertaking constitutes a total misapprehension of the domain. On the contrary, the concept of "genetic epistemology" should be disembarrassed from the unhappy fusion it has undergone, in recent times, with Piaget's specific attempt to orient that discipline along certain lines.

The goal of epistemology is to provide a theory of knowledge in whatever form it occurs. This aim has traditionally been conceived as a matter of logic rather than psychology, of abstract norms rather than concrete facts, as a normative discipline, regulative of inquiry, rather than a positive discipline shaped by the results of empirical investigation. But the demarcation of epistemology from empirical inquiry involves a decision and not a description of "the way things are". This decision is not regulated simply by the character of the concept to be defined, but depends also on the soundness of the interest it is designed to serve, so that the proceeding is partly normative. On the other hand, between the conception and the creation of such a logic falls the shadow of a presupposed psychology, because every epistemology is shaped by underlying conceptions of the mind and conduct of which cognition is a product.

This dual characteristic of thinking as both a process and a product was clearly understood by Baldwin and by most of the early genetic epistemologists. Hence, the recurrence in Baldwin's writings of such reversals of terms as "worths as thoughts" and "thoughts as worths". This passage from facts to norms and vice versa is indeed central to any epistemology and especially to genetic epistemologists who agree in recognizing that any form of knowledge is triple: (a) a social system; (b) a group of psychological behaviours; and (c) a system *sui generis* of signs and cognitive activities. But they do not all agree on Piaget's solutions to these two main issues: the relationship of facts to norms cleverly eschewed as "normative facts" (*faits normatifs*) or the consideration of science as the form of knowledge *par excellence*.

Cassirer, for instance, would consider Piaget's emphasis upon the scientific forms of knowledge as extremely limitative, and Baldwin as simply preposterous. The "fusion" of norms and facts under the heading of "normative facts" would be considered as muddy by most of the genetic epistemologists mentioned here.

Besides limiting genetic epistemology to the sole attempts of Jean Piaget, there is another confusion generally made by philosophers and scientists alike, that of fusing Piaget's epistemology with his psychology. Numerous examples can be given of people who sincerely think that genetic epistemology is the title Piaget bestowed upon his theory of intellectual development in human ontogeny, although it should have seemed unlikely that a person of Piaget's considerable historical erudition and critical acumen would conflate individual developmental psychology and genetic epistemology. In fact, Piaget defines genetic epistemology as "the study of the mechanisms of the growth of knowledge" (Piaget 1957 p. 14). In addition to this general and broader form of genetic epistemology, there is a more specific notion of genetic epistemology:

> Under its limited or special form, genetic epistemology is the study of successive states of a science as a function of its development. Thus conceived, genetic epistemology could be defined as the positive science, empirical as well as theoretical, of the becoming of positive sciences *qua* sciences. (Piaget 1957)

Once again, other genetic epistemologists would disagree with the idea that genetic epistemology could be a positive science only. They would include in it a normative aspect. They would not, as has been seen, share the same fascination for science.

Piaget's fascination is easily explainable in terms of the original purpose of genetic epistemologies, according to which, as has already been seen, any form of knowledge is triple. Science is indeed so social that it has become a social institution, so psychological as to engender specific forms of behaviour, and such a complex and coherent system of signs and cognitive activities that it requires a long and difficult training to be practised. The coherent system of signs and cognitive activities evolves with time and has to be explained. Piaget assumes that the explanation of this development of scientific knowledge comes from its psychological and sociological aspects which are thus indissociable from the epistemic aspect. Indeed, Piaget goes so far as to maintain that a:

> systematic study of the development of any sector of scientific knowledge will necessarily be led, in attempting to disengage the sociogenetic and psychogenetic roots of this form of knowledge, to push the analysis of its formative mechanisms to the terrain of prescientific and infra-scientific common beliefs in the history of societies . . . , in the development of the child and even to the frontiers of physiological processes. (Piaget 1957 p. 13)

The implicit assumption of this statement by Piaget is that knowledge can be attained through the pre-

suppositions, methods, procedures, and resultant findings of empirical sciences such as history of ideas, history of science, sociology of knowledge, developmental psychology, psychophysiology even. No special place is given, in this context, to epistemology itself as a separate way of knowing or of assessing, at least, the validity of claims to knowledge. Thus, it may be argued that such positive inquiries into the history, sociology, and psychology of epistemic claims to knowledge presuppose, as Piaget explicitly stated several times in his paper "*De la psychologie génétique à l'épistémologie génétique*" [stupidly translated into English as "Genetic Psychology and Epistemology" (Piaget 1952); see especially the two examples of number concept and conservation], incontrovertible resolutions of ontological and epistemological issues. Piaget can be apodictic about these resolutions, because he believes that the experimental method renders findings incontrovertible.

> From the University of Louvain to Soviet laboratories, psychologists agree today upon a number of issues (perception, habit formation, intelligence development, etc. . . .) without making it possible, while reading an experimental report, to recognize the philosophy of its author. (Piaget 1947 p. 118)

1. Is Genetic Psychology Relevant to Epistemology?

Since it is beyond the scope of this article to examine the relations of all genetic psychologies to all conceptions of epistemology, this article will be limited to two questions dealing with Piaget's genetic psychology: (a) is this psychology relevant to philosophical epistemology? And (b), is Piaget's psychology of intelligence relevant to Piaget's epistemology?

Piaget's answer to the first question is clear:

> Genetic psychology is a science whose methods are more and more closely related to those of biology. Epistemology, on the contrary, is usually regarded as a philosophical subject, necessarily connected with all the other aspects of philosophy and justifying, accordingly, a metaphysical position. In these circumstances, the link between the two subjects would have to be considered either as illegitimate or, on the contrary, as no less natural than the transition from any scientific study to whatever form of philosophical thought, less by way of inference than by inspiration and involving, moreover, the addition to the latter subject of considerations beyond its scope. (Piaget 1952 p. 51)

This disclaimer takes part in Piaget's general depreciation of philosophy (see Piaget 1971a). As an empirical researcher, Piaget distrusts armchair psychologists: "The unfortunate thing for psychology is that everybody thinks of himself as a psychologist. As a result, when an epistemologist needs to call on some psychological aspect, he does not refer to psychological research and he does not consult psychologists; he depends on his own reflections" (Piaget 1970a p. 8).

As far as the second question is concerned and to the extent that the reader accepts Piaget's claim of not being himself a philosopher, Piaget has pointed out many times that "specialists in genetic psychology, and especially in child psychology, do not always suspect what diverse and fruitful relationships are possible between their own subject and other more general kinds of research, such as the theory of knowledge or epistemology" (Piaget 1952). The preliminary condition for their "diverse and fruitful relationships" is indeed the acceptance by philosophers and developmental psychologists of Piaget's own idea of what epistemology really is all about; which answers positively the second of our two questions, but leads to a new question, in turn. What is epistemology for Piaget? As has already been seen, the central task of genetic epistemology is the study of "knowledge, and in particular scientific knowledge, on the basis of its history, its sociogenesis, and especially the psychological origins of the notions and operations upon which it is based" (Piaget 1970a p. 1). The common denominator of the history, sociogenesis, and psychogenesis of knowledge is, for Piaget, the stages of scientific thought which are the answer to what Piaget considers as the fundamental question of a truly experimental epistemology, namely: "By what process does a science pass from one determinate form subsequently held to be inadequate to another determinate form afterwards held to be superior by the common agreement of the experts on this subject?" (Piaget 1952 p. 51).

As can be seen, this particular form of epistemology rules out any form of philosophical criteriology external to the scientific inquiry itself and rules in the reflection of scientists themselves upon their own disciplines. It calls for an epistemology internal to the various scientific disciplines and it justifies, in advance of any empirical testing, the fundamental categories of a discipline as defined by the practitioners of the discipline. This position renders the status of scientific breakthroughs rather hazardous, because, unless they are sanctioned, a posteriori, by the recognition of the scientific community, the categories under which they operate remain invalid. In this exact sense, Piaget is the direct heir of Baldwin, because the emphasis is put, in both epistemologies, on the social dimension in the control of facts and because, in spite of his numerous and vigorous attacks on Darwinism, Piaget seems to accept, here, a form of natural selection of ideas (considered as analogous to mutations in biology) not unlike the natural selection of the fittest. In such a view, truth is conflated to life. In other words, if this viewpoint happened to be correct, errors ought to be lethal. Such an identification of truth with survival is indeed categorically mistaken.

Nevertheless, such a formulation has the important merit of changing global and unsolvable as such philosophical questions into specific, soluble ones. But it is not possible to see clearly how genetic psychology of intelligence can contribute to such an effort. To do so, it is necessary to go back to the thrust of knowledge. No matter how far back a person traces the origins of a scientific concept, the end point is always a con-struction of reality that has emerged from a more primitive one. From early constructs of reality into earlier ones, the starting point is always removed one step further and it is necessary to recognize that there is no absolute zero in knowledge. One collective representation of knowledge always hides another one considered as more primitive. Each of these collective representations entails a specific form of ontology accepted as true by a given social group or propounded by some advanced thinkers. These successive ontologies presuppose correlative forms of understanding ("genetic modes", to use Baldwin's phrase) or systems of concepts that can be characterized and even logically formalized.

For Piaget, the safeguard to maintain in such an inquiry is the consideration that the norms of "scientific" inquiry of a given group at a given moment are facts for the modern researcher; no claim is made about the validity of these ancient norms. Hence, the phrase to designate them: "normative facts". They must be mentioned to account for the beliefs of those investigators who have used them as valid norms, but they cannot be used by subsequent researchers in a more advanced stage of knowledge. This sort of historical and critical effort constitutes the phylogeny of minds and reality. Since no-one leaps from infancy into the adult views of their own society, the phylogenetic research has to be complemented by ontogenetic investigations into the forms of understanding or ontologies of the infants, children, adolescents, and youth who are in the process of becoming full-fledged members of a social order.

In the same way it is not possible to reconstitute the world views of people in different places and times without active research, a person should actually investigate the ways in which growing human beings understand themselves and their world. The form of this investigation is the same as that of the investigation of foreign cultures and past times. The aim is not the knowledge of the actual contents of thought but the architectural organization of thoughts and things.

Moreover, child psychology, à la Piaget, constitutes "a kind of mental embryology in that it describes the stages of the individual development, and particularly in that it studies the mechanism itself of this development" (Piaget 1952 p. 50).

"Once we admit comparisons of this kind, the history of the relations between embryology and other biological studies throws considerable light on the possible and, to a certain extent, the actual relationship between child psychology and epistemology" (Piaget 1952 p. 51). This last statement shows exactly why and how Piaget believes genetic psychology is relevant to genetic epistemology considered as a new scientific discipline.

2. How is Genetic Psychology Relevant to Genetic Epistemology?

The history of scientific thought inevitably poses the problem of changes of perspective and even of "revolutions" in "paradigms". As a student of the French philosopher Léon Brunschvicg, Piaget is aware of the dynamic character of any epistemology that does not put forward either a priorist or empiricist view, where knowledge is subordinated to forms occurring in advance either in the subject (nativism) or in the object (empiricism). In addition, Baldwin's "genetic logic" had given Piaget some penetrating insights, to say the least, into the psychological construction of cognitive structures.

Piaget's concern with this question led him to a two-fold task: (a) constituting a method capable of providing empirical tests and (b) reaching back to the very origins of knowledge. But though this kind of analysis involves an essential element of psychological experimentation, it must not be confused with a study in pure psychology: the psychology dimension inherent in genetic epistemology is nothing but a byproduct of the epistemological research.

There is here a strong belief that psychology or, more accurately, psychogenesis (or formation of knowledge) would give a positive answer to the problems of validity of knowledge, as if this answer were read directly in the empirical observation of reality. In a man who always claimed not to be an empiricist, such an attitude seems rather surprising, because it eliminates the side of the subjective construction in these findings, a side that should be essential to someone who claims to be a constructivist as does Piaget: "Knowledge arises neither from a self-conscious subject, nor from objects already constituted (from the point of view of the subject) which would impress themselves on him; it arises from interactions that take place midway between the two" (Piaget 1972 p. 19). Moreover, Piaget considers, as did Baldwin who coined for this the term "adualism", that "there exists at the start neither a subject in the epistemological sense of the word, nor objects conceived as such, nor invariant intermediaries" (Piaget 1972 p. 20). The initial problem of knowledge will therefore be the construction of such invariant intermediaries. This is the aspect of Piaget's work which is best known: the construction of invariants from the permanence of objects to the most elaborate forms of conservation. Starting from the point of contact between the body itself and external things, Piaget will construct, in the long series of his books on cognitive developmental psychology, the development of these intermediaries in two complementary directions: internal, leading to the construction of the self and its cognitive structures and external, leading to the construction of reality and its properties.

3. The Stages of Development

Here again, there is a common misrepresentation of the importance of stages in Piaget's theory. This misrepresentation is threefold: (a) range of application of the concept of stage; (b) evidence for stages; and (c) function of the concept of stage in Piaget's theory.

Does the stage concept apply only to the three major "periods" of development (sensory motor, concrete operations, formal operations) or does it apply also to the progressive steps or substages in the attainment of a cognitive structure within a stage? It seems self-evident that the idea of conservation of matter rests on and includes the idea of object permanence and, in turn, that the idea of conservation of volume rests on and includes the idea of conservation of matter. So, it is clear that each major period of development prepares the next one logically and materially. But this is not so clear for each of the substages characterizing every major period. However, empirical research seems to agree with the general sequencing observed by Piaget and his collaborators in Geneva. This comparative flexibility of substages seems to be an argument in favour of constructivism, since, if both stages and substages were inflexible, development would be a mere unfolding of genetic competences. On the other hand, if it were possible to speed up cognitive development at the level of basic stages, the sequencing would be unnecessary.

Another question is raised by Piaget's stages: they do not seem to extend beyond the years of adolescence. What happens in the rest of life? Do adults cease to grow? Or do they grow in such idiosyncratic ways that it would be pointless to attempt to trace a coherence in their life? Neither alternative is very satisfying. That Piaget did not address himself to this question very clearly is the reflection of his position in the field of developmental psychology. Be it in his own autobiographical works (*Autobiography*, his "novel" *Recherche*, and other essays) or in his scientific papers, Piaget's categories of understanding human development have not gone beyond the categories of his time, just as Freud's theory of memory does not innovate on Ebbinghaus's. Piaget did not invent a new stage of development after adolescence and youth. In this sense, he was less creative than G. Stanley Hall who revived the notion of adolescence to explain what was happening to young men in America at the turn of the century.

This article will now turn to the second misrepresentation of Piaget's ideas about stages, and show that some critics of Piaget believe that it is not possible to conclude the existence of universal stages on the basis of homely observations of a person's own three children, as did Piaget. After careful scrutiny, this is not exactly Piaget's claim. His contention really is that the sequence of stages is orderly and that this order is necessary because it reflects a "genetic logic" to use Baldwin's phrase.

To show that any sequence is orderly means to show that the observed sequence corresponds in some way to another sequence which is deemed orderly. To show that the logical structures underlying thought grow in an orderly way, it is necessary to have a method for ordering logical structures that is independent of any observations that may be made of children's growth. This independent scale is found by Piaget in the scales of conservations. An example of this method can be given in the field of geometry by Felix Klein's Erlangen programme. This programme orders the different possible geometries according to the number of parameters that are conserved. At the lowest level, there is topological geometry which is strictly qualitative and conserves only the most general properties of space: inside, outside, and vicinity. One cut above, projective geometry is found which conserves straight lines, in addition. Then comes Euclidean geometry which conserves, in addition, distances, angles, and parallel. The order of acquisition of these different geometries parallels their logical order of integration in terms of the number of invariants taken into consideration. But, showing that the thought of the child at a given age (or stage) corresponds to a given logical model is something less than showing orderly growth. As an empirical researcher, Piaget never attempted to go beyond this level of evidence. He never tried to test the reliability of his findings by the standard test–retest procedure.

But he did try to demonstrate the limits of coherence of a stage by his studies of "*décalages*". Horizontal *décalages* are the evidence of the unevenness of stages, since they are the sign that a concept (conservation, for instance) appears in one form at first (conservation of matter, for instance) before being extended over its possible range: weight, volume, and so on. This extension may take many months. For Piaget, this tension between the more advanced aspects and the less highly developed ones is the sign that there is an actual construction of any concept, because this concept does not spring fully formed from the child's mind, as Athena from Zeus' brow. This development of the same concept in its extension is considered by Piaget as evidence for a developmental mechanism that he called "cognitive conflict" among unevenly structured concepts. The dialectical relationship between less and more developed mental structures creates conflicts that foster further growth. But, how much conflict is productive and structuring in the formation of a given stage and how much is destructive and dangerous for further development? This is never clearly specified in Piaget's theory. Apparently, only small and local conflicts are acceptable as factors of cognitive growth.

This question leads to another question, more basic for a good understanding of Piaget's stage theory: the function of the notion within the general theory. Any careful review of Piaget's writings on the topic would show that he wrote very little about stages. This could be considered as evidence for a lack of interest in the subject as well as for the self-explanatory aspect of the concept of stage in Piaget's mind.

From the little writing by Piaget on stages, it is possible to gain the impression that two issues are important to him in this respect: the determination of a developmental level and the way in which cognitive development takes place. Determining developmental level is essentially structural in nature. It requires the recognition of the unity of a certain period of development when it is compared to another one. The order of succession of acquisition must be constant. The structures constructed at a given stage must be integrated in the structure of the following stage and the unity of the stage must be marked by a "*structure d'ensemble*". In order to maintain development on its optimal course, Piaget imagined a complex system of concepts: equilibrium, assimilation and accommodation, adaptation, and so on. But, at this point in the discussion, the concept of "homeorhesis", borrowed from Waddington's work in theoretical embryology, is the relevant one. As its name indicates, homeorhesis is a system regulating the flow of different inputs in the developmental process of an organism. Another concept was also borrowed from Waddington's vocabulary, that of "*creode*", or due course. When the forces making for one choice of developmental pathway (*creode*) are not strong enough, the organism will develop in another way.

Contrary to the conclusions generally drawn in the literature about Piaget's notion of stage, it can be concluded from this brief summary of Piaget's writings on stages that the universality of stages is a claim made more often and more strongly by followers or detractors of the Genevan epistemologist than by himself. The very notion of *creode* indicates the polymorphic character of development for Piaget. So the following sobering view about Piaget's stages has to be taken: they are merely classificatory and hierarchizing devices imported by Piaget from his education in natural history. In addition, stages come handy to fight empiricism, because they preserve the integrity of the organism in the face of environmental pressure.

There are four main periods or levels of development in Piaget's theory: Level 1: the sensory-motor period (in Geneva: birth to age 2 roughly); Level 2: the preoperational thought period (in Geneva: about age 2 to 7); Level 3: the concrete-operational period (about age 7 to 11; and Level 4: the formal-operational period (about age 11 to 15).

The first level is composed of six substages which mark the infant's progress from only performing reflex actions in complete adualism (no dissociation of self and the rest of the world) to a gradual dissociation of the self from the objects and from others (especially the mother). The effects of such a dissociation are: perception of the effects of the infant's own actions upon objects, anticipation of the actions of people and objects and, at the very end of this period, the beginnings of a mental representation of things and thoughts, which existed only in actions so far.

This period is characterized by the passage, in the baby's mind, from action to thought. This means that during infancy, as for animals during all their life, thoughts and things exist only in the course of an action. They do not exist for and by themselves. Hence, no need to conserve them outside of action. There is a tool function, but tools are not kept from one action to the next (no memory). There is space, but only the space of action. Things are located in reference to specific actions that can be performed upon them: vicinity, in and out of the box, the room, the house, finding the cookie jar when mother or father takes it away, and so on. There is time, but it is elastic. Depending on the actions performed during those minutes or hours, they pass by more or less quickly. There is causality, but at first there is one unique causal agent: the child. Then, when objects become permanent, the infant attributes to objects some physical and spatial connections independent of its actions on them.

The second level, preoperational thought, is characterized by the use of language. But language is only one of the signs of the child's mastery of the semiotic or symbolic function. Not only does the child speak, but he or she draws, imitates others intentionally, plays symbolic games (dolls, Indians), becomes capable of minimal forms of cooperation with others (setting the table, carrying things for parents, helping friends), and moral actions (right/wrong).

But there are tremendous limitations to this new form of conduct. First of all, children still use language in an egocentric fashion; they talk at each other and not to each other. True dialogue is not yet possible. Second, they depend on perception in problem-solving situations: if a row of beads is longer than another containing the same number of beads, the child is convinced that the longer row has more beads, and so on, for other quantities.

Between ages 5 and 7, the child undergoes a certain change. The egocentric speech that accompanied the child's actions is becoming focused upon communicating something to others. He or she is more sensitive to contradictions brought about by the heavy reliance upon perception: that a row of beads could be, at the same time, longer than another and still contain the same number of beads becomes puzzling. Children, who used to focus exclusively on one dimension of a situation, begin to recognize that more than one factor at a time has to be taken into consideration to account for an event in a coordinated manner. This increasing coordination leads to the next level, that of concrete operations.

The term "operations", in Piaget's system, means actions that are interiorized, reversible, and coordinated into systems that have laws that apply to the entire system and not just to the single action itself. "Interiorization" means the eventual dissociation between the general form of a coordination and the particular content of an external action. Interiorization leads from "practical" (sensory motor) to operational intelligence and is the precondition for objective knowledge as well as for symbolic representation, by opposition to "internalization" which is the eventual diminution of external movements that become covert and sketchy, illustrated in imitation and language. "Reversibility" is the possibility of performing a given action in a reversed direction. Its two chief forms are negation (not male = female) and reciprocity (not better = worse).

The stage of concrete operations is marked by the acquisition of conservation. Conservation is the maintenance of a structure as invariant during physical changes of some aspects. For Piaget, the stability of an objective attribute is never simply given, it is constructed by the living organization. Conservation therefore implies an internal system of regulations that can compensate internally for external changes. In the case of concrete operations, this system of regulations is made out of three main "groupings" (*groupements*): classification, seriation, and number. Its applicability is limited to objects considered as real (concrete) by opposition to objects considered as virtual or possible (formal).

By the end of the period of concrete operations, children have markedly increased their abilities to account for the cause of physical events so that they are now ready to solve not only problems that involve real objects but also ones concerning hypotheses and propositions about relationships. This readiness to think in hypothetico-deductive terms is the hallmark of the stage of formal operations. It is typically manifested in propositional thinking and a combinatory system that considers the real as one among other hypothetical possibilities. Formal operations are characteristic of the final stage of operational intelligence which "reflects" on concrete operations through the elaboration of formal "group" structures.

4. The Psychological Methods of Genetic Epistemology

The findings of Piaget in the domain of developmental psychology have been obtained by methods that are not standard in contemporary psychology. Piaget's main method for the study of intelligence has been labelled variously by him as "clinical" or "critical". Nothing could be more misleading than these two words for the reader. Clinical or critical investigations à la Piaget mean a free conversation between the child and the investigator when the child is older than 4. It means also a free conversation dealing with a "*matériel*" ("experimental" device) that "does" something in front of the child who has to anticipate what will happen and, then, explain what has happened. This *matériel* can be two clay balls, matches, sticks, erector sets, and so on. Here, Piaget is the true heir to the pedagogical method used, since the eighteenth century, in the little charity schools for the poor and the needy, by Protestant ministers in the Jura chain of mountains. Like these ministers and teachers, he used a *matériel* that was both inexpensive and simple: clay, water, sand, wood, and so on. This *matériel* could be seen and manipulated by the child *ad libitum*. Sometimes, an imaginary child of the same age made countersuggestions and the degree of resistance of the real child interviewed by the investigator is observed. Sometimes, the investigator in person makes countersuggestions to the child. The general idea of this method is clinical in the sense that, like any competent clinician, the investigator probes carefully the extent and the nature of the thought process that produced a child's initial answer. It is critical to the extent that it confronts the child with the consequences of his or her assertions. It depends therefore very much on the argumentative talent of the child and of the investigator alike.

In fact, there are two rather parodoxical aspects in this method: (a) the reliance upon a method that is closer to juridical cross-examinations than to standard experimental methodology; (b) the apparent internal contradiction between the idea that the ultimate stage of cognitive development is hypothetico–deductive thinking and the fact that this method is not used in his research by its extoller.

5. *Piaget's Theory of Intellectual Process*

Each stage of intellectual development may be described as a set of organized structures or schemes. For Piaget, a *"schème"* is the internal general form of a specific knowing activity, be it sensory motor or formal. Note that Piaget distinguishes *"schème"* from "schema" which conveys a figurative, representational outline, by opposition to a *schème* which is related to the operative side of knowledge.

As an individual encounters his or her world, he or she assimilates objects and events to his or her schemes. When this is not possible, because the existing schemes are inadequate, these mental structures modify themselves or accommodate. Assimilation and accommodation form the two poles of adaptation. Adaptation, in turn, is a balanced state of a biological organization within its environment. In behaviour, it is the equilibrium between accommodation and assimilation which is reached only in intelligence by opposition to instincts and other cognitive modalities. Hence, Piaget's effort in this very domain.

Unlike Darwin, Marx, or Freud who were also interested in the problem of dialectics between change and stability, Piaget had to discover and describe the very rudiments of the course of cognitive growth at the same time as he developed a theory to explain it. Darwin did not have to produce evidence for the existence of species or to construct a taxonomy *ex novo*, nor did Marx have to demonstrate the existence of different social forms and classes. Freud's case is somewhat different, since his "stages of psychosexual development" was a rather long-range inference about children, based on his work with adult patients and aimed mainly at developing his psychodynamic ideas; so much so that his stage theory can be easily separated from his psychodynamics.

Piaget had to transform each of the Kantian categories from the philosophical status of first principle into a subject of scientific investigation, in order to prove that there was a positive, experimental solution to epistemological dilemmas faced by philosophers of knowledge. The strategy chosen by Piaget for the solving of

this problem was neither the establishment of laws nor the search of elements constitutive of the universe of knowledge. Unlike the successful physical and chemical scientists, Piaget looked for a third strategy: the search for structures.

Piaget's understanding of structures is somewhat different from that of mathematicians, linguists, and anthropologists. It is closest to Gestalt psychologists, because, as he said once, he was a "Gestaltist with, in addition, the activity of the subject" (personal communication); which does not mean too much, because he also claimed to be a "subjective behaviourist". Indeed, he was neither.

Piaget's use of structures and operations is at variance with what is usually intended by these concepts. The concept of group is a case in point. For Piaget, "A group is a closed circle of operations that return to the point of departure through an operation of the group as a whole" (Piaget 1954 p. 105). Mathematically speaking, the group axioms imply that a sequence of two or more operations can result in a return to the point of departure, but they also imply that there are many more sequences that do not terminate in this way. It is also contrary to mathematical usage to speak of a series of operations as being a group, and still more to speak of two series, involving the same elements, as being two groups. Such a confusion of mathematical groups with the composition of interiorized actions allows Piaget to transform external acts into internal operations. Moreover, this confusion of the global properties of a group with the individual properties of operations pertinent to the group allows the fusion with modern mathematics of the Gestaltist idea that a part of a whole is determined by its relationship to the whole. Finally, the main difficulty of such a treatment of the transformation of object manipulations into mental operations is that there is no explanation for how object handlings see truth values attached to themselves. It seems rather strange that a man who devoted an entire year to the study of negation did not perceive that implications and negations, bearing on propositions to which no action could ever correspond, could not be translated into a combination of acts, as Binet had shown at the time of his opposition to the Wurzburg School and to French empiricism. Nevertheless, such a critique should not be taken too far. By its very structuralism, mathematics is a science for which an operation either exists fully formed or does not exist at all. Genetic epistemology and its main ancillary science, genetic psychology, are genetic and, as such, they displace the emphasis from structures to genesis or development. There is here a strife of systems that should be fully understood.

For structuralism, concepts do not develop; a person just leaps from one form of understanding to another. The articulation between these two forms is never specified. In some forms of structuralism, this articulation cannot be specified in principle. For such a pure form of structuralism, it is obvious that either a concept is in operation or it is not. There is no solution of continuity.

If the child, the "primitive", or the "patient" do not employ the valid criteria for the given concept, they are not manifesting a more primitive form of the concept, they are simply not manifesting the concept at all, period. From this point of view, all of developmental psychology of cognition would be dissolved and especially Piaget's theory of intelligence.

It should be clearly understood, on the other hand, that this general remark about the strife between structuralism and geneticism does not absolve Piaget of two mental confusions: (a) using logico–mathematical concepts in such a distorted way that their formalization becomes virtually impossible, as for the notion of "*groupements*"; (b) trying to unite in one superordinate system structuralism and geneticism, thinking that, by so doing, he could solve the opposition between Gestaltism and behaviourism in psychology, Tarde and Durkheim in sociology, nativism and empiricism in philosophy. There is indeed a world of difference between attempting to solve such contradictions and the legitimate enterprise of a developmental psychology that would try to demonstrate the existence of attenuated forms of a given concept in the child, the "primitive", and the "patient", and would try to show the metamorphoses thereof. Too often, by recourse to mere analogies taken for structural components, as in "Biology and Knowledge" (Piaget 1971b), Piaget has given his readers the impression of overcoming these contradictions too easily. All of the seven methods presented in the second chapter of this very large book are methods to generate analogies, not to explore their meaning.

This question leads to the two other components of Piaget's epistemology: (a) the biogenesis of knowledge and (b) his reconsideration of classical epistemological problems.

6. Biogenesis or the Preliminary Organic Conditions of Knowledge

"Cognitive processes seem, then, to be at one and the same time the outcome of organic autoregulation reflecting its essential mechanisms, and the most highly differentiated organs of this regulation at the core of interactions with the environment so much so that, in the case of man, these processes are being extended to the universe itself" (Piaget 1971b p. 26). But for Piaget, there are some crucial differences between cognition and organic functioning: the completeness, stability, and flexibility of the structures of intelligence, the progressive dissociation of form and content, characteristic of cognitive organizations. This convergence between cognition and organic regulations could be explained, according to Piaget, in three different ways: (a) behaviourism; (b) nativism; (c) interactionism.

Piaget's understanding of what he calls "Lamarckian empiricism" is rather different from Lamarck's ideas, since Lamarckism is here reduced to the heredity of acquired characters. This aspect of his transformism was secondary for Lamarck and pertinent only to what he called "circumstances". His main idea was that of a metaphysical scale of beings that was intangible. Even limited to this form, Piaget's rejection of Lamarckism rests upon the absence of a regulatory mechanism between the stimulation of the environment and the responses of the organism. For him, Lamarckism is the biological version of behaviourism and thus falls under the same criticism.

At the opposite end of the spectrum of epistemological positions, Piaget locates nativism which corresponds to Lorenz's ideas at the level of the physiology of behaviour and to neo-Darwinism at the more general level. Piaget's opposition to Lorenz is focused on Lorenz's attempt to show that Kantian categories are biologically preformed. If these categories are preformed, Piaget argues, they lose their necessity and their unity, which is unacceptable for logical structures.

In spite of its simplism, this difference between Lorenz's and Piaget's geneticisms deserves some attention. Too often, rapid readings of Piaget's ideas have led some of his commentators to think that he was a nativist. His strong rejection of Lorenz's ideas shows indeed the contrary. Without arguing the case in detail, any claim for an invariant sequence or a necessary order of emergence must rest either on a genetic (nativistic) argument concerning a hierarchy of dispositions (evidence showing that putative later forms in the sequence cannot be manifested in the absence or suppression of earlier forms); or, on evidence of a logical order showing that the putative later forms presuppose the "earlier" forms. Clearly, the second alternative is chosen by Piaget.

This criticism of Lorenz is then doubled by a criticism of neo-Darwinism revolving around two key points: (a) random mutations and (b) natural selection. For Piaget, mutations must, somehow, be related to the adaptive needs of the organism. In addition, chance is an improbable candidate to account for the evolution of complex organs and organisms. Natural selection is a process in which the organism is essentially passive. Consequently, Darwinism should be rejected.

Piaget wants a theory in which the initiative remains with the organism: the mutations that occur are part of the total process of organized self-regulation; and an internal process of what Baldwin called "organic selection" plays a major role in determining which variants will be presented to the environment for further natural selection. This is the "phenocopy hypothesis". This hypothesis proposes that there are both exogenous and endogenous variations in phenotypes. Once the exogenous form is established, the organism "re-invents" it by producing endogenously the same phenotypic result. This endogenous or genotypic form is, in some sense, a copy of the phenotypic one; hence "phenocopy". The sort of groping by which an organism senses that something is not working properly is similar to groping in intellectual problem solving; hence the continuity from life to intelligence. Note that this continuity is based on an entirely speculative biology.

7. Classical Epistemological Problems Reconsidered

Once it is accepted that "epistemology is the theory of valid knowledge" (Piaget 1971c), it follows that epistemology is by nature an interdisciplinary subject, since the process of knowing validly raises questions both of fact and of validity. If it were a question of validity alone, epistemology would merge with logic. If it were a question of facts, it would merge with the psychology of cognitive functions. Since it is both, developmental epistemology entails the cooperation (in the sense of Piaget's operations, of course) of psychologists who are studying development as such, of logicians who formalize the stages or states of temporary equilibrium in this development, of mathematicians who would ensure some liaison between logic and the field in question, and of cyberneticians who would connect logic and psychology.

The International Center for Genetic Epistemology in Geneva has been functioning according to this rule since 1955, and has worked on several classical epistemological problems. Some of them will be reviewed critically below.

7.1 Number and Space

Whitehead and Russell sought to make the ordinals equivalent to classes of classes by a one-to-one correspondence, whereas Poincaré considered that the concept of number relies upon an irreducible intuition of $(n + 1)$. In a certain sense, the two Englishmen tried to reduce number to class, whereas the Frenchman attempted to reduce it to series or iteration. By looking at what happens in the child between the ages of 4 and 7, Piaget claimed to have observed the construction of three correlated systems of operations: classification, seriation, and numeration. The concept of number appears then to be the result of the synthesis of classification and seriation, and genetic epistemology has put an end to the endless debate between seriationists and classificationists in an empirical, scientific manner.

As for the problem of space, the Italian mathematician Enriques attempted to reduce different geometric forms to separate sensory categories, whereas others, in the Kantian tradition, thought of it in terms of a priori categories preceding any experience. Piaget shows how space is the result of the sensory-motor construction of a practical group of displacements analogous to Poincaré's group and thus having all the properties of an Abelian group. In addition, he shows why the order of acquisition of different geometries is different in the child and in history. Historically, Euclidean metric preceded projective geometry and topology, whereas developmentally the reverse order is observed.

It has already been shown that this last order is more logical in the sense of the number of parameters to be conserved. Developmental psychology discovers the logical (genetic) order of things rather than their historical (accidental) order which is linked, in this case, to the accident of perception that "sees", according to Piaget, Euclidean forms first. Useless to point out here is that perceptual space is not Euclidean. There are many perceptual spaces corresponding to different geometries.

7.2 Time and Velocity

In classical or Newtonian mechanics, time and space are both absolute, corresponding to simple intuitions (Newton's *Sensorium Dei*), while velocity is merely a relationship between them. In relativistic mechanics, by contrast, velocity becomes an absolute and time, like space, is relative to it. Piaget shows that there exists, developmentally, a basic intuition of speed, independent of any idea of duration and resulting from the primal concept of order: the intuition of kinematic "overtaking". Consequently, the very development of the ideas of space, time, and velocity shows that "there is nothing inevitable about the intuition of universal and absolute time" (Piaget 1971c p. 11).

7.3 Object Permanence, Identity, and Conservation

The idea of permanence seemed to be both self-evident and necessary at the beginning of this century. Then, it had been cast into doubt by atomic physics. Once again, Piaget shows that his developmental researches give an empirical answer to this question by demonstrating the construction of object permanence in the course of the first year of life. Object permanence is, in addition, the first stage of qualitative identity of objects. Then this concept is transferred to quantities and will lead, in turn, to the various forms of conservation.

The fact that the concept of identity is attained before conservation of quantity seems interesting to Piaget from an epistemological point of view, because an epistemological school of thought, represented by Emile Meyerson, in the past, and by Jerome Bruner presently, holds that conservation derives from the concept of identity. In fact, Piaget's own studies show that there is a qualitative jump between identity and conservation. Identity has only qualitative significance; it is obtained by a simple dissociation of constant qualities from variable qualities. Conservation, on the other hand, presupposes operations of quantifying (compensations between the dimension which increases and the dimension which decreases and so on): the concept of quantity therefore requires an act of construction and is not given by simple perceptual verification as is the concept of quality, according to Piaget. Conservation embeds identity in the wider framework of reversibility, quantitative compensations, and the concepts of number and measure. Thus, for Piaget, developmental psychology is the royal road to the solution of all pending epistemological questions.

As has already been pointed out earlier in this article, there is a touch of naïveté in believing this and Piaget's sincerity should be questioned on this central point of the very existence of a positive, empirical epistemology. Two sorts of question are in order here: logical and methodological.

From a logical standpoint, it is clear that Piaget posits a "*telos*" (goal) to development such as to run the risk, in his historico–critical reconstruction of the various stages of a given science, of building up his concepts and beliefs in such a way as to comfort his own views, rather than as "immediate to God" and worthy of consideration independently of his own concerns. The opinion of Vonèche after having read the forthcoming (posthumous) book by Piaget and Garcia, "*Histoire des sciences et psychogenèse*", is that Piaget has not always resisted the temptation to write history in a way pleasing his theory.

From a methodological viewpoint, it is no less clear that sometimes Piaget's evidence is shaky or flimsy. The case in point is the genesis of the various geometries inventoried by Piaget in the child. This inventory rests upon two basic assumptions: (a) children's drawings were completely analysed by Luquet in the 1920s and (b) drawings are the best means to use in order to assess the attainment of geometrical concepts in children. If these two assumptions are carefully examined, it is necessary to recognize that they are a bit abusive. Luquet analysed children's drawings with a strong prejudice: for him, the goal of children's drawings is academic realism. With that "*telos*" in mind, he proceeded to show that the stages of drawing develop from fortuitous realism (found in scribblings) to intellectual realism and then visual realism. This sort of analysis might have been possible in the late 1920s in some uncultivated circles that wanted desperately to "defend" Western art against the invasion of "Negro art" as did the Nazis and the Soviets who invented "socialist realism". Now, after the surrealists' revolution, the rupture with academism instituted by Miró, Picasso, and the like, it is no longer possible to assess children's productions in the same way. This does not mean to say that children do not grow out of scribblings into more realistic drawings. It means that the artistic revolution of the beginning of this century has drawn our attention to the possibility that children's drawings are a language that should not be taken at face value: they might contain some conventions to represent some reality and they might not be read correctly. An example of what is meant here can be given by the stage in which children, incapable of representing perspective according to the rules instituted by the Renaissance, draw very lacy roads to signify perspective. This stage is ignored by Luquet who called it "missed realism" demonstrating only that he missed the point.

Secondly, drawings are not necessarily the best means to represent the progresses in geometry made by chil-dren. If the hypothesis is accepted that drawings are a sort of shorthand for children, that is to say a conventional means of communication, the possibility must be recognized for the child to neglect the uses that the adults who misunderstand this shorthand will make of it. In other words, it is not at all evident that children's drawings are the right way to assess geometrical knowledge in children. Other approaches should at least complement this one. Unfortunately, this has not always been the case. It is so much more regretted that this methodological sloppiness combined with bold theoretical conclusions has cast some doubt on the entire oeuvre of Piaget, whereas, when compared with what was done in the field by others at the same time, his work appears to be so much superior. Think of language and moral development, for instance. At the time when Carmichael's *Handbook of Child Psychology* was happy to account for language by simple word counts at various ages, Piaget presented a complete theory of language. When Hartshorne and May were working on resistance to temptation, Piaget was studying moral judgment. These examples are only two among many possible.

Bibliography

Baldwin J M 1902 *Development and Evolution, Including Psychological Evolution, Evolution by Orthoplasy, and Theory of Genetic Modes*. Macmillan, London

Baldwin J M 1906–1911 *Thought and Things: A Study of the Development and Meaning of Thought or Genetic Logic*. Allen, London

Bosanquet B 1888 *Logic: Or, The Morphology of Knowledge*. Oxford University Press, London

Cassirer E 1903–1920 *Das Erkenntnisproblem in der Philosophie und Wissenschaft der Neueren Zeit*. Cassirer, Berlin

Elkind D 1976 *Child Development and Education: A Piagetian Perspective*. Oxford University Press, New York

Furth H G, Wachs W 1975 *Thinking Goes to School: Piaget's Theory in Practice*. Oxford University Press, New York

Hobhouse L T 1888 *The Theory of Knowledge: A Contribution to Some Problems of Logic and Metaphysics*. Macmillan, London

Hobhouse L T 1912 *Mind in Evolution*. Macmillan, London

Piaget J 1947 Du rapport des sciences avec la philosophie. *Synthèse* 6: 130–50

Piaget J 1952 Genetic psychology and epistemology. *Diogenes* 1: 49–63

Piaget J 1954 *The Child's Construction of Reality*. Routledge and Kegan Paul, London

Piaget J 1957 Programme et méthodes de l'épistémologie génétique. In: Beth E W, Mays W, Piaget J (eds.) 1957 *Epistémologie génétique et recherche psychologique: Etudes d'épistémologie génétique*, Vol. 1. Presses Universitaires de France, Paris

Piaget J 1970a *Genetic Epistemology*. Columbia University Press, New York

Piaget J 1970b *Science of Education and Psychology of the Child*. Orion, New York

Piaget J 1971a *Insights and Illusions of Philosophy*. World Publishing, New York

Piaget J 1971b *Biology and Knowledge: An Essay on the*

Relations Between Organic Regulations and Cognitive Processes. University of Chicago Press, Chicago, Illinois

Piaget J 1971c *Psychology and Epistemology: Towards a Theory of Knowledge.* Penguin, Harmondsworth

Piaget J 1972 *The Principles of Genetic Epistemology.* Basic Books, New York

Sigwart C von 1894–95 *Logic.* Macmillan, New York

Wundt W 1880 *Logik: Eine Untersuchung der Principien der Erkenntniss und der Methoden Wissenschaftlicher Forschung.* Enke, Stuttgart

Basic Concepts of Behaviorism

R. M. Thomas

The word behaviorism identifies a cluster of psychological theories intended to explain why people and animals act as they do. Although there are some differences among the several varieties of behaviorism in this cluster, all have certain characteristics in common. Basically, all behaviorists conceive of learning as the act of establishing a connection between a stimulus (S) and a response (R). As a result, behaviorists are often referred to as S–R psychologists. The goal of child rearing or teaching is to ensure that when the child encounters a particular stimulus (such as a busy street crossing) he or she will emit a particular response (looking both left and right to make sure that no cars are approaching before stepping into the street).

One reason that there are several varieties of behaviorism is that behaviorists have disagreed on whether or not to estimate what occurs within the person between the stimulus and the response. In other words, is it proper to speculate about what the child in the above example thought between the time he or she reached the busy street and the time he or she peered left and right? Some theorists—known as methodological behaviorists—reject the notion that something "goes on" in "the mind" between stimulus and response, and accordingly discount estimates of what occurs between S and R (Watson 1919, Kantor 1959). Others, such as B. F. Skinner (1974), do not reject the idea that people have "thoughts" in mind, but they contend that since a mind and its contents or functions are not observable, it is unprofitable and misleading to waste time speculating about what happens between S and R. While both of these groups just discussed qualify as S–R psychologists, another cluster of behaviorists are better labeled S–O–R theorists, for they speculate about mental processes which they believe to occur in the organism (O) between the stimulus and response. In recent times these S–O–R theorists have been called cognitive psychologists.

Virtually all behaviorists share in common a series of concepts and terms related to these concepts which need to be understood if behaviorism is to be comprehended. These concepts will now be looked at.

The word conditioning in behaviorism means essentially the same as learning. That is, it means the establishment of a connection between a stimulus and a response. The best-known early laboratory experiments with conditioning were those conducted by the Russian psychologist Ivan Petrovich Pavlov (1849–1936) who established procedures for classical conditioning. He put meat powder (called an unconditioned stimulus) on a dog's tongue, which resulted in the dog spontaneously salivating (called the unconditioned response). On a sequence of subsequent occasions (trials), he sounded a bell at the same time as he gave the food to the dog. When the food was accompanied by the bell enough times, he found that he could withhold the food and only sound the bell, which itself would now cause the dog to salivate. The bell became the conditioned stimulus (for the dog learned to equate it with the food) that brought about the conditioned response of salivating to the bell. In sum, classical conditioning (or respondent conditioning) involves substituting a new stimulus for an old one by offering the two at the same time, or nearly the same time, until the new stimulus becomes sufficient to bring about the response that the old stimulus originally elicited.

A second kind of conditioning or learning has been called operant conditioning. It is not concerned with substituting one stimulus for another, but rather with assuring that a particular response is consistently made in the stimulus situation. For example, in a classroom children rarely raise their hands to obtain permission to speak to the class, but instead usually speak without seeking permission. The teacher wants the children to learn to raise their hands every time they wish to talk. It is not that the children lack the hand-raising skill among the various responses they know how to make. Rather, it is that they do not consistently use this skill in preference to other possibilities. And that is what operant conditioning is designed to accomplish—consistency of response in a given stimulus situation. Whether a response becomes consistent or not depends on the consequences the person experiences after making the response. If the consequences are rewarding to the individual, he or she is more likely to give that same response in the future when in a similar stimulus situation. But if the consequences are unrewarding or punishing, he or she is less likely to give that response again. Generally behaviorists do not favor the word rewarding, but rather use the term reinforcing in referring to a consequence that increases the incidence of a response in the future.

From the viewpoint of behaviorists, the task of child rearing or teaching is chiefly one of arranging learning situations and their consequences in ways that reinforce learners for performing the desired behaviors and that punish or fail to reinforce them for undesired acts. Thus, behaviorists have centered a great deal of attention on schedules of reinforcement, that is, on patterns in which consequences can be arranged so as to increase the frequency of desired responses and eliminate or extinguish undesired ones. For example, the effects on performance differ when continuous reinforcement (rewarding every time the desired act occurs) is used rather than intermittent reinforcement (rewarding only certain times the act occurs). Furthermore, different schedules of intermittent reinforcement yield different results. A fixed-ratio schedule (such as rewarding every third or every fifth response) has a different effect than a fixed-interval schedule (rewarding every two minutes or every five minutes). These types of schedule can be combined in various ways to achieve different learning results. For instance, when the children are being taught to raise their hands to speak in class rather than to shout out an opinion, they can profitably be rewarded on each occasion that they raise a hand. But after the habit has become well-established, intermittent reward will likely maintain the habit against extinction better than will continuous reinforcement.

To explain more complex patterns of learning, behaviorists have proposed the concepts of shaping and chaining. Shaping consists of first reinforcing or rewarding any gross approximation the person achieves of a desired refined act. Then, after the gross form of the behavior has been well-established, the teacher can shape it by gradual steps into the ultimate refined form by requiring better and better approximations before reinforcement is provided. To illustrate, in teaching people to play tennis, the coach can first praise them for even hitting the ball toward the net, no matter how faulty the direction the ball takes. As soon as the player can hit the ball consistently, the coach offers praise only when the ball passes over the net, or nearly so. After mastering this second refinement, the player is reinforced only when the ball both crosses the net and falls within the boundary lines in the opposite court. This process of gradually placing more precise limits on the kinds of acts that are reinforced will continue until the player has shaped the skill sufficiently to win matches in competition with other players.

Chaining enables a person to link together a sequence of small, individual conditioned acts to compose a complex skill. The process of chaining begins at the final end of the chain rather than at the beginning. Each preceding link of the chain is hooked on by associating it with the link that has already been established through reinforcement. For instance, consider the complex skill known as "having good table manners." The parent starts with a child who yearns for both food and parental approval. Over a series of days the child is permitted to eat and is told "That's fine" and "How nicely you eat" each time he or she uses a fork rather than fingers for lifting small pieces of meat to his or her mouth. When

the pattern of using the fork is established, the parent adds a new requirement. The child must use a knife and fork to cut large pieces of meat into smaller pieces before being permitted to eat or complimented for his or her actions. After these two habits have been mastered—eating with a fork and cutting up the meat—the parent imposes a new requirement. The child must tuck a napkin into his or her shirt before he or she cuts up the meat, picks up the pieces with the fork, eats, and is complimented. By such a process an extended set of habits can be linked together into a complicated skill.

For the parent or teacher practicing behaviorism, one important problem is that of selecting types of consequences that will serve as efficient reinforcers (rewards) and efficient aversive consequences (punishments). The problem, stated in the parlance of fishermen, is that "not all fish rise to the same bait." Hence, the practitioner seeks to find reinforcers that both increase the desired behavior and do not produce undesirable side effects. The matter of undesirable side effects can be illustrated in the use of candy as a reward for a child's learning a list of spelling words or for his or her helping with work around the home. The candy may stimulate the desired behavior, but it also may foster decay in the child's teeth and also may cause the child to avoid eating a protein-rich food, such as cheese or nuts, which would be better for the child's health. Certain forms of punishment may decrease or extinguish an undesired behavior but, in the process, produce undesirable side effects as well. Hitting a child may cause him or her to stop making insulting remarks to the teacher, but it may also cause permanent physical damage and motivate the child to avoid returning to school altogether. Among the reinforcers commonly used are those of social approval (complimenting the person), special privileges, symbols of public recognition and honor (badges, citations of excellence, mention in a newspaper, membership in a society), money, physical objects of value, and such consumable items as food.

At a growing pace during the twentieth century, behaviorism has contributed to child-raising, educational, and counseling practices in a variety of ways.

Bibliography

Bijou S W 1979 Some clarifications on the meaning of a behavior analysis of child development. *Psychol. Record* 29:3–13

Bijou S W, Baer D M 1961 *Child Development*, Vol. 1: *A Systematic and Empirical Theory*. Appleton-Century-Crofts, New York

Kantor J R 1959 *Interbehavioral Psychology: A Sample of Scientific System Construction*, 2nd edn. Principia, Bloomington, Indiana

Skinner B F 1974 *About Behaviorism*. Knopf, New York

Watson J B 1919 *Psychology from the Standpoint of a Behaviorist*. Lippincott, Philadelphia, Pennsylvania

History and Educational Applications of Behaviorism

S. W. Bijou

Behaviorism is a philosophy of science which holds that psychology is the study of the behavior of an individual in interaction with the environment. The behavior of concern is the total, unified functioning of an organism, human and nonhuman; the environment provides the circumstances under which a species evolves (phylogeny) and in which an individual lives and responds from moment to moment (ontogeny). Foremost among the other postulates of behaviorism is that the subject matter of psychology is studied by objective procedures, particularly the experimental method. Some psychologists and educators are convinced that behaviorism is one of the most significant movements in all of modern science; others view it as part of an inevitable trend from subjective investigation of inner states and processes to the objective study of behavior. Whatever the contention, history has shown that behaviorism has significantly changed the course of psychology in the sense that practically all contemporary psychologists are, at least in part, behaviorists; and without question it has served to accelerate applied research, particularly in mental health and education.

1. History and Philosophical Origins

Behaviorism came into being in the early twentieth century as a protest against the two schools of thought prevalent at that time: structuralism and functionalism. To understand the origins of behaviorism, it is necessary to have some appreciation of the nature of these two points of view.

Structuralism, the first systematic position for psychology as an independent science, was formulated in mid-nineteenth century by the German physiologist and founder of experimental psychology, Wilhelm Wundt. Wundt maintained that the subject matter of psychology, in keeping with the *Zeitgeist*, is immediate experience, and the task of psychology is to analyze consciousness into its separate elements. The method of investigation, which was compatible with the writings of the English empirical philosophers and the German experimental psychologists Ernst Weber, Gustav Fechner, and Hermann von Helmholtz, was the experimental method, adapted to accommodate self-observation or introspection. He believed strongly that psychology should study its subject matter in the same way as the natural sciences were studying the natural universe, particularly chemical phenomena.

Wundt's outstanding student, British-born Edward B. Titchener, transplanted the new psychology from Germany to the United States where he extended his mentor's teachings. In addition to reducing conscious experience to its common elements, Titchener believed that psychology should determine the laws of their

combinations and relate them to their underlying physiological processes.

As structuralism was gaining acceptance in the United States, another school of thought, functionalism, was taking form. This view, associated with John Dewey, James Angell, and many others, focused on treating psychological processes as functions and placing them in the context of the philosophy and theory of evolution of Herbert Spencer and Charles Darwin, respectively. To them, functions meant adaptive activities that typically, and in the long run, presumably are or have been advantageous to the maintenance of life in the organisms in which they occur. The functionalists did not object to the kind of research conducted by the structuralists but they did protest against the restrictions on psychological inquiry that they attempted to impose; they wanted to study any and all activities of organisms.

Strongly influencing the functionalists' formulation, in addition to the writings of Spencer and Darwin, were the views of Sir Francis Galton who was concerned with mental inheritance and the measurement of individual differences, George J. Romanes who emphasized the observational method in comparative psychology, and C. Lloyd Morgan who introduced the "law of parsimony" as a safeguard against the then prevalent anecdotal method of studying animal behavior. Interestingly, these influences on functionalism came mostly from British scholars and scientists, yet functionalism was entirely an American movement.

At the turn of the twentieth century, when structuralism was at its height and functionalism was blossoming into maturity, behaviorism made its appearance on the psychological horizon. Its undisputed leader, John B. Watson, an animal experimental psychologist and a "graduate" of the functionalist school, published a paper in 1913 in which he argued that psychology is a purely experimental branch of natural science; therefore psychologists should discard all the mentalistic terms cherished by structuralists and functionalists in favor of concepts like stimulus and response, borrowed from biology. He insisted, further, that the goal of psychology is to predict and control behavior rather than to explore the elements of consciousness in humans by introspection.

The behaviorism espoused by Watson and supported with variations by Edward B. Holt, Albert P. Weiss, and Karl Lashley evolved from the philosophical tradition of objectivism which originated with the French scholar, René Descartes, in the seventeenth century. Descartes' seminal contributions included a dualistic conception of humans (a machine-like body in interaction with a mind); the brain as the mediator of behavior; the reflex as a unit of behavior; internal stimuli as the determiners of body behavior; and built-in internal capacities such as innate ideas. These conceptions were embraced and elaborated in the eighteenth and nineteenth centuries by English and Scottish empirical and associationist philosophers, among them John Locke, Thomas Hobbes, George Berkeley, and David Hume; the German rationalists Immanuel Kant and Johann F. Herbart; and the French positivist, Auguste Comte, who argued that the only valid knowledge is that which is social in nature and objectively observed.

Functionalism, too, had an impact on behaviorism mainly because of its emphasis on evolution and the adaptation of the organism to the environment, its concern with practical outcome and application, and its commitment to the objective study of animal behavior. Still another influence was the rising interest in the study of animal behavior, including animal conditioning. The trend instigated by Romanes and Morgan was accelerated by the German biologist Jacques Loeb, who theorized that psychological behavior could be explained by the mechanical functioning and biochemical processes of the organism, and by the groundbreaking research of the Russian physiologist Ivan P. Pavlov on animal functioning.

Undoubtedly the American *Zeitgeist* at the beginning of the twentieth century was another factor that set the stage for behaviorism. The striking advances in practically every branch of science that took place during the immediately preceding period kindled the prevailing attitude that science, given enough time, could find the answer to any commonplace or extraordinary problem. This was an era in which tender-minded idealism was rapidly yielding to the spirit of tough-minded realism.

Watson, like all systematic theorists, attempted to build behaviorism in accordance with his fundamental postulates. All areas of psychology were to be analyzed in mechanistic stimulus–response terms very much in keeping with Pavlov's conditioning paradigm. There are numerous examples of this singular perspective: he emphasized learning, denied the existence of instincts, postulated that all human emotions evolve through the conditioning of three innate emotions (love, anger, and fear); and viewed thinking as implicit speech movements, with verbal thinking interpreted as subvocal talking involving muscular habits learned in overt speech.

Because Watson attacked the existing order, he was subjected to intense criticism. For one thing, Watson's position on the mind–body problem raised strong antipathy. While he accepted the dualistic concept of humankind, he maintained that mental states and processes, the heart of psychology for structuralists, could not be studied scientifically because they were not publicly observable. Another target was his stance that psychological activities could be explained in terms of physiological structure and functioning (philosophical reductionism). Other points arousing acrimonious discussion were (a) his insistence, in opposition to those who embraced the doctrine of free will, that all psychological phenomena are determined by observable or potentially observable conditions (determinism), and (b) his extreme positions on the active role of the environment and the passivity of the organism, and on the nature of objectivity in research. His conceptualizations on learning, emotions, and thought were also viewed with disfavor because they were extrapolated from very limited data.

Although its life span was a brief 16-year period, Watsonian behaviorism provided impetus for a shift from consciousness and subjectivisim to materialism and objectivism. The rapidity of this transition may be attributed to the fact that the march was already in progress and to Watson's energy, clarity, and force in presenting his position to the profession and the general public.

2. Neobehaviorism

The behavioral movement resulted in a mass of experimental data on learning which in the 1950s prompted such American psychologists as Edwin R. Guthrie, Clarence C. Tolman, Clark L. Hull, and B. F. Skinner to formulate what might be called neobehavioral learning theories. Compared to the schools of the 1920s and 1930s, which attempted to account for all of psychology within a simple framework, the theories of the 1950s were circumspect and restricted and could be described as "miniature" theories.

More than the others, Skinner's theory rapidly evolved into a system of psychology encompassing a philosophy of science (radical or basic behaviorism), a theory of behavior (behavior analysis), a core research methodology, and a program of applications. Radical behaviorism stoutly rejects the body and mind concept of humans and holds that the individual is a unified organism (philosophical monism). The body that ingests food, breathes air, and so on, is the same body that interacts as a totality with the environment. Furthermore, it holds, contrary to Watson's position, that psychology studies inner activities (covert or "private" events) by means of acceptable scientific procedures. And finally, it postulates that interactions between the environment (stimuli) and behavior (responses) are analyzed functionally, that is, in terms of their reciprocal relationships, and not, as Watson would have it, as mechanistic interactions between the physical environment and the physiological activities of the individual.

Skinner's theory, behavior analysis, consists of concepts based on data from Pavlov's conditioning reflex paradigm and Skinner's operant conditioning model, a variation of Thorndike's trial and error formulation. Operant behavior, which includes social language, and cognitive behavior, is modified by the stimuli following behavior, in contrast to reflex behavior, which is modified by the conditions preceding behavior, that is, the pairing of conditioned and unconditioned stimuli. According to this view, the basic unit of psychological analysis, the three-term contingency, consists of a temporal sequence involving antecedent stimuli, operant behavior, and consequent stimuli. The strategy of theory construction is to first study simple concepts like sensorimotor and self-help skills and then proceed to complex adjustments like thinking, problem solving, moral behavior, and creative behavior, all involving large components of language and covert interactions. Thus far, most of the research has been on relatively simple concepts.

Another variation of neobehaviorism, based loosely on the formulations by Tolman and Hull, is cognitive behaviorism which accepts the dualistic concept of humans and contends that mental structures and processes can be studied through research on the interactions between behavior and the environment. This approach is similar to radical behaviorism in that it incorporates concepts and principles based on the classical and operant conditioning paradigms but is different in that it includes hypothetical terms.

Neobehaviorism, in all of its variations, is criticized by some as too scientific and by others as not scientific enough. The former group, primarily humanistic psychologists, reject the notion of psychology wholly as a science of behavior on the grounds that it is too narrow, artificial, and sterile for the understanding of human beings. A human, they aver, is not an animal with behavior determined entirely by mechanical interaction with the environment, a view that seems directed more at Watsonian behaviorism rather than contemporary behaviorism. In line with this argument is the contention by social critics that Western culture is too dehumanized, depersonalized, and deindividualized. Humanistic psychologists have not yet offered a viable alternative approach to the study of human beings.

The other group of critics, the interbehaviorists, contend that cognitive behaviorism is too mentalistic to be scientific, and that radical behaviorism does not adhere to all the basic assumptions of the natural science approach. They agree with radical behaviorism's monistic treatment of humans, its functional definitions of behavior and environment, and its program for the study of covert or implicit activities. They claim, however, that radical behaviorism should extend its experimentation to include all complex human behavior, such as feeling and emotional behavior, the creative processes of imagination, inventing, thinking, problem solving, and reasoning, and should replace its basic psychological unit of analysis with a behavior field concept consisting of a set of interdependent relationships among stimuli, behaviors, mediating conditions, and setting factors.

3. Investigative Methodology

At the inception of Watsonian behaviorism, the subject matter of psychology was to be studied by (a) direct observation, with and without the use of instruments, (b) the conditioned reflex method with secretory as well as motor responses, (c) verbal reports as accounts of behavior rather than as observations of nebulous inner experiences, and (d) objective testing methods to determine abilities and general behavior characteristics rather than innate traits. All these investigative procedures were in use at the turn of the twentieth century; Watson provided emphasis and encouraged their further development.

During the ensuing 50 years, these methods were improved and extended. The direct observation technique was refined by the development of explicit procedures for coding interactions and by the use of statistical procedures for assessing observer reliability. Pavlovian conditioning techniques were augmented by operant conditioning methods and both were enhanced by electric and electronic devices for presenting stimuli and recording responses. Objective testing methods, which were mainly norm-referenced tests of intelligence, aptitude, and personality, were expanded to include criterion-referenced tests, which sampled domains of an individual's functional behavior, such as self-care, communication, socialization, and cognitive behavior.

Mainly through the influence of operant experimentation, single subject designs ($N = 1$) in which each individual serves as his or her own control were introduced and developed, and experimental techniques, traditionally restricted to basic research in perception and learning, were employed in the study of child, social, industrial, and educational problems. Basic and applied experimental research came to differ not so much on the basis of subject matter, but on the kinds of questions posed and the behaviors studied.

4. The Flowering of Applied Behavior Science: Behavior Modification

From its inception, behaviorism adopted the practical orientation of functionalism. This pragmatic inclination was manifested in the 1930s and 1940s by scattered instances of the practical application of a selected learning principle. In the 1950s, along with the initial formulations of empirically based learning theories came applications to a wide range of problems on a concerted basis. The new applied discipline, behavior modification, emerged almost simultaneously in three far-flung geographical locations. In South Africa, Joseph P. Wolpe and his colleagues, disenchanted with the disease model of psychopathology, the assumptions and tenets of orthodox psychoanalysis, and the concept of symptom substitution, ventured into research on the clinical treatment of maladjusted adults, which was based on Pavlov's conditioning paradigm. At about the same time, Hans J. Eysenck and his co-workers in England, also disillusioned with psychoanalysis and its associated practices, embarked on behavior therapy research with adults, patterning their work primarily on Hull's behavior theory. In the United States, two lines of investigation helped to crystallize the new movement: one, the application of Pavlovian conditioning principles to specific problems like enuresis and alcoholism; the other, the application of Skinnerian conditioning principles to general problems such as the education of handicapped children and the analysis of psychiatric diagnostic categories of hospitalized adult patients.

As might therefore be expected, present-day behavior modification reflects its history: it is divided into two subdivisions—behavior therapy, traceable to Wolpe and Eysenck and dominated by models with hypothetical concepts; and applied behavior analysis, associated with Skinner's operant approach which eschews hypothetical terms.

For its relatively short existence, research in behavior modification has had noteworthy impact on diverse fields, among them child and adult clinical therapy, education, health care, community work, criminal justice, business and industry, and the armed services. Also affected have been the clinical and research practices in psychiatry, pediatrics, general medicine, dentistry, nursing, probation, penology, and social work.

Behavioral investigators and practitioners have spawned professional organizations, the largest of which are the Association for the Advancement of Behavior Therapy and the International Association of Behavior Analysis; accelerated the publication of behavioral books and journals; expanded the instrumentation industry; proliferated workshops on an international basis; and introduced behavioral courses and research and service programs in the United States, the United Kingdom, the Federal Republic of Germany, Venezuela, Brazil, Peru, Colombia, Australia, and New Zealand.

5. Principal Findings and Contributions to the Educational Process, School, and Learning

Although both divisions of behavior modification— behavior therapy and applied behavior analysis—have contributed to the field of education, applied behavior analysis has had a conspicuous and more dominant role. The operant paradigm with its emphasis on antecedent conditions (instructions from the teacher, curriculum tasks, etc.) and consequent conditions ("rewards and punishments") is well-suited to studying problems associated with academic achievement and personal– social adjustment. It has been said, with some justification, that the contributions of applied behavioral research to education have not necessarily been new but that they have reemphasized the importance of thorough and consistent application of learning principles, attention to details, and systematic and objective evaluations.

This survey of contributions is organized into two categories: research on the application of single concepts and principles to pupil achievement and adjust-ment, and research on the application of multiple behavior concepts and principles to circumscribed areas of education.

5.1 Research on the Application of Single Concepts and Principles

At the heart of effective application of single behavioral concepts and principles to school achievement and adjustment problems is the knowledge of how the acquisition and maintenance of skills and knowledge work. For this reason it is understandable why most attention has been devoted to specific instances of school learning and adjustment and why so much of this research has focused on the conditions that follow behavior: it is the area with the greatest accumulation of data on the subject based on nonhuman experimentation.

Studied intensively to date have been the stimuli and activities that serve as "strengtheners" for academic learning and adjustment, such as attention, praise, physical contact, consumables, play opportunities, and so on, and the withdrawal of aversive stimuli, such as sarcasm, ridicule, objects of value (fines), and the like. Also appraised in depth have been the conditions that weaken incorrect or undesirable behaviors, namely, the presentation of aversive stimuli and the withdrawal of positive reinforcers. Some of the studies in this category have been aimed at determining alternative and unintrusive techniques for punishment.

Research on the strengthening and weakening of school-related behaviors by managing consequent conditions has also included studies on tokens and token economies, systems in which tangible symbols earned are exchanged for a wide variety of objects and activities. Also, a fair amount of investigative attention has been directed at determining the immediate and long-range strengthening effects of varying the time and/or number of responses required for a given consequence (schedule of reinforcement).

Research findings on the effects of consequent conditions have been applied to reducing or eliminating classroom problem behavior as a prerequisite to academic learning—classroom management. Whether the setting is a preschool, kindergarten, elementary school, or special class, findings have indicated that when a teacher pays any kind of attention to unruly conduct, such behavior tends to increase (reinforcement); when he or she directs attention to desirable personal–social behavior (reinforcement) and totally ignores undesirable behavior, the undesirable behavior tends to decrease (extinction).

Any number of studies have been done using contingent conditions to reduce behavior problems and disorders of individual children. In regular classes, the problems investigated have been mainly of the aggressive and disruptive sort; in special classes they have consisted of these two categories together with those associated with retardation, emotional disturbance, learning disability, autism, social deprivation, and speech problems. Findings have shown repeatedly that problem behavior in individual children is most effectively reduced when the primary treatment emphasis is on strengthening desirable behavior through positive reinforcement, and secondary emphasis is on weakening undesirable behavior through aversive and extinction processes.

Not as much research has been devoted to the conditions that precede academic and personal–social behavior, as, for example, getting the learner's attention, giving instructions, prompting, and sequencing the curriculum materials. The latter category, which subsumes task analysis and programmed instruction, has received the lion's share of attention, some of it devoted to the sequencing of elementary-level reading and arithmetic materials into units but most to the curricula for exceptional children. For retarded children, programmed hierarchies have been developed for teaching gross and fine motor coordination, self-help, language, academic and preacademic knowledge and skills, social behavior, and occupational and work-related behaviors; for behavior-disturbed or disordered children, the programs have been geared to the enhancement of social behavior and the acquisition of academic tool subjects; and for autistic children, curriculum sequences have been prepared to enhance language and social development.

To a lesser degree, research on programmed sequences has been concerned with the development of social and academic programs for socially disadvantaged children, learning-disability children, underachievers, children with speech disorders (particularly stuttering and articulation problems), and for retarded adolescents and young adults with prevocational and vocational problems.

5.2 Research on the Application of Multiple Concepts and Principles

The contributions of behavioral research to specific domains of education include (a) preschool education for handicapped children, (b) elementary-school education for socioculturally disadvantaged children, and (c) college instruction.

(a) *Preschool education for handicapped children.* Research on the education of young handicapped children has moved in two directions: training in a preschool setting (center based) and training at home with the mother as teacher (home based). In a center-based setting, the aim is to prepare a learning environment that will ensure a child's success later on when he or she attends a normal or special kindergarten or first grade. As a general rule, studies have focused on the development and refinement of the essential components of preschool training: (a) criterion-referenced tests (inventories or checklists) to assess a child's behavior repertoire upon admission and upon completion of preschool; (b) instructional programs for teaching self-help, language, socialization, and cognitive skills;

(c) behavioral teaching techniques; (d) monitoring procedures for tracking progress in instructional programs; (e) techniques for modifying instructional programs and teaching procedures to ensure continual progress; and (f) procedures to encourage parent involvement.

Studies have been made on physically and behaviorally handicapped children, culturally disadvantaged children, and retarded children of varying degrees and etiologies. Some investigations have specialized in specific categories of retardation, for example, Down Syndrome. Almost without exception, the results have indicated that children in these programs not only improved significantly in their development and achievement as measured by norm-referenced and criterion-referenced tests, but also that they enjoyed attending classes. Two other findings are pertinent: first, children whose parents participated in their programs made greater gains than children whose parents did not; and second, children continued to make gains in their first regular kindergarten or first-grade placement only when their teachers used individualized instruction, motivational techniques, and systematic evaluation similar to those in the research programs.

Research on the home-based training of preschool handicapped children has shared the same aim as research on center-based programs and has focused on the development and refinement of the same components of preschool training as those outlined for center-based programs. Because the teacher in the home-based format teaches the parent rather than the child and because he or she has contact with both in the home at regular intervals, usually once a week, research has put greater emphasis on parent training and supervision and the development of curricula that can be fractionated into small units, suitable for mastery within a week.

Norm-referenced and criterion-referenced test data have repeatedly shown that the great majority of handicapped children make marked developmental gains in home-based programs. For example, results from the Portage Project, in operation in the United States since 1969, have shown that handicapped children in the Project for an eight-month period made an average gain of more than a year in mental-age scores and in ratings on the Portage criterion-referenced checklist. Furthermore, surveys revealed that the teaching mothers have strong positive reactions about participation in their child's progress. In England, where this study has been replicated, these findings were corroborated. And finally, findings have consistently shown that, in comparison with center-based programs, home-based programs are cost effective.

(b) *Elementary education for socially disadvantaged children.* Since the early 1970s nine approaches to the elementary education of children from socioculturally disadvantaged homes were studied in a United States Office of Education project called Follow Through. The sponsors of each approach trained teachers and established classes ranging from kindergarten or first grade through the third grade in over 100 urban and rural communities throughout the United States. Of the nine, two of the approaches were behaviorally oriented: direct instruction and behavior analysis.

Direct instruction evolved primarily from the research on compensatory education by Wesley C. Becker, Siegfried Engelmann, and Douglas W. Carnine, all of the University of Oregon. Incorporated into the curriculum were meticulously graded sequences in reading, arithmetic, and language which were taught by teachers who were required to follow scripts. The children, five to ten in a group, responded to questions and instructions in unison, the objective being to encourage active and alert participation. To this end the teacher used a high frequency of prompts and reinforcers which he or she gradually reduced as the children progressed. Evaluation of the children in all nine approaches at the end of the third grade revealed that those in the direct instruction project not only made substantial advances in academic skills and knowledge, surpassing all the others, but also that they had scored higher on the cognitive and affective tests. After the projects had been terminated, follow-up evaluations in the fifth and sixth grades showed that the children in this program continued to make satisfactory academic progress.

The other behavioral approach, behavior analysis, which emphasized the role of motivation rather than meticulous programming, was based in large measure on the research of Donald Bushell (University of Kansas) on token reinforcement in the classroom. For the most part, the curriculum was drawn from commercially prepared materials. In the behavior analysis approach, achievement was enhanced through the pairing of tokens with praise, and with the exchange of tokens for games, art projects, stories, playground activities, singing, and opportunities for extra academic performance. Children were taught in groups of six to eight, with academic progress monitored primarily through the number of tokens earned. Parents were encouraged to serve as teachers' aides, not only to assist in the instructional and motivational procedures but also to encourage their active participation in the program. The results of objective tests administered at the end of the third grade, the termination point of the research, indicated that the children had surpassed in academic achievement all the children in all the projects except those in the direct instruction program, and in some instances they had exceeded the national norms. Also, like those children in the direct instruction project, they continued to make satisfactory academic progress in the fourth and fifth grades.

(c) *College instruction.* In the early 1960s, Fred S. Keller and J. Gilmour Sherman of the United States and Rodolfo Azzi and Carolina M. Bori of Brazil collaborated on research on college teaching at the University of Brazilia. Since that time, their approach, Personalized System Instruction (PSI), has been studied at colleges and universities in the United States, Brazil, Mexico, and Venezuela; a center for the study of and training on the PSI approach has been established at Georgetown University, Washington, DC; and a journal devoted to the PSI method has been founded.

The Personalized System of Instruction aims to shift the emphasis of higher education to a goal of teaching for mastery of the subject matter rather than merely passing examinations. It consists of replacing the lecture method with carefully prepared assignments consisting of sections from standard textbooks and articles, together with specially prepared supplements, study questions, instructions, and the like. When a student believes that he or she has mastered a unit assignment, he or she takes a brief quiz which is immediately evaluated by a proctor who critiques the responses. As a student masters an assignment, he or she moves on to the next unit, proceeding through the course at his or her own pace, demonstrating competence each step of the way. Grades are determined solely on how much of the material is finally mastered. Variations of the basic format have included occasional lectures, demonstrations, and audiovisual presentations of course material, multiple choice rather than short essay examinations, and incentive systems to encourage movement through the course at an even pace.

The method has been repeatedly evaluated in its own right and in comparison with the lecture method in terms of data from course grades, final examinations, questionnaires, and personal interviews. The results uniformly indicate that students do better in PSI courses and prefer it to lecture courses despite the added work involved. In addition, follow-up evaluations repeatedly favor the PSI method. Thus far, these findings have not led to wholesale acceptance of the PSI method in colleges and universities, indicating that institutions of higher learning do not modify their practices simply on the basis of empirical data, no matter how compelling.

6. Active and Underdeveloped Areas of Research

Active and underdeveloped areas of research will be considered in terms of the categories used in reviewing behavioral contributions to education, namely, the application of single behavioral concepts and principles to problems of school achievement and adjustment, and the application of multiple concepts and principles to circumscribed aspects of education.

6.1 Application of Single Conceptual Principles

Research on the conditions that follow behavior in the acquisition and maintenance of school achievement and adjustment continues to be one of the most active areas of study. Among the topics requiring further investigation are: techniques for converting extrinsic reinforcers to intrinsic reinforcers, and for transferring reinforcement operations from teachers to peers and to others who play important roles in the lives of children.

As was indicated previously, relatively little research has been done on the conditions that precede behavior, yet it is just as important an area for study as the conditions that follow behavior. It should be noted, however, that an impressive amount of research was devoted to the empirical ordering of instructional material in the 1960s—the heyday of teaching machines—because such material was the "software" for these devices. When teaching machines failed to satisfy the expectations of those educators who envisioned them as the "answer" to unsupervised individualized teaching, research in instructional programming decreased. In more recent times interest in subject matter sequencing has been rekindled through the discovery of "task analysis" and the recognition that reliable ordering of learning materials and tasks can be derived only from systematic experimentation.

Research is just beginning on the conditions that prevail over an episode of acquisition and maintenance. These conditions, called settings or contextual factors, influence the functional properties of the antecedent and consequent conditions in acquisition and maintenance, and they stem (a) from the physiological functioning of an individual, including health and illness states, emotional states, and satiation and deprivation for biological needs, (b) from the social environment or the composition of the social group and the behavior of the teacher; and (c) from the physical environment, or surrounding synthetic and natural objects.

Finally, there is a paucity of research on the conditions that enhance generalization of learning in educational settings. In the past, investigators gave little heed to the process of generalizing, assuming that the learning acquired in the classroom automatically transferred to the home and community—an assumption not borne out by recent research. It is now apparent that there is need for information on how to facilitate generalization by modifying teaching procedures and by training others, particularly parents, to supplement classroom teaching (see *Transfer of Learning*).

6.2 Application of Multiple Concepts and Principles to Specific Areas of Education

Active areas of research include behavioral methods of teaching exceptional children, particularly the retarded, the behaviorally disturbed, and the socioculturally disadvantaged. On the other hand, relatively little research has been directed to teaching the gifted. Research on children at the upper end of the ability spectrum would throw light on stimulating, encouraging, and maintaining cognitive skills not ordinarily treated in educational research, for example, problem solving and creative behaviors.

Behavioral research on college instruction continues to be an active area but research on a closely related

problem, teacher training, has been rather neglected. Although teacher training has received some research attention, it is not nearly enough, considering that the teacher's behavior is by far the most important set of conditions influencing learning and motivation in the classroom. Studies on teacher training have explored, to some degree, among other things, modeling, role playing, reinforcement alone, and reinforcement in combination with other methods. While the results have been mixed, they have indicated that positive reinforcement techniques are the most promising. The identification of effective techniques for teacher training is only the first step in improving teacher performance. Two others, implementation and maintenance of training, are equally important. These phases are difficult to achieve mostly because the major incentive for teachers is not contingent on behaviors that actually affect students' behaviors. Without additional incentives to those now in existence, such as compliance with administrative directives and desperation on the part of individual teachers, it is unrealistic to expect any approach to teacher training to sustain proficient performance.

Since the mid-1960s, research activity on parent training designed to augment the schools' efforts has steadily increased. Interest here has been heightened by the repeated finding that young handicapped and disadvantaged children gain most from preschool attendance when their mothers participate in the programs and by the general belief that parents, when properly trained, can help to prevent mild or moderate retardation and academic underachievement. A review of the literature suggests that research is needed on improvement of investigative methodology and on enhancing generalization of the behaviors acquired by parents in training programs.

Bibliography

Benson H B 1979 *Behavior Modification and the Child: An Annotated Bibliography*. Greenwood, London

Bijou S W, Rayek R 1978 *Análisis Conductual Applicado a la Instrucción*. Editorial Trillas, Mexico

Bijou S W, Ruiz R 1981 *Behavior Modification: Contributions to Education*. Erlbaum, Hillsdale, New Jersey

Kazdin A E 1978 *History of Behavior Modification: Experimental Foundations of Contemporary Research*. University Park, Baltimore, Maryland

Kazdin A E 1981 Behavior modification in education: Contributions and limitations. *Dev. Rev.* 1(1): 34–57

Kazdin A E, Craighead W E 1973 Behavior modification in special education. In: Mann L, Sabatino D A (eds.) 1973 *The First Review of Special Education*, Vol. 2. Buttonwood Farms, Philadelphia, Pennsylvania, pp. 51–102

Schultz D P 1969 *A History of Modern Psychology*. Academic Press, New York

Skinner B F 1953 *Science and Human Behavior*. Macmillan, New York

Sulzer-Azaroff B, Mayer G R 1977 *Applying Behavior Analysis Procedures with Children and Youth*. Holt, Rinehart and Winston, New York

Social Learning Theory

R. M. Thomas

Social learning theory is a way of explaining human development based on the assumption that the pattern of behaviors people acquire as they grow up is chiefly the result of their interactions with other people. Such a social learning perspective is actually not a single theory but, rather, a collection of theories that share several basic features in common (Sahakian 1970). Hilgard and Bower have proposed that:

> social learning theory provides the best integrative summary of what modern learning theory has to contribute to solutions of practical problems. It also provides a compatible framework within which to place information-processing theories of language, comprehension, memory, imagery, and problem solving . . . . For such reasons, social learning theory would appear to be the "consensus" theoretical framework within which much of learning research (especially on humans) will evolve. . . . (Hilgard and Bower 1975 p. 605)

The following review first describes basic tenets on which social learning models are founded, then turns to applications of these models to child rearing, educational practice, and counseling.

1. Basic Tenets

Historically, social learning theory is a derivative of behaviorism. However, in contrast to classical behaviorism, social learning models not only recognize observable behavior as an important factor for explaining development but also include speculation about a person's cognitive functions, that is, about the role that mind or mental processes play in effecting behavior.

Among the basic tenets of the social learning viewpoint is the belief that when a person takes action (or "behaves"), the consequences that follow the action will influence whether the person will try that same behavior again under similar circumstances. If the consequences are experienced as rewarding (reinforcing), the same behavior will probably be tried again in the future. But if the consequences are not rewarding (nonreinforcing) or are experienced as punishment, the behavior is less likely to be used later in similar situations. This principle is a cornerstone of both behaviorism and social learning theory.

However, a second typical belief in social learning theory is one to which traditional behaviorists would not subscribe. It is the conviction that much learning is vicarious—it occurs by means of individuals observing others rather than by their participating directly in activities themselves. They see what other people do and note the consequences of those actions. Then, depending on how desirable they judge the consequences to be, they decide which of the actions to imitate and which to avoid. This is the commonsense notion that people model their lives on the lives of others whose behavior achieves desired results, and they avoid modeling their behavior after that of people whose actions lead to undesired ends (Bandura 1971).

Related to beliefs about the importance of imitation and modeling is the concept of psychological identification, a term referring to a person's assuming that someone else is in some way much like himself (Sears et al. 1965). Identification is not only cognitive, meaning that the person believes he has something in common with certain others he observes, but it also includes an affective component, so the individual feels a degree of emotional attachment to the others. What the others experience—both their successes and their failures—he feels he experiences as well. In this way identification is an investment of one's own self or ego in the fate of others.

The importance of identification for learning is that learners accept as models those people whom they regard as being either much like themselves or else like an ideal they hold for themselves (heroes). Research studies support the commonsense idea of hero worship in the following ways: (a) people are more likely to model their behavior after the actions of others they regard as prestigious than after actions of others who are not highly regarded; (b) people are more likely to adopt behavior patterns from models of their own sex than from those of the opposite sex; (c) models who receive rewards, such as money, fame, or high socioeconomic status, are more often copied than ones who do not, (d) people who are punished for their behavior tend not to be imitated (Bandura and Walters 1963).

In seeking to account for the great influence parents exert over their children, social learning theorists can propose that parents serve as the earliest and most ubiquitous models in the child's life and that the child's identification with, and emotional attachment to, its parents grows particularly strong as the child recognizes the parents as essential instruments for fulfilling its needs.

According to Bandura's (1977) analysis, the process of an individual's learning from observing models consists of at least five components—paying attention to the model, coding the observed information for memory, retaining the information in memory, carrying out an eventual motor action or observable response, and having this entire process fueled by motivation. The nature of each of these components is as follows.

(a) *Attention*. The act of observing a model may consist of directly watching someone carrying out a behavior, such as kicking a football or giving a speech, or the act may involve indirect observation, as in seeing the behavior in a motion picture or reading about it in a book. However, no matter what the observational setting may be, it is essential that the learner attend to the pertinent clues in the stimulus situation and ignore the aspects of the model and the environment that are incidental and do not affect the performance the individual is to learn. A child's later failing to perform the observed behavior correctly, especially if the behavior has been complex, is frequently due to his or her misdirecting attention at the time the model was observed. Teachers often try to prevent this error by eliminating as many as possible of the irrelevant stimuli from the setting and by verbally directing the child's attention to those aspects of the model's performance that are most important.

(b) *Images and semantic codes*. If the learner is to store in memory what he has observed, he needs to cast the observation into a visual or auditory image or into a semantic code, such as a key word or a pattern of words. Without an adequate coding system, a child fails to store what he has seen or heard. There are obvious developmental trends in the ability to profit from models. Older children learn more readily from witnessing others' performance than do young children. This superiority of older children is due in large part to their more advanced ability to use symbols. In illustrating this, Bandura (1977) points out that the infant's use of modeling is confined mainly to instantaneous imitation. The very young child will imitate the adult's gesture or word immediately instead of reproducing it after a period of time. But as children grow up and have more experience in associating words or images with objects and events, they can store these symbols in order to recall and reproduce the events after increasingly long periods of time. In effect, the development of language and of schemes for coding observations enhances children's ability to profit from models.

(c) *Memory permanence*. Much that people learn from observing models is forgotten, so that the learning is no longer available when the individual needs it to solve problems in life. Such memory-aiding techniques as rehearsal (review or practice) and attaching multiple codes to an event (associating a variety of interlinked words or images with the event) serve to keep the stored information at a level that makes it readily retrieved when needed.

(d) *Reproduction*. The ultimate purpose of learning is to make it available for taking action when the need arises. This is the step of accurately reproducing the learning in the form of motor acts—kicking the football, giving the speech, writing answers to the test questions. It is not enough that the observers get the idea of the actions in order to perform them, or that they code and store the idea accurately; it is also necessary for them to get the muscular feel of the behavior. They usually cannot do this perfectly on the first trial. Thus they need a number of trials in which they approximate the behavior, then receive feedback from the experience in order to correct the deviations from the ideal that their early attempts have involved. As a result, it is useful for the learner to try out the observed actions in the form of motor behavior in order to discover those

aspects that have been imperfectly learned and, by diagnosing the nature of the imperfections, to remedy them.

(e) *Motivation*. Traditional behaviorists and social learning theorists both agree that the consequences of one's behavior affect whether that behavior will be learned, with learned in this case meaning using the behavior again in similar circumstances so that it becomes habitual. However, the two schools of theorists do not agree on why consequences produce such an effect. Behaviorists have tended to assume that a rewarding or reinforcing consequence automatically strengthens the likelihood that the behavior preceding that consequence will be used in the future under similar stimulus conditions (Skinner 1974). But such social learning theorists as Bandura (1977) offer a different interpretation. They propose that the consequences serve informational and motivational functions for the learner. In their informational role, the consequences show learners which behaviors have been rewarding and which have not, and this information guides their decisions about how to act in the future. In other words, by inspecting the observed consequences, a person can predict whether a given act will likely lead to pleasant or unpleasant outcomes on a later occasion. Consequences that are observed to be rewarding then motivate learners to perform those same acts in the future.

Both behaviorists and social learning theorists have studied in detail the influence of different patterns of consequences and, on the basis of this research, have produced a series of generalizations to guide child raising, educational, and counseling practices. One group of generalizations comes under the title reinforcement schedules, since they describe the way different schedules of timing and of sequencing consequences can influence the appearance of a behavior or a "learning" in the future. For example, the effects on performance differ when continuous reinforcement (rewarding every time the desired act occurs) is used rather than intermittent reinforcement (rewarding only certain times the act occurs). Furthermore, different schedules of intermittent reinforcement yield different results. A fixed-ratio schedule (such as rewarding the learner's every third or every fifth correct response) has a different effect from a fixed-interval schedule (rewarding every two minutes or every five minutes). These sorts of schedules, combined with a variety of others, can produce an array of different behavior results. For instance, when primary-school pupils are in the early stages of learning to raise their hands to speak in class rather than shout out their opinion, they can profitably be rewarded (reinforced) on each occasion that they raise their hands. But after the habit has been well-established, intermittent reinforcement will probably serve to maintain the habit against extinction better than continuous reinforcement.

One of the strengths of social learning theory has been its fertility in stimulating research. An endless series of empirical investigations are being conducted to test hypotheses derived from such theory and to refine people's understanding of the way learning takes place under different conditions. A second strength of the theory is that it has furnished practical guidance to people engaged in child rearing, education, and counseling.

2. Applications of Social Learning Theory

The value of social learning theory for parents, teachers, and counselors lies chiefly in its offering them both a general model for teaching and specific recommendations for applying this model in everyday situations (Bandura 1969, 1971, Klein et al. 1973).

2.1 A Five-step General Model

The process of teaching or (in behavioristic terms) of modifying the learner's behavior can be divided into five steps. The resulting five-step plan can serve as a general model to guide decisions of those performing the roles of parents, teachers, and counselors.

Firstly, the motor skill, or concept, or moral value that the learner is to acquire should be described specifically in terms of how it is ultimately to be shown in observed actions. This step is sometimes called "stating the learning goal in terms of the desired student behavior." For example, the goal for a child at home may be that he will "pick up his clothes and hang them on hooks in the closet rather than leaving them lying around the room." For a secondary-school student in a geography class, a learning objective could be to "identify the likenesses and differences among the concepts 'island,' 'peninsula,' and 'continent'," or in a mathematics class to "describe steps for solving problems involving quadratic equations." For an adult in a citizenship-education program, the desired behavior might be to "explain ways in which our nation's political system is superior to the systems of certain other nations."

Secondly, a method should be used to ensure that the learner both pays attention to this new, desirable behavior and attempts to perform it. There are several ways this step may be accomplished. One is for the parent or teacher simply to wait for the behavior to occur spontaneously, that is, wait until the child happens to hang his or her clothes in the closet. Another method is to provide a model, as is the case when a teacher or another student demonstrates how to solve mathematics problems. An obvious third method is to explain the desired behavior verbally to the learner, as when the teacher or the textbook explains to the learner the characteristics of islands, peninsulas, and continents. These verbal explanations are sometimes in the form of an order, as when a parent orders a child to hang his or her clothes in the closet.

The third step is to select appropriate consequences that can be provided when the learner either performs the desired behavior or fails to do so. These consequences are the rewards (reinforcers) and punishments that the parent or teacher arranges for the learner to experience. Reinforcers may be of many varieties, including verbal praise, special privileges, objects the learner values (candy or sweets, a toy, an attractive writing pen, an interesting book), symbols of achievement (a badge or ribbon, a gold star placed beside the student's name), or public recognition (the student's name is written on the school "honor roll" or mentioned in the newspaper). Likewise, there are many forms of punishment, such as withholding expected rewards and privileges, criticizing the learner in private, criticizing the learner in the presence of others, removing the learner from the social setting (an example is the time-out procedure of isolating a pupil from the rest of the pupils for a period of time), requiring unpleasant tasks (weeding the school yard, doing extra homework assignments), and administering physical punishment. Frequently several of these reinforcement or punishment options are used in combination.

Fourthly, once reinforcers or punishments have been selected, they need to be organized into a plan or schedule that likely will ensure that the desired behavior will be efficiently acquired.

The final step is that of applying the schedule of consequences to the learning situation and of monitoring the effect of the reinforcement schedule on the learner's progress. The purpose of assessing progress is to determine if the selected consequences actually do motivate the learner as intended. If they fail to motivate the learner, so that he or she does not acquire the desired behavior at the intended rate, then the types of consequences or the way they have been scheduled may well need to be changed.

2.2 Suggestions for Implementing the Model

To supplement the overall model, a variety of suggestions about how to carry out the steps successfully have been produced by researchers and practitioners. The nature of such suggestions is illustrated by the following four generalizations which may help in performing the third step in the above scheme—the step of selecting appropriate reinforcers and punishments.

The first generalization is: the type of consequences that serve as reinforcers and as punishments are not the same for all learners, so that a consequence experienced as a reward by one learner may not be considered as a reward by another. Furthermore, a consequence that serves as a strong reinforcer in one situation may not be so in another. Therefore, in selecting consequences that stimulate learning, it is important for a teacher to estimate which consequences will be most effective for the particular learners he or she now faces and for the teaching situation in which they find themselves.

A second generalization of help for identifying which potential consequences will be suitable reinforcers for which learners has been offered by an American psychologist, David Premack. His generalization, supported by a body of empirical evidence (Hilgard and Bower 1975 pp. 562–66), can be stated as: behaviors that are frequent in a person's set of responses can serve as reinforcers for behaviors that are infrequent. Or, cast in more applied terms: actions in which students often voluntarily engage can be used as rewards for actions teachers want them to learn. To put this principle into operation, a teacher may tell a student: "I see that you like to read science-fiction stories; so if you'll learn to spell correctly these 10 words that you misspelled on your last essay, I'll give you extra time to read a story from a new collection of science-fiction tales I have on my desk." In other words, a student's opportunity to engage in a favorite activity (the frequent behavior in the learner's repertoire of responses) is made contingent on his learning the material the teacher presents (the less frequent behavior). This means that a teacher who analyzes a particular student's pattern of voluntary behaviors may be able to identify which of these behaviors can serve as consequences that will be effective reinforcers for that learner.

A third generalization is: in most instances, reward (reinforcement) is far more efficient in effecting learning than is punishment. The inefficiency of parents' child-rearing efforts and teachers' instructional techniques often appears to result from their failure to apply this principle. Too often they depend on threats and punishment instead of positive reinforcement. In many cases, apparently, parents and teachers commit such an error because they assume that when students perform a learning task correctly, such behavior is simply what is expected and it thus deserves no comment or reward. At the same time, they assume that when students fall short of the learning goal, the best way to motivate them to improve their performance is to apply punishment. As a result, it is possible that the only response learners ever receive from those in charge of their education is punishment.

A fourth generalization is: some forms of reward and of punishment effectively stimulate the desired learning, yet are unsuitable as intended consequences because they also generate undesirable side effects. One example of this phenomenon is the practice of giving children candy or other sweets as a reward for learning. While this sort of reinforcer may indeed motivate the child to accomplish the learning task, the use of sweets produces undesirable nutritional outcomes in the process, such outcomes as increasing tooth decay, satiating the child's appetite with the "empty calories" of the refined sugar found in sweets so that the child does not eat foods containing such proper nutrients as protein, and upsetting the blood-sugar level in children

who are prone to hypoglycemia. A second example is the practice of using sarcasm for criticizing students in front of their peers, with the sarcasm intended to motivate them to learn more adequately in the future. While the students may indeed, as the result of the public criticism, master the next learning task more satisfactorily than they did the last, the use of sarcasm may also generate in them a variety of unwanted outcomes. Such outcomes may include fear of coming to class, hate for the subject matter of the course, loss of self-confidence, and psychosomatic disorders—headaches, stomach pains, or nausea each time the students expect that they may be criticized again in public. Therefore, when parents and teachers select types of reinforcement and of punishment which they contemplate using, they can profitably try to predict the kinds of undesired side effects the various types could produce. On the basis of this prediction, they can then select only those consequences that are unlikely to produce damaging side effects.

In conclusion, social learning theory offers so much practical guidance for improving the learning process that it has become one of the most popular sources of aid in everyday decision making for a growing number of parents, teachers, and counselors.

Bibliography

Bandura A 1969 *Principles of Behavior Modification*. Holt, Rinehart and Winston, New York
Bandura A 1971 *Psychological Modeling: Conflicting Theories*. Aldine-Atherton, Chicago, Illinois
Bandura A 1977 *Social Learning Theory*. Prentice-Hall, Englewood Cliffs, New Jersey
Bandura A, Walters R H 1963 *Social Learning and Personality Development*. Holt, Rinehart and Winston, New York
Hall C S, Lindzey G 1978 *Theories of Personality*. Wiley, New York
Hilgard E R, Bower G H 1975 *Theories of Learning*, 4th edn. Prentice-Hall, Englewood Cliffs, New Jersey
Klein R D, Hapkiewicz W G, Roden A H (eds.) 1973 *Behavior Modification in Educational Settings*. Thomas, Springfield, Illinois
McMillan J H 1980 *The Social Psychology of School Learning*. Academic Press, New York
Rotter J B 1982 *The Development and Applications of Social Learning Theory*. Praeger, New York
Sahakian W S 1970 *Psychology of Learning: Systems, Models, and Theories*. Markham, Chicago, Illinois
Sears R R, Rau L, Alpert R 1965 *Identification and Child Rearing*. Stanford University Press, Stanford, California
Skinner B F 1974 *About Behaviorism*. Knopf, New York

Information-processing Theory

C. Michel

In the last two decades the information-processing approach has spread through the field of cognitive development. Its emergence is linked principally to (a) the

advancement in understanding of the way the nervous system works, and (b) the development of computer-based systems which simulate a number of human functions. In the 1980s, computers perform highly complex human operations. Thus they provide an avenue for research on human capabilities and learning processes.

The metaphor established between the human brain and the computer is useful in that mental operations are to some extent comparable to the workings of a computer since they both take in information (input function), perform operations (throughput function), and display results (output function). More generally, both human beings and computers manipulate symbols and transform input into output.

The general notion of human beings functioning as processors of information is not new. From ancient times, people have speculated about how they receive information, think about it, remember it, reach a decision, and act the way they do. Information-processing theory only provides new insights and adds greater precision in describing the likely parts of the human processing system and their ways of operation.

So far the label *theory* has been used to designate the information-processing approach as if it were a single theory. However, as proposed by developmental psychologists Kail and Bisanz (1982, p. 47), information processing can be considered more as a framework within which a multitude of theories have emerged. In effect, this framework is characterized by a large number of research programs which sometimes offer different views about the types of components comprised in a person's processing system and their various modes of interactions. Our discussion here will focus on the widely agreed upon notions of information-processing models and will identify some of the key issues that are debated. For matters of convenience, the term *theory* will be used along with *approach* and *model* to designate the information-processing framework. The topics reviewed in this essay are organized in the following sequence: general orientation of the theory, modes of investigation, interacting components of information processing, development aspects of the system, and the significance of the model.

1. General Orientation of the Theory

The attraction of information-processing theory can be understood only in the light of events which have marked experimental psychology. First, a crisis occurred in the 1940s and 1950s within neobehaviorism. Many psychologists started questioning whether laboratory experiments actually lead to a real understanding of human thought in natural settings. At about the same time, Chomsky in his now famous review of Skinner's book, *Verbal Learning* (1959), argued that his own research on language acquisition led him to conclude that learning theory is subjective rather than objective in its definitions and observations. Furthermore, the World War 2 had contributed to psychologists viewing human beings as information transmitters and decision makers. Other influences came from communication

engineering, information theory, and computer technology which suggested the notion of "communication channels" as a metaphor for human thought, the idea that people might be considered symbol-manipulation systems and the fact that logical capabilities could be simulated by appropriate computer programs.

In the 1960s a new generation of psychologists willing to talk about the mind emerged. Ten years later, psychologists moved from an emphasis on behavior to a focus on thinking, from a notion of passive learner to one of active learner. More important, they dared to be mentalistic, to consider behavior as merely an indicator of the more interesting underlying mental events (Miller 1983 p. 255). By the 1970s, the information-processing model matured into a well-balanced field; its influence expanded considerably in the 1980s.

2. Modes of Investigation

Information-processing psychologists share several methodological concerns. For instance, they view humans as information-processing devices which effectively organize millions of bits of information; they study the human mechanism to discover how the person treats the information and acts on it; and they make a detailed examination from input to output. At a finer level of analysis, they look at developmental changes for each state of the information-processing system. (The different components involved in this process are reviewed in the following section.)

Information-processing adepts also investigate memory, perception, attention, language, and problem solving, topics traditionally studied by experimental psychologists. However, information-processing experiments tend to be methodologically microscopic in that they focus on brief events and often examine temporal variables. For instance, they may try to determine the circumstances under which a stimulus is perceived and how it is perceived. They may also be interested in ascertaining the number of chunks of information which can be accommodated in short-term memory during an experiment in the general mechanism by which these pieces of information are transmitted to the memory bank. Mostly, however, they are concerned with the analysis of the step-by-step process leading to a given output.

Information-processing researchers utilize the so-called "task analysis process" as a crucial element in understanding human learning. Task analysis refers to the careful inspection of the experimental or real-life task facing the adult or the child. Analysis of the task and its broader environment is essential, because the task and its setting affect the different processing activities.

Experiments often include the use of simulated computer programs devised to monitor different stages of the human processing system in operation. The assumption is that if a computer program is given the same problem-solving input as a human being and the computer produces the same output as the human, then the program may well contain the same sorts of components and processing steps as those in the human processing system. Theorists working in the artificial intelligence field would have taken a significant step toward understanding human thought processes if they could program a computer to produce the same sorts of solutions to problems that a human would produce (Thomas 1985 pp. 338–39). In addition to developing computer simulation, information processing psychologists have utilized another tool, that is, schematic representation. Temporal and functional relationships among several processing stages are typically depicted via diagrams; in most cases they are simple flowchart models but are also often mathematical symbols or propositional logic models.

3. Interacting Components of Information Processing

As conceived today, the human processing system consists of four major elements: (a) sense organs, (b) short-term memory, (c) long-term memory, and (d) muscle systems. The system also involves functions and processes within each element and the interactions among these elements. The following description is one version of such a processing network.

In the hypothetical system displayed in Fig. 1, the large box represents the person's mind and the open regions represent the world outside the person. The person's encounter with the environment is mediated by (a) the senses called the "windows to the world," as input channels, and (b) the muscle systems as output channels or "actors on the world."

3.1 The Sense Organs

The sense organs, such as eyes, ears, taste buds, pressure and pain nerves in the skin, receive impressions from the environment. They serve as input channels which gather information from the environment. Each sense organ is, however, a very specialized instrument, attuned only to one type of stimulation. They gather impressions in a selective way, filtering out much information and allowing only some environmental stimuli to enter the human processing system.

3.2 Short-term Memory

Those stimuli collected from the outside world are initially processed in what different theorists have labelled *short-term memory, primary memory, active memory, or working memory*. Most people consider those terms as being synonymous. The working memory's primary function is to hold limited amounts of information for a very short period of time, evaluated at a few seconds. Its role and functioning can be explained by reviewing its three stages.

(a) *Sensory memory*. This is an unselective type of memory which holds for only one or two seconds all stimuli that strike the particular sense organ within a range of receptiveness. Labels applied to this early stage are *iconic memory, echoic memory*, and *tactile* or *haptic memory*. During this momentary retention an interchange occurs with long-term memory. At this first stage certain gross characteristics of the stimuli are identified.

(b) *Encoding*. This term suggests that at this second stage impressions and stimuli are recast into a form—codes, symbols, representations—that will be later manipulated and stored in long-term mem-

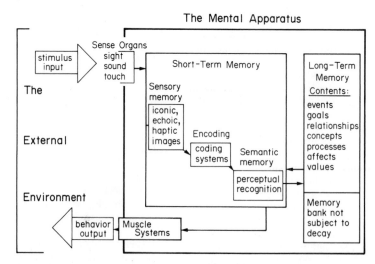

The Mental Apparatus

Figure 1
A hypothetical model of the human information-processing system

ory or else they are lost. This stage lasts one or two seconds and holds very little capacity.

(c) *Semantic memory*. At this point, the person compares the information of stages (a) and (b) with some selected elements of long-term memory. It is a stage of perceptual recognition during which the information is identified for what it represents in terms of the person's past experiences, or long-term memory. It is believed that a mature adult can hold seven "chunks" of information at a time (Miller 1956). A chunk is described as "a portion of a person's knowledge base that is actually activated and deactivated as a unit" (Kail and Bisanz 1982 p. 59). Chunks may be simple, like a name or a date, or complex, such as a concept.

3.3 Long-term Memory

Long-term memory is the portion of the system which stores infinite amounts of information, probably indefinitely, as implied by its name. It has two principal functions: (a) directing the operation of the entire processing system, and (b) storing information or coded material derived from the person's past encounters with the environment. Coded material takes two main forms: (a) *episodic memories* which are memory traces about single events from the past involving specific persons or objects, and (b) *semantic memories* which consist of more generalized instruments of thought, concepts, and processes which are not limited to one place or time. Other elements which also constitute the anatomy of long-term memory are: goals, relationships, affects, and values. *Goals* are motivational components which stimulate the individual to focus attention on certain facets of the environment rather than others. *Relationships* are the connections and rapports existing between one item in memory and another. *Affects* are emotions which are often associated with concepts, certain events, and relationships. *Values* are opinions about the desirability, or propriety, or goodness of something. They, too, are associated with certain elements of the memory bank.

A popular suggestion is that long-term memory is organized like a fishnet, with each node representing an individual memory trace such as an event or a concept. The strands lead to other events and concepts. The links between some nodes are stronger, meaning that linkages are more quickly and strongly established between these memory traces than between others which represent more distant associations. However, such a comparison is inadequate for describing the complex intricacies of human thoughts and the mechanisms of interaction between short-term and long-term memories (Anderson 1983).

One of the most important interactions is that of matching the stimuli received from the environment with the content of long-term memory. Thus, active decision making and problem solving are carried out through semantic short-term memory and long-term

memory during a flow of rapid transactions. Then the person assigns a "meaning" from the long-term memory to each now recognizable sensory encounter with the environment. The main ideas or concepts are then stored in the memory bank. The results of the new encounter may be similar to existing memory traces, or may be new additions to the memory bank. In some instances, new memory traces are recorded in great detail and exact phrasing; at other times they are not. In all cases, old coded traces influence how new experiences are constructed and stored. It may also happen that the new experience casts doubt on the logic of the original memory trace and alters it. The memory-construction process is fed by people's past and present experience—their memory banks. These coded traces and their interactions with short-term memory make up the human processing system.

3.4 Behavioral Output System

The muscle systems constitute the last link of the information-processing chain. Each decision made in semantic short-term memory elicits from long-term memory coded directions for activating the appropriate behavior output. The nerve system transmits these orders to the appropriate muscles which perform the desired behavior. This action ends the information-processing cycle. But this last step need not necessarily be in the form of overt behavior. It may well be acquisition of a concept, coming to a conclusion, or some sort of cognitive development. However, such results will eventually be reflected in future observable acts.

4. Developmental Aspects of the System

Since our concern is with human development, information processing in children should not be overlooked. Information-processing models were first developed as theories of adult thought, then later adopted by developmentalists who were dissatisfied with the explanation offered by other theories of cognitive growth. Most of the early information-processing studies were mere translations of adult research, but using children as subjects. However, over the past decade or so, the number of studies of children's memory—and to a lesser extent, of attention, comprehension, and problem solving—have increased exponentially. The following discussion includes examples of the kind of data supporting the idea that information is processed differently at various stages of children's growth.

Differences are noticeable at three main levels: (a) sensory intake and short-term memory, (b) long-term memory, and (c) interaction of system components.

4.1 Sensory Intake and Short-term Memory

A first difference concerns elements in the environment to which an infant and an older child attends. The infant, with a limited store of experience, is expected to find novelty in elements which are quite usual to an older child. A second difference appears in the three stages of attention-development proposed by Mackworth (1976). First, small infants focus on objects in their sensory environment frequently and at great length. During a second stage (age 1 until 4 or 5), children begin to show acquaintance with patterns they have already seen and focus on features on which to base their decisions. But their attention shifts from one detail to another from one moment to the next. At the third stage, older children and adolescents are capable of searching an environment to acquire all needed information. They are not so hasty and are capable of selecting key features, of altering judgment on the basis of feedback, and of abstracting or modifying a rule. They have acquired better cognitive control over attention.

Another major feature appears to be developmental differences in short-term memory capacity. According to some studies, at 18 months the attention span is one chunk, a capacity that increases to four chunks by age 5 and which reaches seven chunks—the adult span—during adolescence (Thomas 1985 p. 341). The number of chunks affects the operation of short-term memory but so does their structure. A chunk that involves an entire concept "my mother wears her blue dress to go to church" is more encompassing than another referring only to "dress" or "mother." The greater complexity of the chunks in the older child's repertoire of memories facilitates a more efficient functioning of short-term memory than does the younger child's.

4.2 Long-term Memory

The difference in children's information-processing systems is largely due to changes in long-term memory. These modifications are of two general types: genetically determined maturation of the nervous system and alterations of the knowledge base or the contents of memory as a result of experience. In effect, the typical older child has accumulated a greater number of memory traces as a result of more years of experience and a more mature nervous system. Besides having a larger fund of knowledge, older children use a greater number of associations relating concepts and creating more complex thought patterns than do younger children. Furthermore, the processes also advance in sophistication with the advance of age. These include rehearsal and mnemonic techniques. In short, the data and processes of long-term memory grow in quantity, variety, and complexity.

4.3 Interactions of System Components

The inherent complexity of the interaction between short- and long-term memories renders difficult theorizing about the effects of developmental changes on this interactive process. However, it seems that older children's greater ability for coding stimuli into symbols, concepts, or words seems to explain their superiority in perceiving, storing, and recalling information. Another facet of the interactions between the two types of memories which seems to be affected by age is the speed at which information is processed. In conclusion, with the passing of time, the human information system increases in the complexity, speed, and integration of the system's components.

Obvious applications of children's information-processing theory occur in teaching. Teachers acquainted with the theory can better understand students' learning processes and help them develop their metaperception and metamemory, thereby equipping children to "learn how to learn." The model is also a valuable instrument for both parents and teachers as a guide to diagnosis and treatment of learning difficulties. However, scores of unanswered questions about developmental changes in the information-processing system represent some of the challenges that this approach poses for researchers in the field of genetic psychology. At this point all signs point to the continuing rapport between adult information-processing and developmental psychology. It is likely that this exchange will be mutually enriching.

5. Significance of the Model

The theory's ability to stimulate new research and discoveries is undeniable. "For ambitious researchers, there is no lack of threads of investigation to follow and of tangles to unravel in information processing" (Thomas 1985 p. 346). This appears justified considering the increasing accumulation of research related to the senses, to the encoding and memorizing processes, to problems in the retrieval of stored information, to the mechanisms that guide the system's behavioral output, and to computer simulations of information-processing functions.

Other strengths include the theory's ability to express the complexity of thought, ranging from the simple detections of a stimulus to the development of complex rules. Among the highlights of information processing are the specific predictions, based on careful analysis of tasks and of the current state of the subject's cognitive system, that the model offers about a person's moment-to-moment behavior. In other words, the theory attempts to be explicit about *how* people use their cognitive skills in a given situation. As such, it provides a model of performance, which is lacking in many leading theories, such as the Piagetian framework, for instance.

The theory also gets high ratings for its rigorous methodology, marked by stringent and precise experimental methods. The theory is internally consistent and economical, that is, it has few if any apparent internal inconsistencies, and the components and their interactions as proposed by various theories have not appeared unduly elaborate to account for the data they intend to explain. In addition, with the strict requirements demanded by laboratory research and computer simulations, contradictions and vague statements are not permitted.

Weaknesses of the information-processing model include mainly what certain scholars view as the short-comings of the computer model. Critics claim that: (a) the model may adequately describe certain human output (given knowledge of the input), but still differs in important ways from the way people really think; (b) information-processing theorists have been over-enthusiastic about adopting different flowcharts and models, or on the contrary, limited in their thinking by adopting one exclusive pattern; (c) computer-simulation models have technical limitations, such as a "language barrier"; (d) there are difficulties in expanding precise computer models into more general ones that can run successfully.

Other critics question the degree of success of information processing as it addresses developmental issues. Although much research needs to be conducted, it is believed that it is still too early to pass an ultimate judgment on this matter. Also, whereas most theories began with observations of people in natural environments, information-processing models have often begun with research on artificial situations. This shortcoming is, however, somewhat overcome by the addition of the so-called "task analysis" which moves research on information processing into an ecological attitude toward learning and cognition.

Bibliography

Anderson J R 1983 A spreading activation theory of memory. *J. Verbal Learn. Verbal Behav.* 22: 261–95
Chomsky N 1967 Review of Skinner's *Verbal Learning*. In: Jakobovits L A, Miron M S (eds.) 1967 *Readings in the Psychology of Language*. Prentice-Hall, Englewood Cliffs, New Jersey, pp. 85–103
Hale G A, Lewis M (eds.) 1979 *Attention and Cognitive Development*. Plenum, New York
Kail R, Bisanz J 1982 Information processing and cognitive development. In: Reese H W (ed.) 1982 *Advances in Child Development and Behavior*, Vol. 17. Academic Press, New York, pp. 45–81
Kail R V Jr, Hagen J W (eds.) 1977 *Perspectives on the Development of Memory and Cognition*. Erlbaum, Hillsdale, New Jersey
Mackworth J F 1976 Development of attention. In: Hamilton V, Vernon M D 1976 *The Development of Cognitive Processes*. Academic Press, New York, pp. 111–52
Miller G A 1956 The magical number seven, plus or minus two: Some limits on our capacity for processing information. *Psych. Rev.* 63: 81–97
Miller P H 1983 *Theories of Developmental Psychology*. W. H. Freeman, San Francisco, California
Siegler R S (ed.) 1978 *Children's Thinking: What Develops?* Erlbaum, Hillsdale, New Jersey
Thomas R M 1985 *Comparing Theories of Child Development*. Wadsworth, Belmont, California

Psychoanalytic Theory of Human Development

E. Douvan

Psychoanalytic theory was developed at the end of the nineteenth century and in the early decades of this century by Sigmund Freud and his followers. Contemporary theories of development incorporate assumptions and insights from psychoanalytic theory either explicitly or unintentionally as part of the intellectual culture which has absorbed them.

Freud's theories, in their turn, grew out of an encounter between an intellectual giant and a particular set of historical and cultural conditions. Industrialization and the division of classes on grounds of competitive achievement rather than birth and blood lines were firmly established. Physical science had developed rapidly and informed nineteenth-century thought. Darwin's discoveries and theory opened the possibility of a scientific study of the human condition as well as the physical environment.

Freud was raised in a bourgeois Jewish family in Austria under the sway of that set of conventions and ideals we have come to designate as Victorian: strong familistic values, a patriarchal authority system, a sharp division of sex roles in the family, a sentimental view of the domestic wife and mother, adherence to manners and forms dictated by conventional morals, and respect for civility and correctness in public behavior.

Along with all of this order—of industrial society, scientific knowledge, and Victorian morality—class consciousness and revolutionary ideologies were in the wings and very much a part of the intellectual atmosphere in which Freud lived and worked. The image of repressed and downtrodden forces pushing their way through and overthrowing established order and authority occurred in revolutionary social criticism and in literature. In literature it was applied to the individual human psyche: sexual and other hidden and irrational forces were shown to have power in human behavior and to subvert the best laid plans of rational or conventional controls. The elements of a Freudian view were all available in the thought of the time, waiting to be systematized and formulated in a theoretical frame.

The genius of Freud was scientific. He was trained in science and his thought bore the stamp of science. Dostoevsky, Ibsen, Strindberg, and other artists had apprehended the force of the irrational in human behavior. They used the insight to create characters and dramatize situations. They gave concrete form to their insights and used their artistic understanding to appeal to the unconscious in their audiences. But Freud, confronting the same insights, turned them to scientific purposes.

Noting the force of the sexual instinct in his patients, Freud began to formulate a theory and proceeded to extend his bases of evidence, his sources of data, and the breadth of coverage of the theoretical connections he made. He looked at his own dreams, he looked to other cultures, to children's experience and expression, and to myth and fantasy. The further he looked, the more certain he became of the scientific validity and the universality of his theories.

Aside from his discovery of the method of psychoanalysis, Freud's most dramatic discoveries include the unconscious and the large role it plays in all of human behavior, and infantile sexuality, the fact that sex does not arise only at puberty but is a critical part of psychic life and development from the moment of birth and throughout life. His developmental theory is in a very important sense a theory about the sexual development of personality.

Two interdependent aspects of the theory are critical to the understanding of development. These are the structural hypothesis describing the way in which the personality functions are organized and the stages in drive organization.

1. The Structure of Personality

Freud posited three structures or functions of the personality. These are the id, the ego, and the superego. In the mature personality the three functions operate in balance and allow the individual to interact with the environment in ways that produce need satisfaction and acceptable social relations.

The id is the locus of drive or instinct and its function is to realize immediate discharge of tension or energy created by the drives or by external stimulation. When the infant is hungry, a state of tension is created in the organism. When the baby is fed, tension is reduced and satisfaction prevails. The aim of the id is to reduce tension, to seek immediate satisfaction of drive. The id operates according to the pleasure principle, that is, it seeks to realize satisfaction and to avoid pain or tension.

At birth the infant is all drive, but development of other aspects of the personality begins almost immediately. If the baby were able to reduce its own hunger drive automatically through some internal mechanism, or if the mother were immediately available at all times so that no delay ever occurred between the need and its discharge, personality would not develop. Since inevitably in the real world the baby will suffer some delay in the satisfaction of its drives, the consequent frustration leads to the development and employment of new psychic functions.

The most elementary of these functions consists of the substitution of a mental image of food for real food during the period of delay between drive and satisfaction. Since the baby has been fed in the past and has a memory of the state of satisfaction, when food is not immediately forthcoming, the baby will produce this image from memory and will experience satisfaction. This represents the primary process, in which the image of an object or state is not distinguished from the actual object or state. Primary process operates

outside the realm of logic and accords with the pleasure principle. It is the mode characteristic of the id, of infancy, but also of poetry and dreams.

But an image of food cannot substitute for food in the long run, and the baby must come to distinguish between the inner world of images and the outer world of real objects. In the process of nursing when hunger is satisfied and when drive is no longer imperative, the baby looks and touches, perceives and explores the narrow dimensions of its external environment. The baby begins to distinguish between its own body—which yields the double sensation of toucher and touched— from the body of the mother and other aspects of its world. This process enriches the store of images in the infant's memory, leads to the gradual distinction between inner and outer worlds, and lays the groundwork for perception, memory, and cognition, which are among the critical functions of the ego.

To reiterate: the id is the source of all psychic energy. Its function and aim is to realize immediate discharge of tension arising from drive states or external sources. It operates according to the pleasure principle and its tools are motor activity (e.g., crying, flailing) and hallucinatory images. Its mode is primary process. The energy of the id is neither well-organized nor bound but is highly mobile. It operates outside the categories of logic and time.

The ego is the executive of the personality, mediating conflict that arises among the internal functions and negotiating with the external environment to realize the gratification of needs and other aims of the personality. Among the assets the ego has at its command are perception, memory, cognition, and directed action. It operates according to the reality principle, it binds energy which it acquires from the id, and it directs that energy to the realization of need gratification by means of mastery of the environment. To realize gratification the ego must be able to bind energy and postpone discharge until the means of actual gratification are at hand.

The ego distinguishes between the inner and outer worlds, between image and object, between fantasy and reality. Whereas the id operates unconsciously, the ego is largely conscious. It deals with the real world and harmonizes among the functions of the personality. It is not, however, synonymous with consciousness. The ego also has at its disposal certain mechanisms like identification, sublimation, and other defenses for reducing anxiety which operate unconsciously.

The ego operates with secondary process, that mode of thought governed by the laws of logic and a sense of time. Secondary process corresponds to problem-solving thought. The ego makes use of images but now their function is to symbolize and abstract prospective realities and possibilities to facilitate the ego's command of reality and choice. Images do not serve, as they do in the id, as a substitute for reality.

The third structure or set of functions in the personality is called the superego and represents the incorporation by the individual of the norms and moral strictures of society. The superego corresponds to the concept of conscience. It develops between the third and fifth years when the little child, confronted by an insoluble conflict (the Oedipal conflict, discussed in Sect. 2) between sexual desires for the parent of the other sex and fear of retaliation by the like-sexed parent, performs an unconscious act of identification with the like-sexed parent. This identification, combined with unconscious repression of the sexual desire, realizes the child's unconscious sexual aim (i.e., as the like-sexed parent, the child now has sexual control over the love object) and avoids the danger of retaliation. The act of identification also eventuates in the child's incorporation of the like-sexed parent's moral proscription against incest and murder. The superego is thus the heritage of the Oedipal drama.

With the acquisition of the superego, the functions of the personality are now complete. The superego acts as an internal representative of the parents and society and guides the actions of the personality. Just as earlier the little child behaved in certain ways and avoided certain acts to win the approval and love of the parents, he now behaves in order to win approval from the internalized parent or conscience and to avoid the pain of its disapproval or punishment (guilt).

The superego shares qualities with the id. It is largely unconscious, at least in its early form, and since it represents the incorporation of the parent, the objects of the original drive live on in the superego. It is this early and primitive characteristic that we often note in the rigidity and punitiveness of conscience. The superego will sometimes punish the individual for merely thinking about a prohibited act. It does not distinguish between the thought and the act.

Conflict arises between the various functions of the personality. Id impulses obviously come into conflict with superego prohibitions. But impulses also conflict with the ego's ability to think and plan in accordance with reality to gain the best possible need satisfaction. Also, prohibitions of the superego may conflict with the ego's aims and inflict crippling guilt when reality does not justify it. The function of the ego, then, is to work compromises and negotiate conflicts in the interest of harmonious internal functioning and the realization of optimal mastery of the environment. The ego changes and grows in power as the child develops. Freud described the orderly stages of normal growth as stages in the locus and form of drive.

2. Stages of Development

Growth and change occur and are affected by internal (maturational) forces in combination with forces in the environment, but the pattern or sequence of change follows the development of drive, which is governed by maturation. Drive development follows a template, a pattern built into the organism. Although the pattern

governs changes in both libido and aggressive drive, it is most easily observed and understood as it affects the sexual drive.

Freud distinguished three stages in the development of infantile sexuality: the oral, the anal, and the phallic. Sexual energy, sensitivity, gratification, and preoccupation center and are invested in each of these body parts in sequence. Each becomes the focus of sensual pleasure, the medium of drive expression, and the organizing symbol of ideation. The drive, its pattern of development, and its accompanying fantasy sequence—that is, the contents of ideation—are predetermined by the built-in maturational template.

The oral phase begins at birth and extends through infancy. Erotic drive invests in the mouth, and the infant's pleasure derives from eating, sucking, biting, holding in, and spitting out. While these expressions are connected to eating, they are not restricted to the satisfaction of hunger. Sucking has been shown to be a need above and beyond the need for nourishment. Its erotic character can be detected in thumb sucking in little children and in its incorporation into sexual foreplay in adults.

The mouth also functions at this stage as a sensory organ, a means by which the infant comes in contact with and knows the world. Whatever comes within reach is tasted and mouthed by the infant. Nursing provides the first social contact for the baby, a contact repeated thousands of times during infancy; and since it is a system that requires coordination between the infant and the social world, it lays a groundwork of expectations about that world. If nursing or feeding is painful or unpredictable (e.g., because of colic or other dysfunctions), the infant's expectations of the world (which at this stage is indistinguishable from the self) will assume a negative cast.

In addition to focusing drive and serving as a primary contact with the physical and social world, the mouth and oral modes structure fantasy. From fairy tales and dreams, from children's drawings and the fantasy of neurotic patients, images of eating and being eaten can be seen to hold a central position in the nonrational layers of human thought. Adults in traditional and naive cultures often express similar thoughts when they react to the beautiful, soft reality of a baby by saying "I could just eat you" or "Isn't she delicious?" The mouth is the organ of expression for both sensual needs and aggressive needs, and the experiences of the baby around feeding will, in Freud's view, determine adult stances toward such varied psychological characteristics as dependency, acquisitiveness, generosity, criticalness, and verbal aggression.

At the close of infancy, somewhere around the end of the second year of life, libidinal cathexis shifts to a new center in the anal zone. Waste from the digestive system accumulates in the lower end of the alimentary canal and creates tension in the bowel and anus which is released by the reflex opening of the anal sphincter and defecation. Both aspects of this process—the accumulated pressure and the tension release—produce pleasurable sensations, heightened at this stage by the location of libidinal cathexis in the anal region.

Coordinated with this development of the sexual drive the little child also faces its first demand for adherence to social mores at the expense of instinctual pleasure. He or she is toilet trained, that is, asked to bring the reflex action of the sphincters under voluntary control and regulate the time and place of elimination in accord with accepted social practice. The importance of toilet training derives from the fact that it is the first lesson in conforming to social requirements and the fact that the child is asked to give up or postpone the instinctual pleasure associated with defecation.

Just as the oral stage contains two modes of functioning, taking in and spitting out, the anal stage also consists of two modes, the expulsive and retentive. While one child may resist toilet training by defecating at the wrong time and in the wrong place, another will resist by retaining the feces in constipation. Since the parent has a stake in the child's performing toilet functions in a particular way, it is clear that the issue can develop into a battle of wills and lay the foundation for the child's later responses to authority, social convention, and social requirements. Attitudes toward cleanliness and punctuality and toward one's products and one's freedom from constraint by others are also undergirded by developments in this stage.

The third stage of infantile sexuality, the phallic stage, begins at around the fourth year of age when libidinal focus again shifts, this time to the genitals. Here the theory recognizes the anatomical difference between males and females but asserts that it is the phallus (or its embryological equivalent in females, the clitoris) that attracts and focuses drive. The phallic stage and its hypothesized Oedipal conflict are central to psychoanalytic theory. And it is clearly more compelling as a theory of male development than a statement or description of the way in which the little girl's personality develops.

In the little boy the intensification of phallic sensitivity and interest is accompanied by a fantasy that carries the Oedipal theme. His erotic interest and desires focus on the mother—the first love object—and he yearns for total erotic possession of her. He would eliminate rivals, kill or castrate them to break their erotic claims on his beloved. But an irreconcilable conflict arises since his chief rival for her affection is also a beloved object, the father. His father is also more powerful than he is, and the little boy assumes through identification that the father wants to destroy or castrate him. Torn by conflicting passions which cannot be resolved in reality, the little boy resorts to a psychic solution: he "becomes" the father through an unconscious identification. He thus gains erotic control over the mother and takes from the father, through identification, the moral strictures against murder and incest. This, then, is the process by which the superego is formed, the identification with the moral code of society begun. The Oedipal conflict

provides the key to the great question of socialization and education: why does the child choose to grow up or become socialized? It is the centerpiece of the psychoanalytic theory of development.

It is easy to see why the little boy decides to collaborate with the forces of socialization—when not doing so carries the threat of losing his most prized source of pleasure, the focus of his erotic life, his penis. Castration fear is a powerful motive force. It is precisely here, in the provision of a comparably powerful motive, that the theory falls short of explaining development in the female child. For her the mother is also the primary love and she presumably would wish total possession of the mother. But, says the theory, she becomes disillusioned and disappointed with the mother when she compares her body to that of her brother and father. Concluding that the mother somehow failed to provide her with a phallus, the little girl turns to the father in the hope that he will repair the injustice. With her cathexis fixed on the father, she is now in competition with the mother and undergoes a development parallel to the boy's. She identifies with the mother and incorporates the beginning of a superego. While the little boy negotiates an identification to avoid castration, the little girl makes her move toward moral control because of envy and a sense of deprivation. In addition to the relatively pallid motivation provided for the development of the girl, Freud's women students objected on theoretical grounds to the idea that the girl's development should be governed by the boy's body. The criticisms have never been adequately answered and psychoanalytic theory must be judged to have provided a compelling theory of male development and a much less adequate understanding of growth in the female.

Just as the anal period presents a prototype for conformity to social requirements that is fateful for the child's later relationships and interactions in the social world, developments in the phallic period establish prototypes and expectations in the child about his or her ability to affect the social world, to influence others, and to realize gratification of needs. The success of the identification process and its yield in satisfying desires for love are critical to the development of the child's sense of self and morality.

The Oedipal identification with the like-sexed parent that resolves the conflict and brings the phallic period to a close is accompanied and reinforced by repression—that is, by an active unconscious quashing of drive. The identification allows vicarious gratification of the desire for the parent of the other sex, but a desire considerably tamed by repression. The close of the Oedipal period, then, finds the child in a relatively quiescent state vis-à-vis the drives. The period that follows in which repression holds sway is referred to as the latency period, extending from the close of the phallic period to the beginning of puberty. It is a period of relative internal calm and is used by society as a time for initiating the child into the culture through schooling. The attention of the child—relatively freed from internal developments and conflicts—turns to the task of absorbing the knowledge, techniques, and conventions of the society in which he or she will live.

At puberty the balance and calm achieved through repression is disrupted by hormonal changes and the system's infusion with a massively heightened sexual drive. Old conflicts are reopened and old settlements are renegotiated. The Oedipal resolution must be reworked and this time the goal is transfer of cathexis from the parent to an appropriate member of the other sex. While the aim of infantile libido is sensual pleasure, in adulthood this aim is joined by a procreative aim. Whereas infantile libido can be handled by repression and identification, adult sexuality cannot be satisfied in this way without serious cost to the adult personality. The young person at adolescence must effect a resolution of Oedipal issues that transfers libidinal investment out of the family and reunites sex and affection in adult love.

Following the phallic period, the location of drive remains in the genitals. Drive development is relatively complete by the close of the Oedipal period, and it was this fact, in part, which led Freud to the conclusion that all important development occurs and all the prototypes for later behavior and adaptation are fixed by the age of five or six. This position was also heavily influenced by Freud's biological orientation. Since drive represents the biological component of personality, when its development is complete, all critical and critically important development has occurred. The position and its biological bias were among the points that led students and early followers of Freud to criticize and begin to offer amendments to psychoanalytic theory. A few of these amendments and expansions are discussed below.

3. Developments in Psychoanalytic Theory Since Freud

During the early years of the psychoanalytic movement several followers broke from Freud and offered competing theoretical systems which differed from psychoanalysis in important respects. The most famous of these schisms, represented by Jung, Adler, and Rank, all challenged the primacy of the erotic drive in infancy and offered competing sources of motivation—the need for nourishment, the drive to overcome a sense of inferiority, and the need to master the anxiety of separation. Though the theories they offered were highly influenced by the structure and assumptions of psychoanalytic theory, the early heretics formed splinter movements that developed independently and had little influence on later developments in Freud's system.

A second group of critics among members of the Vienna circle consisted of Karen Horney, Erich Fromm, Clara Thompson, and others who came to question the biological assumptions and the metaphors from physical science that underpinned Freud's theory. This group of neo-Freudians, who emigrated from Europe under the threat of Nazism and spent most of their professional careers in the United States, were impressed with cultural differences and the striking findings of modern social anthropology and emphasized the force of the social environment in their theories of personality development. They rejected the notion that drive development was the only critical aspect of personality development and that all important prototypes were complete by the age of five or six. They introduced interpersonal interaction as the critical mechanism by which growth and change are effected, and conceived change as possible throughout life. Cultural and historical forces, in the neo-Freudian view, affect development by establishing ideal concepts of human personality and modal patterns of adaptation. The neo-Freudians eventually established their own training centers and drew away from the orthodox Freudian group.

Within the orthodox mainstream two significant revisions of theory have developed. The first of these, formulated by Erik Erikson in his very influential book *Childhood and Society* which was published in 1950, offers a substantial refinement and extension of our understanding. Erikson integrates biological, personal, and social factors in his theory of personality development, he illuminates the way in which all of these factors enter into the developmental process to influence both the pace and direction of change, and he extends developmental theory beyond childhood to account for changes throughout the life span. Once social roles are accorded reality and power in the processes of personality development, the role transitions of adulthood (becoming a worker, becoming a parent, retiring from employment) become subjects of interest to the theorist. Erikson's analysis of the developmental tasks and processes of adolescence (identity and intimacy) stimulated a great deal of research in the social-science community and became as well a popular symbol and shibboleth for a generation of American youth.

The other significant revision of Freud's theory from within the ranks of his loyal followers fixed on the issue of the origin of the ego. The challenge here is to Freud's assertion that the id is the original source of all psychic energy, that development of the ego and superego depend on a process of borrowing or diverting of instinctual-drive energy from the id to turn to the functions of the other aspects of personality. Hartmann and other psychoanalysts offered the alternative view that the ego has independent energy of its own from the beginning of life. The change in emphasis on the ego represented by this revision is consonant with Erikson's revision and has been very influential in psychoanalytic theory and its development up to the present.

4. The Influence of Psychoanalytic Theory on Education

Psychoanalytic theory has been a major source of cultural change. No area of modern life or thought has remained unaffected by the insights and formulations of Freud. The assumptions made about human behavior, the forces that affect it, the possibilities and limitations of change in the human condition—all of these carry the mark of Freud's thought.

Freud made a decisive contribution—along with the major figures in modern European literature—to a shift in cultural emphasis from traditional morality based on criteria of the social good to the modern "era of psychology" that stresses mental health and judges events and behavior on internal psychological grounds, the extent to which they contribute to individual happiness and "fulfillment." Psychoanalytic theory contributed in this and other ways to the breakdown of traditional authority.

By uncovering and stressing the "dark underside" of human life, motivation, and behavior, psychoanalysis opened the way to interpretation of all human behavior as reflecting hidden motives. Again, this aspect of the theory reduced the special aura of authority possessed by parents and other adults in traditional, particularly Victorian, society.

By focusing attention on childhood and recognizing its continuity with adulthood, the extent to which it shares the main problems and features of adulthood (the sexual instinct, the struggle between impulse and conscience), Freud turned our attention to children and laid a groundwork for sympathetic and child-centered education. Indeed, some critics assert that he so stressed the delicacy and importance of early experience that he made child raising into an awesome and anxiety-laden task, for which parents were inadequate without the aid of expert advice.

All of these changes have affected education. The education of children is no longer conceived to be solely education in skills and moral standards. Education now has the goal of influencing the "adjustment," happiness, and mental health of children as well. While this may in some sense place an unrealistic burden on educational institutions and teachers, there can be little doubt that it has also made our schools more humane and sensitive to children's needs.

Some of Freud's early followers held great hopes for a utopian outcome if only his discoveries could be introduced into our techniques of child raising and education. If repression and guilt over normal impulses were reduced and sexuality accepted as a normal part of life, generations of healthy individuals could be realized, free of neurotic conflict. Freud himself was never sanguine about utopias, and his skepticism now seems judicious. For all the reduction in repressive norms, for all our increased openness about sex, neurotic conflict has not disappeared but seems rather to have changed its form of expression.

Bibliography

Brenner C 1955 *An Elementary Textbook of Psychoanalysis.* International Universities Press, New York
Erikson E H 1950 *Childhood and Society.* Norton, New York
Freud A 1946 *The Ego and the Mechanisms of Defense.* International Universities Press, New York
Freud S 1933 *New Introductory Lectures on Psychoanalysis.* Norton, New York
Freud S 1938 Three contributions to the theory of sex. *The Basic Writings of Sigmund Freud.* Random House, New York
Hall C S 1954 *A Primer of Freudian Psychology.* World Publishing, Cleveland, Ohio
Hartmann H 1958 *Ego Psychology and the Problem of Adaptation.* International Universities Press, New York
Horney K 1939 *New Ways in Psychoanalysis.* Norton, New York

Erikson's Developmental Theory

H. W. Maier

Erik H. Erikson's theory of human or individual development represents much of the psychological hopes of a post-Second World War era. This theory, more than any other formulation of its time, defines human beings as products and shapers of their history. Erikson's psychoanalytic theory breaks with the traditional Freudian emphasis upon life's dangers and deviations by highlighting life's opportunities for success and a positive future within an individual's life synthesis. Human beings "are not only worse, but also better than they think they are" (Erikson 1959 p. 288). Human development, for Erikson, constitutes opportunities for growth; human problems serve as much to mark life's "victories" as to test difficulties. "There is little that cannot be remedied later", Erikson (1950 p. 145) proclaims, and "there is much that can be prevented from happening at all." In the first 25 years following the Second World War, Erikson's concept of psychological dialectics of the individual and society was hailed in psychoanalytic circles for the advancement of ego psychology and was also productively welcomed by educators, counselors, and the public in general. In the final quarter of this century, however, his teachings have been challenged for being outdated. His work unquestionably opened up new vistas, presenting the psychological and social sciences with findings yet to be verified and challenges still to be answered.

1. A Biographical Sketch

The theory's portrayal of human development and the theoretician's participation in his or her own history are intimately interconnected, Erikson teaches us (Erikson 1970, 1974). His observation applies aptly to his own life story.

Erik Homburger (Erikson) was born in Frankfurt,

Germany, in 1902. His later salient work on issues of identity crises had its roots in his personal developmental history. It is interesting to note that he started life in a one-parent family. During his school years he lived with a strong, adoptive stepfather—a pediatrician. His youth was spent wandering around Europe until in his mid-20s, he became a Montessori teacher in Vienna. During his Vienna days he became associated with the Freudian circle, and from this entered into psychoanalytic training under Anna Freud's tutelage. During those Vienna years (1927–1933), he found his work and family commitments: he became a fully trained child analyst with several professional publications to his name and he also married Joan Mowat Serson, occupational therapist and later an author in her own right (Maier 1978 p. 276).

An invitation from Harvard Medical School in 1933 brought the Erikson family to the United States. Six years later, in 1939, the family not only adopted United States citizenship, but also the name Erikson as the family name (Erikson was his original father's family name). A wide range of clinical practice, teaching, and research projects brought Erikson appointments at Yale University (1936–1939), the University of California (1939–1951), and from 1951–1960 a combination of academic commitments at the Austen Riggs Center, Massachusetts Institute, University of Pittsburgh, and, in 1960, again at Harvard University (Division of Human Development). Since 1972, the year of his retirement as professor emeritus, Erik and Joan Erikson have lived in California, continuing their writing, lecturing, and consulting. In fact, in his early eighties, Erikson published an essay, emphasizing his psychosocial theory as cyclic and universal (Erikson 1982). Previously, developmental and historical relativity was interpreted along an intertwined chronological life progression. In his latest book he presented the life cycle in the form of unraveling from old age to infancy—from a never-ending wisdom at maturity descending to birth with its inherent trust in cosmic order. Moreover, Erikson's latest writing articulates his commitment to psychoanalytic inquiry, a perspective which guided him in his life's work; actually, he himself led psychoanalytic theory to a new stratum of thought.

Erikson's major published contributions are in three areas: (a) the human life cycle (1950, 1958, 1959, 1963, 1968), (b) identity formation (1962, 1974), and (c) the synthesis of psychological, historical, political, and ethnic phenomena into a psychohistorical analysis (1943, 1958, 1969, 1974, and Erikson 1973).

2. The Epigenesis of Life

Once a student of Sigmund and Anna Freud, he revolutionized his former teachers' teaching while remaining faithfully in their psychoanalytic camp. Erikson departs from Freudian concepts of the polarity of libidinal forces by proposing that development is as much anchored in a dialectic interplay between individuals and their society as in the interacting internal polarities. Erikson dethrones Oedipus rex. The oedipal child–father–mother triad loses part of its analytic significance because Erikson sees it as the young child's challenge for mastery as he or she joins communal institutions. He sees a similar phenomenon in the adolescent struggles over achieving cultural adaptation, an issue of "personal growth and communal change" (Erikson 1962, Maier 1978 p. 76). Most important, psychoanalytic concerns with the pitfalls and aberrations of development are replaced by a humanistic faith in the elasticity of human beings. In Erikson's words: "Children fall apart repeatedly, and unlike Humpty Dumpty, grow together again" (1950 p. 83).

Unconscious motivation is an accepted fact as evidenced by his clinical work and psychohistoric studies (Erikson 1943, 1950, 1958, 1963, 1969, 1975). His concepts on the cycles of human development, in contrast, establish essentially an ego theory, a theory of reality relationships for the management of daily living (Maier 1978 p.76).

Mutual regulation is central to Eriksonian theory. Erikson explores regulation between biological development and human orientation; between partners; between individuals and their social context, between parent and child; and the manifold mutualities which unite generation with generation, each generation and its culture, and each culture, in turn, with the cosmos (Maier 1978 p. 83). Humans are constantly faced with the promise and threat of synthesis. With Erikson, psychoanalytic theory has become an open system formulation.

Human development is epigenetic. Once born, the human organism continuously unfolds by a prescribed stage-like sequence of locomotive, sensory, and social capacities (Erikson 1950 p. 97). Each individual's culture specifies what that person is to do and to be and determines how she or he should be recognized within the culture as the individual progresses along universal developmental phases.

3. Selected Teachings

3.1 Human Development Within the Context of a Person's Psychohistorical Existence

The analysis of people's political and historic space and time is indigenous to Eriksonian thinking. He has provided a new turning point when, as an analyst, he focuses upon cultural and political issues, and particularly, assumes a strong philosophical bent. The lives of the Yurok (1943), psychohistorical studies of Martin Luther (1958), Mahatma Gandhi (1969) (for which he received a Pulitzer Prize), and Thomas Jefferson (1974) are presented in Erikson's poetic literary style. With the keen eyes of an artist and the inquisitive mind of an analyst, he paints a backdrop of historic issues with broad strokes and fills in a person's life experience in minute detail in order to join historical events and human adaptiveness as the "natural" synthesis of a person's course of life (Maier 1978 p. 75).

3.2 Identity Formation—The Crises of Adolescent Development

Erikson devoted more time and published accounts to the study of identity formation in adolescence than to any of the other seven developmental phases (1950, 1963, 1968, 1970). Prolonged adolescence (as was his own), is seen as a product of a time reflecting rapid social and technological change. It creates opportunities for incorporating the wide array of values, knowledge, and skill expectations at (biological) maturity; simultaneously, prolonged adolescence burdens the developing youth with a residue of emotional immaturity. The latter is aggravated by the inherent identity struggle of adolescence (1963 p. 12).

This identity struggle or crisis brings with it a developmental dilemma, namely, a shift from childhood desires to do and to be to the reality of becoming an actual part of a contemporary adult world. Simultaneously, the personal identity crisis is also a social issue because the youth's society lacks clarity in its expectations for rites of passage. Society and youth seek for moratoria (i.e., prolonged educational opportunities, alternative service years) to ward off too early adult commitment or potential voids in the availability of an expanding future and a more universal identity (Maier 1978 pp. 109–20). "A sense of identity" at the point of passage from adolescence to young adulthood, Erikson (1974 pp. 21–22) explains, "means a sense of being at one with yourself as one grows and develops; and it means a sense of affinity with a community's sense of being at one with its future as well as its history—or mythology."

3.3 A Human Developmental Progression

Erikson's epigenetic life cycle, an easy-to-grasp eight-stage developmental ladder, undoubtedly constitutes Erikson's major and best-known contribution (see below). His developmental chart depicts human beings in their capacity to grow, to overcome personal predicaments, and external obstacles. Sigmund Freud's original five psychosexual genetic stages are revolutionized into psychosocial open-system phases. The Freudian's treacherous psychosexual phases are envisaged for the opportunities they provide human beings to move beyond their present existence. In Shakespearian fashion, Erikson sets forth, from birth to old age, stages of human development. He is the first modern theorist who recognizes that human beings tend to continue to develop as adults.

In the Eriksonian development theory, infants first experience society through their body. Significant bodily experiences are babies' first social events which also then form psychological patterns for subsequent social experience. Erikson contends that inherent sex differences lead to basically different developmental experience, which in turn make the respective sex better prepared for a range of life tasks while less qualified for the other gender's modal tasks (Erikson 1950, 1959). This latter point was later challenged and brought Erikson into stark conflict with feminist concerns of the 1970s (see below) (Millet 1970, Reeves 1971, Smith 1973).

Throughout life, the individual is always a personality in the making, striving to incorporate dialectically irreconcilable opposites. Simultaneously, the ultimate solution of a particular phasal dilemma generates a struggle for the next one. Environmental life events both limit and free the individual. Society and its cultures preserve the unique qualities needed for their survival (Maier 1978 pp. 84–87). The growing human being "must at every step, derive a vitalizing sense of reality from the awareness that his or her individual way of mastering experience . . . is a successful variant of a group identity and is in accord with its space-time life plan" (Erikson 1963 p. 208).

Human development for Erikson is essentially affect development within a tridimensional progression. First, development always proceeds in the same order through a succession of interlinked phases, assuming that such a developmental predictiveness lends caregivers and the community "an almost somatic conviction that there is meaning to what they are doing" (Erikson 1950 p. 107). Second, development moves through a succession of mutualities, starting with caregiver and child, then mutuality between peers, and finally a mutuality between generations. Third, development progresses in phases, but phasal development is relative; previous developmental issues are differentially dealt with anew in each sequential phase.

4. The Eriksonian Life Cycle

Development is an evolutionary process—a universally experienced sequence of biological, psychological, social, and cultural events, including spontaneous recovery from periodic crisis-prone setbacks. Erikson identified eight phases in the life cycle.

4.1 Phase I: Acquiring a Sense of Basic Trust while Overcoming a Sense of Basic Mistrust—A Realization of Hope

After a life of prenatal rhythmic regularity, the achievement of basic trust and overcoming mistrust becomes the critical theme of the first developmental phase (approximately from birth to 18 months of age).

A sense of trust requires a feeling of physical comfort and a minimum amount of uncertainty and discomfort. Thus, bodily experiences provide the foundation for a psychological state of trust. Successful experience of having needs fulfilled increases favorable expectations and the infants' trust in others. The infant begins to learn to what degree hope is realizable. Trust produces inner comfort and interpersonal predictability of mutual adaptaion by care receiver and caregiver, including the permissible degree of trust and mistrust implied to them by their caregivers' culture.

4.2 Phase II: Acquiring a Sense of Autonomy while Combating a Sense of Doubt and Shame—A Realization of Will

With the acquisition of trust and mistrust for the caring persons and their way of life, infants discover that they can pursue their own behavior while their continued dependence creates doubt and shame over their own capabilities. This conflict as to whether people should assert themselves or deny themselves the capacity for self-assertion furnishes the major dialectic phasal crisis between roughly 18 months to 3 years. Newly won motor and mental abilities, as well as the pleasure and pride over these freshly acquired capacities for body management and control, become major arenas for verification of autonomy. For toddlers, the skills needed to feed, walk, dress, toilet, and manipulate objects and people involves much of their own and their caregivers' energy and time. It is the "me do" stage. Mutual regulation—boundary maintenance—between child and caregiver becomes the theme of daily life. This child versus caregiver struggle eventually delineates how strongly and where the young "self" can appear buoyant and where the boundaries are to be drawn in order that the young child can assert herself or himself without shame.

4.3 Phase III: Acquiring a Sense of Initiative and Overcoming a Sense of Guilt—A Realization of Purpose

With the acquisition of a measure of conscious self-control and a clear capacity to imitate as instructed as well as to influence the environment, children move forward to new conquests in ever-widening social and spatial spheres. Children still in the preschool age discover they can imitate actions akin to those of the adults in their world. Incorporating their new prowess for reaching out with inquisitiveness, communicative language, and ever-expanding imagination, children can easily enjoy and fear the thought: "I am what I can imagine I will be" (Erikson 1950 p. 127). Children's conscience increasingly assumes the supporting and controlling functions of significant adults. In a truer sense, conscience is built out of the key adults' sociocultural heritage. Children are now fully on their way from an "attachment to their parents to the slow process of becoming a parent, a carrier of tradition" (Erikson 1963 p. 225). A struggle to move ahead, to be one's own parent, is constantly dialectically constrained by the accompanying sense of guilt for going too far and thereby defeating one's purpose.

Sex roles become markedly defined. Relationships to the parent of the same sex are strongly influenced by the parent of the opposite sex's expectations of attitude and behavior for persons of her or his opposite sex.

Simultaneously, role expectations are also annunciated for girls by their mothers and for boys by their fathers. Children expand their social spheres beyond their family units and become aware of differential family standards. Whether children move on to the next phase with a thrust for initiative and subsequently outbalance their sense of guilt depends largely upon adults' response to their self-starting actions and apparently never-ending inquisitiveness.

4.4 Phase IV: Acquisition of a Sense of Industry and Fending Off a Sense of Inferiority—A Realization of Competence

Children's forward surging necessarily brings a wealth of experiences—many within the realm of their own age group. Their abundant energy is turned towards mastering the tasks within their spheres of activities. A perceived lack of progress in their chosen activities forebodes for the now school-age child a feeling of inferiority. Realization of competence through actual accomplishment—to be able "to do it" predictably is the life thread for this phase.

The world of peers and the institutions where peers can be found (school, playgrounds, street corners, or clubs) assume a position almost equal in importance to that of home life. Out-of-the-home experiences are of parallel importance to the home influence in determining whether elementary-school children incorporate into their life-style the urge to accomplish or whether they settle for a halfway measure and mediocrity. The latter may bring him or her too close to a sense of inferiority, and it remains that the child must both combat and accept this experience as a fact of life in order to move on with a sense of competence toward greater maturity.

4.5 Phase V: Acquiring a Sense of Identity while Overcoming a Sense of Identity Diffusion—A Realization of Fidelity

Identity development is closely linked with the acquisition of competence and a sense of being worthwhile. Once into adolescence in the ages between roughly 12 and 18, an identity struggle carries with it a sense of mastery of childhood issues and an increasing readiness to face the challenges of the adult community as a potential equal, withstanding the confusion of diffuse alternatives.

A struggle over one's identity, or an identity crisis, is neither a fatal event nor a pathological condition. It is instead an inescapable turning point for better or for worse. "Better" means confluence of the energies of adolescents and their particular segment of society; "worse" means a prolonged period of identity confusion for these young individuals and continued confusion for the manifold efforts invested by their communities (Maier 1978 p.111). Adolescents gradually establish a synthesis within this period of self-standardization in the search for identity as an adolescent, as members of a sexual and sociocultural age group, as members of a community, and as persons with a present and future (Erikson 1975 pp. 18–19).

4.6 Phase VI: Acquiring a Sense of Intimacy and Solidarity, While Avoiding a Sense of Isolation—A Realization of Love

As young adults, individuals become full community members in Western society; their energies are thereupon invested in pursuits of career or love. Their major developmental theme establishes psychological readiness for intimate personal partnership and work commitments. Both in the world of work and in love, efforts are directed toward achieving mutuality and solidarity, a sense of shared identity. Intimacy assures mutual verification and shared membership while overcoming the dangers of isolation.

4.7 Phase VII: Acquiring a Sense of Generativity and Avoiding a Sense of Self-absorption—A Realization of Care

Full membership within a societal unit serves also as a prelude to concerns for the unit's maintenance and its perpetuation. An assured adulthood serves as the foundation for the care that the next generation requires. It is a period in the life cycle when individuals are apt to be productive in work or leisure to satisfy themselves, their partnership and, at times, people beyond their own immediate life spheres. Interestingly, it was the period when Erikson himself, in his 40s and 50s, blossomed with his initial major works (Erikson 1950, 1959, 1963).

A sense of generativity includes parental and communal responsibility for society's efforts in supporting childcare, education, the arts and sciences, as well as the traditions which are to nurture the current and next generations' life span. Personal, ideational, and community life become one, to the extent that self-absorption no longer drains so much energy, thereby estranging the individual from his or her own community.

4.8 Phase VIII: Acquiring a Sense of Integrity and Avoiding a Sense of Despair—A Realization of Wisdom

Finally, as adults witness the development of a new generation, they simultaneously enjoy a fuller perspective of their own life history. They realize a generational wisdom, a sense of integrity, while overcoming a sense of despair over what was not meant to be. Substantive integrity rests upon an acceptance of the collective and the individual life cycle of human beings. Some individuals find in their last phase of their own life cycle a philosophical wisdom which extends beyond their own into future developmental cycles; they nurture the roots of a new cycle of life.

5. Implications for Child Rearing, Counseling, and Education

Eriksonian teachings have had profound effects upon the concepts in child caring, psychiatry, social work, and upon other forms of clinical work in the United States and in other parts of the Western world. Standard child development texts published in the 1960s and 1970s tend to incorporate fully his theory as part of the text's content or at least cite his life-cycle formulations. Erikson's propositions are well-reflected in United States government guidelines for day care and nursery programs. His catchy phrases highlighting his readily comprehendable concepts—such as developing basic trust, autonomy, or a sense of identity—have all become common household notions. His concepts and terminology have become ingrained in general psychological thought; psychiatrists, social workers, and clinical and educational psychologists have resolved much of their disenchantment with traditional psychoanalytic thinking by adopting Eriksonian theory as their own and reviewing their cases in Eriksonian terms.

6. Eriksonian Theory Today

Erikson's work has achieved a high prestige and popularity in both the academic and lay world. His work, however, has been acclaimed without the usual critical review and verification by empirical studies. A good number of his studies deal with persons and populations of various cultures. Yet, serious doubt exists whether his formulations are cross-culturally applicable. Whether they are or not remains unanswerable, for neither significant cross-cultural nor unicultural research has been carried out thus far (Roazen 1976).

Eriksonian and Freudian theoretical concepts remain in want of empirical verification at a time when validated theory is preferred. Erikson's theory seems presently to have lost much of its functional attractiveness along with the demise of psychoanalytic theory in general.

Eriksonian concepts have received their sharpest jolt from the feminist movement which poignantly challenges his analytic perceptions of women (Millett 1970, Reeves 1971, Smith 1973). Erikson was especially attacked as one of the leading psychoanalysts for his views on biological determinism, mystification of womanhood, upholding a sex-role hierarchy, and perpetuating the status quo (Smith 1973). Erikson, like most analysts of his time and before him, studied mankind as malekind, and his clinical and historical subjects in the literature are almost exclusively male. His writings belong to an era prior to feminine liberation. Although he himself has responded to these challenges and has tried to explain and justify his writings to the newly emerging position of women in these changing times, it has been almost impossible for him to meet the critical challenges (Maier 1978 pp. 127–30).

While Erikson's star may be fading in the last decades of this century, his contributions remain of substantive and historic significance. He bestowed a psychology of faith and hope for at least two generations of educators, clinicians, and people in general with a complete, internally consistent theory of human development and communal existence. Much of his teaching finds its continuation in new paradigms of psychological thought and in the pragmatics of everyday care, clinical inquiry, and educational wholeness.

Bibliography

Caplan P J 1979 Erikson's concept of inner space: A data based re-evaluation. *Am. J. Orthopsychiatry* 49: 100–08
Coles R 1970 *Erik H Erikson: The Growth of His Work*. Little, Brown, Boston, Massachusetts
Erikson E H 1937 Traumatische Konfigurationen im Spiel. *Imago* 23: 447–516
Erikson E H 1943 Observations on the Yurok: Childhood and world image. *Am. Archaelogical Ethnology* 35: 257–301
Erikson E H 1950 Growth and crisis of the "healthy personality." In: Senn M J E (ed.) 1950 *Symposium on the Healthy Personality*. Josiah Macy Jr Foundation, New York, pp. 91–146
Erikson E H 1958 *Young Man Luther: A Study in Psychoanalysis and History*. Norton, New York
Erikson E H 1959 Identity and the life cycle: Selected papers. *Psychol. Issues* 1: 1–171
Erikson E H 1962 Youth: Fidelity and diversity. *Daedalus* 91: 5–27
Erikson E H 1963 *Childhood and Society*, 2nd edn. Norton, New York
Erikson E H 1968 *Identity, Youth, and Crisis*. Norton, New York
Erikson E H 1969 *Gandhi's Truth. On the Origins of Militant Nonviolence*. Norton, New York
Erikson E H 1970 Autobiographic notes on the identity crisis. *Daedalus* 99: 730–59
Erikson E H 1974 *Dimensions of a New Identity: The 1973 Jefferson Lectures in the Humanities*. Norton, New York
Erikson E H 1975 *Life History and Historical Moment*. Norton, New York
Erikson E H 1978 (ed.) *Adulthood: Essays*. Norton, New York
Erikson E H 1982 *The Life Cycle Completed*. Norton, New York
Erikson K T (ed.) 1973 *In Search of Common Ground: Conversations with Erik H Erikson and Huey P Newton*. Norton, New York
Evans R I 1967 *Dialogue with Erik Erikson*. Harper and Row, New York
Maier H W 1978 *Three Theories of Child Development*, 3rd edn. Harper and Row, New York
Millett N E 1970 Inner space. In: Millett K (ed.) 1970 *Sexual Politics*. Doubleday, New York, pp. 210–20
Reeves N 1971 *Womankind: Beyond the Stereotypes*. Aldine, Chicago, Illinois
Roazen P 1976 *Erik H Erikson: The Power and Limits of a Vision*. Free Press, New York
Smith J M 1973 Erik H Erikson's sex role theories: A rhetoric of hierarchical mystification. *Today's Speech* 21: 27–31
White R W 1960 Competence and the psychosexual stages of development. In: Jones M R (ed.) 1960 *Nebraska Symposium on Motivation*. Nebraska University Press, Lincoln, Nebraska, pp. 97–141
Whitman L E 1968 Adult developmental tasks as suggested by the writings of Erik H Erikson. Masters thesis, University of Washington

Soviet Theories of Human Development

V. V. Davidov

Soviet theories of development can profitably be reviewed from the philosophical and psychological perspectives of activity. In presenting such a viewpoint, the following discussion focuses on the topics of (a) underlying theoretical principles, (b) relationships between psychic development and activity, particularly in terms of the concept of leading activity, (c) the correlation between activity (in the social environment) and heredity in effecting development within the history of society, (d) periods in human development, (e) stable and critical periods in child development, (f) illustrative empirical results from the study of development, and (g) main trends in Soviet theories.

1. Underlying Theoretical Principles

The first theories of child development at the outset of Soviet psychology were presented in the 1920s and 1930s by three Soviet scholars—M. G. Basov, P. P. Blonsky, and L. S. Vygotsky. Later S. L. Rubinstein added further significant proposals about the analysis of development. The result was that the leading developmental theories of the day as conceived by J. Piaget, W. Stern, K. Bühler, S. Freud, and J. B. Watson spiraled up to a new level in the light of Marxist philosophy and new empirical data. The principles thereby formulated as the foundation of a Soviet approach to the theory of child development propose that the ontogenesis of human psychological development should be viewed in terms of: (a) the sociohistoric continuum of the cultural development of society, (b) qualitative transformations in the activity of humans and in the content and structure of human consciousness and individuality, and (c) the context of the individual's interiorizing essential material and spiritual forms of socioculture.

Further advances in developmental psychology as guided by the forgoing principles occurred in the 1940s, 1950s, and 1960s when a number of Soviet psychologists reported the results of studies covering a variety of manifestations of human psychic activity (B. G. Ananjev, P. G. Galperin, A. V. Zaporožets, A. N.

Leontjev, A. R. Luria, S. L. Rubinstein, A. Smirnov, and D. B. Elkonin). An extensive study of the forces that produce psychic development led to the assumption that intellectual development is primarily influenced by the process of children's achieving successive transitions from one main type of activity to another, with the three main activities being playing games, learning, and engaging in creative work.

In the 1970s and 1980s the prime focus of Soviet psychologists has been on such basic psychological problems as human communication, the influence on development of the interaction of the child's social environment and heredity, the effect of teamwork on the development of the individuals who form the team, and the criteria which may be used to reveal the state and the boundaries of developmental age periods.

The nature of such present-day Soviet research on development is perhaps best understood against a background of the following chief postulates that are implied in the work of Soviet psychologists.

2. Psychic Development and Activity

Soviet developmental psychology presumes that psychic functions are specific events in complex structural patterns, events which emerge and are shaped and qualitatively transformed during the course of socially determined object activity. The term activity in this context is a philosophical and psychological concept originating in classic German philosophy and developed further in Marxism. Activity means a person's active engagement with his or her surrounding world, a genuinely industrious, goal-oriented interaction that is reflected in the person. Thus conceived, human activity aims at the active transformation of the environment. Activity as a unit combines four interrelated components—the subject, the object, the goal, and the means of attaining the goal.

Not only may an individual be the subject of activity, but any collective body, including humankind as a unit, may function as the subject. The objects and the means that are components of activity can be either of a material nature or in the form of ideas. In the process of developmental transformations, activity attracts new objects, new goals, and new means.

The focal point of the above approach is the assumption that the functions of human intellect are produced during the developmental transformations of people's activity. Modes of activity that are interiorized by the person become the principal causes behind the development of the structures of psychic functions. Thus, in Soviet theory the ontogenesis of the human intellect reflects the interiorization of the essential modes of human activities. More specifically, whereas psychic development is determined by human activity, the effect is achieved only indirectly as the influence of activity is manifested through historically shaped sign systems that have developed in the process of human communication as essential elements of socioculture.

The main law of human activity was formulated in the 1930s by L. S. Vygotsky as: "Any supreme psychic function emerges on the developmental stage twice—for the first time in the form of collective social activity and for the second time as an individual activity, that is, in the form of an individual mode of thinking" (Vygotsky 1960 pp. 198–99).

Any complex psychic function of an individual primarily emerges in the social context of human communication via sign systems, with the sign systems conveying historically molded meanings. At the beginning of the individual's development the signs are turned "outward" at partners of the communication, but gradually they become turned "inward" and are transformed into the individual's means of psychic self-development. Thus, full-scale social modes of communication, via the process of the person interiorizing these modes, bring forth the development of any individual psyche.

At the foundation of such a theory of development lies the concept of a hierarchy of various types of activities, with the dominating or leading activity at the top. At any age, the individual is involved in many activities simultaneously, yet a person's life is by no means composed simply of the arithmetic sum of different activities. Instead, some types of activities always play a more dominant role than others at a given period of life. Consequently, every period of human development is motivated by a particular leading activity. The change from one leading activity to another brings about a change in the person's attitude toward life and signifies the transition in development from one stage to the next.

The leading activity is characterized by three features: (a) it is the main, basic factor setting off a given period in the person's psychological progress; (b) it is within the realm of this activity that particular psychic processes emerge and are transformed; and (c) from the climax of the activity the prerequisites of the next leading activity arise.

In sum, it is mainly under the influence of the leading activity during a given age period that the structure of psychic functions is formed and altered, and thus it is the leading activity that stimulates the general development of human intellect.

3. The Relation of Social Environment to Heredity in Human Development

Having accepted the view that psychic development is chiefly determined by the form of human activity that is of a sociohistorical nature, most Soviet psychologists no longer seek for the source of development in either physiological mechanisms or in the processes of the maturation of the nervous system. Instead, they seek the source in the social origin of human intelligence, that is, in the social forms of human activity. Thus, when analyzing infancy, a Soviet psychologist will turn his or her attention to the relationship between the baby and the mother. The determining role of this relationship in the child's development is clearly seen in the period when a so-called voluntary—meaning conscious—action is formed in the child.

Normally a voluntary action will begin with the mother's initiating an instruction that results in a corresponding movement of the child's hand. In effect, this action initially requires a social unit—the mutual activity on the part of the mother who begins the action and of the child who continues it. Therefore, the social nature of a human action is the source of the action that later becomes voluntary and conscious. At the beginning the child only follows the mother's instructions, but in time the child helps himself or herself verbally, so that a child's speech first follows the action and then later precedes the action.

> The action emerges in the act of the child's submission to the speech of an adult. Later the action is guided by the child's own speech and becomes self-monitored and voluntary—social by origin and performed indirectly via objects and speech. (Luria 1977 p. 74)

This approach to the analysis of the genesis and organization of a voluntary action is a kind of model enabling Soviet psychologists to study any form of conscious self-regulation. Luria (1977 p. 72) formulated the idea in the following manner:

> The origin of human psychological processes should be looked for neither "inside brains" nor in the nervous system's functions but in the actual relation of the man to the world of objects, in his social activity which is the genuine source of the origin of the most complex forms of conscious activity of man.

While thus analyzing intellectual development in its social context, it is still also necessary to take into account the dynamics of the nervous system's functions. No psychic process can be effected apart from the function of the brain, which forms the substratum of any psychic act of systematic character. However, it is essential to recognize the distinction between the roles of social interaction and of the nervous system in the analysis of psychic development. The development of complex intellectual forms of thinking (perception of categories, voluntary attention, active memorizing, abstract thinking) are brought about by the requirements of the social organization of human life, whereas the dynamics of nervous system processes do not reach beyond the formation of temporally integrated circuits.

While the development of human intelligence is entirely monitored by the social source—the so-called social environment—heredity molds physical systems, which are the substrata of psychic functions. Yet heredity does not launch the formation of essential human faculties. Since human development to a certain extent does take into account individual peculiarities of the organic substratum (for instance, the individual dynamics of nervous function), development necessarily brings up the question of the functional interaction of psychic development and organic advancement. And

there is now strong evidence that this interaction changes considerably over the history of humankind.

Since the early 1970s, Soviet psychology has witnessed the increased popularity of so-called twin-study methodology for answering the question about the extent to which heredity conditions the development of psychic functions. Studies of memory processes with monozygotic twins indicate that interindividual variation in elementary mnemonic skills is to a certain extent under control of the genotype—that is, the child's inherited structure—but that complex forms which are organized via verbalization are rather independent of the genotype. This same tendency of influence of genetic structures has been noted as well in the study of attention and intentional motor reactions.

Luria (1962) and Ravich-Sherbo (1978) hypothesized that the transformations observed today in mechanisms of achieving certain complex psychic functions (achieved indirectly via speech, symbols, and the like) may before long change the now existing relations between these functions and the genotype. Meanwhile, it is appropriate to recognize that the main qualities of nervous system function are determined principally, though not totally, by genetic endowment. Each quality is versatile and therefore displays its nature in a number of ways. In other words, each quality manifests all of its characteristics only in relation to the whole of development and thus cannot be unequivocally defined by itself.

Identical genetically determined qualities of the nervous system in two different people can result in different intellectual characteristics because of the varied circumstances of their lives. As Dubinin and Shevchenko (1976 p. 23) have noted: "Even monozygotic twins born of the same genotype, in spite of their absolute organic identity, may develop into spiritually different individuals if they have been brought up under different environmental conditions."

In brief, all modern psychological, genetic, and physiological data lead us to the conclusion that in ontogenesis the development of human functions is due to the decisive role of the child's initial involvement in social contact with adults, chiefly through verbal communication. The historical character of such social interaction is best understood when the correlation is observed between the organic and sociopsychological maturation of humans. As early as the 1920s, L. S. Vygotsky suggested that in the course of anthropogenesis the nature of general physiological maturity and puberty had undergone significant changes. In the evolution of humankind and with the corresponding extension of the length of infancy and early childhood, the time of puberty was continually extended so as to occur at the end of organic development. Subsequently, in the course of the development of human society, there appeared a new form of individual maturation in addition to the physiological. The new form was the sociopsychological, the termination of which is indicated by the moment a young person is recognized as a fully fledged member of the society. The historic change in the time relationship between the physiological and the sociopsychological aspects can be clearly observed in different types of cultures. In socioeconomically "backward" countries, the termination of sociopsychological development is forced on the child well before the time of puberty. In cultures at a middle socioeconomic level, puberty and social maturity more or less coincide in time, whereas in developed industrialized societies puberty comes before both social and psychological maturity.

Modern ethnographic data on child development in societies at different socioeconomic levels prove that sociopsychological maturity is chiefly determined by the system of social and cultural relations in those societies. It is the society, not organic development, that relegates the child to the appropriate social setting and determines the time and ways the child "needs" to become acquainted with means of production (Tulviste 1978).

The fact that society imposes boundaries on childhood produces the paradox that children belonging to different sociocultures but born equally helpless and immature will pass through childhoods of different content and length. This disparity among cultures suggests that the immaturity and helplessness of the newborn child reflect a great psychic plasticity so that the child is very prone to the functional influence of the social environment.

Such a condition demands that, when considering the problem of the interaction of organic with sociopsychological development, the history of childhood should be kept clearly in mind. The historic changes in the content of sociopsychological development and the changes which take place even in the succession of the child's developmental periods prove that the potentials with which the child arrives in the world are only one condition of his or her future development, a condition that does not determine either the level the child may reach or the stages he or she will pass through. The levels and stages are achieved only in relation to the social environment of his or her particular society and the success the child achieves in adopting the culture of that society.

4. Periods in Human Development

The problem of periodization has been studied in the Soviet Union by B. G. Ananjev, D. B. Elkonin, A. N. Leontjev, L. S. Vygotsky, A. V. Zaporožets, and many other psychologists. The best-known description of periods from birth to age 17 was developed by Vygotsky and Elkonin. The description is based on the assumption that the main criteria for outlining the boundaries of a period are to be found neither in the child's psychological development nor in the growth of his or her intellectual functions, but rather in the way one overall activity is replaced by another (Vygotsky 1972). The overall activity serving as the foundation for a given age was later called the leading activity (Elkonin 1971,

Leontjev 1981). The leading type is always accompanied by other less important activities. Thus, playing games is the leading activity of the preschool years, yet during those years there also may be found elements of the learning and the performing activities.

An analysis of the totality of data from child psychology has provided the means of identifying a group of leading activities, each corresponding to some age period of contemporary childhood. Their genetic succession provides a picture of the inner entirety of psychic development of the child. The following modified scheme of types of leading activities is one based on the theoretical proposals of Elkonin (1971).

(a) *Intuitive–emotional contact.* This occurs between the child and adults (infancy, from birth to age 1). In the course of this activity, many essential types of psychological development take place in the child, including the need for contact with other people, an emotional attitude toward them, a number of perception actions, the act of grasping things, and others.

(b) *Object manipulation activity* (early preschool years, from age 1 to age 3). The child adopts socially developed modes of handling things. Cooperation and interaction with adults develops speech and visual thinking.

(c) *Playing games activity* (later preschool years, ages 3 to 7). The child develops the symbolic function and creative imagination along with the ability to comprehend in human relations those indications of management and social coordination.

(d) *Learning activity* (elementary-school years, ages 7 to 11). Children develop some theoretical approaches to the world of things, a function that involves them in considering objective laws of reality and in grasping some psychological preconditions of abstract theoretical thinking (mental operations of a voluntary or intentional character, mental schemes for problem solving, and reflection).

(e) *Social-communications activity.* This type of activity includes communication involved in organizations, in sports, and in learning settings (adolescent years, ages 11 to 15). Teenagers develop skills of initiating the different types of communication necessary to solve various life problems. They also advance in understanding other people's characters and motives and learn to submit consciously to norms accepted by the group.

(f) *Vocational learning activity* (upper-secondary-school years, ages 15 to 17). The youth develops cognitive and vocational interests, comprehends elements of research work, and constructs life projects.

The forgoing activities fall into two divisions, with three sets of activities in each division. By means of activities in the first division, children learn mostly about the norms, motives, and tasks of human relations and they develop motivation. The second division embraces activities which develop social modes of interaction with the world, of adopting or interiorizing spiritual and material forms of the socioculture. In the process of progressing through these periods, children advance in cognitive functions. The activities of the first division merge naturally with those of the second.

There are three major "epochs" in childhood, with each consisting of two parts. The first part is guided by a leading activity of the first division and the second is led by a leading activity of the second division. As a result, three stages of child development can be identified: (a) early childhood—first from infancy until age 1, then the early preschool years of ages 1 to 3, (b) childhood—the upper preschool years of ages 3 to 7, then the elementary-school years of ages 7 to 10, and (c) adolescence—the school years of ages 11 to 14, then the upper-secondary-school years of ages 14 to 17.

The above scheme brings up the question of why the periods and stages coincide precisely with the stages that already exist in society in the society's child-rearing practices. The answer may be that the historic experience of people educating many successive generations of children has been inevitably "taken into account" by the contemporary system of education and, through people's experience, adjusted to the demands of society. Vygotsky (1972 p. 114), commenting on this point, has written:

> . . . as soon as the stages of child development very closely reflect the stages of social upbringing and the stages of education based on practice, it is only natural that the educational principle of setting up such stages brings us close to the real periods of intellectual development.

The general results in intellectual development achieved by the end of childhood are expected to match the goals the socialist society sets for the education system. These goals are explicated in terms of the socially accepted image of a young person who is to embark on the life of an adult. In terms of psychology, this ideal image contains the needs and capabilities that a contemporary young man or young woman acquires to fulfill, in a creative and productive manner, the individual's job demands and civic responsibilities.

5. Stable and Critical Periods in Child Development

In the transition from one period of development to another, and particularly at the meeting point between "epochs," specific developmental crises arise in the child. Each transition between periods is brought about by the fact that a previous leading activity stops dominating the child's concerns and gives way to prerequisites for the next activity that is to occupy the leading position. The child will inevitably engage in the new activity which, when adopted, will produce a relatively stable period in psychic development. Meanwhile, during the time of transition, the child goes through deep qualitative transformations that are reflected in so-called crises, with the development processes becoming rapid and stormy. "If critical periods had not been discovered empirically, they would have

been indicated analytically and included in the scheme of development" (Vygotsky 1972 p. 121).

It has long been observed that children at ages 3, 7, and 11 are markedly different from children at other ages in their self-awareness and overt behavior. Children at these three transition times tend to demonstrate independence, unable to curb their impulse to act improperly towards adults, and often become what are referred to as "problem children." They lose much of what they seem to have acquired earlier, but then learn much that is new and useful in leading them to further progress in their relations with adults through adopting a new leading activity and discovering new modes of expressing their individuality. The "problem" nature of these children is rather relative, because problems occur only in those settings in which the adult society's established mode of interacting with the child lags behind the rapid changes occurring in the child's personality. The dynamics of each critical period depend on how soon the adults notice and foresee the changes in the child and on how easily the adults adopt new modes of interaction. If the educational approach is adaptive to such changes, the expected crisis does not arise to provoke conflict and pain.

6. Illustrative Results of the Empirical Study of Human Development

In the great surge of empirical studies of development in the Soviet Union since the early 1970s, the most significant have been investigations of child development. Studies of infancy by Zaporožets and Lisina (1974) revealed the basic need in the child to have contact with adults, demonstrating the specific role of this need in promoting self-regulation in the child. Research by Poddyakov (1977) and Obuhova (1972) on children from ages 3 to 7 opened the possibilities of a previously unrecognized reserve of children's ability to advance in cognitive development. These investigators discovered ways to produce in 5- and 6-year-old children the normal concrete operations level of intellectual function not anticipated in Piaget's theory.

A long-term educational experiment on teaching elementary-school children led a group of psychologists to formulate a conception of the content and structure of learning activities. The study revealed ways a learning activity develops the foundations for reflective—that is, theoretical—thinking in 17-year-olds. This discovery is regarded as of major significance for the further intellectual development of the youth (Aidarova 1978, Elkonin 1974).

Furthermore, fresh data shed additional light on the problem of encouraging teenagers' interactions with adults, with the problem of promoting such interactions satisfactorily solved under the conditions of a specially organized social activity with adolescents (Feldstein 1982). Another study focused on the development of self-awareness and moral stability in senior-secondary-school pupils at the time in life when they are searching for standards to follow (Chudnovsky 1981, Shumilin 1979).

7. Main Trends in Soviet Theories

Five principal trends in the progress of Soviet theories of human development can be summarized as follows:

(a) The foundations of the concept of development itself are being studied, with the meaning of the concept in reference both to humans in general and to individuals' intellects being extensively discussed.

(b) Investigators now commonly recognize the necessity of conducting fundamental studies of the correlation between the ontogenetic development of intellectual processes and historical development.

(c) Acute questions are being raised regarding the relationship of psychic development and the process of the formation of the leading activity during different age periods of childhood. There is an urgent need to develop a complete theory of the relationship of intellectual development and leading activities.

(d) New methods are being devised for studying critical periods over the entire span of human development.

(e) Finally, there is a strong feeling in present-day Soviet psychology that investigators should move beyond the boundaries of studying children in order to concentrate more on various aspects of intellectual development in middle-aged and elderly people.

Bibliography

(Whereas the following titles are listed in English, the actual publications are all in the Russian language.)
Aidarova L I 1978 *Psychological Problems of Teaching Russian in Elementary School Grades*. Pedagogica, Moscow
Chudnovsky V E 1981 *Moral Stability of an Individual*. Pedagogica, Moscow
Dubinin N P, Shevchenko U G 1976 *Some Questions on the Bio-social Nature of Man*. Nauka, Moscow
Elkonin D B 1971 On the problem of periodization in childhood. *Quest. Psychol.* 4
Elkonin D B 1974 *Psychology of Teaching Elementary School Children*. Pedagogica, Moscow
Feldstein D I 1982 *Psychology of Social Activity by Teenagers*. Pedagogica, Moscow
Leontjev A N 1981 *Problems of Psychic Development*. MGU Press, Moscow
Luria A R 1962 On the variability of mental functions in the process of the development of a child: On the material from a comparative investigation of twins. *Quest. Psychol.* 3: 15–22
Luria A R 1973 *On the Historic Development of Cognitive Processes*. MGU Press, Moscow
Luria A R 1977 The place of psychology among social and biological sciences. *Quest. Philos.* 9: 68–76
Obuhova L F 1972 *Stages of Development in Child Thinking*. MGU Press, Moscow
Poddyakov N N 1977 *Thinking in Preschool Children*. Pedagogica, Moscow
Ravich-Sherbo I V 1978 The twin method in psychology and physiology. *Problems of Genetic Psycho-physiology of Man*. Nauka, Moscow
Shumilin E A 1979 *Psychological Characteristics of the Personality of a Senior School Child*. Pedagogica, Moscow
Teplov B M 1963 New data on peculiarities of nervous system functioning in man. *Types of Nervous System Functioning in Man*, Vol. 3. APN RSFSR Press, Moscow
Tulviste P 1978 On theoretical problems of historic development in thinking. *The Principle of Development*. Nauka, Moscow
Vygotsky L S 1960 *The Development of Supreme Psychic Functions*. APN RSFSR Press, Moscow
Vygotsky L S 1972 Problems of periodization in child development. *Quest. Psychol.* 2
Zak A Z 1978 Experimental study of reflection in the elementary school child. *Quest. Psychol.* 2
Zaporožets A V, Lisina M I 1974 (eds.) *The Development of Contacts in the Preschool Child*. Pedagogica, Moscow

Ecological Theory of Human Development

R. P. Ross

. . . much of developmental psychology, as it now exists, is *the science of the strange behavior of children in strange situations with strange adults for the briefest possible periods of time.* (Bronfenbrenner 1979 p. 19)

Ecological research contrasts sharply with more traditional psychology research. Proponents of the ecological study of behavior have typically avoided the use of experimental methods involving controlled manipulation of isolated variables in the laboratory. Ecological psychologists have generally laid great stress on the importance of using naturalistic methods, of studying behavior in its situational context, and as a corollary, of careful description of the environment.

In the 1940s, two psychologists working at the University of Kansas, Roger Barker and Herbert Wright, started the Midwest Psychological Field Station as a center for the ecological study of human behavior. Two major strands of ecological research were conducted at the field station. One strand focused on the behavior of individual children in their everyday environments. The other strand examined the influence of the ecological environment on behavior. Methods of identifying, unitizing, and describing the settings of behavior were the focus of this aspect of the research conducted at the field station. In this article, both of these strands will be briefly reviewed.

1. Specimen Record Research

An important part of the early work conducted at the field station was the preparation of a set of records documenting the behavior of individual children in their everyday environments. The records which were collected are known in the literature as specimen records of behavior. These records were termed "specimen records" since they preserve for later study actual specimens of behavior with minimal disturbance to the behavior in the process of observation. One specimen record, consisting of 435 pages, was published commercially as the book *One Boy's Day* (Barker and Wright 1951). This book and other specimen records are stored in an archive at the University of Kansas, and many researchers from this university as well as from other universities have utilized it to answer a variety of psychological questions.

Two kinds of specimen records have been developed. The first, called a day record, extends through an entire day, from the time of waking to the bedtime of a subject. In this type of specimen record, the subject is held constant, but the settings in which he or she participates vary. The second kind of specimen record is called a setting record. Here observers record the behavior and context of an individual for the entire time that he or she is in one particular behavior setting. Subsequent individuals are observed in the same setting. Here, the setting is held constant, but the subjects vary.

Both the day record and the setting record are detailed, sequential, and narrative accounts of behavior and its immediate environmental context. To make a specimen record, a trained observer watches a target individual and records in ordinary, nontechnical language the behavior of the individual and his or her environmental context in concrete, specific terms. The Stenomask is a recording device that is often used by observers. This mechanical aid permits oral note taking without the observer's voice being audible to others. Complete details on how to collect and analyze specimen records, as well as information on the reliability of this method of observation, have been provided by Wright (1967).

As part of the specimen record research, Barker and Wright identified a unit of behavior which they termed the behavior episode. A behavior episode is the smallest ecological unit of an individual's stream of behavior. The basic criterion used to identify episodes is that they have a constancy in the direction of behavior exhibited throughout the unit. Two other defining characteristics of episodes are that they occur within the normal behavior perspective, and that the whole episode has greater potency than any of its parts. Examples of behavior episodes include, "rejecting lemonade," "recollecting pancakes eaten for breakfast," "cutting tomatoes," and "helping self to noodles."

The first major quantitative study conducted at the Midwest Psychological Field Station was based on a set of day records of 12 children between the ages of 2 and 10, and four physically disabled children within this age range. The 12 normal children lived in a small Midwest community in the United States. The four disabled children lived in a private institution for disabled children. Results of this investigation are published in a book called *Midwest and Its Children* (Barker and Wright 1955).

The results of the Midwest study provide important information regarding the structure of children's stream of behavior. Surprisingly, there were not any clear-cut differences between the episode structure of normal and physically disabled children. On a typical day, the Midwest children engaged in between 500 and 1,300 episodes. These episodes ranged in duration from a few seconds to 121 minutes, with more than 70 percent of the episodes lasting less than 2 minutes.

One of the most interesting findings of Barker and Wright's analysis of the structure of the children's behavior episodes was that it changed as a function of age. Younger children did more things in a day and their episodes were generally shorter than those of the older children. Not only did the older children engage more often in episodes of longer duration, but they tended to carry on more than one action at a given time. Conversely, the younger children tended to shift from one action to another, to do things sequentially, one at a time. While about three-quarters of all episodes were carried through to full completion, the younger children stopped short of the goal more frequently than the older children. Age was not related to the frequency of success, failure, or frustration in the episodes. Further, the spontaneity of episode initiation and termination was not related to age.

Although specimen sets have generally been used to record the behavior of children, obviously there is nothing inherent about the methodology which restricts its use to this age group. In fact, in recent years, researchers have used the specimen approach to record the behavior of adults. Scott (1977) used specimen records to investigate the episode structures of "effective" and "ineffective" preschool teachers during two contrasting school activities: morning greeting and large-group instruction. Scott discovered that in both settings the more effective teachers could be differentiated from the less effective teachers by at least three factors. First, effective teachers had fewer episodes which, reciprocally, lasted a longer period of time. Second, effective teachers had more episodes ending in attainment of their goals than did ineffective teachers. Finally, effective teachers had more positive and less negative emotional feeling tone in their contacts with the children. Further, during morning greeting, effective teachers had more episodes lasting at least a minute and had more enclosing episodes than the less effective teachers. In contrast, the ineffective teachers showed more isolated, single episodes than the effective teachers. Kounin (1970) similarly found that the ability to manage overlapping activities was characteristic of effective teachers.

Barker and Wright's (1955) finding that the episodes of young children tend to be sequential rather than overlapping, coupled with the finding that ineffective teachers also tend to have sequential rather than overlapping episodes, suggests that it is the less competent and less experienced individual who is less likely to be able to engage in overlapping activities.

2. *The Same Child in Different Milieus*

One of the most robust and perhaps most important findings of the specimen record studies is that children's behavior predictably changes as they enter different settings. One study which clearly demonstrated this finding was conducted by Gump et al. (1963). The researchers observed one boy, Wally O'Neill, for one full day at home and for one full day at a summer camp. They found that the settings which Wally entered on these two days were quite different. On the camp day, Wally entered 17 different settings including a craft shop, a swimming area, and a cookout. At home, this same child entered only six different settings, and few of them were specifically designed for children's play. The researchers also found that Wally's behavior differed in these contrasting environments. At camp, Wally engaged in a significantly more active, exploratory, constructive, and dramatic play, while at home, he spent more time in passive recreation (including several hours of television viewing), dallying, and formally competitive play.

Wally's associates and social interactions also differed in these two environments. His camp associates included many adults, many peers, and few nonpeer children. The number of different peer and adult associates was twice as great at camp as at home, as was the number of episodes devoted to adults and peers. On the other hand, the number of different nonpeer children and the number of episodes with them was much greater at home than at camp. Wally's associates were more aggressive, resistant, and appealing at home than his camp associates. His camp associates were more nurturant and sharing than his home and neighborhood associates. Camp adults, as compared to those at home, extended more interest-centered, less aggressive, and less resistant social behaviors to Wally. At home, Wally was more dominant, aggressive, and tended to be less submissive than he was at camp. At camp, Wally was more nurturant. The fact that most child associates at camp were peers probably contributed to the more egalitarian social relationships that developed in that setting. Differences in the settings were also related to aspects of Wally's emotionality on the two days. He more often demonstrated strongly positive emotions and more ambivalent emotions at camp than at home.

Ecological psychologists have found that the behavior of children can be predicted more accurately from knowing the situation children are in than from knowing individual characteristics of the children. The specimen record studies revealed that over the course of a day,

each child's behavior varied with the immediate surroundings and that in similar surroundings, different children behaved quite similarly. For example, when children were eating dinner with their families, they behaved differently than when they were playing outdoors with their friends. Further, the way different children behaved while playing outdoors was more similar than the behavior of the same child in contrasting situations. Barker and his colleagues concluded from observing children in their natural environments that it was important to learn more about the contexts in which behavior occurs.

3. *Behavior Setting Research*

The second major strand of research and theory conducted by ecological psychologists involved examination of the ecological environment. Methods of identifying, unitizing, and describing the settings of behavior were the focus of this aspect of the research conducted at the field station. As part of this line of research, a series of behavior setting surveys were conducted in several small towns in the United States, England, Norway, and Africa, in institutions such as high schools, churches and hospitals, and in special environments such as military bases and a mining town in Canada's far north. Procedures for conducting behavior setting surveys have been described by Barker (1968).

A behavior setting is an ecological unit consisting of both a physical milieu (spatial enclosure, facilities) and a behavioral program (a standing pattern of behavior, a regime, a set of procedures). Examples of behavior settings are basketball games, Easter parades, and Sunday church services. Once an individual enters a behavior setting, his or her behavior is markedly influenced by the milieu and program.

In the most extensive study of behavior settings, Barker and Schoggen (1973) measured the environments and the environmental usage of two towns—Midwest in Kansas in the United States and Yoredale in England. Both towns were described with identical methods, at two points in time, a decade apart. These researchers enquired as to what proportion of a community's environment children are free to choose entry or nonentry. Communities have a range of settings with various entrance requirements and obligations. Children discover that they are often restricted from entering certain settings like hospitals, factories, office buildings, banks, or bars. Some restaurants do not encourage families with children to patronize them. Some films may not be viewed by children. In contrast, there are other settings that encourage the participation of children. Zoos, children's rooms in the library, children's museums, child-oriented restaurants, schools, and parks can generally be entered freely by children. Barker and Schoggen's results showed that Midwest allowed children more freedom to choose which of the town's public behavior settings to enter than did Yoredale. In Midwest only 21 percent of all settings required that children enter (e.g., school settings) or stay out (e.g., taverns) whereas in Yoredale the comparable figure was 34 percent. In both communities, the territorial range of the residents (i.e., the actual number of settings entered during the year) increased steadily from the youngest age group (the infants) up to the adult age group. For example, in Midwest, the infants entered only 60 percent of the town's settings, while the adults entered nearly all the settings in the town. However, the elderly (age 65 and up) were found in only 80 percent of the town's settings, a figure which closely matched that for the adolescent age group.

Behavior settings are highly dependent upon people for their operation and maintenance. Behavior settings specify human components for certain positions within them. These are termed the habitat claims for human components. For example, the instructor's position in an academic class is a habitat claim; this position requires an appropriate human component—one with the necessary knowledge and skills—in order for the behavior setting to become operational. The number of habitat claims of a behavior setting is the number of positions of responsibility that must be filled for the normal occurrence of the setting. In settings, persons may be assigned relatively low power (guests, audience persons), moderate power (members, customers), or high power (functionaries, leaders). The leadership range is a measure of the amount of habitat within which members of the age subgroup are very important and responsible persons; for a town's behavior setting the leadership range is the extent to which members of an age subgroup serve as single or joint leaders.

On average Midwest residents spent more time and occupied more positions of leadership in their behavior settings than was true for their Yoredale counterparts. Not surprisingly, infants and small children served in positions of responsibility or leadership in only a very small part of the town's habitats. However, young people in Midwest were more often found in relatively high-power positions than children and adolescents in Yoredale. Midwest's behavior settings produced leaders at a younger age (older elementary-school subgroup) than Yoredale's (adolescent). The towns differed most in the leadership range of adolescents; Midwest's adolescents exceeded Yoredale's adolescents in the number of behavior settings where they were joint or single leaders. Thus, in the ecological sense, children and adolescents were more needed in the American than in the English community. The elderly were also leaders in the behavior settings of Midwest more often than they were in the Yoredale behavior settings.

The English system tended to reserve significant participation in community life for adults. Midwest, on the other hand, used young people in some of the significant action. While this can be expressed as a contrast in values, it is important to consider the accompanying ecological conditions. Compared to Yoredale, Midwest had a substantially larger number of behavior settings but a smaller number of persons to staff and operate

them. Thus in Midwest, there were many more positions of responsibility to be filled than there were in Yoredale and there were fewer residents in Midwest to fill these positions. In fact, there were more than twice as many positions per resident in Midwest than in Yoredale. Midwest, relative to Yoredale, appeared to be short-handed; the behavior settings of Midwest were undermanned. To maintain its settings Midwest had to accept—even instigate—significant contributions from children and adolescents.

As an environment for behavior development, Midwest differed from Yoredale in that the Midwest system required the responsible participation of other than its most able class of human components. In Midwest, the elderly as well as children and adolescents were expected to perform difficult and important functions more frequently than in Yoredale.

This finding and similar ones in other investigations led Barker to develop a behavior setting theory with special reference to the consequences of undermanning on the behavior and experience of the inhabitants (Barker 1968). The main thesis of this theory is that undermanned settings exert more pressure than adequately manned or overmanned settings on potential participants to enter and take part in the operation and maintenance of the setting. If, for example, the high school junior class play has parts for 12 actors and there are only 25 members of the junior class, no member of the class is likely to be exempt from pressure to take a part or at least to help backstage. But if there are 250 juniors, only the more talented and highly motivated are likely to become involved.

The theory of undermanning has been tested in a number of other investigations. The relation of school size to student behavior and experience has been carefully investigated by Barker and Gump (1964). They found that students in small high schools experienced more invitations and more pressures to assume setting work than students in large schools. As a result, students in small schools worked harder and assumed more responsible and difficult setting positions in extracurricular affairs. Students in small high schools who were more active in central positions in an activity had different experiences from those who were merely audience members. Not surprisingly, small-school students also reported different attitudes and feelings regarding their settings than large-school students.

The fact that undermanned schools must utilize all students in order to maintain extracurricular operations has important implications for academically marginal students. Barker and Gump found that in small schools, academically marginal students were very likely to become a part of the enterprise. In large schools, academically marginal students were also marginal in their extracurricular participation and in their feelings of being responsible for their school's settings.

An important finding of the studies reviewed is that the behavior of children depends on the particular environments they enter and on how much these environments need their contributions. While the data collected by Barker and Wright and other ecological psychologists have made important contributions to the developmental literature, the most important contribution of this line of research has been the creation of methods for studying behavior in natural situations and the provision of new units of measurement for analyzing both behavior and the settings in which behavior occurs.

Bibliography

Barker R G (ed.) 1963 *The Stream of Behavior: Explorations of its Structure and Content.* Appleton-Century-Crofts, New York

Barker R G 1968 *Ecological Psychology: Concepts and Methods for Studying the Environment of Human Behavior.* Stanford University Press, Stanford, California

Barker R G et al. 1978 *Habitats, Environments, and Human Behavior.* Jossey-Bass, San Francisco, California

Barker R G, Gump P V 1964 *Big School, Small School: High School Size and Student Behavior.* Stanford University Press, Stanford, California

Barker R G, Schoggen P 1973 *Qualities of Community Life.* Jossey-Bass, San Francisco, California

Barker R G, Wright H F 1951 *One Boy's Day: A Specimen Record of Behavior.* Harper and Row, New York

Barker R G, Wright H F 1955 *Midwest and Its Children: The Psychological Ecology of an American Town.* Row and Peterson, Evanston, Illinois

Bronfenbrenner U 1979 *The Ecology of Human Development: Experiments by Nature and Design.* Harvard University Press, Cambridge, Massachusetts

Gump P V 1975 Ecological psychology and children. In: Hetherington E M (ed.) 1975 *Review of Child Development Research,* Vol. 5. University of Chicago Press, Chicago, Illinois

Gump P V, Schoggen P, Redl F 1963 The behavior of the same child in different milieus. In: Barker R G (ed.) 1963 *The Stream of Behavior: Explorations of its Structure and Content.* Appleton-Century-Crofts, New York, pp. 169–202

Kounin J S 1970 *Discipline and Group Management in Classrooms.* Holt, Rinehart and Winston, New York

Kounin J S, Sherman L W 1979 School environments as behavior settings. *Theory Pract.* 18: 145–51

McGurk H 1977 *Ecological Factors in Human Development.* North-Holland, New York

Schoggen P 1964 Mechanical aids for making specimen records of behavior. *Child Dev.* 35: 985–88

Schoggen M, Barker L S, Barker R G 1963 Structure of the behavior of American and English children. In: Barker R G (ed.) 1963 *The Stream of Behavior: Explorations of its Structure and Content.* Appleton-Century-Crofts, New York, pp. 160–68

Scott M 1977 Some parameters of teacher effectiveness as assessed by an ecological approach. *J. Educ. Psychol.* 69: 217–26

Wicker A W 1979 *An Introduction to Ecological Psychology.* Brooks/Cole, Monterey, California

Wright H F 1967 *Recording and Analyzing Child Behavior with Ecological Data from an American Town.* Harper and Row, New York

Ego Psychology Theory of Human Development

D. P. Ausubel

Ego psychology deals with the development, organization, and functioning, both normal and aberrant, of those core aspects of human personality that account for psychological growth, adaptation, adjustment, and disorder. It is not concerned with the nature of such psychological processes as perception, learning, memory, cognition, problem solving, or creativity in their own right, but only insofar as they are directly implicated in the mechanisms of ego development and functioning. Thus, ego psychology and cognitive psychology constitute two fundamentally independent bodies of knowledge in terms of their respective basic science thrusts and major applications, even though they are obviously related and interdependent at numerous points of intersection, as will become abundantly clear throughout this article. Contrary to the broader implications of its title, however, this article will be restricted to an ego psychology interpretation of only the personality (ego) aspects of human development and will not consider as such either cognitive development or contemporaneous (nondevelopmental) aspects of personality structure and functioning.

To avoid later confusion, the reader should be aware at the outset that there are two completely different major versions of ego psychology in terms of their historical antecedents and theoretical orientation, namely, psychoanalytic ego psychology and naturalistic ego psychology, that have very little in common with respect to philosophy of science orientation, underlying psychological theory, empirical methodology, and accepted database.

Psychoanalytic ego psychology is basically a derivative and extension of orthodox psychoanalytic psychology to problems of ego development and functioning that accepts all of the major tenets of psychoanalysis, although positing some "conflict free" or "autonomous" areas. As a separately identifiable movement within the larger psychoanalytic framework, it was first identified with the work of Hartmann (1958) and Anna Freud (1937), later with such figures as Mahler (1968) and Erikson (1950), and more recently with Kernberg (1967) and Kohut (1971).

Naturalistic ego psychology, on the other hand, is not only nonpsychoanalytic in its theoretical orientation but is also based on a theoretically opposite set of psychological and developmental propositions and on a naturalistic, rather than a largely speculative and impressionistic, approach to theory building and verification. Its principal protagonist, the American psychiatrist and psychologist Ausubel formulated between 1946 and 1952 the first comprehensive and unified nonpsychoanalytic theory of ego development and of its relation to mental disorder. This theory was derived both from his own diverse clinical experience with narcotic addicts and from a broad range of other mentally ill persons (children, adolescents, and adults in both inpatient and outpatient settings), and from the then available naturalistic data in personality and ego development. Much of the initial impetus for the elaboration of Ausubel's ego psychology theory came from his postulated identification of the motivationally inadequate personality as pathognomonic of the predisposing premorbid personality structure of both narcotic addicts and of so-called process schizophrenics, thereby establishing the first significant etiological and psychopathological linkage between narcotic addiction and other major forms of mental disorder.

In this article only the naturalistic version of ego psychology will be considered (except for a brief comparison between the two versions) because (a) it is based on a currently more tenable and generally accepted theoretical approach to personality and developmental psychology; (b) it is related to, and consonant with, findings from methodologically rigorous studies of ego development rather than being derived uncritically from a combination of orthodox psychoanalytic theory and new speculative assertions about the nature and stages of human development which are buttressed only by impressionistic and anecdotal clinical material; and (c) it is more compatible with modern biological and ethnological conceptions of human development and of the interaction between heredity and environment as expressed in such fields as behavioral genetics, embryology, and cultural anthropology.

1. Historical Antecedents of Naturalistic Ego Psychology

Although the modern version of naturalistic ego psychology evolved contemporaneously with psychoanalytic ego psychology, and also antedated it in many significant respects, this fact has tended to be obscured by the dominant position of psychoanalysis in the middle third of the twentieth century (particularly in the United States) in psychiatry; in other mental health professions such as social work, child guidance, and counseling; in other social sciences (e.g., cultural anthropology); and in the social science aspects of more distantly related fields such as pediatrics, education, art, literature, law, religion, history, and philosophy. As a result, it is hardly surprising that psychoanalytic ego psychology came to be perceived in North America as coextensive with ego psychology generally, both by its protagonists and by other mental health professionals, social scientists, and informed laymen.

Paradoxically enough therefore, even though naturalistic ego psychology was rooted both empirically in the longitudinal studies of personality and ego development conducted at American child development institutes [particularly by Gesell and his associates (1946) at Yale University] as well as theoretically in the pre- and non-psychoanalytic speculative mini-self-psychologies developed by such American philosphers and psychologists as Baldwin, Cooley, Dewey, G. H. Mead, G. W. Allport, and Maslow, it tended to flourish more in Europe. This was largely the case because of the less dominant influence of psychoanalysis on European social and behavioral science than on their American counterparts. These latter nonpsychoanalytic trends in American ego psychology, both speculative and empirical, reinforced by several influential critiques of psychoanalytic predeterminism and of psychoanalytically oriented views on sexuality and on the impact of child-rearing practices on personality development in American and primitive cultures (e.g., Kinsey et al. 1948, Orlansky 1949, Sherif and Cantril 1947), set the stage for Ausubel's more definitive, naturalistically grounded ego psychology theory of ego development over the life span and of its relation to mental disorder. Ausubel's stages of ego development were organized around his key concepts of satellization and desatellization and his key distinctions between satellizers and nonsatellizers, on the one hand, and between executive and volitional independence, on the other. These concepts and stages will be delineated below in greater detail.

2. Principal Differences between Naturalistic and Psychoanalytic Ego Psychology

Generally speaking, naturalistic ego psychology differs from the psychoanalytic variety in the following ways.

(a) In accordance with modern trends in genetics, embryology, comparative psychology, primate behavior, and cultural anthropology, naturalistic ego psychology is devoid of any taint of preformationism or predeterminism, eschewing all prestructured and predetermined drives and "stages of psychosexual development," instincts, or innate identifications.

(b) It repudiates the notion of innate, "original" and finite sources of psychic energy (libido) from which all socially acceptable drives are said to be derived, largely through such mechanisms as sublimation, symbolic equivalence, and reaction formation. All drives are held to be acquired, completely undifferentiated at birth, and "functionally autonomous."

(c) All components and functions of the ego are conceptualized as acquired from interaction between relevant genetically determined potentialities, predispositions, and preferences on the one hand, and corresponding interpersonal experience on the other. Neither ego nor character structure is regarded as a precipitate of id or "pleasure principle" drives that are modified by corrective contact with the "reality principle" or with particular child-rearing practices impinging on erogenous activity during successive stages of psychosexual development and resulting in over- or under-gratification with subsequent fixation of libido.

(d) The responsiveness of infants and children to various affective and attitudinal cues is held to be limited by their relative perceptual, cognitive, and social immaturity and also by the primitiveness of their prevailing ego structures. Thus, for example, the alleged qualitative comparability of infant and adult sexuality and the alleged psychoanalytical sensitivity of infants to subtle attitudinal cues of parental rejection, emotional distancing, or guilt are categorically denied.

(e) Armchair speculation about stages of ego development is abandoned in favor of naturalistic longitudinal observation and testing of children, adolescents, and adults for purposes of designating stages of ego development of the life span. Little essential scientific difference, for example, is seen between Shakespeare's poetic characterization of successive stages in the life cycle and Erikson's corresponding developmental stages of personality development.

(f) Naturalistic ego psychology rejects all impressionistic clinical and anecdotal "evidence" as scientifically inappropriate for confirming or disconfirming hypotheses regarding ego development or functioning, insisting on methodologically rigorous data for these purposes.

(g) Emphasis is placed on relating all aspects and dimensions of ego structure and functioning to each other at each stage of development. It does not reduce all of ego development to progress along a single linearly progressive dimension as Mahler (1968), for example, does in describing movement from a symbiotic relationship between mother and infant to a later stage in which ego boundaries are sharpened and a sense of self is individuated out of an undifferentiated and amorphous mother–infant mass.

(h) Naturalistic ego psychology makes no arbitrary distinctions or divisions between aspects of ego that refer to ego functioning generally and aspects having to do with expressions of conscience or sexuality. The ego as an entity is regarded as functioning as a whole. Sexual self-expression or moral self-expression, for example, is not considered to be categorically or qualitatively separate from problems of self-esteem, independence–dependence, or deferred versus immediate gratification of hedonistic needs. Hence, separate personality substructures such as id or superego are not postulated but, rather, are incorporated within the general framework of ego structure.

(i) Finally, unlike psychoanalytic ego psychology, naturalistic ego psychology does not place the role and significance of repression completely out of perspective as a defense mechanism and, hence, elevate it as the principal source of psychopathological symptomatology and/or concomitantly, perceive insight as the cornerstone of psychotherapy. On the contrary, most significant motives and attitudes are generally perceived as being functionally accessible to awareness, at least in their broad outlines, and with respect to their basic essentials.

3. Definition of Ego and Related Terms

The terms self, self-concept, ego, and personality constitute, in the order given, an ascending hierarchy of complexity and inclusiveness. The self is a constellation of generally tangible individual perceptions and memories that have self-reference. It consists of the visual image of the appearance of one's body, the auditory image of the sound of one's name, more amorphous images of kinesthetic sensations and visceral tensions, memories of personal events, and so forth. The self-concept, on the other hand, is an abstraction of the essential and distinguishing characteristics of the self at each stage of development that differentiate an individual's selfhood from the environment and other selves. In the course of development, various evaluative attitudes, values, aspirations, motives, and obligations become associated with the self-concept. This system of interrelated self-attitudes, self-motives, self-esteem, self-values, self-obligations, self-ideals, and self-aspirations organized around the self-concept may be conceptualized as the ego.

Personality is a still more inclusive term than ego. It includes all of the psychological and behavioral predispositions characteristic of individuals at a given point in their life history. Thus it embraces the peripheral, transitory, and trivial, as well as the central ego aspects of their behavioral propensities and their cognitive as well as their motivational, moral, and affective traits.

4. Stages of Naturalistic Ego Development

In Ausubel's naturalistic schema of ego development, three main normative stages are delineated: (a) ego omnipotence during infancy (roughly 6 months to $2\frac{1}{2}$ years); (b) satellization during a childhood (roughly age 3 to puberty); and (c) desatellization during adolescence and early adult life. The key new concept here is that of satellization which will, therefore, first be described briefly before the three stages are examined more closely.

Much conceptual confusion has resulted in the past, and still prevails today, because of failure to distinguish between two essentially different kinds of identification, each of which involves a reciprocal relationship between a relatively dominant and independent individual (or group) and a relatively dependent and subordinate individual. In a satellizing relationship, the subordinate party acknowledges and accepts a subservient and deferential role, and the superordinate in turn accepts the subordinate as an intrinsically valuable "retainer" in his or her personal orbit. As an outcome of this type of dependent process and relationship, satellizers acquire a derived (vicarious, attributed) biosocial status that is wholly a function of the dependent relationship and independent of their own competence or performance ability, and that is bestowed upon them through the fiat of simple intrinsic valuation by a superordinate individual whose authority and power to do so are regarded as unchallengeable.

On the other hand, the two parties to the same "transaction" could relate to each other in quite a different way. The subordinate party could acknowledge dependency as a temporary, regrettable, and much-to-be remedied fact of life requiring, as a matter of expediency, various acts of conformity and deference but, at the same time, not accept a dependent and subservient status as a person. In turn, he or she could either be rejected outright or accorded qualified acceptance, that is, not for intrinsic reasons (as a person for his or her own sake) but in terms of current or potential competence and usefulness to the superordinate party. The act of identification, if it occurs at all, consists solely in using the latter (superordinate) individual as an emulatory model so that the subordinate can learn the superordinate's skills and methods of operation and thus eventually succeed to his or her enviable status. Accordingly, the nonsatellizing child acquires no derived (vicarious, attributed) status. The only type of biosocial status that can be engendered in this situation is the earned status that reflects the subordinate's actual functional competence, power, or control.

This nonsatellizing type of identification occurs for one of two reasons: either the superordinate party will not extend unqualified intrinsic acceptance (as in the case of rejecting parents or those who value their children for ulterior self-enhancing purposes) or, much more rarely, because the subordinate party is unwilling to undergo satellization or is incapable of satellizing.

4.1 Stage 1: Omnipotent Ego Structure (about Age 6 Months to Age 2½ Years)

Paradoxical as it may seem at first glance, the omnipotent phase of ego development coexists with the period of the child's greatest degree of objective helplessness and dependence on parents. Yet this apparent paradox is easily resolved if the nonunitary concept of dependence is divided into its easily discriminable executive and volitional components. When this is done, concomitant self-perceptions of volitional independence and executive dependence are not mutually contradictory at all, but are, on the contrary, very compatible with each other under the pancultural biosocial conditions of infancy. Unlike the psychoanalytic doc-

trine of infantile omnipotence—which unparsimoniously assumes the existence, in part, of a preformed ego and of a sense of volition even before birth—the present theory conceives of omnipotent feelings in infants as a naturalistic product of both actual interpersonal experience (i.e., experienced parental deference) and of their perceptual cognitive immaturity.

At the same time that infants are developing a functional concept of executive dependence from their gradual appreciation of their own inability to gratify their most elemental needs, and of their consequent absolute dependence on familiar competent caretakers to do so, concomitant notions of volitional independence and omnipotence gradually begin to emerge. This is the case because it is precisely when children are most helpless that, almost invariably in all cultures, they are accorded more indulgence and deference by parents than at any other period of childhood. At this time, parents tend to be most solicitous and eager to gratify the child's expressed needs. In general they make few demands upon infants and usually accede to their legitimate requests. If training is instituted, it tends to be delayed, gradual, and gentle. In this benevolent environment, therefore, much support is provided in external interpersonal conditions for a perception of parental subservience to the child's will.

Furthermore, it is unlikely that infants are sufficiently mature, perceptually and cognitively speaking, to appreciate the relatively subtle motivations (love, duty, altruism) underlying this deference. As a result they quite understandably acquire the developmentally autistic misperception that, because of their volitional power, parents are obliged to serve them rather than the correct perception that the superservience is altruistic and practiced in deference to their extreme helplessness. Hence, their appreciation of their executive dependence does not conflict with, or detract essentially from, their self-concept of relative volitional omnipotence and independence inasmuch as volitionally powerful persons do not have to be executively competent and independent as long as they have an executively competent person at their beck and call.

4.2 Stage 2: Satellization (Age 3 to Puberty)

Devaluation of the omnipotent ego structure begins when the infant loses his or her extreme helplessness and acquires sufficient cognitive, motor, and language competence to help in his or her own care, to become responsive to parental direction, and to conform to parentally transmitted cultural norms. The imposition of these new demands and expectations (e.g., for sphincter control and control of aggression), coupled with markedly decreased parental deference and reciprocally increased parental dominance and assertiveness in the relationship, tends to undermine environmental supports for infantile self-perceptions of omnipotence and volitional independence. At the same time, greatly increased cognitive and perceptual sophistication contribute to ego devaluation by enabling children to perceive their actual impotence in the household power structure and to appreciate that they are just as dependent on their parents volitionally as executively. Thus, ego devaluation is characterized by increased executive independence and decreased volitional independence.

Under these circumstances, given a minimal degree of acceptance and intrinsic valuation, most children elect to undergo satellization. Since in no culture can children compete with adults on better than marginal terms, and since they can no longer be omnipotent themselves, the next best thing in terms of their self-esteem needs is to be satellites of persons who apparently are. By so doing they not only acquire a guaranteed derived status which they enjoy solely by the fiat of being accepted and valued for themselves irrespective of their competence and performance ability, but also, by perceiving themselves as allied with their parents—albeit in a subordinate role—they share vicariously in the latter's omnipotence.

In all cultures, however, a variable number of parents are psychologically unable, unwilling, or negatively disposed by circumstances to extend acceptance and intrinsic valuation to their offspring. Under these conditions genuine and thorough-going devaluation of the omnipotent ego structure does not occur; and deprived of intrinsic feelings of security and adequacy on a derived basis, the children have no alternative but to strive compensatorily for their extrinsic counterparts by seeking an earned status based on their own competence, hierarchical position, and power to influence and control their environment. Unlike satellizers who assimilate parental training goals and standards uncritically and unselectively on the basis of personal loyalty, these children merely acknowledge parents as suitable emulatory models for acquiring power and prestige and internalize their values selectively in terms of the expediential criterion of potential usefulness for ego enchancement.

4.3 Stage 3: Desatellization (Adolescence and Early Adult Life)

Before ego development can be completed by the attainment of adult personality status, one more important maturational step is obviously necessary: emancipation from emotionally dependent attitudes towards parents. This essentially involves a process of desatellization that includes not only assuming the role of a volitionally independent adult in society, but also seeking the major source of one's biosocial status and self-esteem from earned rather than derived sources, that is, from one's own competence and achievement. These new ego-status goals of desatellization are self-evidently the opposite of those prevailing during the satellizing period; but the ego-maturity goals necessary for implementing these new adult drives and ego characteristics are identical and continuous with those operative throughout childhood, namely, increased executive independence, frustration, tolerance, responsibility, self-critical ability, and deferral of hedonistic grati-

fication. However, the motivation for assimilating these same trait values, and for acquiring the traits themselves, shifts from the expression of uncritical personal loyalty to parents and desire for parental approval to perceived necessity for, and compatibility with, the acquisition of increased earned status and volitional independence.

Desatellization is precipitated by cultural, parental, and internal individual needs for attaining adult personality status and is supported by corresponding shifts in demands and expectations that are triggered by the onset of pubescence. In Western cultures it is effected through three main mechanisms: (a) resatellization—the replacement of parents by peers as the essential socializing agents of children and as the individuals in relation to whom residual satellizing trends are maintained; (b) the displacement of derived by earned status as the principal source of self-esteem; and (c) the displacement of uncritical personal loyalty to parents by considerations of expediency, ego enhancement, and abstract ideals of equity, virtue, and morality as the basis on which values are assimilated.

Inasmuch as the nonsatellizing child has never undergone satellization, the basic aspects of desatellization are unnecessary and its objectives may be considered as largely accomplished in advance.

5. Implications of Naturalistic Ego Psychology for Child Rearing, Counseling, and Educational Practice

The major implication of naturalistic ego psychology for child rearing, counseling, and educational practice follows naturally from the logical plausibility of the proposition, supported by clinical findings, that the most tenable and felicitous course of ego development—from the standpoint of mature, stable, and productive personality functioning and the avoidance of disabling personality distortions and mental disorders—is the modal type prevailing panculturally, namely, satellization during childhood followed by desatellization during adolescence and early adulthood. Failure to satellize typically results in compensatorily and unrealistically high and tenacious needs for achievement, severe impairment of self-esteem, neurotic anxiety and its various distortive defences, and susceptibility both to conduct and antisocial personality disorders and to such psychotic complications as affective, reactive schizophrenic, and paranoid disorders (Ausubel and Kirk 1977). Failure to desatillize, on the other hand, is associated with a motivationally immature and inadequate personality structure predisposed to chronic academic and vocational underachievement, the amotivational syndrome, substance abuse, and process schizophrenia (Ausubel and Kirk 1977).

Nonsatellization is preventable, at least in part, by educating parents about the causes and consequences of the rejecting and extrinsically valuing parent attitudes that beget it. To some extent it is reversible by treatment of such parents when nonsatellizing children are identified in early childhood education and treatment centers. When parent attitudes are resistive to change (and also in the case of nonsatellizing older children and adolescents, and adults with clinical symptoms), then compensatory satellization to counselors, teachers, spouses, and older relatives can be encouraged, as well as the formulation of more realistic ego aspirations.

Failure to desatellize can be similarly prevented and counteracted, in part, by parent and teacher education regarding the child-rearing and teacher attitudes (overprotecting, overpermissive, overdominating) that promote it, by providing corrective identification with teachers, counselors, and surrogate parents, and, in more serious cases, by appropriate character reeducation in residential centers.

Bibliography

Ausubel D P 1952 *Ego Development and the Personality Disorders: A Developmental Approach to Psychopathology.* Grune and Stratton, New York
Ausubel D P, Kirk D 1977 *Ego Psychology and Mental Disorder: A Developmental Approach to Psychopathology.* Grune and Stratton, New York
Erikson E 1950 *Childhood and Society.* Norton, New York
Freud A 1937 *The Ego and the Mechanisms of Defence.* The International Psycho-analytical Library, No. 30. Hogarth, London
Gesell A L, Ilg F L 1946 *The Child from Five to Ten.* Harper, New York
Hartmann H 1958 Ego psychology and the problem of adaptation. *J. Am. Psychoanal. Assoc.*, Monograph Series No. 1. International Universities Press, New York
Kernberg O F 1967 Boderline personality organization. *J. Am. Psychoanal. Assoc.* 15: 641–85
Kinsey A C, Pomeroy W B, Martin C E 1948 *Sexual Behavior in the Human Male.* Saunders, Philadelphia, Pennsylvania
Kohut H 1971 *The Analysis of the Self: A Systematic Approach to the Psychoanalytic Treatment of Narcissistic Personality Disorders.* The Psychoanalytic Study of the Child, Monograph No. 4. International Universities Press, New York
Mahler M S 1968 *On Human Symbiosis and the Vicissitudes of Individuation.* The International Psycho-analytical Library, No. 82. International Universities Press, New York
Orlansky H 1949 Infant care and personality. *Psychol. Bull.* 46: 1–48
Sherif M, Cantril H 1947 *The Psychology of Ego-involvements, Social Attitudes and Identifications.* Wiley, New York

Existential Theory of Human Development

B. Mohan and B. M. Daste

There are numerous ways to analyze the currents of existential thinking. As a system of philosophy or a school of thought, existentialism is a revolt against traditional metaphysics. As a theory of human development, it is an approach to highlight the existence of being, the process of becoming. Since a person, in the becoming state, always exists in a constantly dynamic phase, "his life may be regarded as a journey on which he finds ever newer experiences and gains greater insights" (Kingston 1961 p. xii).

Existentialism represents a protest against the rationalism of traditional philosophy, against misleading notions of the bourgeois culture, and the dehumanizing values of industrial civilization. Since alienation, loneliness, and self-estrangement constitute threats to human personality in the modern world, existential thought has viewed as its cardinal concerns a quest for subjective truth, a reaction against the "negation of Being," and a perennial search for freedom. From the ancient Greek philosopher, Socrates, to the twentieth century French philosopher, Jean Paul Sartre, thinkers have dealt with this tragic sense of ontological reality—the human situation within a comic context.

1. Existentialism Defined

Various definitions of existentialism have been proposed by different authors. Blackham (1952 p. 150) has described existentialism as a philosophy of being, "a philosophy of attestation and acceptance, and a refusal of the attempt to rationalize and to think Being." The peculiarity of existentialism, according to Blackham (1952 pp. 151–52), is that "it deals with the separation of man from himself and from the world, which raises the questions of philosophy, not by attempting to establish some universal form of justification which will enable man to readjust himself but by permanently enlarging and lining the separation itself as primordial and constitutive for personal existence."

Harris and Levey (1975 p. 911) define existentialism as "any of several philosophic systems, all centered on the individual and his relationship to the universe or to God." Tiryakian (1962 p. 77) defines it as "an attempt to reaffirm the importance of the individual by a rigorous and in many respects radically new analysis of the nature of man."

In the opinion presented here, existentialism is a humanistic perspective on the individual situation, a philosophy of existence, of being, of authenticity, and of universal freedom. It is a quest, beyond despair, for creative identity.

2. Basic Tenets

The main tenets of existentialism involve a kind of subjective and direct approach upholding the emergence of the person in a rather impersonal environment.

The first important tenet is that the essence of humans

is their existence. A synthesis of immanency and transcendency, guided by a primordial sense of ontological wonder and subjective knowledge, constitutes existence. Sartre (1956) wrote that freedom is existence, and in it existence precedes essence.

The cardinal concept of subjectivity essentially concerns a person's openness and uniqueness, their encounter with the "thou," the transcendent. To Sartre, consciousness of freedom relates to "no-thingness." This perspective on existence is inspired by a stance which is against positivism, scientism, and a logico-rational approach to reality.

Other tenets of existentialism relate to human suffering, despair, alienation, and anguish. The events that led to the First World War, followed by Auschwitz, Nagasaki, Hiroshima, and Bangladesh, generated a disillusionment which can lead to detachment and enlightenment. According to existential thought, people are able to appreciate human fortitude only through extreme situations. Sorrow, disappointment, and death enable humans to achieve authentic life. Existential writings—plays, poems, novels—seek to offer experiences of nausea and extremity (Scott 1978).

3. A Perspective Toward Human Development

Human development is seen by existentialists as independent of external forces, guided by the creative forces of the integral self. In other words, development is a self-directed synthesis of self-destined energy, potential, aspirations, and needs. From the existential perspective, the individual has freedom of choice, which implies a capacity to change. It is a freedom that helps with the self-emerging process. Identity and security attained at the cost of freedom constitute bad faith. Likewise, to question the dynamism of the personality is an act of bad faith. Thus, human personality is conceptualized as a transcendental reality that emerges through inner creative forces, with natural growth viewed as an integrative process marked by authenticity. Development consists of a uniquely subjective style by which the individual relates to others and to the processes of being and becoming.

4. Educational Implications

The implications of existentialist formulations for child-rearing, education, and counseling practices are many. Since existentialists behold human life as unique and emerging, a child is to be recognized as a full person and not simply as an incomplete adult. The practices by which the child is socialized varies from one culture to another. If the emphasis in the culture is on mundane security and on the value of worldly essence, then the individual may experience neurotic growth through the conflict between these unsuitable values and the person's inner forces of creativity that continue to aspire for unique emergence and subjective expression. The extent to which a child is accepted or rejected, succeeds

or fails, and develops satisfactorily or is retarded depends on the experiences and processes which explain the meaning of things (persons, objects, situations) in relation to the child's being.

Educational standards and practices that manipulate the child's behaviors in an arbitrary manner violate the principle of free choice. From the existential point of view, many teaching practices, testing procedures, and bureaucratic systems of classifying children may be questioned. Existential critics of these practices say that overstructured public and parochial school systems enslave rather than liberate young souls. Such educational institutions serve a political rather than a truly educational purpose, promoting the manufacture of efficient robots rather than inspired, enlightened, and creative individuals. As a result, various contemporary educational theories are radicalizing the institutionalized structures of learning. Teachers who have learned to provide existential encounters for their students enable the learners "to create meanings in a cosmos devoid of objective meaning, to find reasons for being in a society with fewer and fewer open doors" (Greene 1967 p. 4).

If the purpose of education is to build character, to optimize potential and creativity, and to enhance the quality of life through knowledge, then from an existentialist perspective bureaucratization needs to be replaced by humanization. That the existential goal is not being achieved today is illustrated by such evidence as that produced in a study of students' values indicating that American students predominantly seek to learn survival skills rather than to develop a social conscience, a situation contrary to an existentialist view of satisfactory development (*Chronicle of Higher Education* 1982). This crisis in education is not confined to the West but is observed in Eastern cultures as well (Mohan 1972).

In the realm of counseling, existential intervention is conceptualized as "a conscious attitudinal perspective toward rebuilding the impaired self" (Mohan 1979). The existential influences on counseling practices, though not yet fully acknowledged nor duly assessed, have been far-reaching. Some form of existential intervention is employed by such a range of practitioners as those using gestalt therapy, "antipsychiatry," rational–emotive psychotherapy, psychodrama, transactional analysis, communication and cognitive approaches, encounter groups, and reality therapy.

The existential view of development is not without its critics, many of whom view the theory and its practices as representing a neurotic, narcissistic philosophy of pain and anguish. In contrast, existentialism's protagonists see it as the only hope for human survival.

Bibliography

Blackham H J 1952 *Six Existentialist Thinkers*. Routledge and Kegan Paul, London
Chronicle of Higher Education 1982 April p. 10

Greene M 1967 *Existential Encounters for Teachers.* Random House, New York

Harris W H, Levey J S (eds.) 1975 *The New Columbia Encyclopedia.* Columbia University Press, New York

Kaufmann W A (ed.) 1959 *Existentialism from Dostoevsky to Sartre.* Meridian, New York

Kingston F T 1961 *French Existentialism: A Christian Critique.* University of Toronto Press, Toronto, Ontario

Mohan B 1972 *India's Social Problems.* Indian International Publications, Allahabad

Mohan B 1979 Conceptualization of existential intervention. *Psychol: Q. J. Hum. Behav.* 16(3): 39–45

Sartre J P 1956 *Being and Nothingness: An Essay on Phenomenological Ontology.* Barnes H E (trans.) Philosophical Library, New York

Scott N A 1978 *Mirrors of Man in Existentialism.* Collins, New York

Tiryakian E A 1962 *Sociologism and Existentialism: Two Perspectives on the Individual and Society.* Prentice-Hall, Englewood Cliffs, New Jersey

Humanistic Theory of Development

A. R. Mahrer and P. A. Gervaize

The humanistic theory of development holds that human beings are to be described in terms of potentials which have the capacity for growth or actualization, and the capacity for harmonious or integrative relationships with one another. Human development is understood in terms of plateaus of increasing actualization and integration of these potentials, and of a self which is correspondingly more actualizing and integrating. The wellsprings of the humanistic theory of development lie in three bodies of philosophical thought: humanism, existentialism, and phenomenology. Its conceptual refinement and application, however, occur in such fields as education, psychology, psychiatry, religion, and sociology. Among the major contributors to this theory of development are: G. W. Allport, A. Angyal, L. Binswanger, M. Buber, C. Bühler, F. J. Buytendijk, A. W. Combs, H. F. Ellenberger, H. Fingarette, V. E. Frankl, E. Fromm, E. T. Gendlin, A. Giorgi, K. Goldstein, I. J. Gordon, A. Gurwitsch. L. L. Havens, M. Heidegger, E. Husserl, S. M. Jourard, E. Keen, S. Kierkegaard, G. M. Kinget, R. D. Laing, A. R. Mahrer, A. H. Maslow, R. May, C. Moustakas, C. Naranjo, J. Needleman, F. Perls, C. Rogers, J. P. Sartre, E. G. Schachtel, E. W. Straus, P. Tillich, R. Von Eckartsberg, D. Wyss, and others.

1. Basic Concepts of Humanistic Theory

With regard to the assumed basic nature of human beings, humanistic theory accepts a philosophy of science position known as constructual monism. It is assumed that there is a basic nature to human beings, their personalities, physical bodies, and their behavior. However, the assumed basic nature is no more than that, namely, an assumption. Accordingly, this assumed basic nature is held as open to description by means of concepts or theoretical constructs. Provided that the concepts or constructs meet criteria of rigor and usefulness, the assumed basic nature of human beings is open to description from a variety of perspectives. While humanistic theory describes the assumed basic nature from its perspective, using its own organized body of constructs, it is understood that human beings, their personalities, physical bodies, and behavior, are also open to description from such other perspectives as neurophysiology, sociology, chemistry, and religion.

In adopting this approach, humanistic theory declines an assumption of some irreducible fundamental nature of human beings. It declines an assumption that human beings are fundamentally of a biological nature, or that the bedrock of human beings, their bodies and behavior, are neurophysiological or social or physical or chemical. Nor is it assumed that the basic nature of human beings is comprised of two or more fundamentally irreducible elements such as mental or psychic and physical or biological elements. The rejection of reductionism means that the constructs of humanistic theory are not open to reduction to more "basic" constructs from fields such as biology or physics or chemistry.

Within this approach to the philosophy of science, each human being is described in terms of potentials for being or feeling or experiencing. The more carefully and concretely each person's own potentials are described, the clearer it is that persons differ in the precise meaning of their own potentials. The leaning is toward unique sets of potentials for most persons. Some of these potentials are closely linked to the way the person acts and behaves, while others are described as deeper, with little or no direct connection with the person's actions and behaviors. Whatever the nature or content of the person's own set of potentials for being, feeling, and experiencing, each potential is described as capable of being actualized. While humanistic theorists differ on the question of whether there is any intrinsic force toward actualization, the commonality lies in the capacity for the bringing forth or actualization of these potentials (Bühler and Massarik 1968, Maslow 1968, Rogers 1959).

Of equal importance to inner potentials is the nature of their relationships with one another. When the relationships are integrated, the potentials occur in their good form, and both internal and external relationships may be described as whole, intact, organized, peaceful, harmonious. When the relationships are disintegrated, the potentials occur in their bad form, and both internal and external relationships may be described as disjointed, dead, numb, torn apart, anxious, hollow, disorganized, disjunctive. While relationships may remain disintegrated, the capacity is there for relationships among potentials to be, or to become, integrated.

Basic to humanistic theory is the concept of *Dasein* or "I"-ness or self. This is the center of gravity for one's sense of identity or personhood. To the extent that relationships among potentials are integrated, the *Dasein* is free to move in and out of potentials with graceful ease. However, to the extent that relationships are disintegrated, the *Dasein* is restricted to a few potentials. If relationships among potentials are severely disintegrated, there is essentially no self, and the person exists as an object in the world of other persons.

Whether the external world is described in terms of interpersonal relationships, real objects and things, or institutions and agencies, the human being is assumed to be the one who perceives, organizes, and constructs his or her own meaningful external world (Binswanger 1967, Maslow 1968, May 1967). On the basis of one's own potentials and their relationships, each person's meaningful external world is perceived, organized, and constructed. This may be accomplished by using real parts of the actual world of external reality. It may be accomplished by selective use of external components. It may be accomplished by phenomenological perception. In the same way, human beings work together in dyads and groups to organize and construct complex social phenomena, large-scale objects and things, external agencies and institutions. The worlds in which human beings exist, and the ways in which human beings exist in these worlds, are held as a function of their collective potentials and relationships among potentials.

Furthermore, it is assumed that meaningful external worlds are perceived, organized, constructed, and maintained to serve two conjoint purposes. In one, the external world serves as the medium or situational context for the experiencing or feeling of potentials. Regardless of the nature of the potentials, regardless of whether the accompanying feelings are pleasant or unpleasant, the constructed external world provides a context within which the potentials are experienced or felt. In the second, the external world serves as a context for the experiencing of the nature of the relationships among potentials. If the relationships are integrated and harmonious, or if they are disintegrated and disjointed, the meaningful external world serves as a medium or context for the experiencing of those relationships.

2. Plateaus of Human Development

The humanistic theory of development includes a sequence of three plateaus. The basis for each of these plateaus turns upon the progressive formation and development of the self or *Dasein*. Although theorists are divided on the issue of an assumed set of forces which move the person throughout the course of humanistic development, there is general agreement that a person may remain at any one plateau for any length of time, even throughout his or her entire life.

2.1 The Externalized Self

The development and formation of the first plateau occur predominantly from the first year or so before birth to the first three or four years after birth. On this first plateau, the locus of self is external to the infant or young child, and resides mainly in the parental figures. Accordingly, there is no real internalized self, no genuine *Dasein* or "I"-ness or sense of personal self in the infant or young child. At best, there is a fragmented, illusory sense of self, and, at worst, the infant and young child is an object or pawn of surrounding persons (Laing 1960, Mahrer 1978).

From the work of existential phenomenologists such as Kierkegaard, Heidegger, Husserl, Sartre, Buber, Binswanger and others, the infant is understood as merely another instance of the world building and world construction of parental figures. These parental figures and the infant constitute a system in which the activating and determining forces lie within the parental figures, and not within the infant or young child. Accordingly, it is the parental figures who define the infant, provide it with meaning and significance, encompass it in a role, and serve as its organizing center. On this first plateau, the functional *Dasein* or center of self is external to the physical infant. Whatever potentials may be said to be within the infant, and whatever the nature of their relationships, the determining center of self lies within the parental figures. This means that the parental figures have the predominant hand in defining the very basic foundations of the infant, including the nature of the infant's potentials and the nature of the relationships between and among these potentials.

The human being may remain on this plateau throughout his or her entire life. Although the person may have a fragmentary, rudimentary, or illusory sense of self, the person functions largely as a pawn of external agencies and forces. Such people are defined and determined by parental figures, families, significant other individuals, the attitudes and expectations of others, social agencies and forces, and group pressures and dynamics. Their very identities are determined externally. Not only are their determining forces located in the external world, but their very sense of identity, personhood, and self is determined by external persons and agencies. This is the plateau of the externalized self.

2.2 The Internalized Self

The hallmark of the second plateau is the development of a person's own internalized self. This includes a sense of "I"-ness, of personal identity, a capacity for self-reflection and self-consciousness, a sense of acting upon and effecting and determining his or her own meaningful world. The characteristics of this second plateau have many features in common with other theories of human development.

What is perhaps more distinctive of a humanistic theory of development is the means whereby the person moves from the first to the second plateau. It is here that humanistic theory emphasizes concepts of growth of human potentials, facilitation of actualization tendencies, and the promotion of personal choice. Movement onto the second plateau requires the dissolution of the externalized self, dissolution of the encompassing external world of determining forces and agencies. It requires a letting go and letting be. This is the humanistic emphasis upon individuation, personal growth, and an atmosphere of welcoming facilitation (Bühler and Massarik 1968, Maslow 1968, Rogers 1959, 1970). It also requires an emphasis upon the person's own opportunity to self-reflect, self-experience, and to have a major hand in effecting, building, determining his or her own meaningful world. Accordingly, the infant or child or older person is helped to move onto the second plateau when encompassing persons provide a facilitating atmosphere of letting be, of choice to effect a person's own world, and opportunity to interact with a person's self.

Movement onto the second plateau may occur during infancy, commonly occurs in childhood, or may take place at any time throughout a person's life. Although the development of an internalized self generally occurs in childhood, humanistic theory accepts its occurrence earlier or later, or not at all.

It is on this second plateau that most changes occur distally, behaviorally, interpersonally, and in the modification of a person's world. While the basic personality structure and the internalized self remain fixed, significant changes occur in these other realms. Indeed, it is on this second plateau that changes take place which are ordinarily referred to as maturation and growth, aging and development, cognitive and affective change, psychosocial and biopsychological development. Yet, from the perspective of humanistic theory, all of these changes represent movement along the second plateau.

2.3 The Integrating and Actualizing Self

A third plateau represents the valued pinnacle of humanistic development. The hallmark of the third plateau is the giving up or letting go of the internalized self, and the ultimate attainment of a qualitatively new integrating and actualizing self (Binswanger 1967, Maslow 1968, May 1967).

For a person to let go of his or her internalized self is a courageous and effortful achievement, one which has been attained by few persons. It calls for a radical expansion of consciousness, a disengagement from a person's own continuing, substantive personhood and identity, and a profound willingness to allow the extinguishing of the very core of his or her internalized self. Essentially, the person sacrifices the internalized self which he or she is.

The integrating aspect of the new self means that relationships with both the deeper personality processes and also with the constructed external world are char-

acterized by integration. That is, relationships are characterized by welcoming acceptance, by openness, congruence, and transparency, and by I–thou dual modes of relationships (Jourard 1968, Maslow 1968, Rogers 1970). The actualizing aspect of the new self means that there is a gradually unfolding depth and breadth of experiencing; increasingly deeper potentials are experienced, and there is heightened amplitude of experiencing (Binswanger 1967, Maslow 1968, May 1967, Rogers 1970). Both conceptually and in terms of the value system of humanistic theory, the goal is the development of an integrating and actualizing new self which is in continuous unfolding through the complementary processes of integration and actualization.

3. Implications for Counseling and Guidance

Humanistic counseling and guidance are designed to enable the person to move along the plateaus of development. Accordingly, its methods and procedures may be used with infants, children, adolescents, adults, and persons in the older age groups. For infants and children, the aim is to enable the emergence of the internalized self characteristic of the second plateau. Although the counselor may work directly with the infant or child, the emphasis is upon providing parental figures with the methods and procedures for facilitating the emergence of the internalized self. For adolescents and adults, the aim is to enable the person to move in the direction of the third plateau of development, that of an integrating and actualizing new self. There are two axes of changes, two fundamental ways in which change is facilitated. One is by means of experiencing in which the internalized self is progressively replaced by an integrating and actualizing new self through the carrying forward of increasingly deeper experiences. The second is by means of a counselor relationship characterized by integration (e.g., warmth, empathy) and actualization (e.g., encountering, confrontation). By means of the complementary use of these two axes of counseling change, the person moves in the direction of increasing choice and responsibility to be the new self, increasing internal integration, increasing growth and actualization of the deeper personality processes, and increasing choice and responsibility to live in a world which is congruent with this integrating and actualizing new self.

There is a broad family of approaches which includes client-centered counseling, humanistic counseling, existential counseling, logotherapy, feeling-expressive counseling, Gestalt counseling, *Daseinsanalysis*, holistic counseling, encounter counseling, emotional flooding counseling, and experiential counseling, among others.

4. Implications for Child Rearing and Education

In the earliest years, the objectives of both child rearing and education include the following: (a) the infant and young child are to acquire a sense of self, personal identity, self-consciousness. In essence, the child is to move onto the second plateau of human development. (b) The infant and young child are to acquire a basic personality foundation characterized by a high degree of integration and actualization. In essence, the basic personality structure is to be sound, harmonious, well-organized, free of internal disjunctures and disintegrative relationships among its basic parts.

In order to achieve the first objective, the humanistic theory of development is cordial to prenatal programs, early infancy programs, parent education programs, infant and early childhood education programs, and the like. Whether carried out by parents or educators, the programs emphasize enrichment, effectance training, stimulation, cognitive development, physical–motor development, and other means of implementing the development of an independent and autonomous sense of self and personal identity.

In order to achieve the second objective, the priority is on the presence of parental and educational figures who themselves are in the process of movement onto the third plateau of human development, that is, who are integrating and actualizing persons. Accordingly, the humanistic theory of development calls for parental figures being provided with maximum opportunity to reach the third plateau of human development, and for educators who likewise are attaining this third plateau.

With regard to formal education, the humanistic approach is divided into two wings. One is characterized by the intent to humanize education in accord with humanistic values, philosophy, and theory. Prominent contributors include Combs, Kelley, Ojemann, Maslow, and Rogers. This wing seeks to emphasize the student's own choice, self-worth, interpersonal skills, pacing education according to the student's own emergent needs and rate of growth, carrying forward of the student's own array of potentials, personalized learning, and sensitivity to the human being who is the student. This wing sets itself in opposition to group norms, lock-step marching through school, externally imposed standards, the loss of individuality, the acquisition of brick-upon-brick of knowledge, learning through reward and punishment, education without personal human growth.

The other wing of humanistic approach regards educational institutions as the conjoint construction of collective human beings. To the extent that educational institutions are comprised of persons on the first and second plateaus of human development, the nature and content of these institutions reflect the collective nature and content of those persons. To the extent that educational institutions are comprised of persons on the third plateau of human development, these institutions will be characterized by integration and by actualization. As the field of education includes an increasing proportion of persons on this third plateau, there will occur cordial and concomitant changes in educational methods, procedures, systems, philosophy, administration, and atmosphere.

Bibliography

Binswanger L 1967 *Being-in-the-world: Selected Papers of Ludwig Binswanger.* Harper, New York

Bühler C, Massarik F (eds.) 1968 *The Course of Human Life: A Study of Goals in the Humanistic Perspective.* Springer, New York

Jourard S M 1968 *Disclosing Man to Himself.* Van Nostrand Reinhold, New York

Laing R D 1960 *The Divided Self: A Study of Sanity and Madness.* Tavistock, London

Mahrer A R 1978 *Experiencing: A Humanistic Theory of Psychology and Psychiatry.* Brunner/Mazel, New York

Maslow A H 1968 *Toward a Psychology of Being.* Van Nostrand Reinhold, New York

May R 1967 *Psychology and the Human Dilemma.* Van Nostrand Reinhold, New York

Rogers C R 1959 A theory of therapy, personality, and interpersonal relationships as developed in the client-centered framework. In: Koch S (ed.) 1959 *Psychology: A Study of a Science*, Vol. 3. McGraw-Hill, New York, pp. 184–256

Rogers C R 1970 *On Becoming a Person.* Houghton Mifflin, Boston, Massachusetts.

Attribution Theory of Human Development

D. Bar-Tal

Attribution theory is the term given to the various theories concerned with the study of how people in everyday life figure out what causes their own behaviors and that of others, and what causes events. Social psychologists have typically conceptualized the attribution process as one in which a naive person first observes a behavior or an event and then on the basis of past experience, available information, and/or motivational tendency forms a cognition called attribution about why an event or a behavior occurred. Attributions are considered to be necessary for the understanding, organization, and formation of meaningful perspectives about myriad events which people observe every day. Furthermore, the main tenet of attribution theory is that individuals' emotional, cognitive, and behavioral reactions are based on their causal explanations of why people behave the way they do. This assumption implies that attribution theorists believe that individuals react in accordance with a way they perceive and understand their world.

Attribution theory grew out of the area of person perception. But, whereas person perception deals with the description of the stimulus person, attribution theory focuses on the loci of causality of the person's behavior. Nevertheless, both areas assume that the outcome of perception or attribution is subjective. The contributions to attribution theory have focused on four major issues: (a) What are the antecedents of an attribution? (b) What are the contents of the attribution process? (c) What are the processes through which people make attributions? and (d) What are the consequences of the attributions? During the 1970s the study of attribution became one of the central areas of investigation in social psychology. This growing up occurred since the process of attribution has been related to a wide range of psychological functioning—from interpretation of internal states including perception of emotion, freedom, physiological arousal, and attitudes to strategic choices in interpersonal conflict setting and evaluation of help giving. Moreover, principles of attribution theory have been utilized to analyze different psychological phenomena such as aggression, attraction, moral judgment, learned helplessness, or close relationships (see Harvey et al. 1976, 1977, 1981).

At present, attribution theory consists mostly of a series of fragmented sets of explanations or descriptions pertaining to specific cases of attributions (Kelley and Michele 1980). In this respect the term "attribution theory" may be misleading, since a general inclusive theory has yet to appear. The pioneering work by Heider (1958) and the later works by Jones and his colleagues (Jones and Davis 1965, Jones and McGillis 1976) and by Kelley (1967, 1972a, 1972b) are considered among the most influential contributions to the study of attributions.

1. Naive Psychology of Heider

Fritz Heider is considered to be the father of attribution theory. He was born in 1896 in Vienna, Austria. He studied with several of the major Gestalt psychologists in Germany, and this Gestalt influence is evident in his work. He came to the United States in 1930 and spent many years arguing in vain against the prevailing behavioral perspective within American psychology. First in a paper on phenomenological causality in 1944 and then in an extensive discussion on the phenomenology of social perception published in a book (1958), Heider laid the foundations for many of the basic concepts in attribution theory. His analysis is phrased in commonsense language, and Heider calls his psychology naive because it is based on the phenomenology of the lay person. It is possible to identify three fundamental assumptions that guided Heider's naive psychology of attribution (Schneider et al. 1979). The first is that an adequate understanding of a person's behavior is contingent on the description of how this person perceives and describes his or her social world. Second, Heider assumes that people desire to predict and control their environment. People want to be able to anticipate the effects that their own and others' behavior will have on other people, on the environment, and on themselves. This goal can be achieved if people are able to interpret

and infer the causal antecedents of behaviors. Third, Heider believes that there are some basic similarities between object and person perception. Predictability in the social world is achieved by the same processes that are involved in perception of the physical world. For both cases, people look for enduring or dispositional properties in others to explain particular behavior.

Central to Heider's theoretical position is the proposition that people perceive events as being caused and that the causal locus can be either in the actor or in the environment. In Heider's analysis, an action outcome or effect is perceived to be an additive function of the effective environmental force and the effective personal force. Personal force is seen as a multiplicative function of the actor's power and motivation. According to Heider, power is determined primarily by ability, although other characteristics may affect a person's power. The motivational factor refers to a person's intention (what they are trying to do) and exertion (how hard they are trying to do something). One of the most important decisions the perceiver makes is an estimate of the extent to which the internal rather than the environmental force was responsible for the effects of a person's actions. But Heider further suggests that individuals go beyond the person–environment discrimination to differentiate between personal and impersonal causality. Personal causality refers to those instances of internal causality when a person intentionally produces an outcome. Impersonal causality refers to externally caused effects and to effects that are caused by a person unintentionally. The intentions of the person are important aspects of the perceiver's attribution.

In his theorizing, Heider assumed that lay persons can rationally analyze the causes of their own and others' behaviors. However, he pointed out that sometimes people make attributions that are based on insufficient information or on inadequate analysis of information, or they reflect the person's own psychological needs and motivations as opposed to an objective and logical assessment of available information. The contribution by Heider represents a profound set of observations based on brilliant arm-chair insights about commonsense attributional behavior. Though it has not served as a basis for much empirical work, it had immense influence on more systematic theorizing on attribution by Jones and his colleagues, Kelley, Bem, Weiner, and others whose works have provided bases for specific predictions regarding attributional reactions.

2. Theory of Correspondent Inferences

Jones and Davis (1965) entered their attributional ideas into the realm of person perception: how the perceiver tries to infer what effect the actor intended to produce with his or her acts and how those inferred intentions are used to infer dispositional properties of the actor. In making these inferences, individuals tend to identify different action alternatives that the actor did not choose and compare their possible effects with the effects of the chosen action. The perceiver sorts through those effects of the chosen action which would not have occurred if the actor had chosen any other alternative action. The perceiver assumes that, on the one hand, the actor wanted to avoid the negative noncommon effects of the unchosen alternatives, but on the other hand, the actor especially wanted to achieve the positive noncommon effects of the chosen action. The negative noncommon effects of the unchosen alternatives plus the positive noncommon effects of the chosen action provide much information which serves as a basis for attributing dispositions. In this case, the observer can be to a large extent certain that the actor's behavior reflected an underlying disposition, that is, there is correspondence of inference. To illustrate the process described above, it is possible to consider the case of the teacher inferring why the very good high-school senior has applied to a mediocre college in the vicinity. The teacher may decide that the student could apply to the best colleges in the country which will require much effort in comparison to the selected college. In addition, the selected college enables the student to be close to his or her home. Since mediocre colleges are in other parts of the country as well, the teacher may infer that the student is very attached to his or her family and, therefore, wanted to choose a college close to home. Two factors increase an individual's tendency to make dispositional attributions: (a) hedonic relevance, which refers to the extent to which a person's actions are rewarding or costly to the perceived; and (b) personalism, which refers to the perceived intentionality of a person's actions to the perceiver.

In a more recent theoretical paper, Jones and McGillis (1976) have made some additions to correspondent inference theory. They stress that correspondence will be increased to the extent that behavior departs from what the perceiver expects the stimulus person to do. According to Jones and McGillis, there are two general sources of expectations about others. Category-based expectancies are based on an individual's knowledge about what particular kinds of people are like, similar to the process of stereotyping. Target-based expectancies are gained from knowledge about a particular actor.

3. Covariation Model and Causal Schemata Model

Two particularly influential models were suggested by Kelley (1967, 1972a, 1972b). While the first model, the covariation model, deals with cases in which the perceiver has information regarding the event, or behavior, the second model, the causal schemata model, deals with cases of a single observation with little information.

The first model (Kelley 1967) uses the principle of covariation which states that the effect is attributed to a cause which is present when the effect occurs and is absent when the effect does not occur. This principle

implies temporal contiguity. The notion of covariation was used to examine variations in effect with respect to entities, persons, time, and modalities of interaction with the entity. Presenting his covariation model, Kelley argued that people often make causal attributions as if they were analyzing data patterns by means of analysis of variance, a statistical technique of examining the effect of an independent variable on a dependent variable. On the basis of this technique, Kelley theorized the conditions under which individuals attribute the causes of an event to the person or to the environment. Specifically, he suggested that people assess causality for a particular behavior by using four criteria more or less automatically and simultaneously. They check (a) distinctiveness across entities (was the response made uniquely to this entity and not to others?); (b) consensus (was the response made uniquely by this person, or did others respond similarly?); (c) consistency over time (was the response made consistently over time?), and (d) consistency over modality (was the response made consistently across different modalities of interaction with the entity?). Kelley hypothesized that attribution to the environment rather than to the person requires that the actor respond differentially for different entities, that the actor respond consistently over time and modalities, and that the person's response be in agreement with other people's response to this entity.

This analysis suggests that individuals act like scientists examining the various possible causes for a given effect. They look for a systematic pattern of relation and infer cause and effect relationship from those patterns. However, while the analysis of variance is appropriate for certain cases in which the person conducts a complete causal analysis on a basis of multiple observations, individuals do not always make attributions in this way. Often the individuals have a small sample of data and incomplete data patterns from a single observation. Under these circumstances individuals use more simplistic principles in their attribution process. Kelley (1972a) suggested that in these situations individuals use their causal schemata to infer causality.

A causal schema is a conception of the manner in which two or more causes relate to a particular kind of effect. A causal schema is learned, stored in the memory, and then activated by environmental cues. It answers the attributor's need for economical and fast attributional analysis under situations offering limited information. Causal schemata allow causal sense to be made of the world, and they provide stability and organization to the perceived world. Examples of causal schemata are the multiple-sufficient scheme and the multiple-necessary scheme. The first one indicates that the presence of two or more causes are sufficient for the occurrence of the effect, and the second one implies that several causes are necessary for the effect to occur. Some of the schemas can be formalized in two principles. The discounting principle implies that if an individual perceives several possible causes for the actor's act and all of them are plausible, then he or she is less confident about which cause produced the effect (multiple-sufficient schema). The augmentation principle implies that if there exists an inhibitory cause which prevents the effect from occurring, then the facilitative cause is perceived as very effective, if the effect occurs despite the inhibitory cause (compensatory schema).

4. Self-perception Theory

Bem (1972) has suggested that a person's internal states, such as attitudes, beliefs, or emotions are not directly experienced, but may be arrived at via an attribution process similar in kind whereby the individual infers the internal states of another person. Calling this process self-perception, Bem posited that in situations in which internal cues are weak, ambiguous, or uninterpretable, individuals are in the same position as an outside observer and, therefore, have to rely on external cues to infer own internal states. This theory is in startling contradiction to the usual practice in psychology of assuming that behavior is a consequence of awareness as reflected in attitudes, cognitions, or emotions. In this conception, people are strictly information processors without any motivational drives in their examination of their behavior.

5. Biases and Errors

Although attribution theorists have compared individuals to naive scientists who, for the most part, make systematic use of available information in their attempts to explain their own or another person's behavior, they have also acknowledged a possibility of biases and errors. In recent years empirical research has shown that attributions are often affected by systematic biases and errors. This line of research is based on assumptions that there exist known criteria of valid attributional inference and that there exist psychological factors that bias human attributional inferences from such criteria.

It has been suggested that the various biases of attributional inference be classified as either motivational or cognitive in origin. Motivational biases are characterized by a tendency to form and hold beliefs that serve the individual's needs and desires. Individuals are said to avoid drawing inferences they find threatening, unpleasant, or incongruent and to prefer inferences that are satisfying, pleasing, or need congruent. Depending on the momentary salience of different needs, such motivational influences could presumably yield judgmental biases and errors. A number of motivational biases have been indicated. For example, investigators have argued that individuals are motivated to enhance and protect their egos. Thus, in situations of success they readily attribute it to themselves, but they tend to externalize failure. Also, it has been suggested that individuals are motivated to organize the perceived social events in a predictable and controllable manner. Thus, they tend to overestimate their control over events and to underestimate the role of uncontrollable factors.

Cognitive biases originate in human limitations to process information. These limitations are reflected in the strategies which direct people's attention to some types of information and hypotheses rather than to other types. As a result, individuals underestimate or disregard information relevant to the judgment in question. An example of cognitive bias occurs when individuals rely on information that is salient or available to them at the time they make their judgments. Thus, people may use information that is not representative of the population as a whole, tend to ignore consensus information of how other people act in the same situation, or tend to overestimate the importance of dispositional characteristics in others' behavior. With regard to the latter bias, a theory by Jones and Nisbett (1972) is of special interest. They pointed out that people tend to attribute their own actions to the constraints of the situation but attribute the behavior of others to their personalities. Two main reasons were identified for this bias. One reason is that actors have different information available than to observers. Actors know about their own past history and therefore have more consistency and distinctiveness data available to them, whereas observers typically have only consensus data. Another reason refers to differences in the salience of the various forms of information. The actors view their behavior in the context of their past behavior, so their variations in response to different situations are highly salient, making the possible environmental cause more salient. In contrast, observers view the behavior of any particular actor in the context of how his or her behavior differs from the behavior of other people in that same situation. Therefore, the idiosyncratic factors in the actor are highly salient in explaining this behavior.

6. A Theory of Lay Epistemology

Of special interest for attribution theory is a theory of lay epistemology by Kruglanski (1980). In this theory Kruglanski has attempted to formulate a general framework that allows the various attributional models to be considered in common theoretical terms. According to lay epistemology, attribution making is knowledge-seeking behavior which follows a particular sequence, referred to as the epistemic process. Specifically, Kruglanski suggests that the epistemic process consists of two phases: problem formulation and problem resolution. In the phase of problem formulation the individual is motivated to gain knowledge regarding a specific question, for example, a question about cause. In the phase of problem resolution the individual deduces his or her inferences from certain premises in which he or she already happens to believe. This phase is governed by the principle of logical consistency. The epistemic process may be affected by different needs and/or desires of the individual as well as by the availability of hypotheses and/or information.

Attribution theory constitutes a special case of the epistemic question. A causal inference is rendered exactly in the same way as any other inferences, by the principle of logical consistency. According to lay epistemology theory, various attributional models focus on specific cases of causal inferences without extracting a general principle.

7. Development of Attribution Inference

The study of causal thinking is not new in developmental psychology. Piaget (1930) devoted considerable effort to understanding children's causal thinking. But it was the appearance of attribution theorizing which provided the impetus for empirical research regarding the development of causal perception. It seems obvious that from the first years of life, children infer causality. Their learning about cause–effect comes from two sources. First, agents of socialization communicate cause–effect relationships to children. Second, children themselves observe repeated reoccurrence of events from which they infer cause–effect relationship. But, in spite of the early use of attributions, only in the late childhood do children become capable of comprehending the use of various principles of attribution.

Research has shown that young children are able to attribute an effect on a basis of a single observation. They attribute causality to those factors that are temporally contiguous, spatially proximal, physically similar, and antecedent to the effect. Studies have indicated that from as early an age as 3 years, children can identify causes on the basis of temporal order (covariation principle) as long as the task is simple, familiar, and does not require advanced verbal skills. The use of temporal order precedes the use of spatial contiguity as a basis for causal inference. Specifically, the use of the covariance principle deteriorates in the following situations: (a) when children observe a sequence of events that contains more than one cause–effect instance, (b) when the information is presented in a simple summary form, and (c) when a temporal delay between the cause and effect occurs. Also, they are willing to accept imperfect cause–effect covariation. In addition, it has been found that young children can combine multiple causes when predicting an effect and have less difficulty using an augmenting principle than in using a discounting principle. It is only during the first five years in school that the described difficulties seem to disappear and older children begin to apply various attributional principles with greater reliability and across a large set of task conditions (Sedlak and Kurtz 1981).

On the basis of empirical studies, three levels of development of attribution making have been identified. It has been found that at a very early age children behave as if they comprehend various principles before they can make appropriate judgments using self-report techniques. At the next level, children make schema displaying consistent causal judgment before they can

explain the attributional logic underlying these responses. Finally, at the age of 10 or 11, children become able to articulate the underlying attributional principles (Kassin 1981).

8. Application of Attribution Theory to Education

Because the attribution process is believed to be an integral part of many of the most significant aspects of people's lives, its principles have been applied to the analysis of various real-life situations, ranging from a jury deliberating about whether to attribute the crime to circumstances or to the defendant's disposition to a teacher puzzling about whether the student failed because of lack of ability or lack of trying (e.g., Frieze et al. 1979, Antaki and Breisin 1982). Two attributional models applied to education have instigated much empirical research. The first model deals with the relationship between attribution and achievement-related behavior; the second model focuses on the development of intrinsic motivation by students.

8.1 Attributional Model of Achievement-related Behavior

A model which has a direct implication for education is Weiner's attributional model of achievement-related behavior (Weiner et al. 1972, 1974). A classroom is a place where students' achievements are constantly evaluated and, therefore, the causal explanation of why students have failed or succeeded is an important question. The answer determines to a large extent the behavior of students as well as of teachers. According to Weiner, causal perceptions of success and failure mediate between the antecedent conditions and achievement-related behavior (Weiner 1974, Weiner et al. 1972).

Specifically, in his most recent formulation, Weiner (1979) has suggested that individuals use a variety of causes to explain their success or failure on achievement tasks. These causes can be classified along three dimensions. One dimension, locus of causality, differentiates the causes in terms of their internality/externality. While some causes, such as ability, effort, or mood, might be considered internal because they might be believed to originate within the person, other causes, such as luck, home conditions, or task difficulty, might be considered external because they might be believed to originate outside the person. The second dimension differentiates causes in terms of their stability over time. While some causes, such as mood, effort, or luck, may be considered unstable because they may be believed to fluctuate over time, other causes, such as ability, task difficulty, or home conditions may be considered as stable since they may be believed not to change over time. The third dimension differentiates causes in terms of their controllability. While some causes, such as effort, attention, or others' help, may be believed to be under the volitional control of the person, other causes, such as mood, luck, or ability, may be believed not to be under the volitional control of the person.

The above described dimensions have important consequences. They are related to individuals' cognitive reactions or expectations regarding future outcomes, affective reactions related to self-esteem, and behavioral reactions of achievement-related behavior. Weiner (1974, 1979) has postulated that expectancy for future success is determined by the stability of the causes. Ascription of an outcome to unstable causes produces greater shifts in expectancy of achievement to the desired outcome than does ascription to stable causes. Failure at an achievement task attributed to unstable causes may result in expectations for eventual success, since unstable causes might change. Failure due to stable causes is expected to continue, since these causes are believed to remain. Similarly, if success was attributed to stable causes, continued success would be expected.

The locus of causality dimension is an important determinant of affective reactions. Individuals who attribute their success to internal causes experience affects of pride, competence, confidence, and satisfaction, while individuals who attribute failure to internal causes experience feelings of guilt and resignation.

Of special interest is the link between causal perception of success or failure and achievement-related behavior. There is a substantial amount of evidence indicating that causal perception of success and failure influences the individual's persistence, intensity, and choice behavior of achievement tasks. Individuals who tend to attribute their failure to unstable-controllable causes, such as effort, tend to persist long in failure situations. This attribution of a failure enables them to believe that there is a possibility of modifying the outcome in the future. Attribution of a failure to stable-uncontrollable causes does not leave the possibility of changing the outcome in the future and, therefore, there is no reason to persist. The belief in unstable-controllable causes, such as effort, causes the person to assume that the outcome depends on will. Therefore, these individuals perform with great intensity on achievement tasks. On the other hand, the belief in stable or uncontrollable causes, such as ability or mood, does not motivate the person to perform with intensity, since there is no belief in having control over the causes of success or failure. Finally, it was found that individuals tend to prefer to perform tasks that are compatible with their causal perception. For example, students who generally attribute their achievement outcome to ability are likely to choose tasks in which competence is requisite to outcome. Conversely, students who tend to attribute their success to luck prefer tasks which depend on chance and avoid tasks requiring competence.

Finally, on the basis of Weiner's model (Weiner 1974) it was suggested that two general categories of antecedents influence causal perception of individuals: per-

sonal dispositions and available information. The personal dispositions category consists of three subcategories: (a) personality tendencies; (b) demographic influences; and (c) causal schemata. The available information consists of four subcategories: (a) own performance; (b) others' performance; (c) constraints and nature of the achievement task; (d) others' influence.

Recently, Bar-Tal (1979) extended Weiner's model to explain interpersonal interaction in the classroom. According to Bar-Tal, teachers as well as students make attributions regarding the successes and failures of their students. Thus, in the same way that students' causal perception of their own successes or failures is related to their achievement-related behavior, the teachers' causal perception of their students' successes or failures is related to their behavior towards their students through expectations regarding students' future achievements. Furthermore, the model suggests that teachers' behavior greatly influences students causal perception of their academic achievement, whereas students' achievement-related behaviors influence teachers' causal perception of students' academic outcomes.

8.2 An Attributional Model of Intrinsic Motivation

Lepper and Defoe (1979) applied the attributional model of intrinsic motivation to the classroom setting. This model has been based on Bem's (1972) self-perception theory. According to Lepper and Defoe, students in the classroom make attributions regarding reasons for engaging in various activities. If a student who is engaged in an activity perceives his or her actions to be controlled by salient and powerful extrinsic contingencies such as a promise of tangible reward or the teacher's surveillance, he or she will be likely to attribute his or her behavior to those extrinsic factors. But if such extrinsic constraints are not salient or are insufficient to explain this engagement in the activity, the student will attribute his or her behavior to intrinsic factors. This conception implies that inappropriate use of tangible rewards in the classroom may have detrimental effects on performance and subsequent interest in the task. Offers of rewards in such situations may decrease students' intrinsic motivation to engage in this activity.

Bibliography

Antaki C, Breisin C (eds.) 1982 *Attributions and Psychological Change: A Guide to the Use of Attribution Theory in the Clinic and Classroom.* Academic Press, London
Bar-Tal D 1979 Interactions of teachers and pupils. In: Frieze I H, Bar-Tal D, Carroll J S (eds.) 1979 *New Approaches to Social Problems: Application of Attribution Theory.* Jossey-Bass, San Francisco, California
Bem D J 1972 Self-perception theory. In: Berkowitz L (ed.) 1972 *Advances in Experimental Social Psychology,* Vol. 6. Academic Press, New York
Frieze I H, Bar-Tal D, Carroll J S (eds.) 1979 *New Approaches to Social Problems: Application of Attribution Theory.* Jossey-Bass, San Francisco, California

Harvey J H, Ickes W J, Kidd R F (eds.) 1976 *New Directions in Attribution Research,* Vol. 1. Erlbaum, Hillsdale, New Jersey

Harvey J H, Ickes W J, Kidd R F (eds.) 1981 *New Directions in Attribution Research,* Vol. 3. Erlbaum, Hillsdale, New Jersey

Harvey J H, Smith W P 1977 *Social Psychology: An Attributional Approach.* Mosby, St. Louis, Missouri

Heider F 1958 *The Psychology of Interpersonal Relations.* Wiley, New York

Jones E E, Davis K E 1965 From acts to dispositions: The attribution process in person perception. In: Berkowitz L (ed.) 1965 *Advances in Experimental Social Psychology,* Vol. 2. Academic Press, New York

Jones E E, Kanouse D E, Kelley H H, Nisbett R E, Valins S, Weiner B (eds.) 1972 *Attribution: Perceiving the Causes of Behavior.* General Learning Press, Morristown, New Jersey

Jones E E, McGillis D 1976 Correspondent inferences and the attribution cube: A comparative reappraisal. In: Harvey J H, Ickes W H, Kidd R F (eds.) 1976 *New Directions in Attribution Research,* Vol. 1. Erlbaum, Hillsdale, New Jersey, pp. 389–420

Jones E E, Nisbet R E 1972 The actor and the observer: Divergent perceptions of the causes of behavior. In: Jones E E, Kanouse D E, Kelley H H, Nisbett R E, Valins S, Weiner B (eds.) 1972 *Attribution: Perceiving the Causes of Behavior.* General Learning Press, Morristown, New Jersey, pp. 79–94

Kassin S M 1981 From "laychild" to "layman": Developmental causal attribution. In: Brehm S S, Kassin S M, Gibbons F X (eds.) 1981 *Developmental Social Psychology: Theory and Research.* Oxford University Press, New York

Kelley H H 1967 Attribution theory in social psychology. In: Levine D (ed.) 1967 *Nebraska Symposium on Motivation,* Vol. 15. University of Nebraska Press, Lincoln, Nebraska

Kelley H H 1972a Causal schemata and the attribution process. In: Jones E E, Kanouse D E, Kelley H H, Nisbett R E,

Valins S, Weiner B (eds.) 1972 *Attribution: Perceiving the Causes of Behavior.* General Learning Press, Morristown, New Jersey, pp. 151–74

Kelley H H 1972b Attribution in social interaction. In: Jones E E, Kanouse D E, Kelley H H, Nisbett R E, Valins S, Weiner B (eds.) 1972 *Attribution: Perceiving the Causes of Behavior.* General Learning Press, Morristown, New Jersey, pp. 1–26

Kelley H H, Michele J L 1980 Attribution Theory and Research. *Annu. Rev. Psychol.* 31: 457–501

Kruglanski A W 1980 Lay epistemo-logic-process and contents: Another look at attribution theory. *Psychol. Rev.* 87: 70–87

Lepper M R, Defoe J 1979 Incentives, constraints, and motivation in the classroom: An attributional analysis. In: Frieze I H, Bar-Tal D, Carroll J S (eds.) 1979 *New Approaches to Social Problems: Application of Attributional Theory.* Jossey-Bass, San Francisco, California

Piaget J 1930 *The Child's Conception of Physical Causality.* Routledge and Kegan Paul, London

Schneider D J, Hastorf A H, Ellsworth P C 1979 *Person Perception,* 2nd edn. Addison-Wesley, Reading, Massachusetts

Sedlak A J, Kurtz S T 1981 A review of children's use of causal inference principle. *Child Dev.* 52: 759–84

Shaver K G 1975 *Introduction to Attribution Processes.* Winthrop, Cambridge, Massachusetts

Weiner B 1974 *Achievement Motivation and Attribution Theory.* General Learning Corporation, Morristown, New Jersey

Weiner B 1979 A theory of motivation for some classroom experiences. *J. Educ. Psychol.* 71: 3–25

Weiner B, Frieze I, Kukla A, Reed L, Rest S, Rosenbaum R M 1972 Perceiving the causes of success and failure. In: Jones E E, Kanouse D E, Kelley H H, Nisbett R E, Valins S, Weiner B (eds.) 1972 *Attribution: Perceiving the Causes of Behavior.* General Learning Press, Morristown, New Jersey, pp. 95–120

Developmental Tasks

R. M. Thomas

One way to conceptualize the process of human development is as a succession of problems which the growing person must solve in order to progress from one stage of life to the next. These problems, faced by virtually everyone within a given social context, have been called developmental tasks.

Since the early 1930s, when the notion of developmental tasks was introduced in the United States by a group of progressive educators, several versions of tasks have been devised and applied to the fields of child rearing, education, and counseling. Perhaps the best-known version is Havighurst's (1953), which divides the life span into six stages and proposes between six and ten tasks for each growth period. For the period of infancy and early childhood, encompassing the first six years of life, Havighurst defined the nine tasks of learning to walk, to take solid foods, to talk, to control the elimination of body wastes, to recognize sex differences and sexual modesty, to achieve physiological

stability, to form simple concepts of social and physical reality, to relate oneself to family members and other people, and to distinguish right from wrong and develop a conscience.

For middle childhood, covering ages 6 through 12, Havighurst identified the nine tasks of learning physical skills needed for ordinary games, building wholesome attitudes toward oneself as a growing organism, getting along with agemates, learning an appropriate masculine or feminine social role, developing literacy and numeracy, learning concepts needed in everyday living, developing a conscience and set of values, achieving personal independence, and building attitudes toward social groups and institutions.

Havighurst's 10 tasks of adolescence include achieving more mature relations with agemates of both sexes; adopting a masculine or feminine social role; accepting one's physique and using it effectively; achieving emotional independence of parents and other adults;

attaining assurance of economic independence; selecting and preparing for a vocation; preparing for marriage and family life; developing intellectual skills needed for civic competence; achieving socially responsible behavior; and acquiring a set of values as a guide to behavior.

The stage of early adulthood was assigned the eight tasks of selecting a mate; learning to live with a marriage partner; starting a family; rearing children; managing a home; starting an occupation; assuming civic responsibility; and finding a congenial social group.

The seven tasks of middle age were those of achieving adult social responsibility; maintaining an economic standard of living; assisting teenage children to become responsible and happy adults; developing adult leisure-time activities; relating oneself to one's spouse as a person; accepting the physiological changes of middle age; and adjusting to ageing parents.

For old age Havighurst identified the six tasks of adjusting to decreased physical strength and health; adjusting to retirement; accepting the death of one's spouse; affiliating with one's age group; meeting social and civic obligations; and maintaining satisfactory physical living arrangements.

Developmental tasks are not identical for all societies. Because cultures differ in form and complexity, the list of tasks identified for one society can differ from the list identified for another. Furthermore, the items in a particular list are determined to some extent by the personal value system of the people who have prepared them. Havighurst (1953 p. 26) stated that the list he proposed was "based on American democratic values seen from a middle-class point of view, with some attempt at pointing out the variations for lower-class and upper-class Americans."

Some lists are brief, with relatively few tasks specified for each age level. A European author, Philippe Muller (1969), has cited four tasks for the period of infancy: coordination of eyes and movements; ingestion of solid food; acquisition of initial language skills; and achievement of toilet training. For the primary-school child, Muller has listed ten problems to be solved: those of growing self-awareness; achieving physiological stability; forming simple concepts about physical and social reality; developing concepts of good and evil while developing a conscience; communicating with agemates; assuming an appropriate sex role; mastering physical skills needed to play games; learning literacy and numeracy; achieving a positive attitude toward one's own development; and learning concepts needed for everyday living.

For adolescence Muller has proposed the six tasks of recognizing one's limitations; developing new human relationships; attaining emotional independence from parents; selecting a life partner; choosing a career; and forming a personal philosophy of life.

Other theorists' lists of tasks are more detailed at each age level. Tryon and Lilienthal (1950 pp. 77–89) composed such a more complex scheme by proposing 10 categories of behavior, then specifying one or more developmental tasks at each of five stages of growth between infancy and late adolescence. The 10 categories are those of achieving appropriate dependence–independence relationships with other people; achieving a suitable pattern of giving and receiving affection; relating to changing social groups; developing a conscience; learning a suitable socio-biological sex role; adjusting to a changing body; learning new patterns of motor movement; understanding and controlling the physical world; developing a symbol system and conceptual abilities; and relating one's self to the cosmos.

The manner in which Tryon and Lilienthal defined specific tasks at each stage of growth for the 10 categories can be illustrated with their third category, that of the child's relating to changing social groups. At the first stage, the infant faces the task of becoming aware of the difference between things that are alive and things that are inanimate. At the next stage, the young child must adjust to the role within the family that the rest of the family members assign to the child. The older child must clarify the difference between the adult world and the child world and must also learn to get along with groups of agemates. The young adolescent needs to adjust to a changing peer code, and the older adolescent must begin adopting an adult set of social values.

Some writers have not attempted to encompass all major aspects of life in their lists of tasks. Instead, they have limited their attention to a particular facet. An example is Godin's (1971) succession of five developmental tasks in Christian education. The first task consists of the child's discovering Jesus at the center of God's plan in history, an accomplishment that becomes possible only when the child's historical consciousness is awakened at around age 12 or 13. Second is the task of comprehending that Jesus was not simply an historical figure but is a continuing symbol of God's present-day actions. Such comprehension first becomes possible when the adolescent at around age 13 has reached Piaget's formal-operations level of intelligence and thus can grasp the relationship between a material sign (the image of Jesus) and spiritual meanings (the relationship of humans to God).

Godin's third task is that of gradually abandoning a magical or superstitious view of religion during middle adolescence and replacing it with true faith in God's plan. Fourth is the task of progressively leaving behind the notion that moral behavior earns favors from God. This notion is replaced by a growing desire to do good works, because the works are an expression of humanism, without expecting God to provide gifts in proportion to the works performed. The fifth task, to be accomplished in later adolescence and early adulthood, is that of freeing one's Christian beliefs from the parental images of mother and father, images on which childhood beliefs have so depended. Godin has accompanied his five tasks with suggestions for Christian educational practices that depart markedly from the typical teaching strategies currently found in religious education programs.

For child-rearing and educational practice, an important assumption underlying the developmental-task perspective is that if a child is successful in achieving each task, he or she is happy and is approved by society. Furthermore, success builds a sound foundation for accomplishing later tasks. However, the individual who fails with a task can be expected to feel unhappy, will be disapproved by society, and will face difficulty with later tasks (Havighurst 1953 p. 2). As a consequence, parents and educators are expected to recognize the tasks at each age level and to help the growing child or adult accomplish the tasks.

While developmental-task schemes have stimulated relatively little research (Havighurst 1953 pp. 325–6), the schemes have been widely applied in certain curriculum-development projects and in books explaining child development for parents and educators (Bernard 1970, Muller 1969). The relatively popular acceptance of the developmental-task viewpoint is apparently due to the fact that advocates of a task approach have found this viewpoint to offer an easily understood way of describing to parents and educators why children and adults behave as they do at different stages of life.

Bibliography

Bernard H W 1970 *Human Development in Western Culture*, 3rd edn. Allyn and Bacon, Boston, Massachusetts
Godin A 1971 Some developmental tasks in Christian education. In: Strommen M P (ed.) 1971 *Research on Religious Development*. Hawthorn, New York, pp. 109–54
Havighurst R J 1953 *Human Development and Education*. Longman, Green, New York
Muller P H 1969 *The Tasks of Childhood*. McGraw-Hill, New York
Tryon C, Lilienthal J 1950 Developmental tasks: the concept and its importance. In: *Fostering Mental Health in Our Schools 1950*. Association for Supervision and Curriculum Development, Washington, DC

Ipsative Theory of Human Development

L. Garduque, J. V. Lerner, and R. M. Lerner

Psychologists and educators may seek generalizations or laws of at least one of two types. Nomothetic laws are those that apply to all people; they are believed to pertain to the general human being. Idiographic laws are those that apply to the individual; they are highly specific generalizations, describing or explaining those principles applicable to a given individual. Whereas analyses of behavior derived from nomothetic concerns compare one individual with one or several others, analyses derived from idiographic interests compare the individual with himself or herself. That is, idiographic interests lead to ipsative, or intraindividual, analyses. For example, rather than ascertaining how a person's values for education, sports, family, and religion differ from those of his or her peers, in an ipsative analysis one would assess how much the individual valued each of these concerns. Thus, in an ipsative developmental analysis one is concerned with depicting the individual's attribute repertoire and/or attribute interrelation within and across time (Emmerich 1968, Lerner 1976).

The rationale for an ipsative analysis is that the variables providing the bases of human functioning coalesce in each person in a unique way. As such, laws of behavioral and psychological functioning that apply only to groups may have no direct meaning for a given individual's functioning, although they may constrain that individual's social interpersonal behaviors.

Psychologists from diverse theoretical perspectives have argued for the need for ipsative analyses of human behavior. For example, the need for such analyses may derive from an individual's unique genotype and genotype–environment interaction (Hirsch 1970), from the person's individual reinforcement history (Bijou 1976, Bijou and Baer 1961), or from the person's unique temperament–attribute interrelation (Thomas and Chess 1977) or personality organization (Allport 1937, Block 1971). It should be noted, however, that while all such theorists would agree that ipsative analyses are necessary to describe an individual's functioning, not all would agree that idiographic laws need to be used to account for intraindividual uniqueness. For example, Bijou and Baer (1961) might argue that while each person would have a unique reinforcement history and would therefore have a unique response repertoire, the laws governing the acquisition of any of the responses (laws of conditioning) and applicable to all organisms.

When ipsative analyses are used in developmental research the two key features of an ipsative analysis (the identification of the person's attribute repertoire and the specification of the attribute interrelation) become more complex. That is, once time becomes a parameter of one's assessments many different instances of the two components of individual uniqueness are possible. At each time of measurement the person's attribute repertoire may change. If the repertoire changes, then so too does the interrelation. Moreover, even if the repertoire remains the same the interrelation may change.

Several methods exist for conducting ipsative developmental analyses. Quantitative techniques include Q-sort methodology (Block 1971), P-technique factor analyses (Baltes et al. 1977, Cattell 1965), and the single subject designs found in the conditioning literature (Baltes et al. 1977). More phenomenological, qualitative approaches exist also. For example, Thomas and Chess (1977) have used a longitudinal series of structured, open-ended clinical interviews to describe each of 133 subjects' repertoire and interrelation of temperamental attributes.

There are both scientific and practical issues limiting the use of ipsative analyses. First, scientifically, theorists differ as to the power of idiographic laws to account for substantial proportions of the variance in behavior development, both absolutely and, especially, in comparison to nomothetic laws. A second scientific issue is that the interpretation of the individual differences described in ipsative analyses is open to debate. Do such individual differences reflect qualitatively unique, individual laws, or only quantitative (and perhaps "error") variation around some more general (group or universal) law? If the former is the case, then both basic research and more applied endeavors of assessment and intervention need to focus primarily on the individual and defer, for secondary analysis, any focus on the group or on general laws. If the latter is the case, then given the practical problems (of cost and time) of designing and implementing plans for separate assessment of every individual, it may be that the appropriate role for basic research would be to remain focused on designing research to assess general laws. Similarly, if the latter is the case, then the same practical problems of cost and time would suggest that those interested in applied issues should be primarily concerned with assessments and interventions aimed at the more general components of human functioning.

These issues regarding ipsative research arise in several areas of psychological and educational research. An exemplary case occurs in literature pertinent to the aptitude-treatment interaction paradigm. This article will now look at this literature in order to illustrate both problems with, and potential uses for, an ipsative approach.

1. The Aptitude–Treatment Interaction Approach

Educational research and practice has led to theories of learning and instruction which have much in common with an ipsative approach. Teachers confront on an everyday basis individual differences and the interactions of these differences with instructional techniques, teaching styles, and learning environments. Indeed, it can be argued that classroom organization and management have as their goal controlling for, and mitigating the effects of individual differences. Researchers, on the other hand, are concerned with identifying and measuring individual differences related to performance on learning tasks.

Interactions of student traits and attributes with instructional variables have only recently undergone systematic study (Cronbach and Snow 1977, Gehlbach 1979). Researchers following this line of inquiry have abandoned the search for the single "best" approach to instruction because it has not been useful in determining

those techniques or strategies to most effectively achieve desired outcomes (Berliner and Cahen 1973). Alternatively, researchers have begun to consider simultaneously the attributes and traits of the learner, the instructional goals to be achieved, and the context in which learning takes place. The paradigm for such research has been termed trait-treatment interaction (Berliner and Cahen 1973), or aptitude-treatment interaction, research (Cronbach 1957). The trait-treatment interaction or aptitude-treatment interaction researcher asks questions related specifically to the design of instructional methods: What works best for whom under what circumstances?

The concepts and ideas of aptitude-treatment interaction research reflect less a clearly defined area of learning and instruction than an approach to research. Traits, attributes, and characteristics assume importance when they modify the relationship between "educational treatments" (all related to instruction, including teacher behaviors and characteristics, materials, method, and content) and performance. An important yet unresolved issue is whether "treatment modifies the relation between trait and performance or whether the trait modifies the relation between treatment and performance" (Berliner and Cahen 1973 p. 66). Thus, the researcher's task involves identification of a set of learner attributes relevant to instruction, and a set of characteristics of instructional methods which may be modified or manipulated to capitalize upon the learners' strengths or to compensate for their weaknesses.

Research which follows the general aptitude-treatment interaction paradigm takes several forms. Studies may be grouped together on the basis of the types of attributes that are examined, for example personality (Gordon and Thomas 1967), ability (Stallings 1975), or status attributes, such as sex or age (Case 1978). Alternatively, studies may be distinguished from one another on whether they were specifically designed to test interaction hypotheses; for example, who benefits the most from structured approaches to instruction (for a review, see Cronbach and Snow 1977). Other studies attempt to prescribe differential educational interventions on the basis of differential diagnosis of learning characteristics (for a review, see Arter and Jenkins 1979). Efforts in curriculum development have also shown a concern for individual differences in manner and rate of learning, such as programmed and computer-assisted instruction (e.g., Resnick et al. 1973).

Since the early 1970s, aptitude-treatment interaction research has flourished, although the initial enthusiasm which greeted the paradigm has quieted somewhat (Cronbach and Snow 1977, Tobias 1976). While there have been some promising aptitude-treatment interaction leads, research has uncovered few replicable interactions that would allow us to specify one mode of instruction for a group of learners with one set of characteristics and an alternative method for learners with different characteristics (Tobias 1982). In the area of special education, for example, Arter and Jenkins

(1979) take researchers and practitioners to task for relying on ability tests to classify and place children when the links between assessment, intervention, and improved achievement have failed to be demonstrated.

One possible explanation for the limited success of aptitude-treatment interaction research is definition and measurement of an appropriate set of learner characteristics (compare with Berliner and Cahen 1973). Some researchers have argued that specification of relevant learner attributes and the development of valid measures of those attributes rests upon analysis of learning tasks and the cognitive processes they demand (Resnick 1981). Working backwards from a model of optimal performance, effective and ineffective strategies may be identified and described. Individual differences may arise in either the frequency with which strategies are employed or the particular strategies comprising a response repertoire. Tobias (1982) advocates directly addressing the question: What are the cognitive activities of the learner and are they meaningfully related to individual difference measures and differences in instructional methods? Whether as a strategy for identifying: (a) spontaneous strategies (Case 1978); (b) potentially unique strategies involved in a specific skilled performance (Resnick et al. 1973); and/or (c) the individual and/or universal laws that may be involved in either (a) or (b), an ipsative analysis may be very fruitful in yielding information about the contribution of individuality to performance.

Other uses of an ipsative approach may be noted. First, while researchers have incorporated some features of an ipsative approach in their analysis of human behavior in educational contexts, they have assumed stability in the attribute repertoire and the attribute interrelations, as well as the treatment over time. A sensitivity to ipsative analysis issues would suggest that such assumptions deserve empirical verification. Thus, when an ipsative approach informs aptitude-treatment interaction research, the term interaction assumes importance beyond the statistical sense. Statistically, interaction refers to a stable relationship—between stable individual differences and stable treatment variables. An ipsative approach alerts us to the possibility that stability may not exist. As noted earlier, attributes, their interrelations, hence their interactions with treatment, and, as a consequence, the treatment itself, may change over time. From a developmental perspective, then, changing individual differences are being dealt with that have a changing relationship to changing treatment variables (Peters and Busch 1977).

In sum, ipsative analytic features would give aptitude-treatment interaction research another significant dimension. The result would be an approach to instructional methods and curriculum design potentially more useful (in terms of educational practice) and more powerful (in the statistical sense) than traditional aptitude-treatment interaction research. Yet, problems emerge when the full implications of an ipsative approach are realized.

The issue of structuring the proper relation between learner and instructional method raises important philosophical questions. Should efforts be channeled toward the creation of alternative settings and the design of innovative instructional techniques? Or should steps be taken to modify or to develop traits which would enable the learner to participate in existing settings and benefit from current instructional methods? Further, the time involved in assessment, evaluation, and planning as prescribed by an ipsative approach raises practical problems of costs. Case (1978) views the issue of cost effectiveness as a matter of specifying the groups of students for whom no other alternative strategy is appropriate (e.g., handicapped individuals) and tasks for which the approach is likely to have the greatest impact. However, Berliner and Cahen (1973) take the position that to make such decisions without consideration of the ethics of the approach is dangerous.

2. Conclusion

Both in the abstract and when applied to a concrete research literature, such as aptitude treatment interaction research, the ipsative approach has several compelling theoretical features (e.g., in regard to the conceptualization of individuality) and yet raises important issues pertinent to implementation. However, scientifically and practically appropriate resolutions to these issues may exist. Scientists favoring either a nomothetic-derived or an idiographic-derived approach to research or intervention do not ordinarily disavow the possibility that both general and specific laws apply to the individual. Indeed, some theorists (Emmerich 1968, Kaplan 1983, Werner 1957) have proposed that it may be possible to merge nomothetic and idiographic ideas in a common, integrative conception, the orthogenetic principle. This principle holds that whenever development occurs it moves from a state of globality, or lack of differentiation, to differentiation, integration, and hierarchic integration. There is some evidence that both relatively short-term and long-term developments follow this principle (Lerner 1976, 1979, Lerner and Busch-Rossnagel 1981, Werner 1957).

If the orthogenetic principle was used to guide a merged nomothetic–idiographic approach to developmental research and intervention, then this would mean that despite the unique contents of the attribute repertoire that might exist for any individual at any point in time, the structural changes in the repertoire would follow a general sequence. As such, research aimed at describing both the contents of the repertoire and the level of hierarchic integration that exists, and interventions aimed at facilitating structural change of any repertoire (if such facilitation is valued by the person and by the intervenor), would be both feasible and appropriate. Through such merged endeavours both the uniqueness of the individual and his or her participation in a common humanity would be preserved.

Bibliography

Allport G W 1937 *Personality: A Psychological Interpretation.* Holt, New York

Arter J, Jenkins J 1979 Differential diagnosis and perspective teaching: A critical assessment. *Rev. Educ. Res.* 49: 517–56

Baltes P B, Reese H W, Nesselroade J R 1977 *Life-span Developmental Psychology: Introduction to Research Methods.* Brooks/Cole, Monterey, California

Berliner D, Cahen L 1973 Trait-treatment interaction and learning. In: Kerlinger K (ed.) 1978 *Review of Research in Education*, Vol. 1. Peacock, Itasca, Illinois

Bijou S W 1976 *Child Development: The Basic Stage of Early Childhood.* Prentice-Hall, Englewood Cliffs, New Jersey

Bijou S W, Baer D M 1961 *Child Development*, Vol. 1: *A Systematic and Empirical Theory.* Appleton-Century-Crofts, New York

Block J 1971 *Lives Through Time.* Bancroft Books, Berkeley, California

Case R 1978 A developmentally based theory and technology of instruction. *Rev. Behav. Res.* 48: 439–63

Cattell R B 1965 *The Scientific Analysis of Personality.* Penguin, Baltimore

Cronbach L 1957 The two disciplines of scientific psychology. *Am. Psychol.* 12: 671–84

Cronbach L 1976 Beyond the two disciplines of scientific psychology. *Am. Psychol.* 30: 116–27

Cronbach L, Snow R 1977 *Aptitudes and Instructional Methods.* Irvington, New York

Emmerich W 1968 Personality development and concepts of structure. *Child Dev.* 39: 671–90

Gehlbach R 1979 Individual differences: Implications for educational theory, research and innovation. *Educ. Res.* 8: 8–14

Gordon E, Thomas A 1967 Children's behavioral style and the teacher's appraisal of their intelligence. *J. Sch. Psychol.* 5: 292–300

Hirsch J 1970 Behavior-genetic analysis and its biosocial consequences. *Seminars in Psychiatry* 2: 89–105

Kaplan B 1983 A trio of trials: The past as prologue, prelude and pretext; Some problems and issues for a theoretically-oriented life-span developmental psychology; Sweeney among the nightingales—a call to controversy. In: Lerner R M (ed.) 1983 *Developmental Psychology: Historical and Philosophical Perspectives.* Erlbaum, Hillsdale, New Jersey, pp. 185–228

Lerner R M 1976 *Concepts and Theories of Human Development.* Addison-Wesley, Reading, Massachusetts

Lerner R M 1979 A dynamic interactional concept of individual and social relationship development. In: Burgess R L, Huston T L (eds.) 1979 *Social Exchange in Developing Relationships.* Academic Press, New York

Lerner R M, Busch-Rossnagel N A 1981 Individuals as producers of their development: Conceptual and empirical bases. In: Lerner R M, Busch-Rossnagel N A (eds.) 1981 *Individuals as Producers of Their Development: A Life-span Perspective.* Academic Press, New York

Peters D L, Busch N 1977 Research on early childhood education: The aptitude/treatment approach. Paper presented at the Annual Meeting of the National Association of Young Children, Chicago

Resnick L 1981 Instructional pscyhology. *Annu. Rev. Psychol.* 32: 659–704

Resnick L, Wang M, Kaplan J 1973 Task analysis in curriculum design: A hierarchically sequenced mathematics curriculum. *J. Appl. Behav. Anal.* 6: 679–710

Stallings J 1975 Implementation and child effects of teaching practices in follow-through classrooms. *Monographs for the Society for Research in Child Development* 40 (Serial No. 163): 7–8

Thomas A, Chess S 1977 *Temperament and Development.* Bruner/Mazel, New York

Tobias S 1976 Achievement treatment interactions. *Rev. Educ. Res.* 46: 61–74

Tobias S 1981 Adapting instruction to individual differences among students. *Educ. Psychol.* 16: 111–20

Tobias S 1982 When do instructional methods make a difference. *Educ. Res.* AERA 11: 4–9

Werner H 1957 The concept of development from a comparative and organismic point of view. In: Harris D B (ed.) 1957 *The Concept of Development.* University of Minnesota Press, Minneapolis

Theories Embedded in Religious Traditions

Jewish Theory of Human Development

D. Hartman

In seeking to understand how beliefs about human development and personality can be derived from Jewish religious doctrine, it is helpful first to recognize a distinction between using strictly legal writings as contrasted to nonlegal narrative forms of rabbinic literature for such a purpose. This distinction is made at the outset of the following review. The discussion then proceeds through five phases which treat (a) children's egocentrism and their evil inclinations during the first decade of life; (b) their growing sense of realism that occurs at the time of puberty; (c) the morality of obligation which adolescents face; (d) the importance of controlling one's passions; and (e) a proper role for sexuality during adolescence and adulthood.

The centrality of law and practice in Judaism often leads to the view that Judaism is a self-contained system of precise rules of behavior. Like a formal axiomatic system, Judaism is often understood as a way of life whose norms may be explained as legal inferences from basic premises. Given a person's commitment to the authority of the system, all that is then required is an understanding of the complex process of legal argumentation by which explicit rules are inferred from other rules and ultimately from the legal premises of the system.

The characterization of law as a formal, deductive system is inadequate to explain legal systems in general and Halakhah in particular. Numerous philosophers have argued against the formalistic orientation to law by pointing to the creative role of the judge in rendering decisions where legal norms conflict or are too vague to determine only one solution to a problematic situation. In such situations, considerations other than strict legal consistency guide the judicial decision. Such decisions, whether made by a judge or by an authorized group of people such as talmudic scholars, are ultimately legislative insofar as they become precedents which may justify later legal decisions. The crucial point for the purpose of this article is that considerations other than strict formal consistency (e.g., conceptions of man, ideals of the nature of community, the purpose of human existence, etc.) enter into the development of legal systems.

Without elaborating on the arguments against legal formalism, an attempt will be made to elucidate some of the psychological attitudes of rabbinic teachers which, in part, determined the nature of Halakhah (Jewish jurisprudence). The rabbis of the Talmud were not philosophers or metaphysicians, but keen observers of human beings. Behind many of the rules and regulations of the Halakhah is a framework for understanding the psychological dynamics of human nature. The rabbis were not obsessed with clever legal argumentation; they were committed to formulating a law for human beings according to how they perceived the human condition. Though committed to a framework of norms not subject to change according to individual interest and taste, the rabbis' role in interpreting and developing the written law of the Pentateuch often indicates an underlying philosophy of man.

In this article, various aggadic midrashim (aggadah is a nonlegal narrative form of rabbinic literature), will be examined, which deal with the *yetzer hara* (the evil inclination) as paradigmatic statements that reflect rabbinic psychology.

1. Egocentrism and Evil Inclination in Childhood

The following midrash is related in Yoma (69b):

> "And they cried with a great (loud) voice unto the Lord, their God" (Nehemiah 9:4). What did they cry? Woe, woe, it is he (the *yetzer hara*) who has destroyed the Sanctuary, burnt the Temple, killed all the righteous, driven all Israel into exile, and is still dancing around among us! Thou hast surely given him to us so that we may receive reward through him. We want neither him, nor reward through him! . . .

In contrast to the argument often used in discussions of theodicy that the existence of evil is a necessary condition for human perfection and greatness and therefore people ought to accept and appreciate the "gift" of evil (specifically human evil), the midrash formulates the candid and sensible response: Spare us the suffering and the struggle and we shall willingly forfeit the reward!

In Berakhot (5b), a similar reaction is discussed:

> R. Hiyya b Abba fell ill and R. Hanina went in to visit him.

He said to him: "Are your sufferings welcome to you?" He replied: "Neither they nor their reward."

While acknowledging the great rewards involved in overcoming the test of evil and pain, R. Hiyya, like the people in the midrash in Yoma, weighed the horrors of human suffering, pain, and failures against the rewards and likelihood of success and decided that he would rather withdraw from the entire enterprise. Somewhat like a Pascalian wager which backfired, the justification of evil in terms of its human benefits leads to the position that were the existence of the *yetzer hara* subject to human choice, it would be best to eliminate it—whatever the losses.

The midrash in Yoma, quoted above, continues with God taking up the challenge of the people's response:

> . . . Thereupon a tablet fell down from heaven for them, whereupon the word "truth" was inscribed. . . . They ordered a fast of three days and three nights, whereupon he (the *yetzer hara*) was surrendered to them. He came forth from the Holy of Holies like a young fiery lion. Thereupon the Prophet said to Israel: "This is the evil desire of idolatry. . . ." They said: "Since this is a time of Grace, let us pray for mercy for the Tempter to evil." They prayed for mercy, and he was handed to them. He said to them: "Realize that if you kill him, the world goes down."
>
> They imprisoned him for three days, then looked in the whole land of Israel for a fresh egg and could not find it. Thereupon they said: "What shall we do now? Shall we kill him? The world would then go down. Shall we beg for half mercy?—They do not grant 'halves' in heaven." (Then) they put out his eyes and let him go. It helped inasmuch as he no more entices men to commit incest.

The statement, "They do not grant 'halves' in heaven," affirms the belief that the potential for evil cannot be isolated and eliminated without undermining a necessary component of human society. In Midrash Rabbah (Gen. IX, 7), R. Nahman claims that the phrase *tov me'od* (very good) in the account of Creation in Genesis includes reference to the evil inclination, for without it people would not build homes, marry, or have children. In calling the *yetzer hara* "good", God indicated that human evil has its source in the elemental matrix of needs, wants, and desires which account for human initiative and creativity. The *yetzer hara* is not the name of a particular need or desire like thirst or sex, but is the way certain aspects of man's instinctual passionate nature are characterized. The psychological elements which explain human evil are capable of providing the basis for positive expressions of power and creative assertion.

The midrash in Yoma symbolizes the divine response to the human longing to extricate the *yetzer hara* by the falling from heaven of the tablet inscribed with the word *emet* (truth). A true picture of the human condition contrasts with the childlike wish for a simple world of perpetual satisfaction. The child in man asks the question: "Why did not God create people who would only do good?" Its impulse is to dissect reality in a way that would eliminate struggle and pain and risk. Mommy and Daddy should get along all the time if they really love one another. The natural longing of the child is expressed in the illusion of omnipotence and the wish for an uncomplicated world where passion and desire are only channeled according to the good and the beautiful. Truth shatters the dream of the child by insisting on the impossibility of sustaining a human reality on "half-mercies."

In wishing for a world without risks, the child in man falls victim to illusion and self-deception. One who wishes to build and create must face the fact that the factors which enable one to act constructively are the very same factors which may lead one to destroy. Struggle and the risk of tragic failure are inherent in the human condition.

The rabbis realized that a human being develops the capacity to love and to relate to others—to other persons and to God—within the context of the family. A child is first exposed to others through its parents. The relationships cultivated within the family prepare the child for relationships to persons beyond the self. Egocentricity characterizes early stages in human development; as the child matures, egocentricity is countered by perceiving oneself as one person amidst a universe of other persons whose needs and desires warrant attention whether they serve one's own interests or not. Maturity involves the ability to recognize and respond to the interests of human beings insofar as they are human beings.

The family may aid the child to achieve this level of maturity by cultivating a deep awareness of interdependence. Families ought to convey to the child the consciousness of being a creature, that is, that no mortal is self-made and self-sufficient. The family may be instrumental in eliminating egocentrism if it embodies the notion that without the concern of others and the readiness to assume responsibility for the welfare of others, an individual cannot thrive or develop positively.

Yet, the very same social institution—the family—which can effectively cultivate concern and love for other human beings, can become a framework for extreme egotism and parochialism. Potentially a bridge connecting the self with others, the family can become the psychological extension of the self by enclosing the individual within closed impenetrable borders. The limits of the family may become barriers "protecting" the individual from the dangers of "foreign" contact. Fear of outsiders and suspicion of "strangers" may become a way of life fostered and perpetuated by the family.

> Many times when a person desires to do a *mitzvah* (divine commandment), the *yetzer hara* within him says: "Why do a *mitzvah* and diminish your possessions? Before you give to others, give to your children." And the *yetzer hatov* (good inclination) says to him: "Give (according) to the *mitzvah*. Consider what is written: "For a *mitzvah* is a candle. . . ." (Prov. 6:23). Just as this candle when burning can be used to light thousands of wax and tallow candles while its own light remains intact, so too whoever gives (according) to the

mitzvah does not diminish his possessions. Hence it says: "For a *mitzvah* is a candle and Torah is light" (Prov. 6:23). (Exodus Rabbah 36:3)

The *yetzer hara* as portrayed in this midrash confronts a person's readiness to transcend his or her own needs and to respond to the norm of giving to others by diverting attention to the legitimate needs of the family. "Why give to others, to 'strangers'? attend to your own family first." The *yetzer hara* seeks the dividing line separating the individual self and the smallest social unit with which the individual identifies (the family) from the domain of human beings beyond the self and its social extensions. By focusing attention on this dividing line, the *yetzer hara* attempts to drive a wedge between the self and others so as to justify exclusive concern with one's own family needs.

Thus it can be seen that social institutions, like human desires and passions, can serve various purposes. Heaven does not give "halves"; social and psychological givens may not be labeled good or bad; the potential for good contains within it the potential for evil. The rabbis firmly rejected fatalism and despair as well as passive optimism and complacent hope. Rabbinic activism is expressed in the belief that without conscious active input by human beings, the great potential for good may lead to the brutalization of the human spirit.

2. The Growing Realism of Adolescence

The evil impulse (*yetzer hara*), what is it? It is said: By thirteen years is the evil impulse older than the good impulse. In the mother's womb the evil impulse begins to develop and is born with a person. If he begins to profane the Sabbath, it does not prevent him; if he commits murder, it does not prevent him; if he goes off to another heinous transgression, it does not prevent him.

Thirteen years later the good impulse is born. When he profanes the Sabbath, it reprimands him: "Wretch!" lo it says, "Every one that profaneth it shall surely be put to death" (Exod. 31:14). If he goes to commit murder, it reprimands him: "Wretch!" lo it says, "Whoso sheddeth man's blood, by man shall his blood be shed" (Gen. 9:6). If he goes off to another heinous transgression, it reprimands him: "Wretch!" lo it says, "Both the adulterer and the adulteress shall surely be put to death" (Lev. 20:10). (The Fathers According to Rabbi Nathan 16)

The *yetzer hara* is formed in the womb and is born with the child. The child, according to this midrash, is not the paradigmatic symbol of purity and innocence. The child is subject to the influence of the *yetzer hara* alone; only 13 years later, at the age of bar-mitzvah, does the *yetzer hatov*, the good inclination, begin to affect the young person's choices and conduct. When the youth after the age of 13 sets out to profane the Sabbath or to harm another person, the *yetzer hatov* reprimands him by indicating the consequences of such conduct: "Wretch!" it says, "Every one that profaneth it shall surely be put to death"; "Wretch!" it says,

"Whoso sheddeth man's blood, by man shall his blood be shed."

The child, though not pure or innocent, is not culpable for his actions because immaturity precludes full awareness of the consequences of behavior. The *yetzer hatov* begins to play an effective role in determining conduct when one may be expected to be cognizant of the consequences of one's choices. The *yetzer hara* of the child focuses on immediate gratification, whereas the *yetzer hatov* complicates decisions by declaring: "You pay a price for your actions."

The simplicity of childhood behavior, which is characterized by acting on impulse and by spontaneous, spur-of-the-moment responses to present needs and desires, is often confused with innocence. Cognizance of future consequences forces the adult to deliberate about choices and to consider alternate actions in the light of their repercussions. The psychological maturity to weigh alternative actions in terms of future effects, that is, the ability to transcend exclusive concern with immediate gratification, is a condition for acting according to the *yetzer hatov*.

To go through life seeking spiritual illumination while "Rome burns" is to be like a child in the protective care of his parents who is oblivious to his relationship to a total human environment. Such is the condition of many a naive pseudomystic. One who seeks personal fulfillment in isolation from the active world of everyday human life, no matter the grandeur and sublimity of one's private symbolism, is in effect encapsulated in the childlike domain of the *yetzer hara*. The *yetzer hatov* gains a foothold in one's psyche when one is able to relate the present to the future (a sense of history); when one is enslaved to the *yetzer hara*, one is trapped within the narrow confines of the present moment. The *yetzer hatov* is not simply one reason for action among numerous others; the *yetzer hatov* represents the enlargement of one's perspective on conduct—the psychological broadening of the context of one's choices wherein one discovers responsibility and accountability.

The rabbis, therefore, said that the *yetzer hatov* begins at 13. The age of 13 was not only considered to be the time of puberty, but was also considered the period in human development when one begins to understand the *mitzvot* (divine commandments), that is, when one can transcend egocentrism and pay serious attention to claims emanating from sources outside oneself. Only when one is psychologically able to acknowledge another, to consider another person's interests independent of one's own interests, to feel oneself to be claimed by an external "Thou shalt . . ." which may limit and inhibit one's immediate needs and desires, does one begin to discover the *yetzer hatov*.

The *yetzer hara* is dominant when a person is imprisoned within the self and driven exclusively by private need and impulse. The child is ruled by the *yetzer hara* insofar as the child's world revolves around the child alone. The child is not the lofty symbol of innocence; he is blameless only because he is guiltless. And he is guiltless not because of his being righteous, but because his immaturity precludes blame and censure. The conditions for responsibility are lacking. Childhood is an excusing and not a justifying condition; childhood exempts the child from moral and legal condemnation and such exemption is not synonymous with purity and righteousness.

To be sure, the potential for childlike immaturity is in all of us. Do adults ever fully extricate themselves from being the "child"? Do grown-ups ever escape narcissism or envy of childlike freedom which is impervious to having to consider the consequences of our actions?

3. The Morality of Obligation

It is not accidental that the "birth" of the *yetzer hatov* occurs at the same time as the person becomes responsible for fulfilling *mitzvot*. Mitzvah presupposes some degree of liberation from childhood egocentrism.

Essential to the concept mitzvah is normative obligation. Normative obligation is incompatible with an egocentric world view; receptivity to the normative force of commandments involves one's capacity to respond to another. Commandment involves listening: *Shema Yisrael*—"Hear O Israel." If a person is unable to respond to beings other than himself, he cannot "hear" the commandment and hence he is not accountable.

The legal concept mitzvah has distinct logical connections to the psychological concept *yetzer hatov*. Kant emphasized the logical incompatibility between acting from duty and acting because of pleasure, or need, or utility. In order to characterize actions as moral, there must be among one's reasons for action the response to the moral "ought." Whether one's actions satisfy one's personal needs and desires or whether they promise fulfillment and "self-realization" is secondary; to be capable of moral conduct and to be a responsible person, one must be responsive to the normative force of duty. To be a responsible Jew, therefore, one must feel the weight of mitzvah; to be a responsible Jew, one must be a responsive Jew.

To go to synagogue solely because of feelings of well-being is to miss the element of mitzvah. To observe the Sabbath because of pleasurable feelings of relaxation is not to respond to a commandment. One's children give one pleasure and enhance feelings of self-worth; what if they are not nice kids or if caring for them interferes with one's self-realization? Obligation must continue irrespective of the joys of parenthood.

In Rosh Hashanah (28a), Rashi elaborates on the talmudic principle "Commandments were not given for the sake of pleasure" by explaining that commandments were not given to Israel so that their performance would be a source of pleasure, but rather commandments are a "yoke around their necks." Accepting to live by the commandments is described by the Talmud as *kabalat ol mitzvot*—accepting the yoke of the Commandments.

R. Joseph (who was blind) said: Originally, I thought that if anyone would tell me that the Halakhah agrees with R. Judah, that a blind person is exempt from the precepts, I would make a banquet for the Rabbis, seeing that I am not obliged, yet fulfil them. Now, however, that I have heard R. Hanina's dictum that he who is commanded and fulfils (the command) is greater than he who fulfils it though not commanded; on the contrary, if anyone should tell me that the Halakhah does not agree with R. Judah, I would make a banquet for the Rabbis. (Kiddushin 31a)

The talmudic principle "Greater is the one who acts because one is commanded to do so, than one who acts though not commanded to do so" may strike many people to be counter-intuitive. Such people would insist that doing something because one is commanded lessens the worth of the act performed. ("I go to synagogue solely because I want to and not because I'm supposed to!") The talmudic opinion quoted above turns this reasoning on its head. If one attends synagogue because he believes he ought to or if one gives to the poor in response to the mitzvah or *tzedakah* (alms-giving), the deed is regarded as greater than the same deed performed in the absence of mitzvah.

The reason for this attitude is based on the relationship between a person's response to a normative "ought" and the moral personality of the performer of a mitzvah. When a person acknowledges the force of a commandment, he demonstrates his responsiveness to a reality beyond himself. An act can become moral only when the egocentrism of the *yetzer hara* yields to the self-transcending voice of the *yetzer hatov*; the moral and religious worth of an act depends to a great extent on whether the act takes place within a context of responsive hearing (*Shema*).

Man should not say, "I do not want to eat meat together with milk; I do not want to wear clothes made of a mixture of wool and linen; I do not want to enter into an incestuous marriage," but he should say, "I do indeed want to, yet I must not, for my Father in heaven has forbidden it." (Sifre, Lev. 20:26)

The rabbis insist on retaining the normative force of mitzvah among one's reasons for performing *mitzvot* not because of austere puritanism, but in order to safeguard the responsive feature of normative conduct. Feelings of disgust or of pleasure may determine human actions and omissions, but they cannot justify moral and religious behavior. Disgust at the sight of blood can, without inconsistency, lead to a selective responsiveness that is morally abhorrent or to unjust persecution of people whose life-styles or sexual practices arouse disgust. Disgust and pleasure are neither sufficient nor necessary reasons for determining moral behavior and moral norms.

One is not only permitted to enjoy Judaism, one is often told to experience joy and pleasure: "And you shall rejoice before the Lord your God. . . . And you shall rejoice in thy feast. . . . You shall be altogether joyful . . ." (Deut. 16:11ff.). Pleasure ceases being legitimate, however, when it becomes the sole basis of action. When pleasure (or disgust) replaces normative responsiveness as the ground of action, mitzvah loses its meaning and the basis of the moral personality is undermined.

The Talmud (Shabbat 88a) characterizes the Sinai revelation with the imagery of God suspending the mountain of Sinai over the people like a tank and telling them that unless they accept the Torah they will be buried beneath the mountain. The element of coercion is a necessary component of hearing the word of God. This midrash symbolically captures the idea of the normative force of the divine command by picturing the Sinaitic revelation in terms of brute coercion. Norms have "weight" when one acknowledges their imperative force. Experiencing the "ought" of *mitzvot* is a necessary (though not necessarily a sufficient) condition for accepting to live by *mitzvot*; unless one is capable of transcending egocentrism, one will be deaf to the commanding voice of God.

When a mitzvah involves personal effort and self-transcendence, the *yetzer hara* whispers to the Jew, "Why be compelled to act?—Who needs the pressure and the burden of responsibility?" Like the child, people often choose to live in a narcissistic domain of pleasure and self-indulgence. The significance of bar-mitzvah at age 13 relates to the psychological maturity implied by the formation of the *yetzer hatov*. Today, unfortunately, bar-mitzvah celebrations often reinforce narcissism. Bar-mitzvah often becomes a glorified child's day; everything centers around the youth's ego-needs. Fantasies of self-importance are magnified and intensified; all eyes are riveted on the child who is showered with gifts and attention. It is as if one were celebrating the final victory of the *yetzer hara*.

4. Controlling One's Passions

One who tears his clothes in the heat of anger, and one who smashes his dishes in the heat of anger, and one who throws away his money in the heat of anger should be regarded as one who worships idols. For such is the craft of the *yetzer hara*. Today he (the *yetzer hara*) says to a person "Do this," and tomorrow he says "Do that" until finally he says "worship idols"—and he goes and does it.

Rabbi Abin said: What is the meaning of the verse "There shall be among you no strange god nor shall you worship any alien deity" (Psalms 81:10)? What is the strange god that inhabits a person's body? I would say this is the *yetzer hara*. (Shabbat 105B)

The *yetzer hara*'s presence is indicated by one's loss of self-control. Destroying one's clothes and smashing dishes in the rage of anger are signs of a personality driven by passion and emotion. Like an alien deity beyond one's control, the *yetzer hara* reduces a person to wild fluctuations of mood and conduct. "I was not myself" often expresses the afterthoughts of a person in the grip of violent rage. "Who is valiant? He who conquers his *yetzer (hara)*" (Avot 4:1)—that is, he who controls and is master of his passions.

The *yetzer hara* may be identified in acts of rage, loss of self-control, feelings of being inwardly driven, that is, the *yetzer hara* expresses the psychological condition of a person lacking the resources for self-transcendence.

Maimonides, in the *Mishneh Torah* (Nezikin, "Laws of Robbery and Lost Property," Chap. 1), presents a framework of norms whose relationship to one another indicates the dynamics of the *yetzer hara*. In one chapter he discusses the following commandments: *lo tahmod* (you shall not covet) (Ex. 20:14, Deut. 5:18); *lo titaveh* (You shall not desire or lust) (Deut. 5:18); *lo tignov* (You shall not steal) (Ex. 20:13 Deut. 5:17); *lo tigzol* (You shall not rob) (Lev. 19:13); and *lo tirtzah* (You shall not commit murder) (Ex. 20:13; Deut. 5:17).

According to Maimonides, *lo tahmod* (You shall not covet) includes the case of one who pressures another to sell some possession:

If one covets the male slave or the female slave or the house or goods of another, or anything that is possible for him to acquire from the other, and he subjects the other to vexation and pesters him until he is allowed to buy it from him, then he transgresses the negative commandment, "You shall not covet" (Ex. 20:14), even if he pays him a high price for it. No flogging is incurred for breach of this prohibition, since it does not involve action. Nor does one transgress this prohibition until he buys the object that he covets, as is exemplified by Scripture when it says, "You shall not covet the silver and gold that is on them nor take it to you" (Deut. 7:25)—thus implying that the transgression of coveting is effected only when accompanied by action.

Lo titaveh (You shall not desire or lust) refers to improper desiring per se:

If one desires another's house or his wife or his goods or any similar thing that he might buy from him, he transgresses a negative commandment as soon as he thinks in his heart how he is to acquire the desired object and allows his mind to be seduced by it. For Scripture says, "You shall not desire" (Deut. 5:18), and desire is a matter of the heart only.

The five "You shall not . . ." commandments are related to one another as stages in a process. Beginning with the covetous desire and the psychological inability to accept the limits which others impose on oneself, a chain of events unfolds which leads ultimately to the elimination of the other person through murder:

Desire leads to coveting, and coveting to robbery, for if the owner does not wish to sell, even when he is offered a high price and is greatly importuned, it will lead the coveter to rob him, as it is said, "And they covet houses and seize them" (Micah 2:2). Moreover, if the owner should stand up to him to protect his property and prevent the robbery, this may lead to bloodshed. You can learn this from the story of Ahab and Naboth. (cf. I Kings 21)

According to Maimonides, lust leads to active acquisition of another person's property by theft or robbery or, if these fail, to murder. The justification for this generalization about the connection between the various stages of this process is the psychological insight into the dynamics of a person unable to accept limits to his wants. A person who cannot tolerate having to evaluate his wants and desires in the light of other persons whose presence may thwart the satisfaction of his personal needs and desires, will, under various circumstances, lust, intimidate, rob, and murder. Common to these transgressions is the egocentrism of the *yetzer hara* and the negation of the limits imposed on personal satisfaction by the community of other human beings.

Murder, the elimination of the "other," is, like idolatry, the ultimate expression of the *yetzer hara*. Idolatry differs from true worship of God in that the idol-worshipper aspires to control and manipulate his god. Like the difference between magic and prayer, the difference between idolatry and the religion of Israel is expressed in the latter's ascribing unqualified freedom to God who alone creates and is subject to no power outside Himself.

The *yetzer hara* is the psychological framework of the person imprisoned within the confines of the self—the childlike individual entrapped within personal desires and hungers. The victim of the *yetzer hara* cannot penetrate beyond his own skin; he cannot hear the voices of those beyond himself. There is no love because there is no genuine experience of others. There is no "ought" because there is no experience of objectivity, no outside reality, no creator. The *yetzer hara* encloses one within the perimeter of the self. Idolatry and violence give expression to the psychological dynamics of the child's egocentric world view.

The midrashic equation of the self-inflated arrogant person with the idolator may be understood as reflecting the connection between the above analysis of the *yetzer hara*, idolatry, and violence:

Rabbi Johanan said in the name of R. Simeon b. Yohai: "Every man in whom is haughtiness of spirit is as though he worships idols". . . . R. Johanan himself said: "He is as though he had denied the existence of God, as it is said, 'Thine heart be lifted up and thou forget the Lord thy God.'" (Sotah 46)

R. Eleazar also said: "Every man in whom is haughtiness of spirit is fit to be hewn down like an *asherah* (an object of idolatrous worship)." (Sotah 5a)

R. Hisda said, and according to another version it was Mar Ukba: "Every man in whom is haughtiness of spirit, the Holy One blessed be He declares, I and he cannot dwell in the world." (Shabbat 105b)

The relationship between arrogance, rage, and idolatry reflects the relationship between belief in God and the psychological capacity to be open and responsive to others. One who is subject to the passions of the *yetzer hara*, rage, and arrogance loses the discriminating capacity to affirm the independent dignity of an objective reality.

5. The Proper Role of Sexuality

According to the midrash quoted above from Yoma 69b, the imprisonment of the *yetzer hara* resulted in no

eggs being fertilized. The relationship of the *yetzer hara* to sexuality is a recurrent theme in rabbinic thought:

. . . Abbaye heard a certain man saying to a woman, "Let us arise betimes and go on our way." Said Abbaye, "I will follow them in order to keep them from transgression." And he followed them for three parsangs across the meadows. When they parted company, he heard them say, "Our company is pleasant, the way is long." "If it were I," said Abbaye, "I could not have restrained myself," and so he went and leaned in deep anguish against a doorpost, when a certain old man came to him and taught him: "The greater the man, the greater his evil inclination." (Sukkah 52a)

R. Akiba used to scoff at transgressors. One day Satan appeared to him as a woman on the top of a palm tree. Grasping the tree, he went climbing up: but when he reached halfway up the tree, he (Satan) let him go, saying "Had they not proclaimed in Heaven: 'Take heed of R. Akiba and his learning,' I would have valued your life at two ma'ahs (a small amount)." (Kiddushin 81a)

A great deal of talmudic imagery of the *yetzer hara* (or of Satan) is sexual in nature. The sex drive leads a person to others; inter alia, it makes one conscious of human dependence. This drive, however, may become the basis of human manipulation and domination. Sexual love may express the genuine meeting of two persons or it may be confined exclusively to ego gratification. Sexual passion may reduce others to objects or it may lift a person out of his self and provide for self-transcendence.

Although the rabbis considered procreation to be a normative obligation incumbent on all people and unequivocally negated the value of celibacy, they were fully awake to the potential for evil of sexual passion. Like human assertion and power, sexual passion may blind a person to others and thwart self-transcendence.

6. Summary

Knowing the psychological dynamics of the human condition warrants neither despair nor optimism. Man is by nature neither depraved nor "basically good." Whether the *yetzer hara* or the *yetzer hatov* dominates a person's conduct depends on the picture of life framing one's experience. If the borders of the self are the limits of one's world, if one's needs and wants exhaust what counts as compelling reasons for acting, then norms and love (of man or of God) have no place. "Of every man in whom is haughtiness of spirit, the Holy One blessed be He declares: I and he cannot both dwell in the world" (Sotah 5a).

The notions of the *yetzer hara* and the *yetzer hatov* revolve around the psychological issues of self-transcendence. The rabbis focused on the psychological conditions affecting moral attitudes and moral behavior. Knowing the good alone is pointless if the person is psychologically handicapped and impotent to act on the basis of this knowledge. The *yetzer hara* and the *yetzer hatov* are not symbols of ignorance and knowledge respectively; they represent the psychological outlooks which make knowing-the-good desirable and worth having.

Bibliography

Buber M 1958 The way of man according to the teaching of Hasidism. In: Friedman M (ed.) 1958 *Hasidism and Modern Man*. Horizon, New York, pp. 126–67

Eichrodt W 1961 The place of Man in the Creation. In: Eichrodt W (ed.) 1961 *Theology of the Old Testament, Vol. 2* [Translated by Baker J A]. Westminster, Philadelphia, Pennsylvania, pp. 118–50

Hartman D 1976 Halakhic and Aggadic categories and their relationship to philosophic spirituality. In: *Maimonides: Torah and Philosophic Quest*. Jewish Publication Society, Philadelphia, Pennsylvania, pp. 66–101

Heschel A J 1951 *Man is Not Alone: A Philosophy of Religion*. Farrar, Straus, and Giroux, New York, pp. 207–29

Heschel A J 1966 Sacred image of Man. *The Insecurity of Freedom: Essays on Human Existence*. Farrar, Straus, and Giroux, New York, pp. 150–67

Moore G F 1954 The nature of Man. *Judaism in the First Centuries of the Christian Era, the Age of the Tannaim*. Harvard University Press, Cambridge, Massachusetts, pp. 445–59

Scholem G G 1974 Man and his soul (Psychology and anthropology of the Kabbalah). *Kabbalah*. Quadrangle/The New York Times, New York, pp. 152–65

Soloveitchik J B 1965 Lonely man of faith. *Tradition* 7(2): 5–67

Soloveitchik J B 1978 Catharsis. *Tradition* 17(2): 38–54

Urbach E E 1975 *The Sages, Their Concepts and Beliefs*. Magnes, Hebrew University, Jerusalem, pp. 471–83

Christian Theory of Human Development

R. M. Thomas

The task of extracting a theory of human development from Christian doctrine requires at the outset several methodological decisions. First is the question of what properly constitutes Christian doctrine for such an undertaking. While it is obvious that the Bible is the basic source of Christian belief, there is the problem of which version of the Bible should be used, since different Christian denominations subscribe to separate versions whose contents are not entirely the same. A second question concerns what writings—if any—beyond the Bible can also qualify as doctrine for this purpose. Can interpretations of Biblical passages written by religious scholars in recent centuries qualify? If so, what criteria should be used to separate authentic interpretations from false or doubtful ones? A third issue is that of literal versus symbolic meanings. For example, in Genesis, the first book of the Bible, a description of the origins of the Earth and its inhabitants states that the Lord created the universe and all living things in six days, then rested on the seventh. Is this passage to be interpreted literally as meaning six 24-hour days, or is the term *day* meant to symbolize eons of time and not a 24-hour period? And if certain words are to be regarded as symbols, or if described incidents are to be interpreted as parables that signify broader meanings, how is such interpretation to be validated? In short, who is competent to decide which words are symbolic and what meanings they intend?

For the purpose of this article, the forgoing three issues have been settled in the following manner. First, the Bible translation authorized by King James I of England in the year 1611 has been used for the present enterprise because it continues to be the most widely adopted version in the English-speaking world. As for other sources of Christian theory besides the Bible, extensions or interpretations of basic doctrine have been accepted which have been written since early Christian days if such extensions have been regarded in recent times as authoritative by one or more of the major Christian sects. Likewise, interpretations of symbolism or parables are included if they have been regarded as valid by one or more of the major sects.

It should be apparent that when such a set of ground rules is adopted, the resulting theory cannot be considered *the* Christian model of development but rather must be viewed only as one version of Christian theory, which may even include some variations among its subparts. In recognition of this fact, at several points in the following account opposing beliefs are identified that different Christian denominations may hold regarding a given issue.

It should be recognized at the start that the aspect of human life on which Christian theory focuses is that of moral development, meaning the growth of an individual's relationship to a Supreme Being and to fellow humans. Christian theory gives little or no attention to physical growth or to cognitive development, except as cognition may relate to moral behavior.

The topics to be inspected include (a) personality structure and its origin, (b) the original moral nature of the child, (c) the goals of development, (d) the length of development, (e) stages of development, (f) influences on development, (g) sources of evidence, and (h) implications of the theory for child rearing and education. (Throughout the review, quotations from the Bible are cited in terms of the particular Biblical book's name, chapter number, and verse number in the King James version—for instance: Hebrews 4:12.)

1. Personality Structure and its Origin

The most basic components of human nature, as reflected in scripture from both the Old and New testaments of the Bible, are the physical and the immaterial, that is, body and soul. This bipartite division is initially described in Genesis (2:7) with the creation of the first man: "And Jehovah God formed man of the dust of the ground, and breathed into his nostrils the breath of life; and man became a living soul." The two aspects are recognized again at the time of death: "Then shall the dust return to the earth as it was, and the spirit shall return unto God who gave it" (Ecclesiastes 12:7).

However, Christian interpretations of human nature often go beyond the bipartite concept to propose additional components of the human's immaterial portion, the portion which, for convenience of discussion, will be referred to as personality. One question theologians have long debated is whether soul and spirit are merely different words for the same entity. Or are soul and spirit separate components of the personality, as suggested in such phrases as "your whole spirit and soul and body be preserved" (1 Thessalonians 5:23)? In pursuing this issue, advocates on both sides of the question have argued their positions without being able to adduce sufficient unequivocal scripture or empirical psychological evidence to convince the other side of the validity of their position, so that today the matter remains unsettled. A further problem has been that of determining if spirit and soul are identical to, or different from, heart or mind as in the passage "thou shalt love the Lord thy God with all thy heart, and with all thy soul, and with all thy mind" (Mark 12:30).

The debate about the composition of personality has become even more complex over the centuries as Christian scholars have proposed further divisions of the nonphysical self. By the twentieth century these divisions had emerged as faculties of the mind, with the term faculty meaning a power, capacity, function, or trait of personality. For several centuries past, this faculty psychology has provided the generally accepted view of personality structure for large numbers of Christian theologians and it continues to do so today. Typical faculties within Christian conceptions of personality are intellect, sensibility, will, and conscience.

> Intellect is the soul knowing; sensibility is the soul feeling (desires, affections); will is the soul choosing (end or means). . . . Man has intellect or reason, to discern the difference between right and wrong; sensibility, to be moved by each of these; free will, to do the one or the other. . . . But in connection with these faculties there is a sort of activity which involves them all, and without which there can be no moral action, namely, the activity of conscience. (Strong 1907 pp. 497, 505)

However, these four are not the only powers or divisions of mental activity. Theologians also speak of such faculties as judgment, intuition, memory, imagination, and others. Although Christian scholars may disagree on the exact number and types of faculties, their discussions of human nature reflect a conviction that personality is indeed composed of traits or faculties that operate within the soul, or along with the soul, to make up the nonmaterial individual.

A key element of doctrine for most Christian sects has been the belief that the chief distinction between humans and other living things is in the soul, which only humans have, and it is the soul that gives them a God-like character that makes them supreme among beings. ("And God said, let us make man in our image, after our likeness. . . . [to] have dominion over the fish of the sea, and over the fowl of the air, and over the cattle, and over all the earth. . . ." Genesis 1:26.) Or as an alternative interpretation, plants and animals are credited with immaterial characteristics that can be labeled soul, but the types of souls they possess are not identical to the human soul. From such a perspective, the human soul is a unitary object; but like God himself, it forms a trinity consisting of a vegetative soul, a sensible soul, and a rational soul. The vegetative soul has the powers of nourishing and propagating, two characteristics that people share with the earth's plant life. The sensible soul has not only powers of nourishing and propagating but also additional equipment possessed by animals—external senses as well as an internal common sense and such faculties as imagination and memory, emotions, and the musculature (sinews) that makes locomotion possible. But it is the rational soul, the highest in the trinity, that contains all the powers of the other two, plus the faculties of reason and will and conscience that make humankind more Godly than the beasts.

1.1 The Origin of the Soul

The matter of how and when the soul of the individual person originates is an issue not only of theoretical significance but of practical importance as well. Three main theories about the soul's origin, disputed over the centuries, continue under debate today.

First is the pre-existence theory, the belief that every person's soul existed in the mind of God prior to the creation of the individual's body. Such a theory is proposed to account for what are assumed to be people's intuitive ideas—their sense of space, time, causality, right, and God—with which, ostensibly, they are born. It is reasoned that since these ideas are innate and not the result of experience in the world, they must have existed in a soul or mind prior to the individual's conception and birth.

Second is the creation theory, the proposal that the soul of each human is immediately created by God and joined to the body at conception or at birth, or at some time between the two. The creation theory has been advocated by most Roman Catholic and Reformed theologians who support their belief by "referring to God as the Creator of the human spirit, together with the fact that there is a marked individuality in the child, which cannot be explained as a mere reproduction of the qualities existing in the parents" (Strong 1907 p. 491). In present-day disputes about the practice of abortion, supporters of the creation theory propose that aborting the normal development process of the unborn baby is an act of murder if the abortion is performed after the soul has been entered into the fetus by God.

The question of when between conception and birth the soul is created by God becomes, therefore, an issue of great import to those who subscribe to a creationist view.

Third is traducian theory, a prevailing view of many followers of Martin Luther. From the traducian viewpoint, the human race began with God's creating Adam and Eve—creating them body and soul—and from that original pair all subsequent humans have inherited their characteristics, both material and immaterial. Advocates of the traducian position contend that the scriptural evidence of God's final creative act appears in Genesis (2:1–3): "Thus the heavens and the earth were finished, and all the host of them. And on the seventh day God ended his work which he had made . . . . And God blessed the seventh day, and sanctified it: because that in it he had rested from all his work which God created . . . ." If this was indeed the last of God's creative acts, then individual souls must have been inherited from one generation to the next over the centuries rather than each soul being created anew by God prior to the birth of every new infant.

Nevertheless, while Christian theorists may disagree on the origin of the soul and on exactly what faculties or traits compose the soul, all agree that the key element of human personality is a soul or spirit, which represents God's essence and thereby differentiates humans from other living things.

2. The Child's Original Moral Nature

Intimately linked to notions of the origin of the soul is the issue of whether the newborn is moral (naturally inclined to perform morally correct acts), is immoral (inclined to do evil), or amoral (neutral, that is, inclined neither to good nor to evil acts).

The dominant position on this issue in most Christian sects is that children are naturally inclined to evil. One rationale for such belief is that the original sin committed by Adam and Eve has been transmitted through the souls of everyone born since their time. This conviction derives logically from the traducian theory and has been reflected in such educational material as the New England Primer, which served as the chief primary-school reading textbook in North America from the late seventeenth century through the mid-nineteenth century. To teach children the first letter of the alphabet, the primer used the phrase "A = In *Adam's* fall, we sinned all" (*New England Primer* 1836 p.11).

Even Christians who do not subscribe literally to the inheritance of original sin still typically see humans inclined toward immoral behavior.

> In the sight of God his Judge, man is a sinner. . . . This is not a condition to which God has fatally condemned mankind, but a perversion of the nature and destiny of man as God created him for which man himself is responsible. It is a misuse of the great powers with which God has endowed man, so that he oppresses his fellows instead of loving and serving them, is inwardly at war with himself, and becomes

the slave of those natural and temporal forces he was meant to dominate. So long as man remains impenitently in this condition, he remains under the condemnation of God his Judge. (Dunstan 1961 p.208)

3. The Goals of Development

The goals of human development in Christian theory can be divided into the ultimate and the intermediate. The ultimate goal is to achieve life everlasting in the company of God and Christ in Heaven. The intermediate goal is to do God's will in one's daily life on earth. The behaviors that represent God's will will have been defined in the Old Testament of the Bible mainly in the form of specific commandments and proverbs, often illustrated with examples from people's lives. Most prominent of these are the 10 commandments that warn against such acts as killing, stealing, telling lies, committing adultery, coveting others' possessions, worshiping idols, misusing God's name, failing to respect one's parents, and improperly conducting religious rites (Exodus 20:4–26). God's will is reinterpreted by Christ in the New Testament in the form of more general principles of conduct, the chief of which are to love God and all mankind.

> And thou shalt love the Lord thy God with all thy heart, and with all thy soul, and with all thy mind, and with all thy strength: this is the first commandment. And the second is . . . thou shalt love thy neighbor as thyself. (Mark 12:30–31)

The principle of treating others with love is illustrated with examples in the accounts of Christ's life and with suggestions in subsequent books, most of which consist of letters sent by the apostle Paul to various groups of Christian adherents.

Hence, according to Christian theory, human development can be judged satisfactory when the individual's behavior increasingly matches the behavior described in God's commandments. Or stated differently, because the term sin identifies all behaviors contrary to God's will, human development is progressing satisfactorily when a person increasingly avoids sin.

However, Christian theologians disagree on the question of the connection between (a) the intermediate goals of abiding by God's commandments and (b) the ultimate goal of the soul's ascending to Heaven after the death of the body. The question is: Will a person earn an after-life of everlasting joy in Heaven by having faithfully followed God's commandments while on earth, or earn an after-life of misery in Hell by having lived an earthly life of sin? Or is the soul's destiny after death dependent simply on God's inclination or grace, regardless of one's conduct during the years on earth? Can people who have lived sinful lives attain a Heavenly after-life by, at the time of death, confessing their sins and accepting Christ as their savior? While some Christians would answer yes and others no to such queries, all Christians endorse the belief that humans are obligated to follow the Lord's commandments, and child-raising and educational practices are directed toward such an end.

4. *The Length of Development*

Defining the length of life and of development from a Christian perspective requires that the material being—the body—be considered separately from the non-material—the soul or spirit. For the body, the beginning of both life and development occurs with conception, with the joining of the sperm and egg, and the end comes with physical death as the heart stops beating. For the soul, life is far longer, although the length of development may be the same as for the body. The decision about when the life of the soul starts depends upon which theory of the soul's origin is adopted. To people who subscribe to either the pre-existence or traducian theory, the soul originates at the time of conception, when the sperm and ovum merge. To those who subscribe to the creationist theory, the soul originates at whatever time between conception and birth God places the individual in the fetus. It is not clear in Christian doctrine whether the soul achieves any prenatal development, so the beginning of development of the soul appears indeterminate. However, it is clear that from birth until physical death the soul develops; that is, it changes with experience and knowledge. One of the key tenets of Christian belief is that the life of the soul does not end with physical death but continues on through everlasting time. Hence, the life of the soul extends from the prenatal period into eternity. It is unclear, however, whether any development of the soul occurs after physical death. In the view of Jonathan Edwards, a seventeenth-century American Protestant theologian, "An unbodied spirit may be as capable of love and hatred, joy and sorrow, hope or fear, or other affections, as one that is united to a body" (Simonson 1970 p.163), but the question of whether such an ostensibly sensate soul experiences any development while in its unbodied state following physical death is left unsettled.

5. *Stages of Development*

For present purposes, a stage of development is considered to be a period of life which is marked by characteristics that differ from those of other periods. Passage from one stage to another is often indicated by a society's assigning responsibilities and rights not expected at an earlier stage. Sometimes passage is also signified by a formal ceremony.

In view of this definition, there appear to be at least five stages of development in Christian theory—the prebaptismal, the postbaptismal childhood stage, the age of reason, the years of marriage, and the post-mortem period.

In most Christian denominations the prebaptismal stage consists of the 9-month prenatal period as well as

the early days or early months of infancy until the baby is baptized. During the baptism ceremony, the child is officially assigned the name that he or she will bear throughout life, and the ceremony shows the world that the parents dedicate the child to a Christian life. People who have not been baptized in infancy may be baptized at any later time in life.

During the postbaptismal period of childhood, which typically extends from infancy until around puberty, children are expected to gradually learn how to be good Christians. However, during this first decade of life, children are considered too immature to fully understand Christian doctrine or the consequences of their behavior, so they are not held responsible for moral decisions. But around the time of puberty, they are thought to reach the age of reason and thus become capable of comprehending more completely the significance of Christian commitment. They are now considered to be accountable for their moral decisions and behavior. This passing from the state of irresponsible childhood into the fellowship of responsible, mature Christians is signified by a formal ceremony conducted before the church congregation. The ceremony in the Catholic church is the confirmation rite and in most Protestant denominations it is the ritual of accepting the youth as a full church member with the right to partake of holy communion. During the period immediately preceding the ceremony, the youth usually engages in intensive study of key elements of church doctrine to help ensure that he or she enters the new stage of life with a truly enlightened Christian commitment.

Entrance to the next stage, which traditionally occurs in early adulthood, is signified by a marriage ceremony during which the bride and groom publicly pledge to respect, love, and protect each other, forsaking all other potential mates "until death do us part." An important facet of marriage is that of achieving parenthood.

The final stage of development begins with death. Whereas physical death means the end of the corporeal self, for the soul it signifies the onset of life hereafter. Although there may be no change in the soul's condition during the after-life, passage into the final stage is itself a developmental change. A person's entering this last stage is marked by a funeral ceremony in which the soul of the departed is entrusted to the care of the Lord.

In certain versions of Christian theory an additional stage, or perhaps substage, during the period of adulthood is postulated. It is that of the born-again Christian, a condition achieved when an adult experiences a spiritual reawakening, a revival of Christian insight and commitment, with the spiritual rebirth often occurring during the conduct of a religious ceremony.

6. *Influences on Development*

The four varieties of influence that shape development in Christian theory are heredity, the environment, supernatural acts, and human will.

Heredity, as set by the genes contributed by the two parents at the time of conception, determines the general structure of the human body and the basic pace of its growth throughout life. This is true in all forms of Christian theory. And as noted earlier, in the opinion of Christians who subscribe to either a pre-existence or traducian belief in the origin of the soul, heredity also accounts for the condition of the human soul at the time of birth.

Environmental forces significantly affect the development of the body through nutrition, exercise, illness, and accident. The environment also strongly influences the contents of the soul or mind through the direct instruction of parents and educators, through the examples set by parents and by companions, and through the way life is portrayed in mass communication and entertainment media.

As for supernatural acts, the primary sources of these are God and Satan. Satan or the Devil constantly urges the individual to adopt sinful ways, to behave contrary to God's directives. To combat Satan's influence, God is always available as a guide and supporter for people in moments of indecision, of spiritual weakness, and of temptation. God's guidance and strength may be sought directly through prayer and through reading passages of holy scripture, or sought indirectly through consulting a priest or pastor. Not only do Christians believe God serves as adviser and spiritual supporter, but also that he can intervene to change either the individual or the environment so as to cause an event to turn out as the individual has hoped it would. This conviction that God at any moment can manipulate events to effect a particular outcome is suggested in many passages of the Bible. A familiar example is Psalm 23, which reflects the faith that both the individual's behavior and the influence of environmental elements—such as one's enemies—can be controlled by God on any occasion.

> The Lord is my shepherd . . . . He maketh me to lie down in green pastures; he leadeth me beside the still waters. He . . . leadeth me in the paths of righteousness for his name's sake. Yea, though I walk through the valley of the shadow of death, I will fear no evil; for thou art with me . . . . Thou preparest a table before me in the presence of mine enemies . . . .

A passage from the oft-repeated Lord's prayer (Matthew 6:11,13) reflects this same belief in God's ability to fashion events that influence the individual's development: "Give us this day our daily bread . . . . And lead us not into temptation, but deliver us from evil."

The fourth force affecting development is human will or intention. In contrast to a belief in complete determinism, which holds that a person's development is entirely the result of hereditary and environmental factors that are beyond the control of the individual, Christian doctrine suggests that humans have a free will which permits them to make decisions about how to behave. Hence, people's conscious intentions and determination play an important part in deciding the direction

their lives take. Expressing one common view of will within Christian doctrine, Strong (1907 p.509) has proposed that:

> Man is responsible for all effects of will, as well as for will itself; for voluntary affections, as well as for voluntary acts; for the intellectual views into which will has entered, as well as for the acts of will by which these views have been formed in the past or are maintained in the present.

In summary, then, from conception until death, human development results from the interaction of forces of heredity, environment, God and Satan, and the individual's own will or determination.

7. Sources of Evidence and Investigative Methodology

To answer questions about sources of evidence and types of investigative methods used for generating and supporting Christian theory, it is useful to adopt Dunstan's (1961) three categories of Christians—conservatives, liberals, and mainstream Christians. The categories cut across denominational lines, so that conservatives, liberals, and mainstreamers are found within nearly all large Christian sects—Roman Catholic, Presbyterian, Lutheran, Baptist, Anglican, and others.

Conservatives, who sometimes refer to themselves as evangelical Christians, base their beliefs about human nature and development on the literal word of the Bible. If a theory derived from modern-day science is in conflict with Bible scripture, then there is no question that the scientific theory is false. A case in point is the conflict between (a) the description of the creation of animal life and of human life in the Bible (Genesis 2:7–22) and (b) Charles Darwin's theory that humans have evolved over time from simple forms of animal life. In the view of conservatives, no matter what evidence Darwinian evolutionists present in support of their case, Darwin's theory could not possibly be true because it deviates from the Biblical version of creation.

To conservatives, the truth about any phenomenon is not discovered by humans through their own cleverness or the investigative techniques they devise. Rather, truth is revealed to mankind by God in messages sent through specially chosen people, such as Moses, David, and Solomon among the compilers of the Old Testament of the Bible and such followers of Christ as Matthew, Mark, Luke, John, and Paul for the New Testament. Since earliest Christian times there have also been other people credited with being authentic recipients of divine revelations. These have included Christian saints, the popes of the Catholic church, and such individuals in Protestant denominations as Martin Luther (1483–1546), John Calvin (1509–1564), John Knox (1505–1572), Joseph Smith (1805–1844) as founder of the Mormon Church, and Mary Baker Eddy (1821–1910) as founder of the Christian Science Church.

At the opposite end of the philosophical spectrum from the conservatives are Christian liberals who do not regard the Bible as the literal, infallible word of God.

Rather, they consider the Bible to be an inspired record of a people's search for the truth about the nature and origins of the universe, especially a search for the truth about how a person can most satisfactorily interact with other people, with God, and with the nonhuman world so as to achieve a feeling of contentment and self-worth. Typical liberals subscribe to the principles of living as exemplified in the teachings and actions of Jesus Christ. They regard Christ as certainly the best and most godly of men if not literally the special Son of God.

In regard to methods for learning the truth about human nature and development, liberals do not depend on the authority of any scripture or any individual, past or present, even if that individual is labeled a saint or holds high church office. Liberals believe in giving any "authority" a fair hearing, but they then weigh the authority's evidence and line of reasoning against competing proposals and thereupon draw conclusions that seem logically convincing. A typical liberal contends that:

> Religion is devoted and loyal commitment to the best that reason and insight can discover. The liberal understands what loyalty to the best means as the authoritarian never can . . . . God has to talk our language if we are to understand him, and if we don't understand him I see no use in talking either with him or about him . . . . Every sense experience, value experience, or experience of God must be put through the critical mill, . . . in a good sense rationalized, before it can take its place in the reasonable stream of thought. (J. S. Bixler in Dunstan 1961 pp. 197–98)

In effect, liberals welcome scientific inquiry and seek to accommodate differences between scientific theory and Christian scripture by determining which is the more reasonable or by proposing a line of reasoning that links the two compatibly. Thus, liberals can accept both a Darwinian view of the evolution of humans and a Biblical description of creation by reasoning that the Biblical version is a poetic estimate rather than a literal depiction of what occurred.

Between the conservative and liberal viewpoints are the convictions of mainstream Christians, who believe that humans, like other mortal and finite creatures of God, fit into the order of nature. But humans are special in the sense that they are responsible beings that are:

> capable of personal confrontation with God, and conscious "response" to God. In this basic fact, man's "chief end" is already indicated; he is made for fellowship with God. In the sight of God his Judge, man is a sinner . . . . This is not a condition to which God has fatally condemned mankind, but a perversion of the nature and destiny of man as God created him, for which man himself is responsible . . . . There is thus a considerable agreement among Christians concerning the position of man in God's world, the fact that he tends tragically to miss his high calling, and the centrality of sin among the imprisoning forces from which he needs deliverance, if he is to be restored to his true destiny. (Hodgson 1938 p.224)

As for the proper means of learning about human nature, mainstream Christians subscribe neither to the conservative's accepting the literal statements of the Bible as infallible nor to the liberal's questioning or reinterpreting scripture that conflicts with logical conclusions drawn from evidence gathered by ostensibly scientific methods. Instead, mainstream Christians believe that while the exact phrasing of tenets and incidents in the Gospel should not be considered the literal Word of God, "any teaching that clearly contradicts the Biblical positions cannot be accepted as Christian" (Richardson and Schweitzer 1951 p. 243).

In summary, although differences exist among Christians about the proper status of the Bible as a source of evidence, on the most central issues regarding human nature and development most Christians hold that the Biblical version is paramount and thus takes precedence over opposing views.

8. Educational and Child-rearing Implications

Suggestions about goals and instructional methods in education and child raising can be derived from the views of human development reflected in both the contents and the form of the Bible. The following examples demonstrate how the process of extracting implications can be carried out.

First is the question of who should set the goals of instruction. From a Christian view, because children by their nature are inclined to sinful acts, they should not be the ones to determine the objectives of child rearing or schooling. Rather, the aims should be set by adults who are no longer "childish" but who have advanced well into the age of reason and who know well the teachings of the Lord. As the apostle Paul wrote to members of the church at Corinth (1 Corinthians 13:11):

> When I was a child, I spake as a child, I understood as a child, I thought as a child: but when I became a man, I put away childish things.

The central goal of Christian education in both home and school is to teach the nature of God and his commandments so the learners will understand the consequences of a sinful life in contrast to a virtuous life and will be motivated to adopt the virtuous and avoid the sinful. Consequently, a major portion of educational programs and child care should focus on understanding God's will and on living by Christian principles.

> It cannot . . . be desirable or advantageous that religion should be excluded from the school. On the contrary, it ought there to be one of the chief agencies for moulding the young life to all that is true and virtuous and holy . . . . Therefore, the school, which principally gives the knowledge fitting for practical life, ought to be preeminently under the holy influence of religion. (Brantl 1961 p.202)

The form of the Bible's contents can serve as a model for teaching methods, since the contents illustrate a variety of instructional approaches. The Bible teaches its lessons through descriptions of historical events, proverbs, songs (psalms), parables that point out moral precepts, letters of consolation and instruction, and the direct preaching of moral principles. All of these methods appeal to the intellect, to cognition rather than simply to the emotions, thus implying that people can learn through an appeal to reason to overcome sinful tendencies and follow the path traced in the Lord's word. And the inclusion of these different instructional approaches in the Bible may imply that different people have different learning styles, so that teachers can profitably use a diversity of instructional methods in order to succeed with as wide a variety of learners as possible. Another possible implication of the variety of approaches is that different instructional techniques can reinforce each other, so that when a teacher uses a variety of approaches with a particular learner, the cumulative effect of the several methods can be greater than that of a single method alone.

Finally, consider the question of how to motivate people to learn. Many passages of the Bible reflect the assumption that people can be motivated both by promises of reward and by threats of punishment. This assumption also includes the belief that people are motivated not only by promises of immediate consequences. Instead, the promise of distant consequences—such as during life after death—will motivate learning and behavior as well if the expected rewards are sufficiently magnificent or the expected punishments sufficiently devastating. In promising a distant consequence, Jesus told the multitude in his sermon on the mount, "Rejoice, and be exceeding glad: for great is your reward in heaven" (Matthew 5:12). He later assured his disciples that "In my Father's house are many mansions . . . . I go to prepare a place for you" (John 14:2). The psalmist, addressing God, acknowledged that "at Thy right hand there are pleasures for evermore" (Psalms 16:11). "Again, the kingdom of heaven is like unto a treasure hid in a field" (Matthew 13:44); and faithful Christians, after death, "shall hunger no more, neither thirst any more . . . and God shall wipe away all tears from their eyes" (Revelation 7:16-17).

Frequent mention is also made of punishments to be suffered by sinners, either immediately or in life after death. Immediate punishments to be meted out by society for specific sins include banishment from the community, depriving the sinner of possessions, and death by stoning, burning, hanging, beheading, and crucifying. Then after death "the wicked shall perish; . . . as the fat of lambs, . . . into smoke shall they consume away" (Psalms 37:20), while other sinners "shall go away into everlasting punishment: but the righteous into life eternal" (Matthew 25:46).

In such ways the contents and form of holy scriptures can be interpreted as implying concepts of human development that suggest applications to educational practice.

Bibliography

Berkouwer G C 1962 *Man: The Image of God*. Eerdmans, Grand Rapids, Michigan
Brantl G 1961 *Catholicism*. Braziller, New York
Chafer L S 1947 *Systematic Theology*, Vol. 2. Dallas Seminary Press, Dallas, Texas
Dunstan J L 1961 *Protestantism*. Braziller, New York
Hodgson L (ed.) 1938 *The Second World Conference on Faith and Order*. Macmillan, New York
New England Primer: Or an Easy and Pleasant Guide to the Art of Reading. 1836 Massachusetts Sabbath School Society, Boston, Massachusetts
Richardson A, Schweitzer W (eds.) 1951 *Biblical Authority for Today*. A World Council of Churches Symposium on "the Biblical Authority for the Church's Social and Political Message Today. SCM Press, London
Scofield C I (ed.) 1967 *Holy Bible: Authorized King James Version: The New Schofield Bible*. Oxford University Press, New York
Simonson H P (ed.) 1970 *Selected Writings of Jonathan Edwards*. Ungar, New York
Strong A H 1907 *Systematic Theology: A Compendium and Common-place Book Designed for the Use of Theological Students*. Judson, Valley Forge, Pennsylvania

Islamic Theory of Human Development

R. A. Obeid

While there is no traditional Islamic text that directly describes a Moslem theory of development, it is possible to synthesize such a theory by performing a content analysis of Islamic scriptures. This task involves using questions about development as guides to a study of Islamic sacred writings, then organizing the answers derived from the study into a coherent statement of a Moslem theory of development.

A decision faced at the outset of the content-analysis process is that of determining which are the appropriate scriptures to analyze. Islamic literature, like the literature of other major philosophical traditions, contains writings considered to be of different degrees of authenticity. Some writings are more widely regarded as the true word than are others. In Islam, the one book universally considered the authentic word of God is the Koran. Second only to the Koran is the Hadith (*Traditions*) which contains sayings of the Prophet Muhammad who founded Islam in the seventh century AD. In addition to these two sources, a wide array of writings by Islamic scholars has evolved over the centuries. Certain sects within Islam subscribe to different selections among these writings as valid representations of Moslem doctrine, while other sects consider such additional writings as of doubtful authenticity.

When books that are to be subjected to content analysis are selected for extracting Islamic theory, a conservative approach that may faithfully reflect the beliefs of a wide range of Moslems is that of basing the analysis on those volumes most generally regarded as the actual word of God and his chief prophet. The material presented in the following article reflects such a conservative approach, since the analysis draws solely on the Koran and Hadith.

The questions which the analysis has sought to answer are: (a) What is the length of the human life span? (b) On what aspects of life does Islamic development theory focus? (c) What is the goal or proper direction of development? (d) What is the effect of innate factors as compared with environmental influences? (e) What is the form of the learning process in Islam? (f) What implications for child rearing and educational practice can be drawn from Islamic theory?

1. The Period of Development

An individual's life span, from an Islamic perspective, is a continuous process that begins with biological conception 9 months prior to birth and extends past the death of the body into an infinite future.

Just 120 days after conception, as the foetus is growing in the mother's womb, God sends an angel to embed a soul in the foetal body and to set the lifelong fate of the unborn child in four aspects of existence: the earnings he will acquire, key deeds he will do, the time of his death, and whether he will be happy or miserable.

Following birth, the infant grows through different stages of childhood, adulthood, and old age until death. But the death of the physical body is not the end of the human soul, which continues to live in an invisible state until Judgment Day, at which time all people are judged by God according to the quality of their deeds on earth. On Judgment Day, all learn if they are destined to spend eternity in Heaven or in Hell.

2. The Aspects of Development

Various aspects of human life—the physical, intellectual, social, emotional, moral—receive attention in Moslem scriptures. However, the main focus is on the development of human character, of moral behavior, and of one's relationship to God. All other aspects are expected to interact in a way that contributes to the person's moral growth.

3. The Goal or Direction of Development

Since the chief concern in Islam is with character formation and with establishing a proper relationship with the Supreme Power, the goal or desired direction of development is defined in terms of acquiring such traits as obedience to God, respect for parents, benevolence, patience, forgiveness, courage, firmness in resisting evil, respect for the law, and the discipline that will enforce justice in society. All of these character traits serve the ultimate aim of enabling the individual to earn eternal life in Heaven.

According to Islam, the most general components of a human are the physical and the spiritual. The physical component is tangible: it grows and moves. The spiritual component is abstract: it judges, values, and directs behavior. Each of the components has its needs to fulfill. The physical self needs food, drink, sexual satisfaction, and the like, while the spiritual holds the achievement of moral perfection as its goal. In Islam, a person is entitled to fulfill both the physical and spiritual, without overemphasizing either one.

4. Nature, Nurture, and Free Will

From an Islamic viewpoint, three types of factors interact to form the pattern of an individual's development. First are predetermined factors set by God. Second are environmental influences. Third is the person's free will that enables him to decide on his own which alternative he will select when he has a choice among alternatives.

The exact relationships among these three factors has long been a matter of debate among Islamic scholars, with no real consensus resulting from the debate. However, the scriptures do identify certain characteristics that are established prior to a child's birth. One is the type of physical growth the child will experience. Included in this physical-growth determination is the time of the person's death. A second aspect is the worldly income the individual will receive. A third is the factor of general happiness or unhappiness. The rationale behind God's predetermining such matters is that when people recognize that their fate in these respects has been preset, there is nothing they can do to change them; consequently, there is no need to overindulge in either grief or joy over such matters.

In other aspects of life, however, people are free to choose the path they will take. As a preparation for making wise choices, God's will is represented in the words of the prophets that He has sent to guide people and to warn them of the cost of transgressions. Man's free will is expressed in his choice of which way to follow. The Koran frequently points out that man is then responsible for his own deeds. "Verily never will God change the condition of a people until they change it themselves with their own souls."

Environmental variables interact with a person's will to determine the individual's deeds. The main type of influence identified in Islamic scriptures is the social environment. People are advised to associate with companions who exhibit appropriate behavior as judged by God's standards of morality. While the individual may not be able to alter his condition of happiness on earth by the nature of his deeds, his deeds do determine the condition in which his soul will spend eternity after the death of the physical self.

5. The Learning Process

In Islam, people are expected to develop their characters through a long process of learning. The scriptures identify the kind of learning each Moslem is to pursue and the learning process itself. In addition, the style in which the Koran is written illustrates various ways to stimulate learning.

5.1 Kind of Learning

The type of learning encouraged in Islam is the sort that combines memorization and understanding. To clarify the meaning intended by this kind, it is important to distinguish between rote memorization, which relies on verbatim repetition without thought or understanding, and the kind of memorization recommended in Islam, a type that enables the learner to establish associations between previously acquired knowledge and present situations. Understanding, in this sense, means that the learner judges others' experiences, avoids unverified matters, engages in a wide range of experiences, and then chooses the best path as a result of this combination of activities.

5.2 Aspects of the Process

The learning process is a function of perception and of reasoning. It involves two senses—sight and hearing—that inform the mind of impressions in the environment, and the mind either accepts or rejects the impressions and analyzes them in terms of what is already in memory.

Not only are the Koran and the Hadith the main sources of information about the content to be learned in Islam, but the form of the two works appears to be founded on a set of beliefs about how people learn, a set that could qualify as an implied theory of learning. The aspects of form that suggest such a conclusion are those of: (a) God's directly addressing the reader in a father–child or teacher–student relationship, (b) dialogues to illustrate a train of logic leading to a conclusion, (c) intentional repetition of important principles, (d) parables and life-like examples that both clarify concepts and serve as models for readers to imitate, (e) reinforcement through proposed rewards for desired behavior and threats of punishment to deter readers from undesired behavior, and (f) the use of figures of speech, such as metaphores and similes. Each of these will be considered in turn.

God's direct lecturing or exhortation serves as an immediate link between God and His worshippers, setting forth Islamic laws, warning humans against committing irreligious acts, and encouraging them to adopt desirable behavior.

The discussion or dialogue method consists mainly of posing questions, then supplying answers, apparently to capture the reader's attention and, on other occasions, to challenge the reader's curiosity by bringing up unfamiliar matters. The types of dialogues in the scriptures include the descriptive, the narrative, and the argumentative. In the argumentative variety, the discussion follows a train of logic based on explanations derived from Islamic traditions, such as:

> They will say: "Who will cause him to return?"
> Say: "He who created you first."

A third approach involves the repetition of either ideas or actual words and phrases. A fourth consists of parables, most of them depicting morally noble deeds of prophets who are proposed as models for Moslems to admire and imitate. The scriptures also urge parents to fashion their own lives as models suitable for children to copy.

A fifth aspect of the learning process illustrated in the scriptures is the use of psychological reinforcement, that is, the technique of encouraging a desired behavior by showing the rewarding consequences which that behavior can bring. Just as reinforcement is used to promote desirable acts, so its opposite—punishment—is employed to eliminate transgressions of religious, personal, and social rules. Some passages describe punishments that have been suffered by evildoers in the past:

> Against some We sent a violent tornado
> (with showers of stones), some were caught
> By a mighty blast; some We caused the earth
> To swallow up; and some We drowned.
> It was not God who injured them;
> They injured their own souls.

Other passages predict punishments to be meted out on Judgment Day:

> They shall have layers of fire above them
> And layers of fire below them; with this
> Doth God warn off his servants:
> "Oh, my servants, then fear ye Me!"

A sixth mode of enhancing learning is the use of metaphors and similes which illustrate abstract meanings in materialistic terms, thus aiding the reader in understanding and remembering the intended lesson:

> The parable of those who
> Take protectors other than God
> Is that of the spider,
> Who builds (to itself)
> A house, but truly
> The flimsiest of houses
> Is the spiders' house;
> If they but knew.

6. Implications for Child Rearing and Education

The following suggestions illustrate the kinds of guidance provided in the holy writings for raising children in the home and for teaching them at school.

6.1 Guidance for Child Rearing

Only a few specific recommendations about raising young children (such as, weaning them at age 2) are included in the scriptures. Most advice about child rearing appears in the form of general guidelines. For example, readers are told that infants are born with the innate tendency to do the right thing, but they are apt to be misled into wrongdoing by environmental forces. So it is the duty of parents to direct children in the Islamic way in order to "Save yourselves and your families from a fire whose fuel is men and stones."

Personal qualities that parents should foster in their children are described in the Koran by God, speaking through the tongue of Lugman:

> Establish regular prayer, enjoin what is
> Just, and forbid what is wrong;
> And bear with patient constancy
> Whate'er betide thee, for this
> Is firmness (of purpose) in affairs.
> And swell not thy cheek with pride
> Nor walk in insolence through the earth;
> For God loveth not an arrogant boaster.
> And be moderate in thy pace,
> And lower thy voice.

The Koran also advises parents to be affectionate toward their children and to care for their needs. It is reported that Prophet Muhammad often hugged his grandchildren and the children of friends and said: "Oh, God, have mercy on them as I am merciful to them." Parents are also expected to prepare their children to

make wise selections of friends, for children can be strongly influenced by their peers.

6.2 Curriculum Planning

A school's curriculum can be defined as all those learning experiences the school provides for carrying learners toward the objectives of the education system. From an Islamic viewpoint, these objectives of development are the ones described earlier (see Sect. 3)—proper moral and social behavior, obedience to God, and a healthy physical condition. As a consequence, the curriculum is heavily weighted in favor of teaching moral precepts as found in Islamic scripture, with emphasis upon memorizing the scriptures along with applying the precepts to life situations in order to ensure that they are not only memorized but also understood. The chief teaching materials are necessarily the Koran and Hadith. Instructional methods, as derived from the scriptures, are the ones reviewed above under Sect. 5.

Bibliography

Ali A Y 1979 *The Glorious Qu'ran.* Dar El Kilab Al Masri, Cairo
El Gazali M 1968 *Revival of the Religious Teachings.* Dar Almaarifa, Beirut
Elnahlawi A 1979 *The Basics of the Islamic Education.* Dar Alfiker, Damascus
Taiara A 1974 *The Essence of the Islamic Religion.* Dar Alilm, Beirut

Hindu Theory of Human Development

R. M. Thomas

Embedded within the extensive body of India's Hindu literature are concepts that can be extracted and organized to form a Hindu theory of human development. If it can be assumed that knowledgeable, dedicated Hindus apply such concepts in the conduct of daily life, then an understanding of this theory can help explain such people's child-rearing and educational practices and the modes of counseling they may adopt to aid others who are psychologically distressed.

It would be inaccurate to say that a description of ideas about development drawn from the vast store of Hindu literature represents "the" Hindu theory of development, because the beliefs contained in one set of scriptures are not always consistent with those found in another. It is true that some concepts, such as those of karma and of the transmigration of souls, are universally accepted by the various Hindu sects. However, certain other beliefs have been controversial. Therefore, the following version should be considered "a" Hindu theory, one version consistent with what might be called the most central documents of Hindu tradition.

In deriving the version presented here, the author has used questions about human development as guides

to an inspection of Hindu writings in English translation. The books that proved most useful in this task were *The Laws of Manu* or *Manu Smriti* (Bühler 1886) and *The Grihya-Sutras—Rules of Vedic Domestic Ceremonies* (Oldenberg 1886). Of further use were the *Dharma Sutras,* segments of the *Upanishads,* portions of the *Vedas,* and the epic *Mahabharata* and *Ramayana* (Bloomfield 1908, Nikhilānanda 1956, Renou 1961).

The questions which guided the search through Hindu writings concerned (a) the origin and order of the cosmos, (b) the goal of life and of development, (c) causes of development—heredity, environment, and intention, (d) the learning process and motivation, (e) levels of consciousness, (f) stages of development, and (g) individual differences. The following discussion is organized around these topics and closes with a description of child-rearing, educational, and counseling practices that logically derive from such a theory.

1. The Origin and Order of the Cosmos

Hindu doctrine holds that all things have derived from a Cosmic Soul or Divine Self-existent that over infinite time subdivided in successive stages to produce all the objects of the universe. From this belief arises the concept fundamental to all of Hinduism that Mind or Soul (atman) is the essence of reality and that the physical world of everyday life is a passing thing, a kind of illusion. Thus, Hinduism's key concern is with the development of the human soul rather than with the body.

Three further assumptions central to Hindu theory are those concerning caste, reincarnation, and karma. The caste system which has so dominated social life in India over the centuries is founded on the conviction that a person's social status in the world is properly determined by a divinely ordered hierarchy of social classes or castes. The caste structure in its most basic form consists of four well-defined upper strata, plus an almost ignored lower stratum occupied by the socially despised "untouchables."

The four main castes, ranging from the most privileged and honored at the top to the least privileged at the bottom, are: (a) the Brahmins or priests who exercise spiritual power, (b) the Kshatriyas or warriors and administrators who wield secular power, (c) the Vaisyas or artisans who perform business and production functions, and (d) the Sudras who serve the upper three castes. For understanding development, the caste system is significant in two ways. First, a person is immutably bound to his caste by birth. Second, the rules of living which influence a person's development vary somewhat from one caste to another. Failure to abide by the multitude of rules designated for one's caste results in serious consequences for an individual's development, particularly for his fate in subsequent lives after the present one is over.

A keystone in Hindu theory is the concept of justice. In his development, a person gets what he earns and deserves. Justice operates through the principle of karma, a term which literally means deeds. According to this principle, the acts a person performs in daily life carry with them defined values, either good value or bad value or, sometimes, neutral value. Acts also differ in strength, some being weak, some moderate, and some strong. Under the principle of karma a person accumulates the effects of his acts in the form of an investment account. A person's karma represents a progressive accounting ledger, with the total result of bad deeds balanced against the total result of good deeds. As a consequence, a person's karma at any point in life is the algebraic sum of good and bad deeds.

Associated with the concept of karma is a belief in reincarnation of the soul. Hindus are convinced that when the body they currently inhabit dies and turns to dust, the soul lives on to be encased in a new body for another lifetime on earth. The new body may be that of a human or an animal or an inanimate object. It is a person's karma, or the effect of one's deeds, that determines the nature of the body to be inhabited in the next life. An abundance of good deeds entitles the person to a higher level body in the future or to a higher

social caste. An abundance of bad deeds condemns a person to inherit the body of a lower animal or inanimate object. The cycles of life, of death, and of transmigration into new bodies can be repeated again and again until the individual ultimately is released from the succession of embodiments by the soul's reuniting with the Cosmic Soul or Cosmic Mind from which all things originated in the infinite past.

Not only do the doctrines of karma and reincarnation provide a logic for explaining the justice of an individual's fate in an individual's life, but they furnish as well two ways to calculate the length of development. The period of development for the body extends from the moment of biological conception to the moment of the final heartbeat that signals death, a period of 70 to 80 years or so. In contrast, the period of development of the soul extends from the time the individual soul emerged from the Cosmic Soul in the infinite past (and was placed in an initial body) to the time when the individual soul accumulates sufficient good karma to deserve reunification with the Cosmic Soul at an unforeseeable moment in the future.

2. The Proper Goal of Development

In various Hindu texts the Supreme Being or Omnipotent Force is referred to by different names such as: Cosmic Soul, Brahman, Supreme Power, Cosmic Mind, Divine Self-existent, and Divine Reality. Likewise, the Individual Soul is sometimes called the atman, and at other times is identified as the inner spirit, inner Self, Mind, or Soul.

The desired end of a Hindu's existence is to achieve relief from both the pains and joys of mortality by being united with the Cosmic Soul. This goal of release from life is attained by mastering knowledge of the sacred writings, by practicing austerities, and by performing a multiplicity of rites. Subgoals of development that serve as instruments for achieving the ultimate objective of liberation from rebirths on earth are represented in Hindu literature as character traits and proper behaviors that lead to the desired end.

In terms of traits of desired development, the exemplary Hindu is: (a) studious and knowledgeable in the sacred literature, (b) disciplined, dutiful, devoted, loving, and obedient, (c) humble, unselfish, self-effacing, and self-sacrificing, (d) even tempered, chaste, freed from desire and aversion, exempt from hate and inordinate affection, and pure of speech and thought, (e) trusting in the correctness of Hindu doctrine and "confident in eternity" (Bloomfield 1908 pp. 281–87, Bühler 1886 pp. 29, 59, Iyer 1969 pp. 13–15).

To guide the Hindu's efforts in developing these traits, the scriptures contain detailed descriptions of specific rites and acts that earn positive karma and contain as well descriptions of behavior that is despicable and earns bad karma that will lead to an undesired fate in future lives on earth.

3. Causes of Development—Heredity, Environment, Intention

In Western secular theories it has been customary to analyze the causes of development in terms of the interaction of hereditary and environmental factors. In Hinduism, however, the further factor of personal intention, founded on an implied free will, must be considered the third and the most important component in the interaction.

Heredity, in the sense of a person's genetic endowment that strongly influences the nature and pace of development, does not exist in Hindu theory. Rather, a person creates his own inheritance for his present period on earth by means of the deeds he performed in previous existences. In other words, a person's deeds have determined his karma, and his karma from earlier lives is what he inherits to cause current developmental characteristics. In this sense, an individual becomes both his own progenitor and his own heir.

While the major portion of a person's inheritance comes from self-created karma, a small portion is derived from the parents and is of three varieties. The first arises from punishment earned by parents' misdeeds in their earlier lives on earth. "If the punishment falls not on the offender himself, it falls on his sons; if not on the sons, at least on his grandsons" (Bühler 1886 p. 156). The second consists of deeds parents commit or fail to commit in preparation for the birth of the child, such as eating specified food in a specified manner to determine the sex of the child that they are about to conceive (Nikhilānanda 1956 pp. 374–75). The third variety of parental legacy takes the form of direct bequests of character traits or talents passed on just prior to the parent's death. "A father, when about to decease, summons his son . . . my intelligence in you I would place." And the son replies, "Your intelligence in me I take" (Renou 1961 pp. 100–01).

In summary, then, a person's physical and social condition during the current life span is almost entirely inherited, in the sense of being predetermined. The agents who furnish this inheritance are both the individual and his parents. The process of inheritance consists primarily of deeds of the past generating karma that has fashioned a person's current fate.

Environment, from a Hindu perspective, consists of a person's surroundings that provide opportunities which individuals use to create their own fate. In effect, humans are considered to be internally energized beings with free wills, beings equipped to take advantage of the resources of their locales to shape their own development. So the question is not whether the people and objects around individuals will mold their development, for they will do so if they let them. But the question, rather, is whether individuals will permit them to influence their life. People are free to choose how to think and act. They provide the answer by means of two factors, their level of knowledge and their personal intention. So they may think sinful thoughts or engage in evil deeds through either ignorance or bad intentions. The ignorance can be cured by knowledge of the sacred scriptures and by introspection or contemplation that enables them to comprehend their inner spirit (atman), which is the individual soul derived from the Cosmic Soul known as Brahman. The bad intentions can be controlled by threats of punishment and the practice of austerities and rituals that can stiffen a person's resolve to abide by the teachings of the scriptures.

While most of a person's current development has been determined by deeds during earlier lives, the individual can exert some limited influence over his or her present fate by adhering faithfully to Hindu doctrine. As a modern-day interpreter of Hinduism has explained, if a person has "predestinated himself to be the possessor of a bad temper, he cannot suddenly change it into a good one; but he can gradually alter it by right desire and right thought" (Besant 1908 p. 152).

4. The Learning Process and Motivation

In Hindu theory there are two types of learning, each with its own goal and its own method. The first has the goal of gaining knowledge from the world, so it is outer directed. Its source of knowledge is the environment, and its methodology is twofold—(a) formal study of the sacred writings and (b) informal interaction with the world, known as experience. The second type of learning has the goal of understanding a person's own self, so it is inner directed. Its source of knowledge is the individual's inner spirit or atman, and its methodology is introspection as achieved through meditation.

To motivate students' learning, Hinduism has depended heavily on punishment or the threat of punishment. Thomas (1960 p. 66) has noted that the Hindu maxim "knowledge must be grown in tears" is the equivalent of the Western "spare the rod and spoil the child." This conviction is constantly reflected throughout sacred writings in the multitude of punishments to be suffered by those who, either intentionally or inadvertently, transgress the rules. As the *Laws of Manu* points out:

> The whole world is kept in order by punishment, for a guiltless man is hard to find; through fear of punishment the whole world yields the enjoyments which it owes . . . . The wise declare punishment to be the law. (Renou 1961 pp. 121–22)

The punishment needed to mold people's development is administered by two sorts of agents. First are those persons who wield power over others' conduct— the king over the populace, the parent over the child, the teacher over the pupil. Such punishment is immediate, in that the consequence is administered promptly after the transgression. The second sort of agent is the Supreme Power (Brahman) that governs the universe. The punishment meted out by Brahman is not immediate but, instead, is postponed until after the present life on earth. As such, its power for frightening a person into learning or into proper deeds depends on the Hindu's faith that the world operates on the principle of justice, that people get what they deserve, even if it takes a long time for justice to appear.

In addition to the outer-directed type of learning about the world and about proper behavior, there is the second source that focuses inward. It consists of meditation, best known to the world through the sects that practice yoga. The purpose of meditation is for the person through intense concentration to experience the core of the inner self (atman). The long practice required to achieve successful meditation usually involves specified postures, rituals, and the repetition of mantras, which are propitious syllables intoned by the meditator.

Although in Hindu theory a person at every stage of life is expected to engage in both outer-directed and inner-directed learning, a larger portion of the outer-directed study is expected to take place in adolescence and early adulthood and a larger portion of the inner-directed meditation in middle and old age.

5. Levels of Consciousness

In Hindu theory the universe is composed of two classes of phenomena, the eternal and the transitory. Eternal is the Cosmic Soul (Brahman), whose essence includes Absolute Truth, Ultimate Reality, and Supreme Bliss. The individual person's soul (atman) is of this eternal class. In the transitory class are objects and events of the day, including the human body, representing neither Truth nor Reality but merely illusion.

These two classes of phenomena are associated with three states of awareness: (a) the waking state, (b) dreaming, and (c) dreamless sleep. In the waking state the individual consciously observes the passing of daily events, naively believing them to be reality whereas they are simply illusions. Dreamless sleep, in contrast, involves no awareness at all and thus is considered to be the nearest a mortal can approach that sense of blissful nothingness ultimately to be experienced when the individual soul (atman) finally merges into the Cosmic Soul (Brahman) for all eternity. Intermediate between wakefulness and dreamless sleep is the dream state. The Brihadāranyaka Upanishad proposes that the dreamer is in a condition to survey both the wakeful and dreamless states simultaneously, using impressions from the waking state as materials and using intimations from the dreamless state as the power to create dream experiences of his or her own volition.

6. Stages of Development

Generally, throughout Hindu writings the extent to which the stages of life apply to women is unclear. However, the main tenor of the text suggests that the stages apply to men.

When a child of one of the upper three Hindu castes—

the Aryan castes—reaches puberty or shortly after, he begins to study the ancient scriptures under the tutelage of a guru or holy teacher from the top Brahmin caste. This initiation into the study of the holy books is known as the individual's second birth, so that he has now become a "twice-born man." The four stages of human development begin at this point and extend until death.

The first stage is that of studentship, defined not in years but in mastery of the scriptures, vows, duties, rites, austerities, and techniques of meditation needed to earn the karma for attaining a desired higher condition in subsequent lives on earth.

The second stage is that of householder, which begins with the individual's marriage. Upon entering this stage, the householder assumes a heavy burden of responsibility, since he is expected to support the members of the other three stages—the student, the ascetic, and the mendicant—with food, clothing, and sacred knowledge. Householders keep the workaday world operating through assuming the roles of parents, administrators of government, producers of goods, traders, warriors, and educators.

The third stage is that of the hermit in the forest, a condition that the householder enters after several decades of performing his duties as parent and producer of goods. When the householder "sees his skin wrinkled, his hair white, and the sons of his sons, then he may resort to the forest" (Bühler 1886 p. 198). Living the life of an ascetic, the twice-born Hindu now wears a tattered garment, has unclipped beard and nails, and spends his time reciting the scriptures and performing rites. He is obliged to make no effort to obtain things that give pleasure. Before long the individual abandons his forest dwelling to enter the final stage of development, that of the roving almsman. He forsakes all earthly ties and all concern for his physical self and turns ever inward in final search for union of his inner soul (atman) with the Cosmic Soul. His physical needs are cared for by others. The mundane end to this stage is death, but the inner soul proceeds beyond, its fate for the future determined by the karma accumulated during the life span just completed.

As this sequence of four stages of development illustrates, Hindu theory focuses only on adolescence and the several states of adulthood, virtually ignoring childhood prior to puberty. The only mention of childhood appears as occasional comments about child rearing that appear incidental to other topics.

7. Individual Differences

In Hindu tradition five types of differences among individuals that receive attention are those related to caste, to sex, to age, to physical attributes, and to personal behavior.

Caste determines to a great degree the esteem in which a person is held, the occupation he enters, the privileges he enjoys, the rites he performs, the responsibilities he bears, and the pattern of his social relations. These differences in caste are entirely the result of a person's karma, his own deeds in past existences.

In terms of sex differences, more privilege and decision-making power goes to men than to women. Such differences are produced by the parents' observance of proper rites at the time of conception and by the ratio of male to female essence contributed by the parents during coitus.

Age differences result simply from the passing of time, while physical attributes depend chiefly on one's karma and, to a lesser degree, on parents' deeds.

Differences among individuals in their daily behavior are a result of their own intentions, their own free choice. They themselves determine how they will act from day to day.

8. Implications for Child Rearing, Teaching, and Counseling

Advice about correct methods for raising children appears mainly in the *Grihya-Sutras* (Rules of Vedic Domestic Ceremonies) and the *Manu Smriti* (Laws of Manu). The advice is of two types, proposals for direct treatment and ones for mediated treatment.

Direct treatment means advice about what to do to the child to effect proper development. For example, one source recommends that after the infant has been breast-fed for six months, it should receive its first solid food while the father repeats the prescribed verses. The infant can be fed goat's flesh for promoting physical fitness, partridge for holy luster, fish for swiftness, and boiled rice with ghee (clarified butter) for splendor (Oldenberg 1886 Vol. 1 p. 54).

Mediated treatment means that the child is not treated directly but that a rite is performed to an intermediary force, such as the Supreme Power or a particular god, with the expectation that this force will then effect the desired results in the child's development. Hindu lore offers more advice about mediated than about direct treatment of young children. For example, to enhance a child's intelligence, the father repeats three times in the child's right ear an incantation to the goddess of speech and mind (Oldenberg 1886 Vol. 1 p. 51).

As already noted, when the upper caste child approaches adolescence, he should be assigned to a guru who will guide his education during the years of studentship. Along with memorizing the scriptures so

he can repeat them accurately throughout his life, the student is expected to abide by an extended list of duties and rules of avoidance. The guru's teaching methods consist of drilling the student on the scriptures and of elucidating the implications of the texts. To motivate the learner, the teacher depends primarily on threats of punishment to be experienced now and in lives hereafter and on actual punishments the teacher imposes in the form of criticism, shaming, and blows.

In the Hindu setting the people logically prepared to serve as counselors are men of the priestly caste, the Brahmins, who are thoroughly versed in the sacred writings and experienced in the conduct of rites. To qualify, a Brahmin would need to be past the stage of studentship, well into the stage of householder or hermit. Counseling techniques logically would include giving instruction in the sacred rites and austerities, describing the penances required for canceling the consequences of transgressions, performing rites that promote the welfare of the counselee, and motivating the counselee to adopt the behaviors recommended in the scriptures. Motivation techniques would principally be threats of punishment and, secondarily, promises of an earlier release from the birth–death cycles for assiduously keeping to the path of righteousness.

Bibliography

Besant A 1908 *Questions on Hinduism, with Answers.* Theosophical Publishing Society, Benares
Bloomfield M 1908 *The Religion of the Veda, the Ancient Religion of India (from Rig Veda to Upanishads).* Putnam, New York
Bühler G 1886 The Laws of Manu. In: Muller M (ed.) 1886 *The Sacred Books of the East*, Vol. 25. Clarendon Press, Oxford
Iyer K B 1969 *Hindu Ideals.* Bharatiya Vidya Bhavan, Bombay
Keith A B 1925 *The Religion and Philosophy of the Veda and Upanishads.* Harvard University Press, Cambridge, Massachusetts
Nikhilānanda S 1956 *The Upanishads: Aitareya and Brihadāranyaka*, Vol. 3. Harper, New York
Oldenberg H 1886 The Grihya-Sutras—rules of Vedic domestic ceremonies In: Muller M (ed.) 1886 *The Sacred Books of the East*, Vols. 1, 29, 30. Clarendon Press, Oxford
Renou L 1961 *Hinduism.* Braziller, New York
Thomas P 1960 *Hindu Religion, Customs and Manners; Describing the Customs and Manners, Religious, Social and Domestic Life, Arts and Sciences of the Hindus*, 4th edn. Taraporevala Sons, Bombay

Buddhist Theory of Human Development

J. C. Marek

While the Buddha (born in 623 BC according to Theravāda Buddhists) never specifically developed a theory of human development, his teachings provide a rich collection of insights about the nature of humans, detailing how he believed people do and should develop. Today the millions of Asians who are professed Buddhists apparently base at least part of their perception of human development on these teachings, so that an insight into their perception of child rearing and education may be gained by a study of key concepts of Buddhism.

The Buddha himself left no writings, but his disciples recorded their recollections and interpretations of his beliefs. These records serve as a source from which several variants of a Buddhist theory of development can be generated, with each variant determined by the particular set of Buddhist literature from which the theory is abstracted. The following account is based on the Thai version of the Sutta Pitaka, the second "basket" of the Tripiṭaka (Three Baskets).

Buddhism evolved in a Hindu society and, as such, it adopted certain Hindu beliefs and rejected others. For example, Hinduism subscribes to the notion of reincarnation, that is, the transmigration of the human soul from one body to another after each period of life on earth. In contrast, the Buddha was far more of an empiricist than the traditional Hindus, who were willing to speculate about matters for which they lacked observable evidence. The account below can profitably be viewed against a background of Hindu doctrine. The following description begins with the nature of Buddhist empiricism, then continues with Buddhist ideas of creation, karma and rebirth, personality structure, the goal of development, causes of development, the learning process, and the nature of individual differences. The account closes with implications for educational practice.

1. Buddhist Empiricism

The Buddha was an empiricist who discouraged questions about matters not susceptible to verification by the senses. "What is the *all*? The eyes and forms, the ears and sounds, the nose and smells, the tongue and tastes, the body and tangible things, the mind and mental dispositions. That is the *all*" (*Samyutta-Nikāya* 1957 v. 28 pp. 15, 16). While the senses and the mind are the *all*, the Buddha claimed to have developed his own ordinary senses to a point of extrasensory perception. Thus, the "developed eye" could see the death and rebirth of other beings, and the "developed mind" could know the thoughts of others. However, even such developed sensory knowledge is limited. The senses can never, for example, tell people whether a god or a cosmic soul does or does not exist.

2. Creation and Dissolution of Existence

Through the power of retrocognition, the Buddha claimed to have been able to look as far back as he wished into his own past lives, but nowhere could he see the ultimate beginning (*Samyutta-Nikāya* 1957 v. 26 p. 2). Therefore, the Hindu or Jewish claim that the world was created by a god or that it derived from a cosmic soul was, for the Buddha, mere metaphysical speculation.

The Buddha did, however, say that the world goes through periods of dissolution and re-evolution. The process of re-evolution described in the Agganna Sutta of the *Digha-Nikāya* pictures the world at the beginning as being all water in total darkness. Living things are known simply as beings. Gradually the world takes on form and greater variety, and only gradually do differences among beings develop. Men become differentiated from women, and all people become differentiated by social class and occupation. In effect, the Buddha taught that all people have the same origins and, therefore, no group has the right to claim superiority over others on the basis of birth. This was a direct refutation of the Hindu claim that only Brahmins of the top caste are God's or Brahma's direct offspring and that human development theory is limited to the four upper Hindu castes. In Buddhism, all people are capable of developing to the point of achieving the final goal of life, the end of suffering that is *nirvana*.

3. Karma and Rebirth

Like the Hindus, the Buddha subscribed to the notion of rebirth, with life continuing after death in a different form. The Buddha also subscribed to the idea of karma being the accumulation of credit or blame a person acquires as the result of the deeds he or she commits in life. The result of many good deeds is an accumulation of favorable karma and a subsequent rebirth as a higher being. However, unlike the Hindus, the Buddha did not believe that a particular act necessarily brought a specified result in terms of good or bad karma. Instead, the Buddha was a relativist who contended that the circumstances in which the act was committed influenced as well the effect the deed would produce. To illustrate this concept of an effect depending on the conditions present when an act was committed, the Buddha said that if a grain of salt (the deed) is put into a cup of water, the water will taste salty (the effect). But if the grain of salt is put into a river, the river (representing different circumstances) will not taste salty. Thus, the same evil deed may lead to much suffering for one person and to very little suffering for another (*Anguttara-Nikāya* 1957 v. 36 p. 311, Kalupahana 1976 p. 48). Therefore, it is not the individual act that determines a person's future fate, but rather the act as it fits into the entire life pattern of the individual. The Buddha is quoted as saying:

> [Take the case of] a person who says that just as a man commits an act, so does he experience that act [as effect]. Monks, if such is the case, there is no living the holy life, nor is there an opportunity for the extinction of suffering. [But if] a person says that the effects experienced accord with the acts committed by the person, in such a case there is living the holy life, and an opportunity for the extinction of suffering. (*Anguttara-Nikāya* 1957 v. 36 p. 311)

The Buddhist idea of rebirth is different from the Hindu belief in that the Buddha refused either to admit or to deny the existence of a metaphysical entity called the soul, because its existence could not be empirically verified or rejected. But if there is no eternal soul that is reborn, who or what is it that carries the effect of karma or past deeds into a next life? The answer turns around the distinction between "identity" and "continuity" (Kalupahana 1976 p. 51). The Buddha rejected the notion of a personal, unchanging identity or soul, but he did not reject continuity. To illustrate, he said that just as curds derive from milk and butter from curds, so does the man derive from the boy and the future person from the past person. The butter is not identical to the milk, but there is a continuity leading from milk to butter. Therefore, when the period of human development is computed within Buddhist theory, it can be calculated in two ways. The more obvious way is to consider only the current life span which extends from observable birth until physical death. The second way is to view development as extending over a series of such current life spans that originated at some unknown point in the past and continue until some unknown time in the future. In effect, the Buddha could not identify the beginning of life, and he remained silent about the nature of development after nirvana was attained in the unforeseeable future.

4. Personality Structure

What is the human personality that develops? The Buddha is credited with answering:

> What we designate by the word *being* is nothing but a heap of conditioned factors. Just as we call [a chariot] "a chariot" because the various parts are in place, so we call [a being] "a being" because of the presence of the five aggregates [form, feelings, perception, volitional activities, and consciousness]. (*Samyutta-Nikāya* 1957 v. 24 p. 158)

This collection of aggregates or factors comes into existence by virtue of a type of spontaneous-generation causal principle:

> When this is present, that is present; when this arises, that arises; when this is not present, that is not present; when this ceases, that ceases. (*Samyutta-Nikāya* 1957 v. 25 p. 69)

According to the Buddha, the five aggregates are rupa, vedana, sanna, sankhara, and vinnana.

Rupa is the body or visible form, composed of the four principal material elements (earth, water, fire, air) and of whatever visible shapes as can be derived from the elements.

Vedana refers to feelings or sensations of three types—pleasant, unpleasant, and neutral.

Sanna is perception, which occurs when there is a sense (eyes, ears, taste buds, and others), there is a sense object (items in the environment to be perceived), and there is sense consciousness. If one or more of the three conditions is absent, perception will not take place, as suggested in the universal causal principle's statement that "when this is not present" (the three conditions), then "that is not present" (perception).

Sankhara (volitional activities, dispositions) is used in various ways in the sacred scriptures so that different scholars have translated the term in different ways. In the *Samyutta-Nikāya* the Buddha describes sankhara as including the will for sights, sounds, smells, taste, and touch. The sankhara elsewhere are interpreted as "acts of will" (Jayatilleke 1975) or as "creative activities" (Johansson 1979) which are purposeful and dynamic. In the Chula Vedalla Sutta within the *Majjhima-Nikāya* sankhara are described as activities, with respiration the activity of the body, observation and thinking the activities of speech, and perception and feeling the activities of mind. Sankhara are said to be conditioned by ignorance and to condition consciousness.

> If a person intends something, fixes something, and is engrossed in something, that is a factor for the establishment of consciousness. When consciousness has been established, it grows and rebirth takes place again in the future . . . . Thus arises this entire mass of suffering. (*Samyutta-Nikāya* 1957 v. 25 p. 126)

Thus, such acts of will or creative activities condition how a person's consciousness develops and thereby have great impact on the person's entire future development (Jayatilleke 1975 p. 219).

Sankhara can also be thought of as unconscious dispositions (Kalupahana 1975 p. 128) which function like instincts and lead people to act in certain ways. For example, the fact that a person flees upon seeing a poisonous snake is due to his or her desire to live or, in Freudian terms, due to his life instinct. In sum, sankhara can be either active or passive (walking as contrasted with breathing), they are purposeful (the desire for a better future life), and they may involve unconscious aspects (the instinct to seek safety when threatened).

Vinnana or consciousness is another complex term. As mentioned above, sense consciousness is, in one respect, a particular manifestation arising because of the presence of sense and sense object. In this meaning, consciousness is whatever is being attended to at the moment through using the five senses and mind. But vinnana is also thought to be the link that connects one existence (life span) to the next. The Mahatanha Sankhya Sutta of the *Majjhima-Nikāya* explains that the conception of a new individual or psychological being comes about through the conjunction of three things: coitus of the parents, the mother's period of fertility, and the presence of a rebirth consciousness (gandhabba). Vinnana thus provides the continuity between existences. However, the Buddha did not conceive of the vinnana as a permanent entity that transmigrated from one existence to the next. Such consciousness arises only if the proper conditions are present.

While the five factors described above—body form, feelings-sensations, perception, activities-dispositions, and consciousness—constitute the human personality, the Buddha rejected the notion that a permanent "I" or "self" could be found in any one or combination of these factors. On the other hand, the Buddha did not deny the existence of persons. Persons do exist; that is an empirical fact. But their nature is different from what most people suppose it to be. Rather than having an enduring self, a person is a collection of conditioned processes that will continue to exist as long as the conditions are present.

5. The Goal of Proper Development

At the core of the Buddha's teaching is the notion that existence is sorrow or suffering. Anything that is impermanent brings suffering and, therefore, even the five factors of personality, being impermanent, bring suffering. Because conditioned existence is unsatisfactory, the ultimate goal in Buddhism is to eliminate rebirth and its suffering. When rebirth and suffering have been cut off, the person has reached nirvana, the final goal.

The Buddha did not claim to be a god but only a guide who pointed out the path leading to nirvana. Treading the path is a task that each individual must perform for himself if he is to reach the goal. The road to nirvana is summarized as the Noble Eightfold Path:

(a) Right views—knowledge of the Four Noble Truths, meaning knowledge of the existence of suffering, the origin of suffering, the end of suffering, and the path to the end of suffering.

(b) Right aims—ones that are free from lust or craving, hatred, and cruelty.

(c) Right speech—not lying, not using harsh or dirty language, and not gossiping.

(d) Right action—not killing, refraining from sexual misconduct, and not stealing.

(e) Right livelihood—earning a living in a way that does not harm other living things.

(f) Right effort—mobilizing one's strength to foster right views and to reach the goal.

(g) Right mindfulness—consciously observing all of one's bodily and mental processes so as to focus attention on whatever one is engaged in at the present moment.

(h) Right concentration, consisting of nine levels of concentration extending from the elimination of sensuality and lust (level 1) to the cessation of ideation and feeling (level 9).

The eight steps of the path divide into three parts. The first two steps are concerned with knowledge and understanding of the world, the next three with moral behavior, and the final three with mental training.

In short, all of the Buddha's teachings were aimed at helping people to free themselves from rebirth and continued suffering. But this final goal could not usually be reached immediately. Therefore, intermediate goals on the way to nirvana consist of developing the forgoing virtues and practices in one's life and developing one's power to understand the true nature of life.

6. Causes of Development

Buddhism posits an interaction among heredity, environment, and intention to condition the course of development both in this life and in future lives. As for heredity, the Buddha proposed that all of what a person is today—physical and mental traits, socioeconomic status, emotional condition, and so on—has been inherited. A person is also born with certain latent traits and instincts that unfold or mature as the individual grows older. For example, infants are said to have no sensual desires, lusts, or passions; rather, they have only latent sensual tendencies (*Majjhima-Nikāya* 1957 v. 19 p. 149). The Buddha made it quite clear that the source of these characteristics and traits is the person himself or herself, or, more accurately, his or her past deeds. "All beings are the heirs of their own deeds" (*Majjhima-Nikāya* 1957 v. 19 p. 84). However, while a person's present characteristics are determined by his or her past actions, his or her future life is not predetermined. Even a person with a "dark birth" may carry out "light acts" and attain nirvana (*Digha-Nikāya* 1957 v. 16 p. 254). However, heredity is only one of the factors that condition the person's future life. The others are environmental influences and an individual's intention. The Buddha was more concerned with environment and personal intention than he was with heredity. Personal intention generates particular behaviors which lead to future effects (possibly inherited traits in the next life). It is not possible to change past behaviors but, through will, it is possible to help shape the future. Also, the environment can help shape intentions. Probably for these reasons, the Buddha exhorted people to develop their will and to resolve not to harm others, to develop mindfulness, to seek knowledge, and so on.

The environment is important because it provides conditions that either facilitate or hinder leading a virtuous life and gaining understanding. A verse in the *Samyutta-Nikāya* tells people that they "should associate and be intimate only with men of high moral principles since knowledge of their moral principles will [aid] in being good, rather than evil, . . . and give wisdom" (*Samyutta-Nikāya* 1957 v. 23 p. 262).

A proper environment is, by itself, not enough to ensure proper development. The third factor is personal intention or personal will. Personal will has both a positive and a negative aspect. The positive side is that unless a person has the will to travel the path, the goal of nirvana cannot be reached. The negative side of will is that most people constantly wish for things and plan deeds that, from the Buddhist standpoint, keep them tied to the wheel of suffering. A desire to be rich and a desire for sensual pleasures are examples of the negative aspect of personal will.

In summary, while people can do nothing about their

inherited characteristics, they can choose to lead virtuous lives, to seek out those environments conducive to spiritual development, and to use their talents to progress, however slowly, toward the goal of cessation of rebirth and suffering.

7. Motivation and the Learning Process

From the Buddhist perspective, all that people do in their daily lives is aimed at relieving the unsatisfactoriness or suffering in their lives. However, most behaviors, such as striving to become wealthy, only serve to increase people's ignorance and bind them more closely to the world of continued existence. On the other hand, dissatisfaction with this life and the desire to end suffering motivate people to "find the path and tread it."

The actual process leading to nirvana consists, as shown in the Noble Eightfold Path, of training the physical senses and developing understanding or insight into the true nature of the world (that all things are impermanent and that they arise from causes). To develop tranquility of the senses and to foster insight, the Buddha recommended various meditations to help control the senses. To develop understanding, he recommended practicing mindfulness of body, feelings, mind, and mind states (dharma). For example, one exercise is to be mindful of breathing and bodily postures.

8. Individual Differences

In Buddhist theory, the two differences that receive the most attention are those related to personal behavior and wisdom. Factors such as social status and physical attributes are of little import in treading the path. A person's behavior and understanding are held to be most important because they determine the person's future progress on the path to nirvana. As for the causes behind these differences in behavior and understanding, as has been stressed, all things arise because of conditions. Thus, individual differences in behavior and understanding are a function of one's karma, present environment and, most importantly, personal will.

9. Implications for Education

The literature reviewed here contains few direct references to formal schooling. It does, however, have many implications concerning the role of the teacher, the nature of the learner, and classroom teaching methods. Several of the more important implications are discussed below.

Based on Buddhist theory, the three most important learning objectives are (a) moral development, (b) the development of intellectual autonomy so that students can analyze things for themselves, and (c) the development of mental discipline and proper will.

The development of moral behavior is fundamental. Not only is it the basis for the development of intellectual understanding and insight, but the course of a person's future life is, to a large extent, determined by his or her present behavior. Thus, one of the most important duties of a teacher is to inculcate proper moral behavior among the students. Also, since a proper environment is important for fostering moral behavior, teachers must not only tell students what is right and wrong, but they must also behave properly themselves in order to be good models for their students.

Because each person is responsible for personally verifying the truths expounded by the Buddha rather than simply having faith in the Buddha's teachings, it is essential that individuals learn how to analyze and evaluate ideas and experiences. Thus, the proper role of the teacher can be viewed as that of a "facilitator" rather than as a "provider" (Gurugé 1977). Teachers should guide their students to discover things on their own rather than simply teach facts.

People are different because of their past deeds (heredity), the present environment, and their personal will. Yet all people can eventually reach their goals if they put forth effort. This suggests that, since students differ from each other, teachers should structure the classroom environment to fit the individual learning needs of each student. Then, by putting forth effort, each student can reach the educational goals, even though some may reach them later than others. The Buddha did this for his own followers by recommending particular meditation exercises to meet particular needs. Thus, one important teaching method is to have pupils work individually at tasks given by the teacher. However, before a teacher can know what tasks are appropriate for each student, he or she must first diagnose the present needs of the students. Engaging in class discussions, questioning students, and answering students' questions are important means of determining the needs of the students.

To spread his teachings, the Buddha sent his advanced disciples to instruct others. This suggests that teachers use students to tutor slower students. Also, during his travels, the Buddha gave sermons to both large and small groups. This can be compared to giving lectures. However, the listeners were expected to ponder deeply the ideas present in the sermon; they were not to accept blindly what the Buddha had said. Thus, teachers may use lectures but they must always ensure that the students have a chance to confirm the truth of what has been taught.

Bibliography

Anguttara-Nikāya 1957 Thammaphakdi, Bangkok
Digha-Nikāya 1957 Thammaphakdi, Bangkok
Gurugé A 1977 *Buddhism and Education.* Mahabodhi Society of India, New Delhi
Jayatilleke K N 1975 *The Message of the Buddha.* Allen and Unwin, London

Johansson R E A 1969 *The Psychology of Nirvana.* Allen and Unwin, London
Johansson R E A 1979 *The Dynamic Psychology of Early Buddhism.* Curzon, London
Kalupahana D 1975 *Causality: The Central Philosophy of Buddhism.* University Press of Hawaii, Honolulu
Kalupahana D J 1976 *Buddhist Philosophy: A Historical Analysis.* University Press of Hawaii, Honolulu
Majjhima-Nikāya 1957 Thammaphakdi, Bangkok
Samyutta-Nikāya 1957 Thammaphakdi, Bangkok

Confucian Theory of Human Development

Lin Huey-Ya

Over the centuries in Chinese culture four books have represented the core of the Confucian philosophical tradition. The first of these is the *Analects of Confucius*, a collection of brief proverbial sayings attributed to the teacher and social philosopher after whom the tradition was named, Confucius or Kung Fu-tzu (551–479 BC). Second is *The Book of Mencius,* composed by the sage Mencius or Meng-tzu (circa 372–289 BC), a student of Confucius' grandson. The last two books, *The Great Learning* and *The Doctrine of the Mean*, were written somewhat later but are still considered to be faithful representations of Confucius' beliefs.

In Chinese society prior to the twentieth century, these four classics served as the material to be mastered by candidates for the civil-service examinations that determined who would be awarded positions in the imperial government. Today the four continue to be viewed by followers of Confucian philosophy as the most authentic description of the proper conduct of life in the well-ordered political state. The four can be used as well as the source of a Confucian theory of proper human development.

The version of Confucian theory offered here has been formulated by the writer's addressing a series of questions about human development to the contents of the four books, then organizing the derived answers under four topics: (a) personality structure, (b) the goal of development, (c) learning theory, and (d) implications for child rearing and education.

1. Personality Structure

From a Confucian perspective, human nature is divided into two general types, the physiological and the virtuous. The physiological represents lower level characteristics and is disposed toward certain aspects of the world of behavior—the mouth disposed to tastes, the eye to colors, the ear to sounds, the nose to odors, and the four limbs to ease or rest. The higher level of human nature is that of virtue, which makes the difference between humans and brutes. Unlike animals, humans innately possess a heart that is sensitive to the suffering of others. This sensitive heart is a composite of the four hearts containing virtues—hearts of compassion, of shame, of courtesy and modesty, and of a sense of right and wrong.

In the heart of compassion is the seed of the virtue of humanity (jen). The heart of shame is the basis for righteousness (i). The heart of courtesy and modesty is the source of the observance of the Confucian rites (li). And the heart of right and wrong is the source of wisdom (chih). These four are the origin of all other virtues people develop.

Although human nature consists both of physiological needs and of virtues, in Confucian philosophy the fulfilment of physiological needs is chiefly in the hands of fate, while achieving the virtues depends upon the individual.

According to Mencius, although a person at birth is endowed with a positive human nature (a sense of virtue), he or she does not necessarily preserve it forever. Environmental influence can exert a profound impact on the preservation and nurturing of this nature. Mencius illustrated this point by comparing life to a forest. The trees can be felled by the axe. And even though new seedlings spring up, cattle can consume them, so the hillside remains denuded. It is not because the forest was never there but that it has been cut down. In like manner, each person is born with a virtuous nature, but the circumstances of his or her life thereafter will determine whether he or she will nuture or lose that nature.

However, people are not simply the victims of life's circumstances. External influences are not so crucial in determining a person's development as is self-cultivation. Virtue will be maintained and developed only if the individual continues to cultivate it throughout the life span. Even under difficult conditions, people should not cease cultivating their original nature. Indeed, a person can benefit from unfavorable circumstances, gaining strength of character by struggling against adversity. Mencius wrote: "When Heaven is about to place a great burden on a person, it makes him suffer starvation and hardship, frustrates his efforts so as to shake him from his mental lassitude. It thus toughens his nature and corrects his deficiencies" (Liang Cheng-t'ing 1958 p. 324).

In summary, all people are endowed by Heaven with the same nature at birth. The differences observed among people as they develop are due to how well they nurture their original endowment. People behave badly because they have allowed themselves to lose virtue. However, even when apparently lost, the inner strength of human nature always exists in the mind and is rediscoverable if a person seeks to recover it.

2. The Goal of Development

The goal of development and of life is to maintain and enhance jen, which is the sense of humanity. By achieving jen, the individual becomes a superior person. The key characteristics of jen are sincerity, righteousness, filial obligation, and reciprocal respect in relationships with others. Jen is founded on love—first, love of one's parents, then of neighbors, and ultimately of all humans. Proper social relations are built on li, meaning courtesy and modesty as defined by the rules of traditional social patterns. A person who possesses jen is sincere in speech ánd behavior and without pretense. What he or she says or does is the true expression of what he or she thinks.

Jen is formed by giving attention to two agents, self and others. As for the self, individuals develop their own personalities through recognizing the meaning and value of their own natures and through accepting the responsibilities of life. Then they draw inferences about others on the basis of the way they perceive themselves. In a passive mode of interacting with others, if an individual does not want something done to him or her by others, he or she will in turn not do it to others. In an active mode, he or she not only performs acts of self-development but also helps others develop themselves as well. As Confucius wrote in the Analects, "You yourself desire rank and standing; then help others achieve rank and standing. You want to turn your own merits to account; then help others turn theirs to account" (Ch'ien Mu 1964 Book 6, p. 90).

In summary, the goal of development is jen, the perfection of self-understanding and the extension of this understanding and love to encompass others and their welfare. By achieving these characteristics, it is possible to become a superior person, evidencing all of the human virtues. Thus an individual attains the perfect life.

In pursuit of self-development, a person bears the responsibility constantly to: (a) sharpen sensations—visual and auditory—in order to examine people and events clearly, (b) be gentle and respectful in manner, (c) speak sincerely and with care, (d) ask others' advice on matters about which he or she has doubts, (e) control his or her temper when angry, and consider carefully the likely result of different sorts of reactions when angry, and (f) when seeing an opportunity for personal gain, think primarily about what would constitute righteous behavior in such a situation.

Of overriding concern in a person's social relationships is that of filial obligation—the responsibility to parents. Sons and daughters of all ages are to accept and execute their parents' commands and to support their parents with worldly goods, love, and personal service.

3. Learning Theory

A learning theory derived from analysis of Confucian writings can be viewed in terms of a learning hierarchy,

how a person learns, and the relationship of ability to effort.

3.1 Steps in the Learning Hierarchy

The book *The Great Learning* postulates a learning hierarchy which consists of seven levels, each built on the successful completion of the levels below it. At the top of the hierarchy, the ultimate aim is that of producing peace and enlightenment for all humankind. Starting at the bottom of the hierarchy, it is possible to identify the way each successive level becomes a necessary foundation for the next higher one and thus contributes to the final goal of universal peace and enlightenment.

(a) *Step 1: Investigating objects and events.* The author of *The Great Learning* proposed that everything in the world operates according to principles, and the human mind is formed to understand these principles. The first step of learning is to use the intellect to investigate the principles, to understand the essence of each object and event. This is called knowing the roots.

(b) *Step 2: Extending one's knowledge.* After analyzing the principles of all events perceived over a long period of time, an individual is able to apprehend the quality of every object and event, whether internal or external, refined or coarse. Through such a process knowledge is extended to its limits.

(c) *Step 3: Making the will sincere.* Sincerity or authenticity means no self-deception. It is the process of becoming true to oneself and then of extending this understanding and sincerity to others.

(d) *Step 4: Controlling one's mind so as to cultivate one's life.* According to Confucianism, such emotions as wrath, fear, fondness, and worry or anxiety all exist in people's hearts. When these emotions are kept in balance, the person can control them. But when the emotions are unduly aroused, they control the individual. Thus, by means of sincerity, which enables a person to examine his or her emotions clearly, a person can control the emotions and prevent his or her behavior from being misguided. This ability to control the emotions is called cultivating one's life.

(e) *Step 5: Regulating the family.* When the members of a family achieve each of the first four steps, they are equipped to carry out their individual responsibilities within the group in an amicable manner, with the parents in charge of the group and the sons and daughters willingly performing the tasks they are assigned. In essence, Step 5 consists of the members learning to operate efficiently as a small social system.

(f) *Step 6: Bringing order to the state.* Confucian belief holds that since the state is composed of families, if all of the families are well-regulated, then the state will be properly regulated as well. The individual family members' knowledge, sincerity, self-cultivation, and skills of living within the family social system form the elements that ensure the state operates efficiently.

(g) *Step 7: Achieving world peace and enlightenment.* When each state operates efficiently on the basis of knowledgeable, sincere, and socially skilled individuals, peace and enlightenment for all of humanity are achieved.

As the hierarchy illustrates, the ultimate aim of Confucian theory is the good society and not simply the good or efficient or happy individual. However, since the goal of the good society can be achieved only if the individuals composing it are good, the theory necessarily centers initial attention on developing each individual into a superior person.

3.2. *How People Learn*

The learning process consists of the interaction of "doing" and "thinking". Doing means the learner searches for varied sources of knowledge. For example, the learner first reads books or gains wider personal experiences. However, it is useless merely to memorize what has been read or experienced. Rote memorization is not learning. What is needed in addition is thinking, in the sense of organizing and comprehending how new experiences relate to other aspects of life and knowledge.

Both processes, the doing and the thinking, are necessary for learning. Doing, in the sense of reading widely or encountering life experiences, can result in useless memorization. On the other hand, thinking based on limited reading or experience leads to error, for the individual lacks the breadth of resources to verify conclusions.

3.3 *Ability and Effort*

Confucianism holds that most people are born with similar mental capacity or ability to learn. Therefore, differences among individuals in their knowledge or virtue result chiefly from the effects of learning and, to a lesser degree, from such environmental factors as opportunities to learn or the models of behavior of the people around the individual. In Confucian theory, only a very few "naturally superior persons" have an innate ability to "know" without having to learn what they come to know. And, at the other end of the ability scale, few people are mentally incapable of learning.

Consequently, since it is assumed that most people have similar potential, what they know and how virtuous they are is the result of effort, of how diligently they have dedicated themselves to study. The assumption is that no matter how difficult the task, a person can succeed if he or she tries hard enough. Therefore, failure is not attributed to level of ability or the difficulty of the task, but rather to the amount of effort expended.

The Doctrine of the Mean (Liang Cheng-t'ing 1958 p. 107) urges:

> When there is anything not yet studied, or studied but not yet understood, do not give up. When there is any question not yet asked, or asked but its answer not yet known, do not give up. When there is anything not yet thought over, or thought over but not yet apprehended, do not give up. . . . When there is anything not yet practiced, or practiced but not yet earnestly, do not give up.

4. *Implications for Child Rearing and Education*

Confucian theory does not distinguish between characteristics of childhood and of adulthood. The general process of developing jen and becoming a superior person is essentially the same at all stages of life. Therefore, no special suggestions are offered for child rearing. However, from the theory's postulates about the nature of humans and the goal of life, it is possible to infer several implications for child-raising practices.

First, since children are born with a basically virtuous nature (including the seeds of compassion, shame, courtesy, modesty, and a sense of right and wrong), adults should recognize the child's good nature and further develop it. The child should also be taught such traits as honesty, good faith, and respect for others that are founded on his or her original virtuous nature. More specifically, Confucian writings suggest that the child learn poetry and music to nourish his or her nature, since these arts not only harmonize the emotions but also stimulate the mind.

As noted earlier, Confucianism stresses the development of people as social beings, as elements of the family and of the broader society. As a consequence, the child needs to learn the rules of social relationships (li) so as to become a mature participant in society. This process is called ritualization. For instance, in the parent–child relationship, children are to obey parents in all things. In the sibling relationship, older children take precedence over younger ones, with the older guarding the younger and the younger respecting and obeying the older. In relations with friends, a person should always be sincere and faithful.

While environmental forces are not as crucial in development as personal effort, the environment can exert some influence in terms of the opportunities for learning that are available. Parents and teachers should arrange the child's environments so as to furnish proper models to imitate and a wide range of useful experiences. To illustrate, a well-known story of Mencius' boyhood describes the boy and his mother living near a funeral parlor, and as a consequence young Mencius soon was imitating the way funeral processions were conducted. Since his mother wished to avoid such an influence, she moved their abode to a market district, where Mencius began imitating the buying and selling activities. Again his mother disapproved of the neighborhood's influence, so she moved to a dwelling adjacent to a school where Mencius learned to study. Accordingly,

Confucian doctrine would suggest that a proper environment is one in which people behave according to jen and li.

A further recommendation to parents and teachers is that they urge the growing child to concentrate diligently on learning tasks and not give up readily, since the main ingredient of success in Confucian theory is the amount of effort expended to achieve a goal.

Finally, since rote memorization is regarded as an inadequate form of learning, the growing child should not only be provided with a wider range of experiences to remember (including such vicarious experiences as are found in books) but should also be guided to analyzing the remembered experiences so as to decide what

generalizations can be drawn and what implications they hold for achieving personal jen and a peaceful and enlightened society.

Bibliography

Ch'ien Mu 1964 *Lun-Yo Yao Lueh [A Summary of the Analects of Confucius]*. Shang-wu, Taipei

Kuo Chieh-ming 1969 *San-tzŭ-ching Ching Chiai [An Essential Explanation of the Three Words Classic]*. Hung-yeh, Taipei

Liang Cheng-t'ing 1958 *Kuang Chiai Ssŭ Shu Chin Ku [A General Explanation of the Four Books]*. Hsa-sin, Taipei

Liu I-shêng 1963 *Lun-Yu Piao Chiai [An Illustration of the Analects of Confucius]*. Chinese Publishing Committee, Taipei

Shinto Theory of Human Development

R. M. Thomas and R. Niikura

Shinto or Shintoism is a religion of ancient origin that has exerted a significant influence over the character development of individual Japanese and over the political–social nature of Japanese society. While the influence of Shinto is widely recognized, the nature of Shinto itself is difficult to describe in concise terms because the religion appears in a variety of forms and it has no recognized founder, no established dogmas, no list of ethical behaviors or commandments, and no sacred scriptures, although there are historical accounts that function somewhat as scriptures. Furthermore, the mystical aspects of Shinto cannot readily be conveyed in words.

In attempting the elusive task of defining Shinto, Holtom (1938 p. 6) has described it as "the characteristic ritualistic arrangements and their underlying beliefs by which the Japanese people have celebrated, dramatized, interpreted, and supported the chief values of their national life." Ueda (1972 p. 29) has called Shinto simply "the basic value orientation of the Japanese people." Ono (1962 pp. 3–4) has proposed that "Shinto is more than a religious faith. It is an amalgam of attitudes, ideas, and ways of doing things that through two milleniums and more have become an integral part of the way of the Japanese people."

Historically, Shinto has been affected by other religions imported from China, chiefly by Confucianism and Buddhism. Confucianism appeared in Japan at least by the fifth century AD and perhaps even earlier. Buddhism came first in the sixth century AD, and its more influential Zen version in the twelfth century. Modern-day Shinto consists of an amalgamation of these belief systems and others into what can be considered a Shintoist view of life in modern Japan.

While there are no defined orthodox scriptures from which to extract a Shintoist theory of human development, there is a sufficient body of analytical writing based on past scholarship and present observations of Japanese modes of thought to form the outlines of a

theory. The following description is one version constructed from an inspection of such writing. The issues relating to human development that are treated here concern: (a) the nature of kami, (b) human nature and personality structure, (c) the goal or direction of development, and (d) applications to child rearing and education.

1. The Nature of Kami

The Japanese term kami has often been translated as "gods," with the word Shinto interpreted as "the way of the gods." And, indeed, in Shinto there are many kami that pervade all aspects of life and nature, thus giving the religion a polytheistic and pantheistic character. However, to equate kami with identifiable gods much oversimplifies the matter, for in practice the term implies a good deal more. Essentially it refers to the noble and sacred spirits that make things good, pure, productive, and aesthetically excellent.

> Among the objects or phenomena designated from ancient times as kami are the qualities of growth, fertility, and production; natural phenomena, such as wind and thunder; natural objects, such as the sun, mountains, rivers, trees, and rocks; some animals; and ancestral spirits. . . . Also regarded as kami are the guardian spirits of the land, occupations, and skills; the spirits of national heroes . . . and even the pitiable dead. (Ono 1962 p. 7)

These spirits—the kami—are important in a Shinto theory of development in three principal ways. First, a prime goal of development is to emulate the kami, for humans are regarded as potential kami themselves, able to attain the esteemed characteristics of kami if they lead virtuous lives. Second, honoring the kami through ceremonies at Shinto shrines and in rituals of daily life can enlist the support of the kami in warding off evil forces in one's environment. Third, the polytheistic nature of the kami reflects an essential notion about the individual and the group in Japanese tradition. Group living, group ventures, and group norms have been supreme in the culture of Japan. Just as the universe was created by the group efforts of the many kami, so life in the human world consists of the individual living harmoniously with others, working for the good of the group. Human development has no significance unless viewed as the individual compatibly fitting into society.

> There is no place for egotism in Shinto. Egotism runs counter to the spirit of worship. Worship makes the interest of the community and public welfare paramount. (Ono 1962 p. 104)

2. *Human Nature and Personality Structure*

In contrast to Judaic and Christian tradition, humans are not born in sin with a natural bent for evil. Rather, the newborn is pure and good, so the chief developmental task of the individual and of those who rear children (parents, teachers, the general community) is to sustain and enhance the original goodness. Evil and destructive forces are not part of human nature but arise from the environment, from external spirits which need to be vanquished during the process of development. By scholars of the past, human nature was likened unto a clear pool whose waters may be roiled and muddied by disturbing forces, but the waters will subsequently settle when peaceful conditions obtain, and their purity will return. In a more modern analogy, human nature has been compared to a mirror on which dust may accumulate, but the dust can be swept away and the clarity of images restored.

The Japanese concept of personality is expressed in the word *hito-gara*, which refers to the basic human character. One's personality develops over the life span, beginning with the newborn's fundamental nature as fashioned by the gods and thereafter molded and embellished by family and societal traditions, by the person's own self-training and trials, by the values to which he subscribes, by the position he occupies in the social system, and by the power relationships he maintains with those who help him and whom he helps (Shinto Committee 1958 p. 23).

As already noted, in Shinto the individual cannot be separated from society, nor is there a society transcending or preceding the individual.

> Society is within the individual, and the individual is within society. Man cannot be born unless he receives the body and blood of his parents and ancestors. Similarly, he lives with the support of society, is raised to manhood within the culture of society; and he cannot live in isolation, cut off from human culture. (Shinto Committee 1958 p. 32)

In other words, the individual's nature is bound to others along two dimensions. The vertical dimension is that of historical time, linking the person into the chain of his or her ancestors and of those descendants to be born in the future. The horizontal dimension is that of present-day society, the individual's current social environment. These two dimensions are imbedded in the notion of personality and its development. To the degree that these two dimensions (and the people they represent) are enhanced, so the individual's personality is enhanced. To the degree that they are diminished, so the individual's development is diminished. Thus, concern for others—for the dead, the living, and those to come—becomes an important factor in personality development.

While there are words for soul or spirit in Shinto (such as *tama*), the idea of a separation of body and soul so familiar in Western thought, with body and soul in a state of tension, is not held by Shintoists. Nor is the body viewed as the source of human sinfulness. Rather, Shintoism assumes that body and soul (or spirit) are an indivisible unit and that corporeal/psychological desires are good and deserve satisfaction. Although such desires can become misdirected through the influence of destructive outside forces, the desires themselves are natural and thus virtuous (Spae 1972).

3. *The Goal or Direction of Development*

While some theories of development can be labeled as stage theories, Shinto cannot. It is true that Shinto tradition does cite times in the life cycle that certain events should occur. However, these periodic events are not stages in the sense of being periods of life when the person's capacities and growth are markedly different from those of other periods. Therefore, the goal of development in Shinto cannot be defined as passage from one identifiable stage of life to another. Instead, as mentioned above, the aim of development is to sustain and enhance one's originally endowed good nature. The term enhance is of particular note, for there is the belief in Shinto that the life of both the individual person and society develops in the direction of infinite improvement, toward a never-ending purity and perfection. While it is granted that the individual is born virtuous rather than inclined to evil, it is recognized as well that his or her innate goodness is still less than perfect. Therefore, during one's lifetime an individual has both the opportunity and obligation to pursue perfection.

To adherents of such religious persuasions as Hinduism, Buddhism, and Christianity, the goal of life on earth is to prepare for a life after death, for a future in nirvana or heaven where a perfect existence becomes one's reward. But such is not the case in Shinto. The focus of Shinto is on the present, on life in this world. The Shintoist pursues purity and perfection in this life, with relatively little regard for a life hereafter. Shinto "concentrates on the *naka-ima* or eternal present of the world. . . . Shinto accepts this world; it does not want to change it" (Spae 1972 p. 65).

It has often been remarked that Shinto has no code of ethics, in the sense that Judaism has 10 commandments and Islam has five pillars of conduct. However, this does not mean that Shinto lacks guidelines delineating the direction in which one's development should progress. It means, rather, that the ethics of Shinto are cast as a general principle whose application, in terms of specific actions, is influenced by the particular conditions that pertain to each situation one meets in life. As already suggested, the general goal is to attain perfection and purity in all ways. To do this, it is necessary for the individual "to bring the soul into unison with the Divine [the Kami] and to attain an attitude at one with the divine judgment in each separate action" (Shinto Committee 1958 p. 31). To approach this desired unison, a person performs religious service for the kami and for his or her ancestors:

> ... and from this will be derived all the other things he should do. This is, in the final analysis, the consciousness of responsibility. The actions which we are to perform are the practice, the realization of the things which we have been called into life with the mission and the ability to do by the gods and our ancestors. These actions are service to increase the abundance, harmony, and unity of all things in this world. (Shinto Committee 1958 pp. 31–32)

When Shintoists speak of purifying the soul and of achieving perfection, they refer not only to issues of ethical behavior but also to matters of comprehending the natural world and appreciating its elegance, in other words, a commitment to the pursuit of truth and beauty.

> Both art and religion try "to grasp objects as they are," and for that purpose require perfect tranquility of mind. . . . Both are a conscious, methodological, and stubborn effort to reach perfection in some field or other. And it is a Japanese conception that when a man has attained a high degree of perfection in any one thing, however trivial that thing may seem to be, he has attained a similar level of Perfection pure and simple. Thus the artist who can bring out a faultless sound from his instrument, or write faultless *kanji* (characters), or execute a faultless gesture must be a faultless man, a saint. (Herbert 1967 pp. 90–91)

While purity and perfection are given as general aims of development, a number of constituent virtues common to other ethical systems are also accorded prominent attention in Shinto. Principal among these is sincerity (*makato*), meaning "That which is spoken by the mouth must surely be manifested in actions," which implies an approach to life in which nothing is shunned or neglected (Herbert 1967 p. 71). Coupled with sincerity are purity and cheerfulness of heart, a pair of inseparable factors incorporated in the word *akaki*. Other virtues to be pursued are loyalty to one's society (as evidenced in fealty to the governing powers and to one's employers), filial piety, protecting the honor of one's family, faithfulness to friends, industriousness, aversion toward failure, tenderness, affection, thankfulness, tolerance, honesty, respect and proper etiquette, and benevolence. These guides to social behavior, then, can be considered the more specific goals of development. They chart the direction in which life should be aimed.

4. Applications to Child Rearing and Education

There are at least three ways in which a Shinto view of development offers guidance to those responsible for child raising and educational practices: (a) in setting levels of expectation for performance, (b) in providing the aims of instruction, and (c) in suggesting ways that the aims can be achieved.

4.1 Levels of Expectation

Three core assumptions of Shinto suggest that the learner, as well as the instructors, should hold high aspirations for his or her performance in social relations and productive work and that the success of such performance is properly judged by society's standards rather than by standards the individual might create.

The first assumption is that development of both the individual and society is incessant. Thus, the growing child or youth should realize there is always room for improvement in his pursuit of excellence. It is his or her obligation continually to strive for greater improvement.

The second assumption is that the object of development is not to attain some idealized state in a life hereafter. Rather, the object is to achieve greater purity and perfection at the present time in the world of daily experience. Thus, how well a person is succeeding can be judged in the present in terms of worldly measures, such as in the quality of one's social relations and of the things one produces.

The third assumption is that the individual and society are indivisible, so that what is good for society is good for the individual as well. Hence, society's standards of conduct rather than the individual's own feelings of satisfaction are the proper criteria to use in assessing the individual's development.

In other words, man must strive, in both public and private life, "to serve the gods and the ancestral spirits, and to make contributions and impart blessings to the world through his own work in life. The greatness of the character of a man is based on the greatness of this service and these contributions" (Shinto Committee 1958 p. 32).

4.2 The Aims of Instruction

As noted above, the central goal of life is to achieve purity of soul and perfection in all things. Many of the more prominent traits that compose such a goal have been reviewed above—loyalty, filial piety, industriousness, and so on. These are the characteristics learners are urged to acquire, the traits that parents and teachers are expected to reward and whose neglect they are expected to punish. Character-development classes that are an obligatory part of the school curriculum in Japan are directed toward producing such traits.

4.3 Methods of Achieving the Aims

In addition to the forgoing general educational implications to be inferred from Shinto theory, exponents of various Shinto sects have described specific practices they believe assist an individual toward purification of the combined body–soul. In way of illustration, Herbert (1967 p. 79) has provided a four-stage sequence of practices that he terms "the most methodological description which I could obtain of the whole process," a description furnished by members of the Yamakage Shinto school.

The first stage consists of purifying the body by bathing, by cleansing toxins from the inside of the body through purifying the bowels and blood, by adopting proper diet and sleep habits, and by engaging in prescribed physical movements that confer divinity on the body. The second stage is designed to purify the heart by a person's trying to comprehend the concepts of life, soul, universe, and Deity in order to obtain "basic life" through peace, tranquility, tolerance, and placidity. Meditation activities contribute to attaining the outcomes of this stage. The third stage involves regularizing the environment by cleaning up the physical surroundings, by abstaining from discouraging and useless talk, by using only optimistic or "luminous" words, by serving others, and by helping both oneself and others express greater devotion to the kami. The final stage is the mystical activity of purifying and unifying the "holy soul which sheds light like the sun" and thereby rising into the world of "higher and wider dimensions."

In summary, then, Shinto theory provides general guidelines to anyone responsible for child rearing and education as well as specific directions for those who would dedicate their lives to finding *michi* or "the Way" as conceived in Shinto.

Bibliography

Herbert J 1967 *Shinto: At the Fountain Head of Japan.* Stein and Day, New York

Holtom D C 1938 *The National Faith of Japan: A Study in Modern Shinto.* Kegan Paul, Trench, and Trubner, London

Ono S 1962 *Shinto, the Kami Way.* Tuttle, Tokyo

Shinto Committee for the Ninth International Congress for the History of Religions 1958 *An Outline of Shinto Teachings.* Jinja Honcho and Kokugakuin University, Tokyo

Spae J J 1972 *Shinto Man.* Oriens Institute for Religious Research, Tokyo

Ueda K 1972 Shinto. *Japanese Religion.* Kodansha International, Tokyo

Part 3

Stages and Rates of Development

Part 3

Stages and Rates of Development

Introduction

Books about child development intended for parents and teachers are usually organized according to age periods. In the typical book, an early chapter will describe the prenatal stage, followed by a chapter on infancy, another on early childhood, and still others on middle and late childhood, and adolescence. Likewise, books that encompass the entire life span are also frequently divided into periods, such as childhood, adolescence, early adulthood, middle age, and old age. This organizational style reflects the fact that there is a lot of popular interest in the question of how age is related to people's characteristics. Phrased differently, what does knowing a person's age tell about that person's physical and mental maturity, social skills, interests, emotional condition, and sense of responsibility? The 10 articles that comprise Part 3 offer answers to such questions.

For educators, the practical value of information about age-defined stages is found in the help that such information offers for predicting what can be expected of a newly-encountered learner. If we simply know that a girl is age 5 rather than 12 or 18, we clearly are better prepared to teach her than if we knew nothing of her age. Therefore, descriptions of typical characteristics of people at different stages of development equip a teacher or counselor with an initial estimate of what a newly-met learner of a given age may be like in abilities, interests, and life-adjustment problems. These sorts of age-related information are often called *normative data* or *age norms*, meaning information about *normal* or *usual* characteristics of people in a particular age bracket. While normative information can be helpful in child rearing and in education, it can also do harm when misused. Two common types of misuse result from (a) failing to recognize the way *typical characteristics* are established for an age category and (b) equating *typical characteristics* with *desired characteristics*.

1. Determining Typical Characteristics of Age Stages

Age norms are established by researchers making observations or taking measurements of people who are in the particular age range under discussion. Such norms are most trustworthy when (a) they are based on a sufficiently large and representative number of people from the category, so that the resulting description accurately reflects characteristics of the entire age group, and (b) the great majority of the people in the category display the described traits. Violating either of these principles decreases the value of the normative information.

First, consider the matter of "a sufficiently large and representative number of people." This is the issue of sampling. Since not everyone in an age category can be observed or tested, a representative sample of people from the category needs to be chosen for study. Conclusions drawn from the study of the sample will then be applied to the entire group. However, this principle of representative sampling is sometimes disregarded by people who offer descriptions of developmental stages. For example, the norms in the widely used early books from the Gesell Institute in the United States were based on studies of a few dozen children at each age level, with nearly all the children drawn from one small city in the northeastern section of the country (Gesell and Ilg 1949). Yet the books improperly implied that the physical, mental, and social characteristics found in this small sample of children were true of children everywhere. In contrast to such norms based on small samples are others founded on large numbers of people from a variety of geographical and cultural settings. The authors of the articles in Part 3 have sought to draw their descriptions from such large and representative groups.

Next, consider the matter of basing normative statements on "the great majority of people" in an age category. This is the issue of the extent of individual differences among the people within an age group. When authors seek to depict an age group, their main intention is usually to describe ways that members of the group are alike. Seldom, if ever, are all members of the group alike on any given characteristic. For instance, 10-year-olds differ in height, weight, resistance to disease, intelligence, ethnic origin, social skills, emotional reactions, and so forth. People at all other age levels also display such diversity. Therefore, since authors cannot claim that all people in an age category are the same in terms of any characteristic, they frequently choose to express the status of the group by the use of either mathematical averages or proportions. For instance, they report the group's average height, average weight, and average intelligence. They can also tell what proportion of the group are from a particular ethnic background or have suffered a particular disease. Sometimes this proportion is numerically precise, such as "$\frac{3}{4}$ of the group" or "80 percent of 10-year-olds." But often the proportion is reflected only vaguely, as in the phrase "the typical 10-year-old" or "most of the children", or "the majority." As a result, readers are left unsure about how common the characteristic is at that age level. Even more misleading are reports that omit any such qualifying phrases as "the average child" or "the usual 10-year-old." In effect, some authors simply write that "10-year-olds are" or "a notable trait of 10-year-olds is," thereby giving the impression that everyone in the age group is identical on the trait under discussion. Such an impression can cause readers to carry inaccurate expectations into their encounters with newly-met members of the age group.

Of what significance, then, are the above observations for teachers, parents, counselors, social workers, and the like? Three sorts of significance are reflected in the following generalizations.

(a) Any statement about the characteristics of an age group will have exceptions to it, whether or not the writer has identified the nature or degree of these exceptions. Therefore, readers should recognize that when an author states that 9-year-olds like to play a wide variety of games, at least some 9-year-olds will like to play only a very limited number of games, and others will play no games at all. Likewise, when a writer states that "young adolescents experience a personal-identity crisis," at least some of the adolescents will not experience such a crisis.

(b) A general statement about people who are within a range of ages, such as the age range of 4 to 6 years will usually be more valid than a generalization about people of a single age, such as 6-year-olds. This is true because not everyone develops at the same rate. For instance, studies of mental development by Piaget and his followers show that the ability to solve certain abstract problems in science and mathematics does not occur until the latter years of childhood or early adolescence. Because mental abilities do not mature in all children at the same rate, some children will achieve abstract-reasoning ability at the age of 10, others at the ages of 11 or 12, and still others at a later time. Thus, a generalization about abstract reasoning among children in the age range 10–14 will apply to a higher proportion of children in the group than will a generalization based solely on 10-year-olds or 12-year-olds. In recognition of this fact, none of the seven articles in Part 3(b) that describe age-related characteristics is limited to describing developmental characteristics for only one year of the life-span. Instead, all of the articles, except the article on *Prenatal Development*, range over more than one year of growth. Furthermore, since the most rapid, most dramatic developmental changes occur during the earlier years of life, each of the articles focusing on the earliest growth periods (prenatal development, infancy, and early childhood) encompasses fewer years than do the articles about later periods (adulthood and old age).

(c) Normative information is mainly useful as a starting point for helping a teacher or a counselor predict what a newly-met individual may be like. However, the normative description should only be regarded as tentative, merely an initial estimate that needs to be corroborated or altered on the basis of further information gathered about that particular individual. In other words, normative data should be seen as hypotheses that need to be adjusted in light of more exact information collected about each specific learner.

2. Equating Typical Development with Desirable Development

People frequently use normative descriptions as the basis for deciding whether an individual is developing satisfactorily. Such is true when a boy who is above the average weight is then advised to diet until he is no longer "overweight." Alternately, a girl who has fewer acquaintances than do the majority of girls her age is urged to join social groups that could help her become more like the majority. Underlying this mode of thought is the belief that "what the majority of the group are like" represents "what each individual should be like." In other words, *is* should become *ought*.

This same sort of reasoning is reflected in the claim that a given behavior is quite acceptable if it is displayed by most members of an age group. For example, in certain societies, the majority of youths are reported to have used tobacco, illicit drugs, and alcohol. Thus, the argument goes, because such behavior is so widespread, it should be considered "a natural part of growing up" and therefore "nothing to worry about."

People who depend on normative data for setting their standards of desirable development will often apply these standards differentially to various aspects of growth or behavior. Hence, parents may consider it desirable for their daughter to be average in weight, above average in intelligence, and below average in sexual precocity—a pattern of standards reflecting dominant social values of their culture. So, if such parents are to judge how well their daughter is progressing, they will require normative information about physical, intellectual, and sexual development.

The issue of concern here can be summarized as a question: Under what circumstances is it appropriate to regard typical development as desirable development? Or, stated in another way: To what extent should normative data serve as the criteria for judging how satisfactorily an individual is growing up? For most people, normative descriptions apparently play a part in setting their standards of desirable development. However, such standards also appear to be influenced significantly by people's convictions about the proper goals of human life, the responsibility that individuals owe to their society, and what constitutes personal happiness.

3. The Contents of Part 3

In Part 3(a), the three opening articles are intended to prepare readers for the seven subsequent articles on different stages of growth. In the first article, McHale and Lerner describe ways that developmental stages can be defined and they suggest implications that information about stages can offer for educational practice. The second article concerns trends observed in theorists' conceptions of stages and the third article focuses on the rate at which people advance from one stage to another. For educators and parents, this matter of developmental rate becomes important when it is recognized that people do not all progress through the stages at the same pace. As a result, children who are the same chronological age will not all be ready at the same time for identical learning experiences.

The seven articles in Part 3(b) treat particular stages of development, starting with *Prenatal Development* and continuing through *Infancy*, *Early Childhood*, *Later Childhood*, *Adolescence*, *Adulthood*, and *Old Age*. The author of each article has sought to identify characteristics typically displayed by people at each particular stage and to suggest how educational practices can be suited to such characteristics.

Bibliography

Gesell A, Ilg F L 1949 *Child Development: An Introduction to the Study of Human Growth*. Harper and Row, New York
Piaget J, Inhelder B 1969 *The Psychology of the Child*. Basic Books, New York.

Definitions of Stage and Rate

Stages of Human Development

S. M. McHale and R. M. Lerner

The stage concept is used by developmental psychologists to imply that developmental changes are qualitative. Stage changes in development are conceptualized not merely as increases in the quantity of behaviors or skills, but instead as novel reorganizations or patterns in the way an individual thinks or behaves. As such, new competencies are thought to be qualitatively discontinuous and emergent, and thus not reducible to earlier patterns of an individual's abilities.

Such a view of development contrasts fundamentally with perspectives that describe developmental change as quantitative or incremental—that is, as occurring continually and gradually, and involving the addition of "molecular" (stimulus–response) units into the behavioral repertoire (Bijou 1976, Bijou and Baer 1961). Such mechanistic approaches typically take a functional analysis or learning theory approach to conceptualizing developmental change. In such approaches the processes through which behaviors are shaped, and through which an increasing number of skills are acquired, are seen to involve an individual's response to contingencies in the external environment (Bijou and Baer 1961).

Major stage theorists describe changes across much, if not all, of the life span, and focus on broad-based changes such as the nature of individuals' psychosexual conflicts (Erikson 1950, Freud 1965), or on individuals' cognitive structuring of the world (Bruner 1964, Piaget 1970). More recently, however, theorists have been offering stage-like descriptions of more circumscribed domains of development (Fischer 1980, Kohlberg 1963, Selman 1976, Siegler 1978). These latter conceptualizations are discussed in full below.

Stage theories of development are predicated on a commitment to an organismic philosophical metamodel or paradigm. This philosophy stresses a holistic approach to understanding an active organism's sequential, adaptive, and qualitative changes (Reese and Overton 1970). Within this tradition, stages are used to describe a universal progression of structural reorganizations. This characterization of the nature of development is an idealized one, and provides a formal conceptual metric against which observed behavioral change is compared in order to ascertain whether a given change constitutes development.

There are two key components of a developmental analysis from this perspective. First, a stage theory must provide descriptions of the stages themselves, that is, descriptions of the structural properties of each stage in the sequence. Second, a stage theory must posit mechanisms by which the individual progresses through these stages. It should be noted that these stages and the progression through the stages are explained by concepts different than those associated with the systems of explanation employed in mechanistic views of development (Bijou 1976). Specifically, the stage components are explored from the perspective of formal causality. This is in addition to considering empirically defined, antecedent–consequent relations that are included in mechanistic approaches (efficient causes of events). An example of the way in which formal structural properties may be used to explain developmental status are the structures of grouping in Piaget's (1970) cognitive developmental theory.

1. Issues in the Conceptualization of Stages

As implied in the above overview, there are a variety of key issues associated with the conceptualization of stages. For instance, one major issue is "abruptness versus gradualism." In other words, is the transition from one stage to the next an abrupt, "all-or-none" phenomenon, or do the characteristics of one stage begin to emerge while those of a former stage still exist? Another major issue is a descriptive versus explanatory one. That is, are stage concepts useful only for the description of developmental change, or can stage concepts explain the developmental characteristics they depict (Brainerd 1978b)? In this section some of the major stances developmentalists have taken in regard to these key issues are indicated.

1.1 Abruptness Versus Gradualism

A strong view of developmental stages is one which would characterize such phenomena as abrupt. Such a strong view of the stage concept would depict development as involving extended periods of relative stability in an individual's level of functioning, followed by "an abrupt and synchronized metamorphosis to a decidedly novel set of components and component interrelationships" (Flavell 1971 p. 423). Such transitions are typically held to proceed in a universal sequence because earlier stages are both functional, and often logical, prerequisites of later ones. The functions of one stage are reorganized and integrated into those comprising the structure of a later stage. Thus, developmental changes are seen as qualitative and sequential, and as reflecting a marked degree of discontinuity. That is, given the abruptness of stage emergence, all competencies characteristic of a new stage are achieved concurrently because they are based in the novel structure. A model that portrays developmental stages in this manner would be most useful because, "it lends a meaning to 'stage' that is conceptually clear, theoretically strong, operationally useful, and quite congruent with the ordinary language meaning of the term" (Flavell 1972 p. 428).

Many theorists have pointed out, however, that a more accurate picture of development is provided by a model that portrays transitions in development as gradual and continual processes, with individuals displaying at the same period of time competencies that are characteristic of different stages of development (Fischer 1980, Flavell 1983). As a means of addressing this controversy, Flavell (1972) has outlined three models of qualitative discontinuity which describe possible variations in the degree of abruptness that characterizes stage transitions. Discontinuity between stages will appear more or less marked depending upon: (a) the ratio of developmental changes within stages to developmental changes between stages; (b) the degree of temporal overlap in an individual's exhibition of competencies from different stages; and (c) the speed with which all of the skills characteristic of a new stage are acquired. Thus, discontinuity will be strongly evident when an individual's level of functioning changes between stages but is stable within stages, when an individual displays concurrently only those competencies that characterize one particular stage, and when the onset of each of the competencies characteristic of a given stage occurs at the same point in time.

1.2 Description Versus Explanation

While most developmentalists appreciate the descriptive utility of the stage concept, a number of critics have argued that stage models do not provide an accurate picture of developmental change (Brainerd 1978a, 1978b, Flavell 1983, Wohlwill 1973). Here, criticism has focused on whether the empirical data on children's development are consistent with predictions of a given stage model, that is, whether stages adequately describe observations of development.

In turn, controversy exists about the explanatory status of the stage concept. First, on a metatheoretical level, this controversy involves differences between organismically oriented developmentalists—who make use of stage as both a descriptive and an explanatory concept—and mechanistically oriented developmentalists—who either prefer to focus solely on notions of efficient causality (Bijou 1976, Bijou and Baer 1961) or who cannot appreciate the idea that there may be a useful notion of causality other than efficient cause (Brainerd 1978b).

When these paradigm differences are brought to the level of theory, controversy about the nature of cause is translated into the issue of whether stage models can adequately explain development. For example, consider Piaget's (1970) theory, one which is the exemplar of a structural approach to formal explanation. Structures in this framework are integrated sets of cognitive elements whose organization is relatively stable. These structures are "regarded as the common, underlying basis of a variety of superficially distinct, possibly even unrelated-looking behavioral acts" (Flavell 1972 p. 443). However Brainerd (1978a), for example, argues against Piaget's use of logical structures as explanations of development; and indeed, critics of Piaget have suggested that development may not be reducible to logical and mathematical operations (to the "structures" that Piaget believed were the key feature of cognitive development).

Other criticisms of the explanatory use of the stage concept have involved the argument that competencies which are supposedly interrelated do not display a sufficient degree of co-occurrence in their time of onset to support the existence of unitary stages (Brainerd 1978b, Flavell 1983, Fischer 1980). However, this criticism may be most applicable to structural theories, such as Piaget's (1970), in that the Piagetian structuralist approach to stage theory has been distinguished from other stage models, such as Freudian and Eriksonian ones, precisely on the basis of the view that the latter do not portray stages as integrated structures (Kessen 1962, Wohlwill 1973). Rather, in the latter models, particular themes are dominant at given periods in an individual's life (for example the establishment of self-identity in adolescence), but elements from earlier stages continually pervade the individual's functioning. Similarly, even stage models which are also structurally based, for example, Kohlberg's stages of moral reasoning (1963, 1976), have been distinguished from Piaget's theory in terms of the degree to which and the processes through which the components comprising a structure are interrelated (Wohlwill 1973).

These explanatory issues have, of course, not remained unaddressed. One relatively recent trend in the literature pertinent to stage theories, a trend which may be viewed as an attempt to resolve these explanatory controversies, is the advent of more circumscribed models. As was noted earlier, instead of completely rejecting an organismic, or even more specifically a Piagetian approach, some theorists have opted to investigate relatively specific areas of ability, such as problem-solving skills (Siegler 1981) and social cognitive development (Selman 1976, Turiel 1978). In addition, these theorists have tried to define patterns of change more precisely by limiting their focus of study, by delineating smaller and more circumscribed increments of developmental change, and by identifying procedures for measuring developmental change.

Still other theorists have devised broad-based theories of development, along the lines of the Piagetian model, that describe patterns of development across the range of individuals' functioning (Fischer 1980). These theorists have described specific sequences of development, and argue against the existence of pervasive underlying structures and homogeneities in functioning across different domains of behavior. Fischer (1980), for example, portrays development as the acquisition of sequences of skills in different domains of functioning.

2. Applications of Stage Models

Theorists have discussed the general implications of stage models for clinical interpretation, assessment, and intervention in children's cognitive and behavioral development. One of the most significant implications of stage models is that interpretations about the underlying basis of specific behaviors will vary, depending upon a child's stage of development. If the causes of a behavior vary according to a child's stage, it follows that decisions about whether and how to modify particular behaviors should vary according to a child's developmental level. The negativism exhibited by 2-year-olds, for example, may be based on their drive toward autonomy (Erikson 1950) or their egocentric level of social role taking (Selman 1976) and may be tolerable to adults who see these children as "just going through a stage." The same behavior, however, may not be tolerated in older children who are expected to have qualitatively different social and emotional competencies (an ability to understand others' social perspectives and a "conscience" or personal standards for acceptable behavior).

A stage model of development argues for the interrelationships of a wide range of competencies, and this idea also has significant implications for the clinician's understanding of children's disordered functioning. For example, several writers have noted that lack of synchrony in the rates of development of different competencies may be at the root of some children's disordered behavior (Craighead et al. 1983, Selman 1976). Children may be cognitively precocious, for example, while their social and affective development occur at normal rates. Such a developmental pattern could become problematical if others expect these children to be more mature in general, simply because they are cognitively advanced. In a similar way, children whose physical development is precocious may arouse inaccurate, overgeneralized expectations about their social and emotional maturity because of their appearance.

Lack of synchrony across domains of functioning may

be a problem for children who are more advanced in specific ways, and a delay in one or more aspects of children's functioning may also be problematic. One view of the basis of psychotic children's disordered thought patterns, for example, is that the reasoning abilities of these children are impaired such that they are unable to reason probabilistically (Inhelder 1971). Consequently, when they are confronted by uncertainty, psychotic children may attribute causes of events to magical forces or to an adult who is trying to trick them. In doing so, they mimic the performance of very young children who lack operational intelligence (Inhelder 1971). Children who display symbiotic psychosis exhibit extreme forms of the thought processes characteristic of children in earlier stages of development. Thus these children display extreme forms of egocentric thought in their inability to discriminate inanimate from animate objects and in their failure to distinguish self from nonself (Mahler 1965). Some behaviors of severely handicapped children may also reflect a mismatch between their chronological and mental ages. Mildly retarded adolescents, for example, may have had many experiences comparable to those of normally developing youngsters, but their reasoning about those experiences and their ability to solve problems relevant to those experiences may remain concrete. More severely retarded children, despite their advanced chronological age, may display behaviors comparable to those exhibited during the normal infant's sensory-motor period of development. The diagnosis of early infantile autism, for example, reflects the conception that children with this disorder continue to function in some ways like infants during the normal "autistic phase" of development. In each of these examples, an understanding of the meaning of a specific pattern of behavior in the context of invariant sequences of development may be the first step in determining a course of treatment.

Stage models of development also have implications for assessment techniques. For example, because stages are seen as invariant sequences, developmental assessments of subjects' level of functioning provide implicit information about directions for intervention or treatment. Whereas standardized scores on IQ measures or personality inventories will only indicate that a person is significantly different from the norm, an assessment of the stage of an individual's functioning will supply age normative information as well as information about what competencies come next in a developmental sequence and should therefore be taught or otherwise instilled. In determining the effectiveness of interventions directed toward cognitive or social-cognitive functioning, a stage-based assessment may also reveal whether "structural" (generalized) changes in functioning have taken place (Selman 1976).

In devising programs to promote children's development, workers in the field have relied mainly on the Piagetian cognitive developmental framework. Educators have made use of the Piagetian model in devising early childhood education curricula for both advantaged and disadvantaged children (Furth 1970, Kamii and DeVries 1974, Klaus and Gray 1968, Lavatelli 1970, Lawton and Hooper 1978). Practitioners have incorporated into their curricula both the training of the concepts and logical operations thought to be necessary for solving tasks designed by Piaget, as well as the principles of instruction derived from Piaget's model. Some of these more fundamental principles stress: (a) the differences between stage-based development and incremental learning; (b) the importance of the adaptation and reorganization of experiences as opposed to the simple accumulation of facts and; (c) the importance of children's active involvement in learning as the basis for development.

Although most program-development efforts have focused on children's cognitive development, several programs have been designed to promote children's social and affective functioning. Juvenile delinquents, for example, have been trained in social role taking, and promoting their social cognitive development has led to a reduction in the rate of these adolescents' crimes (Chandler 1973). Investigators have also discovered that role-taking competence is related to children's popularity, and programs have been devised to promote the development of social cognitive competencies in socially isolated children (Gottman et al. 1976). In another line of study, investigators have created programs to foster self-control in young children, and in older children who display hyperactive or impulsive behavior, by developing in these children more advanced means of processing information, using verbal mediation as private speech (Fuson 1979). Although these techniques have been defined by cognitive behavioral theorists who adopt an incremental model of developmental change, a "shift" to verbal mediation, and the concomitant changes in children's ability to monitor their own behavior, have been described as stage-like (White 1965). Moreover, some research suggests stage-like shifts in children's ability to profit from programs designed to promote these verbal mediation processes (Schleser et al. 1981).

In sum, stage models may be employed in a number of ways in educational settings. Given the variety of meanings and characteristics of stages, however, it would seem especially important that practitioners understand the implications of the particular stage models that they choose to adopt.

Bibliography

Bijou S J 1976 *Child Development: The Basic Stage of Early Childhood*. Prentice-Hall, Englewood Cliffs, New Jersey

Bijou S W, Baer D M 1961 *Child Development: A Systematic and Empirical Theory*, Vol. 1. Appleton-Century-Crofts, New York

Brainerd C J 1978a Learning research and Piagetian theory. In: Siegel L S, Brainerd C J (eds.) 1978 *Alternatives to Piaget: Cultural Essays on the Theory*. Academic Press, New York

Brainerd C J 1978b The stage question in cognitive-developmental theory. *Behav. Brain Sci.* 1: 173–82

Bruner J S 1964 The course of cognitive growth. *Am. Psychol.* 19: 1–15

Chandler M J 1973 Egocentrism and antisocial behavior: The assessment and training of social perspective-taking skills. *Dev. Psychol.* 9: 326–32

Craighead W E, Meyers A W, Craighead L W, McHale S M 1983 Issues in cognitive behavior therapy with children. In: Rosenbaum M, Franks C M, Jaffe Y (eds.) 1983 *Perspectives on Behavior Therapy in the Eighties*. Springer, New York

Erikson E H 1950 *Childhood and Society*. Norton, New York

Fischer K W 1980 A theory of cognitive development: The control and construction of hierarchies of skills. *Psychol. Rev.* 87: 477–531

Flavell J H 1971 Stage-related properties of cognitive development. *Cognit. Psychol.* 2: 421–53

Flavell J H 1972 An analysis of cognitive-developmental sequences. *Genet. Psychol. Monogr.* 86: 279–350

Flavell J H 1983 Structures, stages and sequences in cognitive development. In: Collins A (ed.) 1983 *Minnesota Symposia on Child Psychology*, Vol. 15. Erlbaum, Hillsdale, New Jersey

Freud A 1965 *Normality and Pathology in Chldhood: Assessments of Development*. International Universities Press, New York

Furth H G 1970 *Piaget for Teachers*. Prentice-Hall, Englewood Cliffs, New Jersey

Fuson K C 1979 The development of self-regulating aspects of speech: A review. In: Zivin G (ed.) 1979 *The Development of Self Regulation Through Private Speech*. Wiley-Interscience, New York

Gottman J, Gonso J, Schuler P 1976 Teaching social skills to isolated children. *J. Abnorm. Child Psychol.* 4: 179–97

Inhelder B 1971 Developmental theory and diagnostic procedures. In: Green D R, Ford M P, Flaner G B (eds.) 1971 *Measurement and Piaget: Proc. CTB/McGraw-Hill Conf. Ordinal Scales of Cognitive Development, Monterey, 1969*. McGraw-Hill, New York

Kamii C P, DeVries R 1974 Piaget for early education. In: Parker R K, Day M C (eds.) 1974 *The Preschool in Action: Exploring Early Childhood Programs*, 2nd edn. Allyn and Bacon, Boston, Massachusetts

Kessen W 1962 "Stage" and "structure" in the study of children. *Monogr. Soc. Res. Child Dev.* 27(2): 55–72

Klaus R, Gray S 1968 The early training project for disadvantaged children: A report after five years. *Monogr. Soc. Res. Child Dev.* 33(4): 1–66

Kohlberg L 1963 The development of children's orientations toward a moral order: (1) Sequence in the development of moral thought. *Vita Humana* 6: 11–33

Kohlberg L 1976 Moral stages and moralization: The cognitive-developmental approach. In: Lickona T (ed.) 1976 *Moral Development and Behavior: Theory, Research, and Social Issues*. Holt, Rinehart and Winston, New York

Lavatelli C 1970 *Early Childhood Curriculum: A Piaget Program*. American Science and Engineering, Boston, Massachusetts

Lawton J T, Hooper F H 1978 Piagetian theory and early childhood education: A critical analysis. In: Siegel L, Brainerd C J (eds.) 1978 *Alternatives to Piaget: Critical Essays on the Theory*. Academic Press, New York

Mahler M 1965 On early infantile psychosis. *J. Am. Acad. Child Psychiat.* 4: 554–68

Piaget J 1970 Piaget's theory. In: Mussen P H (ed.) 1970 *Carmichael's Manual of Child Psychology*, 3rd edn., Vol. 1. Wiley, New York

Reese H W, Overton W F 1970 Models of development and theories of development. In: Goulet L R, Baltes P B (eds.) 1970 *Life-span Developmental Psychology: Research and Theory.* Academic Press, New York

Schleser R, Meyers A W, Cohen R 1981 Generalization of self-instructions: Effects of general versus specific content, active rehearsal, and cognitive levels. *Child Dev.* 52: 335–40

Selman R L 1976 Social cognitive understanding: A guide to educational and clinical practice. In: Lickona T (ed.) 1976 *Moral Development and Behavior.* Holt, Rinehart and Winston, New York

Siegler R S 1978 The origins of scientific reasoning. In: Siegler R S (ed.) 1978 *Children's Thinking: What Develops?* Erlbaum, Hillsdale, New Jersey

Siegler R S 1981 Developmental sequences within and between concepts. *Monogr. Soc. Res. Child Dev.* 46, Serial No. 189

Turiel E 1978 The development of concepts of social structure: Social convention. In: Glick J, Clarke-Stewart A (eds.) 1978 *The Development of Social Understanding.* Gardner Press, New York

White S H 1965 Evidence for a hierarchical arrangement of learning processes. In: Lipsitt L P, Spiker C C (eds.) 1965 *Advances in Child Development and Behavior*, Vol. 2. Academic Press, New York

Wohlwill J F 1973 *The Study of Behavioral Development.* Academic Press, New York

Stage-theory Trends

J. ter Laak

In order to describe and understand cognitions, feelings, and behaviors over the course of time, they have to be categorized and connected in one way or another. One way to do this is to propose a number of qualitatively different stages of cognitive, emotional, and behavioral development. Another way is to study behavioral stability, asking questions such as: is an intelligent, anxiously attached child also an intelligent, shy adult? A third way is to associate behavioral changes in the course of time with immediate social and environmental causal forces, like modeling and reinforcement.

This article is confined to (neo-)structural and cultural–historical stage theories. Functional and existential stages are not considered. First, two sources of stage theories are identified. Some characteristics of stage theories are then mentioned, and some examples of old and new stage theories reviewed. Finally some trends in stage theories and the significance of stage theories for education are discussed, and some thoughts about the future of stage theories are expressed.

1. Two Sources of Stage Theories

In its beginning as a scientific discipline, developmental psychology borrowed from the life sciences of the nineteenth century. Darwin's theory of the evolution of species and theories of embryological development contributed to the concept of development. Ideas about the evolution of species were applied to individual development; behaviors were considered to evolve from each other by the mechanism of adaptation. Moreover, as in embryology, these changes were conceived as regulated and hierarchically organized. Methods of conducting research also reflected the methods used in biology, with comparative descriptions of humans and animals in their natural habitat constituting the basic materials.

A second, less often mentioned source of stage theories is the Soviet cultural–historical tradition. This tradition is inspired by Marxist sociology and anthropology. It assumes that humans acquire, in the course of their development, the historical and social features of the species. This phenomenon is considered as compelling as the acquisition of the biological characteristics of the species.

The two sources have in common the fact that development is considered as orderly. An individual passes through a number of invariant and distinct stages toward a provisional endpoint.

2. Characteristics of Stage Theories

There are several stage theories, the most influential one being Piaget's structural stage theory. Using elements from the theory of evolution and the embryology of his time, Piaget designed a theory of cognitive development. It was his fundamental intuition that human cognition belonged to the realms of both biology and logic. As in biological growth, cognitive development was conceived as a series of structural changes evolving from each other. These structures were qualitatively different but served the same function of adaptation in a progressively more equilibrated and therefore less vulnerable way. The structures could not return to a genetically earlier form and the higher structures implicated the lower ones. Logic played a double role in the theory. On the one hand it was used as a formal system for depicting empirical relations. On the other it was the description and explanation of cognitive development itself. For example, an 8-year-old, concrete operational child was considered to be a class-and-relation "logician."

These presuppositions about the biological and logical origins of knowledge led Piaget to the conclusion that there must be stages of cognitive development. His stages had the following characteristics: there were "structures of the whole" (*structures d'ensembles*), that is, underlying organizations of an extensive domain of thought. The stages consisted of qualitatively different structures, which served the same function. There was an invariant sequence which no training could change. The stages were hierarchically integrated. With the exception of the sensory-motor period, all stages were modeled with the help of logical and algebraic formulas.

The Piagetian stages have been interpreted, commented upon, and supplemented: the "structure of the whole" was often exchanged for more limited conceptions like cognitive sequences and levels of development. The specific logical and algebraic modeling was not elaborated, because of the frequent use of quantitative multivariate models. On the contrary, procedures for finding sequences were elaborated. Siegel et al. (1983) proposed a structure-function analysis, that is the analysis of several more or less similar behavioral sequences, and the search for parallels and isomorphs in several behaviors. They pointed to the fact that the processes of change were usually limited to differentiation and integration, and suggested more processes like the growth of attentional capacity and self-modification. The same emphasis on content was found in an article by Campbell and Bickhard (1986), who insisted on the active search for necessary and sufficient precursors of behavior.

Fischer and Silvern (1985) formulated empirical criteria for the assessment of levels on the basis of existing stages and sequences. Some of these criteria were: systematic relations between age and achievements, qualitative differences between levels, discontinuous changes, and evidence that what can be learned is limited by the developmental level.

Finally, the developmental paradigm was extended to moral reasoning by Kohlberg (1979) and to the taking of the perspective of other persons by Selman (1980).

Characteristics of stages, sequences, and developmental levels are not clear cut. This is not to say that the concepts are not fruitful. It means that stages, sequences, and levels are open theoretical concepts which can progressively be connected to empirical reality.

3. Examples of Stage Theories

Within structural stage theories there are several varieties of theory. A selection of four will be looked at in this section. The four can be grouped within three categories: Piagetian, neo-Piagetian (or neo-structural), and cultural–historical. Piaget's and Kohlberg's (Piagetian) stage theories are discussed because they are the most researched theories of cognitive and moral development. Case's (1985) theory was chosen because it is probably the most complete neo-Piagetian theory of intellectual development. El'konin's (1972) stage theory is discussed because it stems from an old, but relatively unknown, tradition.

Piagetian theories differ from neo-Piagetian theories in many aspects. A central aspect is that in Piagetian

approaches, underlying structures are assessed, usually by trained interviewers armed with voluminous scoring manuals. The structures are supposed to underly diverse behaviors. In the neo-structural theories, however, there is no search for universal underlying structures. It is accepted that no assessment is context-free. There is, however, resistance to the idea that every task can be carried out at every age. The situational context and features of tasks are analyzed in so far as these contribute to the assessment of a person's developmental level. In El'konin's stage theory the emphasis is on the social origin of knowledge of the world of things and persons. Stages are conceived as dominant activities during a period. A summary is given below of the concrete stages of the four theories.

Piaget distinguished four structural stages: sensory-motor, preoperational, concrete-operational, and formal-operational. The stages refer to ways of dealing with the physical world and to accompanying abilities. The sensory-motor stage is characterized as a spontaneous, practical perceiving-and-doing intelligence. The child acquires insight in means/end relations and in the permanence of objects and persons. During the pre-operational stage the child discovers qualitative constancies: objects are, for example, identical despite differences in form, place, color, and so on. The comprehension of constancies in the concrete operational stage is called conservation. Children at this stage know that number, length, mass, and so on, do not change when perceptual arrangements change. They understand that the changes are reversible and compensatory. In the formal-operational stage, the subject is considered to be able to think inductively and deductively. The person thinks and acts like a scientist.

Kohlberg (1979), on the basis of answers to moral dilemmas, constructed six underlying structures of moral judgment. These stages ran parallel with the Piagetian stages. The first two are called preconventional: actions are either allowed or not because they lead to punishment or enhance personal wellbeing. The second two are the conventional stages: actions are justified because other persons expect such actions or because they are prescribed by social conventions. The last two require insight into the rationale of social contracts or the risks of violations, and into moral/ethical principles and are called "principled" stages.

The neo-Piagetian stage theory of Case (1985) also runs parallel with the Piagetian stages. This theory contains four main stages, each divided into four sub-stages: operational consolidation, unifocal coordination (i.e., a qualitative change within a main stage), then bifocal and elaborated coordination. In the sensory-motor stage, the child acquires successively the following control structures: visual tracking behavior, coordination of visual tracking and hand movements, and means/end relations. The relational stage contains control structures of relations between sensory operations. For example, the insight into simple reversible relations (here up, there down; here high, there low) is acquired. In the dimensional stage the subject applies enumeration. Variables are conceptualized as continuous dimensions. Moreover, two dimensions can be perceived together. Finally, kinds of relations between dimensions, like reversibility and compensation, are understood. In the abstract dimensional stage the relations between dimensions are coordinated as, for example, in fractions and ratios.

El'konin (1972) rejected Western naturalism in which the relation between the child and the physical world was central. In his view the child/thing system is both a child/social-object system and a child/social-adult system. With these presuppositions in mind, El'konin described the dominant activities of six periods. The activities of the child in the first period are dominated by direct emotional contact with adults. Against this privileged background, sensory-motor and manipulative actions take place. The second period is characterized by direct practical actions with objects, which prepare for the emergence of symbolic functioning. The dominant activities of the third period are play, role playing, and imitation. The preschool child imitates the activities and human relations of adults. In the fourth period formal schooling is the dominant factor of cognitive development. The fifth period distinguishes school age from adolescence. Because there is no substantial outward change, the cause of the transition is found in the organism itself: the process of sexual maturation. El'konin pointed also to another transition: the establishment of intimate personal relationships. In the sixth period the relations with society at large are central; including work and career.

4. Trends in Stage Theories

Bergius (1959) summarized stage theories between the two World Wars. Probably because of the conviction of the editor that such diverse theories could not all be true at the same time, he suggested abandoning the stage concept and using the neutral concept of change. It did not work.

In the 1960s associationism declined as the leading theory of behavioral change. Piaget was at the same time rediscovered in the United States. This discovery was an enormous impetus for the study of cognitive development. At the same time there was much criticism, and among others, the stage concept was vigorously attacked. First, the "structures of the whole" suggested a solidity of organization which could not be demonstrated empirically. Futher, there was no place for ubiquitous individual differences. Moreover, very diverse cognitions and behaviors that appeared at different times were reduced to the same denominator, and also the methods for assessing the structures were not clear. Some authors discovered preoperational thought in children at the age of 2, while using seemingly appropriate criteria. Then the explanatory power was rejected: the theory did not define clearly what concrete behaviors changed and it did not manipulate specific antecedent causes for the changes. Further, the logical and algebraic models were criticized. The models were on the one hand incorrect and on the other they reflected a confusion between logical and empirical domains. Finally, equilibration was not considered as central for stage transition. Learning was regarded as more powerful.

Kohlberg's stage theory was thoroughly researched but criticized less than Piaget's because the investigators worked within the paradigm. Some criticisms were, however, put forward. It was found, for example, that sometimes subjects seemed to regress in their moral judgments. Kohlberg had in fact to formulate a new stage to account for this phenomenon. Furthermore, the scoring system was oriented solely to an increasing autonomous morality of the individual. Justice was the only central value and values like interpersonal responsibility were disregarded.

In the 1970s the criticisms of stage theories continued, and a new framework for the study of cognition was developed: the information-processing approach. The interest in different global structures over the course of time almost disappeared. There was, instead, a detailed modeling of what subjects did on various tasks and under various task conditions.

In the 1980s information-processing analyses continued, but neo-structural theories of development also appeared. Some authors attributed this trend to the explosion of data on children of various ages which had to be integrated to form an overall picture. Further, the analyses pointed to parallels of processes and achievements on different tasks. Although some authors (e.g., Case 1986) pointed to new evidence and new methods, such methods and data do not account entirely for the revival of interest in developmental sequences and levels.

5. Stage Theories and Education

The development of an educational curriculum requires a selection of goals, contents, means, ways of learning and teaching, and their organization. Stage theories are about cognitive development, not about educational goals, contents, and the like. But this does not detract from the fact that elements of the theories are used to select goals, contents, and so on. In this sense, stage theories are of significance for education.

Although Piaget was reluctant to admit that his theory had educational significance, its influence was tremendous. The theory was used to define goals: for example, autonomy, ability to decenter, ability to take the perspective of another person, and stimulating operational thought. Contents were adopted: for example children have to classify, to seriate, to enumerate, and so on. As teaching methodology, a Socratic method of teaching was recommended. Finally, many curricula were sequenced in a way that reflected both the global stages and the emphasis on actions as prerequisites for internalizations. Aebli (1963), for example, adopted Piagetian elements for some general internalization steps. The steps were: actions with concrete materials; external representation of the task (e.g., a drawing); carrying out the action in the head with a known beginning-and-end state; the same but only with the end state; and finally carrying out the task without the support of concrete materials.

Kohlberg's stage theory was soon used to stimulate moral development. The goals of the discussions about moral dilemmas were to move the subject to a level higher in the moral judgment stages. An educational presupposition was that training on the next higher level was the most effective. Goals and contents of the curriculum were directly borrowed from the theory. "Is" and "ought" became very close, not to say confused.

The neo-structural stage theory of Case has an explicit link with education. Though the theory does not formulate educational goals or contents, it contains an instructional part. This instruction theory contains three main steps, First, a specific academic task is structurally analyzed: how much and which control structures are needed for solving the problem. Second, the developmental level of the subject is assessed. Third, given the aforementioned knowledge, an instruction is designed.

In the cultural–historical tradition, the link between development and instruction is very narrow. Instruction is a necessary social factor in development. The common goal of development and instruction is the establishment of fully fledged mental acts. The organization of curricula is based on the steps which are necessary for a "complete" mental act. Subjects have to orient thoroughly on all task elements, have to manipulate, and so on. Finally, people can solve tasks "internally" without the help of materials and motor actions. It looks like a shortened repetition of historical materialism.

Stage theories are used very easily in education, they are used without scruple for the selection of goals, means, and so on. This should not blind us to the fact that there is only one criterion for a curriculum: do pupils profit from it, and is it effective given the cost for pupils and teachers?

6. A Future for Stage Theories?

There is a future for stage theories, for there do seem to be some promising facts and possibilities.

First, there has been a revival of stage theories in the 1980s. Among others, the works of Case (1985) and Fischer (1980) are clear examples. Second, the epistemological climate is becoming more willing to accept pattern theories. In stage theories one is searching for organization and patterns of cognitive and behavioral changes over the course of time. The antecedent–consequent causal explanations are too limiting for developmental psychologists. In modern epistemology an open-stage, or rather a sequence or level concept, is allowed. In other words, strict operationalism is rejected. Third, much is known about all kinds of achievements of children and adults. But there is often no overarching picture of cognition and behavior at a certain point in time and certainly not over the course of time. Stage theories are attempts to build such overarching pictures of development. Fourth, the methods of data analysis in psychology are becoming more and more sophisticated in analyzing complex patterns (see, for example, Davison et al. 1980). Fifth, there is a theoretical renewal of developmental level conceptions (see, for example, Campbell and Bickard 1986).

Do the foregoing points possess enough power to build a research program in the sense of Lakatos? Time will tell. Stage theories organize different cognitions, feelings, and behaviors over the course of time. There is always the risk of putting together what does not belong together. Stage theories need critics, because the story of development runs the risk of being told too easily. Kagan (1980) is such a critic. He reproached the developmental psychologists for telling "coherent stories" without attention to immediate courses of behavioral change. It is, however, allowable to tell coherent stories, if the stories have a theoretical basis and relevant empirical referents.

Bibliography

Aebli H 1963 *Über die geistige Entwicklung des Kindes*. Klett, Stuttgart

Bergius R 1959 Entwicklung als Stufenfolge. In Thomae H (ed.) 1959 *Entwicklungspsychologie*. Hogrefe, Göttingen, pp. 104–95

Bloom B S 1964 *Stability and Change in Human Characteristics*. Wiley, New York

Brainerd C J 1978 The stage question in cognitive-developmental theory. *The Behavioral and Brain Sciences* 1: 173–213

Campbell R L, Bickhard M H 1986 *Knowing Levels and Developmental Stages*. Karger, Basel

Case R 1985 *Intellectual Development*. Academic Press, Orlando, Florida

Case R 1986 The new stage theories in intellectual development: Why we need them: What they assert. In: Perlmutter M (ed.) 1986 *Perspectives for Intellectual Development*. Erlbaum, Hillsdale, New Jersey, pp. 57–96

Commons M L, Richard F A 1984 A general model of stage theory. In: Commons M L, Richards F A (eds.) 1984 *Beyond Formal Operations: Late Adolescent and Adult Cognitive Development*. Praeger, New York. pp. 120–40

Davison M L, King P M, Kitchener K S, Parker C A 1980 The stage sequence concept in cognitive and social development. *Dev. Psychol.* 16: 121–31

El'konin D B 1972 Toward the problem of stages in the mental development of the child. *Soviet Psychol.* 10: 225–51

Fischer K W 1980 A theory of cognitive development: The control and construction of hierarchies of skills. *Psychol. Rev.* 87(6): 477–531

Fischer K W, Silvern L 1985 Stages and individual differences in cognitive development. *Ann. Rev. Psychol.* 36: 613–48

Flavell J H 1985 *Cognitive Development*. Prentice-Hall, Englewood Cliffs, New Jersey

Kagan J 1980 Perspectives on continuity. In: Brim O G Jr, Kagan J (eds.) 1980 *Constancy and Change in Human Development*. Harvard University Press, Cambridge, Massachusetts, pp. 26–74

Kitchener R F 1983 Changing conceptions of the philosophy of science and the foundations of developmental psychology. In: Kuhn D, Meacham J A (eds.) 1983 *On the Development of Developmental Psychology*. Karger, Basel, pp. 1–30

Kohlberg L 1979 De continuiteit in de morele ontwikkeling (The continuity in moral development). In: Koops W, Van der Werff J (eds.) 1979 *Overzicht van de ontwikkelingspsychologie* [Review of developmental psychology]. Wolters Noordhoff. The Netherlands, pp. 327–46

Laak J ter 1986 Developmental sequences, some characteristics and an empirical demonstration. In: Van Geert P L C (ed.)

1986 *Theory Building in Developmental Psychology*. North-Holland, Amsterdam, pp. 293–330

Lakatos I J 1978 *The Methodology of Scientific Research Programmes*, Philosophical Papers, Vol. 1. Cambridge University Press, Cambridge

Piaget J 1970 Piaget's theory. In: Mussen P H (ed.) 1970 *Carmichael's Manual of Child Psychology*, Vol. 1, 3rd edn. Wiley, New York, pp. 703–32

Selman R L 1980 *The Growth of Interpersonal Understanding: Developmental and Clinical Analyses*. Academic Press, New York

Siegel A W, Bisanz J, Bisanz G L 1983 Developmental analysis: A strategy for the study of psychological change. In: Kuhn D, Meacham J A (eds.) 1983 *On the Development of Developmental Psychology*. Karger, Basel, pp. 53–80

Developmental Rate

C. Hertzog and R. M. Lerner

A developmental process is a set of systematic, adaptive changes in the quantity and/or quality of a variable. Obviously, for such processes to occur and to be detected time must elapse. Simply, change is a time-bound concept and the detection of change requires at least two and, preferably, more measurement times. However, time may be used in at least two ways to appraise development. As an independent variable, a time$_1$–time$_2$ interval (or a time$_1$–time$_2$–time$_3$–time$_4$, etc., interval) is kept constant, and levels of some dependent variable (for instance a behavior) are measured at each time point. Alternatively, two (or more) different levels of development can be used as a standard, and the time taken to change from level 1 to level 2 (etc.) is then the dependent variable.

The concept of "rate of development" is most meaningfully represented by the second use of time. Thus, rate of development, as a feature of intraindividual development, refers to the magnitude of a time$_1$–time$_2$ interval associated with a fixed level 1–level 2 contrast. Rate of development, as a dimension of interindividual difference, refers to between-people differences in time$_1$–time$_2$ intervals associated with an interindividually fixed level 1–level 2 contrast. In turn, the presence of a particular level of development at a single time point cannot be unequivocally construed as revealing anything about rate of development. Interindividual differences in developmental level at a single time point are similarly equivocal as to their status as an index of interindividual differences in rate of development—a point often misunderstood or unrecognized in developmental research (Baltes 1968, Baltes et al. 1977, Schaie 1965).

1. Rate of Development in Evolutionary Theory

The concept of rate of development is not an organizing concept in major theories of ontogeny, although it is in theories of phylogeny (Gould 1977). Theories of ontogenetic development treat rate of development as a descriptive individual-difference concept; in evolutionary biology interspecies differences in rate of development (that is, heterochrony) is a central, explanatory concept (Gould 1977). That is, in evolutionary biology, heterochronic differences are presumed to account for species differences in plasticity and complexity of final developmental levels (Gould 1977, Schneirla 1957). One form of heterochrony is recapitulation, which refers to the evolutionary compression of ancestral adult stages of development into the juvenile stages of descendants; such heterochronic changes have not been found, however, to be of general explanatory use in accounting for species differences in plasticity or complexity (Gould 1977). Another form of heterochrony—neoteny—has been seen to have such explanatory value. Neoteny refers to the retention of ancestral juvenile characteristics in the adult stages of descendants. Such retention, termed paedomorphosis, is produced by a slowing down of somatic development (Gould 1977). Such a retardation in rate of development allows greater lengths of time for learning and for the organization of the large brain, and especially the neocortex, that humans have evolved.

2. Rate of Development in Ontogenetic Theory

2.1 Organismic Theories

Organismic, stage theories of ontogenetic development see interindividual differences in rate of development as one of the two types of individual differences that can exist (Emmerich 1968, Lerner 1976), "final level of development" being the other. Explanations of interindividual differences in rate of development in such theories usually involve reference to: (a) individually distinct heredity, for example, different maturational "ground plans" (Erikson 1959); (b) facilitating or inhibiting experiences; or (c) some interaction between (a) and (b).

Structural models of cognitive development fare especially poorly with regard to the issue of rate of development. In general, organismic-stage models may conceptualize rate of intraindividual development in terms of the age at which qualitatively different stages of development are achieved, as well as the rate of consolidation (e.g., attainment of equilibrium) within a stage. Examination of the empirical literature on stage models of cognitive development reveals little if any interest in characterizing individual differences in the rate of stage acquisition. Thus, the typical paradigm in studying conservation behavior, for example, is a cross-sectional study spanning some childhood age range (for instance 5 to 9 years). Such studies show attainment of various conservation behaviors between ages 7 to 9 (see Elkind and Flavell 1969 for a review). It is as if individual differences in rate of stage attainment are irrelevant anomalies. For example, Liben (1981), in an essay describing a Piagetian perspective on children's contributions to their own development, emphasized the critical importance of the individual's internal representation of environmental forms. However, in this Piagetian perspective there is no discussion of whether there are individual differences in such representation and, if so, what implications there would be for individual differences in rate of development. Similar problems exist in other cognitive studies examining a variety of skills, even where new perspectives on cognitive development have emerged (Gelman 1979); in sum, interindividual differences in intraindividual development trajectories have not been a primary focus.

2.2 Mechanistic Theories

In mechanistically derived (e.g., behavioristic) approaches to ontogenetic development (Bijou 1976, Bijou and Baer 1961), interindividual differences in rate of development are explained by reference to contrasts in reinforcement history. Here differences in schedules of reinforcement (e.g., a fixed-interval versus a variable-interval schedule), and the types of reinforcing stimuli used therein, lead to interindividual variation in the rate of acquiring a given criterion behavior. In addition, some theoretical discussions have indicated that some organismic attributes (particularly those with evolutionary significance for the organism) potentially constrain the effects of some reinforcers on the acquisition of selected behaviors, that is, those that may interfere with the emitting of evolutionary central behaviors (Breland and Breland 1961, Herrnstein 1977, Skinner 1966, 1977).

2.3 Contextual Theories

In approaches to ontogenetic development derived from a contextual perspective, interindividual differences in rate of development are universally expected. The person and context variables that interact to provide a basis for development do so in a temporally probabilistic manner (Lerner et al. 1983, Lerner et al. 1980, Schneirla 1957, Tobach and Schneirla 1968). Indeed, given the infinity of these variables, no two people are expected to have either isomorphic developmental profiles (at least insofar as the content of one's behavioral repertoire is concerned) or, therefore, identical rates of development. Indeed, since a contextual approach would, in the extreme, indicate that no interindividual isomorphism could exist between level 1–level 2 contrasts, precise interindividual comparisons of rate of development would be precluded.

However, as suggested elsewhere (Emmerich 1968, Lerner 1976), while such singularity of a developmental profile may require an ipsative analysis for complete description of an individual's development, general patterns of change are not logically excluded by the presence of idiographic phenomena. For example, comparable structural changes, for instance, as described by the orthogenetic principle, may occur despite distinct contents of an attribute repertoire. Such interindividual, structural comparability would permit level 1–level 2 contrasts in regard to developmental rate.

In sum, rate of development is a concept pertinent to all major approaches to developmental theory. Yet, the concept has not been a prominent one in any major instance of any type of theory.

3. Bases of the Lack of Attention to the Rate of Development Concept

For a variety of reasons, developmental psychologists have spent relatively little effort identifying interindividual differences in developmental trajectories—so it is not surprising that relatively little is known about individual differences in the rate of behavioral development. Consider the case of psychometric intelligence, which has been extensively studied over the adult life span (Bayley 1970, Horn and Donaldson 1979, McCall et al. 1977, Botwinick 1977, Schaie 1979). The psychometric model for intelligence derives primarily from a mechanistic perspective in which it is deemed reasonable to conceptualize intellectual development as a process of continuous development from young childhood to maturity. To be sure, longitudinal studies have suggested lability in the developmental trajectories of infants and of young children below the age of 3 years (McCall et al. 1973, 1977), but after age 6 the stability of individual differences in psychometric test performance increases markedly. Given, then, the relatively continuous nature of the development "growth" curves in psychometric intelligence from age 6 through adolescence, one might expect that developmental psychologists have attempted to identify the mathematical form of the average developmental function so as to estimate a rate parameter for the function. Certainly, developmental methodologists have provided the requisite mathematical tools (Cattell 1970, Goldstein 1979, Guire and Kowalski 1979).

However, efforts to characterize the mathematical form of the developmental function of intelligence are notably lacking in the literature. From a contextual perspective, this may not be at all bad, since it is unlikely that the averaged growth curve for intelligence would accurately reflect the intraindividual rates of development; the rate parameter of such functions would be representative of all individuals' rate parameters only if there were interindividual differences only in rate parameters, but not in the form of the developmental function (Guire and Kowalski 1979). For instance, it is highly unlikely that an average developmental rate parameter for intelligence across the adult life span would be meaningful, since development during adulthood is critically dependent upon environmental contingencies, for instance, the impact of nonnormative life events and other nonorganismic influences on development (Baltes and Willis 1977, Hultsch and Plemons 1979).

The fact remains, however, that the psychometric literature has focused upon age norms for psychometric performance (Matarazzo 1972)—thereby indirectly measuring normative developmental functions—without addressing directly: (a) the issue of measuring the developmental function or (b) the examination of individual differences in either the focus of the function or the rate parameter of the function. Instead, individual differences are examined solely by comparison to age norms—the individual is characterized by the deviation from the age group's mean (or another measure of central tendency). As discussed above, this is hardly satisfactory, since interindividual differences at point in time—4, say, tell nothing about the rate of change leading up to status at time—4. It could be argued that adequate assessment of the likely educational implications of psychometric assessment of children can only be understood from the developmental context of intraindividual change leading to an antecedent–consequent model for the developmental processes producing the child's status at a fixed point in the developmental sequence (Baltes and Nesselroade 1979).

4. Towards Incorporating the "Rate of Development" Concept into Developmental Research and Intervention

What developmental psychology has to say about intervention or education in respect of the rate of development concept is limited. This omission is due to the fact that theory and research have not focused on the concept, at least in regard to interindividual differences in individual developmental trajectories. This lack of focus is in turn partially accounted for by the fact that developmental researchers have, by and large, not opted to do longitudinal research (Baltes and Nesselroade 1979, Livson and Peskin 1980). Since such

research is necessary in order to have the database requisite for the study of rate of development, such "preferences" have precluded advances in understanding pertinent to the rate-of-development concept. For instance, developmental psychology has not progressed sufficiently to generate functional rate models, an outcome which would accrue if data relevant to "rate of development" had been generated in appropriately designed longitudinal research.

What information is needed to enhance knowledge? Why would this information be important? First, it would be necessary to know what constitutes formally equivalent points of development ("level 1" and "level 2") before rate of development can be studied. Simply put, it is necessary to understand, at least at a descriptive level, the target phenomena of interest before it is possible to begin to understand interindividual differences in developmental trajectories and rates. Perhaps it is the relative paucity of our knowledge about developmental phenomena which has precluded attention to individual differences in the rate of development. To achieve such knowledge about target phenomena, it is necessary to adopt ipsative methods, along with nomothetic ones, in order to study rate of development between multiple levels of psychological structure. One obvious place to initiate such research is where the structures comprising each level are well-understood, as may be argued to be the case in regard to cognitive developmental stages (Piaget 1970).

Knowledge of rate parameters would have import for intervention and educational practice. It might be found that while children develop from one comparable level to another, they do so with lawfully different rates, that is, rates which might require different models of instruction if rate facilitation is desired. Attention to the issue of rates of development would logically lead educators away from global questions like: "Was Head Start effective?" to differentiated questions such as: "For whom was Head Start effective, and why?". Developmental rate might well be a critical preintervention status variable which would predict successful intervention outcomes, and more importantly, might indicate qualitatively different intervention techniques for individuals differing in developmental profiles. In addition, there may exist multiple techniques for altering rates, but each rate involved might be associated with a different cost:benefit ratio. As such, intervenors and educators might have to begin to ask: "What technique is most feasible for altering the development rate of what type of child between what points in his or her life span?"

Bibliography

Baltes P B 1968 Longitudinal and cross-sectional sequences in the study of age and generation effects. *Hum. Dev.* 11: 145–71
Baltes P B, Nesselroade J R 1979 History and rationale of longitudinal research. In: Nesselroade J R, Baltes P B (eds.)

1979 *Longitudinal Research in the Study of Behavior and Development*. Academic Press, New York

Baltes P B, Willis S L 1977 Psychological theories of aging and development. In: Birren J E, Schaie K W (eds.) 1977 *Handbook of the Psychology of Aging*. Van Nostrand Rheinhold, New York

Baltes P B, Reese H W, Nesselroade J R 1977 *Life-span Developmental Psychology: Introduction to Research Methods*. Brooks/Cole, Monterey, California

Bayley N 1970 Development of mental abilities. In: Mussen P H (ed.) 1970 *Carmichael's Manual of Child Psychology*, Vol. 1. Wiley, New York

Bijou S J 1976 *Child Development: The Basic Stage of Early Childhood*. Prentice-Hall, Englewood Cliffs, New Jersey

Bijou S J, Baer D M 1961 *Child Development*, Vol. 1: *A Systematic and Empirical Theory*. Appleton-Century-Crofts, New York

Botwinick J 1977 Intellectual abilities. In: Birren J E, Schaie K W (eds.) 1977 *Handbook of the Psychology of Aging*. Van Nostrand Rheinhold, New York

Breland K, Breland M 1961 The misbehavior of organisms. *Am. Psychol.* 16: 681–84

Cattell R B 1970 Separating endogenous, exogenous, ecogenic, and epogenic component curves in developmental data. *Dev. Psychol.* 3: 151–62

Elkind D, Flavell J H (eds.) 1969 *Studies in Cognitive Development*. Oxford University Press, New York

Emmerich W 1968 Personality development and concepts of structure. *Child Dev.* 39: 671–90

Erikson E H 1959 Identity and the life cycle. *Psychol. Issues* 1: 18–164

Gelman R 1979 Preschool thought. *Am. Psychol.* 34: 900–05

Goldstein H 1979 *Longitudinal Studies*. Academic Press, New York

Gould S J 1977 *Ontogeny and Phylogeny*. Belknap, Harvard University Press, Cambridge, Massachusetts

Guire K E, Kowalski C J 1979 Mathematical description and representation of developmental change functions on the intra- and inter-individual levels. In: Nesselroade J R, Baltes P B (eds.) 1979 *Longitudinal Research in the Study of Behavior and Development*. Academic Press, New York

Herrnstein R J 1977 The evolution of behaviorism. *Am. Psychol.* 32: 593–603

Horn J L, Donaldson G 1979 Cognitive development in adulthood. In: Baltes P B, Brim O G (eds.) 1979 *Life Span Development and Behavior*, Vol. 2. Academic Press, New York

Hultsch D F, Plemons J K 1979 Life events and life-span development. In: Baltes P B, Brim O G (eds.) 1979 *Life Span Development and Behavior*, Vol. 2. Academic Press, New York

Lerner R M 1976 *Concepts and Theories of Human Development*. Addison-Wesley, Reading, Massachusetts

Lerner R M, Hultsch D F, Dixon R A 1983 Contextualism and the character of developmental psychology in the 1970s. *Annals of the New York Academy of Sciences*, 412: 101–28

Lerner R M, Skinner E A, Sorell G T 1980 Methodological implications of contextual/dialectic theories of development. *Hum. Dev.* 23: 225–35

Liben L S 1981 Individuals' contributions to their own development during childhood: A Piagetian perspective. In: Lerner R M, Busch-Rossnagel N A (eds.) 1981 *Individuals as Producers of their Development: A Life-span Perspective*. Academic Press, New York

Livson N, Peskin H 1980 Perspectives on adolescence from longitudinal research. In: Adelson J (ed.) 1981 *Handbook of Adolescent Psychology*. Wiley, New York

McCall R B, Appelbaum M I, Hogarty P S 1973 Developmental changes in mental performance. *Monographs of the Society for Research in Child Development*, 38 (Serial No. 150)

McCall R B, Eichorn D H, Hogarty P S 1977 Transitions in early mental development. *Monographs of the Society for Research in Child Development*, 42 (Serial No. 171)

Matarazzo J D 1972 *Wechsler's Measurement and Appraisal of Adult Intelligence*, 5th edn. Williams and Wilkins, Baltimore

Schaie K W 1965 A general model for the study of developmental problems. *Psychol. Bull.* 64: 92–107

Schaie K W 1979 The primary mental abilities in adulthood: An exploration in the development of psychometric intelligence. In: Baltes P B, Brim O G Jr (eds.) 1979 *Life Span Development and Behavior*, Vol. 2. Academic Press, New York

Schneirla T C 1957 The concept of development in comparative psychology. In: Harris D B (ed.) 1957 *The Concept of Development*. University of Minnesota Press, Minneapolis

Skinner B F 1966 The phylogeny and ontogeny of behavior. *Science* 153: 1205–13

Skinner B F 1977 Herrnstein and the evolution of behaviorism. *Am. Psychol.* 32: 1006–12

Tobach E, Schneirla T C 1968 The biopsychology of social behavior of animals. In: Cooke R E, Levin S (eds.) 1968 *Biologic Basis of Pediatric Practice*. McGraw-Hill, New York

Seven Stages of Life

Prenatal Development

D. Rapson

The term prenatal means prior to birth. Prenatal development is the period of growth and maturation of an organism which begins at conception and continues until birth occurs. In humans the period of prenatal development is approximately nine months long, a period during which a person develops from a zygote (made up of a single cell from each parent) into a complex human being with highly differentiated organs and body parts. The whole process of prenatal development is directed by the hereditary code that not only affects prenatal development but also development after birth. In the following discussion, conception and the hereditary code and its effects are described, then the three periods (germinal, embryo, and fetal) of prenatal growth are examined. The last section briefly lists environmental factors that can affect prenatal development.

1. Conception

The process of prenatal development begins at the moment of conception, which is the result of a male sperm cell uniting with a female ovum (egg cell). After the two cells have joined, they form an organism which is called a zygote whose walls cannot be penetrated by other sperm cells. Each of the original two cells (sperm and ovum) carries genetic material which, at conception, sets in motion a complex series of events that result in the development of a human being.

2. Heredity

The genetic material that each organism carries as a result of conception is made up of chromosomes that make up a hereditary code that is both general and specific in nature. The general hereditary code is shared by all individuals of a given species. For instance, the chromosomes that make up the general hereditary code of the fertilized human egg always lead to the development of characteristics that are strictly human (i.e., a human zygote cannot develop wings, fins, or other nonhuman qualities).

2.1 Chromosomes

The specific hereditary code is related to many characteristics that make individuals within a certain species different from one another, so that humans vary in height, eye color, sex, weight, intellectual abilities, and other qualities.

The 46 chromosomes that make up the hereditary code of every normal human zygote (23 from the sperm cell, 23 from the ovum) are composed of DNA (deoxyribonucleic acid) molecules which are shaped like a double helix, or a twisted ladder. As the cells in the zygote reproduce by dividing in two, the double helix splits down the middle, sending the same genetic code into each cell. Specific sections of the DNA molecules, called genes, often are responsible for the development of a given trait or physical characteristic, such as eye color. There are approximately 20,000 genes in every chromosome.

2.2 Genotype and Phenotype

The unique arrangement of genes and chromosomes in each individual is called genotype, defining a person's potential traits or characteristics. Interaction with the environment determines an individual's phenotype, that is, the actual or observable characteristics and traits. Some characteristics of the phenotype are directly controlled by the genotype (eye color or blood type). Others are less dependent on genotypic instructions and are influenced more by the environment (personality and certain intellectual abilities).

2.3 Dominant and Recessive Genes

Sometimes the genotype has directions for the development of a certain trait which never shows up in the phenotype, and which is not repressed by environmental interaction. This is because that trait is controlled by two genes, one of which is dominant and the other recessive. The instructions of the dominant gene are the ones that show up in the phenotype. An example of this phenomenon can be seen in eye color. If a person inherits one brown-eye gene and one blue-eye gene, the person will have brown eyes because the brown-eye gene is dominant and the blue-eye gene recessive. In order to have blue eyes, one must receive a recessive blue-eye gene from both the ovum and the sperm cell.

2.4 Sex and Sex Linkage

Genes also determine one's sex and control certain characteristics that are sex linked. Sex-linked characteristics are traits more likely to appear in one sex than the other. Color blindness is an example of a sex-linked trait. The 23rd chromosome pair (the one that determines sex) in women is XX. The 23rd pair in men is XY. The Y chromosome contains fewer genes than the X chromosome. If a recessive gene in the X chromosome, such as the color-blindness gene, has no counterpart in the Y chromosome, then that trait will appear in the phenotype. Since women have two X chromosomes, they must receive two recessive genes in order to have color blindness (a dominant normal gene will override the recessive color-blind gene in women). Thus, men are more likely to have color blindness than women. Other sex-linked characteristics are hemophilia and certain kinds of baldness (Gander and Gardiner 1981 p. 34) (see *Color Blindness*).

2.5 Genetic Abnormalities

Abnormal genetic structures can also affect phenotypic characteristics. A miscarriage, or spontaneous abortion, may be caused by defective genes. Syndromes such as phenylketonuria (PKU), Down syndrome (mongolism), and amaurotic idiocy have all been traced to genetic structure.

The genetic structure that one inherits has long-range effects on all aspects of human growth and development, all traceable to the union of one egg cell with one sperm cell.

3. Germinal Period

The ovum is usually fertilized (united with the sperm cell) in one of the female's fallopian tubes as the ovum is traveling from the ovary to the uterus. Fertilization marks the beginning of the germinal period. As the fertilized ovum travels to the uterus, the 23 pairs of chromosomes line up and split as the ovum divides into two cells. Each of the new cells contains 23 pairs of chromosomes structured the same as the original set. For the next 10 to 14 days, the cells in the ovum continue to divide, with each cell having the same chromosomal structure. The ovum will have reached the uterus and become firmly attached to the uterine wall 7 to 10 days after conception. At this time, the cells in the ovum gradually separate into an inner and outer part. The outer part is connected to the uterine wall and later becomes part of the mother–fetus barrier. The inner part develops into the fetus.

4. Embryonic Period

The embryonic period begins around the end of the second week and continues on through the eighth week. During this time, the basic body parts (head, trunk, arms, and legs) begin to take identifiable form. Eyes, ears, fingers, toes, and other finer body parts also become noticeable. Internal organs begin to develop, with some (heart, liver, kidney, circulatory and nervous systems) already functioning to a certain extent by the end of the embryonic period.

During this time the life-support system for the embryo also develops. The placenta develops from the part of the embryo attached to the uterine wall to act as a filter between the bloodstreams of the mother and the embryo. While the placenta keeps the bloodstreams separate, it does absorb oxygen, vitamins, nutrients, drugs, and other substances from the mother's bloodstream and passes them into the embryo's bloodstream through the umbilical cord, which attaches the embryo to the placenta. The umbilical cord also transports wastes from the embryo back to the placenta where they are filtered into the mother's bloodstream.

At the end of this period, the embryo is about 2.5 centimeters (1 inch) long and weighs about 14 grams (0.5 ounce).

5. Fetal Period

The fetal period, the longest stage of prenatal development, lasts approximately seven months, from around the eighth week through to birth. During this time, the fetus grows in size and internal organs develop to such a degree that by the end of the ninth month, the normal fetus is capable of independent life separate from the mother's womb. Monthly development consists of the following sequence of events.

5.1 Third Month (8–12 weeks)

In the third month, the fetus becomes very active, and physical and anatomical features become well-differentiated (Yussen and Santrock 1982 p. 70). The head is large in proportion to the rest of the body (constituting approximately one-third of the total body length), and features such as the eyelids, nose, chin, and forehead are distinguishable. Upper and lower arms, legs and feet, and hands are clearly differentiated. The genitals have also developed to a point where sex can be determined. At the end of 12 weeks the fetus is about 7.5 centimeters (3 inches) long and weighs about 28 grams (1 ounce).

5.2 Fourth Month

During the fourth month, the lower body begins to grow more rapidly, following the rapid head growth of the previous month. Some prenatal reflexes (arm and leg movements) become strong and may be felt by the mother. The child grows to about 15 centimeters (6 inches) in length and 110 grams (4 ounces) in weight.

5.3 Fifth Month

Through the fifth month, skin structures become completely formed, toenails and fingernails appear, and the fetus becomes increasingly more active. The fetus is now about 30 centimeters (circa 1 foot) long and weighs about 450 grams (16 ounces).

5.4 Sixth Month

Irregular breathing movements and a grasping reflex now appear, eyes and eyelids are completely formed, a thin layer of hair develops on the head, and the fetus grows to about 36 centimeters (14 inches) in length and 900 grams (2 pounds) in weight.

5.5 Seventh Month

The fetus reaches the age of viability, meaning the child has a good chance of surviving if he or she is born prematurely. The fetus grows to 40 centimeters (16 inches) and 1.4 kilograms (3 pounds).

5.6 Eighth and Ninth Months

Throughout the last two months of prenatal development, the fatty tissues develop and the functioning of various organs (heart and kidneys) increases. The baby increases in length and weight so that the average North-American child at birth weighs 3.2 kilograms (7

pounds) and is 50 centimeters (20 inches) long (Yussen and Santrock 1982 p. 72).

6. Environmental Influences on Prenatal Development

The periods of development outlined above describe normal prenatal development. There are a number of environmental factors, however, which affect prenatal development and can have a severe impact on a newborn's appearance and abilities. A mother's advanced age, poor health, inadequate diet (nutritional intake), and distressed emotional states during pregnancy have all been shown to have a negative effect on the physical and psychological functioning of the newborn. Alcohol, cigarette, and drug use during pregnancy can also exert a severe negative effect on fetal development.

Bibliography

Gander M J, Gardiner H W 1981 *Child and Adolescent Development.* Little, Brown, Boston, Massachusetts

Miller O L 1973 The visualization of genes in action. *Sci. Am.* 228: 34–42

Mussen P H, Conger J J, Kagan J 1980 *Essentials of Child Development and Personality.* Harper and Row, New York

Pikunas J 1976 *Human Development: An Emergent Science.* McGraw-Hill, New York

Yussen S R, Santrock J W 1982 *Child Development: An Introduction*, 2nd edn. Brown, Dubuque, Iowa

Infancy

D. Rapson

Infancy is a term used by developmental psychologists to denote the period of development that begins at birth and continues on through the second year of life. The word "infant" has its roots in a Latin word which means "without language" (Schell 1975 p. 143). Although the historical definition of infancy relates to language development, today infancy is a term which includes development in the areas of cognition, perception, motor activity, emotions, sociability, and language. Development in each of these areas affects development in the other areas, so that although it is possible to talk about development in each area separately, it must be understood that each facet of development is part of the growth of an integrated unit made up of many facets. For example, physical growth combined with development of motor coordination lead to a child's being able to walk. Development in locomotion, in turn, affects a child's cognitive development by providing a larger variety of experiences and objects to explore. Development in cognitive skills (especially symbolic representation) affects language development, which in turn affects how children interact with those around

them. With this understanding in mind, each of the following areas will be discussed: (a) physical growth and motor development, (b) perceptual development, (c) concept development, (d) language development, and (e) attachment and social development. In order to understand the significance of growth in each of these areas, however, it is important to know what capabilities and characteristics are present in the neonate. Therefore the logical place to begin the description of infant development is with the newborn child.

1. The Neonate

A newborn infant is usually referred to as a neonate for the first 2 to 4 weeks following birth. At birth the neonate's appearance can be quite a surprise for new parents. The head is large in proportion to the rest of the body (comprising approximately one-quarter of the total body length), and may be misshapen as a result of passage through the birth canal. The skin is soft and wrinkled and may be covered with vernix, a light body coating which lubricated the infant for passage through the birth canal (this coating will disappear after a bath or two).

The newborn's eating and sleeping patterns can also be surprising and require new adjustments on the part of the infant's parents. Neonates sleep around 19 hours a day. Although approximately 80 percent of the infant's day is spent sleeping, parents tend to feel that their newborn child is always awake. This is because during the neonatal period the infant takes seven or eight naps a day. As the child develops, this pattern changes so that by 28 weeks of age the infant will sleep through the night and will need only two or three daytime naps (Mussen et al. 1980 p. 82).

The newborns' eating patterns are similar to their sleeping patterns in that the neonate takes seven or eight feedings a day. The number of feedings, like naps, decreases with age; however, the amount of food ingested remains relatively unchanged.

The neonate's preoccupation with eating and sleeping lead many people to the belief that newborns are totally dependent beings that only sleep, eat, cry, and fill their diapers with waste. Recent research has shown this to be untrue. Newborns are active beings that perceive and respond to events going on around them. The senses of taste, touch, hearing, smell, and vision are all present and functioning at birth. An example of neonatal sensory capabilities can be shown by infants' abilities to differentiate between two notes that are only one step apart in a musical scale. Another example is the newborn's ability to differentiate the tastes of sweet and salty fluids (Mussen et al. 1980 p. 80).

Besides having well-developed senses, infants also are born with a number of reflexes. Reflexes are built-in body and behavioral responses which are generally believed to have evolved in humans because of their survival value. "This is apparent in the rooting, sucking, and swallowing reflexes. For example, the mother's breast touching the newborn's cheek stimulates reflexive turning of the head; the nipple touching the lips brings reflexive sucking; the milk stimulating the throat brings reflexive swallowing" (Gander and Gardiner 1981 p. 113) Another reflex present at birth is the palmar grasp. This reflex can be elicited by touching an infant's palm. Infants will respond to this by closing their fingers tightly around the object touching their palm. Pricking an infant's foot results in the foot being withdrawn to the body. This is the flexion reflex. Lightly stroking the sole of an infant's foot brings about the Babinski reflex, which involves the foot being flexed and the toes being spread apart. The Moro reflex is a response to being startled or to sudden shifts in position. Infants will respond to these occurrences by throwing their arms out to the side, extending their fingers, and then quickly drawing their arms and hands back to their chests. Other reflexes include coughing, yawning, sneezing, and vomiting.

As infants develop muscle control, certain reflexes that are present at birth will begin to fade. Certain reflexes which persist can be indications of brain damage. This is why pediatricians routinely check the reflexes of infants.

2. Physical Growth and Motor Development in Infancy

Development in the cerebral cortex of the brain and in the central nervous system during the first 4 to 5 months results in the decrease of many reflexes (e.g., the Babinski and Moro) and the evolution of many physical skills (lifting the head and chest and visually following moving objects). Much of early physical development involves functioning in the head and neck regions. The reasons for this are that physical and motor development follow cephalocaudal and proximodistal patterns. Cephalocaudal development is a term that refers to the fact that growth begins in the head and continues on down through the torso, arms, and legs to the feet (hence the proportionally large head in the neonate). Proximodistal development involves growth which begins at the center of the body and then progresses out toward the extremities. Thus, muscle control in the shoulder regions precedes arm and hand coordinations. Since infants develop in cephalocaudal and proximodistal directions, sequences of development can be studied and described. Table 1 provides some examples of motor abilities attained at various ages during infancy by American children. It is important to understand that not all children will develop the abilities mentioned at the ages mentioned. Genetic factors (hereditary make-up) combine with environmental factors (culture and economic status) to create children with individual characteristics and developments which differ not only between cultures but also within cultures and even within families. Table 1 only shows general developmental trends in American infants that may or may not apply to specific children.

3. Perceptual Development

People gather information about the world around them through the senses of touch, taste, smell, vision, and hearing. Perception is the interpretation of information gathered by the senses. For example, the ear picks up certain vibrations in the air through the sense of hearing. Perception is the interpretation of these vibrations as being voices, musical notes, or other sounds.

Perceptual development, like physical development, is an area of immense growth during infancy. However, studying perceptual growth is more difficult than studying physical growth. Determining sensory responses in newborns is difficult because they cannot reach, crawl to, or talk about what they see, hear, smell, touch, and taste. Although children cannot describe the way they perceive things in the world, their perceptual abilities can be studied by observing bodily responses to various stimuli. The senses are examined by observing body movements and by monitoring breathing and heart-rate

Table 1

The development of motor ability with age

Age	Motor ability
1 month	Lifts head and turns head when on stomach. Visually follows slowly moving objects.
2–3 months	Holds chest up when on stomach. Can raise head up while held in a sitting position. Begins to swipe at objects in visual range.
4–6 months	Follows objects with eyes in different directions and planes. Sits up with some support. Reaches for and grasps objects. Holds head erect in sitting position.
7–9 months	Sits without support. Rolls over in prone position. Crawls (moves with abdomen on the floor). Stands up using furniture. Transfers objects from one hand to another.
10–12 months	Creeps (moves on hands and knees). Walks by grasping furniture or if hands are held. Stands without help. Squats and stoops.
13–15 months	Walks without help. Stacks two blocks. Puts small objects into containers and dumps them. Climbs steps. Rolls ball to adult.
18–24 months	Shows hand preference. Stacks 4–6 blocks. Turns pages of a book one at a time. Walks sideways and backwards.

changes in response to certain stimuli. Research in infant perception has focused on vision because it is much easier to measure than the other senses (Mussen et al. 1980 p. 93).

3.1 Touch

Newborns' reflexive responses to tactile stimulation show they possess the sense of touch. Various studies show that infants respond to touch in other ways too. Studies report that infants are responsive to mild electric shock, that females are more sensitive to gentle touch than males, and that tactile sensations are important in promoting social growth (Yussen and Santrock 1982 p. 102).

3.2 Smell

Studies of the sense of smell show that neonates have variable responses to odors of sweet and sour. They will turn their heads toward sweet smells, and their heart and respiration rates will slow down. Sour odors will cause infants to turn away and will result in increased heart and respiration rates. Infants also learn to distinguish between the odor of their mother's milk and that from another woman (Gander and Gardiner 1981 p. 128).

3.3 Taste

Infants are sensitive to various tastes. Newborns have shown the ability to differentiate between sugar, salt, lemon, and quinine (Yussen and Santrock 1982 p. 103). Breast-fed infants also show a distinct preference for their mother's milk over prepared formulas. Gander and Gardiner (1981) describe a study in which breast-fed newborns showed strong negative responses to a preparation of sweetened cow's milk.

3.4 Hearing

In the area of auditory perception, researchers have found that newborns attend most to patterned, rhythmic sounds; show preferences for some voices (e.g., the major caregiver's voice) over others; and have some ability to discriminate between sounds coming from the left and the right (Yussen and Santrock 1982 p. 101). Infants also have been reported to be able to distinguish between various consonant sounds that are similar, such as the sounds of the letters b, d, p, t, and g (Yussen and Santrock 1982 p. 102).

3.5 Vision

Research with young infants has shown that they respond to variations of light–dark contrast, color movement, and brightness (Yussen and Santrock 1982 p. 102). However, the neonate's perception of the world differs significantly from that of older children and adults. One reason for this is that newborns cannot focus on objects as well as adults. In order to focus on an object, the eyes converge (turn inward to view objects that are close) or diverge (turn outward to view objects that are far away). Young infants do not have coordinated eye movement, and this results in poor binocular convergence. Another factor that affects infant vision is their ability to accommodate visually. Visual accommodation is the regulation of the shape of the lens in each eye to adjust for the distance between the eye and the object being viewed. Newborns are unable to do this. Their lenses are set to focus on objects that are 8 to 12 inches away. Limitations in convergence and accommodation have a significant impact on the child's ability to focus on objects and to perceive depth. However, in the first three to four months of infancy, children's abilities in both of these areas show remarkable improvement. By this time an infant's focusing capacity is about as flexible as an adult's (Yussen and Santrock 1982 p. 105).

Gibson's research using a visual cliff with 6-month-old children has shown infants' abilities to perceive depth. The studies were done using a table which had a clear-glass surface. On one side of the table a pattern was placed several feet below the glass to give the impression of a sharp drop. On the other side the pattern was placed directly under the glass, giving the impression of solidity or a shallow drop. When infants were coaxed to one of the two sides, Gibson found that children moved readily to the shallow side but avoided the cliff side (Gander and Gardiner 1981 p. 132).

Other research with infants has focused on visual preferences. These studies show that what a child chooses to attend to determines what a child knows and how the child constructs reality. The general results of research in this area show that infants prefer contour, pattern, and movement, and they desire more complexity as they grow older (Gander and Gardiner 1981 pp. 140–42) (see *Perception*).

4. Concept Development

In order for a person to solve problems in his or her head or to use abstract symbols, it is necessary to be able to form concepts. A concept is a mental representation (memory) of some object or experience. Jean Piaget spent a great deal of time studying cognitive development in children. He described an infant's cognitive abilities in terms of the way they operate on and explore various objects in their environment. He saw this as a precursor to thinking in terms of mental images (Gander and Gardiner 1981 pp. 148–49). An example of cognitive growth in infancy is the development of the concept of object permanence (the idea that an object exists even though it cannot be readily perceived). Up to 4 months of age, children will not search for an interesting object (e.g., a rattle) that is hidden under a cloth. It is as if the object no longer exists once it is hidden. Between 4 and 8 months, infants may reach for the rattle if they can see part of it. This is the beginning of object permanence. As children progress through infancy, they will search for completely hidden objects (8 to 12 months of age) and eventually search for objects when the hiding includes multiple displacements under more than one cloth (12 to 18 months of age). By the end of infancy a child will have a well-developed concept of object permanence. Having a mental image of an object that is not present is a necessary prerequisite to solving problems mentally and using such abstract symbols as words (see *Cognitive Development*).

5. Language Development

Language development is a complex process that involves more than just pronouncing words. Being able to communicate a thought is dependent upon using vocalizations that mean something. Therefore, language can be seen to be directly linked to cognitive development. Children from all cultures and language backgrounds seem to follow a specific sequence in their development of speech. Gander and Gardiner (1981) delineate five stages of language growth that children go through during their first 2 years of life. The first stage, which begins at birth, involves crying. Newborns may utter a few other sounds, but crying is their major form of vocalization.

Around the second month, infants begin making sounds like "oooh," "aaah," or gurgling sounds. This is the second stage of speech development, sometimes referred to as the "cooing" stage. Muscle coordination of the lips, teeth, tongue, and throat provide infants with the ability to produce a greater variety of sounds. By the age of 6 months this increased coordination leads to the third stage, which is babbling. In early babbling, infants may frequently produce sounds that are not a part of the language which is spoken in their environment. In the later part of the first year, infants make sounds that are most often heard. They also tend to unite syllables with vowels (sounds like "ga ga ga" or "ba ba ba"), and use intonation, rhythm, and stress patterns in their native language.

Around one year of age, infants enter the fourth stage. This stage is marked by the use of one-word sentences to express a thought of desire. For example, a 1-year-old child may say the word "ball." By this the child may mean "Get me the ball," or "There is a ball," or "Make the ball move." The meaning of a one-word sentence may be clarified by the child's intonation and gestures. Most of the words used during this stage are words which refer to classes of things (cat, truck, baby).

The fifth stage, using two- or three-word sentences, appears near the end of the child's second year. During this stage, children will use mostly nouns and verbs. For example, a child might say "Mommy glass" or "Mommy give" instead of "Mommy, please give me a glass of milk." During this stage children use words that are most important in getting their thought across and leave out words that are not as useful in conveying meanings.

It is important to note that throughout language development in infancy, children's comprehension of language precedes their ability to vocalize thoughts. Thus, a 1-year-old may pick up a doll when told "Go get your doll" but be unable to tell a person "Go get my doll" (see *Language Acquisition and Human Development*.

Deaf children vocalize in the same manner as hearing children do through the stage of babbling, after which their vocalizations fade (Gander and Gardiner 1981 p. 159).

6. Attachment and Social Development

In early infancy, children develop significant emotional and social ties with the person or persons who provide for their basic needs. These ties are called attachments and are the result of two processes: "(a) the interaction that occurs between the infant and the caretaker (looking, vocalizing, smiling), and (b) the association the infant makes between feelings of pleasure stemming from relief of distress and the presence of the caretaker" (Mussen et al. 1980 p. 139). The development of attachment affects social development in a number of ways. Persons with whom infants have an attachment relationship are more likely to be approached for play or help. These persons are also more likely to be able to calm and comfort an infant. A third way attachment affects infants is shown by children's lack of fear when exploring strange situations in the presence of a person to whom they are attached.

Cultural child-rearing values also have an effect on social development. In some cultures, infants are left alone in a dark room most of the day with few toys and little verbal interaction. In other cultures, children are with one or more caregivers most of the day and receive many toys and much attention. Some infants are raised in environments independent of other children. Other infants are raised in environments where other children are present all of the time. Each of these factors affects how a child responds to unfamiliar and familiar children and adults.

Cultural child-rearing practices, attachment relationships, and cognitive development combine to cause the onset and resolution of various social fears during infancy. Three of the most common fears are of unfamiliar adults, of unfamiliar children, and of separation when caretakers are not present (Mussen et al. 1980). Fear of strangers and separation anxiety begin to appear around 8 to 12 months after birth. Fear of unfamiliar children arises between 12 and 20 months of age. These fears can be related to the infant's development of mental images and the ability to compare various stimuli with one another. Experience with uncertainties and

growth in the ability to solve problems mentally and to make predictions help the child overcome these fears as infancy draws to a close.

In summary, infancy is a time of immense growth in the areas of physical appearance, motor coordination, perception, cognition, language, and sociability. While growth in each area can be studied separately, one must remember that development in one area affects capabilities and growth in other areas. Children develop from infants whose motor responses are chiefly primitive reflex reactions, and whose vocalizations are chiefly crying. Newborns seem to have little interest in those around them except in so far as these people provide food, comfort, or something interesting to look at. At the end of infancy children walk and talk and enjoy exploring the world around them.

Bibliography

Cohen S, Comiskey T (eds.) 1977 *Child Development: Contemporary Perspectives.* Peacock, Itasca, Illinois

Gander M J, Gardiner H W 1981 *Child and Adolescent Development.* Little, Brown, Boston, Massachusetts

Lerner R 1976 *Concepts and Theories of Human Development.* Addison-Wesley, Reading, Massachusetts

Mussen P, Conger J, Kagan J 1980 *Essentials of Child Development and Personality.* Harper and Row, New York

Pikunas J 1976 *Human Development: An Emergent Science.* McGraw-Hill, New York

Schell R E (ed.) 1975 *Developmental Psychology Today*, 2nd edn. CRM/Random House, New York

Thomas R 1979 *Comparing Theories of Child Development.* Wadsworth, Belmont, California

Yussen S R, Santrock J W 1982 *Child Development: An Introduction.* Brown, Dubuque, Illinois

Early Childhood

J. B. Hendrick

Preschool children are generally thought of as being children who are between 2 and 5 years old, and although there are pronounced differences in the developmental characteristics of 2-, 3-, and 4-year-old children and of children who live in different parts of the world, there are also some general characteristics that apply to the overall preschool period and to children from a widespread number of cultures.

One of these characteristics is that preschool children grow and change with astonishing rapidity, for it is during this brief period that they acquire language, achieve a sense of who they are and what constitutes their appropriate role as a boy or girl in a particular culture, and begin to move from the sheltered life of the family group to existence in the larger world of a more extended society. In the entire span of human life, the dynamism of the preschooler's growth is exceeded only during the years of infancy and toddlerhood that immediately precede it.

Another characteristic of these youngsters is that their growth is orderly and sequential. There are predictable stages of development through which they pass. Children learn to stand before they are able to walk and use single words before using complete sentences. It is also true, however, that the exact time such events take place varies from culture to culture because of environmental and cultural influences (Werner 1979). Malnutrition, for example, retards the rate of physical growth, and social isolation slows down the time in which language is acquired.

Still another characteristic of preschool children is that they occupy themselves with play when provided with this opportunity. This play varies in kind and quantity from culture to culture (Whiting et al. 1975), often incorporating imitation of the surrounding adult activity, but play *is* a universally typical occupation of young children (Sutton-Smith and Roberts 1981).

During this period, too, children are engrossed in the

acquisition of language. The work of Slobin (1972) who studied cultures as diverse as the English, Finnish, Luo, Russian, and Samoan reveals that children from all these cultures begin to talk at about the age they begin to walk and by age 3 have acquired a vocabulary of around 1,000 words as well as the basic ability to use the grammatical structures of their language. An additional universal phenomenon related to language development is that adults from many cultures have been found to use special forms of simplified speech when conversing with these young beginning talkers (Ferguson 1977). (For a more extensive review of current cross-cultural research on language development, refer to Bowerman 1981.)

The final characteristic preschool children have in common is that they vary not only according to their own individuality but also according to the cultural milieu from which they come. Regrettably, the comparative study of such cross-cultural developmental variation (termed developmental ethnopsychology) is still in its own infancy, and knowledge about 2- to 5-year-olds from various cultures and across cultures is just coming to light. At the present time the most comprehensive developmental studies are still those focusing on children from specific cultures, most notably those from the United States exemplified by the work at the Gesell Institute (Ames et al. 1979) and by the Piagetian group at Geneva (Gruber and Vonèche 1977). For that reason, the following material draws frequently upon these sources.

1. Characteristics of Physical Development

Werner (1979) reviews numerous studies of infants living in the traditional, preindustrial regions of Africa, India, and Central America which demonstrate that the psychomotor development of these children is superior to that of infants from more developed countries. By age 2, however, this early superiority has disappeared, the decline being attributed to poorer nutrition following weaning combined with less maternal stimulation as the mother turns to the care of the next infant.

Among children of the poor in developing countries, this slackening of growth becomes even more apparent during the following years so that by age 4, Meredith (1968) reported that the shortest and lightest youngsters were found in South, Central and Southeast Asia and in Africa. By that age, there was as much as 7 inches and 13 pounds average difference in height and weight between these groups and children in Europe and the United States. The likelihood that these differences are poverty related and due to diarrhea, measles, tuberculosis, and malnutrition rather than to genetic causes is substantiated by other studies which show that only small growth curve differences exist when economically favored children of differing ethnic groups are compared.

It is suggested that the reader bear the prevalency of such physiological lags in mind during the following discussion of various preschool characteristics since the lassitude and apathy resulting from such illness and malnutrition affect so many of the world's children and cannot help but exert a generalized, deleterious effect upon their entire development.

For the more privileged children of the world who have enough to eat and who live in reasonable conditions of sanitation, the age of 2 is one of vigorous physical activity. Two-year-olds are tireless climbers and runners about. Their performance of fine muscle tasks may seem frustratingly clumsy to the adult, but they will work at these with absorbed and dedicated persistence until mastery is achieved. Their world is full, not only of tasting and feeling, but also of manipulating objects in order to explore and determine their properties.

By the age of 3, children have mastered basic physical skills—they balance well, walking and running come as second nature to them, and by the age of 4, they are genuinely accomplished as they turn to ever greater physical challenges—enjoying the temptations of physical risks, and moving on to increasingly difficult fine muscle tasks such as holding writing implements and fastening clothing.

2. Characteristics of Emotional Development

Most of the work on emotional development comes from the pens of Western writers, the foremost theoretician being Erikson (1963), a child psychoanalyst, who maintains that the early preschool years are characterized by a drive toward strong self-assertion. This may be seen by weary parents as sheer contrariness, but it is more helpfully characterized by Erikson as the stage of "autonomy versus shame and doubt." He sees this behavioral stage as being a healthy effort on the child's part to attain an independent identity (see *Erikson Developmental Theory*).

In Eriksonian theory, around the age of 4 or 5, preschoolers move on to the third stage of development termed "initiative versus guilt." This is the period of undertaking independent action and reaching out to the world beyond the family. Children at this stage become interested in the use of tools, and, in many cultures, are assigned care of their younger siblings (Whiting et al. 1975).

There appears to be a growing possibility that these stages may not be characteristic of all cultures, however. For example, one study of Japanese and American 2½-year-olds has demonstrated that Japanese children showed considerably more dependency-related behavior than American children did (Caudill and Schooler 1973).

Erikson's stages parallel the stages of emotional development hypothesized earlier by Freud who placed preschool youngsters mainly in the "anal" (approximately 18 months to 3 years) and "phallic" stages of development (age 3 to 7). Freud saw each of these stages as being fraught with possibilities for emotional conflict. Conflicts during the anal stage arise primarily from difficulties resulting from inappropriate toilet training, and conflict in the phallic stage results from the necessity that boys and girls surrender their wishful sexual fantasies toward parents of the opposite sex and identify, instead, with the parent of the same sex. Freudian theory maintains that inability to resolve such conflicts in a satisfactory manner is the cause of later personality difficulties and reduced capacity to function in an emotionally healthy way (see *Psychoanalytic Theory of Human Development*).

A somewhat different approach was taken by Gesell who noted that the emotional development of young American children seems characterized by alternating periods of emotional stability and instability. Children aged 2½ years old were seen as emotionally labile; 3-year-olds were in steadier control; 4-year-olds were more likely to act out their feelings; and 5-year-olds were once again on a more even emotional keel (Ames et al. 1979).

3. Characteristics of Social Development

The social world beyond the family is only beginning to dawn for 2-year-olds. The Gesell Institute reports that 2-year-olds, although enjoying the presence of other children, typically play alone or beside, rather than with other youngsters. There is little cooperative or dramatic play in evidence. Moreover, 2-year-olds lack strategies for peaceful social approaches to other children and tend to pre-empt whatever they wish to play with.

By the age of 3, preschoolers have begun to gain rudimentary social skills and ploys, and, since they enjoy pleasing adults at this stage, are often responsive to adult suggestions about appropriate social behavior. Around this age, children begin to form friendships, though these are often shifting and of short duration. Three-year-olds play together, but fight frequently albeit briefly.

Four-year-olds really enjoy playing with other children and often do so in larger groups than do 3-year-olds. Their play is mutual, imaginative, and interactive. The vitality of 4-year-olds combined with their increased self-assurance leads them to try out daring stunts, and borderline acting-out behavior which becomes most challenging at 4½ years old subsides about the time children enter kindergarten (Ames et al. 1979).

The work of the Whitings in their studies of children from six cultures presents an interesting comment on preschool children and the socially important world of work. They analyzed the differing kinds and amounts of work expected of children as young as 3 or 4 years old, by families from various cultures and found that parents in simpler societies assigned more tasks earlier to 3- and 4-year-olds than parents in more complex societies did (Whiting et al. 1975). This finding is thought to be related to the development of some pro-social behaviors since Whiting et al. also reported that nonegoistic, altruistic, helping behavior by children was typical of those societies where children had such assigned tasks, and that egoistic behavior (seeking help more frequently, being dominant, and demanding attention) was seen more frequently in children who did not have the welfare of others depending on them.

4. Characteristics of Cognitive Development

One of the most significant aspects of preschool cognitive development, the acquisition of language, has been discussed already so the reader will only be reminded here of its importance.

Perhaps the other most important point to understand about the cognitive development of preschool children comes from the work of Piaget (Gruber and Vonèche 1977). It is that children pass through a number of stages of cognitive development as they grow and that their thought processes are actually different in kind from those of the adult (see *Piaget's Theory of Genetic Epistemology*).

During the preschool years, the child is likely to be in the preoperational stage. This stage is characterized by the dominance of perception over reason, a truth Piaget demonstrated by means of many ingenious experiments. The preoperational, perception-bound child cannot mentally reverse a situation, that is, he or she cannot conserve or hold two ideas for comparison in the mind at the same time. This inability to draw mental comparisons restricts the child's power to perform certain reasoning tasks, among these being classification, seriation, and perception of part/whole relationships.

It is only as the child passes through this stage and has many real opportunities for interactions with reversible materials that he or she acquires the ability to conserve, and it is the ultimate acquisition of this ability which enables the child to advance to the next stage, that of concrete operations at around the age of 7.

Piaget stresses that play, which presents so many opportunities for interaction with people and materials, is a very effective medium for conveying such learning and that the acquisition of language, which permits the substitution of symbols for objects, is another important factor in the child's progression from one stage to the next.

Whether these stages of cognitive development are invariant or even present among children of all cultures remains a matter of continuing investigation and debate. At present data indicate that the basic tenets of the theory and the sequence of developmental stages are supported by the majority of cross-cultural studies, but there may be considerable variation between cultures in the time taken for the child to reach a particular stage and the length of time it takes to pass through it (Ashton 1975, Dasen 1977, Dasen and Heron 1981).

5. Implications for Child Rearing and Education

A number of implications can be drawn from even this brief article about what constitutes sound developmental and educational practice when adults work with preschool children in the home or at school.

The most vital implication is that, although much progress has been made, there remains a pressing need to improve health and nutrition services for many young children in the world. Without this foundation of good health and the adequate potential for growth it confers, other recommendations concerning good child-rearing practice cannot be effectively implemented.

In addition, parents and teachers of young children should remember that children change rapidly, and that it is necessary to be alert and sensitive to these changes as they occur in order to keep up with them and to provide the effective job of teaching that will promote children's development. Fortunately, the fairly regular patterns and sequences of growth found in early childhood make it possible to predict in a general way the next developmental step the child is likely to take and to prepare for it accordingly.

Knowledge of developmental stages and how children learn is also helpful when adults are identifying which learning materials and methods are appropriate to use with a particular age group. Teachers who understand that preschool children learn best through direct experience and by means of play will base their curriculum upon these principles just as they will include many opportunities for children to talk and be listened to in order to facilitate their development of language skills.

Since the preschool years are characterized by emotional ups and downs and also by a great deal of social learning and experimentation, it is also evident that adults will need to draw on reserves of patience, understanding, and firmness if they wish to help the child develop well throughout this rich but challenging period of life.

The final implication to be drawn from the forgoing material is that much remains to be learned about how the developmental patterns of children are similar in various cultures and about how they differ. This raises fascinating and, as yet, unanswered questions. How much does the development of young children really vary around the world? How could environments be modified to provide optimum conditions for development? What *are* optimum conditions for development? What could one culture learn from another that might improve the well-being of that culture's children? *Could* such cultural practices be transplanted with success?

In coming years, these questions and more remain to be answered by developmental ethnopsychologists.

Bibliography

Ames L B, Gillespie C, Haines J, Ilg F (eds.) 1979 *The Gesell Institute's Child from One to Six: Evaluating the Behavior of the Preschool Child.* Harper and Row, New York

Ashton P T 1975 Cross-cultural Piagetian research: An experimental perspective. *Harvard Educ. Rev.* 45: 475–506

Bowerman M 1981 Language development. In: Triandis H C, Heron A (eds.) 1981 *Handbook of Cross-cultural Psychology*, Vol. 4: *Developmental Psychology*. Allyn and Bacon, Boston, Massachusetts

Caudill W A, Schooler C 1973 Child behavior and child rearing in Japan and the United States: An interim report. *J. Nervous and Mental Disease* 157: 323–38

Dasen P R (ed.) 1977 *Piagetian Psychology: Cross-cultural Contributions.* Garden Press, New York

Dasen P R, Heron A 1981 Cross-cultural tests of Piaget's theory. In: Triandis H C, Heron A (eds.) 1981 *Handbook of Cross-cultural Psychology*, Vol. 4: *Developmental Psychology*. Allyn and Bacon, Boston, Massachusetts

Erikson E H 1963 *Childhood and Society*, 2nd edn. Norton, New York

Ferguson C A 1977 Baby talk as a simplified register. In: Snow C E, Ferguson C A (eds.) 1977 *Talking to Children: Language Input and Acquisition.* Cambridge University Press, Cambridge

Gruber H E, Vonèche J J (eds.) 1977 *The Essential Piaget.* Routledge and Kegan Paul, London

Meredith H V 1968 Body size of contemporary groups of preschool children studied in different parts of the world. *Child Dev.* (39): 335–77

Slobin D I 1972 Children and language: They learn the same way all around the world. *Psychology Today* 6: 71–74, 82

Sutton-Smith B, Roberts J M 1981 Play, games and sports. In: Triandis H C, Heron A (eds.) 1981 *Handbook of Cross-cultural Psychology*, Vol. 4: *Developmental Psychology*. Allyn and Bacon, Boston, Massachusetts

Werner E E 1979 *Cross-cultural Child Development: A View From the Planet Earth.* Brooks/Cole, Monterey, California

Whiting B B, Whiting J W M, Longabaugh R 1975 *Children of Six Cultures: A Psycho-cultural Analysis.* Harvard University Press, Cambridge, Massachusetts

Later Childhood

Zhuang Jiaying

Children in the primary-school years, between ages 6 and 12, display physical, intellectual, and social characteristics that have important implications for educational practice. While each child during this period of life is a unique personality, differing in overall composition from every other child in the age range, nearly all children at this stage also have certain traits in common. The following discussion identifies a variety of these common traits and suggests how understanding such characteristics can aid parents and educators in performing the tasks of child rearing and schooling.

1. Physical Growth

Physical growth follows an asynchronous pattern, in that different parts of the body grow at different rates, as shown in Fig. 1. In terms of height and weight, both boys and girls advance at a relatively steady rate during later childhood, with the average child annually increasing in height by 2 or 3 inches and in weight by 5 or 6 pounds. Likewise, their internal organs develop at only a moderate rate compared to the more rapid growth of organs during infancy and at the start of adolescence. For example, the brain has 50 percent of its adult weight at 6 months of age, 90 percent by age 5, and 95 percent by age 10 (Sarafino and Armstrong 1986).

Differences between children in height and weight are caused by such factors as genetic endowment, nutrition, and living conditions. During this time of life, there are only slight differences between the average boy and the average girl in height and weight.

As children's height, weight, and internal organs grow, their motor skills also improve. During the elementary-school years, running speed and jumping agility increase significantly. The ability to throw a ball accurately and for a distance also increases, as does balance. In effect, children become stronger, faster, more agile, and more graceful. Boys are usually slightly stronger and faster than girls, but girls tend to be slightly better than boys in measures of flexibility, that is, in the ability to bend and contort the body and limbs into a variety of positions.

As maturation progresses, school-age children can execute finer, more precise movements. They are able to combine simple movements into complex, smoothly coordinated acts. For example, in hand-writing, typical 4-year-olds print letters and numbers with slow and deliberate actions. Each letter is put together with several separate strokes, and the letters are printed large and may be placed anywhere on the page. By the time children enter school at around age 6 or 7, they print more quickly and often with a continuous stroke. By age 9, most can write quickly, can space the letters evenly, and, in cultures that use European writing traditions, can give up printing in favor of cursive writing.

Motor skills develop out of the interaction between internal maturation and learning experiences. When children are physically ready to perform a complex activity, the rate and quality of their motor-skill development are influenced by their motivation and their opportunities to learn and practice a skill.

Scientists have discovered that children who are physically fit are healthier and more resistant to fatigue and stress. Physical activities increase bone width and mineralization, and they may help prevent such disorders as later adult heart trouble (Kaplan 1986). Exercise also has social benefits and a positive effect on learning.

Information about the physical attributes of children during this stage of life suggests several implications for school practice. Because of their increased strength, size, and agility, pupils can successfully engage in a wide variety of games and other physical pursuits. They profit from classes in physical education and from studying health and nutrition. However, because they are still growing and their bone structure, musculature, and circulatory systems are not yet mature, it is unwise for children of this age to engage in athletic events that involve frequent body contact or long periods of strenuous exertion.

2. Intellectual Growth

A child's intellectual growth is gradual and continuous. One of the most influential theories of how intelligence evolves in children is Piaget's cognitive development theory. Piaget proposed that cognitive development is a progressive elaboration of schemes (the techniques of adaptation to the world) or of knowledge (a process of acting on things either physically or mentally) by means of two mechanisms: assimilation and accommodation. In Piaget's system, the intellect develops through four successive levels. The third of these levels, labeled the concrete operations stage, occurs during the elementary-school years.

During the preschool years, children's thoughts are not yet integrated into a full and rational system. Their conclusions about their sensory experiences may be irrational, but during the concrete operations period of the early primary-school years, children become capable of devising a rational explanation of why the world operates as it does. However, children usually need concrete materials that are at hand or in sight in order to produce their explanation. In effect, they are not yet capable of constructing explanations from abstract evidence or relationships.

The major features of concrete operational thought are conservation, decentration, classification, and seriation (Hanson and Reynolds 1980). Conservation refers to those aspects of events that remain constant when other changes are produced in objects or situations. The concept of conservation is important in understanding number, weight, and volume.

Decentration refers to children's ability to notice transformations. Prior to the elementary-school years,

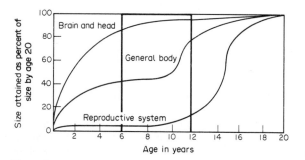

Figure 1
Differential growth rates of body systems

children often center their attention on only one aspect of an event. For example, when they see water poured from a tall glass into a wide bowl, they fail to recognize that the greater width of the bowl compensates for the bowl's lack of height, so that the short bowl can hold all of the water that was in the glass. But by the concrete operations stage, children are able simultaneously to take more details into consideration and integrate several aspects of an object or event to form a more complete picture of what is occurring. Decentration also helps children master classification and seriation by equipping them to recognize the principles of placing objects into different classes and arranging objects to form a series. School-age children are able to classify objects not only on the basis of one or two obvious characteristics, such as color or size, but also on the basis of more subtle characteristics such as combined shape and color, or in terms of descriptive words.

During later childhood, children also develop rapidly in the cognitive processes of perceiving, remembering, and reasoning (Mussen et al. 1980). Perception is the process by which people detect and interpret information from physical stimuli. Several changes in the nature of perception occur during these years. As pupils have now learned more about the world, they can conduct a more specific search of their environment, guided by their knowledge of what they want to, or are likely to, perceive. Their selective attention also improves. A child can listen to a variety of sounds or look at a number of objects and perceive each one separately. As a result, their perception is faster, more efficient, and more accurate than it was during early childhood.

Memory, as the ability to recall and recognize previously learned information, can be divided according to how long the information is kept in mind. First, sensory memory occurs in the sense organ itself, rather than in the brain. It operates unconsciously, like a reflex, and lasts only a brief instant. Next comes short-term memory, the awareness of information just perceived, which is lost after a few moments unless transferred into long-term memory. The phrase long-term memory refers to the permanent, or nearly permanent, retention of information. As children grow older, their ability to remember improves. This is partly because the amount of knowledge they retain from the past is increasingly large, so that it is easier for them to relate new events to their existing knowledge and thus to store the new material more readily. Furthermore, children improve in their use of strategies to code and store information. Such strategies include those of organization (putting bits of information into meaningful groups), rehearsal (repeating to themselves the information to be remembered), and association (recognizing connections among the information items to be remembered).

School-age children also improve in reasoning ability, meaning the process of drawing inferences from pre-

viously learned information and of finding an explanation for the problems encountered. They also become more adept at reasoning to categorize new objects or ideas. With their increased ability to distinguish the critical features of phenomena, they can understand the relationships among more complex phenomena. Thus, it becomes easier for them to explain why things happen in particular ways.

Because schooling dominates children's mental life during later childhood, pupils' intellectual progress is heavily influenced by the nature of teacher–student relationships, peer-group activities, school curricula, and parents' attitudes toward schooling. One apparently strong motive that stimulates older children to acquire skills and knowledge is an intrinsic need to deal effectively with their environment. This motivation—often referred to as curiosity—is also affected by children's assessment of their own cognitive competence, an assessment greatly influenced by how children's parents, teachers, and peers evaluate their abilities (Sarafino and Armstrong 1986).

The foregoing characteristics of intellectual development during later childhood hold several implications for school practice, as Piaget's conception of the cognitive abilities suggests. Educators, guided by research findings based on Piagetian theory, can design the sequence of instruction to suit children's cognitive-development patterns. For example, during the early school years teachers can profitably design activities that promote children's skills of classification and seriation (Kaplan 1986). Piaget's theory also encourages teachers to provide activities in which children learn through direct experiences. In short, teachers are responsible for diagnosing the current stage of a child's mental development and for offering learning activities that challenge the child to advance to the next higher step in the sequence of cognitive growth (Thomas 1978).

3. Social Development

As children are developing motor capabilities and greater cognitive skills during later childhood, they also change their patterns of socialization. Socialization, in this context, means the process by which children learn to conform to the expectations of the culture in which they grow up. During this period, their social world expands rapidly as a result of their attending school. The number of acquaintances and the importance of friendship increase, while at the same time children's relationship with their parents undergoes a subtle but definite shift toward greater independence (Kaplan 1986).

A child's self-concept or self-esteem is considered of great importance for social development. The term self-concept here refers to an individual's judgments about himself or herself relative to other people. Self-concept is central to good psychological adjustment, personal happiness, and effective functioning, because it affects how people interpret situations and thereby influences their attitudes and behavior. Children who have high self-regard are self-assured. Because they expect to be well-received and successful, they are not afraid to express their ideas or to follow their own judgments. Ones who lack self-confidence, on the other hand, tend to be apprehensive about voicing unusual ideas. To avoid attracting attention, they choose to be alone rather than to interact socially with others, or may be extremely aggressive or rebellious as a reaction to their lack of self-confidence (Mussen et al. 1980).

Children's self-concepts evolve from a combination of the assessment or feedback they receive from others and from their own evaluation of their experiences. During later childhood, boys and girls get feedback from an increasing variety of sources, not only from their parents and other family members, but also from peers and teachers. Those children who were the center of attention at home may find this is not the case in school, and the evaluation they receive from others may not always please them. At the same time, children continually compare their experiences against standards set by their society, parents, peers, teachers, and themselves. Therefore, during the transition into later childhood, honest and supportive feedback from adults is of great assistance in children's adjustment to a larger world and in their establishing an accurate self-concept.

Although the family's influence on school-age children is great, one of the most important features of later childhood is the growing influence of others, including peers, friends, and teachers. In the early years of later childhood, boys and girls derive great pleasure from reaching the goals set for them by parents and teachers and from acting in ways that meet adults' standards. Later in this stage, however, children's peers become more important, so that fitting into the group's expectations takes center stage. In other words, children begin to identify less with adults and more with peers (Kaplan 1986).

Peer groups play many important roles in an individual's social development. Through social interaction and comparing themselves with others, children learn skills and develop a view of where they fit within groups. Two other functions of peers are those of providing social support and friendship.

During the primary-school years, children often play games which promote both cognitive and social skills. Games serve several purposes. They allow children to deal with anxieties about their social acceptability through practicing roles in the simplified life situations that games can represent. In addition, games often provide children with the means of expressing their feelings. Games also allow them to exercise power and control over their world. But perhaps the most obvious advantage of games is that they provide opportunities for children to interact with their peers, thereby helping them learn cooperation, goal-oriented behavior, and individual responsibility (Hanson and Reynolds 1980).

School experiences also affect children's perceptions of appropriate gender roles. Included among these experiences are ones that contribute to sex-role stereotyping, as many teachers react differently to boys and girls. Teachers typically expect pupils to sit still and be neat, polite, and quiet. These qualities are in conflict with the traditional stereotyped sex roles of males in many societies. As a result, boys behaving in such traditional ways frequently receive more criticism and harsh discipline than do girls. Furthermore, boys' failure in school is often interpreted as due to lack of motivation, while girls' failure is attributed to lack of ability. Such treatment in school can affect their later development (Kaplan 1986).

Since school is the center of pupils' lives outside the family, the kinds of teachers they face, the teaching methods they encounter, and the types of games they play all have a strong impact not only on their school performance but also on their general adjustment to society. Appropriate social activities and educational games which are compatible with the developmental characteristics of school-age children are important for building social skills and promoting adjustment.

4. Emotional Development

Children's emotions are displayed in a variety of ways: as internal feelings and thoughts, facial expressions and body postures, and by such physiological changes as a rapid heartbeat. As children progress in cognitive and social development, their emotions become more complex and they become adept at displaying mixed emotions. New emotions that coordinate two or more basic feelings, such as guilt and shame, also develop during the school years (Sarafino and Armstrong 1986).

As children grow older, they learn which expressions of emotions are acceptable within the culture and they become aware of many subtle rules regarding the expression of emotions. During later childhood, as children begin to take responsibility for their own daily lives, they express their emotions with greater control because they seek to function as socially acceptable human beings. However, some children are unable to cope with unpleasant emotions, so that negative feelings become dominant characteristics of their personalities and create serious personal adjustment problems. Such a phenomenon is often referred to as a neurosis.

Sigmund Freud's psychoanalytic theory of development suggests that adults' neurotic behavior may be caused by their primitive urges and by traumas from their past, that is, traumas of which the adults are not aware. In Freud's model of psychosexual growth stages during childhood, he proposed that the personal–social relationships children develop—including their feelings about themselves and others, as well as their ways of treating themselves and others—are founded in the experiences they had at each growth stage. Children's failure to satisfy the needs related to a given stage will have a destructive influence on their development in later stages. In Freud's system, school-age children are in a latency period. Throughout this period, children prefer to work and play with others of their own sex. According to Freud, working through the latency period successfully is a difficult and stressful task. Children who fail at this task may become fixated at the latency stage, so they do not relate to the opposite sex appropriately later in life (Thomas 1985).

In contrast to Freud's emphasis on the appearance and cure of neurotic behavior, Erik Erikson emphasized the development of a healthy personality and proposed that children progress through a series of innately determined psychological stages as they adjust to their particular culture. At each stage, the individual strives to achieve ego identity or a sense of self by solving the particular crisis which characterizes that stage. In Erikson's system, during later childhood the individual faces the crisis of achieving an industrious personality or, in contrast, suffering a sense of inferiority. Although primary-school children still profit from hours of make-believe games and play, they also become dissatisfied with too much of this as they grow older and wish to engage in worthwhile productive activities. If adults can thus pose appropriate tasks that children recognize as interesting and worthy, then children gain the satisfaction of completing work by perseverance, which improves their chance of passing through Freud's latency period with a sound sense of industry. However, if children are not ready for school and cannot accomplish the tasks posed by adults, they may develop a sense of inadequacy and inferiority. Feelings of inferiority may also occur when children's efforts are not appreciated by teachers and peers. How well children solve the crisis at this stage influences how well they solve future crises (Thomas 1985).

During later childhood, the school provides many of the most significant experiences of that period of life. For some children, this is the first time they face intellectual competition with peers and, as a result, perhaps experience failure. The failure often leads to feelings of shame, distress, embarrassment, and incompetence. Such negative feelings usually exert a negative effect on children's intellectual and social development. Therefore, supportive attitudes expressed by teachers and parents help children cope with their experiences in school and thereby form a positive self-concept.

Although this discussion has separated children's development into several realms (physical, intellectual, social, emotional), it is important to recognize that these realms are interdependent. Treating one of these aspects influences the development of the others as well. Furthermore, it is important to recognize that even though children during the school-age years share certain general characteristics, they also can differ from each other in their rates of maturation and in the patterning of the several realms of development. Hence, it is inaccurate to assume that children should all be expected to grow and behave alike. Not only do children differ from each other in their genetic inheritance, but their growth patterns are affected as well by their society: their families, schools, neighborhoods, peer groups, and mass media.

Bibliography

Hanson R A, Reynolds R 1980 *Child Development: Concepts, Issues and Readings.* West, St Paul, Minnesota
Kaplan P S 1986 *Child's Odyssey: Child and Adolescent Development.* West, St Paul, Minnesota
Mussen P H, Conger J J, Kagan J 1980 *Essentials of Child Development and Personality.* Harper and Row, New York
Sarafino E P, Armstrong J W 1986 *Child and Adolescent Development.* West, St Paul, Minnesota
Thomas R M 1978 *Comparing Theories of Child Development.* Wadsworth, Belmont, California

Adolescence

A. C. Diver

Adolescence can be defined as the period of time during which individuals change from children to adults. In Western culture, it is a continuous process, not marked by true rites of passage that in some cultures definitively inform a young boy that he has passed into manhood and has taken on the responsibilities of an adult, or that greet a young girl's first menstrual cycle, the signal of the advent of womanhood, as a cause for celebration. Adolescence is marked by physical, mental, and emotional change. It is the physical changes that can be thought of as connoting the passage from childhood into adulthood in any culture whether or not this passage is overtly recognized.

1. Biological Functions

The beginning of adolescence, heralded by biological change, is more easily defined than its termination which is controlled by the cultural and societal factors that determine when an individual has attained adult status. Adolescence begins with the onset of puberty, the time when sexual maturity is reached. Prior to this, children go through approximately a two-year span called pubescence which encompasses the physical changes leading to puberty. A part of the brain called the hypothalamus controls the pituitary glands and initiates the production of sex hormones: progesterone and estrogen in females and testosterone in males. During the time of pubescence, both primary and secondary sexual characteristics begin to develop. Both males and females experience the appearance of pigmented pubic hair which is initially straight and later becomes kinky. Both experience the growth of axillary hair. Females begin to develop breasts, and their hips become wider. The most significant signal that physical maturity is being reached in females is menarche, the first menstrual period. Males experience an enlargement of the testes, rapid growth, growth of facial (and in some cases chest) hair, a lowering of the voice, growth of the size of the penis and scrotum, and first ejaculation.

These changes lead to sexual maturity, but adolescents are not sexually mature simply because they have the ability to ejaculate semen or because the menstrual cycle has begun. Males do not reach full sexual potency at the first emission, and females are not able to reproduce until one or two years after their first menstrual period. Pubescence is considered terminated when the full adult level of sexual potency is reached, meaning that the individuals have the adult ability to reproduce.

Some aspects of adolescence have remained unchanged through time. Girls still mature before boys by approximately two years. A wide scope of individual differences remains in both sexes in the timing of pubescence culminating in full sexual maturity, and the sequence of biological events remains the same. However, the process itself begins earlier now than in the past, with, for example, the average age of menarche dropping by one year for every 20-year span of time. The causes cited for this change are better nutrition and better health. The biological aspects of human development during adolescence remain the same across cultural lines, although the timing can vary from culture to culture, as it does from individual to individual.

2. Physical Individual Differences

In observing a group of same-age adolescents, individual differences are obvious in the physical and mental realms. A physical growth spurt is common in adolescence, with girls experiencing this growth spurt between the ages of $10\frac{1}{2}$ and 13, and boys between the ages of $12\frac{1}{2}$ and 15. This difference in timing accounts for girls being bigger than boys between the ages of $10\frac{1}{2}$ and 13. Later, the boys catch up and continue to grow until they are approximately 10 percent larger than are their female counterparts (Tanner 1969). The psychological implications of this delayed growth in boys sometimes take the form of feelings of inferiority, with boys acting in an aggressive manner to compensate for their lack of physical stature. Girls may suffer from maturing too quickly so that, in essence, their physical maturity is not in keeping with their less mature emotional needs. Girls who are late bloomers may also suffer some adjustment problems in comparing them-

selves to their more physically mature age-mates. Thus, the concept of physical attractiveness is a pervasive one in adolescence.

Physical attractiveness, though differing in standard dependent upon the society, can be a valued commodity. During adolescence, when importance is placed on relationships with members of the opposite sex, the ability to attract becomes overwhelmingly important. Peers' responses to attractive individuals are positive, so being considered attractive and striving to that end is not an illogical goal for adolescents. Consequently, they may spend a seemingly inordinate amount of time concerned with their physical appearance. In part, this can be a difficult time for them as they learn to accept the physical pluses and minuses of their own bodies. Self-image is wrapped up in this concern, and the adolescents who do not fit into the mold of an attractive individual may suffer from feelings of inadequacy and inferiority. To overcome these feelings, they must learn to accept who and what they are and to learn to make the best of what they have. This concept of self-image is not helped by the fact that as adolescents' bodies change, they are susceptible to facial blemishes, acne, and oily skin.

Two areas in which body type dramatically influences psychological adjustment are obesity and anorexia nervosa. Caloric requirements vary from individual to individual. What is a normal meal to one person could be a case of extreme overeating to another. In view of societal expectations of, and adolescents' preoccupation with physical attractiveness, obese adolescents frequently suffer from a negative self-image and experience a great deal of anxiety which can lead to adjustment problems. Treatment of chronically obese individuals is difficult, and not only does the caloric intake have to be reduced, but entirely new patterns of eating and dealing with stress and boredom have to be forged.

On the other hand, anorexic individuals seem to have a phobia of food. They take it far beyond dieting and can cease eating or induce vomiting after having eaten. This leads to an emaciated physical condition and can result in extremely ill health and even death. Anorexic individuals are generally white girls in early to middle adolescence. Doctors are reporting more and more cases of anorexia nervosa, and as with obesity, it is difficult to treat. Although both obesity and anorexia nervosa are extreme examples of individual deviation from the physical norm, they occur with a high enough frequency to warrant concern.

The implications of the changing bodies of adolescents and the individual differences in the timing of these changes suggest that in dealing with young people, educators must be aware that no two youths will necessarily be at the same stage of growth at the same time. Physical education programs must take these differences into consideration so that those who are not maturing as rapidly as others do not feel they are inferior but that they are competing with themselves to better their own bodies in strength and coordination. In the classroom, teachers must be aware that students who are in the process of reaching puberty are in a state of physical upheaval and consequently can be affected in their behavior, attitudes, mood swings, and ability to concentrate. As sexual maturity is reached, educators are competing for top priority against a new and intriguing world, and they cannot always be successful in their attempts. They must also attempt to be sensitive to those whose physical differences set them apart from the rest.

3. Adolescence and Sex

In various societies around the world, the 1960s are often cited as having started a sexual revolution, yet there is no hard evidence that young people have become more promiscuous than their previous counterparts. Attitudes toward sex have become more liberalized today as young people have begun to talk more openly about their views (Rutter 1980). As stated earlier, adolescents are faced with bodies that have matured to their full adult sexuality. The desire for sexual outlet is not an unnatural one at this time, but the physical need does not necessarily coincide with the psychological one.

Societies that are sexually restrictive either frown upon or actually punish any signs of sexuality in children. Autoerotic activity, that is, masturbation, and sexual play among same-sex or opposite-sex children are punished if observed by adults. Children in these societies are kept ignorant of any sexual functions. Premarital affairs are not allowed. Nonetheless, even in these restrictive societies, adolescents still find ways around these rules and do frequently engage in some form of sexual interaction (Ford and Beach 1969).

Most Western cultures are considered restrictive in the sense that sexual intercourse is not actively encouraged or allowed to pass if observed as it is in permissive and semirestrictive societies. However, adolescents do engage in sexual activities ranging from masturbation to kissing, genital petting, and actual intercourse. As adolescents become involved in dating and the establishment of transitory couples, they begin to explore and experiment with the realm of human sexuality. Sometimes pressures are exerted from peers to gain sexual knowledge. If adolescents are not psychologically prepared to accept an adult sexual role, the result can be guilt, anxiety, and frequently unwanted pregnancy. At a time when they are faced with a fragile sense of themselves, with easily shattered identities, the fear of the loss of a boyfriend or girlfriend can be enough of an impetus to force them to engage in sexual intercourse before they are ready.

The ability to copulate does not necessarily imply knowledge of sexual functions and reproduction. Many adolescents hang on to myths about sex which causes unnecessary problems. Some believe masturbation can cause blindness, the loss of the ability to function sexually, or other disorders, and they feel guilt and fear

associated with masturbation. A pervading myth is that a girl cannot become pregnant the first time she engages in intercourse. Some believe that the absence of orgasm will insure safety from pregnancy. Finally, the last vestiges of egocentricity appear in the form of adolescents believing that pregnancy could not happen to them. Unplanned pregnancy is generally unwanted and a cause of severe emotional crisis for both the girl and boy. Adolescent pregnancy is on the rise, and these young people are faced with difficult decisions. Their options are threefold: abortion, adoption, or marriage. In societies where emphasis is increasingly placed on education and the skills needed to function in a highly competitive job market, dropping out of school to have a child and support a family causes a severe disturbance in an individual's potential earning power. Adolescents, who are still going through a period of change and the establishment of their own identities, do not make the most stable of spouses, especially when the marriage has been forced by the prospect of legitimizing a child. Obviously, many of these marriages cannot stand up to the stress and thus fail. Those that do survive can still result in one or both individuals experiencing dissatisfaction and anger at having been forced to accept an adult role before they were ready.

While many forms of contraception are available, to seek a contraceptive device is tantamount to admitting to having a need for it, that is, an admission of planning to engage in sexual intercourse. This, combined with the vast amount of misinformation circulating among adolescents about love relationships and sex, can account for the large numbers of adolescents who are currently sexually active and who use no form of contraception. Sex-education programs frequently do not address the issues that worry adolescents and are often quite nebulous. The need for clear-cut and easily understood information is obvious, especially since many adults are uncomfortable discussing sexual issues with their children.

Homosexual experiences, not an unusual part of prepubescent and early adolescent growth, can have definite ramifications if the adolescents are intercepted in their activities by adults and labeled homosexuals. These encounters are relatively common and do not constitute the definition of an actual preference. The labeling may force questioning adolescents to assume that they are indeed homosexuals. Some adolescents do establish this preference, and in many societies a social stigma surrounds homosexuality. One school of thought says that homosexuality is deviant, and many religious groups feel these people should be "cured." Another says that both homosexuality and heterosexuality are acceptable, preferring a "live and let live" philosophy. The adolescents who are confronted with this choice are subject to many societal and peer group pressures (see *Homosexuality and Human Development*).

Rather than allowing misinformation to flourish, educators need to address the issue of human sexuality with adolescent students. Sex-education courses rarely suffer from attendance problems, pointing to the fact that adolescent interest is high and that they do have a desire to learn the facts. Schools run into problems in this area because of the religious attitudes and moral reasoning of parents, administrators, and the communities. Hence, misinformation continues to exist, resulting in many situations that could have been alleviated by information about biological functions and human sexuality.

4. Adolescence and Cognitive Abilities

One manner in which to view the cognitive processes of adolescents is through the theories of Piaget. Adolescents have arrived at Piaget's formal operations period and are no longer bound by their perceptions (see *Basic Concepts and Applications of Piagetian Cognitive Development Theory*). They can become involved in abstract thought about things that are not immediate to their environments. They can perceive relationships among abstract concepts and conceptualize problems involving transitivity. The basis for intellectual functioning is complete by adolescence, but intellectual growth will continue through adulthood. With their new intellectual abilities, adolescents are able to perceive the past, the present, and the future, and to note how the three interrelate. They are able to see that actions taken in the present have an effect on the future. They can perceive the differences between what is actually real and what is not, between what is and what could or should be. It is this new ability that perhaps leads them to the characteristic adolescent trait of idealism (Lefrancois 1973).

Adolescents are cognitively able for the first time in their lives to develop a real picture of how the world functions. They are able to become involved with political thought rather than parroting ideas they have heard. Much of the political activism often found in later adolescence is attributable to the fact that adolescents can not only perceive that things could be better, but they are equipped to perceive that changes initiated now could perhaps make life better in the future. They are able to see that they have inherited a far from perfect world. Typically, they feel anger over this, and they formulate an idealistic vision of how they will change the world for the better for their children. They tend to think of the world in an introspective manner, envisioning a world without hate, without violence, without war, and, currently, without the threat of extinction from nuclear attack. A certain amount of cynicism inevitably results in a generation of young people who have grown up with the threat of total destruction. They may become involved in projects involving ecology or peace, and this can be viewed as healthy in terms of Eriksonian theory: these young people are defining their own ideologies, associating themselves with a cause, and thus defining their own identities. On the other hand, some youths become so disenchanted with the state of the world and the quality of life, they find ways of shutting off to everything

through drugs, antisocial behavior, and sometimes through suicide (see *Eriksonian Development Theory*).

At this point in time, adolescents change dramatically in the types of information with which they can cope. The subject matter to which they are exposed in school pulls on their new abilities. They can draw logical conclusions and can formulate an hypothesis from data they have collected or that have been presented to them. They are able to work with concepts that do not exist in the real or physical world. All of these abilities are new, and educators frequently confront the joys of intellectual discovery in adolescents as the latter are able to grasp concepts that alluded them before their cognitive processes had matured sufficiently.

5. Theories of Adolescent Crisis

In urbanized societies, adolescent crisis in varying degrees is an accepted norm. Adolescents are faced with the realization that the next step of growth for them is adulthood, and society asks that they begin to prepare for their new roles. No longer are they dependent children within a directed world of their parents' making. They approach independence while receiving guidance from their parents. They begin to take an inventory of themselves, attempting to understand who they are, from where they originated, and where they are headed in the future. They are attempting to integrate themselves and their new insights into society to find a niche for themselves that is culturally, socially, and sexually acceptable (Frisk 1975).

Adolescence is popularly thought of as being a time of crisis. Freud saw adolescents as going through a difficult transition from same-sex interests in the latency period to opposite-sex interests and a desire for copulation that can be hindered by cultural taboos against premarital sexual relations. Erikson expands on Freud's theory in the sense that he sees adolescents as going through enormous physical and emotional changes during puberty, a time when they are forced to question themselves and their roles in society. This can lead to what Erikson terms as an "identity crisis." This crisis can be resolved by adolescents adopting a role and defining their own ideology. If this is not accomplished, identity diffusion will result (see *Psychoanalytic Theory of Human Development*).

Adolescence has been referred to as a time of turbulence, an expansion of Freud's and Erikson's theories. Young people are popularly viewed to be idealistic, frustrated, and at odds with the older generation from whom they are struggling to be freed in their quest for independence. This view of adolescence as a time of turmoil could be not so much the norm as a deviation from the norm. The picture of the belligerent young man who defies authority, has no respect for his parents, and runs wild is the exception to the rule. The opposite side of this view of adolescence as a time of confusion is the theory that most young people have indeed incorporated the belief systems and ideals of their parents and are functioning with them in an environment of ever-decreasing parental authority and direction as parents see their children take on more and more of the roles of adults. According to this viewpoint, most parents begin to function as guides and counselors, and the relationships between parents and youths are marked by mutual respect and caring (Bandura 1969).

So much variation exists in theories of adolescent development because so much variation exists among adolescents and because human development is continuous rather than discontinuous. People do not awaken one day to discover they are suddenly very old, grey, and arthritic. Neither do adolescents awaken to find they have been transformed overnight into adults. The transition into old age is a very gradual one. The transition from adolescence to adulthood occurs in less than a decade. It occurs at a time when adolescents have developed the mental abilities to perceive the world in reality as opposed to their more childish and limited perceptions of how it functioned. They begin to deal with people of all sorts outside of the home environment and have realized that they will have to adopt a role that fits in a harmonious fashion with their natures. With one foot still in the secure, tested world of childhood, they begin to try on the different roles of adults to find one that is comfortable. This adjustment can be difficult and painful, or it can progress smoothly with only minor hitches.

Adolescents can be helped through any troubled transition they might experience at this time by their exposure to the school environment. Because they are moving away from their parents so as to establish independence, they can benefit from adults who are removed from the home setting and who will listen to their concerns. Life-adjustment, family-planning, and social studies courses can give them the opportunity to begin to cope with their fears and problems and to meet the world of adulthood with realistic expectations. Sympathetic counselors, advisors, and teachers can help to cut down any friction felt in their transition from children to adolescents to young adults.

6. Peer Groups

Adolescence is frequently referred to in literature as a time of dilemma when the young person is neither an adult nor a child. This "in-between" stage is referred to as an awkward one, and many of the problems of growing up are popularly attributed to the basic non-status of adolescents. It is also possible to take a more positive approach to adolescence, viewing it as a time when young people develop and try out their looming adult functions. It can be thought of as a time when they can become emotionally mature and learn adult behaviors. The question of peer groups and peer acceptance is an integral part of this issue.

Peer groups, though commonly referred to as a negative influence in adolescence, are actually an essential proving ground for adolescent relationships and

behaviors. Adolescents, as they move from the world of sole parental influence, must find companionship and acceptance elsewhere. The circle of friends which adolescents cultivate becomes increasingly important as a support system, a place where they can confront values and issues in their attempts to join the ranks of socialized adults. The relationships in adolescence may begin with same-sex groups, leading to mixed groups, and finally resulting in the coupling which is the first step towards adult hetero-sexual relationships. Eventually, it is important that young people let go of their need for peer group approval and become independent. This process is usually served by the pairing of individuals in late adolescence.

Any deviation from the norm in this time of peer group relationships can lead to isolation and result in severe psychological ramifications for the individual. Adolescents who are physically different in regard to possessing a physical defect or having a chronic disease, have a difficult time gaining acceptance from their peers, and this problem is compounded by the fact that they must also learn to cope with their own deficiencies. These individuals may have problems separating themselves from their parents, and displaying strong self-image and self-confidence. This can lead to their feeling depressed and angry (Friedman 1975).

Adults recognize the strength of the influence of peer groups on adolescents. The concept of "white flight" in the United States, a social class issue, is an example wherein people moved from certain neighborhoods so as to remove their children from exposure to certain types of young people in particular schools. Those adolescents who are not secure in themselves find a sense of security and solidarity in gangs, and the pressure to do what the rest of the gang is doing is intensely strong. Schools generally become the meeting place for these young people, so the social aspect of school becomes more important than (what becomes) the inconsequential educational aspect.

7. Drug Usage

The drug problem in adolescence received wide attention during the 1960s. It is a misconception to believe that the use of drugs either started or stopped with that particular decade, though the most prolific coverage of drug usage among adolescents occurred during that time, especially in the United States. Adolescents in many societies today experiment with all manner of drugs, including hallucinogens, stimulants, and depressants. Drugs are still easily available in secondary and even primary schools. Peer pressure and a desire for altered states of consciousness figure strongly, as does the adolescent need to experiment, to try new things, and eventually to make a decision as to their worth (see *Drugs and Human Development*).

Alcohol is commonly used around the world. Drinking is considered an adult activity, so its attraction for adolescents is easily noted. Especially in cultures that hold no real rites of passage for adolescents, drinking can serve as the marker that they have passed into adulthood. Adolescents do not generally have the body weight of adults and are thus less able to "handle their liquor." Nicotine, also a drug, is also widely used around the world, and it is difficult to dictate to adolescents that they should refrain from smoking cigarettes when they are surrounded by adults who smoke. Adolescents are still growing, so the dangers to them physically from the usage of such common drugs as alcohol and nictotine are even greater than for adults.

The primary point in viewing the usage of drugs is that experimentation is most probably a natural adolescent phenomenon. However, a large difference exists between drug usage or experimentation and drug abuse. Probably the biggest hope for adolescent experimenters is clearly defined, nonjudgmental information and education that recognizes the social forces operating upon young people, that can point out the continuing scientific research as to the hazards of drug usage, and that sees experimentation as a normal adolescent activity as youths sort through all the possibilities of adulthood and make decisions for themselves. Certainly, young people who become involved with drugs of any sort show a marked change in their performance in school.

8. Adolescence, Education, and the Future

In societies that are highly or moderately literate, an emphasis is placed on the individual being able to perform a function that will equally benefit the society and earn a living for the individual. Young people in school are increasingly prepared for life after school in the subject matter they are taught and the skills they learn. If a student is not academically oriented, an emphasis is placed on the individual learning a skill that will be marketable. Dropping out of school in these societies means that individuals are unable to get useful, interesting, or well-paid jobs. Some societies place value on a well-rounded education, including mathematics, the sciences, foreign languages, and writing ability. Others establish minimum competencies for adolescents to achieve before they leave the formal education environment, and beyond that, an attempt is made to train them in a marketable skill.

One misfortune in the educational experience of many adolescents is that the school does not fit them well. Clearly, all youths are not equally intelligent. Consequently, it is frequently found that some individuals are forced to fit into a scholastic mold that is not comfortable for them, turning them against the entire educational process. A continuing movement in many countries establishes a competency-based education so that all people leaving secondary schooling will have at least a minimum competency in such areas as mathematics, reading, and writing. Some countries impose a minimum age requirement for mandatory school attendance. This can result in adolescents attending school who are not interested, who perhaps bring to the school a wide variety of personal problems with which the school system is poorly equipped to deal. Frequently, schools have been cited as being negligent in their duties to the young, and, just as frequently, schools respond that they cannot perform both the educational role assigned to them and the nurturing role that has fallen on them in the wake of the disintegrating family unit.

In summary, it is well to recognize that many young people do pass through all manner of psychosocial and psychosexual crises unscathed, finding the years between 12 and 20 to be rewarding ones. These young people pass through what is considered a time of emotional instability and find emotional balance in late adolescence and early adulthood, along with altered perceptions of themselves, the world around them, their new roles, and their fully developed mental capabilities.

Bibliography

Bandura A 1969 The stormy decade: Fact or fiction? In: Rogers D (ed.) 1969 *Issues in Adolescent Psychology*. Appleton–Century–Crofts, New York, pp. 187–98

Ford C, Beach F 1969 Development of sexual behavior in human beings. In: Grinder R E (ed.) 1969 *Studies in Adolescence: A Book of Readings in Adolescent Development*, 2nd edn. Macmillan, London, pp. 447–58

Friedman S 1975 Emotional maturation and behavior In: Berenberg S R (ed.) 1975 *Puberty: Biologic and Psychosocial Components*. Stenfert Kroese, Leiden, pp. 253–55

Frisk M 1975 Puberty: Emotional maturation and behavior. In: Berenberg S R (ed.) 1975 *Puberty: Biologic and Psychosocial Components*. Stenfert Kroese, Leiden, pp. 236–47

Lefrancois G 1973 *Of Children: An Introduction to Child Development*. Wadsworth, Belmont, California

Rutter M 1980 *Changing Youth in a Changing Society: Patterns of Adolescent Development and Disorder*. Harvard, Cambridge, Massachusetts

Schofield M G 1965 *The Sexual Behavior of Young People*. Little, Brown, Boston, Massachusetts

Tanner J, Eveleth P 1975 Variability between populations in growth and development at puberty. In: Berenberg S R (ed.) 1975 *Puberty: Biologic and Psychosocial Components*. Stenfert Kroese, Leiden, pp. 256–74

Adulthood

C. E. Kennedy

Poets, novelists, and artists down through time have been faithful chroniclers of the patterns and portents of change in adulthood. Although adults have managed the affairs of all societies through the generations, it was not until the last quarter of a century that the changes and individual experiences after adolescence started to be delineated as a major area of scientific study. Indeed, it is only in recent research that specific work on adulthood will be found. Adulthood comprises life from 18 years of age to death. The period from mid-60s to death, identified as old age, is discussed in the following article and will, therefore, largely be omitted here.

1. Stages of Adult Development

Changes during adulthood are often viewed in terms of life stages. Neugarten suggested that life stages reflect a social clock set by society. The changes through which an adult moves are prompted in some measure by biological processes, but also, in a proportionately much larger measure than during childhood, they are prompted by psychological and social influences.

The term development refers to any change in the adult and does not indicate a predetermined direction such as toward greater complexity, as it does in child development. Conceptualization in the study of stages of adulthood reflects constructs from Erikson's developmental stages, Havighurst's developmental tasks, and Kohlberg's stages of moral development. Much of the popular awareness of adult life stages comes from four studies of different groups of persons as they moved through stages of adulthood. Each of these studies has been published in books appearing since 1975, along with Sheehy's *Passages* (1976), a widely read popularizing synthesis of data from these studies and other sources. Vaillant (1977) followed a group of college men until they neared 50 years of age; Gould (1978) studied a cross section of men and women between ages 16 and 52; Levinson (1978) interviewed four groups of men: industrial workers, business executives, novelists, and biologists. Lowenthal (1975) initiated her study with adults in four life transition stages: graduating from high school; getting married; having their last child leave home; and preparing for retirement. The classifications in each of these studies differ somewhat, but the general patterns of normative transitions are reflected in the outline that follows. Neugarten (1977) indicates that there are normal expectable events that serve as markers along the life cycle calling forth changes in self-concept and in sense of identity.

1.1 Young Adulthood

Young adulthood spans approximately the ages between 18 and 35. The beginning years of this period are occupied with separating, searching, and preparation. The later years are involved with tentative commitments and testing. It usually takes an individual five years or so to move out from his or her family of origin into a somewhat independent status, to choose a career direction, and to begin preparation for that career. Simultaneously with career concerns, young adults are learning more about themselves in relation to others and they are also considering future styles of family living. Erikson has described the searching going on during these years as gaining a sense of identity versus confusion and gaining a sense of intimacy versus isolation.

During the next 10 years of this period the young adult is verifying and becoming established in career and interpersonal identities that will serve as the foundation for succeeding stages of adult life. The decisions made at this time regarding jobs, values, and family relationships are not permanent, but formative. This is not the last time the individual will choose directions or consider the meaning of intimacy, but the place arrived at during these years will establish the basis from which he or she moves forward in succeeding stages of life.

A pattern prevails through each of the periods of adulthood. Young adulthood begins with testing and searching and tentative commitment, leading to a more intense involvement. This is followed by a transition period of review. Often this is a time of values clarification or an affirming of a particular aspect of career identity. In the Catch–30 transition, as Sheehy terms it, some young adults decide that their career or marital choice was not the right one and take action to move toward another alternative before becoming too deeply immersed. For others who may have been briefly trying out a number of different roles, the review at around the age of 30 affords the occasion for more lasting commitments. Questions raised around 30 begin to be resolved or put aside as 35 approaches and the individual moves into a new, busy, and usually one of the most productive periods of life—the middle adult years.

1.2 Middle Adult Years

This is a time of complete absorption in career, family, and community affairs. Middle adults are aware of having set aside, for a time, their vacillation and doubts and are now committed to proving to themselves the full abilities and potential they have. These years, from the mid-30s to the mid-40s, are the most pressured of adult life. The pressures involve gaining advancement in a career, time demands for care of family, and for community responsibilities.

Erikson's developmental stage, generativity versus stagnation, characterizes the growth potential of this period. Generativity involves developing a capacity for caring about others: children, adults, culture, and the continuation of society. It means a growth in personal maturity so that people no longer feel themselves children to be nurtured or young people seeking approval from their mentors. Levinson suggests that having a mentor (role model and guide) during young adulthood is important in laying the affective foundation in the self for the later maturing of generativity. While growth in generativity versus stagnation is the prevailing task of middle adulthood, earlier developmental accomplishments, such as intimacy, will require reworking in the light of new growth and circumstances. In some instances, such as with single, divorced, or widowed persons, intimacy becomes a major developmental task. During the mid-40s individuals stop counting age in terms of years they have lived; instead they think in terms of time left to live. It is a transition time that some refer to as middlescence. Middlescence has been compared to adolescence because of its bewildering blend of physiological changes (e.g., menopause) and new responsibilities for determining one's own future. The variety of commitments which have held the adult's world together are no longer so fixed. With the children about ready to leave home and his position in his job nearing its peak, the husband of age 45 is faced with an opportunity to make new, or to reaffirm previous life commitments concerning who he is and where he is going. This is true also for women, but in a somewhat more complex fashion. Much of the research to date has been with women whose primary identity has been that of homemaker, even though they may also have been working outside the home. As children leave home, the prospect of an "empty nest" holds mixed messages for women. Some may view it as a threat to their identity and reason for being; others may view it as an opportunity for new identity. Research is just beginning on the meaning of this period for the woman who has more explicitly thus far in life pursued a career outside the home, either as a single woman or in a dual career marriage. Educational implications of this period are that it is important for men and women in late middle adult years (45 to 50) to have the opportunity to think about family communication, alternatives for second careers, and matters of health regarding themselves and their aging parents. Strength groups, self-discovery workshops, supportive and educational groups for adjustment to widowhood and divorce are illustrative of the developmental resources needed during this period.

1.3 Maturity

Until recently adults went directly from the struggles of work to the status of old age, at 50 plus. Lengthened life coupled with social changes enables adults to experience new social and psychological dynamics. It is possible to think of the range from mid-30s to mid-60s as one period and call it middle age. However, there are sufficient differences in the preoccupation of the 40s and the 50s, so that a designation of a distinct period, maturity, is justified. Maturity begins at around age 50 and continues to retirement or about 65. In this period adults exercise a greater freedom and a greater degree of power than at any other period of their lives.

The soul searching of middlescence has resulted in a new clarification in identity, and new approaches to career and life-style. In maturity, men begin to relax in their jobs, where they may have achieved managerial or other senior status. Women, with reduced family responsibility, have begun to move into second careers, either in paid employment or in community work. There is a greater percentage of women of this age in the labor force than of any group except young adult women just out of school. Adults usually have greater income during this time than at any other period; they also have fewer

financial obligations. The adult is also more free to accept or reject community and family tasks.

Somewhat different things happen during this period. Men become somewhat more relaxed, more introspective and mellow, more oriented to personal interests and to socializing with others. Women become somewhat more oriented toward productivity in new careers and inclined toward more assertive roles. Developmentally, the interests of generativity occupy most people. As the period ends the adult is beginning to be oriented toward the last of Erikson's stages, integrity versus despair, which is the developmental stage of old age. Neugarten has described this blending of the two psychodynamic stages in her observations that individuals in their 50s and 60s develop an increased "interiority" while at the same time maintaining an active, effective instrumental dealing with life.

The years of maturity are much more comfortable years for both men and women than the preceding middle adult years. Where men in their 40s expressed considerable boredom and frustration with their work, even as they pressed hard to get on, men of maturity are much less preoccupied with financial concerns or advancement. Women, though experiencing some of the tensions of emerging aggressive and achievement orientations, are much less hostile and depressed than in their frustrating years of middle adulthood. The woman's uncertainty immediately preceding the empty nest is replaced with self-affirmation as she experiences new opportunities with new freedom.

New relationships are being formed by the adults with their grown children even as they are developing new relationships also with their own increasingly elderly parents. The expression "woman in the middle" is sometimes used to describe the superwoman role that employed women in their 50s take on as they care for an elderly parent, are active grandparents, and still manage their own home. Many women freed from family responsibilities, and some perhaps from a husband's domination, formulate new life goals. New forms of expression emerge for women of maturity which carry them forward to positions of increasing power. This power manifests itself in their marital relationships and/or in more active social roles. Shortly after 60 the consideration of retirement occupies considerable time as the adults plan the details of the transition that moves them toward the fastest growing group in adult life, the period of old age.

2. Intellectual Development

Research by Schaie (1977/78) indicates that intellectual competence continues to increase through most of adulthood. Different kinds of intellectual processes are needed to accomplish the goals of different age groups. The intellectual style of young adulthood is characterized as "achieving"; it is a task-related, competitive, cognitive style. Middle adulthood intellectual style is described as "executive" and "responsible"; in these years the intellectual task is to integrate long-range goals with the solution of current real-life problems which call for organizational, integrative, and interpretive intellectual skills. Later adulthood calls for a "reintegrative" style characterized by the need to attain a sense of meaning in experience; this requires the ability to retrieve and attend selectively to information from the abundance of information that has been accumulated over the life span.

The three phases of intellectual development relate to the different areas of problem solving associated with different stages of adulthood. The first phase emphasizes the attainment of intellectual skills and application to personal and societal goals needed in establishing family units and entering the world of work. The second period is one of relative stability and integration. It is accompanied by some reduction in response speed. The security of the middle adults' social position and their wealth of experience provide adequate compensation for the loss of speed. Theirs is a style appropriate to the solution of practical problems that occur for persons performing the generative tasks of caring, and of being responsible for others. In the final cognitive style of older years there is more selectivity; the focus of intellectual activity shifts from content to context.

Continuing research in educational measurement involves the differentiation between intelligence and competence. Schaie describes intelligence as an inference of underlying traits coming from many observations; competence is a more situation-specific combination of intellectual traits, which, with adequate motivation, will permit adaptive behavior. Schaie's position is that traditional measures of intelligence are not likely to be very useful for predicting many of the more situation-specific skills of the older learner.

3. Moral Development

The study of adult moral development is extending the conceptual frameworks of Kohlberg and Piaget to include stages influenced by "contextual relativism" (Murphy and Gilligan 1980). This reflects a step that accompanies the adult's change from concern about identity to a concern about intimacy. In adulthood the formal categories of moral development are transcended and the adult gains a new awareness of the interdependence of self and others. The ethic of justice gives way to the ethic of responsibility in the maturing development that Erikson labeled sense of generativity.

In the study of moral and cognitive development during adult years, a Piagetian-type stage is being recognized as problem finding, to distinguish it from the problem-solving orientation of formal thought. It is employed in the "contextual relativism" that results in moral development beyond Kohlberg's principled moral judgment. Education and life processes that lead adults to question that which was taken for granted are the catalysts for continued moral and cognitive development during adult years (Murphy and Gilligan 1980). It is through the understanding of other persons' lives, both past and present, that the adult's concern moves from identity to intimacy and then to generativity as manifest in continuing moral development.

4. Social Norms and Role Transitions

In simple societies, life may be divided into two periods—childhood and adulthood. Other societies may include three: childhood, adulthood, and old age. Neugarten (1977) has pointed out that where the division of labor is simple and the rate of societal change is slow, a single age-grade system functions well. There, as individuals move from childhood to adulthood, they simultaneously take on new roles. There is a close match between social age grades and chronological periods in the life course. In more complex societies there are multiple systems of age grading. In the United States people are adults in the political system when they are 18 and allowed to vote. They are adults in the family system when they marry and become parents. They are adults in the economic system when they become full-time workers.

There are in each culture and period of history generally recognized age norms. In her study of middle-class American men and women, Neugarten found they expressed a general consensus about the best age for men to marry; when they should be settled in a career; when they should hold their top jobs; when they should be ready to retire, and so on. Adults experience two types of transition—normative and idiosyncratic. Normative transitions are changes expected by social norms such as graduations, marriages, births, and retirement. Idiosyncratic transitions are changes that do not happen in everyone's life or at expected times. Social timetables serve to create a normal, predictable adult-life course. Although role transitions require adjustments, they are not traumatic if they occur "on time," because they have been expected and prepared for. Distress occurs with idiosyncratic transitions, role changes that are unexpected and without preparation. Death of a loved one is accompanied by grief at the loss, but if the death is of an elderly person and in a normal fashion it is "on time" and not devastating. The death of a child or an accidental death is "off time" and creates much more difficult adjustment.

5. Educational Applications

Adults perceive events and are motivated differently at different life stages. Effective development requires that they consider the characteristics of their life stage and have access to information needed for decision making. In addition to adult development courses, other areas for program planning include: family communication, career alternatives, health information for self and aging parents, and adjustment groups for widowhood and divorce. Effective educational planning requires the development of criterion variables relevant to the cognitive styles, life roles, and societal requirements of competent adult functions (Schaie 1977/78).

Bibliography

Chickering A W, Havighurst R W 1981 The life cycle. In: Chickering A W (ed.) 1981 *The Modern American College.* Jossey-Bass, San Francisco, California
Erikson E H 1968 *Identity: Youth and Crisis.* Norton, New York
Gould R L 1978 *Transformations: Growth and Change in Adult Life.* Simon and Schuster, New York
Levinson D J 1978 *The Seasons of a Man's Life.* Knopf, New York
Lowenthal M F, Thurnher M, Chiriboga D 1975 *Four Stages of Life: A Comparative Study of Women and Men Facing Transitions.* Jossey-Bass, San Francisco, California
Murphy J M, Gilligan C 1980 Moral development in adolescence and adulthood: A critique and reconstruction of Kohlberg's theory. *Hum. Dev.* 23: 77–104
Neugarten B L 1977 Personality and aging. In: Birren J E, Schaie K W (eds.) 1977 *Handbook of the Psychology of Aging.* Van Nostrand Reinhold, New York
Schaie K W 1977/78 Toward a stage theory of adult cognitive development. *J. Aging Hum. Dev.* 8: 129–38
Sheehy G 1976 *Passages: Predictable Crises of Adult Life.* Dutton, New York
Vaillant G E 1977 *Adaptation to Life.* Little, Brown, Boston, Massachusetts

Old Age

C. E. Kennedy

Old age is a period of adulthood of indeterminate length for two reasons. One is that its ending varies with the length of life of the person. The second reason is that there are differences among researchers' definitions as to when old age begins. Its beginning is most generally identified as age 65, reflecting the legislated age for retirement. Neugarten has conceptualized two groups of persons, the young-old and the old-old. She sees the young-old (perhaps beginning in the 50s with early retirement) as representing a rapidly expanding sector of our society with tremendous energies and resources for social influence and contribution. Entry into the old-old phase is usually in the 70s, depending on health considerations.

There has been a prevailing impression in popular thought that all old people are alike and that old age is synonymous with weakness and lack of creativity. However, research contradicts this stereotype. There is greater diversity among the elderly than among any group of persons. This period poses important developmental tasks, the solution of which comes from the combination of resources from earlier life-styles, from the availability of social, psychological, and economic resources in the community, and from the individual's health and physical energies. Many of the negative values associated in the public mind with old age come from a tendency to confuse the effects of illness and poverty with the effects of the aging process. Illness and poverty bring with them significant limitations, whether the individual is young or old. For much of the period of old age, the majority of people experience relatively good health and satisfactory incomes.

1. Demographic Information

In the 15-year period, 1963–1978, the number of people in the United States who were 65 or older increased by 40 percent, from approximately 17 million to 24 million.

About 11 percent of the American population is over 65. Every day more than 1,000 Americans celebrate their 65th birthday. The average lifetime a century ago was less than 50 years; today it is over 70 years. This increased life span is due to the fact that there are fewer deaths among children, and also because of better health and lower death rates of young and middle adults. The smallest decline in death rate has been in the group where the population growth rate is most rapidly increasing, those in old age. It is the fact that more people are living to reach the period of old age that accounts for the noteworthy population growth of the old age group. However, improved health care in earlier life and during old age also increases the possibilities for satisfying life during old age.

2. Developmental Processes in Old Age

At the turn of the century, the family life cycle was quite different from today. Then, the last child did not leave home until about the time that one or both of the parents were nearing death. Today, the last child leaves home at about midpoint in the parents' marriage. There are usually as many years ahead for the couple alone as there are behind them with children in the home.

The fact that some people choose to withdraw from active life and some strive to maintain the activity level of earlier years as long as possible has led to two theories of aging: disengagement theory and activity/compensation theory. Current research indicates a more general perspective that accommodates both processes. In old age the individual continues the mode of behavior begun in early life. Except where financial or health factors intervene, the person continues to choose alternatives in accord with the individual's established lifelong pattern of needs. There is usually no abrupt personality shift in old age, but rather the principle of integration promotes increasing consistency within the individual's life. This means, also, that individual differences continue to increase among older persons as they continue to add to their individual collections of unique life histories (Maas and Kuypers 1974).

For both sexes, with increasing age there appears to be an increased interiority, that is, preoccupation with inner life. They are more introspective; they tend to respond to inner stimuli rather than to what the social environment would dictate. They are less likely to respond to new challenges or to be self-assertive. While increased interiority is characteristic of both sexes, there are differences in the patterns that develop for men and women. Men in old age are more responsive to their affiliative, nurturant, sensual promptings and women move toward more expression of their aggressive, egocentric impulses (Neugarten 1977). Since this difference is found in many different cultures, one explanation is that social assignments in most cultures require men to be the breadwinners and women to nurture the family. With old age the assignments are relaxed and the complementary aspects of their personalities are allowed to emerge (Guttman 1977).

Erikson (1978) described two developmental stages of old age—generativity and integrity. Generativity versus stagnation is the stage initiated in middle years in which the individual strives to provide for the coming generation. This continues with the young-old, as they establish family and community resources and train the young to take over in their place. The last of Erikson's eight stages, that of integrity versus despair has increasing prominence with increasing age. Gaining a sense of integrity is the developmental process in which individuals begin to recognize the patterns of their life and affirm the meaning of one's total existence. Older people looking back upon the years accept their strengths and their limitations and in this process express hope and gain wisdom. The individual who does not achieve this sense of integrity experiences despair, tending to reject one's past life and to fear death.

3. Biology of Old Age

Very few people die of old age. Death usually comes from disease. Heart disease is the primary cause of death of people over 65. Aging is associated with gradual decline in the performances of most organs of the body. The amount of blood pumped by the heart falls from 6.5 liters per minute at age 20 to 3.5 liters at age 85. This means that less blood flows through the kidneys and through other organs and muscles, causing them to be increasingly vulnerable to disease. However, there is great individual variability and many old people have circulatory performances of young persons. With the exception of sexual hormones, the endocrine glands retain their ability to produce hormones into advanced ages. In the elderly, tissues that respond to the hormones may require a greater supply of hormones than they do in the young. As a result, responses in the elderly are often slower than in the young. Exercise

and life-style influence the effective functioning of the biological system.

4. Intellectual Development

Aging causes some degree of physical and psychological change in everyone. In the intellectual area there are changes in visual and auditory acuity and in perceptual speed that cause older persons to be at a disadvantage in intelligence testing. Some age-related decline in ability may be attributable to an increase in cautiousness in older persons. Substantial associations have been found between hearing loss and intellectual functioning, as measured by subtests of the Wechsler Adult Intelligence Scale. Also, old people process information received from the senses more slowly (Schaie and Parr 1981).

People growing up at different periods of history learn different kinds of information and use different approaches to learning. An examination of generational differences in level of function shows that much of what has been thought to be intellectual deficit in older people is not deficit, but rather the effect of older people using skills that are inappropriate in the current educational environment. Improved functioning for older adults can be assisted through helping them develop new learning skills and techniques. Old adults are also limited at times by the conventional values assigned to them by our age-graded society. While there is some decline in the perceptual functions with age, there is much compensation. Often the perceived deficit is the result of a lack of self-confidence or lack of intellectual exercise, resulting from stereotypes that limit opportunities for the elderly to be intellectually active. Effective academic endeavors can be carried on by most adults well into their 70s. Motivation is different for older learners, however. Novelty is of less value to older learners; new skills and information are interesting insofar as they enable learners to cope with present life situations.

5. Environmental Influence

Life-style and personality patterns of earlier years set the stage for the functioning of old persons. Individuals with a life-style of conflict or perceived vulnerability often find retirement debilitating. Individuals experienced in a life-style of adaptation and effectiveness in problem solving, and who have some choice in planning their later years, usually find retirement a satisfying experience. Sudden or severe loss of environmental support—through death of a spouse, being moved from a familiar community and friends, or lack of income—may have major negative effects on the individual, resulting in lowered morale and increased susceptibility to physical illness. Environmental conditions that have been found associated with longer lives include a history of satisfactory work experience, high intelligence, sound financial status, intact marriages, lower food intake, and abstinence from smoking (Botwinick 1973). In earlier stages of life, role exits lead to valued new roles, for example, from school to job. With increasing age, role exits are less likely to lead to socially valued roles. Retirement and widowhood are role exits in which morale and physical health are significantly influenced by how the individual deals with these exits, whether the individual is able to experience these as transitions into new roles (Rosow 1976).

5.1 Retirement

In earlier periods of history, only the wealthy could afford to retire. In 1900, two-thirds of the men over 65 were working; in 1960 it had dropped to one-third. The manner in which retirement comes about influences its effect on the individual. If the individual can choose his or her own time and pace of retirement, adjustment is usually a smooth transition. Finances may be a cause of concern; retirees often move from a period of highest earnings to positions where their income is the least it has ever been during adult life.

Health tends to improve rather than decline following retirement. The individual's earlier life pattern offers the best predictor of how that person will experience such later life transitions as retirement. For some the interruption caused by retirement brings frustration and a pressured searching to find new ways of self-expression. For others, the decreasing importance of economic achievement frees them to focus on long-desired interpersonal experiences. Many retired persons spend part of their time in travel and other leisure pursuits. For some, social isolation may be a problem in life.

5.2 Widowhood

Although the majority of people in the beginning years of old age are living with their spouses, widowhood increases during this period. It is rare that both spouses die simultaneously. With increasing length of life, widowhood can be expected to last for a longer time. Because women tend to live longer than men, it is unlikely that the rate of remarriage will increase. Nearly five out of six widowed persons in the United States are female. About 60 percent of widowed persons over 65 live alone; 30 percent live with family; 10 percent live with nonrelatives or in institutions (US Bureau of Census 1979). When widowed people live with relatives, it is more likely to be with a daughter than with a son.

In widowhood, old statuses and roles are lost and new relationships must be substituted in order to effect a satisfactory adjustment. Transition to widowhood is made difficult by the lack of clearly defined cultural expectations and by the loss of supportive relationships (Lopota 1973). The loss of a spouse puts a strain on other relationships the individual has with family, neighbors, and community groups. Women tend to maintain family ties somewhat better than men. Suicide is more prevalent among widowers than among widows.

6. Family Life and Leisure

It is an erroneous notion that people in old age have little contact with family. Although the extended family with several generations living under the same roof is not the norm in Western nations, modern communications and transportation make possible frequent contact among family members. There is an increase in families of three and four generations. A young-old person is quite likely to have at least one surviving parent and one married child and one or more grandchildren. Grandparenting is identified as one of the primary satisfactions of old age.

There are often various combinations of intergenerational exchanges of psychological support and other kinds of assistance. Some elderly are involved in assisting grown children and caring for grandchildren; other old people have responsibilities for their even older, and often frail, parents. Many older women are part of the labor force and also have family responsibilities that involve both their children's families and their own parents' needs.

While there is generally a high level of assistance from parents to children, older persons—at least in industrialized Western nations—often prefer to live separately from the younger generations. This is manifest by the growing number of retirement communities. The majority of old people, however, live in two kinds of settings: the inner city and rural/farm areas.

In the years to come, the educational level of elderly people will continue to increase, as persons who grew up after compulsory education laws were in place reach retirement years. Education is likely to be a major leisure-time activity, since those with advanced education are inclined to seek more education.

People in old age continue to eat out and attend concerts, sports events, and church services, following interests characteristic of their earlier life-style. Factors such as education, finances, and transportation figure predominantly in their choice of activities. Those who belonged to country clubs, participated in music guilds, or were frequent users of the library continue this pattern in old age. Senior centers provide a resource for many older persons, particularly those from low-income groups. About one-fourth of those over 65 indicate that they provide active volunteer service. Many older persons state that if a job is worth doing, it is worth having a salary. Political activism, such as Grey Panthers, and involvement with church and social group projects, are also a part of the self-expression of people in old age. In attitude studies older people express more interest in religion than young adults do. However, this is more in the personal domain. They participate in church activities at about the same level as other adults.

7. Educational Implications

The fact that people, as they grow older, process incoming stimuli more slowly suggests that they need to be given the opportunity to absorb information at their own pace. Schaie and Parr (1981) recommend that educators distinguish between those aspects of the older learner's intellectual competence that are related to perceptual speed and those that are related to sensory activity. Prosthetic devices and appropriate classroom sound and lighting can greatly improve the learning experience for the elderly. Also important is the recognition that older learners strive to integrate new information within the pattern of meaning from their lifelong experience. They focus selectively, emphasizing context over content (Schaie and Parr 1981). The fact that individual differences increase among the elderly underscores the importance of individualized counseling in planning educational programs for them. Effective education for people in old age requires programs and teachers that are prepared with their uniqueness in mind.

The following are some of the reasons for having education programs for, and about, old age:

(a) Intelligence is a developmental factor requiring continuing exercise, however, in the average community there is little stimulation or opportunity for older persons to be involved in intellectual activity.

(b) The prejudice of agism expresses itself in misinformation and lack of information about old age. Even the elderly themselves agree with the negative stereotypes associated with old age, although they exclude themselves (Harris et al. 1975).

(c) While many persons enjoy their most satisfying sexual experiences in old age, others are deterred by misinformation and fear that sexual capacities will fail them.

(d) Guidance in reminiscence and life review can assist the elderly to gain a sense of well-being associated with Erikson's last developmental stage, integrity.

(e) Information and encouragement can help the elderly to have better exercise, improved nutrition, and a healthy life-style.

(f) Education and social support assist individuals to prepare for role changes such as retirement and widowhood.

The elderly in the 1980s will be of a cohort that is more inclined to seek education and other support services than were previous groups (Gatz et al. 1980). They will also be more inclined to provide services to peers through paraprofessional services, self-help groups, and peer counseling. Therefore, there will be a demand for training programs focusing on the skills of the helping relationship and built on a foundational understanding of the developmental processes of old age.

While only about 5 percent of the elderly are in nursing homes at any one time, in certain Western countries there is an increasing expectation that families of the future will care for their older members in their own homes, as has been the practice in most societies in the past. With the increasing frequency of four-generation families, many young-old will assume special responsibilities as their parents become frail. These new family constellations underscore the family's need not only for education about the characteristics of old age but also for family-life education that helps the family clarify and develop skills in new role relationships in the family.

Bibliography

Botwinick J 1973 *Aging and Behavior*. Springer, New York

Chickering A W, Havighurst R W 1981 The life cycle. In: Chickering A W (ed.) 1981 *The Modern American College*. Jossey-Bass, San Francisco, California

Erikson E H 1978 Reflections on Dr. Borg's life cycle. In: Erikson E H (ed.) 1978 *Adulthood*. Norton, New York

Gatz M, Smyer M, Lawton M P 1980 The mental health system and the older adult. In: Poon L W (ed.) 1980 *Aging in the 1980s: Psychological Issues*. American Psychological Association, Washington, DC

Guttman D 1977 The cross-cultural perspective toward a comparative psychology of aging. In: Birren J W, Schaie K W (eds.) 1977 *Handbook on the Psychology of Aging*. Van Nostrand Reinhold, New York

Harris L et al. 1975 *The Myth and Reality of Aging in America*. National Council on the Aging, Washington, DC

Lopota H Z 1973 *Widowhood in America*. Schenkman, Cambridge, Massachusetts

Maas H S, Kuypers J 1974 *From Thirty to Seventy*. Jossey-Bass, San Francisco, California

Neugarten B L 1977 Personality and aging. In: Birren J W, Schaie K W (eds.) 1977 *Handbook of the Psychology of Aging*. Van Nostrand Reinhold, New York

Palmore E B 1975 *The Honorable Elders: A Cross-cultural Analysis of Aging in Japan*. Duke University Press, Durham, North Carolina

Rosow I 1976 Status and role change. In: Bainstock R, Shanas E (eds.) 1976 *Handbook of Aging and the Social Sciences*. Van Nostrand Reinhold, New York

Schaie K W, Parr J 1981 Intelligence. In: Chickering A W (ed.) 1981 *The Modern American College*. Jossey-Bass, San Francisco, California

United States Bureau of the Census 1979 Marital status and living arrangements: March 1978. *Current Population Reports*, Series P-20, No. 338. US Government Printing Office, Washington, DC

Part 4

Intellectual Development

Part 4

Intellectual Development

Introduction

When attempting to understand a person's development it is necessary to contend with the problem of seeking to view the individual as a unified organism, yet at the same time having to analyze the person part by part. This problem arises because each human being is comprised of so many components that interact in such complicated ways that no one can comprehend all these complexities simultaneously in order to understand the person as a whole. As a result, researchers have been obliged to inspect the components separately and to analyze the ways they interact in producing a being who behaves as a single, unified person. The articles in Parts 4, 5, and 6 reflect the necessity to dissect people into separate components in an effort to comprehend human development.

An initial step of dissection and analysis is that of identifying the kinds of components into which a human can profitably be analyzed. Over the centuries, the most common division has been the bipartite division of body and mind. However, in some religious traditions the distinction has been tripartite—body, mind, and soul. Within each of these principal categories, subdivisions have often been distinguished. At the most detailed level, the body has been analyzed into hundreds of subcategories, as books on human anatomy and physiology attest. While there is relatively little controversy over what components make up the physical being, there has been great controversy over what components make up the rest of a human. Debate continues over the question of whether such concepts as *mind, personality, ego, self, soul, intellect*, and *emotion* represent suitable constructs to be employed for the analysis of human development.

As the articles comprising Parts 4, 5, and 6 were organized, the problem of choosing the manner in which humans may most usefully be divided to reveal relationships between development and education arose. An inspection of the article titles reveals that a single systematic taxonomy was not adopted for this purpose. Rather, the components were chosen on pragmatic grounds. The primary division of the person follows a rather traditional pattern that centers on mental aspects (Part 4: Intellectual Development), physical aspects (Part 5: Psycho-physical Development), and social aspects (Part 6: Social and Cultural Interactions with Development). Within each of these major categories, articles were selected either because they appear frequently in textbooks on human development, or because they represent aspects of development which received little attention in the past but have become prominent in recent times. Examples of traditional subjects are: intelligence, motivation, memory, transfer of learning, language acquisition, and physical fitness. Examples of subjects of recent prominence are: social cognition, field dependence, one-parent families, child abuse, and children's effects on adults.

Part 4 is comprised of 27 articles, divided into four sections. The first section, Mental Development in General, introduces traditional general concerns in the realm of intellectual development, namely *Cognitive Development, Abilities and Aptitudes*, and the nature of intelligence. In the opening article, Murray traces the growing use of the term *cognitive development* and then reviews ways in which Piagetian theory has contributed to the understanding of children's progress in cognitive tasks. *Abilities and Aptitudes*, and their relationship to major current theories of intelligence, are analyzed by Pellegrino and Varnhagen in the following two articles. The final article in this section reviews studies of the influence of hereditary and environmental factors on measured intelligence, including the effects of such environmental conditions as children's schooling and socioeconomic status.

Part 4(b) consists of seven articles dealing with Learning Processes. The first two articles discuss *Basic Concepts of Learning Theories* and *Historical Backgrounds of Learning Theory*. These two articles appear here rather than in Part 2 under General Theories of Human Development, so that readers will have an immediate overview of learning theories before examining separate aspects of the learning process treated by the remaining five articles in this Part. These articles include entries on *Motivation, Perception, Memory, Transfer of Learning*, and the relationship between *Cognitive Style and Learning*.

Analyses of intellectual development often divide mental life into varieties of cognitive activity. Part 4(c) includes 12 entries organized in such a fashion. The first three center on general *Communication Skills Development, Language Acquisition and Human Development*, and *Bilingualism*. The remaining articles describe *Attitude Development, Mastery Motivation, Social Cognition, Social Perception, Creativity, Creativity and Individual Development, Spatial Cognition, Drawing and Individual Development*, and *Humor*.

In scholars' struggle to understand humans as unified organisms in contrast to analyzing them as a combination of separate parts, some theorists have sought to solve the problem by focusing on what they conceive to be the essence of the individual person. In other words, they seek to understand the nature of an individual's central unifying, coordinating function. This essence has most often been called the *self*. The final section in Part 4 is concerned with The Self in the Environment. The first two articles deal with matters of *Self-concept* and *Self-control*. The third focuses on humanistic psychologists' notion of *Self-actualization*. The last article, entitled *Field Dependence* and *Field Independence*, concerns the degree to which an individual's judgments are influenced by factors in the environment as contrasted with his or her own self-determined perceptions.

Mental Development in General

Cognitive Development

F. B. Murray

The term cognitive development scarcely appeared in the psychological or educational literature until the early 1960s. By 1970 it had become one of the principal ways psychologists, particularly developmental psychologists, organized their discipline. One of the five parts of the definitive *Carmichael's Manual of Child Psychology* (1970) and 35 percent of its content, for example, were devoted to cognitive development. Some reasons for this rapid and pervasive assimilation of a term into the discipline are given below.

The term refers to the changes in the act of knowing that occur throughout the human lifespan. Whether all the changes in knowing are developmental remains a matter of debate between developmental theorists, but there is consensus that the changes in cognition to which the term refers should be stable and occur over relatively long periods (months and years). Apart from this limitation the meaning of the term is tied to particular theories of cognition and models of human development.

1. Changing Conceptions of Cognition

Cognition is the act of knowing and the analysis of the act and its components has become the core of psychologists' and educators' attempts to understand the mind. Cognition is a troublesome term in psychology, because it has no clear referent. It has been defined so narrowly as to refer only to "awareness" (Guilford 1967) and so broadly by others as to include all higher mental processes (perception, thinking, attention, language, reasoning, problem solving, creativity, memory, and intelligence). Even though the term cognition was not used until the early 1960s, it is still fair to say that the concern of psychology has always been about cognition.

When William James (1890) proposed the new discipline of psychology as "the science of mental life," it was clear then, as it is now, that the mind was the proper object of study for the new discipline. The science James and others inaugurated before the turn of the century was more a hope for a science than a science, since the available research methodologies amounted to little more than having people report the activities of their own minds. This introspective method yielded little

information that met the scientific criterion of replicability, although over the years matters improved on this account as researchers learned that replicability could be had by carefully contriving and controlling the situation in which the introspections occurred (Lachman et al. 1979).

Throughout its relatively short history as an experimental science, psychology, which had no theoretical model of its own for the mind, borrowed major concepts and models from other disciplines. Borrowing initially from atomic theory and Lockean epistemology, psychologists searched for the mental atoms that were bonded by the principles of association (proximity, temporality, similarity) first laid down by Aristotle. These efforts to identify the atomic structure of the mind gave way somewhat, under the influence of the theory of evolution, to considerations of the mind's functions rather than its structure. Whatever its structure, what it does is what required explanation. Until quite recently the question of the structure of the mind was answered inevitably by the postulation of association mechanisms and structures that mediated or stood between the stimulus and the person's response to it. The examination of the functions of mind in the survival of our species through learning and problem-solving mechanisms dominated psychological research until the 1960s, particularly in the United States.

During the same period the rapid advances of field theory in physics found its counterpart in the Gestalt psychologies of perception. The invention of topology in mathematics led again to considerations of structure, this time the "topological" structures of personality. More recently the Bourbaki group of logicians provided Jean Piaget with a model for the development of children's reasoning, and advances in linguistic theory by Noam Chomsky supported the contemporary notion of the mind as an innate system of plans and rules which underlies our competence to know things, particularly language.

The work of Piaget, although largely ignored in the United States until the 1960s, and the work of Chomsky beginning in the late 1950s paved the way for the contemporary study of cognition. (For an elaboration of their opposed points of view, see Piatelli–Palmarini

1980.) From the First World War until 1960, United States psychology in particular was dominated by a behavioristic approach which focused on learning, and held that a science of mind was not possible except insofar as it was a science of behavior. Furthermore, the principal theoretical factor in the explanation of a behavior was the consequence of the behavior, whether it was reinforced positively or negatively (see *History and Educational Applications of Behaviorism*). The work of Piaget, for example, showed that the child's acquisition of certain logical–mathematical ideas (such as if A = B and B = C, then A = C) was not so simply explained by reinforcement principles. For example, by using reinforcement procedures, it proved difficult (some said impossible) to teach the child that A had to equal C, given their relationship to B. Chomsky and others showed that the language the child acquired, particularly during his or her first two years, seemed entirely too complicated to have been shaped simply by environmental events which followed the child's babblings. The child's language competence seemed generated by elaborate rules that the child simply would not have had time to master if they had to be acquired in accordance with the prevailing learning theories.

When the post-Sputnik curriculum reforms were being designed and applied in the 1960s, many psychologists and educators turned away from the then current learning theories, which emphasized the reinforced associations between stimuli and responses, and turned toward the study of cognition, which was emerging as a new approach to the study of the higher mental processes.

Although earlier attempts to specify the mind's inner workings had failed, what now convinced psychologists that their new approach—a renewed attack on so-called cognitive processes—would succeed was the development of computer programs. The new model, borrowed this time from computer engineering, was the model of a mind as an information processor that does many of the things computers do (accept information, manipulate and transform it, store it, retrieve it). As Neisser (1976) points out, the fact of computers gave psychologists reassurance that cognitive processes were as real as the muscular and glandular responses that comprised behaviors. Moreover the development of artificial-intelligence computer programs, which could do things people do in ways that were indistinguishable from the ways people do them, reinforced the belief that cognitive processes can be understood by the development of computer programs which simulate human higher order behavior (like playing chess, proving theorems, writing poems, diagnosing illnesses, landing airplanes). A computer program that plays chess as well as a person can then serve as a good theory of what the person is doing—whether aware of it or not—when playing chess (see *Information-processing Theory*).

Although the mind as a computer metaphor nour-

ished theories of cognitive psychology, the empirical need to support these theories with precise measures of the flow of information through the mind generated new research techniques and paradigms. Most of these avoided the need for introspection by carefully constructing tasks for research subjects and by precisely timing a person's responses to various tasks (Posner 1978) or by tracking a person's eye movements (Cohen 1978). Newell (1973) cataloged 59 cognitive research paradigms, for example.

These techniques, coupled with models of the mind as an information processor, constitute the approach to the science of the mind known as cognitive psychology. As cognitive psychologists have analyzed how the reading process works or how basic arithmetical operations are or can be carried out, educators have been quick to see the implications for the sequencing of curricular information (Siegler 1981, Shavelson 1981, Farnham-Diggory 1978). Although the "cognitive" approach is not without its critics, it can point to some achievements. The most significant have been in the general field of memory.

Throughout the 1960s and 1970s cognitive psychologists created several models of the mind (Lachman et al. 1979). These all divided up the act of knowing into its component processes, some of which could be reduced to well-established neurophysiological events. The models all stressed mental processes over mental content. The processes are the actions that depend upon biological features and that take place in real time. On the other hand, the contents of cognition (symbol systems, knowledge, etc.) are acquired culturally, not biologically, and have a meaning that is independent of time, as Blumenthal (1977) notes. Although the processes create the content, there is an independence between them as in the classic case of arithmetic in which people's ability to do large-scale mental arithmetic is limited by process constraints that have no counterpart in the content of the discipline of arithmetic itself.

The models were rarely developmental; that is, they attempted to specify only the cognitive capacity of mature persons, and did not account for any changes in the organism's capacity over the lifespan. The models defined the developmental end point of cognitive development; only recently have developmental psychologists begun a systematic exploration of the changes in information processing over the lifespan (Siegler 1981). They have also taken up the question of the child's cognition of cognition (called metacognition) and have found generally that children's ideas about the workings of their own minds are consistent with their developing knowledge about everything else.

The models stressed psychological function over neurophysiology insofar as the behavioral phenomena would be true and meaningful regardless of the neural actions that might "cause" them. Although the model builders have been constrained by neurophysiological findings, most notably by the split-brain research and clinical neurology literature on hemispheric dominance (Cohen 1977, Glass et al. 1979), few features of the models can be reduced directly to brain events (see *Brain Laterality*). Because the complex interconnected firings of 14 billion cells may preclude in principle the prediction of cognitive events in any case, neurophysiological fidelity may not be a significant criterion for adequate cognitive models (see *Brain Development and Function*).

Since the early 1960s the cognition models have shared by and large these features: (a) the components of knowing are thought to be serially connected, although parallel functioning is sometimes thought to occur during the initial knowing stages; (b) information from the environment is generally thought to receive some processing independent of attention to it. This information is collected or aggregated in sensory buffers or collectors for brief periods (0.75 seconds). These buffers cause input delays and are needed in any systems in which the capacity to receive information exceeds the capacity to process it. Most of the information or the experience created in the buffer is lost, but when attentional processing occurs, some of it is transferred to a short-term memory store, where the information quickly decays (in about 5–20 seconds) unless it is continually attended to and reinstated. Here it is recognized or identified for what it is through an interaction of higher level and lower level processing; and sometimes it is recoded in verbal form. Some of the information in the limited short-term store can be shifted with rehearsal and study to a relatively unlimited long-term store, where it can be maintained without conscious attention more or less indefinitely (see *Memory*).

This oversimplified sketch of the dominant information processing models is expanded and critiqued in many current texts (Cohen 1977, Glass et al. 1979, Anderson 1980, Wessells 1982). Despite the tremendous technological progress brought about by the new cognitive methodologies of mental chronometry, eye-movement tracking, computer simulation, and so on, the actual advances in knowledge of cognition have been slight (Cohen 1977). The empirical findings are constantly challenged by new experiments (Glass et al. 1979), and specific theoretical models are so rapidly invented and discarded that firm summaries of the field are not possible.

Information-processing models have allowed psychologists to gain substantial insight into such mental processes as memory, but only the surface has thus far been scratched; and, as in all science, more questions are raised than answered. For educators, the implications of this model are substantial. For curriculum development, the implications rest on the ability to design curricula that maximize the potential storage of information in meaningful and organized fashion consistent with the organizational properties of human memory. For teaching children how to learn, the implications concern the teaching of potentially useful and powerful strategies for efficient storage and retrieval of information and the teaching of different strategies applicable to different purposes of information processing.

2. Models of Human Development

The most primitive, yet essential, kind of scientific law merely states how a behavior or event varies with time. Until quite recently the field of cognitive development consisted, almost exclusively, of such laws and relationships. In these, such cognitive variables as the number of words the child knew, or the number of digits he or she could recall, or the child's susceptibility to visual illusions, or his or her knowledge of some subject matter domain (ethics, physics, arithmetic) or his or her reasoning competence, and so forth were plotted as a function of children's ages, yielding age norms for every conceivable mental ability and achievement.

Apart from readily conceded doubts about the reliability and generalizability of such norms, there was the realization that time is never a cause of anything and that only the causative factors which operated in time were the true objects of study. It was clear that theories of development (that is theories of the causes of how cognition came to be the way the cognitive psychologists were finding it to be) were needed—if only to tell researchers what cognitive variables were worth measuring and counting. Should researchers, for example, keep track of the number of words the child uses, or the type of word, or the number of morphemes, or some ratio of one to another, and so forth? On the one hand, the available theories of cognition provided guidance, but on the other, there were theoretical questions that arose strictly from the consideration of the development of cognitive competence. For example, how was the integrity of the person's way of knowing preserved over time while so much of what he or she knew was changing? Were the changes essentially changes in degree or quantity or were they qualitatively different from what went before? Were there, in fact, stages or breaks in the continuity of cognition over time and so forth? The theories of cognitive development divide themselves along two lines—those focusing on differences in what factors or types of causes provide a complete and adequate account of a cognitive change and those centering on differences in the factors or mechanisms with which each theory endows an organism so that it will end with a human mind.

2.1 Types of Causes or Determiners

Aristotle identified four types of causes or determiners and his analysis, ancient as it is, provides a useful way to distinguish the two principal models of human development. To know and understand an event or object completely one model (the so-called mechanistic model) requires the specification of the first two causes while the other model (the so-called organismic model) requires, in addition, the specification of the third and fourth causes. The four causes, traditionally, have been labeled:

(a) The material cause: the substance out of which the thing is made.
(b) The efficient cause: the agent which made the thing happen or which caused it in the usual sense of the word.
(c) The formal cause: the form or structure of the thing; that which makes it a *this* or a *that*.
(d) The final cause: the purpose, significance, meaning, or final end of the thing.

Thus to explain or know any cognitive change it is necessary to determine the underlying muscular, glandular, neurological activities which comprise it (material cause); the environmental events which stimulate, trigger, and modify it (efficient cause); the name of the change insofar as the name identifies a structure or pattern (the formal cause); and its purpose or how it fits in with everything else (the final cause).

Psychologists, by and large, have restricted themselves to the determination of the efficient causes, which they have tended to think of as the stimuli which cause or elicit the responses and maintain them thereafter. Formal causes are talked about speculatively in various theories in which claims are made that certain responses or behaviors are part of a pattern, form a stage, or have unique characteristics which single them out from all other behaviors; that is, they have a certain form or structure.

The very naming of a response or a collection of responses is the beginning of the specification of the behavior's formal cause. Although highly arbitrary and speculative at the present time, convincing labels or names for cognitive periods and subperiods are an indispensable part of scientific progress. Historians are faced with the same problem in their field. Their effort to explicate our race and culture's past forces them to examine the formal causes of historical events, to see them as part of other structurally similar events, as part of the progressive era, for example, or as part of an age of anxiety, or era of good feeling, and so forth.

Consider the causes of the following simple behavior: when a light comes on, the subject is to remove the ball of his extended forefinger from a stylus; if he does not, an electric shock will be delivered through the stylus to his finger within five seconds. The material cause is fairly clear, namely certain muscles and nerves comprise the response; the efficient cause also is evident, namely the light and the subject's anticipation of the shock. The formal cause is the withdrawal of the finger. To see that it is distinct from the other causes, consider what would happen were the subject to turn his hand upside down so that his fingernail rested on the stylus. When the light came on, the finger would surely be withdrawn, but propelled by the opposing set of muscles or by a very different, in fact opposite, material cause. There is something quite apart from the specific responses themselves which nevertheless indicate that these opposite responses are really the same response. This something is the formal cause. The responses are the same because they have the same form, the same structure; they are a "withdrawal response" for want of a better label. In intellectual tasks, like the Genevan (Piagetian) operativity tasks, it is often the case that opposite responses may in fact indicate the same underlying intellectual structure, operation, or scheme.

The explication of the final cause of the withdrawal response would entail the specification of the purposes of such a response for the organism, how the response was integrated with all the organism's other responses, how the response fits into the lifespan of the organism and perhaps the evolution of the organism. The issue of the response's final cause is raised when the following questions are asked: What is the meaning of this behavior? What significance does it have?

Although psychologists search for efficient causes and speculate about formal causes, they have left the search for material causes to other disciplines, principally biology, and most have argued, along with other scientists, that the search for final causes should be left to philosophy or theology. In fact, new disciplines of physiological psychology and behavioral genetics deal exclusively with the material causes of behavior. Whether it will be possible to reduce all the contents of our minds to various features of brain chemistry is a legitimate question, often called the reductionism issue. The truth of psychological laws, of course, will not be affected in the end by whether or not it becomes possible to link them to physiological processes. For instance, Mendel's discoveries in 1865 of the principles of genetics are true, quite apart from the later linking of his hypothetical constructs with the physical and chemical structure of the hereditary materials. The truth of psychological laws is in no way dependent upon their link to physiological laws, although the establishment of that link would advance both fields immeasurably.

The search for final causes is a different matter and many scientists argue that the consideration of final cause has no place in science. One argument is that final causation violates the fundamental notion that the cause always comes before what it causes. Final causes would seem to come after, since the goal or purpose of an event comes after it. On the other hand, final causes make the phenomena intelligible; so to exclude them from theorizing seems unwise, particularly in cognitive psychology where certain features of early cognitive development make more sense when viewed from the perspective of what comes after them and what they lead to. Thus, the complete explanation of the infant's early language or logic is facilitated by an examination of what it leads to, what the final form of language and logic turn out to be. The contents and processes of the infant mind may only be understandable in terms of their contribution to and link to the adult mind.

The field of cognitive psychology, like other parts of

psychology, is divided upon the question of whether final causes, even formal causes, are a legitimate, nonparsimonious part of psychology. The conservative position is that an adequate discipline can be based solely on the specification of efficient causes. Theories in this tradition, as has been noted, are often viewed as mechanistic (e.g., Skinner, Bandura) while those that demand consideration of the full range of Aristotelian causality have been termed organismic in the sense that an individual behavior can only be understood as part of a system, as part of a totality of the organism's behavior (e.g. Werner, Piaget) and all other organisms with which it interacts. There exists an ecology of behavior in other words, a macrosystem of behavior which transcends each individual.

This division persists throughout the discipline of psychology, and a good deal of controversy in the discipline reduces itself to debates, usually fruitless, between those who view human behavior from a mechanistic perspective and those who take an organismic perspective. The debate is fruitless only because each judges the other to be attempting to answer the wrong questions, no matter how well; in fact, each does answer the questions. (See Reese and Overton 1970 for an elaboration of this point.)

The psychological study of infant cognition is permeated with this division, for example, and it has generated fascinating research results which all point to the fact that the infant is much more cognitively competent than most researchers had previously thought. From the mechanistic viewpoint, the infant is essentially a bundle of reflexes and all the infant will become is largely the effects of the basic learning and imitation mechanisms on his initial responses. Behaviors would be expanded, strengthened, or weakened as a function of their consequences, and the infant is thought to add still other behaviors to his or her repertoire by imitating certain behaviors performed by models. Researchers with an organismic perspective, while not denying the obvious truth of conditioning and imitation, were directed to search for the underlying form and structure of the infant's cognitive competence. In the process, new research techniques were invented which enabled researchers to probe the structure and content of the infant's mind (see *History and Educational Applications of Behaviorism; Social Learning Theory*).

2.2 Two Models of Cognitive Development

The assumptions researchers and theorists make about the nature of cognitive changes leads some to reject formal and final causes as an indispensable part of a complete theory of cognitive development (see Reese and Overton 1970). Such theorists tend to view a cognitive change (such as the child's eventual awareness that 2 + 3 not only equals 5, but that it must equal 5, that it has to equal 5, that it could not equal any other number) as a response event which (a) is understandable and predictable by itself, (b) is reducible to links of prior cognitive events which determined it, (c) is largely

under the control of events outside the organism, and (d) is best understood as a change in a response.

While not denying the truth and need of material and efficient causal factors in their account of cognitive development, other researchers and theorists focus on the change or activity itself and see it as not wholly reducible to prior events; that is, they see the emergence of the child's appreciation of necessity as a somewhat spontaneous event, qualitatively different from his or her prior way of thinking, under the control of internal structures and regulations, as part of a system of events which determines its form and emergence. It is a change that is not entirely predictable from earlier developments. It is not just that a response changes, but rather a structure or pattern or an organization changes. Most importantly the changes are unidirectional, always in the direction of more general, more coherent and consistent systems which progressively enhance the competence of the individual and species to know.

2.3 Theories of Cognitive Development

Theories are shaped by the assumptions mentioned above and to some extent by the particular aspects of cognitive development explained by the theory—language, concepts, logical reasoning, and so on. The class of theories which make mechanistic or exclusive efficient cause assumptions, provide tolerably good explanations for many concept-formation and learning phenomena. To the extent that cognitive developments (changes that occur in periods of months or years) are looked at as the accumulated result of many small changes due to learning which each took place in minutes, hours, or days, then cognitive developmental theories can be viewed as a special case of learning theory. On the whole cognitive development theories of this sort (mechanistic) need only postulate the existence and functioning of the following competencies: (a) basic reflexes, (b) the ability to be conditioned, (c) principles of association (proximity, contiguity, and similarity), (d) imitative and modeling mechanisms and (e) mediational mechanisms. Theories which stem from models which require formal and final causes (organismic) postulate the existence of a system activity which has mechanisms which preserve or conserve the system (e.g., assimilation), mechanisms which promote modification and flexibility in the system (e.g., accommodation), and a regulatory principle by which the system is made more coherent, consistent, and general (e.g., equilibration). These theories provide tolerably good explanations for language development and the development of logical thought.

3. A Specific Organismic Theory: Piaget's Developmental Theory

The theories of Jean Piaget and his Genevan colleagues are the most mature of the organismic theories of cognitive development, both from the perspective of the specificity and completeness of the theoretical mechanisms and from the perspective of the richness of the empirical findings the theories have generated (see *Piaget's Theory of Genetic Epistemology*).

Despite his death in 1980, it is clear that Piaget's account of intellectual development still progresses, and Piaget, near the end of his life, only claimed that he had:

> . . .laid bare a more or less evident general skeleton which remains full of gaps so that when these gaps will be filled, the articulations will have to be differentiated, but the general lines of the system will not be changed. (Sinclair-deZwart 1977 p. 1)

That the theory would be open ended and tentative and subjected to major revisions is in part a validation of it as a developmental theory that is developing. For example, the work, *The Equilibration of Cognitive Structures* in 1975 replaces and contradicts the earlier 1957 work, *Logic and Equilibrium* (Sinclair-deZwart 1977). Equally forceful are the forthcoming modifications in the theory required by the research findings of hundreds of researchers, with the result that, if anything, the surprising competence of the younger child and unevenness in adult thought has blunted the distinctions between the classic stages and softened the claims of the differences between children, adolescents, and adults (Vuyk 1981).

Still, the general lines of the system remain, and to understand the implications of Piaget's theory of intellectual development for educational practice, it is first necessary to understand that the theory is not, strictly speaking, a psychological or educational theory. It is not concerned primarily with the explanation and prediction of psychological or educational phenomena, although it may illuminate these phenomena. The theory has its origins in certain classic epistemological questions that it proposes to resolve through a treatment of how these philosophical concepts, dilemmas, and paradoxes have evolved and developed in thought. The point is that Piaget's work seeks to resolve through a method of "experimental philosophy," as Elkind (1976) has called it, certain philosophical issues, such as the reduction of causality to correlation, the priority or absoluteness of time or velocity, or the essence of number as a class or set or a relation.

The theory that results is a theory of human behavior in exactly the same sense as grammar is a theory of language behavior or the program of a chess-playing computer is a theory of how humans play that game. The theory is, in other words, a competence model or theory and tells only that people behave *as if* they were constructing the structures that Piaget claims define each of the stages. The properties of stages are in fact more properly properties of the theory than behavior and indicate only that the explanation for concrete operational thought (or period), for example, will not suffice for the kind of reasoning done later in life.

The basic theoretical constructs Piaget proposes for intellectual functioning are (a) a system of schemes or patterns of activity—not the activity or response itself—but rather its form, pattern, or structure, and (b) the balancing or equilibration of two mechanisms—one to conserve or preserve the system of schemes (assimilation) and the other to modify and transform the system (accommodation). It is a common mistake to think of these mechanisms, especially accommodation, as responses to "reality" as if there were some external reality independent of the reality embedded in the structural system and constructed by it. From this perspective, it may be clearer why or how Piaget claims that while maturation, learning, and imitation are necessary for cognitive change, they are insufficient for it; and why Piaget's constructs should not be reified. They do not really exist as material or efficient causes, and they have the same relation to intelligence as grammar does to speaking.

The appropriate model of equilibration is not the beam balance, but the analytical balance in chemistry. It is a balance of a self-regulated set of simultaneous interactions between the elements of the system in which, so to speak, the swings of balance continually increase in amplitude and power and do not dampen to a prior equilibrium. The theory suggests that the difficulties in school learning are more likely to be consequences of incomplete structure than faulty or distorted information. A major contribution of Piaget's viewpoint to education is merely the provision for a way to conceptualize the instructional problem as the interaction and integration of perceptual and linguistic content (images, figures) with a system of cognitive or intellectual operations or structures. These seem to be best described as a mathematical group because of their ability to produce any member of the system from any two and to convert any member to an identity element.

Education or schooling is largely, and perhaps to some extent mistakenly, concerned with the acquisition of information (what is the country's population or capital?) and skills (3 Rs), while Piaget's theory is concerned with the development of knowledge and thinking, that is, things that are known to be true because they *must* be true, and they have to be true because they are consistent, have coherence, and can be deduced from other things. The relationship between information and knowledge, content and structure, is subtle and profound. Whatever implications there are from genetic epistemology for education, they deal only with the knowledge of things that are necessarily true, that are always true, that have to be true, and the process by which such knowledge develops. The relation and dependence of this knowledge upon information and fact, arbitrary as it might be, is the major research and theoretical problem of the decade for the behaviorial sciences and education. The range of concepts the Genevans have researched since the early 1930s has sampled the major curriculum areas well. Even though the Genevan intention was not to provide such a corpus, one by-product of their research of necessary knowledge is this corpus on the development over the school years of many important concepts in mathematics, logic, social studies, ethics, politics, physics, chemistry, biology, psychology, language, and fine art.

Another important claim in this theory, and perhaps its most controversial one, is that knowledge develops out of systems of action and not language. Language is taken to be a poor medium for developing knowledge, especially before adolescence. This leads to the obvious, although not original or unique, educational implication that teaching by telling is inadequate unless a provision for the acquisition of the linguistic referents has been made previously.

In the main, the practical implications of Piaget's theory for education have already been made by others. In fact, what has really happened is that the theory has provided a theoretical justification for a number of long-standing educational innovations. For example, any instructional innovation, like progressive education, Montessori, open education, or discovery learning, for example, that makes a major provision for the self-initiated and self-regulated activity of the pupil can be justified in the theory. On the other hand, one over-riding curricular recommendation from the theory is that the demands of the curriculum sequence should match the competencies of the pupil's stage of cognitive development. That the curriculum sequence should be based upon the psychology of the developing child is not a novel idea, of course, but what makes it interesting in this case is that Piaget and his colleagues have made specific claims about the order in which specific curricular concepts and competencies develop.

For example, by the time children are 7 years old, they can respond to a number of problems more or less as an adult would respond to them. Before that time children tend to give quite surprising responses, such as that their brother has no brother (egocentrism); that a flattened clay ball has more clay, weighs more, and takes up more space than it did before it was flattened (conservation); that the water level in a tilted glass is parallel to the bottom of the glass (absolute space); that there are more girls in the class than children (class inclusion); that if John is older than Jim, and Jim is older than Bob, John may or may not be older than Bob (transitivity); that a person cannot be two things at the same time like an American and a Catholic (centration); or that a rearranged group of objects has more objects than it had before the objects were moved about (number conservation). These children under 7 tend also to focus their attention on only one aspect of a situation, such as noticing that a milk bottle and juice glass differ only in height while ignoring the difference in width. Similarly they seem incapable of ordering a set of 10 or so sticks according to their lengths (seriation) because, presumably, this would require thinking of the same stick as both longer than the stick to its right and shorter than the one to its left. As well, all kinds of sorting and classification tasks from simple sorting on one dimension to more complex two-by-two (or more)

classifications, are incorrectly performed by these children. Moreover, when they are pressed for their reasons for responding as they do, they resort finally to elaborate and preposterous justifications (justification at any price). All of these peculiarities in the young child's responses are characteristic of the preoperational stage of reasoning and place limitations upon comprehension. In the space of 3 or 4 years, however, the child's responses in these areas become very much like the adult's.

Piaget hypothesized that the ability to give adult-like responses in these instances rests upon the development of a system of operations. It is a system of reversible internalized actions that allows the child to mentally reconstruct the flattened ball as the original round ball (to reverse mentally the flattening transformation), to see himself as his brother's brother, to view the same object from more than one perspective or as on more than one dimension, and so on. This system of operations, furthermore, has the properties of a mathematical group (closure, associativity, identity, and inversion) and is both Piaget's description and explanation of the qualitative changes in the child's thinking that are found between 5 and 10 years of age.

These operations are taken to operate distinctly upon different content areas so that there appears to be little transfer between the child's solutions to problems. Thus, the child typically conserves number (that the number of objects in a set is unaffected by their spatial arrangement) before he conserves weight or volume. Or he may be able to classify animals before vehicles, although the principles of classification and deduction are the same in each case. The operations are said to be content, determined, or bound to specific *concrete* situations (hence, concrete operations).

A more comprehensive model of formal operations was proposed as the developmental end-point for logical thought and to provide an explanation for cognitive changes that occurred after the concrete operational period. Initially, it was felt that the formal operations would be relatively content and context free but there is now ample evidence that these operations are not applied uniformly across all knowledge domains but only across those in which the person has some expertise, familiarity, or training. The system of formal operations was proposed to account for the young adolescent's emerging competence in combinatorial reasoning, scientific hypothesizing, holding all factors constant but one, probabalistic reasoning, concepts of proportionality, syllogistic reasoning, and so forth.

4. Implications of Piagetian Theory for the Curriculum

A major issue in curriculum design is the sequence of subject matters since, if for no other reason, everything cannot be learned at once. On this issue Piagetian theory would appear to be most useful, containing, as it does, strong claims about the invariant sequence of intellectual development. While the dual recommendations of matching curricular demand and cognitive development or recapitulating that development in each learning episode are commonly made, the long span of time in the major stages can of necessity give little guidance to sequences within grade levels in any case. The well-known horizontal decalage phenomena, in which, for example, the concrete operations are successfully applied in a reliable order in subject matter domains (e.g., number, length, mass, weight, time, volume, density), do mark sequences within the stages. These could be of some use, but they cannot be derived from the theory because no theory at the moment explains them. The horizontal decalage phenomena are theoretical anomalies and threats to most structural theories as they are presently formulated. The theories are by this fact of little use in the sequencing of the parts of new subject matters except to caution the educational planner to expect these structural anomalies.

These within-stage lags or sequences of conceptual attainment are reliable but not predictable a priori. They are chiefly testaments to a well-known instructional phenomenon in which students' mastery of a principle in one area of the subject fails to transfer to other areas, even to those strikingly similar to the mastered area. While Piagetian research has delineated a number of such arresting sequences, which in fact define the concrete operational period, without a theory to link them, their significance for education remains clouded.

While the sequencing of curricular content is an inescapable matter, the prior issue of curriculum development is, of course, the nature of the content itself. No psychological theory has statements in it that prescribe curricular content. To the extent that the Piagetian tasks themselves become curricular elements, the theory contributes, along with the results of correlated research, to an understanding of the factors that are related to the child's performance on the task. At the very least the theory describes the intellectual problems and constructions on which the child is working at various ages. Should the school view its role as an assistant to natural conceptual development, the theory provides guidance for that role (Varma and Williams 1976) by identifying the contents and course of that development. To make the Piagetian tasks part of the curriculum is probably misguided as these tasks are mere diagnostic techniques for revealing the schema or operational structures that give the child's thought coherence. It is analogous to teaching intelligence-test items in an attempt to develop intelligence. To teach the properties of the logical models that describe intellectual operations as an attempt to foster intellectual development is equally wrong-headed in that it confuses competence and performance models.

No doubt much of the attention Piaget has received has been due to the surprising errors he discovered in children's conceptions. Presumably equally arresting errors remain to be discovered in children's understanding of other concepts in the traditional curriculum. The continued diagnosis of these peculiarities is recommended along the same clinical and critical exploration method lines that Piaget and his collaborators initiated and employ.

This approach provides no prescription to the curriculum writer for correcting these misconceptions; rather, it merely points out that these errors exist and that perhaps they should be treated.

5. Implications of Piagetian Theory for Instruction

Since 1961 over 150 research studies have been published that were designed specifically in one way or another to train young children between 4 and 7 years old to solve the problems the Genevans posed for children. Quite apart from the theoretical reasons that may have motivated and legitimized the attention scientific journals give to this issue, the thesis of this concluding section is that in these studies a number of precise teaching techniques were created and, more importantly, were evaluated. Moreover, the extensive experimental literature on conservation, of which the training literature is a small part, provides serendipitously a model for programmatic research in educational psychology.

A number of reviews of the conservation training literature exist (Beilin 1971, 1977, Brainerd and Allen 1971, Glaser and Resnick 1972, Goldschmidt 1971, Peill 1975, Strauss 1972, 1974–75, Murray 1978). Because Piagetian theory had claimed that conceptual development was under the sufficient control of unique and largely unmodifiable structural mechanisms, the intent of the early studies was to demonstrate that conservation could be trained and was amenable to conventional learning procedures. The failure of the first dozen training attempts (Flavell 1963) undoubtedly motivated the subsequent attempts with the result that there is no longer doubt that conservation can be taught (Beilin 1977). Still, there is an overwhelming and somewhat pessimistic result that training—even highly individualized training—is only successful (by whatever criteria) with about half the children in the sample, or, more precisely, that the children make about half the gains in conservation performance that could be made, although the gains are stable for as long as a month and are significantly different from pretest or control group subjects' performance (Murray 1978). This result seems to be as true for procedures that take as little as 5 minutes as it is for those that take an hour.

It also seems to be a well-supported, but not surprising, principle in this literature that the training effort needed to bring a behavior to criterion is most successful with behaviors that were initially closest to the criterion. The evidence for aptitude treatment interactions in this literature is scant, but there remains the theoretical issue of whether training is constrained by the child's developmental level.

It should be noted that many of these training strategies have face validity as classroom techniques and in many instances would seem to be a teacher's first response to a child who thought, for example, that the number of objects in a patterned array changed when the pattern changed.

The chief legacy of Piagetian theory for instruction has been and will continue to be the development and evaluation of specific training techniques for various school concepts even if the success of the technique may be more parsimoniously explained by another theory. The value of a theory, and ultimately its truth, is in the uses to which it is put. Piagetian theory's value to education is, by this criterion, not in dispute if even specific educational practices are not deducible from it. Such logical entailment is rare in science and virtually absent in the behavioral sciences, which leaves the discipline of education with a number of practices that are, while not derivable, at least consistent with the theory insofar as their not being specifically proscribed by it.

In summary, the only certain educational recommendation from a theory such as Piaget's is that schools should simulate "natural" human development; not that schooling is unnatural but, rather, that it promotes intellectual growth best when it is based upon natural mechanisms of intellectual development. These Piaget has tried to describe, and they suggest that schools are good when they place a high instructional premium upon self-initiated and self-regulated "discovery" learning activities in situations that demand social interactions and a higher curricular premium on thinking and knowledge than on learning information and skills.

Bibliography

Anderson J R 1980 *Cognitive Psychology and its Implications*. Freeman, San Francisco, California

Beilin H 1971 The training and acquisition of logical operations. In: Rosskopf M F, Steffe L P, Taback S (eds.) 1971 *Piagetian Cognitive-development Research and Mathematics Education*. National Council of Teachers of Mathematics, Washington, DC

Beilin H 1977 Inducing conservation through training. In: Steiner G (ed.) 1977 *Psychology of the 20th Century*, Vol. 7. Kinder, Bern

Blumenthal A L 1977 *The Process of Cognition*. Prentice-Hall, Englewood Cliffs, New Jersey

Brainerd C J, Allen T W 1971 Experimental inductions of the conservation of "first order" quantitative invariants. *Psychol. Bull.* 75: 128–44

Cohen G 1977 *The Psychology of Cognition*. Academic Press, New York

Cohen K M 1978 Eye activity in the study of the reading process. In: Murray F B (ed.) 1978 *Models of Efficient Reading*. International Reading Assocation, Newark, Delaware

Elkind D 1976 *Child Development and Education: A Piagetian Perspective*. Oxford University Press, New York

Farnham-Diggory S 1978 How to study reading: Some information processing ways. In: Murray F B, Pikulski J J (eds.) 1978 *The Acquisition of Reading: Cognitive, Linguistic and Perceptual Prerequisites*. 2nd Delaware Symposium on Curriculum, Learning and Instruction, Newark, Delaware, 1975. University Park Press, Baltimore, Maryland

Flavell J H 1963 *The Developmental Psychology of Jean Piaget*. Van Nostrand, Princeton, New Jersey

Glaser R, Resnick L B 1972 Instructional psychology. *Ann. Rev. Psychol.* 23: 207–76

Glass A L, Holyoak K, Santa J 1979 *Cognition*. Addison-Wesley, Reading, Massachusetts

Goldschmidt M 1971 The role of experience in the rate and sequence of cognitive development. In: Green D R, Ford M P, Flamer G B (eds.) 1971 *Measurement and Piaget: Proc. CTB/McGraw-Hill Conf. Ordinal Scales of Cognitive Development*. McGraw-Hill, New York

Guilford J P 1967 *The Nature of Human Intelligence*. McGraw-Hill, New York

James W 1890 *The Principles of Psychology*. Holt, New York

Lachman R, Lachman J L, Butterfield E C 1979 *Cognitive Psychology and Information Processing: An Introduction*. Erlbaum, Hillsdale, New Jersey

Murray F 1978 Conservation training and teaching strategies. In: Glaser R, Lesgold A, Pellegrino J (eds.) 1978 *Advances in Instructional Psychology*. Erlbaum, Hillsdale, New Jersey

Neisser U 1976 *Cognition and Reality: Principles and Implications of Cognitive Psychology*. Freeman, San Francisco, California

Newell A 1973 You can't play 20 questions with nature and win. In: Chase W G (ed.) 1973 *Visual Information Processing. Proc. 8th Symposium Cognition, Carnegie-Mellon University, 1972*. Academic Press, New York

Peill E J 1975 *Invention and Discovery of Reality: The Acquisition of Conservation of Amount*. Wiley, New York

Piatelli-Palmarini M 1980 *Language and Learning: The Debate Between Jean Piaget and Noam Chomsky*. Harvard University Press, Cambridge, Massachusetts

Posner M I 1978 *Chronometric Explorations of Mind: The Third Paul M. Fitts Lectures, University of Michigan, September 1976*. Erlbaum, Hillsdale, New Jersey

Reese H, Overton W 1970 Models of development and theories of development. In: Goulet L R, Baltes P B (eds.) 1970 *Life-span Developmental Psychology: Research and Theory*. Academic Press, New York

Shavelson R J 1981 Teaching mathematics: Contributions of cognitive research. *Educ. Psychol.* 16: 23–44

Siegler R 1981 Information processing approaches to development. In: Mussen P (ed.) 1981 *Carmichael's Manual of Child Psychology*. Wiley, New York

Sinclair-deZwart H 1977 Recent developments in genetic epistemology. *Genet. Epistemol.* 6: 1–4

Strauss S 1972 Inducing cognitive development and learning: A review of short-term training experiments, Vol. 1: The organismic-developmental approach. *Cognition* 1: 329–57

Strauss S 1974-75 A reply to Brainerd. *Cognition* 3: 155–85

Varma V P, Williams P 1976 *Piaget, Psychology and Education: Papers in Honour of Jean Piaget*. Hodder and Stoughton, London

Vuyk R 1981 *Overview and Critique of Piaget's Genetic Epistemology, 1965–1980*. Academic Press, New York

Wessells M T 1982 *Cognitive Psychology*. Harper and Row, New York

Abilities and Aptitudes

J. W. Pellegrino and C. K. Varnhagen

While some people distinguish between the terms ability and aptitude, in typical educational practice the two are used synonymously to mean an individual's potential for acquiring new knowledge or skill. In the field of education, information about a person's potential is useful in setting reasonable expectations for what he or she can accomplish and in diagnosing learning difficulties individuals may exhibit.

When aptitude is thus defined as a person's potential for learning, it may be apparent that the term intelligence, as commonly used, refers to a general sort of aptitude, one not limited to such skills as those of mathematical or clerical or mechanical performance, but rather treating a widely encompassing ability that influences many sorts of performance. While in educational circles the term aptitude frequently has been used only in relation to specific skills and the term intelligence in relation to more general ability, this distinction is not founded on a true separation of mental abilities into two such categories in most modern-day theories. As a result, discussions of abilities and aptitudes are necessarily enmeshed with considerations of intelligence, so that the articles under the title *Intelligence* in the Encyclopedia are properly regarded as aspects of the following discussion of abilities and aptitudes.

1. Aptitudes, Intelligence, and Achievement

It is commonly accepted that individuals vary with regard to their specific mental abilities. An individual may show superior linguistic or verbal ability while being relatively weak at spatial and mechanical reasoning tasks. The converse is also a common ability pattern. Such variations among individuals have been of concern to those interested in developing theories and tests of aptitude as well as educational practitioners wishing to optimize the outcomes of formal instruction. Unfortunately, there is no universally accepted theory of aptitude. It is not known how many specific mental abilities there are nor their degree of independence. There are, however, a number of tests which attempt to measure individual differences in general and specific aptitudes. This is similar to the situation that exists with respect to the construct of general intelligence. There is no acceptable theory and definition of intelligence, but there exists an elaborate testing technology that attempts to measure individual differences in general intellectual ability.

Aptitudes are psychological constructs about individual differences in learning or performance in situations where individuals are required to learn from instruction. For a test to be an acceptable measure of verbal or spatial aptitude, it must be shown that individual differences in mental-test performance are predictive of an individual's ability to learn in some specific instructional setting.

A distinction is drawn, not without controversy, between aptitude and achievement measures. While both may predict an individual's ability to profit from a specific instructional program or course, the two types of tests are often quite different in content. The essential difference between achievement and aptitude tests is that the former attempts to measure abilities an individual has acquired as a result of specific study in a given instructional sequence. In contrast, an aptitude test attempts to measure what an individual has acquired as a result of more general experience. Both can serve to predict an individual's ability to acquire new knowledge or skill in a given area such as mathematics, mechanics, or foreign-language learning. While prior achievement in an area such as mathematics is a better predictor of subsequent learning and performance, often no formal instruction has previously occurred. In such cases, only aptitude assessment is possible.

2. Theories and Tests

Theories of aptitude have been intimately tied to trends and developments in the area of mental testing. Historically there have been two contrasting viewpoints which emphasize general mental ability versus specific abilities. A combination of both viewpoints is represented in hierarchical theories of aptitude and intelligence such as those advocated by Cattell (1971) and Vernon (1961). An interesting point is that the database for all theories is essentially the same. It is derived from performance scores on a number of specific mental tests administered to a large sample of individuals. Individuals' scores on each test are then correlated with scores on all other tests in the battery, resulting in a large intercorrelation matrix. The values in the matrix indicate how strongly individual differences on one test are related to individual differences on all other tests. Factor-analytic and other multivariate techniques are then used to attempt a mathematical reduction of this data matrix. The goal of such multivariate-analysis methods is to represent the underlying factors or aptitudes responsible for the entire pattern of correlations.

Figure 1 is a graphical representation of a common pattern observed when such a multiple test battery is administered to a sample of over 200 high-school students. Each individual test is represented as a point in two-dimensional space and the closer two points are the more highly correlated is the performance on both tests. In addition, the figure represents tests that form a common factor, as indicated by the heavy solid lines connecting individual points. The capital letter desig-

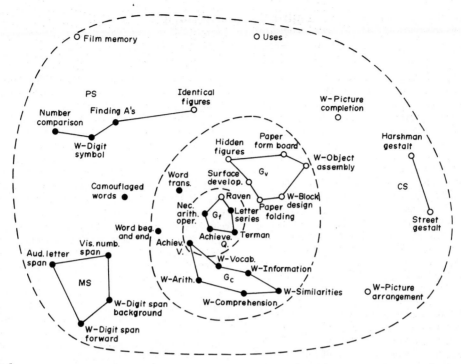

Figure 1
Multidimensional scaling representation of intercorrelations between ability test scores. Tests preceded by a "W" are from the Wechsler Adult Intelligence Scale. From Snow 1980a

nations identify factor labels frequently assigned to these clusters of tests: G_c, G_f, and G_v stand for crystallized, fluid, and visualization factors in Cattell's (1971) theory. Those tests which represent G_c include verbal knowledge, reading comprehension, and prior educational achievement (both verbal and quantitative). The G_c cluster is also similar to the "verbal–educational" factor in Vernon's (1961) theory. The G_f cluster consists of abstract and nonverbal reasoning tests while the G_v cluster consists of spatial relations and visualization tests. The latter two clusters serve to define the "practical–mechanical" factor in Vernon's theory. The remaining factors that exist toward the periphery are memory span, perceptual speed, and closure speed.

Figure 1 also contains contour lines which distinguish central, intermediate, and peripheral regions. Tests in the central region correlate with a wider range of other tests and thus they are presumed to measure more general aptitudes. Finally, it should be noted that a diagonal line drawn from the upper left to lower right corner differentiates two classes of item content—(a) digits, letters, and words (solid points) versus (b) pictures and figures (open points).

The pattern shown in Fig. 1 is consistent with a number of hierarchical theories of aptitude as well as different approaches to aptitude testing. A distinction is often drawn between general aptitudes such as verbal and quantitative ability, inductive-reasoning ability, and spatial ability and much more specific abilities such as perceptual speed, memory span, clerical speed, numerical fluency, and others. Consistent with this is the fact that there are both general-purpose scholastic-aptitude tests and more broad-range differential-aptitude tests. Scholastic-aptitude tests, often referred to as general-intelligence tests, include the Binet and Wechsler individual intelligence tests and numerous intelligence and aptitude tests designed for group administration. General scholastic-aptitude tests emphasize measures of both G_c and G_f and include tasks that appear in the central portion of Fig. 1. Such tests yield the highest correlations with measures of typical academic achievement. Differential-aptitude batteries sample a broader range of skills. Examples are the Differential Aptitude Test in the United States and the Differential Test Battery in the United Kingdom. The Differential Aptitude Test reports scores for eight subtests measuring verbal reasoning, numerical ability, abstract reasoning, clerical speed and accuracy, mechanical reasoning, spatial relations, spelling, and language usage. In addition to multiple-aptitude batteries, tests have been developed for other areas such as musical aptitude and foreign-language learning.

The ultimate goal of differential-aptitude testing was to provide information that would be of more help in educational and vocational planning and guidance. To some extent this has been realized. For example, success in occupations such as engineering and dentistry has been found to be significantly related to spatial aptitude. However, the attempt to further differentiate aptitude patterns that are related to school performance has been largely unsuccessful. In 1964, a careful analysis was done by McNemar of the validity coefficients of certain widely used differential-aptitude batteries. He argued from his analysis that "Aside from tests of numerical ability having differential value for predicting school grades in math, it seems safe to conclude that the worth of multitest batteries as differential predictors of achievement in school has not been demonstrated. . . . It is far from clear that tests of general intelligence have been outmoded by the multitest batteries as the more useful predictors of school achievement" (McNemar 1964 p. 875). More recent work reaffirms McNemar's conclusion (Carroll 1978). Differential-aptitude tests followed the accepted practice of attempting to predict the final outcomes of learning, and did no better than general-ability tests in identifying and measuring abilities and prerequisite skills that could be related to models of learning and the acquisition of specific content. McNemar reflected on a possible reason for this lack of success:

> Abilities, or capacities, or aptitudes, or intellectual skills, or whatever you choose to call them, are measured in terms of response products to standardized stimulus situations. The stimulus is presented to an organism which by some process comes up with a response; thus any attempt to theorize and/or study intellect in terms of a simple stimulus-response (S–R) paradigm seems doomed to failure unless drastically modified and complicated by the insertion of O for organism and P for process. . . . Studies of individual differences never come to grips with the process, or operation by which a given organism achieves an intellectual response. Indeed, it is difficult to see how the available individual difference data can be used even as a starting point for generating a theory as to the process nature of general intelligence or of any other specified ability. (McNemar 1964 p. 881)

3. Aptitudes and Instructional Treatments

Although the measurement of aptitude and intelligence has always been tied to instructional settings, the question about what underlies such relationships has been a persistent theoretical and practical problem. Woodrow (1946) was among the first to demonstrate that while the correlation between scholastic-aptitude and achievement measures was substantial, gains in achievement scores from year to year seemed to be negligibly related to aptitude. Subsequently it was demonstrated that when the easiest items are eliminated from achievement tests, gains on such tests are significantly related to scholastic-aptitude measures. Thus, aptitude appears to be more related to the complexity of the material that is mastered rather than total amount.

Psychologists and educational researchers have continued to be concerned about the relationship between measures of individual differences and learning variables. To a large extent, this work was heralded by the 1957 book by Cronbach and Gleser entitled *Psychological Tests and Personnel Decisions* and its second edition in 1965. This book developed a decision-theory model for the selection and placement of individuals into various "treatments." The word treatment was given a broad meaning, referring to what is done with an individual in an institutional setting. In education it refers to the particular programs or instructional methods a student is assigned to or has the opportunity to select. This theoretical analysis pointed out that aptitude information is useful in modifying and selecting treatments only when aptitude and treatment can be shown to interact. Such research is different from differential-aptitude testing in which emphasis is placed on determining the relationship between measured aptitudes and learning outcomes resulting from relatively fixed curricula. In aptitude-treatment-interaction (ATI) research, the emphasis is on determining whether aptitudes can predict which of several different learning methods might help different individuals attain similar educational outcomes.

Cronbach and Snow (1977) have carried out a very extensive review and analysis of many of the ramifications of the ATI research area. They conclude that, with a few notable exceptions, ATI effects have not been solidly demonstrated. The frequency of studies in which the appropriate interactions have been found is low, and the empirical evidence found in favor of such interactions is often not very convincing. In those occasional instances when positive results have been obtained, no general principles have emerged because of the lack of consistent findings in replication studies and in transfer to new subject matter areas.

While one is struck by the absence of any prescriptive assistance to instruction, certain sections of the Cronbach and Snow book suggest a trend that bears further study. A pattern of more promising results appeared in situations where investigators were forced to construct an aptitude measure because no readymade and labeled aptitude tests were available. There appears to be a tradeoff between the reliability offered by established tests of aptitude and the information about acquisition processes afforded by tests specially constructed for experimental or instructional research. In research using established aptitude tests it seems as though researchers presumed that the label of a particular aptitude measure had direct implications for instructional practice. For example, a spatial-aptitude test was paired with procedures that de-emphasized verbal content in instruction. But the mere absence of words (diagrams, for example) by no means implies the presence of abilities required in these tests.

Such results certainly do not recommend that standardized tests be abandoned as inappropriate measures in ATI research; the fault in these efforts appears to be in the absence of adequate theories of test performance rather than in the tests themselves. Traditional psychometric instruments need to be accompanied by careful analyses of processes that relate aptitude, treatment, and the knowledge or skills to be learned. Testable theories are required that describe abilities measured in the pretest, abilities required for competent task performance, and treatment procedures that connect the two (Snow 1980b). At the present time, generally used aptitude constructs are not productive dimensions for measuring individual differences that interact with different ways of learning. Such measures, derived from a psychometric selection-oriented tradition, do not appear to relate to the processes of learning and performance that have been under investigation in experimental and developmental psychology. The treatments investigated in ATI studies have not been generated by any systematic analysis of the kinds of psychological processes called upon in particular instructional methods, and individual differences have not been assessed in terms of related cognitive processes.

4. Cognitive Process Approaches

The lesson resulting from such endeavors as differential-aptitude testing and ATI research has been learned slowly. In 1957, Cronbach suggested that "Constructs originating in differential psychology are now being tied to experimental variables. As a result, the whole theoretical picture in such an area as human abilities is changing. . . . It now becomes possible . . . ultimately to unite the psychology of intelligence with the psychology of learning" (p. 682). The point was reiterated in 1972 by Glaser who called for research on the "new aptitudes" that would be interpreted in terms of process constructs. However, research has only recently begun to conceptualize individual differences in aptitudes in terms of structure and process constructs of contemporary theories of human cognition and cognitive development.

The global objective of a cognitive process approach is to contribute to an understanding of the ways in which individuals differ in abilities for learning. In the long run, this goal will be achieved if abilities to learn can be specified in terms of the concepts of modern cognitive theory and procedures developed for identifying school-related capabilities based upon these same concepts. The initial step is to accept the fact of a robust correlational relationship between certain abilities measured by tests and school achievement. The next step is to identify classes of test tasks that have consistently appeared on scholastic- and differential-aptitude tests and use current techniques of task analysis to understand the nature of the performance elicited by these tasks. A logical next step would be to relate the aptitude processes to similar task analytic work being pursued in school subject matter areas, such as, beginning reading, text comprehension, elementary arithmetic, and science problem solving. Such an approach should begin to explain the predictive validity of scholastic- and differential-aptitude tests, identify the reasons for limitations in validity, and may suggest how

instruction could affect specific intellectual abilities. As Carroll has written:

The performances required on many types of mental ability tests—tests of language competence, of ability to manipulate abstract concepts and relationships, of ability to apply knowledge to the solution of problems, and even of the ability to make simple and rapid comparisons of stimuli (as in a test of perceptual speed)—have great and obvious resemblances to performances required in school learning, and indeed in many other fields of human activity. If these performances are seen as based on learned developed abilities of a rather generalized character, it would frequently be useful to assess the extent to which an individual has acquired these abilities. This could be for the purpose of determining the extent to which these abilities would need to be improved to prepare the individual for further experiences or learning activities, or of determining what kinds and amounts of intervention might be required to effect such improvements. These determinations, however, would have to be based on more exact information than we now have concerning the effects of different types of learning experiences . . . on the improvement of these abilities. (Carroll 1978 pp. 93–94)

Within this developing area of aptitude research, there appear to be two general research approaches (Pellegrino and Glaser 1979). The cognitive-correlates approach seeks to specify the information-processing abilities that are differentially related to high and low levels of aptitude. Tests of aptitude or intelligence are used to identify subgroups that are compared on laboratory tasks that have cognitive-processing characteristics defined by prior experimental and theoretical research. The cognitive-components approach is task analytic and attempts to directly identify the information-processing components of performance on tasks that have been generally used to assess mental abilities. Performance on standardized tests of aptitude and intelligence becomes the object of theoretical and empirical analysis, and the goal is to develop models of task performance and apply such models to individual-differences analysis.

The two approaches are tied to prevalent theories of human cognition, and both attempt to understand the mental activities that contribute to individual differences as measured by psychometric instruments. In the cognitive-correlates approach, the questions being asked are of the form "What does it mean to be high verbal?" and the answers are sought in the attempt to link experimental tasks and paradigms used in the investigation of cognition with psychometric test-score classification. For the task-analytic approach, the questions being asked are of the form "What do intelligence tests test?" and the answers are sought through rational and empirical analyses of the information-processing demands of the specific tasks that comprise these tests. Having derived models for task performance, it is then possible to investigate sources of individual differences that contribute to overall mental-ability differences. The difference between the two approaches is largely a matter of their focus: the correlates approach uses general models of cognition as its frame of reference, while the components approach uses more specific models of aptitude-task performances. Pellegrino and Glaser (1979) have discussed the advantages of each approach, noting that the analysis of component processes within test tasks circumvents the need to establish a link between performance differences and aptitude-test scores.

5. Analyses of Verbal Ability

Process analyses of verbal aptitude have largely emphasized the cognitive correlates type of approach. This is best typified by the work of Earl Hunt (1978). His research has been set in the context of a general model of memory that depicts the flow of information through a series of sensory buffers into a short-term memory, and then through an intermediate-term memory into a long-term memory. An executive system controls the flow of information and has access to the various levels of memory storage (see *Memory*). With this model as a frame of reference, Hunt has asked a series of questions about the differences between high and low verbal-ability groups that relate to structures, processes, and parameters of the information-processing system.

The intent of this work has been to show that verbal aptitude as measured by conventional tests is related to key constructs studied in modern theories of cognition, particularly the parameters of models that describe the transformation of information in short- and long-term memory. An extensive series of experiments has suggested that university students who score high on a verbal-ability battery show, in contrast to lower scoring individuals, faster performance on tasks that require accessing information in long-term memory and manipulating information in short-term memory. This included: (a) the ability to make a rapid conversion from a physical representation of a letter to a higher level code in a letter-matching paradigm; (b) the ability to retain the order of information in short-term memory as indicated by an immediate serial recall task; and (c) the ability to manipulate rapidly data in short-term memory, as indicated by a memory-scanning task. In general, Hunt et al. conclude that verbal-intelligence tests directly tap a person's knowledge of language, such as the meaning of words, syntactic rules, and semantic relations between concepts denoted by words, and that these tests also indirectly assess more fundamental or elementary information-processing capacities. Although the results obtained by Hunt provide strong suggestions of basic information-processing differences between high- and low-verbal-ability groups, subsequent research has not presented so simple and consistent a picture.

Hunt (1978) has argued that a complex set of factors beyond processing speed may be required to account for individual differences in verbal ability. He suggests three different sources of individual differences: knowledge, information-free mechanistic process, and general strategies. The effect of knowledge has been minimized or held constant in much of the work on cognitive correlates of verbal aptitude through the use of simple verbal materials. The mechanics of information processing are divided by Hunt into two components—automatic and controlled attention-demanding processes. Hunt suggests that the automatic processes appear to be stable individual traits, particularly over the wide range represented by brain-damaged and retardate groups through high verbal-ability adults and outstanding mnemonists. The controlled processes are more labile and thus are not effective long-term predictors of cognitive performance. General strategies include such cognitive performances as rehearsal strategies and metacognitive activities such as the planning, monitoring, and checking involved in problem solving. Carroll and Maxwell (1979) should be consulted for a more extensive discussion of related research on individual differences in verbal ability, including research that focuses on individual differences in reading ability (see *Individual Differences*).

6. Analyses of Spatial Ability

Recently, two reviews have appeared of factoranalytic research on spatial aptitude (Lohman 1979, McGee 1979). Both were clear in noting that all major factor-analytic studies have identified mechanical/spatial factors that are distinct from other general and specific aptitudes. However, both also point out that spatial aptitude is still an ill-defined construct after 70 years of psychometric research. There appears to be little agreement among major studies about the number of distinct spatial abilities that may exist and how best to characterize each one. Lohman (1979) reanalyzed the data from several major studies in an attempt to isolate a common set of spatial factors. The result of these efforts was the delineation of two distinct factors labeled "spatial relations" and "spatial visualization." The spatial-relations factor appears to involve the ability to engage rapidly and accurately in mental-rotation processes that are necessary for judgments about the identity of a pair of stimuli. Spatial-relations tasks can be found in test batteries such as the Science Research Associates (SRA) Primary Mental Abilities Test. The spatial-visualization factor is defined by tests that are relatively unspeeded and complex. Such tasks frequently require a manipulation in which there is movement among the internal parts of the stimulus configuration or the folding and unfolding of flat patterns. For example, test items may require decisions about pictured designs representing different patterns of folded sheets of paper. Spatial visualization tasks can be found in test batteries such as the Differential Aptitude Test.

The differences between and among spatial-relations and visualization tasks seem to reflect two complementary dimensions of performance. One of these is the speed–power dimension. Individual spatial-relations problems are solved more rapidly than spatial-visualization problems and the tests themselves are administered in a format that emphasizes speed in the former case and both speed and accuracy in the latter case. The second dimension involves stimulus complexity. Spatial-relations problems, although varying among themselves in complexity, involve less complex stimuli than do spatial-visualization problems. In terms of a process analysis of spatial aptitude, the important question is whether individual differences in performance on these various tasks reflect differential contributions of the speed and accuracy of executing specific cognitive processes.

Considerable attention has been given to the analysis of performance on spatial-relations tasks (Pellegrino and Kail 1982). Studies have examined sources of sex, individual, and developmental differences in performance on simple mental-rotation problems that require a person to mentally turn the pictured figures that are used as the test items. These studies have applied a process model originally developed for mental-rotation tasks. The results are quite consistent in showing that substantial speed differences exist in encoding and comparison of unfamiliar two-dimensional stimuli and in the execution of a rotation or transformation process that operates on the person's mental image of the stimulus item. Adult individual differences exist in all these components of processing and individual differences mirror overall developmental trends. The limited analyses of age changes in sources of individual differences further suggest that individual differences initially relate to encoding and comparison processes and that the rotation process subsequently becomes an increasingly important source of individual differences. A further potential source of individual differences, one that needs further analysis, involves the strategy for task execution. Systematic individual differences may also exist in the speed and criteria for judging the mismatch between stimuli in different orientations.

The differences in encoding, comparison, and rotation that exist for simple spatial relations tasks are of even greater magnitude in complex spatial-relations tasks employing more abstract three-dimensional stimuli. The complexity and abstractness of the stimuli lead to substantial errors on such problems that are also related to individual differences in aptitude-test scores. The particular errors that seem most important for differentiating among individuals involve the processes associated with making different judgments. The data indicate that individuals experience considerable difficulty in establishing the correspondences between common segments of complex stimuli, leading to several iterations through a sequence of processes, and often culminating in an incorrect evaluation or guess.

It appears that spatial aptitude is associated with the ability to establish sufficiently precise and stable mental representations of unfamiliar visual stimuli that can be subsequently transformed or operated on with a mini- mal information loss. In spatial-relations and visualization tasks, speed of encoding and comparison is significantly related to skill. In more complex tasks, accuracy of encoding and comparison is also significantly related to skill. Thus, individuals who are high in spatial aptitude are faster at representing unfamiliar visual stimuli, and what is ultimately represented is more precise. Differences in representation, most likely qualitative differences, may also give rise to other speed differences, such as the superior rotation and search rates exhibited in different tasks. Problems of representation are most apparent in the more complex tasks that involve the representation and processing of stimuli having several interrelated elements. If it is assumed that stimulus representation and processing involve a visual short-term or working memory, then skill differences may be a function of coding and capacity within such a memory system. Differences between spatial relations and spatial visualization tasks (factors) may reflect a difference in emphasis on coding versus transformation processes within this system. Another difference between the two factors may involve single versus sequential transformations and the ability to coordinate and monitor the latter.

7. Analyses of Inductive-reasoning Ability

The most extensive application of the cognitive-components approach to aptitude analysis has been to inductive-reasoning tasks. There are several reasons why inductive-reasoning tasks have been targeted for such in-depth analysis. First, they constitute prototypical measures of the G_f factor illustrated in Fig. 1. Second, induction problems have been a part of aptitude tests and theory almost from the inception of the testing movement. Spearman and others have argued that inductive reasoning is central to the concept and measurement of intelligence and scholastic aptitude. Third, induction tasks represent more than a psychometric curiosity, for example, Greeno (1978) has classified them as a major form of human problem-solving activity. The importance of inductive thought processes has also been emphasized in science, mathematics, and in classroom learning processes.

Major inductive-reasoning tasks include series completion, classification, analogy, and matrix-completion problems. Various types of content are used to create individual items including letters, numbers, words, and geometric shapes. One or more induction tasks representing verbal and nonverbal content can be found on virtually every test of scholastic aptitude at every developmental level. All induction tasks have the same generic structure. The individual is presented with a set of elements and the task is to induce the rule structure relating the elements so that the pattern can be completed or extended. An example is a letter series-completion problem of the form LQAKRCJSEI– –. Process models and theories have been developed for virtually all the major inductive-reasoning tasks and have been utilized in analyses of developmental and individual differences in inductive-reasoning ability.

Both qualitative and quantitative changes occur in the inductive-reasoning abilities of elementary-school-age children. Qualitative changes refer to the strategies used for task solution and the understanding of task demands and constraints. Quantitative changes generally refer to the efficiency with which a process such as inference, comparison, or evaluation of relations is executed. Efficiency is indexed by the speed of process execution and/or the degree of accuracy. From studies of analogy and classification tasks using verbal, numerical, figural, and geometric stimuli, it can be concluded that the development of inductive reasoning involves all of the aforementioned loci of change. The hallmark of mature inductive reasoning involves the ability to infer, coordinate, and compare multiple relationships that constitute part of a systematic and higher order relational structure. Studies of adult individual differences focusing on both speed and accuracy of processing support the general conclusion that ability differences are primarily associated with processing efficiency. While speed differences are relatively small among college-age individuals, they are nonetheless significant and co-occur with substantial accuracy differences. Studies of individual differences in high-school and elementary-school populations indicate that, like adults, substantial speed and accuracy differences exist among individuals. Less skilled reasoners have difficulties in coordinating and comparing multiple relations among elements of a pattern. In contrast, skilled reasoners are able to manipulate second- and third-order relationships among elements. A major source of variance involves qualitative differences in the strategy used to solve problems and general understanding of the formal constraints on problem solution.

Studies of developmental and individual differences in inductive-reasoning ability indicate that there are impressive parallels in the sources of variability between and within age groups. The processes that are problematic for younger children also appear to be the primary problem areas for older individuals. Processes that deal with multiple relationship comparison and evaluation are consistent sources of differences between high- and low-ability reasoners. This problem manifests itself somewhat differently in adults than in children. Differences among adults are largely efficiency differences. Among children, qualitative differences emerge when comparison and evaluation become extremely difficult. Appropriate inductive reasoning seems to be replaced by a more global associative-reasoning process. Goldman and Pellegrino 1984 should be consulted for a more detailed treatment of the theories, models, and data on inductive-reasoning abilities.

8. Future Directions

When standardized aptitude tests are viewed as samples of knowledge and skills necessary or helpful in contexts such as school learning or job performance, then research can attempt to specify what skills are being assessed, how individuals differ, how such skills are acquired, and how they might be affected by instruction. In contrast to previous psychometric approaches to aptitude and abilities, a cognitive-process conception of aptitude promises to be a dynamic account of individual differences in processes, strategies, and knowledge rather than a static account of amount of a hypothesized entity. Studies of individual differences in specific cognitive abilities have already led to new and productive lines of research on cognitive-process training (Detterman and Sternberg 1982, Feuerstein 1979).

A cognitive conception of aptitude can also lead to forms of assessment that would use existing tests in different ways. It should be possible to distinguish between two levels of performance: a level that individuals can independently achieve on tests and a level that they can achieve with aid and assistance during the course of testing. Such an approach has been important in the philosophy of diagnostic testing in the Soviet Union (Brown and French 1979). Thus, rather than viewing an aptitude score as a fixed measure of one's ability to learn, the independent level would provide a sample of the individual's cognitive resources, the assisted level would provide diagnostic information about learning potential, and the differences between the two would be indicative of the areas that should become the focus of instruction.

In summary, the conception of aptitudes and abilities being developed by recent cognitive and developmental research is that it is possible to identify the components of individual differences in mental abilities in terms of dynamic process and knowledge structure concepts. Simple and complex performances demanded on aptitude tests, and that assist in the acquisition of academic knowledge and job skill are being analyzed in terms of the intellectual components involved in problem solving, language development and understanding, thinking, memory, imagery, and knowledge representation. These efforts should provide the missing theoretical basis for understanding, assessing, and developing mental abilities.

Bibliography

Brown A L, French L A 1979 The zone of potential development: Implications for intelligence testing in the year 2000. In: Sternberg R J, Detterman D K (eds.) 1979 *Human Intelligence: Perspectives on its Theory and Measurement*. Ablex, Norwood, New Jersey, pp. 217–36

Carroll J B 1978 On the theory–practice interface in the measurement of intellectual abilities. In: Suppes P (ed.) 1978 *Impact of Research on Education*. National Academy of Education, Washington, DC, pp. 1–105

Carroll J B, Maxwell S E 1979 Individual differences in cognitive abilities. *Annu. Rev. Psychol.* 30: 603–40

Cattell R B 1971 *Abilities: Their Structure, Growth and Action*. Houghton Mifflin, Boston, Massachusetts

Cronbach L J 1957 The two disciplines of scientific psychology. *Am. Psychol.* 12: 671–84

Cronbach L J, Gleser G C 1957 *Psychological Tests and Personnel Decisions*. University of Illinois Press, Urbana, Illinois

Cronbach L J, Snow R E 1977 *Aptitudes and Instructional Methods: A Handbook for Research on Interactions*. Irvington, New York

Detterman D K, Sternberg R J 1982 *How Much and How Can Intelligence be Increased*. Ablex, Norwood, New Jersey

Feuerstein R 1979 *Instrumental Enrichment: An Intervention Program For Cognitive Modifiability*. University Park Press, Baltimore, Maryland

Glaser R 1972 Individuals and learning: The new aptitudes. *Educ. Res.* 1: 5–12

Goldman S R, Pellegrino J W 1984 Deductions about induction: Analyses of developmental and individual differences. In: Sternberg R J (ed.) 1984 *Advances in the Psychology of Human Intelligence*, Vol. 2. Erlbaum, Hillsdale, New Jersey

Greeno J G 1978 Natures of problem-solving abilities. In: Estes W K (ed.) 1978 *Handbook of Learning and Cognitive Processes*, Vol 5: *Human Information Processing*. Erlbaum, Hillsdale, New Jersey, pp. 239–70

Hunt E 1978 Mechanics of verbal ability. *Psychol. Rev.* 85: 109–30

Lohman D F 1979 Spatial ability: A review and reanalysis of the correlational literature, Technical Report No. 8. Aptitude Research Project, School of Education, Stanford University, Stanford, California

McGee M G 1979 Human spatial abilities: Psychometric studies and environmental, genetic, hormonal, and neurological influences. *Psychol. Bull.* 86: 889–918

McNemar Q 1964 Lost: Our intelligence? Why? *Am. Psychol.* 19: 871–82

Pellegrino J W, Glaser R 1979 Cognitive correlates and components in the analysis of individual differences. *Intelligence* 3: 187–214

Pellegrino J W, Kail R V 1982 Process analyses of spatial aptitude. In: Sternberg R J (ed.) 1982 *Advances in the Psychology of Human Intelligence*, Vol. 1. Erlbaum, Hillsdale, New Jersey, pp. 311–65

Snow R E 1980a Aptitude process. In: Snow R E, Federico P-A, Montague W E (eds.) 1980 *Aptitude, Learning and Instruction: Cognitive Process Analyses of Aptitude*, Vol. 1. Erlbaum, Hillsdale, New Jersey, pp. 27–63

Snow R E 1980b Aptitude and achievement. *New Directions in Testing and Measurement* 5: 39–59

Vernon P E 1961 *The Structure of Human Abilities*, 2nd edn. Methuen, London

Woodrow H 1946 The ability to learn. *Psych. Rev.* 53: 147–58

Perspectives, Theories, and Tests of Intelligence

J. W. Pellegrino and C. K. Varnhagen

Intelligence and intelligence tests are often in the news, usually at the heart of some controversy. Some arguments concern the ethical and moral implications of, for example, selective breeding of bright children. Other arguments deal with the statistical basis of various conclusions, whether, for instance, tests are really biased if the data are analyzed "properly." What is heard less often, however, is discussion of the construct of intelligence itself. What is intelligence? How does it grow? How do people differ intellectually? Questions like these, which should be central to any discussion relating to intelligence and intelligence testing, are less often raised, much less answered. Psychologists, educators, and lay persons alike seem too quick to accept the cliché that "intelligence is what intelligence tests measure." The definition and view of intelligence emanating from the testing tradition is not the only psychological perspective; there are other complementary and viable perspectives on intelligence.

1. Three Influential Perspectives

The psychometric tradition represents the branch of psychology that has been concerned primarily with the measurement of intelligence; essentially all extant tests of intelligence have been devised by psychologists associated with the psychometric tradition. A second view of intelligence, that provided by cognitive–developmental psychology, stems from Piaget's theory of intellectual development. This tradition is a rich source of information on the growth and development of intelligence. A third view on intelligence, the information-processing perspective, is an outgrowth of work in experimental psychology. It provides elaborate descriptions and theories of the specific mental activities that comprise intelligence and intellectual functioning.

The three perspectives are similar in the general skills and activities that are associated with "being or becoming intelligent." Reasoning and problem-solving skills are the principal components of intelligence. Virtually all psychometric theories and tests of intelligence are based upon performance on reasoning and problem-solving tests. Piagetian theory focuses on the development of the cognitive structures necessary for logical reasoning. Recent work within the information-processing perspective has also emphasized problem solving and reasoning at both a general level and within specific content domains, such as mathematics and the comprehension of text.

A second area of overlap involves adaptability as an aspect of intelligence. In the psychometric tradition this is often implicit in that intelligence tests require individuals to deal with a succession of novel stimuli and tasks; performance depends on the ability to adapt rapidly to the new situations. Such adaptation to changing environmental demands is also a principal component of Piaget's theory, although the period of adaptation and change is more extended, usually being measured in months and years rather than minutes. Finally, both short and more extended forms of adaptation—usually referred to as transfer—also have defined major research and theoretical topics within the information-processing tradition.

As a move is made away from a general description of intelligence, the perspectives clearly differ in their emphases. The psychometric perspective, as the name implies, emphasizes measurement of intelligence and, especially, measuring individual differences in intelligence. Research done within the psychometric framework typically involves testing large numbers of individuals on many different tasks with each person obtaining a score on each task. Theories are based upon statistical analyses of the patterns of test-score relationships. These theories attempt to describe the structure of intelligence by examining the ways in which individuals differ in intellectual performance. Theories developed within the psychometric perspective do not focus on the specific psychological processes that are used when a person solves a particular problem. The emphasis is on the products or outcomes of intellectual activity, rather than the mental processes underlying such products.

The cognitive–development perspective emphasizes general theoretical principles that govern intellectual growth and change. Within this tradition, theory and data focus on the characteristics of intellectual development that are common to different individuals, rather than emphasizing differences as in the psychometric tradition. Compared to the psychometric tradition, cognitive–developmental psychologists have had greater interest in explaining how children and adults solve reasoning problems, but only to the extent that the mechanisms underlying such reasoning are general and not specific to particular problems.

The information-processing perspective emphasizes theoretical and empirical analyses of performance on simple and complex cognitive tasks. Precise theories of the knowledge and cognitive processes necessary for performing a task are emphasized rather than broad principles and theories of cognitive change as in the cognitive–developmental tradition. No attempt is made to test all the different structures and processes that have been hypothesized from analyses of many different tasks. Instead, research involves sampling of knowledge and processes as reflected by a specific task often created to meet the needs of testing a particular theory or model. Finally, like cognitive–developmental psychologists, information-processing psychologists typically show little interest in individual differences, a characteristic revealed in the willingness in both traditions to develop elaborate psychological theories based on the performance of a handful of individuals.

The emphasis on individual differences within the psychometric tradition is certainly relevant to any complete theory of intelligence. A theory of intelligence should take into account similarities and differences among individuals in their cognitive skills and performance capabilities. However, a theory of cognition based solely on patterns of differences among indi-

viduals cannot capture all of intellectual functioning unless there is little that is general and similar in intellectual performance. In contrast, the developmental tradition emphasizes similarities in intellectual growth and the importance of organism–environment interactions. By considering the nature of changes that occur in cognition and the mechanisms and conditions responsible, it is possible to better understand human intellectual growth and its relationship to the environment. This requires, however, that the focus is not just on commonalities in the general course of cognitive growth, but that consideration be given to how individuals differ in the specifics of their intellectual growth. Such a developmental–differential emphasis seems necessary for a theory to have adequate breadth and to move the study of intelligence away from a static, normative view, where intelligence changes little over development, to a more dynamic view that encompasses developmental change in absolute levels of cognitive power. Finally, the information-processing perspective helps to define the scope of a theory of intelligence by further emphasizing the dynamics of cognition, through its concentration on precise theories of the knowledge and processes that allow individuals to perform intellectual tasks. Psychometric and developmental theories typically give little heed to these processes, yet they are necessary for a theory of intelligence to make precise, testable predictions about intellectual performance.

Each of these emphases—individual differences, developmental change, and specific cognitive processes—should be integral parts of any theory of intelligence. A comprehensive theory of intelligence should explain (a) how individuals differ intellectually from one another; (b) how intelligence develops as children grow older; and, (c) the specific cognitive processes that give rise to intellectual activity. No theory developed within any of the three perspectives attempts to address all of these components. However, each perspective has led to theory, research, and methodology that are useful for addressing certain of these aspects of a theory of intelligence. The remainder of this article will concentrate on theory and research emanating from the psychometric perspective. Piagetian and cognitive–developmental theory and research are discussed elsewhere (see *Piaget's Theory of Genetic Epistemology*).

2. Historical Roots

Intelligence testing has its roots in early experimental psychology and psychophysical measurement. Much of the early testing research was conducted primarily in the United Kingdom and the United States and utilized psychophysical methods developed by the German psychophysicists, Weber, Fechner, Müller, and Wundt. Although intelligence testing began as a more-or-less scientific pursuit into the nature of intelligence, it soon acquired practical significance as a tool for predicting school achievement and selecting individuals for various educational programs.

Sir Francis Galton is recognized as the principal figure in pursuing research on intelligence and individual differences. His work in the late 1800s formed the background for much of the research conducted during the last 100 years. Galton believed that all intelligent behavior was related to innate sensory ability. To test this assumption, he used psychophysical methods to measure sensory-motor reaction time and sensory discriminations. These measures were then correlated with various indices of achievement using statistical procedures developed by his student, Karl Pearson. Galton's attempts to empirically validate the supposed relation between sensory ability and intelligence were largely unsuccessful, however. James Cattell, in the United States, held a similar view of the determinants of intelligence. He studied both in Germany under the psychophysicist Wundt and in England with Galton. Cattell developed additional sensory tests based on his conviction that intelligence could be described in terms of sensory-motor function. In 1890 he introduced the term "mental test" to describe his procedures. Cattell also found little relation between sensory-motor functioning and school performance.

The approach to intelligence testing via assessment of simple sensory-motor abilities was widely adopted in Germany, the United Kingdom, Italy, and the United States. However, all attempts to empirically validate such mental tests using conventional measures of intellectual behavior (school performance) failed. Binet and Henri (1896), in France, criticized this approach on the basis that the tests assessed too narrow a range of mental abilities. They argued that appropriate intelligence testing must include assessment of more complex mental processes, such as memory, attention, imagery, and comprehension. Binet and Henri's arguments provided the impetus for a different movement in intelligence testing. This approach, combined with a practical need, provided the basis for the development of the first empirically valid intelligence test in the early 1900s.

In 1904, Binet and his colleague, Henri Simon, were commissioned by the French Minister of Public Instruction to develop a procedure to select children who were not able to benefit from regular public-school instruction for placement in special programs for the retarded. As a result, in 1905 Binet and Simon published an objective, standardized intelligence test based on the concepts developed in the Binet and Henri (1896) article. The test represented the first attempt to quantify the concept of intelligence. The 1905 Binet and Simon intelligence test consisted of 30 subtests of mental ability, including tests of digit span, object and body part identification, sentence memory, and so on. Many of these subtests, with minor modifications, are included in the current Stanford–Binet intelligence test. These subtests were arranged in a crude order of difficulty. The examiner would present each subtest to the examinee in ascending order of difficulty and record the individual's performance. Scoring of the items was based on the assumption that mentally retarded individuals would be unable

to correctly perform the more difficult subtests appropriate to their age level.

In 1908 and again in 1911, Binet and Simon published revised versions of their intelligence test. The revised tests distinguished intellectual abilities according to age norms, thus introducing the concept of "mental age." The subtests were organized according to the age level at which they could be successfully performed by most children of normal intelligence. As a result, children could be characterized and compared in terms of their intellectual or mental age. The Binet and Simon intelligence test was widely adopted in Europe and in the United States. Cyril Burt translated and restandardized the test to be used in England. Lewis Terman, at Stanford University, in the United States, developed the more extensive Stanford–Binet test in 1916. This test has been used extensively in several updated versions throughout the United States.

A major change in intelligence testing involved the development of intelligence tests that could be simultaneously administered to large groups rather than single individuals. Group tests similar to the original Binet and Simon intelligence test were developed in the United Kingdom and the United States. This was particularly important in the United States. During the First World War, group-administered intelligence tests (the Army Alpha and Army Beta tests) were used to assess the abilities of recruits who were then selected for various duties on the basis of this assessment of their intellectual abilities. In England, from the 1940s to the 1960s, intelligence tests were administered to all children near the age of 11 years to select students for different classes of vocational training. Currently, intelligence tests are widely used by most countries for educational selection and diagnosis.

3. Factor Theories of Intelligence

The Binet-type intelligence tests are quite adequate for the purposes of predicting and diagnosing intellectual deficit and selecting individuals on the basis of intellectual ability. But what do these tests actually assess? Although test developers, such as Galton and Binet, had intuitive notions of what constituted intelligence, they made little effort to evaluate their tests in terms of those aspects of intelligence that were actually required for successful performance. Spearman (1904) pointed out the extent of the disagreement between psychologists about what constitutes intelligence. Spearman was reacting to both the sensory-ability position and the higher mental-processes position. He pointed out that differences between definitions could not be resolved on a theoretical level. As a result, he sought empirical tests of the similarities and differences between various mental tests and school-performance measures. He found that many of the seemingly diverse tests were strongly correlated with each other. This led him to postulate a general factor of intelligence (g) that all mental tests measure in common. At the same time, tests also differ in terms of how much the general factor contributes to performance. The relationship between any two tests was attributed to the contribution of the general factor within each test. Systematic differences between tests were accounted for by postulating different specific factors of intelligence (s) that the various tests also measured. This theoretical orientation served as the foundation of factor-analytic theories of intelligence. On the basis of his correlational studies, Spearman argued that intelligence is composed of a general factor that is found in all intellectual functioning plus specific factors associated with the performance of specific tasks. Spearman (1927) later developed a more complex theory introducing more general "group factors" made up of related specific factors. However, he adhered to his main tenet that a common ability underlies all intellectual behavior. For lack of a better definition, he referred to this as a mental force or energy.

The concept that intelligence is characterized by a general underlying ability plus certain task-specific abilities constitutes the basis of major theories of intelligence developed by British researchers. Burt (1949) suggested that intellectual abilities might be hierarchically organized. From his factor-analytic studies, he argued that a comprehensive general factor could be used to represent all intellectual performance. This general factor could also be subdivided into several group factors accounting for different broad classes of intellectual behavior. These broad group factors, according to Burt's conception, can be further subdivided into narrower group factors, then down to numerous, very specific factors. Burt's hierarchical theory of intelligence was elaborated by Vernon. Vernon's (1961) theory of intelligence begins with a centrally important general intellectual factor (g) which, like Burt, he found to account for most of the relations between intelligence tests. At a lower level, he posited two major group factors, verbal–educational and practical–mechanical abilities. These group factors are subdivided at the next lower level into minor group factors. At the lowest level, Vernon breaks down minor group factors into specific intellectual abilities.

Quite distinct from the British theories of intelligence are those developed by American theorists. Whereas the British theorists represent intelligence in terms of a general factor that can be broken down into more specific factors, the American theorists emphasize specific abilities that can be combined to form more general abilities. Thurstone (1924, 1938) developed factor-analytic techniques that first separate out specific or primary factors. Among the most important of Thurstone's primary mental abilities are verbal comprehension, word fluency, numerical ability, spatial relations, memory, reasoning, and perceptual speed. Thurstone argued that these primary factors represent discrete intellectual abilities, and he developed distinct tests to measure these primary mental abilities. As a result of Thurstone's work, various tests of primary

mental abilities have been developed and widely administered in the United States.

Raymond Cattell (1963, 1971) attempted a rapprochement of the theories of Spearman and Thurstone. In an attempt to produce a general (g) factor, he combined Thurstone's primary factors to form secondary and higher order factors. From this analysis, Cattell found two major types of general factors and three minor ones. The major factors he labeled fluid and crystallized general intelligence (gf and gc respectively). Cattell argued that the fluid-intelligence factor represents an individual's basic biological capacity and can be measured as perceptual ability. The other major factor, crystallized intelligence, represents the types of abilities required for most school activities, and is measured by most general intelligence and achievement tests. Cattell labeled the minor general factors gv, gr, and gs for visual abilities, memory retrieval, and performance speed, respectively. Cattell's initial theory has been extended by individuals such as Horn (1979).

Guilford (1967) argued against the concept of a single general intelligence factor proposed by Spearman, Burt, and Vernon. He also disagreed with Cattell and Horn's notion of a small group of general abilities (Guilford 1980). Instead, he posited 120 distinct intellectual abilities representing the structure of intellect. Guilford organized these factors along three dimensions that interact to determine different specific factors. The three dimensions consist of five types of mental operations, four types of content areas in which to perform the mental operations, and six products resulting from the application of different mental operations to different content areas. Each intellectual ability results from a unique combination of some mental operation being applied to some content area and resulting in some product. These dimensions do not represent higher order factors but simply provide an organizational framework for Guilford's structure-of-intellect theory. Guilford has attempted to create individual tests to specifically measure each of his posited 120 factors (Guilford and Hoepfner 1971). Although it has not been adequately validated empirically, Guilford's structure-of-intellect theory has led to the development of many educationally appropriate measures, particularly in the area of creativity.

In summary, the two major orientations in factor-analytic theories of intelligence have been to emphasize a general factor representing intelligence or to emphasize very specific factors of intelligence. The British approach to intelligence research has predominantly been concerned with the former orientation; the American approach has mainly considered the latter orientation. Whereas the British factor out a general factor first, then consecutively factor major and minor group and specific factors, the Americans factor out specific abilities and consider general factors as of secondary importance. These differing theoretical orientations of the British and American researchers have strongly affected the composition of various types of intelligence tests. In particular, it has led to a predominance of general aptitude testing in the United Kingdom versus a predominance of differential aptitude testing in the United States.

4. Individual and Group Tests

An enormous number of "mental" tests are available today. People interested in the various tests available and their respective properties should consult Buros (1974, 1978). Intelligence tests are typically divided into those involving group versus individual administration. In North America, the most frequently used individual intelligence tests are the revised version of the Stanford–Binet (Terman and Merrill 1960), the Wechsler Adult Intelligence Scale (WAIS), and the downward extension of the WAIS for children known as the WISC—Wechsler Intelligence Scale for Children (Wechsler 1974). A Wechsler Preschool and Primary Scale of Intelligence (WPPSI) for children aged 4 to 6 was introduced in 1967. Studies have shown that children's scores on the Stanford–Binet and WISC are highly correlated, with correlations ranging from 0.43 to 0.94, although the Stanford–Binet yields higher absolute intelligence quotients. The Stanford–Binet scales are arranged in order by ages, and the examiner finds the age level at which the examinee passes all tests. Testing then continues until the examinee reaches the test level at which none of the tests are passed. The major difference between the Stanford–Binet and Wechsler Intelligence Scale for Children is that the latter is organized into separate subtests which represent verbal and performance scales. The Wechsler Intelligence Scale for Children yields three separate IQ scores: verbal, performance, and full scale (Sattler 1974).

Whereas IQ (the intelligence quotient) was originally reported as the ratio of an individual's mental age to chronological age multiplied by 100 ($100 \times MA/CA$), IQ is now based upon normative score distributions for particular age groups. All individual and group tests currently in use yield such deviation IQs. The IQ is an indication of relative position within a given age group, with an IQ of 100 representing the 50th percentile.

There are many widely used group intelligence tests, the majority of which are targeted for children of school age. Group intelligence tests typically yield a single overall score as well as separate scores for verbal, quantitative and nonverbal scales. Frequently used group intelligence tests in North America include the Lorge–Thorndike, Otis–Lennon, California Tests of Mental Maturity, Kuhlmann–Anderson, and Cognitive Abilities Test. In addition to "general" intelligence tests, there are also specific abilities batteries such as the Science Research Association (SRA) Primary Mental Abilities Tests, the Differential Aptitude Tests, and the General Aptitude Test Battery. The specific abilities batteries include subtests measuring many of the same abilities assessed on "general" intelligence tests. All of the commercially published general and specific abilities

tests include extensive data on the psychometric properties of the test and various validity coefficients, including correlations with other intelligence tests and measures of achievement or school performance. In general, intelligence tests yield high correlations with each other and correlations between 0.4 and 0.8 with measures of academic achievement.

Most general intelligence tests include similar types of items. For example, the verbal item types most frequently found on such tests include vocabulary problems such as synonym and antonym items, classification items requiring the individual to select a word that is consistent with a group of words such as orange, apple, peach, and analogy items requiring the selection of a word to complete an analogy, for example, bird is to robin as fish is to —. Quantitative subtests include simple calculational problems and number–arrangement problems such as number series, for example, 3 7 11 5 7 12 7 7 —. The nonverbal subtests often parallel the verbal tests and include classification and analogy items. The selection of items found on tests is based upon various statistical properties with respect to the age range to be tested. Children of ages 8 and 9 are typically tested on different specific items than children of ages 14 and 15, although the general problem types may be identical, that is, both age groups solve verbal and nonverbal analogies and classification items and vocabulary items.

5. Uses and Abuses of Tests

Earlier it was noted that testing was developed in response to pragmatic concerns regarding educational selection and placement. The use of intelligence tests for educational selection and placement proliferated during the decades from the 1930s through 1960s as group tests for children became readily available. In recent years, however, general intelligence testing has declined in public educational institutions. One reason for diminished use of such tests is a trend away from homogeneous grouping of students and attendant educational tracking. A second reason is that achievement rather than aptitude testing became increasingly popular for educational assessment in various countries. Whereas children used to be administered aptitude tests at various points during the school year, they now more often receive end-of-year achievement tests as a regular part of educational assessment. Research has indicated that achievement tests tend to be better predictors of subsequent achievement than aptitude or intelligence tests.

Intelligence and aptitude tests are still used with great frequency in military, personnel-selection, and clinical settings. There are two major uses of intelligence tests within educational settings. One of these is for the assessment of mental retardation and learning disabilities. This particular use of tests is reminiscent of the original reason for development of the Binet and Simon scales in the early 1900s. The second major

225

use is at the postsecondary level. College entrance is frequently based upon performance on such measures as the Scholastic Aptitude Test (SAT) which was first adopted in the United States by the College Entrance Examination Board in 1937. Performance on the SAT, together with high-school grades, is the basis for admission to most colleges and universities in the United States.

Throughout the history of the testing movement, dating back to the early 1900s and extending to the present day, there has been controversy concerning test use. One of the earliest such debates was between Lewis Terman, who helped develop the revised Stanford–Binet and other tests, and the journalist Walter Lippman (see Block and Dworkin 1976). A frequent issue in debates about the uses and abuses of intelligence tests in society is that of bias. It is often argued that most standardized intelligence tests have differential validity for various racial, ethnic, and socioeconomic groups. Since the tests emphasize verbal skills and knowledge that are part of Western schooling, they are presumed to be unfair tests of the cognitive abilities of other groups. As a response to such arguments, attempts have been made to develop culture-fair or culture-free tests. The issue of bias in mental testing is beyond this brief review and Jensen (1980, 1981) should be consulted for highly detailed treatments of this topic. For a brief history of test use see Carroll (1978) and a discussion of social issues see Kamin (1974).

6. Factors Affecting Test Scores

Much of the research on intelligence has focused on specific factors affecting test scores. The majority of such research has centered on environmental versus genetic contributions to IQ scores and related issues such as race differences in IQ.

One issue that bears mention is age changes in IQ. Although most intelligence tests are targeted for school-age populations, there are instruments developed for younger age groups. Such tests emphasize the assessment of perceptual and motor abilities. Unfortunately, measures of infant and preschool intelligence tend to correlate poorly with intelligence tests administered during the school years. However, there appears to be a high degree of stability in the IQ scores obtained in the early primary grades and IQ scores obtained at the high-school level and beyond. Often this is misinterpreted as indicating that an individual's intelligence does not change as a function of schooling or other environmental factors. What such results actually indicate is that an individual's score relative to his or her age group remains fairly constant. In an absolute sense, an individual of age 16 can solve considerably more difficult items and problems than an individual of age 8. Comparing IQ scores obtained at different ages is akin to comparing apples and oranges since the composition of tests changes markedly over age levels.

Research has also been pursued on changes in IQ

following early adulthood. A frequent conclusion from research examining age groups ranging from 21 to 60 and beyond is that there is an age-related general decline in intellectual functioning. However, there are serious problems with many such studies since they involve cross-sectional rather than longitudinal contrasts. In those cases where longitudinal data are available, it is less obvious that intelligence declines with age. Horn and Cattell (1967) have presented data indicating a possible differential decline in crystallized and fluid intelligence measures. Crystallized intelligence measures focus on verbal skills and knowledge whereas fluid intelligence measures focus on reasoning and problem solving with visual and geometric stimuli. The latter also often place an emphasis on performance speed. Fluid intelligence measures tend to show declines as a function of age whereas crystallized intelligence measures show little or no decline.

7. Definitional Problems and Future Prospects

At the beginning of this article it was noted that after 100 years of research and theory on the nature of intelligence, there is still no clear definition of intelligence. Although it appears trite, a frequently used operational definition is that "intelligence is what intelligence tests measure." Even with this as a starting point, it is possible to go further and pursue this definition within the context of the tests themselves. Various related definitions of intelligence have been offered, including (a) the ability to adapt to the environment, (b) the ability to deal with symbols or abstractions and (c) the ability to learn. Intelligence tests tap all of these aspects of cognition since they typically assess what an individual has learned already and his or her ability to apply it in novel situations with both concrete and abstract materials. It is incorrect to assume that performance on intelligence tests is independent of prior learning or experience. The reason that intelligence tests predict future learning and achievement is that they sample how much an individual has already learned and how well that knowledge can be utilized for solving simple problems. It must be remembered that items included on intelligence tests are there for pragmatic rather than theoretical reasons. Intelligence tests do not typically emanate from a theory of cognition or intelligence but are based upon an atheoretical technology of measurement designed to optimize (a) the differentiation of individuals of the same age and (b) the prediction of some criterion performance, typically academic achievement.

The use of intelligence tests for educational selection and placement has declined in recent years, partly reflecting the torrent of criticism about the validity and utility of such tests. Some criticisms are well-founded, while others involve overblown rhetoric which lacks an understanding of the tests themselves and the limits on their validity. One reason for the current disfavor over intelligence testing in educational settings is that they are not diagnostic in nature and provide minimal information for adaptive educational programs. Intelligence tests yield relative rather than absolute assessments of an individual's cognitive abilities, thus providing little information about an individual's cognitive strengths and weaknesses. The trend in education has been away from norm-referenced assessment toward criterion-referenced assessment, and many achievement tests tend to offer both forms of assessment for guiding educational practice.

While the current trend is away from general intelligence testing, researchers working within the field of cognitive psychology have begun to explore issues concerning the cognitive processes and knowledge underlying performance on tasks found on intelligence and aptitude tests. This research reflects an attempt to understand what intelligence tests measure and how individuals differ, but within the general framework of theories of human memory and information processing. This relatively new area of research on the nature of intelligence and aptitude is considered in more detail elsewhere.

Bibliography

Binet A, Henri V 1896 La Psychologie individuelle. *Année Psychol.* 2: 411–65

Block N J, Dworkin G 1976 *The IQ Controversy: Critical Readings.* Pantheon Books, New York

Buros O K (ed.) 1974 *Tests in Print II: An Index to Tests, Test Reviews, and the Literature on Specific Tests.* Gryphon, Highland Park, New Jersey

Buros O K (ed.) 1978 *The Eighth Mental Measurements Yearbook.* Gryphon, Highland Park, New Jersey

Burt C L 1949 The structure of the mind: A review of the results of factor analysis. *Br. J. Educ. Psychol.* 19: 100–11, 176–99

Carroll J B 1978 On the theory-practice interface in the measurement of intellectual abilities. In: Suppes P (ed.)

1978 *Impact of Research on Education.* National Academy of Education, Washington, DC

Cattell R B 1963 Theory of fluid and crystallized intelligence: A critical experiment. *J. Educ. Psychol.* 54: 1–22

Cattell R B 1971 *Abilities: Their Structure, Growth and Action.* Houghton Mifflin, Boston, Massachusetts

Guilford J P 1967 *The Nature of Human Intelligence.* McGraw-Hill, New York

Guilford J P 1980 Fluid and crystallized intelligences: Two fanciful concepts. *Psychol. Bull.* 88: 406–12

Guilford J P, Hoepfner R 1971 *The Analysis of Intelligence.* McGraw-Hill, New York

Horn J L 1979 The rise and fall of human abilities. *J. Res. Dev. Educ.* 12: 59–78

Horn J L, Cattell R B 1967 Age differences in fluid and crystallized intelligence. *Acta Psychol.* 26: 107–29

International Review of Applied Psychology 1975 Vol. 24:2 (Special issue on intelligence in applied psychology)

Jensen A R 1980 *Bias in Mental Testing.* Free Press, New York

Jensen A R 1981 *Straight Talk About Mental Tests.* Free Press, New York

Kamin L J 1974 *The Science and Politics of IQ.* Erlbaum, Potomac, Maryland

Sattler J M 1974 *Assessment of Children's Intelligence.* Saunders, Philadelphia, Pennsylvania

Spearman C 1904 "General intelligence," objectively determined and measured. *Am. J. Psychol.* 15: 201–93

Spearman C E 1927 *The Abilities of Man: Their Nature and Measurement.* Macmillan, London

Terman L M, Merrill M A 1960 *Stanford-Binet Intelligence Scale: Manual for the Third Revision Form L–M.* Houghton Mifflin, Boston, Massachusetts

Thurstone L L 1924 *The Nature of Intelligence: A Biological Interpretation of the Mind.* Harcourt, Brace, New York

Thurstone L L 1938 Primary mental abilities. *Psychometric Monogr.* No. 1

Vernon P E 1961 *The Structure of Human Abilities*, 2nd edn. Methuen, London

Wechsler D 1974 *Manual for the Wechsler Intelligence Scale for Children.* Psychological Corporation, New York

Heredity–Environment Determinants of Intelligence

P. E. Vernon

To what extent human qualities are innately given or determined by upbringing and environment has long been a source of dissension between radical reformers and the conservative establishment. In England in the nineteenth century, it was taken for granted that the upper classes inherited abilities superior to those of the lower classes and required a better education to fit them for their position in life. Conversely in the United States all people were believed to be created equal, and to deserve equal educational opportunities (though this did not apply to the black slaves and their descendants). Such a polarity of ideologies does not necessarily coincide with political attitudes, though it is true that extreme hereditarian and racist views were held in Nazi Germany and extreme environmentalism prevailed in Soviet Russia.

The early pioneers of mental testing, particularly Terman in America and Burt in the United Kingdom, were convinced that their versions of the Binet–Simon Scale were measuring inborn ability, conceived as almost wholly determined by the genes, and developing with age irrespective of the environment in which children are reared. Hence the intelligence quotient (IQ), measured quite early in life, showed the level of education and occupation each child would be able to achieve. However, even in the 1920s, critics argued that the Army Alpha Test results of different national groups of recruits reflected the economic and educational environment of these groups, not innate ability. Several studies showed that children reared in deprived environments obtained low IQs and that, if adopted by well-educated foster parents, the scores tended to improve.

From the 1950s attacks on intelligence tests as measures of innate capacities mounted, and reached their climax in the years following the publication of A. R. Jensen's article supporting hereditarian views (1969). There was a violent reaction by radical student groups, black activists, and many social scientists against his suggestion that black–white differences in intelligence in the United States might be largely genetic in origin. This increased the distrust of intelligence testing amongst the general public. Also, in several legal contests the application of such tests for assigning dull children to special education programmes, or restricting entry to college or to various employments, was challenged, often successfully. However, the majority of psychologists rejected both extreme views, and admitted that both genetic and environmental factors are necessary for human intellectual growth, and that these interact with one another from conception onwards. Yet views still differ widely on the relative importance of these factors, with estimates of "heritability" of intelligence ranging from 40 percent or less to 70 percent or more. These figures represent genetic variance, that is, the extent to which genetic differences between people account for high or low intelligence scores. They do not imply that 40 percent or any other percentage of a person's intelligence is of genetic origin, for genetic potential is only realized in combination with appropriate environmental conditions. Also heritability is a population statistic, not an attribute of the particular ability. Nevertheless, it is possible to use the statistical technique of analysis of variance to estimate the major underlying factors in intelligence, and it is found that very little distortion occurs in assuming an additive model, where the total genetic and environmental components add up to 1.0 or 100 percent. Several subcomponents have also been investigated—(dominance, assortative mating, genetic–environmental covariance)—but there is little consensus among genetic statisticians regarding their relative importance.

1. Evidence of Genetic Determination

The bulk of evidence for genetic factors in intelligence derives from kinship studies, where correlations are found between parents and offspring, or between siblings, and particularly between twins. Monozygotic or identical twins are known to carry the same genes, whereas dizygotic or nonidenticals have only half their genes in common. First cousins share one eighth, and so on. The obtained correlation coefficients (r) between IQs of monozygotic twins do approximate to 1.0, as would be expected if intelligence was wholly genetic. Similarly the correlation coefficient for siblings, or for a child with one of his or her parents, approximates to 0.50. But some correlations do not fit closely, and different studies of the same kinship often give widely varying results. Bouchard and McGue (1981) have collated 111 studies, and the following are some of their average correlations: (a) for monozygotic twins reared together, the obtained figure of 0.86 falls below 1.0, partly because of test unreliability, but also probably because the twins' environments (including prenatal conditions) and upbringing have differed to some extent; (b) when the environments are more dissimilar, as with such twins reared apart, the correlation coefficient drops to 0.72; (c) dizygotic twins give a lower average of 0.60, as expected; but it is higher than the 0.47 for siblings, probably because they are brought up more alike; (d) pairs of unrelated children should give zero correlations, but two in the same home show 0.29, and an adopted child with one foster parent averages 0.19.

However, environmental similarities and differences cannot wholly account for the higher correlations between closely related pairs, as L. J. Kamin and some other critics argue. For example, it is most improbable that the environments of monozygotic twins reared apart (0.72) could be more alike than those of dizygotic twins reared together (0.60). There is evidence that monozygotic twins reared together are commonly treated more alike than dizygotic twins and siblings. But some writers suggest that identicals often strive to emphasize their differences and assert their individualities. Kamin has drawn attention to weaknesses in many of the studies that support genetic influences, though his arguments, according to some reviewers, are often based on dubious statistical analyses. In particular Kamin criticized the work of Cyril Burt, who was the leading figure in educational, child, and statistical psychology in the United Kingdom from 1909 to 1971. Burt claimed to have tested 53 pairs of separated monozygotic twins, obtaining a correlation coefficient of 0.88 between their IQs and also to have compared 826 persons in all who were variously related. This analysis led him to the extremely high estimate of 80 percent or more for the heritability of intelligence. A close examination of his published correlations by Jensen revealed numerous inconsistencies, and his methods of testing were open to criticism. But it was not until 1979 that L. S. Hearnshaw, having studied all the available personal documents, showed beyond any doubt that Burt had fabricated at least some of the twin data. Probably this occurred chiefly in the years following his retirement (i.e., aged 65 to 88); but it is impossible to determine how far earlier investigations were also flawed. Actually, most of his published findings have been replicated by the work of other, more scrupulous psychologists.

Another valid point raised by Kamin is that separated twins are unlikely to be placed randomly over the whole range of different environments. One or both usually go to the homes of relatives or to foster parents of education and socioeconomic status similar to that of the true parents. This would spuriously increase any intertwin correlation.

More generally, genetic–environmental covariance arises because the parents of children with superior genes usually provide better environments for stimulating intellectual growth. Also, such children are not only moulded by environment but also manage to improve it, by reading and seeking out stimulating experiences, for example. Most statisticians have ignored these possibilities, but others report covariance estimates of about 10 to 20 percent. This complicates the interpretation of the average parent–offspring or sibling correlation of about 0.50. Few writers, other than Burt, have realized the paradox that the resemblances between children's intelligence and that of their parents do not yield evidence of genetic influence, since it might also be explained by the environmental influence of parents on child upbringing. It is the fact that children often differ considerably in ability from their parents and siblings, which is really significant, since this would be expected on the grounds of genetic theory, but could hardly be accounted for environmentally.

2. Adoption Studies and Other Evidence

Adopted children obviously carry genes different from those of their foster parents, but are likely to be affected by the foster-home upbringing. Several studies have found a tendency for foster-child IQs to rise above the level expected in their true-parent homes, though the maximum gain seems to be about 10 IQ points. Alternatively, correlations are calculated between children and foster parents, and these tend to be lower than the correlations with true-parent ability (if known). However, different studies vary, and the data are often unsatisfactory for various reasons, including selective placement, where the adoption agency tries to place the child with foster parents of education and socioeconomic status similar to those of the true parents. This tends to boost child–foster parent correlations, and would partly account for the unexpectedly high correlation of 0.29 between unrelated children in the same home.

Another line of evidence is provided by the known dependence of certain mental deficiencies—such as those of Down syndrome and Turner's syndrome—on specific gene anomalies. It has been claimed, too, that close inbreeding, ranging from incestuous matings to first-cousin marriages, tends to increase the number of low-intelligence children. However, the published studies on this point are open to criticism.

Genetic theory is also supported by the appearance of special talents at a very early age, such as Mozart's genius, which could not possibly be explained by the influence of a musical home upbringing. J. Stanley makes similar claims for mathematical prodigies, whose ability much exceeds what could be ascribed to environment. Though much disputed, many psychologists would consider the superior numerical and visuospatial abilities of boys, and the superior linguistic abilities of girls, as having some genetic basis, and not wholly attributable to cultural expectations of the two sexes.

The fact that the total size of the brain (not the skull) has correlations approximating 0.30 with IQ further suggests a biological basis for intelligence. In the late 1970s, Jensen, H. J. Eysenck, and others investigated the relations between IQ and certain measures of mental speed. Although simple reaction time gives very little correlation, choice reaction—where the subject has to respond to any one of eight stimuli—is more strongly related, as also is low variability of response times. Inspection-time tests—discriminating which of two lines, shown very briefly, is the longer—are also indicative. A combination of several such tests of information processing speed gives multiple correlations of 0.6 to 0.8 with IQ. Eysenck has claimed similar validities for the speed of evoked potentials in brain waves.

Apparently, then, the intelligence of adults and children can be measured with some accuracy without using tests that are affected by cultural background. These cognitive tests are not dependent on past experience, language, training, or motivation. However, caution is needed before assuming that they represent genetic intelligence. Experiments on baby rats by M. R. Rosenzweig showed that stimulation by handling improved their later maze learning. Thus, it is possible that environmental stimulation of humans brings about brain growth, rather than the other way round.

3. Ethnic and Racial Group Differences

The claim for genetic differences in intelligence between racial or ethnic groups is highly unpopular since, throughout history, supposedly inferior groups have been the victims of discrimination, hostility, repression, and even genocide. Though there is evidence both for and against the notion of genetic differences, there are no satisfactory methods of separating genetic from cultural influences. A very thorough survey of black–white differences by Loehlin et al. (1975) concluded that they are partly attributable to "inadequacies and biases in the tests themselves", partly to "differences in environmental conditions", and partly genetic. But it is not possible to tell "the relative weight to be given to these three factors".

Since there are obvious physical differences between races, there is no a priori reason why there should not also be neurological (mental) differences, especially when, as Jensen points out, there are large genetic individual differences. If unfavourable environment was the main factor underlying the 15-point difference in IQ between American blacks and whites, it is surprising that this has remained almost constant from 1918 to the present, despite considerable advancement in the economic and educational status of blacks. On the other hand, the descendants of immigrants who were of poor peasant stock and presumably below average genetically, do not seem to retain this low level. Rather, they catch up with American-white norms in a couple of generations.

In Klineberg and Lee's frequently quoted studies, black children whose parents migrated from the south to the more favourable environment of New York and

Philadelphia, showed significant gains, as was also the case in some rather unsatisfactory studies of black children adopted by white foster parents, though the gains in both cases were still much smaller than the conventional 15 points. A striking finding by Jensen, which seems to defy any simple environmental explanation, was that Hispanic American and American Indian children, who were living under even worse environmental conditions than blacks, nevertheless surpassed them in mean scores on nonverbal intelligence tests. Again, Chinese and Japanese immigrants in the nineteenth and twentieth centuries were subject to severe discrimination, but have nevertheless come to exceed whites in educational and occupational achievement. Oriental children's nonverbal scores are higher than the white norms, and though their performance on verbal tests was lower at first, they now approximate those of whites. However, it is more plausible to account for their progress in terms of family upbringing, and the values held by Oriental parents. This might also hold for Jews, who consistently average higher than Caucasians on verbal intelligence tests.

The black–white issue is complicated by the facts that most blacks have some white ancestry due to cross-breeding in the past, and they also share a great deal of the American culture, for example, schooling, language, and television. With more distant cultures, such as those of Africa or Asia, the languages, concept development, upbringing, and norms of behaviour are so different from those of whites that testing them with American tests (even if translated) gives very little information on genetic differences. Nonverbal or performance tests have often been applied, but here, too, remote peoples may perceive and interpret shapes or pictures very differently from Americans. Many tests adapted for use in foreign cultures can be validly used for selection or assignment within the culture, though not for making intercultural comparisons.

The only reasonable conclusion from such conflicting evidence is that no dogmatic statements are justified, either that one racial group is innately inferior to another in intellectual potential, or that improved health, social, and educational conditions would wipe out all intellectual differences between groups. Further, it is untrue that all members of any one group are inferior to another, either in potential or performance. There is much overlapping. Thus, some 15 percent of blacks obtain higher IQs than the average white, and 15 percent of whites are lower than the average black. Clearly, each individual should be judged on his or her own merits and not on a racial–ethnic label.

4. Constitutional Factors

There are numerous physiological conditions which affect intellectual growth adversely. These are usually present at birth, but they are constitutional, not genetic, in origin. They occur much more frequently in low-social-class and ethnic-minority families. Dull and poorly educated parents often live in poverty. The mother's health is weakened and she is likely to incur "reproductive casualty" (to use Pasamanick's term). Infant mortality is high, and surviving children may be unhealthy, inadequately cared for, or malnourished. They achieve poorly at school and are fit only for unskilled jobs. So the cycle repeats itself and it is difficult to say which features of this syndrome are causes and which effects.

Mothers who take drugs or alcohol, or undergo physical or emotional stress during pregnancy, are especially apt to produce premature or unhealthy babies. Prematurely born children and those with a difficult delivery tend to be below average in intelligence, though this adverse effect seems to decrease as they grow older. Retardation, learning disabilities, and dyslexia are often attributed to minimal brain damage. But this is an unsatisfactory diagnosis, since it is not usually possible to tell such damage exists, nor its location in the brain, and it is of little help in planning remediation. Poor nutrition is known to affect the growth of brain cells, particularly over the period between 3 months before and 6 months after birth. When severe, as in many African countries, it leads to deficiency diseases, such as marasmus and kwashiorkor. But in technologically developed countries, although the diet of the poorest classes is often defective, the effects on children's mental development are usually slight.

Family size, birth order, and spacing also have minor but significant effects on intelligence. A negative correlation of 0.2 to 0.3 has frequently been found between numbers of children in a family and their average IQ; the deficit increases if they are born in quick succession. According to Zajonc's "confluence theory", this occurs because the parents' care and attention are spread more thinly than in small families. This would account, too, for the lower average IQ of twins than of singletons, though the frequency of prematurity among twins may also be involved. First-born children tend to be superior in educational and occupational achievements, since they receive more parental care and stimulation than those born later. However, only children are somewhat lower than first-borns, possibly because they lack the stimulus of interacting with younger siblings. The theory that the lower intelligence of large families will lead to a decline in the average IQ of the next generation is not confirmed. Moreover, the relative fertility of upper-, middle-, and lower-class parents fluctuates in different countries and at different periods.

5. Early Stimulation and Deprivation

Remarkable advances in knowledge of early child development, made in the 1970s, have shown that young children are active in their own mental growth, and not merely shaped by the environment. They appear to have inborn dispositions to be selectively attentive to human visual and auditory stimuli, and to react particularly to any novel experiences. Quite early in the first year, children and their mothers engage in what might be called prelinguistic conversations, that is, activities in which each stimulates the other in turn. The mother's talking encourages the infant's vocalizations and later speech. However, there is little direct evidence of lasting effects on the children's intelligence, and it would be difficult to follow up these ephemeral interchanges. Thus, more information has been obtained from studies of children reared under conditions of severe deprivation and lack of stimulation.

Several instances have been reported of children brought up for years with virtually no human contact or experience of the world outside their own room. When discovered and rescued, they had no speech and their intelligence, in so far as it could be measured, was at imbecile level. Some never recovered fully, but others, placed in good foster homes, made rapid progress, becoming socialized, speaking fluently, and approximating to normal intelligence in a few years. Thus, early damage to mental development is not irreversible. Other work, such as that of Spitz, has shown retarded physical and mental growth among babies in institutions where there is minimal human care and visual stimulation. Similar findings on the effects of restricted versus enriched environments on the mental development of rats and dogs have been reported by D. O. Hebb.

A striking investigation by H. M. Skeels of 24 orphans (aged 7 to 30 months) in a highly unstimulating institution, showed that those transferred to a hospital, where they received better care and attention, improved greatly in IQ. When traced 25 years later, he found that the transferred cases were normal, self-supporting adults, many of them in skilled employment, whereas the nontransferred were all either still institutionalized or in very low-grade jobs.

In the Milwaukee Experiment, Garber and Heber (1977) provided 20 Negro babies from poor backgrounds with a highly stimulating upbringing for six years. This was designed to develop their sensory-motor, language, and thinking skills. Numerous tests from 2 to 9 years of age showed them to average some 24 points higher in IQ than matched controls reared in their own homes. Complete details are not yet available, and it is possible that the stimulated group, in ordinary schools, may lose some of their advantage. Note should be made that gains of up to 30 points, claimed by Skeels and Garber, fall within the range to be expected on Jensen's or other theories which allow 20 percent of environmental variance.

It is generally agreed that the formation of close mother–child bonds in the early months is crucial to normal cognitive growth. The father is also important in providing a male model to boys. If he is absent for prolonged periods during early childhood, whether because of job demands, marital disharmony, or other reasons, the sons tend to show poorer self-esteem and are more given to antisocial activities with peers. Their abilities come to resemble the female pattern, with lowered mathematical and visuospatial scores.

6. Other Intervention Studies

Several studies have found that attendance at day care centres or other kinds of preschool from about 2 to 5 years of age does not produce IQ gains. On the other hand, this separation from home does not appear to be harmful if the centre provides good mother substitutes. Bronfenbrenner summarized several investigations of psychologically designed programmes, such as Levenstein's, which obtained average improvements of 10 to 20 IQ points. Though there has been some later follow-up, it is not clear how lasting the gains are. With children under the age of 2, the most successful schemes involve visits by psychologists or social workers to the homes and giving the mothers practical instruction in how to interact with and stimulate their babies. Weekly attendance of mothers and children at a centre also helps, but the mere provision of classes in child rearing seems ineffective.

Much the largest intervention scheme was the Head Start experiment in the late 1960s and the 1970s. Approximately half a million children each year, from unfavourable home backgrounds, received some 5 to 10 months of schooling before entering grade 1. This was designed to compensate for their handicaps and to help them to adjust better to ordinary schooling. The earliest follow-up studies found that such programmes yielded IQ gains, but within another year or two this superiority disappeared, and the children achieved no better than others of similar background who had not attended. However, additional "follow-through" programmes in grades 1 to 3 produced more lasting effects. As described by Zigler and Valentine (1979), the main benefits were socioemotional rather than intellectual. The children's health improved, as did their self-esteem and confidence at school. Up to grade 8, significantly fewer had to repeat grades or be assigned to special-education classes. In many ways, also, the parents and the community profited. Some differences were observed as a result of different types of programme: students in highly structured schools showed more positive achievement gains than those in strongly child-centred schools.

7. Effects of Schooling and Socioeconomic Status

Reports on inequalities of family background and education by J. S. Coleman and by C. Jencks in the United States concluded that differences in quality or type of schooling made little difference in achievement. However, M. J. Rutter in England claimed that performance on objective achievement tests is too narrow a criterion of effective schooling. He found significant differences at grade 9 between 10 secondary schools on a variety of outcomes, including conventional written examinations, delinquency rates, and behaviour at school, even when holding constant the ability level of the students entering each school. Some of the influential school characteristics were size and age of school, academic emphasis in the instruction, differences between teachers, and especially the overall climate of the school and student–teacher relationships (Rutter et al. 1979).

A wide range of environmental variables correlate positively with child IQ, though this does not prove that they are causative. Thus, the typical correlation with parental socioeconomic status of 0.30 to 0.35 is probably partly genetic. Parents in high-grade jobs are likely to pass on genes underlying high intelligence to their offspring. This by no means denies that children reared by well-off and well-educated parents receive better stimulation than poorer children, nor that high-soc-ioeconomic-status parents can often exert influence to get their offspring good jobs. Additional evidence comes from Cox and Terman's study of geniuses, which found that about one-fifth of them came from lower-middle- or lower-class homes. J. H. Waller showed that sons whose adolescent IQs surpassed those of their fathers tended to achieve higher socioeconomic status jobs than the fathers, whereas those with lower IQs were more likely to be downwardly mobile. This could hardly be explained environmentally.

Socioeconomic status itself is a poorly defined variable, some of its components being more relevant to child IQ than others. Thus, the educational level of both parents correlates more highly than family income. Bloom and his students found that parents' educational aspirations, and the linguistic and cultural stimulation they provided, correlated as highly as 0.76 with a child's intelligence at grade 5. Some of the most influential work has been that of B. Bernstein on differences in language usage by social class. He distinguishes the "formal or elaborated code" from the "public or restricted code". The former, which is mostly used in middle- and upper-class homes, is more precise and analytic. The latter is more ungrammatical and expressive of emotions and personal relations. Formal language is generally necessary for conceptual thinking, and the organized planning of activities, and it is linked with middle-class values. Since school teachers chiefly use it, children from lower-class homes are handicapped by having to learn what is almost a new language.

It is generally more difficult to prove the effects on intelligence of environmental factors than of genetic factors because of the complexity and diversity of environments and the variability of people's responses to the same environmental pressure. Frequently, therefore, plausible suggestions regarding environmental influences fail to be confirmed by validatory studies (for instance the alleged effects of broken homes on the development of black children). Jensen has pointed out that environmentalists are apt to put forward ad hoc hypotheses for which there is little or no evidence, and he calls these "X-hypotheses", because it is obvious that a person can explain anything by factors that he or she knows nothing about.

8. Criticisms of Intelligence Tests, and Conclusions

The commonly alleged weaknesses in intelligence tests are discussed elsewhere, and most of these criticisms can be answered fairly effectively (see Vernon 1979). However, it is true, as J. McV. Hunt and B. S. Bloom pointed out in the early 1960s, that children are more variable and plastic in their mental growth than is generally realized. Intelligence is certainly not predetermined at birth. Such fluctuations probably arise from internal maturational changes as well as from changes in external environment.

In view of the theory of interaction between genes and environment, the frequent objection that tests only measure "learned skills" is a misconception. Most critics also assert that intelligence tests are culturally biased, and, therefore, are unfair to children who do not have the same cultural advantages as middle-class whites. But the mere fact that children or adults from lower-class homes or minority groups score below average does not prove that the tests are biased. Such persons also perform poorly on any other criterion of intellectual achievement, for example, at school, or in jobs that depend on complex thinking. Thus it has been shown repeatedly that the test scores of minority-group students correctly predict their likelihood of success in college, just as do the scores of majority-group students. Jensen (1981) has analysed the various implications of the term "test bias" and provided evidence to counter this criticism. One interesting finding is that people (whether psychologists or not) are unable to distinguish between test items that are more, or less, "unfair" to disadvantaged groups. However, some groups, such as Hispanic Americans or new immigrants from foreign countries, are much handicapped by lack of knowledge of English, and in their case, scores on American tests must be distorted or biased.

These attacks on intelligence testing, whether justifiable or not, have been of benefit to psychology in showing that no type of psychological enquiry exists in a social vacuum. All types reflect to some extent the ideologies, the culture, and the thinking styles of their authors, and all have social consequences or side effects—often unforeseen. In his book, *The Ecology of Child Development*, Bronfenbrenner brings out the interaction between children's behaviour and the wider social context of home, school, and the political–economic system. A simple example is the different behaviour of children (including test responses) when observed in an unfamiliar experimental laboratory, as against their behaviour in their own homes. Tests themselves may not be biased, but the uses to which they are put do involve ethical considerations and social values.

Several writers have criticized the commonly accepted view that low-socioeconomic status and minority children do badly on tests because they are deficient in some respects, whether this arises from their deprived environment or from genetic causes (the deficiency hypothesis). In other words, the victims are blamed for their lack of ability, rather than asking whether the educational or social systems are responsible. All the important decisions about educational policy are taken by middle-class whites, with a view to helping their own children's progress. They assume, perhaps unwittingly, that children from other subcultures are, and always will be, inferior. The results from mental tests are, in effect, being used to preserve the status quo.

Thus, the protagonists in the heredity–environment controversy are at cross-purposes, neither side accepting the kind of evidence that is cited by the other side. Fortunately, though, most psychologists have more moderate views, and agree that both sides have made useful contributions. They see the issue as a matter of theoretical interest, but not necessarily of much practical importance. The hereditarians (apart from a few diehards) do not advocate reduction of any measures designed to benefit the disadvantaged, nor do they support discriminatory practices. Jensen, for example, believes that the question of hereditary or environmental determination could be ignored if mental tests were used for their proper purpose, namely as a guide to psychologists, teachers, and parents in planning the most suitable type of education for the individual child. The recognition of genetic differences also implies that educational programmes should be diversified to suit different students instead of, as at present, submitting all disadvantaged children to the same monolithic education which inevitably dooms large numbers to failure.

Bibliography

Bouchard T J, McGue M 1981 Familial studies of intelligence: A review. *Science* 212: 1055–59

Bronfenbrenner U 1974 Is early intervention effective? *Teach. Coll. Rec.* 76: 279–303

Eysenck H J, Kamin L J 1981 *The Intelligence Controversy.* Wiley, New York

Garber H, Heber R 1977 The Milwaukee project. In: Mittler P J (ed.) 1977 *Research to Practice in Mental Retardation: 4th Congress of the International Association for the Scientific Study of Mental Deficiency.* University Park Press, Baltimore, Maryland, pp. 119–27

Husén T 1974 *Talent, Equality and Meritocracy.* Nijhoff, The Hague

Jensen A R 1969 How much can we boost IQ and scholastic achievement? *Harvard Educ. Rev.* 39: 1–123

Jensen A R 1981 *Straight Talk About Mental Tests.* Free Press, New York

Loehlin J C, Lindzey G, Spuhler J N 1975 *Race Differences in Intelligence.* Freeman, San Francisco, California

Rutter M J, Maughan B, Mortimore P, Ouston J, Smith A 1979 *Fifteen Thousand Hours: Secondary Schools and Their Effects on Children.* Open Books, London

Vernon P E 1979 *Intelligence: Heredity and Environment.* Freeman, San Francisco, California

Zigler E F, Valentine J (eds.) 1979 *Project Head Start: A Legacy of the War on Poverty.* Macmillan, New York

Learning Processes

Basic Concepts of Learning Theories

R. M. Thomas

In a broad sense, learning can be defined as the process of effecting change in a person's thoughts and observable actions as the result of experience. Therefore, learning contrasts with maturation, which typically is defined as the process of change resulting from the internal growth and ripening of the person's nervous system and musculature. Learning and maturation are thus complementary processes, each depending on the other. A child cannot profit from the experience of trying to read until a certain level of neural maturation has already taken place. Likewise, experience or practice is necessary for maturation to blossom into useful thought and action. Hence, human development—in the sense of progressive changes in a person's physical characteristics and mental functions—results from the coordinated advance of maturation and learning.

If facts are defined as "reports of observed phenomena," then theories can be defined as "interpretations of how the facts interact." Learning theories are therefore psychologists' attempts to explain how the facts of people's experiences alter their knowledge and their behavior.

The main purpose of this article is to introduce five central concepts that theorists employ in their explanations and to illustrate ways in which one theorist's views of these concepts can differ from another's. A further purpose is to suggest what each concept can imply for educational practice.

As the discussion proceeds, it should become apparent that theorists usually do not disagree entirely with each other about all components of the learning process. For example, there is general agreement that learning requires that the individual (a) be motivated, (b) interact with the environment, (c) incorporate or interpret the results of this interaction, (d) remember or store past experiences, and (e) when the occasion calls for it, display the learning in observable action. However, theorists disagree over which components deserve the greatest emphasis and how the various components operate.

1. The Breadth of Learning Theories

One way to compare theories is in terms of what range of learning they attempt to encompass. In the past it has often been the hope of theorists to discover a set of principles that will explain all types of learning under all conditions. However, those models intended to perform this ambitious function have tended to explain some types of learning far better than others. As a consequence, a more recent trend has been toward devising narrower and more formal theories so that there is a great variety of theories available today. To account for such diversity, Hill (1980 p. 254) has proposed that:

> There are two generalizations that we can make with a good deal of confidence. One is that narrow theories have a greater chance to be precise than do broader ones: the more situations one tries to encompass in a theoretical system, the more likely it is that one's predictions will apply more-or-less to many situations but not closely to any. The other generalization is that theories can be more precise when they deal with controlled experimental situations than when they deal with the variable situations of everyday life. Theories developed in the laboratory are, of course, applied to everyday life, but in this application they lose some of the precision that is their greatest asset.

For teachers and curriculum planners, Hill's remarks suggest that the learning theory of most practical aid is one that is based on learning situations much like those faced in the classroom, in the vocational-education shop, in the home economics laboratory, in the typing and shorthand class, or on the athletics field.

2. Cognition versus Behavior

An important distinction among theorists is the degree to which they focus attention on overt action as contrasted with covert thought. Behaviorists, such as Skinner (1974), consider it unprofitable to speculate about what goes on in a person's "mind," so they limit their attention to overt actions and to ways that other people, such as parents or teachers, can influence those actions. For behaviorists, the evidence that something has been learned is found solely in the changes seen in a person's actions.

In contrast, cognitive psychologists believe it is important to speculate about what goes on in people's minds. On the basis of people's actions and introspective reports, the cognitive psychologist tries to discover the structures and functions of the intellect. For example, Piaget (Piaget and Inhelder 1969) proposed that the contents of people's minds were patterns of thought and of physical action he called schemes. People facing new situations either assimilate the situation (match it to an existing scheme), or if no existing scheme seems to fit the new situation, they accommodate the situation (reform existing schemes so as to create new ones that will fit). Thus, according to Piaget's speculation, learning consists of revising and multiplying schemes so people can adapt to an increasingly wide varieity of life situations.

Information-processing theorists, as another group of cognitive psychologists, postulate a series of mental functions intended to explain learning and memory. They speak of such functions as sensation (stimuli impinging on sense organs), perception (the interpretation of the stimuli), short-term memory (a brief retention of the interpretation), long-term memory (the storage of interpretations and of goals), memory contents (facts, concepts, procedures, affects), associational linkages (relations among memory contents), and more.

Unlike behaviorists, cognitive psychologists assume that learning does occur "in the head" even when it is not evidenced in overt behavior, so that people do acquire new facts, concepts, and skills without publicly displaying such learning.

We may now ask: Of what significance for educators is this debate between cognitive theorists and behaviorists? For classroom practice it is likely that both sorts of theories will appear much the same, since both require the same kind of evidence for judging whether students have properly learned what was taught. Even though the cognitivist assumes that students have acquired much "in their minds," it is still necessary for both the cognitivist and behaviorist to obtain from students some kind of behavioral evidence (oral reports, test answers, written descriptions, physical actions) to show how well they have achieved the instructional goals.

3. Comprehension versus Habit

Another way learning theories can differ is in the attention they give to the initial perception or first comprehension of a concept or action as compared to the habitual application of the action in life situations.

As an example of emphasis on initial comprehension, a popular form of social learning theory holds that a great many of the new concepts and actions people acquire are first gained through imitating models (Bandura 1977). When children observe other people, they learn by copying the speech patterns, beliefs,

and actions of those models they would like to emulate. Such models can either be people in the children's immediate lives or those seen on television or described in books. As a consequence, learning for such theorists can mean both the initial understanding of a new idea or action and the continued use of it thereafter.

Radical behaviorists, on the other hand, pay little or no attention to how an individual first grasps an idea or action. Instead, they concentrate on how a new behavior pattern becomes well-established, that is, how it becomes habitually used in similar stimulus situations. Hence, learning for traditional behaviorists means essentially the habitual display of a particular action rather than its first comprehension (Skinner 1974).

4. Associational Links versus Proclivities to Organize

A further issue that can divide theorists is the question of whether learning consists of new experience simply hooking itself onto the individual's chain of past perceptions so as to form one added link in the individual's knowledge network. In effect, is a person's store of learning determined entirely by the sequence in which new stimuli are met in life and by the duration, salience, and after effects (reward or punishment) of each stimulus? Or, instead, do stimuli not automatically link onto past experiences but, rather, the person's mind casts an intuitive organizational pattern on stimuli, thereby predetermining how each new event will be comprehended and stored in memory?

Psychologists who emphasize the linking process have been known as associationists. Those who stress the influence of intuitive organizational proclivities have been called rationalists or structuralists. Rationalists have included Gestalt psychologists (the German noun *Gestalt* means "pattern" or "form,") such linguistic theorists as Chomsky (1972) and McNeill (1970), and the genetic epistemologist Piaget (Piaget and Inhelder 1969).

What, then, might these two conflicting conceptions of the learning process imply for educational practice? We might assume that a teacher operating from an associationist perspective would pay special attention to the order in which new ideas or actions are presented. By offering students the material in a properly linked sequence, the teacher would expect to control the way the learning becomes organized in the student's mind or behavior system. But for a teacher of a rationalist bent, the order in which material is served might not be so important as the level of maturational readiness of the learner. Such rationalists as Piaget assumes that the mental structure or mental lenses through which the learner interprets stimuli are not all present at birth. Instead, over the first two decades of life the

structures change, becoming ever more sophisticated,
A 4-year-old's interpretive structures differ from
those of a 15-year-old. Thus, if teachers are to succeed, it is not so important that they sequence the
stimuli in the linkage order that they want it to assume
in the learner's mind. Rather, it is more important
that they suit the complexity of the stimuli and its
presentation to the learner's current mode of perceiving
the world.

It should be clear, however, that a theorist need not
be entirely an associationist or a rationalist. As Gagné
(1965) has proposed, some measure of both associationism and rationalism can be incorporated into a
theory.

5. The Role of Reinforcement

Theorists and practitioners alike have been keenly interested in the controversy over the effect that consequences have on learning. Cast as a question, the
issue becomes: How do the events that follow a learning
incident influence what the person will learn from that
incident? Among teachers and parents, this issue is
usually considered to be one of reward versus punishment. Among psychologists the issue is often referred
to as a debate over the role of contiguity and of
reinforcement.

Theorists known as stimulus–response psychologists
are ones whose explanations of learning focus primarily
on the relationship between an event in the environment
(a stimulus) and a person's reaction to the event (an
associated response). The question of interest here is:
How does a given stimulus become connected to a given
response so that in the future when an identical—or
highly similar—stimulus appears, the person reacts with
the same sort of response? In other words: How are
habits learned? The most common answer from the
distant past is expressed in the principle of contiguity—
that ideas or events experienced together tend
to become associated (Bower and Hilgard 1981). For
some theorists, such as Guthrie (1952) and Tolman
(1959), the fact that the two things happen at nearly
the same time is sufficient for them to become
connected. However, for others, such as Skinner
(1974) and Bandura (1977), the key to establishing
a lasting association between the two events or ideas
lies in the consequences attendant upon the association between the two. In layperson's terms, a lasting connection is established if the pairing of the
two events results in rewarding consequences for the
person, but the connection is lost or at least is weakened if the consequences are either unrewarding
or are punishing. Behaviorists, when speaking of
such matters, usually substitute the word *reinforcer*
(meaning a consequence that strengthens the bond
between stimulus and response) for the layperson's
term *reward*.

Not only is there debate over the contiguity-

reinforcement issue, but theorists who subscribe to the
reinforcement position may disagree with each other
over how reinforcement operates. Skinner (1974) has
suggested that the reinforcement occurs automatically
so that when a response (a pigeon taps a lever) is
followed by a reinforcing consequence (a kernel of corn
appears), the tendency is automatically strengthened
for the pigeon to act the same way when in the same
kind of stimulus situation in the future. However, such
cognitive psychologists as Bandura (1977) disagree with
this automatic-strengthening notion. Instead, they propose that the consequences of the contiguity of stimulus
and response simply give the learner information about
how to act in the future. If the response has been
followed by a rewarding consequence, the individual
expects the same to happen in the future, so it would
be well to try that same response on future occasions.
But if the consequence on this occasion was nonrewarding or punishing, the learner realizes that it would
be unwise to respond that way again under similar
conditions.

Thus it is that learning theorists have not entirely
agreed on how and why associations develop between
two or more events. However, both empirical evidence
and common sense suggest that consequences do indeed
influence learners' future actions. Rewards do increase
the chance that the behavior preceding the reward will
occur again when the learner is in a similar circumstance,
and punishment will decrease that chance. However,
for the teacher or parent it is often difficult to determine
which kind of consequence the child or youth will regard
as a sufficient reward (reinforcer) or a sufficient punishment, because there are differences among learners
in the sorts of incentives they find attractive. Identifying
what will serve as a sufficient reinforcer often requires
some trial and error experimentation on the part of the
teacher or parent.

Bibliography

Bandura A 1977 *Social Learning Theory*. Prentice-Hall, Engle-
wood Cliffs, New Jersey
Bower G H, Hilgard E R 1981 *Theories of Learning*, 5th edn.
Prentice-Hall, Englewood Cliffs, New Jersey
Chomsky N 1972 *Language and the Mind*. Harcourt Brace
Jovanovich, New York
Gagné R M 1965 *The Conditions of Learning*. Holt, Rinehart
and Winston, New York
Guthrie E R 1952 *The Psychology of Learning*, rev. edn.
Harper and Row, New York
Hill W F 1980 *Learning: A Survey of Psychological Inter-
pretations*, 3rd edn. Methuen, London
McNeill D 1970 *The Acquisition of Language*. Harper and
Row, New York
Piaget J, Inhelder B 1969 *The Psychology of the Child*. Basic
Books, New York
Skinner B F 1974 *About Behaviorism*. Knopf, New York
Tolman E C 1959 Principles of purposive behavior. In: Koch
S (ed.) 1959 *Psychology: A Study of a Science*, Vol. 2.
McGraw-Hill, New York, pp. 92–157

Historical Backgrounds of Learning Theory

J. W. Cotton

Learning is a process of gaining new knowledge or skill. In order to qualify as learning rather than just temporary gain, this process must include retention of the knowledge or skill so that it can be displayed at a future time. Learning may be more formally defined as a relatively permanent change in behavior or potential behavior resulting from experience. The purposes of learning theory are to describe, predict, and explain learning in human beings and in animals. As these purposes are attained, the practical work of teaching others or even oneself also becomes easier.

Though early learning theory sought to be comprehensive, interpreting most of the existing data and observations about learning processes, later work has tended to be more specialized. The major categorization of learning is twofold: (a) the study of choice behavior, such as the choice of a rat to press or not to press a lever in a cage right now or the choice of an author to write or not to write part of a short story today, and (b) the study of changes in the knowledge that a person has memorized and can repeat or the kinds of questions to which a person can infer appropriate answers even if those answers have not been memorized. The first kind of learning has a large component of motivation; a researcher wants to know why the organism being studied engages in one activity rather than another. Motivational effects of the latter kind of learning do exist but are often mediated by the choices that are made. Later parts of this article will call attention to the ways that rewards and similar events called reinforcements affect the acquisition of habits such as bar pressing and writing novels.

Although choice behavior can be studied in most species, it is easier to study the acquisition of knowledge in humans than in other organisms. Therefore, theories dealing with the first topic are based both on studies of animal (i.e., nonhuman) behavior and studies of human behavior. Theories dealing with the second topic are primarily based on studies of human behavior.

A difference in philosophy corresponds to the difference in research topics just noted. This difference is dependent upon a distinction between two kinds of responses which can be learned. An observable or overt response to the question "What is 2 plus 1 plus 9?" might be "12." A covert or mental response to that question might be "2 plus 1 is 3, and 3 plus 9 is 12." A psychologist who studies animal behavior has no way of finding out the internal or covert responses of the animal and so must study overt behavior, possibly supplementing it with observations of physiological behavior such as changes in heart rate or respiration. A psychologist who studies humans can ask a person to report what he or she is thinking when answering an arithmetic question or some other question which is presumed to involve covert responses in addition to overt ones. Therefore, it is more convenient for the latter psychologist to develop a learning theory which discusses internal mental events as well as directly observable responses. Persons who incorporate internal mental events into their theories are called cognitive theorists. Those who do not are called behaviorists.

Note that the choice of a cognitive versus a behavioristic theory is not simply a function of the kind of organism a person decides to investigate. There are important reasons why many psychologists who study humans take a behavioristic position. When a person is asked to report on what he or she is thinking or experiencing, as well as to report on the solution of a problem, that person may not want to tell the whole truth for some reason. Furthermore, that person may not even be conscious of all the reasons for a particular overt response to a problem or other stimulus event. Accordingly, the psychologist knows what the person reported the mental processes to be, but can never be certain that those exact processes did in fact occur. The behaviorist chooses to treat such reports as further overt behavior and not as indications of something going on in the mind of the learner. On the other hand, the cognitive theorist believes that the intermediate steps in an arithmetic problem are vital to the solution of that problem. While there may be some inaccuracy in a student's report of those steps, the cognitive theorists use that report as an indication of what the student may have been thinking and also as a guide to experimental procedures that might influence both the overt solution and the internal responses reported by the student.

An authoritative source of information on theories of learning (Bower and Hilgard 1981) has been extensively used in preparation of the present essay. Interested readers are encouraged to examine that book for further information. Examination of a sizeable compendium of original writings in this field is also recommended (Sahakian 1976).

The theories of learning discussed in this article are associated with six psychologists out of many whose work could be emphasized: Pavlov, Skinner, Tolman, Guthrie, Hull, and Estes. Although all continue to have some influence on the field, only two (Skinner and Estes) are now living. Hence, the discussion of four of these theorists is largely an historical analysis rather than a statement of current trends.

1. Pavlovian Conditioning Theory

The earliest behavioristic theory of learning was developed by a Russian psychologist, Ivan Pavlov (1849–1936). This theory, often called the theory of classical conditioning (as opposed to instrumental or operant conditioning to be discussed later), was an interpretation of a large number of experiments (e.g., Pavlov 1927) on the acquisition of various voluntary and involuntary responses.

The prototypical classical conditioning experiment is a demonstration that a dog learns to salivate whenever a bell is rung, provided the following training has occurred: many trials have been given in each of which the bell is sounded and simultaneously (or slightly later) food is presented. Certain terminology is standard for use in discussing studies of classical conditioning: the conditioned response (CR) is the response developed during training, and the conditioned stimulus (CS) is the stimulus which through training comes to evoke the CR. In this example, the CS is the sound of the bell, and the CR is salivation. The unconditioned response (UR) is the same or almost the same response as the CR, but it exists prior to training, normally being given whenever a certain stimulus, the unconditioned stimulus (US), is presented. Therefore, the US is food presentation and the UR is salivation in our prototypical conditioning experiment. Learning may be said to be conditioned (or conditional) on the pairing of CS and US; hence the use of the terms conditioned stimulus and conditioned response. Conditioning may also be interpreted as the association of CS, UR, and CR.

Classical conditioning has a counterpart process called extinction. Extinction is the loss of a previously conditioned tendency to make a CR in the presence of a CS. This extinction occurs if the CS is repeatedly presented without being followed or accompanied by the US. Note that extinction is not equivalent to forgetting or permanent elimination of the response, or else the following phenomenon could not occur. Spontaneous recovery is a tendency for reoccurrence of an extinguished response after passage of a short period of time without presentation of the CS. Pavlov interpreted extinction as the result of an internal inhibition of the conditioned response. Although other explanations (such as counter-conditioning, discussed later) have some usefulness, many extinction data still support Pavlov's view.

Pavlov called attention to the process of discrimination. Sensory discrimination may be said to be the experience of noting differences between two or more stimuli. Conditioning studies cannot identify this experience and so concern themselves with behavioral discrimination—typically the development of a different overt response (or nonresponse) to each test stimulus. For example, conditioning of the salivation response to a bell (S+) and concurrent extinction of that response to a bright light (S−) is a discrimination procedure. Pavlov made a controversial interpretation of one kind of discrimination experiment: a dog was taught to salivate in the presence of a circle but not in the presence of an ellipse. When further training employed successively more circular ellipses as S− stimuli, the dog made fewer and fewer correct responses and began to respond

emotionally, barking and trying to stay out of the laboratory. Pavlov thought of this behavior as a conditioned neurosis; the neurological hypotheses he offered for this behavior have not been widely accepted.

The inverse of discrimination is called stimulus generalization—the tendency of an animal to respond to a new stimulus as if it were a similar stimulus which is already a CS for a certain CR in that animal. Pavlov hypothesized that the nervous system has an irradiation process in which excitation of certain cells in the brain's cortex spread to other cells. If these cells are later indirectly stimulated by slightly different stimuli from the original CS, the CR would now be evoked because of the irradiation of excitation. Thus irradiation would explain stimulus generalization.

2. Skinner's Positivistic Behaviorism

From his early research with rats (Skinner 1938) to a recent summary of his position (Skinner 1974) following a distinguished career which has influenced society as a whole rather than psychology alone, B. F. Skinner (1904–) has espoused a consistently behavioristic position and disavowed theory. He views his work as the demonstration and summary of observable relations between stimulus events and observable responses, rather than as the statement and testing of hypotheses about relations between psychological events (some of them possibly unknowable except by inference from observed events plus the hypotheses held by the psychologist). This makes him philosophically a positivist, that is, a person dedicated to the gaining of knowledge through observation rather than through rational inference; so his orientation toward science is much like that of Mach(1914).

Despite his positivistic commitment, Skinner is universally recognized as a psychological experimenter, systematist, and theorist. Much of his systematization organizes the results of experiments by himself and his associates; it becomes theory on the rare occasions when he introduces a concept not directly defined by observations (e.g., "reflex reserve" in Skinner 1938 pp. 26–28) or the more frequent occasions when he states an empirical hypothesis or states that certain interpretations by other theorists are unallowable.

Skinner will be long remembered for his distinction between operant and respondent behavior. Operant behavior does not require a specific and identifiable eliciting stimulus, it is strengthened by reinforcements such as food presentation after the behavior has occurred, and it is commonly associated with "voluntary" responses. Instrumental behavior, an approximately equivalent term for operant behavior, is also a widely used term. Respondent behavior is originally elicited by its unconditioned stimulus or reinforcement but comes to be elicited by the conditioned stimulus paired with the unconditioned stimulus. It is strengthened by repeating such pairings, and it is commonly associated with "involuntary" responses. Bower and

Hilgard (1981 pp. 199–203) have commented on recent erosions of the operant–respondent distinction.

Skinner made major contributions in the fields of conditioning, extinction, education, and therapy. Much of his research on schedules of reinforcement, originally performed with rats or pigeons, has been a guide to the study and treatment of patients who need to modify their behavior in order to learn normally or to lose weight, stop smoking, avoid further family conflict, and stay out of trouble with legal authorities. Skinner's emphasis upon the beneficial effects of immediate reinforcement of desired responses, of shaping desired behavior by rewarding successively closer approximations to the response desired, and of chaining individual responses into complex groups of responses, formed some of the basis for teaching machines, programmed instruction, and related educational innovations developed by him and his followers.

3. Tolman's Cognitive Behaviorism

In *Purposive Behavior in Animals and Men*, Edward C. Tolman (1932) expressed many of the distinctive views about learning for which he is justly famous. As the title of that book suggests, his theory was a mixture of two potentially contradictory approaches: cognitive psychology and behaviorism. During his long life (1886–1959), he emphasized the purposes and goals directing the activities of various living organisms, as well as the knowledge they acquired in such activities. This knowledge may be characterized either as an expectancy of association between two or more stimulus events (S_1–S_2 connections) such as the ringing of the bell (S_1) and the presentation of food (S_2) or as an expectancy that the making of a certain response after presentation of one stimulus would lead to the presentation of a new stimulus (S_1–R–S_2 connections), as in the case where S_1 is a T-maze, R is running to the goal box in its right arm, and S_2 is the presentation of food there. However, Tolman was not willing to assume cognitive events without evidence for them. He emphasized the necessity to infer expectancies or other cognitive processes from overt behavior in controlled experiments. This emphasis marked him as a behaviorist, albeit an unusual one. Although modern cognitive psychologists focus on more complex intellectual tasks than those studied by Tolman, their point of view is quite compatible with his.

Unlike reinforcement theorists such as Skinner and Hull, Tolman believed that food reward was important to learning only because it changed expectations about the effects of the rewarded responses. Latent learning experiments confirmed this belief by showing that learning occurred during practice periods in which mazes were explored but no reward given; minimal improvement in maze traversal was shown during those periods, but very rapid improvement after introduction of the reward suggested that (latent) learning had been occurring earlier. Thus, learning is a necessary but not suf-

ficient condition for good task performance. Similarly, previously trained animals placed in an empty goal box apparently learned not to expect food there in later extinction trials, for they decreased their speed of approach to the empty goal box more rapidly than members of a control group without the prior latent extinction trials in the goal box.

Probability learning, a procedure in which people guessing which of a group of optional events will occur on the next trial tend to match their guessing rates to the actual rates of occurrences of the events, is similar in its effects to partial reinforcement with food reward. Humphreys (1939) found that a reversal of a tendency to guess Event A upon a switch to presentation of Event B was faster if preceded by less than 100 percent reinforcement of "A" guesses than if preceded by 100 percent reinforcement. This result was consistent with Tolman's conviction that the meaning of a reinforcement was more important than its frequent occurrence in determining future behavior. Occasional failure of reinforcement during training had become a cue that reinforcement would come again; this delayed extinction effects later in the experiment because the person retained an expectancy of reinforcement of the "A" category response for a longer time than if the first nonreinforcement occurred at the beginning of extinction.

Consider a new experiment with a maze shaped like a cross: suppose a rat is placed in the east end of the maze and allowed a choice of turning right (north) or left (south). Once the right hand turn has been well learned by training with food reward, the animal is placed in the west end and allowed to turn right (south) or left (north). This produces a test of whether the rat has been learning to go to a certain place (place learning) or to turn right (response learning). Blodgett and McCutchan (1947) found that in a dim room with few extramaze cues, most animals exhibited response learning rather than place learning. Other studies showed place learning, especially in the presence of extramaze cues. Although place learning has a more cognitive aura, both types of results can be interpreted as consistent with Tolman's theory that animals and people have cognitive maps of noteworthy situations they have encountered.

An early investigation of all-or-none learning supported the Tolman theory. Krechevsky (1938) studied rats trained to choose S_1 rather than S_2 for a few trials but not meeting criterion on that discrimination before reversal to a task in which S_2 should be chosen rather than S_1. He found that with only an intermediate amount of prior training (20 trials), these reversed animals were no slower in learning the latter discrimination than animals without the earlier task, suggesting that no unlearning of the previously practiced task was required. (Animals with 40 trials of prior training gave opposite results.) Krechevsky inferred that the animals with less prior training were testing a variety of hypotheses and would perform at chance level until the correct response was chosen, whereupon they would always perform correctly. This emphasis upon an internal cognitive process called hypothesis selection has proved very important in recent studies of human concept learning.

Tolman also welcomed the finding of secondary reinforcement—the capacity of a stimulus such as a bell preceding food reward to strengthen responses preceding the food reward. Early secondary reinforcement studies showed that animals would work to attain balls or other tokens which could later be exchanged for food. In Tolman's terminology, the ball gained a positive valence or appeal because of its relationship with another highly valenced object—the food. Later studies showed that signals such as bells could serve just as tokens had, presumably because they caused the organism to expect food or other primary reinforcement.

Finally, the concept of learned helplessness (Maier and Seligman 1976) developed after Tolman's death, seems wholly compatible with his views. Dogs subjected to inescapable shocks early in an experiment may never learn to escape or avoid punishment when it is possible later in the study. This research plus related findings with humans are consistent with the view that organisms can develop expectancies that no responses can be successful, leading to maladaptive behavior.

4. Guthrie's Contiguity Theory

Edwin R. Guthrie (1886–1959) advocated a form of behavioristic learning theory in which a single principle of stimulus and response contiguity was dominant. According to this principle, whenever a certain stimulus configuration is present, the response that has previously been made in the presence of that configuration tends to be made again. This theory has the merit of simplicity; it became influential in part because Guthrie wrote so clearly and gave many interesting examples of its implications. Yet there are three questions to be raised about the principle of stimulus and response contiguity.

Firstly, although there are many situations in which a person seems to respond consistently, there are others in which response variability seems to be the norm. A soccer player usually kicks the ball with appropriate force and direction, but sometimes he makes a very bad kick. Why is this so? Guthrie would say that the two kinds of situations are very different. Possibly the bad kick results from the opposing player being so close as to distract the kicker or restrict his movements. In such a case the external stimuli are not the same as before, and so the response could be expected to be different. However, sometimes moving pictures or video tapes of the stimulus situation just before a kick may show no difference between external stimuli preceding a good and a bad kick. Does this contradict the contiguity principle? Guthrie would say, "No," arguing that internal stimuli such as a stomach cramp or a movement-

produced stimulus may be different before a good and a bad kick occurs.

Bower and Hilgard (1981 p. 77) cite empirical objections to the use of movement-produced stimuli to explain apparent failures of the contiguity principle. Yet it is hard to disprove the hypothesis that some internal or external stimulus difference must accompany any difference in responding to a certain situation. One reason the Guthrian position still finds some favor among psychologists is that it is compatible with strict determinism—the conviction that every causal event, properly described, has a unique effect.

Secondly, if there is a tendency for the same response to occur the next time the same stimulus configuration is present that previously evoked the response, how can learning occur? This objection seems quite telling, for it does seem as if people should hardly ever exhibit behavior change in response to a given, precisely defined stimulus situation. It has been shown that responses may differ because apparently identical situations are actually different in some external or internal details. But what causes other behavior changes?

Guthrie answered this question by adding a principle of postremity to his theory: the last response made in a situation will be protected from change. For example, in the Guthrie and Horton (1946) study of cats trying to escape from a box, the animals could only gain release by pushing against a pole inside the box. Pictures taken at the time of this release showed that one cat would have a particular stereotyped way of pushing the pole—possibly with its hindquarters—while another would have quite a different, equally stereotyped response. Thus, different specific movements apparently had been learned by different cats even though a variety of movements could have been used to push the pole. This evidence, although later questioned by Moore and Stuttard (1979) on the basis that pole rubbing is an innate response of cats, was consistent with the postremity principle. Whereas other theorists use reinforcement as the basis for learning, Guthrie concluded that reinforcing events such as food presentation were only effective because they removed the learner from a situation, thus activating the postremity principle.

Now there is a problem. The last response made in a situation is protected from change, but the contiguity principle implied that all responses were protected from change: "A combination of stimuli which was accompanied by a movement will on its reoccurrence tend to be followed by that movement" (Guthrie 1935 p. 26). How does the postremity principle add to the contiguity principle? The answer seems to be that the contiguity principle is probabilistic whereas the postremity principle is absolute: except when a situation changes drastically following a response, that response may have a 90 percent likelihood of reoccurrence but is not certain. The next time the exact stimulus is presented again, there would be a 10 percent chance, then, of making a different response and having the contiguity principle apply to it. But, if the situation changes drastically when the different response takes place, then the postremity principle will apply, and the new response will have a 100 percent chance of reoccurrence when the same stimulus situation is repeated later. The change from one response to another is an all-or-none change in Guthrie's theory because it either occurs or does not occur. What looks like gradual learning to other theorists is explained as the all-or-none acquisition of individual responses which combine to make a complex act such as hitting a ball or solving an equation.

Finally, does Guthrie's theory make specific predictions which can be verified or contradicted with experimental data? Most psychological theories are modified as their advocates and opponents conduct tests of their predictions, finding ways in which those implications of the theory are inaccurate. To some degree, this has occurred with Guthrie's theory as well. However, because the definitions of "stimulus" and of "response" are empirically ambiguous, it has been difficult to make precise predictions from that theory. Many features of Guthrie's theory, such as an interpretation of extinction as the learning of new responses, have been influential in recent years. But the theory as a whole is no longer fashionable. Perhaps it survives most effectively as an influence upon Estes' stimulus sampling theory, discussed later in this article.

5. Hull's Behavior System

Clark L. Hull (1884–1952) developed a quantitative theory interrelating a massive set of experimental variables and behavior measures. This theory emphasized biological bases of psychology such as bodily needs and refractory periods for certain responses. Hull (1943, 1951, 1952) stated successive versions of his theory as postulate sets with most postulates relating either (a) stimulus events and theoretical constructs, (b) three or more theoretical constructs, or (c) theoretical constructs and response measures. For example, Postulate 4 (Hull 1952) stated an exponential equation relating number of reinforcements, N (a stimulus event), to amount of habit strength, $_sH_R$ (a theoretical construct). Similarly, Postulate 8 stated that $_sE_R = DV_1K_sH_R$, thus saying that the theoretical construct of reaction potential, $_sE_R$ was equal to the product of four theoretical constructs: drive (D); the dynamism of the signalling stimulus trace (V_1); incentive motivation (K); and habit strength ($_sH_R$). The third type of hypothesized relation is illustrated by Postulate 15, stating that $_sE_R = 0.02492A$, thus implying that the amplitude (A) of a galvanic skin reaction is proportional to the value of the theoretical construct $_sE_R$ mentioned earlier. These postulates were generally inferred from empirical equations of a fourth type relating stimulus events and response measures. However, as both Koch (1954) and Cotton (1955) have detailed, the mathematical equations of the theory were inconsistent, making it frequently impossible to reproduce equations of the fourth type by combining the three types of postulates just discussed.

Despite the difficulty just noted, workers in the tradition begun by Hull and extended by his brilliant and prolific disciple, Kenneth W. Spence (1907–67) quite properly dominated the field of learning theory for many years, attaining this influence because of their ingenious hypotheses, deep commitment to simultaneous growth of experimental knowledge and psychological theory, and the large number of energetic research workers whom they attracted to their theoretical position.

The Hull–Spence system (see also Spence 1956) may be viewed as assuming a single type of learning—reinforcement-based learning—encompassing both classical and instrumental (operant) conditioning. The system was clearly behavioristic in its early days; more recent developments (Kendler and Spence 1971) have been called neobehavioristic because internal mediating responses included in recent theories of this type relax behaviorists' constraints against assuming internal unobservable events. The resulting modifications of the Hull–Spence system bear some resemblance to cognitive models such as Tolman's theory or information-processing theory; for example, in a size discrimination task, older children and adult humans are hypothesized to make a mediating response of size identification, examine the stimulus generated by the mediating response (which a cognitive theorist might call a stored memory item), and then respond to the generated stimulus overtly. Ingenious test procedures have provided evidence that such mediation is less likely in younger children and in animals (Kendler and Kendler 1962).

The central concepts of Hull's system were the growth of $_sH_R$ as a function of reinforcement of the response R having that habit strength, the parallel growth of K with such reinforcement (the maximum K value being larger with a large magnitude of reinforcement per response and smaller with a long delay of reinforcement after the response), and an increase in drive or motivation (D) with increased amounts of deprivation of some (but not all) substances needed for individual or species survival. A distinction between learning and performance emphasized by Tolman was explained within the Hull–Spence system by Postulate 8, mentioned earlier: even when learning is substantial, as indicated by the value of $_sH_R$, performance can only be strong if the other components of reaction potential, $_sE_R$, are also high; because of the multiplicative nature of the reaction potential equation, a near-zero value of any component can make overall performance weak. Other important Hullian concepts were the stimulus-intensity dynamism V_1 mentioned earlier (a tendency for increased intensity of stimulation to lead to greater reaction potential); inhibitory potential I_R (a combination of temporary fatigue effects of responding and inhibitory effects of nonreinforcement during experimental extinction); and stimulus generalization, a process discussed earlier in this article.

More recent Hullian approaches have included work by Logan and by Capaldi. Taking a position related to Skinner's emphasis upon the specificity of reinforcement effects, Logan (1956) first proposed a micromolar theory in which "microscopic" features of responses such as medium intensity of response could be built up as a consequence of reinforcing precisely those features. Equations much like those of Hull incorporated the specific effects to which Logan called attention. More recently Logan (1979) has proposed a hybrid theory which combines principles from the Hull–Spence tradition with the more cognitive principles of Tolman and his successors. Whereas learning for an early Hullian was habit strength, that is, a stored tendency to make a certain response in a given situation, to a hybrid theorist learning is the storage of associated stimuli, thus the contents of memory rather than its behavioral effects.

Capaldi (1967) has produced a neo-Hullian theory of partial reinforcement effects on extinction which emphasizes the problems of an organism in discriminating between a partial reinforcement situation and an extinction situation. Stimulus after effects of reinforcement and nonreinforcement can carry over to new trials, even 24 hours later, thus permitting the organism to associate past nonreinforcement cues to responses on trials which are reinforced, thus maintaining behavior strength during partial reinforcement. When, however, the sequential patterns of stored cues of reinforcement and nonreinforcement become too similar to those of extinction procedures, a discrimination can be made that leads to cessation of response in the test situation.

6. Estes' Stimulus Sampling Theory

William K. Estes (1919–   ) founded and guided the extensive development and testing of the mathematical models of learning known collectively as stimulus sampling theory. This theory focuses upon the sampling of stimulus elements among those presented on a trial of an experiment. These elements, partly internal and partly external to the learner, are each presumed to be conditioned to some specific response. As new stimulus elements are sampled on successive trials and specific reinforcement is given, the proportion of elements conditioned to a certain response changes, with a corresponding change in probability of that response. Partly because of the precision with which its axioms have been stated and the rigor with which theorems have been derived from those axioms, stimulus sampling theory has been extremely influential in psychology. However, the theory could not have gained wide acceptance without frequent empirical verification of its theorems (predictions about behavior).

Early versions of stimulus sampling theory (for instance, Estes 1959) and closely related theories (for instance, Bush and Mosteller 1955) were primarily applied to animal learning, avoidance conditioning, extinction, discrimination, motivation, and spontaneous recovery plus human probability learning and discrimination learning. Later, this theory was also applied

to such fields as verbal learning and memory, letter identification, concept identification, eyelid conditioning, and decision making.

Stimulus sampling theory has been formalized (Estes and Suppes 1974) using five primitive notions:

(a) The possibly unobservable set S of stimulus elements available in a situation.

(b) The number r of different responses that can be made in the situation.

(c) The number t of possible outcomes, such as food or no food and "correct" or "incorrect."

(d) The sample space, consisting of a conditioning function (a listing of the response to which each stimulus element is conditioned), a subset T (of S) that is actually presented, a subset i sampled from T, the outcome j following the response, and the reinforcing event k that occurs.

(e) A probability measure P.

Outcomes and reinforcements are often, but not always, identical. The theory includes explicit axioms (Estes and Suppes 1974 pp. 171–72) about learning, sampling, responding, reinforcement, and stimulus presentation. The less technical parts of representative axioms are quoted below:

> . . . if reinforcement occurs . . ., all stimuli sampled becomes conditioned to the reinforced response . . .
> . . . samples of equal size are sampled equally often . . .
> . . . the probability of any response A_i is the ratio of sampled elements connected to A_i to the total number of sampled elements . . .
> . . . the probability of a reinforcing event depends only on the response $A_{i,n}$ and the outcome $O_{j,n}$ of the same trial . . .
> . . . the probability of a stimulus presentation set depends only on previous observables . . .

A mathematical change in Estes' theory somewhat paralleled the subject matter change noted earlier: originally stimulus sampling theory assumed an infinite size for the set S of available elements, leading to gradual learning processes much like those of Hull. However, experimental evidence consistent with an assumption of instantaneous learning in certain situations such as discrimination learning and paired associate learning led to an assumption of a finite sized S (Estes 1959, Estes et al. 1960). Currently an enlarged theory is employed in which certain phenomena are described with finite sized S and others with infinite sized S. The former subtheory is particularly amenable to mathematical analysis based on the theory of so-called Markov chains (Kemeny and Snell 1960), but Markov chains with infinite numbers of states can be used to describe the latter case.

A further development leaves the mathematical characteristics of stimulus sampling theory essentially unchanged but makes its orientation more cognitive, thus reducing its similarity to the theories of Pavlov, Skinner, Guthrie and Hull and increasing its similarity to that of Tolman and to the currently dominant information-processing theory. This change is the expansion (Estes 1972, Estes and Suppes 1974) of the simple notion of an association of a stimulus and a response into the notion of a complex memory structure that focuses upon details of storage, rehearsal, and recall or recognition of information rather than upon S-R connections alone. This approach is particularly important in the interpretation of complex responses, such as spelling polysyllabic words, where a high level control unit activates lower level control units for individual syllables and the lower level units activate individual letters.

It should be mentioned that some workers in the field of mathematical learning theory have used assumptions which do not emphasize the selection of stimulus elements central to Estes' theory. However, it is clear that stimulus sampling theory continues to be the principal approach to mathematical learning theory. Readers are referred to three books (Laming 1973, Norman 1972, Wickens 1982) for further information about mathematical learning theory as a comprehensive area of study.

In conclusion, it has been stated earlier that a new class of learning theory, currently information-processing theory, is superceding stimulus sampling theory as the most influential kind of learning theory. Estes (1975 p. 279) has noted that computer simulation, a favorite tool of the new theory, is taking over many of the tasks previously performed by mathematics. He points out, however, that mathematical approaches have advantages in the specification of the fundamental psychological laws operative in ideal situations: ". . . mathematics remains our principal vehicle for the flights of imagination that smooth our experiences and extract from varying contexts the relationships that would hold among events under idealized noise-free conditions." For this reason, it is to be hoped that information-processing theory and mathematical learning theory will effect some kind of merger in which each takes advantage of the strengths of the other.

Bibliography

Atkinson R C, Shiffrin R M 1968 Human memory: A proposed system and its control processes. In: Spence K W, Spence J T (eds.) 1968 *The Psychology of Learning and Motivation*, Vol. 2. Academic Press, New York, pp. 89–195

Blodgett H C, McCutchan K 1947 Place versus response learning in the simple T-maze. *J. Exp. Psychol.* 37: 412–22

Bower G, Hilgard E A 1981 *Theories of Learning*, 5th edn. Prentice-Hall, Englewood Cliffs, New Jersey

Bush R R, Mosteller F 1955 *Stochastic Models for Learning*. Wiley, New York

Capaldi E J 1967 A sequential hypothesis of instrumental learning. In: Spence K W, Spence J T (eds.) 1967 *The Psychology of Learning and Motivation*, Vol. 1. Academic Press, New York, pp. 67–156

Cotton J W 1955 On making predictions from Hull's theory. *Psychol. Rev.* 62: 303–14

Estes W K 1959 Component and pattern models with Markovian interpretations. In: Bush R R, Estes W K (eds.) 1959 *Studies in Mathematical Learning Theory*. Stanford University Press, Stanford, California, pp. 9–52

Estes W K 1972 An associative basis for coding and organization in memory. In: Melton A W, Martin E (eds.) 1972 *Coding Processes in Human Memory*. Winston, Washington, DC, pp. 161–90

Estes W K 1975 Some targets for mathematical psychology. *J. Math. Psychol.* 12: 263–82

Estes W K 1976 Structural aspects of associative models for memory. In: Cofer C N (ed.) 1976 *The Structure of Human Memory*. Freeman, San Francisco

Estes W K, Suppes P 1974 Foundations of stimulus sampling theory. In: Krantz D H, Atkinson R C, Luce R D, Suppes P (eds.) 1974 *Learning, Memory and Thinking, Contemporary Developments in Mathematical Psychology*, Vol. 1. Freeman, San Francisco, pp. 163–83

Estes W K, Hopkins B L, Crothers E J 1960 All-or-none and conservation effects in the learning and retention of paired associates. *J. Exp. Psychol.* 60: 329–39

Guthrie E R 1935 *The Psychology of Learning*. Harper and Row, New York

Guthrie E R, Horton G P 1946 *Cats in a Puzzle Box*. Rinehart, New York

Hull C L 1943 *Principles of Behavior: An Introduction to Behavior Theory*. Appleton-Century-Crofts, New York

Hull C L 1951 *Essentials of Behavior*. Yale University Press, New Haven

Hull C L 1952 *A Behavior System: An Introduction to Behavior Theory Concerning the Individual Organism*. Yale University Press, New Haven

Humphreys L G 1939 Acquisition and extinction of verbal expectations in a situation analogous to conditioning. *J. Exp. Psychol.* 25: 294–301

Kemeny J G, Snell J L 1960 *Finite Markov Chains*. Van Nostrand, Princeton, New Jersey

Kendler H H, Kendler T S 1962 Vertical and horizontal processes in problem solving. *Psychol. Rev.* 69: 1–16

Kendler H H, Spence J T (eds.) 1971 *Essays in Neobehaviorism: A Memorial Volume to Kenneth W Spence*. Appleton-Century-Crofts, New York

Koch S 1954 Clark L. Hull. In: Estes W K, MacCorquodale K, Meehl P E, Mueller C G, Schoenfeld W N, Verplanck W S (eds.) 1954 *Modern Learning Theory*. Appleton-Century-Crofts, New York

Krechevsky I 1938 A study of the continuity of the problem-solving process. *Psychol. Rev.* 45: 107–34

Laming D R J 1973 *Mathematical Psychology*. Academic Press, London

Logan F A 1956 A micromolar approach to behavior theory. *Psychol. Rev.* 63: 63–73

Logan F A 1979 Hybrid theory of operant conditioning. *Psychol. Rev.* 86: 507–41

Mach E 1914 *The Analysis of Sensations and the Relation of the Physical to the Psychical*. Open Court, Chicago, Illinois

Maier S F, Seligman M E P 1976 Learned helplessness: Theory and evidence. *J. Exp. Psychol. Genet.* 105: 3–46

Moore B R, Stuttard S 1979 Dr. Guthrie and *Felis Domesticus*, or: Tripping over the cat. *Science* 205: 1031–33

Norman M F 1972 *Markov Processes and Learning Models*. Academic Press, New York

Pavlov I P 1927 *Conditioned Reflexes: An Investigation of the Physiological Activity of the Cerebral Cortex*. Oxford University Press, London

Sahakian W S 1976 *Learning: Systems, Models, and Theories*, 2nd edn. Rand McNally, Chicago, Illinois

Skinner B F 1938 *The Behavior of Organisms: An Experimental Analysis*. Appleton-Century-Crofts, New York

Skinner B F 1974 *About Behaviorism*. Knopf, New York

Spence K W 1956 *Behavior Theory and Conditioning*. Yale University Press, New Haven, Connecticut

Thorndike E L 1903 *Educational Psychology*. The Science Press, New York

Tolman E C 1932 *Purposive Behavior in Animals and Men*. Century, New York

Wickens T D 1982 *Models for Behavior: Stochastic Processes in Psychology*. Freeman, San Francisco, California

Motivation

H. I. Day

The term motivation, as defined by psychologists, refers to the causes for the initiation, continuation (or cessation), and direction of behaviour. It is assumed that every behaviour is motivated and begins, continues, and is directed towards some goal. The study of motivation is the study of inferred causes for behaviour for actual causes cannot be known with certainty. Thus a limitless number of theories can be generated each of which attempts to explain and predict some aspects of an individual's behaviour or attempts to account for behaviours of groups of people. The application of motivational principles in education lies in an understanding of some of the many theories that attempt to rationalize behaviour in specific educational situations.

1. The Nature of Motivation

Despite the protestation of teachers that it is possible to identify "unmotivated students", it is as well to recognize that all people are always motivated to some extent. The intensity and direction of the motivation may vary so that a particular student may be motivated to daydream in class, or to behave in a way that distracts other students and irritates the teacher, when the teacher would prefer that the student be motivated to perform certain behaviours, such as to attend to the task designated by the teacher as most important, to learn something specific, or to inhibit disruptive behaviour. The study of motivation is therefore the examination of factors in a person–environment interaction that allow an understanding of why certain behaviours are performed over others.

Since motivation is an attempt to explain why certain behaviours occur and become predominant, the scope of theorizing can be as broad as the differences among theoreticians in psychology. These differences of opinion range with attitudes towards the nature of humankind and the bases for learning, growth, and thinking. Common to most theories of motivation are a number of premises, namely that humans begin life with a plastic armoratorium and that this can be shaped by events both intrinsic and extrinsic to the individual. Disagreement tends to centre on the relative importance of each of the influencing factors (such as pregenital dispositions), intrinsic factors (such as expectations, hopes, and challenges), and extrinsic reinforcing or punitive events, and in their interactions.

No current theory of motivation is able to explain and, what is more important, predict the behaviour of an individual consistently. At best, theories predict group behaviour at some level of probability and at worst, weave fanciful theories, replete with exotic hypothetical constructs to explain past behaviour. Most of the current theories tend to be versions of an approach which argues that two opposing forces inhere in an individual's life and interact to motivate that person. The first is the force towards equilibrium (stability, homeostasis, constancy, congruity, balance, consonance). The second force—one much harder to identify—appears to be one that drives the individual to seek change or disequilibrium (uncertainty, excitement, activity). The variations in descriptions, bases for, and explanation of this second motivational force are greater and lead to more controversy. Thus it would be possible to subscribe to a theory that suggested that this force was innate (e.g., Freud, White), physiological (e.g., Berlyne, Pribram), or acquired (e.g., Murray).

Interaction between these two forces—the drive for stability and the need to expose oneself to instability—can be explained by an infinite array of theories. This article will concern itself only with a few, those that seem to contribute especially to an understanding of the educational process.

2. Varieties of Theories

Historically, motivational theories have been expounded, accepted, rewritten, and finally have given way to other theories that seem to account for a greater number of facts and empirical findings. No one theory has ever been universally accepted, and at present no one theory is even commonly held. At best, it is possible to see that families of theories, that is, a group of theories having common roots, become popular.

Early theories tended to explain the causes of behaviour in terms of instincts. People were said to display specific behaviour patterns because of a set of inborn motives. When this approach proved unconvincing because it failed to account for variances in time and space and failed to be predictive, a shift in theorizing took place. The new approach attempted to specify to a greater extent the roots of the behaviours and to seek physiological bases for their instigation. Specific drives were identified, such as Freud's drives towards life and death or Hull's set of primary drives that include hunger, thirst, sex, and pain avoidance. But once again discontent with drive theories led psychologists to postulate a set of needs that inhere in the newborn and grow differentially in importance (e.g., those of Murray). Others assumed a hierarchical order of importance of a large set of needs or concentrated their research and exposition on a single or a small number of needs (e.g., Maslow's theories).

Since the Second World War there has been an explosion in the number of theories of motivation. The plethora of theories available today can be categorized into families by fitting them into distinct dichotomies. While few of the theories fit the categories absolutely, their main thrusts can usually be identified.

First of all, theories tend to be proactive or reactive, that is they tend to stress that behaviour is initiated outward from within the individual or that people tend to react to external forces that disturb their equilibrium. Both types of theory accept the notion that the result of the person–environment interaction is never a return to a previous state but rather the progression to a "higher" or more sophisticated state.

Another way of dichotomizing motivational theories is along a time dimension: some theories argue that people are impelled to act mainly for immediate consequences, such as tension reduction (although eventual consequences are not to be denied), while other theories concern themselves with extended outcomes (such as academic achievement) while not negating immediate consequences.

Finally, theories tend to be intrinsic (autotelic) or extrinsic (exotelic). The former are concerned with self-rewarding behaviour; the latter with satisfaction delivered by external agents. But even the notion of intrinsic motivation is complicated, as will be seen later, by the need to define whether intrinsic is meant intrinsic to the task or intrinsic to the person.

Most of the theories to be introduced as educationally relevant are intrinsic theories. The one extrinsic theory, behaviour modification, is presented in more detail elsewhere.

3. Curiosity

Probably the best developed and most clearly enunciated reactive–intrinsic motivational theory is that of D. E. Berlyne (1963). Berlyne postulated a motivation that drives individuals to react to environments moderately high in uncertainty with approach and exploratory behaviour. He called this drive an exploratory drive and the state curiosity. Thus, he argued that curiosity is a state of tension induced by an environment high in uncertainty and response conflict that leads to many possible forms of exploration.

Environmental factors that induce curiosity, he held, were those high in collative variability—such variables as incongruity, novelty, complexity, difficulty, and contradiction—which require the individual to collate or compare either different parts of an incoming stimulus or an incoming stimulus with memory traces of previous stimuli. Where a mismatch occurs response conflict and uncertainty are produced and tension is induced. The mechanisms of the process reside mainly in the "reticular activating system" of the brain, but also in other physiological and biochemical processes, similar in nature to Pavlov's "orienting reflex."

The affect associated with the curious state is held to be mixed, for some degree of anxiety is considered to be present in the excitement. Thus positive affects, linked with approach tendencies, are countered by negative affects, linked with withdrawal and avoidance tendencies. The relationship between the two is best expressed in a graph first expounded by Berlyne in which he argued that the two tendencies interact to produce the "Wundt curve" (see Fig. 1). Variations of this approach have been expounded by a number of psychologists, but the main features are similar—that moderate discrepancies in the environment lead to approach and exploration, but extreme discrepancies lead to withdrawal and avoidance (Hunt 1971, Day 1981).

Of interest to education is the notion that collative variability not only induces a motivation to explore (curiosity) but also directs that motivation towards those features in the environment which are high in collative variability. Thus, if some aspect of the environment is novel or complex, the individual will be attracted to it rather than to other parts of the environment, and will explore it until uncertainty has been reduced. Clearly, the goal of the exploration is information acquisition, and the result is learning.

Educators, who are interested in promoting learning in students, are therefore instructed to manipulate the level of collative variability in the environments of their

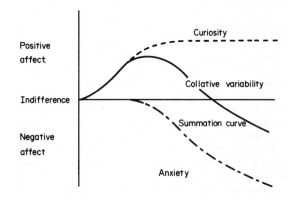

Figure 1
The interaction of curiosity and anxiety to produce a "Wundt" curve

classrooms to facilitate curiosity and exploration. Thus, educators could introduce a novel topic with incongruities and contradictions and then encourage students to explore the nature of the topic so as to reduce the tension aroused within them (Day and Berlyne 1971, Day 1981).

Curiosity has also been studied as a personality variable, for it is clear that people vary in their willingness to tolerate or react favourably towards situations fraught with uncertainty. Highly curious students would be expected to prefer less structured environments while students low in curiosity would be expected to work best in situations where instruction is clear, precise, and unambiguous.

4. Achievement Motivation

While curiosity can be considered an immediate, autotelic motivation because it is immediately reinforcing and the reinforcement lies in the interaction between person and task (in uncertainty reduction), achievement motivation can be considered an extended person-intrinsic motivation because its reinforcement is delayed and arises from an interaction within the person. This motivation is:

> a pattern of planning, of actions, and of feelings connected with striving to achieve some internalized standard of excellence, as contrasted, for example, with power or friendship. (Vidler 1977 p. 67)

Over time, the individual assesses his or her behaviour and evaluates the result. Achievement motivation is also called need for achievement (nAch). Important is the attitude to achieve rather than the achievements themselves.

Early interest by McClelland in the 1950s was directed towards broad questions such as how need for achievement is reflected in societies and how, as a societal value, it affects the economic and political growth of a nation. His work had its source in that of Murray who had listed the need to achieve as one of 27 acquired human motives.

Thus the need to achieve appears to be a need that becomes part of an individual's personality and affects that person's behaviour in every facet of life including education. Individuals with a high need for achievement are people interested in excellence for its own sake rather than for the extrinsic rewards it can bring such as money, or prestige. They prefer situations in which their personal responsibility affects the outcome. They tend to prefer to control their destinies and to make independent judgments based on their own evaluations and experience. They choose challenging goals (McClelland 1958) and prefer delayed, larger rewards to immediate, smaller rewards.

Educationally, work in need for achievement and achievement has been sparse and only moderately successful. It was demonstrated that under some circumstances high need-for-achievement people will persist longer at a challenging task (unless alternative tasks become more challenging). Challenge, especially that of marks or grades in school, has been investigated; but since need for achievement is considered to be an intrinsic motivator and independent of external reinforcers such as grades and prizes, it cannot be expected that there should be a high correlation between it and school achievement. Yet, a number of studies have found some support for this position (McClelland 1958).

Since need for achievement is regarded as a learned motivation, training programmes have been developed for children to enhance their levels of it, and encouraging findings have demonstrated that even though academic grades may not have improved greatly, purposeful planning and action in many phases of life have resulted.

5. Anxiety

One of the important motivators in an educational milieu is anxiety. Like curiosity it tends to be intrinsic but it can be viewed both as task intrinsic and person intrinsic. In the first instance, it can be contrasted with curiosity and can be viewed as arising in an individual when external stimuli become overwhelming. If, for example, an individual is confronted with an excess of variability and becomes overwhelmed with uncertainty, arousal increases to a high level (see Fig. 1) and negative affect together with avoidance and withdrawal ensue. Some psychologists (Day and Berlyne 1971) prefer to label this situation as fear rather than anxiety, for the source of the emotion is fairly clear. These psychologists hold that when the source of arousal is specific, curiosity is induced at moderate levels but fear overwhelms at excess levels of arousal. When the source of tension is obscure or diverse, such as in an unchanging environment, or an understanding one, boredom or diversive curiosity may be aroused at moderate levels. Anxiety, on the other hand, arises when arousal becomes high and when the negative affect overwhelms the individual because no source of tension nor course of action to reduce the arousal can be identified.

Anxiety as a person-intrinsic motivation is frequently viewed as ego threatening. It is felt by many psychologists (Spielberger et al. 1981) to reflect a condition wherein a person perceives a threat to his or her ego rather than a physical danger. This reflects the notion that people can punish themselves for failure to prepare adequately as well as reward themselves for achievement. Such anxiety can be pervasive and can affect an individual's behaviour across many facets of life.

To avoid undue confusion, the terms anxiety and fear can be equated, for in practice it is almost impossible to distinguish between the two. The terms will be used interchangeably here.

The term "test anxiety" has been introduced to describe the fear of taking tests and argued that some students are affected adversely by any test situation so that the outcome of any threatening, externally judged act is poorer than when that act is not evaluated externally. It has however, been argued that anxiety (also called "achievement anxiety") can be either facilitating or debilitating. In an unpublished study, Day found that facilitating-achievement anxiety correlated positively with a measure of curiosity and with a measure of intelligence while debilitating-achievement anxiety correlated negatively with these two measures as well as with facilitating-achievement anxiety.

Most paper and pencil measures of anxiety tend to measure fairly stable dispositions and so should be considered personality rather than motivational tests. This distinction has been emphasized by Spielberger who developed a state–trait anxiety inventory in which both state and trait measures were developed in parallel. The former require the respondents to describe themselves in a situational sense, the items requiring the individuals to recognize a current state of tension coupled with feelings of ego threat, while the latter presents items that, though similar in content, require the respondents to recognize a pervasive disposition to react with tension and arousal.

Much research has been done correlating anxiety measures with academic behaviour. In most cases, moderate correlations were found between scores on anxiety tests and intellectual performance, school achievement, lab work, and choice of highly complex alternatives for exploration. But the levels of correlation suggest that the relationships are really quite complex and are affected by such factors as rate of input of stressful stimulation, other environmental conditions that are arousing (such as bright or noisy classrooms), level of complexity or novelty of the material, and ability of the individual to process complex stimulation and to react to stress in a facilitating manner.

6. Competence Motivation

In 1959 Robert W. White published a paper which he felt had grown out of his grave discontent with psychological theories in which the person was treated as the result of the influences acting upon him, rather than as an effective agent in events. White argued that the motivation to become competent or effective in dealing with the environment is a biological drive that leads to such behaviours as grasping and exploring, crawling and walking, attention and perception, language and thinking, and manipulating and changing the environment. He argued that this motivation leads to behaviour that is directed, selective, and persistent. Thus competence motivation acts to drive an individual to take the initiative and act on the environment. This theory could therefore be termed proactive, person intrinsic, and extended over time.

White argued that competence motivation, although genetically disposed, grows with learning and achievement. The infant's first interaction with its environment, if rewarded with success, will become stronger and endure. Exploration is also manifest with positive effect

and leads to positive self-regard and confidence. Confidence leads to continued engagement in exploration which, when successful, continues to enhance positive self-regard. In some way, the concept is similar to that of curiosity in that tasks may be reinforcing, but in other ways it is similar to need for achievement in that an individual becomes his or her own reward agent, signalling successful interactions with the universe, evaluating his or her performance, and enhancing self-esteem.

Competence is not a dichotomous trait, but one along which people vary. People can be more competent in some facets of their lives than in other facets, and more competent in some situations than in others. Competence develops in many areas and in different stages. The age of 2, for example, seems to be one of the important ages. It is one in which a spirit of experimentation occurs, one that could be trying to parents who often react in a restrictive and decisive manner, one that may frustrate the growth of competence. Similarly, teachers who are not attuned to the concept may impede the strivings of a child who is performing in some areas at a level of competence deemed insufficient to the teacher.

On the other hand, the individual who explores and is rewarded for that exploration by understanding, learning, and feelings of mastery will become inner directed, independent, and continue to strive towards competence. Such individuals become intrinsically motivated.

Of course the opposite may occur. An individual may attempt to explore but the behaviour may result in failure to understand and to learn, and thus to reduction in feelings of mastery. Such conditions might occur in a classroom where a teacher is intent on introducing high levels of complexity to the class, disregarding the effectiveness level of each of the students. Under such conditions, it is the teacher who has imposed collative variability upon the class rather than allowing each student to choose that individual's optimal level; so the extreme conditions illustrated in Fig. 1 may operate and anxiety with its associated feelings of negative affect may ensue.

7. Extrinsic Motivation

Until this point this article has been dealing with intrinsic motivators of behaviour, either task intrinsic or person intrinsic, immediate or extended, proactive or reactive. One other important motivating influence in education is the set of motivators subsumed under the rubric extrinsic motivation.

Extrinsic motivation inheres when the source of reward or punishment lies external to the individual and in the control of other people who determine the appropriateness of the behaviour of the individual. People are motivated to maximize satisfaction and minimize dissatisfaction; when they obtain satisfaction from others, those others become agents of control.

The nature of the reward or punishment may vary greatly, including verbal statements of praise or contempt, physical rewards or punishments, or signs of approval or disapproval (such as diplomas, licenses, and parking tickets). All of these motivate because they serve to initiate or terminate some behaviour, change its frequency of occurrence, cause it to intensify or weaken and, hopefully, direct it towards some satisfying goal.

Behaviour modification is the best known, immediate, reactive extrinsic motivation, and its application in the educational milieu has been researched thoroughly. Behaviour modification allows the teacher to respond with immediate and appropriate feedback to students in order to shape acceptable behaviours and eliminate undesirable ones. These responses by teachers serve as reinforcers or punishments that modify operant behaviours of students. More space would be required to introduce all the concepts and explain their interactions, so this section can only serve to identify behaviour modification as one of the inferred causes of behaviour change. Of the utmost importance to the teacher is the need to recognize that behaviour modification acts in both directions. That is, while the teacher is controlling and shaping the students, they are also controlling and shaping the teacher. Efficient learning by students will induce teachers to teach rapidly and focus on the task, while evoking positive regard for the class and feelings of satisfaction and well-being in the teachers.

8. Conclusion

Motivational theories have proliferated in the last few decades to the point where any attempt at an overview must perforce omit many of them. Most theories tend to deal with narrow aspects of behaviour, such as exploration, achievement, and persistence at a task. They also tend to be descriptive and explanatory rather than predictive; when prediction is attempted, it is usually presented as a probability of occurrence by some of a large number of individuals.

Since motivation has also the inference of causality, one specific theory need not be adopted over another. Rather a person should be acquainted with a large number of theories and try to choose the most relevant for specific situations. However, it is important to note that the adoption of a theory shapes a person's behaviour. If, for example, a teacher assumes that curiosity induction is most appropriate in a classroom, that teacher will adopt a teaching format designed to manipulate the uncertainty level in the students. The teacher using curiosity as the teaching style will act on the environment directly and thus on the students indirectly. A teacher adopting an extrinsic motivational theory of learning, on the other hand, will act to reward or punish students directly for their efforts.

Bibliography

Berlyne D E 1963 Motivational problems raised by exploratory and epistemic behavior. In: Koch S (ed.) 1963 *Psychology: A Study of a Science*, Vol. 5. McGraw-Hill, New York
Day H I 1981 Neugier und Erziehung. In: Voss H G, Keller H (eds.) 1981 *Neugierforschung*. Beltz, Weinheim, pp. 226–62
Day H I, Berlyne D E 1971 Intrinsic motivation. In: Lesser G (ed.) 1971 *Psychology and Educational Practice*. Scott, Foresman, Chicago, Illinois, pp. 294–335
Hunt J McV 1971 Toward a history of intrinsic motivation. In: Day H I, Berlyne D E, Hunt D E (eds.) 1971 *Intrinsic Motivation: A New Direction in Education*. Holt, Rinehart and Winston, Toronto, Ontario
McClelland D C 1958 Risk-taking in children with high and low needs for achievement. In: Atkinson J W (ed.) 1958 *Motives in Fantasy, Action and Society*. Van Nostrand, Toronto
Spielberger C D, Frain F, Peters R 1981 Neugier und Angst. In: Voss H G, Keller H (eds.) 1981 *Neugierforschung*. Beltz, Weinheim, pp. 197–225
Vidler D C 1977 Achievement motivation. In: Ball S (ed.) 1977 *Motivation in Education*. Academic Press, New York, pp. 67–90
White R W 1959 Motivation reconsidered: The concept of competence. *Psychol. Rev.* 66: 297–333

Perception

A. D. Pick

Perception can be considered as the first-hand acquisition of information from the environment. Thus perceiving is acquiring information via sensory systems about the objects, places, and events of the world. This view of perception is broad, but the discussion of perception that follows will be selective. The selection is guided by some presumptions of what aspects of perceptual development might be usefully considered in regard to school learning and problems in school learning. This discussion will begin with a consideration of the course of perceptual development during infancy. If perceptual functioning is implicated in the problems

that some children have with early school learning, then knowledge of the course of early normal perceptual development is relevant for clarifying what might be the bases for those problems. Next, the direction of perceptual development during the preschool and early school years will be reviewed briefly. Although a high level of perceptual functioning characterizes infants at the end of the first year or so of life, there are still important changes in their perception during the next few years, and the relevance of these changes for the tasks children encounter in school will be considered.

1. Perceptual Development During Infancy

Many discussions of perceptual development during infancy have begun with reference to William James's description of the infant's visual world as a blooming buzzing confusion, and many recent writers on the topic have taken note of the fact that James's description, though vivid, is inaccurate. As investigators have become ever more clever at inventing and refining procedures for assessing infants' perceptual sensitivity, it has been learned that many basic perceptual competencies are present and functional early in life (Bower 1981). A reasonable summary of current evidence is that the world is quite well-articulated for the newborn infant but it becomes more differentiated with time.

It is important to note that more evidence than a simple demonstration of sensitivity or responsiveness to a stimulus is necessary as a basis for inferring mature perceptual functioning. In discussing specific aspects of perceptual development during infancy, particular attention will be paid to the kinds of behaviors that provide good indices of that perception. For perceiving depth, distance, and space, such behaviors include grasping, reaching, and crawling.

1.1 Spatial Perception

Reaching and grasping have been observed in rudimentary form in newborns and their development traced over the first months of life. Babies can reach quite accurately by 5 or 6 months of age (Yonas and Pick 1975), so at least by this age reaching and grasping provide appropriate indices of infants' perception of relative distance. Using reaching as a criterion, it has been found that by 5 months of age, babies demonstrate surprisingly well-developed visual–spatial perception (Yonas 1979). At this age, their accuracy of reaching to a visible object is much greater than their accuracy of reaching to a noisy unseen object—perhaps implying that visual–spatial perception develops to a high level earlier in life than does auditory–spatial perception. However, there is only scanty evidence available at present about the development of auditory–spatial perception.

Avoiding an object that is approaching on a collision course is another behavior that reflects quite accurate spatial perception by the second half year of life. Babies have been reported to draw back their heads in reaction to stimulus information for impending collision as young as 1 and 2 months of age, and the reaction is clearly developed by 5 or 6 months. A related reaction to a rapidly approaching object is an eye blink, and this is more clearly developed at an even earlier age—by about 3 months.

Once infants are locomoting, there are new means available for evaluating their perception of space beyond the immediately surrounding reachable or avoidable environment. Experiments with an apparatus known as a visual cliff (Walk and Gibson 1961) have provided a great deal of information about the development of depth discrimination during the second half year of life. A baby is placed on a center board in the middle of a glass-topped table. A textured surface is directly under the glass on one side, and far below the glass on the other side. Babies who can locomote will rarely venture out onto or cross over the glass on the "deep" side where the textured surface is far below. However, there also is further development of depth discrimination beyond the age when babies are first able to crawl, probably reflecting the continued development of the use of motion parallax information for depth perception through these months (Walk 1978).

Infants younger than about 6 months, that is, pre-locomotor infants, demonstrate differential sensitivity to the two sides of the cliff. For example, the heart rate of younger babies decelerates more when they are placed on the deep side than when they are placed on the shallow side. Such differential sensitivity by itself is not sufficient to inform us whether the babies perceive the depth in the way that appropriate behaviors like reaching and crawling or refusing to crawl do. Nonetheless, such differential sensitivity may be an early phase of the development of depth perception.

1.2 Perception of Motion

Even though infants may not use motion-parallax information for making fine depth discriminations by the time they can crawl, they perceive the motion of moving objects at a very young age. Even newborns visually follow moving objects, and their visual pursuit typically is smooth by the age of about 2 months. Infants as young as 5 months are sensitive to the difference between the motions that reflect changes in rigid objects as compared to nonrigid objects (Gibson 1982). Perceiving rigid objects moving implies also perceiving them as solid, three-dimensional objects, and from very early ages infants demonstrate the ability to discriminate between three-dimensional and two-dimensional displays, that is, between a sphere and a circle. That there is important information in the motion of a moving object is attested to by the fact that 3-month-old babies distinguish between the shapes of two objects when they have only seen those objects in motion (Gibson 1982).

1.3 Pattern Perception

Young babies discriminate among a wide variety of two-dimensional patterns. Among the features of patterns that infants of 2 or 3 months of age discriminate are curvature or straightness of contour, curvature or straightness of elements, regularity or irregularity of arrangement of the elements, presence of many or few angles, presence of many or few components. A preference for curvature of form over straight lines has even been demonstrated for newborn infants.

Much more is known about infants' perception of nonmeaningful patterns than of their perception of meaningful patterns such as faces. Walk (1981) summarized evidence about when babies recognize their mothers, and he concluded that auditory recognition of the mother's voice occurs at an earlier age than does visual recognition of the mother's face. Babies can discriminate among at least some portrayed facial expressions at 3 months of age; 5-month-old babies can recognize photographs of live faces they have just seen, and by 7 months of age, babies can recognize different photographed poses of the same face. It may be that infants' increasing specificity of facial recognition reflects an increasing tendency to process pattern configurations rather than isolated elements.

1.4 Intermodal Integration in Infancy

Some of the procedures used in studying perception and learning presuppose intermodal functioning, that is, perceiving information from two or more senses at the same time. For example, one investigator used a complex, presumably interesting visible object to reinforce infants' localizing the direction of the source of a sound (Wilson 1978). The success of such procedures implies that intermodal functioning may characterize the infant's ordinary learning environment, and other findings suggest directly that this is so. For example, 4-month-old infants shown two movies simultaneously and a sound track appropriate to one, will look more at the movie specified by the sound track than at the other one. Furthermore, these young infants will search visually for an event they hear (Spelke 1979). Infants as young as 3 weeks will increase their visual scanning of faces that talk compared to faces that do not (Haith et al. 1977). All of these behaviors imply that babies can integrate very complex visible and audible information emanating from the same event. Sounds and their spatial properties influence visual scanning even in newborns, thereby demonstrating functional relations between the auditory and visual systems at birth.

1.5 The Senses and Intermodal Functioning

Infants' visual acuity normally improves as a quite regular function of chronological age during the first few months of life and nears adult level at around 6 months of age. Among the early abnormalities that affect the eventual level of adults' acuity are astigmatism, myopia, and cataracts. In addition, some abnormalities of binocular vision (specifically, of stereopsis) are the result of early and uncorrected strabismus (cross-eyed or wall-eyed), and this condition also results in decreased vision in one eye. Apparently even several weeks of deprivation of vision in one eye during the first few months of life can result in eventual reduced visual acuity of that eye (Mitchell 1978). Thus, assessing infants' visual functioning is important for early detection of such conditions.

Some of the abnormalities that can occur early in one of the senses also affect intramodal and perhaps even intermodal coordination. For example, strabismus develops if the two eyes are not synchronized, and eventually vision in at least one eye is affected adversely. In a sense strabismus may be thought of as adaptive,

for if instead of strabismus one experienced retinal rivalry or double imaging, directional information for localizing objects in space would be imprecise or absent. Other early sensory problems clearly have maladaptive outcomes, however. For example, infants who have chronic ear infections may experience prolonged periods of distorted or discontinuous hearing. In principle, such distortions might affect their acquisition of speech, or, later on, their ability to follow precise verbal instructions or directions about where and how to carry out many tasks in school.

1.6 Perceptual Development During Infancy and School Learning

Since perception of depth and space as well as motion are developed to a high degree early in life, and because difficulties in these aspects of perception do not generally characterize the problems of children who have school-learning difficulties, these areas do not currently present unresolved issues of pressing educational import. However, pattern perception is an aspect of infant perception with obvious educational relevance, and its subsequent development during the preschool years could profitably be investigated more thoroughly than it has been. Although the basic capacities for pattern perception are developed early in life, a great deal of perceptual learning occurs during the first few years of life, and much of this perceptual learning has to do with the perception of patterns, particularly the kinds of patterns that are relevant for reading (Gibson 1969, Gibson and Levin 1975). Since difficulty in learning to read is almost a defining criterion of learning disabilities, it is important to learn more about the development of pattern perception during the first years of life. This topic will be discussed in more detail in the following section.

2. Perceptual Development During Early Childhood

There are important developmental changes in perception after infancy that are not primarily changes in basic competencies. These include changes in scanning strategies, efficiency, and self-regulation of perception (Pick et al. 1975), and they are reflected in developmental changes in young children's perception of patterns as well as their perception of other important aspects of their environment. The development of children's pattern perception has been studied with geometric forms as well as with patterns that are more like those they encounter and must learn to use in school—letters, words, and pictures. It is the development of perceiving these latter kinds of patterns that will be focused upon here.

2.1 Perception of Letters and Letter-like Patterns

In an early study of the development of perception of letter-like forms, children from 4 to 8 years of age were shown artificial graphic forms and variants of those forms that were based on features of letters (Gibson, Gibson, Pick, and Osser 1962). The children were asked to say which variants were identical to the standard form and which were not, and the developmental pattern of the children's errors reflected their emerging knowledge of the alphabet. For example, perspective transformations were the most difficult for the children of all ages to discriminate, whereas rotation and reversal transformations were difficult for the younger children to discriminate, but resulted in very few errors by age 7—an age when most children have learned that orientation is an important feature of letters. Perspective differences, on the other hand, do not have the same status as distinctive features. In fact, children must learn to identify a variety of letter productions as being members of the same set (e.g., the different handwritings one must cope with). Young readers as well as adults discriminate among letters of the alphabet on the basis of their distinctive features, and the particular features used may change with the acquisition of reading skill (Pick 1965, Gibson et al. 1968, Gibson, Osser, Schiff, and Smith 1963). Children with problems learning to read English have been found able to discriminate and to learn to recognize letter patterns from other languages, such as Chinese characters and Hebrew letters, which implies that their reading problems may be based not in their perceptual functioning, but perhaps in linguistic translation (Vellutino et al. 1975).

It has been observed consistently that children's knowledge of the alphabet upon beginning school is highly related to their subsequent reading achievement and it is useful to speculate about the basis for this correlation. If it were a question of rote memorization, then drill in learning the 26 letters and their sounds should result in improved reading achievement. However, this is not automatically the case, as reading teachers well know. If the relation were mediated by the children's general visual discrimination skills, then practice in improving any such skills should generalize to better reading achievement. Long experience with perceptual-training programs (Haring and Bateman 1977) has consistently demonstrated that this is not the case. Furthermore, as the research on letter-like patterns has demonstrated, most children, even those categorized as reading disabled, appear to have no specific pattern perception deficit. Another hypothesis about the relation between knowledge of the alphabet and early success in reading is that knowledge of the alphabet reflects acquisition of an alphabetic principle. Children discern that letters are not arbitrary marks, but rather represent speech sounds in consistent ways (Pick et al. 1978). Children as young as 3 years of age can discriminate between marks on paper that are writing, and similar marks that are not (Lavine 1977), yet these children will not learn the alphabet nor begin to learn to read for 1 or 2 more years.

2.2 Perception of Words

Children perceive some aspects of the structure of words even before they begin to learn to read (Pick et al. 1978). As might be expected, the development of perception of words follows a course that is linked closely to acquisition of reading skill. Children who are at a very early phase of learning to read perceive printed words as being similar if the beginnings of the words are alike. Later on, the sounds of the words are also used to decide how similar two printed words are. The constraints in the letter combinations of words are used in perceiving them, for children as well as adults recognize nonsense words with legal spelling patterns more accurately than they recognize nonlegal letter strings (Gibson, Pick, Osser and Hammond 1962, Gibson, Osser, and Pick 1963).

Perceiving the meaning of words also follows a developmental course that is linked to learning to read. By the time children are in the third or fourth grade, inflectional endings can be perceived as units. It may be that beginning readers derive meaning directly from the written word, although this issue is unresolved (Barron and Baron 1977).

2.3 Perception of Pictures

Pictures, drawings, photographs, and other kinds of illustrations are used extensively as pedagogical devices in textbooks and by teachers. Since even a high-fidelity realistic photograph is very different from what it depicts, the development of perceiving the representational information in pictures may not follow exactly the same course as the development of perceiving objects and space. Picture perception has been a topic of cross-cultural study for some time because of the prevalent belief that culture-specific experience with pictures may be important in the development of the necessary skills for perceiving representational information in pictures. (See Hagen and Jones 1978, Pick and Pick 1978 for reviews of the cross-cultural studies.)

Children perceive the identity of a familiar object in a picture at quite a young age and without requiring specific experience with pictures. Direct evidence on this point is from observations of a child who was raised for the first year and a half of his life with very few opportunities to view any pictures and without anyone ever labeling a picture for him (Hochberg and Brooks 1962). When he was shown line drawings and photographs of familiar objects, his recognition accuracy was extremely high for both kinds of representation. There are other observations of very young children, unschooled adults, and people in cultures without indigenous pictorial art, who all recognize pictures of familiar objects with high accuracy (Kennedy and Ross 1975).

How are objects best portrayed for ease of recognition? In high-fidelity photographs? In outline drawings? In caricature? This is an important question to answer in order to know how best to use pictures for illustrative and teaching purposes. Unfortunately, there is not sufficient information on which to base an unequivocal answer. However, outline drawings which depict contours clearly may be better than even fully detailed photographs (Hagen and Jones 1978). When children do encounter difficulty in perceiving a depicted object, the difficulty may be in knowing what is the relevant information to attend to in a picture. If only the most relevant information is included, as in an outline drawing in contrast to a photograph, then such difficulty is precluded. What is needed is systematic information about the relative ease of perceiving familiar objects depicted in various ways.

There is other information in pictures besides that for recognizing objects. Often pictures portray spatial relations among objects as well as depth and distance. Children as young as 3 years of age are sensitive to texture-gradient information for depth (Yonas and Hagen 1973), to linear perspective information for depth, and to overlap or superposition (Hagen 1976). In addition, they are sensitive to shading information for depth when the pictorial display is presented vertically, but not when it is presented horizontally (Hagen and Jones 1978). There may be a phase in the development of pictorial perception when the space portrayed in the picture is not wholly separated from the spatial environment that surrounds the picture. Thus, children presented with pictures containing animals may describe the animals as "standing up" when the picture is presented vertically, and as "lying down" when the picture is presented horizontally.

After the preschool years, children improve in the accuracy with which they perceive pictorial depth information, and the improvement continues throughout the early school years and even into adolescence for some types of pictorial depth information (Hagen 1976). There is also improvement during the school years in using other pictorial information than depth, for example, using lines to convey action of characters.

A useful way to begin to identify the implications for school learning of the development of picture perception would be to analyze the kinds of pictures that are used for assessment and diagnosis in school, and to describe the information they contain. For example, in tests of reading comprehension, or tests of aural comprehension, children are often asked to select from among several pictures the one that "goes with" or "means the same as" a spoken or written sentence. Yet the pictures themselves are often ambiguous and require attention to different aspects in order to understand them. Studies in which information available in pictures is varied, and in which children's attention to different kinds of information or different types of portrayals is assessed, would be important for knowing how to highlight information we want children to acquire and how to direct their attention appropriately.

Bibliography

Barron R W, Baron J 1977 How children get meaning from printed words. *Child Dev.* 48: 587–94

Bower T G R 1981 *Development in Infancy*, 2nd edn. Freeman, San Francisco, California

Gibson E J 1969 *Principles of Perceptual Learning and Development.* Appleton-Century-Crofts, New York

Gibson E J 1982 Affordances and the concept of development: The renascence of functionalism. In: Collins W A (ed.) 1982 *Minnesota Symposia on Child Psychology*, Vol. 15. Erlbaum, Hillsdale, New Jersey, pp. 55–81

Gibson E J, Levin H 1975 *The Psychology of Reading.* MIT Press, Cambridge, Massachusetts

Gibson E J, Osser H, Pick A D 1963 A study of the development of grapheme–phoneme correspondences. *J. Verb. Learn. Verb. Behav.* 2: 142–46

Gibson E J, Shapiro F, Yonas A 1968 Confusion matrices for graphic patterns obtained with a latency measure. *The Analysis of Reading Skill: A Program of Basic and Applied Research.* Final report, Project No. 5–1213. Cornell University and United States Office of Education, pp. 76–96

Gibson E J, Gibson J J, Pick A D, Osser H 1962 A developmental study of the discrimination of letter-like forms. *J. Comp. Physiol. Psychol.* 55: 897–906

Gibson E J, Osser H, Schiff W, Smith J 1963 An analysis of critical features of letters, tested by a confusion matrix. *Final Report on a Basic Research Program on Reading.* Cooperative Research Project No. 639. Cornell University and United States Office of Education, pp. 1–20

Gibson E J, Pick A D, Osser H, Hammond M 1962 The role of grapheme–phoneme correspondence in the perception of words. *Am. J. Psychol.* 75: 554–70

Hagen M A 1976 Development of ability to perceive and produce pictorial depth cue of overlapping. *Percept. Motor Skills* 42: 1007–14

Hagen M A, Jones R K 1978 Cultural effects on pictorial perception: How many words is one picture really worth? In: Walk R D, Pick H L (eds.) 1978 *Perception and Experience.* Plenum, New York, pp. 171–212

Haith M M, Bergman T, Moore M J 1977 Eye contact and face scanning in early infancy. *Science* 198: 853–55

Haring N, Bateman B 1977 *Teaching the Learning Disabled Child.* Prentice-Hall, Englewood Cliffs, New Jersey

Hochberg J E, Brooks V 1962 Pictorial recognition as an unlearned ability: A study of one child's performance. *Am. J. Psychol.* 75: 624–28

Kennedy J M, Ross A S 1975 Outline picture perception by the Songe of Papua. *Perception* 4: 391–406

Lavine L O 1977 Differentiation of letter-like forms in pre-reading children. *Dev. Psychol.* 13: 89–94

Mitchell D E 1978 Effect of early visual experience on the development of certain perceptual abilities in animals and man. In: Walk R D, Pick H L (eds.) 1978 *Perception and Experience.* Plenum, New York, pp. 37–75

Pick A D 1965 Improvement of visual and tactual form discrimination. *J. Exp. Psychol.* 69: 331–39

Pick A D, Pick H L 1978 Culture and perception. In: Carterette E C, Friedman M P (eds.) 1978 *Handbook of Perception*, Vol. 10. Academic Press, New York, pp. 19–39

Pick A D, Frankel D G, Hess V L 1975 Children's attention: The development of selectivity. In: Hetherington E M (ed.) 1975 *Review of Child Development Research*, Vol. 5. University of Chicago Press, Chicago, Illinois, Chap. 6

Pick A D, Unze M G, Brownell C A, Drozdal J G, Hopmann

M R 1978 Young children's knowledge of word structure. *Child Dev.* 49: 669–80

Spelke E 1979 Exploring bimodally specified events in infancy. In: Pick A D (ed.) 1979 *Perception and its Development: A Tribute to Eleanor J. Gibson.* Erlbaum, Hillsdale, New Jersey, pp. 221–35

Vellutino F R, Steger J A, Kaman M, De Setto L 1975 Visual form perception in deficient and normal readers as a function of age and orthographic–linguistic familiarity. *Cortex* 11: 22–30

Walk R D 1978 Depth perception and experience. In: Walk R D, Pick H L (eds.) 1978 *Perception and Experience: Perceptual Development.* Plenum, New York, pp. 77–103

Walk R D 1981 *Perceptual Development.* Brooks/Cole, Monterey, California

Walk R D, Gibson E J 1961 A comparative and analytical study of visual depth perception. *Psychol. Monogr.*

75(15) whole No. 519

Wilson W R 1978 Behavioral assessment of auditory function in infants. In: Minifie F D, Lloyd L L (eds.) 1978 *Communicative and Cognitive Abilities: Early Behavioral Assessment.* University Park Press, Baltimore, Maryland, pp. 135–50

Yonas A 1979 Studies of spatial perception in infancy. In: Pick A D (ed.) 1979 *Perception and its Development: A Tribute to Eleanor J. Gibson.* Erlbaum, Hillsdale, New Jersey

Yonas A, Hagen M 1973 Effects of static and motion parallax depth information on perception of size in children and adults. *J. Exp. Child Psychol.* 15: 254–65

Yonas A, Pick H L 1975 An approach to infant space perception. In: Cohen L B, Salapatek P (eds.) 1975 *Infant Perception: From Sensation to Cognition*, Vol. 2: *Perception of Space, Speech and Sound.* Academic Press, New York, pp. 3–31

Memory

S. M. Thomas and R. M. Thomas

Perhaps in no area of psychology is there less agreement than there is about memory—about what memory is, how and where memorized material is stored, and how such material is retrieved. Some theorists equate memory with learning by reasoning that only when a person is able to remember something can he or she claim to have learned it. In contrast, other theorists see memory as an intermediate process between learning and behavior—information is learned, then stored in memory, and subsequently retrieved to be expressed as behavior. While there are thus various theories of memory that might be analyzed here, the following discussion is limited to one currently popular viewpoint based on an information-processing analogy, a viewpoint chosen because it is in keeping with recent research and offers numerous suggestions of use to educators (see *Information-processing Theory*).

In the daily task of instruction, teachers' concern with memory centers on a pair of interrelated questions. The first is: Why do students forget what they have been taught? The answer, from the perspective being adopted here, is that something could have gone wrong at any step in the process of taking in information, of manipulating it internally, and of expressing the result in some such behavior as writing a mathematical formula, correctly dialing a telephone number, or reciting a poem. The number of steps that compose this process from the initial intake of information to the final behavioral output can differ from one version of the theory to another. So, the seven-step process described below is only one of the available versions of the information-processing model. This version has been selected for discussion because it is particularly useful for guiding teachers in the diagnosis and treatment of learners' memory problems.

The second question is: What can be done to improve students' skills of remembering? The answer depends on which step in the information-processing system is not being performed efficiently. A particular set of remedies is generally needed for each stage of the remembering process.

The following review furnishes answers to these two focal questions by presenting each of seven stages of the information-processing model in turn. The final section of the article offers a brief description of characteristics of memory at different stages of life.

1. Seven Stages in Information Processing

The stages compose a cycle that includes (a) sensing stimuli from the environment; (b) grasping the sensation briefly in sensory memory; (c) perceiving or interpreting the stimuli; (d) retaining the percept in short-term memory; (e) transferring the percept to long-term memory where it is stored until it is (f) retrieved and (g) expressed as a behavior.

1.1 Sensing Stimuli

At this first step, stimuli from the environment in the form of light waves, sound waves, and chemical substances in the air contact the person's sense organs—the eyes, ears, nose, and others. Or in some instances the sensations arise not in the outside world but, rather, within the individual's body, such as in the vestibule of the inner ear where liquid pressures contribute to the person's sense of balance. If something is wrong with these sense receptors, stimuli will be inaccurately transmitted to the central nervous system or perhaps not transmitted at all. So sometimes when a teacher comments that "The child failed to remember what I taught," the apparent memory failure is actually the result of the student's not sensing the teacher's stimuli accurately in the first place.

To discover whether supposed memory problems are seated in faulty senses, teachers can have tests conducted on whichever of the pupil's sense organs is suspected of being defective. Teachers can also observe the pupil's behavior in class to detect symptoms of sensory malfunction. For example, a girl who squints when looking at writing on the chalkboard, who often rubs her eyes, and who does not recognize faces at a distance might be suffering from nearsightedness. Hence, the reason she has not remembered material written on the chalkboard can be because she never saw it clearly in the first place. Likewise, a boy who leans forward and frowns in concentration when the teacher is speaking in front of the class, and who often appears inattentive when classmates talk, may be suffering a hearing loss, so that his apparent poor memory has been caused by his failing to hear much of what has been said in class (see *Vision and Visual Perception; Hearing in the Aging; Hearing in Children*).

An obvious step toward correcting this cause of memory problems is to provide whatever sight and hearing equipment is needed—eye glasses or electronic hearing aids. In addition, teachers can adjust classroom procedures to (a) enhance students' chances of sensing instruction accurately and (b) substitute a different sensory channel for the faulty one.

One way to enhance a learner's chances of sensing accurately is to seat the student at a place in the classroom from which it is easier to hear or see the instruction. The near-sighted girl can be seated close to the chalkboard. The hard-of-hearing boy can be moved closer to the teacher, or a classmate who sits nearby can be assigned to explain to the boy information he has failed to hear accurately. As another possibility, the teacher's lecture can be tape-recorded for the boy to hear privately at a later time.

To substitute a different sensory channel for a faulty one, the teacher can read aloud the material on a chalkboard that the girl cannot see accurately. For the boy who is hard-of-hearing, the key ideas of the teacher's oral instruction can be furnished also in written form, either by the teacher or by a classmate who has made written notes during the lesson. If the instruction concerns physical skills, such as typing or throwing a ball, the teacher can depend less on sight-and-sound explanations and more on haptic sensing; that is, more on the sense of touch in the skin, of balance in the inner ear, and of kinesthetic receptors in the joints and muscles. In this event, the teacher has the learner physically try the movements, with the teacher depending very little on oral and visual explanation.

1.2 Grasping in Sensory Memory

During a geography lesson, as the student observes the teacher pointing to different countries on a wall map, a great host of light waves reach the student's eyes from other areas of the classroom in addition to the waves coming from the map. Likewise, sounds other than the teacher's voice strike the student's ears, odors impinge on the sense of smell, and pressures and heat stimulate receptors in the skin. But from this myriad of stimuli, the pupil attends only to a chosen few—the teacher's voice and selected colored areas on the map. This act of selective attending operates by means of a mode of momentary remembering known as sensory memory, which consists of a stimulus lingering very briefly in the sense organ, such as light waves lingering on the retina of the eye in the form of a picture. Such sensory memory lasts for perhaps a second or less, just long enough for the person to identify the experience.

The factors that guide sensory memory toward grasping particular sensations are incompletely understood, but they appear to include both the salience of the stimulus and the direction of the person's motives at the moment. Some stimuli are more salient than others, in that they stand out from the background of other stimuli because of their brightness, movement, difference in shape, loudness, or such. At the same time, the person searches the environment to fulfill some interest or motive and, in this effort, identifies those stimuli that seem to be pertinent to the motive and worthy of attention. Hence, stimulus salience and internal motive apparently operate together to determine what is caught in sensory memory.

In order to improve student's sensory memory, teachers can seek to make the instructional stimulus of the moment especially salient so it stands out from other sights and sounds by virtue of its distinctiveness or clarity. Simultaneously, teachers can influence the way students search the environment by using such techniques as: (a) employing stimuli that appear to serve motives students normally have—this is the approach of appealing to the learners' "felt needs," (b) prior to offering the instruction, giving assignments that will require the learners to attend to the instruction in order to solve the problems on which assignments focus, and (c) during the instruction, pointing out key elements of the stimuli that match interests or motives the teacher believes are significant to the students.

1.3 Perceiving the Stimuli

The act of perception consists of the person's interpreting the stimuli, that is, of deciding what the stimuli mean. To do this, the learner matches the characteristics of the stimuli against memories of similar past experiences. So meaning, from this perspective, is the process of determining how the new stimuli are alike (compared with) and are different from (contrasted to) the memory of past experiences.

Some learners' apparent inability to remember instruction is caused by problems with their perception system. These are people who have normal general intelligence and normal sight but still experience great difficulty in learning to read, apparently because something is wrong with the neural circuitry system that handles visual stimuli. The label dyslexia has been applied to this visual-perception difficulty. Other kinds of neural-circuitry disorders that relate to different perceptual functions that have been identified by other labels, such as dyscalculia for difficulty in comprehending quantitative ideas and aphasia for problems in understanding speech. Some learners also experience cross-modal perceptual problems, that is, difficulty in matching information arriving from different sensory sources. This disorder is most apparent in the cases of learners who cannot match the sight of a word to its sound, so they cannot adequately pronounce written words nor write down spoken language.

A variety of special instructional techniques have been developed to remedy or to circumvent these perceptual problems and thereby enable students to comprehend and thereafter remember material they have studied.

1.4 Retaining in Short-term Memory

Short-term memory is the next link in the chain. It is of but brief duration, perhaps no longer than one or two minutes or even less, but long enough to enable the mind to select which items it wishes to retain. A popular example is that of remembering a telephone nember. A person may look up a number in the book or obtain it from the telephone operator, then remember it just long enough to dial it. During the interval after first obtaining the number, he or she may rehearse or repeat it several times in order to retain it for a somewhat longer period than short-term memory allows. If it is rehearsed enough times, it may be moved into the next stage in remembering, that of long-term memory.

The normal capacity of short-term memory is limited to an average of seven meaningful units (with a range from five to nine), which are referred to as chunks. For example, a person might directly remember only between five and nine numbers or digits in a series. But if he or she can organize the digits in some meaningful fashion (such as 1492 can be recalled as the year Columbus arrived in the West Indies, and thereby the four digits become a solid chunk), he or she can retain perhaps as many as seven such composite chunks. Thus, a way of improving students' short-term memory is to train them in organizing perceptual chunks in meaningful patterns. Because such training also enhances long-term memory, the training techniques will also be reviewed in some detail under the following stage of memory cycle.

1.5 Storing in Long-term Memory

Long-term memory is represented by the lasting information which stays with us. Researchers do not yet know the capacity limits of long-term memory. Possibly everything once stored is always there. It may be only the inefficiency of the retrieval function that prevents people from knowing the extent of long-term memory and from intentionally recalling all that they ever learned.

One characteristic of long-term memory of particular importance for educators is its modifiability. Stored items do not reside unchanged in memory but may be altered with the passing of time. Certain details of an event may be lost and others retained, and the memory for one event may merge with elements of another. Or else memories, when recalled, may be embellished with new percepts or interpretations and unused memories commonly appear to fade away. As a consequence, teachers can help students keep stored events more faithful to the events' original conformation and readily available for recall by providing periodic rehearsal or review of the material.

There are numbers of techniques for improving long-term memory, with many of them based on the assumption that memories are located in the central nervous system—principally the brain—and that they are reached along neural pathways through the complex nerve–tissue network that makes up the system. Included in this assumption is the belief that new material is most usefully stored if it is associated with a variety of memories or "meanings" already in long-term memory. An item so stored is therefore available for recall via several routes or cues rather than only one. The following are some of the more popular devices teachers can use to help students enhance long-term memory.

One way to establish multiple pathways to an item in memory is that of suggesting multiple associations with the item during the instructional process. For example, a common device for recalling the numbers of days in each month of the year is some version of the rhyme: "Thirty days hath September, April, June, and November. All the rest have 31, except February alone." This rhyme offers one route to recall the lengths of different months. To create a second route to knowledge of at least certain months, a teacher can explain Julius and Augustus Caesar both wanted to have 31-day months named for them, so they inserted July and August in the previous 10-month year as added months, thus moving the month that was named after the Latin 7 (September) up to position nine in the list, month 8 (October) to position 10, and so forth. To provide still another association, the teacher can show how the knuckles on one hand can represent the 31-day months, while the valleys between the knuckles represent the months with fewer than 31 days. Therefore, assigning the names of the sequential months to the knuckles and valleys, back and forth across one hand, identifies which months are longer and which are shorter.

Memory is also enhanced when the material to be stored is cast as a pattern that links various elements together. Sometimes this meaningful form consists of a generalization or principle which structures the learning for the student. Or the pattern may be organized as a line of logic. For instance, the seven steps we are now tracing through the information-processing system are intended to represent a meaningful patterning of items. Displaying the pattern graphically in Fig. 1 provides additional visual associations for these ideas and thereby renders them more easily remembered.

Apparently people store items in short-term memory

verbatim, either in exact words or as visual images. But in the long-term memory information is more often stored by meaning or by paraphrase. Thus, the sentence "The boy brought in the dog" may be recalled as "The dog was brought in by his young master."

While a general principle or a logical outline can give meaning to a collection of items, in some instances the type of scheme that improves memory has no inherent meaning but is more of a trick or a crutch for recalling rote items as contrasted to meaningful information. In rote-memorization, a memory tool or mnemonic device is constructed to connect disparate items that cannot readily be assembled under a principle or by a line of logic. The rhyme about the months of the year is such a mnemonic device. Another popular mnemonic tool can be an acronym produced by creating a word from the initial letters of several terms or phrases to be remembered. For example, in a class studying problems of drug abuse, the letters in the artificial word "moch" can represent the names of the various derivatives of opium—morphine, opium, codeine, and heroin and thinking of the coffee-flavor term mocha may help students recall their mnemonic word "moch." In a study of political–economic coalitions, the creation "TIMPS" can serve as a key to the membership of the Association of Southeast Asian Nations: Thailand, Indonesia, Malaysia, the Philippines, and Singapore. To produce many such useful acronyms during the process of instruction, teachers can first demonstrate how mnemonic words are created, then encourage students to make a game of devising their own words for remembering material in various subject matter fields.

A further mnemonic approach is the keyword method, perhaps most popular for memorizing foreign-language vocabulary but applicable to other curriculum areas as well. It typically consists of a two-stage technique for remembering materials that have an associative aspect. Pressley, Levin, and Delaney (1982 p. 62) have illustrated its operation in the case of an English-speaking student learning Spanish vocabulary. The student

> first derives a key word, which is an English word (preferably a concrete noun) that sounds like part of the foreign word. For example, *cart* is a good keyword for the Spanish word *carta*. Then a meaningful interaction involving the keyword (here *cart*) and the vocabulary word's definition (here *postal letter*) is constructed. This can be in the form of a provided interactive illustration, or the learner can generate an interactive visual image. Thus, for *carta* a reasonable picture/image would be that of a postal letter inside a shopping cart. Alternatively a meaningful sentence can be used to link the keyword to the vocabulary word's definition, as in *The cart transported the letter.*

Another way to improve long-term memory is to overlearn the information—to practice it beyond the initial level of mastery. Periodic practice or review also helps correct slight errors as well as maintain the learning in a fresh, readily available condition. Teachers can also provide varied situations in which students practice so they do not become bored and thus fail to profit from

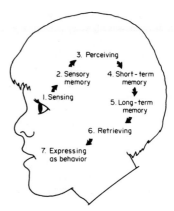

Figure 1
Memory in an information-processing cycle

the review. Games are often good for this purpose, so long as the games do not distort the meaning of the material to be learned and do not require much distracting activity—such as running about or keeping score—that is really not pertinent to the learning goals.

By distributing practice among several sessions, so that not all of the reviewing is done within one long uninterrupted session, the student is less likely to suffer fatigue that reduces the effectiveness of the review. Finally, when practicing complex skills or a great many items, learners can set short-term goals of either quality or quantity of review, then provide themselves with a reward when they reach each short-term goal. This generates motivation to continue practicing energetically.

1.6 Retrieving from Memory

Failure in the memory system may also occur at the stage of recalling stored material. Possibly there is more than one cause of such failure—unused memories decay or are erased, some memories may be buried in ways that make them inaccessible by the usual techniques of recall, or unpleasant associations with certain memories may cause the retrieval mechanism to avoid bringing them to consciousness.

One theory of memory storage proposes that memories are filed in a cross-referenced system by means of multiple associations. To locate a memory in the file, it may be necessary to hunt for associations that will serve as keys or paths to the memory. For example, in order to find a mislaid purse, a woman can retrace her steps since the last time she saw the purse and thereby perhaps encounter a cue to the memory of where she left it. Or, as a man tries to remember what he did on 31 December 1975, he may try recalling what age he was at the time, where the family might have been, and how they celebrated New Year's Day. In effect, by searching through other memories that could be connected with the forgotten material, he may consider an associative link to that material and thus retrieve it.

Memory

1.7 Expressing the Memory as Behavior

The final step in the cycle is to use the recalled information or skill in carrying out the task at hand—spelling a word correctly, swinging the golf club accurately, addressing a former acquaintance by her correct name, answering a test question, or the like.

One way a person can prepare ahead of time for this final step is to practice the memorized material in a form that is as close as possible to the form of behavior in which the material ultimately will be expressed. For example, if the memorized items will be needed later for the purpose of writing an answer to an essay-test question, then during the preceding practice stages it will be profitable to create sample essay questions and to practice writing answers for them. Such practice in the same form as that needed in the ultimate behavior increases the similarity between the two occasions and thus increases the likelihood that the complex of information and skills will be retrieved most satisfactorily.

2. Human Development and Memory

Babies are born with as many as five times more of the billions of brain neurons (nerve cells) as they will have in extreme old age, because such cells continually die over time. However, in the infant the neurons are not fully developed, nor have the associative pathways in the brain and the learned meanings been formed, as they will be throughout the coming years, even throughout the entire period of adulthood in some cases. As a consequence of these two opposing phenomena—the gradual reduction of cells and the regular increase in associative pathways and meanings—memory changes both quantitatively and qualitatively with age.

In studying memory in young infants, researchers are obliged to infer many of their conclusions from simple behaviors. For example, in studying recognition (knowing whether a stimulus has been seen before), which is the simplest form of memory, researchers have assumed that the baby will look longer at something new and look a shorter time at something recognized as familiar. Thus, the time an infant spends looking at an object has been used as a measure of recognition memory. Studies of this sort suggest that infants can recognize a wide variety of stimuli at very young ages. Even newborns can recognize their own parents, as suggested by the infants' behaving differently when offered a toy by their mother than when offered one by someone else. By the age of one week a baby can recognize its mother's voice among other female voices, and by two weeks can associate the mother's face and voice as belonging together. Five-month-olds can distinguish both photographs and drawings of a human face.

An average 4-year-old can recognize as many as 12 pictures he or she has seen before, but when asked to perform the more sophisticated memory function of recall, he or she can only recollect two or three pictures. The ability of 4-year-olds to recognize pictures equals adults' ability, probably because young children tend to think in visual images rather than in words, and pictures capture their attention readily. At ages 4 and 5, children seem to cluster and label objects, but they do not classify them in such groupings as flowers, animals, and the like as 6- and 7-year-olds begin to do. Between ages 5 and 7 or 8, major changes occur in children's thinking abilities in general, and particularly in memory, as evidenced by a growing employment of organizational and increasingly abstract modes of thought which become refined with advancing age.

As noted earlier, rehearsing is an important tool for transferring information to long-term memory. One way to determine whether a child is rehearsing verbal material is to watch for lip movements. Those 5-year-olds who rehearse at all apparently do not rehearse very effectively, but 10-year-olds do it quite well. In one study wherein children were asked to remember a series of words (dog, pen, book, flag, cup) 8-year-olds rehearsed each word aloud (dog, dog, dog, pen, pen, pen); in contrast, 15-year-olds added each successive word to the preceding memorized list and repeated the whole list over and over.

Scores on tests of rote memory, such as for a series of numbers repeated forward and in reverse order, increase progressively by age until about age 20, then gradually decrease until age 60 when the average score is only equal to that of an 11-year-old. This trend is in contrast to memory for meaningful material, called information, which remains fairly constant from age 20 to 60. However, the ability to recall recently learned material declines over the years. Young children possess an advantage denied to older people. The young children are not so much affected by interference from the effect of the sheer amount of already learned material crowding out the acquisition of new items.

Bibliography

Adams J R 1980 *Learning and Memory: An Introduction*, 2nd edn. Dorsey, Homewood, Illinois

Anderson J R 1976 *Language, Memory, and Thought*. Erlbaum, Hillsdale, New Jersey

Brainard C J, Pressley M (eds.) 1985 *Basic Processes in Memory Development*. Springer-Verlag, New York

Cohen G, Eysenck M W, LeVoi M E 1986 *Memory: A Cognitive Approach*. Open University Press, Milton Keynes

Klatzky R L 1980 *Human Memory: Structures and Processes*, 2nd edn. Freeman, San Francisco, California

Melton A W, Martin E (eds.) 1972 *Coding Processes in Human Memory*. Winston, Washington, DC

Murdock B B 1974 *Human Memory: Theory and Data*. Wiley, New York

Norman D A 1969 *Memory and Attention*. Wiley, New York

Pressley M, Levin J R, Delaney H D 1982 The mnemonic keyword method. *Rev. Educ. Res.* 52(1): 61–91

Tulving E, Donaldson W (eds.) 1972 *Organization of Memory*. Academic Press, New York

Transfer of Learning

R. M. Thomas

The meaning of transfer of learning or transfer of training is reflected in the question: how much does learning in one area serve to improve the learner's performance in other areas? Or, stated differently: how adequately does training in one situation generalize to other situations?

When the concept of transfer is applied to specific educational settings, the question assumes such forms as: to what extent does learning one foreign language, such as Latin, affect progress in learning another language, such as French or Mandarin Chinese? To what degree does practice in analyzing literary works enhance a person's skill in analyzing scientific experiments or social conflicts? How much will instruction in the theory of soil chemistry and plant genetics influence a learner's farming methods?

Important early contributions to research on transfer of learning were provided by E. L. Thorndike (1924) and C. H. Judd (1908). Thorndike proposed that transfer between one learning task and a new task depended upon how many elements were alike in the two tasks. Judd's investigations led him to the conclusion that generalizations, and not just specific elements, could transfer from one learning situation to another.

The matter of transfer has been investigated for much of the twentieth century, with the studies yielding a series of generalizations of use to people interested in improving the efficiency of instruction. The nature of such generalizations is illustrated by the following six points in which each generalization is accompanied by an example of what it can imply for educational practice.

Firstly, the extent to which learning will transfer is influenced by the learner's age, mental ability, attitude toward learning, and acceptance of the methods of instruction (Orata 1941 p. 83). Older and intellectually brighter students transfer their training more readily than do younger and less intelligent ones. In addition, transfer is improved when students regard what they have learned and the methods by which it was taught as being useful beyond the classroom.

Secondly, transfer is enhanced when students learn not just facts and specific skills but also broad concepts and principles applicable in many different situations. The pupil who learns by rote the multiplication fact of $4 \times 7 = 28$ is not as well-prepared to transfer this knowledge to a variety of mathematical situations as is the pupil who learns the principle that "multiplication facts are simply the answers that result (such as 28) when several quantities (four of them) of the same size (each in the amount of seven) are added together."

Thirdly, transfer is fostered when a variety of life-like examples are used in teaching skills, concepts, and principles (Harlow 1959 p. 502). The science instructor who systematically illustrates principles with a wide array of applications of these principles in the world improves students' abilities both to recall the principles and to apply them in the future.

Fourthly, the greater the number of similarities the student perceives between the original learning and other situations in life, the more the original learning can improve performance in the other situations (Harlow 1959 p. 502). To foster learners' ability to perceive transfer opportunities, teachers can provide students with a diversity of problems in which they practice the application of newly learned skills and principles to varied life situations. Such practice problems can profitably include three types: (a) those in which similarities are rather apparent, (b) those in which appropriate similarities exist but they are not so readily identified, and (c) those in which there are essentially no useful similarities. Confronting learners with all three types sharpens their skills of distinguishing situations that involve suitable transfer conditions from situations that do not.

Fifthly, concepts and generalizations which the learner derives from personal experiences (observing, gathering data, analyzing, drawing conclusions) transfer more adequately than ones the learner has been taught in the form of verbal definitions and examples (Suchman 1961 p. 149). Learners can accurately apply an insight or generalization to new situations without having to verbalize it (Hendrix 1947 p. 200, Harlow 1959 p. 502). As a consequence, inquiry modes of instruction that place learners in problem situations in which they are expected to "work their way out" can be expected to promote transfer better than lectures, explanations, and demonstrations by the instructor.

Finally, guided practice in heuristics—that is, in general problem-solving skills and methods of inquiry—can enhance students' performance in a broad range of new situations (Biehler 1978 pp. 481–90). Teachers can furnish such practice by instructing students in problem-solving steps and then offering frequent problem situations in which to master these procedures. Various theorists have analyzed problem solving and have proposed steps followed, either intuitively or purposely, by people in the past who have proved to be skilled at devising solutions. For example, one set of steps consists of (Thomas and Brubaker 1971 pp. 276–77):

(a) Identifying problems or questions to investigate.

(b) Analyzing the problems or questions into component parts so that the kinds of information to be gathered for answering them become apparent.

(c) Planning who will collect what data, where, and how.

(d) Collecting the desired information.

(e) Organizing the information into a comprehensible pattern.

(f) Interpreting the information in a fashion that solves the problems or answers the questions.

(g) Reporting the results.

(h) Evaluating the success of the process. Were all the steps performed successfully? If not, why not?

Bibliography

Biehler R F 1978 *Psychology Applied to Teaching*, 3rd edn. Houghton Mifflin, Boston, Massachusetts

Bigge M L, Hunt M P 1968 *Psychological Foundations of Education: An Introduction to Human Development and Learning*, 2nd edn. Harper and Row, New York

Harlow H F 1959 Learning set and error factor theory. In: Koch S (ed.) 1959 *Psychology: A Study of a Science*, Vol. 2. McGraw-Hill, New York, pp. 492–537

Hendrix G 1947 A new clue to transfer of training. *Elem. Sch. J.* 48: 197–208

Judd C H 1908 The relation of special training and general intelligence. *Educ. Rev.* 36: 42–48

Orata P T 1941 Recent research studies on transfer of training with implications for curriculum, guidance, and personnel work. *J. Educ. Res.* 35: 81–101

Suchman J B 1961 Inquiry training: Building skills for autonomous discovery. *Merrill-Palmer Q.* 7(3): 147–69

Thomas R M, Brubaker D L 1971 *Decisions in Teaching Elementary Social Studies*. Wadsworth, Belmont, California

Thorndike E L 1924 Mental discipline in high school studies. *J. Educ. Psychol.* 15: 83–98

Cognitive Style and Learning

N. J. Entwistle

Cognitive style is the term used to describe different ways in which people process information, including perception, storage, transformation, and utilization of information from the environment. It describes habitual processes of perceiving and thinking which are qualitatively distinct. Cognitive style differs from ability in that it is typically described in terms of contrasting poles, rather than as a single dimension. It is also thought to be associated with personality, affective, and motivational characteristics. Like ability, however, it is considered to be relatively stable, being consistent across both time and task (Schwen et al. 1979, Kogan 1976, Messick 1976).

1. History

The idea that people of contrasting personalities differ not only in terms of behaviour but also in their modes of thinking can be traced back into antiquity (Vernon 1973). Such ideas are also contained in the writings of Jung. He contrasted the empirical, fact-bound thinking of the extrovert with the personal, theory-bound thinking of the introvert. Vernon (1973) traces the idea of cognitive style to an article in 1951 by Klein on "The personal world through perception", but the term itself he attributes to R. W. Gardner in 1953.

Since then many sets of dichotomies have been used to describe aspects of cognitive style with a corresponding variety of methods of measurement. Messick (1976) has described 19 such terms, while Goldstein and Blackman (1977) have summarized the more important approaches to measurement. No attempt will be made here to describe all the categories used; rather, the different types of category will be illustrated, in terms of styles of perceiving, of processing information, of thinking, and of learning.

2. Styles of Perceiving

The best-known cognitive style of all is the field-independence/field-dependence (FI/FD) dimension which was developed and used extensively by Witkin and his associates (1977). This field of research began in the late 1940s with an interest in perceptual processes, and in particular in the extent to which people could detect the gravitational upright in conditions which made it difficult to relate a figure to its background. The rod and frame test was the best-known instrument to assess the ability to identify the gravitational upright, but more recent work has concentrated on the embedded figures test which may be administered to groups or individually. This test presents a series of simple geometrical figures, and the time taken to identify these shapes within complex figures is noted. High field independence is indicated by a short completion time.

Witkin was able to demonstrate that people are likely to be consistent in their preferred mode of perceiving over periods of many years. He argued that this preference was partly inherited and partly the result of child-rearing practices. In industrialized societies sex-role socialization was considered to be responsible for the greater field dependence found among women. Cross-cultural studies showed that such a sex difference was "uncommon in mobile, hunting societies and prevalent in sedentary, agricultural societies" (Witkin et al. 1977 p. 7).

Although his initial work was specific to perception, towards the end of his life Witkin was able to demonstrate such a wide range of correlates of field independence that he argued that his tests were describing a cognitive style which covered preferred ways of processing information in general, and not just a form of visual acuity. He used the terms *articulated* and *global* to refer to these broader conceptions. An articulated approach implied the imposition of structure and the tendency to use narrow, tightly organized sets of concepts in trying to understand new topics, whereas a global approach implied less rigidity. Witkin was able to show that teachers differed in the way they organized course material, with field-independent teachers imposing structure, and preferring more formal, impersonal modes of presentation. Field-dependent teachers used looser structures, were less organized, and were more likely to adopt discussion methods. Witkin pointed out that areas of study differed in the extent to which they were tightly structured and used formal analytic procedures. As a result field-dependent students were expected to prefer, and were found to be more successful in, arts and humanities courses rather than the sciences. These students also preferred the more informal teaching methods adopted by field-dependent teachers.

Although Witkin described clear, logical, and consistent sets of relationships between cognitive style and educational variables, other researchers' findings have been less convincing. There is even doubt whether field independence can be treated as a cognitive style at all, as it contains elements of both general and spatial ability (Vernon 1973). In addition the positive characteristics of field dependence can be inferred only from incidental relationships, not from the defining method of measurement (Entwistle 1981).

The other main perceptual test used to identify a cognitive style is matching familiar figures, developed by Kagan, which distinguishes between *reflective* and *impulsive* styles (Messer 1976). The test presents a target drawing, followed by a set of up to eight drawings, all of which are very similar to the target, but only one of which is identical. The respondent is required to make the match as quickly as possible, but has to make another attempt after each incorrect response. There is thus pressure to find the correct answer, but also to decide quickly. This situation creates competing anxieties between correct and fast responses (Kogan 1976). The average time to answer (response latency) is measured, and also the number of errors. Impulsive people succumb rapidly to the need to identify the matching figure; they choose hurriedly and make mistakes. Reflective individuals treat the task more analytically and cautiously; they are more accurate, but slower.

There is some evidence that difficulties in learning to read may be related to impulsiveness. Reflective individuals are more successful at problem-solving tasks, show higher levels of attention to cognitive activities, and are more concerned with the quality of their answers. Reflectiveness can be seen as a more mature intellectual strategy which children can, to some extent, be helped to acquire (see Schwen et al. 1979 for references).

Again, there is a difficulty in interpreting this dimension as a style. Some people are both fast and accurate while others are slow and inaccurate. Reflectiveness can

be seen, in part, as an ability and, in part, as a personality trait (Guilford 1980).

3. Styles of Information Processing

The information processing model of cognition describes a long-term memory made up of a large number and variety of schemata, concepts, ideas, and facts against which incoming information is compared and into which aspects of it are coded and stored. An effective cross-referencing system is required both for storage and recall and this demands categories which are distinct, clearly defined, and interconnected. Coding incoming information depends on identifying defining characteristics, and then analysing similarities and differences. Recall involves searching among the stored categories, which may be done in a manner that is broad and leisurely, or narrow and fast (Entwistle 1981). Cognitive styles can thus be described in terms of the emphasis on either similarity or difference (levelling vs. sharpening and breadth of categorization), the number of attributes used in comparing objects or people (cognitive complexity) or a preference for abstract or concrete referents (see Messick 1976 for further details).

Besides investigating breadth of categorization, Wallach and Kogan (1965) also distinguished differing styles of conceptualization by showing children pictures of familiar objects which had to be put into groups. The children were also asked why the objects belonged together. They found characteristic differences between children according to whether they made predominant use of concrete, relational/thematic, or abstract analytic properties.

This last set of distinctions highlights the recurring problem in interpreting cognitive style data from children. To what extent do the differences reflect developmental differences rather than stylistic preferences? The categories described by Wallach and Kogan bear a close resemblance to those used in describing stages in conceptual development. Style of conceptualization implies the preference for, say, concrete properties even though abstract properties are also recognized. But children have to "construct their alternatives" before they can choose between them.

4. Styles of Thinking

The main part of Wallach and Kogan's study was an exploration between what they referred to as intelligence (measured by conventional reasoning tests) and creativity (indicated by responses to open-ended questions requiring imagination and fluency, rather than analytic skills). Wallach and Kogan contrasted the children high on intelligence, whom they saw as "addicted" to school achievement, with those highly creative children in whom school produced feelings of frustration and inadequacy. A similar distinction, in terms of scores on tests of convergent and divergent thinking, was made by Hudson (1966) who coined the terms *convergers* and *divergers* to describe styles of thinking related to contrasting preferences for subject areas and personality attributes. Convergers tended to be cautious, emotionally inhibited, and to choose science; pupils taking the humanities were more impulsive, expansive, uninhibited, and provided a large number of sometimes bizarre "uses for objects" in that test of divergent thinking.

As with impulsiveness, however, there must be four styles which can be derived from contrasting scores on convergent and divergent thinking. In describing styles of thinking both high/high and low/low categories tend to be ignored, although those categories are still interesting and important.

5. Styles of Learning

A more recent way of describing differences in cognitive style is that proposed by Pask (1976). He has used problem-solving tasks to contrast holist and serialist strategies of learning. The holist tends to view the task as a whole, to seek interconnections between even tenuously connected ideas, and to make avid use of illustrations, anecdotes, and individualistic analogies. The serialist has a narrower focus in carrying out the learning task, prefers cautious step-by-step procedures, and relies more on detailed fact and evidence in building up an argument. Pask describes learning pathologies associated with the consistent use of a particular strategy (hence learning style). Holists, in their search for interconnecting ideas, exhibit globetrotting, through failure to make proper use of evidence, while serialists become improvident as they fail to make use of valid analogies and relationships.

Pask has used teaching materials based on extreme holist or serialist principles to demonstrate that students who are mismatched with materials learn slowly and inaccurately, while those who experience materials matching their own learning style assimilate the ideas quickly and remember them well. Besides the two contrasting styles, Pask also describes versatile learners who are able to adopt either style as demanded by the task and to alternate between the styles in building up understanding. Rote learning, on the other hand, seems to involve neither style. There is now some tentative evidence that holists have a personality pattern that includes thinking introversion, impulse expression, emotionality, aestheticism, cognitive complexity, and flexibility, while serialists are mainly distinguished by a practical, as opposed to a theoretical, outlook (Entwistle and Morison 1983).

6. Conclusion

One of the striking features of the literature on cognitive style is the use of dichotomies to describe individual differences. Is the use of dichotomous classification an oversimplification of more complex typologies, or is it fundamental to some underlying neurological property? Ornstein (1977), in describing the functions of the left (analytic) and right (expressive) hemispheres of the brain, parallels many of the distinctions made between cognitive styles. Some attempts have been made to link styles to cerebral dominance, but the results are still inconclusive (Springer and Deutsch 1981). If there is this neurological explanation, then it is clear that we should expect not just the two distinct styles of information processing, but also the two levels which imply the capacity to use each style effectively, or use neither of them. Yet the neurological explanation would also imply that every normal individual should have the capacity to use both modes of thinking to some extent, and to use them in alternation. Indeed, the alternation between focusing on detail and on the interconnections between ideas may be fundamental to building up understanding in any subject area (Entwistle 1981).

How then can the different styles described above be summarized and the idea of levels be introduced at the same time? Table 1 provides a tentative framework,

Table 1
Views of cognitive style[a]

Style type	Integrated A + B	Style A	Style B	Underdeveloped	Author
Perceiving	—	Field-dependent	Field-independent	—	Witkin
	Fast, accurate	Impulsive	Reflective	Slow, inaccurate	Kagan
Information processing					
Categories	—	Broad	Narrow	—	Wallach and
Concepts	—	Relational	Analytic	Descriptive	Kogan
Thinking	Both strong	Divergers (Imaginative)	Convergers (Logical)	Both weak	Hudson
Learning	Versatile	Holist	Serialist	Rote	Pask
Personality	Integrated	Expressive, emotional, cognitively complex	Self-contained, inhibited, practical	—	Hudson Entwistle and Morison

[a] Adapted from Entwistle 1981 p. 218

although there is still little empirical evidence of the interrelationships between the different descriptive categories. An impression of what may be stereotypes of the basic underlying cognitive styles can be obtained from reading off the characteristics listed in the appropriate columns of the table.

The insistent message from all the literature on cognitive style is that teachers should take account not only of the range of styles exhibited by their students, but also recognize that their way of teaching is likely to be an expression of their own cognitive style. The decision to adopt an extreme teaching method, or to espouse a particular philosophy of education to the exclusion of any other, could be seen as an unjustifiable self-indulgence. That style of teaching might well be personally satisfying to the teacher and to like-minded students, but would impose on other students an alien way of learning. Of course, a majority of teachers and students are not extreme in their styles, but the dangers of insisting on one or other mode of organization or presentation of material should be recognized. It is also possible that by helping students to identify their own style of learning, it may be possible to train them to capitalize on their strengths and develop the weaker parts of their repertoires of learning strategies.

Bibliography

Entwistle N J 1981 *Styles of Learning and Teaching.* Wiley, London

Entwistle N J, Morison S E 1983 Personality, and cognitive style in studying. In: Entwistle N J, Ramsden P (eds.) 1983 *Understanding Student Learning.* Croom Helm, London

Goldstein K M, Blackman S 1978 *Cognitive Style: Five Approaches to Theory and Research.* Wiley-Interscience, New York

Guilford J P 1980 Cognitive styles: What are they? *Educ. Psychol. Meas.* 40: 715–35

Hudson L 1966 *Contrary Imaginations: A Psychological Study of the English Schoolboy.* Methuen, London

Kogan N 1976 *Cognitive Styles in Infancy and Early Childhood.* Erlbaum, Hillsdale, New Jersey

Messer S B 1976 Reflection–impulsivity: A review. *Psychol. Bull.* 83: 1026–52

Messick S (ed.) 1976 *Individuality in Learning.* Jossey-Bass, San Francisco, California

Ornstein R E 1977 *The Psychology of Consciousness,* 2nd edn. Harcourt, Brace, Jovanovich, New York

Pask G 1976 Styles and strategies of learning. *Br. J. Educ. Psychol.* 46: 128–48

Schwen T M, Bednor A K, Hodson K 1979 Cognitive styles: Boon or bane. *Viewpoints Teach. Learn.* 55 (4): 49–65

Springer S P, Deutsch G 1981 *Left Brain, Right Brain.* Freeman, San Francisco, California

Vernon P E 1973 Multivariate approaches to the study of cognitive style. In: Royce J R (ed.) 1973 *Multivariate Analysis and Psychological Theory.* Academic Press, New York

Wallach M A, Kogan N 1965 *Modes of Thinking in Young Children.* Holt, Rinehart and Winston, New York

Witkin H A, Moore C A, Goodenough D R, Cox P W 1977 Field-dependent and field-independent cognitive styles and their educational implications. *Rev. Educ. Res.* 47: 1–64

Varieties of Intellectual Development

Communication Skills Development

P. A. Drum

Communicative competence refers to the effective use of language in social contexts. A social context describes any situation in which two or more persons are engaged in a conversation in order to exchange information, to share feelings, and/or to express desires. Basically, the first speaker makes a comment that has some content relative to the purpose for the utterance. The act of speaking has an effect upon the listener, who then responds in speech, action, or thought to the content of the message. Any of the four parts of the utterance can be successful or unsuccessful. Using Austin's terms (1962), the locutionary act can be heard or misheard; the content of the message can be garbled or clear; the speaker's intent (the illocutionary force) may or may not be appropriately signalled for the situation; and the effect upon the receiver (the perlocutionary force) can either be the one intended or a mismatch. However, the quality of the message is only part of what a language user must know.

Any community establishes social conventions over time that include rules for speech. The rules are seldom codified, nor, in most instances, are they directly taught. A speaker unconsciously acquires the rules of when to say what to whom because he or she is a member of that community. For instance, in English, the utterance "you must" means it is a required action, while "you may" indicates permission from the speaker to do something. However, as a guest at a dinner party in someone's home, the rules change (Lakoff 1973). "You must have some of this cake" becomes the most gracious form from your host, and "You may have some of this cake" is almost rude. "Must" shows attention to the guest, but "may" can be paraphrased as a reluctant inclusion toward the addressee. A child who grows up in the community will eventually learn the social-style shifts, but there is much to be learned.

1. Language in Use

Language in social use has certain key determinants which implicitly dictate the structure of communication. Hymes (1972) describes certain general factors: (a) the time and the place of the physical setting; (b) the characteristics of the participants, including age, sex, role relationships (minister and parishioner, teacher and pupils, lovers); (c) the desired outcomes of the participants, which can be identical or diverse; (d) the structure of the speech act, such as the abbreviated phrasal retorts of good friends talking about daily events versus the more precise enunciation and reference of strangers discussing abstract topics (restricted speech versus elaborated speech discussed by Bernstein 1967); (e) the tone or seriousness, playfulness, or irony of the psychological setting, often conveyed by gestures and intonation patterns (a wink, syllabic stress, etc.); (f) the dialect and register divergence among speakers; (g) the conversational norms for the community (for instance, "children should be seen and not heard"); and (h) the type of speech act, such as jokes, persuasive speeches, sermons, or lectures.

The rules vary from country to country, and even in subtle ways from community to community. The attainment of an advanced degree often requires that the new physician, doctor of philosophy, or army general immediately change his or her mode of address to those who were his or her teachers or his or her superior officers prior to the moment of advancement. Every profession has its jargon; every group of people has its "in" language. To be a member, it is necessary to be able to conform to the specific speech structures of that community. Once membership is acknowledged, freedom to vary in individual ways is implicitly understood. Thus, an ability to conform to the social conventions involved in speech acts includes an unconscious appreciation of all levels of these factors crossed with one another that are pertinent for a particular community, seemingly an inordinately difficult task when the infinite possibilities are considered.

The general steps in which children acquire competence in the execution of speech acts and in signalling the dual functions of these acts (message meaning and social convention) are described here. There seems to be a continuous stream of development along both dimensions without the somewhat definite demarcations of mean length of utterance and/or inflectional acquisition. Conversation evolves toward the adult model, but the why and how of this process are not well-delineated as yet.

2. Precursors of Conservation

A baby's scream which subsequently brings comfort is a precursor for communication, for a vocalization has provoked a response in a listener. A more inclusive term than "speech act" is Dore's "conversational act" (1979a p. 342), which encompasses any utterance that "conveys information and expresses an attitude (intention, expectation, belief, etc.) relative to that information." Conversational acts are always embedded in sequences with two or more respondents sharing a common topic. Each act is regulated by both topic and communicative intent. As long as there is some means to correlate intent, conversational acts can refer to certain infant utterances.

Bates, Camaioni, and Volterra (1979) have proposed a three-stage model for the development of communication in the infant's first year. Stage one consists of the infant's vocal and physical reactions to his or her own physiological conditions, such as crying, gurgling, and burping. The infant's caretakers often assume that they recognize subtle distinctions in cries as having different meanings, but if there is intent, it is not accompanied by any eye contact with the adult or other gestures that could help in confirming it. However, the repetitive patterns of vocalization and response could serve as rudimentary models for a later period. In stage two, at 9 to 10 months, the child uses some objects and gestures, such as pointing, reaching, eye contact, and others, in order to make requests. Toward the end of this period, the gestures are used by themselves with less and less direct contact with an object—almost an unconscious sign language. In the third stage, the child's gestures are accompanied by vocalizations; for instance, as the child reaches for a rubber duck, he or she says "qua-qua." This developmental analysis points out that an infant's use of vocalizations, then gestures, and finally the coupling of gesture and vocalizations to make a request illustrate embryonic characteristics of future dialogues. At least the infant is learning to attend to the receiver of the comment as evidenced by repetitive eye contact and other physical manifestations.

By the time the child is 2 years old, it both imitates and sequences action responses but apparently does not use language to either accompany or regulate actions. Pairs of children playing together will seem to be holding conversations, but if one listens closely, each child is apparently talking to himself or herself most of the time. One child's comment is not generally responsive to the preceding remark of the other child. There is no common conversational topic though their play indicates some physical commonality in the actions. On the other hand, 4-year-olds also use action in child–child interactions, but the action is generally initiated by and concomitant with language (Camaioni 1979). Dialogues are now apparent, but the questions remain as to how successful the children are in signalling their intent, in encoding their messages, and in following the rules of conversational interactions.

3. Speaker Intent

Any language learner must not only learn the form of the language of the cultural milieu, but how and when to use language to achieve his or her goals, his or her intent. The goals, according to Halliday (1978), have two interrelated functions in the child's speech. One is a pragmatic intent, whereby language is used (a) to obtain desires whether they be physical or psychological (instrumental use), (b) to control the actions or feelings of the receiver (regulator use), or (c) to express solidarity within the speech dyad (interpersonal use). The other is a mathetic purpose (a) to express deixus—the relationship between the speaker, the listener, and what is said—(interpersonal use), (b) to comment on the world (heuristic use), and (c) to interpret the world according to one's perspective (imaginal use). Thus, child communication consists of two components, an intent or a pragmatic function and comments on the world or a mathetic function.

Here both the development of requests in speech acts (an intent purpose) and the development of speech routines (an interpersonal mathetic goal expressing social learning) are examined as two exemplars of communicative competence which the child must attain.

3.1 Requests

Requests to do something have been studied in 3- to 5-year-olds (Garvey 1975). The speaker's purpose is to obtain some specific response by the listener. There are at least three forms for requests: (a) direct requests, such as "Shut the window"; (b) indirect requests, such as "See if you can shut the window"; and (c) inferred requests, such as "It is cold in this room." This direct form without some polite adjunct, such as "please," is often used when either the speaker is ignorant of speech courtesy (a young child) or the speaker is in a power relationship to the addressee (a sergeant to a private). Also, a direct request is the simplest form, in English and similar languages consisting of a verb in imperative voice and an object and often an indirect object, such as "Hand me the pencil" and "Put it on." Indirect requests are generally longer; for example, "Why don't you put this jacket on, okay?" and "Will you put this box away for me?" Indirect forms are somewhat politer, for the listener seems to have a choice in responding. But there is no ambiguity about what is wanted. Inferred requests are quite subtle. The speaker often does not state the request; instead, a need condition is mentioned in which the response will alleviate the need. The listener has to infer, from the need condition, what is being requested.

In Garvey's study, the 12 younger children, aged between 3.6 years and 4.4 years, made 225 direct requests and 15 indirect requests to one another. The 24 older children, aged between 4.7 years and 5.7 years, made 340 direct requests and 52 indirect ones to one another. Only two episodes were discussed as representing inferred requests, and the need condition was quite specific in both: "I need that pencil" and "I want a purse." In a little over one year's time, children increase in not only the number of exchanges but also in their ability to use more complicated, less direct forms. Another interesting difference that was common across ages is that the child respondents were more likely to comply with the indirect forms (75 percent of the time) than to the direct requests (53 percent of the time).

3.2 Speech Routines

Ritualized speech routines (greetings and farewells) are characteristic of all communities (Ferguson 1981 p. 22). They are "possible innate predispositions to the use of interjections and ritualized exchanges in which a given formula triggers an automatic response." The formulas change across languages. In Moroccan Arabic, the higher status person says the greeting first, while in Gonja, the lower member initiates speech. The length (number of words) and the formality ("Hi" versus "How are you") also vary. These utterances carry little message meaning, as the content is predictable in the physical context of human encounters. However, if no speech acknowledgement is uttered, then the listener may worry that something has gone awry.

Unlike most message-related speech, children may learn these routines as unanalyzed ritual formulas through direct instruction. Very early, mothers are likely to tell their children to "Say bye-bye" or "Say hello to grandmother." According to Gleason and Weintraub (1976), the direct instruction consists of "say" for very young children, and as the child grows older, the prompt becomes "what do you say?" The utterances are not explained, but are used in specific situations. For instance, the child may learn "Thank you very much" as if it were a long, one-word unit that should be uttered after receiving gifts or assistance. In a study of Japanese and certain European languages, Coulmas (1981) notes that ritual expressions for thanks and apologies are generic across cultures, but specific cultures, such as Japan, have more types of expressions for the various rituals which have to be learned "in order to say the right thing in the right place." Similar requirements for specific utterances, such as "howdy" versus "how do you do" or "morning" versus "good day" seem to indicate that speaker characteristics and situational formality also operate in English (Laver 1981). However, children are not likely to learn the alternations to such forms until they are well into their school years. Until then, the basic routines suffice.

4. Who is Talking to Whom?

Interpersonal relations are conveyed in both the manner of speech and the structure of conversations. Such factors as reciprocal familiarity (how well the conversants know and like one another) and power (the social and psychological distance between the conversants) are often consciously or unconsciously exhibited in conversational situations. Who has the right to initiate and to end a conversation, whose interruptions will be acknowledged and whose will not, and how topic switching and turn taking are demonstrated depend on the sociocultural aspects of the situation (Hymes 1974). Both the language content and the implicit rules for conversation are quite varied in the formal and often delicate situations of diplomacy versus the informal and intimate conversations of close friends.

The child must learn how to talk in formal and informal settings. The child begins to learn the social conventions for speech at about age 3 (Bloom and Lahey 1978), that is, how to talk with different people. Children ask more questions of adults than they do of their peers even in mixed-age situations. Also, 4-year-olds change their speech structures when talking to younger children. They are likely to use direct imperatives and concrete verbs with 2-year-olds and more embedded imperatives (indirect requests) and abstract verbs with adults and their peers (Shatz and Gelman 1973). Many young children seem shy, or at least quiet, in the presence of strangers. If the direction of learning to speak is from the here-and-now to the abstract, unbounded by time, the child may simply either not realize that speech is not constrained to the intimacy of familiars or not know how to proceed with strangers. Berko-Gleason (1973) notes that children do change their manner of speaking with parents as opposed to other adults, whining only with their caretakers.

Children will change their message style to adapt to perceived differences in the listeners. Maratsos (1973) asked 3- and 4-year-old children to describe toys to both blind and sighted listeners. The children included many more details for the blind listeners. Children of deaf parents use more speech with hearing adults than with their parents, and they do so as young as 2 years of age (Schiff 1976 as reported in Bloom and Lahey 1978). The necessary condition for the child's style shifts is the physical saliency of the situation. The differences due to age (infants versus 4-year-olds), familiarity (strangers versus caretakers), and physical differences (deafness and blindness) are all readily apparent to young children. They will accommodate to such distinctions very early, but it takes more time and experience from them to note more subtle differences in what their listeners know or do not know.

5. Speaker Presuppositions

The presuppositional prerequisites for successful speech are to present new information with sufficient clarity so that the hearer can interpret the comments. In an ideal informative utterance, according to Grice (1975), there are four general categories of cooperative principles for speech. First, the message will contain all necessary information but will not refer to the perceptually obvious nor be redundant. Two, the speaker will say only what he or she believes to be true. Three, the message will be relevant to the topic under consideration. Finally, the utterance will be both clear and precise. Thus, a speaker needs to estimate what his or her listener already knows in order to determine the information that should be included in the message.

Young children have difficulty in either realizing the necessity for such estimation or in determining what it is that others know. Glucksburg and Danks (1975) report on examination of the ability of pairs of 5-year-old children to communicate with one another when the children were visually separated by screens. The task was to stack a set of blocks. One child would verbally describe in order each of six building blocks with abstract designs on them, and the alternate child would try to follow the directions. The children could not succeed with this task, though they were able to give and to follow directions in a similar task with animal pictures. The speaker child would use such descriptions as "sheet" to describe the design. Later, the child explained "Have you ever noticed when you get up in the morning the bed sheet is all wrinkled." Of course, the listener child did not know the particular referent for "it looks like a sheet." The description may have been both accurate and imaginative. But the problem was that there was insufficient information for the listener to share the image.

Children are also inclined to discuss the obvious, thereby ignoring the requirement that speech should be relevant. The statement that "this is a dog" is obviously unnecessary in most situations. Young children often ask questions when they know the answers (Lewis 1938), but they may be imitating typical adult questions addressed to them. In other words, decisions about who-knows-what take practice with many speech acts before the child masters the art of what to encode in a message.

6. Turn Taking

Successful dialogues require both speakers to address the same topic and to listen to the comments made so as to respond appropriately to what is said. Turn taking is a major component in this process. If both participants speak at once or overlap one another, then no-one is listening and no interpersonal message communication occurs. The general characteristics of turn taking for adult conversations are summarized by Ervin-Tripp (1972), Overlaps are infrequent, occurring less than 5 percent of the time during normal conversations. Most of the overlaps that do occur come because of the secondary requirement to avoid gaps in the dialogue (periods of silence). The overlaps often come when the listener notes that the speaker is about to stop at tag points, such as, "Don't you think so?" When, from the speaker's point of view, important information has been obscured through an overlap, the tendency is to speak more loudly and more distinctly, to repeat the utterance, or possibly to stop speaking.

By age 2, children often do respond verbally to prior comments, rituals of greetings, thanks, goodbyes, and

replies to various types of questions and commands. But the utterances may not be directly relevant to the preceding utterance. If the child's response is not relevant, then other speakers often ignore the child's message. The child may thus learn to listen so that, in turn, others will listen to him or her. Also, children are not necessarily quick to reply, so the speaker is not sure whether the child misunderstood the utterance or whether the child was not paying attention. In any case, other than a child's talking with a caretaker, young children either are not cognizant of the turn-taking rules or are not capable of performing them successfully. Turn taking requires listening and interpreting the message while at the same time preparing a response appropriate to the topic.

Older children, aged 4 years and beyond, are more generally ready to reply and to complete the speech of others. Preschool children can conduct conversations with one another on imaginal tasks, such as making a sandwich out of cleaning sponges (Dore 1979b). In Dore's study, the topic was introduced by one child, but three others participated in turn with topic-directed remarks and actions. Thus, children could insert their contributions into ongoing conversations quite successfully. They also could redirect the conversation to their topics through reassertions after interruptions. However, they were still much more likely to be successful in directing the content of speech with their peers than with adults.

A few of the myriad ways in which communicative skills could be examined have been presented, essentially in a parochial manner concentrating on English. What is needed is a series of cross-language and/or cross-community studies following the form analyses of Slobin (1967). A question is: should such studies focus on the universals of ritualized expression, where the commonalities of the situational matrix could be explored; or should they focus on the development of presuppositional knowledge—knowledge-based skills that may be much more culture specific but eventually adding to our knowledge of how people learn.

Bibliography

Austin J L 1962 *How to Do Things with Words.* Oxford University Press, London

Bates E, Camaioni L, Volterra V 1979 The acquisition of performatives prior to speech. In: Ochs E, Schieffelin B B (eds.) 1979 *Developmental Pragmatics.* Academic Press, New York

Berko-Gleason J 1973 Code switching in children's language. In: Moore T E (ed.) 1973 *Cognitive Development and the Acquisition of Language.* Academic Press, New York

Bernstein B 1967 Elaborated and restricted codes; Their social origins and some consequences. In: Gumperz J J, Hymes D (eds.) 1967 *The Ethnography of Communication.* American Anthropological Association, Menasha, Wisconsin

Bloom L, Lahey M (eds.) 1978 *Language Development and Language Disorders.* Wiley, New York

Camaioni L 1979 Child-adult and child-child conversations:

An interactional approach. In: Ochs E, Schieffelin B B (eds.) 1979 *Developmental Pragmatics*. Academic Press, New York

Coulmas F 1981 Poison to your soul. Thanks and apologies contrastively viewed. In: Coulmas F (ed.) 1981 *Conversational Routine*. Mouton, The Hague

Dore J 1979a Conversational acts and the acquisition of language. In: Ochs E, Schieffelin B B (eds.) 1979 *Developmental Pragmatics*. Academic Press, New York

Dore J 1979b Conversation and preschool language development. In: Fletcher P, Garman M (eds.) 1979 *Language Acquisition: Studies in First Language Development*. Cambridge University Press, Cambridge

Ervin-Tripp S 1972 On sociolinguistic rules: Alternation and co-occurrence. In: Gumperz J J, Hymes D (eds.) 1972 *Directions in Sociolinguistics: The Ethnography of Communication*. Holt, Rinehart and Winston, New York

Ferguson C A 1981 The structure and use of politeness formulas. In: Coulmas F (ed.) 1981 *Conversational Routine*. Mouton, The Hague

Garvey C 1975 Requests and responses in children's speech. *J. Child Lang.* 2: 41–63

Gleason J B, Weintraub S 1976 The acquisition of routines in child language. *Lang. Soc.* 5: 129–36

Glucksberg S, Danks J H 1975 *Experimental Psycholinguistics: An Introduction*. Erlbaum, Hillsdale, New Jersey

Grice H P 1975 Logic and conversation. In: Cole P, Morgan J L (eds.) 1975 *Syntax and Semantics: Speech Acts* Vol. 3. Academic Press, New York

Halliday M A K 1978 A sociosemiotic perspective on language

development. In: Bloom L (ed.) 1978 *Readings in Language Development*. Wiley, New York

Hymes D 1972 *Towards Communicative Competence*. University of Pennsylvania Press, Philadelphia, Pennsylvania

Hymes D 1974 *Foundations in Sociolinguistics: An Ethnographic Approach*. University of Pennsylvania Press, Philadelphia, Pennsylvania

Lakoff R 1973 Questionable answers and answerable questions: *Papers in Honor of Henry and Renée Kahane*. In: Kachru B B, Lees R, Malkiel Y, Pietrangeli A, Saporta S (eds.) 1973 *Issues in Linguistics*. University of Illinois Press, Urbana, Illinois

Laver J D M H 1981 Linguistic routines and politeness in greeting and parting. In: Coulmas F (ed.) 1981 *Conversational Routine*. Mouton, The Hague

Lewis M M 1938 The beginning and early functions of questions in a child's speech. *Br. J. Educ. Psychol.* 8: 150–71

Maratsos M P 1973 Nonegocentric communication abilities in preschool children. *Child Dev.* 44: 697–700

Schiff N 1976 The development of form and meaning in the language of hearing children of deaf parents. In: Bloom L, Lahey M (eds.) 1978 *Language Development and Language Disorders*. Wiley, New York

Shatz M, Gelman R 1973 The development of communication skills: Modification in the speech of young children as a function of listener. *Monogr. Soc. Res. Child Dev.* 38(5): 1–37

Slobin D I (ed.) 1967 *A Field Manual for Cross-Cultural Study of the Acquisition of Communicative Competence*. University of California, Berkeley, California

Language Acquisition and Human Development

P. A. Drum

The following article traces the growth of children's command over the language's sound system (phonology) and over words as they evolve into sentences (vocabulary and syntax) from birth until the child enters school. The opening section on phonology first centers on the young child's development in understanding speech, then turns to the child's early growth in producing sounds. Section 2 describes successive stages in the child's use of words and sentences.

Normal children acquire the language spoken by others in the environment in which they are nurtured. There is no innate predilection for one language over another. At birth, a child cannot either comprehend or produce any language. By age 5 to 6 or on entry into formal schooling, the child has acquired much of the phonological and grammatical systems of the specific language or languages to which he has been exposed, though both systems will continue to expand throughout the school years. The number of words known (the internal lexicon) and the meanings to which these words refer (the semantic system) continue to expand throughout life.

The general purpose for language acquisition research is to describe the stages from birth to ages 4 or 5 years in children's comprehension and production of their

native language. Theoretical positions and language foci change with time, as illustrated in the change from Jakobson's universals of phonemic contrast for acquisition of the sound system (1968) to Halliday's socioeconomic explanation for the acquisition of the meaning system (1975, 1978). But the common factor for acquisition studies is the change from month to month or even day to day in the child's mastery over the phonological, grammatical, and semantic language characteristics.

1. Phonology

Acoustic phonology describes the means by which speech sounds are transmitted through the air. Individual sounds are not segmented in the acoustic waves, but are embedded into chains of sounds. How the child learns to segment the continuous stream of speech into phonemic (sound) categories is not known, but young infants do respond to speech sounds.

1.1 Speech Perception: Birth to 3 Years

Newborns less than 10 days old time their reflexive movements with the breaks in adult speech in such languages as English or Chinese, but not with nonspeech rhythmic sounds (Condon and Sander 1974). Since the early 1970s, several ingenious techniques have been used to determine infants' discriminatory powers. If an infant of one month is interested in a sound or a visual stimulus, he will increase his sucking energy. If the same stimulus continues, the sucking energy abates as the baby loses interest. Increase in heart rate and head turning have also been used successfully with infants of 3 months and older.

Morse (1979) reviewed the infant discrimination research and concluded that infants' speech perception is similar to that of adults. Infants younger than 8 weeks habituate and reactivate sucking for categorical contrasts in place of articulation, /ba/ versus /ga/, and to voicing changes, /ba/ versus /pa/. Vowel contrasts are not perceived as categorical by either infants or adults. Almost the only difficult English perception for infants is that of contrasting the fricative /f/ and /θ/.

The database for infant-speech perception is small, and there are differences for infants within a language as well as for different languages. The voiced/voiceless distinction of English and the prevoiced/voiced boundary of Kikuyu were both salient for 2-month-old Kenyan infants (Streeter 1976), but 6½-month-old Guatemalan infants could not distinguish the Spanish voicing boundary (Lasky et al. 1975). More work needs to be done before generalizations can be made about the types of speech discrimination that infants can make. The phonemic contrasts have always been presented to infants in the same phonetic contexts, which does not describe when or how the child perceives the commonality of a sound type in different linguistic contexts.

A few studies have examined speech perception in children from 9 months to 3 years. Menyuk and Menn (1979) summarize some of the findings by Garnica (1973) and Edwards (1974). Gross initial consonant contrasts in nonsense syllables are correctly identified in object association tasks between the ages of 10 to 22 months, but not voicing changes to which much younger infants responded in sucking responses. However, by 35 months, most minimal-pair contrasts of words in English are perceived. Infants also have a general meaning for sets of words within specific physical contexts, but they cannot attach the meaning to the utterance in different contexts.

1.2 Productive Sounds: Birth to the First 50 Words

Articulatory phonology is the study of the ways in which speech sounds are made. The major speech organs include the lips, the tongue, the vocal chords, the nose, and the lungs, with combinations of voicing, the position of the tongue, the closing or partial closing of the breath channel, the use of the oral or nasal cavity, and the rounding of the lips producing varied speech sounds.

The newborn child uses all of the various speech organs in his or her productions, but the time when identifiable language is noted depends on the methodology available and the theoretical position of the investigator. Infant sounds during the babbling stage,

approximately 6 months to 18 months, were considered almost random play where the infant practiced all possible speech sounds. True speech sounds specific to the infants' language began after a discontinuity, a time break, when babbling sounds lessened or disappeared (Jakobson 1968). Currently, researchers attempt to establish the continuity of infant production from one time period to another (Menyuk 1977).

The five stages of preword sounds identified by Stark (1979) are described in terms of articulatory characteristics during approximate time frames. The birth cry is part of the respiratory, reflexive system which accompanies the infant's oral sounds for the first eight weeks. These sounds typically are described as crying, fussing, burping, swallowing, and spitting up, often labeled "discomfort" sounds. Both voiced (vibration of the vocal chords) and voiceless sounds are uttered, but the former predominate. The sounds are judged to be similar to mid- or low-front vowels (Lieberman et al. 1971). Around eight weeks, or stage two, a baby begins to coo, and soon after to laugh with a decreased frequency of sustained crying. In the contentment sounds of stage two, nasal consonants and vowels predominate, with the mouth more closed and some control over voicing. In the third stage, 16 to 30 weeks, the baby's oral cavity, in which many articulatory movements are made, increases in size, providing more room for mapping the sounds made to different positions of the speech organs (Bosma 1975). At this time, the cooing sequences shorten. The baby seems to play with alternate features, one at a time, such as prolonged vowels or consonants, high or low pitch, and introduces a greater variety of vowel sounds. Toward the end of stage three, longer segments, which include combinations of these features, appear. A prolonged vowel might also contain changes in pitch from high to low. Repeated series of consonant–vowel syllables characterize stage four, at ages 25 to 50 weeks. This reduplicated babbling lacks the play with different linguistic segments and the prosodic features of the previous stage. The vowel sounds are now fully formed, and syllable duration is similar to that of adults, except for the final syllable which is shorter than previous syllables or adult speech. The final stage, 9 to 18 months, before the onset of words, combines the stress and intonation prosodic features with different syllable patterns across and within babbling sequences. The characteristics of sounds at this stage are markedly similar to those of the adult phonological system. At this fifth prespeech stage, the infant is prepared for the quick vowel to consonant shifts necessary for speech.

Generally, children's perception of sounds precedes their ability to produce them. Children distinguish /l/ versus /r/ earlier than /w/ versus /y/, but the order for correct production is often reversed. Articulation for liquids (r and l) probably requires more muscular control than that for glides (w and y). If an adult imitates the child and says "wabbit," the child is likely to respond by saying, "No, wabbit." The child distinguishes the appropriate sound, but cannot produce it in the particular context required. Jesperson (1922) noted that children produce particular sounds in babbling play that they cannot articulate by self-command in uttering words.

The child begins to use speech meaningfully when a particular utterance, which may or may not be a recognizable word, is only used for a particular situation. "Dada" used for people, animals, and goodbye is a reduplicated CVCV (consonant-vowel-consonant-vowel) sequences. It is only when the utterance is consistently associated with the same referent (object) that the child has acquired the relationship between word and event. On the basis of the criterion of 10 meaningful words as the measure for speech, most children are found to attain this number by 15 months (Nelson 1973). The words are one- or two-syllable CV forms similar to stage-four babbling, but now used in meaningful ways.

An attained production of 50 words often signals the beginning of two-word relationships, an overt child grammar. The general phonological characteristics of the 50-word corpus for children acquiring such languages as English, Chinese, French, and Hebrew include: (a) assimilation of sounds where the child uses the same place to produce all the vowels or consonants within a word, imitating either the initial or final consonants (*goggy* for *doggy*); (b) deletions or reductions of clusters (*tring* and *string*) and final consonants (*da* for *dog*); and (c) substitution of voiced for voiceless in initial or final positions (*bie* for *pie*), exchanging stops /p/ for fricatives /f/ in first position and vice versa for last position, changing liquids to glides (/l/ to /y/), and preferring front consonants to back consonants (/p/ versus /q/) (de Villiers and de Villiers 1978).

2. Lexical–syntactic Stages

Prior to a child's uttering recognizable words, it is possible to use real time in months in organizing the linguistic comprehension and production of infants. As soon as the analysis turns to syntactic and lexical development, the linguistic units may be less limited by physical constraints and more by situational ones. Individual differences, both within a language and for different languages, create a need for another organizational device than just the age of the child.

Lexical–syntactic stages from one-word to sentence coordination and clausal structures are used here to describe the continuity of language acquisition. The stages are not discrete. Three-word utterances occur in the one-word stage, and a vocabulary or lexicon of 50 words can occur at 1.2 years or not until 1.10 years. The stages are simply an attempt to impose order on what is a comparatively small and fragmented database.

2.1 One-word Stage

The first words are described by Clark (1979) as expressing the "here and now" of the child's world: words about food, body-parts, clothing, animals, vehicles, household items, and the people who take care of the child as well as words referring to the child. These words are quite similar to the baby talk lexicon described by Ferguson (1971), consisting of the words used by parents to talk to their infants in six different languages. Benedict (1979) classified the types of words that appeared in the 50-word lexicons of young children according to Nelson's system (1973). The nominals or object-naming words outweighed all other categories at 61 percent, followed by 19 percent for action words, and then approximately 10 percent each for modifiers and social words.

The child's underlying meaning for his first words can differ from that of the adult's. Often children overextend the word by applying the utterance to a feature of the thing they are referring to and using the word any time that feature appears. For instance, in a Russian diary study of a child's growth in language (Shvachkin 1973), *dany* originally referred to the sound of a bell, then to a clock, to a telephone, and to doorbells. The overextension of a single feature does not last long, and it could result from the lack of an appropriate word for a given object rather than a confusion that the word stands for a perceptual feature. Children also overrestrict the meaning by using the utterance as a name for a particular referent rather than as a label for all applicable referents, such as *table* used only for the kitchen table. The two other possibilities, that the underlying meaning is either appropriate to or totally different from adult meaning, also occur.

The linguistic intent behind the single-word utterance has been debated from de Laguna's holophrastic interpretation (1927) (that each word conveys the meaning of an adult sentence) to Bloom's carefully delimited semantic interpretation of Alison's use of relational and substantive words (Bloom and Lahey 1978). It is likely that the child does comprehend more than he or she can utter, but only the child's caretakers are sure that they understand the semantic intent behind the child's word. Brown's caution (1973) about being careful in seeking to provide either syntactic or semantic interpretation of a one-word utterance still seems the most reasonable position.

However, two features of the single-word stage may indicate attempts at establishing relationships, or at least be precursors to the relationships established in the following stage. First, with a single context, two words with a time interval between them will be said, with both words converging on the topic (Bloom and Lahey 1978). Second, nonmeaningful forms of various kinds described by Dore et al. (1976) occur with other words and may be presyntactic devices for the next stage.

2.2 Two Words to Simple Sentence Strings

Age can vary from 19 months to 28 months or more before the first recognizable two-word utterance is noted. The children do not shift into only two-word utterances; instead, there is a combination of two-word, one-word, and spaced-word utterances with the proportions changing into the longer, more connected types. Researchers have described early sentences in terms of concatenated morphemes, with concatenate meaning linked together in a speech and a morpheme being a minimal unit of meaning, such as *cats* equals two morphemes—*cat* and the plural *s*. The mean length of utterance (number of spoken morphemes) described by Brown (1973) does not change much early in the two-word stage, but there is a substantial increase in the child's lexicon or total number of words (Smith 1926). For instance, there were relatively few verbs within Benedict's action words of Stage 1 (1979), but Goldin-Meadow et al. (1976) found more verbs in the production of 2.0-year-olds than in the 1.7-year-old children. Bloom (Bloom and Lahey 1978) describes the order of acquisition for categories of verbs from actions (*get, play, eat*), to locative actions (*put, take, fall*), and then statives (*that's, it's, there's*).

Smith (1926) noted that the increase in vocabulary slows down from 2.0 to 2.6 years, but at the same time, the children are increasing their mean length of utterance substantially, from an average of 1.7 morphemes to 2.7. The children are also using an impressive number of different meaning or semantic relations in their two- and three-word utterances. Bloom counted the use of 18 different semantic–syntactic relations in the speech samples of four children from 19 to 25 months. She noted a progression from object relations (existence, nonexistence, and recurrence) to verb–object relations, to either modification relations or progressive relations occurring somewhat later. A partial list of two-word semantic relations in the early speech of children across different languages include the following: recurrence (more cake), attribute (broken car), possessive (chair father), action–locative (sofa sit), agent–action (doll comes), action–object (hit ball), and question (where papa). Slobin describes the commonalities across languages at this stage as reading "like direct translations of one another" (1970 p. 177).

Telegraphic speech is often used to describe the two- and three-word utterances, for there are few inflections, though the number differ by languages. English does not inflect for agent, object, or other major semantic roles. Bowerman (1973) notes the prevalence of the nominative case (subject or agent forms) for all forms of syntactic roles in the early speech of her Finnish children. Since articles, auxiliaries, prepositions, and other indicators of syntactic class are generally not included, the case labels of action–locative, possessive, and others are adult interpretations of the child's underlying meaning. Whether these two-word relations are truly productive for the children is somewhat moot. They, instead, may have learned the stressed content words that they have identified with particular physical objects, which they then conjoin in specific contexts.

2.3 The Emerging Sentence

Between 2 years and 4 years of age, children expand their telegraphic speech into sentence structures that, over time, more closely approximate adult forms. Brown (1973) used Jacobs and Rosenbaum's description of transformational complexity (1968) to classify and rank order the appearance of 14 grammatical forms in three children's utterances. The 14 morphemes were also classified into 10 types of semantic meaning with four pairs labeled as semantically identical: past tense, third person, copulas, and auxiliaries. Both of the complexity designations and their order of appearance are shown in Table 1.

Seven of the 14 morphemes refer to the verb system. Fletcher (1979) describes the development of the verb system in Leopold's diary of his daughter, Hildegarde, and that of a young boy named Daniel. For Hildegarde, the unmarked form *eat* was followed by the progressive -

Table 1
Ordering of 14 morphemes from Brown's study (1973)

Grammatical morphemes	Morphemic meanings	Order of acquisition	Examples
Present progressive	Temporary duration	1	eat*ing*
On	Containment	2.5	*on*
In	Support	2.5	*in*
Plural	Number	4	eat*s*
Past irregular	Earlierness	5	*went*
Possessive	Possession	6	daddy*'s* coat
Uncontractible copula	Number, earlierness	7	*is, are*
Articles	Specific–nonspecific	8	*the, a*
Past regular	Earlierness	9	walk*ed*
3rd person regular	Number, earlierness	10	she walk*s*
3rd person irregular	Number, earlierness	11	she *has*
Uncontractible auxiliary	Temporary duration, number, earlierness	12	I *will* go
Contractible copula	Number, earlierness	13	*I'm* tired
Contractible auxiliary	Temporary duration, number, earlierness	14	*I'll* go

ing form. The early auxiliaries were *won't* and *can't* with *will* and *can* appearing soon after. Strong past tenses, such as *went*, occurred before the weaker forms such as *talked*. In a similar description of Daniel's development, Fletcher found that adverbial time specifiers, such as *yesterday* and *once time*, and the strong (irregular) past tenses preceded the weaker (regular) past tenses. The auxiliary *did* was transferred from simple occurrence and use in questions and negatives to an unstressed past tense marker, such as "My balloon did pop." The auxiliary *be* in both present and then past was followed by the past tense of modals, such as *could* or *would*. The verb data cannot be generalized to other languages, of course, but eventually, verb systems, pronomial systems, and free and bound morphological systems will be collected with sufficient data so that patterns of development can be compared.

The development of both question and negation systems are examined in some detail to illustrate the general process of acquiring aspects of the grammatical systems. Other aspects, including the pronomial system (when to use *him*, *he*, *his*, for example), the use of articles and demonstratives, prepositions and conjunctions, and others, are assumed to follow the same general acquisition principles. The child's first utterances require the fewest manipulations of grammatical order to express a question or negation meaning. Subsequent utterances either increase syntactic manipulations or express more abstract, less context-specific meanings. The child's procedures for speech-acts change from requiring the fewest manipulations of order to express a common meaning, to increasing syntactic manipulations and more abstract less context-specific meanings.

Control over the auxiliary system is also reflected in the child's production of negatives and questions, which generally follow similar patterns. Both negation and *wh* forms (what, when, why) occur in isolation, *nein* at 1.6 years and *why* at 1.10 years for Hildegarde (Leopold 1939). By the two-word stage, certain primitive transformations appear in telegraphic speech, including the additions of a "no" marker to an object or a verb to express denial or nonexistence, the use of *what* or *where* before an object, and the rising intonation for a yes–no question in the two- to three-word sentence string. Next, as the child acquires various grammatical morphemes, including auxiliaries, the negative word is embedded within the sentence before the verb, though generally without the requisite auxiliary, such as "he no bite" rather than "he doesn't bite." According to Bellugi (1967), the forms *can't* and *won't* are unanalyzable wholes and not indications of an auxiliary system. As the sentence strings approach four morphemes in length, most of the auxiliaries appear in both positive and negative forms. At this time, the negation system for definite forms often resembles the adult system, but there seems to be an overgeneralization in indefinite forms. In a number of utterances, both the auxiliary and the object will be negated; "he not doing nothing"

is a typical example. Conscious control over this aspect of negation will not occur for many children until they are well into the school years.

Question-form development is quite similar to that of negation. The rising intonation and *wh* words of stage one are followed by *wh* words in first position, such as "why you mad?" and "where my doll?," and then verb and auxiliary inversions for yes–no questions. However, the requisite inversion for *wh* questions, along with the addition of the *do* auxiliary, do not appear until later. Instead, such forms as "What he can ride in?" and "What we saw?" co-occur with appropriate yes–no forms, "Can't you get it?" and "Am I silly?" (Bellugi 1965). More complex questions, such as negative tag questions (You can get it, can't you?), will not be produced by many children until much later.

Children gradually gain control over different aspects of language in the early years. For example, children use the auxiliaries in declaratives and simple inversion forms, so they can produce such words in appropriate places. But at this initial auxiliary stage, they rarely use the auxiliary along with the *wh* insertions. The general principle may be "one thing at a time." The acceleration and leveling off in vocabulary learning in Smith's report (1926) seem to alternate with increases in structural manipulations in the mean length of utterance within the periods of leveling off of vocabulary growth. Essentially, there are two somewhat independent systems, the semantic and the syntactic, with each expanding in a cyclic manner. When new syntactic forms appear, there is likely to be a fairly steady state of practice on these forms for some period of time. This syntactic practice may, in turn, be accompanied by a growth in the semantic system, where the child uses the acquired forms first on old words and then with new words.

In any case, the English grammatical morphemic systems are acquired in a somewhat reasonable order, but whether the morpheme acquisition is determined by the syntactic complexity of English, the relational complexity of the semantic system, or some combination of both, is not known. In depth, cross-language studies of acquisition of varied morphemic systems will help determine the answer.

The development of more complex structures is summarized by Dale (1976). Simple agent–action–object sentences (Daddy get car) appear quite early in child language, almost as soon as the child is able to say three consecutive words. Of course, these sentences are in telegraphic forms. However, by 3 years of age, many children construct declaratives (I like candy), direct and embedded imperatives ("lift me" versus "I want up"), as well as many question types, and can negate either the whole sentence (Mary is not crying) or certain parts within the sentence (Mary is unhappy). Some 4-year-olds will even alternate forms for different situations, using direct imperatives with their peers and politer (embedded) forms with adults. Object noun-phrase complements are generally the first complex additions to simple sentences, such as "I see you sit down," where the clause *you sit down* serves as the object of *see*. Generally locative (where it is) and temporal (when I get big) clauses precede the appearance of the other *wh* clause (what I got). When the *wh* words are used in clauses, they are found in initial, final, and center-embedded positions; an example is "I show you what I got." The relative clauses are used first to modify objects and predicate nouns and then subjects. The use of a relative clause to modify a subject is usually embedded in the center of the sentence (the man who came to see you is thin) and may be more difficult for that reason. At approximately the same time as the relative construction, simple sentences are likely to be conjoined into compound forms by inserting *and*.

There has been relatively little research in this area, so that this order of complex and compound sentence acquisition is quite tentative. Also, though the child may utter the various sentence types, complete control over their meaning and when it is appropriate to use each type may not occur until the child is 10 to 12 years old (Ingram 1975).

3. Language Development at School and Beyond

From infancy through early childhood, children attain control over much of the phonological system. Any listener knows which language the child is using. The morphemic and syntactic systems are sufficiently evolved to convey the major meaning functions of language communication. Children express emotions, refer to both concrete and abstract events, and use language to find out about their world. But the process of acquiring language does not stop. According to Carey (1978), by age 6, the child has learned approximately 14,000 words (8,000 root words). By the time the child enters college, he or she will have a recognition vocabulary of over 150,000 words (Seashore and Erckerson 1940). Obviously, lexical learning continues.

Though children apparently know the major rules for the inflectional systems for plurals and for tense, they still often overgeneralize in the case of strong verbs and nouns, such as *goed* and *childrens*. They also have problems with inflecting derivational forms; at least they do in a nonsense word task (Berko-Gleason 1958). Derwing and Baker (1979) examined English derivational morphology for preschoolers up to college-age subjects using a nonsense-word task. They found that even a substantial number of their adult subjects had not mastered noun compounds, the instrumental change with *er* (*teach* + *er*), and only a third of the adults knew the addition of *ie* or *y* for the affectionate-diminutive (*dog* + *ie* or *doggie*).

In sentence development, the child has already learned some ways to expand the parts of the sentence: modification words, prepositional phrases, relative clauses, and others. However, specific syntactic expansions can only be used with certain words within the grammatical class, for instance, animate versus inanimate nouns. Now, many of the selectional restrictions

for the semantic system need to be acquired (Menyuk 1977).

Thus, at school entry, the child can understand a great many language utterances and can also be understood most of the time, but there is still much to be learned about language.

Bibliography

Bellugi U 1965 The development of interrogative structures in children's speech. In: Riegel K F (ed.) 1965 *The Development of Language Functions*. University of Michigan, Ann Arbor, Michigan

Bellugi U 1967 The acquisition of negation. Ph.D. thesis, Harvard University

Benedict H 1979 Early lexical development: Comprehension and production. *J. Child Lang.* 6: 183–200

Berko-Gleason J 1958 The child's learning of English morphology. *Word* 4: 150–77

Bloom L (ed.) 1978 *Readings in Language Development*. Wiley, New York

Bloom L, Lahey M 1978 *Language Development and Language Disorders*. Wiley, New York

Bosma J F 1975 Anatomic and physiological development of the speech apparatus. In: Bosma J F (ed.) 1975 *Human Communication and Its Disorders*. Raven, New York

Bowerman M F 1973 Structural relationships in children's utterances: Syntactic or semantic? In: Moore T E (ed.) 1973 *Cognitive Development and the Acquisition of Language*. Academic Press, New York

Brown R W 1973 *A First Language: The Early Stages*. Harvard University Press, Cambridge, Massachusetts

Carey S 1978 The child as word learner. In: Halle M, Bresnan J, Miller G A (eds.) 1978 *Linguistic Theory and Psychological Reality*. MIT Press, Cambridge, Massachusetts

Clark E V 1979 Building a vocabulary: Words for objects, actions, and relations. In: Fletcher P, Garman M (eds.) 1979 *Language Acquisition: Studies in First Language Development*. Cambridge University Press, Cambridge

Condon W S, Sander L W 1974 Synchrony demonstrated between movements of the neonate and adult speech. *Child Dev.* 45: 456–62

Dale P S 1976 *Language Development: Structure and Function*. Holt, Rinehart and Winston, New York

de Laguna G A 1927 *Speech: Its Function and Development*. Yale University Press, New Haven, Connecticut

Derwing B L, Baker W J 1979 Recent research on the acquisition of English morphology. In: Fletcher P, Garman M (eds.) 1979 *Language Acquisition: Studies in First Language Development*. Cambridge University Press, Cambridge

de Villiers J G, de Villiers P A 1978 *Language Acquisition*. Harvard, Cambridge, Massachusetts

Dore J, Franklin M, Miller R, Ramer A 1976 Transitional phenomena in early language acquisition. *J. Child Lang.* 3: 13–28

Edwards M L 1974 Perception and production in child phonology: The testing of four hypotheses. *J. Child Lang.* 1: 205–19

Ferguson C A 1971 *Language Structure and Language Use: Essay*. Stanford University Press, Stanford, California

Fletcher P 1979 The development of the verb phrase. In: Fletcher P, Garman M (eds.) 1979 *Language Acquisition: Studies in First Language Development*. Cambridge University Press, Cambridge

Fletcher P, Garman M (eds.) 1979 *Language Acquisition: Studies in First Language Development*. Cambridge University Press, Cambridge

Garnica O K 1973 The development of phonemic speech perception. In: Moore T E (ed.) 1973 *Cognitive Development and the Acquisition of Language*. Academic Press, New York

Goldin-Meadow S, Seligman M E P, Gelman R 1976 Language in the two-year-old. *Cognition* 4: 189–202

Halliday M A K 1975 *Learning How to Mean: Explorations in the Development of Language*. Arnold, London

Halliday M A K 1978 A sociosemiotic perspective on language development. In: Bloom L (ed.) 1978 *Readings in Language Development*. Wiley, New York

Ingram D 1975 If and when transformations are acquired by children. In: Dato D P (ed.) 1975 *26th Georgetown University Round Table on Languages and Linguistics. Developmental Psycholinguistics: Theory and Applications*. Georgetown Press, Washington, DC

Jacobs R A, Rosenbaum P S 1968 *English Transformational Grammar*. Blaisdell, Waltham, Massachusetts

Jakobson R 1968 *Child Language: Aphasia and Phonological Universals*. Translated by Keiler A R. Mouton, The Hague [First published 1941 as *Kindersprache, Aphasie und Allegemeine Lautgesetze*. Almqvist and Wiksell, Uppsala]

Jesperson O 1922 *Language, Its Nature, Development and Origin*. Allen and Unwin, London

Lasky R E, Syrdal-Lasky A, Klein R E 1975 VOT discrimination by four to six and half month old infants from Spanish environments. *J. Exp. Child Psychol.* 20: 215–25

Leopold W F 1939 Speech development of a bilingual child: A linguist's record, Vol. 1: Vocabulary growth in the first two years. In: Bloom L (ed.) 1978

Lieberman P, Harris K S, Wolff P, Russell L H 1971 Newborn infant cry and nonhuman primate vocalization. *J. Speech Hearing Res.* 14: 718–27

Menyuk P 1977 *Language and Maturation*. MIT Press, Cambridge, Massachusetts

Menyuk P, Menn L 1979 Early strategies for the perception and production of words and sounds. In: Fletcher P, Garman M (eds.) 1979 *Language Acquisition: Studies in First Language Development*. Cambridge University Press, Cambridge

Moore T E (ed.) 1973 *Cognitive Development and the Acquisition of Language*. Academic Press, New York

Morse P A 1979 The infancy of infant speech perception: The first decade of research. *Brain, Behav. Evol.* 16: 351–73

Nelson K 1973 *Structure and Strategy in Learning to Talk*. University of Chicago Press, Chicago, Illinois

Seashore R H, Eckerson L D 1940 The measurement of individual differences in general English vocabularies. *J. Educ. Psychol.* 31: 235–47

Shvachkin N Kh 1973 The development of phonemic speech perception in early childhood. In: Ferguson C A, Slobin D I (eds.) 1973 *Studies of Child Language Development*. Holt, Rinehart and Winston, New York

Slobin D I 1970 Universals of grammatical development in children. In: Flores d'Arcais G B, Levelt W J M (eds.) 1970 *Advances in Psycholinguistics*. Elsevier, New York

Smith M E 1926 An investigation of the development of the sentence and the extent of vocabulary in young children. In: Baldwin B (ed.) 1926 *University of Iowa Studies in Child Welfare*. University of Iowa City, Iowa

Stark R E 1979 Preschool segmental feature development. In: Fletcher P, Garman M (eds.) 1979 *Language Acquisition: Studies in First Language Development*. Cambridge University Press, Cambridge

Streeter L A 1976 Language perception of two-month old infants shows effects of both innate mechanisms and experience. *Nature* 259: 39–42

Bilingualism

M. Paradis

Bilingualism is generally defined as the ability to use two languages in one of several ways: both languages as a native speaker ("true" bilingualism), neither like a native speaker (semilingualism), or one language in one cultural context and the other language in another (diglossia). Speakers' proficiencies in their two languages are situated on a two-dimensional continuum going from the native-like mastery of each language, that is, from (a) passing for a native speaker among unilingual speakers of each, to (b) using a second language with a foreign accent and/or involuntarily but systematically incorporating syntactic, morphological, and/or semantic elements of the mother tongue as well as other nonnative elements, to (c) systematically incorporating elements of the incompletely mastered second language when using the first. Independently of the native or non-native-like characteristics of their languages, bilinguals may have more or less occasion to use each language in similar circumstances and hence may possess a larger or more specialized vocabulary and/or exhibit faster access to some lexical items and phrases in one language than in the other. Of course, variations in size, specialization, and availability of vocabulary exist among individual unilinguals as well, depending on level of education and fields of work and interest.

A bilingual, like Chomsky's "ideal speaker–listener" who knows his or her language perfectly and lives in a completely uniform speech community, is an abstraction, a hypothetical construct, but a necessary one for practical purposes. Bilinguals do not form a homogeneous group. They vary along all the dimensions mentioned above. However, the variables are too numerous to be effectively taken into account. They should nevertheless always be kept in the back of the experimenter's mind, and the more obvious ones should be reckoned with.

In addition to differences in fluency and context of use, speakers of two languages differ with respect to age, context, and manner of acquisition. All of these factors may contribute to differences in linguistic behaviour by fostering unidirectional, bidirectional, or no interference. It has been suggested that individuals are more likely to speak each language as natives do (coordinate bilingualism) when they learn their two languages in different contexts than when they acquire the two languages in the same context at the same time (compound bilingualism). In the latter case bidirectional interference will be evidenced. When the second language is learned through translation (subordinate bilingualism) unidirectional interference is likely to emerge.

It is widely believed that there is a critical period for fully acquiring a language (ranging roughly between ages 2 and 6) and it is further thought that a second language learned after this critical period will contain nonnative features, particularly a foreign accent. Even though adults may learn a second language more quickly than young children, they may never master it as completely as children eventually will. The older the individual is when the second language is encountered, the greater the chances that nonnative elements will be manifested, though, to some extent, individual differences in cognitive style, rate of maturation, and/or motivation may reduce the number of nonnative elements.

The rising awareness since the 1960s of "ethnic identity" has led to a growing concern for matters pertaining to individuals and societies that partake of two or more cultures and languages. Questions such as what effects bilingualism may have on the languages used, on the users of these languages, and on the society in which they are concurrently used are being asked with increasing insistence and frequency. Not only is the topic of bilingualism becoming the focus of attention in Canada and the United States, as new legislation challenges age-old well-ingrained policies, but it is also very much in the fore in all nations where more than one language is spoken—or where another language is being revived—and these nations may well represent the majority of nations in the world today.

Bilingualism is a multidisciplinary field of study. Linguists examine its effects on the structure of the languages involved and on the grammatical constraints on switching and mixing two languages within a sentence. Anthropological linguists inquire into the effects of bilingualism on culture, and of culture on bilingualism. Applied linguists explore bilingual education and second language teaching methodology as a way to becoming bilingual. Psycholinguists concentrate on problems of perception, learning and memory in bilinguals, and on the mechanisms allowing the maintenance of both languages separately or the switching from one to the other. Politicians involved in language planning must make decisions about official languages and literacy. Sociolinguists examine the relative status of the two languages in a bilingual community and its manifestations in language use. Social psychologists examine how individuals express their ethnic identity, how group allegiance is manifested in the choice of language in particular circumstances, in patterns of switching, and in speaking one of the languages with or without a foreign accent.

Two aspects of bilingualism which have been the object of a considerable increase of interest since the early 1970s, and which may ultimately provide valuable suggestions for second language teaching methodology, have been the psycholinguistic and neurolinguistic. For comprehensive treatment of more general aspects of bilingualism the reader is referred to Grosjean (1982), Vildomec (1963), and Weinreich (1953).

Psycholinguistic studies of bilingualism have concentrated on the question of whether bilinguals have one set of meanings for words in both their languages (compound bilingualism) or a different set of meanings for each of their languages (coordinate bilingualism). A subset of compound bilingualism, in which the meanings are those of the mother tongue irrespective of the language used (subordinate bilingualism) has not systematically been considered. In the mid-1950s it was hypothesized that context of acquisition would influence the type of storage of the two languages. It was assumed that two languages learned in the same context would be stored in a compound fashion whereas two languages learned in separate contexts would be stored separately.

More than 60 studies have been devoted to bilingual linguistic memory since the late 1960s. The question generally asked is whether bilinguals possess two memory stores or one. Two mutually exclusive hypotheses have been formulated in the literature: (a) all information is kept in a common store, and subjects have access to it equally with both languages; (b) information is stored linguistically in separate stores (Kolers 1968). However, these studies have several shortcomings and it should come as no surprise that experimental results have been contradictory—some interpreted as supporting the two stores hypothesis, others as evidence of one common store.

In addition, psychologists have failed to differentiate between recent memory for words (i.e., meaning + form) and long-term retention of the message. They have relied on experiments that have focused on the retention in recent memory of words outside any meaningful context. Therefore results cannot be generalized to the organization of either the language system or the information acquired verbally. There is ample clinical evidence to the effect that access to a linguistic system (ability to use language) and verbal memory (ability to remember words) are distinct from experiential memory (ability to remember events) and conceptual memory (memory for information). For example, global aphasic patients retain access to experiential and conceptual memory even for items acquired verbally (Hécaen 1973, Lecours and Joanette 1980).

Moreover, these word experiments have not controlled for the semantic overlap that exists between lexical items of the two languages tested, nor for the different types of semantic organization of the two languages that may (as in compound bilinguals) or may not (as in coordinate bilinguals) introduce idiosyncratic semantic overlap. Yet the connotative and referential meanings of morphemes in one language differ from those of (more or less) equivalent morphemes in another language. Some words share more features of meaning than others across languages. Hence responses to free-association tests, lexical-decision tasks, word-recognition tasks, similarity judgments, free recall, paired associates, avoidance of electric shock experiments and the like, will depend in part on the degree of semantic overlap between translation equivalents. In addition, bilingual subjects may have parts of their semantic networks organized in at least three basic ways. Insofar as their semantic system is organized in a coordinate manner and the test words have little semantic overlap, subjects will tend to give different responses to translation equivalents. In as much as their systems are compound or subordinate, they will give similar responses to both words. In fact, translation equivalents have been shown to trigger responses not quite like repetitions of the word itself in the same language, nor like altogether different words in the same language, but rather like synonyms of the words within the same language.

It may thus be postulated that bilinguals possess one common conceptual system differentially organized depending on which language is used to verbalize a given experience, feeling, or idea. They are thus able to organize their mental representations in different ways, in the manner that two aspects of Boring's (1930) ambiguous figure can be perceived. This ability to adopt two perspectives might account for the greater cognitive flexibility and superior performance of bilinguals on divergent-thinking tasks, concept-formation and general-reasoning tests, verbal and metalinguistic tasks, as well as in the discovery of underlying rules in the resolution of problems.

Neurolinguistic research too has focused on investigating the way in which languages are represented in bilinguals. Clinical (Paradis 1977, 1983) as well as experimental (Albert and Obler 1978, Vaid and Genesee 1980) studies of bilingualism have spawned a number of hypotheses about the storage and processing of two languages in the same brain.

From the end of the nineteenth century, aphasiologists have argued for or against a different locus for the representation of each language in the bilingual brain. More recently, some authors have postulated a greater participation of the right cerebral hemisphere in the language functions of bilinguals than of unilinguals. However, their conclusions have largely been based on insufficient clinical evidence from cases of aphasia in polyglots and on inconclusive experimental evidence from dichotic listening and visual half-field tachistoscopic tests. Before speaking of greater participation of the right hemisphere in bilinguals, it is necessary to be more explicit about the participation of the right hemisphere in unilinguals. In the normal use of language (i.e., in nonartificial experimental contexts) by individuals with normal (i.e., nonpathological) brains, the

processing of the grammar (phonemic, morphemic, syntactic, and some semantic analysis) is subserved by activities of the left hemisphere. But other aspects of language use, such as the processing of nonliteral meanings (jokes, proverbs, figurative meanings), the use of affective suprasegmental components, and the linguistic and nonlinguistic contextualization of an utterance (presuppositions, implications, pragmatics) are subserved by activities involving the right hemisphere. It also appears that the extent to which areas of the cortex—including areas of the right hemisphere—are active is proportional to the difficulty of any cognitive task at hand. Hence, speaking a second language less than fully fluently would involve more right hemisphere participation in proportion to the amount of mental effort required; but this would be no indication of second language storage or of language-related processes per se in the right hemisphere.

It is necessary to be very cautious with respect to suggestions about teaching a second language through techniques emphasizing the use of the right hemisphere. Some learners tend to obtain better results when using right hemisphere strategies but others do better with left hemisphere strategies. The efficiency of reliance on a particular hemispheric mode of processing information varies with age as well as with inherent individual preferences. These might in turn result in success in acquisition of a second language in a natural communicative environment or, on the contrary, in success in learning in a formal, deductive, analytical framework.

With respect to the participation of the right hemisphere in the language functions of bilinguals several hypotheses have been proposed: (a) the second language is represented in the right hemisphere; (b) the second language is represented bilaterally; (c) both languages are represented in the left hemisphere but the second is less lateralized than the first; (d) both languages are less lateralized; (e) both languages are represented in the left hemisphere and there is no difference between bilinguals and unilinguals with respect to lateralization.

Moreover, at least four hypotheses have been suggested to account for the alleged differential lateralization: (a) the age hypothesis according to which a language acquired after puberty will be less lateralized; (b) the second language effect hypothesis, according to which a second language (L_2), learned once a first has been acquired, will have greater representation in the right hemisphere; (c) the stage hypothesis, according to which the right hemisphere will be maximally involved in language processing at the beginning of L_2 acquisition, and will then gradually shift to the left hemisphere as fluency in L_2 improves; (d) and the bilingual type hypothesis, according to which coordinate bilinguals, keeping their two languages more separate than compound bilinguals do, will store them in different ways, with a greater involvement of the right hemisphere for one of the languages.

However, the coordinate–compound–subordinate

distinction, which refers to the organization of the grammar as evidenced by the individual's linguistic performance, may have no bearing on the neural substrate underlying the respective languages. Here again at least four hypotheses must be considered: the extended system hypothesis, the dual system hypothesis, the tripartite system hypothesis, and the subset hypothesis.

(a) *The extended system hypothesis.* Additional phonemes (i.e., phonemes of L_2) are processed as allophones; morphemes of L_2 are processed like allomorphs (to be used only in the context of L_2); and new syntactic rules behave like different rules within the same language, such as may be found within different registers, or simply different patterns for realizing similar meanings within the same register, for example an active and a passive construction. Thus a bilingual subject may possess a stock of 60 phonemes instead of 36, each supported by the neural mechanisms that underlie phonemes of the languages in unilingual native speakers of those languages, and *mutatis mutandis* a similarly increased stock of morphemes, syntactic structures, semantic representations, and so on.

(b) *The dual system hypothesis.* Phonemes of L_2 are stored separately in a system of connections independent of the first language (L_1). There are different networks of neural connections underlying each level of linguistic structure for each language. The two linguistic systems are thus separately represented in the brain.

(c) *The tripartite system hypothesis.* Those items which are identical in both languages are represented by one single underlying neural substrate common to both languages, and those which are different each have their own separate neural representation. Thus whatever two languages might have in common would be represented only once, and whatever would be specific to each language would be represented separately.

Each of these three hypotheses is compatible with each of the three types of bilingual linguistic organization (coordinate, compound, subordinate). Hypothesis (b) assumes redundancy of representation of those elements that could be common to both languages, on the grounds that each language forms a system independent of the other, whether those languages share few or many features, and whether some of those features are bona fide members of the language(s) concerned or the result of unidirectional or bidirectional interference. The synchronic competence for each language, whether idiosyncratic or consistent with the norm of the respective unilingual speech community, is represented in a separate system. Hence compound or subordinate bilinguals would nevertheless have separate neural substrates for each of their language systems. Hypothesis (a), on the other hand, assumes a single neural system for both languages, even in an (idealized) coordinate bilingual. Hypothesis (c) assumes a single representation for items common to both languages in coordinates as well as compounds. The only difference is, trivially, that for compounds, by virtue of the fact

that their grammars exhibit a greater overlap, the languages would share a larger portion of the neural substrate.

Evidence from aphasia tends to support a dual-system hypothesis, irrespective of the type of bilingualism. Some patients have been reported to have selectively lost comprehension as well as expression in one or more of the languages spoken fluently before onset. In cases of successive recovery, patients do not regain access to a second or third language until a first has been well-recovered. In cases of reciprocal antagonism, one of the patient's languages becomes inaccessible as the other is recovered (Paradis 1977). More recently (Paradis et al. 1982), two patients with alternate antagonism have been observed. That is, for alternate periods of time they suffered word finding difficulties so severe that they could not name objects, describe pictures, or speak spontaneously in one language while they remained relatively fluent in the other. This clinical evidence tends to show that a language can be selectively inhibited and therefore must be represented functionally as a system, separate from the other system to which the patient has access. Moreover, this seems to hold, regardless of age or manner of acquisition of the two languages: one patient had learned Arabic after the age of 12 with a very traditional grammar–translation method; the other patient had acquired English from his environment during infancy.

On the other hand, the ease with which a person may put on a foreign accent and speak L_2 with the phonemes of L_1 or vice versa, or intentionally use syntactic rules of L_1 when speaking L_2 or vice versa, or insert words and phrases of L_1 when speaking L_2 or vice versa (with or without a corresponding switch in phonology), as well as add L_1 inflexions on L_2 words and vice versa, speaks in favour of the extended system hypothesis. Evidence that there is no need for an input switch (Obler and Albert 1978)—that in fact it could not be turned off and that the processing of words in either language is unavoidable under any condition—can also serve as an argument in favour of one extended system.

Electrical stimulation evidence from Ojemann and Whitaker (1978) would tend to support a tripartite system, since within the language area for each of the two patients examined there appeared to be "sites common to both languages as well as sites with differential organization of the two languages". However, in this experiment the areas of stimulation were much too extensive and imprecise for a person to ascertain whether the same system of neurons had been disrupted on two separate occasions.

(d) *The subset hypothesis.* This postulates that hypotheses (a) and (b) need not be mutually exclusive but represent two aspects of the same phenomenon. Both languages might indeed be stored in identical ways, in a single extended system, though elements of each language, because they normally appear only in different contexts (elements of L_1 in the environment of other elements of L_1, and likewise for elements of L_2), would form a de facto separate network of connections, and thus a subsystem within a larger system (that comprises both). According to this hypothesis, bilinguals have two subsets of neural connections, one for each language (and each can be activated or inhibited independently because of the strong associations between the elements) while at the same time they possess one larger set from which they are able to draw elements of either language at any time. Each subset, as a system, is susceptible to selective pathological inhibition, yet individuals with intact brains may alternately use elements from one and the other subsystem depending on the verbalizability (or ease of encoding) of any given notion in either system.

Clearly, more accurate techniques will be necessary to determine the precise location of specific language substrates. It is likely that both languages (of some bilinguals at least) are subserved by neural circuits in the same areas and that they are so intricately interwoven that it is not possible with available techniques to interfere with one and not the other. At a gross anatomical level it is possible to find substrates in identical areas. Only at microanatomical levels is it possible to identify separate circuits.

Eventually, the outcome of psycholinguistic and neurolinguistic research is bound to have a considerable impact on second language teaching methodology and bilingual education. However, it is too soon yet to try to apply any of its tentative assumptions to classroom strategies. Many issues remain unsolved. The most important contribution of these studies to date has perhaps been to draw attention to the existence of extreme subject variability along numerous dimensions.

Bibliography

Albert M L, Obler L K 1978 *The Bilingual Brain: Neuropsychological and Neurolinguistic Aspects of Bilingualism*. Academic Press, New York
Boring E G 1930 A new ambiguous figure. *Am. J. Psychol.* 42: 444–45
Grosjean F 1982 *Life with Two Languages*. Harvard University Press, Cambridge, Massachusetts
Hécaen H 1973 La méthode neurolinguistique dans l'étude des aphasies. *Cinquantenaire de l'Hôpital Henri-Rousselle*. Paris, pp. 218–24
Hornby P (ed.) 1977 *Bilingualism: Psychological, Social, and Educational Implications*. Academic Press, New York
Kolers P A 1968 Bilingualism and information processing. *Sci. Am.* 218: 78–86
Lecours A R, Joanette Y 1980 Linguistic and other psychological aspects of paroxysmal aphasia. *Brain Lang.* 10: 1–23
Obler L, Albert M 1978 A monitor system for bilingual language processing. In: Paradis M (ed.) 1978 *Aspects of Bilingualism*. Hornbeam, Columbia, South Carolina, pp. 156–64
Ojemann G A, Whitaker H A 1978 The bilingual brain. *Arch. Neurol.* 35: 409–12
Paradis M 1977 Bilingualism and aphasia. In: Whitaker H A, Whitaker H (eds.) 1977 *Studies in Neurolinguistics*, Vol. 3. Academic Press, New York, pp. 65–121
Paradis M 1983 *Readings on Aphasia in Bilinguals and Polyglots*. Didier, Montreal
Paradis M, Goldblum M, Abidi R 1982 Alternate antagonism with paradoxical translation behavior in two bilingual aphasic patients. *Brain Lang.* 15: 55–69
Vaid J, Genesee F 1980 Neuropsychological approaches to bilingualism: A critical review. *Can. J. Psychol.* 34: 417–45
Vildomec V 1963 *Multilingualism*. Sythoff, Leyden
Weinreich U 1953 *Languages in Contact: Findings and Problems*. Linguistic Circle, New York

Attitude Development

L. J. Keil

Attitudes are positive or negative feelings that an individual holds about objects, persons, or ideas. They are generally regarded as enduring though modifiable by experience and/or persuasion, and as learned rather than innate. Attitudes are also seen as predispositions to action. That is, if it is known that a child likes a teacher, it might be expected that the child will smile at the teacher, try to please the teacher by being helpful and cooperative, and in general to express an attitude of liking toward the object of that attitude—the teacher. Actual behavior, however, is influenced by many things, attitudes being only one of these factors. Thus it is important, as Fishbein and Ajzen (1975) have noted, to separate the concept of attitudes from behavioral intentions and actual behaviors, both of which are open to a variety of sources of influence. The study of attitude development thus focuses on how children acquire positive and negative orientations towards persons, objects, or ideas.

1. Measuring Attitudes in Children

To be able to evaluate the development of attitudes empirically requires that they be measured. Techniques for measuring attitudes can be classified into two general categories: direct measures and indirect measures. Research on the attitudes of adolescents and adults has relied heavily on direct measures which require self-reports of feelings about specified attitude objects. Commonly used attitude measurement scales, such as the Likert scale and the semantic differential, assess both attitudinal direction (positive or negative feelings) and intensity. Typically, a person is asked to rate their attitude toward a particular person, object, or idea on a 5- or 7-point scale ranging from strongly negative to strongly positive. Such direct measurement procedures assume people are both willing and able to respond accurately to inquiries about their attitudes. It is known, however, that in the case of socially undesirable attitudes, such as racial prejudice, people often misrepresent their actual attitudes and/or distort the intensity of their feelings. Thus, indirect measures are sometimes employed in an attempt to measure a person's attitudes without his or her knowing precisely what information is sought. Indirect measures of attitudes include projective tests, various behavioral indicators of attitude, and certain physiological indices such as changes in galvanic skin response and pupillary response.

Measuring the attitudes of children, particularly in the preschool and early elementary years, presents a number of unique problems. Many of the direct measurement scales frequently utilized with adolescents and adults are unsuitable for assessing young children's attitudes. Such measures rely heavily on an ability to conceptualize and verbalize abstract concepts such as racial stereotypes. Further, very young children find it difficult to assign a value to the level of intensity of their likes and dislikes. On the other hand, young children are less likely than adults to hide their feelings about socially undesirable topics when asked about them directly.

Caution is also required in the interpretation of indirect measures of children's attitudes, such as making inferences from play behavior. Researchers have often imposed meaning on children's behaviors which may not be indicative of children's attitudinal dispositions. For example, in a classic series of studies, Clark and Clark (1939) investigated children's racial orientations by asking them to choose between a white doll and a black doll. Critics of their methods have correctly pointed out that it must be determined whether or not children have awareness of racial categories and their cultural significance before using children's choice behavior as an indirect measure of racial preferences. The choice of a white doll by young children might indicate a greater familiarity with the dolls available in the market place or indicate a simple color preference rather than differential attitudes towards racial groups.

1.1 Measuring the Attitudes of Pre-school-age Children

In adapting attitude measurement scales for use with young children, researchers have often simplified the task so as to afford them a simple choice as obtained in the Clark and Clark studies noted above. This procedure measures the polarity or direction of the child's attitude but not the intensity. Examples of attitude measures which have been developed for use with pre-school-age children are found in Brown's (1956) "It" Scale and in both Williams and Morland's (1976) Color Meaning Test (CMT) and their Preschool Racial Attitude Measure (PRAM). Brown's "It" Scale was developed to measure sex-role attitudes in young children by asking them which picture they preferred in a series of pairs of pictures of people and various objects each having specific sex-typed characteristics. Williams and Morland's CMT and PRAM are tests which are used with

preschoolers to measure color preferences and racial preferences respectively. In both tests, children are shown pairs of pictures and are asked to choose between the pictures on the basis of brief descriptive stories. For example, pictures of a Caucasian and a Negro child are shown during administration of the Preschool Racial Attitude Measure and children are asked to decide which is the "kind" child, the "lazy" child, and so on.

Numerous researchers have argued that in order to assess the intensity of attitudes in younger children multiple measures are needed. Kohlberg and Zigler (1967), studying attitudes of 4- to 8-year-olds towards male and female sex roles, utilized a number of separate measurement procedures. In addition to Brown's "It" scale, they included a doll-play test in which the child chooses from a variety of male and female dolls to build a family, a playmate preference measure in which the child is asked for the names of three playmates, and two observational measures of dependency and imitation of male versus female experimenters. Kohlberg and Zigler then combined their observations across these various preference measures to obtain a better estimate of both the polarity (direction) and intensity of the child's sex-role attitudes.

1.2 Measuring the Attitudes of Elementary-school-age Children

Attitude studies with children of elementary-school age combine the measurement procedures used with preschoolers and simplified versions of those used with adults. Lambert and Klineberg (1967), for example, in a massive study of 6- to 14-year-old children's attitudes towards foreign peoples, used an open-ended interview technique. The interview was partially structured so that, for example, all children were asked to name foreign people who are "like them" and "not like them," as well as questions about specific groups such as "What do you know about Brazilians?" Additionally, open-ended, unstructured responses were solicited which were coded in terms of the information they revealed about the depth of the child's knowledge, as well as the polarity and intensity of the attitudes expressed.

Another example of attitude research with primary and junior high-school children is a study by Hess and Torney (1965) of children's attitudes toward government in the United States. Sampling at each grade level from grade 2 (approximately age 7 or 8) through grade 8 (approximately age 13 or 14), these researchers administered a simplified Likert scale to assess children's attitudes. In addition to wording the questions as simply as possible, graphics were used to make the meaning of the scale clearer. The children were asked to check the box which most closely matched their feelings of agreement (yes) or disagreement (no) on a topic. Each box was labeled with "yes" or "no." Both the size of the boxes, and the size of the "yes" or "no" provide a basis for expressing the strength of their agreement or disagreement. For example, strong agreement with the statement "All laws are fair" was indicated by checking the largest box labeled YES while mild agreement could be shown by choosing a smaller box labeled with a smaller yes.

These few examples illustrate the problems of measuring both the direction and intensity of attitudes in young children, as well as the range of techniques developed.

2. Theories of Attitude Development

In general, theories play an important role in guiding research. They focus attention on questions of importance in understanding and predicting the behavior of interest.

Much of the research which has been conducted on the development of attitudes in children over the past 50 years has been atheoretical. Such research has generally been guided by an interest in describing variations in children's attitudes as a function of age level in regard to specific issues, such as racial prejudice. Findings from these descriptive efforts are sometimes utilized to help generate theories about the development of specific attitudes. Thus, there exist a number of theories concerning the development of racial prejudice, sex-role attitudes, and others.

A single comprehensive theory of the emergence and change of attitudes in children has yet to emerge from the specific subtheories concerning particular kinds of attitudes. However, two major approaches to questions of general attitude development do exist and can be distinguished. One approach emphasizes experiential factors occurring during socialization, and the other emphasizes ontological or maturational factors as primary determinants of change during the course of attitude development. Recently, attempts have been made towards integrating these two perspectives into an overall theory of attitude development. Such an effort is confronted with the necessity of describing the complex interactions which occur between experiential and maturational factors and which strongly influence the development of attitudes.

2.1 Socialization

Social learning theorists emphasize the importance of two key concepts in development: reinforcement and imitation. Skinner (1953) has postulated that in addition to primary reinforcers, such as food and water, certain social stimuli, such as affection, attention, and approval, can take on reinforcing properties, and can shape behavior in the developing child. However, as Bandura and Walters (1963) have argued, selective reinforcement, whether social or nonsocial is too inefficient and time consuming to explain the vast behavioral repertoire achieved by children. They argue that the establishment of novel behavior can be achieved much more rapidly and effectively by the process of imitation of modeling, suggesting that children acquire most new behaviors by imitating others, primarily their parents, at early age

levels. Such behavior is then maintained or extinguished by selective reinforcement.

Considering these processes in regard to the development of attitudes, young children would be expected to imitate the attitudinal statements of their parents, of television programs, or of numerous other sources. If an attitude statement from one of these sources is acceptable or valued by the parent, then reinforcement in the form of approval and attention is likely to be forthcoming, thus increasing the likelihood that the attitudinal statement will be repeated. On the other hand, repetition of an unacceptable attitudinal statement is likely to result in negative reinforcement or punishment, and a consequent decline in the likelihood of further repetition.

The principles of imitation and reinforcement can account for the initial acquisition of attitudes. However, it is also important to understand how such attitudes are internalized, that is, how the child accepts an attitude, originally under external control in his or her definition of self, as under internal control. Two processes are assumed partially to account for internalization: identification and classical conditioning. Identification implies a process whereby one person adopts the attributes, prohibitions, and values of a particularly salient other. Although it is closely akin to imitation, the concept of identification has been used in the broader sense. Whereas imitation generally refers to the modeling of particular behavioral responses, indentification refers to a broader and more long-term acceptance of attributes associated with the salient other. Young children generally identify with their parents, especially their mothers, in traditionally organized households. Thus, while they will imitate and subsequently learn attitudinal statements obtained from many sources, one would expect them to be more likely to incorporate into their belief systems statements made by their parents than those coming from other sources. Hence, the identification process can be seen as one factor determining the selection of attitudes to be internalized.

A second major issue in understanding how attitudes and behaviors come under internal control is that of why they persist when direct reinforcement ceases. Classical conditioning is generally believed to account for this persistence. In classical conditioning, a neutral stimulus is paired with a stimulus which produces an emotional or physiological response such that repeating the stimulus increases the likelihood of the response. Attitudes may be conditioned in this way when a child pairs an attitude statement with reinforcements such as affection and approval. Over time and with similar repeated pairings, the child comes to associate the attitude statement with the positive emotional response experienced when approval and affection have been generated. In time, a positive conditioned response is elicited each time the attitude statement is considered, without approval or affection being afforded by an external agent.

The majority of theoretically guided research on attitude development has emphasized the role of a variety of variables that influence the socialization process. Such variables include parental attitudes, the child's sociocultural background, and the influence of mass media, education, and peers in children's socialization in general and their attitude development in particular.

2.2 Theories Stressing Cognitive Development

Less common in the area of attitude development are studies emphasizing the role of children's cognitive capabilities in the formation of attitudes. This approach, originating primarily in the work of Piaget (1952), Werner (1948), and others, rests on three basic ontological assumptions (Cairns 1979). First, the development of cognitive capabilities is assumed to parallel general organismic development and to be governed by analogous principles. Second, it is assumed that cognitive development progresses from dependence on immediately present sensations and perceptions toward achievement of abstract representations of experience. Thus, the infant is capable of responding only to direct stimulation from the immediate environment, whereas the mature person is also capable of responding to purely internal, mental events. The third and final assumption of this approach is that children's cognitive structure or characteristic ways of viewing the world evolve over the course of development in a series of relatively invariant, hierarchical stages in which each earlier stage forms the basis for the next, more complex stage.

Piaget (1952) postulated two interacting processes to account for the child's transition from stage to stage: assimilation and accommodation. Assimilation refers to the incorporation of new experiences into existing cognitive structures. Accommodation refers to the progressive reorganization of the structures themselves which occurs when such new information is introduced into the system. For example, a child may have experience with the family dog which forms the basis of a cognitive representation of the category "dog" as a friendly, furry creature which barks and wags its tail when it sees the child. New information introduced by the experience of being bitten by a strange dog initiates the processes of assimilation and accommodation. The experience with the strange dog is assimilated into the child's existing cognitive category, but the category itself is broadened to include this new aspect of experience—the knowledge that unknown dogs may bite. This example greatly oversimplifies the processes involved in cognitive growth. However, it illustrates the focus on internal, cognitive reorganization which is characteristic of this theoretical perspective.

Although both ontological and experiential factors are seen as important determinants of cognitive growth, Piaget (1952) and others tend to emphasize the parallels between cognitive and biological development to the relative neglect of the role of social learning in the transition from simpler to more complex levels of cognitive functioning. While no comparable stage theory

of attitude development has yet been advanced, some work has assessed the relationship between children's stages of cognitive development and their attitudes toward specific issues [e.g., Kohlberg's (1969) theory of moral development].

2.3 An Integration of Maturational and Experiential Factors

Recent research on attitude development, as exemplified in the work of Williams and Morland (1976) to be discussed subsequently, focuses on the interaction between cognitive and experiential factors. The theoretical bases for such an approach are illustrated in Jones and Gerard's (1967) discussion of the formation of attitudes. To explain why parents have such a monumental influence on the development of children's views, Jones and Gerard describe two important aspects of parent–child interaction: information dependence and affect dependence. Young children are typically dependent on their parents for information about the world, including themselves. Since parents are the earliest providers of such information, the way in which they present it not only influences the substance of a child's thinking but it also has a profound effect on the way the child structures and processes subsequent information. Children also depend on their parents to meet their physical and emotional needs—affect dependence. Such dependence maximizes parental power to reinforce the modes of thought thus established. For example, children may be rewarded by their parents for their abilities to recognize and identify racial or ethnic characteristics which correspond to stereotypes the parents have presented.

In this view, then, information provided to children early in life has important consequences for the course of their mental development. The ways of categorizing persons, objects, and ideas suggested by parental provision of information is a crucial determinant of the child's later thinking patterns. Thus, the consequence of early information and affect dependence is a complex interaction between children's maturing cognitive abilities and their learning experiences in forming their attitudes.

3. Attitude Development: Representative Research

In the following subsections three representative research programs are discussed in detail. First, Lambert and Klineberg's (1967) study of children's attitudes towards foreign peoples presents an example of research guided by a theory stressing socialization. Second, a study of sex-role attitudes by Kohlberg and Zigler (1967) exemplifies work in which cognitive development is stressed. Third, Williams and Morland's (1976) work on the development of racial attitudes focuses on both maturational and experiential factors in attitude formation.

3.1 Development of Attitudes Toward Foreign Peoples

Lambert and Klineberg, in a study representative of research from a socialization perspective toward attitude development and change, conducted a massive investigation of the development of children's views of foreign peoples. The study included 3,300 children at three age levels (6–7 years, 10 years, and 14 years) from 11 cultures (American, Bantu South African, Brazilian, English Canadian, French Canadian, French, German, Israeli, Japanese, Lebanese, and Turkish). Using an interview technique, the researchers evaluated children's attitudes towards foreign peoples. Specifically, they compared across ages and cultures children's tendencies to regard foreigners as similar or different, their feelings of friendliness or affection toward specific groups, and their ethnocentrism in regard to their own culture.

In general, 6-year-olds considered fewer foreign groups to be similar to themselves than children at the older age levels studied. Additionally, the youngest group expressed the least friendliness toward other groups whether they were considered similar to dissimilar. In contrast, the 10-year-olds displayed the most openness on both the similarity and friendliness measures. It is notable that 10-year-olds manifested the maximum readiness to like dissimilar others. There was virtually no increase after age 10 for any of the national groups studied in expressed affection for dissimilars. In fact, there was typically a decrease on this measure between 10 and 14 years of age.

There were cultural differences on these measures indicating the influence of culture-specific socialization practices. For example, French Canadian and Japanese children exhibited a decrease in friendly attitudes towards foreigners from 10 to 14 years of age whereas Americans showed an increase on both the similarity and friendliness measures; Brazilian, German, and Turkish children increased in friendliness toward similar others only. Cultural differences were most pronounced in the measure of ethnocentrism, with Bantu and Brazilian children showing the highest levels of ethnocentricity and Americans, both Canadian groups, Japanese, and French children showing the least.

The authors interpret their findings using the assumptions of a social learning paradigm. They suggest that the development of attitudes toward foreign peoples parallels the way children define people who are "like us" and "not like us." Six- and 10-year-olds think of foreigners as unlike themselves if they possess physical differences which are clearly visible. Fourteen-year-olds base their discriminations on cultural customs and stereotypical personality characteristics they have come to associate with particular foreign groups. In concluding, the authors postulate that children develop particular attitudes toward other cultural groups first as a means of understanding reality as it is defined in their own culture (hence the concentration on visible, objective differences) and later to help them identify with their own reference groups (consequently concentrating on how other groups differ in customs and personality).

3.2 Development of Sex-role Attitudes

An example of research in which the emphasis is on the role of cognitive maturity in attitude development is a study by Kohlberg and Zigler (1967). They examined the relationship between intelligence and sex-role attitudes. Their major hypothesis was that the child's level of cognitive development, as measured by a standard IQ test, is an important determinant of the development of sex-role attitudes. This maturational hypothesis can be sharply contrasted with a social learning theory approach, which would predict such relationships to obtain between chronological age and attitude development, since age implies an increasing exposure over time to socializing agents and life experiences.

Children at four age levels (4, 5, 6, and 7 years) and two levels of intelligence (bright and average) participated in the Kohlberg and Zigler study. In addition, a group of average 10-year-olds were included. Across age levels significant differences between bright and average groups were found on all the measures of sex-role attitudes described earlier except that which measured children's imitation of the experimenter. The response patterns of bright 4-year-olds were similar to those of average 6- to 7-year-olds and bright 7-year-olds showed response patterns similar to average 10-year-olds. The authors conclude that intelligence level plays an important role in the development of sex-role attitudes, with bright children considerably advanced in development over children of average intellectual abilities. They argue that these findings are strong evidence for a cognitive-developmental theory of attitude formation and change rather than a social learning theory. The primary basis for their argument is that whereas one would expect most, if not all, children in a given culture to be exposed to similar socialization messages from parents and others, brighter children develop at an earlier age the cognitive structures necessary for effectively integrating adult-initiated messages concerning sex-role identities and sex-role attitudes. Thus it is the stage of children's cognitive development which produces the differences between bright and average groups rather than differences in socialization experiences.

3.3 Development of Racial Attitudes

The development of racial prejudice has been one of the more heavily researched aspects of attitude development. Representative of this area of inquiry is a program of research detailed in Williams and Morland's (1976) book *Race, Color, and the Young Child*. In a comprehensive series of studies including children from preschool age to adolescence, they have explored children's racial attitudes from a theoretical perspective which incorporates both maturational and experiential factors and illustrates the current trend toward integrating these two perspectives.

Williams and Morland argue that children's early biologically based learning experiences with light and darkness create a universal bias in favor of the color white over black. Humans, as a species that depends heavily on the sense of sight, find darkness inherently frightening. This natural predisposition coupled with various childhood experiences, such as thunderstorms at night, creates this bias strongly in children. Williams and Morland report a number of studies which demonstrate such a color bias which appears to be pan-cultural on the basis of a broad cross-cultural sample.

There also exists a correlated and strong cultural symbolism in virtually all cultures which equates white with goodness and black with badness or evil. Williams and Morland report anthropological data supporting this idea of black(bad)–white(good) symbolism in which very few exceptions to this equation have been found throughout the world. The message children receive about the symbolic nature of black and white reinforces their natural black–white color biases. In studying racial attitudes in children, Williams and Morland argue, great care must be taken not to attribute racially prejudiced attitudes to children who may be merely exhibiting natural color preferences.

In an extensive series of studies assessing both black and white American children, these researchers have explored the conceptually distinct areas of color preferences, racial acceptance, and racial preference. Briefly, their findings indicate that both black and white preschoolers exhibit a bias in favor of light-skinned persons over dark-skinned persons with the degree of bias somewhat lower in black children. This bias appears to continue into early school grades and while diminishing gradually, it is still evident in early adolescence.

Williams and Morland conclude that the developmental course of the acquisition of a color bias, which may transition into negative attitudes towards blacks, is affected by three kinds of determinants: (a) the child's early biologically based experiences with light and darkness, (b) the messages the child receives from the general culture regarding color symbolism and racial stereotypes, and finally (c) the amplification or suppression of the appropriateness of these culturally transmitted messages by the subculture to which the child belongs. Thus, they conclude that "racial bias" which is "exhibited by young children is not primarily racial in its origin, but becomes racial in its effect as children learn about race and their own identity."

4. Implications of Research on Attitude Development

In summarizing the findings of research on attitude development, implications can be drawn from each of the three perspectives discussed in the current article:

socialization, cognitive maturation, and an integration of the two.

Research emphasizing the role of the socialization process has shown the importance of the environmental context in attitude formation. Cross-cultural research, such as that of Lambert and Klineberg (1967), demonstrates the pervasive influence of culture-specific socialization messages on children's attitudes. Additionally, as Hess and Torney (1965) have shown in their study of the development of children's attitudes toward government, some attitudes are imparted primarily by parents while others emanate mainly from other socializing agents such as schools. These findings imply the necessity to distinguish the primary sources of specific types of attitudes in order to better understand the attitude development process, as well as to formulate improved programs for imparting cultural attitudes to our children.

The research which emphasizes maturational factors, particularly cognitive ones, in attitude development points out the importance of individual differences in both the rate and content of attitude formation. These findings imply, for example, that although most school systems are organized by chronological age level, great variations can be expected in the cognitive maturity levels of children of the same age. This fact is well-established in the area of education and cognitive growth, but the findings of attitude research imply an extension of these ideas to social development as well. Thus, both parents and educators should be aware that individual levels of cognitive maturity have an important role in the way children interpret the socialization messages they receive. A better understanding of these maturational factors is needed in order to enable those who are responsible for socialization to effectively impart cultural views.

Finally, research exploring the relationship between cognitive development and social learning implies that very early learning experiences may be more important determinants of later attitude development than was previously thought. Jones and Gerard's (1967) discussion of the influence of early information on the formation of category structures illustrates this point. They note that research has shown that initially formed category schemes are resistant to change, and appear to have long-lasting and pervasive effects on the processing of later information and consequent attitude development. One example of this process is found in Williams and Morland's (1976) theory about the effects of early experiences with light and darkness on the subsequent development of racial bias.

All three theoretical perspectives discussed here thus make significant contributions to an understanding of the development of attitudes in children. The current trend toward emphasizing both maturational and experiential factors suggests that future research will deal more directly with the complexities of the interaction of these two processes as they affect attitude development.

Bibliography

Bandura A, Walters R H 1963 *Social Learning and Personality Development*. Holt, Rinehart and Winston, New York

Brown D G 1956 Sex-role preference in young children. *Psychol. Monogr.* 70 (14) (Serial No. 287)

Cairns R B 1979 *Social Development: The Origins and Plasticity of Interchanges*. Freeman, San Francisco, California

Clark K B, Clark M P 1939 The development of consciousness and the emergence of racial identification in Negro preschool children. *J. Soc. Psychol.* 10: 591–99

Fishbein M, Ajzen I 1975 *Belief, Attitude, Intention and Behavior: An Introduction to Theory and Research*. Addison-Wesley, Reading, Massachusetts

Hess R D, Torney J V 1965 *The Development of Basic Attitudes and Values Toward Government and Citizenship During the Elementary School Years*, Part 1. University of Chicago, Chicago, Illinois

Jones E E, Gerard H B 1967 *Foundations of Social Psychology*.

Wiley, New York

Kohlberg L 1969 Stage and sequence: The cognitive–developmental approach to socialization. In: Goslin D A (ed.) 1969 *Handbook of Socialization Theory and Research*. Rand McNally, Chicago, Illinois

Kohlberg L, Zigler E 1967 The impact of cognitive maturity on the development of sex-role attitudes in the years 4 to 8. *Genet. Psychol. Monogr.* 75: 89–165

Lambert W E, Klineberg O 1967 *Children's Views of Foreign Peoples: A Cross-national study*. Appleton-Century-Crofts, New York

Piaget J 1952 *The Origins of Intelligence in Children*. International Universities Press, New York

Skinner B F 1953 *Science and Human Behavior*. Macmillan, New York

Werner H 1948 *Comparative Psychology of Mental Development*. Follett, Chicago, Illinois

Williams J E, Morland J K 1976 *Race, Color, and the Young Child*. University of North Carolina Press, Chapel Hill, North Carolina

Mastery Motivation

R. M. Ryan and J. P. Connell

Mastery motivation refers to the general tendency of organisms to be effective or to gain competence in relation to their environment. Mastery motivation theorists argue that this tendency reflects a primary psychological need and is not reducible to drive or reinforcement explanations. Rather, mastery motivation is seen as an intrinsic need, and mastery-motivated behavior is inherently satisfying or pleasurable.

1. History of the Concept

Mastery motivation emerged as a central concept in both psychodynamic and empirically based psychologies following White's (1959) classic paper, "Motivation reconsidered: The concept of competence." In that paper White employed the term *effectance motivation*, and he argued for the recognition of this innate, non-drive-based energizer of behavior. Drawing from the diverse sources of psychoanalytic ego psychology, the developmental theories of Piaget, and neo-Hullian animal experimentalism, he pointed to the generalized propensity of organisms to gain competence in their environments independent of external supports or rewards. He also linked this primary motive with such behavioral phenomena as exploration, play, and curiosity. The importance of his paper and subsequent monograph (White 1963) lies not only in the naming of a new motive, but also in emphasizing the active, purposive nature of organisms and the importance of mastery motivation to development.

White's classic work spawned numerous studies and theories (many within the fields of social-developmental and educational psychology). Included in this category

are the theories of intrinsic motivation, including those of deCharms (1976), Deci (1975), Deci and Ryan (1985), Harter (1981), and Csikszentmihalyi (1975). In these approaches, mastery or intrinsic motivation has been studied as an energizing process in the development of competence in general and more specifically within education; as a motive capable of being either undermined or facilitated by various social contexts; and, finally, as an important source of optimal cognitive performance.

Mastery motivation is evidenced primarily in behaviors which occur in the absence of external controls or reinforcement. Put differently it is "autotelic" (Csikszentmihalyi 1975) or done "for its own sake." Because it is done freely and is spontaneously emitted, it represents an autonomous form of organismic functioning (Deci and Ryan 1985). The primary affective hallmark of mastery-motivated activity is interest. However, mastery-motivated activities are also often accompanied by the experience of enjoyment and/or excitement.

Mastery motivation plays a significant role in developmental processes. In curiously exploring their surroundings and playfully manipulating objects, children not only experience the inherent pleasure of functioning but also exercise and elaborate their own capacities. Thus, mastery motivation underlies the growth of psychological structures and increasing competence.

Similarly, mastery motivation is seen as playing a particularly crucial role in education. In the academic domain it is manifest in students' natural tendencies toward discovery and learning and is seen by many theorists as perhaps the most important source of the motivation to learn (Ryan et al. 1985). Indeed the concept of mastery motivation implies an inherent tendency to assimilate material and tackle challenges. Educators who acknowledge mastery motivation in some form have a long tradition and include Montessori, Dewey, Rogers, Holt, and others. This tradition stands in contrast to the view that the motivation to learn is exclusively a function of external contingencies and controls.

2. Educational Contexts

A large body of research has explored the effects of varied educational contexts and teaching styles on students' mastery or intrinsic motivation. Generally speaking there have been two broad classes of influence that have been shown to affect the degree to which children manifest mastery motivation in school: the level of challenge and the affordance of autonomy or self-determination.

Evidence from many quarters has suggested that mastery motivation is most likely to emerge under conditions of optimal challenge (Csikszentmihalyi 1975, Deci and Ryan 1985, Harter 1981). Students who are provided with tasks and problems just above their current level of competence are more likely to show enhanced interest and persistence. In contrast, challenges that are below optimal levels of challenge lead to boredom and disengagement, while tasks above optimal challenge elicit anxiety and/or lack of interest. An issue related to level of challenge is that of novelty or optimal discrepancy. Kagan (1972), Hunt (1971), and others have argued that novel or optimally complex materials are most likely to facilitate interest and mastery motivation.

The second dimension of importance in contextual studies of mastery motivation is that of autonomy. Mastery motivation is enhanced by environmental affordance and support for autonomous exercise of capacities. Classroom environments that emphasize teacher control, rewards and punishments, and/or evaluation and grades undermine mastery motivation, while teaching styles and feedback structures that are more autonomy-supportive facilitate the occurrence of mastery motivation, persistence, and interest (deCharms 1976, Deci and Ryan 1985, Ryan and Grolnick 1986).

Finally, numerous studies have linked mastery or intrinsic motivation to the quality of learning and performance in educational settings. Amabile (1983), in a series of studies, has shown that environments conducive to intrinsic motivation also promote creativity. More recently, Grolnick and Ryan (1987) have shown how the factors conducive to mastery motivation enhance conceptual integration of material. On the most general level it seems that student interest and mastery motivation need to be encouraged for heuristic and conceptual learning to occur, while strong pressure and external controls are sufficient to promote rote learning and algorithmic types of performance (McGraw 1978).

The concept of mastery motivation thus represents a focus on students' inherent tendencies to learn, and has generated a large body of both theoretical and applied studies of particular relevance to educational contexts. The idea that there is a primary need to master challenges and gain competence suggests an aspect of human nature that can be utilized by educators toward the end of student learning and development. In fact, this notion of mastery motivation fits with the etymological definition of education itself, which is to bring out capacities that lie within the learner. From a mastery motivation view, the role of the educator is that of a facilitator and supporter of students' inherent tendencies to learn.

Bibliography

Amabile T M 1983 *The Social Psychology of Creativity*. Springer, New York

Csikszentmihalyi M 1975 *Beyond Boredom and Anxiety*. Jossey-Bass, San Francisco, California

deCharms R 1976 *Enhancing Motivation: A Change in the Classroom*. Irvington, New York

Deci E L 1975 *Intrinsic Motivation*. Plenum, New York

Deci E L, Ryan R M 1985 *Intrinsic Motivation and Self-Determination in Human Behavior*. Plenum, New York

Grolnick W S, Ryan R M 1987 Autonomy in children's learning: An experimental and individual difference investigation. *J Pers. Soc. Psychol.* 52: 890–98

Harter S 1981 A model of intrinsic mastery motivation in children: Individual differences and developmental changes. *Minnesota Symposium on Child Psychology*, Vol. 14, Erlbaum, Hillsdale, New Jersey

Hunt J McV 1971 Toward a history of intrinsic motivation. In: Day H I, Berlyne D E, Hunt D E (eds.) 1971 *Intrinsic Motivation: A New Direction in Education*. Holt, Rinehart and Winston, Toronto, pp. 1–32

Kagan J 1972 Motives and development. *J. Pers. Soc. Psychol.* 22: 51–66

McGraw K O 1978 The detrimental effects of reward on performance: A literature review and a prediction model. In: Lepper M R, Greene D (eds.) 1978 *The Hidden Costs of Reward: New Perspectives of the Psychology of Human Motivation*. Erlbaum, Hillsdale, New Jersey, pp. 33–60

Ryan R M, Connell J P, Deci E L 1985 A motivational analysis of self-determination and self-regulation in education. In: Ames C, Ames R E (eds.) 1985 *Research on Motivation in Education*, Vol. 2, *The Classroom Milieu*. Academic Press, Orlando, Florida, pp. 13–51

Ryan R M, Grolnick W S 1986 Origins and pawns in the classroom: Self-report and projective assessments of individual differences in children's perceptions. *J. Pers. Soc. Psychol.* 50: 550–58

White R W 1959 Motivation reconsidered: The concept of competence. *Psychol. Rev.* 66: 297–333

White R W 1963 *Ego and Reality in Psychoanalytic Theory*, Psychological Issues Series, Monograph No. 11. International Universities Press, New York

Social Cognition

J. M. Zimmer

The term social cognition refers to a new hybrid field of study that treats matters of how people think about themselves in relation to other people and how they perceive society and its institutions. The field has been labeled "hybrid" because it represents an integration of several scholarly disciplines and investigative persuasions, the chief of which have been social psychology, psychoanalysis, social learning theory, developmental psychology, and anthropology. According to Shantz (1975), who has provided one of the first major reviews in the area, the field of social cognition did not become a focus of major interest and research until about 1965. Prior to that time social behavior had been studied by diverse researchers and theoreticians representing separate disciplines or schools of thought.

At its present stage of development, the field of social cognition is marked more by the questions it poses than by the secure answers it offers. Hence, the concern of this article is with identifying (a) the sorts of contributions that various disciplines and schools of thought have made to this new hybrid and (b) the key issues being studied by means of integrated theory and methodology drawn from such disciplines.

1. Foundation Disciplines and Theoretical Persuasions

Social psychologists have built on the work of Mead (1934), Allport (1961), Kelley (1973), and others to investigate questions about the processes which people employ in perceiving the self, other people, and settings in which people function. While social psychologists have recognized that such processes develop in childhood and adolescence, they have been mainly concerned with adults' perception, assuming that adults function differently at different times and under different conditions and that the complexity of what is perceived changes. The general method for conducting such studies has been that of an investigator observing two other people in social interaction within a controlled environment. Or in other instances data have been collected by means of questionnaires, such as those described by Miller (1981) in studying the conceptual complexity of people's social perceptions.

The psychoanalytic movement since Freud has focused on how thoughts and feelings about the self can be made conscious, rather than held only in the unconscious. Erikson (1968), from a psychoanalytic perspective, studied people's self-identity, concluding that achieving identity requires simultaneous reflection and observation within the context of other people and the particular culture. The processes of reflection and observation are both aspects of cognition which are influenced by the particular social context in which the person is achieving "identity consciousness" or perceiving "who I am." Psychoanalytic researchers have primarily focused on the individual in relationship to deviations from a social standard. The most prominent research technique contributed to the field of social cognition by psychoanalysis has been the case study method, employed for illuminating the processes of making the "self" conscious.

Social learning theory is yet another source of contributions to the field of social cognition. For the social learning theorist, "performance of a skill requires continuous improvisation and adjustment to ever changing circumstances" (Bandura 1981 p. 200). Thus, the "skill" of perceiving one's self in relation to society is altered by influences of the social environment, particularly by the consequences of one's accomplishments (reinforcement) and by vicarious experiences or seeing what happens to other people under various circumstances (modeling). In effect, people's accomplishments and vicarious experiences are thought directly to influence people's judgments about themselves and the transactions they might have with the environment. Mischel (1981) uses the term meta cognition to express the phenomenon of how children understand their own cognitions. He explored the way in which knowledge of psychological principles or rules governs a person's own behavior. This issue of how meta cognition can be used to regulate a people's "own" conduct so they achieve social "mastery and control over their environment" falls within the province of social cognition. A favorite investigative method of social learning researchers is that of conducting controlled experiments.

Developmentalists influenced by the work of Jean Piaget form another group who, in turn, have influenced the way in which the study of social cognition is conceived. Piaget argued that the child begins slowly in early life to construct a mental picture of the world through her or his internal organization. This internal organization is altered as the child interacts with the external environment of people, objects, and events. As part of that construction, the child is thought to develop from an organism centered heavily on "self" to one that is gradually able to differentiate itself from others. From this conception, studies of empathy and egocentrism have become prevalent (Borke 1978). In addition, the organization of thought that is constituted at the various levels of the child's development leads to a definable social and moral consciousness. Piaget (1965) elaborated on the theme of moral consciousness, and Kohlberg (1969) initiated extensive research in the same area to trace the development of moral understanding and action. Developmentalists have attempted to describe levels of thought about social and moral judgments and causal relationships as reflected in the answers which children and adults give to questions about moral dilemmas presented to them in story form.

Anthropology has developed an expanding subdiscipline of cognitive anthropology. Schwartzman (1978) poses the researcher's problem clearly when she states that culture resides in the mind of the informant, and the problem of the anthropologist is how to get into the mind and how to know when one has gotten there. Anthropologists, including Mead (1930), have always been concerned with the "native's" point of view, and cognitive anthropologists have focused on this perspective. As anthropologists have sought to build generalizations from the comparative study of cultures, they have stressed that the habits and thoughts which the researchers bring from their own culture need to be transcended in order to understand the point of view of the people they are currently studying. Goodenough (1964 p. 36) stated that:

> As I see it, society's culture consists of whatever it is one has to know or believe in order to operate in a manner acceptable to its members . . .; culture is not a material phenomenon; it does not consist of things, people, behavior, or emotions. It is rather an organization of these things. It is the forms of things that people have in mind, their models for perceiving, relating, and otherwise interpreting them.

For years anthropologists have studied how a culture and its organization and relationships are thought about by its members. Studies of play, games, and friendships illustrate the ways in which members of a culture understand the various organizations of their culture. An important quality of anthropological research is that the conceptual models or significant categories used in the studies should reveal concepts indigenous to that culture rather than represent models imposed by the researcher or the researchers' culture.

In summary, social cognition as it is presented in contemporary literature can best be thought of as a hybrid, with each investigator drawing upon one or several of the approaches described above and combining research methods and rationales in various ways. Flavell (1981) captured the hybrid characteristics of the field of social cognition when he wrote:

> social cognitive enterprises . . . include all intellectual endeavors in which the aim is to think or learn about social or psychological process of self, individual others, or human groups of all sizes and kinds . . . thus what is thought about . . . could be a perception, feeling, motive, ability, intention, purpose, interest, attitude, thought, belief, personality structure, or any other process or property of self or other(s). It could also be the social interactions and relationships that occur among individuals, groups, nations, or other social entities. A social cognitive enterprise can be very brief or very extended.

2. Current Focus of Social Cognition

Some of the important issues being investigated in the new and hybrid realm of social cognition are the following.

One concern of investigators has been the relationship of the social-cognitive domain to other domains. Chandler (1977 p. 141) has stated "There does appear to be some growing confluence in the findings of these diverse studies." Chandler reports that person perception, social-role taking, and empathy are regulated by a similar "assimilating influence of the child's changing cognitive organization." At the same time that a confluence of findings is beginning to emerge around domains, another group of studies report that other domains are lacking in any significant relationships. Ford (1979), for example, concluded that the variances shown by measures of visual/spatial perspective taking and identification of affect states are small and that the underlying construct is not evident but that these results can "contribute to our knowledge about social cognitive development."

Questions concerning social cognition in relationship to other domains have been investigated to define the characteristics of the known (object) and the nature of the knower (person) as well as the interactions of the two. In reference to the nature of the knower, the following are questions treated in studies of social cognition.

(a) Does social cognition fit a developmental or nondevelopmental model?

(b) Are the structures or mechanisms different for knowing social phenomena than those that function to understand nonsocial phenomena? (In many ways this question is much the same as that concerning whether there is a "g" factor of intelligence or whether there are multifactors of intelligence.)

(c) Are there prerequisites for social cognitions?

(d) Is there an inherent order of social and nonsocial cognitions?

Another set of questions concerns the known or the object that is to be known. Object in this sense refers to persons, including the self, as well as any other social, psychological, or cultural occurrence or concept. The general nature of the questions is centered on whether certain understandings are more privileged than others. Examples of this concern would be:

(a) Are judgments or understandings concerning "necessity of a consequence" more or less easily grasped than consequences that are derived by a "consensus?"

(b) Can that which is to be known be placed on a continuum, such as concrete to abstract or simple to complex?

(c) What is there about objects which allows generalizations to be made?

Finally, a number of questions have been raised concerning the interactions between the knower and what is to be known. Embedded in the question of interactions are also the ever-present questions involving

' the relationships between thinking, feeling, acting, and social cognition. Illustrative questions are:

(a) How does feedback from the environment affect the way in which social cognitions are understood and acted upon?

(b) What is the relationship between environmental feedback and the functional needs or inner state of the organism?

(c) What is the role of reinforcement and vicarious experiences in giving meanings?

In reference to applied issues, the accuracy and processes of judging and acting on social, psychological, and cultural occurrences and concepts have become important to various therapies (Meichenbaum 1977) as well as in education (Rest 1974).

Perhaps Cooney and Selman (1980 p. 351) best describe the state of social cognition when they state, "Our investigations have only just begun. They have left us with more questions than answers, more speculation than fact. We hope that others may find these possibilities as intriguing as we do."

Bibliography

Allport G W 1961 *Pattern and Growth in Personality*. Holt, Rinehart and Winston, New York

Bandura A 1981 Self-referent thought: A developmental analysis of self-efficacy. In: Flavell J, Ross L (eds.) 1981 *Social Cognitive Development*. Cambridge University Press, Cambridge, pp. 200–38

Borke H 1978 Piaget's view of social interaction and the theoretical construct of empathy. In: Siegel L S, Brainerd C J (eds.) 1978 *Alternatives to Piaget*. Academic Press, New York, pp. 29–41

Chandler M 1977 Social cognition: A selective review of current research. In: Overton W, Gallagher J (eds.) 1977 *Knowledge and Development*, Advances in Research and Theory, Vol. 1. Plenum, New York, pp. 93–147

Cooney E W, Selman R L 1980 Children's use of social conceptions: Toward a dynamic model of social cognition. *Pers. Guid. J.* 58: 344–52

Erikson E H 1968 *Identity Youth and Crises*. Faber, London

Flavell J 1981 Monitoring social cognitive enterprises: Something else that may develop in the area of social cognition. In: Flavell J, Ross L (eds.) 1981 *Social Cognitive Development*. Cambridge University Press, Cambridge, pp. 273–87

Ford M E 1979 The construct validity of egocentrism. *Psychol. Bull.* 86: 1169–89

Goodenough W H 1964 Cultural anthropology and linguistics. In: Hymes D (ed.) 1964 *Language in Culture and Society*. Harper and Row, New York, pp. 36–39

Kelley H H 1973 The processes of causal attribution. *Am. Psychol.* 28: 107–28

Kohlberg L 1969 Stage and sequence: The cognitive–developmental approach to socialization. In: Goslin D A (ed.) 1969 *Handbook of Socialization Theory and Research*. Rand-McNally, Chicago, Illinois

Mead G H 1934 *Mind, Self and Society*. University of Chicago Press, Chicago, Illinois

Mead M 1930 *Growing up in New Guinea: A Comparative Study of Primitive Education*. Morrow, New York

Meichenbaum D 1977 *Cognitive Behavior Modification: An Integrative Approach*. Plenum, New York

Miller A 1981 Conceptual matching models and interactional research in education. *Rev. Educ. Res.* 5: 384

Mischel W 1981 Meta cognition and the rules of delay. In: Flavell J H, Ross L (eds.) 1981 *Social Cognitive Development*. Cambridge University Press, Cambridge, pp. 240–71

Piaget J 1965 *The Moral Judgement of the Child*. Free Press, New York

Rest J 1974 Developmental psychology as a guide to value education: A review of Kohlbergean programs. *Rev. Educ. Res.* 44: 241–59

Schwartzman H 1978 *Transformations, the Anthropology of Children's Play*. Plenum, New York

Shantz C 1975 The development of social cognition. In: Hetherington E M (ed.) 1975 *Review of Child Development Research*, Vol. 5. University of Chicago Press, Chicago, Illinois

Social Perception

C. U. Shantz

Social cognitive development encompasses the development of social perception, understanding, and reasoning. Specifically, it is focused on conceptions of other people, self, relations between people (e.g., friendship, authority), social roles and social rules (moral and conventional), and, more recently, the relations of such conceptions to social behavior.

The field emerged within developmental psychology in the late 1960s, probably because the dominant developmental theories of that time dealt either with "the social–emotional child" (psychoanalytic and social learning theories) *or* "the thinking and reasoning child" (Piaget's and Werner's theories). Each set of theories was limited: the former gave no explicit account of the thinking social child, while the latter largely neglected the social thinking child. Most research has been based primarily on early Piagetan research and theory dealing with egocentrism and moral reasoning, and to a lesser extent on Werner's theory and adult social causal attribution theories.

Developmental changes in the way children understand others' behavior (as assessed by their attention to and recall of movies and television), and their ways of conceptualizing people they know well (as assessed by free descriptions) show some general similarities. During the preschool and early school years, children notice and remember primarily the "surface" aspects of behavior such as movement, statements, obvious emotions, and the setting and consequences of behavior. Likewise, they describe people largely in terms of their surface characteristics such as appearance and possessions, and in global evaluative terms (such as good, bad, nice, mean) (Livesley and Bromley 1973). Around the middle childhood years substantial changes occur in children when they begin to make inferences about the psychological characteristics of people, that is, their intentions, attitudes, thoughts, and subtle feelings, and to abstract general traits based on regularities of behavior over time and situations. In early adolescence, usually, people and their behavior are seen as often determined by particular combinations of traits and situational influences. Whereas the young child seems to assume that his/her conception of social reality *is* the reality, the adolescent is much more aware that his/her conceptions are interpretations and that other interpretations are possible. The same relative developmental shift from focusing on obvious behavior, to focusing on psychological aspects, and then to focusing on social relations and social impact can also be seen in children's understanding of social relations. For example, young children think of friendship as playmateship, exchanging goods, and being nice, but by adolescence it is conceived as an attraction of personalities who trust and help one another (Damon 1977).

The young child has difficulty in the self–other differentiation, tending to attribute to others the child's own wishes, thoughts, viewpoints and feelings in situations where they are, in fact, different. This lack of differentiation of self and other is egocentrism, a construct originally proposed by Piaget. Research has revealed less egocentrism in preschoolers than there was originally thought to be (e.g., Flavell 1968, Shantz 1983). However, once a child recognizes that different viewpoints can exist, the ability to then infer what another person sees, thinks, or feels (role taking) has a long developmental course that continues well into adolescence. Some researchers have taken the position that children with advanced role-taking skills or greater empathic abilities behave more prosocially (cooperate, help) and less aggressively with other children and adults (see *Prosocial Behavior*), but the findings of several studies are not supportive of such a direct relation between these abilities and social behaviors (Shantz 1983). In short, this new area has found what older areas of psychology have found: the relationship between thinking and behaving, and between attitudes and behaving are less strong and direct than most assume.

The number of different strategies children use to solve interpersonal conflicts with peers and adults increases substantially between the preschool and late middle childhood years, and has been found to be related often to overall social adjustment, that is, shy and inhibited children, as well as aggressive and impulsive children know substantially fewer strategies than normally adjusted children. After the preschool years, children are quite often accurate in their perceptions of

dominance relationships (pecking orders) and liking relationships in small groups or classrooms of which they are members. These perceptions are quite stable over years or groups that remain largely intact (e.g., classrooms), and tend to agree with adults' perceptions of these relationships.

The research on social cognitive development (including moral reasoning) shows that performance on various tasks is not highly related to psychometrically measured intelligence or IQ. Often no relation is found, or only low to moderate relations (correlations of 0.35 or lower). As such, there is no support for the notion that social cognitive abilities are "nothing more" than a reflection of general intelligence. In some areas such as moral reasoning and perspective-coordination, qualitatively different stages of reasoning have been demonstrated, for example, Damon (1977) and Selman (1980); in other areas, such as person perception and causal reasoning, there is as yet no evidence of developmental stages.

There are a number of studies indicating that it is possible to teach children how to "take the role of the other," or to improve their ability to do so. Small group role-enactment activities (behaving as if one were a story character) and small group cooperative activities both seem effective in increasing children's ability to understand others' thoughts and feelings. Confronting children with the differences between their viewpoint and others' different viewpoints seems to be an effective means of increasing spatial perspective-taking and improving the ability to take the role of the listener in communication tasks.

The field of social cognitive development has many potential applications to the field of education, only a few of which can be cited here. In terms of curriculum, children's understanding of others' behavior in history and in different cultures can be approached more effectively if the teacher has a knowledge of the kinds of abilities and biases children of different ages are prone to, that is, their modes of person perception, role taking, and causal schemes. Likewise, the reasons for which children think they succeed or fail at academic tasks are highly influential for their expectancies and motivations to succeed (Weiner 1974).

Bibliography

Damon W 1977 *The Social World of the Child.* Jossey-Bass, San Francisco, California
Flavell J H 1968 *The Development of Role-taking and Communication Skills in Children.* Wiley, New York
Livesley W J, Bromley D B 1973 *Person Perception in Childhood and Adolescence.* Wiley, London
Selman R L 1980 *The Growth of Interpersonal Understanding: Developmental and Clinical Analyses.* Academic Press, New York
Shantz C U 1983. Social cognition. In: Mussen P H (ed.) 1983 *Handbook of Child Psychology*, 4th edn. Wiley, New York
Weiner B 1974 *Achievement Motivation and Attribution Theory.* General Learning Press, Morristown, New Jersey

Creativity

J. W. Getzels

Although there may be agreement on what constitutes an act of creation as in the case of $E = mc^2$, the *David*, the *Eroica*, or for that matter even lesser works, there is disagreement regarding almost every aspect of its nature and development. Definitions vary; modes of identification vary; theories vary; research methods and results vary. Agreed upon only is that creative thinking is the highest of mental functions and creative production the peak of human achievement.

There is no universally accepted definition of creativity any more than there is of intelligence (Getzels and Dillon 1973, Barron and Harrington 1981). The most widely applied definitions may be classified according to the emphasis placed on the product, the process, or the experience of creativity. Some definitions are formulated in terms of a manifest product: it is novel and useful. The criterion here is a statistically infrequent tangible response or idea that is adaptive and sustained to fruition. Other definitions are formulated in terms of an underlying process: it is divergent yet productive. The focus is on the course of change and development in the psychic life of the creator leading to useful invention. Still other definitions are formulated in terms of a subjective experience: it is inspired and immanent. Creativity is defined by the flash of insight, the transcendent sensation itself, without reference to whether it will result in anything tangible. Definitions have also centered on the quality of the problem rather than the solution, the significant element in creation being the envisagement of the imaginative problem, for it is the fruitful question to which the novel solution is the response.

None of the existing definitions of creativity is immune from the objection that each omits some component vital to the others. A suggested omnibus definition of creative thinking is: the product has novelty and value for the thinker or the culture; the thinking is unconventional, highly motivated, and persistent, or of great intensity; the task involves a clear formulation of an initially vague and undefined problem (Newell et al. 1962).

1. Identification

The indices or measures of creativity are as varied as the definitions (Getzels and Dillon 1973). In general, the numerous modes of identification may be classified into a half-dozen categories: tangible achievement, ratings, intelligence, personality, biographical characteristics, observation of performance, and psychometric assessment.

The most common mode of identification is by achievement. Deeds and thoughts which reflect manifestly superior accomplishments may be determined, especially in the form of prizes, awards, or other marks of public recognition. Under the assumption that an observer can provide a valid judgment of another person's inventiveness and originality, ratings have been used as an index of creative ability. Since creativity is presumably a function of intellect and the intelligence test is the best available measure of intellectual functioning, a superior IQ has been used as an indication of creative potential. An empirically derived profile of the creative personality is formulated, and the closeness of fit of traits of personality is used as a mode of identification. The distinctive biographical characteristics of persons known to be creative are compiled and then used to predict the future creative performance of other persons by matching the biographical characteristics. Tasks requiring creative ability such as writing a story or formulating a fruitful problem are assigned and the observed performance judged for originality. Finally, just as there are intelligence tests, there are creativity tests like the Remote Associates Test, AC Test of Creative Ability, Torrance Tests of Creative Thinking, and other such psychometric instruments.

2. Theory

The predominant conceptions of creative thinking derive from sources as diverse as classical learning theory, psychometric models of intellect, and psychoanalysis, which do not, of course, exhaust the variety of views.

For associationists, thought is a chain of stimulus–response connections. A problem initiates a succession of previously learned responses to try out in the new situation. There is no fundamental difference between the higher and lower mental functions, between trial-and-error, logical, or creative thought. The creative thinking process consists simply of the forming of associative elements into new combinations that are in some way useful; the more mutually remote the combinatory elements, the more creative the process or solution (Mednick 1976).

For Gestalt theorists, thought does not proceed through trial-and-error associations. It proceeds through cognitive reorganization of a problem situation where there is a structural gap into a solution situation where the gap is closed and the structural trouble disappears. In creative thinking, the unstable structure of the problem situation produces tensions which the creator reduces through a solution that meets these conditions: it does justice to the facts, it fits the personalized view of the creator, it presents the simplest possible structure for the complex set of problematic conditions (Arnheim 1966).

The disagreements among psychometric conceptions

of thought and creativity are equally sharp. Terman founded his *Genetic Studies of Genius* (1925, 1926, 1930, 1947, 1959) on the assumption that the source of giftedness is in superior intellect, and since the general intelligence test is the most valid measure of intellect, a high IQ is the most valid index of giftedness. According to this conception, ability to solve the kinds of problems presented by the intelligence test is the principal ingredient of creative thinking, and intelligence as represented by the IQ metric is the primary determinant of creativity and even of genius.

For factor analysts like Guilford (1950), the aspect of intellect represented by the IQ metric is only one of numerous factors, and not necessarily even the most important one. He disaggregated the factors of intellect, distinguishing especially between convergent and divergent thinking. Convergent thinking is the generation of new information maximally dependent on known information as in most intelligence test problems where the only acceptable solution is a single already-known solution. Divergent thinking is the generation of new information minimally dependent on known information, and the acceptable response to a given problem may be a variety of emergent solutions characterized by fluency, flexibility, originality, and elaboration, which are said to be the principal components of creativity.

Despite Freud's (1961) admonition that before the enigmas of creativity even psychoanalysis must lay down its arms, a steady flow of psychoanalytic studies has provided a distinctive and influential conception of creative thinking. There is a psychic cleavage in thought between unconscious nonrational primary processes and ego-controlled rational secondary processes. The source of creativity is in the unconscious primary processes. When these are not repressed but are sublimated and become ego-syntonic, the conditions exist for acts of creation or "special perfection" (Freud 1959 p. 127). The psychic function of the creation for the creator is the discharge of pent-up tension until a tolerable level of equilibrium is reached.

There are disagreements in psychoanalysis too, neo-psychoanalysts shifting the orthodox emphasis on the unconscious processes (Rothenberg and Hausman 1976 pp. 127–61). It is said that when conscious processes predominate, thinking is rigid since the conscious symbolic functions are anchored in the literal relationships of reality; and when unconscious processes predominate, thinking is even more rigid since anchorage is to an unreality not open to the corrective influence of introspection or experience. Creativity depends on the extent to which preconscious processes can function between the oppressive conscious and unconscious processes (Kubie 1958). In this conception, the unconscious is not the source of creativity but a cause of rigidity.

3. Paradox in Creative Thought

The variety of definitions, modes of identification, and theoretical formulations reflect a key paradox of creative thinking (Getzels 1964). Despite the self-evident need of conscious effort and rationality and the development of reality orientation and logic with age, creative thinking entails at least in part child-like playfulness, fantasy, and the nonrationality of primary-process thought. A pertinent and illuminating distinction has been made between the *cogito* and *intelligo* components of creative thought, the one meaning originally to "shake together" and the other to "select among" (Hadamard 1954). Cogitation and intelligence: on the one hand, to let one's memories, conjectures, fantasies rise freely; on the other, to choose rationally from the emerging combinations the patterns having significance in reality. The several theories seem to focus on one or the other of these components, artificially separating processes which in actuality are inextricably united.

The accounts given by creative thinkers of their thought processes are compelling in this respect. Poincaré tells how he struggled with a mathematical problem to no conclusion and finally turned away from it to go on to a geologic expedition. One day, while engaged on other matters, the solution "appeared" in his mind. He writes of this and other similar experiences, "Most striking at first is this appearance of sudden illumination, a manifest sign of long, unconscious prior work. The role of this unconscious work in mathematical invention appears to me incontestable" (Hadamard 1954 p. 14). A. E. Housman (1955) writes of his poetic creation, "There would flow into my mind, with sudden and unaccountable emotion, sometimes a line or two of verse, sometimes a whole stanza at once, accompanied, not preceded, by a vague notion of the poem which they were destined to form a part of" (p. 91).

Two features of these and many other such accounts are notable. One is the similarity of the descriptions in the arts and sciences. The second is the insistence upon the union of spontaneous, almost involuntary imagination with conscious rational effort. Sometimes the process begins with the conscious effort as in the case of Poincaré, which is then followed by a "sudden illumination"; sometimes the process seems to begin with a sudden illumination as in the case of Housman, which is then worked out by conscious effort. But always there is the alternation and combination of elements from the nonconscious sphere, or what Galton called the "antechamber" of thought, and the conscious sphere, or what Galton called the "presence" chamber of thought (Hadamard 1954 p. 25). When communication between the spheres is cut off, there is on one hand the futility of fantasy out of touch with purpose, or on the other, the sterility of mimetic product untouched by imagination.

4. Problem Finding, Problem Solving, and Creativity

Underlying the prevailing conceptions of creative thinking, despite their apparent disagreements, is a common paradigm of human action that has dominated psychology and education. Implicitly or explicitly, all the conceptions are founded on the homeostatic model of self-maintenance and the drive- or tension-reduction principle of behavior.

The organism's natural state is said to be equilibrium, and the organism always acts so as to avoid the tension of conflicts or problems or, if they are unavoidable, to solve them in order to return to the optimum state of rest and equilibrium. Just as hunger is a problem, generating tensions which motivate the organism to seek a solution in food, so do other problems, including intellectual ones, with which the human being is confronted generate tensions which motivate him or her to seek solutions, which may eventuate in acts of creativity. The motive for thinking is the reduction of tensions generated by problems with which one is confronted; the creator is a person especially adept at solving in novel ways the problems with which he or she is confronted.

Herein lies a critical anomaly. The prevailing conceptions of creativity obscure what artists and scientists themselves say is the distinctive mark of their creative work, namely, that it is as much a process of problem finding or forming as of problem solving. Albert Einstein (Einstein and Infeld 1938) goes further and argues that finding and formulating the problem may be more important than attaining the solution. In his words, "The formulation of a problem may be more important than its solution, which may be merely a matter of mathematical or experimental skill. To raise new questions, new possibilities, to regard old questions from a new angle, requires creative imagination and marks real advance in science" (p. 92). This is true not only in science but in art and in all activities calling for creative thought.

Despite the testimony of scientists and artists regarding the importance of formulating the right problem, the assumption seems to have been both in research and in education that fruitful problems are just there. They need not be sought or their formulation given serious attention. Only answers and solutions need be sought and only their attainment deserves consideration and instruction. Although there are numerous theories, instruments, investigations, and educational programs in problem solving, there is no comparable work in problem finding. The prevailing conceptions of thinking and creativity have focused on the problem of the solution and neglected the problem of the problem (Getzels 1979).

It has not seemed sensible to raise any questions about the meaning or nature of problems. A problem is a problem, an obstacle, a difficulty, and it seemed unnecessary to say anything else. Yet closer examination reveals that different and even contrary phenomena are often subsumed under the single term problem. At one extreme, a problem may refer to an undesirable situation the individual wishes to avoid or mitigate; at the other, it may refer to a desirable situation the individual strives to find or create. It is no contradiction when a doctoral student at the dissertation phase of his or her work says that his or her problem is to find a problem.

Three general types of problem situations may be identified: presented, discovered, and created. In a presented problem situation, a problem exists and it is propounded to the problem solver. A teacher teaches that the area of a rectangle is side a times side b, and the pupil is required to solve the problem: what is the area when a is 3 and b is 4? The problem is a given, and in the particular instance, it has a known formulation, known method of solution, and known solution. All the problem solver has to do is plug the numbers into the formula to attain the solution that matches the already-known solution. There is no need or opportunity for imagination or originality. This is the typical problem situation in the school setting.

In the discovered problem situation, the problem also exists but it is envisaged by oneself rather than propounded by another, and it may not already have a known formulation, known method of solution, or known solution. Roentgen saw a fogged photographic plate as others had before him. But while others paid no attention to it, he asked "Why is the plate fogged?" —a self-initiated problem that led to the X-ray and a revolution in atomic science. Here the problem is not presented to the individual by another; he or she discovers the problem himself or herself, and even takes some pleasure in doing so. This problem situation is much less typical of the school setting.

Finally, there is the created problem situation. Here the problem does not exist until someone invents or creates it. A psychometrician invents a series of problems to test problem-solving abilities; the scientist conceives of the problem: what is the nature and speed of light?; the artist creates a still-life problem where no such problem existed before. It makes no sense to think of these situations as merely obstacles one encounters through accident, ill-fortune, ignorance, or ineptitude. Quite the contrary; these are situations people strive to find and formulate. Indeed, a well-formulated problem is at once a result of knowledge, a stimulus to more knowledge, and, most important, is itself knowledge (Henle 1971). It is the created problem situation that scientists and artists describe as at the foundation of their creative work. Yet it is this type of problem that is hardly ever met with in the school setting.

5. Research

In his presidential address to the American Psychological Association in 1950, Guilford (1950) called attention to the circumstance that up to that time only 186 out of 121,000 entries in *Psychological Abstracts* dealt with creativity. Within a decade following the address, several hundred publications were appearing yearly and were increasing at almost a geometric rate. It is obviously impossible here to do more than touch on several of the major issues from the massive, variegated, and controversial literature, namely, the relations between creativity and intelligence, creativity and educational performance, and the development and characteristics of creative persons.

5.1 Creativity and Intelligence

Even before the advent of the intelligence test, studies reported that some persons of "intellectual type" and "logical power" performed poorly on indices of imagination (Getzels and Jackson 1962). With the greater precision provided by the IQ metric, Terman's study showed that a fourth of the gifted children with IQs of 170 or above had only fair to poor achievement, and Hollingworth (1942) reported that some of her children with the highest possible IQs seemed entirely uncreative.

Creative individuals unquestionably perform better than the average on intelligence tests, but the correlation between the intelligence and the creativity tends to be low to moderate. As one illustration (MacKinnon 1964), the correlation between the rated creativity of 60 eminent architects and their scores on an adult intelligence scale was −0.08. Since it is not possible to identify the creative achievement of children, research with them has most often dealt with the relation between performance on divergent-thinking tests and on intelligence tests. Although the hundreds of reported correlations vary from 0 to +0.7 depending on the divergent-thinking tests, the heterogeneity of the sample, and the nature of the testing situation, a recent review of the work (Barron and Harrington 1981) gives +0.3 as a "reasonable estimate" of the central tendency.

5.2 Creativity and Performance in School

The unexpected observation by Getzels and Jackson (1962) that despite a 23-point difference in IQ, their high-creativity and high-IQ groups performed equally well on standard measures of achievement gave rise to a number of studies with similar and discrepant results. Explanations for the diversity of results called attention to the possible effects of relative rigidity and permissiveness in the learning conditions of the schools, and of systematic interactions between convergent and divergent teachers and convergent and divergent pupils.

Three other observations regarding the relation between creativity and school performance are worthy of note. Students with high divergent-thinking scores seem to do better as they progress up the academic ladder; at age 15, the diverger is less academically successful than the converger but by college entrance the balance has tended to redress itself (Hudson 1968). British students in the humanities were found to be relatively weaker in IQ and better in divergent-thinking tests, while those in science were the reverse (Hudson 1966). Although here as elsewhere, there are contrary observations, the preponderance of observations shows that teachers tend to prefer the high-IQ over the high-creative student (Torrance 1962a).

The experience of the creative student in the educational setting is complicated in the extreme. Presumably school is where creative talent should be recognized and nurtured. Yet in practice, educational institutions at all levels may so focus on academic performance to the exclusion of all else that they not only obscure potential creative talent but act as an incubus to its expression.

The experience of some American novelists is instructive (Hattam 1968). James Fenimore Cooper was expelled from Yale. Herman Melville left school before he was 15 years old. Hawthorne, who graduated from Bowdoin, wrote that he was "an idle student, negligent of college rules, rather choosing to nurse my own fancies." Stephen Crane attended Lafayette College but did not graduate. Mark Twain and Sherwood Anderson went to work at the beginning of their teens. William Faulkner's education was irregular after the fifth grade, and he did not graduate from high school. Ernest Hemingway graduated from high school but did not go to college. F. Scott Fitzgerald failed a third of his courses at Princeton and maintained a D average in the rest. After publishing *This Side of Paradise*, he wrote the president, "It was a book written with the bitterness of my discovery that I had spent several years trying to fit in with a curriculum that is after all made for the average student."

Had school achievement alone been used as the criterion of creativity, these individuals would surely have been counted among the uncreative, as no doubt students with talent in other fields have also been. To cite the classic case, Albert Einstein's headmaster told his father that Albert would "never make a success at anything," and Albert was expelled from high school with the admonition, "Your presence in the class is disruptive and affects the other students" (Clark 1971 pp. 10, 12).

5.3 Development and Characteristics of Creative Persons

In creativity as in other aspects of human development, the heredity–environment issue is not yet amenable to fruitful investigation. Studies have instead revolved around such problems as the influence of age, family background, and child-rearing practices. Although none of the results is unequivocal, some generalizations may be ventured if it is understood that there are the inevitable exceptions to what seems to be the rule.

Adult creativity tends to mature early and reach its highest point in the 30s, but there are significant variations by field of endeavor, achievement in mathematics being earlier than in, say, philosophy (Lehman 1953). Since few criteria of creative accomplishment for children are available, their creative development has typically been studied through performance on divergent-thinking tests. Observations in the United States have revealed the following: an increase in divergent-thinking abilities from age 3 to 4½; a drop upon entry to kindergarten; a rise and then a sharp drop at about the fourth grade; and a relatively steady rise, albeit with some gender and test variation, through grade 11. This pattern varies in different cultures and for black American children (Torrance 1962b).

Most of the research has focused on family influences and child-rearing practices (Getzels and Dillon 1973). Significant birth-order effects have appeared with substantial consistency, first-born males being more creative than later-born siblings. Mothers of more creative children were found to be less restrictive and more self-assured. They preferred change, valued autonomy, and were less sociable, conscientious, and inhibited. They were less concerned with making a favorable impression and less nurturant or obliging toward others. These are traits suggesting that the mothers of creative children may themselves be more creative than the general population and foster creativity in their children through the force of their own unstereotyped behavior.

Although studies of single characteristics of creative persons often produced inconsistent observations, certain patterns of characteristics appeared quite systematically. Creative persons in a variety of fields exhibited the same pattern of values and interpersonal relations, including high theoretical and aesthetic values, high self-sufficiency, introversion, greater concern with ideas than with people, and disinterest in social activities. They also exhibited a common pattern of perception and cognition, including preference for complexity, independent judgment, resistance to group pressures, and willingness to take risks. Children who were judged creative were humorous in their free associations and aspired to unconventional rather than conventional careers. Although there is a long tradition that creative performance is related to neuroticism, a number of studies with a variety of children found no relation between measures of creativity and measures of emotional disorder.

With rare exceptions (Torrance and Wu 1981), studies of the development and characteristics of creative persons are retrospective, carried out after the artist or scientist had become worthy of biographical notice. A unique developmental study (Getzels and Csikszentmihalyi 1976) took a different approach; it was prospective, that is, it was a longitudinal investigation of would-be male artists from the time they undertook serious study at one of the leading museum-connected art schools in the United States to the time they became or failed to become professional artists. This permitted the observation of events in the life of the developing artist up close instead of reconstructing them from the hindsight of an already eminent artist, and it permitted the observation not only of those who undertook to become artists and succeeded but also those who, with apparently equal graphic talent, failed, allowing developmental comparison not ordinarily possible.

Instead of the typical retrospective account of art as a calling that attracted the graphically talented person with the finality of a divine order, the prospective investigation revealed an intricate web of actions and reactions which led to a career that was often not so much engineered as fortuitous. The first attempts at drawing were cartoons and copies of comic book figures, which were not substantially superior than those of other children. But their drawings were noticed and praised, and became ways by which the future artists gained attention and demonstrated competence just as other children did through athletics, school achievement, or good looks.

Elementary and secondary school were bleak experiences. Sports, the main way of gaining recognition for most boys, were usually alien and threatening for the future artists. They turned ever more to drawing, which progressively became not merely a demonstration of competence but a means of self-expression and self-affirmation. Even so, the decision to become an artist did not come easily. Many tried other activities before enrolling in art school. The most important determinant of whether to apply one's graphic talent to fine art, art education, advertising, or industrial art was the values that were held. Although all the art students held significantly higher aesthetic and theoretical and lower social and economic values than the norms, those with the highest aesthetic values chose fine art, those with the highest social values chose art education, and those with the highest economic values chose advertising or industrial art.

A number of personal, school, and family characteristics, including lack of concern for social approval, high ratings in originality and artistic potential by their instructors, and family affluence were related to the success of the former art students in becoming successful fine artists after graduation from art school. There was a strong unanticipated and inexplicable effect of sibling position. Eldest sons accounted for 81 percent of the successful artists as against only 33 percent of the unsuccessful ones; 53 percent of the unsuccessful artists and none of the successful ones were middle sons. Perhaps the most intriguing and pedagogically relevant observation pertained to the role of problem finding in creative achievement. Not only was superiority in problem finding related to the originality of a drawing produced at the art school but the ratings in problem finding while in art school were related to success as professional fine artists 5 to 6 years after graduation from the school.

6. Educational Issues

It is evident that no single set of educational principles can be drawn from the extant work on creativity. The definitions, modes of identification, theoretical formulations, and research results are all too diverse to permit unequivocal conclusions. It is, however, possible to raise a number of illustrative issues for further consideration by teachers and investigators.

First, with respect to the kinds of problems dealt with in the classroom, a distinction can be made among presented, discovered, and created problems differing in the opportunity they provide for creative thinking. What is the effect of the quantitatively different representation of those problems in the classroom on the students' modes of thinking and learning?

Second, although such broad categories as convergent and divergent thinking do not exhaust the possibilities, they do suggest the possible existence of different styles of both learning and teaching, the one style focusing rather more on the acquisition of skills and established knowledge, the other on the cultivation of imagination and creativity. What is the effect of the interaction of those different styles among students and teachers?

Third, there is a paradox in teaching for creative thinking. On the one hand, solving problems requires conscious effort, possession of already-known facts, application of well-honed skills, rationality of attack, that is, aspects of so-called secondary-process thought. On the other, creative thinking seems to entail, at least in some degree, regressive childlike playfulness, acceptance of fantasy, toleration of nonrational impulse, that is, aspects of so-called primary-process thought. How can instruction proceed in developing secondary-process thought without thereby irrevocably cutting the person off from all aspects of primary-process thought, and conversely of course, how can encouragement of the acceptance of primary-process thought proceed without thereby derogating the indispensability of secondary-process thought?

Finally, from the inception of interest in fostering creativity in the classroom, two lines of instructional strategy have been proposed. One line bids to foster creative thinking through revising the curriculum material and teaching methods in the specific subjects taught, the other through instituting courses of instruction in creative thinking as such. It would be comforting to be able to say with assurance that the one is superior to the other, or under these conditions this strategy is superior and under those the other. This is not yet possible in any systematic way. The strategies raise once more the age-old unsettled educational issue of learning sets and transfer. Can a set for creative thinking be taught, and if it can, is such a set most effectively taught as a specific skill in a given subject or as a general attitude or talent transferable across the entire gamut of school subjects and beyond?

Bibliography

Arnheim R 1966 *Toward a Psychology of Art: Collected Essays*. University of California Press, Berkeley, California
Barron F, Harrington D M 1981 Creativity, intelligence, and personality. *Ann. Rev. Psychol.* 32: 439–76
Clark R W 1971 *Einstein: The Life and Times*. World Publishing, New York
Einstein A, Infeld L 1938 *The Evolution of Physics: The Growth of Ideas from Early Concepts to Relativity and Quanta*. Simon and Schuster, New York
Freud S 1959 The unconscious. In: Riviere J (ed.) 1959 *Collected Papers*, Vol. 4. Basic Books, New York
Freud S 1961 Dostoevsky and parricide. In: Strachey J (ed.) 1961 *Standard Edition of the Collected Works of Sigmund Freud*, Vol. 21. Hogarth Press, London
Getzels J W 1964 Creative thinking, problem solving, and instruction. In: Hilgard E R (ed.) 1964 *Theories of Learning and Instruction*. Sixty-third Yearbook of the National Society for the Study of Education, Part I. University of Chicago Press, Chicago, Illinois, pp. 240–67
Getzels J W 1979 Problem finding: A theoretical note. *Cognit. Sci.* 3: 167–72
Getzels J W, Csikszentmihalyi M 1976 *The Creative Vision: A Longitudinal Study of Problem Finding in Art*. Wiley, New York
Getzels J W, Dillon J M 1973 Giftedness and the education of the gifted. In: Travers R M W (ed.) 1973 *Second Handbook of Research on Teaching: A Project of the American Educational Research Association*. Rand McNally, Chicago, Illinois, pp. 689–731
Getzels J W, Jackson P W 1962 *Creativity and Intelligence: Explorations with Gifted Students*. Wiley, New York
Guilford J P 1950 Creativity. *Am. Psychol.* 5: 444–54
Hadamard J S 1954 *The Psychology of Invention in the Mathematical Field*. Dover, New York
Hattam E 1968 The school days of our novelists: The case for creativity. *Teach. Coll. Rec.* 69: 459–64
Henle M 1971 The snail beneath the shell. *Abraxas* 1: 119–33
Hollingworth L S 1942 *Children above 180 IQ, Stanford-Binet: Origin and Development*. World Book, Yonkers-on-Hudson, New York
Housman A E 1955 The name and nature of poetry. In: Ghiselin B (ed.) 1955 *The Creative Process: A Symposium*. New American Library, New York
Hudson L 1966 *Contrary Imaginations: A Psychological Study of the English Schoolboy*. Methuen, London
Hudson L 1968 *Frames of Mind: Ability, Perception and Self-perception in the Arts and Sciences*. Methuen, London
Kubie L S 1958 *Neurotic Distortion of the Creative Process*. University of Kansas Press, Lawrence, Kansas
Lehman H C 1953 *Age and Achievement*. Princeton University Press, Princeton, New Jersey
MacKinnon D W 1964 The creativity of architects. In: Taylor C W (ed.) 1964 *Widening Horizons in Creativity*. Proc. 5th Utah Creativity Research Conf. New York, 1962. Wiley, New York
Mednick S A 1976 The associative basis of the creative process. In: Rothenberg A, Hausman C R (eds.) 1976 *The Creativity Question*. Duke University Press, Durham, North Carolina
Newell A, Shaw J C, Simon H A 1962 The process of creative thinking. In: Gruber H E, Terrell G, Wertheimer M (eds.) 1962 *Contemporary Approaches to Creative Thinking*. Atherton Press, New York
Rothenberg A, Hausman C R (eds.) 1976 *The Creativity Question*. Duke University Press, Durham, North Carolina
Terman L M (ed.) 1925–1959 *Genetic Studies of Genius*, Vols. 1–5. Stanford University Press, Stanford, California
Torrance E P 1962a *Guiding Creative Talent*. Prentice-Hall, Englewood Cliffs, New Jersey
Torrance E P 1962b Cultural discontinuities and the development of originality of thinking. *Excep. Child.* 29: 2–13
Torrance E P, Wu T 1981 A comparative longitudinal study of the adult creative achievements of elementary school children identified as highly intelligent and as highly creative. *Creative Child and Adult Q.* 6: 71–76

Creativity and Individual Development

D. K. Simonton

Creativity is usually conceived as a quality possessed by those persons who generate products that are simultaneously original and adaptive. The relevance of originality as a criterion is clear, for few would claim that a product is creative without first noting that it is novel, surprising, or unusual in a distinct manner. At the same time, the requirement that the original product be adaptive is no less crucial; otherwise creativity could not be segregated from the merely bizarre or insane. Much of the research on creativity has concentrated on the creative process, person, or product, although considerable work has been devoted to understanding the acquisition of creative potential. These studies of creative development have tended to pursue one of two major strategies.

1. Research Strategies

The first method begins with the identification of gifted children or adolescents, commonly on the basis of their performance on some "creativity test" or other psychometric instrument. Next, the investigators search for the developmental events that set these select young people apart from their less talented peers. Ideally, gifted children should be followed long enough over time for it to become possible fully to appraise how youthful promise translates into adult accomplishment. A classic illustration of this longitudinal approach may be found in Terman's (1925) *Genetic Studies of Genius*, one of the most ambitious inquiries ever conducted. Terman used the Stanford–Binet intelligence measure to pick a sample of gifted children, and then started to trace their development well into adulthood. At the time of writing, this investigation is still in progress.

The second research strategy works backwards, or retrospectively, by exploiting historical data. The biographies of eminent creators are systematically examined for early childhood and adolescent factors that may have contributed to the development of their creative potential. This alternative historiometric approach is exemplified by Cox's (1926) *The Early Mental Traits of Three Hundred Geniuses*, which comprises the second volume of Terman's magnum opus. She began with a collection of notable geniuses (like Copernicus, Darwin, Descartes, Cervantes, Leonardo da Vinci, and Beethoven), gathered extensive biographical data on their early development, and then assessed the origins of their adult success, with special focus on the role of precocious intellect. To this day, Cox's study is continually cited as the source of estimated IQ scores for various historical personalities.

The longitudinal and historical perspectives on creative development differ immensely in their comparative assets and liabilities. The former method begins with contemporary individuals who can be easily assessed on a wide range of developmental variables, yet the validity of the criteria by which the gifted children are selected cannot be really known for decades. The latter method has no problem demonstrating the validity of the selection criteria, for it begins with universally acclaimed creative geniuses, yet the biographical information is not always reliable enough to gauge some central developmental factors. Despite the obvious contrasts in these two modes of approach, the empirical research has tended to converge on a set of established findings regarding the developmental trends in creativity. The following seven results perhaps stand out.

2. Characteristics of Creativity Development

(a) A series of investigations spanning over a century have consistently demonstrated the impact of birth order on creative development. For instance, first-born children, especially first sons in the family, enjoy higher odds of attaining distinction in the sciences, whereas artistic creativity appears to be more characteristic of later born children. A child's birth order apparently affects the acquisition of creative potential by influencing the course of both intellectual and personality development.

(b) Those who achieve success in creative endeavors tended to have suffered a higher incidence of parental loss, particularly orphanhood, in comparison to the norm. The presence of such early trauma is most conspicuous in those who exhibit artistic forms of creativity, especially poetry. This effect has been attributed to a bereavement syndrome, as well as to disrupted socialization.

(c) Marked childhood precocity is virtually commonplace among those who demonstrate exceptional creativity as adults. Outstanding creative individuals tend to be intellectually precocious, as revealed in high IQ scores and in early voracious and omnivorous reading. Extraordinary precocity is most evident in mathematical and musical types of creative expression.

(d) Early exposure to creative role models contributes to the development of creative potential. Thus, the amount of creativity evinced by one generation is directly proportional to the availability of suitable role models in the preceding generation. Role-model availability, in fact, is positively related to a youthful exhibition of creative precocity. Although excessive identification with a single model can lead to debilitating imitation, this danger is mitigated by selecting multiple models and by favoring those models more remote in time. In the case of models who serve as personal mentors, developing creators gain most from those teachers who are themselves at their creative peak, which is normally somewhere in the late 30s or early 40s.

(e) Creative development is nurtured by the availability of cultural enrichment in the homes of the gifted. The parents of future creators tend to display a broad array of intellectual and aesthetic hobbies and interests, accompanied by a love of learning that encourages the developing child to explore the ample materials available in the immediate environment. Books and magazines of a stimulating variety are common, and family trips to museums, galleries, and expositions frequent. The home atmosphere favors diversity, freedom, and autonomy.

(f) The prevailing political milieu may deflect creative development in either a positive or a negative direction. Political events that enlarge the influx of cultural diversity tend to raise the magnitude of creativity witnessed in the next generation. The beneficial effects, after a one-generation lag, of popular rebellions and nationalistic revolts against the pervasive homogenization of large empires illustrate this point. In contrast, international war, if sufficiently extensive, can thwart creative development, at least to the extent that creativity is most compatible with an individualistic disposition. Most striking, however, is the adverse developmental consequence of political instability—when coups d'état, military revolts, assassinations, and other internecine struggles among the power elite yield a state of anarchy at the top. Those potential creators exposed to these conditions in late childhood, adolescence, and early adulthood are less likely to exhibit creativity in maturity. This negative effect is especially prominent in the more scientific and philosophical fields where a belief in logic and order is essential. By comparison, creative development in the visual arts, which does not require the same acquisition of a rational worldview, seems unaffected by political instability. That the growth of creativity is contingent on the political milieu helps explain why some nations fail altogether to produce creators of the highest caliber.

(g) Education leaves a definite impression on the emergence of creative potential in the child and adolescent. Even if the correlation between scholastic success (as gauged by honors or the "grade point average") and adult creativity is essentially zero, the level of formal education obtained is related to creative potential. Specifically, eventual distinction in a creative endeavor is a curvilinear "inverted-U" function of the final educational level reached. In concrete terms, creative development tends to increase as an individual passes through elementary- and secondary-school training, but begins to turn around in college, and then declines in professional or graduate school. The optimum amount of education appears somewhere in the last two years of undergraduate instruction, albeit the peak occurs somewhat later for the scientific disciplines. Although this curve warns that higher education may

not always contribute in a positive way to the acquisition of creative potential, an optimistic side of this result deserves emphasis: the first dozen years of formal instruction are apparently favorable to creative development. Only when education becomes overly specialized may it become detrimental to such growth.

The precise theoretical meanings of the foregoing findings are still subject to some debate. The most favored explanation is that certain environmental circumstances nurture the development of creative potential. Creativity demands the cognitive capacity to combine ideas in novel ways, an ability that presupposes a memory which consists of richly interconnected concepts. Many measures that purport to tap creativity in fact gauge a person's skill at generating remote associations or some other form of "divergent" thinking. Even if the long-term validity of these tests has yet to be proven, the possibility remains that the intellectual structure requisite for creative thought depends on the extent that an individual was exposed to a diversified array of unconventional experiences. Such developmental antecedents as orphanhood, role model availability, family cultural enrichment, and education represent some of the routes to acquiring the needed exposure.

This nurture viewpoint, on the other hand, is sometimes countered by the nature position which says that such developmental trends and tendencies simply reflect superior genetic endowment. For example, it may be that children and adolescents who are innately gifted with supreme creative powers will instinctively seek out the proper role models and educational level. Even so, despite the fact that certain developmental variables, such as precocity, can be readily explicated in these terms, other factors are much less amenable to this treatment. It is hard to argue, for instance, that the effects of birth order, parental loss, and the political milieu are genotypic rather than experiential.

To some degree, of course, this ancient controversy should be resolved before making practical recommendations. The nurture outlook leads to numerous suggestions about how to construct an environment most sympathetic to creative development, whereas the nature perspective in its most extreme form simply argues that the genes will always win out no matter how dramatic the attempted intervention. It makes an obvious difference whether a creative individual is made after birth or born ready made. Nevertheless, the weight of the evidence seems to side with the nurture explanation for most developmental variables, and even some of the supposed genetic effects are not without useful implications. Therefore, three practical repercussions of the enumerated results can be put forward, however tentatively.

3. Applications of Research Results

To begin with, many of the seven developmental trends listed above can help us identify which young people hold the most promise as future creative adults. Precocity is a case in point; it is a wise practice adopted by some school systems to separate out precocious children and adolescents for special programs for the gifted. The advantage of this criterion is especially evident in those activities where, as noted earlier, precocity is rather common, as in mathematical and musical creativity.

In addition, certain developmental effects suggest means for more actively encouraging creative development rather than merely passively identifying those who have promise. The parents can strive to enrich the home with cultural materials, and infuse their children with the curiosity to freely explore that environment. Also, institutions of higher learning may wish to investigate methods for rendering even advanced graduate training an occasion more akin to the creative development of students. Nevertheless, it must be acknowledged that not all factors conducive to creative development are easily manipulated, the political milieu providing the most obvious example.

Finally, all of these applications, whether identification or encouragement, must take care to distinguish between scientific and artistic modes of creativity. The events and conditions that encourage (or discourage) the creative development of an artist may discourage (or encourage) the emergence of a creative scientist. The differential consequence of birth order for success in the arts and sciences is one example, and the different locations of the optimal educational level for the two varieties of creativity is another. Thus, in some instances a parent, educational system, or society must establish priorities as to which sort of creativity is most desirable, a value judgment which, naturally, lies outside the province of empirical research.

Bibliography

Albert R S (ed.) 1983 *Genius and Eminence*. Pergamon, Oxford

Bloom B S 1985 *Developing Talent in Young People*. Ballantine, New York

Cox C M 1926 *The Early Mental Traits of Three Hundred Geniuses*. Stanford University Press, Stanford, California

Dennis W, Dennis M W (eds.) 1976 *The Intellectually Gifted*. Grune and Stratton, New York

Goertzel M G, Goertzel V, Goertzel T G 1978 *Three Hundred Eminent Personalities*. Jossey-Bass, San Francisco, California

Gowan J C, Khatena J, Torrance E P (eds.) 1979 *Educating the Ablest: A Book of Readings on the Education of Gifted Children*, 2nd edn. F E Peacock, Itasca, Illinois

Hudson L 1966 *Contrary Imaginations*. Methuen, London

Lehman H C 1953 *Age and Achievement*. Princeton University Press, Princeton, New Jersey

Simonton D K 1984 *Genius, Creativity, and Leadership*. Harvard University Press, Cambridge, Massachusetts

Simonton D K 1987 Developmental antecedents of achieved eminence. *Ann. Child Dev.* 5: 131–69

Sternberg R J 1988 *The Nature of Creativity*. Cambridge University Press, Cambridge

Sternberg R J, Davidson J E (eds.) 1986 *Conceptions of Giftedness*. Cambridge University Press, Cambridge

Terman L 1925 *Genetic Studies of Genius*. Stanford University Press, Stanford, California

Spatial Cognition

L. P. Acredolo

The term *spatial cognition* is generally used by developmental psychologists to refer to the knowledge children have about the spatial layouts of the large-scale environments which surround them and within which they move. Encompassed within this definition is the traditional term *cognitive mapping*; excluded, however, are other spatial phenomena such as the development of depth perception, spatial localization of sounds, object integrity, and object permanence. Although these phenomena are obviously relevant to knowledge of one's environment, it is generally held that dealing with the spatial relations characteristic of the environment beyond the child's reach involves concepts and processes qualitatively distinct from those apprehended more locally. The very fact, for example, that many environments must be viewed from multiple vantage points in order to be seen in their entirety yields the possibility that mental representation and integration play a larger role in this type of spatial problem than in other equally "spatial" domains.

Interest in the topic arose in part from Piaget's many formal and informal attempts to assess such knowledge in order to describe the development of abstract spatial notions in infants and children (e.g., topological versus projective versus Euclidean geometries). The field, however, has gone well beyond Piaget in the types of questions asked and methods used to assess spatial cognition. Even excluding some of the more basic spatial capacities listed above, the list of topics which have come under scrutiny by those interested in spatial cognition is long. Questions asked include how and how well infants and children conceptualize their environments, how well they maintain their orientation when moving themselves or being moved, what role self-produced locomotion plays in the development of these conceptualizations, how to account for individual differences in these abilities, what role landmarks play in spatial representations at different ages, how the ability to externalize one's knowledge of the environment develops (i.e., production or use of maps), and whether or not children's representations of large-scale spaces are subject to the same types of distortions typically found among adults.

1. Theoretical Distinctions

Research in this area has been aided immeasurably by the efforts of Liben (1981) to distinguish among three different types of spatial representations and two different levels of inquiry. The former include *spatial products*, *spatial storage*, and *spatial thought*, and the latter include *specific* versus *abstract* questions about development. According to Liben, those who study developments in the child's ability to produce an externalized, concrete representation of a spatial layout (e.g., a model or map) are studying *spatial products*. In contrast, those who seek information about the spatial facts, notions, or propositions stored "in the head" and relevant to environmental behavior or the production of spatial products are asking questions about *spatial storage*. This is essentially the individual's database in memory and, as such, the information need not be available at a conscious level in order to inform behavior, just as explicit knowledge of the rules of grammar is unnecessary for actual speech. It is spatial storage which most closely fits the traditional notion of "cognitive maps." Because it is not always explicitly available to the child, information about spatial storage must usually be inferred from spatial behavior. Finally, the term *spatial thought* is used to refer to attempts by the individual to apply procedures to information from the database so that the information is brought to consciousness and manipulated in some way (e.g., imagined, rotated, measured, compared). Clearly any one or any combination of these types of spatial phenomena can be the object of developmental study. Moreover, each one can be assessed with either the understanding of large-scale environmental knowledge as one's specific goal or in order to yield information about the development of abstract notions of space held independent of any specific environmental encounter (e.g. horizontality versus verticality, topological versus projective versus Euclidean spatial knowledge). Both goals are subsumed under the title "spatial cognition," and it is usually possible to see the results of a given study as applicable at either level.

2. Frames of Reference

Perhaps the most frequently encountered finding in the spatial cognition literature is the observation that older children do better than younger children in their attempts to recall information about large-scale space. Taken alone, this pattern tells us very little about the nature of the development of spatial cognition. What is needed in addition is some explanation for these "ontogenetic" changes—that is, some clue as to the nature of the underlying strategies or capacities which mediate the superior performance of the older child. Of parallel interest are the frequently observed "microgenetic" changes in spatial cognition apparent at every age level. What is being referred to here are the improvements that almost invariably accrue with increased exposure to a specific environment. Familiarity may "breed contempt," but it also breeds greater knowledge of spatial layout, greater confidence in orienting, and more sophistication in mental manipulations of the spatial information available. Such changes over time are also subsumed under the rubric of "development," but the focus is obviously on short-term rather than long-term change, or "microgenetic" rather than "ontogenetic" development.

One attempt to explain the improvements that have been observed within both of these developmental domains involves the delineation of different frames of reference which can be used to help an individual mentally organize the specific information encountered within a space. Used in this way, the term *frame of reference* refers to a set of specific cues or spatial relations which serve to help the individual define or encode in memory the positions of objects within the environment. Three such frames of reference (egocentric, fixed feature, and abstract) have been most frequently mentioned, and there is increasing evidence suggesting that they tend to occur in a particular order across development, thus accounting in part for differences observed both ontogenetically and microgenetically (Acredolo 1981, 1985, Hart and Moore 1973, Pick and Lockman 1981).

This developmental progression begins with preference for reliance on an egocentric system in which positions are encoded with regard to the relation between objects and the individual's body (e.g., left/right of self). Such a system operates quite effectively to structure space, but only as long as the individual remains immobile. This important limitation to its applicability, however, is in part off-set by the ease with which egocentric relations can be detected and retained, thus making it a viable strategy for both infants and for older individuals encountering an environment for the first time. The next step in development is thought to be appreciation of allocentric frames of reference, organizing systems which are independent of the location of the individual's body within the space. Such allocentric systems include frames of reference based upon relations among specific objects, either in very simple forms such as paired associations between a site to be remembered and a specific landmark ("fixed feature"), or a more advanced construction of multiple object–object relations into an overall configuration in which many object–object relations are represented. At an even more advanced level, an allocentric frame of reference can be dependent on completely abstract systems of relations, such as the use of the cardinal directions (north, south, east, and west) to develop a configurational representation of specific locations. Such a system involves levels of cognitive sophistication thought to develop in middle to late childhood as part of the more general trend toward what Piaget refers to as "formal operational reasoning." With this basic outline of developmental change in mind, one can turn to consideration of specific age changes which have been observed in spatial cognition.

3. Developmental Trends

3.1 Birth to 18 Months

The infancy period is generally treated as a distinct developmental phase when it comes to delineating the child's knowledge of large-scale space. The reason lies in the initial immaturity of many of the underlying capacities fundamental to spatial perception as well as spatial cognition (e.g., visual acuity and depth perception). Of equal importance, however, is the fact that the infant is incapable of self-produced locomotion until approximately 7–9 months of age. It is this latter limitation which led researchers to predict that an egocentric frame of reference might be relatively more important during infancy than later in development, a prediction which has been confirmed in many studies of the first 18 months of life (Acredolo 1985). Before the onset of self-locomotion, infants generally seem inclined to encode location based on relations between self and object, probably as a result of accumulated successful uses of the rule "If I turn this way, I can expect to see X again." Such a rule is an example of the type of contingency learning very easily achieved during infancy and serves the infant quite well until the onset of mobility both negates these relations and increases the infant's motivation for retaining accurate location information. In fact, the onset of self-produced location— either in the form of crawling or experience in a walker—has been demonstrated to mark the onset of greater reliance on allocentric information (Bertenthal et al. 1984). It is at this point that we see infants more reliably capable of compensating for a change in their location in space by referring to the objective spatial information available in object–object relations, a change that is often referred to in terms of a developing appreciation for landmark information.

3.2 The Toddler Years

Once the child is mobile, the next advance seems to be a cognitive one, namely an increased mental ability to represent information and a concomitant decline in dependence on immediate perception. The availability of such representations means also that mental manipulation of the information is possible, at least to solve very simple spatial problems. This translates into the ability to make simple detours, to translate simple spatial information obtained from one perspective (aerial) to another perspective (nonaerial), and to point accurately at objects no longer in sight. Each one of these abilities, however, continues to undergo developmental change during this period and the ones to follow, mainly in the direction of application in increasingly complex situations. For example, the ability to point towards out-of-sight objects at 24 months is limited to objects occluded by a barrier within the same room. When asked to point to objects after a walk to an adjacent room, the 2- to 3-year-old instead tends to point at the doorway through which he or she passed. It is not until about $3\frac{1}{2}$ years that this response is replaced by appreciation of the actual spatial relations involved (Rider and Rieser 1988).

3.3 Preschool and Elementary School Years

In general we see during these years increased sophistication in the skills first manifest in the 2- to 3-year-old. The ability to point to objects out of sight improves considerably, although not to adult standards until late childhood (e.g., Pick and Lockman 1979, Hardwick et al. 1976). Increases are also seen in the ability to detect alternative routes to goals and to model familiar environments using three-dimensional materials. Appreciation of maps seems to have its rudimentary beginnings during the preschool years (Bluestein and Acredolo 1979), and increases from then on in knowledge of both cartographic conventions and the ability to abstract location information from aligned and non-aligned maps. Thus, by the end of this period, we see children capable of constructing and using both mental and physical representations of familiar spaces which display coordinated, configurational knowledge of object–object relations.

4. Factors Influencing Spatial Cognition

4.1 Intra-individual Variables

It is true in general that the greater the extent to which an individual explores a new environment, the more accurate and sophisticated (within a given developmental level) will be the resulting spatial knowledge. Thus, factors which influence exploration of a space will, in turn, effect knowledge of that space. The sex of the child is one such factor, with boys being allotted greater freedom to explore unfamiliar environments than girls. Another factor which has been identified is the strength of the attachment between primary caretaker and infant, the logic being that a good relationship provides the child with a secure "home base" from which to explore the world. In support of this theory, Hazen and Durrett (1982) report more exploration of an unfamiliar environment and greater spatial knowledge among $2\frac{1}{2}$-year-olds with a history of a secure attachment than among a comparable group with a history of insecure attachments. Finally, it is quite conceivable that innate differences in temperament might influence exploration through the operation of mediating variables such as activity level, ability to adapt to novelty, and sensitivity to changes in stimulation. Research in support of this hypothesis, however, has yet to be carried out.

4.2 Effect of Active versus Passive Exploration

It is a common observation that one recalls more about a route when one is driving the car than when one is merely a passenger. This phenomenon has been the focus of research aimed at delineating the advantage that active exploration gives over passive exploration at various points in development. The results of this research are fairly straightforward. Even from its beginnings in infancy, self-directed movement yields better spatial knowledge than other-directed (passive) movement when the task requires integration of multiple perspectives of an environment. The reason is that self-directed travel increases even an infant's attention to relevant spatial information. However, if the spatial relations necessary to solve a problem are all visible from a single perspective, then active movement within the space detracts from rather than enhances performance because the movement from point to point necessitates an effort to integrate the different viewpoints encountered. In such situations, "passive" viewing from a single vantage point yields better results (Acredolo 1985, Cohen 1982). Finally, the act of completing functionally related activities within an environment apparently yields better knowledge of the spatial layout of the activity sites than does random, unorganized activity (Cohen 1982). Thus, the *type* of experience is as important as the *amount* of experience in predicting effects on spatial knowlege during infancy and childhood.

5. Educational Implications

The research results outlined above provide educators with useful information both about ways to promote and ways to use the child's spatial cognition skills. Curricula designed, for example, to make explicit the types of implicit knowledge children have about space would seem worthwhile. This might include introduction of the notion of reference systems and active versus passive exploration. Games could be devised to promote reliance on one system rather than another, to compare self-directed and other-directed movement, or to practice pointing at unseen objects in other parts of the environment. The ways in which hills, fences, and other obstacles divide space and distort our impressions of distance and direction could easily be demonstrated, as could the power of landmarks to clarify one's location in space. Discussions of what constitutes a good landmark, what kinds of activities promote spatial knowledge, and what possibilities for pleasure exist in exploring the unknown would all be worthwhile. All of these would constitute stimulating additions to the traditional emphasis on cartography already present in most curricula.

Bibliography

Acredolo L P 1981 Small- and large-scale spatial concepts in infancy and childhood. In: Liben L S, Patterson A H, Newcombe N (eds.) 1981 *Spatial Representation and Behavior Across the Life Span.* Academic Press, New York, pp. 63–81
Acredolo L P 1985 Coordinating perspectives on infant spatial orientation. In: Cohen R (ed.) 1985 *The Development of Spatial Cognition.* Lawrence Erlbaum, Hillsdale, New Jersey, pp. 115–140
Bertenthal B, Campos J J, Barrett K C 1984 Self-produced locomotion: An organizer of emotional, cognitive, and social development in infancy. In: Emde R N, Harmon R J (eds.) 1984 *Continuities and Discontinuities in Development.* Plenum, New York
Bluestein N, Acredolo L P 1979 Developmental changes in map-reading skills. *Child Dev.* 50: 691–97
Cohen R (ed.) 1982 *Children's Conceptions of Spatial Relations,* New Directions for Child Development No. 15. Jossey-Bass, San Francisco, California
Cohen R (ed.) 1985 *The Development of Spatial Cognition.* Lawrence Erlbaum, Hillsdale, New Jersey
Hardwick D A, McIntyre C W, Pick H L Jr 1976 The content and manipulation of cognitive maps in children and adults. *Monogr. Soc. Res. Child Dev.* 41, No. 3 (Serial No. 166). University of Chicago Press, Chicago, Illinois
Hart R A, Moore G T 1973 The development of spatial cognition: A review. In: Downs R M, Stea D (eds.) 1973 *Image and Environment.* Aldine. Chicago, Illinois, pp. 246–88
Hazen N L, Durrett M E 1982 Relationship of security of attachment to exploration and cognitive mapping abilities in 2-year-olds. *Dev. Psychol.* 18: 751–59
Liben L S 1981 Spatial representation and behavior: Multiple perspectives. In: Liben L S, Patterson A H, Newcombe N (eds.) 1981 *Spatial Representation and Behavior Across the Life Span.* Academic Press, New York, pp. 3–36
Pick H L Jr, Acredolo L P (eds.) 1983 *Spatial Orientation: Theory, Research, and Application.* Plenum Press, New York
Pick H L Jr, Lockman J J 1981 From frames of reference to spatial representations. In: Liben L S, Patterson A H, Newcombe N (eds.) 1981 *Spatial Representation and Behavior Across the Life Span.* Academic Press, New York, pp. 36–61
Rider E A, Rieser J J 1988 Pointing at objects in other rooms: Young children's sensitivity to perspective after walking with and without vision. *Child Dev.* 59: 480–94
Siegel A W, White S W 1975 The development of spatial representations of large-scale environments. In: Reese H W (ed.) 1975 *Advances in Child Development and Behavior,* Vol. 10. Academic Press, New York, pp. 9–55
Stiles-Davis J, Bellugi U, Kritchevsky M (eds.) 1987 *Spatial Cognition: Brain Bases and Development.* Lawrence Erlbaum, Hillsdale, New Jersey

Drawing and Individual Development

J. Matthews

Many accounts of drawing development describe children as moving through a series of age-related approaches to drawing in which the child's understanding and use of drawing media changes according to his or her cognitive and emotional development. Though some writers have emphasized cultural influence (Wilson and Wilson 1984) many studies suggest that children, regardless of race, class, or gender, move spontaneously through a series of distinctive responses to graphic materials. Initially, infants (about 1–3 years of age) investigate the nature of the mark-making media itself, and begin to perceive the relationship between their body actions and the resultant traces in pigment. Later (about 2–4 years of age) a relationship is perceived between drawn shapes or configurations and the shapes and forms of objects and events. At first, only simple features and forms are encoded into drawing, but as children grow older (about 4–8 years of age) drawings reflect their changing conceptions of phenomena. Whilst comparatively few people learn to map the third dimension coherently into their drawings, many children will, in later infancy through to teenage life, make attempts to capture more complex spatial relations and convey, unambiguously, volumetric solids.

1. Characterization of Development

The pattern of development has been characterized in different ways by different authors. In Kellogg's (1969) account, for example, children are described as acquiring, in a rather formal way, a vocabulary of geometric shapes from their early "scribbling". The child is thought to attribute meaning to these shapes only when they are combined to form depictions: two-dimensional configurations in pigment that encode the shapes and forms of things and people. Initially this is achieved by the child perceiving and naming a relationship between the shape of a random mark produced and the shape of an object. With increasing visual differentiation and motor control, the child is gradually able to produce these configurations purposely and extend them.

Other accounts (Smith 1979, Wolf 1983, Matthews 1984), whilst acknowledging a level at which graphic structure is investigated for its own sake, independent of representational value, credit the child with attributing meaning to marks and shapes near the onset of mark-making (about 1–3 years of age) long before clear depictions can be purposely made. Children at this stage use drawing not only to represent simple shape, but also to represent an object's movement. They use drawing as part of a holistic attempt to understand and represent both the dynamic and configurative aspects of phenomena.

2. Stages of Development

By about 4 or 5 years of age, the child can produce lines and shapes of several kinds. These are now grouped in a variety of ways. Straight lines may be produced in parallel series. Swirling continuous curves, loops, and zig-zags are associated with each other or contrasted with other forms. Dots or blobs may be clustered or scattered in rhythmical patterned sequences of actions.

The child makes increased differentiation and synthesis of shapes, and of the movements which produce them. Selections and combinations are made which reflect the simple relations to which the child is attending within the environment. From rotational scribbling the closed shape is selected which enables the child to specify either the holistic form of volumes, or the faces of objects. In the act of placing dots inside and outside closed shapes, the child encodes inside/outside relations. By attaching lines to the perimeter of a closed shape, the child represents connected forms of many kinds. Connectivity is further explored by the attachment of different types of lines and shapes to each other. Higher/lower relations are also mapped onto the drawing surface during this period. The beginnings of projective relations like in-front-of/behind may make an appearance in drawing, though these latter relations do not usually become part of a more coherent drawing system until several years later.

These relationships are often commented on by the child and further investigated in symbolic play. In drawing, they constitute important discoveries about form. From a simple synthesis, a wide range of two-dimensional constructions proliferate. Shapes are accreted one to another to create articulated representations of a wide variety of entities and phenomena.

As children grow older (about 5–8 years of age) they feel the need to encode more information about scenes and objects in their drawings. They do not use perspective—a system which depicts a scene from a fixed viewpoint—but discover other quite legitimate drawing systems (Willats 1985). These are not usually imitated from cultural models, but are arrived at as original solutions to representational problems. In an effort to convey their increasing knowledge of the structure and function of objects, children during this period may show many aspects of an object or scene simultaneously. Whilst these drawings may appear strange to some adults, recent research suggests that these are attempts to show the structure of an object irrespective of viewpoint (Willats 1985). Such drawings are referred to by some psychologists as object-centred depictions.

Later (from about 8–12 years of age and onward) the need is felt by the child to resolve indeterminacies and ambiguities of line and shape and to map coherent three-dimensional arrays onto the two-dimensional drawing surface. This move from object-centred to viewer-centred depictions (drawings which specify the spectator's viewpoint relative to a scene) necessitates the child making further stipulations about the meaning or denotational values of lines (Willats 1985). Willats's experiments suggest that drawing development is, in some respects, similar to language acquisition. According to this view, children as they grow older gradually formulate increasingly complex drawing rules, moving through a series of transformation systems (Willats 1985) in which earlier ambiguities about the meaning of lines and shapes are resolved, and which eventually allow for the encoding into two dimensions of the third dimension. The employment of diagonal lines to represent horizontal edges receding in space is one achievement during this time, and the child is better able to specify such spatial relations as in-front-of/behind.

3. Process of Development

Whilst children do seem to move spontaneously toward the representation of the third dimension in their drawings, many writers now reject the Western ethnocentric notion that this development is a fixed, hierarchical series of steps toward an ultimate goal of perspective drawing. Recent research supports the feelings of some educators that descriptions of children's drawing are not to be couched solely in terms of supposed deficits, a result of regarding drawing as just the reproduction of a visual array seen from a fixed viewpoint. Children may have an array of representational strategies at their disposal (Freeman and Cox 1985). The selection and use of these may be driven by the child's feelings as to what constitutes essential information to be encoded in a drawing. These priorities change as the child moves through successive approaches to graphic representation. Each mode of representation has its own uses, no single one being superior to the others. Each system preserves some features of the world whilst simultaneously sacrificing others.

It follows that people make different approaches to drawing and representation, attending to different aspects of reality as they grow. Teachers and parents can support and foster drawing development by learning to identify the representational modes through which children move. Teachers are then in a position to respond sensitively to children's graphic representational behaviours and needs, in terms of appropriate language and provision.

Evidence suggests that the child actively seeks out basic structures and relations within the environment. Drawing is a useful tool in this programme which incorporates linguistic, spatiotemporal, and logico-mathematical understandings. Teachers should beware of imposing on children limiting definitions which see drawing only as a method of recording a scene from a fixed viewpoint. These are models either loosely derived from the Western perspectival tradition, or from the more vague position of "naive realism" in which the art-object is presumed somehow to replicate or copy the original object. Such notions of drawing, rigidly held, can be destructive to children's development.

Arnheim (1974) pointed out in the 1950s that development in drawing is not triggered simply by better observation of nature, but by children detecting indeterminacies and ambiguities within their own drawings, and seeking solutions to them in terms of a visual language.

At certain times in the development of drawing children need help in moving from one representational approach to another. Intervention, rather than interruption, has to be guided by the teacher's understanding of the uses to which drawing is being put by the children themselves, and some knowledge of the other representational options available.

Bibliography

Arnheim R 1974 *Art and Visual Perception: A Psychology of the Creative Eye*, rev. edn. University of California Press, Berkeley, California

Freeman N H, Cox M V (eds.) 1985 *Visual Order: The Nature and Development of Pictorial Representation*. Cambridge University Press, Cambridge

Gardner H 1980 *Artful Scribbles: The Significance of Children's Drawings*. Norman, London

Golomb C 1974 *Young Children's Sculpture and Drawing: A Study in Representational Development*. Harvard University Press. Cambridge, Massachusetts

Kellogg R 1969 *Analyzing Children's Art*. National Press Books, Palo Alto, California

Matthews J 1984 Children drawing: Are young children really scribbling? *Early Child Dev. Care* 18: 1–39

Smith N R 1979 Developmental origins of structural variation in symbol form. In: Smith N R, Franklin M B (eds.) 1979 *Symbolic Functioning in Childhood*. Lawrence Erlbaum. Hilldale, New Jersey, pp. 11–26

Willats J 1985 Drawing systems revisited: The role of denotation systems in children's figure drawings. In: Freeman N H, Cox M V (eds.) 1985 *Visual Order: The Nature and Development of Pictorial Representation*. Cambridge University Press, Cambridge, pp. 78–98

Wilson B, Wilson M 1984 Children's drawings in Egypt: Cultural style acquisition as graphic development. *Visual Arts Res.* 10(1): 13–26

Wolf D 1983 The origins of distinct symbolic domains: The waves of early symbolisation, the example of event structuring. In: *The Development of Early Symbolic Skills*. Transcript of symposium presentation, Project Zero, Longfellow Hall, HGSE, Cambridge, Massachusetts

Humour

P. Woods

Humour is the term applied to a "mood or disposition characterized by a sensitivity to, or appreciation of, ludicrous, absurd, incongruous, or comical events" (McGhee 1979 p. 6). Forms of humour vary, but one very common form identified in this quotation focuses on incongruity: something illogical, unexpected, or surprising. This in itself, however, will not necessarily be perceived as humorous—it must be seen in a spirit of "play". More developed forms of humour also involve "resolution", that is, the ability to account for the incongruity and see "the point of the joke". However, the appreciation of humour is not always simply a mental process. It may depend on the emotional investment a person has in a subject. Following Freud (1976), many have seen humour and laughter as a means of releasing excess nervous energy, especially related to unconscious sexual and aggressive urges. The humour allows the expression of these urges in a socially acceptable way. Humour, therefore, is both a cognitive and affective experience, which can act as a powerful regulator of reality. Mary Douglas has described the humorist as a "minor mystic . . . one of those people who pass beyond the bounds of reason and society and give glimpses of a truth which escapes through the mesh of structured concepts" (1966 p. 373).

1. The Development of Humour in Children

The appreciation of incongruity-based humour requires a certain level of cognitive or intellectual development, though the physical and emotional changes that accompany puberty enable the further appreciation of sexual and aggressive themes that produce the most uproarious laughter. Studies of the growth of children's humour have invariably centred around the developmental theories of Piaget and Kohlberg.

One influential model for early childhood in Western industrial society has been proposed by McGhee (1979). In young children, fantasy and a playful set of mind are central to an appreciation of humour. During the second year, in the course of play with others and with objects, the child comes to appreciate that events can exist in fantasy. It is the stage when sensory-motor schemes first become available on a symbolic basis. The child, while perceiving something as humorous, pretends that certain properties are present that are not—the typical game of "make-believe", though it will not be seen as humorous without a "playful" mood. Children then pass through a series of stages (though at varying rates) which McGhee (1979) identifies as (a) incongruous actions towards objects; (b) incongruous labelling of objects and events; (c) conceptual incongruity; (d) multiple meanings.

1.1 Incongruous Actions Towards Objects

Eighteen-month-old children can represent objects in their absence, and treat "pretend" objects as faithful replicas, while fully realizing the difference. Piaget gives the example of the child who picked up a leaf and held it to her ear, using it as a telephone. Such pretences gradually increase in complexity.

1.2 Incongruous Labelling of Objects and Events

With the development of language in the second year of life, words come to replace actions in the experience of humour—the first step towards increased abstraction. There is much delight in calling things what they are not, or attributing incongruous functions to objects as in the first observed joke of one author's daughter, "Daddy, oggie-miaow" (McGhee 1979 p. 70). There is,

in a sense, some celebratory experimentation with words, as in simple riddles, nonsensical rhymings, guessing games, and distorting the sounds of words. With the development of language, humour begins to become more of a social, and less of a personal phenomenon, though humour is still largely self-generated, for the child can still only be confident of the fantasy nature of its own proposed incongruities.

1.3 Conceptual Incongruity

At about 3 years of age, the child embraces the whole feature of classes of objects, rather than just naming the object, and appreciation of humour becomes considerably more complex. Thus, humour may ensue with perceived discrepancies at a fantasy level in one or some of the features. McGhee (1979) gives the example of a cat, seen in reality as an animal with fur, four legs, a tail, and so on, which when met in fantasy without fur, two tails, and so on, is perceived as humorous. Wolfenstein (1954) has argued that at this stage children enjoy distorting familiar concepts. For example, as they are just becoming conscious of gender, they delight in calling each other by different names, often of the opposite gender.

1.4 Multiple Meanings

At about 6 or 7 years of age, the child progresses to the stage of "concrete operational thinking". Instead of fixing on one meaning, or feature of an object, the child is able to "conserve" one in mind while thinking about another. This allows the child to consider relationships between events, rather than simple end states. The child also develops "reversibility" of thinking—the ability to go back over events. All this facilitates the appreciation of jokes based on ambiguity and humour in more abstract forms of incongruity. Shultz (1976) argues that at this stage the child acquires the ability not only to see an ambiguity, but also to appreciate its resolution. From henceforth this is essential for the perception of humour; previously, the incongruity alone sufficed. This partly accounts for the popularity of the riddle in the early school years, since the riddle requires conservation, reversibility and an appreciation of multiple meanings. Shultz and Pilon (1973) have noted four different levels of linguistic ambiguity—lexical: "Order, order, in the court! Ham and cheese on rye please Your Honour"; phonological: "He saw three pears" (pairs); surface-structure: "I saw a man eating shark in the aquarium"—"That's nothing, I saw a man eating herring in the restaurant"; deep-structure: "Call me a cab"— "You're a cab". Shultz's evidence suggests that phonological ambiguity is the first form to be considered funny at about age 6 or 7. Appreciation of lexical ambiguity soon follows, though surface and deep structure is not commonly recognized until age 11 or 12.

The above model is based on the incongruity aspect of humour and omits the tendentious qualities of sex, aggression, and so forth, which give much humour its edge. The earliest forms of tendentious humour are concerned with urination and defecation—functions which the child soon learns are surrounded by taboos. The form of humour is at first very direct, consisting of simply a declaration of a taboo word or function such as "wee-wee" or "poo-poo" (Wolfenstein 1954). With the development of language, this develops to attributing naughty deeds to others: "You poo-poo"—or "Hello Mr Poo-Poo". In the early years of school, children learn to disguise the sexual or aggressive nature of humour with a "joke facade", which develops in complexity as the child, and the child's critical problems and conflicts, develop. The joke facade allows expression of growing feeling while disclaiming responsibility for it.

Between the ages of 6 and 11, children become increasingly concerned with knowledge, hence the popularity of riddles, moron jokes, and other knowledge games, obsessions with brightness and dumbness, and the tensions caused by pressures of learning at school.

Beyond the middle years of childhood (10–11 years) and into adolescence, the appreciation of humour becomes more sophisticated. Spontaneous wit and humorous anecdotes are more evident than simple puns and riddles (McGhee 1979). Analysis goes further, beyond the surface and concrete description or manifestation which the younger child concentrates on. Cartoons and jokes are better understood. As for subject matter, many of the topics of humour are concerned with their sexual, physical, and emotional development. Sexual differences are a popular topic of humour from the point when children are first aware of them during the preschool age. But now the actual sexual changes of puberty add piquancy. Adolescent girls, for example, find most humour in matters like their changing physique, relationships with boys, and developing femininity (Chapman and Foot 1977). Boys in early and preadolescence tease each other about girlfriends. Naughtiness of one kind or another also figures prominently as a topic of humour (deviant behaviour, sexual matters) which generally shows a great deal of disguised aggression. On occasions, delight in aggression is undisguised. "Black" or "sick" jokes are also in vogue during early adolescence, "What is red and screams?"—"A peeled baby in a salt pot". The "control" function is strongly evident in the teasing and joking along gender lines, particularly among young males. Signs of weakness, for example, may be declaimed by demeaning accusations like "You're a woman!" Thus, with the hammer blows of humour, are sex-identity stanchions firmly implanted. This is a reminder that humour is a social act, and for a full understanding, knowledge is needed of its social referents and functions.

2. Functions of Humour

Sociological accounts of humour centre on the three broad functions of conflict, control, and consensus.

Conflict humour is a weapon, or an act of aggression used to damage or to establish superiority over an enemy. Sarcasm, ridicule, and caricature are typical of this form, which can boost a person's morale and undermine the opponent's. It can be used by large groups, such as a nation during wartime, when the humour also serves a unifying function; or by individuals in personal battles.

Control humour obviates conflict by helping to establish and maintain order. Anthropologists have noted how, among primitive societies, joking seems to maintain equilibrium among persons and groups who, because of their relative positions and social ties, might otherwise feel antagonism toward each other and threaten the disruption of the society. In the ritual clowning among North American Indians, for example, the clown can invite people to throw off restraints and engage in activities normally strongly tabooed. This has been related to the ritual lampooning and satirizing of the powerful that takes place in Western society, that functions, arguably, to keep the powerful in check. Similarly, Greenland Eskimos resolve intractable quarrels by duel by laughter, hurling insults at each other and trying to win the most audience laughter (Chapman and Foot 1977). The same function has been noticed in institutions in more advanced communities. In hospitals, for example, joking characterizes the negotiation of a private agreement to suspend a general guideline of the institutional setting, bargaining to make unofficial arrangements about taboo topics. And it cements relationships, encouraging a colleague-type of relationship between nurses and doctors rather than one of service—hence the banter and joking which help to cancel out status differences (see Woods 1979). Studies of collections of jokes in the United States have shown a set of values identified as the "traditional American creed, (which) . . . minimizes the importance of economic differences, stresses the notion and value of equality, ridicules the concept of any basic conflicts, asserts the soundness of the American system, and emphasizes the virtues of charity, initiative, and ambition" (Stephenson 1951 p. 574). The same control function, therefore, can be seen operating in widely differing societies, and at various levels.

The third broad function emphasizes solidarity and friendship. In this, the "pleasure principle" or play aspect of humour is uppermost. It may occur in group activity for the sake of the group and for no other purpose than the enjoyment of comradeship. This may be witnessed in many institutions such as bars, servicemen's messes, clubs, staffrooms, and common rooms. But again, it is a function apparent in primitive societies. For example, the men and women of the Ndembu of Zambia have a ritualized "joking relationship", the aim of which is to arouse sexual desire by stressing the differences between men and women by humorous antagonistic behaviour, characterized by a ribaldry and licence far removed from normal behaviour (Turner 1969).

Any humorous act or event could involve one or more of these functions. Some ethnic humour, for example, may serve the interests of acculturating an immigrant community into a new society, particularly if the members of that community poke fun at themselves. But it can equally be a weapon used in conflict against the dominant culture. Some humour may carry contrary tendencies at the same time. Thus, while the manifest function of televised ethnic situation comedies may be to illustrate the extent of tolerance in society, its latent function may be to exacerbate racial disharmony (Chapman and Foot 1977). Another example of multifunctional humour is the calypso humour of Trinidad (Chapman and Foot 1977). There, humour is a way of life, a cornerstone of the culture. It originated (during the nineteenth century) among the slaves as an antidote to suffering, and has become woven into all aspects of Trinidadian culture, serving several functions. A Freudian analysis would seem most appropriate for these calypsos which contain sexual or aggressive themes; a social control function in those that comment on aspects of social and political life, and establish norms and values; a conflict function where humour is used to try to establish superiority. Among these, control is uppermost, for "humour *has become* the stabilizing system and the basis of control in the society" (Chapman and Foot 1977 p. 281). However, all of these functions are subordinate to the great sense of play and pleasure.

3. Cultural Determinants of Humour

Though a case can be made for the structural similarity and the presence of one or more of the functions mentioned, in all forms of humour that have been identified, there are profound cultural differences in content, priority, and development. Social class, for example, will influence what a person perceives as humorous. The bawdy humour of some groups and clubs will be frowned on in other circles. Two groups might find the same event humorous, but for different reasons. The example of Charlie Chaplin is given in Chapman and Foot (1977). Some might laugh at his attacks on the capitalist system (humour as conflict), others because he falls ludicrously far short of the requirements of such a system (humour as control). Among some groups, humour may have acquired a particular importance as an agency of conflict or control, other resources not being available to them. Thus, the calypso in Trinidad is largely the weapon of the lower class, their targets being the ruling class and its agencies, such as the police. Willis (1977) argued that class was the strongest influence operating on the humour of a group of working-class pupils in an English comprehensive school. These "lads" deviated from the official norms of the school, but conformed to their own class culture, which had its roots in the factory shop floor, and which promoted a very distinct form of humour oppositional to the culture of bosses and teachers.

There is also a large sex difference in humour. It has been argued that joking is predominantly a male activity. A study, for example, of the humour of students in Belgium, Hong Kong, and the United States found that males in all three cultures initiated joking, laughed at female mistakes, and joked equally in the company of other males or females (Chapman and Foot 1977). The females, however, did not tell aggressive or sexual jokes in the company of males, and appeared less knowledgeable about jokes. McGhee (1979) in fact suggests that the greatest single source of individual differences in humour may be whether the child is male or female. This could clearly be related to social inequalities between the sexes. Humour can be an instrument of attack and threat, and those who use it well, and often, have power. Thus, sex differences in humour may be a commentary on the lower status of women in society. There are, too, distinctive generational cultures: much children's humour, for example, is traditional, and, like their games, passed from one generation to the next through an informal social network.

There are differences in humour between different races and different countries, though physiological processes and perceptual–cognitive principles appear to be similar across cultures. Shultz (1977), for example, has found a similarity in all forms of humour of many cultures in the basic structure of incongruity and resolution. Forms may largely be the same, but content differs. Humour has been matched among a number of isolated societies (e.g., the Kwakiutl, Eskimos, and Navaho Indians) with particular problems of social relationships. This connection seems to hold for all societies. Thus, sex and aggression are common topics in the West; while students in Senegal, West Africa, and Japan appreciate nonaggressive more than aggressive forms of humour (Chapman and Foot 1977). The Chinese seem more concerned with social relationships; and in certain nonliterate societies humour focuses more on the immediate physical environment. The content of humour will inevitably reflect the concerns of the society involved. The structure of the family in the West, for example, has created tensions within marriage and a profound disjuncture in the woman's career when her children leave home and marry, yielding the "mother-in-law" syndrome. Hence the proliferation of mother-in-law jokes. There are no such jokes in matriarchal societies, or in societies like Japan, where age is esteemed above social role.

4. Implications for Child Rearing and Education

It is clearly very desirable to have a sense of humour. As a psychological regulator, instrument of power and influence, social control mechanism, teaching and learning aid, socializer, and means of delight, it is a highly useful resource both for the individual and for society. Parents can aid the development of humour in their children by providing an appropriate physical and social environment. McGhee (1979 p. 57), for example, mentions the following circumstances as helpful to the child's development of fantasy orientation and creativity: (a) an opportunity for privacy and for practice in a relatively protected setting; (b) availability of a variety of materials in the form of stories told, books, and playthings; (c) freedom from interference by peers or adults who make demands for immediate motor or perceptual reactions; (d) the availability of adult models or older peers who encourage make-believe activity and provide examples of how this is done; (e) cultural acceptance of privacy and make-believe activities as a reasonably worthwhile form of play.

The parent can also play an important role in helping the child's humour to become less personal and more social. The child wishes to share his or her new-found humour, and if this is done with a parent, it reinforces the emotional bond between them. A parent's reactions might be to ignore or reject such overtures as "child's play". Certain forms of humour may be discouraged as offending societal norms. This will cause the child to spend less time in such fantasy play or to avoid others while doing it. On the other hand, parents who play with their children and delight in their humorous inventions, encourage a positive attitude towards humour.

The full benefits of humour as a teaching aid have yet to be realized. If humour is pleasurable, the stimuli associated with it should have greater reward. The example is sometimes given of the popular American television series "Sesame Street", which uses humorous incongruities to teach basic concepts. But it is not known for sure how humour teaches—whether it is simply a facilitator, a therapeutic agency, an entertainment, or whether it contains more pedagogical stimuli. However, it is known that humour is very important in schools. For teachers, jokes help to establish personal relationships with students, and "short-circuit" social situations in a way that allows them to become personal and unique (Walker and Goodson 1977). That pupils appreciate this is shown by their testimony that they like teachers who, above all, can both control them and "have a laugh" with them (Woods 1979). Pupils have little time for humourless teachers. Stebbins (1980 p. 86) has identified a function of humour in schools which he calls "social comic relief". This "offers a momentary respite from the seriousness of lengthy concentration on a collective task, a respite that facilitates the completion of that task by refreshing the participants, [reducing] fatigue which, if allowed to increase, threatens role performance and motivation".

All forms of humour abound in schools. The gaity and frivolity of pupils "mucking about", or of teacher laughter in staffrooms permits tension release and promotes solidarity. It is used by pupils as a device to explore norms with new teachers; and it is used as a weapon to secure ends by, for example, "subversive ironies" (such as name calling), "confrontational laughter" (impacting the cruder elements of one's own culture against the dominant one), or "symbolic rebellion" (such as spoiling school property or insignia, such as school uniforms). Sometimes, pupils seek delight in humour and laughter as a reaction to boredom, and at other times they are simply acting out forms of their own cultures. Correct identification of forms of humour can aid teaching; incorrect identification can seriously jeopardize it.

Not for nothing are schooldays considered "the happiest days of your life", though clearly humour, even apparently frivolous forms, is a very serious business.

Bibliography

Chapman A J, Foot H C (eds.) 1976 *Humour and Laughter: Research and Applications.* Wiley, London

Chapman A J, Foot H C (eds.) 1977 *It's a Funny Thing, Humour.* Pergamon, Oxford

Douglas M 1966 *Purity and Danger: An Analysis of Concepts of Pollution and Taboo.* Routledge and Kegan Paul, London

Freud S 1976 *Jokes and Their Relation to the Unconscious.* Penguin, Harmondsworth

McGhee P E 1979 *Humour: Its Origin and Development.* Freeman, San Francisco

Shultz T R 1976 A cognitive-development analysis of humour. In: Chapman A J, Foot H C (eds.) 1976 *Humour and Laughter: Research and Applications.* Wiley, London

Shultz T R 1977 A cross-cultural study of the structure of humour. In: Chapman A J, Foot H C (eds.) 1977 *It's a Funny Thing, Humour.* Pergamon, Oxford

Shultz T R, Pilon R 1973 Development of the ability to detect linguistic ambiguity. *Child Dev.* 44: 728–33

Stebbins R 1980 The role of humour in teaching. In: Woods P (ed.) 1980 *Teacher Strategies: Explorations in the Sociology of the School.* Croom Helm, London

Stephenson R M 1951 Conflict and control functions of humour. *Am. J. Sociol.* 56: 569–74

Turner V W 1969 *The Ritual Process: Structure and Anti-structure.* Routledge and Kegan Paul, London

Walker R, Goodson I 1977 Humour in the classroom. In: Woods P, Hammersley M (eds.) 1977 *School Experience: Explorations in the Sociology of Education.* Croom Helm, London, pp. 196–227

Willis P E 1977 *Learning to Labour: How Working Class Kids Get Working Class Jobs.* Saxon House, Farnborough

Wolfenstein M 1954 *Children's Humour: A Psychological Analysis.* Free Press, Glencoe, Illinois

Woods P 1979 *The Divided School.* Routledge and Kegan Paul, London

The Self in the Environment

Self-concept

J. W. McDavid

Self-concept refers to the experience of one's own being. It includes what people come to know about themselves through experience, reflection, and feedback from others. The self-concept is an organized cognitive structure comprised of a set of attitudes, beliefs, and values that cut across all facets of experience and action, organizing and tying together the variety of specific habits, abilities, outlooks, ideas, and feelings that a person displays.

The discussion that follows addresses first the origin and history of theoretical analysis of the self, self-concept, and self-esteem; this is followed by a review of psychological aspects of the development of self-concept, and an overview of methods of assessment of self-concept.

1. History and Theory of Self-concept

The concept of self has origins in the earliest history of personality theory. In the seventeenth century, the philosopher René Descartes discussed the "cognito" (awareness of one's own being) as the core of human existence. Sigmund Freud and the early psychoanalytic theorists used the term ego to refer to this organized aspect of personality, and many have followed that tradition. Other theorists, such as William James, used the term self to describe essentially the same processes, and that usage also continues into the present.

An important distinction is recognized between, on the one hand, the notion of self as a set of organizing processes (defense mechanisms, perceptual habits, or attitudes) that bind the personality into a coherent and integrated system, in contrast to the notion of self as perceived object, something of which the individual is aware in his or her conscious experience. Gradually it has become conventional to refer to this latter notion of self (as object of perceptual experience) as self-concept. Thus, while the self system and self-concept may be differentiated, it is almost impossible to discuss one aspect without reference to the other.

The psychoanalytic concept of superego concerns evaluative and judgmental aspects of the self, providing the theoretical nucleus for a third related concept, self-esteem, referring to those aspects of self-perception that concern the degree to which one likes or dislikes the content of what one perceives in the self.

Theory of self-concept was elaborated in the 1940s by Prescott Lecky and Carl Rogers, focusing attention upon the perceptual aspects of self-concept and the evaluative elements of self-esteem. Rogers proposed a distinction between the self-as-actually-perceived (self-concept) and the self-as-ideally-desired (ideal self), suggesting that both are measurable and diagnostically useful notions. Discrepancy between self-concept and ideal self represents an index of personal psychological adjustment, with the optimum condition placing self-concept slightly (but only slightly) inferior to ideal self—resulting in happy levels of self-regard, optimism about goal setting, and appropriate incentive for achievement and adjustment to the world.

The concepts of "self" and "society" are mutually interrelated so that one almost calls for the other. The British theorist, Charles Cooley, drew early attention to the important relationship between self and society in his idea of "looking glass self," proposing that the content of self-perception is derived largely through the mirror of interaction with other people, whereby one assumes the role of another in order to have a look back at oneself. George Herbert Mead, an American, extended the same ideas into a more elaborate description of feedback from others who are especially important or meaningful individuals ("significant others") and composite feedback synthesized from collective interaction with many other people ("the generalized other").

The notion of self-concept emphasizes the psychological significance of one's subjective experience, so that it is more congruent with scientific philosophies of existentialism and phenomenology than with logical positivism and scientific empiricism. Since these latter philosophies underlie the behaviorism that dominated American psychology through most of the middle third of the twentieth century, the study of self-concept has been more theoretical than empirical, producing a wealth of anecdotal description and conjecture, but a scarcity of empirical data. The wave of humanistic psychology (reflecting existential philosophies) that came into American psychology during the 1970s generated a surge of renewed interest in both theoretical and empirical exploration of the concepts of self, self-concept, and self-esteem.

2. Development of Self-concept

Many factors contribute to the development of self-concept. Overall, it is related to the scope of experience one accumulates with oneself. It is at first a simplistic awareness of oneself and one's capacities generalized across all situations, but as one grows older, the self-concept becomes more complex and differentiated into subfacets that have to do with the self in different situations, such as the "social self," the "academic self," or the "physical self."

Among the many forces that help to organize this accumulated experience with oneself, four are especially notable: language, personal success and failure, social feedback, and identification.

Language enables one to label experiences and actions, organizing experience into integrated conceptual categories. Some of the earliest words in a child's vocabulary have to do with the self and the physical body (me, my name, toe, finger, etc.); soon the child begins to label things and people that are especially important extensions of him/herself (Mama, Daddy, toy, etc.); finally, the child learns to label thoughts and actions with such evaluative terms as good, bad, naughty, nice, and so on. These labels facilitate organization of experiences pertaining to the self.

The forces of personal success and failure involve ideas and feelings arising out of rewards and punishments. The pleasure and satisfaction that accompany personal success (or the pain and distress that accompany personal failure) become cognitively associated with all of the activities and experiences accompanying such situations, including perception of oneself. Attainment of self-set goals, improvement over past performance, or measuring up to one's own standards all contribute to the consolidation of self-concept and self-esteem. When objective standards for defining success and failure are missing, social comparison with the performance of others may define success or failure.

Social feedback enables one to incorporate what others perceive as a part of the impression of oneself. This rests upon role-taking ability, and is therefore related to the acquisition of social skills in perceiving other people as well as oneself. In order to fully appreciate another's perception of oneself, it is necessary first to learn what it is like to be in the position of the other. As this develops, those elements become incorporated into the self-concept.

Identification is a process through which beliefs and values are incorporated by young children into their own personalities from exposure to such agents of the society as parents, teachers, or heroes. Beliefs about oneself (self-concept) and values for oneself (self-esteem) are generated through the identification process, which includes introjection (assimilating

another's values as one's own) and imitation (copying actions, beliefs, or judgments of others). Among the many conditions determining the effectiveness of one person as a target of identification for another, special attention is given to the importance of love and affection (anaclitic identification) and of power (defensive identification) as bases that particularly influence the development of self-concept.

A very primitive aspect of self-concept involves perception of the physical self, or body image. This important initial core of early development of self-concept continues throughout the life span. The degree to which one's body is found to be serviceable and reliable to oneself, as well as attractive to others, influences the content of self-concept and level of self-esteem. Adolescence is a time of rapid change in physical aspects of the body (along with rapid shifts of social role as well), and this is reflected in instability of self-concept—the so-called "adolescent identity crisis." The same is true in the declining years as people age and their bodies become less attractive, less reliable, and less adequate to support activities. Likewise, people whose bodies are impaired by disease, injury, or deformity tend to suffer corresponding inadequacy in self-concept and self-esteem.

The degree of consistency or stability of self-concept may vary considerably. Cognitive processes that organize all other aspects of perception as well operate to shape the self-concept. One tends to be perceptually selective about incorporating new experiences into revisions of self-concept and self-esteem, filtering through a screen of sets, expectancies, and defenses. These natural tendencies preserve the stability of self-concept by being more receptive to new information consistent with the existing self-concept, and less so to discrepant information. In general, the self-concept tends to stabilize with increasing age, but this is not a uniform growth process. For some people, each new success (or failure) yields an exaggerated boost (or drop) in self-esteem even from an isolated experience, but others are more resistant to such changes. The dimension of rigidity–flexibility describes this aspect of self-concept. The psychoanalytic description for a condition of extreme flexibility and instability of the self-concept is called "low ego strength" or "weak ego structure." Generally speaking, higher levels of self-esteem accompany greater stability of self-concept.

Inappropriate development of self-concept may be associated with dysfunctions of personal psychological adjustment. Failure to evolve a well-integrated self-system leads to a fragmented and disorganized self-concept—the condition diagnosed as schizophrenia, a broad term that in turn includes a variety of further characterization depending on the specific nature of the disorganization present. Even when the self-concept is reasonably orderly and coherent, one may feel very disapproving about the content of the self-concept, reflecting low self-esteem—a condition characteristic of depressive personality disorders. Low self-esteem tends to make people set low goals for themselves, resulting in poor achievement motivation, lack of persistence and ambition, and even social withdrawal or isolation. Poor self-concept and low self-esteem often result from excessive failure and punishment, and are associated with belonging to social minorities (ethnically, sexually, or socioeconomically). Other familial variables such as parental characteristics, parent–child interaction patterns, and even birth order and spacing of siblings, may influence self-concept. But these effects are complex, and several variables often interact with each other in shaping the self-concept.

3. Assessment of Self-concept

Lack of suitable methods for assessment of self-concept has restricted the range of empirical research, especially with young children. Procedures for investigating self-concept necessarily depend upon self-report. Behavioral observations or reports made by others (such as rating scales) refer only to behavioral products of the self, but not to the subjective experience that comprises self-concept itself. Projective tests, especially drawings, may allow inferences about the quality and nature of self-concept, but these are only indirect. Direct evaluation of self-concept requires one to report and describe the content of his/her perception, thus ordinarily requiring words to communicate, thus reflecting the verbal ability of the subject, and in turn, resting upon such factors as age, intelligence, education, and socio-economic status.

Because they are not adept with words, young children cannot be evaluated with such verbal instruments. Some investigators have therefore attempted to adapt these ideas to nonverbal or pictorial procedures, but with only limited success yielding crude and imprecise measures.

Moreover, people differ in the degree to which they are willing to reveal themselves to others: some are extroverted and transparent, displaying themselves readily to anyone; others are introverted, guarded about their revelations, and reluctant to communicate their perceptions of themselves to others.

There are even individual differences in the ability to form a self-concept! Jane Loevinger (1966) has proposed that there is a measurable dimension of personality related to the ability to conceptualize oneself, to assume distance from oneself, and to describe oneself precisely, and that this variable itself is dependent upon age, intelligence, education, and socioeconomic status.

Bibliography

Cooley C H 1902 *Human Nature and the Social Order*. Scribner, New York
Coopersmith S 1967 *The Antecedents of Self-esteem*. Freeman, San Francisco, California
Freud S 1933 *New Introductory Lectures on Psychoanalysis*. Knopf, New York
Hamachek D E 1971 *Encounters with the Self*. Holt, Rinehart and Winston, New York
James W 1980 *The Principles of Psychology*, Vol. 1. Holt, New York
Lecky P 1945 *Self-consistency: A Theory of Personality*. Island, New York
Loevinger J 1966 The meaning and measurement of ego development. *Am. Psychol.* 21: 195–206
Mead G H 1934 *Mind, Self, and Society from the Standpoint of a Social Behaviorist*. University of Chicago Press, Chicago, Illinois
Rogers C R 1951 *Client-centered Therapy: Its Current Practice, Implications, and Theory*. Houghton Mifflin, Boston, Massachusetts
Shavelson R J, Bolus R 1982 Self-concept: The interplay of theory and methods. *J. Educ. Psychol.* 74: 3–17
Strong D J, Feder D D 1961 Measurement of the self concept: A critique of the literature. *J. Couns. Psychol.* 8: 170–78
Ziller R C 1973 *The Social Self*. Pergamon, New York

Self-control

C. Wenar

The concept of self-control can be described in at least two ways. In the first and more traditional way, the child behaves in a socially acceptable rather than in a socially unacceptable manner when the two behaviors are in conflict. The second concept emphasizes the child as an active agent who is in control of the environment. The following discussion analyzes conditions fostering or undermining these two forms of self-control.

1. Two Varieties of Self-control

As a toddler reaches for a vase on the living room table, his mother comes over, says "No!" and gently slaps his hand, so the child withdraws. After this sequence is repeated on subsequent occasions, the toddler can be observed to reach for the vase, then spontaneously withdraw his hand, perhaps after slapping it himself and saying "No." With the passing of time he avoids approaching the vase altogether.

An 8-week-old infant, whose crib has a special electrical instrument underneath the pillow, learns that every time it turns its head to one side (thereby pressing on the pillow and activating the instrument) a mobile toy overhead begins to dance. It turns its head again and again, laughing with glee.

Traditionally, self-control has been epitomized by the first example. In the conflict between antisocial or asocial behavior and socially approved behavior, the child chooses the latter. Society itself defines the specific content of the two terms in the unacceptable–acceptable equation: the former often includes certain kinds of sexual, aggressive, exploratory, and appropriative behaviors; the latter involves total inhibition of the forbidden behavior or disguised and displaced outlets. Authoritative adults—typically but by no means exclusively the parents—are charged with socializing children so that they will come to monitor their own behavior and make acceptable choices. How the socialization is done varies widely as do the adults' standards of what comprises satisfactory self-control.

The above is familiar territory which will subsequently be explored in detail. More recently, the concept of self-control has been expanded so as to emphasize the child-as-agent. The fountainhead of this expansion was White's classical article (1959) showing that effectance, or producing an effect on the environment, is as basic a motive as are the traditional physiological drives such as hunger, thirst, and sex. The second example, that of the 8-week-old infant's delight in making the mobile toy dance, strongly supports White's contention (Watson and Raney 1972). Effectance includes exploration and manipulation of the physical environment along with child-initiated interactions with the interpersonal environment. As such ventures are successful, children develop a general sense of being effective agents of change. If the process goes awry, however, children develop a perception of their fate as being determined by forces beyond their control or, more ominously, they develop a pervasive sense of helplessness. This newer concept of self-control has little to do with the choice between socially acceptable and unacceptable behaviors; rather it has to do with the child's feeling able to control his or her own destiny. Self-control is equated with self-being-in-control.

2. Traditional Self-control

While the first example of the achievement of self-control in the toddler could not be simpler, the psychological variables involved are complex (Kopp 1987). (Here, "parent" is used synonymously with "socializing adult.") First, there is reward and punishment which serves to encourage appropriate and discourage inappropriate behavior. These rewards and punishments may be physical or psychological, the latter involving either the granting or withdrawal of love. In rewarding and punishing, the parent also serves as a model either of controlled or uncontrolled behavior; for example, by explaining in a gentle way why a punishment was necessary, or angrily shouting "Stop that!" Thus, imitation enters the picture, at times underscoring and at times undermining socialization as in the case of the father who loses his temper and spanks his child for fighting with a younger sibling.

A host of cognitive variables are involved in self-control. At the simplest level, the toddler must be able to grasp cause and effect relations and to remember what behavior leads to reward or punishment, so that past experiences can be applied to the situation at hand.

The child must also be able to integrate piecemeal experiences into guiding principles, so that, "Don't touch that" and "That's Jimmy's, not yours" becomes integrated into "I must not take things which belong to others." As the cognitively developing child can say these increasingly complex directives to itself, inbuilt controls become increasingly effective. "Saying things to oneself" is an aspect of thinking which is a strong ally of control. The very fact that the child must stop and think means that immediate action is delayed, while the child's thoughts serve to guide subsequent behavior into socially acceptable channels.

Interpersonal trust is important in those cases where self-control requires a delay of gratification, epitomized by the parental directive of "Wait." Children's capacity to wait is enhanced if promised rewards are consistently forthcoming, while their tolerance of tension is undermined if parents are unreliable or the environment is disorganized and unpredictable. Finally, the availability of substitute gratifications helps children master the frustration of being forbidden to pursue a given goal. First it is the sensitive parent who offers the substitute but, with age, children themselves become capable of redirecting their activities. At times the substitute involves relinquishing the original goal, so that after being forbidden to look at an adult TV program, a 9-year-old goes and listens to favorite records; at times the substitute involves socially acceptable ways of at least partially achieving the goal, so that the child who is forbidden to fight with peers on the playground can learn judo in the gym. Play and fantasy may also serve as safe substitutes; the child recently punished by its mother can spank a doll for being a "mean old mommie." (For a more detailed account of the variables involved in self-control, see Wenar 1982).

Recently, behaviorally oriented psychologists have become interested in the concept of self-control. This interest derives from two sources: first, from the more venturesome social learning theorists who were eager to expand the domain of behavioral theorizing and research to include covert variables such as cognition, expectancies, and images, along with the traditional overt ones; and second, from behavior therapists who found that, while environmental manipulations could induce changes, these changes often were not sustained when the manipulations ceased. One solution to this therapeutic dilemma was to enhance the child's capacity to control its own behavior.

Understandably, the concept of self-control has been translated into behavioral terms. It refers to specific responses not under immediate or explicit external direction, which alter the conflicting temporal contingencies of a target response, called a to-be-controlled response (TBCR). The two typical temporal conflicts involve behaviors which elicit immediate rewards but eventual punishment, such as excessive drinking or smoking, and behaviors which have short-term aversive but long-term positive consequences such as doing homework or dieting. Thus, self-control enables the child to resist immediate pleasures or sustain immediate displeasures in order to achieve desirable long-range goals (Karoly 1977).

3. Self Being in Control

The newer concept of self-control which centers on the self-as-agent does not seem to be compounded of as many variables as the traditional concept. The desire to explore and the need to master are the major ingredients. Rather, interest has centered on the various manifestation of the self-as-agent throughout childhood. Infants not only want to control their physical environment (as illustrated in the 8-week-old infant's delight in making the mobile toy dance) but also their social environment; for example, by the end of the first year of life, they may be so adept and insistent in their demands for attention that some mothers become resentful. And certainly the willfulness and negativism of the "terrible two's" can be understood as the need of toddlers to be totally in command of even the most minute aspects of their daily lives. Older children's generalized sense of being in charge of their own destiny has been investigated under the heading of locus of control. Children who perceive events as contingent upon their own behavior or some traits in their own character have an internal locus of control; children who believe that events are due to factors other than themselves, such as luck or chance or fate, have an external locus of control. Such perceptions may affect academic achievement; for example, children who believe they can use education to make a difference to their future do better academically than those who believe that education does not matter since they will never have a chance to make anything of themselves (Phares 1976). Such learned helplessness represents the nadir of the self-as-agent. When individuals perceive that they are ineffectual either to relieve pain or obtain gratification they in essence abandon the effort; instead of being an agent, the self is viewed as essentially helpless to produce change (Huesman 1978).

4. Facilitating and Undermining Self-control

Before discussing conditions which facilitate or undermine self-control, it should be noted that most of the literature deals with those ageless, sexless, mythical entities—"parents" and "children"—rather than taking age and sex into account. In addition, most studies are designed only to show the effect of parental behavior on children rather than recognizing that causation may go in both directions. Thus the literature lags behind current thinking and current research on parent–child interaction. To cite only a few illustrations: opposite sexed parent–child interactions are characterized by more benevolence and less strictness than same-sex interactions; parental permissiveness tends to lead to aggressiveness after the preschool period but not before; girls at all ages are generally more obedient and self-

controlled than boys; and maternal caretaking may be significantly affected by whether the infant is easy or difficult to care for (Martin 1975). Finally, it should be remembered that stylistic difference in self-control should not be confused with differences in degrees of self-control; for example, the stereotypical Latin family allows for a greater expression of affect than the stereotypical Nordic family, yet both may have the same degree of self-control.

In general, conditions facilitating or undermining the traditional concept of self-control derive logically from the variables comprising it. The warm parent who explains the reason for discipline and who rewards and punishes consistently, not only nurtures the affective and cognitive elements in self-control but also provides a model of reasonable, controlled behavior. Extreme deviations either in the direction of laxness or punitiveness are apt to undermine control particularly in the area of aggression; for example, hostile, vindictive, authoritarian discipline provides neither the affective bond nor the rationale for controlled behavior while often modeling aggressiveness. The combination of laxness and punitiveness either in the same parent or between parents also undermines control. Relatively little is known about the conditions producing excessive control, but a son who has a close relation with a dominant mother and whose father is remote and unaccepting is apt to be withdrawn and neurotic. More recently, it has been found that the authoritative mother tends to engender qualities of self-control, independence, and expansiveness in preschool children. Such a mother is highly nurturant, but also demanding of age-appropriate behavior, controlling, encouraging of give-and-take, and, while respecting the child, reserves the ultimate decisions for herself (Hetherington and Parke 1979).

Conditions reinforcing and undermining the development of the self-as-agent are more speculative than those summarized above. As developing children experience success with their attempts to control the environment, they gradually come to perceive themselves as competent agents. This development is abetted by reinforcement from adults and peers, by labels implying that they are competent, and by an environment which is orderly and predictable, which not only values initiative but also holds realistic promise of future rewards.

By the same token, the self-as-agent is undermined by conditions more frequently, although not exclusively, associated with poverty: harassed and overburdened caretakers who regard initiative as "getting into mischief"; haphazard administration of praise and punishment; labels designating the child as "stupid" or "bad," a disorganized environment in which consequences have little consistent relation to the child's activities and which contain little evidence that postponement of immediate pleasures—say by studying—will be rewarded in the future—say by job or financial security. Custodial institutions may also systematically reward docility, overdependence, and helplessness while punishing any sign of initiative. Parents of any social class can undermine the self-as-agent by disparaging labels, by setting unrealistically high goals while being cold and critical of failure, and by taking over the decision-making process in everything from what clothes the child should wear to what vocational goals should be set (Wenar 1982).

These general guides to enhancing self-control have recently been augmented by behavioral techniques (Karoly 1977). The four steps involved in a change in self-regulation have tentatively been identified as follows: (a) problem recognition, which is a recognition by the child rather than by others (as so often is the case with children) of the temporal conflicts within his or her current behavior; (b) commitment, which means that the child must not only know the problem but must prefer self-control over the perceived altenatives; (c) extended self-management, which involves self-monitoring, self-management, and self-reinforcement (it is this step which has received the greatest attention from behaviorally oriented therapists); and (d) habit reorganization, which is the end product of the other three stages.

A number of strategies have been employed to remedy self-control deficiencies. Through the use of modeling, self-imposed delay of reward can be instilled in otherwise impulsive children. Self-instructional training is a process by which the realistic instructions of the therapist are first imitated by the child and then transferred to the realm of inner speech. Thus, instead of behaving "thoughtlessly" and impulsively, the child now has well-planned guides with which to regulate and control behavior. Component skills training, instead of concentrating on a specific aspect of self-control, provides a set of conceptually or empirically related self-

control skills. Instead of instructing a child how to solve a particular problem, for example, one such program teaches how to go about problem solving in general by, say, generating alternatives rather than mindlessly repeating a maladaptive behavior.

Work on adapting the above strategies to the classroom has already begun. While initial results show promise, the venture is too new to assess its accomplishments. The strategies could also be adapted for parent training but even less has been done here than in the classroom. Given the vigor of the behavioral movement, there may well be in the near future a significant increase in self-management programs for children in both the home and the school.

Bibliography

Hetherington E M, Parke R D 1979 *Child Psychology: A Contemporary Viewpoint*, 2nd edn. McGraw-Hill, New York

Huesmann L R (ed.) 1978 Learned helplessness as a model of depression. *J. Abnorm. Psychol.* 87: 1–98 (special issue)

Karoly P 1977 Behavioral self-management in children: Concepts, methods, issues, and directions. *Prog. Behav. Mod.* 5: 197–62

Kopp C B 1987 The growth of self-regulation: Caregivers and children. In: Eisenberg N (ed.) 1987 *Contemporary Topics in Developmental Psychology*. Wiley, New York, pp. 34–55

Martin B 1975 Parent–child relations. *Rev. Child Dev. Res.* 4: 463–540

Phares E J 1976 *Locus of Control in Personality*. General Learning Press, Morristown, New Jersey

Watson J S, Raney C T 1972 Reactions to responsive contingent stimulation in early infancy. *Merrill-Palmer Q.* 18: 219–27

Wenar C 1990 *Developmental Psychopathology from Infancy Through Adolescence* 2nd edn. McGraw-Hill, New York

White R W 1959 Motivation reconsidered: The concept of competence. *Psychol. Rev.* 66: 297–333

Self-actualization

L. M. Brammer

The purpose of this article is to review the historical developments, cite representative research, and describe current applications of the self-actualization concept. A brief survey of the root term self is also undertaken.

Self-actualization refers to achieving one's highest potential of development. The term is used widely in American educational and psychotherapy settings as a desirable outcome of a personal growth experience.

1. Development of Self-actualization

Credit for first using the term self-actualization is given to Goldstein (1940). It was picked up quickly by phenomenologically oriented psychologists. Gestalt therapists, such as Fritz Perls, used the term freely in lectures and workshops. Self-actualization is close to

terms such as individuation of Carl Jung (1928), maturation of Charlotte Buhler (1972) and Fritz Perls (1973), full functioning of Carl Rogers (1961), and self-realization employed by American humanistic psychologists. Maslow (1970) is the best known American writer to use self-actualization as a descriptor for high-level functioning and for his basic research on characteristics of self-actualized people.

2. Development of the Concept of Self

Basic to understanding self-actualization is knowledge of the development of self-concept. This concept has a long history and is very important to modern education and psychotherapy. Epstein (1973), in a critical review, asserts that not only is self a useful concept but it is central to understanding individual behavior.

References to self describe the basic identity of the person. In common usage, various descriptions of self, such as work and family roles, answer the question "Who am I?" William James (1891) describes the social me as "an awareness of self as others saw me." Thus, self is a fragile concept dependent largely on the opinions of others for stability.

Much of the usage of self in literature centers around the integrity of the person, and is used sometimes as a synonym for soul. Polonius's advice to Hamlet, for example, emphasized "To thine own self be true . . ." The Italian psychiatrist Roberto Assagioli (1973), refers to the transpersonal self, which is manifested through creative acts or spiritual events. The concept of a higher self even transcends self-actualization.

Carl Rogers (1961), writing from the 1940s through to the present about counseling and psychotherapy, marshalled much evidence to support the idea that one goal of counseling was to close the gap between people's concepts of themselves and themselves as experienced.

Sigmund Freud's ego has much in common with definitions of self in the sense of conscious awareness. Carl Jung (1928) spoke of self as if it were an experiential entity rather than an explanatory concept. Long before, J. S. Mill (1865) wrote about the self as an experiencing agent.

Many writers in the European existential tradition stressed capacity for self-growth and taking personal responsibility for growth. Numerous American writers in counseling and psychotherapy emphasized self-growth also. These traditions resulted in the attachment of the concept of actualization to that of self in order to describe the committed and responsible person's potential for growth and the process of seeking higher levels of functioning.

After the first two decades of using self as a descriptor, the term went into eclipse under positivism and the behavioristic thrust for objectivity. Self-concepts were considered too vague and subjective to be useful. Yet, this accusation spurred considerable writing and research by such eminent self-theorists as Carl Rogers and Abraham Maslow. During the 1950s and 1960s, cracks appeared in the behaviorists' armour and self came back into favor as a descriptor or was hyphenated with another term such as esteem, revelation, realization, and actualization.

A key thrust to usage of self-actualization was given by humanistic psychology and the encounter group movement of the 1960s. On American college campuses in the 1970s this emphasis turned outward to protest and social change. In the late 1970s and early 1980s, the focus reverted largely to individual growth. Self-actualization in the American context is still under suspicion in large, conservative segments of the population because of its connotation of rebellion and narcissism.

The notions of self and self-actualization are ideas largely germane to the Western hemisphere. Self implies a separation from others, deities, and nature. Some cultures do not have a concept of self. Dorothy Lee (1959) writes, for example, that the California Wuntu Native Americans do not have a word for self. They see self and nature in a blend. A dominant theme of some Asian worldviews is the subjugation of self and oneness with nature. So, a large part of the world does not share basically European and American cultural views of the nature of the self and the value of self-actualization.

When Kurt Goldstein introduced self-actualization, it meant developing one's potential to the maximum possible. This self development would then lead to greater satisfaction than if one had not followed the actualization process. Later, the term took on a special creative meaning that required risk and some pain or discomfort. It certainly implied that giving up the comforts of present thinking and acting for some possibly greater satisfaction meant a gamble (Brammer and Shostrom 1982).

Self-actualization is the term used to describe the process of achieving higher levels of function and satisfaction. Abraham Maslow (1970) placed self-actualization at the top of his hierarchy of human needs. This meant that more basic life-sustaining needs, such as security, must be satisfied before self-actualization needs could be fulfilled.

A more recent expansion of the self-actualizing concept is described by Everett Shostrom (1976) as an integration of thoughts, feelings, and bodily processes into one fully functioning being. The concept of full functioning, as opposed to fractionation and internal conflict, is a key facet of self-actualization as a growth goal.

3. Research on Self-actualization

Two lines of basic research on self-actualization will be described. The first was conducted by A. H. Maslow (1970) on actualizing people during the early 1950s. The second focus is E. L. Shostrom's (1966) work with his Personal Orientation Inventory.

Maslow was interested in studying psychologically healthy people. He selected the first subjects from his circle of friends, public figures, and historical persons. From this informal study he evolved a list of characteristics that he applied to a sample of 3,000 college students. The criterion for selection within this group was absence of psychopathology; but more importantly, the list of characteristics for selection included qualities which indicated that these subjects were fulfilling themselves at high levels of achievement. Maslow finally selected a group of young people with qualities setting them apart from what he considered to be the ordinary adult (Maslow 1970). These qualities were:

(a) *More efficient perception of reality*. This was an ability to detect spurious and dishonest aspects of personality, and to judge people and events accurately. This quality emerged as one of good taste and judgment.

(b) *Acceptance of self, others, and nature*. Self at the animal level was the first stage of self-acceptance. These self-actualized types had lusty appetites for sensory enjoyment and respect for their bodies. They lacked defensiveness and disliked artificiality in others. They could live comfortably with their own shortcomings.

(c) *Spontaneity*. In addition to spontaneous inner life and behavior, Maslow's self-actualizing people behaved with simplicity and naturalness. Their codes of ethics were more individual than conventional. The motivational patterns of the self-actualizing subjects were markedly different from ordinary people. Self-actualized people expressed desires to develop their own styles of being rather than fulfilling deficiencies in the expectations of others. They were more interested in living than in preparing to live.

(d) *Problem centeredness*. The self-actualized subjects were focused on problems outside themselves, rather than on themselves.

(e) *Detachment and the need for privacy*. Maslow's subjects sought solitude and privacy to a greater degree than ordinary people.

(f) *Autonomy and independence*. Self-actualized people were relatively independent of their physical and social environment, and were motivated by growth rather than by filling deficiencies through outside sources. They depended on intrinsic rewards. They could take rewards offered by others, but were relatively independent of these social stimulations and extrinsic rewards.

(g) *Freshness and appreciation*. Self-actualized people had a capacity to appreciate repeatedly the basically good and simple things of life. Their reactions were characterized by awe, wonder, pleasure, ecstacy, and freshness.

(h) *Mystic experiences and oceanic feelings*. A common experience of self-actualized people was their strong emotions and visions of being transformed into more meaningful, appreciative beings. Their acute mystic experiences took them into feelings of pleasure, expansiveness, and momentary loss of self-consciousness.

(i) *Interpersonal relations*. Self-actualized people were more capable than ordinary people of relating meaningfully to others, such as giving more love, experiencing more fusion, having keener social skills, and having more extended boundaries of self. Usually their circle of friends was small but relationships were more intense. They felt deeply about people and desired to help them.

(j) *Democratic character structure*. They tended to lack class attitudes, respected differences, and were willing to work with anyone. They were open to learning from anyone willing to teach.

(k) *Sense of humor*. This quality was common in all of Maslow's subjects. They could poke fun at themselves and people in general when they acted foolishly. They enjoyed repartee and witty remarks.

(l) *Creativeness*. This was also a universal charac-teristic. All subjects were inventive, original, and energetic with a freshness and sharpness of perception. They were less inhibited by convention and culture than ordinary people. They resisted enculturation. In this sense they were not well-adjusted because their behavior was sometimes disapproved by society.

While these characteristics are descriptive of high-functioning people, Maslow is quick to point out that self-actualizing people have the usual shortcomings of all human beings. Thus they also exhibit silly, wasteful, thoughtless, and irritating behavior.

A second line of research on self-actualization is Shostrom's work with the Personal Orientation Inventory (1966). This is a well-standardized approach to measuring characteristics of self-actualized people. It consists of 150 paired choices of values related, in part, to Maslow's concepts of self-actualization. There are two basic scales of inner directedness and present-time competence. The remaining scales measure traits of self-regard, spontaneity, sensitivity to feelings and needs, a constructive view on the nature of humanity, ability to transcend dichotomies with commonalities, acceptance of natural aggressiveness, and capacity for intimate contact. This inventory has been used in many research projects when a measure of self-actualization has been desired (Shostrom 1976).

4. Summary

Self-actualization is a well-established educational and counseling outcome. It describes the person who is functioning more fully and lives a richer life than the ordinary person. Self-actualized people report also that they experience high levels of satisfaction and productivity.

Bibliography

Assagioli R 1973 *The Act of Will*. Penguin, Baltimore

Brammer L M, Shostrom E L 1982 *Therapeutic Psychology: Fundamentals of Counseling and Psychotherapy*, 4th edn. Prentice-Hall, Englewood Cliffs, New Jersey

Buhler C, Allen M 1972 *Introduction to Humanistic Psychology*. Brooks Cole, Monterey, California

Epstein S 1973 The self-concept revisited: Or a theory of a theory. *Am. Psychol.* 28: 404–16

Goldstein K 1940 *Human Nature in the Light of Psychopathology*. Harvard University Press, Cambridge, Massachusetts

James W 1891 *The Principles of Psychology*. Holt, New York

Jung C G 1928 *Two Essays on Analytical Psychology*. Dodd Mead, New York

Lee D D 1959 *Freedom and Culture: Essays*. Prentice-Hall, New York

Maslow A H 1970 *Motivation and Personality*, 2nd edn. Harper and Row, New York

Mill J S 1865 *An Examination of Sir William Hamilton's Philosophy and of the Principal Philosophical Questions Discussed in his Writings*. Longman, London

Perls F 1973 *The Gestalt Approach and Eyewitness to Therapy.* Science and Behavior Books, Ben Lomond, California

Rogers C R 1961 *On Becoming a Person: A Therapist's View of Psychotherapy.* Houghton Mifflin, Boston, Massachusetts

Shostrom E L 1966 *Manual: Personal Orientation Inventory.* Educational and Instructional Testing Service, San Diego, California

Shostrom E L 1976 *Actualizing Therapy: Foundations for a Scientific Ethic.* EdITS, San Diego, California

Field Dependence and Field Independence

D. R. Goodenough

The terms field dependence and field independence refer to opposing poles of an individual-difference dimension. They have been most closely associated with the work of H. A. Witkin (1916–1979) on styles of cognitive functioning, and have been used in several different ways by Witkin and others during the period since their introduction in the 1940s.

Field dependence was first defined in terms of the relative importance of visual, as against proprioceptive, cues in perception of the vertical direction. An individual's location on the individual-difference dimension is still commonly measured by a rod-and-frame test in which the individual, as an upright observer is asked to vertically align a rod that is surrounded by a tilted visual field in the form of a large square frame. Under these conditions, the conflict between orientation cues from the body and the frame is typically resolved by a compromise in which the axes of perceived space are rotated in the direction of frame tilt. Dependence on visual-field cues can be measured by the objective tilt of the rod that looks vertical to the observer.

When relationships were found between tests of visual effects on orientation perception and the ability to locate camouflaged forms, Witkin suggested that the same analytical process is required to tease out both proprioceptive cues to the vertical direction in the rod-and-frame test and target forms in camouflaging patterns. He redefined the individual-difference dimension in terms of a capacity to disembed task-relevant information from stimulus contexts, and then used an embedded figures test as a convenient measure of field independence. However, some recent findings on orientation perception are hard to understand in these terms, and he has subsequently favored a form of the initial cue-conflict theory of field-dependence–independence. In this view, the embedded-figures test measures a separate, but related intellectual ability to manipulate or restructure an initial organization of cognitive elements. Visual–spatial materials have been used in most research on the cognitive correlates of field independence, and some critics have attributed the observed relationships to a general visualization ability.

Field-dependence–independence measures have also been interpreted in a broader sense. Research on orientation perception was stimulated by findings that people who are highly influenced by their visual environment also tend to be highly influenced by their social environment. In contrast, people who rely more on proprioceptive cues in orientation perception appear to have internalized values and standards that allow them to function with a greater degree of autonomy in their social–interpersonal behavior. The increasing degree of self–nonself differentiation and accompanying internalization of behavior-regulating mechanisms during the growth years are key concepts in Witkin's attempt to account for the observed perception–personality relationship. The terms field dependence and field independence are sometimes used to refer to developmental and individual differences in these processes.

1. Developmental Trends

While the course of individual development generally proceeds toward greater field independence from childhood to young adulthood, the occurrence of dramatic individual and group differences in growth trends offers many opportunities to study factors that may influence the developmental process. With respect to child-rearing practices, families that emphasize obedience tend to have relatively field-dependent children, while relatively field-independent children are more often found in families that emphasize separation from parental authority. Data from cross-cultural studies of subsistence-level people also show relationships with ecological and economic variables. Agriculturists, for example, tend to be relatively field dependent. Moreover, farming cultures are typically characterized by a sedentary village life with strong political and/or religious authorities who enforce compliance with elaborate rules of conduct. Hunters and gatherers in contrast are often among the most field independent of people, particularly on the rod-and-frame test. They typically live in smaller, nomadic groups that foster greater self-reliance. These findings suggest that parental and cultural factors may play some role in the development of field independence.

Performance on disembedding tasks appears to improve with practice and certain educational programs. The evidence for training effects on field independence in orientation perception is inconsistent, but the finding that visual effects on orientation perception are relatively small in unacculturated hunter–gatherers suggests that formal education is unnecessary for the development of field independence.

2. Educational Applications

Proponents of field-dependence theory have proposed a variety of educational and vocational applications based on the idea that satisfaction and/or achievement can be improved by choosing methods of instruction, curricula, and occupations that are as compatible as possible with the personality and cognitive style of the student. The contrasting characteristics of people at opposite poles of the field-dependence–independence dimension, suggest that interpersonal teacher-structured methods and socially oriented topics would be particularly congenial for more field-dependent students, while self-structured methods and more abstract topics requiring analytical and/or visualization abilities would be more congenial for field-independent students.

The educational implications of field-dependence theory have been developed most fully in the area of academic and vocational choice. Many studies, for example, have shown that more field-independent students graduate with abstract, analytical majors such as mathematics, engineering, and physics, while field-dependent students tend to have majors that deal more directly with people such as social work, nursing, and the humanities. While applications to guidance problems appear particularly promising, their value in practice has not yet been clearly established.

Bibliography

Goodenough D R 1976 The role of individual differences in field dependence as a factor in learning and memory. *Psychol. Bull.* 83: 675–95

Witkin H A, Berry J W 1975 Psychological differentiation in cross-cultural perspective. *J. Cross Cult. Psychol.* 6: 4–87

Witkin H A, Goodenough D R 1977 Field dependence and interpersonal behavior. *Psychol. Bull.* 84: 661–89

Witkin H A, Goodenough D R 1980 *Cognitive Styles: Essence and Origins.* International Universities Press, New York

Witkin H A, Dyk R B, Faterson H F, Goodenough D R, Karp S A 1962 *Psychological Differentiation: Studies of Development.* Wiley, New York

Witkin H A, Goodenough D R, Oltman P K 1979 Psychological differentiation: Current status. *J. Pers. Soc. Psychol.* 37: 1127–45

Witkin H A, Moore C A, Goodenough D R, Cox P W 1977 Field-dependent and field-independent cognitive styles and their educational implications. *Rev. Educ. Res.* 47: 1–64

Witkin H A, Moore, C A, Oltman P K, Goodenough D R, Friedman F, Owen D R, Raskin E 1977 Role of field-dependent and field-independent cognitive styles in academic evolution: A longtitudinal study. *J. Educ. Psychol.* 69: 197–211

Part 5

Psycho-physical Development

Part 5

Psycho-physical Development

<hr />

Introduction

Textbooks describing human development often include a section entitled Physical Development, with articles appearing under this designation usually focusing on observable changes in overall body size and in the complexity and function of body organs. However, limiting the title to Physical Development may prove misleading by its seeming neglect of the psychological factors involved in body growth and motor activities. Consequently, to signal recognition of psychological aspects of physical growth in this *Encyclopedia*, Part 5 has been given the title Psycho-physical Development.

Part 5 consists of 15 articles divided into three sections. The first section includes seven articles on general psycho-physical growth and function. The first two articles in this section review research findings on *Physical Development and Fitness* and on growth and *Motor Development*. The second pair of articles deal with brain development and right-brain, left-brain functions. The last three articles describe ways that nutrition and drug-use can affect psycho-physical functions, including educational performance.

Part 5(b) consists of four articles dealing with the operation of vision and hearing, as the two sense modalities most important for students' educational progress.

The last section, Special Issues in Physical Development, consists of four articles the subject matter of which have been of particular interest in recent years. The first two articles inspect *Sex Characteristics and Roles*, including homosexuality. The third article examines the concepts of *Body Image and Body Language*. The final article reviews the educational functions of *Play, Games, and Toys*, illustrating their functions with examples from various societies around the world.

Influences on Psycho-physical Development

Physical Development and Fitness

E. D. Michael Jr.

Usually the terms growth and development are used differently, with growth referring to the inherent genetic changes that occur with time (such as changes in height), and development referring to the functions of the body. Here, development will be used to mean both the growth and functional changes seen in school children.

The growth and development of children differs between the sexes and between individuals; however, there are similar patterns of development that relate to the changes occurring during the elementary-school years—ages 6–12—and those years spent in secondary school—ages 12–18. Since the individual and the environment are continually interacting, there are environmental as well as hereditary factors influencing the child's physical development. Though heredity has the greatest influence on growth of the size of a body, the physical activity and environment, including nutrition, have a greater influence on fitness or health.

Fitness is defined as the ability to carry out daily tasks with energy left over to enjoy leisure and meet emergency situations. The basic components of fitness are listed by the President's Council on Physical Fitness and Sports (1971 No. 1) as: (a) cardiorespiratory endurance; (b) muscular strength; and (c) muscular endurance. These components of fitness are related to physical development and physical activity. They will be discussed relative to the educational setting and the prepubescent steady growth period of elementary-school children and the rapid growth period of adolescence. The important influence of nutrition is covered elsewhere.

1. Muscular Strength

The strength of a muscle is related to its cross-sectional area and its composition. The changes in strength that occur during early childhood follow the changes in body size. Sex differences are minor, though boys are slightly taller and heavier. The steady gain in height and weight parallels the muscle mass and strength changes between ages 6 and 10. The linear change with strength levels off in females at about age 15, while in males there is a sudden acceleration at age 13 through age 20 (Malina 1978). Height and weight follow the same path, with

adult males taller and heavier due to the longer growing period.

The increased strength of the male is seen in the muscle mass change. Five-year-old boys and girls have 40 percent of the body weight in muscle mass and at age 17 the muscle mass is 42 percent of the body weight in females and 53 percent in males. The sex difference occurs at around age 11 (Malina 1980 p. 453). Along with this increased strength and size of the muscle in the male in the secondary-school years, there is an increase in the fat composition of the female on the limbs so the total body composition of the male reflects greater lean body mass. The increased muscle mass of the male is reflected in grip strength, pulling strength, jumping ability, and throwing ability (Malina 1980 p. 463).

The body composition or the proportion of lean and fat tissue is of concern for fitness since overweight individuals are usually less fit in the ability to exercise over a long period of time. This may relate to the extra weight carried or to some relationship to cardio-respiratory fitness. Work performance is related to the low fat proportion found in the early years of life and decreases with age and the increase of fat (Parizkova 1973).

Systematic physical activity can result in a reduction in the fat and an increase in the lean body mass. This is particularly true in the rapid growth years when the fat metabolites act as a fuel and increase the metabolic turnover in adipose tissue. When energy output is reduced, fat is laid down (Parizkova 1973).

Children today are taller and heavier than children of the same age a few generations ago. Adults are also taller at maturity. This trend is seen in studies from Europe, Australia, Canada, Japan, and the United States (Malina 1979). Since strength and performance are related to body size, this trend in biological changes is of interest to human biologists.

Information on height and weight changes has been synthesized in reviews by authors in Australia, Scotland, Poland, Russia, Canada, Norway, the Netherlands, and the United States (blacks and whites); the greatest increase in size of children is seen until age 12–14 or during the pubertal years (Malina 1979). This increase in size is not seen in studies of the underdeveloped areas of Asia, Africa, and Latin America.

The increased size has resulted in strength changes increasing over the years with little change in strength per height or weight. However, the absolute increase in strength is certainly somewhat related to increased interest in fitness, and the improved performance at the Olympic Games must also relate to the increased number of performers.

Ethnic factors also have been studied relative to development and muscular strength. In the United States there have been many studies of whites, Negroes, Mexican–Americans, and Puerto Ricans (Malina 1973). The strength of Negro compared to white children is greater between 6 and 12 years, while the Mexican–American children had the lowest strength measured. It is not known how much this is related to socioeconomic differences, however.

2. Muscular and Cardiorespiratory Endurance

Physical training results in the hypertrophy or increased size of muscles. The increase in size is accompanied by increased strength changes along with changes in the biochemical responses and possible improved functioning at the molecular level. Though the number and type of muscle fiber is fixed by the time a child reaches school age, there are certain improvements seen in the enzyme activity of the muscle when training is undertaken.

One of the accepted tests of cardiorespiratory fitness is the maximal oxygen uptake or the aerobic power. In early childhood this increases with age and height. Between ages 8 to 14 when the maximum oxygen uptake is expressed as amount of oxygen (in milliliters) per body weight there are no increases seen with changes in size (Malina 1980).

Heredity has been shown to be the most important factor in the limits of the maximal oxygen uptake. Klissouras et al. (1973) showed, with identical twins, that heredity alone accounts for differences in functional adaptability at all ages. Even so, there are several twin studies showing 10–15 percent increases in maximal oxygen uptake levels following training. Thus, the limits of improvement may be fixed but the level of fitness is dependent on the activity during the school years. The measurement of maximal oxygen uptake often increases 15–20 percent with physical training.

Possibly due to the fact that growth and size increases are reflected in the aerobic capacity, or that elementary-school children are more active, change in the aerobic power is slight between the ages of 6 and 10. During the secondary-school years, there are large differences seen between children, with trainability apparently enhanced in adolescence (Malina 1980).

There have been few studies of the cardiac function during the entire adolescent growth period. One such study was reported (Seely et al. 1974) and it is of interest to see the changes found in this rapid growth period

related to cardiorespiratory function. The subjects were lower- and middle-class North Americans living in Montreal, Canada. A stratified sample of 168 students between 13 and 18 years of age was studied. Significant sex differences were seen by age 13. Respiratory function was mature by age 14 in girls and age 18 in boys. By age 18 boys had matured in cardiac function while hematocrit was still rising. With girls, the cardiac function did not reach maturity by age 18 and the maximal oxygen level increased with age with the girls, while with older boys there was no increase.

Muscular endurance has been shown to improve with training in the early years—ages 9–11. Age-group swimmers were tested following an intensive program for seven months and the arm endurance levels increased while strength and body composition did not change (Clark and Vaccaro 1979). The great intensity of the training program may have been necessary to improve the muscular endurance over and above the changes of the control group in this study. Further study of the preadolescent may also show such early changes since intense training is underway at very young ages in America. It remains to be seen whether the improvements seen at this early age are as great as with training at later ages when rapid growth has taken place.

The maintenance of strength and endurance is dependent on the continued activity of the individual. Weight training has been shown to increase strength and cessation results in decrease. The time period for retention is usually equal to the time of training. Maintenance of strength requires exercise as infrequently as once every two weeks. With endurance training, the decrease in fitness occurs more rapidly so that within a week, there are reduced capabilities. The maintenance of cardiorespiratory fitness requires exercise to continue at least twice each week to prevent the detraining effect (Astrand and Rodahl 1977 pp. 389–446).

The evidence supports the concept that endurance athletics is age related to the extent that the cardiorespiratory system matures after adolescence.

3. Measuring the Fitness and Developmental Level

The size of an individual is easily measured by the height and weight. The body composition relative to percent of fat and lean body weight can be found by underwater weighing or by skinfold and girth measurements. The most common skinfold measurements are: (a) back of the arm; (b) the abdomen; (c) the upper back; (d) the front of the upper leg; and (e) the side of the ribs (Mathews 1978). The girths of the chest, arm, and leg and the width of the wrist, knee, chest, and hip will estimate the nutritional status when used in the proper formulas (Mathews 1978).

Strength is easily measured by using standard hand, back, and leg dynamometers or a tensiometer (Mathews 1978).

Muscular endurance is best measured using the body

parts as the resistance, measuring the work done against this resistance. Typical tests are the pull-up, the push-up, and the sit-up.

Cardiorespiratory tests can be done in the laboratory measuring the maximum oxygen uptake and lung volume measures. These methods take time and expensive equipment, therefore it is more practical in a school environment to measure the pulse rate following a standard step test. Children enjoy these tests and most can be taught to count the pulse rate using the fingers placed at the wrist or neck. Also used is a distance run such as the mile run, or a test of the distance covered in a particular time such as a 6- or 12-minute period. A recent study (Krahenbuhl et al. 1978) found a good predictor of maximal oxygen uptake to be a 1,600 meter run for primary-school children 6 to 9 years of age.

4. Developing Fitness

The cardiorespiratory fitness level of elementary-school children is similar to strength changes and related to changes in body size during the six to ten year age span. Heredity factors evidently are of primary importance in the early years (Malina 1980).

Activities for the development of muscular and circulatory fitness in early childhood should relate to general daily activities of running, jumping, climbing, and throwing seen in elementary physical education programs. The California Physical Education Framework for California Public Schools (1973) suggests that a daily program of total participation should be set up for each primary-grade student aged 6–9 years. Cardiorespiratory endurance in these early school years is developed by suggested participation in continuous exercises, such as rope jumping and running for intervals of several minutes. Today, many schools are adding cross-country running and games such as soccer in early school programs. Muscular strength and endurance are developed and maintained by activities such as increased resistance stunts, gymnastics, and weight training. The California Physical Education Framework (1973 p. 45) suggests rope jumping and jogging around the playground to develop cardiorespiratory endurance in primary and intermediate grades (ages 6–11 years). Muscular strength and endurance is developed by such activities as suspending body weight on arms and crossing apparatus and climbing on apparatus for extended times.

Between the ages of 10 and 18 years the rapid change in growth and the increasing effects of environmental factors influencing fitness make this period of time very special. Sex differences become apparent, beginning with the early growth spurt in height and weight of girls, which comes approximately two years before the boys. During the adolescent years, the activities suggested are ones which involve fitness and carry-over activities following the school years.

The secondary-school years include the age group with the greatest variability in maturity and fitness levels. The change in development that occurs between ages 10 and 18 is different for each child and the relationship between age and performance during adolescence is less than in the earlier years where development and age are closely related.

The fitness level of the secondary-school child is related to sex and size, therefore these are the bases for comparison of individuals. The suggestion (California Physical Education Framework 1973 p. 44) to develop cardiorespiratory endurance is to participate in vigorous games such as soccer and cross-country running.

Muscle strength and endurance for the secondary-school child comes about by activities requiring stunts using the legs, arms, shoulders, and abdominal strength. Also suggested is the use of weights and weight machines.

The upper arm strength in boys increases more rapidly than in girls during the adolescent period. It is not known whether this is due to the interest of boys in arm strength or the sex difference related to sex hormones. In a number of nations, there has been a recent increase in the interest of girls in athletics. The result is that there are a large number of secondary schools with weight lifting machines, and an increased interest in running, gymnastics, and swimming programs for girls. The result of this interest in fitness will be revealed over the next few years. The probability is that sex differences will be less in future generations, particularly in strength and muscular endurance measurements.

5. Summary and Conclusions

It has long been recognized that in early childhood, changes in size parallel improved fitness levels. The role that exercise plays in these early years (6–10 years) is not clear since normal healthy children have a basic hunger for movement. Though it has been shown that prepubertal children can improve their strength and endurance with intense work, there appears to be a specific effect of early training that does not affect the linear growth, and has only slight effects on general strength and endurance.

With the beginning of the rapid growth period of school children (10–18 years), exercise appears to have a greater influence on size, strength, and endurance. The environment or extrinsic factors thus have a greater influence on the secondary-school child than on the elementary-school child.

While the limits of physical fitness are set genetically, the capability one achieves within those set limits is determined environmentally, that is, by nutrition and physical activity. The developmental pattern of growth and fitness is similar for all races, though the average size and fitness of a given ethnic group can differ from those of another group.

Both muscle strength and endurance that are due to the oxidative-enzyme change brought about by training are related to the intensity of the exercise undertaken. However, changes in fitness of an individual that are the result of physical activity are only temporary. Since one's level of fitness is retained for not more than a week or so, continued fitness requires continued exercise and proper nutrition.

Bibliography

Astrand P O, Rodahl K 1977 *Textbook of Work Physiology*, 2nd edn. McGraw-Hill, New York

California State Department of Education 1973 *Physical Education Framework for California Public Schools*. Bureau of Publications, California State Department of Education, Sacramento, California

Clark D H, Vaccaro P 1979 The effect of swimming training on muscular performance and body composition in children. *Res. Q.* 50: 9–17

Klissouras V, Pirnay F, Petit J M 1973 Adaptation to maximal effort: Genetics and age. *J. Appl. Physiol.* 35: 288–93

Krahenbuhl G S, Pangrazi R P, Petersen G W, Burkett L N, Schneider M J 1978 Field testing of cardiorespiratory fitness in primary school children. *Med. Sci. Sports* 10: 208–13

Malina R M 1973 Ethnic and cultural factors in the development of motor abilities and strength in American children. In: Rarick G L (ed.) 1973 *Physical Activity, Human Growth and Development*. Academic Press, New York, pp. 333–63

Malina R M 1978 Growth of muscle tissue and muscle mass. In: Falkner F T, Tanner J M (eds.) 1978 *Human Growth*, Vol. 2: *Postnatal Growth*. Plenum, New York, pp. 273–94

Malina R M 1979 Secular changes in growth, maturation, and physical performance. *Exercise Sport Sci. Rev.* 6: 203–55

Malina R M 1980 Physical activity, growth and functional capacity. In: Johnston F E, Roche A F, Susanne C (eds.) 1980 *NATO Advanced Study on Human Physical Growth and Maturation: Methodologies and Factors*. Plenum, New York

Mathews D K 1978 *Measurement in Physical Education*, 5th edn. Saunders, Philadelphia, Pennsylvania

Parizkova J 1973 Body composition and exercise during growth and development. In: Rarick G L (ed.) 1973 *Physical Activity: Human Growth and Development*. Academic Press, New York, pp. 97–124

President's Council on Physical Fitness and Sports 1971 *Physical Fitness Research Digest*, No. 1. Washington, DC

Seely J E, Guzman C A, Becklake M R 1974 Heart and lung function at rest and during exercise in adolescence. *J. Appl. Physiol.* 36: 34–40

Motor Development

R. M. Thomas

Motor development is the term commonly used in referring to the growth and improved functioning of body movements—of arms and legs, of hands and fingers, of tongue and lips, and of the torso. However, some writers prefer the term psychomotor development, since they believe it more accurately indicates the way body movements take place. They reason that seldom do body movements occur automatically, but, rather, the muscles operate the body at the bidding of the intellect, so they find it desirable to indicate this psychic participation through using the word psychomotor.

Another term commonly used in describing movements is motor coordination, which implies that a muscle never operates alone but only in combination with other muscles. Driving a car, playing basketball, preparing a meal, painting a picture, playing the trumpet—all require simultaneous, multiple muscular movements that must occur harmoniously in a proper sequence if the task is to be performed. One measure of motor development is the extent to which such separate movements compatibly cooperate to accomplish an act.

The participation of the sense organs in motor development is suggested by such phrases as eye–hand coordination, which is necessary for a child to learn to write or tie a shoe, or eye–foot coordination, which is needed to kick a rolling ball to a designated spot. Likewise, ear–finger coordination is required in playing the violin, while the sense of hearing normally must be coordinated with muscles of the throat and tongue when a person learns to speak or sing.

All of the forgoing factors are involved in the complex process of motor development. The nature of such development is summarized in the following paragraphs in terms of (a) sequences of development, (b) important influences on development, and (c) two principles of training.

1. Motor-development Sequences

The sequence in which motor development occurs has been studied in great detail, perhaps because motor skills are more easily observed and measured than are mental skills. In the infant and young child, motor control proceeds from the head downward (the cephalocaudal direction) and from the center of the body out toward the extremities (the proximodistal direction). Thus, the control of head movements comes earlier than that of the lower trunk and legs, and arm coordination is earlier than that of the fingers.

The general sequence for the development of different aspects of motor coordination is the same for all normal children, regardless of the culture in which they grow up. However, the exact time that a child gains a particular skill—such as that of walking alone—will differ from one child to another.

An example of the sequence for one set of motor movements is that of manipulating objects with the hand and fingers. The sequential skills, and approximate times that many children first attain these skills, are as follows: picks up cube from table when hand happens to touch cube (5 months); grasps with simultaneous flexion of fingers and briefly holds one cube in either hand (6 months); scoops hand to secure a pellet, and picks up cube easily from table (7 months); picks up pellet with partial finger prehension (8 months); opposes thumb and fingers in picking up cube (9 months); grasps pellet with precise pincer prehension (10 months); scribbles with crayon in imitation of adult writing (1 year); scribbles with crayon spontaneously and vigorously (1½ years); copies vertical line with crayon (2½ years); draws circle from model (3 years); traces diamond figure (4 years); draws triangle and prism from models (5 years) (Gesell 1928).

The sequence of movements leading to walking and running begins around age 5 months with the infant's gaining the skill of rolling from the stomach to the back and, later, from the back to the stomach. By age 8 or 10 months, most infants either crawl by wriggling on their stomachs and pulling themselves along by their arms, or they creep by moving ahead on hands and knees with their trunk lifted off the floor. At about this same age most children can stand when an adult holds them by the hand or when the infant holds onto furniture. Many can walk at age 10 to 12 months while holding on to an adult, then walk unsteadily alone around age 13 to 15 months. Within a few months they can run, though rather stiffly (see Table 1).

While these early sorts of motor activities proceed in an identical or similar sequence in all normal children, the sequences by which a person acquires more complex skills at later times of life can differ from one individual to another as a result of their receiving different amounts and kinds of training. For example, the sequence of acquiring the subskills that compose gymnastic performance can vary with different training routines.

2. Influences on Development

There are two principal sources of influence on motor development—genetic (biological inheritance) and environmental.

The genetic source can be divided into two varieties. First is the potential for the structural composition of the body as determined by the genes inherited from parents. The pattern of genes establishes the basic height, skeletal formation, general musculature, acuity of sense organs, and neural-system coordination that the individual will attain as he or she grows up. Second is the rate at which these elements and the resulting motor skills will mature, a rate heavily dependent on a genetically governed calendar. As a child grows up, the genetic factors combine with at least four types of environmental factors to determine how the genetic potentials will emerge as observable motor skills. One factor is nutrition, which in this instance refers both to what a person eats or drinks and to toxic substances which may be either intentionally consumed (drugs, alcohol, tobacco smoke) or else unwittingly assimilated (pollutants from the air or water). A second factor, closely linked to the first, is that of rest and fatigue—motor skills obviously diminish with fatigue. A third highly significant factor is practice or training. A fourth is disease or accident.

Throughout life the two genetic and four environmental elements interact to determine the motor skills the individual exhibits at a particular time. We shall consider each factor in turn.

2.1 Inherited Body Structure

Gene patterns establish the basic skeletal size and proportions (ratio of trunk length to arm and leg length, shoulder and hip width, size of fingers, and the like) that the individual will develop in growing up, and these proportions significantly affect the motor skills the person will possess. In addition, genes set the basic pattern of hormones that help determine the masculine and feminine physical characteristics a person will display. The hormones, in turn, influence the strength and coordination a person can develop while growing up. Thus, to the degree that inherited traits contribute in these ways to motor skills, a person can be—partially at least—a "naturally born" athlete, dancer, musician, typist, sculptor, or sleight-of-hand magician (see *Genetics and Human Development*).

Table 1
The development of motor ability with age

Age	Motor ability
1 month	Lifts head and turns head when on stomach. Visually follows slowly moving objects
2–3 months	Holds chest up when on stomach. Can raise head up while held in a sitting position. Begins to swipe at objects in visual range
4–6 months	Follows objects with eyes in different directions and planes. Sits up with some support. Reaches for and grasps objects. Holds head erect in sitting position
7–9 months	Sits without support. Rolls over in prone position. Crawls (moves with abdomen on the floor). Stands up using furniture. Transfers objects from one hand to another
10–12 months	Creeps (moves on hands and knees). Walks by grasping furniture or if hands are held. Stands without help. Squats and stoops
13–15 months	Walks without help. Stacks two blocks. Puts small objects into containers and dumps them. Climbs steps. Rolls ball to adult
18–24 months	Shows hand preference. Stacks 4–6 blocks. Turns pages of a book one at a time. Walks sideways and backwards

2.2 Rate of Maturation

The term maturation refers to changes in bodily structure or function caused by genetically timed, internal growth factors rather than by training or experience. The concept of maturation is of particular importance in psychomotor development during the earliest years of life, since the most basic landmarks of motor development during infancy and early childhood are determined far more by maturation than by training or practice. For the infant, this is true for such skills as grasping objects, sitting up, turning over, crawling, standing alone, and walking. Trying to teach an infant these behaviors before he or she is maturationally ready is of little or no use. The untrained child will attain the skill as soon as, or nearly as soon as, the child who has undergone training. And as the years pass, maturation continues to play a significant role—though not as dominant a role—in determining when a child will master such skills as jumping, skipping, handwriting, tying knots, manipulating toys, and the like. However, with the passing years, training plays an increasingly important part in psychomotor skills, particularly when complex motor behaviors are involved, as in the games of tennis and football, in the arts of ballet and playing the piano, and in the manual dexterity required of the expert office-machine operator, seamstress, or cabinet maker (see *Maturation and Human Development*).

Just as the genes determine the times at which physical abilities can arise and profit from training, so also the genes influence the deterioration of motor abilities in later life. Heredity, in combination with nutrition and exercise, affects how long bodily organs will function efficiently. Partly because of the human genetic time clock, the hand of the very elderly quivers, reaction time is slowed, muscle strength decreases, and locomotion agility declines.

2.3 Nutrition, Drugs, and Toxins

The food and other substances that humans ingest as the fuel for growth and action throughout life obviously exert a strong influence on motor skills. Since the effects of nutrition and of drugs on development are described in detail elsewhere, they are not discussed here.

2.4 Rest and Fatigue

With fatigue, motor coordination and strength decrease, to recover spontaneously only after rest. Proper training, as in athletics, consists of balancing the amount of practice against the amount of rest. Overtraining, without permitting sufficient time between training sessions for rest periods that permit muscle and nerve coordination to recover, results in a decrease in psychomotor performance. To determine what the proper balance may be for a given individual who is practicing a given skill, the performer or the instructor can keep records of the ratio of practice to rest in relation to level of performance and by means of such monitoring establish a productive regimen for the learner.

2.5 Training and Practice

While an advantageous genetic structure and sound nutrition form a basis for motor ability, it is clear that skilled performance depends in most instances on proper training and practice, particularly in the cases of complex motor activities. Today, more than ever before, marked advances are being made in refining training methods. Perhaps the most dramatic research conducted in this area has been on the improvement of athletic performance and on motor tasks carried out under such extreme circumstances as those faced by astronauts, underwater explorers, and antarctic scientists. The growing body of knowledge from such studies often appears in the form of guidebooks and training programs for specific combinations of motor skills. Instructors and students can turn to these sources for training suggestions. A large body of research also exists on methods of teaching handicapped children and adults.

2.6 Disease and Accident

How permanently disease or accident will affect motor skills depends to a great degree on the types and extent of body tissues damaged and on the age of the person suffering the damage. Certain body tissues—such as muscles, tendons, and bones—can regenerate themselves or be repaired with manufactured body parts. A damaged hip joint may be replaced with an artificial joint, and metal pins may serve to mend a damaged leg bone. In such cases, the patient can regain much, if not all, of the motor skill which was lost. However, if nerves, rather than muscles or bones, have been severed, as through an accident that cuts the spinal cord, the damage cannot be repaired. Nerve cells do not regenerate, nor can a severed nerve be successfully stitched together and thereafter operate as before. For example, damage to the lower spinal column leaves the patient without control over his legs for the rest of his life.

Age influences the effect of disease and accident on motor skills in at least two significant ways. First, damaged tissues in the young heal more rapidly than in the old. Second, elderly people who suffer the despair that can come with the deterioration of physical and mental abilities and with the expectation of life's end often lack the motivation to engage in the exercise needed to recover lost motor abilities. In contrast, the young may feel they have more to look forward to in life and may, therefore, exert the effort required to perform the regenerative exercises.

3. Two Principles of Training

Training procedures for enhancing psychomotor skills are quite specific to the particular skills involved. Obviously, the exact ways to improve one's ability to play the cello differ markedly from the ways to improve ice skating, juggling, or assembling a wrist watch. Thus, for aid in fostering a particular skill, students need information about the precise training techniques for that skill. However, in addition to specific directions, there are general principles that can serve as guidelines for promoting motor abilities of nearly any variety. The following are examples of two of the most important principles.

3.1 Maturational Readiness

As noted earlier, sufficient maturation of the underlying physical structures is necessary before training can profitably be undertaken. If the structures are not mature enough, the learner not only will fail to gain the skill, but physical or psychological damage may result. To illustrate this principle, consider the examples of toilet training infants and of teaching older children physical-contact sports.

In certain cultures, parents are anxious that infants learn as early as possible to retain urine and feces and only to urinate and defecate in a toilet and not in their clothing. However, the ability to retain feces and urine first depends on the maturation of the neural system that controls the sphincter muscles in the bowel and the urinary tract. Such maturation is absent in the newborn child. It is necessary to await the passing of many months for this maturation to occur and the child can gain conscious control over the muscles. Furthermore, even after the young child at ages 2 or 3 or older gains such control during his or her waking hours, he or she may not be able to maintain the control at night, and thus may unintentionally wet the bed. These accidents may also occur when the child is under emotional stress. Parents who fail to understand or accept this fact of maturation may use harsh physical punishment or verbal abuse to enforce early toilet training. Such treatment not only fails to achieve the goal of early bowel and bladder control, but it may damage the child physically or cause fears and a sense of personal worthlessness that persist for years to come. In contrast to such unreasonable expectations is an approach which recognizes the maturational factors underlying bowel and bladder functions. A reasonable attitude to adopt consists of (a) accepting a child's early lack of control as normal and nothing of which the child should be ashamed and (b), when sphincter-muscle control has matured, encouraging the child to use the toilet and praising him or her for doing so.

In some societies, boys and girls from ages 5 or 6 through ages 15 or 16 are urged to engage in strenuous physical activities that can unduly tax children's capacities. The activities may be in the form either of heavy adult labor or of contact sports, such as football, boxing, competitive wrestling, and ice hockey. What is not recognized by those who sponsor such events is that as children grow, not all of their body organs develop at the same rate, so imbalances among separate body functions may occur. In early adolescence, when rapid growth in bone length takes place, there may be insufficient muscle and heart growth to fully support the skeletal changes during vigorous sports or physical work. The adolescent whose height gives the impression of adult status may well be physically immature in other respects. Consequently, parents, athletic coaches, and employers who supervise children's physical activities need to be aware of growth imbalances, thus suiting physical endeavors to child growth patterns and avoiding undue strain on the child's capacities.

3.2 Individual Differences

In motor-ability potential, as in other aspects of development, no two individuals are exactly alike. This fact suggests at least two implications for parents and instructors.

First, the published studies of size and motor performance in children and adults at different age levels are not absolute standards which everyone of that age should attain in order to be considered "normal." Rather, these "norms" of heights, weights, shapes, measures of strength and endurance, and scores on performance are simply the result of averaging the measures of a group of individuals on such characteristics, with most of the individuals falling above and below the exact norm score, yet most of these individuals can still be considered growing at a satisfactory pace for their individual pattern of development. In short, age norms of size and motor ability are merely general guides to help parents, teachers, and medical personnel establish a general notion about where children of a given age may be located on a trait. But the decision about whether a child or adult is growing in a satisfactory way should be made on the basis of (a) whether the deviation from the average does not prevent the individual from fulfilling typical responsibilities in his or her life and (b) how reasonably an observed deviation from an average fits into the person's overall growth pattern. For example, a child's less than average eye–hand coordination as displayed in handwriting may fit reasonably into the general slower than average development pattern evidenced in the child's overall growth in height, weight, and coordination and thus be considered acceptable for that slower maturing child.

A second educational implication of individual differences is that the training program best for one child may not be the best for another. Therefore, a teacher may serve learners' needs most adequately (a) if the teacher has available more than one variation of training so that if one approach does not succeed well with a given student, another may be attempted and (b) if the teacher does not expect the same rate of progress from all students but allows for individual variations in performance appropriate to the students' differing levels of potential.

Not only are there individual differences in aptitude, but there are also discernible group differences. Perhaps the most obvious are sex differences, with the physical construction of the two sexes, along with their society's expectations, making one sex more expert at certain motor movements than the other. For example, males in general are more adept than females at feats requiring greater height and gross body strength, while females have been found generally more adept in finger dexterity, as in tasks of assembling small parts of scientific instruments.

Certain racial differences in body composition also appear to give one race an advantage over another in performing particular feats. In commenting on racial differences in body proportions, Tanner (1978 p. 98) has noted a characteristic difference between Europeans and Africans in the relation of shoulder width to hip width. The African has slimmer hips for a given shoulder width in both sexes. The proportions of the Asiatic in this respect are similar to those of Europeans. There are differences in body composition also, Africans having more muscle and heavier bones per unit weight, at least in males. These differences confer advantages and disadvantages in certain sports, with results that may be seen in Olympic records. Africans have an advantage in many track events, especially the high hurdles, and the Asiatics an advantage in gymnastics and weight lifting. Consequently, instructors of mixed-race groups should not be surprised if such body-structure characteristics show up as differences in performance of individuals in psychomotor activities.

Bibliography

Cratty B J 1979 *Perceptual and Motor Development in Infants and Children*, 2nd edn. Prentice-Hall, Englewood Cliffs, New Jersey

Eveleth P B, Tanner J M 1976 *Worldwide Variation in Human Growth*. Cambridge University Press, London

Falkner F T 1966 (ed.) *Human Development, by 29 Authorities*. Saunders, Philadelphia, Pennsylvania

Gesell A L 1928 *Infancy and Human Growth*. Macmillan, New York

Tanner J M 1978 *Education and Physical Growth: Implications of the Study of Children's Growth for Educational Theory and Practice*. Hodder and Stoughton, London

Brain Development and Function

J. A. R. Wilson

The human brain is rather like a soft, thick helmet of grey nerve tissues (the "new brain" connected to the helmet's inner contents of other sorts of nerve tissues, the "old brain"). The thick helmet portion is referred to as the "new brain" because it developed most recently in the evolutionary process. It consists of the cerebrum and its wrinkled covering, the cerebral cortex. Beneath the cerebrum, the inner contents of the helmet consist of elements that developed earlier in the evolutionary scheme and are thus known as the "old brain." These contents include such elements as the thalamus, the pons, and the cerebellum, and they connect directly to the spinal column, which is the shaft of nerve bundles that pass down the spine to carry messages to and from the network of smaller nerves that extend to all parts of the body.

Neural systems start to develop almost immediately after conception. Disease, diet, drugs, and disasters all influence brain development. Affective learning is primarily a function of the old brain and involves balanced systems involving neurotransmitters and hormones. Cognitive learning interprets and categorizes sensory input, coordinates this information with the affective input, and organizes output responses. The two halves of the brain operate together but have different primary responsibilities which should be considered by educators as they plan curricular and instructional strategies.

The nervous system consists of neurons, supporting neuroglia or Schwann cells, and neurotransmitters. The system is extremely complex with some 20 billion neurons, more supporting cells, and neurotransmitters available to make connections at any of the thousand or so junction points for each neuron. There can be as many as 10,000 neurons packed into a cubic centimeter of brain tissue; hence tracing pathways is an inexact process. In less compacted areas connections can be followed by killing a neuron, staining it, and observing the trail of the death, or, by stimulating a neuron and observing where the stimulation produces an effect.

Major subdivisions of the nervous system include: the peripheral system that brings in messages from all parts of the body and also takes messages to the muscles, glands, and other organs; the spinal cord that organizes these messages; and the brain that interprets and develops responses to the incoming messages. The brain is an interacting system that can be described in many ways. One set of subdivisions might include: (a) the cerebellum which functions primarily in controlling automatic movements; (b) the brain stem—including the mesencephalic area—which shunts messages through both the emotional and cognitive areas; (c) the thalamus which is a major junction for messages coming in from the sensory transducers; (d) the limbic system which, along with the hypothalamus, has major importance in affective control; (e) the cerebrum, that is the overarching wrinkled "brain" that sorts, interprets, and integrates sensory input and also organizes output messages; and finally (f) the hippocampus which acts as an interface between the affective and the cognitive systems.

1. Neural Development

The nervous system is of supreme importance throughout the life of any individual. By the eighth day after conception cell division has progressed far enough to have a separation between the ectoderm, which will become the nervous system, and the endoderm, which will become the complex digestive system. A week later, the mesoderm appears. The mesoderm will become the skeletal, muscle, and circulatory system.

By the end of the first trimester, when the fetus is only about two inches long, a healthy fetus will show reflex action to touch. The rapid development of the nervous system foreshadows the controlling function that this system will have over all of the operations of the body as well as the mind. The rapid period of development during the first trimester exposes the future child to a number of serious dangers since any one of some dozen viral infections during this period can have disastrous effects on the new life. Rubella, or German measles, has been closely studied. This virus stops the development of whatever is due for a growth spurt when it strikes, and it can result in the non-development of an arm, leg, or other part of the body. Often when the neural system is growing most rapidly the result of rubella is spontaneous abortion. Certain drugs, such as thalidomide, also cause damage that is obvious and disastrous. More subtle effects result from oxygen shortage that comes with the mother's smoking and other common practices.

During the second trimester, the neural system becomes sufficiently sophisticated to permit truly reflexive activity. The responses are coordinated, and by the end of this period it is possible for the potential infant to survive outside the womb if sufficiently sophisticated special care facilities are available. There are some problems, since by the end of the sixth month the cortex is still practically unwrinkled, with only the major fissures in place. Drillien (1978) studied 110 children in Edinburgh (UK) who were under three pounds in weight at birth, usually considered a sign of prematurity, and found that even after four or five years, only 9 percent scored over 100 on an intelligence test. By the end of the study period, a third were in special classes for the ineducable and a third were retarded in their normal classes. Of course, a few were doing very well.

Growth of the nervous system during the third trimester is spectacular. It is a period when a great deal of protein is needed by the developing fetus, particularly for the growing brain. During this period oxygen deprivation to the brain is particularly dangerous. Prescription and nonprescription drugs can be a serious hazard to the new life. Infants of mothers who are addicted to heroin show withdrawal symptoms and require special treatment after they are born. Anoxia, or oxygen starvation, is suffered by many infants either during or immediately after birth. In such cases it is the brain cells that suffer most since they require a continuous oxygen supply in order to survive.

The neural systems that control breathing, hearing, movement, and balance are in place and stabilized by the time of birth. Visual development is rapid immediately after birth. Hormone balances are established prior to birth and result in infants with characteristically different ways of responding to the strains of living outside the womb. To an unknown extent the hormone balance reflects the moods and mental health of the mother during the time she is carrying the child. Considering all the things that can and do go wrong during pregnancy and birth, it is truly remarkable that so large a percentage of children are born happy and healthy infants.

Of particular importance to educators is the need for protein in the diet during pregnancy if the nervous system is to grow and develop as well as it could, given its genetic potential. The amino acids that are not produced in the human body need to be supplied by the diet. The danger of viral diseases is great, particularly rubella during the first trimester of pregnancy, before most mothers-to-be are aware that they are pregnant. A case can be made for inoculating girls against rubella before they reach child-bearing age. In the second trimester, influenza viruses are particularly dangerous to the fetal development. Unfortunately there are many strains of influenza and the protection that inoculation offers is short lived.

Drugs, alcohol, and smoking all have damaging effects on neural development and should be avoided. A regular, serene life-style provides an environment that is likely to become a prototype for the new life. Long continued heavy emotional crises generate hormone balances that tend to become part of the life-style of the developing child. While these crises cannot be entirely avoided, awareness of the damage that over-response can cause may make it possible for the parents to reduce unnecessary strain.

2. Affective Learning

Educators are particularly concerned with affective neural patterns since so many students fail to respond to instructional procedures because of emotional or attentional problems. Olds and Milner (1954) located what they called pleasure centers in the limbic area of the old brain. Electrical stimulation in these areas led to active responding that superseded hunger or sex drives in rats, monkeys, and even in human beings. At about the same time as Olds was starting his work on pleasure centers, Delgado, Roberts, and Miller (1954) found punishment centers where continued electrical stimulation led to avoidance and, if continued, to death. The continued exploration of the pathways that were involved in pleasure and punishment stimulation led to greater understanding of: (a) the affective pathway; (b) the functioning of the hypothalamus and its relationship to the pituitary gland; and (c) the ways in which the affective loadings are associated with cognitive learnings.

Brain Development and Function

2.1 The Affective Pathways

The different senses, with the possible exception of smell, have quite streamlined and direct routes to the thalamus and from there to the cerebral cortex. As they pass through the midbrain area, the multitude of neurons that together are spoken of as touch, pressure, pain, hearing, sight, and the other senses, each sends collaterals into the mesencephalic reticular formation.

The neurons of the reticular formation are small, many branched, and nonspecific in their functioning. Many of them will respond to such diverse stimulations as a flashing light, a sound of a siren, or the prick of a pin. Following pathways through this maze is very nearly impossible. However, there are clusters of neurons called bundles or fibers that run from the mesencephalic area into the hypothalamus, on to the other limbic parts of the brain, including the hippocampus and, in some cases, on to the forebrain area of the cerebrum. As part of the study of pleasure stimulation, the pathways that use norepinephrine (noradrenaline), dopamine, and seratonin as transmitters have been studied intensively. While it would be satisfying to know that each of these systems had a clear and precise function, reality seems to be that not only these systems but many others are involved in pleasure, motivation, avoidance, and other emotional states. Balance seems to be the watchword, with too much of one system just as bad as too little. The fibers and bundles, including the medial forebrain bundle, provide systems connections important to affective learning.

2.2 The Hypothalamus/Pituitary Complex

The center piece of the affective system is the hypothalamus/pituitary complex. The hypothalamus feeds into the pituitary in two different ways. The hormones vasopressin and oxytocin are produced in the supraoptic and paraventricular nuclei respectively. They travel down the axons of the neurons and are released as neurotransmitters into the capillaries of the posterior pituitary. Vasopressin acts on the kidney to conserve water and oxytocin stimulates the contraction of the smooth muscle of the uterus and the muscles that release milk in the breast. Bohus (1971), working in Hungary, found that vasopressin also made avoidance learning long lasting, particularly in fear situations. The precise mechanism by which the vasopressin accomplishes this result remains unclear but the implication for educators is clear enough. If children are made fearful, they are likely to avoid the learning situation that is associated with the fear, and the avoidance is likely to be long lasting and very difficult to overcome. The vasopressin effect may explain why it is so difficult to remediate reading difficulties when children are frightened as they begin their reading experience.

The hypothalamus produces neurotransmitters that act on the anterior pituitary through a system of capillaries rather than directly as in the case of vasopressin. The neurotransmitters are hormone-releasing factors that control the secretion of growth hormones, thyroid hormones, adrenocorticotrophic hormone (ACTH), and most of the other hormones controlled by the pituitary. Multiple feedback loops to the hypothalamus control the amount of a hormone fed into the circulatory system, acting as a messenger to the glands usually associated with specific hormones. The balance of the hormones determines whether an individual will be happy and outgoing, or hyperactive. Based on hormonal controls, the emotions are much slower to start or to stop than are muscle movements but they are also much longer lasting. The importance of the balance can be shown by examining the effect of dopamine, a neurotransmitter that is very important in pleasure pathways. If the production of dopamine falls off in the substantia nigra, a way station from the mesencephalic area to the hypothalamus, Parkinson's disease develops. Often the symptoms of Parkinson's disease can be alleviated by increasing the supply of dopamine through providing L-dopa, a precursor of dopamine. However, if an excess of L-dopa is given, thus abnormally increasing the level of dopamine, symptoms of schizophrenia are likely to develop. The ways in which the different neurotransmitters and hormones interact are largely unknown.

2.3 Affective and Cognitive Interactions

The emotional toning of pleasure, avoidance, fear, and other reactions is associated with particular experiences. For educators these are usually learning experiences that are being established. The cognitive aspects of these learnings usually have followed a much more direct route to the cerebrum than is taken by the emotional component. The two parts of the experience, the cognitive and the affective, probably are brought together in the hippocampus where memory is being produced. There seems to be a comparator and a recycling of the cognitive and affective segments until they have been unified into a recognizable whole.

A part of the affective system is the analgesic handling of pain. The body produces encephalins and endorphins that act at the same sites and in much the same way as analgesics such as morphine. These are neurotransmitters with particular physical characteristics so that they bind in definite ways to receptor sites. These natural analgesics seem to explain why acupuncture relieves many pains and why placebos often relieve pain symptoms. Just how these natural painkillers interact with pleasure systems or other emotional states is not yet clear.

3. Cognitive Learning

The brain has sources of information, the senses, about the outside world that transform various kinds of energy into electrochemical impulses that can be used by the nervous system. The brain acts on the outside world through muscles that control speech, arms, legs, and other bodily parts. In addition, it acts on its own distant parts, controlling smooth muscles and glands. The main input systems are relatively direct, consisting of a neuron that runs to the spinal cord, another that runs up through the spinal cord to the thalamus, and a third that runs to the cerebral center. The output system is somewhat similar in reverse. There is a difference between the output to the voluntary muscle system and the output to the involuntary or autonomic system. In the latter case, there is one extra junction in the neurons that lead from the spinal cord to the muscle or gland. In part, this extra junction largely insulates the muscles and glands of the autonomic system from conscious control by the individual. Although the system is relatively simple, there are complex feedback loops at the muscle sites, at the spinal cord junctions, within the cord, and within the old brain. The relatively large size of the neurons (it is a long way from the toe to the spinal cord and from the lower end of the spinal cord to the roof of the mouth) makes study of these pathways easier than study of the affective system with its tangled system of small neurons.

Major transformations take place at the transducers—the Organ of Corti for hearing, the rods and cones for vision, and the Krause bulbs for temperature change. These changes make it possible to radically transform the nature of the impulse more or less as a television camera takes light impulses and changes them to broadcast waves.

In the auditory system, the outer ear with the ear drum and the middle ear with the hammer, anvil, and stirrup concentrate and magnify sound waves, producing motion in the liquid of the inner ear where the hairs of the Organ of Corti are bent by these waves. Low sounds produce long waves and high sounds short waves. The electrochemical impulses that are generated by the Organ of Corti keep their identity on the way to the cerebral cortex. Ninety percent of the input to each ear reaches both sides of the medial geniculate body, part of the thalamus, and from there to both hemispheres of the cerebral cortex. Because the ears receive the sounds at slightly different times and because the ipsilateral and contralateral paths are of somewhat different lengths, the slightly different arrival times at the cortex provide a basis for complex calculations that provide directional information about the source of the sound. In the unusual situation of dichotic listening, where different sounds are fed to each of the ears, the ipsilateral pathways to the cortex are shut down and only the contralateral pathways function. Much of the knowledge about processing in the cerebral cortex has come from studying inputs that went directly to a contralateral hemisphere and contrasting them with inputs that had to make the extra journey through the contralateral cortex to the ipsilateral cerebral cortex.

In vision the information picked up by the 120 million rods and cones is sorted and consolidated as it passes through the retina so that it can leave the retina in the optic tract consisting of only about six million neurons. The visual fields are separated so that the information in the right visual field of both eyes (roughly to the right of a perpendicular to the nose) goes to the left lateral geniculate body of the thalamus and on to the left hemisphere of the cerebral cortex. The information from the left visual field goes to the right hemisphere of the cortex. Land (1977) found that colors come from comparisons of shades of lightness picked up by different rods and cones. Since the cones can be traced separately to the lateral geniculate body (part of the thalamus) but not beyond, it is possible that the processing in the thalamus generates the basis of color vision. Other senses seem to go through similar complex processing in the area of the thalamus. The thalamus has direct connections to different areas of the cerebral cortex, and it has complex feedback loops from many different areas of the cortex as well as to different parts of the limbic, or emotional, system.

3.1 The Cerebral Cortex

The cerebral cortex is the part of the brain that is most uniquely human. It has a very large surface area, so large that it has wrinkled into many folds and creases in order to fit into the skull space. Much of what is known about the functions of different areas of the cerebrum has come from electrode stimulation. Penfield (1959) in Canada used this technique to determine which parts of the brain could be removed safely in patients who had tumors, epileptic seizures, and other problems that made brain surgery necessary although risky. A. R. Luria (1975), in the Soviet Union, developed a useful description of the functioning of the cerebral cortex both for processing sensory input and for processing motor output.

The visual input to the cerebral cortex arrives at the lower back of the brain (Fig. 1) on the occipital lobe. Part of this primary visual reception area is tucked into the fold between the hemispheres. Electric probes of this area result in light flashes in specific visual fields.

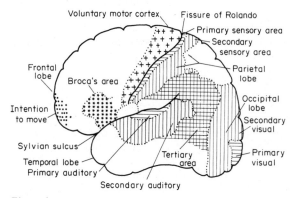

Figure 1
Areas of the brain

Adjoining this primary visual area is a secondary area where electric probes cause the formation of visual pictures filling the whole visual field. This secondary area apparently takes the raw data from the primary area and processes it into meaningful forms.

The primary auditory area is tucked into the fold of the Sylvian Sulcus on the temporal lobe. Electric probes of this area produce clicks and sounds that are tonotopically arranged. In other words as a probe is moved from a point where a low note is produced, each new stimulus will produce a higher note. Surrounding the primary auditory area is a secondary area on the temporal lobe. Stimulation of this area produces words in the left hemisphere and sound patterns in the right.

A similar arrangement exists along the posterior Fissure of Rolando where electrode stimulation produces sensations in different bodily areas arranged according to the sensory sensitivity of the bodily parts. The mouth area takes up much more space than the back but the arrangement of stimulus points is in order of the bodily arrangements from head to toe. The secondary somatosensory area adjoins the primary area on the parietal lobe, and stimulation in this area produces meaningful sensory patterns. Where the parietal, occipital, and temporal lobes come together is an area where stimulation may produce auditory, visual, or sensory patterns and occasionally all three at once. This tertiary area is an important integration area for sensory input. It is particularly important in integrated functions such as spelling, which requires both visual and auditory components.

Movement patterns start in very general terms as an intention to do something. This intention can be investigated by probes into the forebrain area; the intention becomes more specific in a secondary zone, such as Broca's area, and then becomes specific in the motor output area that lies along the anterior edge of the Fissure of Rolando, just across the fissure from the sensory input area. Commands from this motor cortex can be shown to be specific to precise muscle groups.

4. The Dual Brain

While the cerebral cortex has been described as though it were a single entity, it is in fact two halves which interact through a bundle of fibers called the corpus callosum. The thalamus is also dual in nature. The pathways into the cerebral cortex go first to the same side as that of the thalamus that feeds into it and then through the corpus callosum to interact with the input from the other side. The two sides of the cerebral cortex are not mirror images of each other and are specialized for particular functions. In the popular literature they are being called "the right brain" and "the left brain." It cannot be too strongly stressed that they are interacting parts of a whole system, even though there are

functions that are primarily the responsibility of one side or the other.

Well over a hundred years ago Broca (1863) found that damage to a frontal area on the left side of the brain led to expressive aphasia while similar damage on the right had little apparent effect on the ability to express speech. About 10 years later Wernicke (1874) found that damage in the left auditory area made it difficult to understand incoming speech. People with damage in the secondary auditory area often could talk quite fluently but the talk was without meaning. While the damage is nearly always on the left, there are some cases of left-handed people for whom the damage occurs on the right. Discussions of "right" and "left" brains always have to point out that there are some people, most often left-handed people, for whom the systems are reversed. Since the left hemisphere of the brain controls the muscles of the right side of the body, the discovery of speech in the left hemisphere led to the idea of a dominant hemisphere. Comparatively recently the functions of the right hemisphere of the cerebral cortex have been recognized as important.

In order to control severe epilepsy, a group of Californian scientists (see Gazaniga et al. 1962) sectioned the corpus callosum that joined the two hemispheres. Language was found to be largely confined to the left hemisphere, but the right hemisphere was better at music recognition, constructing spatial patterns with blocks, creating architectural patterns and, in general, holistic functions. The right brain had some language recognition, since if the word "spoon" were shown only to the left visual field and thus to the right hemisphere, the subject could pick out a spoon from a pile of objects.

If damage is done to one hemisphere of the brains of young children, the other hemisphere will take over the functions that are usually the province of the damaged area. For reasons that are not clear, women seem to be able to function better than men in using one hemisphere for functions normally performed in the other. Women are likely to have a higher recovery rate for language when the left hemisphere is damaged by a stroke than are men with similar damage.

To a very large extent, words are changed from the electrochemical code needed for transmission to discrete words in the left auditory (Wernicke) area. The Wernicke area is larger on the left hemisphere than it is on the right in most adults (Geschwind 1971). Even in newborn babies the larger size of the Wernicke area is observable in 65 percent of the individuals (Wada 1975).

Most school work has centered on operations that are primarily the province of the left cerebral cortex. The "back to basics" movement stresses reading, writing, and arithmetic, all of which are predominantly left hemisphere functions. Even when emphasis is placed on music, art, creative synthesis, and other functions that are primarily right brain in nature, the emphasis has often required the learner to use left-brain approaches to right-brain functions. Since music is learned most easily as patterns of sounds, successful music teachers have helped children and adults learn these patterns before they required them to read the notes. Probably many of the children who take music lessons and never succeed would do better if they were taught to play by ear before they were asked to play by note. This emphasis on imitation is the essence of the Suzuki method for teaching the violin to very young children which was developed in Japan. It is not to suggest that the notes are not important, but rather that the reading should have a meaning before it is taught.

In art, language often gets in the way of artistic production. Turning a picture upside down before it is copied often results in much better reproduction than copying the same picture the right way up. A head seems as though it should be much bigger than it actually is. If the word "head" is avoided even subconsciously, the lines can go together better.

In medical education the stress has been on verbal facility—memorizing materia medica, for instance. But medical practice diagnosis is very likely to be more of a right-hemisphere activity than a left-hemisphere one. Are potentially good doctors eliminated because of the education process followed? Education would apparently be stronger if more systematic attention were paid to teaching creative synthesis—a right-hemisphere activity—and not quite as much to verbal gymnastics—a left-hemisphere activity.

5. Memory

Most educators think of learning Shakespearian sonnets, multiplication tables, or history dates when memory is mentioned. However, 6-month-old babies will accept a blue bottle that has contained sweetened formula in the past and will reject a red bottle of the same size and shape that formerly contained bitter aloes. The only cue is color. These 6-month-old children have learned to associate color with taste and have remembered which color goes with which taste. Probably more human memory is at the level of recognizing the significance of a color difference than is involved in memory for verbal materials.

At the very basic level, the developing life remembers the genetic instructions to produce blue eyes and red hair. At a more sophisticated level, the embryo produces a breathing system and practices using it with amniotic fluid so that when the air makes breathing necessary for survival, then the necessary muscle synchronizations can be remembered and used flawlessly. Genetic codes for color selection and developmental processes needed for breathing are not usually considered memory but, in neurological terms, these processes are probably part of a continuum that includes memory for sonnets.

The genetic memory is carried in the deoxyribonucleic acid (DNA) that finds expression in ribonucleic acid (RNA) molecules. Considerable, although not conclus-ive, evidence points to RNA molecules as the basis for verbal memory.

A great deal of research activity has gone into a fruitless search for engrams or discrete bits of neurological memory. It may be that there are no discrete bits of memory but only processes capable of recreating patterns, much as a calculating machine stores, potentially, all the "memories" for addition. Penfield (1959) found that stimulating different points on the cerebral cortex would cause an individual to remember an incident of his or her past life as vividly as though he or she was reliving the incident. For them, time passed in real time and not in the instantaneous manner of ordinary memories.

Memories take time to become established. They can be broken up by an electric current during the first minutes or even hours after they are formed, but once consolidated they are very long lasting. Older people, who have not seen each other for half a century, can sit and talk and remember the kind of sandwiches eaten, and by whom, on a picnic 50 years earlier.

The hippocampus, where input from the affective and also from the cognitive systems is processed, has a definite but not well-understood role in memory formation.

Bibliography

Bohus B 1971 Effect of hypophyseal peptides on memory functions in rats. In: Adam G (ed.) 1971 *Biology of Memory: Proceedings of the Symposium Held at the Biological Research Institute in Tihany, 1–4 Sept 1969*. Plenum, New York, pp. 93–100

Broca P 1863 Localisation des fonctions cérébrales: Siège du language articulé. *Bull. Soc. Anthro.* 4: 200–04

Delgado J M R, Roberts W W, Miller N E 1954 Learning motivated by electrical stimulation of the brain. *Am. J. Physiol.* 179: 587–93

Drillien C M 1978 The growth and development of the prematurely born infant. In: Stone L J, Smith H T, Murphy L B (eds.) 1978 *The Competent Infant: Research and Commentary*. Basic, New York, pp. 220–21

Gazaniga M S, Bogen J E, Sperry R W 1962 Some functional effects of sectioning cerebral commissures in man. *PNAS* 48: 1765

Geschwind N 1971 Language and the brain. *Sci. Am.* 226(4): 77–83

Land E H 1977 The retinex theory of color vision. *Sci. Am.* 237(6): 108–30

Luria A R *The Working Brain: An Introduction to Neuropsychology*. Basic, New York

Olds J, Milner P 1954 Positive reinforcement produced by electrical stimulation of the septal area and other regions of the rat brain. *J. Comp. Physiol. Psychol.* 47: 419–27

Penfield W, Roberts L 1959 *Speech and Brain Mechanisms*. Princeton University Press, Princeton, New Jersey

Wada J A, Clarke R, Hamm A 1975 Cerebral hemispheric asymmetry in humans: Cortical speech zones in 100 adults and 100 infant brains. *Arch. Neurol.* 32: 239–46

Wernicke C 1874 *Der Aphasische Symptomkomplex: Eine Psychologische Studie auf Anatomischer Basis*. Cohn und Weigart, Breslau

Brain Laterality

J. A. R. Wilson

Laterality is a term with imprecise usage. Neurologically, it means the control of language and muscle groups by one side of the brain. The term is often used interchangeably but inaccurately with dominance which implies superordinate power of one hemisphere over the other. In special education, mixed laterality has been posited as a major cause of reading difficulty, although better understanding of brain functioning has raised serious doubts about the validity of certain testing procedures and also of the reality of mixed laterality as this term has often been used.

1. Empirical Basis

Dating from Broca's work more than one hundred years ago (Broca 1863), clinical studies have shown that damage caused by broken blood vessels, tumors, or other disasters was more likely to cause loss of language functioning if it occurred in the left hemisphere than if the same damage occurred in the right. Broca's area for expressive speech and Wernicke's area for receptive speech are well-defined in the left although, in some left-handed people, there is a reversal to the same areas in the right hemisphere.

Sperry (Gazaniga et al. 1962) found that the two hemispheres of a cat could be separated by cutting the optic chiasm and the corpus callosum, and that the two hemispheres could then learn separately. Working with Boden and Gazaniga, he used this technique on human subjects suffering from serious and disabling epileptic seizures. The operation cured the seizures, and extensive psychological tests were made to see what, if any, effects the operation had on the subjects. Language was found to be in the left hemisphere, although if the word spoon was flashed to the right hemisphere the subject could pick a spoon out of a pile of objects. The right hemisphere was important for music and for spatial relations, and although tasks such as building block designs on a Weschler test were not very well done by either hemisphere alone, the right-hemisphere production was much better than that of the left. The implication was that for some, and perhaps all tasks, interaction between the hemispheres was important. The complete separation of the hemispheres provided definitive data about functioning of each. Such commisurotomy was discontinued after a relatively small number of operations but did provide a great deal of information.

About the same time as Sperry was working on cats, Wada developed a sodium amytal injection technique for humans which anesthetized the hemisphere of the brain on the same side as the sodium amytal was injected into the carotid artery in the neck. Using this method it was found that more than 95 percent of right handers

have language in the left brain; from a half to two-thirds of the left handers and ambidextrous people also have language in the left hemisphere, but about 15 percent have some language on both hemispheres, and the rest have language on the right hemisphere. The injections are painful, and so less invasive techniques have been sought.

Blood flow, as measured by small increases in temperature, seems promising as an investigative technique but is not yet used on any large scale. Dichotic listening, where competing sounds are fed to the two ears, have been used extensively. On these tests only about 80 percent of right handers show up as having a right ear/left hemisphere preference. Since over 95 percent of physically separated hemispheres show this preference, it seems that ipsilateral suppression of the pathways is not always complete. Left visual field and right visual field presentations yield results similar to those for dichotic listening. Orton suggested the technique of eye preference or ear preference using simple tests as indicative of laterality (Orton 1937). However, each eye feeds into both hemispheres and each ear presents 90 percent of its input to both hemispheres, so these preferences are meaningless as indicators of hemispheric processing.

The indications from the empirical studies are that nearly all right handed people have language in the left hemisphere; that most left handed and ambidextrous people have their language in the left hemisphere but some have language in the right; and about 15 percent of people have substantial language processing in both hemispheres. However, a great many of the people with language in both hemispheres have no problems in reading or speech so mixed lateralization as an hypothesized cause of reading problems is suspect.

2. Lateralization: Ontogenetic or Phylogenetic?

In a study of the brains of 100 still born infants Wada (1975) found that at least 65 percent had a larger Wernicke area (which is used for receptive speech) on the left hemisphere than on the right. This difference paralleled similar findings by Geschwind for adults (1972). It seems that children begin life with speech areas on the left. Using electroencephalograms, a number of researchers have found greater responses to speech on the left and to music on the right even in very young children. These and other similar recent findings seem to indicate that infants are born preprogrammed for speech in the left hemisphere. These and other data contradict Lenneberg's (1967) thesis that the establishment of lateralization for speech is progressive until about 10 years of age. He based his theory on the finding that damage to the brains of infants results in little long-term speech disability—a finding with which most neuropsychologists would agree. He further claimed that right-hemisphere damage resulted in some speech impairment in children much more commonly than in adults. Krashen, among others, was unable to substantiate Lenneberg's findings and wrote that at the very latest, language lateralization was complete by 5 years of age and probably much earlier (Krashen 1973).

Related to the idea that incomplete lateralization causes reading difficulty, is a finding by a number of researchers that women are less completely lateralized for speech on the left than are men. Women tend to recover speech after damage to the left brain better than do men with similar types of damage. If imperfect lateralization were a major cause of reading difficulty, girls and women should outnumber boys and men in dyslexic studies. Actually, boys outnumber girls four or five to one in classes for remedial reading.

Bibliography

Broca P 1863 Localization des fonctions cérébrales Siège du language articulé. *Bull. Soc. Anthro.* 4: 200–04

Gazaniga M S, Bogen J E, Sperry R W 1962 Some functional effects of sectioning cerebral commissures in man. *PNAS.* 48: 1765–69

Geschwind N 1972 Language and the brain *Sci. Am.* 226(4): 76–83

Kinsbourne M, Hiscock M 1978 Cerebral lateralization and cognitive development. In: Chall J S, Mirsky A F (eds.) 1978 *Education and the Brain*. National Society for the Study of Education (NSSE), Yearbook 2. University of Chicago Press, Chicago, Illinois, pp. 169–222

Krashen S D 1973 Lateralization, language learning, and the critical period: Some new evidence. *Lang. Learn.* 23: 63–74

Lenneberg E H 1967 *Biological Foundations of Language*. Wiley, New York

Orton S T 1937 *Reading, Writing and Speech Problems in Children: A Presentation of Certain Types of Disorders in the Development of the Language Faculty*. Norton, New York

Wada J A, Clarke R, Hamm A 1975 Cerebral hemispheric asymmetry in humans: Cortical speech zones in 100 adults and 100 infant brains. *Arch. Neurol.* 32: 239–46

Wernicke C 1874 *Der Aphasische Symptomkomencplex: Eine Psychologische Studie auf Anatomischer Basis*. Cohn und Weigert, Breslau

Nutrition and Human Development

S. R. Schultz

The function of nutrition is to meet the energy and body-building needs of the human organism at any particular point in the life span. The needs for different nutrients vary along this span and, if not sufficiently met, growth and developmental deficits are potential consequences. There is a wide range of flexibility throughout the developmental process in regard to which nutritional deficits can be overcome by appropriate rehabilitation efforts. If rehabilitation takes place early enough, and if the original nutritional deficiency was not too severe, then relatively normal development is possible. There are, however, certain critical points in development at which a nutritional insult has an extremely high potential to produce permanent developmental deficits. These critical periods occur, for the most part, in the earlier phases of the life cycle during which the basic developmental plan is unfolding. The interaction of nutrient needs with the prenatal and early infancy periods is the main focus of this article. Poor nutrition during these periods can significantly influence children's performance during their later years in school.

1. Nutritional Needs

Nutrients as supplied by food support all life activities which take place in the cells of all organisms. The nutrient needs vary, within any species, according to gender, age, individual genetic make-up, various stages of the life cycle, and the demands placed on the organism by a particular environment. The nutrients are used to satisfy the organism's need for energy (calories) and the demands of growth and maintenance. In the latter category are included all of the synthetic and regulatory processes that require protein, vitamins (thiamin, niacin, pyridoxine, folic acid, vitamin C, vitamin A, vitamin D, etc.), and minerals (calcium, phosphorous, iron, zinc, etc.). In general, the more protein, vitamins, and minerals there are in a mixture of food for each calorie consumed, the more nutrient dense the food is. A high proportion of nutrient dense food is desirable at all stages of the life cycle to support human growth and development most effectively.

2. Nutrition and the Developmental Process

The process of human development involves complex genetic and environmental interactions that are dependent on a steady supply of nutrients for energy needs and for synthetic (tissue-building) needs. Under normal conditions, the extent to which the very early stages of development are impaired can be taken as a gross approximation of the genetic contribution to developmental problems. The imprecision as to the absolute contributions of either the genes or the environment centers around the definition of "normal" conditions. Usually this would be taken to mean conditions of good health, sanitation, housing, high-quality medical care, unimpaired access to high-quality food, and so on. These are conditions associated with affluent sectors of developed countries. However, even under these "ideal" conditions, there are many environmental factors that affect development. Among the suspected risks of pregnancy are tobacco, alcohol and caffeine consumption, and poor nutritional status, due to poor or uneducated food choices. For example, recent nutritional surveys (Abraham et al. 1979, Appel and King 1979) indicate that a significant portion of pregnant women, at all economic levels in such a nation as the United States, suffer marginal iron, folic acid, vitamin B6, zinc, and energy status. Thus, financial well-being does not ensure good nutritional status or freedom from other negative environmental influences.

Not only does the developmental process demand a continual supply of energy and nutrients, but there are also certain times during the course of development when nutrient needs are special, and/or the process is especially sensitive to disruption by a poor nutritional environment. To understand these periods of special needs it is important to understand some more of the details of growth and development. This process comprises alternating and partially overlapping cycles of proliferative growth and synthetic growth. These cycles hold true if one is speaking of the early fertilized ovum, or of the later growth of a particular organ. The proliferative phase is a period during which the rate of cell production is highest and the organ or organism attains the optimum, in terms of genetic potential for number of cells. This phase is termed hyperplasia. If key nutrients are not fully available for the demands of hyperplastic growth, permanent reduction of the possible total number of cells is the outcome. This, in turn, leads to diminished size of organs, with functional reductions when compared to norms (Winick 1976). Interference with normal hyperplastic growth is of great concern when one considers human brain development. The most rapid proliferative growth in the brain is during the third trimester (the last three months) of pregnancy and early infancy (Winick 1976, Lloyd-Still 1976) and is potentially a time of high impact of nutrition.

The second phase of the growth cycle involves increase in cell mass (or volume) by synthesis. This phase is termed hypertrophy, and the increase of cellular materials is dependent on a constant supply of nutrients provided by food. In terms of organ development, this phase takes hold after the phase of hyperplastic growth, and after the qualitative arrangement of the cells has taken place (Winick 1976, Worthington-Roberts 1981). Brain development, for example, is now thought to proceed well into adolescence and perhaps longer. Most postnatal development involves neural process elaboration and is hypertrophic. Although this is seen as a quantitative process, there are many qualitative changes taking place in this synthetic phase of growth. This is a period of formation of large numbers of connections among the brain cells. The relative attainment of the level of this "dendritic arborization" is thought to correlate with the level of brain function. In addition to nutrition, the quality of the sensory environment is quite

important in this latter phase of brain development, in that sensory stimulation, or the lack of it, has consequences in terms of future brain function (Worthington-Roberts 1981, Lien et al. 1977). In this sense the needs for proper nutrients and sensory stimulation are equally "critical" during this phase of growth as they are during a hyperplastic phase.

There is another phase of development that can also be considered as "critical." This is the period of organogenesis, when the basic organ plan is established. In humans organogenesis occurs during the first trimester and involves complex interactions of the three primary germinal tissue layers—ectoderm, mesoderm, and endoderm. If the program of timing of movement of these tissue layers is disrupted, or if the developmental messages between the tissue layers is disrupted, the outcome is impaired development. This period has the highest potential for poor nutrition resulting in teratogenesis and subsequent fetal malformations. Thalidomide serves as a good example. It is a minor tranquilizer with no apparent ill effects when taken by pregnant women in their second and third trimesters, that is, the last six months of pregnancy. Consumption during the first trimester (first three months), however, results in disastrous outcomes, in that a high proportion of offspring are born with severe limb deformities. In summary, all of these growth and developmental phases are periods of special needs in terms of nutrition (and social stimulation), and these special needs are manifested at many different points in the life cycle.

The functional significance of nutritional deficits during the early part of the life cycle has been studied in many different countries. Long-term studies carried out in Mexico, Guatemala, and South Africa (where there are significant levels of malnutrition), indicate that growth and developmental deficits correlate with nutritional deficits during pregnancy and infancy (Lloyd-Still 1976, Rosso and Cramoy 1979). The growth deficits measured were those in weight, height, height–weight index, and head circumference. A few studies have indicated that brain weight and the number of brain cells are reduced to the extent of 30 percent or more under conditions of severe malnutrition. The developmental deficits measured were those of motor and cognitive skills and general intelligence (Winick 1976). A number of studies combine a retrospective analysis with a prospective approach and suggest that it is possible to overcome some of these deficits with nutritional interventions. Results from a Guatemalan study indicate that a nutritional supplement of 20,000 calories during the course of pregnancy improves birth outcome (Dobbing 1981, Worthington-Roberts 1981). In addition there is some evidence that children born to these supplemented women attain better intellectual achievement levels.

In summary, it is clear that if the energy and other nutrients for synthesis are not supplied, or supplied in limited quantities, then some form of impairment to development is a certainty.

Table 1
Distribution of weight gain at the end of pregnancy[a]

Tissue	Weight (kg)
Fetus	3.5
Amniotic fluid	0.6
Placenta	0.8
Uterus	0.9
Mammary	0.4
Intracellular fluid	1.2
Blood	1.8
Maternal stores	3.3
Total	12.5

a Adapted from Appel and King 1979 p. 9

3. Nutritional Needs of Pregnancy

The extra nutrient requirements of pregnancy are used for tissue deposition and increased oxygen consumption of both mother and fetus. The course of development in the mother's uterus takes about 40 weeks. In addition to fetal development, the mother's body is also developing specialized structures. The first half of pregnancy is sometimes termed the maternal phase. This usage is intended to denote that the majority of nutrient needs are to support growth of maternal tissues such as placenta, blood, and storage compartments. The second half of pregnancy is termed the fetal phase and indicates that the majority of growth is by the fetus itself and is not of the supporting tissues. It is important to emphasize all of these growth needs so that the nutrient requirements at all stages of pregnancy are understood. In the early stages the fetus (or embryo) is quite small and therefore growth needs are small. The maternal body is, however, preparing itself to accommodate the pregnancy, and the demands are high. It is, therefore, desirable to maintain good nutritional status from the first day of pregnancy. The maternal body is also preparing for producing breast milk (lactation) from the first day of pregnancy—a fact not often stressed to pregnant women by health professionals. This is another reason to maintain a high level of maternal stores throughout pregnancy.

A total weight gain that supports the functional needs of pregnancy and the needs for good maternal stores is, on the average, 12.5 kilograms (kg). The distribution of this weight gain in maternal and fetal tissues is illustrated in Table 1. It can be seen that the weights of the fetus at the end of pregnancy and of the maternal stores are nearly the same. While the pattern of weight gain is highly variable, an ideal pattern is 1 to 2 kg in the first trimester and 0.5 kg per week thereafter until the birth of the child. Inadequate weight gain is defined as less than 1.0 kg per month during the last two trimesters. Weight gains of this magnitude increase the risks of delivering low-birth-weight babies and of reduced milk-producing performance. Since prepregnancy weight and gain in weight during pregnancy are independent and additive in their effects on birth weight (Appel and King 1979, Rosso and Cramoy 1979), an obese woman should not undertake a weight reduction diet at this time.

Some of the nutrients that support the desired pattern of weight gain of pregnancy are illustrated in Table 2. The Recommended Dietary Allowances (RDA) for nonpregnant and pregnant women in the United States are shown in columns 1 and 2. The Canadian and Food and Agriculture Organization/World Health Organ-

Table 2
Recommendations for daily intakes of nutrients during pregnancy

Sources of Recommendation: Nutrient	National Research Council/ National Academy of Sciences, 1980 Nonpregnant (1)	Pregnant (2)	Canadian Department of National Health and Welfare, 1975 Nonpregnant (3)	Pregnant (4)	Food and Agriculture Organization/World Health Organization, 1973 Nonpregnant (5)	Pregnant (6)
Energy (Kilocalories)	2,000	+300	2,100	+100 1st trimester +300 2nd and 3rd trimester	2,200	+150 1st trimester +350 2nd and 3rd trimester
Protein (grams)[a]	44	+30	41	+20	36	+11
Calcium (milligrams)	800	+400	700	+500	400	—
Iron (milligrams)	18	+18[b]	14	+1	19[c]	—
Folic acid (micrograms)	400	+400	200	+50	—	—
Vitamin A (Retinol equivalents)	800	+200	800	+100	750	+450
Vitamin B-6 (milligrams)	2.0	+0.6	1.5	+0.5	—	—
Zinc (milligrams)	15	+5	9	+3	—	—

a High quality protein   b It is recommended that increased iron needs be met by 30–60 mg of supplemental iron   c Mixed diet from plant and animal sources

ization (FAO/WHO) recommendations are shown in columns 3 to 6.

The total energy cost for a full-term pregnancy is about 80,000 kilocalories (Appel and King 1979, Rosso and Cramoy 1979). This averages 300 kilocalories per day over the normal allowance, and supports the increased respiratory demands and needs for tissue deposition of the mother and fetus. The latter category includes the maternal energy storage depots. Studies indicate a progressive accumulation of maternal energy stores to about 32,000 kilocalories under conditions of adequate weight gain. This stored energy is utilized in the last part of the third trimester (when food consumption declines due to the crowding of the gastrointestinal tract by the fetus) and to subsidize lactation (see below). The World Health Organization recommendations are for 150 extra kilocalories per day during the first trimester, and 350 per day thereafter (Food and Agriculture Organization/World Health Organization 1973 pp. 35–36). Dietary surveys conducted in the United States indicate that energy intake of pregnant women is less than recommended, whereas intakes in countries such as the Soviet Union are at, and above, the recommended levels (Appel and King 1979).

Protein intake during pregnancy is quite important as it provides the basic building blocks (in the form of amino acids) for growth. The increase of the element nitrogen, which is provided by the amino acids, is used as a measure of growth. The relative protein status at any time is dependent upon the energy status; and if energy is low, protein is utilized for energy functions rather than synthetic tissue-building functions (National Research Council/National Academy of Sciences 1980 pp. 47–49). If energy intake is adequate, protein is "protected" in that it is utilized primarily for synthesis. The daily intake recommended in the United States for a nonpregnant female is 44 grams of high-quality protein, with an extra allowance of 30 grams for pregnancy. This brings the total to 74 grams of protein per day (National Research Council/National Academy of Sciences 1980, Rosso and Cramoy 1979). The World Health Organization requirement is 41 grams of moderate quality protein for the nonpregnant female with an added allowance of 13 grams for pregnancy (Food and Agriculture Organization/World Health Organization 1973 p. 74). The reasons for the discrepancy between the National Research Council/National Academy of Sciences allowance and the Food and Agriculture Organization/World Health Organization requirement are not clear, but could involve differences in techniques for measuring protein utilization. Quality of protein is a reflection of the pattern of essential amino acids in that protein. Foods such as eggs, milk, beef, pork, fish, and soybeans contain proteins with a pattern of essential amino acids best suited to human needs. Foods such as grains and certain beans and peas contain proteins which are relatively low in one or more of the essential amino acids. These low-quality protein foods can be mixed in a "complementary" fashion to provide a protein mixture of adequate quality. This complementarity is the basis for adequate protein status in vegetarian populations throughout the world. Numerous studies have demonstrated that vegetarians can attain very good protein status and support a normal pregnancy (Worthington-Roberts 1981). The key here is a well-chosen diet from a variety of foods. Practically, the increased daily energy and protein needs of pregnancy can be met by a glass of milk and a peanut butter sandwich on whole wheat bread. Surveys in developed countries indicate that pregnant women consume protein in adequate amounts to meet their needs (National Research Council/ National Academy of Sciences 1980 p. 80). As discussed above, there is an interdependent relationship between energy status and protein status. This relationship is reflected in the condition of protein–energy malnutrition (PEM), where one usually observes a shortage of calories for energy combined with poor protein supply. There is usually an elevated incidence of poor birth outcomes under conditions of protein–energy malnutrition.

Calcium is important for proper development of bone and teeth. The extra needs are greatest in the second half of pregnancy when the rate of fetal bone growth markedly increases. Calcium needs should not come at the expense of maternal stores; therefore, an extra allowance of calcium is added on a daily basis (see Table 2). There is some evidence that different populations have variable calcium needs, depending on certain dietary practices. For example, the high protein and phosphorous consumption in the United States seems to increase the need for calcium, explaining, in part, the higher recommended levels as compared to the World Health Organization standards. Whole cow's milk cannot be considered the universal source of calcium in the diet. Differences in populations show varying degrees of deficiency of the enzyme lactase in certain groups, such as Asian, black, and Middle Eastern peoples. This deficiency is termed "lactose intolerance," and signifies incomplete utilization of lactose in milk. Since the lactose cannot be broken down into its components to be absorbed, the lactose passes into the large intestine. Bacterial action then produces the symptoms of abdominal cramping, bloating, flatulence, and diarrhea. Alternative calcium sources are dark green leafy vegetables, certain seeds (sesame), canned fish, and fermented dairy products in which the lactose is predigested, such as cheese and yoghurt.

Maintaining proper iron stores is essential to meet the increased maternal respiratory needs and fetal development needs. The average diet in certain developed nations does not provide adequate iron to meet these needs (see Table 2); therefore, a daily supplement is recommended. Both Canadian and World Health Organization recommendations take into account maternal stores and the type of diet consumed. This involves certain iron-enhancing properties such as the "meat factor", and the presence of ascorbic acid. Other factors such as the use of cast iron cookware also enhance the availability of iron. If possible, blood-composition values should be monitored during pregnancy and adjustments made accordingly. The dietary level should be around 18 milligrams of iron per day from a mixed (plant and animals sources) diet.

Needs for folic acid during pregnancy are very high since this vitamin is involved in cell proliferation. There is evidence to suggest that folic acid deficiencies are associated with problems of labor, delivery, and fetal malformations (Worthington-Roberts 1981). The importance of this nutrient is indicated by the recommended intake which is doubled in pregnancy (see Table 2). Good sources of folic acid are wheat germ, legumes, dark green leafy vegetables, oranges, and eggs. Surveys indicate that deficient intake of folic acid is widespread in such nations as the United States. This situation is due to a change in diets away from the whole grains, legumes, and leafy vegetables rich in folic acid. As a result, a daily vitamin supplement of 800 micrograms of folic acid is recommended for pregnant women in such countries. A number of nutritionists view this strategy as limited and prefer an educational approach, aimed at promoting better food choices among this population.

Vitamin A is another key nutrient in terms of importance in cell development and growth of bone and teeth. The recommendations in all cases (see Table 2) are for a substantial increase in the diet of a pregnant woman. Good food sources of vitamin A are butter, cream, and green and yellow vegetables.

Both vitamin B6 (pyridoxine) and zinc are important to the growth process in general and for proper brain development in particular. The specific recommendations are shown in Table 2, and surveys (United States Department of Health, Education, and Welfare 1977) indicate that pregnant women often can be deficient in these nutrients. Vitamin B6 and zinc are present in whole grains, legumes, liver, pork, and beef. Processing of whole grains extracts these nutrients to a great extent.

The general dietary recommendations for a pregnant woman are for a varied diet, well-chosen from unrefined grains, legumes, vegetables, fruits, lean protein sources and dairy products (or other calcium sources). Attention should be given to adequate caloric intake and to the nutrients described above. Many nutritionists call for greater efforts in the area of nutrition education and counseling for this target group as well as for the health professionals who serve them.

4. Nutrition and Birth Outcome

Birth outcome is measured by the infant's birth weight, infant death rates, infant disease, birth-labor and delivery complications, malformations, and other developmental problems. The optimal birthweight is in the range of 3 to 4.5 kg (Dobbing 1981, Rosso and Cramoy 1979). The chances for poor birth outcome rise dramatically at birth weights below 2 kg. The three main predictors of poor birth weight are prepregnancy maternal nutritional status, maternal weight gain during pregnancy, and maternal socioeconomic status (Rosso and Cramoy 1979).

As discussed above, there are numerous studies which associate low birth weight with poor birth outcome. There are also selected studies which suggest improved birth outcome when maternal nutrient intake is improved, although the evidence for ascribing improvement to nutrition alone is not without controversy (Dobbing 1981). In spite of this uncertainty, it seems prudent for a pregnant woman to aim for an optimal birth weight. In addition to proper health care and good nutrition, the avoidance of alcohol, tobacco, and drugs is desirable.

There have been recent reports that certain brain and neural-tube developmental deficits can be overcome by supplements of vitamins and minerals in large doses when taken by pregnant women (Smithells et al. 1981). Other studies have claimed that a vitamin–mineral supplement given to children with Down syndrome improves their general intelligence and in some cases normalizes the facial features of mental retardation brought about by this condition (Harrell et al. 1981). But most researchers in this field urge extreme caution in interpreting these isolated and poorly controlled studies.

5. Postnatal Growth and Development

Most of what has been discussed in terms of prenatal development holds true for the postnatal period. The Jellifes point out that the months following birth form the most crucial period in terms of susceptibility to the immediate environment, and they label the neonate an "exterogestate fetus" (Jellife and Jellife 1979). It is the period of greatest risk in terms of mortality, morbidity, and developmental deficits. Not surprisingly, the first year of life requires the highest level of nutritional input, on a body weight basis, of any period (see Table 3).

The question that most often arises during this period of development is that of reversibility of any nutritional shortcoming. This issue has been researched most intensely in the area of brain development and subsequent intellectual performance. As a general rule, the less severe, shorter in duration, and later in the developmental sequence the nutritional shortage, the better the chances for subsequent normal development through nutritional rehabilitation. Any number of studies point to protein–calorie malnutrition of great severity, long duration, and occurring early in the postnatal period as leading to poor brain growth and poor developmental outcomes (Lloyd-Still 1976). A long-term study in South Africa, for example (Stoch and Smythe 1976), demonstrated that children from a population of low socioeconomic status who were severely malnour-

Table 3
Nutrition recommendations (United States)[a]

Ages (years)	Infants–children					Nonpregnant women 23–50	Pregnant women 23–50	Lactating women 23–50
	0.0–0.5	0.5–1.0	1–3	4–6	7–10			
							(In addition to nonpregnant allowance)	
Energy (kilocalories)	Kg × 95–145	Kg × 80–135	1,300	1,700	2,400	(Kg × 36) 2,000	+300	+500
Protein (grams)	Kg × 2.2	Kg × 2.0	23	30	34	44	+30	+20
Calcium (milligrams)	360	540	800	800	800	800	+400	+400
Iron (milligrams)	10	15	15	10	10	18	18+	18+
Folic acid (micrograms)	30	45	100	200	300	400	+400	+100
Vitamim A (retinol equivalents)	420	400	400	500	700	800	+200	+400
Vitamin C (milligrams)	35	35	45	45	45	60	+20	+40
Vitamin B-6 (milligrams)	0.3	0.6	0.9	1.3	1.6	2.0	+0.6	+0.5
Zinc (milligrams)	3	5	10	10	10	10	+5	+10

a National Research Council/National Academy of Sciences 1980

ished and who were rehabilitated after 2 years of age, still manifested growth and developmental deficits, when measured 5, 10, and 15 years after rehabilitation. These outcomes were in comparison to a matched group of children who were not malnourished. If nutritional rehabilitation is early (before 18 months in the chronically malnourished and coupled with an adequate level of social stimulation), it is possible to normalize development (Worthington-Roberts 1981).

6. Postnatal Nutritional Needs

The neonatal period is the most energy demanding for the mother–infant dyad than any other period of the life cycle. Table 3 shows a number of nutrient requirements for the infant, nonpregnant, pregnant, and milk-producing (lactating) women. It can be seen that the lactation period requires an additional 500 kilocalories per day. The actual energy cost of lactation is likely to be 800 to 1,000 extra calories per day. The surplus calories (300–500 per day) come from the maternal energy stores which were being deposited from the first days of pregnancy.

It was stated previously that the female body is preparing for postbirth needs of giving milk from the first day of pregnancy. The importance of this need is not often stressed in counseling of pregnant or nursing women. The demand on the body of an extra 1,000 calories of output is enormous. Most new mothers are unprepared for the overbearing sense of fatigue in the first few months after giving birth. Often the expectations are that a woman be able to handle a newborn

nursing child, tend to the needs of the other members of the family, and carry out all other household responsibilities with efficiency and good cheer. When the energy demands of lactation overcome and conflict with these expectations, the result is often self-blame and depression. These feelings are often responsible for many women giving up breast-feeding in the first few months. If the potential nursing mother and the health professionals who serve her were more aware of the extreme demands on the female body at this time, better management of this period would be possible.

In terms of the nutrient needs other than energy during lactation, these are increased in relative proportion when compared to the nonpregnant state (Table 3). The question arises as to the best source of these nutrients to meet the needs of the infant. In spite of a number of generations, worldwide, of declining incidence of breast-feeding, recent reviews of all the information point to the desirability of breast-feeding as the sole or major source of the infant's nutrients for the first 6–10 months of life (Jellife and Jellife 1979, American Academy of Pediatrics 1982, Ogra and Greene 1982). The adequately nourished lactating woman will consistently produce 750–1,000 milliliters (ml) of milk of proper energetic and nutrient balance to promote the optimal growth and development of the infant. Lactation once established successfully can continue for years with little or no loss in quantity or quality (providing the mother's diet is adequate). If maternal nutritional intake is inadequate during the course of lactation, the output and the quality of milk will deteriorate. If the infant is being exclusively breast-fed, the reduced maternal nutritional status will be reflected in a decreased rate of child growth. In this case, improved nutritional intake for the mother and/or a nutritional supplement for the infant is recommended. Unfortunately, supplementing the infant's diet is usually the only course recommended by the health professional. With a minor effort toward counseling mothers in nutritional principles and with proper breast-feeding technique, adequate production of human milk can be quickly reestablished.

In addition to nutrient adequacy, there are many other suggested health, developmental, and psychological benefits of breast-feeding. Some of these are: (a) fewer gastrointestinal and upper respiratory infections in the infant (due, in part, to the presence in human milk of certain immunity factors and other protein factors which promote conditions favorable to bacteria which crowd out the more infective strains; (b) the composition of human milk in terms of the carbohydrates, proteins, and lipids favors the digestive and absorptive mechanisms of the infant's immature gastrointestinal tract and also provides components of these nutrients not found in formulas based on cow's milk (e.g., the rare amino acid taurine which is required for early growth of the nervous system); (c) there are selective absorption factors in human milk for vitamins and minerals, hence the bioavailability of these nutrients is optimal; (d) the incidence of infant mortality, diarrhea, allergies, and dental caries are lower in breast-fed babies; (e) maternal–infant bonding is enhanced by breast-feeding—this bonding is the total effect of constant skin-to-skin contact, eye contact, smells, and sounds of the shared emotional experience which promotes psychological trust between mother and child (Klaus and Kennell 1976); (f) the cost of the extra maternal nutrients needed for lactation is far less than costs for commercial formula. Also, human milk is a living, nonhomogeneous product. In addition to containing live cells which confer immunity, the proportion of lipid changes during the course of a feeding. Later milk (hind milk), therefore, is 3 to 5 times more concentrated in lipids than early milk (fore milk), making it progressively more difficult to draw from the nipple. Such a mechanism is thought to promote a natural process for causing the child to feel satisfied and account for the lower incidence of obesity in breast-fed infants.

The relative psychological and developmental benefits of breast-feeding to the mother–infant dyad make it important that greater efforts are made in the education of health professionals, and the public, and in regulating the mass marketing and promotion of commercial baby food.

7. Postinfancy Development and Nutrition: Implications

Although much of the developmental plan has taken hold by infancy, the needs for adequate nutrient intake continue throughout the life cycle. These varied needs are usually minor modifications of the patterns of nutrient intakes in pregnancy, lactation, and infancy. The persistent problem is one of identifying those factors which might interfere with adequate nutrition, and, in turn, interfere with development.

Bibliography

Abraham S et al. 1979 *Dietary Intake Source Data, 1971–1975,* Report No. MD DHEW PHS 79-1221. National Center for Health Statistics, Hyattsville, Maryland
American Academy of Pediatrics 1982 The promotion of breast-feeding: Policy statement based on Task Force report. *Pediatrics* 69: 654–61
Appel J, King J 1979 Energy needs during pregnancy and lactation. *Fam. Commun. Health* 1: 7–18
Canada Department of National Health and Welfare 1975 *Dietary Standard for Canada,* rev. edn. Department of Public Printing and Stationery, Ottawa, Ontario, pp. 70–71
Dobbing J (ed.) 1981 *Maternal Nutrition in Pregnancy: Eating for Two?* Academic Press, London
Food and Agriculture Organization/World Health Organization 1973 *Energy and Protein Requirements.* Technical Report Series No. 522. World Health Organization, Geneva
Harrell R F, Capp R H, Davis D R, Pearless J, Ravitz L R 1981 Can nutritional supplements help mentally retarded children? An exploratory study. *Proc. Natl. Acad. Sci. USA* 78: 574–78
Jellife D B, Jellife E F P 1979 Early nutrition: Breastfeeding. In: Winick M (ed.) 1973 *Human Nutrition,* Vol. 1. Plenum, New York, pp. 229–59
Klaus M H, Kennell J H 1976 *The Impact of Early Separation or Loss on Family Development.* Mosby, St. Louis, Missouri
Lien N M, Meyer K, Winick M 1977 Early malnutrition and "late" adoption. *Am. J. Clin. Nutr.* 30: 1734–39
Lloyd-Still J D 1976 Clinical studies on the effects of malnutrition during infancy on subsequent physical and intellectual development. In: Lloyd-Still J D (ed.) 1976 *Malnutrition and Intellectual Development.* Publishing Sciences, Littleton, Massachusetts, pp. 103–59
National Research Council/National Academy of Sciences 1980 *Recommended Dietary Allowances,* 9th edn. Committee on Dietary Allowances, Food and Nutrition Board, Washington, DC
Ogra P L, Greene H L 1982 Human milk and breastfeeding: An update on the state of the art. *Pediatr. Res.* 16: 266–71
Rosso P, Cramoy C 1979 Nutrition and pregnancy. In: Winick M (ed.) 1979 *Human Nutrition,* Vol. 1. Plenum, New York, pp. 133–228
Smithells R W, Shepperd S, Schorah C J, Seller M J, Nevin N C, Harris R, Read A P, Fielding D W 1981 Apparent prevention of neural tube defects by periconceptional vitamin supplementation. *Arch. Dis. Child.* 51: 911–18
Stoch M B, Smythe P M 1976 A 15-year developmental study on effects of severe undernutrition during infancy on subsequent physical growth and intellectual functioning. *Arch. Dis. Child.* 51: 327–36
Winick M 1976 *Malnutrition and Brain Development.* Oxford University Press, New York
Worthington-Roberts B S 1981 *Contemporary Developments in Nutrition.* Mosby, St. Louis, Missouri

Nutrition and Education Interactions

R. M. Thomas

In studies of the interactions between nutrition and education, three central questions that have been investigated are: (a) How does nutrition influence educational achievement? (b) What is the relationship between education and health? (c) What information about nutrition can aid educators in guiding students' health practices? These questions form the focus of the following review.

1. Nutrition and Achievement

In the typical education system, good health is viewed both as a desirable objective in itself and as an important influence on how well students achieve the objectives that make up the study program. Nutrition, as one of the essential contributors to good health, is therefore a factor worthy of educators' concern.

While the connection between nutrition and learning success would appear obvious, it is very difficult to establish. Undernourished populations are usually not only lacking in food but also in a great number of other variables which affect educational achievement directly or indirectly. This makes it difficult to design a research project which can isolate malnutrition as a factor and show that it reduces educational achievement. One study which attempted to do so compared the school performance of supplemented and unsupplemented children from a poor rural area in Mexico. The sample size in this study, however, was only 17 (Chavez and Martinez 1981).

Very good review articles on nutrition and educational achievement have been written by Mushkin (1979) and by Pollitt and Lewis (1980a, 1980b). The latter deal not only with the effects of energy–protein malnutrition, but also with the effects of iron, iodine, and vitamin A deficiency. Other studies have suggested a relation of both chronic undernutrition and severe clinical malnutrition in childhood to scholastic retardation (for example Richardson et al. 1972, Tizard 1974), but in interpreting the results one is always faced with the problem of causal attribution.

Studies suggest that the student who suffers from a diet markedly deficient in nutrients will lack the energy needed to engage in sustained physical or mental tasks. Poor nutrition can contribute to irritability, to lack of attention or concentration, to early fatigue, to vision disorders, to difficulty in memorizing and recalling information, to inaccuracy in motor skills, and to a variety of physical pains that can distract students from their learning tasks. In addition, poor nutrition may also decrease pupils' learning opportunity by contributing to illness that forces pupils to stay home from school.

The question can be asked, then: what can educators do to promote better nutrition among learners? One

answer, as detailed below, is that they can first recognize the importance of education for promoting good health and can next identify specific differences between nutritious and unhealthy diets.

2. Education and Health

A matter of much concern in recent years among people engaged in national planning, particularly in developing nations, is the question of what connection, if any, exists between the amount of education within a society and the level of health of the populace. In other words, does a nation's investment in widely distributing educational opportunity yield benefits in terms of the health of the people? Since proper nutrition is one of the most significant elements of good health, this question of the relationship of education to health also becomes a question of the relationship of education to diet.

Studies centering on these issues have generally involved correlational analyses between such health indices as infant mortality or life expectancy and such educational variables as level of literacy or amount of schooling in a population (Colclough 1980, Cochrane et al. 1980). Data collected from various nations of the world show a consistent positive relationship between literacy and health. The more education a population has, the better its health. Analyses suggest that this positive relationship results from a complex of factors linking education and health. For example, more education leads to greater productivity in a society, and this in turn leads to higher earnings so that people can purchase more health-related goods and services, such as food and medical attention. However, education also promotes health directly through nonmarket channels. For example, instruction about nutrition in home-economics classes influences the quality of meals prepared in the home rather than improving health indirectly by raising the family income. Analyses of data from as many as 29 developing countries

> . . . show that infant and child mortality are lower, the higher the mother's level of schooling. The evidence that a wife's education has a larger total effect on mortality than that of her husband, but that the combined effects of both parents being literate (as compared to having no schooling) may be such as to reduce mortality by up to 27 per 1,000. Finally, there is evidence that maternal education not only reduces child mortality but also improves the health of the survivors: children of more schooled mothers tend to be better nourished. (Colclough 1980 p. 15)

A further way education promotes health is by both (a) raising productivity and thus increasing the money available for public services and (b) raising the awareness of the populace regarding what public services the government might offer to enhance health—such services as pure and fluoridated water supplies, consumer nutrition information, and regulations governing sanitation in food-processing establishments.

In short, investment in education enhances the nutrition and resultant health of a society in multiple ways (Cochrane et al. 1980).

3. Nutrition Information for Educators

It is not enough for educators to recognize the kinds of contributions nutrition can make to education or that education can make to health. It is important also that they know how to identify specific foods that compose a healthy diet. Such specific knowledge is required if curriculum planners, textbook authors, and teachers are to perform their health-education assignments efficiently.

For nutrition education to be effective, however, it needs to take into account the specific needs of a given population and local social, economic, and cultural conditions. In many countries offices of nutrition, departments of public health, nutrition societies, or other institutions periodically issue nutritional guidelines. These guidelines vary from country to country and are a valuable complement to the more general information which can be found in textbooks and which is summarized here.

3.1 A Nutrition Rationale

While the details of human nutrition are still incompletely understood, a general rationale for planning diets which promote health (and consequently help foster learners' educational achievement) can be founded on studies of diet and health carried out in recent decades. The suggestions about specific desirable and undesirable foods from the viewpoint of nutrition listed in Sect. 3.2 below are founded on a rationale which includes the following convictions.

(a) A well-balanced diet includes high amounts of protein, low-fat carbohydrates, vitamins, and minerals.

(b) A diet high in protein furnishes both the body-building material and sources of energy that promote health.

(c) Fibrous foods aid digestion, while diets high in fats (either saturated or unsaturated) can increase the chance of bowel and breast cancer. In particular, diets high in saturated fats (from animal meats other than fish or fowl) are likely to increase an undesirable form of cholesterol in the blood vessels thereby increasing the risk of coronary heart disease.

(d) Whole-grain foods, beans, nuts, and seeds (unpolished brown rice, unwhitened wholegrain wheat, rye, oats, corn) are good sources of fiber, carbohydrates, vitamins, minerals, and protein.

(e) Sugar contributes to tooth decay and weight gain and, at the same time, decreases the intake of constructive body-building foods by satisfying the appetite before proper nutrients are received from desirable foods. Furthermore, children and adults who tend to suffer from hypoglycemia (low blood sugar) often crave sugar products and thus eat large quantities of sweets, with the result that undue amounts of insulin from the pancreas are injected into the blood stream to metabolize the sugar, with the insulin causing the blood sugar level then to decline too rapidly and set off the craving for sweets once again. The blood-sugar deficit is accompanied by a variety of symptoms—irritability, lack of energy, and difficulty in concentrating on such tasks as school assignments.

(f) Most vegetables and fruits, particularly when eaten raw or only lightly cooked, are good sources of vitamins (especially A and C) and fiber.

(g) Too much salt (because it contains sodium) can contribute to high blood pressure that raises the risk of heart attack and of bursting blood vessels in the brain. Many seasonings or condiments can add undesirable amounts of salt, sugar, and fat to the diet.

It is important to recognize that not all of the convictions listed above are agreed upon by everyone in the field of nutrition. For example, the belief that eating foods high in saturated fatty acids contributes to cholesterol in the blood stream has been contested by some workers in the field who believe one's cholesterol level is more influenced by genetic factors than by diet. Whether or not this claim is true, avoiding large amounts of saturated fats in the diet is a safety precaution that will far more likely foster good health than cause damage.

3.2 Specific Food Suggestions

As a guide to specific foods that promote good health in keeping with a rationale similar to the one described above, the Center for Science in the Public Interest (Washington, DC) has published a chart containing ratings of highly desirable foods to include in a balanced diet. The following are a few examples from the chart's extensive lists of vegetables, fruits, dairy products, grains and beans, beverages, poultry, fish, meat, and eggs (Jacobson et al. 1980).

Vegetables rated highest in nutrients include spinach, sweet potato and yam, white potato, kale, squash (vegetable marrow), broccoli, brussel sprouts, tomato, carrot, green peas, green pepper, and sweet corn. Fruits with highest ratings include watermelon, papaya, cantaloupe, mango, orange, grapefruit, banana, and honeydew melon.

Dairy products rated highest are plain low-fat yogurt, skim milk, buttermilk (1 percent), soymilk, and low-fat cottage cheese. Products rated as comparatively undesirable are processed cheese, cream cheese, and cheddar cheese.

Among the most desirable grains, beans, nuts, and

seeds are black beans, chickpeas (garbanzo beans), lima beans, lentils, kidney beans, soy beans, and tofu (bean curd). Relatively low ratings are given to English walnuts and sesame seeds.

The most healthful beverages are unsweetened fruit and vegetable juices such as carrot juice, orange juice, grapefruit juice, apple juice, and grape juice. Coffee and tea and diet sodas are nutritionally not desirable, but far more undesirable yet are soft drinks containing large quantities of sugar, particularly cola drinks that contain both sugar and caffeine.

In the category of poultry, fish, meat, and eggs, the most nutritious foods include waterpack tuna, cooked lobster, roasted chicken (without the skin), salmon, roast turkey, other fish, leg of lamb, baked ham, and rump roast. Least desirable are canned luncheon meat, beef bologna, hot dog, pork sausage, and hard salami.

3.3 Chemical Additives

Commercial food processors typically add chemicals to their packaged or canned products in order to enhance the foods' appearance and taste as well as to preserve the products from spoiling with the passage of time.

Studies of such additives have shown that certain of them pose health risks. Some people are allergic to particular chemicals and, as a result, suffer symptoms ranging from headaches and skin rash to breathing difficulties and loss of energy. For example, clinical evidence suggests that some children who appear to be hyperactive and unable to concentrate on learning tasks at school can gain relief from such symptoms by the removal from their diets of foods containing the suspected additives. Other undesirable substances do not cause immediate symptoms but possibly are conducive to the gradual development of cancer when ingested in large amounts over an extended period of time.

Additives cited as among the most serious offenders are certain artificial food colors (red 2, violet 1, green 1, orange B) and sodium nitrite. Food shoppers can inspect the contents of packaged foods as described in the small print on the package and thereby perhaps determine whether potentially offending substances are included in the product's ingredients.

In contrast to these dangerous chemicals are a variety of other additives that have been tested extensively and appear to be safe, including such substances as ascorbic acid (vitamin C), sorbitol as a sweetener, gelatin to thicken fluid foods, citric acid as a flavoring, and sodium benzoate as a preservative in juices and soft drinks.

To conclude, in view of the information reviewed above, educators can adopt several measures to enhance the health of learners and thereby increase educational achievement: (a) include the study of nutrition in the curriculum of formal and nonformal programs at all levels of the educational ladder; (b) analyze the diets that pupils eat at home and at school in order to advise pupils and their parents on ways to improve the pupils' nutrition; (c) and monitor school-lunch programs to ensure that a nutritious diet is provided for pupils and staff members.

Bibliography

Chavez A, Martinez C 1981 School performance of supplemented and unsupplemented children from a poor area. In: Harper A E, Davis G K (eds.) 1981 *Nutrition in Health Disease and International Development*. Liss, New York, pp. 393–402

Cochrane S H, Leslie J, O'Hara D J 1980 *The Effects of Education on Health*. World Bank, Washington, DC

Colclough C 1980 *Primary Schooling and Economic Development: A Review of the Evidence*. World Bank, Washington, DC

Fredricks C 1976 *Nutrition Handbook*. Major Books, Chatsworth, California

Heyneman S P, Jamison D T 1980 Student learning in Uganda: Textbook availability and other factors. *Comp. Educ. Rev.* 24: 206–20

Jacobson M, Zimmerman J, Kahn K 1980 *Nutrition Scoreboard*. Center for Science in the Public Interest, Washington, DC

Mushkin S J 1979 Educational outcomes and nutrition. In: Klein R E, Read M S, Riecken H W, Brown J A, Pradilla A, Daza C A (eds.) 1979 *Evaluating the Impact of Nutrition and Health Programs*. Plenum, New York, pp. 269–308

Pollitt E, Lewis N 1980a Nutrition and educational achievement. Part I. Malnutrition and behavioural test indicators. *Food Nutr. Bull.* 2(3): 32–35

Pollitt E, Lewis N 1980b Nutrition and educational achievement. Part II. Correlations between nutritional and behavioural test indicators within populations where malnutrition is not a major public health problem. *Food Nutr. Bull.* 2(4): 33–37

Richardson S A, Birch H G, Grabie E, Yoder K 1972 The behaviour of children in school who were severely malnourished in the first two years of life. *J. Health Soc. Behav.* 13: 276–84

Tizard J 1974 Early malnutrition, growth and mental development in man. *Br. Medical Bull.* 30: 169–74

Williams R 1971 *Nutrition Against Disease*. Bantam, New York

Drugs and Human Development

K. E. Thomas

While it is widely recognized that drugs can exert a significant influence on human development, it has been difficult to specify the nature of this influence because (a) the term drug has not been defined in a consistent manner over the centuries, (b) a variety of conditions determine how a given drug will affect a particular individual's development, and (c) the influence of drugs can differ from one period of a person's lifespan to another. These three matters of definition, influential conditions, and stage of life of the individual are the central concerns of the following review.

1. Definitions and Backgrounds

The term drug can be defined as any substance other than food for use in diagnosing, curing, relieving, or preventing disease. Additionally, a drug can be defined as any narcotic or chemical agent other than food that is taken for other than medical reasons to produce a special physiological effect or to satisfy a craving.

Drug use is not simply a present-day phenomenon but, rather, it has a long history. In China, marijuana was used 20 centuries ago as an anesthetic in surgery, while even earlier, in Egypt, opium was used to hush crying babies.

In ancient times the purpose of a drug or potion was usually to cure people's physical illness, to help them bear pain, or to poison them. But over the past 200 years, with the rapid growth of scientific knowledge, new drugs and new properties of old ones have been discovered, radically altering people's ideas of drug use. The most dramatic modern-day change occurred around the 1950s with the discovery of tranquilizers to help the mentally ill become a functioning part of society again. This development was important for two reasons. First, psychiatric medicine was greatly improved by the fact that the mentally ill could be treated with drugs. Second, drugs were now going beyond assisting with physical disorders and were entering the realm of intentional alteration of mental states. As a consequence, the role of drugs has been extended from the ancient meaning of treating physical problems to that of using them in an attempt to cure social and psychological problems as well (Girdano and Girdano 1976).

As a consequence of these developments, people have begun taking drugs to fulfill needs which the drugs cannot pharmacologically fulfill, a function that has been called drug misuse. An endless cycle of misuse can be termed drug abuse. As Farmer (1978 p. 364) has defined it, abuse is "persistent or sporadic excessive drug use inconsistent with medical practice where a drug is taken to such a degree as to impair the ability of the individual to adequately function or cope."

The recently discovered capacity for drugs to alter the mind has caused experts to reevaluate drug definitions. Originally, the World Health Organization (WHO) defined drug addiction as "a condition in which the addict was committed to his or her drug physically and mentally, had progressed steadily along the tolerance ladder, and was a societal problem" (Farmer 1978 p. 365). However, many of the new drugs were found not to cause physical dependence, but rather to create a strong mental drive. Consequently, the World Health Organization had to create a new definition for all conditions that were formerly called drug addiction or habituation: "Drug dependence is a state, psychic and sometimes also physical, resulting from the interaction between a living organism and a drug, characterized by behavioral and other responses that always include a compulsion to take the drug(s) on a continuous or periodic basis in order to experience its psychic effects, and sometimes to avoid the discomfort of its absence. Tolerance may or may not be present, and a person may be dependent on more than one drug" (Farmer 1978 p. 365).

Drugs may cause psychological dependence, physical dependence, or both. Physical dependence occurs when the drug has altered the biological state of the body so that continuous use of the drug is necessary for the person to avoid withdrawal or abstinence symptoms specific to that drug. If there are no withdrawal symptoms, there is no physical dependence. Withdrawal symptoms are defined as those physical effects resulting from the discontinuation of a drug that are relieved either by time or by using the drug again (Girdano and Girdano 1976).

Tolerance often occurs with the chronic use of a drug. This means that repeated equivalent dosages of the drug have less and less effect, so that the individual needs to take increasingly larger amounts in order to produce the desired euphoria. Eventually the dosage required to attain the euphoric effect becomes an overdose, that is, it is sufficiently toxic to cause coma or even death. Tolerance develops relatively quickly for such drugs as opiates and amphetamines, but it is also lost quickly so that a person might take a dose formerly tolerable for him or her but which, after a period of abstention, serves as an overdose.

Psychological dependence occurs when a person feels a compelling desire to use a drug and cannot reduce either the frequency or the dosage. Such people feel they need the drug in order to continue functioning in life or to maintain a feeling of well-being. Dependence can be located any place along a continuum from mild desire to an all-consuming craving for the substance.

2. Conditions Affecting Drug Influence

There appear to be three main sets of factors leading to the use or abuse of drugs: the social setting, the personality or attributes of the individual, and the attributes of the drug itself.

2.1 Social Setting or Environment

The environment which influences how drugs may affect development can be analyzed according to several factors. One is the community in which a person lives. For instance, in some ghetto areas in the United States, exposure to drugs and the pressure to try them are so constant that drug use is almost inescapable for the child or youth.

A second factor—and one of the most powerful—is the peer culture. If a young person's agemates encourage drug use, the youth will likely try drugs. Rebellion against the established adult social system is often part of the motivation for the peer group's turning to drugs,

Table 1
Uses and effects of common drugs

Drug type	Trade or street names	Used to produce:	Physical dependence	Psychological dependence	Tolerance developed?	Effect duration	Typical mode of use	Possible immediate effects	Possible later effects	Withdrawal symptoms	Overdose effects	Physiological dangers
Alcohol Wine, beer, whiskey, gin, vodka, rum	Booze, hootch, sauce, juice	Euphoria, sedation, hypnotic state, pain relief	High	High	Yes	4 to 12 hours	Swallowed	Distorted judgment, perception, coordination, reflexes, speech, numbness, inhibition loss	Headache, nausea, depression, fatigue, dehydration, yearning for alcohol	Chills, tremor, appetite loss, seizures, hallucinations, paranoia, delirium	Chills, tremor, coma, seizures, perhaps death	Damage to liver, kidneys, heart, pancreas, stomach
Cannabis Hashish, hash	Hash, goma de mota, soles	Euphoria, escape from life's problems, no medical uses	Degree unknown	Moderate	Yes	2 to 4 hours	Swallowed, smoked	Inhibition loss, euphoria, short-term memory loss, disoriented thought and action, passivity, distorted sensations, panic, heightened appetite	Sleeplessness, restlessness	Undetermined	Possible but rare, cannabis psychosis: paranoia, depression, hallucinations	In constant users, lung and bronchial disorders, altered endocrine functions
Marijuana	Pot, weed, grass, jay, hemp, joint, smoke, acapulco gold, herb, sativa, colombian, yerba, cannabis, stick, sinsemilla, panama red, reefer	Euphoria, mental-pain relief, medical uses under study	Degree unknown	High to moderate	Yes	2 to 4 hours						
Tetrahydro-cannabinol	THC	Euphoria, medical uses unknown	Degree unknown	High to moderate	Yes	2 to 4 hours						
Depressants Barbiturates	Amytal, Seconal, Amobarbital, Butisol, Phenobarbital, Tuinal, Nembutal, Secobarbital, barbs, downers, pinks, reds and blues, rainbows, yellows	Euphoria, sedation, hypnotic state, relief	High to moderate	High to moderate	Yes	1 to 16 hours	Swallowed	Sedation, drowsiness, slurred speech, distorted judgment and coordination, loss of sensation and inhibitions, depression, loss of consciousness	Depression, slowed movement, weariness, yearning for drug	Weakness, fever, tremor, anxiety, disturbed sleep, rapid pulse, seizures that can be fatal	Confusion, staggering, rage, coma, cold skin, dilated pupils, weak and rapid pulse	Slowed body functions, damage to central nervous system, breathing and heart may stop
Benzo-diazepines	Ativan, Azene, Valium, Clonopin, Librium, Serax, Tranxene, Diazepam	Sedation, hypnotic state, euphoria, less anxiety, anticonvulsive condition	Low	High to low	Yes	4 to 8 hours						

348

Drugs	Trade or Other Names	Medical Uses	Physical Dependence	Psychological Dependence	Tolerance	Duration (hours)	Usual Method	Possible Effects	Effects of Overdose	Withdrawal Syndrome
Chloral hydrate	Notec, Somnos	Sedation, hypnotic state, relief from anxiety or insomnia	Moderate	Moderate	Possibly	5 to 8 hours	Swallowed or injected			Sleeplessness, acute anxiety, yearning for drug
Glutethimide	Doriden, doors	Sedation, hypnotic state, euphoria	High	High	Yes	4 to 8 hours	Swallowed			
Methaqualone	Optimil, Parest, Sopor, Somnafac, Quaalude, soapers, quads, sopes, ludes	Sedation, hypnotic state, euphoria	High	High	Yes	4 to 8 hours				
Other depressants	Equanil, Miltown, Noludar, Placidyl, Valmid	Sedation, hypnotic state, euphoria, reduced anxiety	Moderate	Moderate	Yes	4 to 8 hours				
Hallucinogens										
Amphetamine variants	DMA, DOB, DOM, MDA, MMDA, PMA, STP, TMA	Euphoria, altered mental state, no known medical use	No	Unknown extent	Yes	8 to 12 hours	Swallowed or injected	Distortions in visual, auditory, kinesthetic perception, panic, loss of inhibitions and coordination, illusions, hallucinations	Fright, acute emotional pain, loss of physical control, possible death	Under investigation
Lysergic acid diethylamide (LSD)	Acid, big D, cube, microdot, mike, trip	Euphoria, altered mental state, no known medical use	No	Unknown extent	Yes	8 to 12 hours	Swallowed			
Mescaline, peyote	Mes, mesc, mescal, buttons, cactus	Euphoria, altered mental state, no known medical use	No	Unknown extent	Yes	8 to 12 hours	Swallowed or injected			
Phencyclidine	Angel dust, PCP, fuel, crystal, herms, hog, shermans, supergrass, killerweed, "embalming fluid"	Euphoria, altered mental state, anesthesia for animals in veterinary practice	Unknown extent	High	Yes	Hours to days	Swallowed, injected, or smoked	Loss of hold on reality, distorted thought and speech, anger, violence		Under investigation
Phencyclidine analogs	PCE, PCPY, TCP	Euphoria, altered mental state	Unknown extent	Unknown extent	Unknown extent	Perhaps	Varies	Swallowed		
Other hallucinogens	Bufotenine, DMT, Ibogaine, Psilocybin (mushrooms), psilocyn	Euphoria, altered mental state, no known medical use	No	Unknown extent	Perhaps	Varies	Swallowed, injected, smoked, or sniffed			
Inhalants										
Aerosol products, benzene, gasoline, lead-base paint, lighter fluid, nail-polish remover, nitrous oxide		Euphoria, altered mental state, no known medical use	High to moderate	High to moderate	Yes	Moments to hours	Sniffed (inhaled)	Appetite loss, irritated eyes and nose, chest pain, double vision	Seizures, nausea, chest pain, coma, death; many brain cells destroyed, pulmonary bleeding	Anxiety, depression, vomiting, muscle pain, diarrhea, cramps

Table 1 *(continued)*

Drug type	Trade or street names	Used to produce:	Physical dependence	Psychological dependence	Tolerance developed?	Effect duration	Typical mode of use	Possible immediate effects	Possible later effects	Withdrawal symptoms	Overdose effects	Physiological dangers
Narcotics Codeine	Codeine, Empirin Compound with codeine, Robitussin AC	Euphoria, pain relief	Moderate	Moderate	Yes	3 to 6 hours	Swallowed or injected	Pain relief, euphoria, drowsiness, nausea, itching, loss of appetite, constricted pupils, poor vision, infected sores and needle scars	Depression, constipation, yearning for drug	Nausea, irritability, itching, nasal discharge, cramps, chills, sweats, tremor, intense anxiety	Nausea, seizures, slow breathing vomiting, coma, death	Convulsions, coma, death
Heroin	Big H, boy, brown, H, heroina, horse, junk, smack, stuff, Diacetyl-morphine	Euphoria, pain relief	High	High	Yes	3 to 6 hours	Injected, smoked, or sniffed					
Hydro-morphone	Dilaudid	Euphoria, pain relief	High	High	Yes	3 to 6 hours	Swallowed or injected					
Meperidine, Pethidine	Demoral, Pethadol	Euphoria, pain relief	High	High	Yes	3 to 6 hours						
Methadone	Dolophine, Methadone, Methadose	Pain relief (substitute for heroin)	High	High	Yes	3 to 6 hours						
Morphine	Cube, firstline, morfina, morfo, muo, pectoral syrup	Euphoria, pain relief, cough relief	High	High	Yes	3 to 6 hours	Swallowed, smoked, or injected					
Opium	Dover's Powder, Paregoric, Parepectolin	Euphoria, pain relief, diarrhea relief	High	High	Yes	3 to 6 hours	Swallowed or smoked					
Other narcotics	Darvon, Dromoran, LAAM, leritine, Lomotil, Numorphan, Pentanyl, Percodan, Tussionex	Euphoria, pain relief, cough relief	High to low	High to low	Yes	Varies	Swallowed or injected					
Stimulants Ampheta-mines	Benzedrine, Biphetamine, Desoxyn, Dexedrine, beans, bennies, black mollies, copilots, crank, crystal, Christmas trees, dexies, doxies, hearts, meth, mollies, pep, pills, roses, speed, truck drivers, uppers	Heightened mood, reduced fatigue, reduced appetite, counteraction to depressant drugs, reduced hyperactivity in children, reduced sleepiness, weight control, reduced bedwetting	Perhaps	High	Yes	2 to 4 hours	Swallowed or injected	Sense of clarity energy, euphoria, insomnia, loss of appetite and memory, raised blood pressure, dilated pupils. Heavy use over long period may cause temporary psychosis and schizophrenia symptoms	Depression, fatigue, irritability, cramps, yearning for drug	Depression, anxiety, fatigue, loss of hold on reality, suicidal tendency	Headache, dizziness, tremor, hostility, chest pain, delusions, convulsions, heart failure	Undue stress on heart and body endurance. When alternated with depressants can cause nervous-system, liver, and heart damage

350

Drug	Slang/Trade Names	Medical Uses	Physical Dependence	Psychological Dependence	Tolerance	Duration (hours)	Method of Taking	Possible Effects	Effects	Withdrawal Syndrome	Effects of Overdose	Long-Term Effects
Caffeine (in aspirin, coffee, cola drinks, tea)	No-Doz, Tirend	Reduced fatigue, headache relief	No	Moderate	Yes	2 to 4 hours	Swallowed	Reduced feeling of fatigue, sense of clarity	Similar to amphetamines	Irritability, anxiety, yearning for drug	Rapid heart, trembling, ringing in ears	Heart and blood vessel damage, digestive disorders
Cocaine	Blow, C, coca, coke, dust, flake, heaven, lady, nose candy, paradise, perico, rock, snow	Euphoria, reduced coughing, local anesthesia	Perhaps	High	Yes	1 to 2 hours	Sniffed or injected	Similar to amphetamines	Similar to amphetamines	Like amphetamines	Like amphetamines	Like amphetamines
Methyl-phenidate	Ritalin	Reduced hyperactivity in children, weight control	Perhaps	High	Yes	2 to 4 hours	Swallowed or injected	Similar to amphetamines	Similar to amphetamines	Like amphetamines	Like amphetamines	Like amphetamines
Nicotine (in tobacco)	Various trade names, smokes, weeds, fags	Reduced tension and uneasiness	Perhaps	Unknown	Yes	Varies	Smoked or chewed	Constricted blood vessels, greater bowel activity	Similar to amphetamines	Like caffeine	Nausea, stomach pains, dizziness	High blood pressure, cardiovascular damage
Phenmet-razine	Preludin	Reduction of appetite, fatigue, hyperactivity	Perhaps	High	Yes	2 to 4 hours	Swallowed or injected	Similar to amphetamines	Similar to amphetamines	Like amphetamines	Like amphetamines	Like amphetamines
Other stimulants	Adipex, Bacarate, Cylert, Didrex, Ionamin, Pondimin, Pre-Sate, Sanorex, Tepanil	Reduced appetite and fatigue, reduced hyperactivity in children	Perhaps	High	Yes	2 to 4 hours	Swallowed	Similar to amphetamines	Similar to amphetamines	Like amphetamines	Like amphetamines	Like amphetamines

although this rebelliousness may be short lived and more in the spirit of adventure than of breaking with the adult culture. Lettieri (1980) reported that the majority of Americans between ages 16 and 25 had tried drugs at least once or twice, though most did not repeat the experience further.

The child's family is a further important influence. A study by Dunette (Lettieri 1980) showed that parents of drug abusers were frequently people who abused alcohol, fought often, and were divorced or separated. The family's ethnic and social-class values can also be significant. Kandel (Lettieri 1980) reported that white adolescents were more likely than blacks in America to have tried alcoholic beverages, marijuana, various pills, psychedelics, and inhalants, and less likely to have tried cocaine or heroin. Hispanic secondary-school students were less likely than either whites or blacks to have tried alcohol, cigarettes, or marijuana and more likely to have tried cocaine. Youths of Oriental heritage showed dramatically lower rates of drug use than all other ethnic groups.

2.2 Individuals' Personality Attributes

Drugs affect all people somewhat differently, as determined by individual biological disposition, psychosocial characteristics, and skills for coping with problems.

In regard to biological differences, some theorists hold that drug addiction involves a "deficiency disease" in brain function, and that those suffering this deficiency turn to drugs as a form of self-medication (Farmer 1978). Thus, one issue which has long plagued researchers is whether the psychopathological behavior of drug addicts develops because of a biological predisposition for the disorder before the drug's use. Studies show that adolescents who use drugs manifest more psychopathology than nonusers. The users' symptoms often include depression, immaturity, self-alienation, poor relations with others, major deficiences in ego structure and functioning, poor impulse control, and feelings of inadequacy, of frustration, and of helplessness. But whether biological composition has contributed to such characteristics and thus has encouraged overuse of drugs is not yet known (Breschner and Friedman 1979).

Social characteristics that contribute to personality and are related to drug use include gender, social class, sexual behavior, and delinquency. Studies have shown that more males than females use drugs and that drug users are more likely to be from upper-income families than from lower socioeconomic levels. Furthermore, drug use is higher among adolescents who engage in more sexual behavior and who are involved in delinquency and school misbehavior (Chitwood et al. 1981).

Individuals who have poor skills for coping with life's problems and who display a lack of self-esteem use drugs to excess as an escape from either daily stresses or from boredom. Among regular users, "getting high" on drugs is a primary coping mechanism that begins to dominate the individual's life as he or she turns to drugs

with increasing frequency. Then the person's energies may be almost completely consumed by the drug life. At this point there is a noticeable decrease in overall functioning of the individual and a high risk of overdoses. Many rehabilitation programs are aimed at the formation of a positive identity within the individual so he need not seek to escape reality through drugs (Hundleby et al. 1982).

2.3 Properties of Drugs

Each drug has properties that produce particular psychobiological effects. Thus, reasons for a person's turning to certain drugs are directly related to the specific effects those drugs offer. For example, alcohol, marijuana, or heroin may be used to produce feelings of pleasure. Barbiturates, amphetamines, or sedative-hypnotics are used to help a person cope with moods he or she wishes to escape, such as depression, tension, or anxiety. Psychodelic drugs are usually taken in an attempt to expand awareness or to achieve a personal identity. Drugs also differ from each other in their potential for overdose, dependency, withdrawal symptoms, and tolerance. (See Table 1 for particular effects of specific drugs.)

3. Drugs and Age Levels

In addition to the factors related to drug use reviewed above, the influence of drugs on development can be viewed from the standpoint of four stages of the lifespan: (a) prenatal life, (b) infancy and childhood, (c) adolescence, and (d) adulthood.

3.1 From Conception to Birth

When a pregnant woman takes a drug, it circulates not only through her body but also through that of the fetus. And since the fetus develops very rapidly, drug use by a mother can have severe consequences for the unborn child's growth.

Some drugs are teratogenic, meaning they cause malformations in the fetus. One such drug is thalidomide, a tranquilizer, which can cause flipper-like appendages rather than arms and legs to develop on the baby. Long-term use of antibiotics can cause abnormalities ranging from stained teeth to jaundice and bone deformities.

Alcoholic women can give birth to infants who go through withdrawal symptoms in the first few days after birth, and such women can bear babies who display vitamin depletion, biochemical imbalances, and low birth weight. A further danger is that excessive use of alcohol may produce premature birth and even intrauterine death of the fetus. Heroin and morphine addiction can lead to similar results, with the babies going through withdrawal symptoms following birth (Heath 1979).

Other drugs create specific effects. For instance, a mother's smoking cigarettes can retard growth of the fetus, causing low birth weight and premature birth.

Steroids can cause birth defects, synthetic hormones can cause masculinization of female fetuses and feminization of male fetuses. Diethylstilbestrol (DES), which was often given to mothers in the 1950s to prevent miscarriage, has since been seen as a possible cause of cancer in young daughters whose mothers were injected with the drug. Corticosteroids can produce jaundice, low birth weight, cleft palate, and stillbirth. Alexania (1982) reports recent studies showing that marijuana may cause birth defects, and there is evidence that lysergic acid diethylamide (LSD) can cause chromosome changes that result in malformed infants.

Even such common medications as aspirin and antihistamines have been cited as causing malformations.

These discoveries about the influence of drugs on the unborn child suggest that by avoiding such substances during pregnancy, women enhance the chances of producing a healthy baby.

3.2 Infancy to Puberty

Newborn infants are particularly susceptible to the effects of drugs because they have not yet developed the enzymes necessary to metabolize the drugs (Alexania 1982). Thus, special caution is warranted in prescribing drugs for babies. After infancy and throughout the years of childhood, the likelihood that a boy or girl will begin to use drugs is strongly influenced by the model of drug use offered by members of the family. The child who sees his father drinking beer each night to relax from the day's labors, or the girl who sees her mother constantly taking diet pills in order to lose weight, is apt to follow the parental model and be more susceptible to accepting drugs offered by peers.

Childhood is pictured by developmentalists as a time of industry, of striving for mastery of skills, or learning society's rules, and of developing peer relationships. Introducing drugs during this period can disrupt the need to develop skills and can upset the emotional equilibrium and intellectual striving needed for the achievements expected by late childhood. While the effects of drugs vary with different children, in general they produce apathy, listlessness, and impairment of memory and of the processing and retrieval functions of the brain. The child influenced by drugs may fail to succeed normally during this goal-oriented stage of life because of a lack of will and a resultant lowered sense of self-esteem.

At this period of life certain drugs can influence children differently from adults. An example is the effect of Ritalin when used as a medication for hyperactive children.

3.3 Early Adolescence to Later Youth

Adolescence has been seen as an important time for developing a person's sense of self-identity, a process that involves separating from parental attachments and values and establishing new social ties, values, and ideals. In separating from parents, the youth needs to form other meaningful relationships. Sometimes the peers with whom the growing youth associates influence him or her to adopt drugs as an important part of their social behavior. However, the effect of drugs may not be to enhance social relationships and self-identity. Rather, the drugs may cause the growing girl or boy to become apathetic and emotionally detached and, consequently, to face problems of establishing social bonds, with the result that the youth becomes increasingly isolated emotionally and socially.

Drugs can decrease cognitive operations, making it difficult for the youth to develop a functional set of values and ideals. Reduced cognitive efficiency also leads to poor academic performance and a resultant decrease in self-esteem, contributing to instability of the individual's sense of identity.

Besides such psychological effects, normal hormonal changes at the time of puberty, combined with drug use, can result in drastic chemical imbalances that negatively affect the youth's physical and psychological well-being.

3.4 Adulthood

Frequently adults who become heavily involved with drugs find that their main interest in life becomes that of drug procurement and use. The self-absorption and emotional detachment resulting from drug use frequently makes it impossible for the individual to form adequate intimate relationships with others. Soon the only friends the drug user has are others using drugs themselves, and the friendship often dissipates once the drugs are gone. Since drugs are expensive and the drug abuser usually cannot hold down a job due to the drug habit, the individual frequently turns to crime, either stealing objects to sell or else selling drugs to support the drug habit.

In conclusion, the general effect of different drugs as reviewed in Table 1 is usually much the same across all age levels. but as noted earlier, drugs affect different people in somewhat individualistic ways. An amphetamine which animates one person may depress another, depending upon their individual biological and psychological composition. While certain drugs can have a salutary effect on development when properly administered as medications, they exert such deleterious effects as those reviewed above when they are abused.

Bibliography

Alexania K 1982 *Workbook and Readings for Health and Safety No. 456.* California State University, Los Angeles, California

Breschner G M, Friedman A S (eds.) 1979 *Youth Drug Abuse: Problems, Issues, and Treatment.* Heath, Lexington, Massachusetts

Chitwood D D, Wells K, Russe B 1981 Medical and treatment definitions of drug use: The case of the adolescent user. *Adolescence* 16: 817–30

Farmer R H 1978 Drug-abuse problems. In: Goldenson R M (ed.) 1978 *Disability and Rehabilitation Handbook.* McGraw-Hill, New York, pp. 363–80

Girdano D D, Girdano D A 1976 *Drugs: A Factual Account.* Addison-Wesley, Reading, Massachusetts

Goldstein M J, Baker B L, Jamison K R 1980 *Abnormal Psychology: Experiences, Origins, and Interventions.* Little, Brown, Boston, Massachusetts

Heath H 1979 Drugs of abuse. *Drug Enforcement* 6(2): 2–41. Drug Enforcement Administration, United States Department of Justice, Washington DC

Hundleby J D, Carpenter R A, Ross R A, Mercer G W 1982 Adolescent drug use and other behaviors. *J. Child Psychol. Psychiatry Allied Discip.* 23: 61–68

Lettieri D J (ed.) 1980 *Predicting Adolescent Drug Abuse: A Review of Issues, Methods, and Correlates.* National Institute on Drug Abuse, Rockville, Maryland

Parish P 1977 *The Doctors and Patients Handbook of Medicines and Drugs.* Knopf, New York

Developing Vision and Hearing

Vision and Visual Perception

W. L. Hogan Jr.

At all stages of life, infancy through old age, the development of a person's visual abilities strongly influences his or her educational experiences. For convenience of analysis, these visual abilities have traditionally been divided into two phases, those of visual sensations and of visual perceptions.

The visual-sensation phase takes place in the eye when the retina (composed of optic nerve endings that line the rear portion of the interior of the eye ball) is stimulated by light waves entering the eye through the opening (pupil) at the front of the eyeball. In short, visual sensation occurs within the eyeball itself. In contrast, the visual-perception phase occurs within the brain after the sensations from the eye have been transmitted as electrochemical impulses along the optic nerve to the brain. Perception consists of the person's interpretation of what the visual sensations mean in terms of past experiences. For example, when a child looks at a printed page, the pattern of the black print on the white paper is transmitted into the eye as light waves that pass through the pupil and lens at the front of the eye to cast a pattern on the retina at the rear. This pattern triggers a chemical alteration in the receptor cells, producing coded impulses that are transmitted along the optic nerves to the brain where the child perceives (interprets) the impulses as meaning "The cat was drinking the warm milk." Consequently, if the process of reading is to be successful, both the child's sensing mechanism (the eye) and his or her perceptual mechanism (the interpretation function in the brain) must be in proper order.

The purpose of the following overview is to describe some of the most common defects of the eye and of the visual-perception mechanism that influence the efficiency of people's learning in educational settings. The description includes suggestions about ways such disorders can be identified and corrected or, at least, ways their negative influence on learning can be diminished.

1. Problems of Visual Sensation—Disorders of the Eye

The most common disorders of the eye are those of near-sightedness (myopia) and far-sightedness (hyperopia).

The near-sighted person sees close-by objects clearly, but objects at a distance are blurred. The far-sighted person sees distant objects sharply, but finds close-by objects—such as small print in a book—to be blurred. These two visual malfunctions are caused by the shape of a person's eyeball in relation to how adequately the flexible lens at the front of the eye is able to bend incoming light waves so they focus sharply on the retina at the rear of the eyeball. In near-sightedness, the eyeball is unduly long from front to back and the lens cannot bend the light waves sufficiently to bring images of distant objects to focus sharply on the retina, so the result is an unclear image. In far-sightedness the opposite condition exists—the eyeball is unduly short from front to back and the lens cannot sharply focus light waves from nearby objects on the retina, so the image recorded on the retina is blurred. The most common method of treating both myopia and hyperopia is to equip the person with an artificial lens which produces the sharp focus that the person's own flexible lens within the eye is unable to produce by itself. Artificial lenses are of two general types. First are the traditional eyeglasses, worn in front of the eyes in a metal or plastic frame. Second are the more recently developed contact lenses, which are small rigid or soft lenses worn directly on the surface of the eye, giving the impression to other people that the individual is not wearing artificial lenses at all.

Both near-sightedness and far-sightedness are found among young children and adolescents, so that the success of pupils in school can be significantly affected by these disorders. Because people's general developmental tendency is toward becoming more near-sighted with advancing age, a young child's farsightedness often corrects itself with the passing years. However, the near-sighted child's disorder usually does not improve with age but becomes more pronounced.

A form of far-sightedness that commonly occurs in people past the age of 40 is called presbyopia, a condition resulting from the lens of the eye becoming less flexible and unable to bend light waves so as to bring close-by objects into focus. As a result, many elderly people wear glasses for reading, writing, sewing, and other close work. Frequently two (bifocal) or even three

355

(trifocal) different curvatures are built into the artificial lens to enable the elderly to see both near and far objects clearly.

Another common disorder of the eye is astigmatism, an uneven curvature of the cornea (the transparent tissue covering the eyeball) or of the lens, causing a blurring of the image cast on the retina. Typically when the brain interprets the image it makes a mental adjustment for the distortion. Artificial lenses can be prescribed by an eye doctor to accommodate for the disorder if the distortion is quite pronounced.

Sometimes the muscles controlling movements of the eyeballs fail to direct the eyes to operate together as a coordinated unit. The most common variety of muscular imbalance is strabismus, meaning a failure of the two eyes to direct their gaze at the same object. The child with internal strabismus or esotropia is popularly termed cross-eyed, because one or both eyes point inward toward the nose. The child with external strabismus or exotropia is said to be wall-eyed, because the eyes point outward in different directions. A pupil with slight internal strabismus will have little or no trouble reading. But a pupil with external strabismus will find it to be a major effort to turn both eyes inward to read a book, so will constantly experience nervous strain. This may result in headache, nausea, or a general feeling of discomfort and an unwillingness to do close work. If the strabismus is very marked, the child must suppress the image from one of the eyes, since it is confusing to have two uncoordinated images reaching the brain simultaneously. Therefore, unless the strabismus is remedied through muscle exercises, eye glasses, or surgery on the muscles, the individual eventually loses the function of the less dominant eye and consequently does not develop the binocular vision on which depth perception heavily depends. However, the function of the less dominant eye can be recovered through exercises provided under the guidance of an ophthalmologist, a medical doctor specializing in eye disorders.

In the school setting, strabismus is easily detected in those children who suffer a serious imbalance of the eye muscles, because it is obvious to the observer that the two eyes do not aim at the same spot. However, less obvious but still of marked significance for pupils' learning success are mild cases of strabismus called convergence insufficiency in which the pupil can, by straining the eye muscles, direct both eyes properly for a short time, such as during the early part of a reading assignment. However, before long the pupil begins to feel sleepy and finds it difficult to pay attention to the reading task. Consequently, teachers who are aware that sleepiness and distractibility can be symptoms of convergence insufficiency are prepared to refer such pupils for vision testing by a specialist.

In some children the right eye records an image that is a different size to that recorded by the left eye, causing a problem of stereopsis, that is, a lack of coordination of the images of the two eyes. The relatively small number of pupils who suffer this defect often miscall words in reading because so many words look alike to them.

Two other disorders that frequently occur with advanced age are glaucoma and cataracts. Glaucoma results from a malfunction of the valve system that releases excess fluid from within the eyeball, so that the eyeball's internal fluid pressure builds up and eventually can damage the retina and thereby cause increasing loss of sight. In its early stages, glaucoma is identified by an eye specialist using a pressure-measuring instrument. In its advanced stages, the defect can cause headaches and blurred vision as well as progressive loss of sight. Glaucoma is typically treated with local medication or by surgery to correct the valve mechanism. Although most glaucoma patients are adults, the condition is sometimes found in children, with the eyeball enlarged by the increasing pressure. Such cases need periodic tension checks by an eye doctor, and care should be taken to avoid a blow to the child's eye during play activities.

Cataracts are cloudy, grey-colored growths that develop in the lens of the eye, increasingly preventing light waves from entering, so vision becomes blurred and blindness may result. Generally, the only method of removing a cataract is by surgery which eliminates the lens. In the past, the individual who had a cataract removed would thereafter have to wear strong convex glasses (unless he or she suffered marked myopia), because the loss of the lens causes a great degree of farsightedness, usually accompanied by astigmatism. Since he or she can no longer accommodate to seeing both close and far-off objects, the child might need bifocal glasses. In recent years, however, eye surgeons have succeeded in implanting plastic lenses within the patient's natural eye lenses following the removal of the cataract, so the patient finds it much easier to adapt to the change in his or her visual condition. While most cataracts occur in the elderly, sometimes they do develop in children. Therefore, teachers should be alert for the appearance of the gradual growth of a cloudy film on a child's eye and to evidence that the child's ability to see clearly is decreasing.

1.1 Vision and Life-styles

Eye defects not only influence how accurately students view their environment, but can also significantly affect students' general styles of life. The near-sighted person may prefer reading activities and tasks performed at close distance. Since many tasks, including reading, are solo activities that do not involve outside intervention, the person's habitual behavior may become increasingly of an introspective type. In contrast, far-sighted individuals find close work uncomfortable so that they may engage increasingly in activities suited to sharp distance vision, such as sports and spectator activities, thus encouraging them to become more gregarious and extroverted. Presbyopia, the far-sightedness of the elderly, can affect the precision with which an individual performs close work, such as reading. A scholarly person who in his or her younger years was willing to study documents for long hours may in later years become hasty and imprecise, lacking the patience to continue habits of careful research because the eyestrain from presbyopia causes discomfort.

The effects of cataracts on an individual's view of the world has been dramatically reflected in paintings produced by artists who suffer cataract growth. Because their vision grows progressively cloudy, the intensity of the colors they use in painting increases without the artists realizing it.

Astigmatism produces some blurring of vision and thus requires the eyes to work harder to clarify images, making reading more difficult and causing headaches. A person suffering marked astigmatism may thus tend to avoid reading and similar tasks that require precise, comfortable vision.

People with strabismus cannot focus both eyes on the same spot, so that their depth perception is impaired. This defect can limit their success in sports and in occupations that depend on accurate depth perception. Poor color vision affects people's success in art activities, limits their ability to engage in certain occupations, and influences how effectively they select clothing and decorate their living quarters.

2. Teachers' Roles in Eye Care

There are four main ways that teachers can help students who suffer eye disorders—by helping identify defects, by adjusting school activities to the disorders, by teaching general eye-care practices, and by cooperating with an eye doctor's program of treating students who suffer faulty vision.

2.1 Identifying Eye Defects

In regard to identifying disorders, the actual diagnosis of an eye defect is best made by a doctor who specializes in such matters. However, a classroom teacher who is alert to behavioral symptoms of eye problems can aid in this process by making a preliminary estimate of which children should be examined by a specialist. For example, typical symptoms displayed in school that suggest sight defects include the pupil's: (a) frowning, squinting, or rubbing the eyes when reading or doing other close work; (b) acting irritably or complaining of sore eyes during an extensive period of close work; (c) holding a book close to the face while reading; (d) complaining of blurred vision during reading or writing activities; (e) squinting or rubbing the eyes when trying to read material on the chalkboard or the figures on the wall clock; (f) stumbling over small objects; (g) having trouble participating in games requiring distance vision.

2.2 Adjusting School Work

To adjust school activities to the eye conditions of pupils who suffer disorders not yet corrected by glasses, teachers can seat the near-sighted pupil close to the front of the room so that writing on the chalkboard and items the teacher displays during lessons are close by. Far-sighted pupils should not be required to do close work for extended periods without occasional opportunities to rest their eyes by looking at objects at a distance. Children with marked astigmatism will often find it easier to do their studies if they are in one of the best-lit sections of the classroom. Some children's eyes do not accommodate rapidly to a change from focusing on a close object to focusing on a distant one. Those who experience such difficulties can be aided by the teacher's not requiring them to do much copying of material written on the chalkboard or on charts at the front of the room. If a student has undergone surgery for cataracts, he or she should not be expected to carry the same load of reading or of shifting focus for different distances that is borne by classmates with normal vision.

2.3 Teaching Eye Care

Including material about eye care in the schools' health-education program contributes as well to better vision for students. For example, teachers can stress the importance of a well-balanced diet, particularly the inclusion of foods rich in vitamin A, such as carrots, green string beans, broccoli, green peas, red peppers, yellow squash, and fish-liver oil. In communities without adequate sanitary conditions, such insects as flies can spread infectious diseases from the eyes of one child to another. Therefore, children should be cautioned to protect themselves from flies and not to rub their eyes a great deal. If dirt particles enter the eye, the eye should not be rubbed, but rather be washed out with clean water, preferably administered with a bulb syringe. Or if a syringe is not available, the upper lid of the eye can be pulled forward by the eye lash as the child looks down, so a particle lodged in a fold under the eye may drop out.

To prevent damage to the eyes, pupils should be cautioned not to play with sharp objects, such as knives and sticks, nor should they throw pebbles or shoot rubber bands at each other. Any child who has lost the vision of one eye should be provided with a protective lens to cover the other eye so that the remaining eye is not accidentally damaged.

2.4 Cooperating in Vision Treatment

Teachers can also help students by cooperating with the sight-saving program the student's eye specialist has recommended. Perhaps the most obvious type of cooperation is that of reminding children who have corrective glasses to wear their glasses at the times they are most needed, especially in reminding the far-sighted child to wear the lenses for close work and the near-sighted one to don the glasses for activities requiring distant vision. In addition to cooperating in sight-saving programs designed for particular children, teachers can adopt general classroom practices that promote eye care for all students. For example, a general vision goal is the prevention of eyestrain. This is not because straining the eyes to see in poor light or to read for long periods causes disorders like astigmatism, near-sightedness, or far-sightedness. Eyestrain does not even make such defects worse when they already exist. But eyestrain does cause general fatigue, irritability, inefficiency, and dislike for the kinds of schoolwork that bring it about. One obvious way to reduce eyestrain is to ensure that there is sufficient light in the classroom for pupils to read comfortably. For children who are working at their desks, it is best to have a diffused light source or to have the light coming from the left and slightly to the rear for the right-handed child and from the right rear (such as over the right shoulder) for the left-handed child. Thus, when the pupils writes, his or her hand does not cast a shadow over the material on which he or she is working.

Furthermore, chalkboards, bulletin boards, charts, and demonstrations should be located so they are free from glare. Writing on the chalkboard should be large and done with soft yellow or white chalk that makes clear letters. It is generally a poor idea to write poems, lengthy tests, or long outlines on the chalkboard for pupils to copy on paper, because the continual looking up and down from board to paper strains the eyes. Also, when teachers are talking to a class, they should not stand in front of the windows. If they stand silhouetted against the sunlight, the pupils' eyes must strain in trying to adjust to both the teacher's dark figure and the bright background.

3. Problems of Visual Perception

As was noted earlier, the process of visual perception consists of the person's comparing the visual sensations from the eye with memories of past experiences. Whereas visual sensation depends on the proper construction and operation of the eye and of the nerves carrying messages from the eye to the brain, visual perception depends also on the complex nerve network of the brain and on the condition of memories from the past.

Although great numbers of experiments have been conducted in the realm of visual perception, the way perception operates is still inadequately understood. After an exhaustive review of studies in this field, Uttal (1981 pp. 895–986) concluded that "We know shockingly little about the mechanisms underlying the powerful ability of the nervous system to integrate various aspects of a stimulus scene, to extract invariances, and to construct or infer what might be a plausible solution to the problem so posed." For example, perception is thought to take place in the brain, though the exact location has not yet been pinpointed. According to one theory, there may be many areas within the brain where perception takes place, and these may change depending on the neurological input. Therefore, educators are left without clear guidance concerning the causes of students' misperceptions and concerning what to do

about them. However, in the practical conduct of classrooms, there are three general sources of misperceptions that can be identified. An awareness of these can aid school personnel as they help pupils who suffer learning difficulties.

The first source is the eye itself, the second is the circuitry of the brain, and the third is the set of past experiences the pupil uses for interpreting new visual stimuli. As a practical way of separating these three in educational settings, teachers can begin by assessing the first and third sources—the eye and the memories. If these two sources are not deficient, then the cause apparently lies in the second—the circuitry of the brain.

How to assess the accuracy of the eye has already been described. It consists of vision testing by an eye doctor or by school personnel and of the teacher's watching for symptoms of vision difficulties. If the perceptual fault lies in a defect of the eye, then treating the defect obviously helps correct the visual perception problem.

To estimate whether misperceptions are caused by pupils' inadequate memories, teachers can ask pupils questions designed to reveal the nature of their past experiences needed for making an accurate interpretation of present visual stimuli. For example, when a pupil in an African school misinterprets the picture of a chimney on a house in a story book, the teacher may ask the child how his or her own home is heated or where food is cooked in houses the child has visited. The child may also be asked to explain the concepts "fireplace" and "furnace." If the child's answers suggest that he or she has never had experiences with fireplaces, furnaces, or chimneys, or at least that he or she cannot recall such experiences, then the misinterpretation of the picture and of the word "chimney" may well be caused by the third source of misperception, an inadequate store of appropriate memories. The most direct method of correcting this shortcoming is to provide the pupil with the sort of experiences—with the sort of teaching—that fills in the missing memories or that corrects misconceptions the child has acquired in the past.

However, if the child's eye mechanism and store of memories appear adequate, yet the child continues to misperceive visual stimuli, then the fault may lie in the electrochemical circuitry of the brain network. How this network operates has not yet been discovered in any degree of completeness, despite the great quantity of data already compiled on the functions of the brain. At best, specialists in the field have identified symptoms of common disorders and have labeled combinations of certain symptoms with such terms as dyslexia. In spite of their lack of precise knowledge of the causal mechanisms, educators have discovered some teaching methods which may help pupils learn despite the apparent circuitry disorder.

In conclusion, the education of learners who experience visual-perception difficulties can be promoted in several ways. First, educational personnel can help identify the source of misperceptions—in the eye mechanism, in the learner's store of memories for interpreting visual stimuli, or in the operation of the brain network. Second, teachers can reduce the influence of a visual-perception disorder by such techniques as those mentioned above. Third, teachers can employ instructional methods that supplement or circumvent the visual mode. The most common circumvention is that of presenting subject matter in auditory as well as visual form. A child with serious visual impairment can still grasp the subject matter if the teacher explains it orally, if a classmate can read aloud to the child from a textbook, or if the pupil can listen to an audiotape recording of the lesson. With such instructional help, the learner's progress in school is not unduly hampered by his or her visual-perception problems.

Bibliography

Gregory R L 1978 *Eye and Brain: The Psychology of Seeing.* McGraw-Hill, New York
Kaufman L 1974 *Sight and Mind: An Introduction to Visual Perception.* Oxford University Press, New York
Uttal W R 1981 *A Taxonomy of Visual Processes.* Erlbaum, Hillsdale, New Jersey
Wertenbaker L 1981 *The Eye: Window to the World*, The Human Body Series. US News Books, Washington, DC

Color Blindness

R. M. Thomas

Color blindness is a disorder of the cones in the retina of the eye that prevents a person from perceiving colors normally. About one person in 40,000 is totally color blind. Far more common than total color blindness is partial color blindness, a condition that affects about 5 percent of the population (Wertenbaker 1981). In this case, the person sees only certain colors in a normal manner. The most common type is red–green blindness, where the sufferer is unable to distinguish between colors that normal people experience as red and green. However, individuals who are red–green color blind see yellow and blue in an almost normal way. A smaller number are blind for hues other than red and green. Some people do not experience an actual absence of color, but rather, their color perception is unbalanced so, for instance, they may experience bright red as orange and blue as violet.

Most total or partial color blindness is hereditary, where the individual inherits a faulty genetic plan for the structure of the cones in the eye. However, in some instances the cause lies in the way that visual impressions are processed to the brain. The great majority of totally color-blind people are albinos who, for genetic reasons, suffer a lack of pigment throughout their bodies including the cones. A few of the remaining totally color-blind people were not born with the defect but have lost the ability to distinguish colors as a result of disease or poisoning by such pollutants as lead or carbon disulfide. Some of these environmentally damaged people can recover at least part of their color vision after proper therapy, which often includes large doses of vitamin A.

There is a far higher frequency of color blindness in males than in females, with about 8 to 10 percent of men and only about one in 190 women experiencing marked color-vision deficiency.

The significance of color blindness for educational practice can be found in such diverse fields as art, safety education, mathematics, and science.

Perhaps the most obvious influence is in art, where color-blind pupils use colors in patterns considered unsuitable by others. Or else such pupils unknowingly use two colors—such as red and green—interchangeably, since they cannot distinguish them.

In safety education, pupils can experience difficulty interpreting signs whose colors convey different messages. When the child who is red–green color blind is taught about traffic lights, he or she needs to learn the meaning of the placement of the lights rather than their colors (i.e., "stop" is indicated by the top light rather than the red light). When a color-blind driver sees a single light or flag by the roadside, he does not know whether it is red for "danger" or green for "all clear."

Color-blind individuals also have difficulty performing mathematical activities that employ colored counters—beads or sticks—for teaching such concepts as place value and sets. Charts and graphs that depend on colors for distinguishing functions may also prove confusing.

In science, color-blind students of biology will experience difficulty when they are expected to identify structures under the microscope by color. Such students will also encounter difficulty in chemistry classes where color is a distinguishing property of many chemical compounds.

In conclusion, teachers who recognize that some of their students—particularly the males—will be blind to certain colors can help them to circumvent the problems that arise. Such aid may include attaching labels to colored objects and training students to discover characteristics other than color for identifying the objects.

Bibliography

Gregory R L 1978 *Eye and Brain: The Psychology of Seeing*, 3rd edn. McGraw-Hill, New York
Wertenbaker L T 1981 *The Eye: Window to the World*, The Human Body Series, Vol. 3. US News Books, Washington, DC

Hearing in Children

R. W. Keith

Hearing, the sense by which sounds are appreciated, is a sensory function that is poorly understood and often taken for granted by the lay public. Yet, disorders of hearing in children have significant implications for speech, language, social, and personality development. In addition, the implications for academic and vocational training of children with hearing disorders require all persons related to the educational field to be familiar with these children's special needs.

1. Hearing and Auditory Perception

1.1 Anatomy of the Ear

The ear and the auditory pathways of the brain are marvelous structures with a remarkable range of abilities. The ear itself is made up of three basic components—the outer, middle, and inner ear (see Table 1). The outer ear includes the visible pinna and ear canal, while the middle ear includes the tympanic membrane, the three bones of the ossicular chain (malleus, incus, stapes), and their muscles and suspensory ligaments. The middle-ear space is normally filled with air supplied through the Eustachian tube that is connected to the nasopharynx, an area high in the back of the throat. The innermost bone, the stapes, connects to a window into the inner ear, or cochlea. The 20,000 fibers of the auditory nerve leave the cochlea and begin the complex neurological pathway of the brain.

1.2 Auditory Abilities

With this structure the normal human is capable of hearing a wide range of frequencies from 20 to 20,000 Hz over a wide range of intensities, with the loudest tolerable sound about 10^{12} times the weakest detectable sound. This range of intensities is more conveniently expressed using a logarithmic scale called the decibel (dB). With the threshold of hearing at zero dB, ordinary conversation at three feet is 65 dB, while hammer blows on a steel plate rise to 115 dB. A descriptive relationship between hearing-threshold levels and probable handi-

cap and needs is shown in Table 2. The hearing levels in this table are based on average thresholds at 500, 1,000, and 2,000 Hz, the frequencies usually considered most important for hearing and understanding speech. The table does not take into account speech discrimination ability and other dimensions of hearing and is, therefore, dangerously simplistic. Nevertheless, it offers some basis upon which audiometric results can be interpreted. The psychological correlates of frequency and intensity are pitch and loudness. Another important dimension of sound is its duration. The ability to hear small differences in all of these aspects of sound is necessary to hear differences among phonemes, words, and sentences.

Other auditory abilities include the ability to localize the source of sound, to direct auditory attention and to discriminate speech in the presence of background noise, to attend to one speaker while ignoring others, and so on. These perceptual skills require a minimum of cognitive skills. Other auditory abilities require interpretive skills. These language-based auditory abilities include auditory analysis, auditory synthesis (often called sound blending), auditory memory, closure of an incomplete auditory message, association of sound and its written symbol, and many other cognitive skills.

1.3 Maturation of Auditory Abilities

The perceptual auditory abilities of children develop over many years, reaching maturity in the 11th to 15th year near the time of puberty, although auditory language abilities continue to develop for several decades. For example, newborn infants respond only to loud sound in a reflexive manner, even though their auditory thresholds are similar to those of older children. Within the first year the infant learns to discriminate among voices and will attend to parents while ignoring strangers. At the same time, finer discrimination among sounds are made as expressive language emerges into words. The older child continues to mature both physiologically and intellectually, and, at the same time, increases performance in the perceptual and cognitive auditory skills described earlier.

Table 1
Anatomy of the ear

Outer ear	Middle ear	Inner ear	Neural pathways
Pinna	Tympanic membrane	Cochlea	Auditory nerve
Ear canal	Middle-ear space		Brainstem
	Ossicular chain		Auditory cortex
	Malleus		Association projections
	Incus		Interhemispheric connections
	Stapes		
	Muscles and ligaments		

Table 2
Relationship between hearing threshold level and probable handicap and needs[a]

Hearing threshold level in decibels (dB) (1969 American National Standards Institute Reference)	Descriptive term	Probable handicap and needs
0–15	Normal	No difficulty with faint speech
16–26	Slight	Difficulty with quiet speech. May need favorable classroom seating
27–40	Mild	Frequent difficulty with normal speech. Need favorable seating; may need hearing aid and tutoring
41–55	Moderate	Conversation must be loud to be understood. Difficulty following group and classroom instruction. Need for all of the above plus speech and language therapy
56–70	Moderate to severe	Cannot follow auditory instruction without help. May need a special class for hearing-impaired, or an integrated program
71–90	Severe	Need special educational programs. May enter regular classes at a later time
>90	Profound	Do not usually rely on hearing as primary channel for communication. Need special programs for the deaf; some of these children can eventually succeed with help in the regular classroom

a Modified from Goodman (1965) and Hardy and Hardy (1977)

2. Disorders of Hearing

It is said that the only true and unique disorder of humankind is a disorder of language (Travis 1971). An auditory disorder can prevent or interrupt the normal maturation of auditory abilities and the normal development of speech and language. Hearing disorders are usually placed in one of three basic categories according to the location of the impairment in the auditory system. The categories include conductive, sensory-neural, and central auditory disorders.

2.1 Conductive Hearing Loss

The first category occurs as a result of any dysfunction of the outer or middle ear. These hearing losses usually can be corrected either medically or surgically. The most common conductive hearing loss in children results from accumulation of fluid in the middle ear, called otitis media, that usually accompanies a cold or allergy.

Otitis media is particularly common among children with clefts of the palate, and also in children with Down Syndrome, cerebral palsied children, and other children found in special classes. Chronic otitis media can lead to perforations of the tympanic membrane, erosion of the ossicular chain, and other serious medical problems, including otitic meningitis. While these complications occur rarely, they pose serious hazards to health and to hearing.

Educationally, the presence of fluid in the middle ear can cause a hearing loss resulting in significant sensory deprivation. The primary-school teacher can expect to find upwards of 10 percent of children in kindergarten through third grade with otitis media at any given time, but especially in the fall and winter. The prevalence of otitis media drops in older children. The teacher should look for signs of daydreaming, frequent repetition of "huh" or "what," missed auditory instructions, and other signs of inattention in a previously achieving child. Some physical symptoms of children with this problem include mouthbreathing, draining ears, and earaches. The hearing loss associated with otitis media can fluctuate or remain constant until treated. K. Murphy of the Auditory Research Unit in Reading, England, describes the conductive loss as fluctuating, attenuating, and distorting (FAD). Aside from the known effects of hearing loss on academic performance while the fluid is present, the long-term effects on auditory processing skills are not clearly understood and require additional documentation through research (Ruben and Hanson 1979).

2.2 Sensory-neural Hearing Loss

Sensory-neural hearing loss is a disorder of the cochlea or the auditory nerve. These hearing losses result from prenatal, perinatal, and postnatal causes including hereditary factors, maternal rubella or other viral infections, anoxia or jaundice at birth, meningitis, head trauma, noise, and multiple other causes. This disorder usually cannot be reversed medically or surgically; and the educationally significant hearing loss must be managed through use of amplification and other special techniques.

2.3 Central Auditory Disorders

Previously, there has been emphasis on describing the child's deafness rather than what the child hears; and though it is possible to say a child responds at normal levels, it does not necessarily follow that a child hears normally. The third category of hearing disorders, central auditory dysfunction, can be defined as any breakdown in the child's auditory abilities that results in diminished learning through hearing, even though peripheral auditory sensitivity is normal (Keith 1981). Hardy and Hardy (1977) state simply that "we hear with our brains, not with our ears alone."

Behaviors of children with auditory-processing problems are similar to those of other specific learning disabilities, including problems with attention and impulse control. They may also have problems in following verbal commands or instructions, although they appear to be listening, they often request that information be repeated, cannot remember information presented verbally, and other related behaviors (Keith 1981). Many of these children have difficulty processing auditory information in the presence of competing noise.

The prevalence of central auditory disorders among children is not definitely known because of poor agreement among professionals as to the specific behaviors to be included under this designation. Clearly, mild cases of auditory perceptual deficits are easily compensated for when educational demands are minimal. With increased pressure for academic achievement, mild problems become more significant. In addition to educational pressures, other aggravating factors include teaching methods, motivation, and poor social conditions or health. It is helpful to the child when teachers are aware of the possible existence of a central auditory problem and are willing to seek confirmation of their suspicion and provide positive support in the classroom.

3. Assessment of Hearing

Various types of hearing tests are available that fulfill different needs. The typical pure-tone screening test done in schools is designed to identify educationally significant hearing losses. Unfortunately, however, because screening tests are often conducted in noisy environments, these tests miss mild hearing losses that go unidentified until the pupils encounter academic problems. Recently, the addition of tympanometry to pure tone screening has enabled identification of otitis media with fluid in the middle ear. Because screening tests have a high false positive and false negative rate, a teacher who continues to suspect a hearing loss is

justified in seeking additional testing even if the child passed the screening test.

The pure-tone air and bone threshold test done under quiet conditions by an audiologist will help the physician to determine both the type and degree of hearing loss. These results provide basic information as to whether a hearing loss is educationally significant and whether it is to be treated medically or with amplification.

The presence of a central auditory disorder can be determined only through special audiological test batteries, and cannot be determined through routine pure-tone threshold tests. Therefore, a teacher may again be justified in requesting additional tests for a child whose hearing sensitivity has been determined to be normal but who behaves as if a mild hearing loss was present.

4. Implications for Child Rearing and Educational Practice

The previous paragraphs indicate that the presence of a hearing loss requires intervention in order to optimize hearing and to facilitate the communication process. The conductive hearing loss may be amenable to improvement through medical or surgical intervention. Fluctuating or progressive sensory-neural losses need to be evaluated medically to determine their cause and possible treatment.

During the time a child has a hearing impairment, whether it is temporary or permanent, special audiological, speech/language, and educational treatments (noted on Table 2) may be required. Any intervention requires the total involvement and cooperation of the parents in order to be successful. Hardy (1965) reviews the need to provide parents with information about the effects of hearing disorders, since most parents give little time or thought to the way children learn speech and language. He states that "in many ways the psychosocial involvements between parents and language (and hearing) disordered children are possibly the most important aspects of the matter, once a reasonably sound evaluation of the child's problem has been accomplished."

No-one should underestimate the emotional impact that the presence of a hearing loss has on a family, with its effect on parental hopes and aspirations and consequent discouragement, anger, and blame. Recalling that communication is so unique to humankind, any interruption in the speech chain resulting in a disorder of the communication act can have profound effects.

Since the Education for All Handicapped Act (PL 94-142) was enacted into law in the United States in November of 1975, educators in this country have had a legal responsibility to provide an appropriate education in the least restrictive environment to hearing-impaired children. Even without this legal mandate, good educational practice dictates recognition of hearing impairment as significantly interfering with educational achievement, requiring services and programs that will benefit the child. Consideration should be given to a child's need for favorable classroom seating, amplification, and monitoring of hearing levels through rescreening. Educators should be aware of research that indicates that approximately 50 percent of hearing aids worn by children do not function appropriately, and require constant monitoring. Other considerations include the need for any of the following (adapted from Amon 1981):

(a) recommendations for classroom management;

(b) adaptation of the physical environment;

(c) training in use of residual hearing;

(d) modification of academic curriculum;

(e) initiation of speech and language therapy or tutoring in content areas;

(f) investigation of social–emotional needs;

(g) counseling of vocational goals and avocational activities.

The child with normal hearing sensitivity and central auditory dysfunction will require many of the same considerations.

In summary, the presence of a hearing impairment in a child is often a chronic condition requiring many years of treatment. These children present a special set of educational concerns because their problem involves a unique quality of human behavior: communication. With a professional understanding of the multiple facets of this disorder and a sensitivity to each child's special needs, they can be educated to live a useful, happy, and productive life.

Bibliography

Amon C 1981 Meeting state and federal guidelines. In: Roeser R J, Downs M P (eds.) 1981 *Auditory Disorders in Children*. Thieme-Stratton, New York, pp. 18–31

Goodman A 1965 Reference zero level for pure tone audiometers. *Asha* 7: 262–63

Hardy W 1965 On language disorders in young children: A reorganization of thinking. *J. Speech Hearing Disord*. 30: 3–16

Hardy W G, Hardy M P 1977 *Essays on Communication and Communicative Disorders*. Grune and Stratton, New York

Keith R W 1981 *Central Auditory and Language Disorders in Children*. College-Hill Press, San Diego, California, pp. xii and 61–76

Ruben R J, Hanson D G 1979 Summary of discussion and recommendations made during the workshop on otitis media and development. *Annals of Otology, Rhinology and Laryngology*, Suppl. 60, 88 (5, Pt. 2) pp. 107–11

Travis L E 1971 *Handbook of Speech Pathology and Audiology*. Appleton-Century-Crofts, New York

Hearing and Aging

J. F. Maurer

The term presbycusis, derived from the Greek (*presby*: old, and *akousis*: hearing), is commonly associated with the loss of hearing sensitivity that accompanies the aging process. Audiometric investigations of various cultures, modern and primitive, collectively indicate that hearing loss is a characteristic of senescence. Laboratory studies of temporal bone specimens taken from older adults reflect various anatomical sites of damage or atrophy within the human hearing mechanism, ranging from inner-ear structures to auditory-processing centers and waystations in the central nervous system. Unfortunately, structural alterations attributable to biological aging are often compounded by a lifetime of physical abuses and chemical insults to audition that also influence the detection, recognition, and interpretation of acoustic events, such that presbycusis is often defined medically as any irreversible sensorineural hearing loss found among elderly patients.

There is less than complete agreement on the age-related causes of presbycusis. The loss of sensory cells and neural fibers in the auditory mechanism has been attributed to reduced blood supply accompanying senescence (Jorgensen 1961, Fisch 1970, Schuknecht 1974). Research in Yugoslavia has linked the loss of hearing function with the gradual compression of arteries and nerve bundles by the growth of bony "cuffs" which ultimately reduce blood circulation and neural transmission (Krmpotic-Nemanic 1971). However, the extent to which various causal factors are related to genetically programmed obsolescence in certain cells and how their biological lifespan interacts with degenerative forces and agents which also hasten their demise is a continuing area of investigation.

1. Heterogeneity of Old-age Deafness

The binaural loss of hearing sensitivity associated with presbycusis typically involves depressed hearing for high-frequency pure-tone stimuli. Large-population audiometric surveys conducted in industrialized societies of the world yield remarkably similar results, according to a summary from the Netherlands. There is an increasing high-tone loss for succeeding age decades, with males generally more adversely affected than females (Spoor 1967). Hearing-level surveys of highly selected samples of the aging population, such as non-noise-exposed individuals (Hinchcliffe 1959) and culturally primitive societies (Rosen et al. 1962), have revealed that the severity of the deficit is less pronounced in such groups and the disparity between hearing-threshold levels for men and women is less apparent.

Moreover, a longitudinal study has shown that a small percentage of the population demonstrate flat audiometric configurations instead of the sloping, high-frequency loss of sensitivity (Dayal and Nussbaum 1971).

These data would suggest that there is considerable variance in the severity of hearing-level changes within the older population. In general, older persons who have remained healthy and who have somehow avoided traumatic, acoustic, or chemical abuses to the hearing mechanism during their lifespans demonstrate increased hearing sensitivity in later years. In contrast, the incidence and severity of hearing impairments has been shown to be greater among elderly people in nursing homes, convalescent facilities, and hospitals (Kronholm 1968, Decker 1974, Chafee 1967). Similarly, lower income aging persons demonstrate more reduced hearing sensitivity as a group, probably because of greater exposure to vocational noise, poorer nutrition, and reduced medical care (Roberts 1968, Maurer et al. 1974).

Old-age deafness is frequently accompanied by a loss of understanding for spoken messages. This is due in part to the fact that speech sounds that contribute measureably toward the intelligibility of human communication, that is, voiceless consonant sounds, have their primary energies in the higher frequencies of the speech spectrum. Since the relative phonetic power of lower pitch vowels, dipthongs, and voiced consonants remains more intact than voiceless sounds in the aging ear, this pitch imbalance accounts to some extent for the common complaint among older listeners that spoken messages are heard but not understood. The progressive nature of the deficit over time also contributes to the listening dilemma in the sense that some older persons unknowingly adapt their lifestyles to a hearing impairment that may be entirely unsuspected. A symposium in Munich, in the Federal Republic of Germany, also revealed that senior adults tend to tolerate greater hearing impairment than younger persons before seeking audiologic assistance for their problems (Haggard 1980).

The incidence of tinnitus, a perceived noise or ringing sensation in the head or ears, increases with chronological age as does the frequency of reported dizziness or balance problems (Roberts 1968). Damage within the inner-ear sensory mechanisms for hearing as well as the attrition of cells within neural structures likely account for these symptoms.

The cellular dropout within the central auditory nervous system that accompanies biological aging (Brody 1970) contributes to a slower conduction of messages from the ear to the brain. Increased time may be needed for the older person to process and respond to verbal information. Speakers that talk very rapidly, exceeding the normal rate of 150 to 160 words per minute, are an enigma to older listeners. While spoken conversation has considerable extrinsic redundancy, the depletion of neurons in brain stem and brain tissues contributes to a loss of internal redundancy, such that the central processing system can no longer effectively compensate for messages that are spoken too rapidly or are degraded in some other aspect. The aging listener may have difficulty in particular in background noise reverberation, such as in auditoriums, churches, or cafeterias. The ability to inhibit a secondary message, or an interfering noise, while attending to a primary listening task is especially taxed in situations where the interfering message has semantic or meaningful content.

The depletion of central auditory neurons also affects memory processing. Short-term memory, recall of acoustic events in the recent past, has been shown to be reduced in the performances of older listeners (McGhie et al. 1965). The often-present peripheral loss of hearing sensitivity likely interacts with central-neuron attrition, compounding the impairment of auditory-cognitive skills (Granick et al. 1976).

Older persons within the same chronological time frame evidence various levels of proficiency on tasks involving auditory awareness, speech discrimination in quiet and in noise, verbal recall, degraded or distorted message comprehension, and sound localization. The hearing-impaired aging population cannot be stereotyped. Consistent with this biological and experiential variance, the behavioral consequences of deafness also may range from subtle to profound (Maurer and Rupp 1979).

2. Psychosocial Problems of Hearing-impaired Aging Persons

Individuals who experience better health during the later years demonstrate greater life satisfaction (Edwards and Klemmack 1973). Since hearing skills are an important aspect of mental health, the presence of a significant sensorineural impairment may exert considerable influence on both life-style and life satisfaction. The problem is compounded by other handicaps such as arthritis, visual limitations, and lack of mobility; conditions which appear epidemic among the very old. The insidious onset of the auditory impairment often is accompanied by a gradual disengagement from social activities, cultural events, and educational experiences that are heavily weighted toward oral communication. Such activities soon lose their positive valence when the older person is constantly straining to hear or understand. The disengagement may take the form of a simple decrease in attendance at certain events, such as club meetings or religious services. In the rare extreme, there may be a global withdrawal from all social communication activities. Frequently, the older individual does not assume the responsibility for the listening impairment, but challenges others for not "speaking clearly" or other environments for being "too noisy" and "too confusing." The unfortunate paradox is that too few geriatric facilities are acoustically designed for the hearing-impaired elderly, and many public meeting places, including churches and theaters, are not architecturally designed for speech intelligibility. The worldwide paucity of nursing homes especially designed and staffed for the deaf elderly who can only communicate manually also attests to the lack of advocacy for the aging (Flood 1971).

3. Intervention for Presbycusis

Presbycusis is not a medically treatable problem, and the alternative of wearing hearing-aid amplification may not be looked upon with anticipation. The present generation of aging people is able to recall the stigmata associated with deafness, including bulky hearing-aid appliances, uncharitable jokes about hearing loss, and the recurring association between deafness and growing old. It is understandable why attitudes toward intervention may be counterproductive. Other factors contribute toward this avoidance, including the initial cost of hearing aids, the amount of perceived benefit to the listener, and transportation problems in getting services. Most older persons can benefit from appropriately tested and fitted hearing instruments, although the financial barrier remains very real for individuals on fixed incomes. In countries where hearing aids are provided at little or no charge by government programs, such as Denmark, there is evidence that older persons can achieve the same life satisfaction benefits from wearing hearing aids as younger individuals (Nielsen 1974).

The success of amplification among senior adults also depends to a great extent upon the neurological potential of the individual and his/her ability to physically manage the prosthesis. Elderly persons with central-auditory processing problems, as in difficulties occurring following cerebro-vascular episodes, are often not excellent candidates for hearing aids. One characteristic of a neural lesion is that amplification of the speech signal may further degrade the older person's ability to understand oral communication (Jerger and Jerger 1971). It becomes apparent that not only is a comprehensive audiologic assessment mandated prior to the decision regarding amplification, but the audiologist must also devote considerable time toward training the older person in the management skills associated with the appliance (Miller 1967). The success of such intervention may often be increased by involving the aging individual in group aural rehabilitation, which involves auditory training with the hearing aid, lipreading or speechreading instruction, and counseling.

While presbycusis is the most common communication problem among the aging as well as being the most common hearing disorder in the world population, the majority of older persons do not suffer from an auditory impairment until the seventh or eighth decade of life. Most of those who do can be helped significantly with appropriate audiologic intervention.

Bibliography

Brody H 1970 Structural changes in the aging nervous system. In: Blumenthal H T (ed.) 1970 *Interdisciplinary Topics in Gerontology.* Karger, Basel, pp. 9–21

Chafee C 1967 Rehabilitation needs of nursing home patients: A report of a survey. *Rehabil. Lit.* 18: 377–89

Dayal V S, Nussbaum M A 1971 Patterns of puretone loss in presbycusis: A sequential study. *Acta Oto-Laryngol.* 71: 382–84

Decker T N 1974 A survey of hearing loss in older age hospital population. *Gerontologist* 14: 402–03

Edwards J N, Klemmack D L 1973 Correlates of life satisfaction: A re-examination. *J. Gerontol.* 28: 497–502

Fisch L 1970 The selective and differential vulnerability of the auditory system. In: Wolstenholme G E W, Knight J (eds.) 1970 *Sensorineural Hearing Loss.* Churchill, London, pp. 101–15

Flood J T 1971 *National Association of Homes for the Aged Deaf: Services for Elderly Deaf Persons.* Deafness Research and Training Center, New York University Press, New York, pp. 63–71

Granick S, Kleban M, Weiss A O 1976 Relationships between hearing loss and cognition in normally hearing aged persons. *J. Gerontol.* 31: 434–40

Haggard M P 1980 Six audiological paradoxes in the provision of hearing aid services. In: Berlin C I, Haggard M P, Schwartz D M, Berger K W, Webster D B (eds.) 1980 *Studies in the Use of Amplification for the Hearing Impaired.* Excerpta Medica. Zenetron, Chicago, Illinois, pp. 1–14

Hinchcliffe R 1959 The threshold of hearing as a function of age. *Acustica* 9: 304–08

Jerger J, Jerger S 1971 Diagnostic significance of the PB word functions. *Arch. Otolaryngol.* 93: 573–80

Jorgensen M B 1961 Changes of aging in the inner ear: Histological studies. *Arch. Otolaryngol.* 74: 164–70

Krmpotic-Nemanic J 1971 A new concept of the pathogenesis of presbycusis. *Arch. Otolaryngol.* 93: 161–72

Kronholm A 1968 Auditory problems in a home for the aged. In: Liden G K O (ed.) 1968 *Geriatric Audiology.* Almqvist and Wiksell, Stockholm, pp. 58–62

Maurer J F, McCartney J, Sorenson F 1974 Some characteristics of hearing impairment among the low income elderly. Paper presented at 26th Annual Scientific Meeting of Gerontological Society, Miami Beach, Florida

Maurer J F, Rupp R R 1979 *Hearing and Aging: Tactics for Intervention.* Grune and Stratton, New York

McGhie A, Chapman J, Lawson J S 1965 Changes in immediate memory with age. *Br. J. Psychol.* 56: 69–75

Miller M 1967 Audiologic management of presbyacusic patients. *Fenestra* 14: 29–32

Nielsen B H 1974 Effect of monaural versus binaural hearing aid equipment. *Scand. Audiol.* 3: 183–87

Roberts J 1968 Hearing status and ear examination: Findings among adults. *Vital and Health Statistics.* (United States Dept. of Health, Education and Welfare, Series 11, No. 32) Washington, DC, US Government Printing Office, 1968, p. 13

Rosen S, Bergman M, Plester D, El-Mofty A, Satti M H 1962 Presbycusis study of a relatively noise-free population in the Sudan. *Ann. Otol.* 71: 727–42

Schuknecht H F 1974 *Pathology of the Ear.* Harvard University Press, Cambridge, Massachusetts, pp. 388–414

Spoor A 1967 Presbycusis values in relation to noise induced hearing loss. *Int. Audiol.* 6: 48–57

Special Issues in Physical Development

Sex Characteristics and Roles

D. D. V. Bielby and S. E. Doherty

Biologically, whether a person is considered to be male or female depends on the pattern of the individual's inherited sex chromosomes, with the XY pairing of chromosomes producing the male and the XX pairing producing the female. This biological status has been called the person's sex or, less frequently, gender. The phenomenon of biological maleness and femaleness is referred to as sex dimorphism.

In each culture, certain personality and social characteristics are attached to each of the sexes, with some of the characteristics assigned to the particular sex by tradition rather than an inherent result of a person's being biologically female or male. The assigned or ascribed characteristics figure prominently in how a culture defines the roles people perform, including both the duties and rights associated with such roles. A given culture's definition of the proper roles for each sex is based upon the common image in that culture of the ideal or normal set of characteristics necessary for satisfactory role performance. For example, the typical Western-society image of femininity has included the traits of passivity, emotionality, warmth, deference, cooperativeness, and low intellectuality. In contrast, the traditional image of masculinity has included the traits of competitiveness, rationality, confidence, assertiveness, and instrumentality.

In each society, some people identify with their own biological sex more than do others, with the extent to which a person establishes such identification being called the degree of gender identification or, in earlier research, the degree of sex-role identity (Kagan 1964).

Issues related to sex characteristics and roles are reviewed in the following pages, first in terms of research from the disciplines of anthropology, sociology, and psychology and then in terms of implications such findings suggest for the conduct of education.

1. Anthropological Research

Anthropology views sex characteristics and roles as social and cultural inventions and examines both cultural universals and variations in them. Recent findings about economic patterns, status and role variables, and family structure necessitate reassessing the universal cultural division of labor by sex. Stereotypes of "man the hunter" and "woman the economic dependent" have been revised to acknowledge the role of "woman the gatherer's" foraging activities in subsistence economies. Subsequently, re-evaluations of simplistic, evolutionary accounts of male and female divisions of labor focus on the status of women as a complex cultural product. Efforts toward understanding the general status of women coupled with concern to change women's position in society are directing research to the study of universal subordination of women, cultural variations in their treatment, and conceptions of femininity, and toward alteration of the male-centered bias that devalues women's affairs.

1.1 Division of Labor

Traditionally, biological differences in primary sex characteristics (such as the penis in the male, the vagina in the female) and secondary sex characteristics (such as the different patterns of body hair in males and females) have been used to explain universal culture patterning of sex-typed roles. In all societies males and females differ in both types of sex characteristics but these differences are not fixed and absolute. Universally, males tend to be taller, have more massive skeletons and more body hair, and to have a higher ratio of muscle to fat, but these characteristics are affected by both culture and environment.

Universal sex characteristics are assumed to account for consistencies in tasks that men and women perform. D'Andrade's cross-cultural survey of 224 primitive societies revealed that when society's subsistence depends on pursuing sea mammals, hunting, metal working or weapon making in preparation for war, men always perform these tasks. Women perform tasks of tending children and domestic duties including carrying water and cooking (Maccoby 1966 pp. 174–204). The traditional anthropological explanation is that men perform physically strenuous and dangerous activities like hunting and warfare, involving long periods of travel and a high degree of cooperation. Women, because they bear and breast-feed children, are primarily responsible for child-rearing.

The sexual division of labor which was adaptive in primitive cultures prevails in modern technological societies. Safilios-Rothschild's (1975) survey of 23 modern societies observed the following patterns in division of labor. In the Soviet Union, Poland, Hungary, and Finland, half the women work, primarily in formerly male-dominated occupations; but men do not perform domestic tasks. State-supported child care and a national ideology that supports communal child rearing help women assume work roles but require no changes of men. In Scandinavian society, one-third of the women work. Although ideology favors equality and Sweden is one of the few societies where "househusband" is a socially acceptable role, the actual division of labor is little different from other societies. In Argentina, Japan, Greece, and Turkey, a third of women work, although fewer of them are married. Little child care is provided; wealthy families hire maids and the less well-to-do rely on grandmothers to do housework and child care. In the United States, Canada, and, to some extent, the United Kingdom, France, the Federal Republic of Germany, and Australia, one-third to one-half of women work. The prevailing ideology that child care is a full-time occupation requires mothers to serve children's needs. No systematic child care is provided for working mothers. Women in these countries have not entered the traditionally male-dominated occupations in significant numbers.

1.2 Social Status

In every culture's division of labor there is a distinction between masculine and feminine tasks and, strikingly, between the value attached to those tasks. Men's work is universally regarded as more valuable than women's work. If the women of a tribe grow sweet potatoes and men grow yams, yams will be the tribe's prestige food, the food distributed at feasts (Rosaldo in Rosaldo and Lamphere 1974 pp. 17–42). Further, in societies in which women take over a formerly male occupation, this occupation loses status as happened with secretarial and clerical work, and teaching in the United States, medicine in the Soviet Union, and cultivating cassavas in Nigeria.

The differential cultural evaluations assigned the two sexes has led to studies of universal cultural patterns of sexual asymmetry, male supremacy and dominance, and female subordination. The search for exceptions to the universal male-dominated society was initiated by Bachofen's *Das Mutterrech* (1851); but to date, his model of matriarchy has remained an illusive myth for there has not been an undisputed case in which women as a class controlled the strategic resources of a society and its men (Bamberger in Rosaldo and Lamphere 1974 pp. 263–80). In the egalitarian North American Indian tribe of the Iroquois, women achieved a measure of power and influence through food production and distribution,

and played a role in tribal lineage, yet could not join the ruling body of the "council of elders."

In all known societies, males hold the most prestigious offices and control the basic resources of public life. Male supremacy is strongest in those societies where men have the greatest control over the distribution of scarce commodities outside the family sphere and, thus, have the greatest participation in resulting political and economic alliances and obligations (Friedl 1975). Males achieve status through striving for rank in the social hierarchy controlling male activities. Women's status is ascribed and remains relatively undifferentiated. Their roles are defined largely by age or relationships with males.

1.3 Domestic and Public Domains

A major focus on sex roles concerns relative dimensions of men's and women's social worlds. Women's roles as child bearers and rearers typically restrict them to a narrower social sphere characterized as "domestic" whereas men actively predominate in the wider circles of "public" life. In initiation ceremonies men are initiated into the community as a whole, whereas women's initiations involve incorporation into restricted domestic groups. Other studies have demonstrated the existence of differential distribution of knowledge essential to attain power and prestige in society. Men's wider access to socially strategic information allows them to operate in a more extensive range of social settings. When men have a monopoly on sacred knowledge, it is used to maintain male supremacy. Among the South American Yanomama Indians, access to the spirit world is through the use of hallucinogenics (mind-altering substances) controlled by men.

1.4 Authority, Power, Influence

In analyses of social relationships, women's roles are viewed as less formally defined as well as less public. They differ from men's roles in authority, power, and influence. "Authority" is the exercise of control when culturally recognized as legitimate. "Power" is the exercise of control that is culturally unrecognized or covert. "Influence" is using others' best interest as the means of convincing or affecting their behavior. Women's roles are granted the exercise of power and influence but are denied overt, legitimate authority. Women's exercise of power usually takes the form of subversion, sabotaging plans of those in legitimate authority, or working indirectly through others such as sons and husbands. Thus, family power structure is examined for women's manipulative strategies (Lamphere in Rosaldo and Lamphere 1974 pp. 97–112).

1.5 Sexual Asymmetry

Present anthropological research focuses on in-depth investigations of specific cultural contexts or on the effects of change in specific societies. Regarding universal sexual asymmetry or inequality, a complex model is sought to incorporate evidence on cultural diversity. Individual contexts of sexual subordination are providing more subtle understandings of the variety of female experiences both within and between cultures and improved descriptions of cultural evaluations of masculinity and femininity. A new model must include history, region, class, family structure, and ideology in explaining differences between men's and women's roles.

Investigations are also directed at analyzing modernization, development, and revolution and the impact of these changes on the family and women's position in society. Studies of change demonstrate that traditional reproductive criteria for sexual division of labor have disappeared; yet, sexual asymmetries persist in those societies. These studies suggest that if the positions of men and women in society are to become equal, men should be integrated into the domestic sphere, particularly into the role of child rearing, while women should be integrated into the world of work, particularly into control of resources and products of economic production.

2. Sociological Research

The changing role of women in Western nations has resulted in unparalleled numbers of women in all stages of the family life cycle entering the labor force. Accordingly, sex roles are undergoing redefinition. Coupled with the rise of the women's movement, these trends have drawn sociologists' attention to the unequal status of women in society. In the current emphasis on the study of women, concomitant study of changing male roles is neglected, accounting for this section's singular focus on women.

Sociological research on sex roles seeks identification and interpretation of roles in all structured settings. It focuses almost exclusively on norms, roles, and socialization governing performance in those settings, the correlates of role location and performance, the special situation of deviant roles, and the mechanics of role change. Sociologists are also concerned with women as a minority and associated issues of discrimination, prejudice, and segregation, and the politics of minority status, particularly power differences (Lipman-Blumen and Tickamyer 1975, Hochschild 1973).

2.1 Socialization

Sex-role socialization, beginning in infancy and continuing throughout adulthood, is the outcome of pressures—rewards, punishments, ignoring, and anticipating—by influential individuals, institutional and organizational contexts, and the mass media which direct children to acceptable behaviors. Behavioral norms, values, and expectations are interpreted by primary caretakers, especially parents, and effect differential treatment of male and female infants from birth, resulting in early manifestations of "masculine" and "feminine" patterns. Parents directly and indirectly

influence children to fit sex-appropriate gender stereotypes before children develop a sexual identity or awareness of sex-role standards (Kagan and Moss 1962 in Hochschild 1973). Consequently, the mother–child relationship has been studied extensively. According to Maccoby and Jacklin (1974), this socialization is fundamental for adult self-socialization of sex-role identification. In infancy, parents elicit gross motor behavior more from sons than daughters (Lewis 1972, Moss 1967 in Maccoby and Jacklin 1974), with girls treated as if they were more fragile than boys. During the preschool years, parental behaviors of warmth, restrictiveness, dependency weaning, management of aggression, and competitiveness become salient, show no consistent patterns of differential socialization, but differ in reinforcement of instrumentality or goal-directed behavior which is encouraged in boys but not girls. Different patterns of socialization due to affectional interaction or parental warmth, according to Maccoby and Jacklin (1974), seem related to sex of child by school age. Trends in sex-role socialization differences are also clear cut in the encouragement of sex-typed activities, such as toy selection and stronger restrictions on boys' venturing into female sex-typed activities. Girls' behavior is noticeably more dependent and less exploratory, and their play behavior indicative of a quieter style than boys (Goldberg and Lewis in Maccoby and Jacklin 1974). Boys tend to receive more physical punishment than girls, but the reason they do is not clear. They also receive more praise. Pressure to achieve is not sex-linked until expectations for college attendance emerge, where boys clearly receive more pressure to attend.

Through immediate and anticipatory socialization that prepares the individual for adult roles, sex differences in infancy and childhood are continually enlarged with age. Parents are devoted to defining sex-appropriate behavior and guiding children by differentially "shaping" those behaviors. Currently there is limited exploration of parental factors in shaping sex-role behaviors.

By primary school, sex-role stereotypes are fully developed and influence children's behaviors in patterns of play, peer selection, and vocational choice. Peer choices and play groups are based on sex. Play groups function as subcultures, their norms and roles reflecting the broader culture. Through adolescence, girls engage in relatively uncompetitive play requiring minimal team effort and less elaborate rules. Through more organized play, males learn group procedures, preparing for adult role performance in the labor force. Female vocational aspirations as extensions of sex-role identity are susceptible to foreclosing at an early age.

With the onset of adolescence, female socialization becomes restricted and male socialization directed (Brim 1968). For females, puberty marks initiation of stringent, clear-cut sex-role distinctions. Normative femininity becomes a highly stereotyped attribute that must be acquired. The search for identity, which is the essential developmental task of adolescence, is diffused and delayed for females. Role socialization culminates in emergence of the "contingency orientation" in female adolescents, whereby they prepare for marriage and the marital role as an affirmation of femininity. The female adolescent is socialized to maximize her eligibility. Consequently, career decisions tend to be postponed until mate selection is resolved. In adulthood, females tend to be faced with a role choice of whether or not to work; men are expected to work. Limited female role choices in the work world are a major research focus

2.2 The Role Perspective

Sociological research focuses on the consequences of socialization—women's roles in the family and the economy, role strain accompanying simultaneous involvement, and structural barriers to women fulfilling instrumental, achievement-oriented participation in the labor force. Normative or typical socialization for women is to provide expressive functions in the family and for men to provide instrumental functions in the family, but primarily in the labor force. The career wife is dysfunctional according to this perspective. Research examines her impact upon marital roles, power relationships, and parent–child relationships, and includes examination of societal and psychoanalytic production of the "need" to mother (Chodorow in Rosaldo and Lamphere 1974 pp. 43–66). Consequences of sex-role socialization are analyzed in terms of internalized barriers (e.g., perceptions of deviance, motives to avoid success) and structural barriers (e.g., occupational discrimination) to entering the labor force and mobility in it, especially in the male-dominated professions. Explanations are sought for the predominance of women in low-status, low-paying jobs and female-dominated professions and occupations. Research focusing on school- and college-aged girls, females holding doctorates, and census and employment data allows examination of occupational behavior, understood to be the complex consequence of being born male or female in our society, and factors such as economic resources and the sex-role ideology of spouse.

2.3 Women as Minority

Women's societal roles underwrite their status as an outgroup or minority which is a group who, because of their physical or cultural characteristics, are singled out from others in the society for differential and unequal treatment, and who therefore regard themselves as objects of collective discrimination. Research focuses on polemics of sexual inequality, the determination of social roles by ascribed sexual status, and the "minority mentality" accompanying groups oppressed by limited access to unlimited social roles. Feminist scholarship, responding to the minority status of women, seeks explanation of the complex interplay of biology, socialization, and society, and emphasizes the linkage of sex differences to status and power in society.

3. Psychological Research

Psychologists seek discovery and explanation of individual differences in behavioral performance between men and women in terms of learned sex roles and biological substrates. Research is dominated by both biological and sociocultural explanations of sex differences, notably cognitive–developmental, social learning, and psychosexual approaches.

3.1 Behavioral Differences

Differential sex characteristics have been investigated through the study of intellect and achievement, including perception, learning, memory, intellectual abilities, cognitive styles and achievement, and through the study of social behavior, including temperament, social approach–avoidance, and power relationships (Maccoby and Jacklin 1974). Contrary to popular myth, research on the intellectual processes of perception (sensory intake), learning (or the ways in which individuals acquire information), and memory (or the set of processes filling intellectual capacity) reveal a lack of difference between sexes. Differences exist between males and females in the domain of intellectual abilities and cognitive style, with males demonstrating more variability than females in numerical and spatial but not verbal abilities, where females excel. Characteristics associated with use of intellectual abilities in social contexts are commonly believed to be highly sex-linked but are, instead, related in a complex way. Males and females do not differ significantly in achievement motivation except under sex-typed situations.

Research on social behavior, the complex domain of behaviors manifested when interacting with other individuals, does not substantiate the common assumption that females are more passive than males. Males become more physically active than females after infancy, where few differences exist. Similarly, there is a sex-linked divergence in frustration behavior and to some extent the fear response. Social approach–avoidance behavior (including dependency, nurturance, and helping) are not always differentiated by sex. All children seek close contact with attachment objects. Affiliation and positive interactions stemming from nurturance and empathy show equally high levels of sociability, but differences exist in power relationships and social domination. Overtly aggressive, competitive, dominating behavior becomes charactersitic of males by early childhood and remains throughout adulthood.

3.2 Biological Differences

Investigations of genetically based differences originally analyzed transmission of general intelligence but more recently have analyzed inheritance of specific cognitive abilities (e.g., depth perception in spatial mazes, picture completion, map reading, and mental rotation of objects in space.) Research suggests some degree of sex-linked genetic superiority for males in spatial ability. Verbal ability is heritable but not demonstrably sex-linked.

Sex hormones are presumed to assist in the manifestation of sex-linked traits. In the study of spatial abilities, complex findings indicate an association between highly masculine physical and personality characteristics and low spatial scores. The differentiation between males and females in spatial ability beginning in adolescence, when androgen (the male sex hormone) levels rise, suggests an unknown counterbalancing sex hormone accounting for males' increased ability.

Study of brain lateralization and organization explains sex differences in intellectual abilities by cerebral dominance. Females are likely to have verbal and spatial abilities duplicated on both sides of the brain. Right-handed males are likely to have the speech center on the left, spatial skills on the right. Although the two hemispheres of the brain seem less specialized for females than males, distribution of other mental functions is the same. The sexes differ in hemispheric arousal, with females more adept at activating brain zones required for the task (Witelson 1976). Females are less capable of simultaneously performing distinctively different tasks but more capable of focusing cognition on one activity.

3.3 Sociocultural Approaches: Cognitive-developmental Theory

Kohlberg (in Maccoby 1966 pp. 84–173) argues that the process of forming a gender identity is part of the process of conceptual development and a product of the child's active structuring of his or her experiences. Gender role acquisition relies on the construct of gender constancy. An individual may change in nonessential attributes, such as hair length or clothing, but as long as the criterion attribute, the genitals, is unchanged, gender remains unchanged. Kohlberg predicts that children will reliably sex type and attend to same-sex models after achievement of gender constancy about age 5. Subsequently, sex-role behavior is acquired through the mechanism of cognitive consistency which leads to the formation of values consistent with self-conceptual cognitive judgments of gender identity.

Sex-role preferences are now known to exist during infancy, prior to attainment of gender constancy. According to Lewis and Weinraub (1979) sexual dimorphism imparts information to the infant who constructs schema or mental representation for differentiating others and self from others. Through complex experiences and cognitive development, the child gains an increasingly sophisticated knowledge of sex role and gender. Cultural meanings and values associated with sexual differences provide further information for differentiation. Simultaneously, the principle of attraction ensures that the developing infant acts in a manner consistent with "like" objects. Thus, the child moves toward conformity with cultural sex-role stereotypes.

3.4 Sociocultural Approaches: Social Learning Theory

According to social learning theorists, children's behaviors and values are determined not by their own gender role but by their social learning history (Mischel in Maccoby 1966) in social context and historical time. Sex-typed behaviors elicit different rewards for one sex than for the other and are learned through reinforcements from adults and peers through specific processes of discrimination, generalization, and performance and practice. Cultural meanings and values of sex differences are acquired by the same principles of conditioning. Social learning is facilitated by sex-role stereotypes involving "expectations about the dispositions and typical behaviors supposedly displayed by members of a category" and providing ways of organizing large amounts of information. Complex sex typing, as opposed to simple responses, is also achieved through the mechanism of identification with a model, typically the same-sex parent, whereby the child attempts to duplicate complex behavioral patterns of actions, feelings, ideas, and attitudes. Currently, the social learning assumption of unidirectional influence of parents on children is being revised to account for findings of the effect of child temperament and development on parental patterns and the differential effect of parental treatment on boys and girls.

3.5 Sociocultural Approaches: Psychosexual Theory

Freud's view of gender identity is embedded within his broader conception of sexuality, with its emphasis on bisexuality whereby masculine and feminine elements are to be found in different proportions in all individuals. Freud viewed sexual or libidinal energies as emerging at birth and remaining essential while changing form at each subsequent stage of development (oral, anal, phallic–urethral, and genital). Freud believed "anatomy is destiny," that psychological sex-role development begins with unconscious reactions to anatomical differences precipitated by the critical discovery of the male penis. This event initiates the phallic stage between ages 3 and 6 and the Oedipal complex with subsequent development of castration anxiety in boys and penis envy in girls. Revisions of psychoanalytic theory have maintained that the concept of penis envy is male oriented and have demonstrated a corresponding "womb envy"—male envy of the female capacity for motherhood (Horney 1926). For boys, the Oedipal conflict is resolved through a mechanism Anna Freud labeled "identification with the aggressor," resulting in the acquisition of the masculine sex role. For girls, the feminine sex role is acquired through the anxiety-reducing mechanism of "anaclitic identification" with the mother (see *Psychoanalytic Theory of Human Development*).

371

A revised theory by Simon and Gagnon (1969) states "sexual behavior is socially scripted behavior and not the masked or rationalized expression of some primordial drive. The individual learns to be sexual as he or she learns sexual scripts, scripts that invest actors and situations with erotic content." Finding that boys masturbate more than girls, Simon and Gagnon argue that differential adolescent experiences resulting from both anatomical and social forces produce differential psychosexual patterns in adults.

4. Education Implications

The educational relevance of anthropological, sociological, and psychological research on sex roles and characteristics emerges through examination of sex-role socialization, the process by which cultural contexts and rationales, the acquisition of social scripts (event-specific behaviors) and gender identities, and the mechanisms of shaping or reinforcing produce sex differences. Socialization, the continual social process that fits individuals for participating in societal roles, supplants earlier explanations of sex role based on Freud's "anatomy is destiny." Early sex-role socialization is studied within both the family context and the social context of educational institutions. Such research has profound but complex implications for child rearing and educational practices.

Schools, reflective of the prevailing culture, promote predominant sex stereotypes through instructional texts, achievement tests, sports programs, vocational training, and sex-differentiated curricula. Educators, both as individuals and as products of organizations, are themselves products of cultural expectations about sex roles. Trained in institutions in which are embedded sex-role biases, educators unconsciously model cultural expectations in both their personal and educational practices. Consequently, as agents of socialization, teachers may direct children toward socially preferred sex-role performance and expect different achievement and competency from males and females.

A common belief about classroom organization because of the predominance of female teachers in some societies is that classrooms are feminized environments with feminizing effects. Evidence indicates that within the classroom, boys become practiced at sex-typical competitive skills which enhance their academic performance. Far less is known about the impact of classroom organization on females or the effect of coeducational classrooms, at least until adolescence, upon either sex.

Evidence of sex differences in intellectual abilities is often assumed by educators to generalize to sex differences in learning processes, such as problem solving, memory strategies, and paired associate learning. However, there is no evidence to support that generalization. Educators acting under such an assumption are pro-

viding unequal quality of education for males and females and perhaps creating sex differences where they might not otherwise exist. Finally, the trend in sex differences on visual–spatial tasks has implications for women's access to training and entry into male-dominated occupations. The extent to which male-dominated fields require visual–spatial ability is unclear. When educators discourage female entry into those fields, they exaggerate what is merely a statistical tendency into a sex difference.

Given the reduced cultural need in many present-day cultures for a clearly sex-linked division of labor, educational practices that create sex differences beyond social utility would appear to inhibit human potentials. The multidisciplinary findings reviewed here suggest that if educators wish to provide equal opportunities for children of both sexes to achieve their individual potentials, schools will integrate the sexes into greater role diversity.

Bibliography

Brim O G 1968 Adult socialization. In: Clausen J (ed.) 1968 *Socialization and Society.* Little, Brown, Boston, Massachusetts

Friedl E 1975 *Women and Men: An Anthropologist's View.* Holt, Rinehart and Winston, New York

Hochschild A R 1973 A review of sex role research. *Am. J. Sociol.* 78: 1011–29

Horney K 1926 The flight from womanhood. In: Miller J B (ed.) 1973 *Psychoanalysis and Women.* Brunner/Mazel, New York, pp. 3–16

Kagan J 1964 Acquisition and significance of sex typing and sex role identity. In: Hoffman M, Hoffman L (eds.) 1964 *Review of Child Development Research,* Vol. 1. Russell Sage, New York, pp. 137–67

Lewis M 1972 State as an infact-environment interaction: An analysis of mother-infant behaviour as a function of sex. *Merrill Palmer Q.* 18: 95–121

Lewis M, Weinraub M 1979 Origins of early sex role development. *Sex Roles* 5: 135–53

Lipman-Blumen J, Tickamyer A 1975 Sex roles in transition: A ten-year perspective. *Annual Review of Sociology,* Vol. 1. Annual Reviews Press, Palo Alto, California, pp. 297–337

Maccoby E E (ed.) 1966 *The Development of Sex Differences.* Stanford University Press, Stanford, California

Maccoby E E, Jacklin C N 1974 *The Psychology of Sex Differences.* Stanford Press, Stanford, California

Rosaldo M Z, Lamphere L (eds.) 1974 *Women, Culture and Society.* Stanford University Press, Stanford, California

Safilios-Rothschild C 1975 A cross-cultural examination of women's marital, educational and occupational options. In: Mednick M T S, Tangri S S, Hoffman L W (eds.) 1975 *Women and Achievement: Social and Motivational Analyses.* Halsted Press, New York

Simon J H, Gagnon W 1969 On psychosexual development. In: Goslin D A (ed.) 1969 *Handbook of Socialization Theory and Research.* Rand McNally, Chicago, Illinois

Witelson S F 1976 Sex and the single hemisphere: Specialization of the right hemisphere for spatial processing. *Science* 193: 425–27

Homosexuality and Human Development

R. M. Thomas

In the field of human development, there has been considerable confusion about homosexuality, a confusion deriving from several factors. First, not everyone uses the term homosexual with the same meaning. In addition, there is disagreement about the causes of homosexuality and about what social attitudes or norms should be applied to homosexuals. Finally, there is confusion about the amount and variety of homosexuality in different cultures, since the stigma attached to it has made research difficult to pursue and the findings of questionable accuracy.

The following discussion opens with an inspection of these sources of confusion and then turns to ways in which homosexuality can relate to child rearing, education, and counseling.

1. Definitions

Definitions of homosexuality range from the broad to the narrow. One broad definition holds that homosexuality means simply a preference for companions of the same sex. In further refining this definition, distinctions can be drawn about the type of behavior the companionship involves. For example, the preference may be of the kind exhibited by preadolescent children who, in most if not all cultures, spend their time chiefly with same-sex companions and display a measure of disdain for the opposite sex. This behavior seems to occur mainly around ages 7 through 14, representing a period referred to as the homosexual stage or gang age in contrast to the heterosexual stage that follows in later adolescence when more interest is directed at the opposite sex. The term homosexual when used in this broad sense, is not necessarily intended to imply physical contact among the companions. And if physical contact does occur, such as their holding hands or wrestling, it does not necessarily extend to mutual manipulation of the primary sex organs (vagina and clitoris in the female, penis in the male), although it often does include such manipulation. This child-growth stage, when it involves essentially platonic relations, has sometimes been called normal or naive homosexuality.

While the foregoing broad-range definition is not uncommon among human development theorists and professionals, it is seldom the meaning assumed by the general public. In everyday parlance, homosexual typically means two people of the same sex engaging in "lovemaking," particularly lovemaking that involves use of the primary sex organs leading to orgasm.

The problem of definition is complicated by the fact that sometimes the physical appearance, mannerisms, or interests of an individual are interpreted by others as being "sexually inappropriate," that is, more representative of the opposite sex than of the person's own sex. For instance, a young woman may have noticeable hair on her upper lip and walk with long strides, which are traits considered in the local cultural tradition as those of masculinity. In a similar way, a young man may prefer the hobby of sewing to that of playing football and move his hands in a manner considered more typical of women's movements. So both the young woman and young man may be called homosexuals because of their ostensibly sexually inappropriate traits, whereas in actual lovemaking behavior both may be entirely heterosexual. One authority has estimated that only about 15 percent of male homosexuals can be identified as such by their appearance (Hyde 1979 p. 319).

Cross-culturally, determining who is homosexual is made difficult by the fact that the traits considered masculine and feminine can differ from one culture to another and from one era to another in the same culture. In one society the people who paint their faces and wear elaborate hair styles can be warriors and the epitome of masculinity, while in another society the most feminine of women are the ones distinguished by facial paint and fancy coiffures.

Throughout the following discussion, in order to avoid confusion, use of the term homosexuality will be limited to its more popular meaning—a relationship of lovemaking that involves use of the primary sex organs. It is this variety of homosexuality that poses the most serious problems for child rearing, education, and counseling.

2. Theories of Cause

Theories which attempt to explain the cause of homosexuality can be divided into three types: biological, sociopsychological, and interactionist.

Biological theories assume that a person's homosexual traits are the result of some characteristic of the physical organism, such as a person's ratio of male hormone (androgen) to female hormone (estrogen). A typical supposition is that the greater the proportion of androgen in a female's system, the more she will be homosexual. Likewise, the larger the proportion of estrogen in the male, the greater will be his homosexuality. Such theories may include a belief in the genetic basis for the hormonal ratios. In other words, the balance or imbalance of hormones has been caused by gene patterns inherited from parents. However, a biological theory need not presume that gene patterns are the underlying cause. Instead, a theorist can place responsibility for the hormonal ratio on physiological changes in the individual's life before or after birth, changes perhaps influenced by such things as climate, diet, illness, or injury.

In contrast to biological theories are sociopsychological ones which propose that it is not physiological factors, but rather the quality of an individual's relationships with other people during childhood and adolescence that determines whether the person becomes homosexual or heterosexual—or even asexual (not interested at all in physical lovemaking). So, from the sociopsychological perspective, homosexuality is a learned or acquired characteristic. Diverse people and events can influence a person to adopt homosexuality. For instance, according to psychoanalytic theory, a boy may become homosexual if he fails to copy the model of masculinity provided by an older male in the family. This could occur if there is no father in the home and the boy is raised solely by his mother who becomes the model he copies. A second influence can be peers, such as fellow students in a male boarding school or, in the case of a sailor, shipmates on a long sea voyage that offers no opportunities for heterosexual relationships. A third influence—though apparently less common—can be an older adult, such as a girl's governess or a boy's uncle, who introduces the child to sexual acts.

Interactionist theories draw upon both biological and sociopsychological factors in the belief that some combination of body chemistry and environmental factors accounts for the development of homosexual behavior. In one common version of interactionism, differences between people in body chemistry or genetic inheritance will make some people more prone than others to homosexual practices. But whether such practices are actually adopted depends on sociopsychological factors such as the models of behavior that parents provide; the influence of peers; standards of conduct taught by the church, school, and other social institutions; and the opportunities available, at the moment, to engage in heterosexual rather than homosexual acts. Supposedly, people who have a greater biological predisposition to homosexuality will adopt such behavior even under social conditions that strongly discourage it. At the opposite extreme, people with little or no biological inclination to homosexuality will resist homosexual behavior even under environmental circumstances which encourage it. In effect, an interactionist approach views sexual behavior in different people as the result of different combinations of causal factors. Thus, one person becomes homosexual for a different pattern of reasons than does another.

Because there is such a variety of causal theories, the key question becomes: Which theory is correct? As yet there is no clear answer, and so the issue remains a matter of much debate. Additional research is needed, but in light of currently available evidence, perhaps the safest position to adopt is that of interactionism—the belief that biological and sociopsychological factors combine to form an individual's sexual preferences, with the patterning of these factors differing from one individual to another.

3. Attitudes and Social Norms

For the individual who is homosexual, the prevailing attitudes toward homosexuality in the individual's social environment are highly important. At the core of this social-norms issue is the question of whether homosexuality should be considered a physical illness, a crime, a psychological disorder, or an acceptable alternative life-style (Bergler 1956).

The answer to the social-norms question has varied significantly from one society to another and within the same society at different periods of time. Likewise, the matter of consensus has varied as well. In some cultures the commanding majority of people have agreed on what attitude to adopt toward homosexuality, with this attitude sometimes expressed in the form of laws covering homosexual relations. However, in other societies there has been much disagreement about how homosexuals should be viewed, with the result that an open turmoil continues about what are proper norms.

In ancient Greece, both heterosexuality and homosexuality were regarded as normal behavior. In traditional Polynesian cultures of the South Pacific, male homosexuals who display obvious feminine traits are not only openly accepted members of society, but some parents even raise boys from childhood as girls to fulfill special feminine roles. In contrast, many other societies maintain negative attitudes toward homosexuality, with the degree of disapproval varying from one culture to another. For example, a comparison of the Netherlands, Denmark, and the United States showed that homosexuality was generally disapproved in each of these countries; stricter disapproval in the United States was revealed by the fact that legal statutes in most states identified homosexual behavior as a punishable crime, whereas in neither the Netherlands nor Denmark was it regarded as such (Weinberg and Williams 1974 p. 13).

The social and psychological problems which these differences in attitude cause for homosexuals seem rather obvious. Individuals can hardly live in an environment of widespread social rejection and condemnation, wearing a brand of pathological deviance, without their personalities being affected, especially if, as homosexuals, they accept society's assessment of their condition as valid. Thus, homosexuals can look forward to easier social and psychological adjustment in those societies that accept their sexual preference as a reasonable way of life.

4. The Incidence of Homosexuality

The amount of homosexuality in different societies is unknown, since, in some, the disgrace associated with its practice has caused many homosexuals to hide their condition, thus making surveys difficult to conduct and their results imprecise. However, in recent decades more refined survey techniques and a greater willingness of homosexuals in several societies to report their experiences have furnished some knowledge about the incidence of such practices.

In terms of child-development stages, during later childhood and preadolescence, sexual play with companions of the same sex is apparently rather common in many cultures, more common than such play with the opposite sex. These childhood activities typically involve no more than fondling each other's genitals. Studies in the United States suggest that these sorts of encounter increase gradually during later childhood so that by age 14 about 35 percent of girls and 50 to 60 percent of boys have engaged in the activities at some time (Broderick 1966, Martinson 1973). Such adolescent play does not seem to predict adult sexual preference, since in many cases the early experimentation is dropped and attention thereafter is directed toward the opposite sex.

Part of the problem of determining the extent of homosexuality arises from a failure to distinguish between amounts, life stages, and types of sexual behavior.

In regard to amount, some people, after experiencing one or two homosexual encounters, continue the rest of their lives as heterosexuals; at the other end of the spectrum are those who daily engage in homosexual behavior. Thus, computations of the incidence of homosexuality badly distort the picture of the amount when people from these two extremes, as well as people from all degrees in between these extremes, are placed in the single category of homosexuals.

Similarly, distortion occurs if data are not reported according to different stages of life. As noted above, homosexual encounters—particularly those which do not result in sexual orgasm—are frequent in preadolescence but decrease significantly thereafter. As a result, there are many people who have experienced such encounters in late childhood but are not homosexual as adults. Likewise, some men during their service in the army have engaged in homosexual behavior, but they abandon such practices when they return to civilian life.

Furthermore, some people are bisexual, engaging in both heterosexual and homosexual acts. To label them simply as homosexual conceals the fact of their bisexuality.

In summary, although the precise extent of homosexuality has not been determined, and confusion still exists about the most suitable way to compute its incidence, it seems apparent that homosexual behavior exists in a variety of forms in all cultures and that it significantly affects the lives of many people.

5. Implications for Child Rearing, Education, and Counseling

The implications of homosexuality for child rearing, education, and counseling depend on the values held by those who intend to take action. Thus, the implications drawn by people who consider homosexuality a disorder will differ from those drawn by people who accept homosexuality as a respectable alternative life-style.

Throughout the following discussion, two contrasting sets of illustrative applications are described, one set deriving from the view that homosexuality is an undesirable deviation and the other set from the view that homosexuality is as proper as heterosexuality. For convenience of reference, these sets are labeled the deviation and the acceptance viewpoints.

5.1 Child-rearing Practices: Deviation Viewpoint

Parents who are intent on raising their children as heterosexuals, and who subscribe to an interactionist theory of causation, can find child-rearing guidance in psychoanalytic and social-learning theories. In doing so, they will provide in the home attractive models that represent the surrounding society's notion of masculine behavior for boys and feminine behavior for girls. The term attractive here means that the father and mother models should be people that the child of the same sex will admire and wish to emulate. If the home does not contain such models, as would be true where a girl has no mother or a boy has no father available, efforts can be made to provide suitable models from other sources, such as an older friend, a teacher, or the leader of a club which the child joins.

Furthermore, parents can encourage their child to adopt interests and behavior that are regarded in their culture as proper for the child's sex. This encouragement can take the form of suggesting sexually appropriate activities and rewarding, through compliments or special privileges, the child's engaging in such activities. At the same time, the child is discouraged from adopting interests regarded as more proper for the opposite sex. On the assumption that children are increasingly influenced by peers as they grow older, parents can encourage the child to establish friendship with peers who display the desired sex characteristics and can discourage friendship with peers who display sexually inappropriate behavior.

If the foregoing techniques do not suffice in guiding a child toward a heterosexual preference, and if a physiological condition is suspected as the cause of a homosexual tendency, then parents may seek medical help, which might involve an examination of the child's hormone ratios in order to estimate whether hormonal treatment might alter an incipient homosexual preference.

In short, parents will endeavor to help the child avoid homosexuality or, if it has not been avoided, to help cure it or at least to hide it from discovery by others.

5.2 Child-rearing Practices: Acceptance Viewpoint

Parents who consider homosexuality an acceptable way of life and who subscribe to an interactionist theory of causality may be expected not to make sex-based distinctions in the kinds of activities toward which they direct their children's interests. Both boys and girls can be encouraged to play with all sorts of toys, engage in all kinds of games, and establish friendships with peers of both sexes, with the parents drawing no attention to the peers' characteristics that might be regarded as more masculine or more feminine by cultural standards.

If parents believe there is a biological component in a child's homosexuality, they will do nothing to alter the physiological condition. Nor will they propose to such children that they are psychological deviants or criminals. These kinds of parents accept their homosexual children as worthy members of the family and try to protect them from ridicule and rejection by others.

5.3 Educational Practices: Deviation Viewpoint

Educators who regard homosexuality as a disorder can be expected to adopt the same basic practices at school as those described above for parents who operate from a deviation viewpoint. Furthermore such school curriculum materials as textbooks will depict people engaged in sexually suitable activities. It is also possible, but not really necessary, that in vocational education only boys will be accepted into industrial and technical courses, while only girls will be enrolled in homemaking classes. Separate athletic activities may also be maintained for boys and girls. Such provisions may be seen as suitable devices for encouraging young people to adhere to traditional sex-role distinctions, including sex preference. Furthermore, to influence students' attitudes, units of study that focus attention on sex as a sociological or psychological phenomenon will depict homosexuality as a disorder—a condition to be cured.

In educational administration, the school becomes responsible for monitoring pupils' behavior to prevent homosexual contacts in such settings as the gymnasium locker room or the drama-club theater. Pupils apprehended in homosexual acts are punished more severely than those apprehended in heterosexual behavior. Faculty members known to be homosexuals, and particularly ones who engage in homosexual encounters with students, are dismissed from their jobs.

5.4 Educational Practices: Acceptance Viewpoint

Educators who consider homosexuality a proper alternative can be assumed to follow practices similar to those identified for parents who exhibit an acceptance viewpoint. In addition, curriculum materials may (though not necessarily) make little or no distinction between the sexes in picturing the occupational roles that people pursue. Enrollment in all types of classes and clubs will probably be equally open to both sexes. In classes where sex is studied as a topic under sociology or psychology, homosexuality will be depicted not as a deviation but rather as a suitable life-style for people so inclined, a life-style toward which certain societies have displayed an unreasonable prejudice that has caused emotional maladjustment for those members having a homosexual preference.

In school administration, the rules governing homosexual conduct by either students or staff members will be identical to the rules governing heterosexual behavior.

5.5 Counseling Practices: Deviation Viewpoint

The goal of counselors who consider homosexuality as a disorder is to aid the client in abandoning this behavior. From a psychoanalytic perspective, the treatment will traditionally consist of uncovering from the client's unconscious mind the events in his or her family relationships during childhood that produced the homosexual preference. The client is then guided towards adopting a mentally healthy view of these relationships by reliving them during therapy sessions and thereby curing the homosexuality. From a behavior-therapy approach, a cure can be attempted by furnishing the client with desirable models of heterosexual behavior and then rearranging consequences in the person's life in a way that causes heterosexual thoughts and acts to be experienced as rewarding, and homosexual acts and thoughts as nonrewarding or punishing. From an eclectic counseling approach, therapy could mean combining one of the foregoing sorts of psychological treatments with hormone injections.

From a deviation viewpoint, the degree of success of the counseling effort is determined by the extent to which the patient abandons homosexuality and feels satisfied with the result.

5.6 Counseling Practices: Acceptance Viewpoint

For counselors operating from an acceptance stance, the goal is to aid the homosexual in achieving satisfactory personal–social adjustment within whatever form of sexual preference he or she desires, whether this involves remaining homosexual, or abandoning it for heterosexuality, bisexuality, or even asexuality. Studies have shown that while some homosexuals regret their homosexuality and consider it a disorder which they wish could be cured, many others accept their condition as proper and not a problem except in the way they are treated by other people who disapprove of their life-style (Bell and Weinberg 1978 p. 128).

Since the counselor's goal is designed to suit the client's aim, the counseling techniques adopted need to be adjusted to this aim. Thus, if the client seeks help in changing from a homosexual to a heterosexual, the most reasonable approach may be behavioral therapy or reality therapy. But if the client wishes to remain homosexual, but with less social and psychological distress than in the past, then some form of humanistic therapy may be judged more appropriate.

Finally, the success of such counseling will be determined by how well the individual accepts himself or herself and his or her personal–social relations. Success is not judged on the basis of whether homosexuality is continued or abandoned.

Bibliography

Aardweg G J M van den 1986 *On the Origins and Treatment of Homosexuality: A Psychoanalytic Reinterpretation*. Praeger, New York

Bell A P, Weinberg M S 1978 *Homosexualities: A Study of Diversity Among Men and Women*. Simon and Schuster, New York

Bergler E 1956 *Homosexuality: Disease or Way of Life?* Hill and Wang, New York

Broderick C B 1966 Sexual behavior among preadolescents. *J. Soc. Issues* 22(2): 6–21

Ellis A 1965 *Homosexuality: Its Causes and Cure*. Stuart, New York

Hart J 1981 *The Theory and Practice of Homosexuality*. Routledge and Kegan Paul, London

Hyde J S 1979 *Understanding Human Sexuality*. McGraw-Hill, New York

Martinson F M 1973 *Infant and Child Sexuality: A Sociological Perspective*. Book Mark, St. Peter, Minnesota

Masters W H, Johnson V E 1979 *Homosexuality in Perspective*. Little, Brown, Boston, Massachusetts

Paul W (ed.) 1982 *Homosexuality: Social, Psychological, and Biological Issues*. Sage, Beverly Hills, California

Rosen D H 1974 *Lesbianism: A Study of Female Homosexuality*. Thomas, Springfield, Illinois

Weinberg M S, Williams C J 1974 *Male Homosexuals: Their Problems and Adaptations*. Oxford University Press, New York

Body Image and Body Language

R. M. Thomas

The concept of body image can be defined from two perspectives, one internal and the other external. From the internal viewpoint, a person's body image is the way he or she conceives of his or her own physical self. He or she can picture himself or herself as inhabiting a body that is either strong or weak, large or small, healthy or unhealthy, well-formed or misshapen, agile or clumsy, slim or fat. From the external viewpoint, the individual's body image is the way others perceive him or her: erect or slouching, handsome or ugly, lithe or stiff, large or small. The internal and external perspectives are related, in that what other people tell a person about his or her appearance typically influences his or her own image and thus affects his or her self-concept. Such influences are not merely passing impressions but may have long-term effects. For example, studies of adults' memories of their adolescence have shown that comments made by others about an adolescent's appearance strongly influenced the adolescent's feelings of adequacy, not only at the time of the comments, but for years afterwards (Berscheid et al. 1973 p. 122). Body language is a type of nonverbal communication, a mode of informing others through posture, movement, and gesture rather than speech.

Body language and body image are often closely related, since an individual's concept of his or her physical adequacy can influence his or her posture and movements, and these actions can, in turn, be interpreted by others as reflecting something about his or her personality. In some cases body language accurately reveals a person's abilities, feelings, and level of self-confidence. In other cases body language serves as a facade designed to mask the "true inner self," so that an open display of bravado may cover up feelings of inferiority, and a humble appearance may hide a sharp and confident wit.

Studies of both body image and body language yield implications for child rearing, education, and counseling, as the following observations illustrate.

1. Aspects of Body Image

This review begins with a summary of findings from research on body image, then closes with a series of applications of the findings for educational practice.

1.1 Generalizations from Studies of Body Image

A person's internal body image is a conception rather than an accurate visual perception. As Gorman (1969 p. 17) has explained, one's notion of physical self is composed not only of perceived appearance before a mirror or in photographs, but is influenced as well by hopes and fears about appearance, by what is overheard from others about oneself, and by the impressions one experiences from the senses (sight, sound, touch, posture, pain, pressure, smell, and taste). It is not just the individual's unclad body that makes up his or her body image, but clothing, hair style, posture, and facial expression contribute as well. While a person's body image can significantly affect feelings of self-worth at all periods of life beyond early childhood, body image attains its greatest importance as a symbol of self during adolescence, when puberty alters the body in remarkable ways and when the desire of youths to be accepted by their peers is especially strong. A key factor in developing an internal body image is the impression individuals have of how closely their appearance matches their image of an ideal body. Generally, the closer their body image approaches to their ideal, the more adequate they feel and the more confidently they face the world.

Ideals of appearance are not identical for all societies. The facial and body contours widely admired in one culture can differ from those admired in another. What passes for middle-aged feminine beauty in a Polynesian-island culture is considered obesity in upper-class French society. In many cultures there are social institutions and traditions which promote certain body and facial characteristics as models to be emulated. India,

Thailand, Indonesia, Tahiti, and Greece are examples of countries in which young women who perform traditional dances are models of feminine beauty that adolescent girls can view as ideals. In Westernized societies the cosmetic and diet-food industries urge women to purchase products that ostensibly equip them to achieve the idealized appearance pictured in the industries' advertising. Those societies which promote rather uncommon body and facial types as ideals (such as the ultra-thin female models in modern fashion magazines), and which place great value on physical appearance, are societies in which feelings of inadequacy can be widespread because so few people can attain the ideals.

Just as ideal body types can differ among cultures, so also can the degree to which people are satisfied with their appearance. By way of illustration, Lerner and his associates (1980 pp. 847–55), in a study of Japanese and American adolescents, concluded that the Japanese displayed lower self-esteem and less favorable opinions of their bodies' attractiveness and effectiveness than did the American adolescents.

People's conceptions of their bodies may be either vague or precise, with greater precision thought to be associated with a more positive self-concept. In one study of child-raising practices in nine cultures, where the Rorschach Test was used to measure people's body concepts, the investigators concluded that a precise, clear body image was related to parents' "permissive acceptance of impulse release in young children" (Samuels 1977 p. 90). The investigators theorized that the more a parent inhibits a child, the harder it is for the adult and child to work out a close communication style, with the result that the child achieves an indefinite body image.

1.2 Educational Implications of Body-image Knowledge

The foregoing generalizations, combined with principles from social learning theory, suggest such implications as the following for child rearing and educational practice. Parents, teachers, and counselors can:

(a) provide children with opportunities to engage in physical activities that enhance agility, muscle tone, and awareness of body appearance—such activities as dance, creative dramatics, physical exercises, and athletics (Salkin 1973);

(b) avoid making unfavorable remarks about a child's physical features which the child has no ability to change. Adults properly can comment favorably about a child's physical characteristics that are valued by the surrounding society;

(c) furnish a diet for the child that promotes physical fitness, and set an example for the child by eating such foods themselves;

(d) arrange to remedy any of a child's unattractive physical features that can be corrected or de-

emphasized by means of surgery, dentistry, diet, or grooming;

(e) dress and groom the child in a fashion that enhances his or her appearance in the eyes of admired peers and of others whose opinion he or she respects.

2. Aspects of Body Language

Only in recent years has the study of body language become a scientific pursuit, creating a discipline known as the science of kinesics, which has produced the following observations.

2.1 Generalizations from Studies of Body Language

Research has suggested that eight segments of the body are the most important for expressing body language: (a) the head and its postures; (b) the face and its expressions; (c) trunk and shoulders; (d) arm and wrist; (e) hands and fingers; (f) hip, leg, and ankle; (g) foot; and (h) neck. Movements within these segments can convey messages to an aware viewer (Birdwhistell 1963). Some movements express meaning, either intended or unintended, and are therefore termed significant. Other movements express no meaning but are simply "kinesic noise"; being thus insignificant, they fail to qualify as body language.

Most, if not all, significant body language is learned. There is some dispute among investigators about whether smiling is an innately determined expression or simply a learned reaction. But other than smiling (and possibly weeping in grief), researchers generally agree that people acquire body language from models in their environment, from either consciously or unknowingly imitating people around them (Birdwhistell 1970 pp. 29–38, Ekman et al. 1969).

Some body language is intentional, and some is not. Gesturing to emphasize a point in conversation is usually intentional. Clenching one's fists, frowning, and tightening the jaw while being criticized by a superior is usually unintentional, and a person is usually unaware of displaying such behavior. Yet the unintentional behavior still reveals the individual's internal state and therefore qualifies as body language.

Body language can differ from one culture to another. Nodding the head when passing someone on the street is a greeting in North America, whereas raising the eyebrows is a more typical greeting in the South Pacific. Confusion or offense can result when a person from one culture sees someone from another culture use a gesture or posture that carries different meanings in the two cultures. Pointing one's toe at another person is interpreted as an insult in certain Moslem societies, whereas biting one's thumb towards another is an insult in Italy, and gesturing with the raised middle finger is considered offensive in America. The meaning conveyed by body movements is dependent also on the social context in which the movements appear. Weeping upon receiving an award in a beauty contest carries a different meaning from weeping at a funeral. Hence, it is important to understand both the general culture in which the person has been raised and the specific social context in which he or she is now reacting in order to interpret what his or her body language means.

While some elements of body language are common to most people in a given culture, other bodily expressions are unique to individuals. Therefore, it is often necessary to know individuals intimately over a period of time to understand what their particular postures or expressions mean. Sometimes body language supports and complements what a person is expressing orally. On other occasions, simultaneous verbal and bodily expressions convey opposite messages. A girl shakes her head from side to side as she says, "I deeply respect my father." Or a counselor yawns as he assures the client, "I really care about the way you feel."

Finally, Fast (1970) has postulated that "The difference between maturity and immaturity is often telegraphed by body language. Too much body movement without real meaning is immature. A mature person moves when he has to, and moves purposefully."

2.2 Educational Implications of Body-language Knowledge

To foster an understanding of body language, schools' learning activities can include analyses of body language in different cultures, with the instructional media including photographs, films, creative dramatics, and demonstrations by people from those cultures. Based on the analyses, students can use role-playing sessions to practice new modes of body language which they wish to adopt, with their classmates and teacher aiding the performers by assessing how successfully they have conveyed the impression they hoped to communicate. To help newly arrived foreign students adjust to the community, a teacher can observe their body language and then inform them of the ways such gestures and postures are likely to be interpreted by the local residents.

Teachers who wish to improve their instructional style can aid each other by visiting each other's class sessions to identify body language that detracts from the instructor's effectiveness, to point out instances of conflict between a teacher's verbal and body languages, and to recognize effective body language that could profitably be increased. A mother who has difficulty communicating with her child may be aided by a teacher who explains how conflicting verbal and body messages that the mother may unconsciously exhibit might confuse and antagonize the child. Marriage counselors may provide similar explanations to married couples who seek help in understanding each other.

Bibliography

Berscheid E, Walter E, Bohrnstedt G 1973 The happy American body, a survey report. *Psychol. Today* 7: 119–31

Birdwhistell R L 1963 The kinesic level in the investigation of the emotions. In: Knapp P H (ed.) 1963 *Expression of the Emotions in Man*. International Universities Press, New York, pp. 123–39

Birdwhistell R L 1970 *Kinesics and Context: Essays on Body Motion Communication*. University of Pennsylvania, Philadelphia, Pennsylvania

Ekman P, Sorenson E R, Friesen W V 1969 Pan-cultural elements in facial displays of emotion. *Science* 164: 86–88

Fast J 1970 *Body Language*. Lippincott, Philadelphia, Pennsylvania

Gorman W 1969 *Body Image and the Image of the Brain*. Green, St. Louis, Montana

Lerner R M, Iwawaki S, Chikara T, Sorell G T 1980 Self concept, self esteem, and body attitudes among Japanese male and female adolescents. *Child Dev.* 51: 847–55

Salkin J 1973 *Body Ego Technique: An Educational and Therapeutic Approach to Body Image and Self Identity*. Thomas, Springfield, Illinois

Samuels S C 1977 *Enhancing Self-concept in Early Childhood: Theory and Practice*. Human Sciences, New York

Play, Games, and Toys

I. M. Maimbolwa-Sinyangwe and R. M. Thomas

Although everyone seems to know in general what is meant by play, scholars attempting to specify the exact characteristics of play have failed to produce a universally accepted definition. For example, Vander Zanden (1978) has proposed that play consists of voluntary activities not performed for any sake beyond themselves, voluntary activities outside the serious business of life. But by such a definition, football games which youths consider the most "serious business" of their lives should not qualify as play, nor should a child building a model airplane he or she hopes to sell or a person painting a portrait for a friend, since such projects, while both voluntary and enjoyable, are performed for a "sake beyond themselves." Yet there are people who would say all three of these activities—football, model building, and painting—do indeed qualify as play according to a different definition, that of "occupying oneself in amusement, sport, or recreation." Still other authors have sought to distinguish play from work by limiting the designation play to activities for which the participants receive no money. But such a definition eliminates from play all professional athletics or any game on which participants place wagers as they engage in their amusement, sport, and recreation.

In the following discussion, rather than dispute the above distinctions in defining play, a broad view is adopted that can encompass a wide range of events which people in general might consider playful. Play, in this sense, consists of activities participants enjoy, engage in voluntarily, and would pursue whether or not they received pay for taking part.

The term games, like play, can be defined in various ways. In a broad sense, games have been described as "ways of amusing oneself" or as "pastimes and diversions." Under such usage, games becomes synonymous with play. But more often games are considered a subcategory of play, a type that follows a set of rules, aims at a definite goal or outcome, and involves competition against other players or against barriers imposed by the nature of the game itself. Games included in the following discussion are diversions displaying the three characteristics of rules, a goal, and competition. It should be recognized, however, that by designating these particular games as ones providing diversion or recreation, one broad class of activities is being eliminated that is becoming increasingly important as an educational tool. It is the class of simulation games which people seriously pursue to solve problems or to understand the operation of some realm of life. An example of this class is a war game played by military personnel as practice in battle strategies. Another example is that of political simulations people in diplomatic service play to predict the likely outcome of international relations. In like manner, students in school may engage in games that imitate political, economic, and personal-relations problems of real life. Only when participation in such activities assumes the quality of amusement or diversion do they qualify as the sorts of games treated in the following paragraphs.

A toy, as intended here, is a plaything, a piece of equipment serving as the chief object or focus of play.

The following discussion will first consider functions that play performs in people's lives. It then describes relationships between play and human development, considers ways that different types of play promote educational goals, and the appropriateness of toys as instruments of learning. Finally, a recent development in the field is described.

1. Functions of Play

Perhaps the most obvious function of play in people's lives is that of recreation, of providing relief from responsibilities or from the strain and boredom of work. Play also helps people pass the time pleasantly while they await expected occasions.

But besides its frivolous uses, play serves diverse serious purposes, especially in the life of a growing child. At each stage of growth, play activities enable the child to try new physical, mental, and social skills and to perfect the skills by practicing them over and over. Embedded in this practice is an important element of safety for the child, since by attempting new skills in make-believe form, children can commit the novice's normal learning errors without suffering the criticism, embarrassment, and more serious consequences of making the same errors in real-life situations. Fur-

thermore, play broadens people's range of experience by enabling them, in imagined settings, to try on a great array of roles they would otherwise never understand. This role-taking function of play also enables the young to prepare for positions in life they will assume in the future and to comprehend something of the tasks performed and the viewpoints held by the older youths, parents, or job holders who now occupy those positions. Finally, Gordon (1975) has proposed that play is important for the child's developing a personal identity or knowledge of self through investigating areas of interest and trying on different roles.

Within different theories of human development, play is pictured as serving particular functions. In psychoanalytic theory Freud (1924) and Erikson (1950) have seen play as helping the child work through conflicts between inner drives (from the id) and restrictive rules (from the environment and superego), thereby developing greater capacity to cope with conflicting demands in real-life situations, a capacity known as ego strength (see *Psychoanalytic Theory of Human Development*). Play is also conceived as serving a cathartic function, enabling the child to release tension and to express fears overtly and thereby cope with them more adequately.

In addition to the aid play offers people in conducting their lives, play is a useful tool for psychologists and educators as they seek to understand the development of children and adults. For example, in infants and young children, play can serve as a nonverbal means of reflecting stages of intelligence or ability. Also, by observing children at play, adults can detect children's social attitudes, such as ethnic prejudices, and their skills of social interaction, such as their leadership qualities and their ways of resolving interpersonal conflicts. Play that involves the dramatic enactment of social relations can reveal how children perceive significant people in their lives—parents, siblings, teachers, peers—and can show how children interpret such environments as school and church and such events as a visit to the dentist or to grandmother's home.

2. Types of Play and Child Development

For several decades researchers have studied children's play in order to identify types and their relationship to stages of development.

In a well-known early study, Parten (1932) observed nursery-school children, ages 2 through 5, under free-play conditions to identify the sorts of social relationships children's activities represented. She concluded that the activities could be placed in six categories:

(a) Unoccupied, unengaging acts: the child shifts readily from one action to another with no apparent purpose—sits a moment, stands around, touches something, briefly looks at others.

(b) Onlooking behavior: the child studiously observes others play and may speak to them, but does not personally engage in play.

(c) Solitary independent play: the child plays alone with toys different from those used by nearby children, and he or she pays no attention to their activities.

(d) Parallel play: the child plays alone but next to others who are using the same kind of equipment and are playing in essentially the same way.

(e) Associative play: the child plays with other children, chatting about their common activity and borrowing and lending equipment, with everyone in the group involved in similar actions. There is no division of labor and no subordination of individual interests for the good of the group.

(f) Cooperative play: a group of children organize to pursue a defined goal, as in creating a product (a sand castle, a make-believe airplane), dramatizing a life situation (imitating adults in occupations or in family situations), or playing a formal game. The membership of the group is controlled by one or two members who assume leadership responsibilities, divide up the tasks, assign duties to the others, and give them directions. Members display obvious feelings about who belongs in the group and who does not.

While Parten proposed that the six forms of play represented a succession of stages, with children progressing from one stage to another as they advanced in age and maturity, subsequent investigators have concluded that the situation is far more complex. For instance, a child's engaging in larger amounts of solitary rather than cooperative play does not necessarily signify less maturity. Instead, it may reflect the influence of such factors as habits common in the culture in which the child has been raised, a child's individual interests that differ from the interests of others, or a mature sense of independence (Smith 1978, Rubin et al. 1976).

In addition to Parten's social relationship perspective, many investigators have studied play as a function of steps in mental development. The most prominent findings have been ones published by Piaget (1951), who traced types of play as they relate to stages of mental growth that he identified. During the sensory-motor stage, from birth to about age 2, children carry out repetitive body movements, with or without the use of such objects as toys. As they gain language skills and the accompanying symbolic ability during the preoperational stage (age 2 to around age 7), children can engage in dramatic play, imagining that an object is something that it is not (a wooden block is a car) and assuming roles (mother, father, a cat) in simple dramatic situations they invent. In the concrete operations stage (age 7 to about age 11), children can engage in formal games, in play that has established structure and goals and is governed by rules. When they advance to the final, formal operations level of cognitive development (about age 11 and beyond), children are able to engage

in play which involves complex rules, skill in predicting ultimate consequences of present actions (as in chess or card games), and a repertoire of strategies for achieving the goal under various circumstances (see *Piaget's Theory of Genetic Epistemology*).

Some researchers have confined their studies of intellectual growth to types of play that involve toys. For instance, from observing infants aged 9 to 15 months, Zelazo and Kearsley (1980) identified three levels of toy play. As the most primitive stage, stereotypical play consisted of babies fingering and banging toys and putting toys in their mouths. At the next higher level, relational play involved putting two or more toys together, but not in a manner implied by the toys' design. At the most advanced level, functional play consisted of using toys the way adults intend, such as placing small dishes on a table or babbling into a telephone. The researchers interpreted the transition to functional play as a major cognitive metamorphosis, signifying that the infants had newly acquired the ability to generate ideas.

Other investigators have studied language play as an indicator of cognitive development. An example is children's reactions to riddles. A riddle, as defined in a study by Shultz (1974), consists of a misleading question followed by an incongruous answer, with the listener's task being that of making sense out of such an answer. Shultz posed to elementary-school pupils a series of riddles, each with three possible answers, in order to discover which type of answer was most enjoyed by children of different age levels. A typical riddle was: "Why did the farmer name his hog Ink?" The three answers from which children could choose their favorite were: (a) because he kept running out of the pen, (b) because he kept getting away, and (c) because he was black. Shultz found that typical 6-year-olds thought the nonsensical second answer was the funniest, while 8-year-olds preferred the first answer, which required an appreciation of the double meanings that can be attached to running and pen. In a similar study, Yalisove (1978) found that 6-year-olds preferred riddles with answers based more on reality than on a play with words or absurdity, whereas 10-year-olds liked riddles involving the linguistic ambiguity of double meanings, and 14-year-olds enjoyed absurd riddles most.

In summary, different forms of play are popular at different stages of child development, with the succession of forms reflecting the cognitive, emotional, and social growth changes that occur with advancing maturity.

3. Varieties of Play

For purposes of education, types of play can be analyzed from the perspectives of two questions: which kinds of play are educational and, what types of learning are fostered by different kinds of play? The following review answers these questions by examining examples of play drawn from a variety of the world's cultures.

3.1 The Nature of Educational Play

Some play is educational and some is not, in that some types promote worthwhile learning, while others simply help pass the time without improving a participant's skills or knowledge. Educators wishing to determine if a particular type of play is educational can do so by identifying the degree to which success at playing depends on skill rather than luck (with luck defined as "factors outside the control of the player"). Examples of games depending entirely on luck are ones in which success is determined by rolling dice, by blindly drawing a card from a deck, by tossing a coin, or by spinning a wheel or arrow to numbers that indicate whether the player wins or what the player is to do next. Games of this type are not considered educational since they contribute nothing to the players' skills.

In contrast is play that depends on participants' mental or physical abilities, so that engaging in the activity serves as an opportunity to acquire and to refine knowledge and skill. By this definition, a great variety of play qualifies as educational: (a) physical activities—running, climbing, swimming, playing ball, wrestling; (b) table games—chess, checkers, dominoes; and (c) verbal games—20 questions (contestants are allowed to ask as many as 20 questions in their attempt to guess what object the leader has in mind), information quizzes (contestants answer questions asked by the quiz master about various fields of knowledge), tongue twisters (participants orally try to repeat verses that are difficult to say rapidly, such as, "Peter Piper picked a peck of pickled peppers"), riddles, and jokes.

Some games are only partially educational, in that their outcome depends on luck as well as on skill or knowledge. Such card games as bridge and poker are of this sort, since it is by luck that each player is dealt a particular selection of cards to begin the game, but skill thereafter influences the way a player combines and exchanges cards. In like manner, the table game of Monopoly, which simulates the buying and selling of land and buildings, depends on both luck (the throw of dice to determine how far players move their markers through the plots of land on the playing board) and skill (decisions about when to purchase property in order to maximize earnings and eliminate other players from the game).

Educational play can be either competitive or non-competitive. In noncompetitive play the purpose is neither to beat an opponent nor to beat the game itself. Rather, noncompetitive educational play has the purpose of passing the time while developing a skill or creating a product. The skill may be that of throwing a ball, jumping rope, rolling a hoop or a wheel with a stick, juggling balls, spinning a top, singing, playing a musical instrument, and the like. The product resulting from play may be a doll, a model boat or airplane, a painting, a piece of furniture, a poem or story, an item of clothing, or such.

In competitive play the object is to determine which participant performs the activity best or, in the case of a single participant, whether the player can defeat the game itself, as is the case in solitaire card games. Competitive play usually involves more rules and is more complex than noncompetitive play. Any noncompetitive activity can become competitive either by: (a) making it a contest to determine who performs it best, or (b) incorporating the play skill into a formal game, as when running, ball throwing, ball hitting, and ball catching are combined to form such games as cricket, rounders, kasti, or baseball. In Indonesia, kite flying becomes competitive by assuming a form of aerial combat when children treat their kite strings with a glassy substance that sharpens the string enough to cut down another child's kite when the strings cross each other in the sky.

3.2 Types of Learning in Types of Play

Educators who wish to use play as a means of promoting learning are usually interested in determining what specific skills and knowledge are fostered by different types of play. The following examples illustrate the diversity of learning goals promoted by various kinds of activities. Each set of examples consists of a phrase identifying a main educational outcome or kind of learning followed by illustrative play activities which contribute to that outcome.

(a) *Simple physical coordination*, including practice at spatial visualization and eye–hand or eye–foot coordination: bouncing a ball, fitting diversely shaped wooden pegs into holes of the same shapes, climbing over objects on the ground or through a jungle gym (framework of metal pipes), kicking a stone along the ground, hitting a ball with a stick.

An example of a game of simple eye–hand coordination is kuyata, an African pastime similar to the game of jacks in Europe and North America. In kuyata, the player's task is to toss a small ball in the air, then remove a pebble from a hole in the ground and catch the ball before it can fall onto the ground. After the player removes all stones in this manner, she then replaces each one in the hole by the same ball-tossing process. The game is thereupon repeated removing two pebbles at a time, then three at a time, and so on. When the game includes chanting the number of stones removed, the activity fosters the skill of counting as well.

(b) *Simple physical fitness* by increasing speed, strength, stamina, and fluidity of movement: repetitions of running, starting and stopping, stretching, twisting, jumping, climbing, pushing, pulling, lifting, swimming, tumbling. Yoga exercises from India are of this type.

(c) *Moderately complex physical coordination*: activities requiring somewhat varied movements, as in playing a musical instrument, dancing, skiing, tennis, volleyball, and such combat sports as boxing, wrestling, fencing, oriental judo, jujitsu, and karate.

(d) *Complex physical coordination*: games requiring multiple physical skills, such as football, basketball, baseball, field hockey, ice hockey, lacrosse (a North American Indian game in which teams armed with long-handled webbed sticks compete to advance a ball across a playing field). In these games, complex skills for each player are promoted only when each player performs all functions in the game and is not limited to a single specialized role, such as being limited to the role of goal keeper in football or hockey, of fielder in cricket, or of batter in baseball.

(e) *Memory*: activities requiring short-term or long-term recall of visual or auditory experiences. As an example, practice with short-term recall of a visual experience is provided by a game in which players are asked to inspect the objects in a room. Then the players are removed from the room and asked to list as many objects as they can recall. As a further example, short-term recall of an auditory experience is fostered by the game of "I'm taking a trip," in which the first person in the group mentions an object beginning with the letter A (such as an apple or airplane) that he would take on a trip. The next player mentions an object beginning with the letter B, and must also repeat the object mentioned by the first player. In such a pattern, each player adds a new object to the list according to the next letter in the alphabet, then must repeat from memory all the items mentioned by players before him. Short-term memory practice is provided as well by card games in which it profits a player to recall the names of the cards she has seen the other players draw.

Long-term memory is tested by quiz games in which knowledge from the past is required for answering the quiz master's questions. Since quiz games can be constructed for all subject matter areas taught in school, they can be used as ways to help students rehearse knowledge learned in the past and thereby enhance the efficiency of their long-term memory. In cultures that have depended primarily on oral rather than written traditions for history and literature, the pastimes of telling stories, of reciting poems and songs, and of performing dramas serve as practice in the long-term recall of auditory experiences.

(f) *Creativity*, in the sense of devising a novel variation of an activity. It is apparent that types of play differ from each other in the degree to which originality is encouraged or even allowed. Some types stress adhering closely to tradition and a strict set of rules, with excellence of performance judged by how faithfully players keep to the rules. For instance, little or no creativity is encouraged in highly structured traditional dances, in such heavily rule-governed games as baseball, in horse and dog racing, or in contests of rifle marksmanship and animal husbandry.

In contrast, novelty and freedom of expression are valued in young children's make-believe activities while "playing dolls," "playing house," and "playing soldier." The same is true of the spontaneous dramatics and charades devised by older children and adults. Verbal games played at parties also often foster creativity. An example is the game in which participants are shown an object, such as a light bulb or strangely shaped rock, and are asked to conceive of as many uses as possible for such an object. The winner of the game is the person who has suggested the greatest diversity of uses. Another example is the game in which participants are told the answer to a question without being informed of what the question was, so that the players' task is to tell what the question could have been. The winner of this contest is the player who has suggested the most unusual, yet logical, question to fit the answer. Other varieties of play well-suited for evoking creativity are the pastimes of drawing and painting, writing stories and poems, composing songs, improvising melodies on a musical instrument, making up dances, devising puns and riddles, and describing imaginary inventions.

(g) *Prediction skills*, meaning the ability to estimate the array of possible future actions in a situation and to estimate what factors determine the possibility that will most likely occur: chess, checkers, complex card games, and a host of newly created simulation games. Skill at billiards requires predictions based on estimating geometric angles and on understanding the effect top-spin or bottom-spin on the cue ball will have on where that ball will come to rest.

(h) *Deception skills*, meaning the ability to mislead other people by appearing to plan one action, while actually taking a different one. This ability is an extension of the skill of predicting events, in that it requires an estimate of what sorts of cues one might display in order to mislead the opposing players into making an incorrect prediction of one's future moves. Deception contributes to success in such diverse forms of play as hide-and-seek, magic tricks, card games, football, basketball, treasure hunts, fencing, and self-defense sports.

An example of the use of deception is the Samoan game of toginanonu, which consists of two teams of youths gathered in a palm-tree clearing on a moonlit night, when a leader throws a marked nonu (a fruit from the nonu tree) into the clearing and the youths scramble to find the nonu and race with it to a goal before being caught by opposing players. Experienced nonu players develop various strategies to deceive opponents. A player who finds the nonu may hide the fruit in his waistband, then continue to search the ground as if he had not found it. He slowly edges away from the crowd, then dashes suddenly to the goal before being caught. Or, as another ruse, a player who, unnoticed, finds the nonu will secretly signal his team mates. By prearranged plan, the team mates move to another part of the field and shout that they have found the nonu, so the opponents are attracted away from the one who found the fruit, and he can run unmolested to the goal (Thomas 1976).

(i) *Cooperation*, in the sense of fitting one's own specialized role into an overall pattern of roles that other players perform in order to achieve a group goal. Cooperation of this type involves subordinating one's own welfare to the welfare of the group. Nearly all group games of any complexity foster such learnings.

(j) *Rule-guided behavior*, meaning that the individual understands the rules governing an activity, abides by the rules, honors agreed-upon sanctions that are imposed for infractions of the rules, and follows agreed-upon processes for settling differences of opinion about rules or for changing rules. All games can promote progress toward these objectives.

(k) *Attitudes toward success and defeat*, meaning that the individual adopts socially acceptable responses to winning and to losing. Any activity in which there is a goal to achieve or an opponent to defeat provides opportunities to acquire these attitudes.

(l) *Identification and empathy*, in the sense of imagining oneself in the position of someone else. Acting in formal dramas or engaging in spontaneous dramatics contributes directly to these skills. Furthermore, any game in which a spectator can imagine how a participant feels may promote the ability to identify with others.

(m) *Diligence, self-sacrifice, and bravery*, as exhibited in any activity that requires extended periods of hard work, the renunciation of immediate pleasures, and the risk of danger, pain, and embarrassment. Any play activity in which the perfecting of difficult skills is required can contribute to the acquisition of the above traits.

Such, then, are educational goals that can be fostered through play. While the foregoing samples fall far short of exhausting the list of learnings achieved in play, they do suggest something of the diverse ways play serves educational purposes.

4. Toy Appropriateness

Earlier, toys were identified as playthings that function as the focus for play. A toy may be as simple as a stick or a ball which the infant manipulates, or may be as complex as an electronic computer the older child or adult uses for sophisticated games.

The issue of whether a toy is appropriate can be viewed from two perspectives: (a) Is the toy being used correctly, meaning, is it being used in the way its builder intended? (b) Is the toy suited to the developmental level of the person playing with it? The two questions are related, in that one reason a child may misuse a toy is because the toy is not proper for his or her stage of physical or mental growth, so that even with instruction he or she will be unable to operate the toy properly. In such cases, the problem is solved by substituting a developmentally appropriate toy for the unfitting one. Other times, however, misuse occurs not because the demands of the toy exceed the child's level of development but, rather, because the child has not been instructed correctly in how to operate it. In this case, the solution is to furnish proper instruction. Consequently, if parents and teachers are to be most effective in using toys to promote child growth and education, it is important that they recognize both how to provide developmentally appropriate toys and how to prepare children to use the toys profitably.

The decision about whether a toy is appropriate as an educational plaything can be guided by three considerations, as follows.

Firstly, will the toy teach the child a desirable skill or type of knowledge—one that the child has not already mastered? Or at least will the toy help the child maintain a high level of mastery? In seeking an answer, a parent or teacher can first estimate what skills and knowledge are taught by, or required for, the operation of the toy. If those learnings are deemed desirable, then observations of the child in daily-life activities can suggest to the parent or teacher whether the child already has mastered such learnings. If the child has not, then the toy could contribute to his or her education. Or if the child has already reached mastery, the toy might help him or her maintain that mastery. However, in some instances the estimate of the child's mastery cannot be made until the child is observed using the toy. In such an event, if the child immediately shows mastery of the skills that the toy promotes and then loses interest in playing with it further, the toy can be judged too simple and thus inappropriate for advancing his or her education.

Secondly, is the child's present level of physical and mental maturity sufficient for the child to learn readily: (a) how to operate the toy as it has been intended; and (b) how to maintain the toy in proper working condition? To predict whether a child is sufficiently mature, an adult can compare the skills required by the toy with descriptions in child-development books of the physical and mental skills that an average child can perform at various age levels. These descriptions provide a general notion of how well the toy may match the child's ability level. However, because most children deviate somewhat from the reported average, it is useful as well to have the child try the toy. If, when the operation of the toy is clearly explained, the child fails to grasp the concepts readily, displays frustration, or loses interest, then the toy is judged inappropriate, since toys are playthings intended to bring pleasure, not distress or boredom.

Even if the child is mature enough to operate a toy, that toy still may be unsuitable if the child does not learn to maintain it in acceptable working order. The child who uses a plastic doll as a hammer or who pours hot wax into the engine of an electric train is ending the toy's useful life. If such a child is not easily taught how to care for the object, then the child deserves a different type of toy that can accept such treatment without harm—a toy hammer or a mold for casting figures in wax.

Finally, can the child use the toy safely, not endangering himself or herself or others and not damaging property? To meet this goal of safety, parents sometimes need to arrange the child's play area so that the toy can be used without danger. As an obvious example, placing the child in an open field to bat a ball rather than permitting the activity inside the house is such a precaution. In other cases, safety is fostered by providing the child not only with the toy but also with protective gear, such as a helmet and knee pads for a child who is learning to use a skateboard. In still other instances, training in safety measures is required, as with the adolescent who has received a bow and arrow, a gun, a motor bike, an electric saw, or a toy chemical set.

5. Further Developments in Play Literature

One of the most recent developments in the play literature has been a growing number of studies concerned with school play, that is, the play of students at school (see Block and King 1987). This literature has helped reveal elementary, secondary, and special school students' perspectives on what makes certain school activities "play," namely, that the activities are ones which students perceive they do not have to do, but they want to do them because they are fun. Moreover, the school play literature has helped document the role of the school in shaping the form and substance of students' play as they age. Apparently, schools eventually impress on students the notion that there is little official room at all for play in school. While early on, schools seem to allow students numerous opportunities to play as part of their instruction, these opportunities for instructional play are then systematically withdrawn and students must seek other opportunities for play. Recreational play activities, especially extracurricular activities such as sports, provide some students with legitimate opportunities for play outside their instruction. However, most other students are left with only illegitimate oppor-

tunities for play despite their instruction. Illicit play activities, sometimes referred to as "goofing off," "having a laugh," and "mucking about," provide these opportunities.

Bibliography

Block J, King N 1987 *School Play: A Resource Book*. Garland, New York

Erikson E H 1950 *Childhood and Society*. Norton, New York

Freud S 1924 *A General Introduction to Psychoanalysis*. Boni and Liveright, London

Gordon I J 1975 *Human Development: A Transactional Perspective*. Harper and Row, New York

Parten M B 1932 Social participation among preschool children. *J. Abnorm. Soc. Psychol.* 27: 243–69

Piaget J 1951 *Play, Dreams, and Imitation in Childhood*. Norton, New York

Rubin K H, Maioni T L, Hornung M 1976 Free play behaviors in middle- and lower-class preschoolers: Parten and Piaget revisited. *Child Dev.* 47: 414–19

Shultz T R 1974 Development of the appreciation of riddles. *Child Dev.* 45: 100–05

Smith P K 1978 A longitudinal study of social participation in preschool children: Solitary and parallel play re-examined. *Dev. Psychol.* 14: 517–23

Thomas R M 1976 Changing patterns of Samoan games. *South Pac. Bull.* 26(2): 18–23

Vander Zanden J W 1978 *Human Development* Knopf, New York

Yalisove D 1978 The effect of riddle structure on children's comprehension of riddles. *Dev. Psychol.* 14: 173–80

Zelazo P R, Kearsley R B 1980 The emergence of functional play in infants: Evidence for a major cognitive transition. *J. Appl. Dev. Psychol.* 1: 95–117

Part 6

Social and Cultural Interactions
with Development

Part 6

Social and Cultural Interactions with Development

Introduction

In its most general sense, the term *culture* can be used to identify those patterns of thought and action that are common to a group of people. The process of *enculturation* or *socialization* is the means by which children and youth acquire the cultural patterns of their original society. In contrast, the process of *acculturation* is the means by which people adopt cultural patterns of a society that is different from their original one.

The importance of understanding how socialization operates lies in the fact that the main purpose of child-rearing and educational practices is to guide the development of the young toward the approved beliefs and behavior of a particular society's cultural tradition.

The 24 articles that comprise Part 6 are divided into three sections. The first section includes eight articles concerned with general matters of Socialization and Acculturation and with the emotional development that is associated with socialization processes. Within this section, the opening article identifies general *Cultural Influences on Human Development*, the second considers problems of *Multiculturalism* as they affect educational practice, and the third inspects factors in a child's life that influence *Socialization*. Then, issues of *Social Assimilation*, *Social Role Understanding*, *Social Competence and Individual Development*, and *Achievement-Orientation* are reviewed. The final article focuses on *Emotional Development*.

The second section consists of six articles dealing with Prosocial and Antisocial Behavior. The section opens with a review of research on *Moral Development*, followed by a description of recent work on *Prosocial Behavior*. The final four articles involve the development of socially disapproved behavior such as *Aggression and Development* and *Delinquency*, and of ways in which parents and teachers seek to control childrens' and adolescents' social behavior via *Discipline and Development* and *Punishment*.

The final section directs attention to a variety of forces that can exert important influences on the socialization of the young. The opening article analyzes the socializing role of the family. The next two articles focus specifically on mothers' and fathers' roles, followed by three entries treating the issues of *One-parent Families, Adoption and Development*, and *Foster Care Influence*. The next three articles are dedicated to topics often featured in the public press in recent years—*Child Abuse, Social Discrimination*, and the influence of television on the development of children and adolescents. The closing article, *Child Influence on Adults*, analyzes a factor in child-parent interaction that was generally neglected in studies of development until the 1970s—the factor of how childrens' behavior can affect adults, and how this influence can affect the way those adults subsequently treat the children.

Socialization and Acculturation

Cultural Influences on Human Development

J. P. Milon

Although social scientists do not all agree on the precise meaning of the term "culture," it is possible to abstract from their writings a definition that represents key elements on which many scholars would agree. When Kroeber and Kluckhohn (1952 p. 181) performed this task of abstraction by analyzing over 100 authorities' works, they produced the following definition:

> Culture consists of patterns, explicit and implicit, of and for behavior acquired and transmitted by symbols, constituting the distinctive achievements of human groups, including their embodiments in artifacts; the essential core of culture consists of traditional (i.e., historically derived and selected) ideas and especially their attached values; cultural systems may on the one hand be considered as products of action, on the other as conditioning elements of further action.

As for the term development, LaBarba (1981 p. 514) defines it as "The series of changes that occur in an organism over the course of its life as a result of growth, maturation, and learning." The definition of human development thus entails all the changes which take place in the human organism between conception and death, with the exception of one area of change, that of the direct biological consequences of genetic inheritance.

Combining the Kroeber and Kluckhohn concept of culture with LaBarba's concept of development produces a sense of the scope of the topic "cultural influences on human development." All aspects of the total environment in which a person lives—physical, social, and conceptual—are included. Birth order, clothing worn when living on an arid plain, the soccer team of which a person is a member, and the Talmud that a person reads are all examples of cultural entities which affect development. Only the genetic particulars derived from biological parents, such as blood type and skin color, would in themselves be considered noncultural influences. But even such biological characteristics can indirectly exert cultural effects by triggering different reactions to their presence in different societies. For example, people of a particular skin shade may be given preferential treatment in a society. However, skin color in itself is not a cultural influence.

It is well to recognize also that the physical environment itself is not a part of culture. Instead, it is people's response to their physical surroundings that qualifies as culture. For instance, in the Scandinavian countries, the winter's snow and ice and the few hours of daylight are not parts of culture. Rather, the cultural elements in those societies are the housing, modes of transportation, clothing, occupations, and topics for poetry and songs which Scandinavians have devised in response to such physical surroundings.

Oftentimes an adjective is attached to the word culture to identify the particular group of people who share the cultural elements. The term "Chinese culture" denotes those behaviors, values, symbol systems, and physical artifacts shared by people whose cultural roots derive from China. In other cases, an adjective identifies acquired characteristics of a subgroup of people within a broader cultural setting. This is illustrated in the terms "upper-class Austrian culture," "Spanish–American culture," and "black South African culture." In other instances the adjective denotes the particular subrealm of the broad field of culture under consideration, as in the phrases "Papua New Guinea art," the "Russian language," and "traditional Arabian occupations."

The following review treats (a) themes commonly found in studies of cultural influences on development; (b) prominent agents of cultural influence; (c) some effects of culture on physical, psychological, and social development; and (d) interactions of culture and development in school settings.

1. Themes of Studies

Two categories of themes are found in studies of cultural influences on development. The first concerns the relationship of universality to specificity. The second concerns different stages of life at which culture exerts its effect.

The universality theme occurs in research concerned with the way people resemble each other because of their shared cultural setting—the language they speak, implements they use, religion, laws, values they hold in common, and the like. Research of this nature is often cross-cultural, comparing the shared characteristics of one group of people with those of another, illustrating that cultural influence is universal but may vary in form between one setting and another.

The specificity theme is found in studies which demonstrate that cultural influence, while universal, is also unique for each individual. Any set of cultural influences will have at least a slightly different effect on each person in that environment. There are two reasons for this. First, the genetic makeup of each person is unique, except in monozygotic twins. Second, any two organisms—even twins—will begin to diverge at an early stage in their response to what is nominally an identical environment. This divergence of response, in turn, causes the environment to respond differently to each of the organisms. The amount of differentiation increases with each of these cycles of interaction.

The second set of themes in research on cultural influences treats different stages of life at which these influences occur. The greatest quantity of studies has centered on the effects of cultural settings during infancy, early childhood, and youth. Far less attention has been directed at the periods of young adulthood, middle age, and old age. However, as a higher percentage of people in virtually all societies are living longer due to advances in sanitation and medical practices, populations include more elderly people so that more attention is being directed to the latter stages of the life cycle. Certain concepts associated with adulthood have been examined rather extensively—work, courtship, marriage, and child bearing—but the stages of adult life themselves have not been studied in great detail.

2. Prominent Agents of Cultural Influence

Studies of cultural influence typically focus on particular agents in the society and how they affect development. The agents most frequently examined are the child's caretakers; who, for the young child, are usually the biological parents and other family members. Beyond the immediate family, other agents whose influence becomes more prominent as the child grows older are neighborhood companions, such mass communication media as television and newspapers, such community groups as clubs and gangs, and formal educational institutions. When the school assumes responsibility for a child's welfare, school personnel then qualify as caretakers who contribute to the learner's acculturation in ways described in the final segment of this review.

3. Cultural Effects on Physical, Psychological, and Social Development

One of the most common schemes for imposing organization onto the vast collection of facts available about acculturation involves dividing development into three categories. The first is ordinarily labeled biological, physical, sensorymotor, motor development, or some combination of these. The category includes such biological factors as birth weight, skeletal maturation, and age of the onset of the first menstrual period in girls. The second division is ordinarily labeled psychological, mental, cognitive, perceptual, or some combination of the latter two. It includes such topics as language use and color classification. The third is usually called social, cultural, ecological, or some combination of the three. It includes such topics as children's sex differences in play patterns and the effects on adolescents of their membership in groups. The following examples illustrate the nature of investigations under the three categories.

3.1 Influences on Physical Development

Among the nonhereditary or cultural factors affecting development are socioeconomic status, environmental stress (both physical and psychological), and nutrition (Munroe and Munroe 1975). For instance, favorable socioeconomic conditions are positively correlated with favorable physical growth patterns and appear more strongly associated than are ethnic status and certain physical attributes. As examples, height, weight, and rate of bone ossification have all been shown to be lower among both urban and rural poor than among more affluent members of the same ethnic categories. Landauer (1972) has shown that stress early in life (stress associated with tattooing, immediate postnatal separation from the mother, and innoculation) seems to increase adult height. In young children, head control, sitting, crawling, walking, and smiling are also psychomotor characteristics affected somewhat by nonhereditary factors. While it is clear that cultural influences do not uniquely determine conditions in these types of development, they nevertheless have some impact on the direction and rate of development.

3.2 Influences on Psychological Development

This category consists of perceptual and cognitive aspects of development which are affected by nonhereditary influences. Examples of differential perceptual development are found among the data on people's susceptibility to illusions and on their interpretation of three-dimensional stimuli. Research suggests that at least some of the differences between individuals in these matters can be attributed to differences in urban versus rural environments, degree of technological sophistication, and socioeconomic condition. People's ways of categorizing phenomena and their concepts of number and space are also culturally influenced. For example, different cultures divide up the color spectrum differently.

One of the most important aspects of psychological development affected by culture is that of language. Two questions in this realm that are still unresolved are those of how a person's language influences his perception of the world and how perception of the world affects his language. Whorf (1956) has proposed that all speakers of a given language, because they label the experiences with the external world in a similar way, likewise share a similar internal mental organization of the world. In other words, people speaking the same language tend to think more alike than do people speaking different languages. In opposition to Whorf's strong environmental position are theorists who propose that language is merely a medium which can be manipulated to describe conceptual organization and that consistent differences in perception across speakers of different languages are not the result of their different language backgrounds. That is, differences in thinking patterns are held to be reflected in, but not determined by, different languages (see *Language Acquisition and Human Development*; *Cognitive Development*).

3.3 Influences on Social Development

Social development is the least studied and least understood of the three categories. Topics falling into this class cover a wide and ill-defined range of social processes and concepts. The class treats development which results as a person progresses through the various developmental stages in a successful manner. Such success is in terms of the individual's being able to negotiate the "patterns, explicit and implicit, of and for behavior acquired and transmitted by symbols, constituting the distinctive achievements of human groups" (Kroeber and Kluckhohn 1952 p. 181). The breadth of issues in this area is very extensive, covering such a variety of phenomena as personality traits, aggressivity, altruism, dependent and assertive behavior, motivation incentives, the assumption of rights and responsibilities, sex and ethnic differences in temperament and social responsiveness, and many more (see *Social Cognition*; *Social Perception*).

4. School as a Cultural Influence

All three categories of development described above are related to schooling, with the school exerting the least direct influence on physical growth and the most direct on psychological development.

Studies of physical growth suggest that there is a correlation between people's physical characteristics and the amount and kind of schooling they receive. However, the school cannot be said to be the direct cause of differences in height and weight or in health between two cultural environments, such as urban versus rural areas or modernized industrial settings versus traditional agricultural settings. But it is true that, for a multiplicity of reasons, children who have access to schooling tend to be healthier than ones who do not. The principal overall reason is that the existence of schools usually reflects a sociopolitical system with the interest and resources to maintain a significant level of social support for the population. Families with an awareness of the values of formal education and with the resources to send their children to school are also apt to have the resources to meet the children's nutritional needs. In addition, the school supports this general

societal interest in promoting health with its own programs of health and physical education.

More important than its direct influence on physical development is the school's effect on learners' social skills. Schools tend to place great value on certain kinds of social behavior and to reward these kinds while punishing other varieties of social development. As a result, a significant part of the teacher's efforts in most schools is directed toward promoting pupils' character development and maintaining discipline in the classroom. When the standards of social conduct and the methods of fostering this conduct are the same in the home as they are in the school, the child grows up with a consistent set of forces directing him or her toward a given pattern of social habits. But sometimes the standards or methods of training in the home differ from those in school. Under these circumstances, conflicts arise between the pressures exerted on the child at home and those exerted at school, with resulting difficulties for the child in developing an acceptable pattern of social behavior. The roots of this conflict lie in the differences between the subculture represented by the home and the one represented by the school. For instance, the modes of social behavior acceptable in a lower-class home subculture may be at odds with those acceptable in a middle-class school. In other cases the conflict may arise from the difference between home and school in the religious convictions being taught. Or, as is increasingly happening with the greater movement of ethnic groups from one society to another, the conflict may be seated in the differences between the dominant indigenous population of a region and the people who have recently migrated into that area from another nation or ethnic region.

An example of a conflict between home and school social standards is the issue of assertive versus submissive behavior. In many modern Western schools, assertiveness is encouraged in students in the form of competition among peers in academic performance as well as in social behavior as found in organized sports and debating societies. However, fostering peer competition can yield disruptive consequences in a society organized around mutual nurturing among peers rather than around one child publicly trying to better another in his or her endeavors. Related to such conflicts is the press for "modernization" that has affected so many societies in recent decades. In many traditional cultures, a person's faithfully maintaining the practices of the past is more highly valued than is searching for innovations. Likewise, respecting the opinions of the elders is more highly regarded than is encouraging youths to judge the merit of an opinion on objective evaluative criteria. Modern schooling (in the sense of schools which encourage experimentation and judgments of merit founded on objectively collected evidence) characteristically brings a degree of social turmoil into any cultural group to which it is introduced. Schooling thereby affects the process of social development for members of that group. From a survey of research on modernization,

393

Werner (1979 p. 289) noted that "Education was found to be the most powerful factor in determining the degree of modernization in the attitudes, values, and behavior . . ." of the groups studied. Thus, in developing nations, conflict between the younger generation and older generation frequently arises from a clash between non-traditional beliefs the school has taught the young and the traditional beliefs held by their parents.

While the culture of the school exerts some influence on both physical and social characteristics of the learners, it is in the realm of psychological development that the school makes its greatest impact. There is little serious challenge to the contention that schooling strongly affects the learners' cognitive structures. Few traditional societies are consciously concerned with fostering cognitive abilities, that is, of consciously devising methods for forming people's thought processes. In traditional societies the formal instruction that does take place tends to be task oriented—instruction in applying a skill to a specific situation. In contrast, in industrial societies it is not unusual for a child to spend 15 percent of his or her waking time in a formal school where the learning system stresses such constructs as classification, rule seeking, problem solving, concept formation. In other words, the school emphasizes the development of powers of abstraction, that is, the ability to carry on mental processes in a relatively context-free mode. It is not surprising, then, that children who have successfully undergone such schooling are inclined to be better at mental imagery and rule making as well as at performing such tasks as pictorial depth perception and the manipulation of such concepts as diagonality.

The effect of schooling is not invariant in these areas of cognition. It is true that spatial perception, like pictorial depth perception, is usually linked to educational history, with illiterate adults not doing as well in some instances as primary-school children. However, certain cultural groups, illiterate and unschooled, do as well as or better than the schooled at certain tasks, apparently because of a unique environmental setting that encourages practice of such cognitive skills. An example is the ability of certain unschooled Eskimo groups to achieve as high scores in spatial-perception tests as do Europeans who have had up to 10 years of formal education.

Questions about the impact of schooling on development are intertwined with the questions Berry and Dasen (1974 pp. 11–12) have identified as the major themes in research on culture and cognition.

Firstly, are there *qualitative* differences in cognitive processes among different cultural groups or are the processes identical (or almost so) throughout the species, with the apparent differences attributable to the different cultural materials entering into the processes? . . . Secondly, are there *quantitative* differences in cognitive processes among cultural groups? . . . Thirdly, are the characteristics of *growth* in cognitive operations (both qualitative and quantitative) similar in all cultural groups?

In summary, the role of schools in affecting individuals' development is complex. It is extraordinarily difficult to sort out the interrelationships among such factors as economic condition, ethnicity, degree of urbanization, and schooling. The complexity is increased by the fact that schooling is not only one of a wide range of cultural influences on development, but it is also a major channel by which other cultural influences are distributed to a population. Because schools are essentially conservative in nature—passing on to new generations that culture which the political and social rulers of the present and past generations prefer—the schools are a combination of caretaker, storehouse, and communicator of cultural values. At the same time, the dominant variety of school today also encourages characteristics of modernization and in this sense is a force toward cultural change in traditional societies.

Bibliography

Berry J W, Dasen P R (eds.) 1974 *Culture and Cognition: Readings in Cross-cultural Psychology.* Methuen, London

Cole M, Scribner S 1974 *Culture and Thought: A Psychological Introduction.* Wiley, New York

Kroeber A L, Kluckhohn C 1952 *Culture: A Critical Review of Concepts and Definitions.* Peabody Museum, Harvard University, Cambridge, Massachusetts

LaBarba R C 1981 *Foundations of Developmental Psychology.* Academic Press, New York

Landauer T K 1972 *Psychology: A Brief Overview.* McGraw-Hill, New York

Langer J 1969 *Theories of Development.* Holt, Rinehart and Winston, New York

Munroe R L, Munroe R H 1975 *Cross-cultural Human Development.* Brooks/Cole, Monterey, California

Price-Williams D R 1975 *Explorations in Cross-cultural Psychology.* Chandler and Sharp, San Francisco, California

Werner E E 1979 *Cross-cultural Child Development: A View from the Planet Earth.* Brooks/Cole, Monterey, California

Whorf B 1956 *Language, Thought and Reality.* Wiley, New York

Multiculturalism

R. M. Thomas

Among the hundreds of ways scholars have defined culture, the omnibus definition offered by E. B. Taylor in 1871 remains sufficiently clear and inclusive to serve in an analysis of the relationship of multicultural-

ism to education:

Culture or civilization, taken in its wide ethnographic sense, is that complex whole which includes knowledge, belief, art, morals, law, custom, and any other capabilities and habits acquired by man as a member of society. (Singer 1968 p. 527)

Multiculturalism, then, consists of the meeting of two or more such complex wholes and their coexistence in the same society. Since the culture of a people is passed from one generation to the next through the young participating in family and community life and in attending schools, education plays a very large role in the maintenance and change of cultures. The following discussion treats the topics of (a) agents and consequences of cultural confrontation, (b) child-rearing implications of multiculturalism, (c) educational implications of multiculturalism, and (d) roles for counseling in multicultural societies.

1. Agents and Consequences of Cultural Confrontation

Over the centuries various agents have introduced cultural elements from one society into other societies. In some cases the agents have been people travelling alone or in small numbers from one society to another—traders, adventurers, tourists, explorers, missionaries, and inquisitive scholars. On their travels they encounter a few members of other societies to whom they introduce elements of their home culture, either by intent or only incidentally through their behavior and through objects they carry. In other cases, the agents represent a massive invasion of the society, as occurs in military conquest, in major missionary efforts, in widespread tourism, in large-scale importations of technical specialists, or in the influx of refugees from areas suffering political and economic disorder. Such agents not only influence the society they enter, but they may later influence their home society by bringing back cultural elements from the society they have visited, so that a cultural exchange has taken place.

Often the agents of cultural change are not people, but communications media such as books, magazines, films, and radio and television broadcasts. It is apparent that in recent decades as communication and transportation technologies have advanced at an accelerating pace, the rate of cultural exchange has quickened, increasing both the opportunities and problems that cultural confrontations involve. Both formal and informal educational institutions have played a growing role in fostering cultural exchange and in promoting the society's strategies for solving problems of multiculturalism. Schools have been heavily engaged in teaching about other cultures and in providing the settings in which political–social experiments concerned with solving cultural conflicts have been conducted. Issues of segregating pupils according to their language and ethnic backgrounds, integrating students in schools dedicated to cultural pluralism, and favoring one set of cultural elements over another in the curriculum are among the most disputed problems in modern-day education throughout the world.

In attempting to understand the relationship of education to multiculturalism, it is useful to consider the sorts of adjustment that are possible when two or more cultures meet and mingle. One type of adjustment is parallel accommodation, in which each group retains much of its original identity and advances alongside the other culture(s). For example, a nation may adopt two instructional languages in its schools, with each language respected as the mother tongue of a significant segment of the population, and with neither of the languages or ethnic groups dominating the other.

A second form of adjustment is elimination. One of the contending cultures effectively eliminates the other(s). In its most dramatic form this entails one cultural group entirely wiping out another by means of genocide in warfare or by requiring the weaker group(s) to adopt the traits of the dominant group in all segments of life. More commonly this form of adjustment entails the elimination of only some aspects of the subordinate culture in favor of some aspects of the dominant culture. For example, in Indonesia the introduction of writing paper a few centuries ago eliminated the ancient palm-leaf stationery that had traditionally been used to prepare letters and books.

A less dramatic form of adjustment is domination. One culture overshadows the other, as the two advance in a sort of uneven parallel accommodation.

A fourth type of adjustment is integration. The two cultures merge to form a single new culture, which combines the characteristics of the two. This cultural amalgam is often composed of a greater proportion of the characteristics of one culture than of the other.

Often the type of adjustment seen during a particular historical period is not a set condition that will last a long time, but rather is a transitional condition through which the society is moving on its way to some different type of adjustment. For instance, a plural society which may appear to have achieved a relatively stable parallel accommodation may actually be moving toward a condition of domination by one culture; a domination that may become so complete as to eliminate the weaker of the contenders in the intercultural struggle.

Cultural confrontations do not usually result in one culture completely eliminating the other. More commonly, certain elements of a new culture are adopted by the members of the recipient society, while other elements are not adopted, or else they remain as alternative choices or life-styles in a plural society; that is a society which maintains several forms of culture in parallel accommodation. The decision about whether a foreign cultural element will be adopted, and the degree or generality of its adoption, is influenced by such factors as: (a) the power of the introducers of the element to require the people of the society to accept the new element and to renounce the traditional ways that it is intended to replace—such as the power exerted by a dominating military force to change the language of instruction in schools; (b) how well the new element meets the people's needs, as compared with the effectiveness of traditional elements—such as the superiority of photocopying manuscripts over handcopying, or the superiority of computer data processing over hand calculating; and (c) general attitudes of the populace toward innovation and toward the maintenance of tradition—such as the greater willingness to accept new ideas in societies containing a large percentage of people with a "modernization attitude", compared with the reluctance to accept cultural imports in societies dominated by a "traditionalist attitude" (Inkeles and Smith 1974, Kahl 1968).

Both informal educational or informational media (newspapers, trade books, films, radio, television) and formal institutions (schools' curriculum content, textbooks, teachers) serve as important instruments for affecting the foregoing modes of influence. The political leaders of a nation who seek to promote the adoption of a new cultural element can require that this element be promoted in the curriculum and text materials, and they may control the presentation of the element in the mass-communication media. Schools and communication media can likewise be used to demonstrate to the populace the superiority of an innovation over traditional practices. Education has also been shown to promote modernization attitudes in contrast to traditionalist attitudes (Inkeles and Holsinger 1974).

To illustrate in more detail the implications of multiculturalism for the broad sphere of education, this article will now turn to examples of effects of multiculturalism in child-rearing practices, in schooling, and in counseling.

2. Multiculturalism and Child-rearing Practices

Three ways in which multiculturalism and child-rearing practices interact are (a) in the attitudes that parents want their children to adopt towards elements of cultures other than their own; (b) in the techniques parents use to guide or control the influence of other cultures on their children; and (c) in the reaction of parents to their children's behavior.

2.1 Choosing Which Attitudes to Influence

Whether they do it purposely or through unconscious intent, parents continually seek to influence their children's attitudes toward elements of culture. In monocultural societies which display to the young only one option of a cultural element, such as a single religion or a single language, the task of the parent in deciding what attitude to adopt toward this element is usually quite simple. In plural cultures which display various alternatives, such as several religions and two or more languages of daily discourse, the task can be complex. In recent decades the complexity has increased as improved transportation and communication have speeded the dispersion of cultures throughout the world.

Typical kinds of attitudes parents may choose to encourage in their children are those of: (a) tolerance—having children respect the characteristics of other people as being equally desirable to one's own; (b) superiority tempered with tolerance—having children consider their own cultural characteristics as superior to those of other people, yet not objecting to others maintaining their own characteristics; (c) superiority coupled with intolerance—having children consider their own characteristics as the only acceptable options, so that they feel obligated to dominate or eliminate those of others or to exert influence on others to adopt their own characteristics; (d) inferiority—having children regard the cultural elements of others as superior to their own, so the children will seek to adopt these different traits or customs.

2.2 Selecting Ways to Influence Children's Attitudes

The two main ways in which parents try to affect their children's attitudes are through (a) directly interacting with the children and (b) seeking to control children's access to other sources of influence.

The direct interaction can be either intentional or unconscious. It is intentional when parents instruct their children in what to believe and how to act, or when they deliberately reward children if they display desired attitudes and punish them if they display undesired ones. The interaction is unconscious when the parent does not intend to reflect an attitude toward another culture but inadvertently shows the attitude by his or her behavior. A mother may reflect her attitude toward dress styles by the clothes she wears and the ones she buys for her children. Sometimes parents' instructions to their children about attitudes conflict with the attitudes implied in the parents' actions. A father may preach religious tolerance to his adolescent son, yet prevent the son from keeping company with girls of religious faiths other than his own. Such "double messages" about attitudes can confuse the youth and cause him to distrust his father's advice.

The second way of seeking to influence children's attitudes is by controlling their access to experience with other cultures. This control can be composed of both positive and negative facets. A parent's positive act consists of directing the child towards a source of influence that will promote the desired attitude. This type is revealed in such remarks by parents as "At that private school she will learn to speak properly" or "this is really a fine book—it will do you a lot of good." A negative act is one intended to prevent a child from encountering sources of influence that might encourage the child to adopt attitudes which the parent considers to be undesirable. Parents' statements that qualify as negative acts include such examples as "You are not to look at that kind of television program again" or "Don't spend any more of your time at that girl's home; they aren't our kind of people" or "Living in the city will just get you into trouble; stay here with us in the village."

Much of the pressure that parents and political groups bring to bear on the school is motivated by their desire to control children's access to other cultural ideas or customs. The pressure includes efforts to control the contents of textbooks, the policies toward admitting pupils of various cultural backgrounds, and teachers' personal habits and social–political–religious convictions.

2.3 Reacting to Children's Behavior

Often parents themselves do not initiate deliberate steps to fashion the attitudes of their children towards other cultures or cultural elements, but rather an attempt at attitude formation occurs as a reaction to what they believe to be improper beliefs or behavior on the part of their children. Only when the child begins to smoke marijuana and use slang expressions learned from companions of another cultural group do the parents intentionally instruct the child and control his or her access to other cultures.

3. Multiculturalism and the Schools

Multiculturalism becomes involved in all aspects of schooling. Like parents, schools can provide access to many different options by introducing students to alternative cultures, or they can limit and direct the students' access. Like parents, schools can promote attitudes of tolerance toward other cultures or foster beliefs in the superiority of one culture over others. The methods which schools use to effect their cultural aims are their student-admission requirements; their rules for student behavior; the language of instruction they employ; their provisions for accommodating to individual differences among students; the content of textbooks; the subject matter of the curriculum (particularly the content of the social studies); their requirements for graduation; and the aptitude and achievement tests they use.

Within all plural societies, there is often competition among political groups to require the schools to favor cultural elements and attitudes of particular interest to the groups. Among the elements that have engendered widespread controversy in various nations in recent years are those of: languages of instruction in school rooms, religious beliefs, sexual behavior, political theory, economic systems, abortion, and explanations for such phenomena as the creation of the human race (see *Bilingualism*).

4. Multiculturalism and Counseling

The confrontation of cultures is a factor contributing to many peoples' personal–social adjustment problems. As a consequence, cases faced by counselors often involve multicultural overtones. The refugee who flees to a foreign nation finds it difficult to learn the language and customs of the host society and discovers that people in that society consider him or her odd and unacceptable. The second-generation children of immigrants find themselves torn between the culture which their parents brought from "the old country" and the culture of the new land in which they are growing up. Village youths who migrate to the city in search of employment and the excitement of modern metropolitan life discover that the reality of city living differs so greatly from what they expected that they cannot readily adjust to their new environment. The Hindu man and Moslem woman who fall in love are distressed by the differences in their religious convictions and by the disapproval their families express over their proposed marriage. Counselors are expected to assist such clients.

With the accelerating pace of cross-cultural exchanges in the present-day world, those people who assume the role of counselor find it increasingly necessary to become versed in cultural diversity and its effects if they are to perform their role effectively.

Bibliography

Cortes C E 1980 Global perspectives and multicultural education. *Soc. Stud. Rev.* 20(2): 55–60
Inkeles A, Holsinger D B (eds.) 1974 *Education and Individual Modernity in Developing Countries*. Brill, Leiden
Inkeles A, Smith D H 1974 *Becoming Modern: Individual Change in Six Developing Countries*. Harvard University Press, Cambridge, Massachusetts
Kahl J A 1968 *The Measurement of Modernism: A Study of Values in Brazil and Mexico*. University of Texas, Austin, Texas
Perlmutter P 1981 Ethnicity, education, and prejudice: The teaching of contempt. *Ethnicity* 8(1): 50–66
Robinson E H 1981 Multicultural education: Present scope and future directions. *Humanistic Educator* 19(4): 146–208
Singer M 1968 Culture: The concept of culture. *International Encyclopedia of the Social Sciences*, Vol. 3. Macmillan, New York

Socialization

J. M. Zimmer and S. J. Witnov

Socialization is the process whereby human beings "take on" the values, customs, and perspectives of the surrounding culture or subcultures. Recent thinking has characterized socialization as an interactive communication system between the individual and the society. With this conceptualization, it becomes evident that cultural influences and individual patterns of development need to be considered simultaneously. Research in cognitive development has indicated that growing children will experience and interpret the world around them differently at different ages. Thus, any definition of socialization needs to include the individuals' patterns of development as well as the patterns and values which society or social groups transmit. Furthermore, one should note that cultural influences are not static but should be viewed within an evolving context.

Investigations and theories of socialization have included variables representing individual variations, agents, methods of transmission, and patterns and values which are the effects of socialization. The variables of individual variation would include: age, sibling order, geography, sex, development, maturation, personality, intelligence, race, and ethnicity. The variables categorized under agents would include: culture, nations, family, formal organization, technology (television, computers), literature, and leaders. The variables grouped under methods of transmission would include: language, mechanisms of control, social class, rituals, law, identification, discipline, psychosocial dynamics, and child-rearing practices. Lastly, the variables of patterns and values would include: sex role, aggression, morality, achievement, altruism, attachment, work ethics, and political persuasions.

The above list is not exhaustive; it merely demonstrates the diversity of variables which are investigated. Additionally, the extent of variations can be further appreciated when the variables are considered as interactive.

This article will explore three agents of socialization: culture, family, and organizations. The categories of sex role, aggression, morality, and achievement will be used to organize and present selected findings. During the course of discussion, specific references will be made to methods of transmission and individual variation. The purpose of this exploration is to alert the reader to the diversity and complex nature of the variables that are associated with socialization research and theory.

1. Culture

Kessen (1982) has stated that the child is essentially and eternally a "cultural invention." In this context, children are thought to be shaped by the larger cultural forces of political maneuverings, practical economics, and implicit ideological commitments. In addition to the cultural forces that shape children, the ways in which children are thought about—by psychologists, sociologists, and anthropologists—can also be viewed as cultural inventions.

Investigators exploring socialization have been most interested in both the variations and commonalities among cultures. The most consistent finding in cross-cultural studies of socialization is that child-rearing practices are diverse. LeVine (1970), in a review of cross-cultural studies, stated that "although cultural diversity is worldwide, there appears to be a number of especially sharp discontinuities in the treatment of infants and young children between cultures, particularly those of northern European origin and non-Western cultures, especially those of agriculturalists." Some cross-cultural variations include, but are not

limited to, punishment, toilet training, weaning, and tolerance for aggression.

Factors such as family composition and hierarchies also seem to vary. For example, while families in certain cultures are matriarchal, other cultures exhibit family patterns which are patriarchal. Some cultures evidence extended kinships while others may have limited kinships. Other cultures, such as that of the United States, have such mobility that it is common for a single family unit to exist in geographical isolation from "blood" relatives. With regard to punishment, some families consider it the responsibility of aunts or uncles, whereas in others it is the responsibility of the mother and/or father. Other types of cultural variations include socializing institutions and agencies which reflect a complex network of cultural patterns. Such cultural patterns are influenced by economic, religious, and political systems. In turn, variations in socialization practices and variations in socialization agents are thought to be related to the behavior and values that are sanctioned and desired by the culture. This discussion will examine a few of the cultural influences which socialization research considers.

1.1 Sex Role

Perhaps nowhere are the complexities of cultural influences more obvious than in expectations concerning sex roles. Lambert et al. (1979) report that there are no universal trends but rather regional patterns of child-rearing orientations. What they mean is that North American parents differ from West European parents, who differ in turn from Mediterranean parents. Regional patterns "override and cut across clusters of nations linked by language and ethnicity, such as 'French' people in France, Belgium, and Canada." In terms of sex-role expectations, researchers report an important interaction between national background and social-class standing.

Maccoby and Jacklin (1978), in an extensive volume on sex differences, present the possibility that the first and strongest attachment figure for both sexes is probably the mother. If this is the case, then the function of differentiation of sex roles becomes more critical as children age. Maccoby and Jacklin (1978 p. 280) describe a study by Minturn and Hitchcock of the Rajput in India, where:

women are confined to a courtyard. Children also spend most of their time in the courtyard when they are very young, while they are still dependent upon the care-taking of their mothers and other female relatives, but as soon as they are old enough to escape from the courtyard, they can go to the fields with their fathers . . . . Although girls can leave . . . they have less freedom of movement and are less likely to go to the men's platform. . . . both sexes of children initially have primarily female models available, but . . . with increasing age each sex is exposed more and more to same-sex models.

This is in contrast to other cultures where both sexes

are primarily under the care of female adults. British and American preschools are an apt example.

Cook-Gumperz (1973), building on the work of Bernstein, argues that there are "sub-cultural constraints upon familial processes of communication and control." Cook-Gumperz presents evidence to support the notion that there is a differentiation in communication and control according to the sex of the child and between social class. In essence, the child's gender, social class, and cultural values interact and manifest themselves in variations of child rearing, prohibitions, and expectations in reference to sex-role socialization. In addition, Rogoff et al. (1976) clearly point out that age is also an important variable determining the assignment of roles and responsibilities for boys and girls. For example, the Dusans of Borneo assume adult roles during the seventh and eighth years of life, with girls working with their mothers and boys with their fathers. Clearly, Western cultures are not as precise in identification of the age at which boys and girls assume their respective male and female roles.

1.2 Aggression

One universal observation seems to be that children in all cultures exhibit some form of aggressive behavior. Also, each society deals with aggression in reference to its own values and socialization practices. Mead (1935) stresses the malleability of human nature which allows children to respond "accurately and contrastingly to contrasting cultural conditions." Thus, while aggression is observed in all cultures, the norms concerning aggression and the orientation towards others varies from culture to culture and from society to society. Mussen and Eisenberg (1977 pp. 2–3), in describing the work by anthropologist Colin Turnbull, clearly show the malleability of people and the variations in cultural norms that affect the "expression" of aggression. They describe the Ik mountain people of Uganda and the Hopi in Arizona. The Ik, a:

> small tribe of hunters, once had an established social structure, with laws, morals, and customs until political and technological changes deprived them of their hunting grounds. Then their social organization disintegrated and they broke into small ruthless bands concerned only with personal survival . . . . No one seemed to have any compassion for anyone else . . . . Caring for others, generosity, kindness simply did not seem to exist for this group.

With the Hopi, community cooperation is regarded as essential for survival:

> From the earliest childhood onward, nothing is more important to the Hopi than having a "Hopi good heart" defined as trust and respect for others; concern for everyone's rights, welfare, and feelings; inner peacefulness and avoidance of conflict.

Aggression has also been examined from other perspectives. In an attempt to define human aggression in terms of biological instinct, generalizations have been made from studies of ethology and animal aggression.

The evidence for the biological determination for aggression (or for its converse: altruism) is not convincing. Nongenetic explanations, especially those that describe the manner in which functioning societies survive, provide equally plausible explanations for altruism as well as aggression.

1.3 Morality

Gregory Bateson (1944) has attempted to explain the relationship between culture and the development of different forms of mental and behavioral "aberrations," including those concerned with morality. He explored why each succeeding generation acts in harmony or disharmony with the dominant cultural patterns of interpersonal relations. He concluded that mother–child interaction was instrumental in establishing how children came to perceive and act upon contradictory cultural themes. Others have stressed that morality is transmitted through the culture and is relative to that particular culture. Social relativity assumes that a consensus is possible concerning the moral value of a particular culture or nation taken as a whole. Skinner (1971 p. 28) succinctly describes the position of social relativity in relation to moral development when he states, "Each culture has its own set of goods, and what is good in one culture may not be good in another." Within such an "operant" context, investigators explore the transmission of the "good" or "moral" in reference to controlling contingencies (see *Basic Concepts of Behaviorism*).

Extending Piaget's (1965) work on moral development, Kohlberg (1976) postulated that moral behaviors and understandings are not just a case of culturally given rules. Instead, the internalization of moral standards comes about by transforming perceptions and inputs from the social world. These transformations are thought to be related to cognitive growth. From Kohlberg's point of view, ethics and morality are constructed internally, and can on occasion override cultural norms and values. The defiance of persons against "regressive" values of a culture are illustrative of reflective moral formulations.

2. Family

The family has been viewed as having primary responsibility for the care and raising of children. Though there might be tremendous diversity in what constitutes a family, the actions of family members and the environment which a family creates are believed to exert a powerful influence on children. Because of its crucial place as the first setting for interaction between the child and its culture, investigators have looked closely at structure, social-class standing, and kinship relations.

Even within a culture, one finds tremendous variation. In the United States, Sears et al. (1957) did an extensive study of 379 mothers. At the outset of their book, *Patterns of Child Rearing*, they state that "the commonest phrase in the book is 'the mothers varied widely'" (p. 467). Differences in care patterns have been found among mothers in the same community, mothers of the same age, mothers of similar social position, mothers of the same religion, and mothers of similar ethnicity. The status of the family due to geography, income, and occupation creates differences. Separation and divorce, as well as the health of family members, are other contributing factors.

In viewing the family as a primary agent for socialization, a number of factors will be discussed in the categories of sex role, aggression, morality and achievement.

2.1 Sex Role

Sex roles concern the appropriate and distinct actions of boys and girls or males and females: performing tasks, securing employment, manifesting mannerisms and attitudes that are considered by society to be "appropriate" for one sex rather than the other. While the issues concerning sex roles might be in a transition within certain groups, the distinction of sex roles in most cultures has been maintained in a rather stable fashion. The family has been identified as having a major influence in socializing children and adolescents toward what is thought of as "proper" sex roles.

Research of sex differences can be seen as pursuing two paths. One path concerns the differences which have genetic antecedents, while the second path explores differences that grow out of socializing influences. Obviously, there is going to be some interaction between these two positions which obscures analyses. However, assuming these positions has resulted in important research which has isolated specific differences. For example, at young ages, certain types of cognitive abilities seem to develop earlier in females than in males (such as certain spatial reasoning skills). With regard to the family role in socialization, mothers and fathers seem to engage in specific types of parental action which are dependent upon the sex of their children. Certain actions are reserved for boys, while others are for girls. Typically, boys are allowed greater independence of action.

2.2 Aggression

Feshbach (1970 p. 214) has stated that "the socialization practices directly relating to aggressive responses of children represent only part of the influence upon the child's aggressive behavior. Many family interactions occur, which, although not directly connected with specific training of aggression, may have a profound effect upon the development of aggression. While the larger culture is concerned with the regulation and modification of aggression, the relationship between family variables and aggression has been the subject of extensive study. Feshbach (1970) goes on to identify specific influences upon aggression:

(a) generalized parental attitudes and behaviors: permissiveness restrictions, emotional stability/instability;

(b) socialization of specific behavior systems: weaning, toilet training, independence training;

(c) permissiveness and reinforcement of aggression;

(d) punishment of aggression;

(e) aggressive versus nonaggressive parental models.

Depending upon such factors as sex, these influences are thought to vary within individuals. For example, "Kagan and Moss suggest that early and later restrictiveness have different effects upon the development of aggression in boys" (Feshbach 1970 p. 220). Other variables considered by Feshbach are social class and age. Additionally, cognitive skills, such as fantasy, are thought to affect the influence of parents and the aggression a child might be exposed to.

2.3 Morality

Moral beliefs and actions are considered to reflect the consensus of a social group in reference to what is considered correct. Studies of moral development explore transgressions from the group consensus of what is "right" and "wrong." Also within this context, the resolution of conflict has been examined. Conflicts are thought to occur because of two distinct reasons. First, they occur as a result of the discrepancy among an individual's needs, cognitive competency, or the moral demands of the moment. And secondly, moral conflicts arise as children discover values which might be incompatible with values held by groups they belong to. The first type of conflict can be exemplified by an adolescent's sex drive coexisting with a family prohibition against sexual behavior. The second kind of conflict is evident in the situation where group morality might require people to support one another, even if it involves lying, while a particular group member may simultaneously reside in a family where lying is not considered an ethical practice. This juxtaposition creates a moral conflict.

Regardless of the theoretical framework of moral development (Kohlberg 1976) the family is considered a critical reference point with respect to how moral conflicts are resolved. Important aspects in socialization of moral attitudes and behaviors would include: (a) the child's identification with its parents; (b) parental attitudes and actions in reference to control (e.g., autonomous versus heteronomous or democratic versus authoritarian); and, (c) the nature of punishment.

It is further thought that social class is related to moral development as it refers to the rate of acquisition (Kohlberg 1976). It is also important to recognize that among families, moral obligation and imperatives vary not only along dimensions of social class, but also due to religious, political, and occupational characteristics of family members.

2.4 Achievement

Education has been viewed as a process by which culture (as knowledge) is transmitted. In fact, a great deal has been written on this topic. Though the causal connections seem reasonable from a global perspective, the actual way in which family patterns foster academic achievement is not clear. While research has established many relationships between child and parent activities and certain skills a child must acquire, very few of these relationships represent a definitive understanding of the underlying dynamics. For example, families place various emphasis on children doing things "well" and on children doing things by themselves. It is assumed that families who use motivational procedures that stress excellence should produce children with high achievement motivation. It is also assumed that child-rearing practices whch stress independence should produce children who are self-reliant. Though some studies support these relationships, often methodological problems cloud the results and the amount of influence by families accounted for is disappointingly small. This area of research is in need of more precise measures and longitudinal studies.

There also appears to be a relationship between social-class variables of families and the achievement and self-reliance of their children. Research indicates that not only are there differences between social classes, but also that middle-class fathers might have a positive impact on their children's school achievement. Jencks and his co-workers (1979) conclude: "We began this chapter by asking how much effect family background has on economic success . . . . We concluded that family background as a whole explained 48 percent of the variance in occupational status . . . and 55 to 85 percent of their earnings advantage to family background." They go on to state:

other unmeasured background characteristics that vary among families with similar demographic profiles seem to account for significant amounts of variance in occupational status and earnings . . . (unmeasured characteristics) seem to be "advantageous" for one purpose (e.g., earnings) but not for others (e.g., test performance). These family characteristics could be genetic. Alternatively they could involve subtle differences in the habits and values that parents inculcate in their children. Or they could involve local differences in intellectual or economic opportunity. Or brothers could influence each other on some outcome, but not others. (Jencks et al. 1979 pp. 81–82)

Though research might lack a clear explanation of the specific mechanisms of socialization, there are a number of relationships which appear tenable: (a) families do affect how children are socialized toward achievement and work; and (b) the relationship between families and the socialization of children is interactive with demographic variables (such as geography and social class), and more subjective variables (such as child-rearing practices and parental expectations).

3. Organizations

Organizations can act as settings which socialize children in competencies that are considered necessary for present and future roles in the wider cultural domain. Sieber and Gordon (1981) have described socializing organizations as ranging from "total institution," such as prisons and military and boarding schools, to organizations that are less total in their regulations, which include schools, institutions established for various therapies, summer camps, and such organizations as the YMCA (Young Men's Christian Association) and Scouting groups. Naturally, the duration and intensity of a child's involvement with a given organization will vary and thus the impact of the experience will vary accordingly. Goffman (1961) discusses the way institutions with long duration and high intensity have pervasive socializing influences. Schools, meanwhile, are thought to have less influence. This is because schools, though their durations are long, often prove to provide interrupted impact that is generally of low intensity. Nevertheless, both kinds of settings contribute to the socialization of children in terms of culturally relevant values, norms, expectations, and competencies. Therapeutic settings can also be viewed as having a socializing influence. Such settings are characterized as being of short duration and high intensity.

Researchers have explored a wide range of factors that are transmitted, at least partly, through formal organizations. These factors include behaviors and attitudes appropriate to class, sex, ethnicity, and race. Additionally, one must consider values of the culture, such as individualism or collectivism, competitiveness or cooperativeness, autonomy or heteronomy, and orientation toward work, politics, and religion.

3.1 Sex Role

One function of organizations such as schools, scouts, and camps is socialization into sex roles. As Denzin (1977 p. 118) stated, "Girls must be taught how to be girls and boys must learn what a boy is". Socialization towards differential sex roles is thought to occur because of various mechanisms. For example, organizations attempt to provide same-sex models, with the assumption that same-sex models will be imitated more than opposite-sex models. This assumption has clearly been supported in practices in which boy groups most often have male adult leaders and girl groups female adult leaders.

In Kohlberg's (1976) view, sex-role identification does not occur until after the establishment of "gender constancy." He believes this to be dependent upon cognitive development typical of a 5- or 6-year-old. It is at that age that the preference for same-sex peers and models (provided by organizations) becomes important in sex-role differentiations. It is also necessary to consider that sex roles vary among cultures and that organizations such as schools reflect cultural expectations for appropriate sex-role behavior.

Additionally, the influences which role "models" may exert are quite complex. Besides the issues discussed, it is important to consider the curriculum activities which might define a school setting, since, after all, social models must act within the social context. Adult models will make differential use of reinforcements and punishments; and thus, even though two adult or peer models may be members of the same organization, the possibility exists that they will communicate and portray different messages with respect to the socialization of sex roles.

3.2 Aggression

In considering school responsibilities and aggression, the work in Sweden of Olweus (1978) is most instructive. After conducting research in both Solna and Stockholm, he concludes that personality factors rather than situational factors explain "whipping boy/bully problems." The basic problem is thought to exist at an early age but is often not recognized until a child begins school. So, while the school is not viewed as a causal agent, it is considered an important socializing agent which has the power to make the "bully" less aggressive and the "whipping boy" less vulnerable. Bronfenbrenner (1970) supports the view that it is important to ameliorate the tension between these two factors: by fostering an atmosphere of friendliness and cooperation.

Within a classroom setting, a number of mechanisms are considered instrumental to a child's socialization. The discipline or management techniques implemented by a teacher are perhaps the most influential. Though the wide use of such methods helps establish and maintain "orderly" pupil behavior, there is also a strong socializing effect.

Control and compliance are at issue in school discipline, and a concern for discipline is an often-taken precedent for teaching and learning. This is especially evident in the classrooms of many lower-class and minority-group children.

Generally, it is thought that various organizations might be instrumental in ameliorating aggression. From the classic studies of White and Lippit (1960), in which they studied clubs which were subject to three different types of leadership (democratic, authoritarian, and laissez-faire), the researchers concluded that authoritarian atmospheres were instrumental in eliciting more aggression as well as passivity. In another study of children's groups (Sherif et al. 1961) it was suggested that when frustration and competition are shared within a group in order to overcome something, there tends to be a sense of cooperation rather than the displacement of aggression. Other research has contrasted the traditional classroom, which fosters competition, to small-group learning where cooperation can prove beneficial.

3.3 Morality

Nelson (1980 p. 259) has stated that:

Schools, of course, are not the only agents of socialization. A variety of formal and informal institutions influence the values, attitudes, and behaviors of youth with regard to citizenship and morality. Certainly the family educates in both realms; religious institutions, mass media and peer groups also exemplify prominent agents of political and moral socialization. Schools are, however, the most consistently organized, experienced and controlled of the socialization agents.

Durkheim (1956) expressed the view that one role of the school is to regulate the "moral climate of the nation." In the Soviet Union, schools are used to "indoctrinate students into the ways of the communist state, and to ensure full recruitment for essential occupations" (White 1977). The kibbutzim in Israel are also illustrative of socialization through a clearly defined organization. Within certain cultures such as those of the Soviet Union, Israel, and People's Republic of China, the relationships between formal education and socialization of moral values are highly defined. In other cultures, such as in the United Kingdom, Canada, and the United States, the government does not exercise direct control over schools. It is thought, however, that socialization influences in such school systems do, in a broad sense, shape moral thought and behavior.

In countries where church-related schools are set up, the basic claim is made that "schooling in morals is a basic condition for the existence of schools," and those who establish such schools consider instruction in religious beliefs to be the basis of moral thought and behavior (Nelson 1980). Kohlberg's theory of moral development and the use of his theory have been seen as a means of "inducing citizens to move up the stage ladder." In this context, Kohlberg has concluded that "schools would be radically different places if they took seriously the teaching of the good" (Schwartz 1980).

Both psychology and sociology explore the internalization of moral thought and behavior. Psychologists have primarily addressed the issues of development and maturation, whereas sociologists have often ignored the aspects of the individual and focused on the mechanisms by which organizations and agencies transmit social order and moral rules. More recently, an attempt has been made to recognize that socialization (especially of moral rules and obligations) needs to integrate both perspectives and recognize the interaction between the individual and the organization.

3.4 Achievement

Jencks et al. (1972), in the much cited work *Inequality: A Reassessment of the Effect of Family and Schooling in America*, says that he doubts whether schools are capable of socializing children for either success or failure. He concludes "that the major influences on socialization towards success or failure are competence and luck." In a later work (Jencks et al. 1979) he has generally supported the view of his earlier work in reference to schooling and achievement. However, this later work has accorded greater influence to the part family background plays in influencing test scores and education. It appears that family background can influence children to be "achievement oriented." And, while education does not explain much of the variations in social status or earnings, the interaction between family background and higher education does play a role. Bernstein (1972) has made the same point by stressing that social class is the most formative influence upon the procedures of socialization. He has further stated that "the class system has deeply marked the distribution of knowledge within the society." This differential access has led to variations of "knowledge, possibility, and invidious insulation." It is thought that organizations and communities are "sealed" off from each other, and that "differences in knowledge, differences in the sense of the possible combined with invidious insulation" affects the forms of control and innovation in the socializing procedures of the different social classes. Furthermore, it follows that schools, as a form of control, reflect knowledge, engender possibilities for achievement, and define the mobility of students based on the class structure of the culture.

Theoretically, through assigning marks, promotions, and approval for doing well, the child is thought to begin to value achievement and success. However, many factors mitigate against this simplistic formula for success, such factors as social class, family background, and sex, to name a few.

4. Summary

As indicated at the outset, the purpose of this discussion has been to convey the immense complexity related to the topic of socialization. As has been described, the process of socialization is a system of influences that results from the very fabric of our cultures: our families, institutions, language, and interactions with others. It should be pointed out that the research which has been presented does not necessarily represent a cross section of all such research. The area of socialization research and theory is vast. New knowledge is being acquired on many fronts, and the work of traditional disciplines (such as sociology, psychology, and anthropology) is further supplemented by researchers in hybrid areas such as those of social psychologists, psychobiologists, psycholinguists, and sociolinguists.

Bibliography

Bandura A 1977 *Social Learning Theory*. Prentice-Hall, Englewood Cliffs, New Jersey

Bateson G 1944 Cultural determinants of personality. In: Hunt J M (ed.) 1944 *Personality and the Behavior Disorders: A Handbook Based on Experimental and Clinical Research*. Ronald, New York, pp. 714–35

Bernstein B B 1972 Social class, language and socialization. In: Giglioli P P (ed.) 1972 *Language and Social Context*. Penguin, Harmondsworth, pp. 157–68

Bourdieu P, Passeron J C 1970 *La Reproduction*. Edition de Minuit, Paris

Bronfenbrenner U 1970 *Two Worlds of Childhood: US and USSR*. Russell Sage, New York

Bronfenbrenner U, Mahoney M A (eds.) 1975 *Influences on Human Development*, 2nd edn. Dryden, Hensdale, Illinois, pp. 438–50

Cohen G 1981 Culture and educational achievement. *Harvard Educ. Rev.* 51: 270–85

Cook-Gumperz J 1973 *Social Control and Socialization: A Study of Class Difference in the Language of Maternal Control*. Routledge and Kegan Paul, London

Denzin N K 1977 *Studies in the Development of Language, Social Behavior, and Identity*. Jossey-Bass, San Francisco, California

Durkheim E 1956 *Education and Sociology*. Free Press, Glencoe, Illinois

Feshbach S 1970 Aggression. In: Mussen P H (ed.) 1970 *Carmichael's Manual of Child Psychology*, 3rd edn., Vol. 2. Wiley, New York, pp. 159–259

Goffman E 1961 *Encounters: Two Studies in the Sociology of Interaction*. Bobbs-Merrill, Indianapolis, Indiana

Goslin D A (ed.) 1969 *Handbook of Socialization Theory and Research*. Rand McNally, Chicago, Illinois

Hess R D 1970 Social class and ethnic influences upon socialization. In: Mussen P H (ed.) 1970 *Carmichael's Manual of Child Psychology*, 3rd edn., Vol. 2. Wiley, New York, pp. 457–558

Hurrelmann K, Ulich D (eds.) 1980 *Handbuch der Sozialisationsforschung*. Beltz, Weinheim

Jencks C, Smith M, Acland H, Bane M J, Cohen D, Gintis H, Heyns B, Michelson S 1972 *Inequality: A Reassessment of the Effect of Family and Schooling in America*. Basic Books, New York

Jencks C, Bartlett S 1979 *Who Gets Ahead: The Determinants of Economic Success in America*. Basic Books, New York

Kessen W 1982 The American child and other cultural inventions. In: Gardner J K (ed.) 1982 *Readings in Developmental Psychology*. Little, Brown, Boston, Massachusetts, pp. 13–20

Kohlberg L 1976 Moral stages and moralization: The cognitive developmental approach. In: LicKona T (ed.) 1976 *Moral Development and Behavior: Theory, Research and Social Issues*. Holt, Rinehart and Winston, New York, pp. 31–53

Krappmann L, Oevermann U, Kreppner K 1976 Was kommt nach der schichtspezifischen Sozialisationsforschung? In: Lepsius M R (ed.) 1976 *Zwischenbilanz der Sociologie*. Verhandlungen des 17. dutschen Soziologentages, Stuttgart

Lambert W E, Hamers J F, Frasure-Smith N 1979 *Childrearing Values: A Cross-national Study*. Praeger, New York

LeVine R 1970 Cross-cultural study in child psychology. In: Mussen P H (ed.) 1970 *Carmichael's Manual of Child Psychology*, 3rd edn., Vol. 2. Wiley, New York, pp. 559–614

Maccoby E E, Jacklin C N 1978 *The Psychology of Sex Differences*. Stanford University Press, Stanford, California

Mead M 1935 *Sex and Temperament in Three Primitive Societies*. Morrow, New York

Mischel W 1970 Sex typing and socialization. In: Mussen P H (ed.) 1970 *Carmichael's Manual of Child Psychology*, 3rd edn., Vol. 1. Wiley, New York, pp. 3–72

Mussen P, Eisenberg N 1977 *Roots of Caring, Sharing and Helping*. Freeman, San Francisco, California

Nelson J L 1980 The uncomfortable relationship between a moral education and citizenship instructions. In: Wilson R W, Schochet G J (eds.) 1980 *Moral Development and Politics*. Praeger, New York, pp. 256–85

Olweus D 1978 *Aggression in the Schools: Bullies and Whipping Boys*. Hemisphere, London

Piaget J 1965 *The Moral Judgement of the Child*. Free Press, New York

Rogoff B, Sellers S M, Pirrotta S, Fox N, White S H 1976 Age of assignment of roles and responsibilities. In: Skolnick A (ed.) 1976 *Rethinking Childhood: Perspectives on Development and Society*. Little, Brown, Boston, Massachusetts, pp. 249–68

Schwartz E 1980 Traditional values, moral education and social change. In: Wilson R W, Schochet G J (eds.) 1980 *Moral Development and Politics*. Praeger, New York, pp. 221–36

Sears R R, Maccoby E E, Levin H 1957 *Patterns of Child Rearing*. Row and Peterson, Evanston, Illinois

Sherif M, Harvey O J, White J, Hood W L, Sherif C 1961 *Intergroup Conflict and Cooperation: The Robbers Cove Experiment*. University of Oklahoma Book Exchange, Norman, Pennsylvania

Shweder R A, Turiel E, Much N C 1981 The moral intuitions of the child. In: Flavell J H, Ross L (eds.) 1981 *Social Cognitive Development: Frontiers and Possible Futures*. Cambridge University Press, London, pp. 288–305

Sieber R T 1981 Socializations implications of school discipline, or how first graders are taught to listen. In: Sieber R T, Gordon A J (eds.) 1981 pp. 18–43

Sieber R T, Gordon A J (eds.) 1981 *Children and Their Organizations: Investigations in American Culture*. Hall, Boston, Massachusetts

Skinner B F 1971 *Beyond Freedom and Dignity*. Knopf, New York

White G 1977 *Socialization*. Longman, London

White R K, Lippit R 1960 *Autocracy and Democracy: An Experimental Inquiry*. Harper, New York

Social Assimilation

R. H. Billigmeier

The terms acculturation and assimilation have been used by scholars in examining the ways outsiders become members of a dominant culture. Some scholars conceive of these terms as essentially synonymous. Others see them as referring to processes that overlap but are still distinguishable.

Acculturation is typically considered to be the acquiring of an understanding of those aspects of culture particularly significant to the dominant ethnic element in the society. Such aspects include language, religion, values, *Weltanschauung*, patterns of institutional behavior, and other aspects of life. Acculturation may occur without the shift to a new ethnic identity. Indeed, members of an ethnic group may alter their culture in substantial measure yet long retain their sense of separate identity. This kind of transformation involves a series of cumulative adjustments by members of minority ethnic groups to the dominant community and, secondarily, to other minorities in the society.

Assimilation is often defined as the final stage of acculturation. As groups assimilate, their members increasingly participate in institutional relationships, voluntary organizations, and informal social networks outside of their minority community and within the larger society. Assimilation includes acquisition of a new sense of ethnic-group membership and personal identity with concomitant subordination of old ethnic ties.

The following article centers mainly on problems of immigrant groups becoming assimilated into a dominant society. The review treats (a) some key aspects of assimilation, (b) degrees of assimilation, (c) social distance, (d) acculturation and internal factionalism, and (e) movement toward assimilation. Connections between the education system of a society and problems of assimilation are identified within each of the five sections.

1. Key Aspects of Assimilation

An essential aspect of assimilation is the dominant ethnic group's accepting the immigrant population as part of its own ethnic community. That acceptance signifies that whatever cultural or physical marks or sense of origin remain among members of the assimilating population, these no longer warrant their exclusion from the social "we" of the prevailing population. The remaining social, cultural, and physical characteristics are now regarded as being within the range of variability acceptable to the dominant ethnic group. The culture of the dominant group is thereby enlarged. While this is occurring, new ethnic groups, or new cohorts that have the same origin as that of groups already assimilated, generally proceed through the same kinds of transformation at various tempos.

The direction of the cultural adaptations resulting from interethnic contact represents a balance of contending influences. The ultimate direction of acculturation depends heavily on the relative prestige of the contending cultures in that particular social environment as well as on the political and economic power one group may exercise over another. One way that groups with greater power help maintain their power into the future is by furnishing favored educational opportunities for their children so as to provide the skills, social connections, and prestige that such education offers. Likewise, education is used by members of the immigrant population to acquire skills and social characteristics that enable them to compete successfully in the dominant society for power and privilege.

The absorption of large minorities by dominant ethnic groups involves a measure of reciprocal influence, though not always perceived, through which the majority may themselves be significantly affected in their cultural characteristics as groups merge with them.

2. Degrees of Assimilation

Over the centuries, migrations of people into established societies have been an important part of human experience. Some social scientists have concluded that the most common result of this meeting of peoples has been that the less dominant group comes to conform almost completely to the culture of the dominant society. This process has sometimes been pictured as progressing from initial contact to competition and conflict, then to accommodation, and finally to assimilation. In effect, there has been a widespread impression that acculturation and assimilation are a more-or-less inevitable consequence of interethnic contact, with the process for the most part being completed within several generations.

However, in some societies, historical minorities have existed in regional concentrations for many centuries without their absorption into major cultural communities surrounding them. Armenians, Basques, Welsh, Catalans, Bretons, Romansh, Sorbs, and many others have survived through centuries of contact as distinguishable cultural minorities. The structure of their communities, their institutions, and their social networks have evolved over many generations. How they will fare in the future in retaining their identity in a world of rapid communication and transportation and highly mobile populations is an issue of interest to social scientists. The matter is also of concern to educational planners, for it influences the questions about centralization versus decentralization of school administration, about teacher training, and about the language of instruction and the kinds of curriculum materials needed by the schools.

3. Social Distance

The efforts of people within the ethnic communities to maintain the stability of their culture serve to reinforce the system of stratification into which they have been incorporated. In the early stages of their accommodation to the new social environment, they usually lack the skills and power to challenge the social-class system, so they tend to turn inward into their narrowly confined community life. Their social cohesiveness contributes to the stability of the stratified system and continues to leave them outside of the dominant culture. The social distance between such minorities and the dominant ethnic element is maintained by a variety of conventions limiting the extent and intimacy of interaction between members of the two groups as well as by the minority's preferences for associations largely within their own ethnic community. Social distance is furthered by whatever limits are imposed on their full access to education, occupational training and job mobility, and housing. Parents within both the dominant and minority ethnic groups contribute to maintaining this social distance when they enroll their children in schools that generally exclude children of varied ethnic origins.

4. Acculturation and Internal Factionalism

Not all people of an ethnic group acculturate at the same rate. Great differences often exist in the access various segments of an ethnic group have to those experiences which quicken assimilation. Often such differences provoke intensive strife within the group. The more traditionalist segments perceive those who are acculturating rapidly as traitors, or at least as lacking in wisdom by "thoughtlessly throwing away" previous heritage, values, and symbols of identity. On the other hand, those in the vanguard of acculturation often see the traditionalists as holding the group back from progress advantageous to all members of the group. Their opponents appear to personify outsiders' stereotypes of the group. Most minority members are likely to find themselves somewhere between those two extreme groups, but ultimately moving toward acculturation. A growing number, then, find that old definitions no longer seem valid, traditional standards lose their consensus, old necessities appear less urgent, and old symbols fail in their ability to bind the group together.

Children of immigrants are often raised in an environment representing a mixture of their parental culture and that of the world about them. They frequently acquire an understanding of the values of the social world beyond their ethnic community more readily than their parents. But children confined to large ethnic concentrations are largely sealed off in schools and elsewhere from the kind of informal contact with children of the dominant culture, the sort of contact through which an "intuitive" understanding of perspectives of the surrounding society is most readily acquired.

Where generational differences in experience are not greatly different, members of both generations largely share the same perspectives and the same kinds of contact with the society around them. When this is true, intergenerational conflicts are likely to be minimal. But when acculturation is occurring more rapidly among the younger generation, there are often substantial contrasts in perspectives and values which lead to persistent conflicts. Under these circumstances, communication between the generations is difficult. The parents remain strongly attached to family traditions. It is often difficult for the parental generation to accept with equanimity the abandonment of cherished traditions. For the youths these traditions may seem meaningless, even ludicrous, and parental attachments to tradition may be interpreted as embarrassing indications of their backwardness.

Such intergenerational conflicts frequently affect the school. The frustration youths bring from home can be expressed in conflicts with such authority figures as teachers and headteachers. Or the young may be ashamed of their parents and thus try to keep school personnel from contacting their home at a time when such contact might help teachers and parents understand each other better.

Many features of such intergenerational stress appear with remarkable regularity in widely different social settings. As children reach adolescence, issues arise regarding their obligations to parents and to the extended family and community, their dating and courtship practices, the meaning of work, and their choice of friends and use of leisure time. Conflicts over spending money on items valued in youth subcultures, as opposed to family-oriented use of money, are often sharp. Youths frequently fail to understand the symbolic importance that traditional parents are likely to attach to such events. What makes such conflicts painful to everyone concerned is that, despite the bitterness and apparent irreconcilability of the differences, a deep sense of love and obligation on the part of both parents and children generally persists. Breaches of the relationship cause guilt and shame. As a result, the minority student's attention may be distracted from school work by worry, a condition sometimes rendered less painful by a teacher or counselor who understands the frustrations suffered by the student who is caught in such a marginal cultural status.

5. Movement Toward Assimilation

As acculturation becomes extensive, minority members are increasingly able to acquire those skills which enable them to compete successfully for desirable positions in the economy. Both the formal and informal educational opportunities available to the minority members significantly influence how well they acquire such skills. Often the sharpest dissent between members of the dominant culture and the minority members arises not when the barriers of the stratified system are strongly defined, but, rather, when the barriers are weakening and considerable progress has already been achieved by the minority. Remaining limitations on their opportunities seem inappropriate to the minority in the light of their new competitive strengths and their rising aspirations. At the same time, the dominant group now finds the barriers harder to justify and enforce. As certain members of the minority group make progress, social-class-level differences within the minority population arise, and the advancing classes come increasingly to share interests with people of similar class levels in the dominant community and in other minorities. As social contacts for the advancing members widen beyond their own group, the assimilation of these advancing members is advanced. The public education system is particularly important in this process, since it can put children of minority groups in daily contact with those from the dominant culture and from other minorities, thereby providing social models and direct experiences with the dominant culture in terms of language, values, and topics of interest. In various nations, the government has sought to promote assimilation by requiring that the enrollment in a school represent a mixture of children

from the dominant and minority social groups. At the informal education level, mass communication media, such as television and radio, likewise provide opportunities for immigrants to observe cultural traits of the dominant culture.

However, frequency of contact across ethnic lines, even when it endures over an extended period of time, does not necessarily reduce the social distance between the dominant and minority groups. If relationships remain highly impersonal, with little first-hand contact between the groups, a person's knowledge of individuals in the other group remains partial. However, reduction cannot readily be achieved if the context of association is tension laden. Indeed, ethnic divisions may well deepen through more extensive contact if such contact serves to reinforce stereotypical ideas of the other group or if the contact is viewed only in terms of opportunities for competition and direct antagonism between the groups. Thus, physically integrating ethnic or religious groups in school does not ensure progress toward assimilation. The quality of the students' relationship with groups other than their own strongly determines the attitudes resulting from the contact. Movement toward assimilation occurs in circumstances where personal reserve is relaxed, where individuals may be seen in terms of their unique individual qualities rather than in categorical terms. Under such circumstances personal ties emerge which lead to fruitful cultural interchange and assimilation.

Bibliography

Abramson H J 1980 Assimilation and pluralism. In: Orlov O, Handlin O (eds.) 1980 *Harvard Encyclopedia of American Ethnic Groups.* Harvard University Press, Cambridge, Massachusetts

Bash H H 1979 *Sociology, Race and Ethnicity: A Critique of American Ideological Intrusions upon Sociological Theory.* Gordon and Breach, New York

Castles S, Kosack G 1973 *Immigrant Workers and Class Structure in Western Europe.* Oxford University Press, London

Esman M (ed.) 1972 *Ethnic Conflict in the Western World.* Cornell University Press, London, p. 72

Gordon M 1978 *Human Nature, Class, and Ethnicity.* Oxford University Press, New York

Greeley A M 1974 *Ethnicity in the United States: A Preliminary Reconnaissance.* Wiley, London

Kluckhohn F R, Strodtbeck F L 1961 *Variations in Value Orientations.* Row Peterson, Evanston, Illinois

Newman W M 1973 *American Pluralism: A Study of Contemporary Minority Groups and Social Theory.* Harper and Row, London, p. 182

Park R E 1958 Human nature as elemental communication. In: Thompson E T, Hughes E C (eds.) 1958 *Race: Individual and Collective Behavior.* Free Press, Glencoe, Illinois, pp. 462–64

Peterson C L, Scheff T 1965 Theory, method and findings: The study of acculturation: A review. *Int. Rev. Comm. Dev.* 13–14: 155–71

Shibutani T, Kwan K 1965 *Ethnic Stratification: A Comparative Approach.* Macmillan, London

Thomas W I, Znaniecki F 1927 *The Polish Peasant in Europe and America.* Knopf, New York

Social Role Understanding

M. W. Watson

According to role theory (Sarbin and Allen 1968), a social role is determined by the expectations from a complementary role. For example, a husband role is defined in terms of a wife role so that one cannot be in the category of husband without having a wife. Role theories have proposed that we construct concepts of social roles to help us predict what another person will do and what the other person will expect of us in return. Because we all occupy several roles, we must also learn to deal with these role intersections and the sometimes conflicting expectations of various complementary roles. For example, a person can be both a husband and physician, and though the demands of these two roles may sometimes conflict with each other, most people are able to function in both roles simultaneously.

What happens to children who may not understand the complementary nature of roles, let alone that roles can intersect? Will they understand that a father does not cease being a father and behaving in a certain way toward his children when he also occupies the role of physician and behaves in a different way toward patients? The purpose of this review is to summarize the research findings that provide us with a picture of the developmental trends in children's understanding of social roles. There have been three major tracks of research regarding children's role concept development, which are briefly reviewed below.

1. Acquisition of Kin Terms

In perhaps the first study of the acquisition of kin terms, Piaget (1928) assessed how children defined various family roles. In a similar study, Chambers and Tavuchis (1976) simplified the tasks and found children performing better at younger ages than Piaget had found. Nevertheless, both studies suggest the same sequence of development. In the early preschool years, children defined family kin terms as absolutes (e.g., a brother is simply a little boy); in the later preschool years, they included a one-way relation in their definitions (e.g., the oldest boy is a brother but does not have a brother himself); and at slightly older ages, they defined family roles in terms of reciprocal relations (e.g., a boy can both be a brother and have a brother).

Other studies assessed family role understanding in terms of related tasks and skills. For example, Haviland and Clark (1974) showed that an understanding of kin terms depends in part on the semantic complexity of the terms. Greenfield and Childs (1977) found that in a Mexican Mayan culture children understood how kinship roles are reciprocal before they expressed understanding of reciprocity in other domains.

2. Development of Conservation

Other researchers, interested in how the notion of conservation underlies social concepts, discovered similar trends in role concept development to those reported above. Sigel et al. (1967) found that preschoolers did not believe that a person would stay in one role when another role was added (i.e., the first role would not be conserved when it was changed by adding new roles). For example, if a father became a doctor, young children would say that he was no longer a father. In another study, Jordan (1980) found that several types of transformations of roles (i.e., changes over time, in relationships, and in gender) made role conservation difficult for preschoolers. However, these studies also showed that children began conserving roles (understanding that a person can occupy several roles simultaneously) sometime between 5 and 7 years of age.

3. Role-appropriate Speech

Role understanding is reflected to some extent in the way children talk when pretending to be in various roles. Anderson (1977) found that by age 4 most children could differentiate between roles and change their speech accordingly. Snow et al. (1986) provided an excellent review of the research on children's development of role-appropriate speech and then tested the effects of role exposure on children's discrimination and use of the appropriate speech register for a given role. Children who were hospitalized did indeed increase their playing of hospital-related roles; however, the exposure did little to help them change their speech to a more nurturant style, as is used by parents and medical personnel when talking to children in hospitals.

Together, the studies cited above indicate that children are indeed attuned to learning about social roles and the complexities associated with them. Children seem to progress from understanding roles as absolutes to understanding roles in terms of role relationships to an eventual understanding of multiple role intersections. Nevertheless, different components of this understanding, such as complexity of kin terms and appropriate speech register, may take longer to develop.

4. Sequence of Steps in Role Understanding

Based on the general sequence noted above, Watson (1984) and colleagues predicted a specific developmental sequence of steps in which children would construct social role concepts by adding new levels of understanding to those already obtained, at the same time reorganizing their previous level of understanding.

As a precursor to any understanding regarding roles, children must develop the recognition that agents, who are sources of action, can act independently of the child's own actions. At that point, children begin to attend to the way certain persons can be categorized together based on looks and behaviors. This first step of role understanding is called a behavioral role. For example, a child may see that some people are called fathers when they share the following behaviors: they are men who drive to work, read the newspaper, work in the yard, and play with their children.

The second step, called a social-role relation, involves children combining two or more behavioral roles such that each role is primarily determined by complementary expectations and relations, not simply by looks and behaviors. For example, the child now sees a father role as defined by the father having children and being expected to take care of the children, regardless of the variations in looks and behaviors of fathers. In other words, one cannot have a father without children because these two roles have been combined.

The third step, called a role intersection, involves children combining two or more social roles such that a person can simultaneously occupy more than one role in relation to complementary roles. For example, children can understand that a person can be a father to his children at the same time that he is a physician to his patients or at the same time that he is a grandfather to his grandchildren.

The fourth step, called a role network, involves children combining at least two role intersections to form an entire network of related roles. For example, children can think about the combination of family roles— father, mother, children, grandfather, grandmother, grandchildren—that form what most of us think of as a traditional family. In another case, children can see the relation between the roles of physician, patient, nurse, and so forth to form a medical network.

The fifth step, called a network relation, involves children combining various role networks to understand role relations on a level of abstraction at which all forms of families and occupations can be related. For example, children can understand the similarities and differences between a two-parent family, a single-parent family, and any other kind of family.

In summary, children were predicted to develop through these five major steps that began with a role understanding based on concrete behaviors and ended with an understanding that roles were socially determined, simultaneous, relative, and reciprocal.

In a series of studies, Watson (1984) tested the validity of this sequence, which also included several transition steps between the steps outlined above. A total of 258 children, ranging in age from 1 to 13 years, were assessed for their level of understanding in two domains: understanding medical roles and understanding family roles. In some studies children were coded as to the level of role understanding that they demonstrated in their elicited and spontaneous role playing. In other studies

children were asked questions regarding a doll family to elicit definitions of roles.

Not only was there a strong relation between the age of the children and the highest step of understanding that each demonstrated, but most children showed the steps in the exact order that was predicted. In other words, no higher step was shown by a child unless the child had already shown all previous steps. Children, for example, did not show an understanding of role intersections unless they also showed an understanding of behavioral roles and social role relations. This was true even when children had different configurations in their own families. Thus, this sequence seems to describe the orderly development of children's role concepts. Generally, 3-year-olds demonstrated an understanding of behavioral roles; 4-year-olds demonstrated an understanding of social role relations; 6- to 7-year-olds demonstrated an understanding of role intersections; 9-year-olds demonstrated an understanding of role networks; and by 13 years of age many children demonstrated an understanding of network relations.

5. Significance for Child Rearing and Educational Practice

Just as with adults, children's understanding of role relations can have an impact on their adjustment to changes in the roles they occupy and their ability to control the outcome of social interactions. The following two examples should be illustrative.

Mehan (1976) argued that elementary-school children who were rated as good students by their teachers were those who had gained competence in discriminating the expectations in a teacher–student role relation from the expectations in a student–student role relation. Experimenters surreptitiously observed the children in class and found that the "good" students demonstrated just as much "bad" behavior as did their less competent classmates, but they had learned how to keep it out of the sight of the teacher and how to meet the teacher's expectations. The findings suggest that an important component in children's prediction and control of social interactions is being able to conceptualize roles in terms of how one role (e.g., teacher) affects the behavior of a complementary role (e.g., student).

In studies of the effects of divorce on children (e.g., Hetherington 1979), probably more important than the influence of the child's age by itself is the child's level of role understanding, which might determine in part how a child will interpret the divorce. For example, a child who cannot understand how roles intersect and how a person can be both a husband and a father, may see the dissolution of the spousal relation as being the dissolution of the parent–child relation as well. In addition, when the two role relations are not fully differentiated, the child may think that he or she in some way caused the break in the spousal relation.

When educators take account of children's level of

role understanding and the typical course of development that is expected for children, they will have another tool in understanding and influencing children's social competence.

Bibliography

Anderson E S 1977 Young children's knowledge of role-related speech differences: A mommy is not a daddy is not a baby. *Pap. Rep. Child Lang. Dev.* 13: 83–90

Chambers J C Jr, Tavuchis N 1976 Kids and kin: Children's understanding of American kin terms. *J. Child Lang.* 3: 63–80

Greenfield P M, Childs C P 1977 Understanding sibling concepts: A developmental study of kin terms in Zinacantan. In: Dasen P R (ed.) 1977 *Cross-Cultural Contributions Piagetian Psychology.* Gardner, New York, pp. 335–58

Haviland S E, Clark E V 1974 "This man's father is my father's son": A study of the acquisition of English kin terms. *J. Child Lang.* 1: 23–47

Hetherington E M 1979 Divorce: A child's perspective. *Am. Psychol.* 34: 851–58

Jordan V B 1980 Conserving kinship concepts: A developmental study in social cognition. *Child Dev.* 51: 146–55

Mehan H 1976 Students' interactional competence in the classroom. *Q. Newsletter Inst. Comp. Hum. Dev.* 1: 7–10

Piaget J 1928 *Judgment and Reasoning in the Child.* Kegan Paul, London

Sarbin T R, Allen V L 1968 Role theory. In: Lindzey G, Aronson E (eds.) 1968 *The Handbook of Social Psychology,* 2nd edn. Vol. 1. Addison-Wesley, Reading, Massachusetts, pp. 488–567

Sigel I E, Saltz E, Roskind W 1967 Variables determining concept conservation in children. *J. Exp. Psychol.* 74: 471–75

Snow C E, Shonkoff F, Lee K, Levin H 1986 Learning to play doctor: Effects of sex, age, and experience in hospital. *Discourse Processes* 9: 461–74

Watson M W 1984 Development of social role understanding. *Dev. Rev.* 4: 192–213

Social Competence and Individual Development

K. A. Park and E. Waters

Asked for a brief definition of psychological health, Freud suggested that the psychologically healthy individual is one who loves well and works well. Whitehorn (cited in Garmezy 1973) elaborated on this view to define the socially competent individual as one who loves well, works well, plays well, and expects well. Other definitions of social competence have emphasized the organism's ability to interact effectively with the environment (White 1959) or to generate and utilize a set of problem-solving strategies (Goldfried and D'Zurilla 1969).

Another important component of social competence is reduced vulnerability to stress and environmental disadvantage. As Garmezy (1973) notes, research on children from the most disrupted and disturbing backgrounds invariably turns up a few who overcome their circumstances and achieve far beyond what could have been expected of them. According to Garmezy, competence develops slowly, as an individual acquires different skills, and over time these skills build on one another. This does not imply that less competent individuals cannot acquire new skills or overcome disadvantage. But it does mean that increasing levels of competence gradually inoculate a child or adult against negative influences and support development toward even higher levels of adjustment and achievement.

A number of social and behavioral scientists have gone beyond general definitions of social competence in order to catalog specific skills that competence rests on and that might be important for therapeutic interventions. Anderson and Messick (1974) identified 29 areas of social competence, including the development of a self-concept, self-efficacy, sensitivity and understanding in relationships, positive behavior toward others, and flexible thinking. In addition, they suggested that viewing competence as a general characteristic of a person is misleading, because individuals may function effectively in one area yet not function effectively in another. Rather, an individual is more or less competent with respect to a given situation.

The tendency in the 1980s has been for social competence to be linked to children's cognitive abilities. For example, children's knowledge of social problem-solving skills and strategies has been considered one index of a child's social competence. A child must detect and accurately interpret others' social cues before producing a competent response (Dodge et al. 1986). Inappropriate or incorrect inferences will lead children to perform inappropriate behavior (Dodge 1980).

1. Competence as a Developmental Construct

It is much easier to define social competence as it refers to a particular age group than it is to understand the concept as it applies across the lifespan. For example, the cognitive/social problem-solving model of competence by Dodge et al. (1986) does not explicitly indicate how it might be applied to children of different ages, or how problem-solving skills at one age lead to competence at later ages. Indeed, as Gottman (1986) points out, such theories do not explicitly distinguish between children of different ages, except to imply that skill increases with age. This is an important oversight because in order to assess competence or to intervene and increase it, one must recognize that the tasks children and adults face are different at different ages, and that competence therefore involves a changing array of skills.

Waters and Sroufe (1983) presented an explicitly developmental view of competence: "The competent individual is one who is able to make use of resources within the environment and within himself to achieve a good developmental outcome" (p. 81). By "good developmental outcome" they meant the ability to succeed at the tasks posed by a particular age. They further qualified this by noting that coping with problems at one age should not be considered competence if today's solutions simply delay or complicate problems that will have to be met tomorrow.

One of the key tasks of infancy is to establish a working and trusting relationship with a primary caretaker (usually the mother). A key challenge during the preschool years is to establish quite a different kind of relationship with peers. During the school year issues related to self-esteem and independence are faced. Then during adolescence and adulthood, issues related to intimacy, achievement, and family responsibility loom large. A developmental perspective indicates how these issues are related to one another and how mastering each one lays the foundation for mastering the next. Thus a developmental view of competence goes beyond a theory of mere skills to include a theory of the contexts in which they will have to be applied across age.

This perspective has two implications. First, it helps people recognize that the same behavior may reflect competence at one age and incompetence at another. For example, clinging to mother when a stranger approaches points to an underlying competence in using the mother as a secure base in infancy. But the same behavior in later childhood is more likely to reflect failures in the attachment, peer group, and self domains. Second, a developmental perspective helps explain the otherwise puzzling fact that competence in one domain at one age is often predictive of competent functioning in a different behavioral domain at a different age. For example, security of attachment to mother is related to social competence with peers (Lieberman 1977, Jacobson and Wille 1986, Pastor 1981, Waters et al. 1979).

A developmental view also highlights the relationship between specific skills and the competence construct. The competence construct refers to the organism's ability to meet the current developmental task. Thus, a competent preschooler is one who can effectively interact with peers. Specific skills are needed for the organism to behave competently. The competent preschooler may need leadership skills to achieve peer acceptance (Hartup 1983). Labeling a child as socially competent implies that the child has the relevant specific skills.

2. Competence from a Dyadic Perspective

Traditionally, the term competence describes the behavior of an individual child. More recently, however, there has been the recognition that social competence can only be defined with reference to a child's interactions with a particular partner. Often what makes the social behavior of an individual more or less competent is how that behavior fits into the overall situation or interaction. As stated by Furman (1984 p. 19): "Social competencies are usually conceptualized as characteristics of the individual, and yet what is usually observed—patterns of social interaction—are characteristics of the dyad or relationship. This difference in the level of conceptualization seriously complicates the assessment of social competency."

This problem is illustrated in a study (Pastor 1981) comparing the interactions of toddler dyads in which the children in the dyads received different attachment classifications (c.f. Ainsworth et al. 1978). In some dyads, a secure child was paired with a resistant child: in other dyads, a secure child was paired with an avoidant child. Children in secure–resistant dyads rarely demonstrated aggression. By contrast, both secure and avoidant children, when paired together, showed increased rates of aggression. Thus, resistant children, who on an individual measure had been labeled incompetent, were more competent in pairs than the competent, secure children who were matched with less competent children. To the extent that individuals serve as contexts for one another's behavior (Hinde 1979), it may be necessary to define competence with respect to a particular relationship.

Bibliography

Ainsworth M D S, Blehar M, Waters E, Wall S 1978 *Patterns of Attachment.* Lawrence Erlbaum, Hillsdale, New Jersey

Anderson S, Messick S 1974 Social competency in young children. *Dev. Psychol.* 10: 282–93

Dodge K A 1980 Social cognition and children's aggressive behavior. *Child Dev.* 51: 162–70

Dodge K A, Pettit G S, McClaskey C L, Brown M M 1986 Social competence in young children. *Monogr. Soc. Res. Child Dev.* 51(2, Serial No. 213)

Furman W 1984 Issues in the assessment of social skills of normal and handicapped children. In: Field T, Roopnarine J L, Segal M (eds.) 1984 *Friendships in Normal and Handicapped Children.* Ablex, Norwood, New Jersey

Garmezy N 1973 Competence and adaptation in adult schizophrenic patients and children at risk. In: Dean S R (ed.) 1973 *Schizophrenia: The First Ten Dean Award Lectures.* M.S.S. Information, New York, pp. 168–204

Goldfried M R, D'Zurilla T J 1969 A behavior-analytic model for assessing competence. In: Spielberger C D (ed.) 1969 *Current Topics in Clinical and Community Psychology.* Vol. 1. Academic Press, New York, pp. 151–96

Gottman J M 1986 Commentary. *Monogr. Soc. Res. Child Dev.* 51(2, Serial No. 213)

Hartup W W 1983 Peer relations. In: Hetherington E M (ed.) 1983 *Handbook of Child Psychology,* Vol. 4, *Socialization, Personality, and Social Development,* 4th edn. Wiley, New York, pp. 103–96

Hinde R A 1979 *Towards Understanding Relationships.* Academic Press, New York

Jacobson J L, Wille D E 1986 The influence of attachment pattern on developmental changes in peer interaction from the toddler to the preschool period. *Child Dev.* 57: 338–47

Lieberman A F 1977 Preschoolers' competence with a peer:

Relations with attachment and peer experience. *Child Dev.* 48: 1277–87

Pastor D L 1981 The quality of mother–infant attachment and its relationship to toddlers' initial sociability with peers. *Dev. Psychol.* 17: 326–35

Sroufe L A, Waters E 1977 Attachment as an organizational construct. *Child Dev.* 48: 1184–99

Waters E, Sroufe L A 1983 Social competence as a developmental construct. *Dev. Rev.* 3: 79–97

Waters E, Wippman J, Srouf L A 1979 Attachment, positive, affect, and competence in the peer group: Two studies in construct validation. *Child Dev.* 50: 821–29

White R W 1959 Motivation reconsidered: The concept of competence. *Psychol Rev.* 66: 297–333

Achievement–Orientation

B. G. Klonsky

In the literature, the term *achievement orientation* has been used to refer to achievement motivation and achievement behavior. Even though different investigators have employed varying definitions of these terms, a common emphasis appears to exist among these definitions. Most theorists would agree that the kinds of situations which typically evoke achievement motivation and in which achievement behaviors occur, are those in which competence of performance is emphasized. Achievement-oriented behavior may occur then in any human endeavor that involves a level of competence. Achievement situations typically contain cues pertaining to some standard of excellence which will indicate degrees of competence or incompetence. There are two major types of competence-related goals. These are (a) learning goals, in which individuals try to increase their competence, to understand or master something new and (b) performance goals, in which individuals try to earn favorable judgments of their competence in performing a particular task (Dweck 1986, Dweck and Elliott 1983).

The background literature on achievement orientation is quite extensive. The establishment of achievement orientation as a viable research area with much to offer to educators, clinicians, and parents came primarily from the work of Murray et al. (1938), and McClelland and his colleagues (McClelland et al. 1953) on the need for achievement and achievement motive.

The following review will explore achievement orientation within a developmental framework. The major theoretical views on achievement orientation will first be presented. The developmental sequence for achievement orientation, and the impact of familial, educational, and demographic influences on the development of achievement orientation will then be described. Finally, the significance of the theory and research on development of achievement orientation for educational practice, and needed contributions from future research on such development will be highlighted.

1. Theoretical Perspectives on Achievement Orientation

Each of the three major theories to be described offers its own unique contribution to our understanding of achievement orientation.

1.1 Need for Achievement Theory

Stimulated by Murray's work on the need theory of personality, McClelland and his colleagues (1953) developed a theory of achievement motivation which focused on the role of an underlying achievement motive (need for achievement) in determining achievement behavior. McClelland and his colleagues viewed the need for achievement as a conscious attitude and orientation that could be learned. More specifically, the central constructs in the theory were the motive to achieve success and the motive to avoid failure. Those who have a stronger motive to achieve success tend to take on challenging but feasible tasks (i.e., ones of moderate difficulty). In contrast, those with a stronger motive to avoid failure will avoid such tasks (Atkinson 1964). Need for achievement theory stimulated much research focusing on individual differences in achievement orientation, and the role of parental practices in such development.

1.2 Social Learning Theory

The second major theoretical position is the social learning approach based upon the work of Rotter (1954). This approach represents achievement behavior as a function of (a) value placed on attaining competence, and (b) expectancies of success, and locus of control (Crandall et al. 1960). Locus of control is a pivotal construct in this theoretical position. An internal locus of control (feeling personally responsible for one's successes and failures) is said to be more conducive to achievement than an external locus of control (feeling that one's successes or failures depend on external factors such as luck and fate rather than on one's efforts and abilities). Supporters of this theoretical position have carried out substantial research on the child-rearing antecedents of achievement tendencies.

1.3 Attribution Theory

The third major theoretical position is the attributional approach which places even greater emphasis on one's cognitions than the social learning position. The attributional approach to achievement motivation is based upon the assumption that people's beliefs about the outcome they experience guide their behavior in that and similar situations. The focus here is on specific

411

cognitions about success and failure that mediate persistence on achievement tasks. Different causal attributions are viewed as implying different probabilities of future success. One such prediction is that when a person attributes failure to a lack of ability, achievement expectancies and task persistence will decrease more quickly than when failure is attributed to a more controllable factor such as effort (Weiner and Kukla 1970). Those adopting this social–cognitive perspective have done research on topics such as why people expect to succeed (or fail), and age-related changes in achievement cognition, affect, and behavior (Dweck and Elliott 1983).

2. The Developmental Sequence for Achievement Orientation

According to Veroff (1969), there are three major stages in the development of achievement orientation/motivation: autonomous competence, social comparison about achievement, and autonomous achievement motivation integrated with social comparison strivings.

2.1 The Autonomous Competence Period

This period encompasses approximately the first six years of childhood, and involves internalizing personal standards of competence. It is believed that infants display mastery (competence or effectance) motivation. This represents inborn intrinsic motivation to master one's environment. Children derive pleasure and a sense of effectiveness in exploring and attaining mastery over their environment (White 1959).

During early childhood (at about age 3), the child develops a concept of self. The emergence of self and achievement orientation (i.e., the purposeful pursuit and evaluation of competence) seem to go hand in hand. By such an age, children can (a) cognitively represent and react to self-related competence goals and try to bring them about, (b) evaluate the outcomes of such actions against standards of competence, (c) view outcomes as reflecting one's self, and (d) experience self-related emotions such as pride and shame (Dweck and Elliott 1983).

2.2 Social Comparison Period

At about age 6, with exposure to the school environment with its new goals and standards, children become more likely to evaluate their competence with reference to the performance and standards of others (social comparison). It appears that a certain amount of personal success in reference to such standards is necessary for the child to develop motivation to strive for achievement in social settings (Veroff 1969).

By about age 7, children begin to view ability (intellectual competence) as a more global, stable psychological trait. They also tend to view their ability as very high, underestimate task difficulty, and hold and maintain high expectancies of success. The under-

standing that achievement has multiple causes develops gradually. Most children, before ages 7 or 8, attribute achievement entirely to effort and failure to a lack of effort. By the middle elementary-school years, children understand limitations on the extent to which effort translates directly into achievement (Dweck and Elliott 1983).

2.3 Integration Period

In the third and final stage, which takes place during adolescence, children must learn how to integrate the autonomous and social comparison achievement orientations. They must discern when to rely on internal standards and when to be responsive to external standards. Satisfactory development in each stage depends upon the successful completion of the preceding stage (Veroff 1969).

Recent social–cognitive research (Dweck 1986) provides support for Veroff's (1969) contention that a successful integration of autonomous and social comparison motivations requires children to regain a strong sense of their own independence (i.e., a sense of effectiveness independent of the social groups to which they belong). A child who regains that sense of independence and who believes that intelligence is a malleable characteristic will tend to show an adaptive mastery-oriented pattern characterized by challenge-seeking and high persistence in the face of obstacles.

3. The Influence of Significant Others on the Development of Achievement Orientation

This section will focus on the influence of parents and teachers.

3.1 Familial Influences

Much of the research on antecedents of achievement orientation has concentrated on two aspects of parental influences: parental attitudes and child-rearing practices. Such research indicates that independence training, direct achievement training (Rosen and D'Andrade 1959), reward for effort, and encouragement of intellectual pursuits (Crandall et al. 1960) are associated with achievement striving. It should be noted that independence training refers to encouraging children to do things on their own, while achievement training refers to encouraging children to do things well. More importantly, early independence and achievement training will not be effective if parents accentuate the negative by punishing failures and responding neutrally to successes. Children who show the highest level of achievement motivation are those who (a) are encouraged to "do their best" by parents who reward success intermittently rather than continuously, and (b) respond neutrally to failures. The use of authoritative control techniques (i.e., principled or reasoned discipline), and the provision of opportunities for the child to participate in the family's decision-making processes and be delegated major responsibilities also appear to be associated with the development of achievement orientations and achievement behavior, such as attaining a leadership position (Klonsky 1983). An intellectually stimulating home environment (i.e., emotionally responsive caregivers providing the child with developmentally appropriate opportunities to manipulate and control the environment in play) in the first year of life may also have a favorable impact on the development of achievement orientation.

Research reviews (e.g., Manley 1977) have examined differences in the parental socialization of girls and boys with respect to achievement orientation. Moderate but not high maternal warmth, or even slight hostility, plus an achieving parental model were related to a strong achievement orientation in girls, while more intense socialization (e.g., high maternal nurturance, affection, and achievement demands) was related to a strong achievement orientation in boys.

Further, parents often have different expectations for type and amount of achievement for sons and daughters. More specifically, parents seem to expect more in the way of academic achievement from adolescent sons than from adolescent daughters. They also tend to attribute their daughters' performances to hard work and their sons' performances to high ability. With this attribution pattern, parents may be teaching their sons and daughters to draw different inferences about their abilities from equivalent achievement experiences. These differential expectations appear to have an impact on the child's self-concept and achievement orientation. Other work suggests that parents expect boys to develop a more competitive achievement orientation than girls.

Firstborn children tend to have higher achievement motivation and to achieve more than their later born counterparts. This firstborn advantage may stem from the fact that firstborns tend to receive more direct achievement training.

Family socialization practices can probably best be conceptualized as potential facilitators of the development of achievement orientation. Appropriate family socialization practices could create a type of "readiness" that would make one more responsive to environmental models (e.g., teachers and peers), opportunities, and supports.

3.2 Teacher Influences

Research reviews (e.g., Eccles et al. 1984) indicate that (a) teacher support is correlated with students' mastery and career motivation, and (b) there is a positive correlation between opportunities for autonomy, responsibility, and control in the student role and internalizing academic motivation. Eccles et al. (1984) point to a link between grade-related changes in school experiences and drops in achievement motivation. They feel that this finding is due to the increasing emphasis on relative ability assessments and on decreases in practices which provide students with some sense of autonomy and control at a time when the child's competency and social

maturity are actually increasing (i.e., lower secondary-school age).

Teacher expectations and reinforcement practices also have important effects on a student's achievement orientation (Dweck 1986, Dweck and Elliott 1983). The teacher expectancy effect refers to the phenomenon whereby teachers' impressions about student ability (e.g., manipulated with test information) actually affects student performance. Research on this effect suggests that intellectual gains and achievement orientation were produced in part by "challenging" the students. The teachers seemed to be giving students for whom they had low expectations little work and work that was too easy. However, success in personally easy tasks is ineffective in producing stable confidence, challenge-seeking, and persistence.

Teachers serve their students better when providing positive reinforcement intermittently for major accomplishments on challenging tasks than with continuous reinforcement (i.e., very frequent praise) for short, easy tasks. Intermittent reinforcement for major accomplishments on challenging tasks is more likely to create a learning goal orientation rather than a performance goal orientation.

4. The Impact of Demographic Factors on the Development of Achievement Orientation

This section will review the impact of sex, social class, culture, and race on the development of achievement orientation. It should be noted that while differences between such groups are highlighted, there is a substantial amount of overlap in the level and quality of achievement orientation.

4.1 Sex

While literature reviews (e.g., Deaux 1977) indicate that males and females tend not to differ consistently on achievement motivation, differences on a number of other achievement-related indices (i.e., expectancies of success, level of aspiration, and evaluation of performance) suggest that females are less self-confident about their abilities to achieve and have more feelings of personal responsibility when failure occurs. Such reviews also suggest that females and males have achievement strivings which are often oriented toward different goals (i.e., females being more relationship-oriented and males more task-oriented). As discussed above, sex differences in achievement orientation have been related in part to parental socialization practices.

4.2 Social Class

Among the most consistent findings in the achievement literature are those indicating social class differences. More specifically, higher levels of achievement motivation have been associated with higher socioeconomic status. These class differences in achievement orientation are generally thought to be indicative of class differences in child-rearing practices. The higher

413

achievement motivation among those of higher socio-economic status is seen as stemming from greater emphasis on achievement, mastery training, delaying gratification, and self-direction.

4.3 Culture

Research concerning the impact of culture on achievement orientation has concentrated on child-rearing antecedents. For example, cross-cultural research has indicated that parents in nonindustrialized countries place a lower value on socializing their youth for achievement and independence and a higher value on obedience and responsibility. It should also be noted that the class differences described above appear to hold across many cultural and ethnic groups. Research also reveals that the United States and Japan have particularly achievement-oriented cultures.

Researchers have also found that culture affects the relationship between sex and locus of control. Such studies found that while females in general had a higher belief in external control of their lives than males, the level of belief in externality varied from country to country.

4.4 Race

The majority of research on racial differences in achievement orientation has focused on black/white differences. When story completion measures of achievement motivation are administered to black children, they generally score lower than white children. Black children, in comparison to white children, have less sense of personal control (i.e., more external locus of control) and more anxiety in testing and school situations. It should be noted, however, that young black females show significantly more internal locus of control than their male counterparts. It may be because the authoritarian discipline administered to black females tends to be coupled with the delegation of important family responsibilities. It is not yet clear why black children in general have lower achievement motivation, less of a sense of personal control, and poorer performance on indices of school achievement. Some reasons suggested by the literature have been lack of teacher encouragement, greater likelihood of living in impoverished environments, and greater exposure to authoritarian discipline at home. Finally, it should be emphasized that some researchers are concerned that blacks are at a disadvantage in such studies due to ethnocentric assumptions and a lack of consideration of achievement orientation outside of the classroom (e.g., with peers and family).

5. The Significance of Theory and Research Concerning Achievement Orientation for Educational Practice

Achievement orientation theory and research provide educators and parents with greater understanding of the nature and origin of achievement orientation and achievement-related behavior. With a greater understanding of reasons why some students persist and make the most of their skills and others do not, and explanations of how students react to their successes and failures and different achievement goals, parents and teachers can perhaps create educational systems which nurture achievement orientation and diminish fear of failure. Information on individual and group differences in achievement orientation should make educators more sensitive to student needs.

6. Future Research Needs on the Development of Achievement Orientation

Further research should help pave the way for educational interventions. Research focus should be sharpened to identify specific teacher-related beliefs, expectancies, and behavior; and classroom structure variables that foster adaptive and maladaptive achievement orientations and attributions. Research focus should also be broadened to identify and explain (a) the developmental changes in the quality and level of achievement orientation beyond childhood and adolescence (i.e., investigating achievement orientations throughout the lifespan); (b) how achievement orientation varies with the nature of developmental tasks (e.g., educational, occupational, social, and athletic); and (c) variations in achievement orientations of children from nontraditional families (e.g., single parent and blended). There is also a need for methodologically sound and detailed research comparing the development and maintenance of achievement orientation across cultures which differentially value, express, and socialize achievement behaviors.

Bibliography

Atkinson J W 1964 *An Introduction to Motivation.* Van Nostrand, Princeton, New Jersey

Crandall V J, Katkovsky W, Preston A 1960 A conceptual formulation for some research on children's achievement development. *Child Dev.* 31: 787–97

Deaux K 1977 Sex differences. In: Blass T (ed.) 1977 *Personality Variables in Social Behavior.* Lawrence Erlbaum, Hillsdale, New Jersey, pp. 357–77

Dweck C S 1986 Motivational processes affecting learning. *Am. Psychol.* 41(10): 1040–48

Dweck C S, Elliott E S 1983 Achievement motivation. In: Hetherington E M (ed.) 1983 *Handbook of Child Psychology*, Vol. 4, *Socialization, Personality, and Social Development*, 4th edn. Wiley, New York, pp. 643–91

Eccles J, Midgley C, Adler T F 1984 Grade-related changes in the school environment: Effects on achievement motivation. In: Maehr M (ed.) 1984 *Advances in Motivation and Achievement: The Development of Achievement Motivation*, Vol. 3. JAI Press, Greenwich, Connecticut

Klonsky B G 1983 The socialization and development of leadership ability. *Genet. Psychol. Monogr.* 108: 97–135

Manley R O 1977 Parental warmth and hostility as related to sex differences in children's achievement orientation. *Psychol. Women Q.* 1(3): 229–45

McClelland D C, Atkinson J W, Clark R W, Lowell E L 1953 *The Achievement Motive.* Appleton-Century-Crofts, New York

Murray H A, Barrett W G, Homburger E 1938 *Explorations in Personality*, Oxford University Press. New York

Rosen B C, D'Andrade R 1959 The psychosocial origins of achievement motivation. *Sociometry* 22: 185–218

Rotter J B 1954 *Social Learning and Clinical Psychology.* Prentice-Hall, New York

Veroff J 1969 Social comparison and the development of achievement motivation. In: Smith C P (ed.) 1969 *Achievement-related Motives in Children.* Russell Sage, New York, pp. 46–101

Weiner B, Kukla A 1970 An attributional analysis of achievement motivation. *J. Person. Soc. Psych.* 15: 1–20

White R W 1959 Motivation reconsidered: The concept of competence. *Psychol. Rev.* 66: 297–333

Emotional Development

W. Draper

Emotion may be defined as a complex phenomenon, comprising at least three aspects: (a) the experience or conscious feeling of emotion; (b) the processes that occur in the brain and nervous system; and (c) the observable expressive patterns of emotion, particularly those on the face (Izard 1977). Each of these aspects has important implications for educators.

The first aspect refers to what transpires deep inside a person, hidden from the view or perceptions of others. The child feels something such as frustration, dread, revulsion, or affection. He or she may not be able to identify the cause for this feeling and may be unable to describe it in words; nevertheless, the feeling exists and it affects how the child will respond in certain situations that generate that feeling.

Emotions also involve activity in the brain and nervous system. When a person is under pressure or experiences stress, the limbic system becomes highly activated and learning is subsequently inhibited. As children seek to compensate for their inadequacies, whether real or imagined, they may exhibit behaviors that bring further pressure to bear and consequently continue the cycle of brain patterns that impede both the learning process and control of emotional behavior.

Finally, the third aspect of emotion refers to the intimate connection that prevails between inward feelings and outward expression. Ordinarily, emotional feelings manifest themselves in some form of observable external expression. Sackheim and Gur have reported that at least six emotions can be reliably recognized on the human face: happiness, surprise, fear, sadness, anger, and disgust (Bellak and Baker 1981).

1. Common Types of Emotions

Both the emotions themselves and their patterns of expression change with age and the child's overall development throughout infancy, childhood, youth, and adulthood. The most frequently expressed emotional reactions and expressions of feelings will generally settle into habits that become driving forces in a child's life.

Affection involves the expression of feelings which reflect concern, warmth, regard, caring, sympathy, and helpfulness. Young children are especially open about their feelings of affection toward others. As they reach preadolescence they show less physical affection but demonstrate their feelings through social interaction, confiding in one another, and participating in activities together.

Love is a feeling of deep personal attachment and commitment, a much stronger and more complex emotion than affection. Love may be openly expressed or communicated in subtle ways. Child psychologists appear to agree that children need to feel loved in order to have adequate emotional development.

Joy, happiness, and contentment are similar emotions. Joy is a feeling of gladness and delight; happiness is a sense of well-being that generates attitudes of good fortune and satisfaction. Contentment is a sense of satisfaction, peace of mind, and a feeling of being in tune with the universe.

Grief and sorrow are strong emotions that reflect distress at losing a loved person, animal, or object. Persons experiencing grief and sorrow feel somewhat helpless and they sense a great emptiness. Grief and sorrow are important in early childhood experiences that help build the foundation for future experiences. Adults can help children with grief and sorrow when they are open and honest about a tragic event, yet are sensitive and understanding. Simple statements often help children feel free to ask questions and clarify mistaken or confusing ideas, especially in the case of death.

Fear is marked by such feelings as alarm, dread, anxious concern, fright, terror, and panic. Infants generally experience fears related to loud noises, strange persons and objects, unfamilar surroundings, pain, and sudden changes in lighting or temperature. As children grow and develop, experiencing life more fully, they come into contact with situations that bring about a broad range of feelings related to fear. Worry is a form of fear in which the child imagines that something dangerous or unpleasant will happen. Anxiety is an intense fear or worry that causes the child to feel helpless, uncomfortable, and nontrusting. Children who experience anxiety over a long period of time may become emotionally disturbed.

Anger is an emotion that children learn very early

serves many purposes. It is an expression of intense displeasure, rage, or fury. While fear generally decreases in intensity with age, anger often increases both in forms of expression and intensity.

Jealousy is the thought or perception of possibly losing approval, affection, or love. This emotion can result in anger or resentment toward a loved one as well as toward one who gets attention from the loved one. Children are likely to experience deep feelings of jealousy around the age of 2 or 3 years while they are forming their independence. Another stage when children become jealous is at about age 10 to 12 when they begin to make the transition from childhood to adolescence.

2. Role of Emotions

Blaise Pascal was very perceptive when he wrote: "The heart has reasons the head knows not of" (Bartlett 1882 p. 363). Humans are feeling beings as well as thinking beings. Indeed, human emotions sometimes take control over reasoning. Primarily for this reason, the ancient Stoics advocated a life of *apathos*—emotion free—because the emotionless person does not suffer disappointment, sorrow, anger, or unhappiness; the Stoic was expected to rise above these mundane feelings. Unfortunately, neither does the Stoic experience joy, happiness, or pleasure—which may be one of the causes for the demise of Stoicism as a way of life.

Emotions play a vitally important role in ordering human experience. Without them life would be flat and devoid of excitement. Emotions often provide the stimulus or motivation to act in a certain way. They provide the inner force that attracts one person to another, or that repels one person from another. Emotions provide a sense of feeling with and for others (*Gemeinschaftsgefuhl*). They provide a sense of security, help persons cope with frustration, alert them to dangers, and prod them into action.

At the same time, emotions are also the cause of certain problems. Sometimes, for example, people say or do things they might later regret—primarily because they were acting on the basis of emotion rather than a reasoned response. Often when children do poorly in school, it is because they suffer the emotional trauma of problems at home or in their social life. Feelings of fear, anger, threat, or insecurity can often diminish a child's ability to respond in appropriate ways.

Emotions influence the child's view of the world and the role of the self in society. As children grow into adulthood they carry memories of their childhood with them. Emotional warmth, feelings of love and caring from others, and the appropriate expressions of both positive and negative feelings help children establish affectional relationships with others that reflect fulfillment and social skills.

Unfortunately, the systematic study of emotions in children has not kept pace with the vigorous studies of other aspects of human development, such as Piaget's work on intellectual development. It is possible to speculate that this omission may be due to the enormity of the task. That is, in the absence of the child's ability to articulate what he or she is feeling at a particular moment, the empirical scholar is left with little to report that is both observable and verifiable. It may also be the case that inasmuch as emotions are experienced at a precognitive level, they do not readily lend themselves to description according to the strict canons of scholarship.

3. Factors Influencing Emotions

3.1 Maturation

Rates of biological maturation vary from child to child and therefore influence their emotional development. As the brain and body mature, the child's functions become more sophisticated and differentiated. For example, as the memory improves and the ability to imagine and anticipate increases, children's emotional responses take on new dimensions. Children reactivate feelings of excitement and joy by repeating play activities that previously brought delight. Children who remember frightening experiences may show manifestations of fear when in similar situations.

The endocrine system helps to regulate bodily functions and plays a significant role in emotions. Soon after birth the adrenal glands decrease in size; they begin to increase rapidly up to about age 5, and then slow until about age 10 to 12. Rapid development of these glands occurs from about age 13 to 16. While the glands are active, surges of energy are brought on by the release of body fluids and the child is likely to show feelings through body movements as well as speech and mood states (Hurlock 1972).

3.2 Environment

A healthy "emotional climate" is a physical and psychological setting in which the child feels safe, develops trust in others, and builds relationships with a sense of confidence and trust. Opportunities to explore life and learn in an atmosphere of love and concern provide a sense of comfort and place the child at ease. Safe and healthy surroundings, adequate amounts of nutritious foods, and daily health habits add to the quality of life and, hence, to the child's sense of well-being.

Childhood experiences, both in the family and community, that are filled with genuine affection, happiness, and caring set the tone for healthy emotional development. Children feel free in expressing their feelings when appropriate limits are established and enforced. They learn to control, yet express, strong feelings, such as anger, disgust, and jealousy when adults provide guidance that reflects sensitivity to their individual needs.

The child's own perceptions of "how things are" influence personal feelings and the manner in which those feelings are expressed. The child who consistently sees himself or herself as esteemed and accepted by others will likely form a positive self-image and a sense of personal worth. In contrast, children who perceive others as consistently rejecting, neglecting, or ridiculing them may become less socially acceptable themselves, modeling the behaviors they most often experience and forming less than desirable self-images.

3.3 Cognition

Every emotion has a cognitive component, and every thought is influenced by emotional factors. Both emotion and thought are basic attributes, which in the human being are intimately meshed in a dialectical unity (Thomas and Chess 1980 p. 152). Differentiated psychological traits of older children and adults clearly reflect the interactive processes that involve emotion and thought. Feelings reinforce ideas, and ideas in turn reinforce feelings.

Emotions are categorized by adults in terms of feeling states which are linked with specific cognitive meanings. The identification of emotions requires a combination of subjective feelings and cognitive processes, supplemented by inferences from facial expressions, voice tone, and body gestures. In contrast to adults who can report a combination of subjective and objective data, the young infant's emotional inferences are limited by objective and observable data consisting of vocal, facial, and body movements that express what appear to be positive or negative mood states.

It is not possible to actually learn to control an emotion, per se. For example, a person who experiences fear cannot eliminate fear itself. Rather, what a person learns is how to cope with that fear by expressing appropriate behavior, whether it be by taking flight or by stating, "I am afraid." With maturation of the brain, nervous system, and muscles, the child increases the potential for a broad range of emotional reactions through various forms of learning—imitation and modeling, trial and error, conditioning, and insight.

3.4 Language and Communication Skills

Through the course of normal development children improve their language and communication skills. While early expressions are somewhat random and uncontrolled, infants soon learn a variety of ways to let their feelings be known. They gradually progress from such responses as laughing or crying to waving arms, jumping up and down, smiling, and simple words. As children develop verbal skills, they talk more about their feelings. Even so, throughout childhood body language along with speech is natural and prominent. Until children are about 7- or 8-years old, most are quite frank in letting others know how they feel. As children get older, they learn to control their feelings and to be more discreet about expressing them. Forms of verbal expression and use of body language to express feelings are also influenced by social and cultural patterns of behavior.

3.5 Socialization

Children's emotional responses, although spontaneous, are influenced by their social interactions. When there is someone present who is interested in how a child feels, emotions are usually freely expressed. Appropriate limits and exemplary models help children learn to express their feelings in ways that are socially acceptable. Children who are restricted or prevented from openly expressing themselves may repress or harbor feelings that eventually lead to serious emotional problems.

Emotional deprivation, the prolonged absence of sufficient stimulation from personal interactions and experiences of attachment and affection, inhibits the child's overall development. Children who are denied opportunities to experience love, joy, happiness, and contentment during infancy and in the early years have less opportunity for optimal physical, mental, and social development, resulting in possible delay of motor, language, and intellectual skills. When intimate social interactions are denied, the child has little basis on which to build a repertoire of positive emotional experiences that lead to healthy personality formation and a sense of self-esteem. Furthermore, the child tends to be self-centered and demanding, with a poorly developed self-concept formation.

Behavioral outcomes of prolonged emotional deprivation include listlessness, emaciation, undue quietness, general apathy, loss of appetite, and a variety of psychosomatic illnesses. Young children deprived of love and caring in their daily lives tend to exhibit manifestations of disturbed interpersonal relationships and inadequate social skills such as avoidance of others, aggression, and hostility.

3.6 Personality and Temperament

Personality characteristics vary with each individual in relation to time, place, and circumstances. It is therefore inappropriate to label a child on the basis of an emotional judgment that carries a global inference about one's personality, such as "she is an angry child," "he is a hostile boy," or "she is a happy baby." A school-age child may appear to be angry in the school setting when experiences are threatening, yet appear pleasant while playing with peers. A parent may be firm and forceful with a child in certain family circumstances, yet be gentle and warm in other instances.

Different infants exhibit different rates, ranges, and tempos of internal states that will, in turn, affect the outcome of interactions from individual to individual. These individual differences in infants, together with differing experiences and styles of mothering, contribute to the nature of the emotional interaction that occurs.

3.7 Motivation

Motivation, as a psychological construct, refers to the internal state of the individual which, under certain circumstances, appears to move the person toward a particular action or behavior. Emotion and motivation are bound together in human interaction. In a social context, the strength of the motivating force depends on how the child views the self and his or her needs in a given situation. Although perception may initiate the emoting process, the emotion that follows may, in turn, affect the perceptual process. With emotion there is usually an impulse to act. Feelings, essential to all human conduct and predominant factors in emotion, serve as underpinnings that not only bring about motivation to act but also influence the form that action will take.

4. The Brain and Nervous System

The early work of Papez and later the neuroscientist, Paul MacLean, advanced the concept that certain subcortical regions are involved with emotional behavior. MacLean emphasizes the role of the paleocortex and of the nuclei of the limbic system in relation to intense emotions and drives (Henry and Stephens 1977).

Evidence that the brain's right hemispheric complex is most closely related to the emotional response system and hence to the limbic structures is presented by Flor-Henry and co-workers who speculate that connections from the new association cortex in the right parietal and frontal regions to the limbic system determine affective responses. Sifneos draws a distinction between feelings and emotions: Experiencing emotion can be recognized by a person's behavior and its confirming neuro-endocrine changes. Feelings, by contrast, involve subjective thoughts and fantasies and require neocortical activity (Henry and Stephens 1977).

The limbic system, comprising roughly one-fifth of the brain's area, surrounds the brainstem and is surrounded by the cerebrum. Extensive neural links with the brainstem help maintain a state of emotional balance. Connections with the cerebrum permit interplay between reason and emotion. The neocortex, the newest evolutionary part of the human brain which comprises almost five-sixths of the whole, functions less efficiently under pressure. Pressure of an emotional or psychological nature places greater stimulation on the limbic system and learning is subsequently inhibited (Henry and Stephens 1977).

Stress and pressure from various life experiences can therefore cause a person to function less effectively in the realm of rational thought. An example is the school-age child who is anxious about performing adequately on a given examination, resulting in the inability to think clearly and process the information needed to complete the task. As the child seeks to compensate for inadequacies, whether real or imagined, behaviors may be exhibited that bring further pressure to bear and therefore continue the cycle of brain patterns which impede the learning process.

Nerve pathways, interwoven throughout the limbic system, send electrochemical impulses that direct human drives and emotions. A small cluster of nerve cells called the hypothalamus serves as the center out of which arise feelings of pleasure, punishment, hunger, thirst, sexual arousal, aggression, and rage.

Certain physiological changes also accompany emotion. At times, these changes may be intensive and extensive, altering regulation of the bodily systems, including the respiratory, digestive, circulatory, and nervous systems and glands of internal and external secretion. In the case of fear and anger, for example, these physiological changes have been described as the body's mobilization of resources for "fight or flight" responses (Henry and Stephens 1977). First to react is the hypothalamus, which organizes a series of defenses to prepare the body for handling an emergency. Hypothalamic chemicals cause the pituitary to release a stress hormone through the bloodstream to the adrenal glands which, in turn, produce an adrenal chemical for converting fats and proteins into sugar. Adrenalin and noradrenaline cause the heart to pump faster, blood pressure to rise, and pupils of the eyes to dilate. The combined surge of hormones relaxes bronchial tubes for deeper breathing, increases blood sugar for greater energy, slows down digestive processes to conserve muscular energy, and shifts blood supplies for easier clotting in open wounds. In a matter of seconds the body is prepared to perform with strength and endurance far beyond its normal capacity.

5. Stages of Emotional Development

Overall, emotional development from infancy onward can be characterized by: (a) initial simple emotions becoming increasingly differentiated and elaborated, and (b) new, complex emotions coming into existence. Qualitative differences in the meaning of emotional terms must be considered at different developmental stages. For example, pride and guilt may begin to crystallize during the preschool years and are clearly different from pleasure or distress of the young infant. Emotions with highly developed cognitive components like empathy may not appear until middle childhood or adolescence.

Emotional development is primarily a result of maturation and learning, although manifestations of diffused emotional responses may appear soon after birth. Variations in the frequency, intensity, and duration of different emotions are generally a combination of heredity and maturation, environmental circumstances, and daily living experiences and personal health.

A brief summary of the child's emotional development from birth through adolescence has profound implications for educators. As the child progresses from one stage to the next, each subsequent stage is supported by a cumulative reservoir of past experiences, whether they be adequate and appropriate or lacking and inappropriate. The child's view of self and the world is greatly influenced by the emotional experiences that take place in each stage. These stages, for the most part, are consistent with Piaget's stages of cognitive development (see *Cognitive Development*).

5.1 Infancy (Birth to 2 Years)

During the infant stage, the mother serves as the child's main source of energy, power, possibility, and safety (Pearce 1977). The quality of the mother–infant relationship sets the tone for subsequent emotional development. Emotions are the child's language system during this period, for through the expression of feelings of distress or delight, the child is able to communicate needs and wishes as well as satisfaction or the lack of it. As the child makes a transition from the early parent–infant attachment to interest in other family members, expressions of emotions are manifested in behaviors toward others such as avoidance and approach.

5.2 Early Childhood (2 to 8 Years)

This is the stage during which the child becomes grounded in the experiences of everyday life within and beyond the immediate family. The child's world becomes the center of activity for exploring and discovering both human interactions and physical and material components of the environment. The child still needs the emotional support of the mother, but meaningful interactions expand to persons beyond her, with the father or other significant person serving as the pivotal opportunity to move beyond the mother and into the greater community. The child is very subjective, exhibiting the emotionally based egocentrism typical of this stage. Mastery of the body and emotions is a task during this time. The child's place is "here," the time is "now," and the center is "me." Emotional control begins to take shape, but the child remains open in expressing strong feelings. Mastery of language skills and increasing cognitive abilities help the child develop capabilities for socially acceptable ways of expressing emotions.

5.3 School-age Child (8 to 12 Years)

The child begins to rely on the self as the main source of possibility, energy and safety, yet remains emotionally grounded in the previous stages. This is a period of search for self-identity and use of the body and brain together as a resource for functioning on a concrete level. Emotions are expressed with greater control as the child seeks to function as a socially accepted human being, interacting with others and interdependent in relationships. The child assumes an objective interest in the world, experiencing delight from gathering facts and information, such as how many legs are on a caterpillar. Attachment to the world in a broader sense brings another shift in the child's emotional underpinnings.

5.4 Young Adolescent (12 to 16 Years)

The adolescent progresses to the application of abstract thought, no longer limited to concrete avenues of logic, trial and error, and cause and effect for discovery and learning. Still supported emotionally by the sense of self, the child now begins to rely more on abstract thought and internalizing feelings, capable of controlling emotions in order to interact appropriately as a social participant, accepted by peers and society in general. During this stage of transition from childhood into adolescence, hormonal changes occur and the individual becomes more sensitive to his or her own sexuality, with subtle outward behaviors as manifestations of inner feelings and concerns. By this time, the child is capable of reporting and describing personal feelings; even so, there is a tendency to withhold sharing real feelings.

5.5 Older Adolescent (16 to 20 Years)

Persons at this stage are inclined to want to practice their social and intellectual skills in ways that are personally gratifying to them. They are less interested in the study of how scholars think or feel and more interested in experiencing their own feelings and intellectual competencies. This is a stage of exploring more intimate relationships and new emotional attachments. The emotions are often expressed in artforms and cultural traditions. By this time the adolescent makes an attachment to the world in a broader sense, through private contemplation about the self and its relationship to others, to life itself, and to the universe.

6. Expressions of Emotions

Charles Darwin, for more than 40 years, gathered material on expressive movements and facial expressions of emotion in people around the world. His book, *Expressions of the Emotions in Man and Animals* (Darwin 1872), contained minutely detailed descriptions of the physiological and muscular changes involved in the expression of emotion. In his "Biographical Sketch of an Infant," published five years later, Darwin centered on the expression of emotion in infants as seen in one of his own children. Fear, he stated, is probably one of the earliest feelings that infants experience, shown by "their starting at any sudden sound when only a few weeks old, followed by crying." He observed expressions of "affection" before age 2 months, manifested by smiling at "those who took care of him." By 6 months the baby assumed a melancholy expression when his nurse pretended to cry; he showed signs of discomfort by age 13 months (Jackson and Jackson 1978).

Gerald Young and Theresa Décarie, at the University of Montreal, found that infant expressions usually affect many parts of the face—changes in the brow, eyes, mouth, cheeks, nose, jaw, chin, and throat as well as varied vocalizations. They observed three categories of expressions: (a) positive, or expressing pleasures (babbles, coos, laughs, squeals); (b) neutral or undifferentiated (attentive, detached, sober stares, and frowns, perplexed and surprised, sigh and yawn); and

(c) negative, or expressing displeasure (disgust, fear, sadness) (Jackson and Jackson 1978).

As children progress in overall development, emotional behavior becomes increasingly directed and less chaotic. Crying and temper tantrums progress to physical aggression toward self and others, such as pulling hair, kicking, and hitting. Name calling and other verbal expressions accompany language acquisition.

The child generates emotions for the achievement of personal goals. For example, temper tantrums are often attempts to attract attention or exert power. One cannot always see the child's motive—only the manifestation of it. The temper tantrum may be the child's aim at obtaining power because of feelings of inferiority. If the child felt sure of his or her power, it would not be necessary to demonstrate it.

Emotions can be observed as expressions or indicators of movement toward or away from other persons. Disjunctive emotions separate a person from others; conjunctive emotions join a person to others. Anger enables the child to oppose and dominate, or to hurt and to get even. Empathy, a conjunctive emotion, manifests itself as an expression of positive social concern in the child's ability to identify with the feelings of another person or persons and to express that concern in some meaningful way either verbally or nonverbally.

7. Theories of Emotional Attachment

Expressive patterns of emotions have their roots in early attachment experiences that infants have with their mothers or other primary caregivers (see *Mother–Child Relations*). Attachment, the emergent social relationship, and the attachment behaviors which function to maintain and modulate the flow of a social interaction, appear to begin taking shape during the first 6 months of life.

British psychoanalyst John Bowlby advanced the ethological theory of attachment, with emphasis on a long period of dependency with the identification of several kinds of infant behaviors. Known collectively as attachment behavior, these include crying, smiling, and vocalizing which attract the mother's attention. The active rooting, sucking, clinging, and embracing initiated by the infant produce and maintain proximity, as do crawling and walking. Cuddling and clinging represent immediate contact between infant and mother. Crying and fussing, orienting with looking, smiling, verbalizing, and cuddling serve as precursors of infant–mother attachment (Bowlby 1969).

Bowlby emphasized that attachment behaviors are controlled by a dynamic feedback system existing between the mother and child, resulting from an inborn biological propensity for the development of social bonds. Daniel Stern, Cornell University Medical Center, declares after extensive observations of infants and caregivers in homes, in laboratories, and in social settings, that the social interaction between the infant and mother is a biologically designed choreography that serves as a prototype for all later interpersonal exchanges (Stern 1977).

A baby's tendency to seek attachments may be increased by fear and also by illness and fatigue (Bowlby 1969). Attachments are most likely to be made to people who bring comfort to the baby, actively interact with the baby, and respond to the baby's cues (Ainsworth 1973). Attachment behavior also includes using the mother as a base from which to explore.

Attachment, from the beginning, must be viewed in terms of participating rather than in terms of two individuals sending discrete messages. Brazelton, in studying infant–mother reciprocity in face-to-face play situations by microkinesic analysis, found that reciprocity of behaving is fundamental to the human species and appears soon after birth. By 3 weeks of age, infants evidence behaviors which are different for objects than for human interactions. Infants engage the mother or caretaker in a rhythmical cyclical pattern of attention and nonattention (Brazelton et al. 1975).

Mary D. Ainsworth distinguished several stages in the development of attachment, according to ethological theory. First, the infant displays a variety of fixed-action patterns of behavior in signalling to and orienting toward other human beings indiscriminately. In the second stage, until about 6 or 7 months of age, infants continue to signal and orient but will respond differentially to the mother and one or two other persons. In a third stage from 7 months through about 2 years of age, infants take more and more initiative in maintaining proximity to the mother—clinging, following, and climbing into her lap (Ainsworth 1973).

In contrast to the ethological theory, in which the infant's attachment to the mother is seen as biologically determined, social-learning theory identifies attachment as a dependency relationship that is established by conditioning (crying by the hungry infant is reinforced by the mother's nurturant behavior) and through stimuli associated with the mother's presence (the infant acquires a drive to be close to the mother) (Jackson and Jackson 1978). In short, a "dependency drive" develops. The infant's "proximity behavior" has been conditioned to occur by the association of the closeness to the mother with rewards, such as food. The strength of attachment to the mother lies in her having more reinforcement control over the infant's "behavioral systems" than any other person in the environment.

Bibliography

Ainsworth M 1973 The development of infant–mother attachment. In: Caldwell B M, Ricciuti H N (eds.) 1973 *Review of Child Development Research*. University of Chicago Press, Chicago, Illinois

Bartlett J 1882 *Familiar Quotations: Being an Attempt to Trace Their Sources Passages and Phrases in Common Use*. Little, Brown, Toronto, Ontario

Bellak L, Baker S S 1981 *Reading Faces*. Holt, Rinehart and Winston, New York

Bowlby J 1969 *Attachment and Loss*, Vol. 1: *Attachment*. Hogarth, London

Brazelton T, Tronick E, Wise S 1975 *Parent–Infant Interaction*. Associated Scientific Publishers, New York

Darwin C R 1872 *The Expression of the Emotions in Man and Animals*. Murray, London

Henry J P, Stephens P M 1977 *Stress, Health, and the Social Environment: A Sociobiologic Approach to Medicine*. Springer, Berlin

Hurlock E B 1972 *Child Development*, 5th edn. McGraw-Hill, New York

Izard C E (ed.) 1977 *Human Emotions*. Plenum, New York

Jackson J F, Jackson J H 1978 *Infant Culture*. Crowell, New York

Pearce J C 1977 *Magical Child: Rediscovering Nature's Plan for Our Children*. Bantam, Toronto, Ontario

Stern D 1977 *The First Relationship: Infant and Mother*. Harvard University Press, Cambridge, Massachusetts

Thomas A, Chess S 1980 *The Dynamics of Psychological Development*. Brunner/Mazel, New York

Prosocial and Antisocial Behavior

Moral Development

K. Bergling

The fundamental question which remains the starting point for any consideration of morality is: what is the meaning of morality? Social scientists differ widely on this issue. According to social learning theory, morality is regarded as "internalized control of conduct," whereas according to the cognitive developmental view dominating this article morality is seen as a moral decision-making process; these two dominating branches of moral development research are presented separately in the article on social-learning theory (see *Social Learning Theory*) and in the present article respectively.

The two research orientations differ in their relationship to moral philosophy. Cognitive developmental theory starts in moral philosophy by making the principle of justice and the concepts of equality and reciprocity the core of morality, whereas these philosophical problems are of minor importance to social-learning theory.

There is also a third orientation of research, the psychoanalytically oriented investigation focusing on the development of conscience, of superego, and its impact on behavior (see *Psychoanalytic Theory of Human Development*).

The main question to be addressed in the present article will be: how can developmental changes in moral judgment from early childhood and throughout the life span be described and interpreted?

Pioneering work in the investigation of moral judgments was conducted as early as 1894 by Earl Barnes and Margaret Schallenberger at Stanford University. Barnes studied the child's conception of justice, and Schallenberger presented the first theory of three developmental stages in moral reasoning. She was the first to describe moral realism, which later on became a fundamental concept of Piaget's theory of moral judgment. The meaning of moral realism is that acts are being judged by their results and not by the motives that gave rise to them.

The second phase of investigation in moral judgment was started by the publishing of Jean Piaget's classical study *The Moral Judgment of the Child* (1932), and the third phase was started by Lawrence Kohlberg's introduction of his theory of moral development in his doctoral thesis in 1958, which has dominated the research as well as the debate on moral education in home, school, and society.

1. Theories of Moral Development

1.1 Piaget's Theory

The Swiss psychologist Jean Piaget (1896–1980) (see *Basic Concepts and Applications of Piagetian Cognitive Development Theory*) has laid the foundation for understanding the developmental phases in the moral judgment of the child. The main areas of his experiments were: (a) how children look upon rules and laws; (b) how children judge bad acts and lies; (c) how children look upon punishment and justice. In each of these three areas he described a developmental sequence, which he built into his formulation of a theory of two stages in moral development.

Stage 1 is usually called heteronomous morality, moral realism, or morality of constraint. It is an intellectually immature morality, affected by a one-sided affectionate respect of adults. The heteronomous morality of the child is an expression of a generally immature structure, which is both egocentric and static. That it is egocentric means that the child lacks the ability to distinguish between aspects coming from his or her own self and aspects coming from the social situation, which results in an inability to take other people's viewpoints in social situations. As a consequence of the egocentricity, the child mingles subjective and objective aspects of experience. This leads to his or her view of moral rules as having real existence and being unchangeable absolutes rather than as flexible instruments for human purposes and values.

Stage 2 is usually called autonomous morality or morality in cooperation. With increasing intellectual capacity the child acquires independency in his or her moral judgments, he or she acquires the ability to take roles, and the submission under the authority of adults is changed into a mutual respect and equality in social cooperation. Morality is no longer based on rules decided by authorities which cannot be changed, but rules are regarded as a system expressing mutual rights and obligations for equals, a system with the purpose of making the social group function intact.

1.2 Kohlberg's Theory

In 1958 Lawrence Kohlberg advanced his theory of moral development, which marks a real breakthrough in research in this field. His theory has subsequently been submitted to successive revisions and enhancements, and it has dominated research and development on moral education as well as international debate. There are five basic postulates of this theory:

(a) the sequentiality postulate: Kohlberg's six stages of moral development form an invariant sequence or succession in individual development;

(b) the universality postulate: the invariant sequence of six stages of moral development is universal, that is, true in all countries and for both sexes;

(c) the structured-wholes postulate: stages of moral development form structured wholes;

(d) the role-taking postulate: stages of moral development represent qualitatively different role-taking abilities and social perspectives;

(e) the cognitive prerequisites postulate: Piaget's stages of operational thinking are necessary, but not sufficient for attainment of the corresponding stages of moral development.

From the beginning of the 1970s Kohlberg's six stages have been grouped into three levels: (a) premoral level, comprising stages 1 and 2; (b) conventional morality, including stages 3 and 4; and (c) principled morality, comprising stages 5 and 6. Each level is dominated by a characteristic social perspective.

The premoral level is basically egocentric. Moral judgments are made exclusively on the basis of consequences for the individual himself or herself. The child judges right/wrong or good/bad according to his or her experience of praise or blame.

The level of conventional morality is dominated by a sociocentric perspective. In moral judgments, consequences for the individual as well as for members of the group, family, and nation are taken into account. Expectations and purposes of the group are regarded as valuable without taking into account the immediate consequences for those not being members of the group. "Conformity" and "maintaining good order" are words of honor. The role of the individual in the group determines what is right or wrong. Social expectations and the security of social order and stability for family, group, and nation are the major aims.

At the level of principled morality, right and wrong are determined without reference to the individual himself or herself or the social situation. Ethical principles of democracy are regarded as universal as well as the principles of justice, reciprocity, and equality of human rights, and of respect for the dignity of human beings as individual persons.

The six stages of Kohlberg's theory are as follows:

(a) Stage 1: Heteronomous morality, or punishment and obedience orientation.

(b) Stage 2: Naively egoistic orientation, or individualism, instrumental purpose, and exchange.

(c) Stage 3: Mutual interpersonal expectations, relationships, and interpersonal conformity.

(d) Stage 4: Social systems and conscience, or the law-and-order orientation.

(e) Stage 5: Contractual legalistic orientation, or social-contract orientation.

(f) Stage 6: Universal ethical principles, or orientation toward the decisions of conscience and towards self-chosen ethical principles. (For a comprehensive review of the changing definitions of the stages of Kohlberg's theory, see Bergling 1981 pp. 26–42).

1.3 Hoffman's Theory

Martin L. Hoffman's theory focuses on the development of altruistic motivation. Developmentally, empathic distress comes first, and is very likely a conditioned affective response based on the similarity between distress cues for someone else in the immediate situation and one's own distress experiences in the past. Then follow three levels of sympathetic distress. First, when person permanence is acquired by the child for the first time, the child experiences a desire to help the other in his or her distress. At the second developmental level of sympathetic distress, the child has begun to acquire a sense of the others, not only as physical entities but also as a source of feelings and thoughts in their own right. The child now begins to make an active effort to put himself or herself in the other's place. At the third level of sympathetic distress, the child is no longer confined to the other's distress in immediate situations but aware of transitory, situation-specific distress as distinct from more permanent distress or deprivation. With increasing capacity of mental representation, the individual develops a sense of plight not only restricted to individuals but extending to entire groups or classes of people in need of help.

2. Methods of Research on Moral Development

Piagetian research on moral development has been dominated by use of problems contrasting damage and intent. Often two persons have been presented, one representing small damage and bad intent, the other representing large damage but good intent. Piaget's semiclinical interview technique as well as objective tests have been used in the Piagetian tradition of research.

Kohlberg invented a structured interview technique called Kohlberg's Moral Judgment Scales in which an introductory moral story, called a moral dilemma, is presented. These stories are developed from those of Piaget that contrast two moral behaviors, and constitute dilemmas characterized by conflicting moral aspects. Of fundamental importance to Kohlberg's method is that there is no consensus in society about how to solve the moral conflict presented. A total of 32 distinct moral aspects are coded in the evaluation of responses. The scoring technique has been revised several times, with the four dominating scoring methods being called "global story rating," "sentence scoring," "structural issue scoring," and "standard form scoring." An individual arithmetic mean of all ratings is called the moral maturity quotient of that individual. The reliability of Kohlberg's techniques varies between studies and methods, but ranges from $r = 0.70$ to $r = 0.94$. The validity of these techniques is still under debate. Correlations with other measures of moral maturity are low, but this does not necessarily mean that Kohlberg's techniques are less valid, but rather could reflect the high complexity of moral reasoning measured by his techniques.

Among objective tests of Kohlberg's moral reasoning, the Defining Issues Test, constructed by James Rest, is the most important as it allows large-scale surveys. The main difference between Rest's and Kohlberg's techniques is that Kohlberg measures spontaneously produced answers to complex moral dilemmas, whereas Rest presents a moral dilemma accompanied by a set of responses of which the individual has to rank his or her preferences among these responses. It has been shown that preference measures are constantly higher than spontaneously produced answers. Various scholars have recently produced objective tests for both the Piagetian and the Kohlbergian approaches to moral reasoning.

3. Research Findings

3.1 Developmental Sequence

As Piaget, Kohlberg, and other theorists in the field of moral development research describe a developmental sequence in terms of stages, criteria are needed to decide whether developmental stages are present or not. By definition stages are relatively stable and consequently produce definite patterns of behavior. Thus one criterion is that development in different moral dimensions describing the stage should reach similar levels, resulting in fairly high measurable correlations between the dimensions. Another possible criterion is that the change from one consequent pattern into another pattern described as the next stage might be confined to a certain age period.

After 50 years of research based on Piaget's theory of moral development, it can be concluded that moral development progresses from heteronomous morality to autonomous morality. However, such a development cannot be described as two distinct stages, but rather as one developmental dimension. Unfortunately, very few studies in the Piagetian tradition are truly longitudinal, and thus much too little is known about developmental changes in individuals.

Some major developmental dimensions in Piaget's work that have been verified and further extended are: (a) that with increasing age, the moral perspective of the child is shifting from looking upon rules as absolute and unchangeable into consciousness of varying viewpoints; (b) that with increasing age the child's conception of changeability of rules shifts from looking upon rules as unchangeable to seeing them as flexible; (c) that with increasing age the concept of justice shifts, from immanent justice to justice based on reality. (In his studies of the concept of justice, Piaget told a story of a boy who had stolen money. When soon afterwards this boy ran over an old wooden bridge, he fell into the water. Small children usually interpret the boy's falling in the water as punishment for the theft. Two occasions with nothing else in common than having occurred close to each other in time have thus been assigned a causal relationship by the child. Such a belief that there is an innate justice in things was called immanent justice by Piaget.); (d) that with increasing age the child's conception of responsibility changes from the objective (focusing on the consequences) into the subjective (focusing on intentions).

Twenty-five years of research on Kohlberg's theory of moral development can now be summarized based on a recent intense synthesis and reanalysis of accumulated published research (Bergling 1981). The most famous longitudinal study on moral development is Kohlberg's 20-year longitudinal investigation of 79 boys from working-class and middle-class families in Chicago, started in the mid 1950s and finally reported in 1975 (Kohlberg and Elfenbein 1975). In the final report the results of 30 men retested every three years from age 10 to 30, are presented. Of these 30, there are no regressors who fall back into lower stages of moral reasoning when compared to the previous testing. There is also a majority of progressors and a few remaining stable over three-year periods. The study shows a constant progress in children and adolescents and a plateau in adults. No single individual reached stage 6, and only one reached stage 5. In 1978 Kohlberg himself abandoned stage 6 as a separate developmental stage, and turned it into an alternative form of stage 5.

Another true longitudinal study conducted by D. Kuhn (1976), testing children of mean age 6 years 9 months over a one-year test–retest period, shows that children after one year are either staying stable or progressing to the next higher substage, and that there is no stage skipping at this age level. Other longitudinal studies, of adolescent boys and girls, show more progressive than regressive changes in moral development in the stages 1 to 4, whereas longitudinal studies on adults show equal probability of progression and regression.

3.2 Universality of Moral Development

Cross-cultural investigations of Piaget's theory of moral development have verified his findings on immanent justice in studies from Europe, Africa, and North America. But the cognitive developmental interpretation of the growth of the concept of justice has to be modified, as it has been shown that situational factors, cultural factors, and religious factors as well as mental illness can change the developmental sequence.

The development from moral realism (objective responsibility) to subjective responsibility has attracted most cross-cultural interest in the Piagetian research tradition on moral development. Numerous replications in various countries substantiate Piaget's findings, but it has also been shown that social circumstances can affect the development of responsibility.

The universality postulate of Kohlberg's theory, claiming that the invariant sequence of stages of moral development is universal (true across all countries and for both sexes) has to be rejected. It has been shown that the theory holds true for Western industrialized countries but studies from Nigeria, the Bahamas, and British Honduras show the influence of religious and other cultural factors. An interpretation of the accumulated evidence points to a combination of cognitive developmental and social-learning perspectives on moral development.

In the first major cross-national study of three Western European countries (Federal Republic of Germany, Italy, and the Netherlands), Bergling (1981) showed, using his Moral Development Scales, that over a three-year period from 10 to 14 years of age significant change in the expected direction was found in German and Dutch boys as well as in girls from all three countries, while the Italian boys remained stable over that period. There is need of large-scale cross-cultural surveys of moral development.

3.3 An Alternative View of Kohlberg's Theory

With discouraging evidence for the existence of the two highest stages of Kohlberg's theory as reviewed in the last two sections, a major revision of this theory is called for if the philosophically most important parts are not to be lost or discarded.

From the perspective of existential psychology, John C. Gibbs (1977, 1979) has analyzed the Kohlbergian literature and advanced an alternative model: Gibb's Two-phase Model. He makes a distinction between the naturalistic themes of the first four stages, describing the development of human spontaneous reflection and interpretation of how human life in general is functioning. As shown above, the successive development through these four naturalistic stages has been empirically demonstrated in childhood and adolescence in Western countries. As distinct from naturalistic themes, Gibbs argues that the two highest stages (stages 5 and 6 of Kohlberg's scheme) answer a fundamentally different type of question, namely the why and where in the

person's interpretation of his or her life situation. Gibbs calls these existential themes meta-ethical, as they are not primarily an attempt to answer questions on how human interaction is working but, on the contrary, they are an attempt to answer questions about the meaning and content of human existence. Thus, stages 5 and 6 of Kohlberg's scheme form phase 2 in Gibbs' model. Further, Gibbs takes another step, in accusing Kohlberg of mingling naturalistic and existential perspectives in all his six stages and in calling for pure definitions of naturalistic and existential themes.

The consequences for instructional planning, child rearing, and counseling of such a reformulation of Kohlberg's theory is profound. Gibbs suggests that acquisition of stage 2 is necessary but not sufficient for stage 5 thinking, and that the social perspective of stage 3 is necessary for the meta-ethical orientation in stage 6. In practice, this will imply that naturalistic and existential themes can be stimulated in parallel.

4. Implications for Child Rearing, Education, and Counseling

Kohlberg's theory has dominated the international debate on moral education over recent decades. His motives for introducing moral education in school are based on his contention that there is empirical support for the consequences of changes in moral reasoning for moral behavior in such areas as honesty, noncriminality, refusal to violate human rights, and activity for human rights. The real break-through on how to apply Kohlberg's theory in the classroom came in the 1975 curriculum work, with didactic experiments attracting great interest among educators.

For child rearing, education, and counseling, the finding of a fixed sequence of development in moral reasoning has been of the greatest importance. In issues of moral content, it has produced an awareness of a dynamic process. Three major aims of moral education have been advanced: (a) the facilitation of development as far as possible, even though not all will reach the highest stage; (b) the prevention of fixation at a lower stage—in the case of a certain individual who cannot be stimulated in the direction of the next stage, it is important to help him or her to remain flexible so that development can potentially occur later on; (c) the encouragement of both "horizontal" and "vertical" development, that is, not only to strive for new structures but also for full employment of present structures in new areas.

Bibliography

Bergling K 1981 *Moral Development: The Validity of Kohlberg's Theory.* Stockholm Studies in Educational Psychology, No. 23. Almqvist and Wiksell, Stockholm

Gibbs J C 1977 Kohlberg's stages of moral judgment: A constructive critique. *Harvard Educ. Rev.* 47: 43–61

Gibbs J C 1979 Kohlberg's moral stage theory: A Piagetian revision. *Hum. Dev.* 22: 89–112

Hoffman M L 1970 Moral development. In: Mussen P H (ed.) 1970 *Carmichael's Manual of Child Psychology*, Vol. 2. Wiley, New York, pp. 261–359

Hoffman M L 1975 Developmental synthesis of affect and cognition and its implications for altruistic motivation. *Dev. Psychol.* 11: 607–22

Kohlberg L 1969 Stage and sequence: The cognitive-developmental approach to socialization. In: Goslin D A (ed.) 1969 *Handbook of Socialization Theory and Research*. Rand McNally, Chicago, Illinois, pp. 347–480

Kohlberg L 1978 Revisions in the theory and practice of moral development. In: Damon W (ed.) 1978 *Moral Development. New Directions for Child Development*, Vol. 2. Jossey-Bass, San Francisco, California, pp. 83–88

Kohlberg L, Elfenbein D 1975 The development of moral judgments concerning capital punishment. *Am. J. Orthopsychiatry* 45: 614–40

Kuhn D 1976 Short-term longitudinal evidence for the sequentiality of Kohlberg's early stages of moral judgement. *Dev. Psychol.* 12: 162–66

Lickona T (ed.) 1976 *Moral Development and Behavior: Theory, Research, and Social Issues*. Holt, Rinehart and Winston, New York, pp. 1–401

Nisan M, Kohlberg L 1982 Universality and variation in moral development. A longitudinal and cross-sectional study in Turkey. *Child Dev.* 53: 865–76

Piaget J 1932 *The Moral Judgment of the Child*. Routledge and Kegan Paul, London

Prosocial Behavior

D. Bar-Tal

Prosocial behavior is a general category of positive forms of social behaviors which aim to benefit another person. These behaviors are expected to produce, to improve, or to maintain the physical and psychological well-being of the other person or persons. They are the antithesis of the negative forms of behaviors such as aggression, harm, destruction, or selfishness. Prosocial behavior encompasses such behaviors as helping, cooperation, exchange, or maintaining friendship. Psychologists have especially focused on the study of helping behavior. Thus, the present review will concentrate on this behavior.

Helping behavior is defined as an act which benefits others for which no external rewards were promised a priori, in return. Helping behavior includes sharing, giving, aiding, and comforting. Sharing is defined as giving up part of the object or objects in the individual's possession to another person; giving is giving up the whole object or all the objects in the individual's possession to another person; aiding is defined as alleviation of another's nonemotional needs through verbal or motor behavior; and comforting is defined as alleviation of emotional needs of another verbally or physically.

Thus, helping refers to an act with a goal from the helper's perspective to benefit another person and can result from numerous motives such as feelings of obligation, compliance with a request or threat, expectation of rewards, indebtedness, or compensation. The motives for helping behavior can be classified on the moral quality dimension. On this dimension, an altruistic motive is positioned on one end as the highest moral-level helping behavior. An altruistic act is defined as voluntary and intentional behavior carried out for its own end, to benefit a person, as a result of moral conviction in justice or caring for other's welfare, without expecting external rewards.

Although psychologists have been interested in the study of prosocial behavior for decades, only since the late 1960s has the study of helping behavior become one of the central areas of research in social and developmental psychology. Social zeitgeist, characterized by the preoccupation with improvement of life quality in the 1960s and early 1970s, as well as the pioneering studies of Leonard Berkowitz about socially responsible behavior of individuals towards others who were dependent upon them for their goal attainment (Berkowitz 1972) and of John Darley and Bibb Latané about bystanders' intervention in emergency situations (Latané and Darley 1970), directed psychologists' attention to the study of helping behavior.

1. Performance of Helping Behavior

1.1 Situational and Personality Variables

The majority of helping behavior studies have investigated the conditions under which specific situational and personal variables facilitate or inhibit helping acts. Among the situational variables most investigated have been types of verbal requests, prior helping, observation of helping behavior, observation of harm doing, presence of other people, ambiguity of the situation, size of the request, degree of the dependency of the person in need, characteristics of the person in need, cost involved in helping, a physical distance between the person in need and the potential helper, and similarity between the person in need and the potential helper. Among the most frequently investigated personal variables have been age, sex, race, socioeconomic status, birth order, social approval, mood, need for justice, level of moral development, self-esteem, locus of control, role-taking ability, guilt feelings, social responsibility, and empathy. In these studies, many situational conditions and personal tendencies that facilitate or inhibit prosocial behavior have been identified, but the interrelationship among their influences is still relatively unexplored. It has become obvious that prosocial behavior is multidetermined and the determinants do not relate in one way, but relate in different ways contingent on the specific situation and the specific personality tendencies.

It is not surprising, thus, that in addition to the focus on the isolated variables which affect helping behavior, few elaborated models have been proposed to explain how individuals decide to engage in helping behavior. These models usually have taken an interactionistic position by suggesting that helping behavior is determined by a combination of a personal tendency and situational influences.

1.2 Decision-making Models

Latané and Darley (1970) proposed a decision-making model of the helping process, specifically for the cases of emergency situations. Their model consists of five sequential decisions. First, the bystander has to notice that something is happening. Once the person is aware of the event, the event must be interpreted as emergency. If the person infers that there is an emergency, he must next decide whether it is his personal responsibility to act. Once the person decides to help, he must decide what form of assistance he can give. Finally, he must decide how to implement the decision to help. Out of the Latané and Darley (1970) work, a whole line of research has emerged which has focused on conditions which facilitate bystanders' intervention in emergency situations. With few exceptions, one finding was consistent across many studies, namely, that the likelihood that any given bystander would intervene in an emergency decreased, if other bystanders are, or are believed to be, also available to act (Latané and Nida 1981). This phenomenon has been called "diffusion of responsibility." That is, while the presence of one bystander focuses all the responsibility on this one person, the presence of several bystanders diffuses the responsibility among all the present people.

Piliavin, Davidio, Gaertner, and Clark (1981), also dealing with emergency situations, suggested that observation of this situation elicits a state of physiological arousal in the bystander. Helping behavior may reduce this aversive arousal, but whether an individual decides to help depends on the calculation of costs and rewards involved in helping and not helping.

Bar-Tal (1976) suggested a model which extends the cost–reward calculation and adds the consideration of attribution of responsibility—the decision why the other person is in need. In addition, four types of variables were suggested by Bar-Tal to affect this judgmental process: personal, situational, cultural, and variables related to the characteristics of the person in need.

Recently, Staub (1978) proposed a model which specifies the manner in which situational and personality factors jointly affect helping behavior. According to Staub, helping behavior occurs as a function of personal goals (motives); however, the activation of the behavior depends on the importance of the goal relative to other goals, and on the characteristics of the situation.

Schwartz and Howard (1981) presented a five-step sequential model which involves: (a) the perception of someone in need, as well as identification of potential helpful actions and recognition of one's own ability to engage in these actions; (b) generation of feelings of moral obligation; (c) assessment of the costs and benefits of potential actions; (d) evaluation and reassessment of potential responses; and (e) selection of an action. In general, the model illustrates the specific steps which occur in the decision-making process by taking into account the effect of the specific situational conditions and personal variables that influence the perception, interpretation, and defensive redefinition of a situation that calls for helping responses.

1.3 Mediating Variables

In an attempt to elucidate specific mechanisms which foster the performance of helping behavior, psychologists have suggested a number of emotional-motivational variables which mediate helping acts. In this vein, a study of empathy received special attention, since a number of psychologists suggested that empathy is a necessary condition for the performance of altruistic behavior. Empathy defined as affective response to someone else's situation rather than one's own, is aroused by another's misfortune and motivates the person to perform altruistic acts to reduce the other's distress (e.g., Batson and Coke 1981, Hoffman 1981). In situations in which individuals help to compensate for a previous harm done, a feeling of guilt is suggested as a mediating emotion which motivates performance of the helping act (Hoffman 1984). Guilt defined as unpleasant feeling when one deviates from one's own values is experienced in situations of harm doing and transgression. To reduce the guilt feelings, individuals engage in helping behavior to undo their previous behavior and to punish themselves.

Another attempt to account for helping behavior was made by Walster, Walster, and Berscheid (1978) who proposed an equity motive as mediating helping behavior. According to this conceptualization, individuals in any interpersonal interaction compare their own and their partner's relative gains as a consequence of the relationship. If a person discovers that his relative gains are larger than those of his partner (inequitable relationships), he will experience distress which will motivate him to reduce it by engaging in helping behavior. The performance of helping behavior may increase the relative gains of the other person, thus changing the relationship to equitable. A similar concept was proposed by Lerner (1977) who postulated that individuals have a justice motive which serves as the basis for the person's motivation to see that others get what they deserve. People help others in need whenever they believe that the others do not deserve their fate. Also, a motivational state of indebtedness was proposed to account for those situations in which individuals reciprocate a help received previously (Greenberg 1980). Recently, Reykowski (1984) has proposed a cognitive-mediating mechanism which affects helping behavior and has suggested that helping behavior is related to the cognitive organization of the concept of self and others. According to Reykowski, altruistic behavior can occur when a person is able to suppress self-centered reactions and represent a dissimilar person in his own cognitive network.

1.4 Maintenance of Helping Behavior

Two approaches have been suggested to account for the maintenance of helping behavior. The first approach, the exchange approach, proposes that helping behavior is guided, as are all the other acts, by the principle of maximizing rewards and minimizing costs in order to obtain the most profitable outcome in interpersonal interaction. Helping behavior is considered to be instrumental in receiving rewards which can take materialistic, social, or even self-reinforcement form (Blau 1964). The second approach, the normative approach, suggests that prosocial behavior is regulated by societal norms. Thus, according to this approach, individuals help because they conform to norms which prescribe helping. They follow the prescription of prosocial norms not only because of external pressure, but also because they internalize the norms. Three norms were most frequently cited: the norm of social responsibility which prescribes helping dependent others (Berkowitz 1972); the norm of giving which prescribes helping for its own value (Leeds 1963); and the norm of reciprocity, which prescribes that individuals should help those who have helped them (Gouldner 1960).

2. Development of Helping Behavior

2.1 Theories

Four major approaches have attempted to explain the development of helping behavior, especially of high moral quality: evolutionary, psychoanalytic, social learning, and cognitive development.

The evolutionary approach looks for the biological and social conditions that may facilitate the development of altruistic behavior. Two views are presented in this approach. The first assumes that altruistic behavior has been developed through sociobiological evolution, that is, through the selective accumulation of behavior as a result of social conditions, via a transmission in the genes. This view holds that altruistic behavior is functional for human survival and therefore genes for altruistic behavior were favored and were multiplied in the population. The second view postulates that altruistic behavior has been developed through sociocultural evolution, that is, through selective accumulation of behavior retained via purely social modes of transmission. This view holds that human beings are innately selfish, but social evolution through cultural indoctrination has countered the individual's selfish tendencies to promote altruistic behavior which has a survival value for a group or a society.

The psychoanalytic approach emphasizes the enduring effects of early experiences, especially the experiences of the child with his parents, as determinants of development of prosocial behavior. According to the psychoanalytic approach, human beings are born selfish, but through the process of identification with the parents, the child becomes able to control the impulses and behave altruistically. The experiences are subjectively interpreted, and the prosocial behavior often reflects the unconscious motives of the individual.

The social learning approach suggests that helping behavior is learned, as other behaviors, via interaction with the social environment. This approach emphasizes mainly reinforcement and modeling, but induction and role playing also serve as conditions which foster the acquisition of helping behavior.

The cognitive developmental approach stresses the qualitative changes resulting from cognitive, social perspective, and moral development as necessary conditions for the development of high-quality prosocial helping behavior. This approach focuses on the individual's motivations for helping behavior as reflecting the quality of the act. It posits that the altruistic behavior, as the highest quality helping behavior, is a developmental achievement.

Recently, an integration of the two latter approaches was proposed within a cognitive learning framework. This approach, while recognizing the influences of the cognitive, social perspective, and moral judgment development on helping behavior development, also emphasizes the development of a self-regulatory system as a determinant of the development of altruistic behavior. According to this approach, it is the self-regulatory system that produces self-control, the ability to perform sacrificing behavior without expecting external rewards.

2.2 Research

Only the social learning and cognitive developmental approaches have generated empirical studies which have investigated hypotheses derived from these two approaches (Eisenberg-Berg 1982). On the basis of the social learning approach, researchers have shown how children acquire helping behavior through classical conditioning, which involves empathic conditioning procedures of a helper's positive affect to the recipient's positive reactions to the helping act. The researchers have also shown that children acquire helping behavior as a result of being reinforced with material or social rewards. In addition, evidence has indicated that vicarious rewards also play an important role in learning helping behavior. Through external and vicarious rewards, the child acquires the capability of self-rewarding for helping acts.

Other directions of research have shown that children who have observed a helping model can learn what is appropriate to do and how it is possible to carry out the helping act. Later, the model reminds the children that the helping behavior is the desirable one and strengthens the already existing disposition to carry out helping acts. Besides reinforcing and modeling helping behavior, socializing agents also spend much of their time preaching and giving instructions. According to the results of several experiments, although preaching and instruction do increase the performance of helping behavior, their effect is smaller than that of either the observation of a model or reinforcement.

A cognitive developmental approach has instigated numerous studies whose results have served as empirical support of this approach. Thus, several researchers have found that the frequency and quantity of helping behavior increases with age during the first 10 years of life. Several studies have found that helping behavior is positively related to the level of development of cognition, social perspective, and moral judgment. Also, studies have investigated the relationship between the expressed motives for helping behavior and the quantity of helping behavior. The findings indicated that the higher the moral level of the motives the children expressed, the more helping behavior they exhibited. Finally, findings showed that as children grow older the quality of their helping acts changes. That is, the older the children, the greater the extent of imitation of prosocial behavior without any promise of external reward. Conversely, the younger the children, the more they helped under the conditions of request and/or a promise of reward in return.

In view of the evidence that the social environment influences the development of helping behaviors, researchers have attempted to identify child-rearing practices which facilitate the development of helping behavior. Studies have shown that children's consideration for others tends to develop under the following conditions: when parents provide them with affection; when they use an inductive disciplinary technique which emphasizes the consequences of the child's behavior and is oriented towards the needs of others; when parents emphasize what the children ought to do and not only what they should not do; when the parents serve themselves as models performing prosocial acts; and when parents encourage autonomous behavior and demand high standards of social behavior stressing self-control.

3. Helping Behavior and Schools

Although helping behavior is a social interaction which enables humans to overcome their physical and biological limitation in order to function more effectively in society, relatively little has been done with regard to teaching helping behavior in educational settings. Helping behavior can be encouraged either through direct teaching, as social learning theory advocates, or through facilitation of a cognitive social perspective, and moral development as suggested by cognitive developmental theory. With regard to the first direction, studies which have used a reinforcement method, attribution of prosocial characteristics to children, reasoning as a punishment, moral exhortation, direct instruction, or modeling have shown helping behavior can be trained (Grusec 1982). Few studies have been done to examine

the facilitation of helping behavior development from the cognitive developmental perspective. The few studies that have been performed show that by increasing empathic or role-taking skills, children also enhance their capability to perform helping acts (Bar-Tal and Raviv 1982, Staub 1981).

Of special interest are the recent attempts to organize classroom instruction in a way that supports the development of helping behavior among students. For example, small-group teaching projects in Israel that emphasize cooperative efforts in learning have been found to promote the performance of helping behavior (Hertz–Lazarowitz and Sharan 1984). Also, the tendency to use peer-tutoring procedures in work with underachieving students demonstrates the growing awareness among educators of ways to encourage the use of helping behavior in educational settings (Allen 1976).

Bibliography

Allen V L (ed.) 1976 *Children as Teachers: Theory and Research on Tutoring.* Academic Press, New York

Bar-Tal D 1976 *Prosocial Behavior: Theory and Research.* Halsted Press, New York

Bar-Tal D, Raviv A 1982 A cognitive-learning model of helping behavior development: Possible implications and applications. In: Eisenberg-Berg N (ed.) 1982 *Development of Prosocial Behavior.* Academic Press, New York, pp. 199–218

Batson C D, Coke J S 1981 Empathy: A source of altruistic motivation for helping. In: Rushton J P, Sorrentino R M (eds.) 1981 *Altruism and Helping Behavior.* Erlbaum, Hillsdale, New Jersey, pp. 167–87

Berkowitz L 1972 Social norms, feeling, and other factors affecting helping behavior and altruism. In: Berkowitz L (ed.) 1972 *Advances in Experimental Social Psychology*, Vol. 6. Academic Press, New York, pp. 63–108

Blau P M 1964 *Exchange and Power in Social Life.* Wiley, New York

Derlega V J, Grzelak J (eds.) 1981 *Cooperation and Helping Behavior: Theories and Research.* Academic Press, New York

Eisenberg-Berg N (ed.) 1982 *Development of Prosocial Behavior.* Academic Press, New York

Gouldner A W 1960 The norm of reciprocity: A preliminary statement. *Sociol. Rev.* 25: 161–78

Greenberg M S 1980 A theory of indebtedness. In: Gergen K J, Greenberg M S, Willis R H (eds.) 1980 *Social Exchange: Advances in Theory and Research.* Plenum, New York, pp. 3–26

Grusec J E 1982 The socialization of altruism. In: Eisenberg-Berg N (ed.) 1982 *Development of Prosocial Behavior.* Academic Press, New York, pp. 139–66

Hertz-Lazarowitz R, Sharan S 1984 Enhancing prosocial behavior through small-group teaching in schools. In: Staub E, Bar-Tal D, Karylowski J, Reykowski J (eds.) 1984 pp. 423–43

Hoffman M L 1981 Is altruism part of human nature? *J. Pers. Soc. Psychol.* 40: 121–37

Hoffman M L 1984 Parent discipline, moral internalization, and development of prosocial motivation. In: Staub E, Bar-Tal D, Karylowski J, Reykowski J (eds.) 1984 pp. 117–37

Latané B, Darley J M 1970 *The Unresponsive Bystander: Why Doesn't He Help?* Appleton-Century-Crofts, New York

Latané B, Nida S 1981 Ten years of research on group size and helping. *Psychol. Bull.* 89: 308–24

Leeds R 1963 Altruism and the norm of giving. *Merrill-Palmer Q.* 9: 229–40

Lerner N J 1977 The justice motive: Some hypotheses as to its origins and forms. *J. Pers.* 45: 1–52

Mussen P H, Eisenberg-Berg N 1977 *Roots of Caring, Sharing, and Helping: The Development of Prosocial Behavior in Children.* Freeman, San Francisco, California

Piliavin J A, Davidio J F, Gaertner S L, Clark RD III 1981 *Emergency Intervention.* Academic Press, New York

Reykowski J 1984 Spatial organization of a cognitive system and prosocial behavior. In: Staub E, Bar-Tal D, Karylowski J, Reykowski J (eds.) 1984 *Development and Maintenance of Prosocial Behavior: International Perspectives.* Plenum, New York, pp. 51–74

Rushton J P 1980 *Altruism, Socialization, and Society.* Prentice-Hall, Englewood Cliffs, New Jersey

Rushton J P, Sorrentino R M (eds.) 1981 *Altruism and Helping Behavior.* Erlbaum, Hillsdale, New Jersey

Schwartz S H, Howard J 1981 A normative decision-making model of altruism. In: Rushton J P, Sorrentino R M (eds.) 1981 *Altruism and Helping Behavior.* Erlbaum, Hillsdale, New Jersey

Smithson M, Amato P R, Pearce P 1983 *Dimensions of Helping Behaviour.* Pergamon, Oxford

Staub E 1978 *Positive Social Behavior and Morality: Social and Personal Influences*, Vol. 1. Academic Press, New York

Staub E 1979 *Positive Social Behavior and Morality: Socialization and Development*, Vol. 2. Academic Press, New York

Staub E 1981 Promoting positive behavior in schools, in other educational settings, and in the home. In: Rushton J P, Sorrentino R N (eds.) 1981 *Altruism and Helping Behavior.* Erlbaum, Hillsdale, New Jersey

Staub E, Bar-Tal D, Karylowski J, Reykowski J (eds.) 1984 *Development and Maintenance of Prosocial Behavior: International Perspectives.* Plenum, New York

Walster E, Walster G W, Berscheid E 1978 *Equity: Theory and Research.* Allyn and Bacon, Boston, Massachusetts

Wispé L (ed.) 1978 *Altruism, Sympathy, and Helping: Psychological and Social Principles.* Academic Press, New York

Aggression and Development

T. Tieger

Since the early 1960s, psychologists have generated an enormous wealth of research on the determinants of aggressive behavior in humans. This article reviews various theoretical approaches in the field and describes their implications for efforts to reduce aggressive behavior. While many absorbing theoretical questions remain, it will be seen that the social learning theory of aggression has generated a substantial empirical basis for strategies of control of individual aggressive behavior, as well as prevention of aggression in the society at large. It may now be possible to plan a cultural curriculum to control the destructive capacity of the human species, although this will not be an easy task.

1. Theories of the Development of Aggression

The earliest significant theoretical approach to the study of aggression emerged within the Freudian psychoanalytic school. In the later period of his life, Freud came to view aggression as a manifestation of the death instinct: thanatos. Instinctual impulses seeking destructive expression were viewed as important determinants of the psychic balance of power in the human unconscious (Freud 1933). Freud felt that society could not thwart aggressive impulses entirely, but could only channel their expression in more acceptable directions. This pessimistic view of human nature generated heated debate among psychoanalysts and split Freud's followers. Yet, the psychodynamic theory has had little impact on contemporary research on aggression.

In the United States, a significant effort was made to expand and rewrite Freudian ideas of instinctual aggression in terms acceptable to the prevailing learning theory. Dollard and his colleagues (1939) theorized that aggression was caused by the build up of frustration within the individual. According to this theory, frustration experiences generated a drive state whose principal means of expression was aggressive behavior. The frustration–aggression hypothesis continues to generate research on the physiological substrate of aggressive behavior and the hypothesized cathartic effect of aggression. However, most researchers now feel that frustration is neither necessary nor sufficient as a causal explanation of aggressive behavior (Bandura 1973).

More recently, another instinct theory of aggression was presented from an ethological perspective by Lorenz (1966). From his observations of animal behavior, Lorenz concluded that aggression was an instinctual pattern that served well in attaining needed resources such as access to a mate or food. According to this theory, selective pressures during evolution have thus conferred an advantage to successfully aggressive individuals. Apart from fueling a new cycle of popular views of "man the beast," the impact of the ethological perspective in contemporary research on human aggression is harder to discern. However, one positive effect has been that an important evolutionary perspective has been brought to studies of the development of aggression.

By far the greatest stimulus to the growth of research on aggression since the early 1960s has been the development of a social learning theory approach to the issue (Bandura 1973). Social learning theory views aggression as a learned behavior subject to the "laws of learning." Within this framework, the development of aggression is viewed as a series of learning experiences in the life

431

history of the individual. The social learning theory differs from more mechanistic classical, or operant learning approaches by distinguishing between the acquisition and the performance of aggressive behavior. The acquisition of behavior involves the full range of information processing and integrative capacities of the individual while the performance of a given behavior sequence is viewed as depending on the more immediate contingencies of reinforcement present in the environment.

According to this theory, individuals confront a range of experiences in their development that shape their future likelihood of responding aggressively. For example, a child may gain access to a favorite toy after aggressively hitting another child. Enjoyment of the toy will reinforce the aggressive behavior. Direct learning experiences such as this certainly increase the probability of future aggression. Social learning theory also suggests that these experiences become integrated in the development of abilities, attitudes, expectations, and information-processing styles that, in turn, influence the likelihood of later aggressive behavior. For instance, it has been shown that aggressive children seek out games and play activities that involve a higher likelihood of producing aggression. In this and in other ways, the individual is an active agent in the learning processes that underlie the development of aggression.

Aggression can be fostered in ways other than direct reinforcement of individual behavior. Social learning theory recognizes that humans learn new aggressive skills by observation alone. Observation also teaches expectations about the likely outcomes of aggressive behaviors. Thus, without ever engaging directly in violent and hurtful behavior, a young child can observe others who do so and learn the probable consequences of the actions. In these ways, observation of aggression reliably increases the likelihood of aggression in observers' later behavior.

Since the social learning theory approach views aggression as a learned set of behaviors, the process of reducing aggressive behavior in individuals, or in the society at large, entails changing the factors that influence its development. The social learning approach is thus inherently "optimistic" in suggesting distinct educational practices for treatment and prevention of antisocial behavior. It is this optimistic facet of the approach that justifies its importance for educators and social planners. That is, regardless of how the final causes of aggression are viewed in psychodynamic or phylogenetic terms, educators still need to know how to address the learned, and therefore modifiable, component of aggressive behavior.

2. Reducing Aggression: Some Research Findings

The social learning approach suggests remedies for aggression in the alteration of environmental factors that cause the behavior. Within this framework, the change effort can be focused on individuals, groups, or on the society at large.

2.1 Reducing Aggression in Individual Behavior

Patterns of aggression in individual behavior can be altered by careful application of learning principles derived from extensive research in the context of the family and the classroom (Patterson et al. 1975). The first step in a change plan involves careful observation of the environment in which aggressive behavior naturally occurs. This observational step allows the teacher, parent, researcher, or policy maker to determine the factors instigating aggressive behavior, and the patterns of reinforcement that maintain it. Change involves an intervention to suppress the more immediate patterns of injurious behavior. Often, a "time-out" procedure is used to deter the possibility for any special attention or reward for aggressive behavior. With time-out, individuals are removed from the classroom or play activity when they exhibit unacceptable antisocial behavior (Wilson et al. 1979). Several studies have shown that time-out procedures are more effective than punishment in reducing aggression. As the family or classroom environment becomes more manageable, an effort is made to alter existing patterns of reinforcement for aggression. Specifically, the change agent (i.e., parent, teacher, or researcher) tries to shift observed patterns of attention or indirect reward for aggression to a focus on positive reward for socially desirable behavior.

Many studies have found that aggressive individuals are deficient in cognitive and social development. Thus, compensatory training in language and prosocial assertiveness skills is often a component of the intervention. Deficits in areas of interpersonal skills contribute to aggressive behavior to the extent that successful experiences with aggression have effectively supplanted the learning and use of prosocial means of attaining goals. Aggressive individuals tend to benefit from learning simple and effective means of attaining goals without resorting to antisocial tactics.

2.2 Reducing Aggression in the Society at Large

Beyond these strategies for treatment of aggressive individuals, there is a greater possibility for preventing aggression within the larger context of normal social development. The principles of learning that underlie modification of problematic antisocial behavior in individuals also inform the attempt to create socially desirable patterns of behavior in society in the first instance.

One area of particular interest to researchers in recent years has been the effect of televised violence on the behavior of viewers. Television provides a rich source of vivid information about aggressive behavior, according to analyses of television program content conducted over the last decade in the United States. Televised aggression appears as a frequent, highly visible, and highly rewarded behavior. In the opinion of most researchers, the pattern of research findings suggests that violent televised material increases aggressive behavior among viewers (Comstock et al. 1978). Clearly, then, one aspect of an effort to reduce aggression in the society at large would be reduction of televised aggression, and a greater effort to integrate television as a prosocial educational vehicle.

A second recommendation emerges from research on sex differences in aggression. While theorists dispute a possible biological basis for greater aggression among males (Tieger 1980), there is clear recognition that sex differences in aggression contribute to and are affected by traditional sex-role stereotyping. In the normal course of events, boys are sanctioned in the development of aggressive skills by cultural expectations for masculine behavior. Girls, on the other hand, are taught a range of nonaggressive cooperative and nurturant skills in preparation for expected adult mothering roles. At least one researcher (Eron 1980) has suggested that boys should be encouraged to learn emotional sensitivity, cooperation, and nurturance as a form of skills training to reduce tendencies towards aggression. One way to achieve this goal is suggested by anthropological observations of sex-role development in diverse cultures. Cultures with different expectations for work roles for young boys and girls seem to generate different patterns of sex typing of aggression. Specifically, when boys are given child-rearing responsibilities (not the typical pattern), they tend to be less aggressive (Whiting and Edwards 1973). One obvious suggestion then, in light of this finding, is to give boys greater child-care responsibilities within the family.

Research also suggests that segregation of play groups and activities by sex of child exacerbates the sex typing of aggression. All-male play groups generate higher levels of aggressive behavior than all-female or mixed-sex groups. Thus, within the family and preschool settings, efforts should be made to structure play activities to encourage mixed-sex interactions wherever possible. These and other findings suggest that a contribution can be made to the reduction of aggressiveness by reducing polarized patterns of early sex-role socialization. Since the connection between masculinity and

aggressiveness is learned by children as early as age 3, attempts to intervene in this learning process must also occur early in development.

While research on the development of aggression has generated some tangible results for immediate application by educators and parents, the larger issue of preventing aggression in the society at large involves many practical and political difficulties. Pervasive problems such as aggression will not be whisked away with simple solutions. However, changes in educational practices such as those described above may begin to alter the conditions that encourage the development of aggression.

Bibliography

Bandura A 1973 *Aggression: A Social Learning Analysis*. Prentice-Hall, Englewood Cliffs, New Jersey

Bandura A 1977 *Social Learning Theory*. Prentice-Hall, Englewood Cliffs, New Jersey

Comstock G A, Chaffee S, Katzman N, McCombs M, Roberts D 1978 *Television and Human Behavior*. Columbia University Press, New York

Dollard J, Doob L W, Miller N E, Mowrer O H, Sears R R 1939 *Frustration and Aggression*. Yale University Press, New Haven, Connecticut

Eron L D 1980 Prescription for reduction of aggression. *Am. Psychol.* 35: 244–52

Freud S 1933 *New Introductory Lectures on Psycho-analysis*. Norton, New York

Lorenz K 1966 *On Aggression*. Harcourt, Brace and World, New York

Patterson G R, Reid J B, Jones R R, Conger R E 1975 *A Social Learning Approach to Family Intervention*. Castalia, Eugene, Oregon

Tieger T 1980 On the biological basis of sex differences in aggression. *Child Dev.* 51: 943–63

Whiting B, Edwards C P 1973 Cross-cultural analysis of sex differences in the behavior of children aged 3 through 11. *J. Soc. Psychol.* 91: 171–88

Wilson C C, Robertson S J, Herlong L H, Haynes S N 1979 Vicarious effects of time-out in the modification of aggression in the classroom. *Behav. Modification* 3: 97–111

Delinquency

S. Mitchell

Delinquency may be defined as law-breaking behaviour on the part of those who, by virtue of their youth, are not yet seen as being fully responsible for their actions. The range of behaviour covered is often wide, including not only infractions of the criminal laws, which would apply equally to adults, but also failure to comply with rules pertaining specifically to them as nonadults. Because of the special position of children and adolescents, processing of delinquents is often strongly influenced by considerations of the child's welfare as well as justice. This further blurs the boundaries of "delinquency" in terms of a child's acts and introduces

the notion of the child's needs in terms of assistance toward a nondelinquent future.

Despite the many papers which have been written about delinquents and delinquency, however, surprisingly little is known about it, its causes, and its prevention. One reason for this may lie in the extent to which attention has been concentrated on the attributes and activities of "officially recognized" offenders. The recognition that such people constitute only a small proportion of those actually committing delinquent acts has led to considerable speculation and controversy as to how far the "official" delinquents can be seen as representing the others. Such doubts have considerable methodological, theoretical, and practical implications and, in this article, some of the key issues are briefly discussed. For a more thorough coverage readers should consult specialist publications such as Gibbons' (1981) comprehensive survey; references covering specific aspects may be obtained by consulting abstracting journals.

1. Problems of Measuring Delinquency

Since the early 1950s juvenile delinquency has been presented as an increasing problem by the media in most parts of the world, and this picture is apparently supported by the official statistics. It is necessary, however, to proceed with extreme caution in trying to make assessments of changes in the incidence of delinquency over time in the same country, let alone comparisons between countries. Even within a single country, a change in policy with respect to lawbreakers (or certain categories of them) might lead to an apparent rise or fall in the delinquency rate without any real change in the extent to which the relevant behaviour was occurring. The introduction of police warnings as an alternative to juvenile court proceedings (as happened in England in 1969) might, for example, reduce the number of juveniles appearing in court for minor offences. Conversely, a drive by authority against, say, truancy, could increase numbers of truants appearing in court without any accompanying increase in numbers actually truanting.

The figures that appear in official statistics reflect not only what young people are doing but also the legal provisions in force, the activity of law enforcement agencies, and the organization of the juvenile justice system. This makes it extremely difficult to compare the situation in different countries. Not only does the actual coverage, in terms of acts prohibited, differ from country to country (so that the Netherlands, for example, takes a much more lenient view of soft-drug use than most of her European neighbours), but so does the age range of offenders who are seen as juveniles. Thus, in Europe alone, the minimum age for processing as a juvenile delinquent and, hence, inclusion in the statistics, varies from 7 in Greece to 10 in France and England, 14 in Switzerland and the Federal Republic of Germany, and 15 in Finland and Sweden (most Swedes under 18 appear to be dealt with by child welfare boards rather than the courts).

Differences in law enforcement also assume considerable importance when comparing highly policed areas with those in which social control is mainly in the hands of family or community. In many countries this means that formal methods of processing juvenile delinquency—and hence the figures shown in the statistics—relate only, or mainly, to urban environments.

A major problem in basing a picture of delinquency in any area purely on official statistics is that one has no way of assessing how far these statistics reflect the actual amount of delinquency which is occurring. Self-report studies, where they have been carried out, indicate that official delinquents form only the tip of a much larger iceberg (see Hood and Sparks 1970 for a summary of relevant research in 1950s and 1960s) and that substantial proportions of "normal" adolescents admit to participation in illegal activities, such as theft. Moreover, all these studies agree that the vast majority of those making such admissions have remained undetected by the police. Nor does this picture hold only for the United States (where most studies were carried out): it has also been found in other parts of the Western world, including the United Kingdom and Scandinavia, and is probably worldwide.

2. Types of Delinquency

To speak of juvenile delinquency as a single entity is misleading. The range of behaviour covered can range from murder to defying one's parents, from armed robbery to petty pilfering. Most instances of delinquency, however, seem to fall into four main categories: theft, violence towards property, contravention of status laws (truanting, drinking) and behaviour, in groups, which has a high nuisance value for fellow citizens and which may appear menacing because of the noise and physical activity involved. The idea of violence towards other people as a major aspect of juvenile delinquency appears to owe more to the high publicity given to such happenings in the media than it does to the frequency with which they actually occur (Cohen 1980). The evidence of enquiries both by police and social scientists into football violence in the United Kindgom, for example, has indicated that, in the main, it is limited to remarks and gestures with remarkably little bloodshed. Furthermore, the increase in violent crime attributed to "young people" throughout Western Europe in recent years appears to relate much more to young adults, aged 17 to 21, than to juveniles.

The main cause of court appearances in younger age groups is undoubtedly theft. In Western Europe this accounts for 60–70 percent of officially recognized juvenile crime (European Committee on Crime Problems 1979) and in Japan 77 percent. The involvement of young people in thefts that do not result in a court appearance is even greater. Stealing from shops is widespread among children and adolescents in many countries, including Japan and the United Kingdom (where 70 percent of 13- to 16-year-old "nondelinquent" boys in a recent survey admitted to this). Evidence from self-report surveys and from the shop staff also indicates that girls are equally involved. In highly industrialized countries such escapades appear to be related to a search for "kicks" rather than material gain, and the same is true of the (usually temporary) removal of motor vehicles.

Most juvenile delinquency appears to occur in public places—on the street, in shops, sports stadiums, dance halls—but this may merely reflect the tendency for such public behaviour to come to official and media attention. There is little information available about antisocial or illegal behaviour carried out by children in their own homes, for example, so that while self-report studies have indicated that stealing within the home is not uncommon, parents seldom see this as delinquency and very rarely report it to the police. The extent of violence shown by young people within the home has been considered only in Japan where it has been identified as becoming a problem (Kazuhiko 1981), particularly in middle-class, education-oriented homes where the pressures to succeed in the highly competitive school system are extreme.

The issue of violence within schools is one which has had more publicity recently in various countries, including the United States, France, Japan, and the United Kingdom. Again, however, this is an area where it is difficult to assess the actual situation in any country or any school, as vandalism and physical violence towards teachers may be seen as matters to be dealt with by internal means (e.g., excluding the pupil from the school) rather than by referral to the police. Most of the evidence available is therefore impressionistic. The Safe School Study carried out in the 1970s by the United States Department of Health, Education and Welfare did, however, supply some factual data. This suggested that the problem was declining after reaching its peak in the 1960s and that, while vandalism was highest in suburban schools, interpersonal violence was concentrated in secondary schools in large cities. In those schools, however, the extent of violence, in terms of attacks on teachers, was considerable, with 1.8 percent of teachers reporting that pupils had made a physical attack on them within the period of one month and 1.3 percent that they had been robbed with force or threats (Rubel 1978).

3. Attributes of Delinquents

The picture emerging from the official statistics (and again this is found worldwide) is that the typical delinquent is male, comes from a low socioeconomic background and is resident in a materially, or socially deprived district in an urban area, usually a large city.

The data obtained from self-report studies, however, often show a different picture. Thus, while most self-report studies have tended to accept the nondelinquency of girls as given and, therefore, limit their coverage to "normal" boys, those that have included girls have found that the gap has been reduced considerably. Not only do the girls confess to more law-breaking behaviour than is indicated by their marked underrepresentation in official figures, it has also been found that both boys and girls show similar patterns of delinquency. The often accepted picture of girls as predominantly involved in sex offences and not in theft or vandalism was not supported.

The long-accepted link between juvenile delinquency and low socioeconomic status has also been challenged.

Self-report studies have raised the important issue of middle-class delinquency and why, when differences have ceased to exist in some self-report studies, the official figures should still show such a marked relationship. This has stimulated sociological speculation, and empirical studies have been made into the phenomenon of bias in the processing of deviants. An alternative explanation, however, is that the delinquencies exposed in the general population are qualitatively different from those of official delinquents in terms of type of act and of frequency of participation (Hindelang et al. 1979). Many investigations have tried to map the attributes of delinquents more closely by looking within a social class or areal group and comparing the attributes of youths who had an officially recorded conviction with those that had none. Such studies have revealed that the official delinquent tends to suffer from a multiplicity of adverse factors. He (because such studies have concentrated on boys) is more likely to live in poor housing, to come from a family whose income is low and which relies on support from social agencies; his father is likely to be in unskilled manual work and to work erratically; his parents and/or siblings are more likely to have criminal records; marital disharmony is more likely, as is separation from one or both parents; discipline in the home is seen as unsatisfactory, inconsistent, too harsh, or too lax; and the parents themselves may suffer from mental or physical handicaps. Relationships between the delinquent and his parents may also be worse with less warmth and more rejection on both sides. At school, his measured intelligence is likely to be lower, as is his attainment level both in primary and secondary schools; he is more likely to be seen as troublesome by his teachers and his classmates. In temperament he is more likely to be impulsive and active, to like excitement and competition; to be more extrovert and/or neurotic; to plan less for the future and to have less realistic goals; and to have a different self-image. This is by no means a comprehensive list but details the relationships which have been found most often or most strongly established. The picture is a depressing one, showing the delinquent boy as subject to multiple problems. Girl delinquents are no more fortunate since, in addition to familial and educational problems, the few studies devoted to them have tended to emphasize their lack of feminine qualities. Such findings are, however, based on studies of officially processed delinquents. It is not known whether the attributes relate to the tendency to break the law or to an increased likelihood of being perceived by others as a lawbreaker. The difference becomes crucial when we try to use such descriptive data to explain delinquency.

4. The Search for Causes

Much of the work which has been published on juvenile delinquency has concerned itself with causes—either the causes of delinquent acts ("What makes these people break the law?") or the determinants of official delinquency statistics ("What makes certain categories of people more likely to be arrested and tried?"). These two approaches should not be confused as they involve very different ideological perspectives. Those who are looking for the causes of delinquent behaviour concentrate on the social background and personal characteristics of the offender, taking the law-enforcement process as given. In other words, once the youngster has committed a delinquent act, the forces of law and order are seen as coming into operation with complete impartiality. If this is so, the explanations of delinquency can be based on the characteristics of officially recognized delinquents.

This assumption of the impartiality of the law-enforcement agencies is not shared by the second group of criminologists. Citing the results of self-report studies, they suggest that the groups featured in official statistics are there because their personal characteristics cause them to be seen as particularly "dangerous" by social-control and law-enforcement agencies. Thus the same adverse features (for example, living in a deprived area, belonging to a minority group, or being a migrant) which are seen by the first group as causing criminal activity may be seen by the second as making their major contribution in terms of producing differential outcomes in the interaction between juvenile and authority. The suggestion here, is that the picture of delinquency given in official statistics will be determined by the attitudes and actions/reactions of policemen, judges, and so on, as much as it will be by the actions of young people themselves. Looking first at the studies which have concentrated on the offender, it is possible to differentiate between those which try to explain delinquency in terms of the individual delinquent's psychological characteristics and primary experiences (in the family, school, and peer group) and those that see delinquency as the result of social forces operating differentially within the population.

The search for criminogenic attributes usually involves comparison of those with criminal records (representing delinquents) and those who have no official record (representing nondelinquents). This presents us with two problems. The first has already been mentioned. In the light of self-report studies, the nondelinquent status of the control group is open to doubt: it is not possible to know whether differences between the groups relate to a greater propensity to commit delinquent acts or merely to a greater propensity to be caught while doing so. Secondly, even if the control group is accepted as genuinely nondelinquent, it is still only possible to know that certain characteristics occur more, or less, often in the delinquent group. This does not prove that the relationship is a causal one. For example, the association between delinquency and broken families does not necessarily mean that lack of a parent is the direct cause of delinquency. It could be, for example, that broken families tend to live in areas or subareas where neighbourhood characteristics are particularly conducive to delinquency and/or where

there is a strong police presence. Too often causal explanations are presented because they fit in with the preconceptions of the investigator and not because they have been properly established from the data. Another, perhaps more promising, approach at the individual level, sees delinquency as related to learning theory. Conformity is learned by conditioning, with the withdrawal of parental approval as the stimulus. Delinquency can occur when conditioning is unsuccessful either because the child has an inbuilt resistance (for example, Eysenck's cortical inhibition) or because the parents adopt ineffective techniques. Problems can also occur, of course, when the learning process is perfect but the content of the learning is not socially approved (see *Historical Backgrounds of Learning Theory*).

This idea that faulty learning underlies delinquency has been particularly influential in Eastern Europe. Since the classical Marxist–Leninist view is that crime is a by-product of the excesses of the capitalist system and the oppression of the masses, there should be no crime in a truly socialist society. As there demonstrably is a certain amount of delinquency in the countries of Eastern Europe, however, this must be explained in terms of relics of the capitalistic system which have affected people's attitudes either because they are suffering from a time-lag in social consciousness or because they have been subjected to external (Western) values. Thus, writing from the German Democratic Republic, Buchholz and his co-workers (1974 p.48) say categorically that one of the main determinants of delinquency is "the lack of a fundamental political and ideological attitude" stemming from defects in "the education and upbringing of juveniles and children by parents, school, and social organizations, by groups in which individuals live wholly or temporarily, the negative influences of the West, etc."

Here two new themes are introduced: first, delinquency can involve learning just as much as conformity and, second, learning can take place outside the home. These themes have been developed also in Western criminology. Peer groups have been shown to play an important part not only in teaching delinquent skills and fostering appropriate attitudes but also through reinforcement by providing rewards, in terms of status or popularity, for delinquent activities. Much delinquency, particularly that carried out for fun, has been shown to involve group support. The most common types of juvenile theft—shoplifting and taking motor vehicles—are seldom solitary enterprises. Damage to property usually involves two or more people as does use of soft drugs and glue sniffing. Almost by definition, "rowdyism" is clearly a group activity. Such peer-group support is not limited to the working-class delinquent. The middle class also, according to self-report studies, may be supported in their delinquent acts by their friends. Whether or not more indirect influences, such as those of the West on East European youth or of television in the Western world, have any deleterious effects on those exposed to them is much more difficult to ascertain. The effects of television violence have been studied in various settings, in various ways, and with various age groups but, perhaps because of methodological differences, the results are not consistent. In general it appears that, in the very short term, violence on the screen may produce aggressive behaviour in the young viewer but that longer term effects have not been established.

At a more general level, some sociologists have suggested that delinquents are neither the victims of faulty socialization nor have they been seduced by alien influences. They say, rather, that delinquents are the well-socialized products of lower-class urban subgroups who have their own way of life. In other words, the delinquent is a conformist in terms of a minority subculture and only to be seen as a rule breaker by the standards of a different subgroup. In a hierarchically arranged society where some subgroups have more power than others to enforce their norms, this can lead to certain forms of minority subgroup behaviour becoming classified as illegal.

This type of reasoning has been applied in attempts to explain the concentration of officially recognized delinquency in "lower-class" areas in Western society. Its originator, William B. Miller (1958), for example, suggested that male adolescent groups in such areas displayed (perhaps in a rather overstressed form) the focal concerns of lower-class urban culture, such as trouble, toughness, excitement, smartness (ability to manipulate people and situations to your own advantage, not book-learning), fate, and autonomy. In the gang, then, the boy is learning the conventional lower-class male role, and it is the reactions of such "outsiders" as the police, which bring the attributions of delinquency.

This approach provides insights into some aspects of some kinds of delinquency in some areas, namely lower-class, urban, gang-based delinquency. It is arguable, however, whether the differences in values which exist between "lower-class milieus" and other areas are sufficiently marked to warrant their being viewed as subcultures.

The idea that the school might play a part in causing delinquency is a relatively new one. Officially the role of the school is to socialize children, compensating if necessary for defects in home training, and turning out good citizens at the end of the process. Recent studies in the United Kingdom, however, have shown that in the same or similar areas, different schools, ostensibly of the same type, have very different rates of official delinquency among their pupils and that these rates are stable over time (Rutter et al. 1979).

To some extent these differences appeared to reflect different attributes in the pupil intake. For the children considered as a whole, regardless of school, father's occupational status and the child's verbal-reasoning scores were found to be the best predictors of delinquency. Even allowing for this, however, differences between schools were such that a boy (girls were excluded from later analysis) with a favourable personal prediction and attending a high-delinquency school would have a higher likelihood of becoming delinquent than one with unfavourable characteristics attending a school with a low delinquency rate. The schools, themselves, must therefore play some part in generating or inhibiting delinquency among their pupils. How this happens is not yet clear. Variables found to be associated with low delinquency rates in school included a range of intellectual ability among pupils, a school ethos which stressed pupil responsibility, and teacher actions which provided a high level of pupil praise and reward. Why these factors should relate to delinquency outside school is not yet explained so that further research is clearly needed. Studies within schools have provided evidence that bad behaviour in the classroom relates to factors such as high staff turnover, ineffectual teaching, lax or overauthoritarian discipline, and adverse pupil perceptions of teachers; but as yet it is not known how, or if, such factors affect out-of-school activity.

One link which has been suggested is that some delinquency, particularly that of lower-class boys in groups, may be an attempt to compensate for the low status conferred on them in school. By setting up their own culture with values opposed to those of the school, participation in delinquent acts becomes a source of in-group prestige. Some empirical evidence in support of this idea has emerged from studies of schools which are divided rigidly on grounds of pupil ability and where the ethos overtly favours the most able groups. Under these circumstances it has been shown that the least able pupils, grouped together by the school and aware of their low status, develop an antiauthoritarian, anti-establishment and antiacademic way of life within the school.

Control theory is an attempt to write all these partial explanations of delinquency into one consistent whole. Instead of asking: "Why are some people delinquent?", the new question is: "Why do people conform?". Control theory suggests that deviance will occur when people have little to gain from conformity and little to lose or much to gain from deviation. Conformists are constrained by the bonds which link them to society; delinquents are freed from such restraints. Hirschi (1969) suggested that these bonds were of three types:

(a) Attachment in terms of one person being linked to others by affection. The more young people are linked by such bonds to conventional others—parents, other relatives, teachers, friends—the less likely they will be to commit delinquent acts.

(b) Commitment which refers to having a vested interest in conformity, seeing it as part of a master-plan for life, and making a rational assessment of what losses may be incurred by involvement in delinquency. Conformity will only be abandoned if expected rewards are seen as high enough to justify the risk.

(c) Involvement which describes the extent to which youths are caught up in conventional activities occupying their time and energy. As both time and energy are in limited supply, heavy involvement in legitimate activities will obviously militate against finding opportunities to indulge in the illegitimate, whereas long periods of "hanging around" lend themselves to delinquency.

In control theory, then, there is an explanation which has much more universal applicability than the others. It is not limited to the delinquent activities of lower-class males but can be applied equally well to girls, middle-class delinquents, and "good" adolescents in bad areas. It is sufficiently wide to include earlier partial explanations.

So far, in the search for causes, focus has been on the child's immediate environment of home, neighbourhood, and school since these make up the child's social world. It can be argued, however, that these little worlds cannot be viewed independently as they, in turn, are produced by wider social forces. War and civil unrest have been related to higher delinquency rates as have industrialization and migration to towns. All produce situations in which customary values become inapplicable and old bonds are attenuated or cease to exist. Poverty has been cited as a cause but in industrialized countries the delinquency rate has risen as poverty drops. Long-term unemployment is currently being cited as an impetus to crime in Europe, and, although this applies more directly to young adults, it may be that perceptions of an unemployed future are also affecting those in their last year at school. Implicit in much of what has already been said is also the assumption that delinquency and the adverse factors associated with it are all the products of an unequal social system. Many sociologists would argue that in a society where economic opportunities, power, and prestige are unequally distributed, those who are at the bottom on some or all of these counts may find themselves also at a disadvantage in relation to the criminal law and its enforcement.

5. Creation of the "Official" Delinquent

So far the concern has been with factors seen as drawing individuals towards law-breaking or conformist behaviour. In recent years, however, more attention has been devoted to consideration of the processes by which certain people become officially identified as delinquents while other law breakers do not. This has been seen as involving interaction between the young people concerned and agents of social control.

Empirical studies have shown that officials tend to use considerable discretion in deciding how to classify and process individual law breakers. For example, while the police do not show much variation in the way they process juveniles involved in serious offences, their reactions toward minor offenders have been found to

be influenced by their perceptions of the "kind of person" they were dealing with. Making quick decisions on the spot, they have been shown to be more lenient with girls, with younger children, and with boys who were conventionally dressed and who spoke to them respectfully. Detection of instances of juvenile law breaking can also reflect police discretion. Areas where trouble is expected may be policed more intensively, leading to more arrests, leading to confirmation that the area is a bad one. Certain categories of people may become more liable to be stopped, questioned, or searched.

The actions of the policemen on the street constitute only the first moves in the process which takes a young person from law-breaking act to officially certified delinquent. In the intermediate stages there usually lie several possibilities of diversion both formal and informal.

Formal methods of diversion occur when certain social-control agencies are given the right to take action to halt or to defer the child's progress towards the court. For example, the police might be given the power to dismiss certain categories of offenders after issuing them with a formal warning (as in the United Kingdom) or to refer them to specialized helping agencies such as the youth service bureau and university counselling schemes sponsored by the California police in the United States. Such diversionary decisions are usually made by special officers at police headquarters and do not rest on the discretion of the officer making the charge.

Diversionary programmes may also be implemented at court intake level. Thus, in Canada and some areas of the United States the probation officer acting as intake official can initiate short-term diversionary counselling programs with offenders and their families. If this is successful, the case will never go to court. The guidelines for selection for diversionary counselling are, however, such as to allow some discretion to the intake officer concerned. In general, severity of offence and recidivism would seem to be contra-indications, but in other cases choice appears to relate to the intake officer's views on the type of person the offender is and whether or not counselling would be successful (Needleman 1981). People with suspect personal qualities and/or perceivedly bad social backgrounds may therefore not only be more likely to be referred to the court by the police, but they are also less likely to be diverted once they reach there.

Diversion from court proceedings, however, does not always mean an escape from official processing. It may mean diversion to another type of agency, one concerned with welfare. In Norway, for example, all children were removed completely from the justice system as early as 1896, and young offenders became the concern of local child welfare boards set up in each area to deal with all children with problems whether they were law breakers or the victims of deprivation. This became the model for the other Scandinavian countries so that, though young people certainly continue to break the law, there are no delinquents in the sense of those found guilty in court. Sweden has moved even further from the conventional pattern so that the youth welfare boards have, since the 1970s, taken no action in the great majority of cases of delinquency referred to them, arguing that most children grow out of their delinquency and may do so more successfully if left to themselves and their families since most measures of compulsory intervention are ineffective and may even be counterproductive.

Even in countries where a juvenile court system is operative, it would be a mistake to see welfare considerations as necessarily subordinate to justice. The reverse often appears to have been the case. In the United States, for instance, decisions in the Supreme Court made in the late 1960s indicated that juvenile courts, in their determination to do what was best for young offenders, had succeeded in removing most of the legal rights of the accused which are taken for granted in adult courts. It has been argued that legal safeguards involve formality, legal representation, cross-examination of witnesses and a general atmosphere of learned argument and points of law which would be confusing and frightening for a child. On the other side it can be said that guilt has often been accepted by the court without adequate proof, that the accused were often ignorant of the evidence against them and therefore could not challenge it and that, even if the proceedings were informal, they were still confusing so that the accused and the accused's parents might be unable to correctly determine when, how, and to whom to put their case.

Such criticisms are not limited to American courts. They have been given force in the United States, however, because they have been made by the Supreme Court hearing appeals against specific judgments. The effect on juvenile justice has been considerable. Status offences, such as running away from home, have been removed from the statute books, and therefore from the courts, and are now seen as welfare problems. Legal representation of the accused has also led to more involvement of prosecution attorneys both in deciding which cases are to come to court and in presenting the case when it gets there.

Concern about the extent to which justice and welfare considerations can be observed within a single institution, combined with doubts about the suitability of legalistic court measures for all offenders, has led to considerable worldwide interest in the dual system set up in Scotland in the early 1980s (Martin et al. 1981). This centres on children's hearings staffed by lay members of the community who deal with all cases of children, including delinquents, who are seen as in need of compulsory care. The decision about the child's need is made by a local authority official, called the reporter, to whom all cases are referred, except those involving very serious crimes. Clearly this gives the reporter considerable powers of discretion, and investigations show that, like the intake officers in American courts (though perhaps with more justification in a tribunal concerned

with "care"), they base their decisions not only on the nature of the act but, most strongly, on whether or not the child has family problems or a good report from school (Martin et al. 1981). At the hearing, those who deny their involvement in the acts charged are sent to court for the facts to be judged, returning to the children's hearing for disposal. If the facts are admitted, there is discussion round the table between the three panel members conducting the hearing, the child, and the parents. The case is then disposed of in accord with the child's perceived needs by (a) sending the child home with no supervision order; (b) sending the child home but subject to a period of supervision by a social worker; or (c) sending the child away from home for residential supervision. These remedies differ little from the sanctions available to juvenile courts.

What factors influence the outcome? Here, again, courts and welfare tribunals do not appear to differ radically. The seriousness of the offence perhaps assumes more importance in court but, once guilt has been established, the decision on disposal appears to reflect the judge's view of the offender as an individual in the light of reports on family background, behaviour and attainment at school, and so on. In other words, the bases for decision are individualized in courts as well as in welfare tribunals. To obtain the relevant information on which to base the decision, judges must therefore rely on the reports of others (social workers, teachers) or must make snap judgments on the basis of clues available to them from the offender's appearance and demeanour. The same may be true of welfare tribunals, and in each case, concern has been expressed about the power given to those who supply information. Social workers, for example, can influence the outcome of cases by the way in which they present their social background reports. Instant judgments about type of person, on the other hand, can lead to stereotyping and possible racial, ethnic, or class bias. Decisions about disposal also involve beliefs about the efficacy of certain kinds of experience for certain kinds of children. As these views are intensely subjective, the results can be surprising, with relatively minor offenders on their first appearance being sent to residential establishments. These beliefs can also provide fuel for accusations of bias against certain groups who may be seen as being most at risk and hence in need of the most radical intervention.

6. Disposal and Outcome

Most delinquent children and adolescents who come before juvenile courts or other agencies do so only once. Relatively few return to court again, either as juveniles or as adults (if minor traffic offences are excluded). As a result, it has been argued that disposal of first offenders should involve minimum official intervention—a warning, a "conditional discharge", or a "no action" decision. Such a policy of nonintervention is well-illustrated in Sweden where the child welfare boards take action concerning only a relatively small proportion of juvenile offenders referred to them. This has now spread to the 15- to 18-year-old groups also. Even though older juveniles are officially dealt with by courts, the child welfare boards can intervene and, even though they take no action themselves, the intervention causes suspension of prosecution.

At the opposite extreme is the action which is seen as the most punitive by the child—sending him (or, less often, her) away from home. Such measures are expected to achieve two different goals. One is to protect society by incarcerating dangerous offenders. More often, however, the move is said to be for the children's own good—to provide an environment and experiences which will lead them away from delinquency. There is, however, little evidence that residential establishments achieve this aim. Indeed, the failure rate, in terms of reappearance in court within two to five years of release, has been found to be depressingly high. As a result, many attempts have been made to find alternatives which rather than segregating delinquents will attempt to integrate them more closely with the conventional community.

7. Practical Implications

For those involved in child rearing—as parents or as teachers—the crucial issue in juvenile delinquency is almost certainly prevention. Because the causes of delinquency are not yet understood, despite the efforts of many researchers and theorists, the best methods of prevention are also in dispute. Perhaps the best guideline at the individual level is provided by the very general precepts of control theory with its emphasis on bonds linking the young person to conventional life. Children living in a happy, united, conventional family where they have many activities and interests to occupy them are unlikely to become delinquent or, if they do become involved once, will not persist with a delinquent career. Some parents, however, cannot provide such an ideal environment, and this may well be for reasons beyond their control. Material assistance, provision of community facilities, and housing policy all have their part to play. A deliberate policy of housing all "problem families" in one area, for example, may contain the situation geographically but is unlikely to decrease the rate of delinquency among the children living there.

For teachers there is the suggestion that the pupil least likely to be delinquent is the one who is happy at school, has good relationships with teachers, feels that the curriculum is relevant and feels personally involved in school life. In other words, good classroom management and school administration can encourage conformity. Again, however, this can be of little comfort to teachers in schools where violence and alienation are already widespread. The provision of opportunities to use classroom skills to advantage may be determined by financial and political considerations outside the school itself.

One preventative measure is, however, within the reach of individual teachers—that of avoiding premature labelling and prediction. The attributes of delinquents which were outlined earlier relate to variables which are more likely to occur in relation to delinquents than to other children. This does not mean that all those who show the attributes will be delinquents nor that all delinquents will show them. To attempt prediction of delinquency potential in individual cases is risky. The literature on "self-fulfilling prophecies" in the classroom shows clearly how fast children can pick up clues to the teacher's view of them so that the child who feels he or she is expected to become delinquent may well act accordingly, having little to lose by it.

A similar message can be passed to those who have to identify lawbreakers in public places or to process them once identified. The police have the unenviable task of maintaining public order by prevention of crime as well as by dealing with lawbreakers. In each case, they may have to make decisions on little evidence as to whether to intercept some individual or not. Such intervention may result in the detection of delinquency or its prevention. It may also, if demonstrating systematic bias, be counterproductive, leading to increased delinquency and even to harassment of the police in return by those who see themselves discriminated against. Such reactions can stimulate further police action, so leading to a vicious spiral.

For those processing delinquents, however, perhaps the most important implication is that, in the present state of knowledge, there is no hard evidence about what kind of official action will provide the best outcome. Many children get better without any intervention; many get worse after a period of residential re-education or care. For the individual concerned, however, the choice of action clearly has important and far-reaching implications. In view of this, it is important that considerably more hard evidence should be gathered about the relative success rates, in terms of putting an end to delinquent activities, accruing to different types of treatment for different types of delinquent. This may not stop children and young people breaking the law, but might at least prevent young offenders from developing into adult criminals.

Bibliography

Buchholz E, Hartmann J, Lekschas J, Stiller G 1974 *Socialist Criminology: Theoretical and Methodological Foundations.* Lexington Books, Lexington, Massachusetts

Cohen S 1980 *Folk Devils and Moral Panics.* Martin Robertson, Oxford

European Committee on Crime Problems 1979 *Social Change and Juvenile Delinquency.* Council of Europe, Strasbourg

Gibbons D J 1981 *Delinquent Behaviour,* 3rd edn. Prentice-Hall, Englewood Cliffs, New Jersey

Hindelang M J, Hirschi T, Weis J G 1979 Correlates of delinquency: The illusion of discrepancy between self-report and official measures. *Am. Sociol. Rev.* 44: 995–1014

Hirschi T 1969 *Causes of Delinquency.* University of California Press, Berkeley, California

Hood R G, Sparks R F 1970 *Key Issues in Criminology.* Weidenfeld and Nicolson, London

Kazuhiko T 1981 Changes in traditional society and "delinquencization". *Japan Q.* 28: 362–69

Martin F M, Fox S J, Murray K (eds.) 1981 *Children Out of Court.* Scottish Academic Press, Edinburgh

Miller W B 1958 Lower class culture as a generating milieu of gang delinquency. *J. Soc. Issues* 14: 5–19

Needleman C 1981 Discrepant assumptions in empirical research: The case of juvenile court screening. *Soc. Prob.* 28: 247–62

Rubel R J 1978 Analysis and critique of HEW safe school study report to the congress. *Crime Delinq.* 24: 257–65

Rutter M, Maughan B, Mortimore P, Ouston J, Smith A 1979 *Fifteen Thousand Hours: Secondary Schools and Their Effects on Children.* Open Books, London

Discipline and Student Development

R. L. Curwin and A. N. Mendler

One of the major concerns of public education is managing student behavior. A series of studies (Cichon and Kloff 1978, NYSUT 1979, Bloch 1978) have found that teachers consistently rate "managing disruptive students" to be the leading stressor in their professional lives. According to O'Malley and Eisenberg (1973), for example, 5 to 10 percent of school-aged children are diagnosed as hyperactive. Fourteen consecutive Gallup polls have shown discipline to be the public's number one concern regarding its schools.

1. Causes of Misbehavior

Why do children misbehave? Many explanations have at one time or another been put forward as the primary causes of misbehavior: children wanting attention, being bored, feeling unfairly treated, not trusting adults or other children, experiencing school failure, being treated like spoiled brats, wanting power or control over others, having to prove something to friends, fearing, feeling rejected and/or frustrated, having poor nutritional habits and biochemical or neurological disorders. Probably some or all of these reasons are valid in certain cases.

The biochemical/neurological model postulates that misbehavior is related to neurologic or chemical imbalance problems, and treatment is often directed at altering the internal state of the child through diet and/or medication. The behavioral model suggests that all behavior is learned and that more appropriate behavior can be trained through the use of reinforcement. Cognitive theorists attend to faulty beliefs or self-statements and work at helping children to gain self-control by modifying their thinking. Affective approaches point to the necessity of an acceptant, nonjudgmental environment that encourages children to express their feelings. Misbehavior, according to this view, is caused by frustration when "significant others" fail to attend to the child's needs.

2. What is Discipline?

Curwin and Mendler (1980) define a classroom discipline problem as a situation in which the needs of the individual conflict with the needs of the group or authority who represents the group. When an individual behaves in a way that meets his or her needs, or at least that he or she perceives meets his or her needs, and these behaviors prevent the group from meeting group needs, then a discipline event occurs. In school, this typically means that a discipline event occurs when a student's behavior prevents other students from learning, or the teacher from teaching.

Self-discipline means that an individual is able to select which appropriate needs will be met at a given time, and is able to express those needs with regard to the social context in which they occur. Thus, a self-disciplined student is able to focus his or her attention on the task at hand, and reserve focusing his or her attention to other stimuli until a more appropriate time.

3. Theories of Discipline

The work of most theorists can be viewed as a continuum that ranges from those who favor an internal-control approach that tends to view the individual's needs as more important than those of the group or authority, to those who favor strict and complete control in which the needs of the group or authority are emphasized.

3.1 Internal Control

One set of theorists proposes that the more the school attempts to coerce, manipulate, control, and shape the behavior of students, the greater is the likelihood of discipline problems. The cause of discipline problems is seen as the result of the school's interference with the natural growth process of the child. The seeds for this position, which holds that there is a necessity to structure the learning environment so as to attend to the individual needs of each learner, can be traced to Plato. . He discussed differences among individuals and recommended that steps be taken to discover each child's outstanding aptitude so that education and training along the lines of his or her particular talents might begin early. Rousseau suggested that no great harm to the child or to society will result if the child grows with little adult supervision and direction. Much later, John Dewey, a New England-born philosopher, said that children must have an opportunity to make their own choices, and then to try their choices for themselves so that they can give them the only final test—that of action. He thought this to be the only way to learn, which leads one to discover actions that lead to success and those which lead to failure. Snygg and Combs (1949) see learning as a natural and normal activity which is not dependent upon the stimulation of the teacher. It is their notion that adults actually interfere with much childhood learning through attempts to substitute their goals in place of those already possessed by the children.

All of these theorists would argue the virtues of approaches to education that minimize the role of the school as an agent for external control. Since learning is viewed as intrinsically rewarding, outside interference with this process might stimulate the child to resist the efforts of others to shape him or her in a way that is not natural. Discipline problems are therefore attributed to a poorness of fit between the natural growth processes of the child and the demands of the institution. One of the most widely known examples of this approach is A. S. Neill's Summerhill school in England (Neill 1960). Summerhill exemplifies the belief that the school should "fit the child," and Neill notes that in his school "lessons are optional. Children can go to them or stay away from them for years if they want to." He clearly places the needs of the individual above those of the group or authority and cautions against "imposed authority." Implicit in Neill's approach is that when children work joyfully and find happiness, they do not need to misbehave.

3.2 Strict External Control

A contrasting view of the purposes of school, and by implication the discipline methods to be employed, holds that the pleasantness of school is irrelevant and that schools should engage students in a mental toughening process which is of value in itself. The mind is strengthened through a series of difficult and frustrating experiences. John Locke (1934) was committed to the ultimate rationality of humans. He viewed education as a process to promote self-discipline, self-control, and the "power of denying ourselves the satisfaction of our own desires, where reason does not authorize them. From their very early cradles," he argued, "parents must begin instructing children in self-denial." Standards of achievement and behavior are therefore best left to "rational" institutions.

4. Methods of Discipline

Each behavioral school of thought has a set of methods of discipline based upon its theories. Some of these methods are also related to broader psychological principles.

4.1 Client-centered Therapy

This is a therapeutic method developed by Carl Rogers (1969) which involves listening in a reflective way to a person's thoughts and feelings, and then feeding back the message that was heard. The client (student) has the option of agreeing with the feedback if it "fits," or clarifying for himself or herself what it is he or she means. The key concept is that growth occurs in an acceptant, warm, empathic, nonjudgmental environment that allows students the freedom to explore their thoughts and feelings and to solve their own problems. Schools which lack these characteristics are breeding grounds for discipline problems.

Haim Ginott's work extended that of Rogers through the introduction of the concept of limits. Ginott (1972 pp. 147–48) stated that "the essence of discipline is finding effective alternatives to punishment. To punish a child is to enrage him and make him uneducable. He becomes a hostage of hostility, a captive of rancor, a prisoner of vengeance. Suffused with rage and absorbed in grudges, a child has no time or mind for studying. In discipline, whatever generates hate must be avoided. Whatever creates self-esteem is to be fostered." Ginott's model calls for firm limit setting on behavior but never on feelings.

Abraham Maslow constructed a hierarchy of human needs. This is a developmental model suggesting that growth occurs by having sufficient environmental support. The support gradually shifts in emphasis to an individual's ability to nourish and support himself or herself within his or her environment. Maslow (1954) constructed a pyramid that illustrates this shift. At the base of the pyramid are the basic human needs for food, clothing, and shelter. Survival comes first. A child who comes to school hungry will spend most of his or her time thinking and dreaming about food, not mathematics. In other words, this hierarchy of needs proposes that some needs must be met before others because they are more urgent and basic to our life function. People who have needs for security and safety must have these needs satisfied before they can move on to satisfy other needs. A child whose parents are frequently fighting and who threaten to divorce is often preoccupied with fantasies of abandonment. He or she is often motivated to seek security from others; if he or she becomes stuck in this pursuit, then much of his or her energy will be directed toward finding others to take care of him or her. The first two needs at the base of the pyramid are considered "outer needs" and are almost completely dependent upon being received from the environment outside. The next need is for love and belonging, and Bessel spells out four ways in which this need is met. They are (a) "attention" (young people must be aware that others know they exist); (b) "acceptance" (you have a right to be here); (c) "approval" (I like this about you); and (d) "affection" (I like you). Abidin (1976) has discussed the importance of a person's feeling worthwhile, lovable, competent, and responsible in order to develop a positive self-concept.

Factors that contribute to the needs for respect and self-esteem include recognition from others, accomplishments, having goals or a sense of worth, gaining influence, independence, and self-control.

Knowledge and understanding are important in order to help children to make decisions which allow them to live their lives more effectively. The final human need is for beauty and self-actualization which is a need to experience the world directly and to be open to it. Maslow described self-actualized people as having their faults, but as perceiving reality more clearly. He viewed them as more creative, tolerant, and spontaneous. They accept themselves and others as they are.

Rudolph Dreikurs (Dreikurs and Soltz 1964) stated that misbehavior occurs because children have developed faulty beliefs about themselves which lead to their having goals which may lead to misbehavior. The goals for misbehavior include attention, power, revenge, and display of inadequacy. Children seek attention when they believe that they belong only when they are being noticed or recognized. Such children are often calling out answers in class, despite repeated admonitions, or cracking jokes which disturb the teacher or the other children. Parents sometimes say that their children will not do their homework unless they are right there. Students make their need for power felt through their faulty belief that they belong only when they are in control or are the boss, or when they are proving that no one else can boss them. Children who refuse to do their homework because it has been assigned by a teacher, or who are always in the middle of disputes and arguments with other students, are showing their need for power. Children want revenge when they believe that they belong only by hurting others as they feel hurt. Such students often see themselves as unworthy and unlovable. Unruly students who are angry with others who have repeatedly let them down may show their hurt through antisocial action. The delinquent population have often developed this belief about themselves. The final faulty belief discussed by Dreikurs is the child who believes that he/she belongs only by convincing others not to expect anything from him or her. This belief is frequently experienced by those who feel hopeless or helpless, by the student who is always at the teacher's desk asking for help and who is mostly pleading ignorance by convincing others that he or she is incapable or stupid. The goal here is the display of inadequacy.

Dreikurs suggests the use of natural or logical consequences for dealing with misbehavior and advises against engaging in power struggles with children. Simply stated, this amounts to making sure that the punishment fits the crime.

4.2 Values Clarification

This is a process that helps youngsters answer some of their questions and build their own value system. It is based on an approach formulated by Louis Raths (Raths et al. 1966). His focus was on how people come to hold certain beliefs and establish certain behavior patterns. He looked at specific behavior problems related to students with unclear values. He found that students with unclear values had one or more of the following characteristics: apathy, flight, uncertainty, inconsistency, drifting, overconforming, overdissenting, or role playing.

According to this model, discipline problems are caused by two factors. Students with unclear values are often experiencing considerable inner turmoil which leads them to engage in a variety of behaviors in an effort to restore themselves to more fluid functioning. In the process of restoration, they may "try on" behaviors that may lead them to conflict with the prevailing school system. The second cause of discipline problems, as viewed through the values-clarification model, occurs when both the identified misbehaving student and the school (teacher, administrator) have clear but different values and when either or both are unable to accept each other's differences.

The importance of values clarification is its emphasis on communication in a nonjudgmental, acceptant atmosphere. All participants, including the teacher, are to be free to share their thoughts, values, and feelings and to learn the values of recognizing and accepting their differences.

4.3 Transactional Analysis

This is concerned with analyzing transactions: analyzing, understanding, and paying attention to what goes on between two or more persons. According to this model, each person has three existing ego states. Even young children have each ego state, although the degree of functioning or voice that each is given is dependent upon one's age, past experiences, and current situation. There is the "parent ego state" which develops through the recordings of "all the admonitions and rules and laws that the child has heard and learned from his parents," parent surrogates, or other authority figures. The parent ego state is subdivided into the critical parent which is righteous, judgmental, and moral, and the nurturant parent, which is giving, loving, and caring. The "child ego state" relates to the feelings of the person and records the feelings of frustration, anger, and hurts in response to parental demands, as well as "creativity, curiosity, the desire to know and explore, and the urge to touch, feel, and experience." Both of these ego states begin at birth. The third ego state is the adult, which acts as a computer, making rational decisions after considering information from the parent, the child, and the data which the adult has accumulated. The adult begins to emerge as people begin to control and manipulate objects in their environment. As the adult develops, it begins to discard some of the messages from the parent that are experienced as inapplicable.

According to the view of transactional analysis (TA), discipline problems are to be viewed in terms of the transactions that occur between people. Discipline problems can be avoided by understanding how a teacher gets hooked into playing a game with a disruptive student, and by being sensitive to his or her own ego state and that of the student at any given moment. The TA model considers both the student and his or her environment as responsible for discipline problems, as well as the interaction of environmental factors.

4.4 Teacher-effectiveness Training

Thomas Gordon's approach to discipline places the focus upon communication as being of primary importance. Gordon (1974) considers his method to be democratic. He suggests that the primary reason that teachers spend so much classroom time with discipline is because of the emphasis on "repressive and power-based methods." These methods include "threats of punishment, actual punishment, and verbal shaming and blaming." He claims that these methods invite "resistance, retaliation, and rebellion" in students. His alternative is to provide teachers with a model of communication that includes "active listening," "I-messages," "problem ownership," and "negotiation."

Glasser (1969) believes that students misbehave as a result of a lack of involvement in the school process. School failure is the cornerstone of his theory of student misbehavior, which can be prevented through involvement, responsibility, and success experiences. He also stresses the importance of success experiences, believing that a child forms his or her self-concept of being a success or a failure between the ages of 5 and 10.

His plan for dealing with misbehavior includes an emphasis on behavior rather than on feelings. His approach is a rational, cognitive one which encourages problem solving by the student and elicits a plan for behavioral change that encourages a commitment from the student. He believes it necessary to reinforce appropriate behavior when the student is being successful. The teacher is advised to have clear rules which are firmly enforced and which are nonpunitive in that blaming and threatening are eliminated. Teachers need to provide students with a friendly greeting and classroom tasks that show the teacher's belief in the student's ability to be responsible.

4.5 Moral Reasoning

Lawrence Kohlberg has made a major contribution to the understanding of "moral development." His model is based on cognitive-developmental theory which suggests that moral reasoning progresses in stages. Kohlberg pays some attention to affective factors, such as guilt and sympathy in decision making, but emphasizes that moral decisions are cognitively developed by the judging individual. Consequently, intelligence and the individual's ability to reason abstractly are important factors in the attainment of an advanced morality.

Kohlberg (1968) defines moral development as occurring and progressing through six stages. Stage 1 is a morality based on an orientation to punishment or reward and to physical and material power. Stage 2 is defined as "social contract orientation" which involves an exchange of favors between people. Stage 3 is called the "good boy" orientation, in which the individual's actions are geared to pleasing others and thereby gaining acceptance from them. Stage 4 is a morality based upon the respect for those in authority. At stage 5, the individual is motivated through the recognition that all individuals have rights, and that each individual has a right to exist regardless of his or her social orientation, status, role, sex, race, or importance. Stage 6 is the "morality of individual principles of conscience" which have "logical comprehensiveness and universality." The highest value is placed on human life, equality, or dignity.

Kohlberg would probably argue that most school discipline problems can generally be viewed as a conflict between the school's stage 1, stage 3, and/or stage 4 morality and the student's stage 2 morality. Less frequently, the student's stages 5 and 6 morality can also lead to conflict for him or her.

4.6 Behavior Modification

This is among the most widely known and extensively researched approaches to classroom management. The basic tenet of behavior modification is that learning depends on events that occur after a certain behavior. E. L. Thorndike (1905), a pioneer learning theorist, developed his law of effect which states that "Any act which in a given situation produces satisfaction becomes associated with that situation, so that when the situation reoccurs, the act is more likely to reoccur. Conversely, any act which in a given situation produces discomfort becomes disassociated from the situation so that when the situation reoccurs, the act is less likely than before to reoccur."

Later on, B. F. Skinner (1968) developed extensive principles of operant conditioning which state that the events which follow a given behavior either strengthen or weaken that behavior. He used the term "reinforcement" to mean those events that follow a behavior and cause that behavior to increase in frequency. Skinner's theory suggests that all behavior is learned, and it is the outside environment that either strengthens or weakens a given behavior. In his paradigm, punishment describes a procedure in which a behavior is followed by an aversive or unpleasant event.

A classroom reinforcer can take several different forms, such as a concrete reward (pieces of candy, money, a small toy), an activity reward (10 minutes of free time for completed work), or a social reward (teacher praise, classroom monitor, etc.); or it can take a negative form, such as the removal of an unpleasant stimulus (the teacher who stops yelling, a loud interfering noise that stops, or the removal from the classroom of a child who hates the class).

Misbehavior occurs because it is reinforced by the environment. The antithesis is to change the child's behavior through a manipulation of his or her environment which reinforces or rewards "good" or socially appropriate behavior. This shaping process occurs through rewarding successive approximations (behaviors which gradually come closer to the desired outcome) of the target behavior. Reinforcement is contingent upon the student's emitting behaviors that are closer to those desired by the teacher. Reinforcement can be given continuously (for each and every appropriate student response) or periodically. Periodic reinforcement can be given on a fixed schedule (i.e. after every fifth appropriate response or after each 5-minute interval of appropriate behavior) or on a variable schedule (i.e. after approximately every fifth appropriate response or approximately 5-minute interval). Research indicates that in the initial phase of behavior shaping, continuous reinforcement is needed until the student gradually progresses to one of the intermittent schedules, which appears to ultimately have the strongest effect.

Proponents of behavior modification suggest the reinforcement of behavior that is incompatible with the student's misbehavior. A person cannot be behaving well and misbehaving at the same time, and by rewarding desired behavior, the probability of that behavior occurring again increases. Most behavior modification proponents advise against the use of punishment because of its well-documented deleterious side effects. If punishment is to be used, it should be done selectively and cautiously. Becker (1971) offers the following outlines:

(a) Effective punishment is given immediately.

(b) Effective punishment relies on taking away reinforcers and provides a clear-cut method for earning them back.

(c) Effective punishment makes use of a warning signal, usually words ("No," "Stop that") prior to punishment.

(d) Effective punishment is carried out in a calm matter-of-fact way.

(e) Effective punishment is given along with such reinforcement for behaviors incompatible with the punished behavior.

(f) Effective punishment is consistent. Reinforcement is not given for the punished behavior.

4.7 Drug Therapy

Proponents of drug therapy in the schools tend to see impulsive youngsters who do not fit any acceptable norm as lacking "self-discipline," "self-control," and the power of self-denial. Whether for biochemical, neurological, or environmental reasons, the goal of drug therapy is to have the child fit within the socially acceptable norm. Its use is designed to control misbehavior that the individual either cannot or will not control. The diagnosis that usually leads to drug therapy is based on parental or school complaints of distractibility, overactivity, inattentiveness, impulsivity, difficulty in disciplining, poor social controls, and academic problems in school. These complaints, coupled with the

physician's clinical opinion, may lead to a prescription for psychoactive drugs.

The outcome of most studies indicates that stimulant drugs are generally effective in making the child less distractible, more attentive, less active, and better behaved. Research has generally failed to show positive scholastic results with children who are medicated. Despite numerous studies which have attempted to identify a target population for whom drugs are particularly effective, outcomes suggest that both drug responders and drug nonresponders come from a heterogeneous population that cuts across socioeconomic status and psychiatric or medical diagnoses.

4.8 Three-dimensional Discipline

Curwin and Mendler (1980) suggest a model for discipline which includes helping teachers to choose methods of behavior management based upon their philosophy of education and style of instruction. These authors emphasize the importance of discipline prevention which includes the teacher becoming aware of his behavior, values and attitudes; aware of his students' preferences; able to adequately identify and express feelings; able to participate with the students in formulating classroom rules and consequences; fully knowledgeable of the many theories of discipline and of methods based upon these theories. Prevention is highlighted, and methods of effective action to stop misbehavior when it occurs as well as techniques to help resolve conflict with children who chronically misbehave are offered.

Research with teachers in inner-city environments (Mendler 1981) has shown this program of discipline to be effective in reducing stress associated with disruptive student behavior.

5. Conclusion

Broadly speaking, discipline interventions are conceptualized as those which attempt primarily to alter either behavior (i.e., behavior modification, drug therapy, reality therapy), cognition (Kohlberg, transactional analysis), or affect (Ginott, Maslow, Gordon).

More recently, there have been efforts at integrating pieces of different theories (Meichenbaum and Goodman 1971, Homme et al. 1969, Curwin and Mendler 1980) in efforts to help teachers and students live more compatibly with each other. In each case, the intent is to provide the teacher with a set of skills that either define or facilitate ways to reduce disruptive student behavior so that more time is available for instruction.

Bibliography

Abidin R R 1976 *Parenting Skills: Trainer's Manual.* Human Science Press, New York

Becker W C 1971 *Parents are Teachers.* Research Press, Champaign, Illinois

Bloch A M 1978 Combat neurosis in inner-city schools. *Am. J. Psychiatry* 135: 1189–92

Cichon D J, Kloff R H 1978 The teaching events stress inventory. Paper presented at the annual meeting of the American Educational Research Association, Toronto, Ontario, March 27–31 1978

Curwin R L, Mendler A 1980 *The Discipline Book: A Complete Guide to School and Classroom Management.* Reston Publishing, Reston, Virginia

Dreikurs R, Soltz V 1964 *Children: The Challenge.* Duell, Sloane and Pearce, New York

Ginott H G 1972 *Teacher and Child: A Book for Parents and Teachers.* MacMillan, New York

Glasser W 1969 *Schools Without Failure.* Harper and Row, New York

Gordon T 1974 TET: *Teacher Effectiveness Training.* Wyden, New York

Holmes M, Holmes D, Field J 1974 *The Therapeutic Classroom.* Aronson, New York

Homme L, Csanyi A P, Gonzales M A, Rechs J R 1969 *How to Use Contingency Contracting in the Classroom.* Research Press, Champaign, Illinois

Kohlberg L 1968 The child as a moral philosopher. *Psychol. Today* 2(4): 25–30

Locke J 1934 *Some Thoughts Concerning Education.* Cambridge University Press, London

Maslow A H 1954 *Motivation and Personality.* Harper, New York

Meichenbaum D H, Goodman J 1971 Training impulsive children to talk to themselves: A means of developing self-control. *J. Abnorm. Psychol.* 77: 115–26

Mendler A N 1981 The effects of a combined behavioral skills/anxiety management program upon teacher stress and disruptive student behavior (Doctoral dissertation, Union for Experimenting Colleges and Universities). Dissertation Abstracts International, 1982, 42, 3917A. (University Microfilms No. 82-05171)

Neill A S 1960 *Summerhill: A Radical Approach to Child Rearing.* Hart, New York

New York State United Teachers Research and Educational Services (NYSUT) 1979 *New York State United Teachers Stress Survey Bulletin.* New York State United Teachers Research and Educational Services, Albany, New York

O'Malley J E, Eisenberg L 1973 The hyperkinetic syndrome. *Semin. Psychiatry* 5: 95–103

Raths L E, Harmin M, Simon S B 1966 *Values and Teaching: Working with Values in the Classroom.* Merrill, Columbus, Ohio

Rogers C R 1969 *Freedom to Learn: A View of What Education Might Become.* Merrill, Columbus, Ohio

Skinner B F 1968 *The Technology of Teaching.* Appleton Century Crofts, New York

Snygg D, Combs A 1949 *Individual Behavior.* Harper, New York

Thorndike E L 1905 *The Elements of Psychology.* Seiler, New York

Punishment

D. L. Duke

Consensus regarding the nature, purposes, and effectiveness of punishment in educational settings does not exist. Some clinicians might accept Redl's conceptualization of punishment as a planned attempt to influence either behavior or development through exposure to an unpleasant experience (Redl 1980 pp. 251–52). Theologians could counter, however, that such a definition ignores the notion of retribution—negative consequences that may occur without specific planning. Criminal justice experts might add that Redl overlooks the possibility that punishment may be intended to vindicate the victim as well as correct the behavior of the wrongdoer.

Confusion regarding the concept of punishment is exacerbated by the existence of a variety of related terms. Some appear to have been used primarily because punishment is perceived to carry too punitive a connotation. Behavioral psychologists and educators, for example, often employ aversive consequences, a term presumably more in line with educational purposes. Organization theorists speak of sanctions and disincentives. Some psychoanalysts prefer natural or logical consequences (Dreikurs 1968 pp. 100–13).

Because punishment is a multifaceted concept, it may be useful to focus on several key dimensions. Intentionality refers to the purposes for which punishment is designed. Thus the assumption will be made that punishment is the product of a conscious decision by some person or group. Actions that are not intended to punish, but which are perceived as punishing by those subject to them, will not be addressed. Effectiveness concerns the extent to which the intended purposes of punishment are actually realized. Conceivably, of course, punishment may be effective, yet violate established norms or laws. Legality and morality pertain to the normative dimensions of punishment.

1. Intentionality

Punishment may be intended to accomplish a variety of purposes, depending on the circumstances under which it is administered, characteristics of the person or persons punished, and the beliefs of the punisher.

One of the most obvious purposes of punishment is to effect an immediate behavior change in an individual, either by stopping an unwanted behavior or prompting a desirable behavior. In school settings teachers, for example, frequently employ a variety of punishments—ranging from embarrassing remarks to detention—to correct the conduct of misbehaving students.

Deterrence is a second goal of punishment, one closely related to the first. The mere existence of punishment is hoped to discourage the onset or recurrence of misconduct. When awareness of the existence of punishment is judged insufficient alone to prevent behavior problems, punishment may be meted out for exemplary reasons. Tradition has it, for instance, that in certain Irish parochial schools, on the first day of class, teachers made a point of upbraiding the largest boy in class, thereby serving notice to all pupils that they might expect similar treatment if they misbehaved. It is conventional wisdom that a punishment's effectiveness as a deterrent is directly proportional to its severity.

The purpose of punishment to an organization theorist is to permit the organization to accomplish its objectives and to prevent entropy, or the tendency within all collectivities to disintegrate in the absence of controls. Other control mechanisms besides punishment include incentives, performance evaluation, and supervision.

In primitive societies, punishment frequently is intended as retribution—a means by which "justice can be done," victims can be vindicated, and the consequences of a wrongful act can be ameliorated. For example, a person caught stealing might have to replace the stolen item in addition to suffering some other fate (Malinowski 1976). This justification of punishment has little to do with the pragmatic notion of prevention nor does the expectation exist that the culprit will be a better person as a result of being punished.

In contrast to such a punitive view of punishment is the so-called detergent theory of punishment (London 1969 pp. 139–40). Present in many Western religions and societies, the detergent theory holds that punishment should be designed ultimately to benefit culprits by providing an opportunity for them to pay their "debt" to society. Having been cleansed of guilt through suffering, the individual supposedly is free to return to a normal life.

Educators, at one time or another, have used all five rationales to justify their punishment of students. How effective the use of punishment has been in school settings is the subject of much research and conjecture. Obviously the basis for determining effectiveness will vary from one rationale to the next. Studies of schools suggest that the effectiveness of punishment may also depend on a variety of other factors, including the form of punishment, how it is perceived by the person to be punished, and how the punishment is administered.

2. Form of Punishment

London (1969 p. 135) observes that there are basically two ways to punish: frustration and pain. The first typically deprives the individual of something; the second causes palpable discomfort.

Educators in recent years have tended to make greater use of frustration, though corporal punishment and psychological abuse, such as ridicule and public embarrassment, are major elements of the folklore of schooling throughout the world. As of 1980 many nations had declared corporal punishment illegal. The United States is a notable exception. There are still indications, however, that students continue to be subjected in various nations to the pain of ridicule and embarrassment.

Among the frustration-producing punishments used by educators, detention (loss of free time) and withdrawal of privileges (membership of school teams, participation in games and field trips) are among the most common. Questions have been raised concerning the value of certain punishments, such as suspension or expulsion from school, assignment of extra classwork or homework, and lowering of student grades. Critics contend that these punishments may hurt students by depriving them of schooling and reinforcing the idea that schoolwork is aversive. Rather than producing respect for authority and productive behavior, they may lead to avoidance of school and diminished student self-image (Duke and Meckel 1980 pp. 120–25).

One form of punishment that is difficult to classify is parental contact. Presumably because students fear what their parents will say or do, the threat of a parent conference or phone call home has been reported to be one of the most effective punishments available to educators.

Particular forms of punishment may be effective with some students, but may not be used because they are also punishing to teachers or school officials. Detention, for example, may require teachers to use valuable free time to supervise students. The impact of punishment on the punisher as well as the subject thus must be assessed before determining its true effectiveness.

3. Perception of Punishment

How a student perceives a particular punishment may influence its effectiveness. For instance, some students may actually find a punishment rewarding. Suspending a chronic truant from school may neither be painful nor frustrating, especially if the student has found school sufficiently unpleasant to avoid in the first place. "Time out"—a technique whereby an uncooperative student is removed from the mainstream of class activity until his or her conduct improves—may be viewed by certain students as a welcome respite from teacher demands.

The effectiveness of punishments that are intended to deprive students of something valuable cannot be assessed without weighing the negative value of the loss against the positive value of misbehaving. Attending detention hall may be an insufficient deterrent if a student believes that the benefits of missing a class (i.e., seeing a friend, going fishing) outweigh the liability of spending several afternoons in detention after school.

How a student perceives a punishment may depend on various factors, including age and sex, what else is going on in the student's life at the time, and the nature of his or her relationship with the punisher. Educators who employ punishment need to develop a sensitivity to these factors when considering whether or not what they intend to be punishment actually will be perceived as such.

4. Administration of Punishment

Much has been written about the value of consistency in school discipline. Not only is consistency in rule enforcement regarded as vital, but consistency of punishment is cited as an important consideration for educators. One way to undermine the credibility of school discipline is to employ different punishments for the same offense.

Another issue concerns the level of impersonality that should characterize the administration of punishment. Psychologists generally feel it is more effective for punishment to be administered in a way that avoids highly personal references to students, their character, or their past history. Punishment should be "situation specific," a consequence of certain events rather than the deserved fate of a particular person.

Punishment which is meted out in too vindictive or unfair a manner may well lead to worse, rather than better, behavior. The lessons learned in the international arena by those who study how victors deal with the vanquished probably apply equally well to instances involving individual punishment. Research indicates students are quick to distinguish punishment that is fair from that which is arbitrary or based on an inaccurate assessment of events.

Because of these and other problems with the administration of punishment—problems which create the potential for doing more harm than good—individuals from Rousseau and Froebel to Skinner and Glasser have urged educators to stress positive reinforcement rather than punishment. They contend that punishing inappropriate behavior fails to demonstrate to students how they should behave and may lead to avoidance of school. Providing positive reinforcement in the form of praise and recognition when students observe classroom rules is regarded as a sounder investment of teacher time.

5. Legality and Morality

Whenever one individual attempts to inflict pain on or induce frustration in another person, questions of legal authority and moral justification may be raised. Traditionally in most societies, parents enjoyed virtually unlimited rights to punish their children. Acting in loco parentis, educators similarly possessed broad discretionary powers to punish students. In recent years many nations have acted to protect the rights of the young. In the United States, for example, students accused of serious offenses must be accorded due process, including a hearing. Court cases in which students bring suit against school authorities for improper punishment have been steadily increasing.

The morality of punishing students is a much-debated topic. Critics contend that there is a qualitative difference between the need to punish criminals and the need to maintain order in classrooms. They argue that behavior problems in schools are often indications of inadequate instruction, inappropriate curriculum, and errors in judgment on the part of educators. In recent years, however, student behavior problems in urbanized societies have begun to include more criminal acts such as attacks on teachers, drug use, and vandalism. Adjustments in curriculum and instruction may be unable to counteract the historical shift in the locus of youthful crime from the streets to the schools. Such a shift has occurred, in part, because of the expansion of mandatory school attendance laws.

Another moral issue concerns the use of punishment when there is no victim or when no harm is done to anyone other than the subject. Truancy and smoking cigarettes are two offenses that engender much controversy. Some educators maintain that these offenses actually may affect others, since truancy reduces school revenue in places where appropriations are based on attendance and smoking serves as a harmful model for young students. Others contend that trying to enforce these so-called "victimless" offenses requires energy that is needed more for instructional objectives.

6. Issues

In order to assess the appropriateness of punishment for school settings, it is necessary to consider several issues in addition to those already raised.

6.1 How is Punishment Related to Culture?

Different cultures treat punishment in different ways. Some condone corporal punishment in schools; others proscribe it. Some assume that young people will always misbehave and advocate punishment as an essential component in the development of self-discipline. Other cultures, such as those of Melanesia and the American Indian, are characterized by relatively little punishment of the young.

Cultural differences can also be found when one investigates the form punishment takes and how it is administered. School cleaning, for example, is a basic part of the educational experience of youngsters in much of Asia. In some Western countries where janitors are employed, however, cleaning school is assigned to students only as a punishment. Bronfenbrenner (1970) contrasts school discipline in the United States and in the Soviet Union. While educators are mostly responsible for determining punishment in the former, students handle many disciplinary duties in the Soviet Union.

6.2 Should Punishment be Individualized?

Educators are faced with a dilemma when it comes to punishing students. Educators are both professionals and civil servants. As civil servants, they are expected to treat all clients (students) the same. As professionals, they are expected to treat each client individually. In no area of school operations does this dilemma pose more problems than in discipline. Should teachers punish in the same way all students disobeying a given rule? To act in this manner may erroneously assume that all students are similarly motivated and equally likely to respond to the punishment. Should a student with a serious behavior disorder who is mainstreamed in a regular classroom, for example, receive the same punishment for talking out of turn as a normal student? Should the chronic offender be treated the same as the good student who has a bad day? If, on the other hand, teachers use different punishments for different students, they risk claims of discrimination from segments of the community. Evidence can be found in the United States and the United Kingdom, for example, that minority students are more likely to be punished by suspension from school than nonminority students.

In conclusion, it is safe to say that more questions than answers exist concerning the use of punishment in schools. No single punishment appears to be universally effective with all students. The conventional response to increased behavior problems—namely, to increase the severity of punishment—has not always proven to be an effective strategy. At the same time, eliminating punishment altogether appears unrealistic, given the size of schools today and what seems to be a growing tendency on the part of students around the world to challenge authority.

Bibliography

Bandura A 1969 *Principles of Behavior Modification*. Holt, Rinehart and Winston, New York

Bronfenbrenner U 1970 *Two Worlds of Childhood: US and USSR*. Russell Sage Foundation, New York

Clarizio H F, McCoy G F 1976 *Behavior Disorders in Children*, 2nd edn. Crowell, New York

Dreikurs R 1968 *Psychology in the Classroom: A Manual for Teachers*, 2nd edn. Harper and Row, New York

Duke D L (ed.) 1979 *Classroom Management*. University of Chicago Press, Chicago, Illinois

Duke D L, Meckel A M 1980 *Managing Student Behavior Problems*. Teachers College Press, New York

London P 1969 *Behavior Control*, 1st edn. Harper and Row, New York

Malinowski B 1976 *Crime and Custom in Savage Society*. Littlefield, Adams, Paterson, New Jersey

Redl F 1980 The concept of punishment. In: Long N J, Morse W C, Newman R G (eds.) 1980 *Conflict in the Classroom*. Wadsworth, Belmont, California

Factors Affecting Socialization

Family Influences on Human Development

R. M. Thomas

The term family is usually applied in both a narrow and a broad sense. In the narrow sense it refers to the nuclear or immediate family, meaning parents and their children. In the broad sense it refers to the extended family, meaning not only parents and their children but also such other relatives as grandparents, uncles, aunts, cousins, nieces, and nephews that are either closely related or only distantly connected "by blood" (genetically) or marriage to members of the nuclear family. While the word family usually identifies people who are related by genetics or marriage, in some societies it means as well a group of people who live together, whether or not they have marital or genetic bonds.

Among the units or institutions that compose a society—such as church, school, community, governmental bodies, clubs, and family—the family is universally regarded as exerting the most significant influence on child development, since the child's earliest and most intensive experiences typically take place within the family. Obviously, as the child grows into adolescence and adulthood, other societal institutions increasingly compete with or supplement family influence. However, a person's original family still continues to affect the individual significantly throughout the life span.

It is obvious as well that as the years pass, the individual's role within the family changes—new responsibilities and rights replace or augment earlier ones: the helpless infant becomes the mobile and talkative child; the school-age child grows into the adolescent who gains more privileges and is increasingly influenced by peers; the youth leaves the home to assume a vocation and become economically independent of parents; the young adult weds to begin a new nuclear family; the middle-aged adult bears responsibility for supporting and guiding a new generation; and the elderly grandparent retires from work and—in many societies—from directing the affairs of the family.

The purpose of the following discussion is not to inspect in detail the entire array of family variables that affect development from birth to death. Rather, the purpose is to identify only eight variables that illustrate something of the diversity of family influences. These aspects of family to be inspected include (a) family

functions, (b) authority hierarchies, (c) family size, (d) age roles, (e) sex roles, (f) caretaker roles, (g) birth order, and (h) individual family differences.

1. Family Functions

A family's functions can be regarded as those responsibilities the family accepts for the care and guidance of its members. Different societies hold different expectations for the nature of these responsibilities. For instance, the typical family in a nonindustrialized, rural society that lacks mechanized transportation and electronic-communication facilities will usually perform a far broader range of functions than will a family in a highly industrialized, urban society that depends heavily on advanced technology. The rural family that depends on agriculture, herding, or fishing for its livelihood provides its members with food, shelter, clothing, health care, protection from attack by human or beast, aid in the face of such disasters as fire or flood, love and affection, psychological support at times of emotional distress, companionship, entertainment, spiritual and religious guidance, moral and values training, educational and vocational counseling, social and vocational education, employment or job placement, financial backing for investment ventures (as in the purchase of a farm), and perhaps the selection of a marriage partner.

In contrast, in a variety of modern-day, highly industrialized, urban societies, a great many of the forgoing responsibilities have been transferred, at least in part, to other agencies, including the schools. This is particularly true in those societies that consider lifelong education to be a public responsibility, so that educational agencies extend from infant-care centers and nursery schools for the very young to nonformal education programs for the elderly. Schools have become responsible for teaching literacy, science, the structure of society, health practices, vocational skills, and moral behavior. Schools also provide entertainment, training in social skills, educational and vocational guidance and placement, medical care, and personal counseling. Some schools furnish, as well, food and clothing to needy children. Besides the schools, industrialized societies maintain an array of other agencies to carry out functions formerly performed by the family—police and fire departments for the protection of person and property, hospitals and clinics for medical care, social-welfare organizations for aid during natural disasters and unemployment, counseling and psychiatric services for personal- and social-adjustment problems, entertainment facilities (radio, television, theaters, sports centers, nightclubs, gambling casinos), churches for spiritual guidance, banks and loan companies for financial assistance, and many more.

Clearly, family functions are not limited to responsibilities toward growing children. In each society, husbands and wives are expected to fulfill responsibilities to each other, such as to meet sexual needs, carry out a share of productive work and child rearing, and offer emotional support to each other. The nature of these responsibilities varies from one culture to another. For example, in traditional Moslem societies a husband may have as many as four wives at one time. In Western societies, polygamy of this sort is generally forbidden.

Furthermore, societies hold different expectations for the relationships between the young and old. In many societies, as in traditional China, the young are obligated to display great respect for their elders, to care for the elderly and do their bidding without question. But in a growing number of industrialized societies, the responsibility to care for the elderly is shifting to the state or to private bodies, so that fewer old people live in the homes of their children. In addition, the opinions of the elderly in matters of decision appear to be respected less than in earlier times.

If the typical family in industrialized, urban societies has lost so many of the traditional functions, what roles remain for it? Duvall (1971 pp. 4–5) has proposed that "The new image of family life is that of the nurturing center for human development," a responsibility that includes at least six functions: "(a) affection between husband and wife, parents and children, and among the generations, (b) personal security and acceptance of each family member for the unique individual he is and for the potential he represents, (c) satisfaction and a sense of purpose, (d) continuity of companionship and association, (e) social placement and socialization, and (f) controls and a sense of what is right."

Not only do societies hold expectations about what functions families should perform, but they define as well what families should not do. Perhaps most obvious are strictures against certain sexual relations. Across cultures there appears to be a universal condemnation of incest, that is, of sexual relations between parent and child and between brother and sister. In many societies there is also condemnation of adultery in the sense of sexual relations between a married person and someone other than the marital partner, often with wives being condemned more than husbands for such behavior.

The forgoing review of family functions carries several important implications for human development. First, when a family deviates noticeably from any of its

expected responsibilities, members of the family are likely to suffer social disapproval and be denied the social and vocational opportunities they desire. Children who have not been taught in their family to abide by their society's moral standards may be rejected in their awkward attempts to fraternize with children from "normal" families.

Second, when a family fails to perform an expected role, there may be no adequate substitute agent to pick up that role, so the function remains neglected and can result in personal distress for the affected family members. Such is often the case in families that fail to offer children a proper diet, health care, affection, and understanding.

Third, as family responsibilities in a society change from traditional to modern forms, confusion often results about who is to perform which function. Is the family solely responsible for sex education, or is the school responsible? Is instruction in moral values chiefly the task of the home, of the church, of the school, of mass-communication media, or of all these? Thus, during periods of rapid transition in the social system, the division of responsibilities among the agencies of society in such realms as child rearing and care for the unemployed, the infirm, and the aged is often unclear and leads to anguish and social conflict. This is particularly true when various institutions—family, school, church, mass media—offer the growing child conflicting suggestions about desirable moral behavior, life goals, rights, and responsibilities. Yorburg has noted key interactions among societal change, family structure, and education:

> Societies with high levels of technological development change rapidly and require highly educated, psychologically flexible, and mobile populations. The higher levels of education and the breakdown of extended family and community controls characteristic of modern societies promote a greater tendency to think critically and to use rational means for achieving goals, a decrease in ethnocentrism and an increase in tolerance of human differences. . . . When norms are constantly changing, general principles as guides to behavior become more realistic and appropriate than specific rules and regulations. (Yorburg 1973 p. 185)

2. Authority Hierarchies

In any organization, including the family, there is a pattern of authority—an expected or official structure for who has what kinds of power over whom. The term patriarchal identifies a system in which the father of the family is the chief authority. A matriarchy is a family in which the mother is officially in charge. These terms, however, usually fail to reflect accurately the precise pattern of administrative power in a family. Typically, policy making and executive power is divided among family members according to different tasks they are expected to perform. In a family structure that ostensibly is patriarchal, the father may be responsible for providing the income, for deciding the main division of expenditures, for disciplining the older children, and for guiding their vocational and marital choices. The mother, on the other hand, may be responsible for preparing food and clothing, for housekeeping, for rearing the younger children, and for maintaining a liaison relationship with the school the children attend. Older girls in the family may bear delegated authority for rearing younger siblings. In effect, authority hierarchies typical of a society are often quite complex, and such hierarchies can differ from one culture to another.

From the viewpoint of child rearing and education, the family-authority structures of a society yield several implications. First, the basic model of family authority which children tend to carry through life is the example provided by the family in which they were raised. If that model is faulty, in the sense of deviating from the approved pattern for their society, the children are likely to apply this deviant pattern when they become parents. To illustrate, statistics on battered children show that the parents who abuse their children were often themselves battered children, so that they now are repeating as adults the same violent exercise of authority they experienced when young.

A second implication concerns the outcomes of rapid change in the modal authority patterns of a society. Sociologists investigating social change and family authority in Japan have proposed that such personal–social maladjustment as increased juvenile delinquency and suicide are due, at least in part, to changing family–authority relationships that include an increasing role for mothers and a decreasing importance of fathers in urban families, a loss of traditional values regarding home training, increasing self-centeredness of mothers, and inconsistent home discipline (Caudill in Hill and Konig 1970 pp. 3–11). In short, shifting patterns of family authority due to broad changes in the society can cause confusion within families and result in undesirable child-rearing and educational practices.

A third implication is that a loss of traditional authority in the family may influence authority patterns in the school. When youths lose regard for parents' authority, this disrespect may transfer to the youths' "surrogate parents" at school (teachers and headmasters), with a resultant deterioration in the control that school personnel need over students in order to conduct the typical educational program.

3. Family Size

As more societies enter the stream of increased industrialization and planned social change, families are diminishing in size. Not only are kinship groups being separated through greater geographical mobility, but nuclear families are having fewer children. Several forces have operated to decrease the number of children in families. For example, as industrialization grows, large numbers of children are no longer needed for the family farming and herding tasks of traditional agricultural societies. In addition, pressures of rapid popu-

lation growth find societies ill able to feed, house, and employ the growing millions, so that governments not only are encouraging family planning but often impose penalties on parents for having more than two or three children. Furthermore, in recent decades increasing numbers of women have practiced birth control in an effort to gain freedom from long years of child care and thereby pursue social and occupational ambitions of their own outside the home (Aires in Anthony and Chiland 1980 p. 23).

Accompanying these trends in family size are a number of educational consequences. One relates to the finance of schooling. With fewer children per family, parents and governments can more easily afford the expense of providing universal schooling, that is, of educating all children at least through secondary school in order to prepare them for the complex social and occupational roles required in advanced technological societies.

A second consequence concerns early childhood education. When children enter kindergarten from small nuclear families, one of the chief aims of their early schooling becomes that of peer socialization, of teaching the child how to get along well with other children, an aim that in earlier times was achieved at home in the family of many children.

Family size also influences the amount of direct parent–child interaction, which in turn has consequences for children's learning opportunities. Obviously, a mother and father with one or two children have far more time to spend with each child than parents with nine or ten. This means that in the smaller family, children not only may gain the emotional benefit of feeling important to their parents, but the children have more chances to experience directly adult-level conversation. And if parents use this opportunity to discuss matters that challenge children's growing capacity to understand more complex issues, the children may experience more rapid cognitive development than might be the case if their time were more fully engaged only with other children. Clearly, however, whether this potential for intellectual growth is realized depends upon the quality of the interaction of parent and child.

What may not appear evident at first glance is that the number of social relationships to which a child must adjust in a family is not simply the total number of family members besides himself or herself. Rather, as family size increases, the number of social connections the child encounters grows by geometric proportions. In a single-child family, the child must attend to three relationships—(a) his or her relationships singly with mother, (b) singly with father, and then (c) with the mother–father combination. When a second child enters the family, the number of relationships with individuals and with the various combinations of the other family members rises to seven. With a third child it becomes 15, and so on. This mounting progression of social contacts has both advantages and disadvantages. It furnishes the child constant opportunities to experience varied social relationships, and it provides enough potential companions to allow the child to select some that will prove compatible, even if others are not. On the other hand, the rise in number of family members may heavily tax the child's ability to adjust adequately to the varied individuals and combinations of them, particularly if there is much conflict, competition, and jealousy within the family social system. Furthermore, a child in a large family that is housed in limited space often lacks the privacy required for rest and contemplation and lacks a quiet place to study. The child may also lack possessions—books, clothes, keepsakes—that can truly be considered his or her own, since they must be shared with siblings.

So it is that the decrease in family size the world over is significantly affecting both the home and school environments in which children are nurtured.

4. Age Roles

Age roles are defined by the rights and responsibilities of family members at different age levels. Societies vary in the pattern of age-role expectations, with expectations changing over time and by social-class and rural–urban status.

Of particular significance for education are age roles related to employment and schooling. In low-technology agricultural and herding societies, as well as in the early stages of industrial development that involves much hand-labor of a relatively low degree of specialized skill, children are valuable labor commodities. From early ages they are expected to work in family enterprises. As mechanization increases so that one worker can do the work of many, children are not needed in the labor force. Often they form unwelcome competition for adults in economic systems suffering problems of technologically induced unemployment. Furthermore, in jobs that involve higher level cognitive skills and extensive training, children are unsuitable employees. They are unwelcome in the factories and fields, and are sent instead to school for the higher level preparation needed by advanced technological cultures. These several factors, along with a humanitarian sympathy for the plight of the young, has during the past century or more changed age-role expectations for children and adolescents. Over the first two decades of life, children are increasingly expected to be in school or involved in recreation rather than working. There are, however, many societies—particularly in developing nations—that are still in early stages of transition from having children at work to having children in school. Rural families and ones in lower social classes are slower to achieve this transition than urban families and those of middle- and upper-class status.

One obvious educational consequence of these age-role trends is that more children and youths need to be accommodated in schools. A second consequence is that the efforts of governments of developing nations to enforce compulsory-schooling regulations in keeping with a modernist view of child age-roles will run into conflict with parents who desire to maintain traditional family labor assignments in which both children and older youths stay at home to farm, fish, care for younger children, and do housekeeping.

A further problem faced by developed and developing nations alike is that of suiting schooling to the talents and interests of the entire array of students who are enrolled for compulsory education through ages 15 or 18. The curricula of the majority of the world's secular-education systems is strongly academic, with practical vocational studies in the minority and considered by the populace to be less prestigious than the more academic program. However, a substantial proportion of students in many school systems lack the aptitude or interest to succeed with the academic program and, as a consequence, find school an unsatisfactory experience. In earlier times these same students either would never have entered school at all or else would have left after the primary grades to enter the world of work, often taking jobs in a family enterprise to farm, fish, or follow their parents' trade.

Changing adult age-role expectations have also influenced education systems. The notion of lifelong learning has become increasingly popular, so that parents are increasingly viewed as students. This means that parents take time away from other family activities to attend adult education courses or to study via radio, television, and correspondence programs. In such countries as the Democratic People's Republic of Korea (North Korea), the government makes adult education obligatory and furnishes the learning facilities and social pressure intended to ensure that the expectation is realized. Such a requirement has altered Korean family life.

In summary, changes in age-role expectations within families have produced a variety of consequences for education programs throughout the world.

5. Sex Roles

Sex roles are defined by the obligations and privileges expected of females as contrasted to those expected of males within the family. The nature of these expectations differs from one culture to another, as does the degree of consensus within a given society about which sex should perform which duties and enjoy which rights. In recent decades in many societies there has been a marked transition in sex roles, with the main trend being that of females seeking—and increasingly obtaining—more privileges and responsibilities formerly held by males. This trend has become known by such phrases as the "equal rights movement" and the "women's movement." To a lesser degree, males in certain cultures have taken on tasks of child care and home-making that were formerly the main province of females. In each instance, one sex has not replaced the other, but rather, the responsibilities and rights have been shared more than in the past.

These shifts in sex roles within the family have influenced educational programs in several ways. Courses formerly limited to one sex have been made available to both, so that boys enroll in home economics classes and girls in industrial and technical studies. Certain types of athletics previously restricted to males have been opened to females. More institutions designed earlier for one sex have become coeducational. And in educational and vocational guidance, students from each sex have an increasingly broader scope of options from which to choose.

6. Caretaker Roles

All of the forgoing factors, plus others, have influenced ways that families care for their members, particularly the ways they care for children. In many cultures, child rearing is chiefly in the hands of the biological mother. In others, it is shared by the mother and a grandmother or aunts who live in the home. In still others, an older child—usually a girl—is assigned a younger child to tend much of the day, with the infant riding the older sister's hip or back or trailing along behind as the older girl goes about her chores and play. However, in some cultures, as in parts of Polynesia and Indonesia, men traditionally have shared in the supervision of the young. In others, such as in upper-class British and continental society of the past, mothers often had little—and fathers had practically nothing—directly to do with child raising, since nurses or "nannies" took chief charge of the children, and boys in middle childhood were sent away to boarding school until grown.

In complex societies, there are often several caretaking patterns, with each pattern representing an identifiable subtype of family for that culture. For example, black families in the United States generally lack a patriarchal tradition, so that mothers tend to be the dominant authority in the home and are "more pragmatic, more resourceful, and more flexible than women who have been protected within the patriarchal structure for centuries." At the same time, black fathers, compared to fathers of other American ethnic groups, are "more expressive in their marital and parental roles and are more helpful and willing to share in childrearing and homemaking chores" (Yorburg 1973 p. 143). A type of family that is rapidly on the increase in North America, as in other parts of the world, is the one divided by divorce, so that child care falls chiefly on a single parent, with the children occasionally visiting the other parent for short periods.

These variations in caretaking roles affect child development in significant ways. The caretaking-role assignments a child experiences can be expected to influence which adult or older child models the child seeks to imitate in his or her ideals and style of social interactions. The role assignments also help determine which kinds of people the child will trust, to whom he or she gives affection, and the way the child in later life will behave as a parent.

Yorburg, in discussing child-rearing trends evolving

in cultures marked by advanced technology, has proposed that:

> Declining authoritarianism in childrearing by parents who have more flexibility and more choices and alternatives in their own lives produces children who are more tolerant of outgroups, more honest and psychologically introspective, less sexually repressed, and less hostile. At the same time, the greater availability of objective educational and occupational opportunity, the greater need for drive and talent, and the decline of nepotism tend to promote emphasis on achievement in childrearing in all classes, all ethnic groups, and in all regions and locales—urban, urbanizing, and rural. (Yorburg 1973 p. 186)

7. Birth Order

Whether a child is the first-born to the family, the second, or later in the order of birth can have biological, sociological, and psychological consequences.

Statistics on biological growth indicate that first-born children grow somewhat faster than later born children, though when fully grown there are no significant differences among siblings in such characteristics as height. Tanner (1978 pp. 113–14) suggests that "The more mouths to feed, it seems, or simply children to look after, the slower the children grow."

Sociologically birth order can make a great difference, since privilege and responsibility in many cultures have been doled out differently to the first-born than to those who come later. In traditional societies of both the Orient and Occident, the primogeniture principle has been widely honored, providing to the eldest son (or lacking a son, to the eldest daughter) the choice family titles and estates along with the responsibility to be a faithful steward of the inheritance and the family reputation. However, this pattern is changing, so that opportunities—including chances for schooling—are less likely to depend as much on birth order as on children's individual initiative and on parents' attempt to distribute privilege and duty evenly among their offspring.

Studies have also revealed a variety of psychological correlates of birth order. An investigation of 400,000 Dutch men tested at age 19 showed that the earlier a man was in the birth order, the higher his intelligence-test scores tended to be (Belmont and Marolla 1973). Likewise, first borns tended to have the best psychological adjustment and last borns the poorest (Belmont 1977). The superiority of first borns in mental skills has been found in a variety of other nations as well.

It seems likely that such results are not just the consequence of birth order but are the effect of an interaction of such factors as social class and family size and configuration. Glass, Neulinger, and Brim (1974) found that first born and only children were better readers and set higher educational goals only among the upper social classes; in the lower social classes this relationship did not obtain. Papalia and Olds (1982 pp. 222–23) speculate that "Middle-class parents may be more likely than other parents to treat first-born children different from the others. . . . The crucial factor might well be the time that parents have available to give to each individual child, which is affected by the number of other children close in age who demand their attention."

In effect, it seems apparent that the child's personality characteristics are determined by a constellation of factors within the family rather than the existence of a particular factor, such as family size, the spacing between children, and the order of birth.

8. Individual Family Differences

Up to this point we have focused on typical kinds of families in various societies and have illustrated some ways that characteristics of these types can affect child rearing and education. But the danger in limiting attention to types is that it tends to obscure the fact that no two families are precisely alike, even though they qualify on the surface as being of the same general "type." It is useful to understand trends in family types within a culture in order to generate hypotheses about the way families in that culture likely influence the development of their members. However, in order to estimate how a particular child or adult has been affected by the family, it is necessary to study the constellation of forces operating within the specific family.

Bibliography

Anthony E J, Chiland C 1980 *Preventive Child Psychiatry in an Age of Transitions: The Child in His Family*, Vol. 6. Wiley, New York

Belmont L 1977 Birth order, intellectual competence, and psychiatric status. *J. Individ. Psychol.* 33: 97–104

Belmont L, Marolla F A 1973 Birth order, family size, and intelligence. *Science* 182: 1096–101

Duvall E M 1971 *Family Development*, 4th edn. Lippincott, Philadelphia, Pennsylvania

Glass D C, Neulinger J, Brim O G 1974 Birth order, verbal intelligence, and educational aspiration. *Child Dev.* 45: 807–11

Hill R, Konig R (eds.) 1970 *Families in East and West*. Mouton, Paris

Papalia D E, Olds S W 1982 *A Child's World: Infancy Through Adolescence*, 3rd edn. McGraw-Hill, New York

Tanner J M 1978 *Education and Physical Growth: Implications of the Study of Children's Growth for Educational Theory and Practice*. Hodder and Stoughton, London

Yorburg B 1973 *The Changing Family*. Columbia University, New York

Mother–Child Relations

L. V. Harper

The phrase mother–child relations refers to the quality of the emotional and/or caregiving interchanges between mothers and their children. Interest in the topic stems largely from the assumption that the kind of parenting children receive affects their adult intellectual and emotional functioning, and that mothers usually are the central figures during their offsprings' formative stages. In the last few years, developmentalists have begun to view mother–child relationships as the outcome of interactive processes to which both parties contribute from the outset, and global terms emphasizing the mother's contribution (e.g., warmth, control) have given way to more detailed, quantifiable descriptions of the specific activities constituting exchanges (Bell and Harper 1977, Schaffer 1977a, 1977b).

1. Contextual Determinants

Often underestimated determinants of mother–offspring relationships are the number, sex, and spacing of children. Fewer children and longer interbirth intervals typically mean more sensitive attention from mothers. Individual offspring also differ in terms of a number of attributes which affect parenting such as activity level, attentiveness, and responsiveness to parental ministrations. Furthermore, cultural beliefs concerning the meaning of these child attributes may affect how mothers react to such differences in child behavior. For example, sex differences in children's responses to variations in parenting may be mediated or intensified by cultural expectations for gender-appropriate behavior (Bell and Harper 1977, Lytton 1980, Schaffer 1977a). A mother's own prior experiences in being mothered will affect her relations with her child, but the final outcome will also depend upon her physical condition, her husband's or her family's support, and the cultural/economic milieu in which she finds herself, as well as her offspring's characteristics (Rutter 1979).

2. Development

On average, mothers are the primary caregivers in their children's early years and they usually are the foci of their offsprings' initial emotional attachments; however, they are not the only sources of influence. Grandparents, fathers, and siblings, among others, typically contribute to the development of the young; furthermore, a consistent, harmonious relationship with another adult may compensate for inadequate mother–child relations.

The mother–child relationship may be considered to originate with the implantation of the fertilized egg; subsequent events, including parturition, also involve exchanges between the mother and her developing baby. In the first few hours after birth, mother and infant seem to be uniquely ready to attend to one another. If all goes well, and neither member of the pair is physically debilitated or suffering from the effects of medication, perinatal contact can set the stage for later harmony. But even if contact is not established early, a positive relationship can still form later on, so long as the baby is normal (in particular, if its behavior is predictable) and the mother is physically able to respond (Bell and Harper 1977). The infant and the relationship may be considered "at risk" if the baby has suffered physiological insult during the birth process and/or the mother is suffering from physical or psychological disabilities. The outlook becomes less favorable if the mother does not have a husband or other family members to provide her with support, or if the family is in economic difficulties (Leiderman et al. 1977, Schaffer 1977b).

In the first year, mothers play the more active role in the development of social give-and-take by attempting to pace their activities to synchronize with their babies' receptiveness. Such pacing is accomplished by "reading" babies' facial expressions, hand movements, and vocalizations. Successful communication of this sort is thought to typify harmonious relationships. It seems that imitating a baby's actions or vocalizations provides a particularly effective way of establishing early social interchanges. Some feel that the critical feature in developing mutual social exchanges is the provision of repeated, predictable contingencies between mothers' activities and those of their babies (Schaffer 1977a, 1977b).

Close monitoring of, and responsiveness to babies' signals are not only associated with the development of elaborated communicative routines between mothers and their infants, but also to the development of secure attachments of the children to their mothers wherein the babies seem to trust their mothers to care for them without fear of abandonment. When mothers are inconsistently responsive or otherwise inattentive, their babies may be either very demanding or apparently aloof (Leiderman et al. 1977).

Once they become capable of independent locomotion, babies may be responsible for initiating up to 80 percent of the potentially educative situations that they experience. Maternal encouragement and facilitation, as opposed to direction, seem to best promote the development of capacities which are typically valued in Western, industrial societies. Such early competencies may also be fostered by high levels of maternal responsiveness, especially by conversation related to the toddler's focus of attention and by relatively few restrictions (such as play pens) on opportunities to move about and manipulate objects. Helping toddlers to develop communicative skills which permit them to use

their mothers as resources also seem to facilitate later development; ignoring even 3½-years-olds is a sure way to elicit demands for attention and/or reassurance (Lytton 1980, White et al. 1979).

However, after a child becomes capable of locomotion, the majority of mother–child exchanges focus on disciplinary matters, including the child's development of responsible initiative. Even among families in which the mother–child relationship would be judged harmonious, children up to 2 years of age often fail to comply with requests or directions they receive, and mothers' requests are more frequently ignored than are fathers'. Whereas maternal scolding, abrupt commands, or other forms of power assertion may be relatively effective in the short run, explanation of rules and the reasons for them result in better long-term compliance among young children. Often, however, when children are more compliant initially, their parents use less reasoning on subsequent disciplinary occasions (Lytton 1980, Martin 1981, White et al. 1979).

Whining, aggressiveness, and violation of prohibitions on the part of children are potent elicitors of maternal disapproval or criticism. Under normal conditions, when mothers react in these ways, their children usually shift to more acceptable behavior. However, when mothers respond to their children's transgressions with negatively toned commands or physical punishment, their youngsters' negative behavior tends to persist, and a vicious cycle may thereby be set in motion (Lytton 1980, Patterson 1980).

When their offspring are in middle childhood and preadolescence, mothers of highly aggressive sons may be victimized by their youngsters. Such mothers are often subjected to humiliating remarks, general negativism, and persistent demandingness. In such families, mothers are often burdened with the dual roles of caretaker and crisis manager. It is likely that an early combination of deficient maternal controlling skills and an unusually demanding and recalcitrant son lead to a "negative set" on the part of the mother and ever increasing demandingness and negativism on the part of her son. In such disturbed relationships, the mother often seems to try to avoid confrontation and frequently acquiesces to her child's aggressive insistence on his own way (Patterson 1980).

The quality of mother–child relationships thus develops through a long and complicated chain of interactions that involve, on the mother's part, her early willingness to respond to her offspring's demands and her overall involvement in social exchanges with her baby. The child's contributions involve its levels of demandingness in infancy and rates of compliance in toddlerhood. The picture is further complicated by the finding that later compliance has somewhat different early antecedents for girls and boys (Martin 1981). Studies of socialization also indicate that maternal sensitivity and acceptance typically are positively related to offspring obedience in middle childhood. When mothers of school-aged children expect age-appropriate, responsible behavior;

when they respond consistently and do not give in to nuisance behavior; and when they use reasoning, allowing their children to voice their opinions, their offspring tend to be friendly, self-reliant, and generally well-behaved. Conversely, rejection, punitiveness, or permissive noninvolvement seem to relate to problem behavior (Martin 1975).

3. Implications for Child Rearing

Several issues must be resolved before strong recommendations can be made concerning child-rearing techniques. There are extensive cross-cultural variations in mothering practices which, nevertheless, produce "good citizens." Thus there may be more than one route to a successful relationship. Moreover, it is not yet possible to specify how different children will react to various mothering styles; there may be significant individual differences among children in terms of their responses to what seem to be the same maternal behaviors (Martin 1981, Munroe et al. 1981, Schaffer 1977b).

Given the forgoing disclaimers, the evidence at hand, gained largely in Western industrialized societies, does lead to a few tentative conclusions. The more responsibilities a mother has, be they other children or adults to care for, housekeeping chores, or subsistence-related duties, the less time and energy she will have for her offspring. When mothers have such multiple demands made upon them, they appear to cope most successfully if they have some kind of support or assistance, whether from their spouses or extended families, or in the form of outside caregivers. On average, the more that young children are ignored by their mothers, the more demanding they will be. Contrary to popular folklore, there seems to be relatively little danger of spoiling infants, at least during the first year. On the contrary, when mothers are sensitive to their infants' signals, respond promptly and appropriately, and allow their youngsters to pace social exchanges, their babies are more likely to become securely attached, spontaneous, self-reliant, and cooperative (Lytton 1980, Schaffer 1977b). Furthermore, during the latter part of the first year and into the second year, curiosity and general well-being will be promoted by allowing mobile infants to explore more or less freely, and the provision of a variety of manipulable objects, at least some of which provide feedback, in a safe context which does not require much adult intrusiveness. Mothers also may facilitate their offsprings' linguistic-cognitive development (and further forge positive bonds with their youngsters) by ensuring that a significant proportion of the speech they direct toward their young is relevant to the child's interests. As control or discipline become issues, compliance from children seems to be facilitated by the appropriate use of explanation for demands or prohibitions, by consistent but gentle firmness, and the avoidance of harsh or physical rebuke.

4. Educational Implications

Current research suggests that environmentally induced cognitive deficits in children can be overcome even as late as the age of school entry, but that general interpersonal skills, the capacities to form close emotional bonds, and the ability to use adults effectively as resources may develop best during the preschool years (Rutter 1979, White et al. 1979). Therefore, for practical purposes, the evidence points to the importance of early parent education. White et al. (1979) demonstrated that early instruction in parenting techniques leads to some real (albeit modest) changes in maternal practices during the preschool years. However, these changes were evident only for mothers of first-born children; mothers of later-borns did not seem to be equally likely to put such instruction into practice. Thus, parent education is likely to be most effective if it begins by or before the time the first-born child is 6 months old.

An effective curriculum would involve sensitizing mothers to the significance of their babies' facial expressions, their hand movements, and the meaning of their cries. It would highlight the cues that can be utilized to predict changes in a baby's state and demonstrate techniques for controlling state changes, especially tactics for soothing upset babies. (Insofar as most normal mothers seem to be remarkably accurate at interpretation, emphasis for parents whose babies are not "at risk" might best be placed on the advisability of monitoring and acting upon such cues and of respecting the young infants' rhythms of receptiveness). The curriculum would outline procedures for capitalizing upon young children's inherent curiosity, for timing information to correspond to moments of receptiveness, and for ensuring that children have ample opportunity to become aware of the consequences of their actions and reactions with their environments. The curriculum should emphasize the ideas (a) that parents can make a difference in a child's growth but that they need not intrude into the child's activities, and (b) that much of the child's social and nonsocial education is self-generated so long as the surroundings offer variety, responsiveness, and safety (Munroe et al. 1981, Lytton 1980, Rutter 1979, Schaffer 1977a, 1977b, White et al. 1979).

Bibliography

Bell R Q, Harper L V 1977 *Child Effects on Adults*. Erlbaum, Hillsdale, New Jersey

Leiderman P H, Tulkin S R, Rosenfeld A 1977 *Culture and Infancy: Variations in the Human Experience*. Academic Press, New York

Lytton H 1980 *Parent–Child Interaction: The Socialization Process Observed in Twin and Singleton Families*. Plenum, New York

Martin B 1975 Parent–Child relations. In: Horowtiz F D (ed.) 1975 *Review of Child Development Research*, Vol. 4. University of Chicago Press, Chicago, Illinois, pp. 463–540

Martin J A 1981 A longitudinal study of the consequences

of early mother-infant interaction: A microanalytic study. *Monogr. Soc. Res. Child. Dev.* 46(3): Ser. no. 190

Munroe R H, Munroe R L, Whiting B B 1981 *Handbook of Cross-cultural Human Development.* Garland STPM Press, New York

Patterson G R 1980 Mothers: The unacknowledged victims. *Monogr. Soc. Res. Child Dev.* 45(5): Ser. no. 186

Rutter M 1979 Maternal deprivation, 1972–1978: New findings, new concepts, new approaches. *Child Dev.* 50: 283–305

Schaffer H R (ed.) 1977a *Studies in Mother–Infant Interaction,* Proc. of the Loch Lomond Symposium, Ross Priory, University of Strathclyde, September 1975. Academic Press, London

Schaffer R H 1977b *Mothering.* Harvard University Press, Cambridge, Massachusetts

White B L, Kaban B T, Attanucci J S 1979 *The Origins of Human Competence: The Final Report of the Harvard Preschool Project.* Heath, Lexington, Massachusetts

Father's Role in Development

W. Draper

Fatherhood is a highly individualized experience. The father's role is an active one, but distinctly different from the mother's in the development of their children within the family network. In the following, the father's role in development is presented in the light of cultural and historical perspectives, the direction of research in the area of parenthood, the father's influence on development, and the father's perception of his role.

1. Cultural and Historical Perspective

Cultural ideas influence the conceptualization of the father's role. Fathers reared in one type of family setting but who later move into another culture, or who are caught up in a transitional attitude within a given culture, may experience difficulty in fulfilling the father role conceptualized by peers and even by spouses.

Great variation across cultures characterizes contributions of fathers to early infant and child care. The definitions of sex roles vary with the social, ideological, and physical environmental conditions in different cultures. Fathers share a more equal role in caring for young children in some cultures than in others. Among the Trobrianders of Melanesia, for example, the father has a considerable share in the feeding, transporting, and general care of young children. The Taira of Okinawa, the Nyansongo of Kenya, and the Ilocos of the Philippines are cultures in which the father and mother share equally in infant and child care. Recent trends in Sweden and the United States are evidence of more active paternal involvement in child care (Parke and Sawin 1976).

The role of father has been prescribed primarily in Western, industrialized society as having a minor part in the care of infants and young children. Traditionally, the father has been conceptualized as the provider and head of the family group. Emphasis has been placed on his prescribing activities for the child's good and on doing things for the child, with primary interest in the child's accepting and attaining goals he has established. However, the historical view of the father as being less involved than the mother can be challenged. Evidence clearly indicates that fathers are not consistently assigned a secondary role in all cultures. A con-

temporary view has defined the father as one interested in what his child does, encouraging the child to be interested in what he as father does, and helping the child attain his or her own goals (Parke and Sawin 1976).

Historical, social, and economic arrangements do not necessarily imply that fathers are incapable of assuming a caregiving role. Changes in technological and economic spheres suggest the possibility of changed roles for both males and females. It is important to monitor those shifts in the larger social and economic structure which have a tendency to alter the definition and allocation of sex roles. Shifts in behavior and medical developments also influence parent roles. For example, a trend toward bottle as well as breast feeding makes it possible for fathers to offset the biological difference in this area of child care.

In this connection, patterns of father–child interaction are highly susceptible to shifts in work schedules, family living arrangements, and role expectations. However, because these shifts affect individuals in different ways, general social trends cannot be isomorphically applied to individual families or parents.

2. Research

In contrast to the wealth of data on mothering, a dearth of data exists on fathering, and on the isolation of those behavioral variables which make the father's role take on its significance (Bigner 1970). Since the emphasis in research has been focused on the maternal aspects of parent–child relations, theoretical frameworks in early social development have tended to limit our view of the father–child relationship. By the mid-1960s, theoretical shifts finally legitimized the active investigation of the father's role in early infant social and cognitive development. The work of Schaffer and Emerson in the 1960s helped to bring about this shift, as they demonstrated that human infants showed "attachment" to fathers who may have never participated in routine caregiving activities. They reported that the social stimulation and responsiveness of the father to the infant's behavior was an important determinant of attachment (Schaffer and Emerson 1964).

Increasingly, a shift from "mother as stimulation" and

"infant as contributor" to the dynamics of interpersonal synchrony is becoming the aim of research on parent–infant interaction. This places the focus on the reciprocal nature of the process in which parents and infants mutually regulate and stimulate each other. More recently, focus on a developmental orientation to father–child interaction tracks the continuities and discontinuities across time in the nature of the father–child dyad and in the family triad. Implicit in this developmental approach is a recognition that all members of the interactive network—father, mother, and child—are changing over time (Parke and Sawin 1976).

3. Influence on Development

The father influences his children's social, emotional, and cognitive development by drawing them into a world beyond the intimate relationship with the mother. The father becomes the pivotal person who represents the outside world. He stimulates the child's interest in the world and promotes the child's reality testing (Forrest 1967, Pearce 1977).

Sensitive, nurturing caregiving by the father enables the infant to develop trust in the world as a warm and caring place that functions in an orderly manner. Sensitive caregiving is responsive and, therefore, communicates that the child's actions have consequences, thus motivating subsequent activity. Conversely, restrictions squelch the curiosity that motivates learning and that thrives in a stimulating environment.

Children whose caregivers, including fathers, are sensitive to their cues, responsive to their actions, and stimulating but not too restrictive, are likely to develop optimally during the first years of life.

From the very beginning of attachment relations, infants appear to form attachments to both parents and not to the mother alone. In studies reported by Jackson and Jackson (1978), the Israeli developmental psychologist Rivka Landau found that infants, regardless of age, showed no preference for the mother over the father, even when they differentiated between visitors and their parents by their display of attachment behavior. Moreover, the infants in Landau's research were found to direct significantly more affiliative behavior toward their fathers than their mothers. They smiled, vocalized, looked, and laughed more in the father's presence. In more relaxed atmospheres, babies fussed to their fathers as much as to their mothers and their fathers soothed them as often as did their mothers.

Fathers generally play with their babies more often and for longer periods than do mothers. Positive responses are more intense when playing with fathers even though babies play with both parents (Jackson and Jackson 1978). Fathers are more likely to pick up babies to play with them while mothers pick them up more for caretaking purposes. This practice may explain the greater affiliative responses to fathers than to mothers and the more positive character of these responses.

During the second year of life, the child's relation to the father becomes especially important because the child is in the process of "separating and individualizing" from the mother (Mahler et al. 1975). The father's interest in and response to the child, as well as the nature of his interactional behavior, also has an impact on the child's social and emotional development during the transitional period from early to middle childhood.

At about 7 years of age, the child psychologically reaches out beyond the mother for other close relationships. By this time, the child is more stable, relaxed, and cooperative than during the earlier childhood years. The child thrives on praise and is sensitive to criticism and disapproval. Introspection begins to have more meaning as the child begins to fill out his or her concept of self and of the world. Father–child relationships during this transitional period set the stage for maintaining stable relationships with others through the adolescent years. A sympathetic understanding of what goes on in the mind of the child, therefore, is at the heart of good fathering.

3.1 The Father as Role Model

Fathers serve as models of behavior which reflect a system of values and attitudes that will affect their children's behavior. Examples of the power of such models can be observed as young children imitate and mirror their parents' actions. As children develop cognitively and acquire social experience, they demonstrate the significance of their parent models by (a) performing similar tasks, and (b) reflecting the concepts modeled.

Kagan (1958) delineated masculine identity as being dependent on three conditions: (a) the father as model must be perceived as nurturant to the child; (b) the model must be perceived as being in command of desired goals—such as gaining power, receiving love from others—and as being competent in tasks which the child regards as important; and (c) the child must perceive some basis of similarity between himself and the model (Bigner 1970 pp. 359–60).

Neubauer (1960) and Money (1965) report that sex-role concepts appear to be difficult to change after the third year of life, thus suggesting that the father's presence is critically important during the early years. Future difficulties experienced in sex-role identity by boys whose fathers were absent are supported by the data of Whiting, Kluckhohn, and Anthony (1968) and of Burton and Whiting (1961). These data also reflect that both male and female children experience deleterious personality development when presented with the combined factors of father absence and a shift by the mother to a more authoritarian child-rearing pattern (Bigner 1970 pp. 357–62).

3.2 Absence of the Father

Child rearing in father-absent families is often associated with poor performance on cognitive tests. This also holds true in families in which fathers have little supportive interaction with their children. Research findings are generally consistent with the hypothesis that children's interaction with their parents fosters cognitive development and that a reduction in interaction hinders it. Anxiety and financial hardship in father-absent families may also contribute to these detrimental effects (Chess and Thomas 1972).

Factors resulting from father absence may contribute more to delinquency of children than the actual absence of the father. For example, the mother's ability to maintain effective supervision and a harmonious home climate may be hindered by the father's absence. Such factors include stress and conflict within the home, inability of the mother to exercise adequate supervision, depressed income and living conditions, the mother's psychological and behavioral reaction to the separation from the husband, social and economic difficulties of her situation as a sole parent, and community attitudes toward the child and family (Herzog and Sudia 1973).

Two typical tendencies are noted in the child's response to a parent leaving home: (a) the child idealizes the absent parent, or (b) the child devalues that person completely. Devaluing may help the child to retain a sense of loyalty to the remaining parent, thus attempting to earn the good graces of that parent.

The child may seek to maintain an image of the absent father as a positive figure, using the fantasy of a "good" father to help him or her to comprehend the father's departure, separation, and nonresidency. The child can then express the wish to reclaim the father as a "good" figure who is consistently present in his or her life. In this way the child uses the fantasy father in the continued movement away from the mother toward greater autonomy (Grossberg and Crandall 1978). Similarly, the child may avoid the pain of loss of the father by identifying with or incorporating the image of the father into his or her self and behavior. Some children have a need to believe that the father left as a means of punishment. They may feel that they caused the parents to separate and the father to leave. Children may, in such cases, become active in their behavior with power-centered goals. For as long as a child believes he or she caused the parents to divorce, it is easy to believe he or she has the power to reunite them (Grossberg and Crandall 1978). Boys usually have more difficulty adjusting to divorce situations than do girls. It may be difficult for a boy to identify with the absent father whom the mother dislikes or with a father who was perceived as being hostile to his mother (Grossberg and Crandall 1978).

Death, an event which influences development, shows its effect not only at the time of occurrence, but frequently creates a disturbance at later stages of the child's development. Mourning, including the initial grief reaction to the loss and the resolution of that grief, is dependent on the child's ability to comprehend the meaning of death. In the loss of a father during the early years, the child generally becomes totally dependent on the mother. The expression of anger is often repressed, frequently resulting in aggression turned against the self and increasing attachment to the mother. In such cases the conflict between dependence and defiance may remain unresolved (Grossberg and Crandall 1978).

During the early years, girls who lose their fathers often experience impaired relationships with men because no "real" man can compete with the idealized image of the absent father. During this period, boys may fantasize that the father has been removed by the mother because of the father's masculine aggression, thus acting as a disturbance to the boy's normal heterosexual wishes (Grossberg and Crandall 1978).

4. Father's Perception

The father's world view (*Weltanshauung*) influences how he perceives his role in relation to his children. His image of being a father is formed largely by the way he was fathered, and this image will, in turn, be passed on to his children. The feelings he experiences about being a father will be reflected in the emotional tone of his interactions with the child and in the psychological atmosphere that he helps to create within the family network.

Bibliography

Bigner J 1970 Fathering: Research and practice implications. *Fam. Coord.* 19: 357–62
Biller H B 1971 *Father, Child and Sex Role: Paternal Determinants of Personality Development.* Heath, Lexington, Massachusetts
Chess S, Thomas A (eds.) 1972 *Annual Progress in Child Psychiatry and Child Development.* Brunner/Mazel, New York
Forrest T 1967 The paternal roots of male character development. *Psychoanal. Rev.* 54: 51–68
Grossberg S H, Crandall L 1978 Father loss and father absence in preschool children. *Clin. Soc. Work J.* 6: 123–34
Herzog E, Sudia C E 1968 Fatherless homes: A review of research. *Children* 15: 177–82
Herzog E, Sudia C E 1973 Children in fatherless families. In: Caldwell B, Ricciuti H (eds.) 1973 *Review of Child Development Research,* Vol. 3. University of Chicago Press, Chicago, Illinois, pp. 141–232
Jackson, J F, Jackson J H 1978 *Infant Culture.* Crowell, New York
Lynn D B 1974 *The Father: His Role in Child Development.* Brooks/Cole, Monterey, California
Mahler M S, Pine F, Bergman A 1975 *The Psychological Birth of the Human Infant: Symbiosis and Individualization.* Basic Books, New York
Parke R D, Sawin D B 1976 The father's role in infancy: A re-evaluation. *Fam. Coord.* 25: 365–71
Pearce J C 1977 *Magical Child: Rediscovering Nature's Plan for our Children.* Dutton, New York
Schaffer H R, Emerson P E 1964 Patterns of responses to physical contact in early human development. *J. Child Psychol. Psychiatry* 5: 1–13

One-parent Families

B. T. Eiduson

The one-parent family is defined as the family in which at least one child resides with a single parent. The one-parent family is generally regarded as a modification of the traditional family which in most societies consists of the nuclear unit, as defined by mother, father, and children.

The one-parent family is created in a number of ways: through the death of one parent; through the formal dissolution of marriage, divorce; through informal breakups of the marital relationships, as in separation or desertion; and through single parent status, or intentionally or unintentionally having a child outside of wedlock. Widowhood, desertion, and separation were the primary contributors to one-parent families until the 1970s, when the rise in divorce rates in most countries in the world, and the growth of family units that were not legalized, became major population trends.

Most of the contemporary unwed one-parent households occur by default; however, others are elective. The availability of abortion has made single mother status elective for many women. However, studies suggest that the decision to have a baby is more often made at a postconception, rather than a preconception, stage. The age of the mother seems to be directly associated with the lack of prepregnancy planning, with the adolescent girl being overrepresented in this group.

In addition, a number of one-parent families have emerged as examples of the development of nontraditional alternative life-styles. In these cases, women have opted to become pregnant and raise their children without the support of a male partner. They are considered "alternative" because many of the values of these women are consonant with those of other nonconventional family styles such as cohabiting couples and living groups or communal families. Alternative family styles are conscious departures from the legal traditionally married nuclear units. These alternative families often consider traditional families to be too materialistic, not sufficiently interested in humanistic relationships, too dependent on science and technology, too exclusively oriented toward logic and rationality in problem solving, and too sex stereotypic in assignment of family roles and responsibilities. The elective single parent vacillates in his or her identification with such perspectives, at times assuming alternative positions, but at other times being very traditional, as, for example, in regard to setting conventional goals for achievement for self and offspring.

1. Trends in the Growth of the One-parent Family

Sociological changes affecting family composition point to a worldwide drop in marriage rates during the 1960s and 1970s, a doubling of the number of divorces, a rise in the number of one-parent households (mostly headed by females), and an increase in the number of children born out of wedlock.

In countries reporting annual statistics (Kamerman and Kahn 1978), the number of one-parent families appears to involve between 5 and 15 percent of households. In the United Kingdom, where, in 1975, 50 percent of families were composed of parents with children, slightly more than 6 percent were one-parent families. At about the same time, Poland reported 13 percent one-parent families, mostly headed by women. In the Federal Republic of Germany over 7 percent of all family groups in 1975 were single-parent units. In the United States, 16 percent of all children, involving over five million families, lived with one parent. Nine percent of all Canadian families in 1971 were one-parent, with death of spouse accounting for 47 percent of these, divorce 12 percent, separation 34 percent, and unwed mothers 8 percent. In some countries the lack of a conjugal relationship has become legitimized for all strata of the population. Two-thirds of women having out-of-wedlock children in Sweden in 1971, for example, were cohabiting with the child's father.

Illegitimate births in Denmark, which in 1940 comprised 8 percent, increased to 11 percent in 1970, and to 22 percent in 1975. In Norway, birth rates declined in the period 1965–75, the number of divorces doubled, and the number of children born out of wedlock increased. In the United States, the divorce rate in 1976 was the highest of all time at over one million, affecting 1.25 million children; and the number of marriages, over two million, was the lowest ever. One-parent (mother) families totaled over five million and contained over 10.3 million children; however, in 1976, 80 percent of all American children lived with both parents. Most of the one-parent families in the United States are female headed, with less than 7 percent of one-parent families being male headed. Joint legal custody arrangements are increasing; in these, children have two active parents, but live with only one parent at any one time.

Because of the trend toward restructuring or reconstituting new families through remarriage (in 70 percent of the families with children in the United States, in 1975, for example), single parenting is being regarded increasingly as a temporary or transient phenomenon that will be faced by one-third to one-half of the child population at some time of their lives.

2. Child-Rearing in One-parent Families

The way a child is reared in a one-parent unit would seem to be influenced by a number of factors: the parent's economic wherewithal, employment status, personal and psychological satisfactions, value systems, status in the community, and available support networks.

In most countries, one-parent families are overrepresented in the low-income family bracket. In the United States, one-half of the 11 million families in poverty were female-headed, one-parent families. The United Kingdom's Finer Report (1973) proposed that a special guaranteed maintenance allowance be set up in order to provide some minimum level of income for single-parent families, a recommendation that still remains to be implemented. The plight of those one-parent units, in which a change of family status—as by divorce or desertion—results in sharp downward economic mobility, is often compounded by poor housing and moves into deteriorating and high-stress neighborhoods.

Mothers in one-parent families are overrepresented among employed females, as are women in minority populations and in economically deprived groups. When single mothers seek employment, they often display little experience, and minimal vocational skills. Few opportunities for schooling or occupational retraining exist. Thus such women are relegated to low-paying, unstable positions, and are the most expendable in times of economic recession.

With many single parents in the work force, the availability of appropriate child caretaking arrangements in the early years of infancy and childhood, and for pre- and after-school arrangements for the school-aged child, becomes a major issue. Such needs also exist in the two-parent family in which both parents are employed; yet the inflexibility of the single parent's role is made more compelling by the data (Glick 1979) showing that the number of one-parent families who have second adults living with or near them who are available to share caretaking responsibilities, has generally decreased during the 1970s. Thus the lone parent is stressed with heavy work burdens as well as with the sole responsibility involved in providing psychological and personal supports for children.

Many countries have as yet to make formal commitments to meet the needs of child and parent in one-parent families. Day care, after-school care, and substitute homemakers when a parent is ill or must go to work before children have left for school, are requisites for effective family functioning. In some countries where policy in these areas has been legislated, implementation has resulted in limited and inadequate facilities. In many countries, even where children of single parents have been given priority over two-parent families, the demands of all single mothers for day care are not met.

Having available time for children is a serious problem for the lone parent. Faced with the multiple demands of work, household, and interdigitating adult and child activities, the parent is confronted with the problem of "overload." Dissatisfactions arise over the limited time with children, as well as over their own social isolation. Recriminations and disappointments over "fate" can invade child–parent relationships and color the emotional ambience of the home. With a reduced level of participation in the community, the single-parent feels a lack of social support and a sense of powerlessness. These attitudes condition a negative self-image, reduce ability to be a competent parent, and may lead to long-term pessimism, distrust, and alienation.

Single parent status may generate social censure by the community or criticism of deviancy. Although tempered by the changing values of the modern age, many societies still regard all single parents as nontraditional, and raise questions about the developmental and moral implications for the child. In actuality, child rearing in one- and two-parent families shares many features. Studies of feeding, eating, or sleep patterns of the child show few significant differences between one- and two-parent families. In many of the psychological aspects of caretaking studied in infancy and early childhood—such as affective interactions between parent and child, verbal interchanges, intellectual stimulation, attentiveness—there are few significant differences in one- and two-parent families.

The child-rearing practices of all single parents are no more alike than those of traditional two-parent families and both styles are marked by a large range of parenting behaviors. There are some highly competent single parents, as well as some less competent ones. However, single mothers as a group show more concern about psychological or behavioral problems than do parents in other life-styles. Their children are referred to physicians or child guidance facilities with significantly greater frequency than are children in traditional homes. This may reflect greater frequency of problems on the one hand, but may also indicate the single parents' limited psychological support, and their tendency to become anxious about their ability to handle problem behaviors when they occur. Discipline practices of single parents seem somewhat more restrictive and more punitive than those found in two-parent homes. Divorced single parents report problems disciplining children. Studies suggest that divorced parents make fewer demands than do married controls, communicate less well, are less affectionate, and more inconsistent. Sex and age of child affect child-rearing behaviors, with divorced mothers communicating less well, and using more negative sanctions with sons, as compared to daughters.

In self-chosen single mother households, child rearing is marked by a conscious desire to change the traditional sex stereotyping of children's interests, activities, and propensities.

3. Child Development in One-parent Families

In past studies where father absence has occurred by divorce, death, desertion, or long separations occasioned by war or distant employment, single parenthood has been associated with maladjustment and deviance in the child. Both cognitive and intellectual sequelae as well as emotional problems have been associated with the father's absence; the negative effects on children's intellectual performance and academic attainment were particularly stressed. Changes in the nature of analytic thinking patterns in the direction of characteristics identified with girls (i.e., high verbal and low spatial and quantitative development), were shown in father-absent boys. Gender identity difficulties were hypothesized, and problems in assuming appropriate psychosexual roles during adolescence were noted, with some question about father absence fostering homosexual leanings. Studies showing greater involvement in delinquency of father-absent boys suggested deficits in moral development. Girls were not exempt from such problems, but greater effects in the absence of father as a role model have been postulated. Introversion and depression have been described in the emotional patterns of both sexes.

The validity of such early data have been thrown into question since the studies did not accommodate for such pertinent contributing variables as socioeconomic status of the family, reasons for father's absence, availability of parent substitutes, presence of other siblings who also share father absence, parent's attitude toward the absentee parent, and age of child at time of absence.

More recent studies have identified different types of single-parent families. Some one-parent units show sequelae which put children "at risk." For example, low birth weight, with associated physical anomalies in the child have been found in children of teenage mothers; offspring fail to meet developmental milestones in early years. This is not the case for babies of elective single mothers who were themselves reared in middle-class families.

Other cognitive studies have noted distractibility, impulsivity, short attention span, and lack of task persistence in one-parent children, which in turn were associated with drops in scores on performance and quantitative tests and certain problem-solving tasks. However, these were noted when parenting practices were poor and therefore do not seem to be attributable to the single-parent family style as such. Although being a competent parent is more difficult for all lone parents, some single parents are very effective: in a longitudinal study, children of elective Caucasian middle-class single parents have shown good adjustment, and appropriate signs of maturity. In the group as a whole, children were intellectually as well as socially competent, being appropriately cooperative, creative, and assertive at age 3 and at age 6.

Studies of the single-parent child's attachment or bonding to the mother have shown the same range of behaviors found in two-parent-family children. None of the hypothesized overattachment between single parent and child, nor the rejection of the parent by the child, has appeared at 1-year or 3-year age periods.

The social and emotional data on children who are in one-parent units because of divorce suggest that the child's age at the time of family disruption, the child's sex, number of siblings experiencing the disruption simultaneously, and availability of the noncustodial parent to the child influence child adjustment.

There is growing evidence that in every single-parent family, the imprint of the personality, resources, and limitations of the sole parent becomes markedly stamped on the child, as compared to the two-parent family where the child's sense of identity is shaped by two sources of input. Thus, the single parent's resources, stability, and styles of coping seem critical for the child's personality development.

As yet there has been a dearth of studies showing the strengths and resources a child can gain in having to adapt to a one-parent household. Development of independence in thinking, tolerance for stress and frustration, strong fantasy potential, and early development of personal skills are being studied in this regard.

4. The Role of Education for One-parent Families

Questions educators face include the following: can schools and other educational institutions supplement the one-parent family, to ensure that the needs of the child be adequately met? To what extent should or can schools absorb family functions that single parents have no time or personal resources to meet? Will policies and practices in this direction weaken the already stressed role of the family in children's lives? Will such responsibilities overload the schools unduly, and prevent them from performing their primary functions?

As a corollary, if schools and other institutions begin to serve children of one-parent families in new ways, do issues of privacy and confidentiality arise? What should schools be told about family matters? Especially in regard to the children of elective single parents, will children be exposed to conscious or unconscious discrimination?

The role of educational institutions to date has focused on both parent and child training. For single parents, and for women in particular, effective job training is essential. It is generally agreed that women need the background to undertake work that will make them self-supporting. At the same time, policies of most countries encourage single parents to have choices about whether to work, go to school, or stay at home with children.

Education must also adapt to the pluralism and diversity in contemporary families. Many instances can be cited in which the school curriculum has not accepted single parenthood as an ordinary (although not necessarily preferable) type of family. Teachers, school nurses, and principals must be trained to deal with the needs of children of lone parents just as they have been trained to deal with the needs of children from two-parent families. Report cards may have to be made available to both custodial and noncustodial parents. The handling of the usual "father–son" activities or "parent night" has to be reconsidered.

In addition, the practical problems confronted by a single-parent family, such as needing to get the child home from school when the parent is ill or in a difficult work situation, must be recognized and understood, and perhaps the school needs to offer assisting resources. The development of school emergency services has been suggested. Temporary transportation to and from work and even some kind of temporary accommodation for when a parent is hospitalized or is ill, are characteristic of the kind of facilities that would ensure that the child's normal school routines are not disrupted at such critical, anxiety-producing times.

Single parents often fear that children will be socially segregated in obvious or nonobvious ways and perceived as different from two-parent children by teachers or classmates. They consider that such experiences would be counterproductive to the child's effort at feeling and being regarded as "normal." They therefore discourage identification of the child as coming from a one-parent home, and insist that the child's classroom assignment and participation in all school activities be made without regard to his or her family structure.

Another role suggested for educational resources is the development of a repository of information that provides parents with knowledge that will reduce anxieties and give them some feeling that support is available. Excellent examples of direct, simple question-and-answer pamphlets have been developed to meet the many questions about housing for one-parent families which often involve significant legal issues. The availability of such booklets and the opportunity to discuss implications of one's personal situation with appropriate counseling persons is proving to be a very important strengthening mechanism to the parent who is managing alone and who has customarily not been the person in the relationship who has dealt with such issues.

Bibliography

Eiduson B T 1981 Contemporary single mothers as parents. *Current Topics in Early Childhood Education*, Vol. 3. Ablex, Norwood, New Jersey

Eiduson B T, Forsythe A 1983 Life change events in alternative family styles. In: Callahan E J, McClusky K A (eds.) 1983 *Life-span Development Psychology: Non-normative Life Events*. Academic Press, New York

Eiduson B T, Cohen J, Alexander J 1973 Alternatives in child rearing in the 1970's. *Am. J. Orthopsychiatry* 43: 721–31

Eiduson B T, Kornfein M, Zimmerman I L, Weisner T S 1981 Comparative socialization practices in alternative family settings. In: Lamb M (ed.) 1981 *Nontraditional Families*. Plenum, New York

Glick P 1979 Children of divorced parents in demographic perspective. *J. Soc. Issues* 35: 170–82

Hetherington E M, Cox M, Cox R 1978 The development of children in mother-headed families. In: Hoffman H, Reiss D (eds.) 1978 *The American Family: Dying or Developing*. Plenum, New York

Kamerman S B, Kahn A J (eds.) 1978 *Family Policy: Government and Families in Fourteen Countries*. Columbia University Press, New York

Smith M J 1980 The social consequence of single parenthood: A longitudinal perspective. *Fam. Relat.* 29: 75–81

Wallerstein J S, Kelly J B 1980 *Surviving the Breakup: How Children and Parents Cope with Divorce*. Basic Books, New York

Adoption and Development

E. V. Mech

Adoption is defined as a process whereby persons achieve parenthood through legal and social procedures rather than through a biological process. In adoption a child of one pair of parents legally becomes the child of other parents.

Adoption is an ancient practice. Egyptian, Roman, and Greek societies sanctioned adoption. In earlier periods, adoption was arranged primarily to acquire heirs and to provide continuity for a family line. Modern adoption practice emphasizes giving adopted children the same inheritance rights as a biological child. Because of interference with the inheritance rights of natural heirs, adoption was unrecognized in English common law and not considered legal in England until the early 1900s. Adoption legislation in England, Wales, Northern Ireland, and Scotland was passed in the late 1920s. Even then, Scotland's adoption law did not permit adopted children to inherit from the adoptive parents (Mandell 1973). In the United States, the Massachusetts Act of 1851 was the first adoption statute passed for the main purpose of protecting children and legalizing a new parent–child relationship (Zietz 1959).

Adoptions can be classified as either related or nonrelated. In related adoption, a child may be adopted by a grandparent, step parent, or other family member. In nonrelated adoption, placement is with a couple having neither biological nor family ties to the child. Focus in this summary is on nonrelative adoption. Children placed for adoption with nonrelated persons are thought to be more vulnerable in their development than are children raised with their biological families. Among the reasons cited for the heightened vulnerability of these nonrelated adoptions are: (a) society views adoptive families as a minority group in terms of child rearing and labels adoptive families as being different from normal families; and (b) adopted children are thought to have difficulty with their adoptive status and in understanding why the biological parents "gave them up" for placement.

1. Adoption Outcomes

How do adoption placements work out? Representative follow-up studies over a period of nearly 50 years indicate that nearly three of every four adoption placements are judged as satisfactory (Mech 1973). Recent data from Western Europe corroborate the positive influences of adoption. A follow-up investigation in England indicates that for nearly 85 percent of the adoptive parents studied, that adoption was reported to be a satisfactory experience. Similarly, nearly 80 percent of the adoptees interviewed conveyed satisfaction with the adoption experience (Raynor 1980). In Sweden, a longitudinal study of children registered for adoption reported ". . . at 15 years there was little difference in adjustment between the adopted children and their classmates" (Bohman and Sigvardsson 1980 p. 330). Moreover, the Swedish investigation found considerable maladjustment and school failure among those children reared by their biological mothers who originally registered the child for adoption, but later decided to raise the child themselves.

For the large majority of families, adoption is a successful plan. Adoption has proved to be beneficial for infants, as well as for older children, minority and mixed-race children, and children classified as hard to place. Adoption is associated with positive gains in the development of adopted children, including IQ scores and school performance (Schiff et al. 1978, Winick 1975). The environmental advantages of adoption status apply also to transracial adoptions, and specifically to the adoption of black children by white families. When black children, whose natural parents were educationally average, were adopted by economically advantaged white families, black adoptees " . . . scored above the IQ and the school-achievement mean of the white population" (Scarr and Weinberg 1976 p. 726). What remains at issue about transracial adoptions is the extent to which minority children are able to develop a distinct racial/ethnic identity when raised in white adoptive homes. Various segments of the black community question whether white families can provide proper identity role-models for black children (Hill 1977).

2. Adjustment of Adoptees

Considerable interest has been expressed in the emotional adjustment of children who are adopted. A number of investigators have contended that adoptees are more susceptible to emotional disturbance than are children raised in biological families. Studies of adoptees indicate that slightly more than 4 percent of the children who receive treatment at mental health facilities are adopted. Since the percentage of children placed in nonrelated adoption is approximately 1 percent, the estimate of 4 percent as those served in mental-health facilities seems to indicate that adoptees are over-represented in clinic facilities. A number of

reasons have been offered for this finding. One possibility is that because adoptive parents tend to be older when assuming the parent role than is the case for biological parents, and because the adopted child is more apt to be a first child, more emphasis is placed on seeking help when a potential problem arises. A not unusual response from a middle-class family is to seek expert help from a mental-health resource. Moreover, that 95 percent of all adopted children are not referred to mental-health facilities is a statistic that requires emphasis.

The intense interest in the emotional adjustment of adopted children apparently was not envisioned even by Bowlby, who stated "So far as it is known the proportion of successful and unsuccessful adoptions does not seem unsatisfactory. This result is in accordance with clinical experience which does not suggest that an undue proportion of adopted children are referred to child guidance clinics" (Bowlby 1951 p. 108).

Investigators have studied the emotional adjustment of adoptees from a number of angles and the results reported have been variable and often inconsistent. Some have studied clinic samples only, or have compared agency and/or clinic samples of adopted children with nonadoptees sampled from nonclinic populations. Others have studied both adopted and nonadopted individuals selected from nonclinic populations. The problem of comparability is further aggravated by studying adoptees at various ages and developmental levels ranging from elementary school to adolescence, young adulthood, and older adulthood. Moreover, much variation exists in the criterion measures used to assess the emotional adjustment of adoptees. For example, a recent United States study compared the adjustment of adopted and nonadopted children by obtaining teacher judgments on the 55 item Quay Behavior Problem Checklist for children in kindergarten through grade 8 (Lindholm and Touliatos 1980). It was found that adopted children exceeded nonadopted children in frequency of conduct and personality problems, with more problems found among boys than among girls. Another study compared adopted and nonadopted youth aged 18 to 25 who were university students. Comparisons were made on the Berger Self-concept Scale, which consisted of 36 items and used a Likert procedure. Comparison of mean self-concept scores for adoptees and nonadoptees revealed no difference, and the conclusion was drawn that "Adoptive status alone can not produce a negative identity" (Norvell and Guy 1977 p. 445).

In Sweden, an epidemiological study was conducted of the adjustment of more than 2,000 older adults, who were adopted as children by nonrelatives. Information was obtained from national health insurance files and included data on sick leave, hospitalization, and psychiatric diagnoses. The criterion for psychiatric illness was that persons be registered on a sick list for a period of at least two weeks with a psychiatric diagnosis. The Swedish study reported ". . . an over-representation of psychiatric illness, both for adopted males and for females, compared with controls" (Bohman and Von Knorring 1979 p. 110). Overall, studies on the distribution of emotional problems in adoptees are difficult to interpret and should be approached with caution.

3. Genetic Factors

Increasingly, adoption arrangements are being used to study the relative contributions of genetic and hereditary factors on characteristics such as intelligence, temperament, social behavior, and predisposition toward mental illness (see *Heredity–Environment Determinants of Intelligence*). The use of an "adoption design" permits data to be collected on selected characteristics for the adopted child, the biological parents, and the adoptive parents. The adoption design makes possible the statistical separation of genetic and environmental influences on behavior and development. Studies in a number of areas of behavioral genetics continue to point to heredity as a major force in the development of individual differences. A recent interpretation of the linkage between heredity and IQ suggests that genetic differences explain about 50 percent of the variance, whereas environmental factors account for only 10 percent of the variance (Plomin and DeFries 1980).

With respect to personality development, investigators report evidence that suggests temperament has a genetic component, and that adoptees who, as infants, were identified as being "difficult" in temperament, were those characterized by behavior problems in later childhood (Maurer et al. 1980). Genetic factors are associated with antisocial behavior during adolescence among adoptees whose biological relatives exhibited antisocial behavior or alcoholism (Cadoret and Cain 1980). Also, a study in Denmark reported that mental illness (schizophrenia) was found to be concentrated in the biological background of adoptees who later became mentally ill with schizophrenia (Kety et al. 1976). Child-welfare practice, including the speciality of adoption, has placed its confidence in environmental factors as the way to equalize and/or normalize individual variation in development. While the influences of genetic/hereditary factors are accorded some recognition, they are not considered as paramount in adoption practice.

4. Adoption Trends

Increasingly, adoption practice in the United States reflects a judicial-legal stance which is characterized by emphasis on court decisions as a way of settling matters of equity that involve the civil rights of major parties in the adoption equation. Salient among the issues debated includes the rights of putative fathers to be informed that an adoption is planned. Placement may be delayed until the legal rights of the biological father are assured. Another issue is that of moving away from sealed records in which information about biological origins is not readily available to the adopted child, to a practice of open records in which adoptees have access to information about their biological heritage (Kadushin 1978). Overall, adoption has established itself as a highly successful social intervention for children in need of permanent homes. Its merits are no longer in question.

Bibliography

Bohman M, Sigvardsson S 1980 A prospective, longitudinal study of children registered for adoption: A 15 year follow-up. *Acta Psychiatr. Scand.* 61: 339–55
Bohman M, Von Knorring A-L 1979 Psychiatric illness among adults adopted as infants. *Acta Psychiatr. Scand.* 60: 106–12
Bowlby J M 1951 *Maternal Care and Mental Health.* World Health Organization, Geneva
Cadoret R J, Cain C 1980 Sex differences in predictors of antisocial behavior in adoptees. *Arch. Gen. Psychiatry* 37: 1171–75
Hill R B 1977 *Informal Adoption Among Black Families.* National Urban League, Washington, DC
Kadushin A 1978 Children in adoptive homes. In: Mass H (ed.) 1978 *Social Service Research: Review of Studies.* National Association of Social Workers, Washington, DC, pp. 39–89
Kety S S, Rosenthal D, Wender P H, Schulsinger F, Jacobsen B 1976 Mental illness in the biological and adoptive families of adopted individuals who have become schizophrenic. *Behav. Genet.* 6: 219–25
Lindholm B W, Touliatos J 1980 Psychological adjustment of adopted and nonadopted children. *Psychol. Rep.* 46: 307–10
Mandell B R 1973 *Where Are The Children?: A Class Analysis of Foster Care and Adoption.* Heath, Lexington, Massachusetts
Maurer R, Cadoret R J, Cain C 1980 Cluster analysis of childhood temperament data on adoptees. *Am. J. Orthopsychiatry* 50: 522–34
Mech E V 1973 Adoption: A policy perspective. In: Caldwell B M, Ricciuti H N (eds.) 1973 *Review of the Child Development Research.* University of Chicago Press, Chicago, Illinois, pp. 467–509
Norvell M, Guy R F 1977 A comparison of self-concept in adopted and non-adopted adolescents. *Adolescence* 12: 443–48
Plomin R, DeFries J C 1980 Genetics and intelligence: Recent data. *Intelligence* 4: 15–24
Raynor L 1980 *The Adopted Child Comes of Age.* Allen and Unwin, London
Scarr S, Weinberg R A 1976 IQ test performance of black children adopted by white families. *Am. Psychol.* 31: 726–39
Schiff M, Duyme M, Dumaret A, Stewart J, Tomkiewicz S, Feingold J 1978 Intellectual status of working-class children adopted early into upper-middle-class families. *Science* 200: 1503–04
Winick M, Meyer K K, Harris R C 1975 Malnutrition and environmental enrichment by early adoption. *Science* 190: 1173–75
Zietz D 1959 *Child Welfare: Principles and Methods.* Wiley, New York

Foster Care Influence

E. V. Mech

Foster care is defined as out-of-home care provided on a 24-hour basis for children who enter the system under the auspices of child welfare or juvenile justice agencies. Foster family homes, group homes, residential treatment centers, and institutions serve as placement resources for children classified as dependent, neglected, abused, or delinquent. Nearly 500,000 children in the United States are estimated to be in a foster care facility (Shyne and Schroeder 1977 p. 112). Of this number, approximately 80 percent are placed in foster family homes. Bowlby's influential analysis of child care methods in the United Kingdom, the United States, and in other Western countries, emphasized that children who experience parental separation live in a world different from children raised in their own homes. A common concern is that children raised in foster homes are developmentally behind children raised in their own homes. This article summarizes representative studies of the influence of foster home care on the development of children in the United States.

1. Foster Care in Question

The United States has struggled to improve its foster care system. Numerous national-, state-, and local-level studies have been conducted with the goal of achieving responsiveness from elected officials, program administrators, and service workers. Professional fact finding is routine as a basis for influencing public policy. Policy makers do not lack advice and in many respects are overwhelmed by it. Efforts to change foster care have tended to produce a literature that is highly critical of the foster care system. Studies have faulted the system for failing to provide permanence, stability, and proper nurturance for children. Surveys indicate that foster care intended as temporary often turns out as long term, with placements of four years or more not uncommon (Maas and Engler 1959). Changes in foster homes, turnover in service workers, and lack of contact with own homes pose additional hazards for children (Children's Defense Fund 1978). A point repeatedly made to policy makers is that foster care could be averted for many children if supportive services were available in the form of homemaker service or day care. Far greater amounts of money have been spent on foster care than for homemaker service, or for providing financial assistance to the child's own family, even though economic difficulty may have been one of the reasons for the family breakup (Mott 1975 p. 2). The Adoption Assistance and Child Welfare Act of 1980 (PL–96–272) attempts to reform the child welfare system in the United States. It redirects federal financial incentives away from encouraging out-of-home care toward one of preventing unnecessary placement and reuniting children with families. Kadushin cautions, however, that many of the criticisms leveled against the foster care system are overstated. His analysis offers a balanced perspective on the realities of the system and concludes that ". . .the system is better than it is reputed to be and . . . has been unjustifiably derogated" (Kadushin 1978 p. 105).

2. Development of Foster Children

Foster family care is intended to offer to children a close approximation of normal family living and to allow opportunities for satisfactory intellectual, social-emotional, and physical development. A major concern about foster care, particularly in long-term situations, is that placement works against the psychic maturation of children. It has been proposed that a foster child's self-perception is that of a worthless and unloved person. Table 1 cites representative studies on the development of foster children in four areas: intelligence, school achievement, personal–social adjustment, and health.

2.1 Intelligence

Intelligence levels of foster children test in the low average range. Three studies based on individually administered intelligence tests (such as the Wechsler) reported IQ means of 90.2 (Fox and Arcuri 1980 p. 693); 86.9 for boys and 89.0 for girls (Seligman 1979 p. 185); and from 85.7 for black to 108.9 for white school-aged children (Fanshel and Shinn 1978 p. 177). Maas (1969) in his 10-year follow-up reported that nearly 7 out of 10 foster children were of average intelligence. However, of those in long-term foster care only 56 percent were rated average in intelligence.

2.2 School Achievement

Based on a WRAT-reading mean of 95.5, and WRAT-arithmetic mean of 88.5 it was concluded that foster children were significantly lower in arithmetic and computational skill than in reading ability (Fox and Arcuri 1980 p. 495). Seligman (1979) reported Wide Range Achievement Test (WRAT) performance for black children in reading and spelling at about the 25th percentile, and arithmetic achievement at about the 5th percentile. In the New York City longitudinal study 59 percent of the children were functioning below the average for their age in school, at the point of entering foster care; this figure dropped to 55 percent in the second assessment and subsequently to 52 percent in the final evaluation (Fanshel and Shinn 1978 p. 266). In the Pennsylvania survey (Fox and Arcuri 1980 p. 494) nearly one in three foster children were one or more grade levels behind their chronological age or attended a

Table 1
Studies of children raised in foster care

Investigator(s)	Location	Procedure	Measure(s)	Characteristic Finding
Fox and Arcuri (1980)	Pennsylvania	Tested school-age foster children (N = 163)	Intelligence and school achievement —Wechsler —WRAT	". . . foster care in and of itself does not adversely affect cognitive functions and learning ability . . ." (p. 495)
Seligman (1979)	New York City	Tested black foster children ages 4–18 (N = 98)	Cognitive and emotional —Wechsler —WRAT —Projectives	". . . Compared with other minority disadvantaged children who had not had the added handicap of a foster-care placement, it compared rather favorably." (p. 185)
Fanshel and Shinn (1978)	New York City	Five year longitudinal analysis of children in foster care more than 90 days (N = 624)	Intelligence, school achievement, social–emotional	". . . Continued tenure in foster care is not demonstrably deleterious with respect to I.Q. change, school performance, or the measures of emotional adjustment we employed." (p. 491)
Lahti et al. (1978)	Oregon	Follow-up of evaluation of foster children returned to own homes, those adopted, and those remaining in foster care (N = 492)	Family well-being and satisfaction	"Children who returned to their parents did not score as high on measures of adjustment. . . as children in other placements. Their scores were significantly lower." (p. 8)
Bush et al. (1977)	Illinois	Survey of foster children describing their foster placements (N = 125)	Questions about qualities of the foster parents and the placement	"When asked whether they wished to stay in their present foster homes, 78 percent . . . said they did." (p. 499)
Swire and Kavaler (1977)	New York City	Health assessment of foster children (N = 648)	Medical, visual, dental, psychological	". . . Children who stay in the foster care system. . .have significant medical and psychiatric problems. . ." (p. 650)
Jacobson and Cockerum (1976)	Idaho	Former foster mothers interviewed a panel of former foster children (N = 7)	Perceptions of foster care as reported by former foster children	"Not one of the panelists felt he would have been better off had he remained in his own home." (p. 36)
Canning (1974)	Texas	Interviews with foster children and their teachers (N = 25)	Adjustment to the school environment	"Discussions with foster children invariably swept toward one recurring theme: their feelings of being different from other children at school." (p. 584)
Maas (1969)	8 communities from the original foster care project (see Maas and Engler 1959)	Questionnaire follow-up of children in long-term foster care (N = 130)	Intelligence, physical disability, adjustment	". . . Those in long-term care seemed in the most disadvantaged positions. . .most functioned intellectually at a below-average level and some had irremediable physical disabilities." (p. 333)
Meier (1966)	Minnesota	Interviews with adults raised as foster children (N = 66)	Social effectiveness, sense of well-being	". . . former foster children had more problems with the sense of well-being than with social effectiveness. . ." (p. 21)
Weinstein (1960)	Illinois	Interviews with foster children age 5 and over (N = 61)	Identity, well-being	". . . average well-being was higher in the group whose parents visited them." (p. 68)
Kadushin (1978)	Wisconsin	Survey of foster children under age 10 not placed for adoption (N = 136)	Adjustment and integration in foster family	"It is not likely. . .that so many children would show good and fair adjustment unless they were received with some warmth and affection in foster homes." (p. 24)

special education class. School adjustment problems of foster children include nearly 8 in 10 falling behind by one grade at the elementary level, poor attendance, and a pervasive feeling that as foster children they were different from others in the school (Canning 1974 p. 582–87).

2.3 Personal–Social Adjustment

Numerous investigators report that foster children experience difficulty in the interpersonal area. Meier (1966 p. 21) points out that ". . . these former foster children had more problems with the sense of well-being than with social effectiveness . . . ." Maas (1969 p. 326) reported psychological disturbance for more than 50 percent of the foster children studied. Seligman (1979 p. 186) observed that nearly one-third of the foster children studied had trouble in developing social relationships. The most common difficulty experienced by foster children was that of feeling different from others. In the New York City analysis, approximately 25–30 percent of the foster children still in care after five years were rated by psychologists, caseworkers, and school teachers as experiencing emotional difficulty and/ or adjustment problems (Fanshel and Shinn 1978 p. 492).

2.4 Health

A survey of the medical and health status of 668 children in foster homes in New York City (Swire and Kavaler 1977) produced the following results. Nearly one in four children was found to have a significant health abnormality. Foster children were judged as generally less healthy than children from a nonfoster-home population. Almost half (45 percent) of the children had at least one chronic health problem. Approximately 30 percent had defective vision, and a high percentage were in need of dental treatment, with dental need most acute in the adolescent foster child. Finally, psychiatric evaluations reported that 35 percent exhibited moderate impairment while another 35 percent showed marked-to-severe impairment.

3. Assessment

Children come into foster care mainly for reasons beyond their control. Few children are voluntarily placed in foster care. The majority are abandoned or removed from homes by court action because of parental insufficiency. Even though evidence has been presented which attests to the beneficial influences of many foster homes, out-of-home placement still rates second best to own-home care. Research studies cited are primarily retrospective, cross-sectional, and lack comparisons with children who remain with their own families; hence they are weak in terms of revealing the influences of foster home care. The monumental longitudinal study of foster children in New York City under the direction of Fanshel (Fanshel and Shinn 1978) stands as the exception. While foster care is necessary

for thousands of children, and can be beneficial for many, it is evident that out-of-home placement poses special risks for children. Not uncommon is marginal functioning in health and in cognitive and social–emotional development. Increasingly, evidence points to school settings as yet another source of difficulty for foster children. Perceptions of foster children as being treated differently from other children in school have some basis in fact. One report described an elementary-school principal who announced on a weekly basis that all county foster children were to report to the office for their meal tickets (Canning 1974 p. 585). Educators have been on the periphery in understanding the special needs of foster children and in creating opportunities for their positive involvement in school settings.

Bibliography

Bowlby J M 1951 *Maternal Care and Mental Health*. World Health Organization, Geneva

Bush M, Gordon A C, LeBailly R 1977 Evaluating child welfare services: A contribution from the clients. *Soc. Serv. Rev.* 491–591

Canning R 1974 School experiences of foster children. *Child Welf.* 53: 582–87

Children's Defense Fund 1978 *Children Without Homes*. Children's Defense Fund, Washington, DC

Fanshel D, Shinn E B 1978 *Children in Foster Care: A Longitudinal Investigation*. Columbia University Press, New York

Fox M, Arcuri K 1980 Cognitive and academic functioning in foster children. *Child Welf.* 59: 491–96

Jacobson E, Cockerum J 1976 As foster children see it: Former foster children talk about foster family care. *Child. Today* 5(6): 32–36, 42

Kadushin A 1958 The legally adoptable, unadopted child. *Child Welf.* 9: 19–25

Kadushin A 1978 Children in foster families and institutions. In: Maas H S (ed.) 1978 *Social Service Research: Review of Studies*. National Association of Social Workers, Washington, DC

Lahti J et al. 1978 *A Follow-up Study of the Oregon Project: A Summary*. Regional Research Institute for Human Services, Portland State University, Portland, Oregon

Maas H S 1969 Children in long-term foster care. *Child Welf.* 48: 321–33, 347

Maas H S, Engler R E Jr 1959 *Children in Need of Parents*. Columbia University Press, New York

Meier E G 1966 Adults who were foster children. *Child. Today* 13(1): 16–22

Mott P E 1975 *Foster Care and Adoptions: Some Key Policy Issues*. Subcommittee on Children and Youth. Committee on Labor and Public Welfare, United States Senate. United States Government Printing Office, Washington, DC

Seligman L 1979 Understanding the black foster child through assessment. *J. Non-white Concerns Pers. Guid.* 7(4): 183–91

Shyne A, Schroeder A 1977 *National Study of Social Services to Children and Their Families*. Department of Health, Education and Welfare, Publication No. (OHDS) 78-30150, Washington, DC

Swire M R, Kavaler F 1977 The health status of foster children. *Child Welf.* 56: 635–53

Weinstein E A 1960 *The Self-Image of the Foster Child*. Russell Sage Foundation, New York

Child Abuse

R. Vasta

The abuse and neglect of children is a worldwide phenomenon observed in cultures ranging from the primitive and poverty stricken to the highly industrialized and affluent (Korbin 1979). It is at once a shocking and puzzling problem, whose complexities have only recently begun to be appreciated. Unfortunately, certain difficulties inherent in this area have interfered with the development of a clear picture of the phenomenon. Chief among these difficulties has been the inability to obtain accurate information regarding the incidence and circumstances surrounding many of these cases. Child abuse, like spouse abuse, is often as perplexing to the perpetrator as it is to the victim. Shame and embarassment at having been party to such an incident—often combined with rationalizations that the excessive force was warranted, accidental, or an aberration that will not occur again—may characterize both the parent and the child. Thus neither party may wish to admit to or discuss an abusive assault. Physicians, teachers, and other professionals likewise have sometimes been reluctant to get involved in what many consider to be an internal domestic area, or because they fear that antagonizing the parents may lead to even more violence. Finally, there has been a notable failure on the part of judicial and legislative officials to arrive at a clear definition of abuse and to deal with suspected or convicted violators in a consistent fashion. State and national statutes vary so markedly on this question that virtually no summary statement can be made regarding the current status of various types and degrees of child maltreatment.

The question of precisely what behaviors constitute abuse is, of course, a closely related issue. At least four different forms of abuse can be identified that appear to have somewhat independent characteristics. Neglect represents the largest category, subsuming all of the situations where caretakers fail to provide adequate nutrition, clothing, medical needs, social or educational training, and a psychologically stable and stimulating environment. Sexual abuse typically refers to incest by a biological or nonblood parent, but it is also used to describe cases where the child is exposed to or forced to participate in any number of sexual activities. Ritualistic abuse involves cruel and often bizarre torture practices and is frequently characteristic of parents who hold deranged views of the child or children in general. Disciplinary abuse refers to injurious assaults that occur in the course of administering physical punishment to the child. Such attacks often begin simply as disciplinary episodes, but may quickly escalate in intensity and severity once the beating has begun. At times the degree of injury caused in these cases is unintended and such parents may display considerable remorse and guilt following an attack.

The rubric "child abuse," therefore, actually serves as an umbrella label for a group of rather diverse behavioral patterns. Moreover, exactly where the line is drawn between punishment and abuse has been a question on which very little agreement can be found. The extremes certainly are clear and seem to provide the motivation to irradicate this problem, but the reality of the large "gray areas" suggests that considerably more information needs to be obtained before this phenomenon is adequately understood.

1. Historical Perspective

The phenomenon of child abuse is not a product of twentieth-century society. Many of the practices that today would seem appalling, in fact, have been commonplace at various points in history. Infanticide has been practiced by many cultures for thousands of years as a means of easing population problems or of eliminating infants whose physical conditions may place unusual strain on the family or society (Langer 1974). In ancient Greek and Roman societies young children were frequently made to join in adults' sexual activities, including the castrating of infants for later service in brothels. During the Middle Ages, beating children was considered to be a necessary and appropriate means of instilling correct social and moral habits. A variety of near-torture rituals have long been associated with baptismal and other religious rites, sometimes resulting in permanent deformation, injury, or death of the child. Modern Western society sanctions spanking and other corporal punishment as legitimate disciplinary techniques.

Perhaps more important to the continuation of child abuse than even the most shocking torture practice has been the traditional view that children are the property of their parents. As such, the child becomes free to be dealt with in whatever way the parents see fit, without their having to account to or fear interference from any outside authority. Not until early in this century did the concept of children's rights begin to extend to freedom from parental assault and abuse. In some sense, then, child abuse has probably existed in some form as long as the human species has existed.

The modern history of child abuse, on the contrary, has been remarkably short. During the 1940s and 1950s the American medical community began to suspect that maltreatment of children by parents was much more widespread than had been popularly thought. But it was not until 1961 that the problem was conferred the status (albeit informally) of being a diagnostic category into which suspected cases could be classified. In that year C. Henry Kempe, a noted pediatric researcher, organized a symposium at the meeting of the American Academy of Pediatrics entitled, "The Battered Child Syndrome." It soon became apparent, however, that a great number of maltreated children escape actual physical assaults, but nevertheless are clear victims of psychological, sexual, or negligent abuse. Thus the original label for this category is now rarely used.

While child abuse can obviously take many forms and appears to have a number of different causes, some commonalities exist across many reported cases. Researchers are using these common characteristics to develop theoretical models that may eventually explain the dynamics of this problem.

2. Characteristics of Abusing Parents

Perhaps the most widely cited characteristic of the abuser involves a personal history of abuse. In fact some families can trace abuse back for an indefinite number of generations. Exactly why the abused child often becomes an abusing parent has been the source of considerable theorizing. But this characteristic remains as probably the best single predictor of child maltreatment (Spinetta and Rigler 1972).

Abusing parents are also quite deficient in basic child-rearing skills and they also frequently hold very unrealistic beliefs regarding what may reasonably be expected of a child at a given developmental level. The parent who does not feel that a baby should cry or who believes that a 3-year-old can monitor his or her own behavior, may quickly become frustrated with a child who continually falls short of these expectations. A closely related characteristic is the frequent use of commands, threats, and physical punishment to gain compliance from the child, rather than the use of more positive, rewarding disciplinary techniques (Burgess and Conger 1978).

The social environment of the abusing parent is frequently characterized by isolation and the lack of a support network of other concerned adults. These individuals often do not live near family or relatives and they tend to have little contact with neighbors or social groups. Again, it is not clear precisely how this interaction pattern is involved in abuse. It appears to involve a combination of their having few appropriate models or sources of guidance, along with the opportunity of escaping any social or legal ramifications for the abusive behavior.

Finally, the personality of the abuser is generally characterized by a lack of adequate coping and problem-solving skills. Often these individuals have difficulty managing their personal lives, as well as family and household matters, and they seem to display impulsive and often irrational decision-making practices. In addition, recent research has demonstrated that abusing parents are more physiologically reactive to aversive stimuli and they become aroused, and probably angered, more easily than do nonabusing parents (Frodi and Lamb 1980a).

It must be emphasized, however, that these correlates of abusive behavior are by no means firm predictors of child maltreatment. The majority of individuals display-

ing one or more of these characteristics do not abuse their children, and some abusers display pesonality patterns other than those just described. Thus, pinpointing any single "abuser personality" is a task that is unlikely to meet with success.

3. Characteristics of the Abused Child

There is now little doubt that certain children run a greater risk of being maltreated than do others. Many research studies have demonstrated that specific child characteristics correlate significantly with parental abuse and neglect (Friedrich and Boriskin 1976). These data are bolstered by more informal observations that abusing parents rarely spread their violence among their offspring, but instead concentrate on a single child. Likewise, certain children who are removed from abuse situations and placed in foster care subsequently experience similar treatment in the new environment.

In general, abuse is more likely in cases where the child is somehow unattractive or presents aversive characteristics to the parent. This lack of appeal can take a number of forms. Premature infants are particularly prone to maltreatment at a very young age. Two explanations (both probably at least partially correct) have been offered for this finding. The first is that the child's initial medical condition may require separation from the mother during the first days of life, preventing sufficient mother–infant contact to establish a firm attachment relationship. In addition, studies have shown that premature infants have a more unpleasant, aversive cry than do full-term infants, as evidenced by physiological reactions of adult listeners. Hence the mother not only finds it difficult to establish a close emotional tie to the child, but she also finds the child even more difficult to cope with than most (Frodi and Lamb 1980b).

Other more obvious child characteristics that limit their appeal (and increase the likelihood of abuse) include physical deformities, chronic medical conditions, and mental retardation. But behavioral problems can contribute here as well. Children who whine and cry a great deal or who display hyperactive behavior also run a greater risk of being maltreated. Once again, the great majority of physically or behaviorally unattractive children are not abused. But it may be apparent that certain combinations of a particular parent type and a particular child type can markedly raise the probability of a dangerous situation.

4. Social and Environmental Factors

The third piece in the puzzle appears to involve the environment in which the abuser exists. Put simply, stress-filled situations increase the likelihood of abuse. Such stress can have its roots in unemployment, marital difficulties, health-related problems, or virtually any other factor resulting in tension, frustration, or anxiety. The role these difficulties play in abuse is assumed to be one of lowering the overall threshold for aggressive or violent behavior. The child, or sometimes the spouse, in turn becomes the target of this aggression (Garbarino 1980). There is also evidence that child maltreatment is more prevalent in families lower on the socioeconomic scale and the greater economic and social stresses experienced by this group are assumed by many researchers to be the basis for this imbalance.

5. Theories of Child Abuse

In the medical and behavioral research on this issue since the early 1960s, several important theoretical models have been proposed to account for the occurrence of child maltreatment. Initially, a straightforward but rather naive medical explanation laid the blame on a psychopathological disorder in the abusing parent, meaning that a parent must be insane to intentionally and repeatedly cause serious injury to a defenseless child. But it soon became obvious that only a very small portion of child abusers display psychiatric problems and that many otherwise-normal parents perpetrate violence or neglect on their children. The sociological correlates that began to achieve recognition in the early 1970s drew attention away from the abusing parent and focused on the environment as the primary source of abuse provocation (Gelles 1973, Gil 1970).

The conceptualization that currently holds the greatest sway is an interactional approach wherein the parent, child, and situation each plays a role in producing the problem. In essence, the interactional model holds that when an ill-equipped parent is required to deal with an aversive or difficult child under conditions of high stress or frustration, the risk of child maltreatment becomes very high. But when any of these factors is missing, the parent may have sufficient alternative responses or opportunities to avoid violence against the child (Belsky 1980, Burgess 1979, Parke and Collmer 1975, Vasta 1982). Thus, child abuse has no single cause. Rather, it appears to result from an unfortunate combination of several factors in one situation.

6. Effects of Abuse and Therapeutic Approaches

Although some abused children eventually die from their maltreatment, most victims escape with nonpermanent physical injuries. Yet even these children continue to display problems in their day-to-day functioning. One product of abuse is a greater tendency in the victim to display acts of physical and verbal aggression. Such children frequently become serious behavior problems and show marked difficulties in successfully interacting with peers or adult authority figures (George and Main 1979, Elmer 1967, Kent 1976). Abuse and neglect also have effects that go beyond the behavioral realm. Some evidence suggests that developmental delays and difficulty with normal cognitive functioning may result from early maltreatment. Language acquisition and development are likewise often

impaired within this group (Buchanan and Oliver 1977, Morse et al. 1970).

A wide range of therapeutic approaches has been used to treat these cases. Early work focused on more psychodynamic techniques, including play therapy and art therapy for child victims, and psychoanalytic techniques for abusers. Current trends in treatment typically include the entire family unit, with family therapy and more behavioral techniques being the principal forms of intervention. As research demonstrates the problem to be ever more complex, therapy procedures have become correspondingly multifaceted. Modern intervention involves training and education in child management skills, counseling to improve coping and problem-solving abilities, and the development of peer support groups to help these parents share their feelings and common experiences with one another (Wolfe et al. 1981).

Many experts believe, however, that treating abuse cases represents only a short-term goal and that the prevention of abuse will require a large-scale improvement in the economic and social conditions that foster the problem. Until the society is prepared to make a concerted effort to eradicate such conditions, the problem of child abuse is likely to remain (Garbarino 1980).

Bibliography

Belsky J 1980 Child maltreatment: An ecological integration. *Am. Psychol.* 35: 320–35

Buchanan A, Oliver J E 1977 Abuse and neglect as a cause of mental retardation: A study of 140 children admitted to subnormality hospitals in Wiltshire. *Br. J. Psychiatry* 131: 458–67

Burgess R L 1979 Child abuse: A social interactional analysis. In: Lahey B B, Kazdin A E (eds.) 1979 *Advances in Clinical Child Psychology*. Plenum, New York

Burgess R L, Conger R D 1978 Family interaction in abusive, neglectful, and normal families. *Child Dev.* 49: 1163–73

Elmer E 1967 *Children in Jeopardy: A Study of Abused Minors and Their Families*. University of Pittsburgh Press, Pittsburgh, Pennsylvania

Friedrich W N, Boriskin J A 1976 The role of the child in abuse: A review of the literature. *Am. J. Orthopsychiatry* 46: 580–90

Frodi A M, Lamb M E 1980a Child abusers' responses to infant smiles and cries. *Child Dev.* 51: 238–41

Frodi A M, Lamb M E 1980b Infants at risk for child abuse. *Infant Ment. Hlth. J.* 1: 240–47

Garbarino J 1980 What kind of society permits child abuse? *Infant Ment. Hlth. J.* 1: 270–80

Gelles R J 1973 Child abuse as psychopathology: A sociological critique and reformulation. *Am. J. Orthopsychiatry* 43: 611–21

George C, Main M 1979 Social interactions of young abused children: Approach, avoidance, and aggression. *Child Dev.* 50: 306–18

Gil D G 1970 *Violence Against Children: Physical Child Abuse in the United States*. Harvard University Press, Cambridge, Massachusetts

Kent J T 1976 A follow-up study of abused children. *J. Ped. Psychol.* 1: 25–31

Korbin J E 1979 A cross-cultural perspective on the role of the community in child abuse and neglect. *Child Abuse Neg.* 3: 9–18

Langer W L 1974 Infanticide: A historical survey. *Hist. Child. Q.* 1: 353–65

Morse C W, Sahler J O, Friedman S B 1970 A three-year follow-up of abused and neglected children. *Am. J. Dis. Child.* 120: 439–46

Parke R D, Collmer C 1975 Child abuse: An interdisciplinary analysis. In: Hetherington E M (ed.) 1975 *Review of Child Development Research*, Vol. 5. University of Chicago Press, Chicago, Illinois

Spinetta J J, Rigler D 1972 The child-abusing parent: A psychological review. *Psychol. Bull.* 77: 296–304

Vasta R 1982 Physical child abuse: A dual-component analysis. *Dev. Rev.* 2: 125–49

Wolfe D A, Sandler J, Kaufman K A 1981 A competency-based parent training program for child abusers. *J. Consult. Clin. Psychol.* 49: 633–40

Social Discrimination

R. H. Billigmeier

The term "social discrimination" is widely used to refer to the act of (a) making invidious distinctions among various human groups on the basis of age, gender, and other perceived or presumed social, cultural, and physical characteristics, and (b) treating people, whether by intent or not, in inequitable and injurious ways on the basis of such distinctions. Accordingly, members of one group characterize another as being inferior in some significant ways, and individuals associated with the contrasting group are treated in terms of such generalized notions.

Although the term "prejudice" is used in a wide variety of ways, it generally is used to refer to the presence of a well-developed set of negative attitudes towards human categories without substantial basis in fact. Indeed, these attitudes are widely characterized as being essentially irrational and in large part invulnerable to the onslaughts of whatever contrary evidence is available. Along with such attitudes, the term popularly suggests a disposition to act in a hostile manner towards those groups who are the targets of prejudice. Individuals are treated in terms of the group's presumed characteristics despite internal differences and distinctions which may significantly mark the group.

Some social scientists have described a connection that may exist between "prejudice" and "discrimination." The former, they have observed, may serve to legitimate discrimination and discrimination in turn may breed prejudice. "Yet much discrimination," Pettigrew observes, "is not the direct product of prejudice; it often results as an unintended consequence of institutional arrangements designed for other purposes" (Pettigrew 1980 p. 198).

Human society is marked by richly diverse cultural groupings. Even within a given society differences among cultural and social groups are often extensive in terms of values, perspectives, established modes of behavior, and internal cohesiveness. To acknowledge such differences and to take them into appropriate account in our practical relationships with members of such groups cannot be counted as "discrimination," or "prejudice," or "stereotyping."

Generalized notions of other groups are used to provide useful cues in everyday contact with members of other groups who are not known intimately as individuals. The use of such generalized notions is an inevitable necessity in societies in which most of our relationships are categorical rather than personal. Such abstractions help us organize our world. The phenomenon of stereotyping results from the overextension of such conventional orientations and the practice of using them rigidly. This makes it difficult for a person to treat a member of a group as a unique individual even in instances in which the extent and variability of contact permits personal knowledge of the other. Generalized notions are not useful for anticipating the behavior of members of another group if they bear no resemblance, not even a rough one, to actual characteristics of the group. But often stereotypes are formed out of a distorted mixture of inaccurate impressions of outsiders, incomplete or defective perceptions, and gross overgeneralizations which ignore wide internal distinctions. Such popular evaluations are likely to reflect relative positions in the prevailing system of stratification. Where stereotypes are rigid, highly negative, and indiscriminately utilized, members of groups stereotyped are likely to be severely limited in their access to social advantages by the presumptions upon which members of the dominant group base their treatment of them. Thus, such stereotyping tends to have a self-confirming effect. Stereotypes are, nevertheless, subject to change with altering circumstances, becoming more negatively oriented in contexts of hostility and more favorably oriented as social distance declines.

Popular and scholarly concern is almost exclusively focused upon the attitudes and hostilities of the dominant group towards subordinate social and cultural categories. It is clear that these are likely to be of most consequence given differences in access to power. Nonetheless, hostile attitudes and dispositions are often significantly present among minority groups in a society. These may reflect such historical cultural rivalries as those that Turks and Armenians brought to the lands of their immigration. They may also reflect conflicts over access to jobs, housing, education, and political power. Such dispositions may also be absorbed in the process of acculturating into the dominant society where they widely prevail. The notions and dispositions generally associated with the terms "discrimination," "prejudice," and "stereotype," may vary extensively in their character and significance. They may be well-defined or only vague and fragmentary; they may be simple or relatively complex in their elaboration; they may play a minor or a major role in an individual's associations with members of another social and cultural category (Shibutani et al. 1965 pp. 82–115). Behavior associated with these terms is widely condemned as violating both the basic norm of rationality which requires a reasonable basis for human acts and the norm of compassion for others, that is, the humane concern for the effect of one's behavior on other people.

The conviction of being discriminated against and the rise of resentment against differential treatment are not necessarily proportionately related to the actual magnitude of these disparities. Such sentiments are likely to be heightened when a specific group has registered enough progress to become more fully aware of the remaining discrepancies.

1. Social Discrimination in Various Societies

A serious measure of differential treatment of social and cultural groups may be found in virtually all societies—historical and contemporary. Clearly, the extent of such differentiation varies greatly, in different times and places, in its magnitude, its forms, as well as in its social and personal consequences. Any attempt at compiling a list of the principal manifestations of discrimination is likely to reflect the limited perspectives of a particular time, place, and world view. Contemporary concern commonly focuses upon inequities in access to jobs and career advancement, economic security, housing, standards of living, occupational and educational training, legal rights, and political participation. Similar attention is directed towards equal access to social relations irrespective of group affiliation, to religious expression, representation in the media of communication, as well as creative and symbolic cultural expression. Within these broad areas of differential treatment there are many more specific aspects. Numerous other forms are important in varying measures in a variety of social contexts in all parts of the world.

In most of the twentieth century, the system of apartheid in the Republic of South Africa has been regarded as the most extensive and repressive system of discrimination. Elsewhere as well, the consequences of an immense and heterogeneous immigration over centuries has been attended by widespread ethnic conflicts and in some instances pervasive and long-enduring discrimination. In America, these conflicts have been in full view and, as Pettigrew observes, "American society has not tended to deny them" (Pettigrew 1980 p. 1981). The Soviet Union is a political union of large numbers of historic peoples, linguistically, culturally, and physically distinguished from the most numerous ethnic group,

the Russians. It survives as a political unity by virtue of the government's ability to enforce the subordination, in the interest of socialist unity, of the cultural interests and sense of special ethnic identity of the many constituent peoples—Latvians, Estonians, Lithuanians, Ukrainians, Moldavian Romanians, Germans, Armenians, Uzbeks, and other groups.

In Northern Ireland, Lebanon, the People's Republic of China, Israel, and many other societies, internal cultural divisions remain associated with discriminatory treatment. Some splintered peoples, like Armenians and Kurds, continue to suffer repression in a number of neighboring countries in the Middle East.

The importation of large numbers of workers into industrial countries in Western Europe from underdeveloped countries and the manner of their treatment and integration have produced difficult public issues; among the most serious are those relating to the education and acculturation of children of immigrants, as well as to housing and rights to permanent residence and citizenship.

In many countries not widely mentioned in contemporary discussions of ethnic discrimination there are nevertheless groups that suffer extensive disabilities. Ainus and Koreans in Japan, and to a lesser extent also the Japanese Okinawans, still experience competitive disadvantages in economic life as well as in social relationships.

In Africa and Asia, including former colonial areas, numerous societies are marked by an extensive cultural heterogeneity. Some measure of the rivalries which have traditionally divided Nigeria, Ghana, Sri Lanka, Lebanon, and many other societies have survived to the present. Many issues relating to discriminatory treatment are currently of great importance to the social and political stability of the societies. Even in instances in which political regimes and their leaders are genuinely concerned about a more equitable treatment of the various ethnic segments, serious impediments to amelioration remain by virtue of differences in values and world views, as well as internal factionalism within each ethnic community. To these may be added the problems arising from variability in size of ethnic populations, in the extent of their social and physical isolation, in their access to educational and occupational training, as well as in their effective political power.

2. Research on the Effects of Discrimination on Human Development

While sex discrimination is pervasive in all societies, the forms and dimensions vary vastly. In societies in which equality is not highly stressed and undergirded by the prevailing social and political ideologies, sexism is likely to be more overt than in societies which place a higher value on equality. In their socialization, children can be more explicitly and systematically prepared to "fit" into a rigid system of gender stratification. The more a society values equality, "the more sex role socialization and sex discrimination tend to become subtle and disguised under more acceptable pretences" (Safilios-Rothschild 1976 pp. 246–47).

Some studies of schools in the United States report the continuation of extensively differentiated treatment of boys and girls by teachers and other school personnel. Teachers are more likely both to praise and criticize male students than female. More pressure is exerted upon boys than girls to raise the level of their performance. Boys in a variety of ways are provided more stimulation. Poorer scholastic achievement is more widely tolerated among girls than boys who, it is presumed, must be made more competitive in the world. In a variety of ways girls are handicapped in their development of autonomy, personal effectiveness, and achievement.

Studies of textbooks and classroom materials used in various countries reflect the forms and dimensions of sex stratification. Fathers are still depicted as the sole breadwinners; they make the important decisions. Mothers are the homemakers, the nurturers.

Many scholars express the belief that as parents, teachers, counselors, and employers become more aware of the nature and implications of some of the unexamined behaviors and traditional orientations, they will alter their practices.

In contemporary societies, there are significant ethnic minorities, both regional and immigrant, who continue to suffer from the mutually reinforcing effects of poor education, limited occupational training, low income, discrimination in employment and housing and, often, incomplete mastery of language and culture (Castles and Kosack 1973 p. 430). Along with such social vulnerabilities comes a widespread personal sense of individual and group inadequacies. Empirical research in recent decades has given a clear indication that children, by the age of 4, are becoming aware of the salient ethnic distinctions made in their social environment. Such research has also provided additional insights into the personal consequences of such early racial awareness (Williams and Morland 1976, Beuf 1977).

A distinguished contemporary scholar writes that one of the most disturbing and persistent realities in the field of education in many societies is the fact that the academic achievement of children of ethnic and lower status groups is consistently and seriously deficient. "This retardation," he notes, "begins in the early elementary grades and continues at an accelerated rate throughout the upper grades" (Clark 1972 p. 5). In some instances the retardation reaches massive proportions.

The tasks of educational institutions are made more complex where extensive contrasts exist among ethnic and class populations in values, cultural norms, perspectives, motivations, and range of social experience. There has often been some reluctance manifested on the part of scholars and educators to come to grips with the significance of such differences. This reluctance has in part been born of the fear that recognition of their

existence suggests innate inferiority. Another fear often expressed is that if one admits to something like "cultural deficit," this may seem to divert the educational and political institutions from assuming the full measure of their responsibility for inadequate educational provision.

Disparities in culture, along with the heritage of discrimination and hostility, challenge the capacities of educational systems and their personnel. Some scholars have pointed to the widespread view among teachers that minority and lower status children come to school unready to learn, unwilling to engage themselves, and worse, deficient in their capacity to learn (Clark 1972 pp. 76–77). Specific critical references have been directed by some investigators to: (a) the widely characteristic rigid reliance on certain testing devices in estimating academic growth and potentiality rather than developing more accurate measures of evaluation; (b) the prevalence of a school atmosphere of frustration and hopelessness in the wake of unresolved educational dilemmas; and (c) the poor understanding among students, parents, and the community of the mutuality of responsibility for creating effective, peaceful, and orderly educational processes. Criticism is also sometimes directed against the well-meaning intent on the part of some teachers and administrators to counter the consequences of discrimination by shielding students whom they see as vulnerable, thus insulating such children against what they see as the harsh demands of society or against exposure to rigorous standards which, they believe, the children cannot meet.

In many urban areas, migration to suburban peripheries and the increasing reliance upon private schools have added further complexities in planning for the desegregation and integration of schools. Many American school systems are running out of white students to integrate.

3. Some Unresolved Issues

Many studies of widely differing degrees of scholarly substance are directing their attention to the question as to whether ethnic integration in schools, in itself, has a positive effect upon students, especially those from lower-class and minority neighborhoods. They explore what additional measures must be taken by the school, community and family, such as the application of additional resources, the utilization of superior teachers, the creation of specially designed programs, as well as extensive community and family involvement (Klein and Eshel 1980). The educational issues are made infinitely more complex by political and ideological issues.

Despite the extensive funding of some compensatory education programs supported by strong commitments and high initial expectations, results have often been disappointing. Research is being directed to defining more carefully the specific conditions under which compensatory programs can make a significant difference in long-term educational achievement among minority and lower status children (Clark 1972 pp. 73–77).

Bibliography

Beuf A H 1977 *Red Children in White America.* University of Pennsylvania Press, Philadelphia, Pennsylvania

Castles S, Kosack G 1973 *Immigrant Workers and Class Structure in Western Europe.* Oxford University Press, London

Clark K B 1972 *A Possible Reality: A Design for the Attainment of High Academic Achievement for Inner-city Students.* Emerson Hall, New York

Clark K B, Deutsch M, Gartner A, Keppel F, Lewis A, Pettigrew T, Plotkin L, Riessman F 1972 *The Educationally Deprived: The Potential for Change.* Metropolitan Applied Research Center, New York

Klein Z, Eshel Y 1980 *Integrating Jerusalem Schools.* Academic Press, New York

Pettigrew T (ed.) 1980 *The Sociology of Race Relations: Reflection and Reform.* Free Press, New York

Porter J D R 1971 *Black Child, White Child: The Development of Racial Attitudes.* Harvard University Press, Cambridge, Massachusetts

Safilios-Rothschild C 1976 Sex discrimination: theory and research. In: Veenhoven W A, Ewing W C, Amelvnxen C, Glaser K, Possony S, Prins J, Rhoodie N, Suzuki J, Vidyarthi L P (eds.) 1976 *Case Studies on Human Rights and Fundamental Freedoms: A World Survey*, Vol. 5. Nijhoff, The Hague

Shibutani T, Kwan K M, Billigmeier R H 1965 *Ethnic Stratification: A Comparative Approach.* Macmillan, London

Williams J E, Morland J K 1976 *Race, Color and the Young Child.* University of North Carolina Press, Chapel Hill, North Carolina

Television and Development

C. M. Clermont

The rapid extension of television to all parts of the world has stimulated a great quantity of research about the influence of television on the developing child. This issue of influence is reviewed in this article in terms of the types of programs which children watch, the viewing habits of children, and studies of the impact of television on two characteristics of children—their cognitive development and aggression.

1. Types of Programs

Studies show that children are affected by all varieties of television programming—commercial, educational, and instructional.

From the standpoint of the amount of child viewing, commercial television is by far the most important. Commercial television is the type which is broadcast to the general public, chiefly to furnish entertainment and information or news. The term "commercial" derives from the fact that in many nations such broadcasts are financed by including advertisements in the programming which are paid for by businesses. However, in some countries such broadcasts to the general public are not truly commercial, in that the government or private philanthropic agencies rather than businesses provide the financial support. On commercial television, children are influenced both by programs designed especially for them (cartoons, child adventure dramas, puppet shows) and by ones intended mainly for adults (adult dramas, sports, contests, news).

Educational television, in contrast to the commercial variety, is designed to affect viewers' behaviors, knowledge, attitudes, and values in specific ways. Often, educational television programs are broadcast by stations that are basically commercial. In other cases, however, special public-interest or educational broadcast channels are provided for airing such material. Examples of children's and young people's educational programs are Sesame Street in the United States, its counterpart Open! Ponkiki in Japan, and the health-education broadcasts entitled *Tèlè-Docteur* in Haiti. Some programs found to be successful in one nation have been adapted for use in others. An example is Sesame Street, which is designed for children ranging in age from 2 or 3 to 6 or 7. The original English-language version of Sesame Street has been broadcast in over 40 countries, and at least eight foreign-language adaptations have been presented in 19 nations.

Instructional television is a subtype of educational television. The instructional variety is not only designed to influence viewers' knowledge and attitudes, but is also organized much like a class in school, in that it usually consists of a sequence of connected sessions, with viewers responsible not only to attend each session but to carry out assignments or "homework" as well. While instructional television may be viewed in the home, frequently it is associated with the regular school program, so that pupils view a program in the classroom during a particular time period in the school day in order to study a topic that school authorities believe is taught more effectively by television than by the classroom teacher. Typical subject matter programs that may be broadcast to all schools in a region or nationwide are in science, health, history, social studies, foreign languages, music, and art. Or, in other cases, courses are broadcast for out-of-school viewing in such industrialized nations as the United Kingdom and the United States to furnish adults with an opportunity to complete secondary or tertiary education, or in developing nations to extend basic literacy or primary and secondary education to large numbers of citizens.

2. Children's Viewing Habits

In studying the effect of television on child development, it is useful to identify both the amount and type of television that children view.

The amount of time children spend looking at television programs varies from one nation to another, depending upon such factors as the length of time television is on the air each day, the availability of television receivers, the kinds of programs broadcast, the length of the school day, and other obligations children bear in terms of homework and household duties. The following figures illustrate typical amounts of viewing in different societies. The average American child during the first 16 years of life spends more time watching television than he or she spends on any other activity except sleeping (Schramm 1973 p. 167). Shonborn (1976 p. 65) reported that by the time a typical American has reached age 65, he or she will have watched the equivalent of 3,000 24-hour days or about eight full years of television viewing. Preschool children watch more than three hours a day. Viewing time drops off when the child enters primary school, but markedly increases by ages 12 to 14, before it again drops off somewhat in the latter teenage years.

British children average about half-an-hour less viewing time each day than American children, which is slightly more than the average time in most other European countries. Sakamoto and Akiyama (Holtzman and Reyes-Lagunes 1981 p. 40) reported that the average Japanese child looks at television for two or three hours a day, with 16 percent of them viewing it more than four hours a day. In Brazil, Prado (Holtzman and Reyes-Lagunes 1981 p. 44) in 1973 found that between 6 p.m. and midnight, 34 percent of the viewers were children, of which 22 percent were less than 13 years old.

As for the types of programs children watch, studies have shown that Sesame Street is the most popular worldwide. In Australia, 84 percent of all children aged 3 to 6 view Sesame Street frequently, while *Plaza Sesàmo*, a Spanish-language adaptation, is seen in Mexico by over 90 percent of preschool children who have television available (Holtzman and Reyes-Lagunes 1981 p. 28). Among children's programs, Sesame Street has been the favorite of 64 percent of preschoolers in Canada and 45 percent in the United States (Cohen et al. 1981 p. 207). However, during the primary- and secondary-school years, children throughout the world increasingly view programs designed for adults. Netto (Holtzman and Reyes-Lagunes 1981 p. 45), in a 1976 study of Brazilian primary-school pupils, learned that the children's favorite programs were ones designed for adults. Furthermore, half of the children had no parental guidance in choosing programs and thus were able to see anything they wished.

3. Television's Impact on Development

In recognition of the great amounts of time which children spend watching television, parents and educators have expressed deep concern about the influence of programs on the growing child. Although diverse effects can be exerted by television, two that have attracted widespread attention have been the effects on cognitive development and on antisocial behavior, particularly on violent, aggressive acts. The following discussion concerns these two issues.

3.1 Television and Cognitive Development

From the large quantity of research on learning through the medium of television, three conclusions are of particular note.

First, when television programs are analyzed in terms of Piaget's levels of intellectual growth, it becomes clear that there is viewing material which can be comprehended by children at every step of the mental development hierarchy. For example, Williams (1981 p. 185) reported that infants as young as 6 months of age spend time attending to television programs. And in Piaget's scheme, infancy is the sensory-motor period when children are learning to coordinate sight and sound to achieve meanings. Beyond infancy, children begin to acquire those notions of symbolism necessary for language skills so that television can aid in such development. Young children are also animistic and anthropomorphic, attributing life and human qualities to animals and objects. These modes of thought are served by television programs—and particularly by cartoons—that picture animals expressing human thoughts and feelings. During Piaget's next stage, that of concrete operations, the child who is just entering primary school is acquiring the ability to classify objects, including objects seen on television. Children at this age start to enjoy recounting events and predicting their outcome (Noble 1975 p. 97); dramatic shows furnish abundant opportunities to practice such skills. By the close of the elementary school, children have entered the formal operations stage and become capable of the sort of abstract thinking in which adults engage. Adolescents, with these newly acquired mental abilities, begin to comprehend social, political, and religious ideologies and they also become increasingly preoccupied with their emotional lives. Television in nearly all nations offers a variety of programs catering to these more mature intellectual interests and emotional concerns. In summary, both commercial and educational television furnish material on which children at all stages of intellectual growth can exercise their evolving mental abilities.

A second conclusion is that television is an effective medium for teaching concepts and generalizations, even when the audience is watching for the purpose of entertainment rather than instruction. Studies conducted in many parts of the world have shown that preschool children who regularly viewed Sesame Street had a greater command of the cognitive skills treated in the programs than did matched groups of children who did not watch the series. Assessments of instructional television have demonstrated that both the quality of education and the number of children reached have been increased significantly through instructional television in such diverse locations as El Salvador, South Korea, the Ivory Coast, Niger, and American Samoa (Schramm 1977).

A third conclusion is that television's appeal to both eye and ear and its dramatic quality render it particularly effective in capturing viewers' attention and in exerting a strong perceptual impact.

3.2 Television and Violence

There is no doubt that a great quantity of violence is depicted on television throughout much of the world. Netto and Angelini (Holtzman and Reyes-Lagunes 1981 p. 45) reported that in Sao Paulo, Brazil, during a 3-hour period on a single evening in 1977, programs on seven television channels portrayed 64 murders, 38 shootings, 7 types of sexual violence, 22 fights, 3 robberies, and 16 incidents of intimidation and 7 of extortion. Ninety percent of such programs had been imported from the United States, where it is estimated that the average child by age 14 will have witnessed the violent destruction of 13,000 humans, all during the children's typical viewing hours of 4 p.m. to 9 p.m. (Shonborn 1976 p. 65).

Cartoon programs, aimed at the child audience, are generally the most violent of all types, with as many as 34 violent incidents per hour, reflecting the producers' conviction that frequent exciting climaxes are necessary to maintain the attention of young viewers (Howe 1977 p. 25).

The amount of violence on television varies from one nation to another. In the Soviet Union and the People's Republic of China, where mass-communication media are designed to promote values and behavior considered desirable by the government, the amount of violence on television is greatly restricted (Schramm 1973 p. 165). In Sweden there is likewise little violence depicted, and in Israel the amount of aggressive behavior shown has been about one-sixth of the amount broadcast in the United States (Liebert et al. 1973).

While there is no question about the amount of violence children see on television, there continues to be disagreement about its impact on them. On one side in the debate are those who contend that children not only learn techniques of destructive behavior from television, but they also learn that such behavior is often rewarded. On the other side are the defenders of televised violence who propose that such programs afford children a chance to vent their aggressive tendencies vicariously through the actions of the performers, so it is unnecessary for young viewers to engage in violent acts in their own lives.

However, the research evidence favors the critics rather than the defenders of televised violence. A million-dollar study supported by the Surgeon General's Office in the United States led to the conclusion that violent programs "do have an adverse effect on certain members of our society" (Schramm 1973 p. 165). Berkowitz stated that such programs taught techniques of aggression, aroused previously learned habits of violence, and provided moral justification for hostile wishes (Schramm and Roberts 1971 p. 607). A 10-year investigation by Lefkowitz ending in 1972 indicated that children who preferred violent programs at age 8 engaged in more delinquent behavior by age 18 than children who did not prefer such programs. Stein and Friedrich found that pre-school children were more aggressive after viewing programs involving antisocial behavior than they were prior to seeing the programs (Holtzman and Reyes-Lagunes 1981 p. 22).

Such results are in keeping with the observation from social learning theory that most social behavior is acquired through children's observing models in their environment, with television serving as a rich source of potential models. As social learning research has demonstrated, children commonly imitate the acts of people whose behavior leads to attractive consequences. When aggressivity on television results in rewards for the aggressors, then the logical question to ask is Schramm's (1973 p. 166) query: "How can one expect parents to convince their children that violence is not an acceptable way of life?"

While behaviors depicted on television can indeed influence children's social development, it is important to recognize that television is only one of the environmental forces affecting the child. Each child may use television in a unique manner in order to gain satisfactions not afforded by other sources in the environment. For example, children who feel emotionally insecure because of difficulties with parents or peers are likely to be heavy viewers, apparently seeking from television the emotional support they lack in their own social interactions (Schramm and Roberts 1971 p. 599). Consequently, the impact that television will exert in the life of a particular child needs to be assessed in relation to the impact exerted by other significant agents—family, peers, school, church, and the broader society in which the child is reared.

Bibliography

Cohen M E, Brown J D, Clark S 1981 Canadian Public Television and preschool children. Predictors of viewers and non-viewers. *Commun. Res.* 8: 205–31

Holtzman W H, Reyes-Lagunes I (eds.) 1981 *Impact of Educational Television on Young Children.* Educational Studies and Documents Series, No. 40. UNESCO, Paris

Howe J A M 1977 *Television and Children.* Linet, Hamden, Connecticut

Lesser G S 1974 *Children and Television: Lessons from Sesame Street.* Random House, New York

Liebert R M, Neale J M, Davidson E S 1973 *The Early Window: Effects of Television on Children and Youth.* Pergamon, New York

Noble G 1975 *Children in Front of the Small Screen.* Sage, Beverly Hills, California

Schramm W L 1973 *Men, Messages, and Media: A Look at Human Communication.* Harper and Row, New York

Schramm W L 1977 *Big Media, Little Media: Tools and Technologies for Instruction.* Sage, Beverly Hills, California

Schramm W L, Roberts D F 1971 Children's learning from the mass media. In: Schramm W L, Roberts D F (eds.) 1971 *The Process and Effects of Mass Communication.* University of Illinois Press, Urbana, Illinois, pp. 596–611

Schramm W L, Lyle J, Parker E B (eds.) 1961 *Television*

in the Lives of Our Children. Stanford University Press, Stanford, California

Shonborn K 1976 Violence on television: Some cross-time and cross-cultural comparisons. *J. Appl. Commun. Res.* 4–6: 65–74

Williams T M 1981 How and what do children learn from television? *Hum. Commun. Res.* 7: 180–92

Child Influence on Adults

M. Chapman

Until recently, most research on adult–child relations in the home or at school focused on the ways in which adults affected child behavior. This emphasis resulted from pragmatic educational concerns as well as from theories of child development based on environmental influences. Only since the early 1970s has a bidirectional model of adult–child relations begun to replace the exclusive emphasis on adult effects.

Early research on socialization in the family was based primarily on correlations between parent and child behaviors. Consistent with the prevailing unidirectional model of parent–child relations, these correlations were interpreted as reflecting effects of parents on their children. To consider only one example, Hoffman's (1970) review of research on conscience development indicated that parents who used power assertive discipline characterized by physical punishment and material deprivation tended to have children with an externalized moral orientation, motivated by a concern for externally administered rewards and punishments. In contrast, parents who were affectionate with their children and used inductive discipline characterized by reasoning and explanation tended to have children with an internalized moral orientation, motivated more by subjective values than by external sanctions. According to Hoffman's interpretation of these results, power assertion provides children with a model for the expression of anger and focuses their attention on the punitive aspects of parental authority, whereas induction focuses children's attention on the consequences of their actions for other persons and enlists their empathy for others' experience.

It was not until Bell's 1968 paper that a bidirectional model of socialization processes began to be taken seriously. In this pioneering article, Bell pointed out that correlations alone do not imply causality and went on to argue that correlations between parent and child behaviors, previously interpreted as reflecting effects of parents on children, could be reinterpreted in terms of the effects of children on their parents. Citing evidence that children differ from birth in certain congenital characteristics such as assertiveness, activity level, and person orientation, Bell reasoned that parents would surely respond differently to such differences in child behavior. Moreover, the way in which they respond could be predicted from a control systems model based on the assumption that parents possess standards

regarding the range of acceptable child behavior. If children exceed the limits of parental tolerance, parents would be expected to show appropriate control behaviors designed to bring their children's behavior back into the acceptable range. With overactive children, for example, parents should react with upper limit control behavior intended to restrict or limit the children's activity; with underactive children the opposite would be the case—parents show lower limit control behavior intended to stimulate and encourage their activity.

As an example of the way in which correlations between parent and child behaviors may be interpreted as child effects, Bell proposed an alternative explanation for the relations between parental discipline and children's moral orientation reported by Hoffman. Instead of reflecting an effect of parental discipline on child development, such correlations might reflect instead an effect of children's person orientation on their parent's disciplinary behavior. Children congenitally low in person orientation might develop a less internalized moral orientation, presumably because they tend to have less empathy for the experience of others. At the same time, parents might tend to be less affectionate and to use less person-oriented reasoning in their disciplinary interactions with children low in person orientation. Thus, parental discipline and children's moral orientation would be related, not because of any causal effect of the one upon the other, but because they are both affected by a third variable: children's person orientation. Other reported correlations between parental practices and such child behaviors as aggression, sex-role development, and intelligence were similarly reinterpreted by Bell in terms of child effects.

In subsequent publications, this argument was extended and refined. In a book by Bell and Harper (1977), further examples of child effects in socialization were discussed, offspring effects in animal research were summarized, and 17 different research strategies were described and rated in terms of (a) their effectiveness for separating parent and child effects, (b) their generalizability, and (c) the range of behaviors to which they are applicable. Examples of research utilizing these strategies were reviewed and discussed in a symposium (Bell et al. 1981); in particular, support for Bell's predicted effect of child behavior on adult discipline was found among both natural mothers and children and nonbiologically related adult–child pairs (see reviews by Chapman and Keller in Bell et al. 1981). The implications of the bidirectional model for child rearing were discussed by Bell (1979). In contrast to the extreme behaviorist view that parents can mold children in any direction they wish, the bidirectional model assumes that children show marked congenital differences from birth and that these differences influence parental behavior. Against the extreme maturational view that parents should not interfere with children's innate schedule of development, the bidirectional model implies that parents have a genuine role in guiding children's innate tendencies into socially acceptable channels.

Another implication of the bidirectional view is that parents' attitudes, perceptions, and expectations regarding their children play an important role in mediating parental behavior. According to Bell's control systems model, parental ideas regarding what constitutes normal and acceptable child behavior determine the conditions under which upper- or lower-limit control behavior is elicited. Chapman (in Bell et al. 1981) and Parke (1978) cite examples of research in which parental expectations and perceptions were indeed shown to make a difference in parent–child interaction. The controversy regarding the possible effects of teacher expectations in the classroom is relevant in this connection. In terms of the methods described by Bell and Harper, this controversy provides an example of causal influence in nonbiologically related adult–child pairs. Briefly, research initiated by Rosenthal and Jacobson (1968) suggested that teachers' expectations regarding their pupils' future performance can, under certain conditions, affect their behavior toward those pupils and may ultimately influence the pupils' performance in the expected direction. In reviewing the literature on this topic, however, West and Anderson (1976) argued that it is important to consider the role of students' behavior and characteristics in determining teacher expectations in the first place. As in the socialization literature, correlations between adult and child behaviors cannot uncritically be assumed to reflect an affect of the adult on the child, since the child may also influence the adult's behavior. Both in the family and in the classroom, it would appear to be the case that past interaction between children and adults leads to the formation of expectations which then influence the course of future interaction.

Reaction to the bidirectional model has ranged from critical rejection to uncritical acceptance. In a series of logical arguments, Hoffman (1970, 1975) has defended his hypothesis regarding the effects of parental discipline on children's moral development against the alternative child effects model proposed by Bell. In contrast, Parke (1978) argues that the original overemphasis on parent effects has now been replaced with an overemphasis on child effects and that a recognition of balanced reciprocity in parent–child interaction is necessary. Baumrind (1980) calls reciprocal causation within the family a "truism" and doubts the wisdom of even attempting to separate parent and child effects in real-life settings. Bell (1979) has replied to some of these criticisms by arguing that child effects in socialization processes should not be taken for granted. It may seem obvious that adults are influenced by children in general, but the question is, in what areas and under what conditions in particular do child effects or adult effects predominate? Methods such as those proposed by Bell and Harper (1977) for disentangling adult and child influences should be helpful in answering this question. Fourteen studies using such methods are reviewed by Bell and Chapman (1986).

Bibliography

Baumrind D 1980 New directions in socialization research. *Am. Psychol.* 35: 639–52

Bell R Q 1968 A reinterpretation of the direction of effects in studies of socialization. *Psychol. Rev.* 75: 81–95

Bell R Q 1979 Parent, child, and reciprocal influences. *Am. Psychol.* 34: 821–26

Bell R Q, Barkley R A, Keller B B, Chapman M, Bates J E, Pettit G S 1981 Parent, child and reciprocal influences: New experimental approaches. *J. Abnorm. Child Psychol.* 9: 299–345

Bell R Q, Chapman M 1986 Child effects in studies using experimental or brief longitudinal approaches to socialization. *Dev. Psychol.* 22: 595–603

Bell R Q, Harper L V 1977 *Child Effects on Adults.* Erlbaum, Hillsdale, New Jersey

Hoffman M L 1970 Moral development. In: Mussen P H (ed.) 1970 *Carmichael's Manual of Child Psychology*, 3rd edn., Vol. 2. Wiley, New York, pp. 261–359

Hoffman M L 1975 Moral internalization, parental power, and the nature of parent–child interaction. *Dev. Psychol.* 11: 228–39

Parke R D 1978 Parent–infant interaction: Progress, paradigms, and problems. In: Sackett G P (ed.) 1978 *Observing Behavior*, Vol. 1: *Theory and Applications in Mental Retardation.* University Park Press, Baltimore, Maryland, pp. 69–94

Rosenthal R, Jacobson L 1968 *Pygmalion in the Classroom: Teacher Expectation and Pupil's Intellectual Department.* Holt, Rinehart and Winston, New York

West C K, Anderson T H 1976 The question of preponderant causation in teacher expectancy research. *Rev. Educ. Res.* 46: 613–30

Contributors Index

Contributors are listed in alphabetical order together with their affiliations. Titles of articles which they have authored follow in alphabetical order, along with the respective page numbers. Where articles are co-authored, this has been indicated by an asterisk preceding the article title.

ACREDOLO, L. P. (University of California, Davis, California, USA)
Spatial Cognition, 299-302

AUSUBEL, D. P. (City University of New York, Orangeburg, New York, USA)
Ego Psychology Theory of Human Development, 102-07

BAR-TAL, D. (Tel Aviv University, Tel Aviv, Israel)
Attribution Theory of Human Development, 112-18; *Prosocial Behavior*, 427-31

BERGLING, K. (University of Uppsala, Uppsala, Sweden)
Moral Development, 423-27

BIELBY, D. D. V. (University of California, Santa Barbara, California, USA)
Sex Characteristics and Roles, 367-72

BIJOU, S. W. (University of Arizona, Tucson, Arizona, USA)
History and Educational Applications of Behaviorism, 68-74

BILLIGMEIER, R. H. (University of California, Santa Barbara, California, USA)
Social Assimilation, 404-06; *Social Discrimination*, 474-77

BRAMMER, L. M. (University of Washington, Seattle, Washington, USA)
Self-actualization, 314-17

CHAPMAN, M. (Max Planck Institute for Human Development and Education, Berlin, FRG)
Child Influence on Adults, 480-81

CLERMONT, C. M. (University of California, Santa Barbara, California, USA)
Television and Development, 477-80

CONNELL, J. P. (University of Rochester, Rochester, New York, USA)
Mastery Motivation, 285-86

COTTON, J. W. (University of California, Santa Barbara, California, USA)
Historical Backgrounds of Learning Theory, 238-45

CURWIN, R. L. (Discipline Associates, Rochester, New York, USA)
Discipline and Student Development, 441-46

DASTE, B. M. (Louisiana State University, Baton Rouge, Louisiana, USA)
Existential Theory of Human Development, 107-09

DAVIDOV, V. V. (Academy of Pedagogical Sciences USSR, Moscow, USSR)
Soviet Theories of Human Development, 93-98

DAY, H. I. (York University, Downsview, Ontario, Canada)
Motivation, 245-49

DIVER, A. C. (University of California, Santa Barbara, California, USA)
Adolescence, 188-93

DIXON, R. A. (Max Planck Institute for Human Development and Education, Berlin, FRG)
History of Research of Human Development, 9-17

DOHERTY, S. E. (University of California, Santa Barbara, California, USA)
Sex Characteristics and Roles, 367-72

DOUVAN, E. (University of Michigan, Ann Arbor, Michigan, USA)
Psychoanalytic Theory of Human Development, 83-88

DRAPER, W. (University of Oklahoma, Oklahoma City, Oklahoma, USA)
Emotional Development, 415-21; *Father's Role in Development*, 459-61

DRUM, P. A. (University of California, Santa Barbara, California, USA)
Communication Skills Development, 265-69; *Language Acquisition and Human Development*, 269-75

483

Name Index

The Name Index has been compiled so that the reader can proceed either directly to the page where an author's work is cited, or to the reference itself in the bibliography. For each name, the page numbers for the bibliographic citation are given first, followed by the page number(s) in parentheses where that reference is cited in text. Where a name is referred to only in text, and not in the bibliography, the page number appears only in parentheses.

The accuracy of the spelling of authors' names has been affected by the use of different initials by some authors, or a different spelling of their name in different papers or review articles (sometimes this may arise from a transliteration process), and by those journals which give only one initial to each author.

Subject Index

The Subject Index has been compiled as a guide to the reader who is interested in locating all the references to a particular subject area within the Encyclopedia. Entries may have up to three levels of heading. Where the page numbers appear in bold italic type, this indicates a substantive discussion of the topic. Every effort has been made to index as comprehensively as possible and to standardize the terms used in the index. Given the diverse nature of the field and the varied use of terms throughout the international community, synonyms and foreign language terms have been included with appropriate cross-references. As a further aid to the reader, cross-references have also been given to terms of related interest.